Three Classic Volumes
from the Crime Files of

ANN RULE

A ROSE FOR HER GRAVE

YOU BELONG TO ME

A FEVER IN THE HEART

and Other True Cases

POCKET BOOKS
New York London Toronto Sydney Tokyo Singapore

"For the Good Times" by Kris Kristofferson copyright © 1968 Careers-BMG Music Publishing, Inc. (BMI) All Rights Reserved. Used by Permission.

POCKET BOOKS, a division of Simon & Schuster Inc.
1230 Avenue of the Americas, New York, NY 10020

Books by Ann Rule

A Fever in the Heart and Other True Cases
Ann Rule's Crime Files: Vol. 3

Dead by Sunset

You Belong to Me and Other True Cases
Ann Rule's Crime Files: Vol. 2

Everything She Ever Wanted

A Rose for Her Grave and Other True Cases
Ann Rule's Crime Files: Vol. 1

If You Really Loved Me

The Stranger Beside Me

Possession

Small Sacrifices

Contents

Volume 1
A Rose for Her Grave
and Other True Cases · 1

Author's Note	7
A Rose for Her Grave	9
Campbell's Revenge	269
The Hit Person: Equal Opportunity Murder	295
The Runaway	327
The Rehabilitation of a Monster	347
Molly's Murder	373

Volume 2
You Belong to Me
and Other True Cases · 403

Author's Note	409
You Belong to Me	411
Black Christmas	607
One Trick Pony	643
The Computer Error and the Killer	669
The Vanishing	689
The Last Letter	705

Volume 3
A Fever in the Heart
and Other True Cases · 733

Author's Note   743

A Fever in the Heart   745

The Highway Accident   983

Murder Without a Body   1003

I'll Love You Forever   1025

Black Leather   1045

Mirror Images   1063

A ROSE FOR HER GRAVE

and Other True Cases

Ann Rule's Crime Files: Vol. 1

This book is dedicated to women, to the friends I cherish and to the friends I will never know. Too many times I have to write about the tragedies that befall my sisters. *A Rose for Her Grave* is no exception. I am continually amazed at the strength women have shown in the face of catastrophe, particularly the survivors who pick up their lives and go on after losing a child to a conscienceless killer.

I salute all women who have had dreams, for themselves, for their children and for those they love. Their dreams were—and are—as different as the dreamers. Some came true; many did not. Some women found love and some found betrayal. Some were victims and some were heroines.

Some were both.

Acknowledgments

In a book that covers as many cases as *A Rose for Her Grave* does, there are dozens of people to thank. My research begins, quite literally, with a blank page or a short newspaper clipping. If it were not for those who consented to share their experiences, their impressions, their information and their emotions with me, I would be stuck with my blank page.

The names that follow are not in any particular order and they certainly are not alphabetized—but I am tremendously grateful to everyone listed:

King County Detectives Sue Peters, Randy Mullinax, Mike Hatch and Stan Chapin; King County Senior Deputy Prosecuting Attorneys Marilyn Brenneman and Susan Storey; Donna and Judy Clift, Ben and Marta Goodwin, Brittany Zehe, Hazel and Merle Loucks, Jim and Marge Baumgartner; Judge Frank Sullivan, Lori Merrick and Lynn Harkey, Todd Wheeler, Timothy Bergman, and Jeff Gaw; Chris Jarvis, *Journal American*; Richard Seven and Steve Clutter, *The Seattle Times*; Jack Hopkins, *The Seattle Post-Intelligencer*; Eric Zoeckler, *The Herald*; and Rose Mandelsberg-Weiss, *True Detective*.

Hank Gruber, Rudy Sutlovich, Dan Engle, John Boren, Billy Baughman, Gary Fowler, John Nordlund, Al Lima, Richard Steiner, Gene Ramirez and Don Cameron of the Seattle Police Department Homicide Unit; King County Medical Examiner Dr. Donald Reay and Chief Deputy Medical Examiner Bill Haglund; Joe Belinc, Doug Englebretson and Glenn Mann of the Snohomish County Sheriff's Office; Private Investigator Jim Byrnes, formerly of the Marion County, Oregon, Sheriff's Office.

Jean and Warren McClure, Doreen Hanson, Hilda Ahlers, Don Hendrickson.

Gerry Brittingham, Leslie Rule and Donna Anders, my unflinching critics, researchers and friends.

Finally, to my faithful and hardworking agents Joan and Joe Foley

(East Coast) and Mary Alice Kier and Anna Cottle of CINE/LIT (West Coast); to Emily Remes, who thank goodness, knows the law better than I do; to Liate Stehlik and Joe Gramm, editorial assistants; and to my editors, Bill Grose and Julie Rubenstein of Pocket Books, who envisioned this new series and prodded me every inch of the way until my blank pages became a real book.

And, once again, to the members of the oldest living literary group in Washington State: the inscrutable B. & M. Society.

Author's Note

I have always believed that true crime writing should not only absorb its readers but also educate them. There is no need to embroider spectacular cases; human behavior is in and of itself more fascinating than anything to be found in fiction. Those who have read my work before know that I do not stress blood and gore and grotesque details; I focus my research on the *whys* of murder more than on the *how*. Every day perfectly normal-appearing people commit crimes that seem inexplicable, leaving the rest of us to ponder, *"What happened?"* And there are the monsters, too, who make us ask, "Why did it take so long to happen?"

This series will, I hope, break new ground in the true crime genre. Each volume is designed to stand on its own, unveiling the details of aberrant and criminal behavior in the format that suits a particular case best, and yet the entire series will give the reader a deeper understanding of the psychopathology behind many types of crime.

Among the fourteen hundred murder cases I have covered, there are many that I will never forget. They have become so much a part of my life that the families of the victims are still my friends and so are the detectives who caught the killers. I cannot really tell you why these cases are as real to me today as they were the first time I delved into the police files and visited the places where the human beings involved once walked. It may be because these stories are, in a shadowy, frightening way, classics.

In Volume 1 the title story covers the case of Randy Roth, a modern-day Bluebeard whose alleged crimes went unpunished for more than a decade. The Roth case is an original book-length piece written expressly for this anthology. Randy Roth's trial was held in 1992.

You will also find other true cases from my own archives. These have been revised and updated: "Campbell's Revenge," "The Hit

Person: Equal Opportunity Murder," "The Runaway," "The Rehabilitation of a Monster," and "Molly's Murder."

I have selected each case for a special reason. Some I find extraordinary because of the insights they offer into bizarre and unpredictable human behavior. Others follow police investigators as they search for a killer, and provide examples of the most remarkable detective work I have encountered. Some demonstrate the almost space age advancements in forensic science, new techniques in blood work, computerized fingerprints, and in the identification of the most minuscule evidence imaginable. Even a decade ago detectives could never have foreseen these giant leaps in their fields. And some cases point out tragic gaps that still exist in our justice system.

I hope that you will find *Ann Rule's True Crime Cases* a series unlike anything you have read before.

A Rose for Her Grave

Bluebeard—La Barbe-Bleu—*the story of the wife killer of fairy tales and folklore, has been part of the world's popular culture since 1697. There is a murderous husband in every version of the story from* Tales of Mother Goose *to similar stories in European, African, and Asian folklore. The essentials of the oft told horror tale are the locked, forbidden room, the wife's curiosity, and her eleventh hour rescue. Bluebeard is such an antiquated story that it seems strange that it might be played out in real life in the 1980s and 1990s. Down through the centuries the most popular version has a cruel husband who leaves his bride with the keys to all the rooms in his home—but forbids her to open one room. The disobedient wife cannot resist the temptation to see what is in the room denied her. When that door swings open, she is transfixed with horror to see the bodies of her husband's former wives. The wicked husband discovers her treachery when he finds one telltale spot of blood on the key to that room.*

Knowing that she will die, the doomed bride calls out piteously to her sister who is watching from the tower for sign of rescue, "Sister Ann, Sister Ann, do you see anyone coming?"

In fiction the frightened bride is rescued just in time. In real life it is not always so.

He was a man who hated women, truly hated women. Unlike the serial killer who chooses, stalks, and physically destroys women he does not know, this man knew his victims only too well. The serial killer is "addicted to murder"; Bluebeard was addicted to his own greed. He was above all a man in complete control. He had to be, of course, because his plans required timing, charm, charisma, cunning, and a complete lack of conscience or empathy. He was handsome and boyish, and his victims never saw the danger in his eyes until it was far too late.

His victims were many, but he did the greatest harm to women and children. He wanted a family. He insinuated himself into a number of close families and became something of a cross between the young uncle and the

9

oldest son. But when he formed families of his own, he destroyed them. Utterly. Unlike the serial killer whose crimes invariably have aspects of sexual aberrance, Bluebeard was more stimulated by an expensive car than by the women who desired him. He only used their passion to gain those things he wanted more.

"A Rose for Her Grave" is the story of that man and of the King County detectives and prosecutors who sought to stop him from acting on his obsessions.

PART ONE

Janis

1

Janis Miranda was a little bit of a thing. She stood no more than an inch over five feet tall, and she weighed only 98 pounds. The few snapshots of her that remain are blurry. Even so, it was easy to see that she was pretty. She had long glossy brown hair and green eyes and a good figure that she kept by jogging and dancing. She admitted that jogging bored her, but she loved to dance. Oh, how she loved to dance. On the dance floor she could forget the sad times in her short life, too many failed dreams and too many broken promises. Her natural grace and a lot of practice drew admiring glances from other dancers, and she never lacked for partners.

Janis left home young. When she set off on her own, her mother, Billie Jean Ray, was living in Dallas, Texas, and her father was off in Little Rock, Arkansas—at least he was the last time his daughter had heard from him. He had gone off and left Billie Jean with all the responsibility of raising their four kids. As long as Janis could remember, Billy Jean had worked three jobs at a time. Her mother was more philosophical about her husband than Janis was. She saw how exhausted Billie Jean was most of the time, and she would never forgive her father for what she perceived as desertion. When he tried to make up later by sending Janis birthday cards and offering to send small sums of money, she told him, "If you wanta help somebody, start sending checks to Mom. Once you've caught up with all that you owe her, *then* you can think about your children."

There had been many times when food was scarce, and Janis never forgot them. It wasn't easy for her to believe in men after her daddy took off. And yet her emotions were ambivalent; she longed for a good man even as she doubted that such an animal existed.

Nevertheless, Janis married young the first time. She had known Joe Miranda for a year or so and she was eighteen when she and Joe got married on April 17, 1971. Joe was in the army, and they were transferred to Augsburg, Germany, where their daughter, Jalina, was born on October 10, 1973. When they returned to Dallas, Janis worked at several jobs—first as a lab assistant and then for a security firm and a stockbroker.

The romance went out of their marriage too soon, and Joe and Janis separated in late 1975. Their divorce was final on September 16, 1976. There were no bitter recriminations; they simply went their separate ways, and twenty-four-year-old Janis got custody of Jalina. Somewhat reluctantly, according to Janis, Joe paid $250 a month toward Jalina's support. Janis tried to save most of that for her little girl's future. She found herself working as hard as her own mother had just to cover the necessities of life for herself and Jalina. She couldn't hope to get much help from her family; they were working to keep afloat themselves.

Janis Miranda was a young woman of moderate habits. Occasionally she would have a drink or two when she was out dancing, but that was all. Drinking was against her religion, and besides that, the music and the excitement that she always found at a dance were enough of a high for her. Janis fantasized sometimes that she could be a professional disco dancer, and she also loved to dance to the big band sound. She didn't use drugs—except for diet pills once in a while. She was so tiny that her friends wondered why she felt the need to watch her weight, but she complained that every extra pound showed when you were short. If she went over 105 pounds, she worried.

Janis, with Jalina in tow, moved often, looking perhaps for some geographic solution to the melancholy that periodically washed her world in shades of gray. She went from Texas to California and then on up to Washington State. She didn't have anything in the way of earthly possessions, but she had what was most important—her daughter. Jalina's hair was a little darker than her mother's but just as thick and gleaming with highlights. Janis combed Jalina's hair back and caught it up with a ribbon, letting it cascade to her daughter's waist.

Mother and daughter were close—perhaps too close. Sometimes Janis confided too much in her child. She told Jalina almost everything. "That's more than a little kid should know," Janis's friends cautioned more than once. But Janis shook her head. "Jalina and I don't have any secrets between us."

During and after her marriage to Joe, Janis was a Jehovah's Witness. "She was heavy into religion," Joe remembered. "She was always looking for something to belong to. Her family broke up after a divorce, and Janis was kicked around a lot from family to family."

As an adult, Janis was close to her mother, sisters, and brother, and she had one other person she could count on—her friend Louise Mitchell. The women met at their church in Dallas in 1975. Louise was a little older and had kids of her own, but the two women hit it off right away. Janis's size could make her seem almost waiflike sometimes, as if she needed someone who gave a damn about her. Louise did. They had similar problems, and the two women sometimes combined their households to save expenses. They got along fine. They trusted each other so much that they shared a bank account on occasion. Then one or the other would move and their friendship would continue with long-distance calls and letters.

Janis still longed for a man who would truly love her, but now that would mean loving Jalina too. Janis was young and attractive, and most of the time she managed to show the world an upbeat attitude even when she was sad and scared underneath. Half of her believed in fate and in love at first sight. Half of her clung to her own autonomy and made her treasure her independence.

Pressed to reveal her real feelings, Janis admitted that she believed she would have a second chance at love.

Sometimes Janis leapt without thinking, making decisions based on emotion rather than on common sense. She seemed to change her mind as often as she changed her clothes. The one thing she was absolutely steadfast about was her daughter. Jalina always came first. Janis would have given up her life for her little girl.

Louise Mitchell had seen Janis discouraged and depressed, but not often. The only time she was really concerned was when they were living in California. Janis had looked upon the move to California as a whole new start, only to find that there was nothing magical there either. It was still hard to make a living and support Jalina, and sometimes she got so lonely.

When Louise moved to Seattle in 1979, Janis followed a few months later and found an apartment right across the street from Louise's place. She hadn't found happiness in Texas or in California, and she missed having her best friend around. They fell immediately back into their old habit of visiting together every day, either on the phone or over coffee.

Janis soon got a job working in the office at the Richmond Pediatric Clinic on North 185th in the north end suburb of Seattle. The move from Texas had taken everything she had saved, except for Jalina's college money. She wouldn't touch Jalina's savings if she could help it. Janis had only her 1974 Pinto. She had no furniture at all and no clothes for cold weather. One of the other women working at the clinic loaned her a little television set, and she was surprised and shocked when she brought it over to see that Janis and Jalina slept on the floor of their small apartment in sleeping bags because they had no beds. They were using a suitcase for a table. But neither mother nor daughter seemed to feel bad about it; they were "camping out" until they could afford furniture.

Janis was a good worker, and everyone liked her at the clinic. She never complained about what she didn't have. She just worked harder to change things. "She took a job at K Mart in the evenings," Shirley Lenz, the clinic receptionist, recalled. "She wanted Jalina to have whatever she needed. Janis herself didn't even have a winter coat. She *had* to have two jobs to make it."

If only on a subconscious level, Janis Miranda waited for a prince to come along and rescue her. She knew that wasn't likely to happen. Still, she could hope. Every time she went to a dance, she wondered if it might turn out to be her lucky night. She joined Parents Without Partners and attended all their dances. She went to their Halloween party and then to the PWP Thanksgiving dance. Faces in the crowd began to seem like friends.

Janis went to a Parents Without Partners New Year's Eve dance on the last day of 1980. It was held at a dance hall over the Richmond-Highlands Ice Arena. As always, there were four times as many women attending as men. The women brought the chips and dip and cheese trays and leftover Christmas cookies, and the men brought themselves, fully aware that their very scarcity made them more desirable. Most of the celebrants were over forty. Janis didn't really expect New Year's Eve to be any different from the rest of her nights. She just wanted to dance. Jalina was safe with a baby-sitter, and Janis knew she looked especially pretty in one of her few good dresses.

When she heard a soft voice behind her asking for a dance, she turned around and got a pleasant surprise. She had danced with the man holding out his hand before, although they had never really talked. His name was Randy something. He wasn't very tall, but he had a wonderfully muscular physique, warm brown eyes, and a luxuriant mustache. He was handsome and he was young; he looked no more than twenty-five.

He couldn't dance more than rudimentary steps.

But that didn't matter. Suddenly they were talking as if they had known each other for a long time. He made no move to leave her side all evening. Maybe it was the thought that she wasn't really alone on New Year's Eve any longer; maybe it was her sense that the physical attraction between them was very strong. Whichever. Janis was both thrilled and fascinated with Randy Roth. He told her he had just celebrated his twenty-sixth birthday on the day after Christmas. He had been married once, but his divorce had been final on May 20. He said he had a little boy, Greg, who was three. He was raising his son by himself. She was touched by that; right away they had something in common. Janis looked at the picture Randy carried of his son and saw an adorable chubby-cheeked little boy. It was obvious to her that Randy loved his child as fiercely as she loved Jalina.

As 1981 arrived and the crowd whooped and whistled, Janis Miranda was already half in love. Inwardly she marveled at that; she was the woman who didn't trust men. She had been bruised in the wars of love too many times. But this man was different. Somehow special. When Randy Roth asked if he might call her, she agreed enthusiastically.

And then she held her breath until he *did* call. So many men said they would and then never did. Randy did. He seemed to be as interested in her as she was in him.

Her friend Louise and her co-workers at the clinic warned her to be cautious, but Janis just shook her head and smiled. The more time she spent with Randy, the more she thanked her lucky stars. He was the dearest, sweetest, most romantic man she had ever known. His own life hadn't been easy. He trusted her enough to confide in her about his service in the Marine Corps in Vietnam—but only to a point. She sensed he was holding some of the horror back so that he wouldn't upset her. All he seemed to care about was her happiness. She had never known anyone like that before.

"Janis came to work one morning just beaming," Shirley Lenz would recall later. "She was carrying a little bouquet of flowers and a note. Randy had left them on her car. She just couldn't get over that. She thought it was wonderful."

When Randy sent Janis a dozen red roses, she was even more enchanted with him. If she had sat down and written out exactly what she wanted in a man, her list would have described Randy Roth. Except for the fact that he was only a passable dancer, he was perfect. She told Louise that Randy had held a steady job as a diesel mechanic for Vitamilk Dairy for a long time and that he wanted the same things out of life that she wanted—a happy family, a home with a mother and a father to take care of both Greg and Jalina. Randy told her he was renting his house with an option to buy it. He had lived in the Lynnwood, Washington, area most of his life. Randy seemed solid to Janis, not like the fly-by-night guys she had met before.

Although Janis wasn't thrilled with working out and jogging, she accompanied Randy in those pursuits, puffing along behind him but grinning gamely. If Randy had wanted her to, she would have lifted weights and swum the English Channel. He was a stickler for physical fitness, and she wanted to be just the kind of woman he admired. When she saw how he detested smoking, she quickly quit. She hoped he would never find out that she had smoked.

Loving Randy's son, Greg, was easy for Janis. He was a sweet little boy who didn't even remember his real mother. Janis was ready to be Greg's mother if Randy wanted her to be.

Both Louise Mitchell and Shirley Lenz kept warning Janis to slow down. What did she really know about Randy? She just laughed and told them she knew enough to know she wanted to marry him and live with him for the rest of her life.

Shirley had never even met Randy, but he sounded like the perfect man for Janis. Maybe too perfect. She suggested to Janis that a perfect man would be willing to wait a few more months. Real love could stand the test of time. From Janis's description of their dating, it sounded as though they were racing toward a serious commitment.

Shirley's suspicions were right on target. One morning in February, Janis rushed in to work and showed her co-workers her left hand. She wore a ring with a tiny diamond on her third finger. "He's gonna take care of me!" she cried joyously. "Randy's gonna marry me and take care of me!"

Janis Miranda and Randy Roth were married in a civil ceremony in municipal court in Seattle on March 13, 1981. They took a short honeymoon to Victoria, British Columbia, on Vancouver Island. It was only three ferryboat rides away and a short drive from the Lynnwood-Everett area; culturally it was a world away. The historic Empress Hotel where they stayed seemed so grand and European, with its majestic structure and the afternoon high tea it was famous for. Janis was dazzled by the splendor and romance.

After the honeymoon Janis and Jalina moved into Randy's rented house at 4029 42nd Place West in Mountlake Terrace. At his urging, Janis quit her job and stayed home to be a mother to the two children of their new family. She felt a little guilty because Randy was bringing so much into the marriage, at least financially, and she had nothing to contribute but her love. Randy told her he had $250,000 worth of insurance on his life and that he had changed the policy so that she was the beneficiary.

Three weeks after they were married, Janis applied for a day-care license, had the house inspected, and opened a child-care center in their home. The first of her four toddlers came at 6:00 A.M., and Jan was busy all day. She even kept one child from 10:00 P.M. until 4:00 A.M. for a registered nurse who worked a night shift at a nearby hospital. Jan didn't earn very much—$1.25 an hour during the day and $1.50 at night—but she had children there sixteen hours a day for five days a week. Randy worked at Vitamilk from 7:30 A.M. until 5:00 P.M. He made $14.39 an hour, plus time and a half when he worked overtime. He led Janis to believe that he earned close to $30,000 a year.

Janis and Randy hadn't been married long when Janis told Louise that someone had stolen her car. Louise thought that was almost laughable. Seven-year-old Pintos were not exactly the most desirable targets for car thieves—not like Camaros or Pontiac Firebirds. Besides, Janis acted strange when she talked about it. Actually she didn't want to talk about it at all, and she avoided Louise's questions. She had insurance on the car, however, and she and Randy accepted a cash settlement. What was left of the Pinto turned up a couple of months later, stripped and abandoned.

In the beginning, Janis was deliriously happy in her marriage. Everybody who knew her was happy for her. It was Louise Mitchell who first became aware that things in the Roths' marriage might not be as blissful as they had been.

While Randy had been an ardent lover during his headlong pursuit of Janis, she confided to Louise that he had cooled off rapidly. Even their honeymoon had been a disappointment. Randy told Janis that intercourse was painful for him because of an infection that set in after he had had a vasectomy. Janis didn't understand male physiology, and she was puzzled. Still, she accepted his explanation although she was disappointed that the physical side of their marriage was so diminished.

Randy also had a private area of his life that Janis worried about. During their whirlwind courtship, he hadn't talked about other women, but she had been around enough to assume that he'd had lovers in his past, just as she had. She did not expect that he would continue to see his old girlfriends.

Janis was not happy to discover that Randy was still very close to Lily Vandiveer,* a married woman who had been Greg's baby-sitter. He often had lunch alone with her. Indeed, he sometimes still had

---

*The names of some individuals in this book have been changed. Such names are indicated by an asterisk (*) the first time each appears in the book.

her baby-sit with Greg—which was ridiculous, because Janis was available to care for Greg. Jalina told her mother that when Randy went to pick Greg up at Lily's house, he always made her stay in the car.

Randy laughed at Jan's questions about Lily. "She just wants my attention," he explained. "There's nothing romantic about it."

Jan wanted her husband's attention too, and she was not getting much of it. Before her second marriage was three months old, Janis Miranda Roth began to worry that Randy might be seeing other women. And then she berated herself for being so suspicious; it was her own lack of confidence, she reasoned, and nothing that Randy was doing. After all, hadn't Randy brought up the idea of their buying a house? A man who had fallen out of love with his wife wouldn't do that. She tried to tell herself that they were building a future together, that Randy was simply a man who did not desert his old friends.

Sometimes she had to try very hard to talk herself out of the jealous thoughts that crept into her mind. Everything was so different after their wedding. The romantic gestures that Janis had appreciated so much during their courtship had long since stopped. There were no more nosegays or love notes, no more roses. Janis no longer felt as if Randy saw her as the center of his universe. She rationalized that disappointment away too: Randy was working hard and so was she; roses cost money, and they were saving to buy the house; she would be foolish to expect their relationship to continue as it had before they were married.

Still, Randy's tender and impulsive gestures had ended so suddenly that it was almost as if he had thrown cold water in her face. One day she had been basking in his complete devotion; the next, she felt like a baby-sitter. Her husband seemed closed off to her, his face void of expression, his attitude toward her often almost one of annoyance.

She couldn't understand what had happened. Feeling disloyal, she confided again in Louise Mitchell, "Sometimes I wonder if I didn't get married too quickly."

"Does he hit you?" Louise asked.

"Nothing like that. He's just—just different."

Louise ventured her opinion that her friend's husband seemed to be wound up too tight. She felt that Randy was capable of violence, and she warned Janis to be careful.

Janis shook her head. No, it wasn't that. She didn't know for sure what was wrong. They could sit down and talk things out calmly, and they often did.

"I just worry about things," she admitted. "He lives so danger-ously. He drives so fast. And he's so jealous of me. He's got no reason to be. I never even look at anyone else."

Like Jan, who had been slow to tell her family about her marriage, Randy didn't seem anxious to introduce her to his mother or his siblings. In fact, she had no idea where they lived, nor had she heard any details about them. She would have been shocked to realize how close by they lived. However, they did visit Randy's father, Gordon, and his stepmother, Sandy, in southwest Washington in July of 1981. They went camping during their vacation and drove down the coast pulling a trailer. They camped at Ocean Shores in Washington and then at a campground in Astoria, Oregon, before they arrived in the little town of Washougal where Gordon lived.

Gordon was built much like Randy, muscular and compact, and he was a strong man too. The elder Roth had a small farm near Washougal, and Randy helped his father harvest a crop of hay—something he had done often in the past. Janis liked her stepmother-in-law and Randy's step-siblings—Marcie, thirteen; John, nine; and J.R., seven. Jalina was thrilled to learn that Marcie had two horses, Stardust and Dusty.

Randy, Janis, Jalina, who was seven, and Greg, now three, camped at Beacon Rock State Park, about fifteen miles east of Washougal along the Columbia River gorge. Randy suggested that they hike up Beacon Rock itself. Although Janis was not an avid hiker, she was swept up in Randy's enthusiasm—at least until she saw Beacon Rock up close.

Beacon Rock was more of a mountain than a rock. It was a huge monolith that rose up out of the earth more than 500 feet into the sky. High up at its summit it looked forbidding and dangerous. There was only stone up there. Eight or nine stubborn fir trees clung to its inhospitable surface. Janis confided that she was terrified of heights, but Randy assured her there were easy hiking trails that even the children could manage. With his coaxing and soothing, Janis nodded nervously and said she would give it a try.

They took Marcie and John along, and trudged up the huge rock. The kids did just fine—maybe because their center of gravity was so low. The trail was well marked, and it had handrails and numerous switchbacks to ease the uphill climb. Even so, it wasn't for sissies. There were many other vacationers climbing along with them. Randy walked out on one shortcut about two hundred feet from the top, and Janis saw other people ducking under the handrails, but she hung back. She knew she would get dizzy if she looked down. She kept a close eye and grip on Jalina and Greg to be sure they stayed well back from the edge of the trail where the earth ended suddenly in nothing but a few scraggly shrubs and air.

Janis felt much better when they were back down on flat ground. She was relieved when they headed north to Seattle, leaving the looming bulk of stone behind them.

Back home, Janis and Randy went ahead with their plans to buy a house. In August they found a place they could afford—also in Mountlake Terrace. The community was Seattle's answer to the East Coast's Levittowns built during the post–World War II building boom. Just off the I-5 freeway, halfway between Seattle and Everett, it was the first town of any size to the north. Young couples flocked to buy the new homes that sprouted up as quickly as mushrooms, with only the color of the paint and other minor cosmetic differences distinguishing one from the other.

Randy's service in the marines allowed him to get a VA loan to buy the new house at 6207 229th S.W. It cost $59,950, and there was no down payment required—only closing costs. Randy's rent for the old house had been just $250 a month. Now their mortgage payments were almost $900 a month and it would be years before they built up any real equity in the new house, but it was theirs, not a rental.

Janis was so excited about having her own home. Mountlake Terrace wasn't as popular an area as it had been three decades before; there were scores of newer subdivisions around Seattle and Everett now, and the newness had worn off. The house wasn't fancy, but it was a huge step up from an apartment with no beds or tables.

When they bought the little house, Janis felt slightly guilty that she had complained about Randy to Louise. Even though she had discovered that Randy had only a part-time job as a mechanic for Vitamilk, he was the one who had made their buying a house possible. Her baby-sitting chores didn't bring in enough money to make much of a difference.

"It doesn't seem right," Janis told Louise, mentioning again Randy's $250,000 insurance policy, the policy he had stressed was there to ensure that Greg and Jalina would always be taken care of. "Randy has all that insurance, and I don't have any. He wants us both to get a policy, and that seems fair to me. That way I'll be evening up the financial burden a little."

Randy had made an appointment with Darrel Lundquist, an insurance agent for Farmer's New World Life. Lundquist explained that both Randy and Janis were eligible for a VIP nonsmoking policy with a payoff value of $100,000 and that the premiums would be negligible, only $15.90 a month apiece. Since they were both under thirty and lived clean and healthy lives, they were just the kind of clients that insurance companies wanted.

"This way," Randy told Janis, "we will have mortgage insurance. If either of us should die, the other will be able to pay off the house and look after Jalina and Greg without worrying about losing our home."

It sounded reasonable to Janis. On September 26, 1981, identical insurance policies were issued to the Roths by Farmer's New World Life. They would go into effect in early November. Randy's beneficiary was, of course, his wife, Janis. He listed a neighbor couple, Ron and Nancy Aden, who had become close friends, as secondary beneficiaries. Janis listed Randy first and the Adens second. The Adens belonged to the Baptist church in Silver Lake that she and Randy attended, although Randy wasn't as faithful about attending services as Janis was.

Randy seemed to have a real talent for making friends. His longest friendship was with Nick Emondi,* whom he had known since 1977 when Emondi was only nineteen. They had been friends during the time Randy was married to his first wife, Donna Carlson Sanchez, Greg's mother. Donna had lived with Randy in the rented house he later shared with Janis. When Randy and Donna divorced, Nick had helped to move Donna over to eastern Washington. She had a little girl by her first marriage and apparently agreed to let Randy have custody of Greg. Beyond that, Jan knew practically nothing about Donna.

Randy and Nick Emondi punched the same time clock at Vitamilk Dairy, and they both were into fixing up cars and riding motorcycles. Randy seemed to be the leader and Nick the follower. "Randy liked to control me," Nick would recall years later. "He used the carrot-and-the-stick approach. He would either give you something or punish you so you'd do what he wanted."

Nick was married and had a small daughter. Janis and Carrie Emondi* were friendly, but it was mainly because of their husbands' long camaraderie.

Janis hadn't told her family in Dallas that she had married again—not at first. Maybe she was afraid they would question her impetuous decision after such a short courtship. Maybe she wanted time alone with Randy before they revealed their somewhat checkered family histories. She and Randy had been together for months before she broke the news. Once she told her mom, Billie Jean Ray, that she was married, she wrote to her often and seemed eager for Billie Jean and her sisters Cleda and Sharon and the rest of the family to accept and admire Randy.

On October 12, 1981, Janis sent a long letter to Billie Jean: "It was good to talk to you again," Janis began. She told her mother that Jalina was now four feet five inches tall and weighed 65 pounds. Janis explained that she was not working outside the home and that it was good to be there when Jalina came home from school.

She said that she was baby-sitting for a one-year-old and a four-year-old, and hoped to build up to more clients. Greg's fourth birthday was coming up, Janis noted, and he made his own bed and helped her with chores. "He's quite mature because Randy would not tolerate a 'sissy' boy." Janis's affection for Greg was obvious. "He is a good boy most of the time."

Janis's letter was cheerful as she described the aftermath of Greg's attempt to shave, when he cut himself, and how he had come home from playing with dog mess in his hair. "Kids are kids."

Janis told her mother that Greg told her she looked "pretty" as she fixed her hair and makeup every evening before Randy came home.

She told her mother that Randy was five feet seven and a half inches tall and weighed about 155 pounds, and that he was very strong; he was a former karate champion with trophies to prove it. "He doesn't do it much anymore: he'd get so involved that he couldn't sleep . . . "

Perhaps protesting too much, Janis wrote that Randy has *many* very good qualities. "Sometimes his drawbacks are due to the . . . years he spent in Vietnam. He used to have nightmares, some depression after his tour there. You probably wouldn't believe some of the things he had to do there. He isn't proud of them. But it's either you or the enemy. Also, if you don't do what you're told, then you go to the Stockade. If we ever had another war and Randy got drafted, I wouldn't let him go. . . . So many guys get messed up in 'Nam.' That was a dumb war. The world itself can make you a hard, cold person—but so can war. He had to learn to be human again—if you can understand that."

Janis hastened to assure her mother that Randy had never used any type of drug, and when they went out, they drank very moderately. She had never seen Randy even tipsy, and he had never smoked.

As for her love affair with dancing, Janis wrote that she and Randy only went out dancing once every six weeks. She complained jokingly that she was getting old and that at twenty-nine she couldn't keep up the way she could when she was only twenty-five. "I don't take getting too old to disco lightly!"

Janis complimented Billie on getting a good job as a housekeeper for a wealthy couple and wrote nostalgically about the good old Texas home cooking, which she missed. She said Randy didn't care for vegetables much, and she tried to cook only the things he preferred.

Janis wrote about the weather and the beautiful—and hot—summer the Northwest had just had. Temperatures had soared over a hundred degrees.

She was annoyed with her sister Cleda for giving their father her mailing address—which she still listed as Louise Mitchell's house—because she didn't want him to write to her. "If he really ever cared about us, he would have sent you child support when he was working. When he has paid you a couple of thousand dollars of back child support, *then* I'll speak to him. . . . He forgot his responsibility to us and now I forget mine to him, since I don't live a Christian life anymore." Janis wrote that she lived according to her own standards—as most people seemed to.

Although Janis was no longer a practicing Jehovah's Witness, she did attend church and she was living a Christian life. But she was very hard on herself.

"Think I'm bitter?" she wrote. "Damn right I am. I only appreciate those worth appreciating. (That's my own opinion.) It took me years and years to realize all this. . . . He didn't care if we had clothes or food to eat, now did he?"

Whatever her father had done to make amends, Janis felt it wasn't enough. He had once offered to take Jalina to ease her burden. That wasn't the answer. "I was the problem, not Jalina," she wrote, explaining that several times in her life, Jalina was the reason for her to keep trying. "She loves her Mama and I needed that."

It was a strangely ambivalent letter, sounding happy and confident, but with an undercurrent of . . . what? It was more than bitterness over a lost childhood. A kind of dread, perhaps.

It felt good, she wrote, reversing herself again, to know that it was no longer "I, alone" who was taking care of a family. Janis concluded, "I am the most secure and generally the happiest I've ever been, but sometimes I don't know if that's what I want. Sometimes playing housewife isn't always fun. Sometimes I miss my independency. . . . Randy's good to all of us—and fair—but I sometimes remember liking to be my own boss."

Janis Miranda Roth told her mother she had never had so much in the way of worldly goods, even though she and Randy longed for things they couldn't yet afford. They wanted a basement and a second bathroom and money was tight. Their house payments took $871 a month, and the rest went for groceries, utilities, and insurance. "This house is half mine, and if I choose to leave, I forfeit all rights . . . that's how the contract was written." Janis closed her letter, saying, "I DO LOVE RANDY VERY MUCH. However, sometimes I ASK MYSELF, IS LOVE REALLY WORTH IT? I don't know that answer yet. Bye."

Janis enclosed money for her mother's birthday. She didn't explain "Is love really worth" *what?* Billie Jean Ray never got another letter from Janis Roth.

Nor did anyone else.

2

On Halloween, Randy Roth and his friend Nick Emondi took Nick's daughter and Greg and Jalina out trick-or-treating. The men talked as they waited in the road while the excited children ran across the lawns giggling to knock on doors. Afterward Nick Emondi could not recall how they got into a conversation whose topic was macabre enough to fit right in with the foggy, dark Halloween night.

"Could you kill your wife?" Randy had asked Nick suddenly.

"What?" Nick was startled. "What do you mean?"

"I mean, under certain circumstances, if you had to?" Randy gave examples of situations where a man might kill his wife to save her from something far worse. "What if we were invaded?" Randy continued. "What if the Russians were coming and you knew she was going to be tortured or raped? Could you kill her first?"

Emondi shook his head, chilled at the thought.

"Jan asked me if I could kill her if something like that happened," Randy explained, as if they were carrying on the most normal conversation in the world.

Emondi changed the subject and tried to shrug off Randy's

questions as Halloween spookiness, but he remembered the conversation for years.

Randy had an intensity about him, a way of speaking softly and staring at someone with his brown eyes fixed. Sometimes he came up with the weirdest thoughts.

Nick hadn't realized it, but Jan Roth had felt a chill for a long time, a sense of foreboding that drained the sunshine from her heart the way the northwest rains washed the sky of light. In the space of seven months she had gone from a bubbly bride to a woman with circles under her eyes who seemed always to be watching for something behind her, something creeping up on her.

When Louise Mitchell questioned her about what was wrong, Janis just bit her lip and looked away. Her marriage wasn't happy; that was patently clear to Louise. She *knew* Janis and had seen her put up with all manner of disappointments and still hide her pain from the world. This was something different.

Janis didn't talk about Randy the way she had. There was no joy in her at all. Finally she acknowledged quietly to her best friend that she had made a mistake. She had even begun to think of leaving her husband, although she had nothing but Jalina's college fund to see them through. Janis believed that if she left, she would have no claim at all on the property she and Randy now co-owned.

Louise felt her skin prickle with goose bumps. It almost seemed that Janis was afraid of Randy.

By November 1981 Nick Emondi saw the same depression in his friend's wife. One morning Randy asked Nick to drive him to work. He said he was leaving "on a hunting trip" and didn't want to park his car at Vitamilk overnight. Nick obliged, using Randy's car, although he was puzzled. He had never known Randy to hunt. He felt sure that if Randy was staying away overnight, he wasn't going hunting for deer or elk.

After he dropped Randy off, Nick drove the car back to the little house in Mountlake Terrace. He stopped in to say hi to Jan and found a very sad and frightened woman.

"She said she was scared of dying," Emondi remembered later. "I just know she wasn't happy."

Why on earth would a perfectly healthy twenty-nine-year-old woman be afraid of dying? he wondered. Janis was still jogging and exercising. She was in great shape. She had every right to expect to be around for another fifty or sixty years. Nick Emondi couldn't cheer her up, and he left, perplexed.

On November 25 Janis asked Jalina to come into the master bedroom with her. She had something important to tell her, something that no eight-year-old child should ever have to deal with.

"Jalina," Janis said hopelessly, "you know I love you and I want to stay with you forever and ever. But if anything should happen to me—if I'm not here—I want you to know I have some money put away. It's for you."

Janis showed Jalina the hiding place she had selected. She pulled out a drawer in a cabinet built into the wall. There was a white envelope taped to the back of the drawer. She showed her daughter the thick clump of bills inside. "Remember, honey—if I'm gone, I want you to come in here and take this and hide it."

Jalina nodded, but she was worried. Why was her mother talking like that? It scared her.

Worried and frightened enough, Janis might have dipped into Jalina's money to get away from whatever she feared. Janis had promised Billie Ray that she and Jalina would come to Texas for either Christmas or New Year's, but she hadn't said one word about bringing Randy along.

As far as anyone knew, their marriage was still a going concern. Randy gave no indication to anyone that there were problems. On November 7, 1981, Randy's and Jan's identical VIP $100,000 insurance policies had gone into effect. They continued to work at fixing up their new home in Mountlake Terrace.

Janis made no move to leave her husband. It is likely she hoped that her fears were groundless and that things would go back to the way they had been at first. She had loved Randy so much when she married him, and she had loved their life together until all the affection and sharing trickled away.

Jan had no idea what she had done wrong. All the makeup and dressing up for Randy's homecoming and all her efforts to cook his favorite foods were met with a blank stare. Sometimes she thought he hated her. Sometimes she blamed Vietnam and what that terrible war had done to him.

More often she blamed herself.

Randy announced that they would be going down to visit his father and stepmother in Washougal for Thanksgiving dinner. Janis was enthusiastic about the trip when she told Louise about it. Although she didn't look forward to the long drive, she liked Randy's family. Gordon and Sandy Roth were having their own marital problems and had separated, but they lived just across S.E. 380th Avenue from each other; it was an amicable parting. Randy still felt comfortable visiting them in their separate homes. He and Janis would stay at the farm with Sandy, though; Gordon Roth's bachelor cottage was tiny.

Thanksgiving Day went well, the kids had a good time, and no one in Washougal sensed any strain at all between the newlyweds. They all talked about Christmas and where they would spend the holiday.

On Friday morning, November 27, 1981, Randy and Janis prepared to go Christmas shopping. When the kids heard about their plans, they all clamored to go. But Randy said no. This was just for Jan and him; they needed some time to be together. The weather was chilly but sunny, and he wanted to get started at once. He turned down Sandy Roth's offer to make her usual pancake breakfast for company. Marcie Roth and her little brothers were disappointed about that. Sandy didn't bother making pancakes just for the kids. Jalina didn't care; she was excited about spending the day with Marcie and riding the horses.

Jan seemed happy to go shopping with Randy. In fact she seemed to be happy and enthusiastic about the Thanksgiving weekend in general; it was her first real holiday as Randy's wife. And now there was a Christmas coming up when she and Jalina wouldn't be alone anymore. If she still had doubts about her marriage and fears about something unknown waiting to destroy her happiness, she gave no indication of them.

But Randy and Janis didn't go Christmas shopping after all. As Randy explained later, they were barely down the road toward the huge shopping mall at Jantzen Beach on the Columbia River when Janis asked him if they could change their plans. "She suggested we climb Beacon Rock," Randy said. "She thought it would be romantic for us to climb up alone."

Janis wore jeans and a bright pink ski jacket with white fake fur trim; Randy wore his street clothes and a jacket. Neither had shoes meant for rough terrain. It didn't matter. It wasn't as if they would be going mountain climbing. Randy reminded Jan that Beacon Rock had a trail where they could walk side by side—at least as they started up. Last summer's climb hadn't been nearly as scary as she expected, had it?

Skamania County, Washington, is one of the state's least populated counties, with much of its land mass covered over with forests and mountains. The Gifford Pinchot National Forest sprawls across

Skamania County and the Cascade Range, whose infamous Mount Saint Helens erupted on May 18, 1980, thrusts skyward from the land. Here is the Indian Heaven Wilderness and the Trapper Creek Wilderness. Skamania's small towns crouch along the great Columbia River at the bottom of the county: Underwood, Home Valley, Carson, North Bonneville, Skamania, and Stevenson, the county seat. Except for its natural wonders, Skamania is not a rich county; it is a world away from the industry of Seattle and of Portland, Oregon—its income even more depleted with the slump in the timber industry and the battle between the environmentalists and the loggers over the rights of the spotted owl.

With the exception of an occasional drunken shootout and one tragically memorable family mass murder, Skamania County has a markedly low homicide rate. Lawmen are far more likely to have to deal with highway accidents and mishaps suffered by tourists. It is true now, and it was true in 1981.

It was 11:23 on the morning of November 27 when case number 81-3885 began to unfold in the Skamania County Sheriff's Office. The day after Thanksgiving had been quiet for deputies on duty until Deputy E. L. Powell was instructed to respond to a "possible fall victim" at Beacon Rock. There was very little information available on the incident—if, indeed, there had been a fall. Powell asked that a team from Skamania County Search and Rescue respond. "Better roust Ray out, too," he said quietly into his radio mike. Ray was Undersheriff Ray Blaisdell. People didn't fall off Beacon Rock and walk away with a sprained ankle. If the report was true, the news could be bad. They had perhaps four hours of daylight to locate a fall victim.

When Deputy Powell got to the Beacon Rock trailhead ten minutes later, he was met by a worried-looking young woman who said her name was Shelley Anderson. She said her party of climbers—her husband, Steven Anderson, Merle Quarter, and Edward Warfield, all from Vancouver, Washington—had noticed a man running up and down the trail, calling out some name they couldn't understand. "Then he said, 'My God! My wife has fallen!' He wanted someone to come down and call for help," she explained. "So I said I would."

With only second-party information, Powell tried to determine just where the fall victim might have gone off the rock so that the ambulance crew and the search and rescue team could concentrate their efforts. So far, he was told, they had been unable to locate the woman. He figured that it would be best for them to go into the area from the intersection of Little Road and State Road 14.

Undersheriff Blaisdell arrived to take over the scene, and he talked with the distraught man who said his wife had fallen. He gave his name as Randolph Roth and his address as Mountlake Terrace, Washington. Roth pointed out an area about 200 feet from the top of Beacon Rock and said his wife, Janis, had slid over and off at that point. They had been taking a shortcut—one that they had taken on a climb earlier in the summer—and he had climbed over the railing and Jan had crawled under. His wife was in the lead, Roth said. "She made a sharp right turn. . . . She started to slide on something—dried pine needles, loose dirt, leaves—something." He said he tried to reach out for her, but he wasn't close enough to grab her. As he watched in horror, he said, his wife disappeared from sight. He climbed down as far as he possibly could, trying to find her. He looked down from every vantage point possible, but was unable to find her. Roth said he thought maybe he could run down and come up from the bottom to find Jan, but that didn't work either. Desperate, he said he climbed back up and ran down the trail to find the hikers he had seen earlier and ask them for help. He led them up to the spot where he had last seen his wife. None of them spotted her either.

Far down below the spot where Janis Roth had fallen, searchers looked for her in vain. Bill Wiley, coordinator for Search and Rescue in the county and a master at rock-climbing, rappelled down the face 200 feet in his search for the victim. They were able to pinpoint the area where someone would land—but Janis wasn't there. She should have been. Wiley lowered a weighted rope to indicate the direction of fall. It didn't make any kind of sense; the woman could not have bounced so far off the predictable fall pattern.

Two helicopters, piloted by Jack Caseberg and Tom Nolan, were brought in from the 304th Air Squadron. It was a perilous situation for the searchers. The air currents around Beacon Rock were notoriously treacherous, with sudden wind shears that could tumble the copters themselves down the face of the giant monolith. The backwash of the rotors tugged at Bill Wiley, threatening to knock him from his precarious perch. A parajumper, who was also a highly trained paramedic, was lowered by a rope from the copter in a vain attempt to spot the missing woman.

Down in the parking lot by the sheriffs' cars, Randy repeated exactly what Jan had been wearing. Her new jacket was such a bright pink, he said, that she should be easy to spot. He was pale and sweaty as he paced frantically, his face a study in despair.

From time to time he mentioned small things. Climbing Beacon

Rock had been "Jan's idea. It was her day. She could do what she
wanted. I told her it was cold and asked her if she was sure. She was,"
he said hopelessly. "She wanted to be alone with me."

Minutes and then hours passed. A score or more searchers raced
against sundown. Sandy Cobart, Bob Hoot, Corey Dowty, Connie
Davis, Lester MacDonald, and Todd and Sandy McCaldey from the
search and rescue team moved above the trail on the west side of
Beacon Rock. Helping them were personnel from the Bonneville Fire
Department: Greg Hodges, Jay Christiansen, Mike Southard, Doug
McKenzie, and Jim Duff. The Anderson rock-climbing party stayed
on to help search too.

Finally the aerial team and the ground searchers, working on a
concentrated sweep together, caught a glimpse of pink in a dense
clump of timber halfway down the rock. For the missing woman to
have landed in the timber, she would have had to fall at a 45-degree
angle from where her husband said she had gone off. Janis Roth lay
300 feet from the top on the west side of the mammoth rock. The
chance that she had survived was almost minimal. The parajumper
from Tom Nolan's helicopter was lowered on a swaying rope harness
to where the victim lay while her husband waited for some word of
her condition.

Blaisdell's radio crackled, and communication between the paramedics and the ground station was audible. The medics were
requesting IV's!

Blaisdell turned to Randy Roth. "It's possible that she's still alive."

Randy Roth's face showed joy and relief. That was unmistakable.
Policemen are by nature a suspicious lot. Blaisdell studied Randy
intensely. The undersheriff figured that if there had been any foul
play, Roth would have been stunned and horrified to learn his wife
was alive. Randy Roth's expression revealed only elation that his wife
still lived. Blaisdell worried that he might be building up for an
emotional crash. It seemed incredible that anyone could have survived that fall with all the stone outcroppings along the way.

Fifteen minutes passed. The word that came over the radio was
what Blaisdell had expected all along: the small woman in the pink
jacket was dead; there was no longer any question of that. She had
been carried to a level field where medics got only a flat line on their
Life-Pak monitors. They found no signs at all of life. Blaisdell turned
to Randy Roth and informed him of the tragic news.

Roth began to sob. "Then why did they ask for the IV's?" he
demanded. "She *must* have been alive."

"I don't know," Blaisdell answered. And he didn't.

It took a quarter of an hour for the widower to regain any kind of composure. He walked away from Ray Blaisdell to where his car was parked. He was still crying, but he gradually got control of his emotions. When the undersheriff asked if there was anyone he could call, Roth said he would be all right by himself.

"Can I see her body?"

"Yes, that would be all right. If you could identify her . . ."

Janis Roth's shattered body had been carried from a field on the south side of Beacon Rock by Skamania County ambulance crewmen Terry Webber, Duane Hathaway, and Sonny Kadau. They had transported her first to the Pierce ranch and then to the fire hall to await transportation to Straub's Funeral Home in Camas.

"She doesn't look so good," one of the medics murmured to Randy, cautioning him.

Ashen-faced, Randy Roth leaned into the ambulance to view Janis's body. Silently he studied his wife as she lay in the ambulance. "She doesn't look so bad," he remarked quietly. "Her face doesn't seem as badly damaged as I expected." His tone was flat, washed of any emotion at all.

Later Randy remembered that he had to be absolutely sure that Jan was dead, absolutely beyond help, before he could let them take her body to the funeral home. If there was anything, anything at all, that could be done for her, he wanted it done.

But he could see there was nothing to be done. Jan was dead. He turned away, stumbling toward Blaisdell's patrol car. His voice was suddenly full of tears as he said, "I've seen a lot of deceased people when I was in the service, but I've never had to look at a loved one like this. She didn't smoke and she didn't drink. That's the reason I married her. I loved her very much."

He repeated that statement three times. Did he mean that literally? Was it so hard to find a clean-living women that Roth had fallen in love with his wife because she had those attributes? Probably not. He was hurting and he was crying and he probably didn't know exactly what he was saying. The men standing around turned away. What could anyone say? The poor man seemed overwhelmed with grief. Sonny Kadau handed him Janis's engagement ring and wedding band. When Roth asked about the gold necklace that Janis had been wearing, they told him she hadn't been wearing it; it had probably been ripped off as she plummeted 300 feet down Beacon Rock.

"Besides you," Blaisdell asked, "who are her next of kin?"

"She's got a daughter, Jalina. She's back at my mother's house in Washougal." Roth paused, trying to remember. "And she has a mother in Texas someplace, but I don't know her address. I never met any of her folks."

As it happened, the on-call ambulance driver from Straub's Funeral Home in Camas, the first good-sized town along the Columbia River, was ex-homicide detective Dick Reed. Reed had retired in 1979 after working for almost fifteen years in the Homicide Unit of the Seattle Police Department. As he viewed the body of the young woman and listened to the account of what had happened that day, he got what detectives call a "hinky feeling." A dozen years later he still remembered going to the fire hall to pick up the body of the fall victim.

"It bothered me. Something didn't add up. I suggested to Ray Blaisdell that he at least ask the husband to take a lie detector test, but Ray wasn't receptive at the time. He felt that it had been a terrible accident, that the husband was so grief-stricken that it had to be on the up-and-up."

Dick Reed drove Janis Roth's body back to Straub's Funeral Home. It was a little before 5:00 P.M. when he arrived. It wasn't long after that when Randy Roth himself came into the reception area. He was very definite about what he wanted. He paid in full as he insisted that "Jan" be cremated as soon as possible. "She would have wanted that. We've talked about it, and she hated the idea of being in the ground. We promised each other that if anything happened to either of us, the other would see to cremation."

It would not be an expensive procedure. Roth explained that he and Jan had also agreed that lavish funerals were a waste, that money should go to take care of the living. He paid Straub's $541. Ironically it cost him less to dispose of his dead wife's body than it would have to fly Jan and Jalina to Texas for Christmas.

Randy was a well-organized man, even in such bleak circumstances. His wallet was equipped with data he might need. He added the number of Janis's insurance policy to the papers he filled out at the funeral home.

The last time Sandy Roth had seen her stepson and stepdaughter-in-law, they were happily heading off for a day of Christmas shopping. She expected them home for supper any minute. Instead, Randy called and suggested that everyone come to Camas for pizza. They were all sitting in the restaurant before they noticed Janis wasn't with Randy. He evaded their questions about where she was. Finally and almost casually, he pushed a receipt of some kind across the table.

Sandy looked at it and froze, all color draining from her cheeks. She seemed incapable of saying anything. Marcie pulled it over and gazed without understanding at the piece of paper.

"What does this mean?" she asked Randy. "What's cremation . . . and who's Janis Miranda Roth?"

"You know," he answered.

"No, I don't know any Janis Roth."

"Yes, you do. Think about it."

Slowly the thirteen-year-old girl understood. She had never heard Janis called anything but "Jan." She looked at Jalina, but the little girl clearly didn't comprehend what Randy was saying. Marcie couldn't believe it either. It had to be one of Randy's sadistic jokes. Marcie looked at him. He wasn't crying; he wasn't upset in the least. He was gobbling his pizza hungrily.

It was so weird that it couldn't be real. Jan was probably going to walk in any minute with a breathless excuse. Marcie looked at the door as if she could will her new sister-in-law to appear. But the door was closed to keep the cold air out, and nobody appeared.

Feeling nauseated and scared, Marcie excused herself to go to the ladies' room. Jalina followed her, talkative and cheerful as always. She didn't realize that something awful might have happened. Marcie herself was only thirteen; how could she be expected to tell a little kid that her mother might be dead, that she might already be nothing but ashes?

The pizza roiled in Marcie's stomach, and it seemed like hours before the rest of the family finished eating and they headed home to bed.

As unbelievable as it seemed to Marcie, Jan *was* dead. Randy hadn't been teasing in the mean way he sometimes did. He was a widower, his bride gone in the flicker of an eye.

Randy apparently couldn't bring himself to tell Jalina. As he often remarked, he had never been able to deliver bad news, to say it out loud. But Jalina started asking questions about where her mother was. He had to tell her something. He took the little girl aside that evening and told her only that her mother had fallen and was in the hospital. He seemed so calm that Jalina wasn't upset. She expected her mother to come home in a day or so.

3

Randy Roth was up early the next morning, Saturday, November 28. He had several phone calls to make. On his way home from their doomed climb, he had arranged for his dead wife's cremation, but there were other arrangements that he felt should be accomplished as soon as possible.

Who would have ever thought that all the safeguards they had built to hold off disaster would have to be put into play so quickly? As Randy had told Janis only two months before, it was extremely important that their mortgage be paid off if anything happened to either one of them. They had two little kids to think about—two kids who would need their only parent free of financial burdens—and Janis had agreed with him.

Randy ate breakfast and then placed a call to Darrel Lundquist, his insurance agent in Seattle. It was early on Saturday morning. In fact, Lundquist was still in bed when his phone rang. When he heard Randy's voice, Lundquist's first thought was that he wanted to cancel his policy. But it wasn't that. Randy said he wanted to file a claim.

"But there has to be a *death* before you can file a claim in this kind of policy," Lundquist explained.

"My wife died yesterday," Randy said flatly. Randy told Lundquist that Janis had been killed in a terrible accident. He wanted to begin to process his insurance claim at once.

Lundquist woke up in a hurry and muttered condolences. Answering Randy's questions, the agent explained what Randy would need in order to collect on the $100,000 policy that had been written on Janis's life in September. The company would require a certified copy of Janis's death certificate, of course. "And we'll need to have her Social Security number."

Randy promised to get back to Lundquist as soon as possible with the necessary documents and information.

Janis had been dead only twenty hours.

Randy Roth didn't know his wife's Social Security number, but he figured her former employer at the pediatric clinic must have it on record. Shortly after 8:00 A.M. he placed a call to Shirley Lenz, who ran the doctor's office up in Seattle, and asked if she knew Janis's Social Security number.

Shirley explained that she didn't have access to the information that Randy wanted, that it was locked up in the doctor's files. She asked him to call back after 9:00 A.M. when she could talk to the doctor. "Doesn't Janis know it?" she asked belatedly, but Randy had already hung up.

When Randy called back after nine, Shirley Lenz read off Janis's Social Security number to him: 452 06 5537. But she had had an hour to wonder and worry about his request, and she asked him if anything was wrong.

"Yes," he told her. "We had an accident when we were hiking, and they had to fly Janis out in a helicopter."

"How *is* she?" Shirley asked, concerned.

"I don't know," he said.

"You don't *know*?" she persisted. "What hospital is she in?"

He grunted something she couldn't understand. How peculiar, she thought, and how frightening, but before she could question him further, Janis's husband had gone off the line. Shirley held the dead phone in her hand, staring at it.

Randy packed up his family's things, bundled the two children into the car, and headed toward Interstate 5 to Seattle. He had told Jalina that her mother was in the hospital. As they drove out of Washougal, Jalina craned her neck to stare out the back window, and asked, "Couldn't we go just *see* her?"

"She can't have visitors," Randy answered.

They could be home in three and a half hours if traffic wasn't heavy. Despite Sandy Roth's offer to take care of his children until he made funeral arrangements for Janis and recovered a little from the shock of his sudden loss, he insisted on taking Jalina and Greg with him. He told his stepmother he was fine.

The rest of the family was not fine. It was difficult—well nigh impossible—for Sandy and Marcie and the boys he left behind in Washougal to cope with the thought that Jan had been there with them, laughing and smiling, at Thanksgiving dinner and now she was just gone.

Randy called no one in Janis's old world to tell them that she was dead. Not her mother. Not her sister. Not her best friend, Louise. Not Jalina's father, Joe Miranda.

Randy didn't even call his own best friend, Nick Emondi.

He could not stomach being the bearer of sad news. And there could be nothing sadder than the sudden end of his second marriage.

When he arrived in Seattle, Randy stopped by Louise Mitchell's house to pick up Janis's mail. Louise wasn't there, but her children were. He thanked them for keeping the mail. He did not tell them that Janis had fallen to her death the day before. Nor did he ask that they have Louise call him.

Nick Emondi called shortly after Randy got home. He was shocked to hear Randy say bluntly, "Janis is no longer with us."

When he finally realized what Randy was saying, Nick rushed over to Randy's to see if he could help out, but Randy seemed annoyed and sent him away, saying, "Everything is fine." Nick was back in his car before he recognized the smell in Randy's house. It was the aroma of cookies baking.

Randy called the mothers whose babies Janis had taken care of. He didn't tell them that she would never be able to look after their youngsters again; he just said they would need to find someone else to sit on Monday. One mother stopped by to pick up her playpen, and still, Randy never mentioned that Janis was dead.

Shock can do funny things to people. Randy Roth seemed to be in complete denial. He took care of business, and he took care of his children. He considered that Jalina was his, too; her mother was dead, and he was her father now. He baked cookies and tucked the children into bed. Sometime he would have to tell them that Janis had gone away forever. But not right away.

On that Saturday night one of the other receptionists at the clinic called Shirley Lenz to tell her she had just heard about the climbing accident on the radio. Janis wasn't recovering in a hospital; Janis was dead.

The two women could scarcely believe it. "Her husband didn't tell me," Shirley said. "He didn't even sound very upset."

The next day was Sunday, and Randy took Greg and Jalina to church. He saw his friends Ron and Nancy Aden there, friends whom Randy felt so close to that he had listed them as alternate beneficiaries on both his and Janis's life insurance policies.

Ron Aden grinned when he saw Randy and joked, "Where's your better-looking half?"

"She died."

"*What?*"

"She's dead," Randy repeated.

Dazed, Aden realized that Randy wasn't making an exceedingly tasteless joke. Janis *was* dead, and there seemed to be no comforting Randy. He was handling his loss in his own way, sitting there in the congregation dry-eyed as Ron directed the choir with wooden arms.

Randy was grieving stolidly, apparently unable to let himself cry any more. His friends concluded that he was forcing himself to stay strong for the children. They had never seen a human being exercise such control. The Adens were surprised to learn that Randy and Janis had listed them as alternate beneficiaries on their insurance policies. They had not known. It was academic anyway; thank God Randy was alive and well and able to care for the half-orphaned children.

Although Randy would have preferred not to have an autopsy performed on his wife, Skamania County Coroner Bob Leick ordered that a postmortem exam be done. It was standard in violent deaths. Dr. Eugene Blizard of Saint Joseph's Hospital in Vancouver performed the autopsy. There were no surprises. Jan Roth's petite body bore scratches and terrible head injuries, the expected result when a human skull comes into contact with rock outcroppings at the speed generated during a 300-foot fall. It wouldn't have mattered if they had found her a moment after she landed in the dark thicket of evergreens. No medical procedure could have saved her.

After the postmortem, Janis's body was cremated according to her widower's orders. He requested that her cremains be boxed and sent to his home.

Ultimately Jalina had to be told that her mother was dead. The story of the tragedy was headlined in the *Seattle Post-Intelligencer* on Sunday, November 29, 1981: "Hiking Accident Takes Life of Young Mother." Shirley Lenz called Randy on Monday to ask him when Janis's funeral would be. And then she asked him, "Why didn't you tell me she was dead when you called on Saturday?"

"I've never been able to tell bad news," he said quietly.

Poor little Janis, she thought. Poor, poor little Janis. Shirley could close her eyes and picture Janis's blissful face when she had brought in the bouquet from Randy. And now it was all over. So soon.

Randy did not tell Louise Mitchell that her best friend was dead until the Monday after the accident. Louise was devastated—and appalled—to think that he had come by her house, picked up his mail, and never said a word. Confronted, he confessed again that he simply could not bear to deliver such awful news to anyone— especially to Louise; he knew how close she and Jan had been.

It was Louise who notified Billy Jean Ray that her daughter was dead. She called Billy Jean on Monday, November 30, wondering how she was going to explain that Janis had been dead for more than two days already and only now was her mother being notified. "I only found out myself today," Louise explained. "And I was the only one who had your number."

Down in Skamania County, Ray Blaisdell had no way of knowing how strangely Randy Roth was reacting to being an instant widower. Still, Blaisdell tried to look at Janis Roth's death from all angles. Belatedly, he asked Roth to take a lie detector test. He pulled a fresh sheet of paper and printed a heading and a list:

Possible Reasons to Believe Death Was Other Than Accidental

1. No witnesses
2. Married March 13, 1981—Accident November 27, 1981
3. $100,000 life insurance policy—claim already filed for. $7500 under name of Janis Miranda. (No double indemnity.)
4. Refused to take polygraph examination.
5. Conflicting statements. Told me he was behind wife when she fell—told Bill Wiley he was ahead of her.
6. Roth didn't tell vic.'s best friend of her death. (Louise Mitchell very upset.)
7. Ex-husband asked not to attend funeral.

The Skamania County undersheriff had located Joe Miranda, and Miranda told him he was planning to come up and get Jalina. Janis's ex felt that at least half of any insurance Janis had should go to her daughter. "All she had of value in her life," Joe said, "was Jalina."

Jalina Miranda remembered what her mother had told her the day before they left for Washougal, although it seemed like a bad dream now. Janis had gone into the bedroom, pulled the little drawer out from the wall, and shown Jalina where the envelope was taped. She had shown her all the bills and papers and a couple of checks that had not been cashed. With her mother's voice leading her in her mind, the little girl hurried to the bedroom and repeated the same sequence of events.

Jalina held the envelope in her hand. She wasn't sure what she was supposed to do with it; she was only eight years old, and her mother was dead. She was heading toward her room when Randy walked up and asked her what she had in her hand.

Jalina held out the envelope and explained that her mother had told her to find it and keep it if anything bad ever happened. Randy reached for it and looked at the contents.

"This is something else she's been hiding from me," he said quietly. "I think I should take this, Jalina."

Jalina wasn't sure what to do. She liked Randy. He had been very good to her ever since she had known him—almost a whole year—and for an eight-year-old, a whole year is a very long time. But she kept hearing her mother's voice telling her that the envelope was their secret and that she mustn't tell anyone.

Randy still held the envelope. He was smiling when he said, "I'll keep it, and I'll use it to buy you presents."

He wasn't asking her a question; he was telling her what they should do, and that seemed all right to her. He was like her daddy. And he took good care of her.

Randy Roth had become the only security Jalina had, and she felt that she had no choice but to believe everything he told her.

Billie Ray had never met her daughter's new husband. In shock, she prepared to fly to Seattle for Janis's memorial service, which Roth informed her would take place on Friday, December 4. She and her daughter, Sharon Waldrep, arrived in Seattle before dawn on the morning of the service, and they had reservations to fly out the next morning. They were not invited to stay at the Roth home and checked into a motel.

Somehow it seemed as if they could handle Janis's sudden death more easily if they just knew more about it, but Randy didn't volunteer any information about the accident and he answered their questions with the briefest responses. He seemed very calm and under control, but they didn't know the man at all. They had no idea what normal behavior might be for him. Billie Ray knew from Janis's letters that Randy still had flashbacks and nightmares from his marine service in Vietnam; she didn't want to ask him too many questions for fear of making everything worse.

On the Tuesday after Janis fell, December 1, Joe Miranda arrived in Seattle to pick up his daughter. Randy was adamant that he didn't want Joe in his home, nor did he want Jalina to go and live with her natural father.

Jalina didn't want to leave Randy, either; he was the only father she remembered. He had always been kind to her, and she had grown to love Greg like her own little brother. But her father and his new wife wanted her. Her real daddy loved her, although Randy didn't tell her that; he seemed furious as he threw a few of her things in a bag and delivered her to Joe Miranda.

With all he had on his mind, Randy never got around to buying the "presents" he had promised Jalina he would buy with the money that Jan had put aside for her daughter. Nor did he mention the money to Miranda. Randy didn't give Jalina any of her mothers' clothes, jewelry, or keepsakes. He didn't even give her a picture of Janis. He told her to pack what she wanted. She was only eight years old; she didn't know what to take. He sent her down to Texas with little more than the clothes on her back. He later explained that glibly enough: he thought she was only going for a Christmas visit and would be coming back to live with him.

But Jalina never came back. In the years ahead, Jalina Miranda never heard from her stepfather again, and she didn't get one penny of the money her dead mother had saved so carefully for her. If her mother had left her a letter, she never got that, either.

Randy told Billie Ray that Janis had just taken out an insurance policy but he wasn't sure if the face value was enough to cover her funeral. Either he was lying or his memory was clouded, because $107,500 would pay for the most lavish of funerals.

Janis's memorial service at the Silver Lake Chapel was not lavish. The funeral home in Camas had charged Randy only $541 to cremate her. The service in December was simple and tasteful. Randy explained that he had arranged to have a hand-carved wooden chest made to hold his dead wife's ashes, but it wasn't done in time. He broke down at the funeral and sobbed as if he would never get over losing her. Shirley Lenz, curious about Janis's husband, noted that. So did the Adens. They vowed to have Randy and Greg and Jalina over for dinner often in the next weeks and months.

But Jalina was gone, living somewhere down in Texas, and Joe

Miranda wanted nothing to do with Randy Roth. Randy and Greg were alone again, "batching it" and trying to recover from the loss of the woman who had brought warmth and love into their home for such a short time.

Randy was so grateful to the Adens for their support that he took their family along when he and Greg flew to California for a vacation at Disneyland. He insisted on paying for everything. When they saw how much it meant to him to have them share the Disneyland trip, they were touched. Randy seemed to long for a family, and he had almost created one with Janis. The Adens felt sorry for him; he had lost Jan and then Jalina.

A hundred and fifty miles away, Skamania County detective Mike Grossie, Paramedic Duane Hathaway, and State Park Ranger Don Bauer climbed Beacon Rock to the approximate point where Janis Roth was reported to have fallen. It was a shortcut off the main trail, and it led up a small dirt and rock cutoff trail to a second cutoff trail that ran along a rock ridgeline. They could see that if someone went south along the rocky ridge, he or she would have an exposed rock cliff on either side. The climber could go no more than a hundred yards before coming to a sheer dropoff to the southwest. To the northeast, the trail cut up through some small trees and came out onto the main trail close to the summit of Beacon Rock.

Apparently, after getting to the top of the first cutoff trail, the victim had fallen to her death off the left-hand side of the trail. Near the place where they had been told that Janis had fallen, there were several protruding roots and brushy shrubs that she might have grabbed hold of. The mud was hard, just as it had been on November 27, and there was no standing water or ice on the trail. Bauer could walk easily at least twenty feet down the slope that led to the ravine without fear of plunging over.

Odd.

The three investigators had no difficulty keeping their balance on the shortcut, although they did have to crawl on their hands and knees to get to the top. Once they got there, they were able to stand up, although they noted that the slope of the rock made them all automatically bend forward as they turned to the right.

"It sure would be possible," Grossie speculated, "for someone to fall from this spot—if she was accidentally bumped or if her back was to the ravine."

Randy had said something about Janis taking a picture at this height, but he didn't have their camera when the deputies found him, nor had they found a camera on or near Janis. It might have been caught in the trees below, just as her gold necklace probably was.

The investigators now took photographs from both sides of the trail and then aimed their cameras over the edge, catching the trees, the fields, and even the mighty Columbia River far below in their lens.

The view was awesomely beautiful and, given the circumstances, ultimately chilling.

Down and down and down.

4

On January 24, 1982, Detective Mike Grossie traveled to Mountlake Terrace and talked with Randy Roth in the kitchen of the home he had shared with Janis Roth. Mike Grossie could hear a man's voice somewhere in the house, but Roth didn't offer to introduce whoever it was and Grossie didn't ask.

Nick Emondi had come over to entertain Greg at Randy's request. Curious, he shushed Greg and listened to Randy repeat his story of the tragic accident.

The more he had thought about it, Randy told Grossie, the more he blamed himself for letting Jan climb Beacon Rock wearing slippery leather-soled shoes. Sure, it had been at his wife's insistence that they climbed the rock that day after Thanksgiving, but he should have known better than to let her talk him into it. If he had only refused to indulge her crazy romantic impulse to climb the mountain that day, he wouldn't have lost her forever.

Despite Randy's grieved expression, Grossie noted that he kept veering off the subject of Jan's accident, and he would not sit down and talk with Grossie; Randy was continually doing dishes, wiping down counters, and sweeping the kitchen floor as they talked. It was unsettling to talk to a man about his dead wife while he went about his chores. Grossie would remember that Roth had rarely, if ever, looked him in the eye.

Randy Roth's main concern was what he should do with his wife's ashes. Where to store them was his "biggest worry." Grossie had no opinion on that; he was a frustrated detective.

It was a most unsatisfactory interview.

After Grossie had gone, Nick Emondi walked into the kitchen and stared hard at Randy. He had heard everything that was said in the interview with the Skamania County detective.

"What's going on?"

Randy looked away. "Don't ask me to tell you something you'll have to lie about."

Long acquaintance had taught Emondi not to press his luck, and he asked nothing more.

While the officers of the Skamania County Sheriff's Office kept their death investigation file open on the tragic demise of Janis Miranda Roth, they were having difficulty finding evidence that would prove her fall was anything but accidental. They didn't have solid physical evidence, and they didn't have any eyewitnesses to Jan's actual fall from Beacon Rock. They only had witnesses after the fact.

It was quite possible that the case would have to be closed and stamped "Accidental Death."

The early months of 1982 were hard for Billie Jean Ray. She had lost not only her daughter but also her granddaughter; she hadn't seen Jalina since Jalina had left Texas. She wrote to her dead daughter's second husband, and Randy answered quickly: "I received your letter today and felt compelled to respond immediately that the facts might be properly presented. First of all, Joe never asked for any shot records at all; he wanted a death certificate, birth certificate, and a Social Security number. These items are necessary for him to collect monthly payments from Jan's Social Security for Jalina. I informed him that I was aware of how he was handling Jalina and would not help him. The sheriff had already informed me that Joe was trying to get in on insurance money so I was very abrupt. I absolutely will not cooperate with him while he is circling like a buzzard looking for easy money!" But if anyone had been circling like a buzzard, it had been Randy—not Joe.

Randy went on to prophesy that Jalina's life would not be happy with the Mirandas, which didn't ease Billie Jean's mind any, but he ended with a cheery report on the weather in Seattle. He said that he and Greg were staying really busy, "working and playing all day, and cutting wood," he ended, "so life can go on."

He promised to send Billie Ray a picture of Jan and some of Jan's things so that she could save them for Jalina.

He never did. He had so much on his mind.

Randy had cogent reasons to want to block Joe Miranda's application for Social Security survivor's benefits payments for Jalina. He himself had already applied for benefits for Jalina on December 14, a little over two weeks after her mother died, and twelve days after Joe Miranda had taken her back to Texas.

"Jalina is in my custody," Randy had told the Social Security interviewer. "She's with relatives in Texas for Christmas." Although Joe Miranda had given him his phone number in Texas, Randy said he had no way to reach him—no number, no address.

Randy was also applying on Greg's behalf. Although Jan hadn't given birth to Greg, Randy was gratified to learn that she had been Greg's stepmother just long enough for the little boy to qualify for Social Security payments as if she had been his own mother. After the Social Security representative processed the applications, Randy began receiving payments monthly for both Greg and Jalina.

When Jalina never returned from Texas, however, the Social Security Administration learned that she was not living with Randy Roth. He was required to reimburse the government for the benefit checks he had received and cashed for her.

"It was a question of interpretation," Randy explained. "I *was* attempting to get legal custody of Jalina. My intent was to contact the Social Security office and inform them [that she was not living with him]. In *my* mind, I had not relinquished custody of Jalina."

Randy had a great deal of paperwork to wade through. He furnished all the documents that Darrel Lundquist asked for to facilitate the payoff of the $100,000 Farmers VIP policy on Janis's life, and waited months for a decision on that. He had also remembered that he had an older policy with Allstate Insurance; anyone who had a Sears charge card could elect to have a family policy for $7,500 accidental death benefits. Randy had taken it out for himself and Greg, and when he married Janis, she became part of that. He had that policy for years before he met his second wife, but he suddenly remembered it and filed for those benefits, too.

It was ironic. When Jan was alive, they had struggled so hard to meet their financial obligations. Now that she was gone, Randy no longer had to worry about money.

He filed his 1981 tax return as a widower, listing only his own income from Vitamilk. He didn't file for Jan; his late wife had done all her own paperwork for her day-care business, and he said later that he couldn't find it. When the IRS contacted him by mail about the fact that Janis Miranda Roth had not filed a return for 1981, he wrote back, explaining that she was deceased. He heard no more from them.

Even though his friends tried to make things easier for him and for Greg, Randy said he could scarcely bear to live in the home he had shared with Jan for only three months. "I had a lot of bad feelings about being in the house. . . . We bought the house together. It was the house that she wanted," he would say sadly. "It was her dream house. . . . I don't know that I would have been able to feel comfortable and live in that house."

Besides that, he was having trouble making the $871 monthly payments on the new house now that he didn't have Janis's baby-sitting income to add to his paycheck. He couldn't keep up with his utility bills or other pressing commitments, either. He didn't know if he would ever get the $100,000 due him on Jan's insurance. "The thought hadn't occurred to me that I could borrow money [on the insurance policy] to make house payments."

Randy received the $7,500 from the Allstate policy and gave $5,000 of it to a real estate agent to sell the house he could no longer bear to live in. "I felt bad and empty being in the house. . . . This was my first house, and it was her first house to buy."

Because he had no equity built up, it cost him money to sell the house. He sold it to the listing agent.

On March 23, 1982, Randy received the proceeds of Jan's $100,000 policy. Policy #1611546 with Farmer's New World Life Insurance Company paid $100,014.11. The $14.11 was a premium refund for money automatically withdrawn from Randy's bank account after Janis was already dead. With the money, Randy was finally able to move to another house, where he and Greg hoped to patch their lives back together. He had found a house in the Amber Hills district of Bothell, Washington.

Randy put $50,000 of Jan's insurance down on the house, which cost $89,950. His mortgage payments were far lower than what he and Jan had paid on the Mountlake Terrace house, and he had a solid equity besides.

In his loneliness, Randy had turned to Lily Vandiveer, his one-time baby-sitter, for comfort. The question of whether their affair was platonic or intimate is obscured by supposition and gossip. Lily's husband, Karl Vandiveer,* later said they had once been lovers, and he believed they had never stopped. He said he came home early on one occasion and found them stretched out in front of the fireplace in an intimate embrace. He confronted Randy. "I told him to stay away from my house [or] I was going to the [Skamania County] prosecuting attorney."

The relationship, which Lily insisted was only a matter of two old friends having lunch together from time to time, ended abruptly even though Karl Vandiveer never did report it to the Skamania County investigators. In truth, that threat had been a bluff. There was something about Randy Roth that stopped him. "Hell," Vandiveer said, "I was afraid of him."

Even without Lily's emotional support, Randy Roth's life, which had seemed so bleak, was looking up. He put many thousands of dollars and his own sweat into landscaping his new yard. He had the finest roses on the block, velvety grass, and lush evergreens. He might have spent $5,000; it might have been $10,000. He wasn't sure. He turned his Amber Hills home into a showplace.

Randy put the balance of the insurance payoff in the bank to use over the next few years. He had been pinched for money for so long, and suddenly he no longer was. He spent freely. He bought two motorcycles, one for himself and one for Nick Emondi. He loaned Nick and his wife $1,500. He bought two chain saws so that he and Nick could cut firewood for extra income.

Somewhat surprisingly, Randy and Greg didn't live in the new house in Amber Hills for very long—only two years. Randy's money from the insurance settlements hadn't lasted as long as he expected, and his large equity in the home didn't help him with his monthly bills as much as he thought it would.

In May of 1984 he sold the Amber Hills place for exactly what he had paid for it, despite all his landscaping improvements. He had a cash offer and took it. He bought a house at 3012 169th S.E. in Misty Meadows, a pleasant area less than two miles away.

The Misty Meadows home was only in the $70,000–$75,000 bracket, but it was very nice. Randy kept some of his cash-out money for expenses, and he loaned Nick Emondi another $4,000, this time so Nick could buy a double-wide mobile home to put on some property Emondi had purchased.

Emondi, who now worked for a local fire department, remained ambivalent about Randy. Ever since Randy had asked, "Could you kill your wife?" on that Halloween night weeks before Janis died, Nick had tried to pull away from Randy. But that wasn't easy to do. No one left Randy; *he* had to be the one who decided a relationship was over, and quite frankly, Nick needed money badly and Randy had it to lend. They agreed that the Emondis would repay Randy in baby-sitting. Carrie would take care of Greg, and for each week of child care, Randy would reduce the amount of their debt by fifty dollars. In two and a half years they would be even. But then, suddenly, Randy moved Greg to Lily Vandiveer's home. Nick promised to make payments on the debt, but he wasn't making enough to repay the $200 a month Randy demanded.

Randy's newest home was painted brown and cream, a pseudo-Norman split level with massive exposed beams. It was built on a cul-de-sac where Greg could play outside safely. The lot was pie-shaped. Randy planned to landscape this yard and make it the most beautiful on the block. There was a tall stand of fir trees out in back of all the homes on their block and, behind that, an easement where high-power lines hummed and throbbed.

Misty Meadows was a friendly neighborhood. There was an older couple right across the cul-de-sac who doted on Greg and were like foster grandparents. Best of all for Randy, another couple, Ben and Marta Goodwin, whom Randy had known since 1982 through Greg, moved from a rental a few blocks away and became his next-door neighbors. Their son Ryan was Greg's age, and they had an older boy named Travis and a daughter, Brittany. Randy hadn't seen his own brother, David, for a long time, and Ben became like a brother to him, just as Randy became Ben Goodwin's best friend.

Randy was an avid classic car buff, and he had always supplemented his salary by buying older cars, fixing them up until they were in cherry condition, and reselling them. He and Ben Goodwin both admired old Chevy pickups.

Ben, a handsome but laconic Vietnam vet half a dozen years older than Randy, recalls the first time he ever saw Randy Roth: "He was driving down the street in a 1973 Chevy pickup—just like mine, except it was gold—and I said to Marta, 'Now, that looks like my kind of guy.' I guess those old trucks made us friends first. His Chevy was just like mine, only it was a four-wheel drive, and he was pulling a trailer all full of stuff. He missed the turn, and then I saw him coming back, and he turned into our street, and that's the first time I ever saw him."

Ben and Marta Goodwin would become perhaps the best friends Randy Roth ever had in his life. Their closeness would last for almost a decade, and they would share traditions as if they were family and not just neighbors. Randy had no family any longer—not since Jan died—but with the Goodwins he did.

The Goodwins saw a side of Randy that no one else ever glimpsed. Although they never forgot the good times they shared, their closeness would cost them dearly.

Marta was a pretty, slightly plump woman in her late twenties, and Ben was a whipcord-tough six-footer in his mid-thirties when they met. Ben came from a huge family; he'd made his own way, and he had seen a great deal of action in Vietnam. Randy confided that he, too, had been in the thick of battle in Nam and hinted at darkly violent missions that had left him with nightmares.

"He was my best friend for eight years," Ben Goodwin recalls. "But we knew he hated women. He especially hated women who he said 'looked like whores.' He was always nice to Marta, respectful—as if she represented his ideal of what a woman should be."

Perhaps she did. Marta never saw Randy do anything wrong. He seemed to want her to see him as perfect. When she quit smoking, a habit Randy detested, he sent her flowers. But he never even came close to making a pass at her.

She was the perfect wife. The perfect mother.

Ben Goodwin's first meeting with Randy was anything but cordial. Ben Goodwin is a brusque, sometimes artless man. He loves his own kids and is concerned about all kids. Long before Randy and the Goodwins became next-door neighbors, when Ryan Goodwin was six and in the first grade, he asked if Greg Roth could come home with him and stay after school at their house every day.

"Where's his mom?" Ben asked.

"He doesn't have a mom," Ryan explained. "His mom fell off a cliff, and his dad has to work all day. See, here's his picture."

The child in the school picture was adorable, with cheeks like a little chipmunk, and small. He looked about four years old. The Goodwins stared at each other as they realized that six-year-old Greg went home to an empty house every day after school and spent hours alone. Ben marched over to Randy's house and punched him in the chest and demanded, "Look, you s.o.b., what do you mean leaving that little kid all by himself?"

That should not have been the propitious beginning to a friendship, but it was. They worked it out without an argument. Randy said he was a widower who had just moved into the neighborhood, and he didn't know anyone who could look after Greg. Marta felt sorry for him and agreed to look after Greg until Randy got home from work. Ben and Randy soon found they had a lot in common. Cars and rock and roll golden oldies, camping, and, of course, their service in Vietnam.

Randy was a good-looking man with a well-trimmed beard and mustache. He had dark brown eyes, and, although he was short, he had the massive biceps of a weight lifter. There wasn't anything he didn't know about the innards of a car. He was definitely a man's man.

As Randy got to know the Goodwins, he confided in them, sharing memories of his own bleak childhood. He explained that his mother was now very old and bedridden, too senile for him to visit, but he remembered how she had punished him when he was very small. "He said she made him take his pants off and kneel on the tile floor in the kitchen for hours until his father got home from work to punish him," Marta recalls. "He didn't talk much at all about his brother or sisters."

He did not talk at *all* about Janis. They hadn't the vaguest notion that Randy's marital history was complicated. They had heard only that he was a widower and the story Ryan repeated about Greg's mom falling off a cliff.

Ben finally mentioned that story to Randy, and Randy acknowledged that it was true that Janis had fallen, but it was too painful for him to discuss. The Goodwins believed Randy had only been married once. They didn't know that there had been a wife before Janis— Donna Sanchez Roth, who was Greg's natural mother. "He never volunteered *anything* about the women in his past," Marta remembers. "He'd answer questions, but he wouldn't tell you much."

Randy Roth came into the Goodwins' life "like a whirlwind." He was the most energetic man either of them had ever met, and he was a truly good neighbor. After Ben mentioned casually that they had to do something about cleaning out an eyesore area in their front yard, they woke one Sunday at seven to hear the roaring of a Rototiller. Randy tilled the yard and then shrugged off their thanks. When they wanted to cut down a tree that was growing too close to their back deck, Randy said, "You want it down? Let's take it down," and took a running leap off the deck, clung to the fir twenty feet off the ground, rocked it back and forth with ever-widening swings, and rode it to the ground when it snapped at the base.

"That was Randy. If something needed to be done, he did it right now."

He was a little guy, but powerful. In one day, he built a 200-square-foot outbuilding to use as a gym and weight room, amazing Ben Goodwin. He and his friend Nick sawed and split wood all day long to earn extra money, and Randy never tired. He could split a log into five sections at a time for firewood. He looked like a teenager, but Ben knew he had to be older because he'd served in Vietnam.

Ben had a bronze plaque honoring his marine service. On one of his few visits to Randy's house, he was a little surprised to see that Randy had an identical plaque on his wall with his own name emblazoned on it. Randy was totally gung ho about the marines. He had his picture on the wall in his dress blues and innumerable shoulder patches and framed memorabilia. While Ben would just as soon have forgotten Vietnam, Randy was obsessed with his service years, as hellish as they might have been.

"For the eight years I knew him," Ben says, "he wore marine camouflage fatigues, and he had his kid and my boys wearing them. On patriotic holidays he wore his uniform. I told him the only difference between us was I wanted to forget Vietnam and he kept reminding himself about it."

The Goodwins found their new neighbor fascinating. "He kept us active," Marta recalled. "With Randy around, we couldn't stay home and watch television. We had a good time. He would come over and drag us out to go motorcycle riding, river rafting, or out to dinner. He'd call up and say, 'Hey, I got a car for us to look at,' or 'Let's go look at the Christmas lights.' You couldn't say no to him. He could cheer anybody up. Every year he went out and chopped us a Christmas tree—never one for him, but he always got ours."

There was one television show that Randy never missed, however. Every Thursday night, religiously, Randy came over to the Goodwins' to watch "The Cosby Show." He always brought an apple pie and a gallon of vanilla ice cream for them all to eat while they watched.

"I asked him once," Marta says, "why he didn't bring lemon meringue or blueberry pie once in a while, and he just looked at me solemnly and said, 'Ben likes apple.'"

The macho ex-marine was an immaculate housekeeper and a good cook too. A perfectionist. He cooked for himself and Greg most of the time, although they were frequent guests at the Goodwins' table. Randy almost always contributed something. He made the dressing for the holiday turkeys, he baked date cookies, and one year when Ben cooked Thanksgiving dinner, Randy furnished the dessert: a rather bizarre-looking angel food cake with bright blue frosting. Everyone ate it so that his feelings wouldn't be hurt.

He was a paradox, though, and the longer the Goodwins knew Randy Roth, the sharper the dichotomy in his personality became. He would help in any way he could, but there was a quality about him— a "watching sense"; he was someone who stood off to one side and studied people. There was a calculating air about Randy, as if he was always taking someone's measure and thinking his own private thoughts. The Goodwins put it down to some residue of his experiences in Vietnam.

Ben and Marta knew he was strict with Greg and that he thought they spoiled Ryan, Travis, and Brittany. "We let the kids take turns unloading the dishwasher—you know, bottom, top, and silverware—and for some reason that bothered him. He said it wasn't efficient; they should each unload the whole thing for a week. It was a dumb thing, but it drove him nuts. Greg did all the chores by himself and without question."

Randy bought Greg the very latest and most expensive toys. He had a Nintendo and dozens of games to go with it as soon as they came on the market. Greg had new four-wheelers three times a year and expensive bicycles. It was hard for Ben Goodwin to explain to his sons why Greg had so many things; he couldn't hope to keep up, even though he had a good job at Safeway, while Randy never seemed to hold a steady job. In fact, Ben was puzzled at how Randy managed to afford all the toys, especially when he was cut back to half time at Vitamilk.

Randy hugged Greg and often told him he loved him. Greg always called Randy when he got home from school to talk to him. No one could deny that there was a strong bond between the little boy and the only constant parent in his life. Greg rarely spoke of his natural mother, who visited infrequently, and Janis had been in his life for less than a year. His father was always there.

And yet there was a dark side to Randy's parenting. Maybe it was the vicious circle that all social workers recognize: an abused child becomes an abusive parent.

"Greg could say thank you, but he was not allowed to say please," Marta Goodwin remembers. "Randy told Greg that 'please' was a 'begging word' and he must never beg for anything."

Greg was disciplined as harshly as any young marine in boot camp. When he forgot to put the garbage can out one scheduled pickup day, Randy dumped the whole can and spread the trash all over the cul-de-sac. In the pouring rain he made Greg gather the refuse up with his hands. "He was out there on his hands and knees, and he got it all picked up," Marta recalls. "All except for one little scrap of paper. When Randy saw that, he dumped it all out again, and Greg had to start all over."

If anything was out of place in Greg's room, Randy ransacked the closet, the drawers, stripped the bed—everything—and made Greg put every item back in place. Ryan Goodwin had seen that happen, but Marta and Ben never had. They thought Ryan was exaggerating until they saw the garbage can incident.

The worst example of Randy's discipline came when Greg's third grade teacher called him and said Greg hadn't turned in his homework. Randy grounded his son. Greg completed his homework all right, but he apparently was so frightened that it might not be perfect that he didn't turn it in. The third time his teacher called, Randy was livid, so angry he was frightened by his own rage. "He called me at work," Ben says. "He asked if Greg could stay at our house for a few days because he was afraid of what he might do to him. We said fine, and Greg came over with his sleeping bag and his little suitcase."

But Randy called at nine the first night and summoned Greg home. He had changed his mind. Randy told Ben he was fine, all cooled off. Ben questioned him carefully; he wasn't about to send Greg home if Randy was still out of control, and in his own rough way Ben warned Randy that he would have to answer to him if Greg was harmed.

"No, no, I'm fine. No problem," Randy said easily. He sounded perfectly calm.

But he wasn't. That night Greg forgot to flush the toilet, and Randy erupted. He held Greg's head in the toilet and flushed it again and again until the boy almost drowned, and then he kicked him in the stomach until Greg vomited.

Ryan Goodwin heard about it the next morning when he could see that Greg winced with pain and favored his stomach. Eight-year-old Ryan marched into the principal's office at school and told on Greg's father. Randy was reported to Children's Protective Service and put on probation; he didn't speak to Ryan Goodwin for months.

But he still came over to the Goodwins every Thursday night with pie and ice cream to watch "The Cosby Show," about the perfect American family where no one ever got angry and each episode ended happily.

There were so many things about their bachelor neighbor that the Goodwins didn't know, so many little lies and so much cruelty that lay just beneath his almost boyish veneer. Randy did not care for animals. When another neighbor's cat left footprints all over the hood of his newly waxed car, he didn't complain to the owner. Instead, he caught the cat and bound it to the drive shaft of its owner's car with duct tape.

When the car's engine started, the cat was quickly dismembered, its screams muffled by the sounds of the engine.

One of the young women who worked with Randy would never forget Randy's idea of a joke. She had found a little frog and had shown it to Randy. Later he called her into the shop and pointed to a damp spot that no longer resembled anything alive; he had placed the frog under a rotary sander. He laughed when she started to cry.

It might have been Randy's "family" relationship with the Goodwins that made him distance himself from Nick Emondi, or it might have been one of the surest destroyers of friendship: money. Nick and Carrie were unable to repay the money they had borrowed as quickly as Randy wanted, and he bombarded them with letters that had the thinnest edge of threat in them:

The first was scrawled on the back of a torn envelope, "Nick, I received a bankruptcy letter, and if you are treating *me* the same as all your creditors and have no intention of paying back the money, then we have got some serious talking to do. I can't believe you would destroy the most valuable thing I know—faith and trust of friendship. Call me so I know what is goin' on." The letter was signed, "Randy."

When Nick did not respond with payment, Randy wrote again: "Nick and Carrie, I would like you guys to consider—*seriously consider*—payments of $75 a month until the money is repaid. I am somewhat disappointed that you have given me to date only $50 toward the loan. I lent you the money against my better judgement for fear something like this would happen. However, I gave it to you in good faith and trusted you to repay a thousand dollars a year. I believed you, Nick, and that is the only reason I went against my instinct. . . . You have made no attempt to make good. Our friendship is very much cherished by me and I don't want to lose it over this."

Randy went on and on about his hurt and his disappointment that his faith in his old friend had been misplaced. He had always been the dominant man in their friendship, and Nick had walked softly around him. Now Nick had betrayed him where he lived. Money was very, very important to Randy. Even though Randy was the one who changed the terms of repayment, his resentment over Nick's failure to return his money ate at him.

On July 30, 1984, someone spray-painted obscene threats on Nick Emondi's home.

Randy finally recouped his money from Nick after Emondi's home was burglarized in January of 1985. Nick Emondi's insurance was enough to pay back his old friend.

PART TWO

The Second Donna

5

Marta and Ben Goodwin were surprised that Randy seemed in no hurry to remarry. Greg needed a mother, and Randy was certainly attractive to women. He never had a problem getting dates. To begin with, he was a good-looking man and he could flash a heart-melting smile. Beyond that, he had Greg, who was cute enough to do commercials. It was hard for pretty young women to say no to the adorable little boy who approached them and said, "Would you go out with my dad?" At the very least, the majority of women Greg approached—always on Randy's orders—agreed to meet Greg's father. And a lot of them found the father as appealing as the son.

Randy dated, but he moved from one woman to another, changing partners as often as he bought and sold automobiles.

And then, as 1984 came to an end, he met Donna Clift. She was his second Donna. His first wife, Donna Sanchez, seemed relegated to his distant past. Randy explained to Donna Clift that Greg's mother had not been the mother Randy hoped she would be. And Donna Clift respected him because he didn't bad-mouth his first wife beyond that simple statement. He had had a second wife too, he said softly, but he was now a widower. She didn't press him for details.

Donna was twenty-one, a young divorcée (who had taken back her parents' surname) with a three-year-old daughter. She had moved to the Seattle area on December 1, 1984, to be close to her father and stepmother, Harvey and Judy Clift. She was a very attractive young woman with long brown hair and a perfect figure.

Donna had taken a job as a clerk at the Plaid Pantry, one of a chain of twenty-four-hour fast-service markets. This one was in Bothell, close to Randy's Misty Meadows neighborhood. She had only worked there for a day or two before she noticed the darkly handsome man. They made eye contact and smiled a few times. She was five feet four inches tall, and he seemed no more than an inch and a half taller than she was, but he was very muscular and there was just something about him that she liked. "His eyes. When he stared at me with those dark, dark eyes, I was drawn right into them."

Donna didn't realize then that Randy had the large bright eyes that most nearsighted people do, lovely to look at but almost blind. He would not wear glasses, but his vision was corrected with contact lenses.

When Randy sent Greg up to the counter to buy something, Donna looked over at Randy and smiled. Randy and Greg asked her how long she had lived in Bothell, and she explained she was fresh from Arizona and didn't know anyone. Randy asked her if she would like to go out to dinner. He said he belonged to Parents Without Partners, but he hadn't met anyone who was right for him—and for Greg. He suggested that maybe Donna would like to go to a PWP dance.

Just as he had been for Janis Miranda, Randy Roth seemed the perfect man for Donna Clift, the suitor that a young mother alone hopes for but doesn't really expect to find. Donna soon responded to the double whammy of two lovable males, Randy and Greg, a seemingly inseparable duo.

Donna Clift had gotten pregnant right out of high school. "I wasn't prepared for it," she said. "It really devastated me." She married her baby's father, but they were too young. "It didn't work," she recalled. Now Donna was escaping Arizona and the ashes of a burned-out marriage. She was lonely, despite the open-armed welcome she had received from her father and her stepmother.

Brittany was three, a beguiling blond little girl. Greg Roth was seven, a sweet kid who deserved to have a mother. When Randy took Donna to see the house he had recently sold—the Amber Hills home—she was very impressed. It was huge and very expensive-looking. The Misty Meadows home next to Ben and Marta where he currently lived was very nice too, and perfectly kept—if a little Spartan. There no pictures on the wall, no homey touches. Rather, he had a weird medieval-looking weapon hanging on his bed, a chain with two balls. He had a club with nails poking out. Throwing Stars. Macho things.

But all the landscaping Randy had done was wonderful. He seemed to have a real affinity for growing things, and he pointed out bushes and trees that would bloom come spring.

"Randy never came across like he just wanted me to go to bed with him. It didn't seem important to him. He just seemed to like *me* for me."

Nevertheless, he proved to be a wonderful lover. He was sweet and passionate. He called Donna all the time. He sent her a dozen American Beauty roses three or four times a week. He bought her a solid gold necklace and *two* leather coats. "They were exactly my size, and they were *fitted* coats; I don't know how he knew just what to buy.

"I thought he was really handsome and well built. He had a beard and a mustache. I thought his son was really well mannered. I thought it was really neat that a single parent could be a man."

Donna Clift's parents met Randy and they liked him. Randy explained that he was working part-time at Vitamilk Dairy and that he also worked the graveyard shift as a chemist in Lynnwood.

"How can you leave Greg alone all night?" Donna asked, horrified.

"I just tuck him into bed and make sure he's asleep, and then I go to my night job. I have no choice."

Donna already loved Greg, and she hated the thought of his being alone every night. She worked the graveyard shift often herself. She knew Randy was out late at night because there were many nights when he came to her house and threw pebbles at her window at two or three in the morning. When she peered out the window, she could barely see him. He was like a dark ghost, dressed all in black. She could hear him call out softly, but he darted around the yard just out of her line of vision and then another pebble would drop next to her window. It didn't scare her—not really—but it gave Donna Clift a prickly sensation along the back of her neck.

"I told him not to do that because my dad would be mad."

Perhaps not. Donna Clift's father and teenage brother, Todd, found Randy energetic and fun to be with. Randy and Greg were welcomed into Donna's family almost from the beginning.

At Christmas 1984, Randy gave Donna's parents a studio portrait of himself and Greg. On the back, Randy wrote, "Dec–84, Randy (30 years) & Greg (7 years)—To Mom & Dad, Love, The Roths."

It was kind of sad, Randy trying to make himself and Greg sound like a whole big family when there were only the two of them.

Just as he had with the Goodwins, Randy drew Donna's family into his life-style of outdoor exercise, camping, rafting. He *was* fun to be with.

Randy told Donna about his days in the marines, haltingly—as if the memories were so full of pain that he could hardly stand to speak of them. He had been in a Special Forces unit, he explained, with only ten highly trained men. "He told me that one night they had to kill a whole village of women and children in Vietnam. He was so

badly wounded himself that he had to be in a special hospital for
ninety days."

Randy had scrapbooks filled with gruesome pictures, including
photographs of bodies lying in ditches in Vietnam. It helped Donna
to understand why he had such terrible nightmares. He was still
reliving his marine days. He had stacks of military magazines like
Soldier of Fortune, and he once gave her a book on Vietnam, suggesting
that she read it: "If you want to see what I've been through, read this.
The authors interviewed me, and this part in the book is about me. It
is me."

The book explained a lot to Donna. Randy had been through hell.

And his life had continued to be marked by tragedy. Randy
explained to a stunned Donna Clift how his second wife, Jan, had
died. This was why he had been as lonesome as she was, maybe more
so. Donna Sanchez had left him and Greg, and he had lost Jan in a
tragic accident. Painfully, Randy described how he and Jan had been
taking a shortcut down a mountain. "I was in front of her. I heard
gravel . . ."

Donna held his hand as he said that Jan had slipped on pine
needles and rocks, describing how he had grabbed her but couldn't
hold on and had to watch helplessly as she fell to her death.

His memories of the tragedy made Donna cry. What a terrible
thing for him to have gone through—and how awful for Greg too.

Randy never told Donna he loved her—not in so many words. She
was infatuated with him, and she understood that a lot of men never
said "I love you"—even if they did love a woman. Randy seemed to
her a highly educated man; he used big words and spoke in a careful,
almost emotionless manner. What he did say to Donna was, "I want
to make an investment in you."

"Why are you doing all this for me?" she asked. "All these
presents?"

And he answered again, "I want to make an investment in you."

Donna Clift took that as a sign of Randy Roth's love.

Although she had some reservations about Randy, Donna couldn't
help falling in love. She felt Randy was too rough on Greg, his
punishments too harsh in her view, but she thought she could talk
Randy into taking it easier on his son if they were all living together.
She was sure there was a sensitive, loving man under all that macho
veneer.

On Valentine's Day, Randy took Donna out to dinner and dancing at the Top of the Hilton. It was an incredibly romantic evening. At just the right moment he produced a small velvet box. There was a ring inside, gold with a tiny diamond set in a swirl of black onyx. A gold wedding band would nest beside the diamond. She accepted the ring, believing that he truly did love her.

The flowers and the presents continued to arrive, and Randy urged Donna and her daughter to move in with him and Greg. In March 1985 she agreed. "My mom didn't like it at all. She's really my stepmother—but I call her 'Mom.' We're close. She was always telling me to go slow with Randy, but I was infatuated. I guess I shut my eyes to a lot of things I should have seen more clearly."

Shortly after Donna Clift moved in with Randy, she cleared out the floor of the bedroom closet so she could put her shoes away. At the bottom of a jumble of Randy's clothes and shoes she found a black box; at first she thought it was a videotape. She carried it to the light and saw that it was not an overdue movie rental. The name Janis L. Roth was written on the top of the black plastic box. Randy had not even gotten Jan's middle initial right.

Donna had inadvertently stumbled across her predecessor's ashes. The cremains of Janis Roth had been in the closet even as Donna shared the bed with Randy.

"At first I was really upset. Why would he still have them? And then I tried to think of reasons that Randy kept her ashes there. I'd had a friend who kept her husband's ashes near her, and I tried to tell myself that it could just be a loving thing to do. But not like that—not just shoved under everything in the closet. I went over to my mom's house. Randy knew where I'd be—I didn't know anyone else. He came over, and he was sweating bullets. He told me that he 'just forgot' about Jan's ashes. He said, 'I'll take care of them,' and he came home later and told me he had thrown them in Silver Lake. He showed me the box, and it was empty. Later I found he'd thrown the box away in the garbage."

There was another occasion that startled Donna Clift. She and Randy were still just living together when he brought home a stack of papers. He explained they were insurance applications, and Donna somehow got the impression it was something that was being offered as an employee benefit from Vitamilk Dairy. "I remember we were sitting on the bed discussing it," Donna says. "He explained that if anything happened to me, he would be left alone with Brittany and Greg, and we should think about insurance. We had never talked

about it before; he just came home with the information. There was a
$250,000 policy—I remember that—that would pay off if I drowned.
If I lost an arm, it would be so much: if I lost a leg, it would be so
much: and if I died, it was more, but I can't remember how much. I
know I didn't sign anything. And I don't think we talked any more
about that."

Randy and Donna were married at the Chapel of the Bells in
Seattle on May 18. They had a "sweet lady minister," and Donna
wore a burnt amber chiffon dress and a crown of baby's breath. She
carried a bouquet of white roses and baby's breath. Her stepmother,
Judy, was her matron of honor in a pale pink dress similar to
Donna's. Randy and his best man, Donna's father, wore gray
tuxedos, and Greg's was just like theirs, only in miniature. Brittany
wore gray dotted swiss, a picture hat, and a wrist corsage of roses.
The sun shone brilliantly, and it was a lovely wedding.

But it wasn't legal. Randy had pushed and pushed Donna to get
married "now," and she had gone ahead with the ceremony even
though she wasn't positive that she was legally divorced from her first
husband. Actually, her divorce came through three days after her
second wedding. "I went to my lawyer, and he did the paperwork so
Randy and I *really* were legally married. Randy was so anxious that
we were."

They left for their honeymoon in a 1974 two-toned Pinto, one of
Randy's gifts to his bride. Donna had no idea it was identical to Janis
Miranda's car, the one that was stolen, destroyed, and paid off by an
insurance company a few months after Jan's marriage to Randy in
1981. How could Donna have known? She knew virtually nothing
about Janis Miranda, only the way she had died.

The 1974 Pinto was perhaps only a macabre coincidence.

A second coincidence, another that Donna didn't know about then,
was that she and Randy honeymooned in the very same spot where
he had taken Janis: the Empress Hotel in Victoria, British Columbia.

"It might have even been in the same room," Donna said later. "I
felt something wasn't right on our honeymoon night, but I didn't
know what it was. Just an eerie feeling. I suddenly realized I didn't
really know him at all."

Randy's sexual ardor faded shortly after he and Donna became
husband and wife. "A couple of weeks after we got married,
everything changed," Donna said. "*Everything* changed. Sex was
great before we got married. It wasn't long before he didn't want sex

at all. I kept wondering what I was doing wrong. He wouldn't even *kiss* me. . . . I was so young, so stupid."

Donna had married Randy because she loved him and because she was beguiled by his apparent absolute devotion to her. Like Janis Miranda before her, she brought few assets into the marriage. And she soon learned that Randy was in charge of all finances. He did not add her name to his checking account. "If I ever needed anything, I had to go to him."

But she seldom needed anything; Donna wasn't even allowed to shop for groceries. Randy took care of that. He bought the cars, the sports equipment, their clothes. She became completely dependent on his decisions.

The marriage limped into that summer of 1985, and Donna Clift Roth became more and more attached to little Greg; he bloomed under her love and attention—even if his father did not. Although Donna had thought Randy's discipline of his son was a little strict *before* their marriage, she was appalled at how Spartan, even cruel, it was after. "It was as if Greg was in the military," she said. "Randy beat him with his belt or he'd put him under a cold shower. Or he'd make Greg do like a thousand push-ups outside in the cold. One time he knocked Greg so hard in the head that he swelled up so fast. I flipped. I ran out of the house, and Randy was running after me, and I screamed, 'Leave me alone. Keep away from me.'"

That time Randy had hit Greg with a removable shower nozzle, and Donna had inadvertently walked in on the discipline session in the bathroom. She couldn't bear to see the little boy she had grown to love being treated so badly, and she tried to cover up for him. "I didn't know what to think. Greg wet the bed all the time, which wasn't surprising. I used to hide his sheets from Randy so he wouldn't punish Greg more."

It seemed that every day or so Donna would learn something that jarred her. The least of it was that there were no more gifts, no more flowers. The romance was seeping out of her marriage, but she couldn't bear to tell anyone. She felt like such a fool.

On the surface, when things were good, Randy could seem like the old Randy, the one she had fallen completely in love with. Greg loved his father, and Randy coached a Little League baseball team. Their home was neat, their yard was green and perfectly manicured, and Randy's roses bloomed without blight or bugs.

But when Randy was in a black mood, which was more and more often, Donna tiptoed around him. She would go to Marta Goodwin and ask for advice. "I knew something was wrong with our marriage," she explained, "and I'd say, 'Golly, I don't know what to do. I've tried everything.'"

But then things would get a little better, and Randy talked as if they would be together forever. He wanted to adopt Brittany. He was vehement about that, but Donna explained she could not allow that: "Brittany already had a father. Her father was her father."

By July, Randy was unemployed. He explained that he had been working on an on-call basis at Vitamilk and that he had simply told them he needed a regular income. In truth, there had been a severe misunderstanding about Randy's use of company gas in his own vehicles. Donna's father got Randy a job where he himself worked, at Cascade Prestige Ford in Bellevue, and they car-pooled together. Randy had to take a salary cut of almost four dollars an hour.

Donna Clift was barely twenty-one and in way over her head only a few months after her wedding. There were too many secrets, more each day. She knew nothing about Randy's family, and he volunteered little. "You will *never* meet my mother," he said flatly. "She's hooked on Valium." He added that his mother was totally obsessed with rock singer Rod Stewart.

Donna believed that Randy had one sister and thought her name was Lisa. She didn't know about any other siblings. She did meet Randy's father, Gordon, however. Randy looked like his dad, only about twenty years younger. She liked Gordon Roth. He lived in a tiny one-room cabin down across the river from Portland.

Perhaps the most chilling information Randy gave his bride about his family concerned his younger brother, David Marvin Roth. David, Randy said, was in prison. He had run into a girl from their home state, North Dakota, and given her a ride. "Randy said they got in a big old fight and David, who was twenty then, strangled that girl," Donna explained. "Then he put her body in the trunk of her car and filled it full of bullet holes. It was really weird how he told me. In one version he said he helped his brother hide the car for a while before he finally talked him into turning himself in. Then he said his brother stabbed her to death before he put her in the trunk."

Donna didn't know whether to believe him or not. It could all have been some of Randy's weird teasing.

All in all, Donna Clift's perfect bridegroom was turning into something she could never have imagined. She had seen only the mask he wanted her to see, and now she realized that there was horror behind the mask. What horror she didn't fully comprehend. His stories of violence were so troubling. She could deal with the Vietnam memories, but she wasn't sure if he was simply teasing her sadistically with the things he told her about his brother having murdered someone—or if he was telling the truth.

She had learned that he was cruel when he teased. "I had heard about the Green River Killer—the one they never caught who was supposed to have murdered all those girls—before I came up here from Arizona. The police had been looking for him since 1982, and it was still on the news all the time. Randy liked to scare me by teasing me about him."

The secrets multiplied. Randy would never tell Donna how old he was. "You don't need to know," he said flatly.

In the beginning his age had not mattered. He looked to be only a few years older than she was, and he was in excellent physical condition. But then, with all the ugly surprises that kept popping up, Donna became obsessed with finding out everything she could about this stranger she had married. She had begun to feel like the heroine of a Gothic novel. Like Jane Eyre or Rebecca. Did Randy have an insane wife or a psychotic relative hidden away someplace? Or was he planning to do something to *her?* He kept the shed out in back locked all the time. She wasn't allowed to look in there.

Marta and Ben Goodwin had known Randy for a long time, and they thought they knew him well, but Randy had never told them much of substance about his background. They had seen a woman and young children come to his house once on Christmas Eve, watched as she knocked futilely on his front door. When she finally gave up and drove away, Randy and Greg came over to their house to celebrate Christmas as usual. "He told us that was his sister—but he had no intention of letting her in," Marta recalled.

The more secretive Randy became, the more determined Donna was to find out the truth.

"I snooped through a lot of stuff. I found his birth certificate, his military papers, and an old expired driver's license. They all had different birth dates on them. His birth certificate looked as though it had been altered. . . . I did a lot of snooping. I broke into his file cabinet. He kept it outside under lock and key, and I found the key. I went through his papers trying to find out something about him."

She found out a great deal. Although he had warned her they had to be very cautious about spending money, she found a savings account passbook that showed a current balance of $99,000. "I figured it had to have been from when he sold his house," she said. "He told me he had no money, but he had a red Ford panel wagon, all race ready. I knew that was worth at least $20,000. I knew a lot about cars because of my dad; we used to go to the drag races together. Randy had other toys that [cost] a lot of money."

Randy also had a bank account in Arizona, something Donna had had no knowledge of until she found a statement in his papers.

She discovered that Randy had received two Social Security checks a month at one time. From what Donna could make out, he was getting almost a thousand dollars a month from Social Security. "It made me suspicious. He was working. Why would he be getting Social Security checks?" Donna discovered Social Security numbers for two children whose names she had never heard. She had no idea what that could mean.

In what Randy would have called a "reconnaissance mission," his new bride looked through files he had never meant her to see. She found to her surprise that Randy was embroiled in a lawsuit. She hadn't known that, either. He was suing the state of Washington for $1.8 million for negligence in the death of his late wife, Jan. According to the legal papers, Randy was maintaining that the trail had not been marked clearly. How odd, Donna thought. Randy had told her that they weren't even *on* the trail when Jan fell, that they were taking a shortcut off the trail.

Randy and Donna Roth had not even been married three months, and yet the marriage was disintegrating like a cheap condominium in a hurricane. His cruelty to Greg, his lies, and the secret life that Donna was uncovering in her desperate search for answers had well nigh destroyed the love she felt for him.

She also suspected he was being unfaithful to her. If he wasn't, he was living the life of a celibate monk; he certainly wasn't satisfying his sexual needs with her. The woman she sensed was her rival was a most unlikely candidate: Lily Vandiveer, his former baby-sitter, the same woman who had worried Jan so much. Lily was also the mother of one of Greg's best friends, Brad.*

"Lily always seemed to be around," Donna said later. "She used to live near Randy in Amber Hills. He was a widower and she had just gotten divorced, and she seemed to be terribly in love with Randy. He told me he wanted nothing to do with her—he just felt sorry for Brad. She called the house constantly. You know, it was 'Randy, my car needs fixing.' She was a lot older than I was, and older than

Randy—*however* old he really was. Randy didn't drink—except maybe we'd have a Smith and Kerns with dinner—but I found beer in the back of his pickup truck. I knew he'd been over to Lily's. When he took Brad home, he wouldn't come back for hours."

Donna couldn't prove infidelity, though—with Lily or with anyone else. Actually, Randy's being unfaithful would have been easier to deal with than the sense of foreboding that walked with Donna always. Randy still liked to dress in dark clothes, and he often went running at night wearing a full black bodysuit.

Sometimes Donna noticed that his hands were scratched. But he was, after all, an automobile mechanic. It would be natural for his hands to be scratched and bruised.

Their marriage had already begun to wind down when Randy grabbed Donna's three-year-old daughter by the ear and pulled her upstairs. "I couldn't stop what he was doing to Greg, but I wouldn't let him touch my daughter. My mother really told him off too. The only other person who could make him back off was Ben Goodwin. Ben loved kids, and he would get right in Randy's face about how he treated Greg. I thought they would come to blows over it, but they never did."

And then one day Donna went outside and caught Randy coaxing Brittany to jump from the roof. "He said he was going to catch her. He was teaching her to trust him."

It was all too obvious that Randy didn't like little girls.

6

Randy Roth lived a clean life. He was an athlete, an outdoorsman, a jogger, a man who utterly detested smoking and frowned on alcohol. He was apparently not highly sexed, or—at best—he was only sporadically moved by desires of the flesh; both Jan Miranda Roth and Donna Clift Roth could have attested to that. He was, however, thrilled with grown-up toys—cars, beautiful homes, and money in the bank.

And power. Randy Roth exulted in having complete and utter control over people around him, especially over his wives.

Whatever Donna tried, it was never enough to please him. She did agree to change the beneficiary of her one existing life insurance policy, a policy with a payoff of only $3,000. "It was supposed to go to Brittany," she explained, "but I changed it to Randy's name."

It didn't seem that big a deal, not when she knew that Randy had almost $100,000 in the bank.

Donna, and often her parents, too, went on outdoor expeditions with Randy. Her dad and her brother liked him so much that she began to wonder if there was something the matter with *her*. But her stepmother, Judy, agreed with Donna. Randy had a mean streak in him. He certainly showed it with Greg, and despite his entreaties that he still wanted desperately to adopt three-year-old Brittany, he sometimes grabbed at her as if she were a rag doll, lifting her by her cheeks, by her ear. He made the mistake of grabbing Brittany's cheeks one day in front of Ben Goodwin. He never did it again, at least not in front of Ben.

Donna might have taken physical punishment herself, trying to patch up the marriage that had never really begun, but she loved her daughter with a visceral fierceness, and her love for Randy had begun to die.

Randy had bought still another set of ATVs (all-terrain vehicles), and he and Donna went alone to test his newest rig on a steep hill. She was not afraid of taking chances. Indeed, with the encouragement of Harvey Clift, who was a huge Bob Glidden fan, she had participated in Figure 8 stock car races. But riding with her new husband straight up a hill made Donna's stomach contract.

Just as they almost crested the hill, Randy suddenly jumped off. The ATV stalled, rolled over, and Donna tumbled over and over to the bottom of the slope. She looked up to see the ATV bouncing backward toward her as if in slow motion. There was nothing she could do; it landed on top of her, bruising and twisting the lower part of her right leg. She could not stand up, and she ultimately lost sensation in that part of her leg permanently.

Randy laughed at her before he finally came down the hill to help her up.

The Skykomish River courses along the route leading to Washington State's Stevens Pass, a deceptively treacherous waterway full of hidden currents, sudden froths of white water, and undertows that have pulled scores of waders and rafters to their deaths. Snohomish County sheriff's deputies specializing in search and rescue have pulled both living and decaying bodies from its heedless path, but yearly warnings to neophytes seem to do little good.

Randy couldn't swim. He had explained that to Donna, and when they went to the athletic club pool, he always stayed in the shallow end. She had never seen him in water any deeper than three feet. He always stayed in the shallow end with Greg. He was so muscular, always bench pressing in his weight room in the basement, that she wasn't surprised Randy didn't float. She *was* surprised that he was so enthusiastic about going rafting. They had rafted once with her parents, Harvey and Judy, at a Cascade Ford company picnic, but he hadn't seemed to enjoy it that much. Now he bought a cheap raft made of such thin material that it seemed better suited to a backyard pool than to a river.

Donna was a good swimmer. That wasn't why she didn't want to go rafting. It was more than that; she had grown afraid of her husband. Only when Randy suggested that they invite her parents to accompany them on a rafting trip on the Skykomish would Donna agree to go. But she wasn't happy about it.

It was a hot July day, but the Skykomish is always cold, chilled by the snowpack high in the Cascade Mountains. They took two rafts along, the larger raft for the elder couple and the cheap two-man raft for Donna and Randy. Donna's parents had a net bag with life jackets and extra paddles with them, but they left it in the car, taking only a paddle for each raft. Randy and Harvey both had great upper-body strength, and they would paddle while the women enjoyed the scenery along the river. Randy suggested that Brittany and Greg go with the Clifts and that they take the ice chest, too.

Judy Clift whispered to Harvey, "Do not let my daughter out of your sight." Harvey looked puzzled at Judy's insistence, but he nodded.

Keeping Donna and Randy in sight wasn't as easy as it sounded. Although the river was fairly calm that day, Judy and Harvey Clift's raft was caught up in the current and they sped ahead of Randy and Donna. The Skykomish has bends and turns so sharp that there is no way separate parties can travel downriver together or even hope to keep each other in sight. The roar of the water blocks out all but the loudest sounds.

When Judy and Harvey's raft had disappeared from view, Randy suddenly started having trouble steering. Alarmed, Donna turned to see that they were headed toward the huge sharp rocks that wait beneath the Skykomish. Instead of paddling away from the rocks, Randy seemed to be deliberately steering their tiny raft *toward* them. With no paddle, Donna had no control at all.

Far ahead, Judy insisted that Harvey Clift pull their raft over where they could grab on to an overhanging branch and wait for Randy and Donna to catch up. She stared back at the river.

"What are you doing?" Donna screamed, but Randy ignored her as he drew closer and closer to the jagged boulders that could easily pierce the thin raft.

Ahead, Judy Clift turned again to look for Donna and Randy. Five minutes had gone by. She could no longer see them, but she heard something. A bird's screech? Maybe just the slight change in the river's song as it widened, narrowed, and twisted past the land. Judy was worried; she had come to believe Donna when she said there was something strange about Randy Roth, possibly even something dangerous.

"I was afraid my daughter would not come off that river," Judy remembered with a shudder.

"*Listen!*" Judy shouted. "I hear something."

And she did. She heard Donna screaming in complete panic, "*Dad! I'm going to die! Save me! I'm going to die!*"

Judy also heard Randy's voice. He was shouting, "*Shut up! Shut up! Shut up!*"

Harvey Clift kept his raft motionless, waiting helplessly. When the small raft finally rounded the crook in the river, they saw that it was barely afloat, so filled with water that it rode low in the Skykomish River.

Randy seemed calm. Donna was nearly hysterical with fear. They got the two rafts to a spot where they could pull onto the bank of the river. Judy calmed Donna while her husband helped Randy put patches on two holes in the small raft. Nobody knew quite what to say. What Judy Clift suspected was unthinkable, unspeakable.

Donna Roth would not get back into the raft with Randy; she rode the rest of the way back to their cars in her parents' raft, and Randy paddled the flimsy raft alone.

She never lived with her husband again. She had seen something in his face, in the grim set of his jaw as he steered their raft deliberately against the river rocks until water began to seep in through the holes the sharp edges tore. Donna Clift Roth could not prove that her suspicions were correct. Even her own father looked at her a little quizzically when she talked about her fear of Randy. All she really had to go on was the cold feeling in the bottom of her stomach, the stories that she could not prove were lies, the facts that did not mesh with other facts.

Her parents accepted her decision not to go home to Misty Meadows with her husband of three months. She moved into the Clifts' Bothell home with Brittany for a month, and then in September of 1985 she went to Arizona for another month—to think, to find a quiet place where she could sort out what was real, what was only fear, what might be imagination.

When Donna flew back to Seattle, Randy was there at the airport, smiling, at the gate. Everything would be fine, he said. He was still car-pooling with her father. It was all a misunderstanding. He told her that her father had even gone with him on another rafting trip and nothing bad had happened. Randy had come to pick her up and take her home, but she accepted only a ride to her parents' house.

"I couldn't go home with him, not ever. My mother believed me, too," Donna Clift recalled. "She told my dad, 'He's not what he appears to be.'"

When he realized that Donna was not coming back to him, Randy filed for divorce. "I would have," Donna recalled, "but I had no access to money."

It didn't matter who filed, she decided; she would be free of her terror-ridden marriage.

Oddly, Randy did not let his third wife go easily. Even though he had instigated the divorce, he pursued Donna. Rather, he stalked her. He hadn't seemed to want her when he had her, but he refused to let her go. He would come into the 7-Eleven where she had found a job and watch her. Often he wouldn't say anything at all, but she was aware of him as he gazed at her, his face inscrutable.

Donna found flowers and notes from Randy on her car. He seemed to know where she was all the time. It was ironic. In the beginning, less than a year ago, she had been flattered when he stared at her while she worked and thrilled by his notes and bouquets. Now she found the same behavior threatening. He seemed to be everywhere she looked, where she worked, where she ate lunch, in one of his many cars following her as she drove.

"Finally my mom went to him and told him to leave me alone, and he stopped stalking me—for a while. But then he had Greg call me."

Leaving Greg behind had been the hardest thing for Donna to do, and now Greg called her often, crying, and begging her to come back. If she hadn't been so frightened, she would have gone back—if only for Greg's sake.

One day in the fall of 1985 Randy came in once more to the store where Donna worked. He had tears in his eyes as he told her that he had just gotten terrible news. His mother had been killed in a car accident. But that wasn't the worst of it, he continued. "My sister got so distraught in the hospital that she shot herself. She's dead too."

"I believed him," Donna says ruefully. "It was kind of farfetched, but you never know. I told my mom and dad and they didn't believe it."

She almost went back to him, moved by sympathy for his pain and by her concern for Greg. But Judy Clift talked her out of it.

Randy Roth continued to stalk his third ex-wife. In his dark jogging suit or in his mechanic's clothes, he followed close behind her, keeping track of her. She thought she would never be free of him, this man whose attention had thrilled her only a year before.

"He kept it up until I started dating another man. Once that happened, Randy left me alone," she recalled. "I was with Jerry* for four years. Randy just went away, and it was almost as if I'd never known him at all. No, that isn't true—because I really loved Greg, and I missed him and worried about him."

Randy's divorce from Donna Clift was final on September 24, 1985.

PART THREE

1985

7

There is an odd synchronicity in the way parallel lives veer to touch one another, change direction and then come close again and again until they connect and hold for whatever it was that fate intended to happen. Sometimes synchronicity can be heartwarming—when it leads lost lovers back together against all odds. Sometimes it can be starkly tragic.

Nineteen eighty-five was a watershed year in the lives of a number of people who were, who had been, or who would one day be part of Randy Roth's life. Donna Clift was courted by, married to, and divorced from him—all in 1985.

Although Randy had not discussed it with Donna and she found out only through her "snooping," Randy had filed a suit against the state of Washington and the Department of Parks and Recreation of the state of Washington in November of 1984. On January 19, 1985, he signed a formal contract with Lynnwood attorney Ginny Evans, who agreed to represent him and Jalina Amelia Miranda on a contingency basis. Randy maintained that it was negligence on the part of the state and the Parks Department in not providing adequate trail barriers on Beacon Rock that had caused Janis Roth's death. All through 1985 he huddled with his legal advisers in pursuing his claim.

Breaking his financial losses down, Randy asked for the following:

Funeral expenses for the decedent:	$541.00
Cost of selling family home because Mr. Roth could not keep up payments without decedent's contributions:	$5,863.62
Loss of consortium for each claimant, $250,000.00:	$500,000.00
Lost earnings:	To be determined

77

It cost Randy only $500 out of pocket to file the tort claim against the state for $1,186,404.62. If he won, he would have to pay his attorney one-third of his settlement. He really had nothing to lose.

Randy didn't even know where Jalina was living. He had neither written to her nor sent her presents. He had forwarded none of her dead mother's belongings to her, and so she had very little to remember Janis Miranda Roth by. Still, he presented himself as a fighter on her behalf, anxious to see that Jalina got her due from the negligent state of Washington. He gave her address in Texas, but it was really only the last address he had for Janis's mother, Billie Ray.

Neither Randy's second wife nor his third wife had learned much about his history. Both women had met his father, but not his mother or any of his siblings. His mother was apparently dead, either from old age or by suicide; he had told many different stories about her and her demise. If he truly had a brother, David was reportedly in prison for murder. Randy had told both Jan and Donna again and again about his marine service in Vietnam, and both women had heard him scream at night from the grotesque nightmares that haunted him.

Donna Sanchez Roth, Randy's first wife, had apparently slipped completely out of his life, and no one knew where she was.

Anything that might have happened in Randy Roth's life before his marine years was caught somewhere in his memory, either blurred deliberately or repressed when he talked with his ex-wives. In actuality, Randy had never moved very far—at least for very long—from the area just north of Seattle. He had attended Meadowdale High School in Lynnwood, only a few miles from Bothell, Mountlake Terrace, and Mill Creek. Although he moved often, he did not venture beyond familiar territory.

Although there is no evidence that they ever knew each other, a young man named Tom Baumgartner attended Meadowdale High at the same time Randy did. They both graduated in the early 1970s, but they moved in different circles.

During the time Randy married and divorced three times, Tom Baumgartner married only once, and for life. In 1976 he married pretty blond Cynthia Loucks. They became parents of two cherished little boys: Tyson Jeret Baumgartner, born on December 15, 1979, and Rylie Thomas Baumgartner, August 18, 1981.

Tom was a hard worker, taking a job with United Parcel Service and working his way up to provide security for his growing family. He joined the Teamsters Union and with that membership came both medical coverage and death benefits for survivors. Short of an occasional trip to the pediatrician for the boys, neither he nor Cynthia expected to need Tom's teamster insurance. Tom also took out life insurance.

The Baumgartners' marriage ended in 1985 too, about the same time that Donna Clift and Randy Roth were divorced. But Cynthia and Tom Baumgartner did not choose to be apart. Not yet thirty, Tom had contracted Hodgkin's disease, a form of cancer that affects the lymph nodes. Although the often fatal disease was being treated with some success in the mid-eighties, Tom's case was far advanced when he was diagnosed. He was dead in six months at the age of twenty-nine.

The widowed Cynthia Baumgartner and the newly divorced Randy Roth did not meet in 1985, although they shopped at the same stores, their sons were close to the same age, and they traveled the same roads. Had Randy encountered Cynthia, he undoubtedly would have hit on her; his technique for finding women to date was carefully honed to perfection. Randy seemed to prefer divorced or widowed women in their twenties or thirties, and he scarcely looked at women without children. He liked pretty women, obviously, small women, perhaps because he was so short himself, and he invariably approached shy, dependent women—as if he had antennae that could scope that out without ever speaking to them.

Randy Roth must have asked hundreds of women for a date, or rather he sent Greg to ask them, "Would you go out with my dad? He's right over there."

Many women—many, many women—said yes. The kid was so cute, and the father smiled so charmingly.

Cynthia Baumgartner began to put together the shattered fragments of her world. She struggled to cope with raising her boys alone, something she had never expected to have to do. Tom's insurance and Social Security survivors' benefits made it possible for her to stay home with Tyson and Rylie. Many years back, she had worked for Jimbo's Family Restaurant in Lynnwood and later as a legal secretary, but that was before the boys were born. Now she devoted a lot of time to volunteer work at her church. Although her heart was broken, she was comfortable financially and she prayed that time and the strength of her faith would help her overcome her grief. Cynthia had solid family support from her parents, Hazel and Merle Loucks, and from her older brother, Leon.

Cynthia Loucks Baumgartner didn't really think about marrying again; it was much too soon after Tom's death. However, her friends knew that it would take a very special man for Cynthia to fall in love again. Her own morals and her religious beliefs dictated that any candidate would have to be either single or widowed. She would not marry a divorced man.

Randy Roth had a life to rearrange too. His heart was not broken, and his divorce had cost him nothing. However, his "investment" in Donna had not paid off, whatever the payback he had planned on. Donna had once believed Randy's protestations that he was investing his emotions and his future in her. She no longer did.

Randy continued to spend his Thursday nights at Ben and Marta Goodwins', bringing always the apple pie and ice cream, and they all watched "The Cosby Show" together. Randy was still hurt because Ryan Goodwin had turned him in to Greg's principal and the Children's Protective Service had investigated him.

He seemed confused, totally unable to equate his treatment of Greg with the humiliating and painful punishment he told the Goodwins *he* had suffered as a little boy, a little boy kneeling on a hard floor for hours. And yet Randy's discipline of Greg was ultimately demeaning, and with Donna gone, Greg had no one to take his side once the doors were closed.

One night in the fall of 1985 Ben and Randy were in a tavern at Thrasher's Corner when a woman who knew Donna Clift well walked by and recognized Randy. She stopped suddenly, slapped his face, and spat, "You child-abusing son of a bitch!"

For once, Randy was shocked, taken completely by surprise by an enemy he had not recognized.

"Randy and I both got thrown out." Ben grinned. "He was really upset. I had to take him home, wake Marta up, and we both tried to console him. He cried real tears. He said, '*Nobody* is more important in my life than Greg. Greg is my whole life.'"

And, indeed, he seemed to be. The Goodwins had seen that women came and went in Randy Roth's life, but Greg remained the one constant. "I think he really loved Greg," Marta Goodwin said. "He really felt bad when that girl criticized him for being a bad father, but he could not grasp that you didn't discipline children the way he did Greg."

Greg and Randy had shared their last Christmas with Donna and her family, but on Christmas 1985 the neighbors were back together around the Goodwins' tree. Randy would be thirty-one the day after Christmas, but he still looked about twenty-five in the photographs the Goodwins took that year. Their daughter, Brittany, was almost fourteen, and she clearly adored Randy. When Randy teased her about being too heavy, she dieted until she was thin and weak, and her parents were afraid she would become anorexic or bulimic.

Brittany Goodwin would have done anything for Randy.

In the autumn of 1985, Randy Mullinax, a King County Police detective, had never heard of the man who shared his first name. They were about the same age and Mullinax was also compact and muscular, but there all similarities ended. Randy the detective had a deep and resonant voice, and Randy the mechanic spoke in flat, almost expressionless tones. Mullinax was a friendly and easygoing man, sensitive—perhaps too much so for his own good—to the pain of the people whose lives brought them in contact with the King County Police Department's Major Crimes Unit.

Even though he was born east of the Cascade Mountains in Yakima, Washington, Mullinax grew up as a Seattle kid. His parents moved to the Boulevard Park area in the south end, and Randy and his brothers all grew up there and graduated from Glacier High School, whose campus later became the King County Police Academy. Mullinax got married when he was twenty. He went to work for the County Water District just outside Burien, a small town south of Seattle, and stayed there for eight years. "I got tired of using my back and standing outside in the rain," Mullinax recalls. He went to college, fitting in classes when he could. "I just took a few electives in police science courses at first—but I got hooked. I changed my major."

Mullinax majored in police science at Highline Community College, mastering the intricacies of crime scene investigation, arrest, search and seizure, and constitutional law for police. By day he checked for broken water mains, and in the evening he learned how to triangulate a crime scene so perfectly that the location of a body could be absolutely pinpointed long after a victim was removed. He learned that blood droplets that have fallen from three feet look different from those that fell from one foot or six feet, and he learned how to tell if glass has been broken from inside force or outside force. He learned about tool marks and skid marks and tire tracks, about rigor mortis and lividity and the transmogrification of the human body after death. He even had one ex–homicide detective instructor who claimed he had always preferred to work a crime scene alone "so he could talk to the body and find out what happened."

Randy Mullinax was prepared to be a homicide detective, but first he had to pay his dues. He joined the King County Police in January of 1979, and he worked his way through the usual steps like any rookie, patrolling first the sparsely populated southeast part of the county, then working in a proactive unit on burglaries and larcenies. By the fall of 1985, Randy Mullinax was an integral part of the enhanced Green River Task Force. He had worked on the baffling disappearances and murders of almost four dozen girls and women, most of whom had vanished since July 15, 1982, from the strip that runs by Washington State's biggest airport: Seattle-Tacoma International. The first five victims had been found floating in the Green River south of Seattle, hence the name. Once a country river that curved past verdant strawberry fields, the Green River was far less isolated by 1982; Boeing buildings covered the good black earth on its east flank, shopping malls on the north, and roads leading up a steep hill to the west crossed Pacific Highway every quarter mile or so.

The media and a number of insensitive citizens almost always referred to the Green River victims as "prostitutes" or "hookers." The additional pain inflicted on their families by this attitude could not be measured. The missing girls were very young—many of them fourteen, fifteen, or sixteen—the oldest in their twenties. Mullinax had a soft spot for children, and as he carried on an increasingly frustrating investigation, he would describe his job as "trying to locate young ladies." He was not being sarcastic. The victims had become very real to him, and their almost certain fate pitiable. Victims' groups praised Randy Mullinax highly for his tenacity and especially for his caring attitude.

So, in the fall of 1985, Green River Task Force member Randy Mullinax spent his working days and much of his off-duty time following one dismal trail after another, almost all of them in the area south of Seattle. By the time Mullinax found the young ladies assigned to him, however, they had long since turned to bone, hair, and sometimes a bit of connective tissue. It got worse for the Green River Task Force in 1985. Green River victims were discovered as far away as Tualatin, Oregon, almost 200 miles from where they had last been seen alive.

One of them had had her skull bisected, allowing the Green River Killer to play games with the task force by leaving the rounded calvarium in Oregon and the lower mandible in south King County, Washington.

*   *   *

Randy Mullinax would spend three and a half years in the Green River boiler room investigation with pressure from the media, from the public, from the politicos, and, indeed, from within himself. And yet, in 1993 the Green River murders would still be unsolved.

Women all around western Washington walked in fear of the man who had killed so many of their sisters and then disappeared like a wraith. Donna Clift was only one of thousands who shivered at the thought, and Randy Roth had delighted in teasing her sadistically about the Green River Killer.

When he finally allowed Donna to walk away from him, Randy moved on to new conquests. Many women would move in and out of his life in the next five years; he collected them like butterflies, pinning some helplessly on his own display board, discarding others when they did not meet his criteria. He never anticipated that there might be other women down the road, women who would dog his trail, annoy him, perhaps even frighten him, this man who confessed to no fear—ever. Some might say the fact that a certain trio of women awaited Randy Roth was poetic justice. Perhaps it was only a sign of the times.

Gradually in the last three decades the judicial system had changed. Female cops were no longer relegated to glorified secretarial and baby-sitting details. They worked in uniform beside the men; some of them even commanded the men. Female prosecutors were not automatically second-in-command anymore.

Three women he had not met would one day effect not revenge but a kind of ironic denouement in Randy Roth's life story.

King County detective Sue Peters would be first. She would work as Randy Mullinax's partner in an investigation totally different from but just as complicated as the Green River cases. Peters grew up close by that river. All popular cops have nicknames, and she would be called Sue P., pronounced "Soupie" by the officers she worked with. Five feet three and strong but graceful, with a cap of thick brown hair, Peters is a natural athlete who always expected to be a P.E. teacher and who still plays softball in season.

As a child she spent her summers in Adams County, far east of the Cascade Mountains. Ritzville—a town that could have been lifted out of the Midwest with its tree-shaded neighborhoods, Main Street, and hot summer days—depends on wheat farming. It is also the Adams County seat, and Sue Peters hung around the jail where her grandmother, Marie Thiel, worked as a deputy. "I was fascinated with what went on there," Peters recalls. "I asked for all the Wanted posters to take home, and I pored over the accident pictures. Once in a while my grandmother would give me a Wanted poster, but she would never give me one of the black-and-white accident photos."

Peters graduated from Kent Meridian High School, south of Seattle, in 1976 and went to Washington State University, where she majored in physical education. She transferred to Central Washington University in Ellensburg and graduated in December 1981. She soon found that there was no great demand for P.E. teachers. Perhaps the fact that there were already too many P.E. teachers was not as disappointing as it might have been; Sue had always had two interests, each as natural to her as breathing. Although she had never really planned on a career in law enforcement, it had almost literally been bred into her. When Marie Thiel, now eighty-two, was a deputy, there was women's work and men's work. Women deputies worked with women prisoners and often served as jail matrons. They were not half of the lead detective team working a major homicide case. Sue Peters followed in her grandmother's footsteps and became a King County deputy sheriff, graduating from the police academy in May of 1982.

Sue Peters, three years behind Randy Mullinax on the county force, began with basically the same duties he had; she worked three years in uniform in a patrol car out of Precinct Three in Maple Valley, and then in plain clothes in a proactive squad. Proactive squads worked whatever the biggest problem in their district happened to be at any given time. In Maple Valley in the early eighties Peters worked under cover tracking down small-time drug dealers. The fact that she could easily look like a high school girl made her an asset. She also worked the Green River murder cases and in the Special Assault Unit investigating sex crimes.

Looking back to 1985, Peters recalls that she was mostly involved in working on a new house she had bought; other than that, it was not a particularly memorable year. "I didn't even find time to play ball that year."

In October of 1990 Sue Peters moved into the Major Crimes Unit of the King County Police Department. In the old days—the sixties, the seventies—crime in the county was minuscule compared to what the Seattle detectives handled. King County's Major Crimes detectives usually investigated five or fewer murders in a year while Seattle's Homicide Unit averaged forty-five to sixty. Seattle continued to have forty-five to sixty homicides a year, but by the eighties, King County's regular homicides had climbed to twenty to twenty-five a year.

"They didn't count the Green River murders; there were just too many of them," Mullinax says. "It was as if the Major Crimes Unit had its homicides and the Green River Task Force had theirs, even though we were all in the same department."

However they counted, the county homicide rate was rapidly rising to a point where it matched the city of Seattle's. In 1985 both Sue Peters and Randy Mullinax could expect to work their share of murder cases. They would not work as partners for six years.

Neither had ever heard the name Randy Roth.

PART FOUR

Good Neighbors

8

Brittany Goodwin was fourteen in 1986, and she began to baby-sit for Greg. She was thrilled to be asked to help; she had had a crush on Randy since she was thirteen. Nobody thought too much of it. Teenage girls were always mooning over older men. If it wasn't a rock star, it was a teacher or the guy next door. Harmless.

The Goodwins trusted Randy, even though they could see that their teenage daughter adored him. Ben began to feel vaguely uneasy first. He thought Randy was encouraging Brittany's attention a little too much.

Marta thought her husband was imagining things. "We knew that Brittany was madly in love with Randy," she said, "so we went to him and said, 'Look, this kid is really developing a crush on you. We just wanted you to be aware. Don't show her quite as much attention. Hold back. We need your help on this.'"

Randy nodded understandingly. "I will. I will. I wouldn't ever touch Brittany."

But her parents worried when they saw that Brittany was still mooning over Randy, despite Randy's heartfelt promises to his best friends that he was doing nothing to encourage it. One evening Brittany came home with a teddy bear that said "I love you" and went straight to her room. It was a present from Randy.

"Marta trusted Randy," Ben recalls. "She still did at that point."

"When Ben would start to worry about it," Marta says, "I'd look at him and say, 'Honey, Randy is part of our family, and he knows that Brittany is underage. He knows that's illegal. There is no way that Randy would do anything against the law.' I *actually* said that."

"Damn it Marta," Ben would rage. "I'm her father, and I know something is going on. I don't know what it is or how much it is, but there's something."

"Randy must have taken it as a compliment that this pretty little young girl thought he was King Randy," Marta theorizes. "I guess he thought he could train her to be the type of woman he wanted . . . but still, we were in a state of denial. Our lives were so intertwined with Randy's. We really didn't think that there was anything sexual going on. He was our *friend*. Besides that, whenever Randy was with Brittany, Greg and Ryan were always along too."

When Brittany was depressed, Randy could always cheer her up.

Ben Goodwin was torn. Randy was just about the best friend he had ever had, but Brittany was such a pretty girl and she was so innocent. He watched over her the way every father watches his teenage daughter, and he was suspicious. He knew what a ladies' man Randy could be. Ben went out to coach baseball one Saturday. He noted that Randy was working on his car in his driveway and called out, "See ya later."

But Ben had to turn around and go home to get his wallet. As he drove in his driveway, he saw Randy sitting sideways in the driver's seat of his Blazer with the door open. Ben's fifteen-year-old daughter was standing between Randy's legs and leaning her head on his shoulder.

Randy saw Ben coming and tried to push Brittany away, but he wasn't quick enough. Ben jumped over the fence and grabbed his daughter and pushed her toward the house. "I poked Randy in the chest and said, 'If I *ever* see you touching my daughter again, I'll kill you.'"

Randy knew Ben meant every word, and he downplayed his attentions to Brittany. Shortly thereafter, Randy became very cool to Brittany, leaving her devastated and depressed. Marta and Ben still believed that the relationship between Randy and their teenage daughter had been platonic, although they thought Randy had not used good sense in showering so much attention on Brittany. They assumed her depression was just part of the normal mood swings every teenager goes through.

It was not. Years later, when she was an adult, Brittany Goodwin recalled her pain at being abandoned. She had saved one of the many poems she had written for Randy, and rereading it was bittersweet.

My Eternal Love

I loved you then, and now
you're gone.
I love you now, and all is
wrong.

I try to tell you that I
    care,
    but you don't seem to be aware,
    that you've become my Mr.
    Right.
I think about you every night.
Your love for me has faded away.
Now all I can do is pray
    that someday you'll realize
    what you are to me
And together we'll spend eternity.

It wasn't long before there was a new woman in Randy Roth's life. Just before Memorial Day, Mary Jo Phillips, the mother of five, was grocery shopping one evening at an Albertson's supermarket. She soon noticed that a good-looking man with a little boy seemed to be waiting in every aisle she turned into. Flustered, she began to nod and smile at them.

When Mary Jo left the store pushing her loaded grocery cart, the little boy, who looked to be about nine, followed her out of the store calling, "Hey, lady! Hey, lady, would you go out with my dad?"

She did not know that it was a well-worn and effective pickup line. The father, who said his name was Randy Roth, walked up and stood behind his son, Greg. She was charmed, but not enough to give her phone number to a complete stranger—child or not.

Finally Mary Jo Phillips agreed to write down Randy's phone number. She didn't really expect to call him, but she kept it, debating for almost three weeks if she should do something so crazy.

When she finally did call, she got an answering machine. But she began to smile when she heard the message. It was for her. "Mary Jo," Randy's voice pleaded. "Mary Jo, if this is you, please, *please* don't hang up. There's got to be a way for me to meet you!"

Of course, she left her number. Randy called as soon as he got home, and invited her out to dinner.

When they reached the restaurant, Randy asked her to hold still for a moment as she started to get out of his car. He held a camera in his hand. "Baby," he said, "I just want proof that I was with such a beautiful woman." Mary Jo was touched.

Randy didn't even blink when Mary Jo told him about her large family. Rather, he seemed enthusiastic about dating her. She was a beautiful woman, very petite, with long, curly light brown hair, and she usually dressed kind of "country," in a plaid shirt, blue jeans, and tennis shoes. Mary Jo was so young-looking, peppy, and active that it was hard to believe she had given birth to five children.

For their second date he picked her up on his motorcycle and whisked her almost to the Canadian border a hundred miles north. Just for breakfast. Just the two of them. Riding behind him with her arms locked around his muscular torso, Mary Jo couldn't help but think she had found the 1986 version of a knight on a white horse.

Once again Randy became the consummate lover. It was spring, and their courtship was swift and romantic. Mary Jo was as bedazzled as his first three wives had been. There was, of course, the usual proliferation of flowers. Roses and carnations and pots of azaleas. Nosegays and sweetheart bouquets. "He became the man every woman dreams about," Mary Jo remembers.

Randy was totally indulgent with Mary Jo. He combed her hair, he rubbed her back. He even suggested that they try to coordinate their wardrobes so they would match and everywhere they went people would know they were together.

Randy's relationship with Ben and Marta was back on an even keel. He had apparently kept his promise to Ben not to hang around with Brittany, and they were back to their regular "Cosby Show" nights and their outings together. Marta watched in bemusement the first time she saw Mary Jo arrive at Randy's house in a big Chevy Suburban. She counted five kids as they piled out and played in the yard.

After that she saw Mary Jo and her family often. Randy came to Marta and announced, "Mary Jo will be moving in, and we're going to try and make a relationship."

"The children too?" Marta asked. "How are you going to adjust to living with five little children?"

"I know about kids," he said calmly. Besides, he explained, Mary Jo shared custody with the children's father, so they wouldn't be living at his house all the time.

Six weeks after Randy Roth and Mary Jo Phillips met, he asked her and her children to move in with him. She sold most of her furniture, preparing for a new life. She had raised dozens of exotic birds, and she had to sell off most of those, too. Mary Jo's apartment was about two miles from Misty Meadows, and the Goodwins followed Randy and his trailer and helped him move Mary Jo's belongings into his house. Randy had always been tremendously strong and lifted the heavy pieces easily.

Mary Jo brought a few of her favorite birds and her player piano.

The birds were easy to move; the piano was not. Randy and Ben had to rig a pulley setup to move it up Randy's back steps.

Brittany, with her heart barely healing after Randy broke off with her, had to watch him move yet another woman into his house. No one realized just how much she was hurting—or why.

Just as they had when Randy was married to Donna Clift, the two couples socialized a lot. Either Ben and Marta went out to dinner with Randy and Mary Jo, or the Goodwins barbecued in their backyard. They hoped that Randy's relationship with Mary Jo would last longer than his abortive marriage to Donna; only a year had gone by, and it was summer again, but the roster of players had changed. Randy kept recasting the part of his fiancée-wife. Marta worried sometimes about Greg; he had no stability, no mother he could expect to be there for very long.

It wasn't until Mary Jo moved in with Randy that she learned about Janis Miranda Roth's death. Randy told her that the authorities were still investigating her tragic fall. Once again the actual details of Jan's demise changed in his retelling. Randy told Mary Jo that he and Jan had been climbing Mount Rainier. While they were high up on the 14,000-foot snow-capped peak, he said, Jan's ropes loosened, "I was holding her while she tried to retie her ropes. But she slipped out of my arms . . . and fell to her death."

Mary Jo, like all his other women, was shocked and saddened. What a terrible thing it must have been for Randy to see. Randy confided that he and Jan had had a troubled relationship. Although he had loved her, they had fought a lot. "She didn't appreciate me." None of his women had, he confided—until Mary Jo came along. Donna Clift, the third Mrs. Roth, had been "immature," according to Randy.

Randy seemed defiant about the law enforcement authorities who were allegedly still tracking him. (They were not.) "If they intend to charge me with anything, they only have a limited time to do so."

There is, of course, no statute of limitations on murder. If the Skamania County investigators chose to, they could have charged Randy Roth in his second wife's death when he was eighty years old.

Randy told Mary Jo that he had collected insurance money in Jan's death but that he had spent it unwisely. He wasn't used to having money, and he realized that he should have retained a financial planner.

Mary Jo and her children lived with Randy for four months. Once she was in his domain, she found him less romantic and much more dominating. He made it clear to her that certain areas in his home were off limits to her. Perhaps his discovery that Donna Clift had "snooped" into his papers and belongings had made him cautious. He was adamant that Mary Jo keep out of his things. She thought his demands a little odd, but she went along with them. The house was big, and she had no need to go into Randy's forbidden zones. And she still loved him; it was hard to forget the tender and imaginative lover who had courted her so beautifully.

Randy was the boss. He handled everything. He didn't even let her do the grocery shopping. Nevertheless, Mary Jo and Randy made plans to get married. One day, as they parked at one of the huge Fred Meyer stores, he asked her to go to the jewelry department and have her third finger measured so he could shop for a wedding ring. She knew everything was going to be fine with them after they were married.

There *were* a few more things that got in the way of their perfect relationship, however. Mary Jo had owned a rather lucrative day-care center with her ex-husband. After her divorce was final, she explained to Randy that she had handled her own property settlement, including the day-care assets. Randy was furious when he learned that she had not consulted him. He was angry, too, when she gave back to Donna Clift some clothing she had left at the house.

Mary Jo realized that she was not to make any decisions on her own. But she still adored Randy.

Mary Jo had an almost pathological fear of water, yet she let Randy coax her into going on a raft with him—and without a life jacket. The way he put it, it was a test, a way to prove her love for him.

One night Randy explained to Mary Jo that he had adequate life insurance and that she needed some, too. After all, they now had six children to consider if anything happened to either one of them.

Her heart sank.

Mary Jo had one secret she had not told Randy, something she had agonized over. She didn't want to lose him now that her life had suddenly become so full of love. Taking a deep breath, she told Randy her secret: she was not eligible for insurance. Mary Jo Phillips had been treated for cancer. She was not actively ill, and she had every hope that she would never have a reoccurrence. But she was definitely uninsurable. She studied his face and she saw no expression at all. He seemed to take it all right, and he didn't seem concerned about her cancer, either. At least not right away.

But within days Randy began to change toward Mary Jo. Where he had been warm and loving—if controlling—he became icy cold and distant. He never mentioned marriage again.

Mary Jo had kept a journal of their relationship; it was so beautiful in the beginning that she loved writing down all the wonderful surprises he gave her and all the romantic things he said. Later she wrote in it as a way to help her understand what had happened.

When Randy found out that Mary Jo had kept a journal, he told her it was "incriminating" and ordered her to destroy it. She did not.

Finally Mary Jo had no choice but to move out. Randy clearly didn't want her anymore. She had a heck of a time getting Randy to give her piano back.

9

Although Randy Roth almost always had a job—at Reynolds, at Vitamilk Dairy, at Cascade Ford, at Chuck Olson Chevrolet, and later at Bill Pierre Ford in Lake City—his life-style, his lavish homes, and all the adult toys he owned required more than his salary. His W2s for the 1980s indicated income that could not even have begun to cover his expenses:

1980	$22,412.93
1981	$33,100.00
1982	$28,300.00
1983	$16,951.00
1984	$29,201.00
1985	$30,912.00
1986	$24,830.00
1987	$26,432.00

The low figure for 1983 marked the time when Vitamilk put him on an on-call status. But most of Randy's big money had come from insurance payoffs. Within a few months of Jan's death, he had received $107,514.11 from two policies, and each month since her death, he had cashed monthly Social Security benefits checks of $419 for Greg as Jan's "surviving child," collecting almost $35,000 by the beginning of 1988. None of this money was legally reportable income.

Even the money Randy had loaned to Nick Emondi came back to him after Nick had a burglary and collected on his homeowner's insurance.

Randy was disappointed, however, in the outcome of his suit against the state of Washington. He had hoped to collect almost a million dollars, but after giving depositions, submitting to all kinds of questions, and wasting his time with a couple of lawyers, the suit was dismissed in 1988, and he got nothing.

Anyone with an ounce of deductive reasoning could recognize a pattern in Randy Roth's financial affairs. If ever a man believed in insurance, it was Roth. Even when his budget was tight, he had always found money to pay insurance premiums. His thinking was certainly sensible. He was the single father of a little boy, a man who apparently had no idea where Greg's real mother, Donna Sanchez, was. And insurance had paid off for him when he needed it.

After Mary Jo moved out, Randy continued to date; his choices were invariably divorcées or widows with children, and he always met his dates "cute" by sending Greg over as his advance emissary. He still saw Lily Vandiveer, although she didn't seem to be "his type." Those who knew both of them said Lily would have done anything in the world for Randy. But neither Lily nor any of his dates mattered enough for him to move them into his home.

Randy asked Marta Goodwin once if she and Ben would like to go to a dance with him and a new woman he was dating, and Marta threw up her hands and said, "Randy! I'm not going to get attached to any more of the women you meet. I just get so I really like these gals and then you get rid of them!"

Randy laughed.

In the late spring of 1988 Randy was coaching T-ball for boys Greg's age. He was always involved in his son's sports activities—Little League baseball or whatever was in season. Some of the other parents called him "Super Dad" because he got so involved in the kids' games; some thought he was too rough on the boys and that he always forgot that games were only games.

Dina Clark's* son was on Randy's T-ball team. Dina was an extremely attractive young woman, a divorcée who lived in Mill Creek with her four children. She had ended her marriage despite the fact that she was expecting another baby.

"We were roller-skating at my kids' school, and Randy Roth started flirting with me. I was *pregnant,* for heaven's sake, but it didn't seem to bother him at all."

Dina found Randy attractive enough, although he was awfully short. "I remember he was wearing cowboy boots, and even then he was only about five feet six."

He was funny, though, and nice, and he insisted that he wanted to call her. He wheedled her address and phone number out of her. Randy did go to Dina Clark's house. She wasn't home, but the baby-sitter was. Years later Dina recalled what her baby-sitter had reported: "She said he stood in the front entrance, and then the phone rang and my answering machine picked it up. It was my boyfriend calling. I guess when Randy heard that, he decided I wasn't available, and he just backed out the door. He never called me again."

Randy and the Goodwins still lived next door to one another, and as he always had, he occasionally came up with secrets that shocked them. Ben had known Randy five years when he casually mentioned that his brother was in prison for murder.

"For *murder*?" Ben gasped. Randy had told Donna Clift about David, but he had sworn her to silence about his brother, and she had never told the Goodwins. *"Your* brother?"

"Yep."

"I didn't even know you had a brother. Why don't you ever go visit him? What happened?"

"Well," Randy began slowly, "my uncle was driving in Montana, going down the road, and he picked up this hitchhiker. The hitchhiker killed our uncle. About two years later my brother David was driving down I-5 [near Seattle] and he got up to about 128th Street— you know just about where you hit the Everett exit—and he picked up some guy hitchhiking. They were driving along, and this guy starts bragging about some old guy he killed in Montana. And it was our uncle. So my brother killed him, and they convicted David on circumstantial evidence."

Ben didn't know what to think. It was a pretty farfetched story, but then, he'd heard Randy tell some pretty good ones before. That was just a part of Randy he had to accept—wild tales out of left field.

Randy and Brittany Goodwin were still friends. In fact, as she grew from an awkward fifteen-year-old to a high school senior, he seemed to take a proprietary interest in her. He frowned on her dates with boys her age. On at least one occasion he disabled her car by removing the distributor cap so she couldn't join a group of her friends. Finally convinced that Randy wasn't hitting on Brittany, Ben and Marta had relaxed their rules a little. Randy, Brittany, Greg, and Ryan were kind of a foursome.

Whether Brittany and Randy were involved sexually or not—something her parents no longer suspected—they were together a lot. He took her and the boys bowling, swimming, and sometimes to a movie, and she listened raptly to all of his stories. In the summer of 1988 he explained to her exactly how he could rob his own house if he wanted to, collect the insurance, and make sure no one would ever find out. She didn't know whether to believe him or not. Randy liked to shock people.

During that same period Randy discussed a similar insurance scam with Nick Emondi. There were ways to do it and never get caught, Randy insisted. Emondi didn't encourage such conversation. It reminded him too much of the rainy Halloween night when Randy had asked him, "Could you kill your wife . . . if you had to?"

In truth, Nick was afraid of Randy, of the way he seemed to turn his imagination and his plans into reality. Randy Roth, for all his short stature, shared a kind of mystique with Charles Manson. He was smart, but it was more than that; Randy's gaze was so intense that it burned into your brain. He was a puppeteer, too, manipulating just the right strings to make his friends do his bidding or to convince them that things were not what they appeared to be.

Nick had always been ambivalent about Randy; he admired his guts and energy, but he feared him, too. On one occasion when Randy invited Nick to join him for a snowmobile trip into the backcountry, Nick was hesitant about going. He admitted to his wife, Carrie, that he was frightened—he never knew what Randy might do. "If I don't come back," he said, "tell somebody who I went with."

In September of 1988, Ben Goodwin had to go to California on business for a week. Ben was a notoriously light sleeper, perhaps a legacy of Vietnam. "Nobody drives into this cul-de-sac at night without my waking up," he said.

Marta was the sound sleeper, although she never slept very well when Ben was gone. Then she was usually alert to even the slightest sounds in the night. Their three dogs were kenneled out in the backyard, and they barked if a twig snapped, so that was some comfort. Randy had his German shepherd, Jackson, chained in his yard too. The master bedroom where Marta slept was in the rear of the house only eight feet or so from Randy's backyard and the shed where he kept his tools and his weight-lifting equipment.

During the week that Ben was gone, Marta Goodwin and several of the neighbors noticed that Randy backed his truck up to his garage every night between nine and ten—after it was full dark. He loaded it up and then drove off somewhere. No one thought much about it; Randy often spent weekend days at the local swap meet, and Marta just assumed he was planning to sell some of his possessions. Another neighbor saw Randy take several loads away from his house after dark.

On September 17, two days before Ben returned, Randy Roth was the victim of a burglary. He reported to the Snohomish County Sheriff's Office that a truck had backed up to his house and stolen his property: valuable mechanics' tools, sanders, saws, both of his Stihl chain saws, and his Craftsman tool chest. Not only his work tools but also his home appliances were gone—cameras, television sets, Nintendos and other games, a Kenwood stereo, other music equipment. It was the sort of crime that could put a man who was a truck mechanic by trade out of business. In addition, the burglars had ripped his red wall-to-wall carpeting so that it would all have to be replaced.

Snohomish County Sheriff's Deputy Dean Munday responded to the scene. The investigating officer noted a deep groove in the grass of the Roth backyard and figured that the burglar's truck had gone in that way. He saw the broken garage window, the carpet that was stretched and ripped as if something heavy had been dragged across it, scratches on a banister. It looked like a typical residential burglary. There were so many of them in Snohomish County that it was hard for the detectives to keep up with them.

Randy asked Marta the next morning if she had heard "all the commotion" at his place the night before. She had heard nothing at all. He explained that he'd been robbed, and she was shocked. "I was in the bedroom," she said, amazed. "I was watching television until late. I didn't hear a thing. The dogs didn't even bark. That's really scary, to think I was so close."

Randy explained that Jackson was "passed out" on his deck. He was pretty sure somebody had drugged his dog. "He was gone when I got home last night. He came home this morning, dragging his chain. He's just lying there. He won't even respond to me."

When Ben Goodwin got home, he went over to see Randy and found him and Greg working on their motorcycles in the shed. "My God, Marta told me you were robbed! Are you okay?"

Randy was very calm. "Oh, yeah."

"Well, what happened?"

Randy pointed toward his yard. "See that track right there? That's where the truck backed in. They broke that window there in the garage, came in and took everything."

"Randy," Ben began, "that groove in your lawn is where you and I felled that tree."

Randy half smiled. "If that's what the detectives say it is, then that's what it is."

Ben was nonplussed. He had a suspicion that he didn't want to have. He knew Randy was probably hurting for money; he had just been terminated from Cascade Ford "by mutual agreement." And Randy seemed so calm about losing so many of his things. He explained that he and his friend Max Butts* had gone out to dinner and a movie, but that he had gotten home well before midnight. It was too late; almost everything he owned of value was gone.

Sixteen-year-old Brittany Goodwin didn't have to be told the details of Randy Roth's robbery. She already knew. She went to her parents and said, "Don't tell me how Randy was robbed. I'll tell you. Somebody backed a truck into his yard, right? And then they broke out a window in his garage, right? And all of his tools and things are gone? And I'll bet they tore his carpet up, too, didn't they?"

Ben and Marta nodded slowly.

"Well, I'll tell you that there's a storage locker someplace around here that's just packed full of all the things that Randy had 'stolen.' He was so worried about money, and he told me exactly what he could do to get some, but I thought he was only teasing me."

When Nick Emondi heard of Randy's robbery, he wasn't surprised either. But he knew when to keep his mouth shut.

Brittany Goodwin didn't go to the police. She was afraid, and her parents were afraid for her. They were beginning to wonder if the man who had been their friend for so many years wasn't who they thought he was at all. They didn't know what Randy might do in reprisal if they turned him in. Randy had always said, "I don't get mad; I get even," but that threat had seemed to be part of his macho posturing. Now they warned Brittany not to tell. When they thought about it, they realized that bad things seemed to happen to people who crossed Randy. Now they half believed the wild stories that he had told them over the years. He still lived so close to them that they could have tossed a penny onto his back deck with no effort at all.

Two months later Randy told Ben Goodwin that he had totaled up all his losses for his homeowner's insurance carrier, the Pioneer Insurance Company of Minnesota. By his reckoning he was out close to $60,000.

Sixty thousand dollars! Ben felt the hair prickle at the back of his neck. *He* knew Randy's tools as well as Randy himself did—he'd always been free to borrow whatever he needed. And now Ben recognized the tool chest that Randy was using. *It was the same one he had reported stolen.* Ben also noted that Randy seemed to have his tools back.

Ryan Goodwin was puzzled to see that the Roths' "replacement" television set was the same brand, same size, same everything, as the stolen one. More than that, he and Greg had pasted stickers on Greg's Nintendo game. The "new" Nintendo didn't have stickers on it, but it had telltale glue marks in exactly the same places where the stickers had been on the "stolen" game. Besides that, the glue beads were the same shapes as the stickers. Ryan didn't mention this to his parents for a long time. Randy had been so mad at him the last time he told on him.

Randy had new carpeting; the ugly worn red rug that he had hated so was gone.

"At least Randy's got rid of that red carpet," Ben said sarcastically to Marta. She frowned and looked away.

When Randy filed his claim with Pioneer on November 11, he asked Ben if he would describe his missing tools to Pioneer's insurance adjuster. Ben agreed, feeling queasy about it—suspecting what he suspected. He didn't want to get involved at all. He didn't want to lie, but he sure didn't want to get on Randy's bad side.

The adjuster handed Ben pages of lists of tools and Ben spent twenty minutes checking off the tools he remembered that Randy had owned. He answered all the questions asked of him, but he didn't volunteer any information. The Pioneer adjuster was ready to leave when Marta asked him a general question about insurance— she had just lost her grandmother, whose insurance policies made her estate a complicated disaster.

"*I* didn't even talk to him after that first twenty minutes," Ben recalls. "Nobody mentioned Randy's claim after that, but the adjuster was here for over an hour, mostly talking to Marta and her mother. When I went out in the yard later, Randy walked over and said, 'What the *hell* were you talking about for an hour and a half with that guy?'"

"It was only about twenty minutes."

"Bull*shit*—I timed you."

When Ben finally confronted Randy about the fact that he seemed to have "found" all his missing tools, Randy looked at him without a flicker of expression and said, "These aren't the same tools."

They were neighbors still, but they were never close friends again. "He never really spoke to me again," Ben recalls.

Brittany tore up all of the pictures of Randy they had pasted in their albums over the years, all the Thanksgivings, Christmases, picnics, all the outings he and Greg had shared with her family. All those years of being so close.

She still kept some secrets to herself. If her father knew what Randy had done to her, she was afraid he would kill Randy.

Randy didn't seem to notice that the Goodwins avoided him, or, if he did, he didn't care.

The friendship was over. On both sides.

The Pioneer Insurance Company never attempted to prove that Randy Roth had not even had a burglary; they did, however, take issue with the $58,000 plus that he claimed was his loss. Claims adjuster Shelly Bierman first got suspicious when a receipt of sale that Randy provided for a stolen radio turned out to be a credit slip for the *return* of the described radio. Further, Roth was unable to provide documentation for many, many items he had lost. The insurance company felt the claims made were highly inflated over what they felt the actual loss had been. Pioneer filed a declaratory judgment action against Randy, alleging that his insurance claim was fraudulent.

Pioneer eventually settled with him on October 9, 1990, by paying Randy $28,500 and agreeing to dismiss its court action against him. All parties concerned submitted a stipulation and order of dismissal of claims "with prejudice."

Nothing about his "burglary" had gone smoothly for Randy. It had taken two years to collect, and he had to pay an attorney $11,000 of his settlement.

PART FIVE

Cynthia

10

Cynthia Rae Loucks was born a precious gift to her parents, Merle and Hazel. They had prayed for fourteen years to have "a darling little girl" to raise with their son. Her older brother, Leon, was in his teens when Cynthia was born. She was such a tiny little thing; she weighed only three and a half pounds.

One of the delivery room nurses ran down the hall to Merle Loucks and asked him if he believed in infant baptism. "I'm sorry," she said softly, "but we don't think the baby is going to make it."

Merle and Hazel Loucks's church did not believe in baptizing children until they had reached the age where they could make their own commitment to Christ, but he bent his head in prayer, "Lord, don't leave her go now. You have brought her this far. We want her."

The baby lived. After three weeks in an incubator, Cynthia weighed five pounds, and her parents were allowed to bring her home. She brought such joy and happiness to them.

After a scary start, Cindy Loucks thrived. She was a beautiful blond little girl, and she grew up to be a beautiful blond woman. She was raised in the church, and she did not depart from its teachings. They all attended the Westgate Chapel in Edmonds, Washington regularly. Merle Loucks was a deacon.

When Cindy and Tom Baumgartner were married in a church wedding, it was a union blessed by both sets of parents. No one ever dreamed that Tom would be dead of Hodgkin's disease in 1985 before he was thirty. Almost before he and Cynthia could cope with the diagnosis, the lymph node cancer swept all through his system like wildfire and he was gone.

Cynthia Baumgartner had never expected to be a widow, certainly not at twenty-seven. She was, quite naturally, overwhelmed at the responsibility of raising two lively little boys without a father. Her family and Tom's family were there to help, but the enormity of her loss was almost incomprehensible.

After six months Cynthia had to do something to fill up her days. She volunteered at her current church—the Silver Lake Chapel. It was, coincidentally, the same church where Janis Miranda Roth's memorial service had been held four years earlier. There Cynthia met the young woman who was to become her best friend: Lori.

Lori Baker was a pretty young woman, about Cindy's age, with short dark hair and glasses. She was employed at the Silver Lake Chapel as an administrator, and the two women talked a lot when Cynthia did her volunteer work. They had many interests in common. Cynthia wanted to get married again—someday. But it would be a long time before she could imagine finding anyone to compare with Tom. A widow with two children is not every man's dream woman; most men didn't want the responsibility of raising another man's children. Beyond that, Cynthia had restricted the possibilities of whom she might get serious about by ruling out divorced men. She would have to find a Christian man who was single or widowed.

But in 1985 Cindy wasn't looking. She just wanted to make a stable home for her boys who were only four and six. It made sense for Lori to share the house Cynthia owned at 2419 139th Street S.E. in Bothell. She had no mortgage to pay; Tom had seen to that. Both women felt more secure at night, and there was always someone to stay with Tyson and Rylie. A month after they met, the two women moved in together. Lori paid rent, and they shared cleaning and cooking and friendship. They bowled in a league together, and they were pretty good, collecting trophies. They pooled their money to pay the expenses. They opened a joint bank account for convenience, and they also shared a safe-deposit box at the Everett Mutual Bank: box number 2212.

Cynthia had a new will drawn up in December of 1985, and she named Lori the executor and her chosen guardian to raise Tyson and Rylie if something should happen to her. She stipulated that the house they all lived in was to go to Lori, too, so that the boys could be raised in their own home. There were things of Tom's that she wanted the boys to have when they were older—his pocket watch, wedding ring, other jewelry. The will, the jewelry, certificates of deposit, and other important papers went into the safe-deposit box in Everett. Cindy didn't tell Lori about the will; it just made her feel better to know it was taken care of, and she trusted Lori implicitly. She saw no need to mention it; she had every reason to believe she would live to be an old woman and that Tyson and Rylie would be grown men who could take care of themselves.

The two young women and Cindy's two boys lived together in

harmony for over five years. Cindy was active in her church and in Little League. She wanted her boys to be around masculine influence, and they loved playing ball.

Merle Loucks had worried about his daughter ever since Tom died. She was such a young widow, naive and trusting and comparatively wealthy. "Men may court you for your money," he had warned her gently. "Just be careful." She had promised him that she would be. And for five years Cindy was very careful.

Tom Baumgartner's father, Jim, talked to Cindy about her remarrying. "You're too young to raise those boys by yourself," he told her. "You should try to find a nice guy to marry, to raise the boys and provide a father image."

"I'm looking," Cindy would say, smiling, "but I can't find any good guys out there. They're all just looking for the same thing—if you know what I mean."

Cindy Baumgartner and Lori Baker were like family, like sisters. Lori's mom, Dorothea Baker, taught piano, and Rylie had been one of her students for three years. His grandparents had bought him a piano. Dottie Baker found Cindy "very lovely, very pretty, very happy. Wherever she was, laughter just entered the room. She was just—*life.*"

Cindy took good care of herself so that she made the most of her natural beauty; she had her hair lightened regularly and her nails done professionally. She dressed in a very feminine way, and her person was as immaculate as her house was.

Cindy helped out at Little League wherever they needed her, whether it was as a coach or manning the concession stand. In 1990 she took over the stand. She made sure it was fully stocked and that different parents took turns selling hot dogs, cold drinks, popcorn, and potato chips.

Randy Roth was still a coach in the ten-to-twelve-year-old league. Some of the parents really liked his win-win-win attitude. Some called him "Super Dad" because they admired him, and some did it in a sarcastic way and were put off by the way he criticized kids for mistakes and shouted constantly. He took Little League so seriously; he was, in fact, the quintessential Little League parent who seemed to have his child in the game not for the *child* but to fulfill his own needs.

Practice started in March of 1990, six weeks before their first scheduled game. In the ensuing weeks, teams would be set up and players assigned to their positions.

Randy Roth met thirty-three-year-old Cindy Baumgartner the same way he had met almost every woman who would become important in his life—through his son. At first they just made small talk when Randy bought things for Greg at the concession stand. Later it was Randy's turn to help man the concession stand. He and Cindy got along so well that he arranged to work the stand with her every night for a week. The other parents grinned when they saw how attracted Randy was to Cindy.

He almost missed meeting her. In the spring of 1990 Cindy was thinking seriously of selling her home and moving to Arizona so that she could live closer to her parents' winter home. Meeting Randy Roth changed all of her plans.

Cindy liked him right away. He was handsome and he was fun. And, most important, he really seemed to care about his son and about all the kids who'd turned out for Little League. He was a widower, he explained, and Cindy must have smiled inwardly. No matter how much she cared about a man, she would never have married a divorced man.

Randy's approach to Cindy Baumgartner was humble. "I noticed you right from the beginning," he said. "But the way you look, the way you dress, I figured you probably had money. I didn't feel worthy to introduce myself."

Before Cindy could protest, he hurried on. "But then I saw you drove an Escort—and I drive an Escort too, and I figured anybody driving an Escort couldn't be rich, so I felt I *could* introduce myself."

When he asked her out the next week, she accepted readily. Lori Baker and her mother could see that Cindy was really interested in this man. "She told me that she had met Mr. Right, and she was excited," Dottie said. "Her idea of a husband was a man who had to be one that had never been married or who was a widower. He said he was a widower. He was just what she had been looking for."

Lori met Randy when he came to the house to pick Cindy up, and she saw that he was very attractive and very taken with Cindy. He showered Cindy with red roses and phone calls and notes. But Cindy's best friend and her family were concerned. "Cindy did have money," Dottie Baker recalled. "She did own her home, and her husband had left her well taken care of. This man was just coming into her life *way* too fast. Cindy was such a sharp girl—level-headed—and just thought about everything carefully. I wondered why she was rushing into this."

Cindy was amazed at how much she and Randy had in common.

They both had their boys, of course, and the problems of raising them alone. Randy said he'd come originally from North Dakota, just as Merle Loucks had. They were both involved in baseball, neither of them smoke or drank, and they were family oriented. If Cindy Baumgartner had drawn up a blueprint for the kind of man she wanted for a husband, it would have been the Randy Roth she met in the summer of 1990. They dated, but most of their dates included the boys. Randy was always a perfect gentleman with her, affectionate but never aggressive about sex.

They went to the Strawberry Festival in Marysville, just north of Everett, and had a wonderful time. After that, Cindy invited Greg to spend the night at her house. The boys got along. They went skating, to the movies. It seemed the most normal thing in the world for Cynthia to start cooking supper for them all afterward. Somehow they just seemed to fit—as if they were two halves of a family seeking each other.

Haltingly Randy told Cindy about his wife who had died. "She actually died as I was holding her in my arms," he said. "She left me with a three-year-old boy, and I've been alone ever since, looking for someone like you."

Cindy saw they had the same beliefs, the same respect for marriage. Randy told her that he had been thinking about going to church, even though he had turned his back on religion after he lost Janis. "There has to be more to God, but I think I'm getting there."

Cindy explained to Randy that he had just met another of her personal prerequisites. For her to love a man, he had to be a strong Christian. "My church means more to me than any man. If you want to go to church with me, fine."

"I think that's what I've been looking for for so long." He smiled.

Cindy's parents, Tom's parents, and the Bakers all wanted Cindy to be happy. And yet they were worried that things were moving too fast. Cindy had been cautious all her life, and now she was absolutely enthralled with a man she had known only a few months.

The Goodwins saw that Randy had a new girlfriend, but it wasn't like the old days when he would have brought her right over to meet them. His latest girlfriend was a cute little blonde, they noted, and she often called out a friendly "Hi!" over the fence when she visited Randy's home in Misty Meadows. Cindy drove a little black Ford Escort, and they knew Randy had bought one just like it that spring. Randy made no move to introduce them. And there were certainly no more double dates or barbecues.

Randy kept Cindy to himself. By the time he started dating Cynthia Baumgartner in the summer of 1990, the Goodwins were almost completely estranged from him. They believed he had faked the burglary of his own home, and they suspected that he had lied to them about many things. Randy was angry because he thought that they had cooperated with the insurance company against him, a misconception on his part.

The friendship they had once enjoyed had been based—at least on Randy's part—on deceit. The Goodwins would eventually come to learn that he had broken the most sacred trust anyone could with a parent and then lied about it as blandly as he lied about everything else he did.

And so, as he began his intense courtship of Cynthia Baumgartner, his former best friends could only observe from a distance.

"We only met Cindy once over the fence. She was standing in Randy's yard, and he'd gone off to do something. They had just become engaged. She showed us her ring," Marta said. "Ben said something, and Cindy looked surprised and said, 'Well, what's the matter?' and Ben repeated, 'All I want to say is just be very careful. Just be very careful about what you're doing.'"

Cindy Baumgartner looked at Ben Goodwin as if she thought he was crazy. And then she turned and went to find Randy. She undoubtedly found his neighbors a little odd and could understand why Randy wanted nothing to do with them.

When the Goodwins learned that Cindy had two boys, they were worried. They couldn't imagine any mother allowing her sons to be treated the way Randy treated Greg. Did Cindy know about the garbage can incidents, the rages, the military discipline? They couldn't tell her. They could only hope that she would become disillusioned, as Mary Jo had—and as Donna had—and get out before she was in too deep.

But Cindy was in love. She was deeply impressed with Randy's warmth and kindness, with the devotion he showed his son, and with the way he had taken her boys under his wing.

Toward the end of July 1990, Randy asked Cindy if she would like to go to Reno with him for a classic car show and parade. At first she had a sinking feeling. Oh, no. Was he going to turn out to be like all the other guys she'd complained about to her father-in-law—out for only one thing? Probably. He had just taken longer to ask. Knowing that she might see her wonderful romance evaporate in a moment,

Cindy explained to Randy that she would never travel overnight with a man she wasn't married to.

Randy's response was that it wouldn't be a problem. They were all getting along so well, and the boys were getting along so well, that he thought they should think about marriage. She wondered if he was proposing. Randy used so many words to say something where most men spoke in simple sentences, and he sometimes had such a roundabout way of speaking. While she let hope bubble up in her heart, Randy just kept talking about how well their families blended.

Finally Cindy blurted, "Are you asking me to marry you? If you are, the answer is yes!"

Randy grinned and then immediately called an 800 number for a list of wedding chapels in Reno.

They had been dating only a little over a month.

Making such a momentous decision in a heartbeat was completely unlike Cindy, but she felt it was the right one. Her parents were visiting in North Dakota. Even her former in-laws, the Baumgartners, were away on vacation. But this was *her* decision. She wanted to marry Randy, and she wanted to go to Reno with him. It seemed like such a romantic adventure and such a wonderful way to start a marriage.

There probably wasn't a debater in the world who could have talked Cindy Baumgartner out of her decision to become Mrs. Randy Roth. Lori Baker and her mother begged Cindy to at least wait until her parents got home. But it didn't do any good. Cindy believed in Randy and she loved him. She had, of course, no idea that she would be the *fourth* Mrs. Randy Roth. She believed that she had found a man who had suffered the loss of a spouse, just as she had, a man who had never been divorced, a man who adored her and who would care for her forever.

They drove to Reno and walked up and down the street hand in hand admiring the gleaming, perfectly restored cars from other places in time. It was August 1, 1990. Their wedding day.

When they drove home as husband and wife, Cindy tried to find a way to cushion the shock of this sudden marriage for her parents and her former in-laws. The Louckses and the Baumgartners were pole-axed. They could scarcely believe that Cindy had chosen to get married in a gaudy "marriage mill"—a commercial chapel in Reno instead of in a religious ceremony in a church. They barely knew the man she had married. They worried, but most of all, they wanted her to be happy.

Swallowing their disappointment and their concern, Jim and Marge Baumgartner went to Cindy's house to meet Randy and welcome him into the family. Jim moved to give Randy a hug. The older man felt awkward when Randy stood motionless and did not return the greeting. He showed no emotion at all. In fact, he said nothing. A little nonplussed, Jim Baumgartner tried again, inviting Randy and Cindy to come to his house anytime and to bring all three of the boys. Randy brushed off the invitation.

"After that visit, I asked him many times to come for dinner, but he would never come over," Jim said. "Cindy brought the boys, but she always came alone."

Well, maybe it was understandable, Jim decided. Maybe Randy didn't want to be haunted by the memories of Cindy's first husband. Maybe he was just insecure, afraid he wouldn't measure up to the kind of man Tom had been.

They had married in such haste that Randy and Cindy hadn't even decided where they were going to live. Either of their homes was big enough to hold the two of them and their three boys, but Cindy's was a little larger, a little more expensive. Either way, either house, they would have to do extensive remodeling to accommodate all of them. And then, of course, there was Lori, who would have to find another place to live. Cindy didn't want to rush her; Lori and she had weathered some bad times together, and they would be friends for the rest of their lives.

Finally they agreed that it would be best for Randy and Greg to move into Cindy's house. The newlyweds lived with Lori and the three boys until Lori found her own place. They got along well enough. Lori was glad to see Cindy so happy.

After a little painting and refurbishing, Randy put his house in Misty Meadows up for sale, asking $175,000. The figure was way too high for the real estate market in the Seattle area in 1990. Although Randy had added the workshop and landscaped the yard beautifully, he really couldn't expect to get $100,000 more for his house than he had paid for it only six years before. Maybe he just set a high figure so that Cindy wouldn't notice the discrepancy in value between his house and hers. Cindy was far better established financially than Randy was.

11

After Lori moved out, Cindy and Randy lived in her house for a while, but then they decided they wanted a place of their very own, a new house in which to start their new marriage. After church on Sundays, they looked at several places and found exactly what they wanted in Woodinville, a small town just south of the Snohomish County line. Woodinville, once isolated, was being swallowed up in the nineties in the huge urban sprawl on all sides of Seattle. In another era, the house they chose would have been a farmhouse—it even *looked* like a farmhouse—but this house was brand new, a sunny yellow two-story with multi-paned bay windows, brick trim, and a three-car garage. It had a little front porch with a railing, and room for a swing and a rocking chair. The lot was huge and surrounded by trees—alders and, farther back, Douglas firs. There were a few ancient apple trees, the last vestiges of the farm the development had once been.

The house at 15423 232nd N.E, cost $275,000, a big jump up for both of them, but they loved it so, and it would be the perfect place to raise three rambunctious boys. Cindy's home sold almost immediately for $160,000. That sale closed simultaneously in October with the purchase of their new Woodinville house. So it was all Cindy's money that they paid down on the new house. The monthly payment would be $1,400—a hefty amount, but they felt they could manage; Tyson and Rylie's Social Security survivor's benefits of almost $1,500 could take care of it.

When Randy got his insurance settlement from Pioneer, he wrote a check for $11,000 into the house account, but Cindy wrote him one back for $10,000 right away. They were essentially living on Cindy's money. And, in truth, Randy retained control of his insurance payoff from Pioneer, which was only about $18,000 after his lawyer had taken his percentage. It was a big step down from the $60,000 he had sought originally.

Randy's house didn't sell at $175,000 or at $149,000. Eventually he dropped the price to $135,000 and it sold, but he stubbornly refused to throw in the shed he had built in the back. He demanded an extra thousand for the structure, or he threatened to have it moved. The buyer wouldn't budge. Apparently, Randy discovered how much it would cost him to move it, because he made a last visit to the Goodwins. Would they pay a thousand for it? Ben said he could use it, but he couldn't go that high. It was almost Christmas, and he needed the money for other things.

Marta bought the shed from Randy for $500 for Ben's Christmas present, and the two men who had been best friends but were no longer, moved the shed across the property line into the Goodwin's yard. They were like two strangers working together now; it seemed odd to Ben Goodwin to think that their camaraderie was completely gone.

Refusing to throw the shed into the house deal was a spiteful thing to do to the new buyers, but Randy was funny about money. It meant so much to him that he didn't seem to care what lengths he had to go to to get it.

After eight Christmases spent together, the Goodwins celebrated without Randy. It seemed kind of hollow. They kept asking themselves how things could have gone so wrong. They were happy for him that he had a new wife, and they liked Cindy—what they had seen of her—but they were afraid for her too. And they could not even say why or what it was they feared.

Randy had a number of debts—at least that was what he told his bride. Although he realized almost $50,000 after the sale of his Misty Meadows home, he didn't put any of the money toward the mortgage on the Woodinville house. Cindy's money had made the huge down payment, and Cindy's sons' Social Security survivor's benefit was making the monthly payment. Perhaps for the first time in his life, Randy was free to buy all the cars, trucks, motorcycles, and ATVs he wanted.

It didn't matter to Cindy. They were a family now, and her assets were Randy's, just as he had assured her that she now shared in everything he owned. He didn't want her to work outside their home. He would work as much overtime as he could at Bill Pierre Ford.

Lori Baker took her papers and valuables out of the safe-deposit box she had shared with Cindy, and Randy's name was added. Lori noted that Tom's pocket watch and Cindy's important papers remained in the box.

When they moved to the yellow house in Woodinville in the

autumn of 1990, Randy informed Cindy that he didn't want her taking the boxes of things that had been Tom's—clothes, sports equipment, memorabilia, things she was saving for the boys. She asked Jim Baumgartner if she could store Tom's stuff at his house, and of course he agreed. But he felt a chill. He thought it was peculiar that a man wouldn't let his stepsons have the comfort of their dead father's things. Naturally, Jim was afraid of losing contact with his beloved grandsons. But it was more than that. He hated to see Randy Roth calling all the shots. Cindy had been a feisty, happy young woman who made up her own mind. Now she seemed to follow every order her new husband gave her.

The Baumgartners had always gone to watch Tyson and Rylie play in their Little League games, and they continued to do so. Cindy and the boys were always glad to see their grandparents, but Randy scarcely acknowledged them. He spent his time shouting at Greg, Tyson, and Rylie when they made an error or struck out. He routinely refused the Baumgartners' invitations to go out to eat together afterward. It was clear he was deliberately snubbing them.

Cindy took her boys to see their paternal grandparents as often as she could. She always had some excuse why Randy hadn't been able to come with them—but Jim and Marge Baumgartner knew. He obviously wanted nothing to do with them.

During the fall of 1990, despite Randy's sometimes boorish behavior, Cindy Baumgartner Roth was a very happy young woman—happy in her marriage, happy with her new life. She was kept busy decorating the huge house in Woodinville and driving the boys to all of their myriad activities. She and the boys attended the Four Square Church in Everett or the Silver Lake Chapel, and sometimes she persuaded Randy to come with them.

Cindy chose mauve and blue for her basic color scheme in their new house. It went well with the gray carpet. They bought a lot of new furniture, choosing oak for the coffee tables, the wall units, and the display cabinet for Cindy's doll collection. Where Randy's homes had always been clean, but bare of any decorative details beyond marine gear and sports plaques and photographs, Cindy added many homey touches to the new house. She chose comfortable couches with mauve and blue throw pillows, hanging baskets of mauve or blue artificial flowers, blue candles, and framed prints in the same complementary colors. The decor was "country cottage," in keeping with the house, and Cindy delighted in finding new things that made it even prettier, like the straw wall hangings with lace and artificial flowers.

The master bedroom had a king-size bed with a ribbon-edged pale mauve spread with a tiny white flower pattern. The pillow shams and throw pillows matched. Behind the bed, they had a huge wall unit with a mirror and storage units for each of them.

In deference to the men in her life, Cindy was glad to let Randy decide what went into the upstairs recreation room. That would be the "guys' room." There went the console television, the VCR, the Nintendo, the drum set, the Exercycle, the baseball team pictures, the trophies, and of course Randy's Marine Corps memorabilia. On the wall he tacked a bright red Marine Corps banner bearing the legend "FMF, 3 ENGR BN SPT CO." It didn't match anything, but it made him happy, so what did it matter?

In every other house he had lived in, Randy had set about immediately to landscape the yards. Their Woodinville house had no landscaping and offered great possibilities. The yard was scrubby crabgrass, and there was a problem on one side with drainage, but one that could have been fixed with a French drain. There were no shrubs, flowers, or roses. There was only the partial fence of horizontal white boards and two giant rocks that sat on either side of the driveway. But Randy made no effort to work in the yard. He didn't plant grass, and he didn't plant a single rosebush. He complained that the yard was "a swamp," and he seemed to have no interest in changing that.

It was almost as if he didn't plan to be there long enough to bother.

Randy left Bill Pierre Ford for two months in November and December and took a job "in management" with Washington State. "My job requirements mandated that I work with the public—make inspections of vehicles . . . make adjustments."

The job had a rotating schedule. Sometimes he worked eight to four, sometimes noon to eight. "I was uncomfortable with the change of schedule," Randy recalled. "It was creating a hardship on my family. We were newly married, and we had adjustments. I indicated to my employer that I wasn't suited for an office job."

Randy recalled later that they were all "involved with family and the holidays" at the end of 1990. In his memory of the first six months of his marriage, *nothing* was more important than family. He was not about to leave Cindy and the boys alone at night in their semi-isolated country home. Their family time together was so important to him.

They were in their new house for Christmas of 1990, their first as a married couple. Actually, Randy and Cindy hadn't even known each other at Christmas of 1989. Many of Randy's friends were surprised to learn that he was married. The arrival of a Christmas card with a picture of the new family was the first clue for most of them that he *had* married again.

Cindy invited Lori and the Bakers over for Christmas, and they all celebrated together. Things seemed fine.

After Christmas Randy returned to his mechanic's job with Bill Pierre, and to more regular working hours.

Cindy Roth was not the kind of woman to spill private secrets of her married life, but the people who knew her well sensed a quiet unhappiness in her that seemed to begin after Christmas. While she had been blissful in the first few months after her marriage, she no longer was. She still went shopping with Lori Baker every Friday night, but her whole personality seemed muted, diminished. While the women shopped, Cindy's boys went with Greg and Randy and helped clean up the shop floor at Bill Pierre Ford.

Dottie Baker, too, noticed that Cindy seemed changed. When she gave Rylie his piano lesson at four every Wednesday afternoon, as she had for years, she was shocked to see that Cindy was no longer the bubbly, joyful woman she had known. In all the years Dottie had known Cindy, her house had always been spotless. Now, in the first gray winter months of 1991, the house was still neat, but there was dust on the new furniture, and the floors were not as spotless as they had always been. Cindy herself seemed drabber and less well groomed. She was letting her blond hair go, and the roots were her natural brown, and she hardly wore any makeup. Cindy had always worn earrings and other jewelry to match her outfits, but she no longer bothered.

Cindy didn't explain these changes to Dottie, but the truth was that Randy didn't approve of bleached hair, so reluctantly Cindy was letting it go back to its natural color. Also, Randy was outraged when he found out how much she paid to have her nails done. Cindy had always enjoyed having long, perfectly polished nails. She even had a tiny "diamond" applied to one—a custom manicure. After her marriage, she still went to have her nails done, but she paid half by check and half in cash, and the color of the polish had to meet with Randy's approval. She paid partly in cash when she had her hair cut, too. That way, Randy wouldn't know how much it had cost.

If it occurred to her that they were living in a magnificent house paid for with *her* money, that they derived a healthy part of their monthly income from *her* sons' Social Security benefits from their father, and that she had money saved on her own and had every right to spend a little of it on herself, she never mentioned it to anyone.

Cindy seemed chastened, afraid to speak up, always looking to Randy for approval before she spoke. Any woman who had ever been involved with Randy Roth could have warned Cindy that he was *the boss.* Whatever else mattered in any relationship he had, the most important thing the woman had to remember was that Randy ran things. He did not believe in women's liberation, and woe be unto any woman who argued about that.

Cindy was discovering that, just as all the others had. The romance vanished and the dictator emerged. Each time she bent a little to accommodate Randy's views, he pushed her a little further. And, because she believed in being the kind of wife who made her husband happy, she bent still further. She was not allowed to join a health club because she might "meet men there." Randy, however, *did* join a health club where dozens of attractive young women in their teens and twenties exercised with the men. Randy still left the house whenever he pleased without saying where he was going. He still spent long hours at Lily's house whenever he took her son home after he had visited with Greg.

Cindy was allowed to join the North Shore YWCA to take females-only aerobics classes and join walking groups; Randy deplored excess fat on women. Cindy had perhaps five extra pounds around the middle, and Randy never let her forget it. Her walking group met three times a week in the morning, and the women walked four or five miles. To the other members, basically strangers, Cindy seemed cheerful and friendly, and she quickly got into very good shape. She mentioned she was married and had children, but she didn't elaborate.

When Cindy signed up at the Y, she stressed to the business office that all mailings must be in her husband's name. "He has this thing about everything being in his name," she said half apologetically. He had been angry when she received catalogs addressed to Cindy Baumgartner. Even a flier addressed to Cindy Roth rather than Mrs. Randy Roth would upset him.

What a jerk, the girl at the desk thought. *Has to have his name even on some silly little fliers from the Y.* She didn't say anything to Cindy Roth.

Randy Roth recalls early 1991 as a hectic but happy time. "After the holidays, on New Year's, we loaded up the kids and went down to my dad's new place. . . .

"The next baseball season, 1991, was quite a trial for all of us. Three boys, three practices, three different game sites. She [Cindy] would go grocery shopping between dropping the boys off for practice. I would pick up Rylie and take him to piano lessons."

They all went to a couple of weeks of tryouts and then two days of drafting players. They were among the parents who were truly involved in Little League, and they had to cajole and argue to get help from less enthusiastic families. They still needed managers and coaches. Tyson and Rylie played their games at the main field complex, and the older boys, including Greg, played at the field on Highway 9 on the way to Everett. Regular Little League games ended in the middle of June, and All-Stars were picked by the coaches to go on to the championship competition. Greg was chosen as an All Star, and Randy was very proud.

Five of the mechanics from Bill Pierre Ford joined up to work as a pit crew for local car race competition, too. It was indeed a busy spring.

Maybe that was part of the reason Cindy Roth seemed less bubbly and energetic to her old friends and her family. Compared to her old routine, being married to a human dynamo like Randy must have been exhausting. Randy had a schedule that few men could have handled. He wanted things organized, neat, and he was frenetically busy all the time—sports, racing, work. He wanted his wife slim, trim, and obedient. He spent money—*her* money—freely, buying cars and other adult toys. He also bought ATVs, four-wheelers, for all three boys, with helmets and gloves to match.

One of the things Randy had been concerned about soon after his marriage to Cindy was life insurance. They were married on August 1, 1990, and in October of that year Randy approached Cindy about the situation. He was worried about their boys. He told her that he had had $100,000 worth of life insurance with Prudential since 1985. His beneficiary, he said, was his father, Gordon, whom he could count on to care for Greg and, if the worst should happen, for Tyson and Rylie, too. Cindy explained that she already had a $115,000 policy on her life with New York Life, all paid up.

Randy shook his head worriedly. How far would $215,000 go toward caring for and educating three boys? With the rate of inflation and considering the hefty payments on their $115,000 mortgage, Randy felt they were underinsured. The way he explained it, Cindy could see his point.

He told her that he hadn't been very happy with his own insurance agent's performance in the past, and she suggested they call her agent, Bruce Timm, who represented New York Life. She had been very happy with Timm's sensitivity and professionalism when Tom Baumgartner died. Since Tom had died within two years after his policy was issued, there was a fairly thorough investigation before her claim was paid. But it had been patently and tragically clear that Tom had died of rapidly progressing Hodgkin's disease—something the medical records supported—and Bruce Timm had helped Cindy through all the red tape as quickly as he could.

When the Clifts learned that Randy had remarried, Donna and her stepmother, Judy, had an ominous feeling. Although it had been four years since the rafting incident on the Skykomish River, Donna still panicked when she thought about it.

Judy Clift looked at Donna and murmured, "That poor woman. I have a terrible feeling that she'll be dead within a year."

"I wanted to look her name up in the phone book," Donna says. "I wanted to call her and tell her to run, to hide, or just to be careful, or think of some way to warn her. But what would I say? She probably would have thought I was jealous. Oh, how I wish I had."

If Donna Clift *had* called her, Cindy Roth probably would have been mortified. She didn't even know Donna existed. She had no idea that Randy had been divorced after he was widowed. Had she known, she never would have married him. He would have broken the very first rule she had about a potential mate.

But there were so many things she didn't know about Randy. As January and February of 1991 passed, the Gulf War seized the headlines, and there was a war of a different kind in the perfect home in Woodinville, Washington. Nobody knew how bad things were. Nobody knew how many terrible secrets Cindy Roth was learning. Her skin and her hair grew duller and drabber, and her housekeeping continued to falter. She had never been sick, but now she was often ill. She had always been happy and optimistic about life.

She no longer was.

On July 17, 1991, Cindy gave little clue to her real feelings in a letter to Tom's mother. She explained that Randy's uncle—who had just celebrated his fiftieth wedding anniversary—had been killed in a tragic accident. The whole family had been in a "dizzy state."

Randy's father had been working on the hot-tub behind the yellow house, but was having trouble getting it wired so the function switch worked properly, Cindy wrote. She thanked "Dad Baum" for buying all the wires, but insisted that that was far too generous a "house warming gift." Cindy wrote that she and Randy wanted to pay for at least part of the cost.

Cindy closed her letter as effervescently as she always did, "Thanks bunches and bunches. We love you. Give me a call when you get home. We'll work something out to get up to the cabin . . . August 1st or 4th, we're going to Reno for our anniversary."

The Baumgartners were vacationing in the latter half of July, and so were Cindy's parents, Merle and Hazel Loucks—just as they had been the year before when Cindy and Randy eloped to Reno. Now Cindy had suggested that she and Randy should return to the place they had been married. Perhaps she was hoping to rekindle the romantic love that had vanished from their marriage. She had not the faintest notion of how many other women had tried to do the same thing.

Beacon Rock, rising almost 600 feet above the highway. The Thanksgiving Day celebration with Randy Roth's father and family in nearby Washougal, Washington, turned to tragedy the next day when Janis plunged to her death from near the rock's summit.

Janis Miranda Roth as a happy new bride who had found "a man who was going to take care of her."

Randy Roth gave all his women roses *before* they were married. These were given to Donna Clift prior to their marriage. She was so thrilled, she took this picture of them.

Donna Clift Roth and Randy after their wedding ceremony at Chapel of the Bells.

Randy Roth at 30 with his son, Greg, age 7. This photo was given to "Mom & Dad" (Donna Clift's parents) a few weeks after Randy met Donna. It was signed "The Roths."

Randy Roth with Brittany Goodwin behind him; Marta Goodwin; her son, Ryan; and Randy's son, Greg, on a skateboard outing in a church parking lot.

Randy with Brittany Goodwin at a Christmas Eve celebration. Marta and Ben Goodwin didn't know that thirty-year-old Randy had seduced their fifteen-year-old daughter.

Randy (middle) with Ben Goodwin on his left. Randy always had one good male friend. Ben was the only one who wasn't afraid of Randy.

Cynthia "Cindy" Baumgartner—who became Randy's fourth wife on August 1, 1990, in Reno, Nevada—posed next to one of Randy's prize rosebushes.

Cynthia Baumgartner Roth's last address. The Woodinville house belonged solely to Randy after she died.

The master bedroom in Cynthia and Randy's new house. He "hated her pink things."

Photos of Cynthia's two sons, Tyson and Rylie Baumgartner. The day after Cynthia's death, Randy removed all traces of her. These photos were found in a bathroom closet when police searched the house after Roth's arrest in October 1991.

The badges and patches that Randy kept to substantiate all the places he'd been while in the Marines. Beside them are the receipts for purchasing them.

A reenactment of how Randy Roth claimed Cynthia drowned. Even creating water rougher than during the alleged incident failed to tip the raft.

King County detectives Sue Peters and Randy Mullinax with the Roth files in the evidence room. *(Leslie Rule)*

King County senior deputy prosecutors Marilyn Brennenman (left) and Susan Storey conferring on their strategy in the Randy Roth trial. *(Leslie Rule)*

Randy being led by guards from the courtroom. While in jail he went on a diet, lost his muscular build, and became a shadow of his former self. *(Leslie Rule)*

PART SIX

July 23, 1991

12

King County detective Sue Peters was on call for Major Crimes on the evening shift after the hottest day of the summer, July 23, 1991. The temperature had rocketed up to 99 degrees at four that afternoon, an almost unheard of heat wave. In western Washington, summer evenings were usually comfortably cool no matter what the day's heat had been, but at 7:30 P.M. it was still baking. Five minutes later Peters received a call from her sergeant, Spence Nelson, to respond to Idylwood Park on Lake Sammamish on a possible drowning. The victim was a female. That was all the information that was immediately available.

Peters went into service, and a marine unit came on the radio to report that no one involved was left on the scene. Peters drove to Precinct Three, arriving at a little after eight, and called Marine Officer Elaine Hood, who had been on the scene shortly after 911 was notified. Hood said that a woman had drowned in Lake Sammamish. Apparently she had been rafting or swimming with her husband. At any rate, she had been clinging to a raft when a powerboat raced by and its wake overturned the raft. She said, "The victim was blue. The husband refuses an autopsy."

It was the beginning. Sue Peters had no reason to think she was embarking on a particularly unusual case, beyond the fact that the raft had come in to shore with water in it and water-sodden items in the bottom. Hood reported that some of the witnesses had reported that the husband's demeanor was rather strange. Drownings on a hot summer day were tragically predictable around Seattle. Unused to hot, sunny days, northwesterners flocked to lakes and waterways during unusually warm weather, and a lot of them couldn't swim. They leapt into inner tubes, rafts, jerry-built boats or Styrofoam paddleboards without life preservers, and too often they slipped off and drowned in water still cold from mountain snow runoff.

Peters jotted down some notes. The victim's name—not yet released to the media—was Cynthia Roth, no age given. Her husband was known only as Mr. Roth. Driving his own vehicle, he had followed the Bellevue Medic One rig in which paramedics continued giving CPR to his wife. At Overlake Hospital in Bellevue, the victim had been pronounced dead at 1835 hours—6:35 P.M.—by Dr. David M. Roselle.

There were probably a hundred witnesses to the drowning; the park had been packed with people all day. There were lifeguards on duty, sunbathers, swimmers, and fifty to sixty boats zipping around the north end of Lake Sammamish when the drowning occurred. Sue Peters hoped that she could find enough of them to get the true story.

Peters started by placing a call to Overlake Hospital. She learned that Detective Larry Conrad of the Redmond Police Department and Mr. Roth had already left the hospital. It was seventeen minutes after eight. Roth had seemed in control, although the staff on duty had noted that he did nothing to comfort the two weeping children who sat in the quiet room only a few feet from him. The two little boys had been seen by a grief counselor, and it was hoped that they and their father would be able to cope with their terrible loss.

Larry Conrad was easy to locate. He was at Redmond Police headquarters finishing his paperwork. Peters could sense immediately that Conrad was feeling hinky about the case. The Roths had apparently been out on the lake in an inflatable raft, he reported. The woman had gone swimming and developed a leg cramp, the raft had flipped as she clung to it, and she had lost consciousness before her husband could pull her into the raft and row for shore to find help. Officers at the beach had gotten the impression that the raft had been swamped by a speedboat, but in Mr. Roth's first statement to Conrad at the hospital, he said he didn't think the boater was at fault, estimating the speedboat was at least 50 yards away from them.

"Roth said his wife could swim better than he could," Conrad finished.

Sue Peters knew that people expressed grief in different ways, and she knew what shock could do. She hadn't met Mr. Roth yet—but she intended to. For the moment, she arranged to pick up any physical evidence, including the raft, as soon as possible.

Conrad told Peters that Roth was upset when Dr. Roselle explained that his wife's body would have to be held for the medical examiner's office.

But that was the law.

Detective Conrad had taken the first statement from Roth, whose full name was Randolph G. Roth. Roth said he had been waiting for someone "with some authority," and he seemed relieved to meet the Redmond detective. Conrad noted that Roth's vehicle was an Isuzu Trooper II and that the folded-up raft and the paddles were in the rear of the Trooper, and he had seen at least one plastic sack containing wet towels and/or garments. Roth had appeared calm, but both of the boys, who appeared to be about eight and ten, had cried inconsolably.

It wasn't the facts of the tragedy that bothered Conrad, however; it was the affect of the widower. Randy hadn't seemed grief-stricken. The two little boys were hysterical—but not the guy. At the hospital, the raft had been taken into evidence, and this had seemed to infuriate Roth. "He became very agitated and angry," Conrad told Sue Peters. "He said we had no right to take it."

Randy Roth had given a written statement to Conrad at a few minutes after seven, repeating the same basic facts of the tragedy. One minute Cindy had been alive and clinging to their raft, albeit with a cramp. The next, the raft had flipped over on top of her and by the time he had righted the raft and pulled her in, she was no longer breathing. "He wrote out a statement," Conrad told Sue Peters. "I'll get it over to you."

Early the next morning, Sue Peters called the King County Medical Examiner's Office and asked to have a copy of the autopsy report on the victim. And then she started going down the list of possible witnesses. In any shocking event, different witnesses perceived things differently. She wondered what she might hear from those who saw the "blue" woman lying on the beach at Idylwood Park the afternoon before.

The Redmond Police Department had written the case up as Accidental Death—Case 91-4177.

A possible accident? Or a possible homicide? All Sue Peters had to go on at this point was a detective who felt hinky about a widower's demeanor. It wasn't much, but it was enough to keep her from writing the case off as "Accidental" in the county files.

Sue Peters designated it as a "Death Investigation." The King County Police number was 91-225773. Peters would begin by contacting the people who had been at the beach on that tragic Tuesday afternoon, and trying to find the victim's relatives and friends. Peters asked the media relations officers to distribute green fliers on the east side of Lake Washington, particularly in the Lake Sammamish area and beyond. She was seeking anyone who might corroborate Randy Roth's story. It shouldn't be difficult to find witnesses. The tragedy was the talk of the east side.

The *Journal American*, published in Bellevue, the largest city close to Lake Sammamish, ran the headline "Woman Drowns in Lake Sammamish" on July 24. The thrust of the story was that there were so many people in the park that no one realized Cynthia "Ross" had drowned until they saw the aid units arrive. One witness, Pam Chicoine, was quoted: "There were so many people down on the beach, I don't see how anyone could have seen it. It certainly makes you wonder how these three lifeguards will be able to see every accident."

The reporter acknowledged that the drowning had occurred far from the area protected by lifeguards and said that the lifeguards *had* jumped in when the woman was finally brought to shore. Still, there was just the merest suggestion that Cynthia Roth had drowned because the popular park lacked adequate safety precautions and was understaffed.

Redmond Police Sergeant George Potts told the paper that the dead woman and her husband had crossed from Idylwood Park to the east side of the lake in their two-person raft and were swimming when the victim got a cramp in her leg. The husband pulled her into his raft when he got it righted and paddled "for at least twenty minutes back to Idylwood to get help."

No one had stopped to help the couple, Potts said, but the man hadn't tried to flag a passing boat either: "He was intent on getting her back to shore for help as fast as he could. There's a lot of potential here for these kinds of things to happen, especially with a small raft low in the water—they can be easily overlooked by passing boats."

Mike McFadden, nineteen, was one of the guards on duty that afternoon. He told Sue Peters that he had seen the man paddling his raft near Idylwood Park; he was rowing very slowly, facing the beach. "That's not the most efficient method of rowing for maximum speed," the young guard commented. Indeed, the man had come dangerously close to the roped-off swimming area, and McFadden had blown his whistle and waved him off. The man in the raft did not, however, indicate at that point that he was in trouble. McFadden saw no other person in the raft. When the man beached his craft, McFadden noticed that he sat motionless in the raft for two or three minutes.

The first time the lifeguard knew anything was wrong was when one of the two boys who seemed to be with the man ran over to him. They were so polite and subdued that he was about to send them up to the guard shack for assistance, assuming one of them had a minor cut or some small problem.

"Then I saw the body and the hand laying on top of the raft," McFadden recalled. "I called code 88 [emergency alert] and ran to the boat."

The raft had had quite a bit of water in the bottom, perhaps four inches, and the woman's condition looked bad. She was not breathing, and her color was the blue-gray of death. McFadden shouted to the man he would come to know as Randy Roth to help him get her out of the raft and onto the beach so he could start CPR. Initially the man was so detached that McFadden assumed he was in shock. Roth didn't attempt to help resuscitate the woman; he stood off to the side and watched, his face expressionless.

The man muttered that a boat had come close to them and a wave had caused the raft to capsize, and his wife had swallowed water.

Once, when McFadden stepped aside to let another guard spell him on the CPR, he was surprised to see Roth calmly folding up his raft.

Other guards, including Kelli Crowell, immediately closed the beach to swimmers and joined McFadden as he worked over the woman. Crowell, twenty-eight, overheard Roth say that he had already bailed a lot of water out of the raft, leading her to believe that it had been full of water; possibly it had sprung a leak. She was under the impression that Roth had simply found the drowned woman floating in the water; she had no idea that they were together. The man was too removed emotionally. She didn't realize the two little boys were with him, either. He made no effort to comfort them.

Pam Chicoine had called 911 on her cellular phone, and the Bellevue paramedic team had left for the lake at once.

The victim's sons were terribly upset, with tears streaming down their faces.

Patti Schultz and her boyfriend, Michael Mann, were at Idylwood Park that afternoon. It was their day off. And had the woman's condition not been so hopeless, their presence might have changed tragedy into relief. They were both highly trained paramedics with the Seattle Fire Department. As they strolled on the beach, Patti's experienced eye picked up the frenzied activity near the shoreline. A crowd had gathered around someone on the ground, and she saw that the lifeguards were working over a woman in a one-piece bathing suit. Her skin color was mottled and cyanotic, and pinkish froth was coming from her mouth and nose. Both Patti and Mike joined in trying to resuscitate the victim.

When Patti bent to perform CPR she saw blood in the woman's mouth, as well as copious amounts of sticky sweet-tasting pink fluid, which she evacuated from the woman's stomach by forcibly turning her onto her side. Schultz also noticed discoloration around the victim's neck.

Emergency medical technicians from the Redmond Fire Department, under the direction of Captain Rudy Alvarez, arrived first. Paramedics from Medic I in Bellevue received the 911 call at 5:36 P.M. and were out of the firehouse a minute later, arriving at Idylwood Park at 5:49. Paramedic Mike Helboch recalled that he leapt from his van and raced to the woman lying on the sand. But his own heart sank at the sight of her. So did that of his partner, Chuck Heitz, Jr. Her skin had a bluish tint from the top of her head to her chest. He knew this meant she had been without oxygen for a significant amount of time.

"She had a very, very, very low chance of survival when I got there," he said.

While paramedics inserted an airway and tried to clear away more of the pink froth that blocked the passage of oxygen to Cynthia Roth's lungs, other onlookers were stunned to see her husband methodically gather his possessions from the raft—clothes, towels, thongs—and pack them into a number of plastic and paper bags. And then he calmly deflated the raft and folded it up. He seemed utterly dispassionate, almost more concerned that he would lose some of his belongings than that he would lose his wife. Indeed, most people, like Kelli Crowell, didn't realize that the man was even *with* the drowned woman. He seemed to be just another bystander.

For fourteen minutes, the Medic I team from Bellevue worked in vain over the body of Cynthia Roth. She had no heartbeat. No pulse. They gave her one milligram of epinephrine and used a vasoconstrictor three different times, with no reaction. They tried atropine with epinephrine. Nothing. They tried a bicarb injection. None of the chemical methods that sometimes got a patient breathing and her heart beating again worked.

Attaching the leads of the Life-Pak, the paramedics shocked Cynthia Roth's heart. The Life-Pak monitor leads showed asystolic heart activity—absent or incomplete contractions. The shock therapy didn't work either.

Finally they put a cervical collar in place and strapped her to a backboard. They knew in their gut that she was dead, but they continued to do CPR as they lifted her into the paramedic's rig for their speeding trip to Overlake Hospital. The woman was so young, and even in extremis they could tell she was beautiful.

When the Bellevue paramedics arrived, Kelli Crowell took charge of the two little boys, walking them to the guards shack where they couldn't see their mother. Even an adult couldn't have been expected to cope with such a heartrending loss. One minute the family had apparently been on a happy outing, and the next they were torn apart. The little boys, who told Crowell their names were Tyson and Rylie Baumgartner, were clearly in deep shock, their teeth chattering and their skin pallid beneath their sunburns.

It was past six. The boys had apparently been alone on the beach for hours with no supervision while their parents were on the lake in the raft. They had had nothing to eat except a sandwich offered by the father of some boys they knew. They had no idea how long they had waited for their mother and their dad to come back. It had been a long, long time, and they had begun to get really worried.

The Medic I rig was pulling out, and Patti Schultz saw the boys' father walk away from the scene, his raft slung over his shoulder. He was strolling. He still appeared to her to be in shock; there was no expression at all on his face. Tyson and Rylie hurried to be with him, then walked 20 feet or so behind him. He didn't seem to even notice them. Patti offered to help carry the plastic bags of wet towels, which were so heavy that the children couldn't lift them. Randy Roth told her they were all the things that had fallen out of the raft when it tipped over.

She had noticed that the widower had refused to let police drive him to the hospital where his wife had been taken, and Patti Schultz offered to ride to the hospital with the man and his sons; Mike Mann would follow in their car. The man, who she learned was named Randy, agreed. She had been afraid he would drive too fast or erratically as he trailed the van and its wailing siren to Overlake. But he did neither. His driving was fine; he stayed slightly under the speed limit of 55 miles per hour.

Randy explained that he knew CPR and that he had felt for his wife's pulse, but she had none. Schultz wondered why someone trained in CPR hadn't performed it rather than delaying any resuscitation efforts for the twenty minutes it took him to reach shore. Twenty minutes at a time like that could have been important.

"How long does it take a person to die without oxygen?" Roth asked suddenly. "How long can someone survive—you know, come back—without a heartbeat?"

Schultz didn't want to tell him that, realistically, the time was very short—about four to six minutes. She fudged. "With CPR, maybe thirty minutes."

"It's only four minutes," he said shortly.

If he knew the answer, why had he asked?

Sue Peters detected a chilling pattern emerging as she talked to the lifeguards and other witnesses who had been at Idylwood Park on July 23. Not one of them recalled that the man in the raft had *raced* back to shore to get help. Rather, he had seemed to paddle in an almost leisurely fashion, as if he was out for an enjoyable day at the lake.

One witness, Kristina Baker, a thirty-one-year-old housewife, had been at the park that day with her family and her neighbor's two children. She was sitting between the boat launch and the swimming area, watching the lake. About a half hour before the man and the blond woman launched the gray raft, a police boat had come by, directing all the rafts and inner tubes back toward shallow water and away from the dozens of speeding boats far out on Lake Sammamish. She was surprised to see the gray raft head out toward the deep water, and she watched, expecting the police boat to show up and make them go back.

She looked for the couple in the raft off and on, keeping one eye on the children she had brought to the lake. She saw the man and woman dive off the raft and splash around in the water, and she noticed arms waving in the air. She remembered thinking how foolish it was to swim in a lake so full of powerboats.

Kristina Baker's attention was then diverted for about two minutes. The next time she glanced out at the couple, she saw the man standing in the raft, then kneeling as he pulled the woman aboard. Nothing seemed amiss. Then she saw him sit down and row toward shore. Oddly, she could no longer see the woman. The raft made its way slowly to shore. Baker estimated it must have taken about twenty minutes before it pulled into the beach.

Dr. Donald Reay performed the autopsy on Cynthia Rae Roth the morning after she had drowned. Redmond investigators had classified her death as accidental, but Reay was not ready to be so definite. However, his assessment was not much help to King County Police investigators. If they were looking for definite evidence of foul play, they weren't going to find it in the autopsy report.

"The body is that of a normally developed white female five feet two inches in height, weighing 129 pounds," Reay dictated. "She appears to be in the mid-fourth decade of life. Her nutritional status shows mild obesity. Rigidity is 4+ in the upper and lower extremities. Lividity [the pooling of blood in the lowest portions of the body after the heart stops pumping] over the back—not fixed. Light brown to blond finely textured curly hair eight inches long. Brown eyes."

Even in death Cindy wore eye shadow. A nasal gastric tube used by the paramedics was in place. There was also an endotracheal tube in her mouth, left by those who had struggled to force oxygen into her lungs. A bit of beach sand still clung to her face.

Cindy Roth's fingernails were quite long and perfect, neither broken nor split, and painted pink. Three small clear jewels were set in the polish of her left forefinger. Her toenails were painted pink too.

There were old marks on her body—the striated stretch marks of pregnancy, and some minor scars on one shin. Reay bent to examine two fresh scratches on the left side of her neck. He described them as "two obliquely directed scratches measuring up to two inches [in length] and separated . . . by a half inch and each scratch measuring one-eighth inch [in width]."

"The pathological diagnosis is: (1) Asphyxia by freshwater drowning; (2) Visceral congestion; (3) Needle puncture wounds *of therapy*." (Another desperate measure taken by medical personnel— medications injected in a groin artery and in her forearm.)

Dr. Reay, whose expertise is highly respected, wrote, "This woman's death is due to asphyxia due to drowning. She was recovered from a lake where she was rafting. The death is classified as a *possible* accident."

Peters was perplexed. "Basically, the scenario didn't make sense to me," she recalls. She talked with Dr. Reay and with Bill Haglund, his chief investigator. But they could tell her nothing definitive. Even after they heard Randy Roth's explanation of the events of July 23, heard about his delay in getting help for his wife who had stopped breathing, they still had to say the postmortem had shown only signs to be expected in drowning. Beyond the two scratches, everything spelled death by drowning.

And that, of course, was how the rescuers at the beach had treated the emergency situation.

Having spent less than a year in the Major Crimes Unit, Sue Peters had yet to work a truly memorable homicide case. Most of the murder investigations in any department are routine—if murder can ever be considered routine. Motive, means, manner, and opportunity were usually obvious. Spouses and lovers killed each other out of jealousy or in a drunken rage. Gang members killed each other to look like big men. Victims were murdered during the commission of other, lesser crimes.

But this case was already different. Peters requested a computer check on Randy G. Roth, DOB 12/26/54, seeking any criminal history. Either he was the calmest man in the face of a major disaster she had ever encountered or things were not what they seemed.

Peters read the statement that Randy Roth had written out for Redmond detective Larry Conrad a half hour after his wife was pronounced dead. Roth's knowledge of grammar was rudimentary, and he rarely used commas or periods. His handwriting was unusual, the letters tilting in one direction and then in the other.

We arrived at the lake at approximately 2:30 P.M. Then started to inflate the raft and inner tubes for the kids—so it was sometime after 3 when we reached the beach. The two boys were going to float in the swim area as they had done with their Mom twice before. Cindy asked me to row to the east side of the lake where it would be more romantic. I said it looks like a long way. She replied With your strong arms, you can do it. We rowed to the other side and paddled around for awhile and started back. She asked if I would like to cool off with a swim and I said O.K. We swam for almost 10 minutes and she said the cold water is giving her a cramp in her leg. I said let's head back. We were on the side of the raft and she was holding onto the raft and I said Hang on, I'll go around and hold the other side so you can get in. As I was working my way around a wake from a passing boat about 50 to 100 yards away went by and the raft turned over on top of her. She coughed once and I hurried to right the raft which took about

30 seconds. She was already floating face-down and I couldn't get her into the raft from the water. I managed to climb in and pulled her aboard and proceeded to row for the beach side where help could be found. On beaching, a life guard was summoned by my son on shore and they started CPR. I think my son, Tyson, who was on shore—and they started CPR.

Randy G. Roth

Little things niggled at Sue Peters initially, but they soon seemed bigger. Why hadn't Randy tried to get help from one of the passing boats? Why had he rowed for twenty minutes or more to get his drowned wife in to shore? He had told Patti Schultz that he knew a person could go only four minutes without oxygen before it was too late. Why had he sent a child to get the lifeguard? For that matter, why hadn't he started shouting for help the minute he got within hearing distance?

Peters looked for logical reasons. Denial. Roth could have been so stunned that he had tried to pretend it was all a bad dream, that he had just kept rowing, rowing, rowing, hoping that at any moment Cindy would sit up and everything would be okay.

But the discrepancies warred with the easy explanations. Randy told one rescuer that Cindy had coughed, another that she had gulped. In one version, he was sitting in the raft while she swam; in another, he was swimming with her.

On Monday, July 29, Sue Peters placed a call to the Roth residence and left a message on the answering machine. Nine minutes later Randy called her. He explained that this was the day of his wife's memorial service. His voice was flat, but he obligingly gave Peters a short tape-recorded statement of what had happened on July 23. He was very matter-of-fact.

"When you interview someone about the death of a spouse—in an accident, particularly—they're going to be upset, *you're* going to be upset," Peters says. "If someone had called *me* about someone in my family only three or four days after a death, especially on the day of the memorial, I think I would have said, 'Call me later. I can't talk right now.' He didn't. He basically just went along with the program. . . . He answered my questions, gave a scenario of what had happened, and he gave long answers to short questions."

Randy gave Sue Peters information about Cynthia's parents, the Louckses' names, and their phone number. He said she also had a brother, Leon Loucks, in Lake Stevens and gave his phone number.

He repeated the events on the lake without a vestige of emotion in his voice.

He explained that Cynthia had been cremated shortly after the postmortem examination. "It was what we both wanted," he said. The Louckses had been upset about that, but Randy had convinced them that he was sure Cindy wanted that, told them that he had called one of her best friends in another state who said that was what Cindy would want, and her bereaved parents had finally agreed.

Bracing herself for another sad call, Sue Peters called Merle Loucks. This was the second year in a row that Hazel and Merle Loucks had returned from their vacation in North Dakota to learn shocking news. Compared to this year's tragedy, last year's surprise wedding seemed minor now. Losing their precious daughter at the age of thirty-four in a shocking accident was almost more than they could bear. Merle Loucks said that he didn't know of any marital problems that Cindy might have had; he knew that she and Randy had a trip planned to celebrate their first anniversary, which would have been August 1, only two days away. He thought they had tickets to either Lake Tahoe or Reno, and Cindy had been looking forward to their trip.

Peters asked if Cindy had been able to swim, and he said that she was a *very* good swimmer. Merle Loucks said that he would be able to talk with Peters in more detail later on; he just needed a little more time to adjust to Cindy's death.

Shortly after one o'clock on the day of Cindy's memorial service, Sue Peters received a telephone call from a young woman named Stacey L. Reese, who explained that she and Randy Roth were co-workers at Bill Pierre Ford. Stacey, a single mother with a young child, was worried and upset. She felt that Randy's behavior both before and after his wife's death had not been that of a loving husband. In fact, some things had shocked her.

With Stacey Reese's permission, Sue Peters taped the phone call. Stacey said she had hired on to work in the office at Bill Pierre's Ford dealership in February. Starting in May, Randy had begun to spend an inordinate amount of time coming to the office for coffee or just to talk. She figured he must have come into the office three or four times a day. He had invited her to lunch at a local hamburger place and had wasted no time in telling her that his marriage was not happy. It was, in truth, not really a legal marriage anyway—only a "verbal marriage." He told her that Cindy was obsessive and nasty toward him and that he did not expect to be with her much longer. He didn't really see how he could go on in such a stifling relationship.

At that point, Stacey didn't know whether to believe him or not. He seemed very nice and very unhappy. But, on the other hand, married men often played out that kind of line.

Stacey had never dated Randy, nothing more than the quick hamburger lunches, sometimes with him alone and sometimes with other employees. He had told her and other Bill Pierre employees that his "contract with Cindy was up on August 1."

Juanita Gates, the senior cashier and office manager in charge of accounting at the auto dealership, had noticed that Randy was hanging around the office and had teased Stacey about it.

When Juanita asked Randy if he was married, he had answered, "Kind of. Why do you want to know?"

Juanita kidded back, "Well, if you invite Stacey and me to dinner, we need to know whether to bring candy or candles."

Stacey didn't know what to think. One time, she had gone to an auto race in which the company's mechanics had a car, and she had seen the woman she thought was Randy's "live-in." She had pointed the petite blonde out to Juanita and said, "That's the woman who lives with Randy Roth."

On Wednesday, July 24, Stacey had learned that Randy's wife had drowned—the newspaper story had said "wife." Stacey wanted to do something to help. At the very least, she felt she should call. She left a message on Randy's answering machine, and he soon called back. She asked him how he was doing, and he answered, "I'm fine. Why wouldn't I be? It was a horrible thing—but a relief, too."

But that wasn't all. Stacey told Peters she had received a second phone call from Randy Roth on July 26. He talked to her about his upcoming interviews with the police.

"They don't think you murdered Cynthia, do they?" Stacey asked him, somewhat nervously.

"It's all interpretation," he answered smoothly.

On Saturday, July 27, Randy had called Stacey to ask her if she would like to go to Sunday breakfast with him and his boys at the House of Pancakes. Since Cynthia's memorial service had not even been held yet, Stacey declined. Randy seemed a little more worried about what the police were thinking and told Stacey he was afraid the police might be coming to arrest him that very weekend.

Although she didn't say so out loud, that made Stacey Reese even less interested in going to breakfast with him. He was beginning to sound like a man who was coming on to her instead of a grieving widower. She was worried enough that she thought she should contact someone working on the case.

When Sue Peters hung up, she was troubled too. How could a man who had lost his wife only a day before talk about her that way? *A relief?* Cynthia's drowning had been a relief to him?

Marta and Ben Goodwin learned of the death of Randy's fourth wife by reading the funeral notices in the paper. They were stunned, but there was no mention of how she had died in their paper. They attended the memorial service. "Quite frankly," Marta said, "I wanted to know what had happened. Had she had cancer or something?" It was only near the end of the minister's eulogy that Marta felt icy chills as she heard his words: "Who could have known that on that beautiful sunny day Cindy would drown?"

Marta clutched Ben's hand. They didn't dare look at each other. They were both remembering the day Ben had said to Cindy Baumgartner, "Be careful. Just be careful."

After the service, they saw Randy standing at the end of a long hallway, leaning against the wall. He was smiling faintly.

Marta found Greg eating cake in the church basement. She gave him a hug, and he grinned at her. "My new mom and my dad went out on the lake and she drowned." He said it as if it was business as usual; he had become so used to the comings and goings of mother figures in his life that he was inured to the pain of loss.

He has lost so many new moms, Marta thought, that he doesn't even react to tragedy anymore. He just thinks this is the way things are.

13

On July 30 Randy Mullinax joined Sue Peters in the investigation of Cynthia Roth's death. The case was spreading out like a spiderweb. There were far too many strands for a lone detective to follow up. They would work partners on the investigation into what had seemed to be an accidental drowning, but no longer did. They had never worked together before; they would turn out to be naturals.

They went over the case together, memorizing details, highlighting incongruities. On August 1, they would interview Randy Roth in depth—August 1, Randy and Cynthia's first wedding anniversary.

In a matter of a few days Sue Peters had found out things about Randy G. Roth that she suspected he would never have wanted her to know. It wasn't just his blatant flirtation with Stacey Reese and his cold statement about Cindy's death. It wasn't that Randy had not even bothered to notify Cynthia's parents and brother of her death and had let them hear it on the eleven o'clock news. It was more than his almost complete lack of emotion. More than the long, long time he had taken before he called for help for Cynthia.

No, Randy seemed to have had a whole other life that Cindy either did not know about or had found out about in the months before she drowned.

Cynthia Baumgartner Roth could no longer speak for herself, but her friends could, and Peters's phone had begun to ring almost from the moment the first newspaper stories of Cindy's drowning hit the stands. One friend told Sue that Randy had been alone with another of his wives when she died in an accident. She didn't know the details, but she thought Cindy had become aware of the tragic incident.

"Her kids were her top priority and it would be very unusual for her to leave them alone on the shore, playing in the lake without supervision," the woman added. "Very unusual."

Mary Jo Phillips, who had expected to be Mrs. Roth number four, called to tell Sue Peters about the man she had almost married. She said there had been a *first* wife who was Greg's real mother and who might be living in California. Apparently no one had seen or heard from her in years. That wife had come *before* the wife who "slipped off a rope on Mount Rainier," and then there had been Donna Clift, the wife who came after the mountain tragedy. Mary Jo believed that Randy had been investigated in his second wife's death and that he had collected a couple of hundred thousand dollars in insurance over that. Mary Jo and Randy had actually broken up, she said, because she was uninsurable. From the moment he found out she had been treated for cancer, his ardor cooled rapidly.

There was more. "Randy doesn't like women . . . [and] little girls. . . . Randy has a military background . . . he worked in Vietnam and he has gone through three months of brainwashing on . . . killing people and mutilating women and children."

Randy supposedly had a brother in prison for murder, and he himself had been investigated for a tool theft.

Randy Roth was perhaps, Sue Peters pondered, much more than a simple diesel mechanic with a flat personality and a monotonal voice. He had clearly touched many lives and left most of them diminished in one way or another. She and Randy Mullinax could not arrest a man for showing no emotion over his wife's drowning, but they might be able to arrest a man whose past was riddled with blatant lies, bizarre coincidences, and suspicious circumstances.

Sue Peters and Randy Mullinax weren't even positive that Randy Roth *was* Randy Roth. They half expected to find he had half a dozen aliases, that they had stumbled upon a kind of modern-day Blue-beard with a trail of dead wives.

Sue Peters could not find a death certificate for a Jan Roth in either King County or Pierce County. When she called the Office of Vital Statistics in the state capital in Olympia, she learned that there had indeed been a Janis Miranda Roth who had fallen to her death—not from Mount Rainier but from Beacon Rock in Skamania County. It had happened in November of 1981 while the victim was hiking with her husband, Randolph G. Roth. Peters learned that Jan Roth's date of birth was July 26, 1952, her birthplace was Texas, and she had lived at 6207 227th S.W., Mountlake Terrace. That would have made her twenty-nine when she died. According to Vital Records, Jan Roth had died of a depressed skull fracture. Like Cynthia Roth, her remains had been cremated immediately after autopsy.

That death, too, had been classified as an accident.

Either Randy Roth was a most unlucky man when it came to wives, or Peters and Mullinax had found the end of a thread that they could follow to an elusive and terrible truth.

Peters found that Mike Grossie was still with the Skamania County Sheriff's Office. Grossie remembered the case very well indeed. He had interviewed Randy Roth himself in his Mountlake Terrace home, but the widower had been unable to explain just how his wife might have fallen backwards off the trail. Grossie said he and the rescue people had tried to duplicate the circumstances of Jan Roth's fall, but they had had no difficulty at all keeping their balance on the same trail up Beacon Rock. They had never figured out how she had fallen or if she had fallen from the spot her husband pointed out. Grossie promised to forward a copy of his investigation at once.

Peters and Mullinax could not help the excitement they felt. In a detective's world, this case was like finding a pebble, polishing and examining it a little, and discovering that it was a diamond. Certainly they were out to see that Cynthia Baumgartner Roth was avenged—if avenging was indicated—but they also suspected they were on the trail of a man who had gotten away with murder—quite literally—for a long, long time.

One of Sue Peters's callers had mentioned that Cindy's very best friend was a young woman named Lori Baker. In fact, the caller said, Cindy and Lori had lived together for more than five years after Tom Baumgartner died.

On July 31, Randy Mullinax and Sue Peters went to interview Lori Baker at the Silver Lake Chapel where she worked as a church administrator. Lori described her long friendship with Cindy Roth and her dismay—shared by Cindy's relatives—when Cindy decided to elope with Randy only a month after she began dating him. Cindy had always been a cautious woman, and it had been completely out of character for her to elope to Reno. Lori was as devastated by Cindy's sudden death as the rest of the people who had loved her. Like Leon, Cindy's brother, Lori had had to keep calling Randy to learn even the most minute details of the tragedy. Randy hadn't called any of them voluntarily.

Friends had heard a report about the tragedy on the radio, and she had hoped against hope that it wasn't true. She had finally reached Randy at ten o'clock on the night Cindy drowned.

"I called Randy and asked to talk to Cynthia. He said that 'wasn't possible.' I asked him why, and he told me."

Randy told his dead wife's best friend about the wave that had hit Cynthia in the face. "I really got a lot of water out of her," he explained, referring to his efforts to save Cynthia while they were still out on the lake.

The shock was so great that Lori had hardly been able to speak to this man who had been married to her best friend.

Lori explained to the detectives that she had paid Cindy $300 a month rent during the time she shared Cindy's home. They had also shared a safe-deposit box in Everett. After Cindy got married, Randy's name was added to the list of those who could have passkeys. Lori believed there should be a will on file for Cynthia Rae Baumgartner. Cindy was the type who would have seen that her boys were provided and cared for. Lori Baker also provided Mullinax and Peters with a list of Cindy Roth's friends, people who might be able to tell them about the woman she had been.

The two King County detectives headed up to the Snohomish County Courthouse. They read Thomas A. Baumgartner's will and saw how well he had provided for his wife, Cynthia, and for his sons, Tyson and Rylie.

Public records can be a treasure trove for detectives. Peters and Mullinax discovered the million-dollar suit that Randy had filed against the state of Washington in the "accidental death" of Jan Roth and saw that it had been dismissed. They reviewed records, now dusty, on the death of Janis Miranda Roth in November of 1981.

And so, when Randy Roth came into King County Police head-quarters at a quarter to eight on the morning of August 1, 1991, the two detectives who greeted him already knew a great deal about him, far more than he realized.

It was the first time they had seen him in person. They noted that he was a good-looking man, quite short, but very well buffed, with bulging biceps, broad shoulders, and a trim waist. He appeared to have tremendous upper-body strength. He was clearly a man who took good care of his body and was proud of it. He was at least four or five inches taller than Cindy Roth had been and thirty pounds heavier. As always, he wore contact lens in his brown eyes to correct his extreme myopia.

Randy Mullinax asked the questions and Sue Peters took notes as Randy Roth talked about his background and once more repeated the events of nine days before.

"We obviously knew things about him that he didn't know we knew," Mullinax recalls.

Mullinax asked Roth "nuts and bolts, simple questions." But Roth seemed incapable of giving a short answer. "We could ask him one pretty basic question, and ten minutes later he would still be rambling on about it."

Roth had a ponderous way of speaking. If asked a question like "Did you and your family swim often?" he would answer, "That would be the type of activity in which we would participate for our recreational needs." He seemed incapable of a simple yes.

Perhaps he was stalling, filling the air with enough words to block out troublesome questions.

"He didn't realize the extent of what we knew," Peters says. "At that point we knew about Jan's death—we'd already researched all of that. That was one of our things—to ask him real casual questions. Randy [Mullinax] would ask him how many wives he had had and then ask him to talk a little about each wife. So it was just kind of out of the blue, 'How'd *she* die?' and he'd describe it."

It was cat and mouse, but the mouse didn't realize how well prepared the cats were. "He'd lie," Sue Peters remembers, "and we would know it—but he didn't know we knew. There were at least four or five lies that could help us in a trial."

Randy Roth lied particularly about the amount of insurance he had taken out on his wives. He seemed to believe that there was no way for the investigators to check that out. Indeed, Sue Peters and Randy Mullinax did not know just how much insurance was involved—not at that point—but they had every intention of finding out. Some of the subject's evasions and exaggerations were immediately obvious; others would grow like Pinocchio's nose as the detectives continued their probe.

He repeated essentially the same story he had told the Redmond Police. He and Cindy had rowed to the far shore of Lake Sammamish, and she had suggested they go for a swim to cool off. She had had a cramp in her leg, and he had instructed her to hold on to the ropes on one side of the raft while he steadied it from the other so she could climb in. A boat had gone by, and its wake had flipped his raft. Cindy had been trapped underneath for 30 to 45 seconds, he estimated. He had heard her gulp just once. When he got the raft righted, she was unconscious and floating facedown.

Randy was just as calm talking about Cindy's death as he was about describing his occupation. "While they were working on her, there was no oxygen in the building. They couldn't get oxygen to her because it wasn't available. The paramedics took control and I just watched. They gave her a shock. I thought they were going to use cords to jump her or bump her to get her going. I talked to the Redmond police, and then they hauled her away to Overlake Hospital."

Both detectives noted that Randy talked of his dead wife as if she had been an inanimate object—as if he were talking about a car engine that didn't work any longer.

He recalled that he had deflated the raft with the help of one of the boys, and he thought a paramedic had helped too. (That would have been Patti Schultz.) He didn't know her name, but she went to the hospital with them.

"A doctor came in and said they couldn't revive her." He recalled talking to a social worker and a detective, who had taken his raft away.

"We left—and I asked the boys what they wanted to do. I decided to take them to Burger King, and then we went to rent videos to watch at home. The boys seemed to be pretty good, but the little one [Rylie] cried. I didn't want to really talk to them about what happened. I was looking for a distraction. That's why I rented the videos."

"Do you remember what you rented?" Mullinax asked.

"One was *Short Circuit 2* and the other was *Weekend at Bernie's*. I can't remember the third one."

The two detectives exchanged glances. *Weekend at Bernie's* was a black comedy about a wealthy man who dies at his beach home and whose corpse is carried from place to place, propped up, buried in the sand, thrown off a speeding boat, and posed to look as if it is alive. It seemed at the very least a most inappropriate selection for two little boys to watch for "distraction" after having just seen their mother's drowned body.

"We got home around eight-thirty or nine, and we all took showers and then watched TV."

"Did you notify anyone that Cynthia had died?"

Randy shook his head. "Cynthia's parents were on the way back from North Dakota, and I didn't think to call anybody. The next day I was just sitting around the house and Cynthia's girlfriend Lori and her brother called and left messages on the answering machine."

In the same flat voice, Randy Roth said he had called Leon Loucks back. "He said he'd heard it on the radio and wanted to know if it was true. I told him it was and that the services were set for Monday morning. I told him that we both had decided we wanted to be cremated when we died."

Although the Loucks family had wanted to bury their daughter, they went along with the cremation. "Cynthia's dad took her ashes, I think."

"Did you and Cynthia have wills?" Mullinax asked casually.

"No. We didn't have one together. I don't know if she had one. She told me that she didn't, and her friend Lori was there when she said that."

Mullinax and Peters kept perfectly straight faces.

Randy talked on. "We really didn't talk about Cynthia's past—that was her private life. We just talked about softball practice, the kids at school, how she felt bad because the kids had more respect for me than her and because they liked me better. *I* raised the boys," he said with a trace of smugness.

Asked again about life insurance policies, Randy acknowledged they had one—but only to pay off the house if one of them died. Randy thought it was for about $200,000. They owed nearly $120,000 on the Woodinville house. He didn't really know about any other policies that Cynthia might have had, but he said they were each other's beneficiaries, and his father was his alternate beneficiary.

Randy said he had called the life insurance company on Friday, July 26, on Monday, July 29, and again on Tuesday, July 30, to find out what to do to put in his claim. "It was Cynthia's idea, you see, to get life insurance so our home would be paid for in case of an accident."

It was a familiar tune, but Mullinax and Peters didn't know *how* familiar yet. Randy hadn't let any grass grow under his feet before he tried to collect on Cindy's insurance. They listened as Randy explained that their house had cost $275,000 and they had both sold their previous homes to use as the down payment. "The mortgage is in both or our names . . . we have combined finances, a joint checking account since our marriage. I also opened a savings account and put five hundred dollars in. Actually, we didn't talk about our finances much."

Randy told the detectives that he had realized a $50,000 profit from his house, which he had put down on the new house. He wasn't sure how much Cindy's profit from her house had been. But *they* were—it had been $160,000, the total down payment on the Woodinville house. Whatever he had done with his $50,000, he hadn't contributed toward buying the house.

"I plan on raising Cynthia's boys, but it won't be easy because that's two more." Randy sighed.

"You've been married before?" Mullinax asked casually.

"Yes, to Donna Roth in 1975. We were married for five years. Donna just didn't like being committed. She had a daughter from a previous marriage."

This would have been the first Donna—Donna Sanchez Roth, Greg's mother. Randy said he hadn't talked to her in several years, but that she did have visitation rights with Greg.

"Jan was my second wife. We were married for nine months. She died in a hiking accident in Skamania County in 1980 or so."

When they asked him about Jan's fatal plunge from Beacon Rock, Randy described it, stressing that there had been eyewitnesses. He implied that six or seven people had been standing right beside him when Jan fell. He himself had been walking "eight or ten feet behind her. She was dead at the scene."

There had, he admitted, been a police investigation and, he thought, an autopsy: "I felt like I was being watched for about three weeks."

"Did anyone see what happened?" Mullinax asked.

"Well, *yes*. They were right there," Randy answered.

"We *knew* there were no witnesses," Peters says. "So it was 'Okay, here we go. . . .'" Randy Roth was lying again.

Randy's third wife, he explained, was another Donna. He thought he had married her in 1985, but he wasn't sure of her maiden name. He had met her at Christmastime, married her in May, and she left in September. The second Donna, according to Randy, hung around with a wild crowd and was involved in "drug deals. She slapped her daughter around, and I asked her to leave, and we got a divorce. Very immature . . . very. I think she went to Utah or Colorado to live with her former husband."

Until he met Cynthia in 1990, Randy said, he just dated casually and had no thoughts of marrying again. He had had no insurance policies.

"You have male friends?" Mullinax asked.

"My best friend is Max Butts. I met him in 1985 or '86 at the Bellevue dealership where I worked. Cynthia was real social, but I just had a couple of friends."

Randy explained that he and Max, his three "sons," and Brad (Lily Vandiveer's son) all went motorcycling together.

Cynthia's friends had been a woman named Sally who lived in Colorado, the women from her aerobics class, Pam "the fingernail lady," and Lori Baker, who Randy said was probably his wife's closest friend.

Randy said that he grossed about $3,000 a month in his present job at Bill Pierre Ford and had cash assets of about $20,000 and $4,000 in the bank. He added to his income by buying and selling cars. Cynthia had her money "spread around," and he supposed she had perhaps $20,000 or $30,000. He had no idea how to "access" Cynthia's money.

Randy said his only debt was $1,000 on his Visa card. All of his motorcycles and ATVs were paid for. He said he had purchased the last three vehicles after his latest marriage for Cynthia and her sons.

Asked about his criminal history, Randy rambled into a story of a girlfriend he had in 1974 before he went into the service. When he returned, he met Donna Sanchez, broke up with the first girl, and that ex-girlfriend "set him up." Snohomish County Police had charged him with second-degree burglary. "I wasn't locked up and didn't get any jail time. I lost my voting rights."

Mullinax asked Randy about his family. He said his father,

Gordon, lived in eastern Washington, and his mother's name was Liz. He had three sisters: Lisa, Debbie, and Darlene. His brother's name was David. He offered no additional details about his family.

Asked to recall the events leading up to the day that Cindy Roth drowned, now only nine days past, Randy did so in his odd stilted way. He seemed to make a real effort to sound intellectual, but his vocabulary was not unusually large and he crowded as many words into a sentence as possible. He never took the easy way to say anything.

Cindy had been ill, he remembered, the week before she drowned. She had suffered stomach and head flu. She had been either in bed or on the couch through the week, but she felt better by the weekend. She had been anxious for him to take a half day off so that the family could enjoy a picnic at Lake Sammamish.

And that was what he had done on Tuesday, July 23, hurrying to finish up an engine rebuild so he could spend the sunny day with Cindy and their three boys. Who could have believed that Cindy's plans for a wonderful family day could end in such heartbreak?

Sue Peters and Randy Mullinax had picked up quickly on the fact that whatever bad things had happened in Randy Roth's thirty-seven years, they had always been somebody else's fault: Donna Sanchez didn't want a commitment; Jan wanted to go hiking on Beacon Rock because it would be romantic; Donna Clift ran around with a wild crowd and took drugs; Cynthia wanted to go to the lake and row across because it would be romantic. "Whatever it was," Mullinax recalls, "he always tried to diminish his part in it. It was always the women's idea."

It sounded as if all the women in Randy Roth's life had manipulated *him*. He was the innocent single father of a little boy who had only tried repeatedly to build a happy family, only to have all of his "families" break up because the women involved spoiled things.

At the end of the two-hour interview, Mullinax asked Randy Roth if they might take his fingerprints. They needed major-case prints to prove that this man in front of them really was Randy Roth. Fingerprints would answer that question. They could run an AFIS (Automated Fingerprint Identification System) check and find out exactly who he was. Randy readily agreed to be printed, but he balked when they asked him if he would take a lie detector test. That didn't surprise them; they knew he had also refused a polygraph after Jan's death.

"I'd have to talk to my attorney about that," Roth said.

Randy Roth had retained George Cody, one of Seattle's most competent criminal defense attorneys. He was obviously ready to dig in his heels and make a stand.

The interview was over.

But the investigation had really just begun.

14

Randy Roth had told a number of women about his brother, "the murderer." He had not been so forthcoming during his interview with Mullinax and Peters. Sue Peters placed a call to Gary Singer of the Washington Probation and Parole Department. Singer entered the name in their computer system and found a David M. Roth, born on June 6, 1957. Singer said that David Roth was indeed serving time for first-degree murder; the conviction had come out of Snohomish County. David had a brother named Randy and sisters named Darlene, Debbie, and Lisa. David's mother's name was Lizabeth, and his father was Gordon. Either this was a series of amazing coincidences or Randy Roth and David Roth had to be brothers. This was one of Randy's stories that appeared to be true.

While Randy was a very short man, David was extremely tall, well over six feet, and his mug shot showed a face pockmarked with scars from teenage acne. The details of Randy Roth's younger brother's crime were similar—but not identical—to the version of that murder that Randy had described to his wives and girlfriends.

On August 13, 1977, David Roth, who was twenty and living in Lynnwood with his mother, had been stopped for a minor traffic violation in Gold Bar, a tiny hamlet in the western foothills of Stevens Pass. While Officer Fred Vanderpool was searching Roth's 1963 Chevrolet, he found a .22 caliber Marlin rifle and a clip with fifty-nine live rounds in it. David was arrested on a concealed weapons charge. He seemed to be an amiable enough young man and he was booked into the Snohomish County Jail for only two days and then released.

On August 14 a couple waded into a thicket of blackberries near Mariner High School in the 200 block of 120th S.W. in Everett. Intent on filling their buckets with the abundant crop of sweet wild berries, they almost didn't see the still figure lying in the underbrush. It was a woman, fully clothed, and she lay facedown with her arms at her sides.

Snohomish County detectives found she had been strangled, and shot in the head seven times. She had been dead only about twenty-four hours when she was found. Her wounds would make it difficult to identify her. She was young, probably under twenty. Detectives checking missing persons reports and dental records found no matches.

David Roth's arrest on August 13 and the discovery of the girl's body the next day did not seem to be connected. However, David went to a friend's home after his release from jail and talked about how he had killed a girl. He said he had been driving near the Boeing Company's Everett plant when he saw the young woman hitchhiking. He said he picked her up and they bought some beer and then drove to the woods near Mariner High School to drink it. After they had consumed most of the beer, David told his friend he had tried to have sex with the girl, but she had resisted, and he had strangled her with an elastic cord. Then he took the rifle from the trunk of his car and shot her repeatedly in the head.

David Roth's friend went to the Snohomish County Sheriff's Office four days later and told them what he had heard. Because a records check had shown that David was to appear in district court on August 22 for a pre-sentencing interview on a possession of marijuana charge, Snohomish detectives planned to arrest him there.

But David Roth did not appear. In fact, he remained a fugitive for more than a year. He was finally arrested on January 18, 1979, in Port Orchard, Washington, across Puget Sound from Seattle, and he confessed to the arresting detective during the ninety-minute ferry ride back to Seattle. Although he later recanted his confession and pleaded not guilty to first-degree murder, he was convicted in Snohomish County Superior Court in Everett in November of 1979.

The physical evidence against David Marvin Roth was solid. The bullets found during his arrest in Gold Bar were the same make and caliber as the seven slugs in the victim's body. More damning, the bullets' land and groove markings proved that they had been fired from David's rifle and no other. He was sentenced to life in prison.

In Washington State that meant he would become eligible for release in March 1997.

It was apparent that David Roth had not known the dead girl, and no one had ever come forward to identify her. She was still listed in Snohomish County files as Jane Doe, and her body was buried in a pauper's plot at Cypress Lane Cemetery in Everett.

Snohomish County investigators and court personnel recalled that Lizabeth Roth, an avowed devout Catholic, had attended David's murder trial holding her rosary and praying under her breath continually. Lizabeth and one of her daughters were chastised many times by the judge for disrupting the courtroom. Anonymous threats were made against the judge and court officers, who were issued bulletproof vests to wear during the trial. The trial had been so bizarre that Snohomish County authorities had doubled up on guards in the courtroom.

Lizabeth had fired David's court-appointed attorney, Mark Mestel (one of the area's best), after jury selection was complete. Since David had confessed to the murder of the unknown dead girl, Mestel wanted to plea-bargain for second-degree murder, but Lizabeth wouldn't hear of it.

A defense psychiatrist testified that David Roth had an "abnormally" close relationship with his mother.

The King County detectives wondered where she was now. Was she dead, as Randy had claimed? There were no records showing that Lizabeth Roth had been killed in an accident or that one of her daughters had committed suicide by her bedside. There was no male hitchhiker who had bragged about murdering an elderly Roth relative in Montana.

Sue Peters found that Lizabeth Roth was alive and well—and relatively young at only fifty-two; she was not the aged mother that Randy had described to the Goodwins, not the old woman who lived in a nursing home. Nor was she, apparently, the drug addict that he had told Donna Clift about.

One thing was certain: this was turning into the most convoluted, grotesque case that King County detectives had seen in years. Peters and Mullinax were on the run constantly. All the facets of Randy Roth's life were akin to the thousands of beads of mercury that burst from a broken thermometer—slippery, minute, and often impossible to grasp, and when one bead was grasped, it often separated into two or three or four more. The King County detectives wanted to be sure they had all the mercury back in a container.

On August 2, 1991, Randy Mullinax and Sue Peters located Cynthia Roth's will on file on the Snohomish County Courthouse. According to what they had learned so far, Randy Roth had had a Svengali-like control over all his wives. Certainly he would have wanted Cindy to change—in his favor—whatever will she might have had before she met him, but that had not happened. The detectives suspected he had not even known about Cynthia's 1985 will. By the time Randy asked her about a will, she might have already had reasons to be secretive about her financial assets.

Much to her surprise, Lori Jean Baker had been named executor of Cindy's will. She had promised that she would serve as Tyson's and Rylie's guardian, but she had thought that was just one of those things that young parents talked about in abstract terms, not believing it would ever come to pass. The will stipulated that if Lori could not or would not serve as the executor, then Cindy's father, Merle Loucks, would be the backup. Cindy had designated that her silver, china, and crystal was to go to her "beloved mother, Hazel Loucks, or, if my mother does not survive me, I bequeath my silver, china, and crystal to Lori Jean Baker."

Cindy had directed that a trust be set up with the Everett branch of the Seattle First National Bank for her two sons and any other children she might bear or adopt in the future. With Lori designated as guardian, she wanted her boys to have a live-in mom, as they had always had: "It is further my desire that the trust also operate to benefit the legal guardian of my children to provide minimum benefits to said guardian to assure the fact that said guardian be able to stay home with the children and not be forced to work outside of the home full time. It is my express desire that the guardian of the children be able to provide a satisfying, meaningful home life for my children without the duress of working out of the home. However, my primary desire is to provide for the children as the first priority of this trust."

Lori Baker was perfectly willing, *happy*, to take care of Cindy's boys. She loved them, and they had all been like family for many years. The will had been signed on December 12, 1985, and as far as Peters and Mullinax could determine, there had been no subsequent will to replace it, nor had any codicils been added to it.

Glancing over the will, Lori remembered something that she had forgotten in the days immediately after Cindy drowned. "Before they were married," she told Sue Peters, "Cindy asked Randy if he would sign a prenuptial agreement. He wouldn't do it. He said that would show mistrust on her part, and she backed down."

Lori remembered, too, that Cindy had been disturbed because one of Randy's former neighbors had advised her to be "very, very careful" of Randy. (That would have been Ben Goodwin.) She hadn't been deterred from her elopement, but she had wondered why anyone would say such a thing about Randy.

Lori furnished Sue Peters with the name of Cindy's insurance agent, Bruce Timm.

Timm was on vacation until August 6, but Mullinax and Peters were kept busy in the meantime tracking down Randy Roth's other insurance claims over the years and his criminal record. There was nothing big-time—the second-degree burglary charges, a robbery of a gas station where Randy had formerly worked, and an accident investigation. Randy had reportedly been the victim of a few burglaries—notably the $60,000 burglary of 1988. His former best friend, Nick Emondi, had also suffered at least two burglaries of insured items. So had one of Randy's relatives.

One of the vital questions that had to be answered—and soon— was just how easy it would have been for the wake from a passing speedboat to tip over Randy Roth's gray Supercaravelle Sevylor raft. On August 5, Sue Peters, Randy Mullinax, and Detectives Ross Nooney and Mike Hatch went to Idylwood Park. Hatch had his own 17-foot speedboat, and two lifeguards—Greg Isaacson, seventeen, and Linda Baer, twenty, whose height and weight approximated the Roths'—sat in the inflated raft. The investigators located the area on the east side of the lake where Randy said he and Cindy had gone swimming.

With the lifeguards in the water holding on to Randy's raft in the positions that Randy had described, Hatch revved up his Mastercraft water-ski boat until the waters of Lake Sammamish churned into good-sized wakes. "I was trying to create as large a wake as I could," Hatch recalled. "My instructions were to try to flip the raft." Nooney videotaped each pass the speedboat made as it moved closer and closer to the raft. Although the swimmers were buffeted around and took sprays of water in their faces, the rubber raft didn't even come close to tipping over. It remained completely stable even when the boat passed within a few feet of it. In fact, the only way the lifeguards were able to flip it over was to put their full weight on the near side and then reach across and deliberately pull the far side over on top of them.

Linda Baer said later, "I don't believe that raft *could* flip if the boat was even twenty yards away. Even five to ten yards away the wake might have rolled over my head, but it wouldn't flip the raft. In my opinion, the raft was very stable."

Moreover, Linda said, when the raft was purposely tipped over and she was underneath it, there was a large air pocket between the raft and the water; she could breathe just fine. She was a lifeguard, but she was recuperating from an automobile accident, so she wasn't in top shape.

There would be other tests, but this first reenactment left the King County investigators wondering how a boat 50 yards away could have overturned this raft with its wake. And if the raft had tipped over, why had Randy Roth still had three bags of towels and clothes with him when he rowed in to shore? Had he taken time to dive for them when his wife wasn't breathing? Surely not. Also, he had said that Cindy was floating when he managed to flip the raft over. But drowning victims don't float—not at first.

The police were going to need experts in water safety to sort it all out, but for the moment nothing matched up with Randy Roth's version of Cindy Roth's death.

Randy Mullinax talked with New York Life Agent Bruce Timm on August 6. Timm said he had handled Tom Baumgartner's life insurance policy. His company had paid Cynthia $200,000 when Tom died. She had subsequently put down $10,000 to pay up a $100,000 policy on herself, one that would benefit her sons. "That policy is now worth about $115,000," he said.

Bruce Timm said he had gone to the Roths' Woodinville home in October of 1990. He remembered that "Cynthia looked happier than I had ever seen her." What took place during his discussion with Randy and Cindy would be remembered differently by Timm and by Randy Roth.

According to Randy, it was Timm who suggested how much insurance they needed, using a matrix that took into account their income, the mortgage, and the number of children. The amount needed for each of them, was, he recalled, either $250,000 more than they already had, on the low end, or $350,000, on the high side.

Bruce Timm recalls, however, that it was Randy who suggested the amount. Timm agreed that it was Cindy who called and asked him to come out to Woodinville to talk about insurance for herself and her new husband, Randy Roth. They had decided on the $250,000 policies, naming each other as beneficiary. Because they were both young, the monthly premiums were less than fifty dollars apiece a month.

Randy had suggested that his father should be the adult beneficiary who would look after the boys if both he and Cindy should die. "My father is twenty-five years younger than Cindy's," he explained. Later Cynthia had called and asked Timm to put Randy on her $115,000 policy too—in place of Tyson and Rylie. "I want to make Randy my beneficiary," she insisted. Timm was shocked that she would take her sons' names off, and questioned her. "No, no, you don't understand," she said. "I *need* to do it. My husband has already changed his [policy] to *my* name."

Bruce Timm delivered the $250,000 policies on March 11, 1991.

Mullinax totaled up the insurance and found that Cynthia Roth, dead, had been worth $365,000. At this, his calculation was short; Mullinax didn't know that it was really $20,000 more than that. Her husband, Randy Roth, had insured her life for that amount with Allstate using his Sears card.

$385,000.

If Cindy died, Randy was her beneficiary. If Randy died, Cindy believed she would be his. And she was—at least on the larger policy. But Gordon Roth's name had never been removed as beneficiary for Randy's $100,000 policy. Although Randy assured Cindy that he had changed his policy from his father's name to hers, he never had. It was a mistake, he would say later—he had called his agent repeatedly asking for change-of-beneficiary forms, but all he ever succeeded in doing was changing his address from Misty Meadows to Woodinville.

Cynthia's sons stayed with Randy for the first day or so after their mother died, but by early August Tyson and Rylie Baumgartner were staying with Hazel and Merle Loucks in their Marysville home, a quiet little town north of Everett, or nearby with their uncle, Gary Baumgartner. Randy and Greg were living in the Woodinville house.

Mullinax and Peters wanted to wait as long as they could before they talked to the boys. Sometime soon they would *have* to; the little boys, who were now completely orphaned, were eyewitnesses to the events surrounding their mother's drowning.

In the meantime, Randy Mullinax and Sue Peters had more than enough to do. There were dozens, scores, of witnesses, friends, and acquaintances who wanted to talk about Cindy and Randy Roth. For some it was as if they had seen a freight train roaring down the tracks toward an unknowing victim and been helpless to stop it. Others had tenuous ties to Randy Roth and seemed to need to talk about him. Each of his wives had to have talked to *someone*, someone who might remember vital information, and people seemed to be coming out of the woodwork with tips, information, advice, psychic feelings, and remembrances of Cindy and/or Randy.

Donna Sanchez Roth did not come forward, however. She was still missing. She had apparently moved completely out of both Randy's and Greg's life. Peters and Mullinax wondered if she was even alive. Jan Roth was dead. But Randy Mullinax located Donna Clift at a dry cleaning shop where she worked. He found a shy woman, a frightened woman, who was nothing at all like the wild party girl Randy had described. Donna gave him a statement about the wonderfully romantic courtship of Randy Roth, which was immediately followed by an icy cold marriage. "I never went back to live with him after he tried to drown me."

Drown her? Mullinax's ears stood up.

Donna assured him that her mother and father could verify the terrifying incident on the Skykomish River back in 1985.

As, indeed, they did. Judy Clift said she was saddened but "not surprised" to hear that Randy's latest wife was dead—drowned.

So Donna Clift was alive, but where was Donna Sanchez Roth? Had she, too, taken out way too much insurance before she and Randy parted?

Sue Peters canvassed the homes on the east side of Lake Sammamish, hoping to find someone who had seen Randy and Cindy Roth at the far end of their "romantic" raft trip. After twelve contacts, she got only one hit, and that one was indefinite. One man thought he remembered seeing a gray raft 25 or 30 feet from shore with two people sitting in it, but he couldn't say if they had been men or women. He hadn't seen the raft tip over. He was sure of that.

Randy had called Lori Baker and told her that he was "too bummed out" to use the tickets that Cindy had bought for the trip to Reno. Then why had Randy and "a small boy" appeared on July 26 at Mill Creek Travel to pick up the Reno package? Debbie Erickson, the travel agent who had sold the tickets, recalled to Randy Mullinax that it was Cindy who had paid for the tickets on July 12. She had read about Cindy's drowning in the paper and had expected Cindy's widower to ask for a refund. But only three days after her death, Randy Roth had seemed in good spirits—and he never mentioned that he didn't need the tickets any longer. He only asked if the vouchers he received were the equivalent of a ticket.

Cindy Roth's friends remembered how excited she had been about her upcoming wedding anniversary and the second trip to Reno.

Evidently Randy intended to use his tickets. He could no longer celebrate his wedding anniversary, but that did not seem to deter him.

In the offices of Bill Pierre Ford, Juanita Gates heard Stacey Reese answer her phone a few days after Cindy's memorial service. Stacey talked for a few minutes and then hung up, setting the phone back in its cradle as carefully as if she held a snake. She turned to Juanita with a peculiar look on her face. "Oh my God! Oh, my God! You'll never believe it! That was Randy, and he wanted me to go to Reno with him."

Stacey had muttered a shocked no to Randy's invitation.

Detectives learned later that Randy had then called his old standby, Lily Vandiveer, and invited her to go to Reno with him, saying he already had the tickets.

But for once, Randy couldn't seem to get a date. The tickets went unused.

Sue Peters and Randy Mullinax were getting a feel for the kind of existence Cynthia Roth had lived during the last six months of her life. She had been a sweet, vulnerable, trusting woman who believed in God and in her fellow man. She had waited five years for the right man to come along. And she had fallen in love with Randy Roth.

She had to have been a woman of pride; even her own family apparently hadn't known how bad things were. She had talked a little to Lori Baker—but not much—and Dottie Baker had known Cindy well enough to sense trouble.

Pam Neighbors was Cindy's manicurist—the "nail lady" Randy had referred to, and one of the very few people Cindy confided in. Pam had been aware of Cindy's entire relationship with Randy, from its beginning to its sudden ending. Pam told Sue Peters that she and

Cindy had talked as she worked on Cindy's nails, and they had become good friends.

In the summer of 1990 Cindy had raved to Pam about the wonderful new man she had met. He met her criteria; he was a widower who really liked kids. Cindy had decided to date him. After the marriage, Pam met all three of Cindy's boys and assumed that Greg was the child of Randy's wife who had died. Pam remembered Cindy as "darling—a cute little girl. She was adorable, absolutely adorable. Bubbly and happy and she never said anything bad about anybody. Angelic. You can't imagine. Any man in his right mind would have been thrilled to have somebody like her."

The manicurist recalled to Sue Peters that the Roths' marriage had started out wonderfully, that Randy had seemed completely oriented to being a family man. "They went camping. He was going to teach the boys to hunt. Archery. They did everything together. He was basically the kind of man that Cindy had wanted."

"Did Cindy ever mention life insurance to you?"

Pam shook her head.

"How did you find out about her death?"

"The hairdresser who originally referred her to me had read it in the paper. She called me and asked me if I knew, and I started checking around. I couldn't get an answer. I called the house, and all I got was a recorded message for two days. I finally got ahold of him about Wednesday or Thursday of the week after her death. And I just asked him . . . It was a short—short and emotionless—conversation. I asked him if it was true, and he said yes, and I said 'Well, what happened?' and he said, 'Well, she died in a drowning accident.' I didn't know what to say because he was so expressionless."

Pam had offered Randy any help she could give. "He just said, 'No, thanks. Bye.'"

Pam Neighbors, like most of Cindy's friends and relatives, was surprised to hear that Cindy had drowned. She had been a good swimmer, and very athletic.

It was to become a more and more familiar story. Incredible but familiar. Cindy had drowned accidentally; Randy bought the boys hamburgers, rented a movie about how funny a dead body can be, and immediately went on with his life.

On July 26 Randy had turned in three slightly used ATVs to Aurora Suzuki. He bought new Model LT-160 Suzukis for a total price of $5,389.70. He planned to raise all three boys, his own and

Cindy's, and he wanted to start out their new life with the very best toys.

He sold another ATV to a private citizen, explaining that he no longer had a need for it. "My wife was in an accident," Randy said sadly. "She was in the hospital for a long time, but she didn't make it."

If all of Randy's financial juggling had worked out, he would probably never have had to work again. He believed that he was the beneficiary of Cynthia Baumgartner Roth's insurance policies. That was $385,000 going in. He expected the house would be in his name only. A $275,000 house with $160,000 equity was nothing to sneeze at. He already got $419 a month for Greg on Jan's Social Security account. If he could find a way to double-dip so that Greg could get money from Cynthia too, it would be at least that much more. Add to that the $1,500 that Tyson and Rylie got from their father's Social Security and it didn't take an accountant to see that Randy expected to have at least $2,500 a month coming in from survivors' benefits. If he handled the $385,000 in life insurance better than he had managed Janis's insurance payoff, Randy would have it made. He could spend all his time buying and selling cars, auto racing, and whizzing around on four-wheelers.

As Randy geared up for his new life with his three sons, he was totally unaware that Lori Baker had been appointed guardian for Tyson and Rylie and that they would not be coming home to live with him. The $1,500 a month in Social Security survivors' benefits that the two boys collected on their father's account would now go to their legal guardian.

Two weeks after Cindy died, Lori Baker called Randy about getting into their jointly held safe-deposit box. He insisted he knew of no box. With the help of a bank officer, Lori opened box number 2212. It was empty. A copy of Cindy's will should have been in the safe-deposit box in the Everett bank, but it wasn't there. Nor were Tom's wedding ring, his pocket watch, his other jewelry or the CDs Cindy had owned.

A check of bank records showed that the last person to enter the box was Randy G. Roth. He had signed the register two days after Cindy died. Since bank customers are offered privacy as they enter their safe-deposit boxes, no one could say what Randy might have taken away with him.

* * *

Tyson and Rylie continued to stay with their grandparents, but Lori hoped to have them with her as soon as possible. In the meantime, Randy assumed that the boys would be with him. He knew how to raise boys; he had said that often enough. The marines had taught him how to be a man, and he would teach Greg, Tyson, and Rylie.

15

Although Sue Peters and Randy Mullinax were working overtime, they still found it hard to keep up with all the interviews and investigative work that had to be done. They were building an incredibly complex circumstantial evidence case, but they needed more than that. On "Matlock" and "Perry Mason" circumstantial cases don't need to have all that much substance. And invariably, eyewitnesses burst into the courtroom at the crucial moment. In real life, cases without solid physical evidence were squeakers. Even eyewitnesses were not the strongest weapons available to the state's case; they could be wrong or tainted, or they could—and often did—misperceive what they had seen, or thought they had seen. It took prosecutors with real guts to go for a circumstantial case. It was much easier to get a conviction with blood and fiber matches, fingerprints, ballistics, and other convincing kinds of physical evidence to show to a jury. When the suspect was related to the victim, and especially when he lived in the same house with her, most of those prime areas of physical evidence were useless. Circumstantial cases needed three or four times as much backup in court.

The King County team knew where they wanted to go, and they believed they were right in homing in on Randy Roth. When he told his potential girlfriends that police were checking him out, he was telling the truth. The police certainly *were* checking him out. Daily and constantly.

The King County prosecutor's office, headed by Norm Maleng, had been following the Roth investigation avidly. The prosecutors wanted to confront the constant widower in court, but there were still too many unanswered questions. If Roth should be charged with murder and acquitted, double jeopardy would attach and he could never be tried again. If, as Sue Peters and Randy Mullinax suspected, the man was a modern-day Bluebeard who courted, seduced, married, and then killed women all within the space of a year's time, he had years ahead to cause untold tragedy. He was only thirty-seven.

Somebody had to stop him.

The investigation had been difficult from the beginning, and it wasn't getting any easier. "There are times when a case comes in and you say, 'I've got him,'" Randy Mullinax recalled. "I don't think that happened this time. It seemed every step we took opened a door to a lot more questions."

Indeed it did. Insurance questions. Burglary questions. And murder questions.

The King County detectives had had conferences with Lee Yates, a senior deputy prosecutor. In his decades with the prosecutor's office, Yates had prosecuted some of the most difficult homicide cases the county had ever come up against. Indeed, he had once taken a man to trial not once but *twice* for the strangulation murders of his wife and infant daughter. Lee Yates won, but he knew all too well the difficulties encountered in the investigation of an intrafamily murder. When Yates prosecuted race-car driver Eric Haga in 1973 and again in 1975, it was for a double murder that had occurred in the Haga family home. Fingerprints, hair, fibers, even the necktie and the satin ribbon from a teddy bear that were used as garottes, were no good as evidence. They all *belonged* in the home.

Randy Mullinax and Sue Peters went to see Senior Deputy Prosecuting Attorney Marilyn Brenneman. Brenneman's office was sometimes referred to as the "office of last resort"—the Special Operations Unit. Brenneman had been the first woman assigned to the unit, and the possibility that a female would enter such heady territory had obviously been unforeseen; her key wouldn't fit the rest room door. The unit usually dealt with police departments' intelligence divisions, working the most complex and unpredictable cases. Brenneman was in her element. She thrived on cases that challenged her, and she enjoyed walking the tightrope where one misstep could send her plunging down.

Although she had been the first woman assigned to the Special Operations Unit, she was not the last. By 1993 there were three women—Brenneman, Susan Storey, and Kate Flack—and one man, Duane Evans, working cases in Special Operations.

Marilyn Brenneman had paid her dues and could usually decide whether to take on a case or not. She listened as Sue Peters and Randy Mullinax outlined what they had discovered about Randy Roth and his many unfortunate wives. She was fascinated. She wanted it. There were so many hidden areas, and the case offered the possibility of bringing what appeared to be a truly wicked man into the courtroom. Whether the Roth case would be a boon to her career or an albatross around her neck remained to be seen.

On August 7, Detective Joe Lewis and Stan Chapin came on board to lend a hand. Lewis's first job would be to create a comprehensive summary of the investigation for Marilyn Brenneman. Always a hands-on prosecutor, Brenneman wanted to play catch-up in a hurry. The King County detectives had stacks of reports and scores of witness statements. Brenneman would commit them to memory until every detail of the Roth case would become second nature to her.

Joe Lewis would also try to locate Cindy and Randy Roth's bank accounts, CDs, and maybe the missing jewelry from her empty safe-deposit box. Chapin would attempt to determine the whereabouts of the first Mrs. Randy Roth, Donna Sanchez.

Cindy Roth's eagerly anticipated first anniversary had long since passed, but there were no celebrations, only tears. Randy Mullinax and Sue Peters had delayed talking with her orphaned sons as long as they could, but by August 8 it was time.

They arrived at the Merle Loucks residence in Marysville at two-thirty that Thursday afternoon.

They talked to Tyson first. At eleven, he was a slender, handsome boy, and very polite. He wanted to cooperate with the detectives; that was clear from the beginning of their interview. Asked how he felt about Randy, Tyson said he was "pretty nice" and that he had enjoyed playing baseball in Little League and going four-wheeling with Randy, whom he referred to as Dad.

"Do you remember the day you all went to the lake?" Mullinax began.

Tyson did. He recalled that his mom was in the bedroom getting ready to go. He thought the lake trip was his mom's idea, and he remembered that she and Randy had talked about it the day before—Monday. Randy had never been to Lake Sammamish, but he and his brother had gone with his mom a couple of times. He didn't know just who had wanted to take the raft. They had all been rafting in the Skykomish River the weekend before and had even taken Greg's friend Brad with them.

"You wore life jackets on the river?"

Tyson nodded. "All of us did."

They didn't take a picnic the day they went to Lake Sammamish. Their mom had fixed their lunch before Randy came home—peanut butter and jam sandwiches and milk. At first just Randy and their mom were going to Lake Sammamish, but then their mom had asked the boys if they wanted to go, and the boys said they did. Tyson and Rylie had asked if they could take their "little raft" but their mom had said no.

They loaded up their stuff when Randy came home and arrived at the lake, Tyson thought, about two that afternoon. They pumped up their inner tubes and the big raft. He and Rylie stayed in the swimming area, and Randy and their mom told them to keep their inner tubes in the shallow water. "They were going to the other side of the lake and check it out," Tyson said.

He remembered there were some bags in the raft with lotion, towels, clothes, and maybe a diet Pepsi. The boys swam in the shallow water until they got cold, and then they saw a friend and got out to sit in the sun to warm up.

"I saw Randy about halfway out in the lake, and he was coming back," Tyson said, adding that he couldn't see his mother in the raft anymore—only his dad.

When Randy docked the raft, he told Tyson and Rylie to "Get a lifeguard, but don't make a commotion." Their mother, Randy said, had had a cramp in her leg.

Tyson did as he was told, but he couldn't understand. His mother had been a *much* better swimmer than his father. Randy had told them what happened after they got back to the house with the movies he had rented for them. "He said he did CPR on Mom and yelled for help, but no one in the boats would stop to help them."

Peters and Mullinax had now heard yet another version of Cindy's drowning.

Asked what kind of father Randy was, Tyson said he was very strict. He spanked the boys about three times a week with a belt. He often made them do two hundred squat thrusts when they had done something he didn't like. Greg got punished just as often as he and Rylie did, and in the same manner. They usually got in trouble for fighting or for forgetting to put their clothes in the wash. Randy also got mad if they put the silverware in the wrong compartment in the dishwasher.

His mother and Randy had had "fights" about once a month, and once Randy had been angry because his mom had driven the red Trooper.

It was Tyson's feeling that Randy just wanted to forget about what had happened to their mom. On the Saturday after she died, Randy took them to the swap meet and they sold Randy's old couch, a red dresser, a stereo, and a television set. They also sold his mother's bike.

The day after his mom drowned, Tyson remembered, Randy began to get rid of her things. He emptied the refrigerator of all the food she liked, and "He put Mom's clothes in the corner, and he threw out all of her makeup."

Rylie Baumgartner was almost ten, a curly-haired stocky little boy with an outgoing personality. He, too, liked Randy and felt Randy had been good to him: "He takes us four-wheeling and to motorcycle shops." The whole family went to a demolition derby on July Fourth.

Rylie also thought it had been his mom's idea to go to Lake Sammamish on that bad day. He and Tyson had stayed in the swimming area while his mom and dad took the raft out. Their parents hadn't told them how long they would be gone. It seemed to Rylie that they were gone about two hours. His mother was a good swimmer and had never had any problem before. He had seen Randy coming back alone; he was wearing his sunglasses and looking down as he rowed toward shore. Rylie and Tyson ran out to meet them, and Randy let the air out of the raft right away. Rylie didn't know what had happened to his mom until he heard Randy explaining it to a policeman at the hospital. Afterward, it was Randy's idea for them to go out to eat and rent some movies.

The next day, his "dad" started getting rid of his mom's makeup: "He packed it up and had us haul it to the garbage can. Then he made a big pile of Mom's clothes in his room on the floor."

Rylie also related that Randy's punishments were hard. If he did something "bad," he had to do exercises—bends and thrusts. But Rylie admitted that he guessed he usually deserved the punishments that he got.

Sue Peters and Randy Mullinax talked to Leon Loucks next. Older than Cindy by almost fifteen years, Leon was still baffled by what had happened. He thought that his sister was happy with Randy. He had found out about her death when another relative saw the story on the KIRO-TV eleven o'clock news. When he finally got Randy on the phone, Randy had been very calm and said the boys "were doing fine." His voice revealed no emotion, but Loucks didn't believe he was in shock. Randy was the same way at the funeral, he said. No emotion at all. He had given Leon still another story of how Cindy died. He said he hadn't tried to call for help because there was no one around, but he had tried to give Cindy CPR.

"My sister has been swimming since she was eight," Leon said. "She never had a cramp before."

The detectives talked to Merle and Hazel Loucks. The Louckses had been surprised the year before to learn that Cynthia was going to marry Randy Roth in Reno. She had been seeing him only about six weeks. "Randy took care of all the wedding arrangements."

Cynthia had handled all her own finances. The Louckses knew she had set up a trust fund for her boys and had made some investments. They hadn't known about her will, and Randy had told them he didn't think she had one.

Cynthia had told her parents that Randy was a Vietnam veteran and that he had bad dreams at night. Merle Loucks said that Randy had told him he had also served in the marines in the Philippines: "He told me he was trained to be tough and never show emotion."

The Louckses had noticed that Randy became increasingly nervous in the second week after their daughter's drowning. He was convinced that the police were coming to get him. He had been "scared" before his interview with Peters and Mullinax. He had shown up at their house after being out all night. "He told us he didn't want to go home because, if he went to jail, he would have to sit there all weekend."

Hazel Loucks had gotten a phone call from a woman who said Randy had invited her daughter to go to Reno with him: "She said she was afraid for her daughter." Mrs. Loucks didn't know who the woman was, but she knew he had also invited Lily Vandiveer to go with him: "I asked him, 'Why did you do this?' and he said, 'I also asked my mother, I asked Max, and I asked my younger sister to go, but I decided to stick around.'"

Like Janis Miranda, and like Donna Clift, Cynthia had truly cared for Greg and had felt sorry for him because he didn't have his true mother with him. Hazel knew Cynthia had tried to give Greg a hug now and then, and he had appreciated it, but he always pulled away when Randy came into the room.

Randy hadn't had the sensitivity to explain to Greg what had happened to Cynthia. Mrs. Loucks said she heard he had handed Greg a newspaper article about the drowning. "Randy told Greg that if he never saw him [Randy] again, he was to call two telephone numbers Randy gave him."

When the Louckses asked to view their daughter's body, Randy warned them not to "because she looked swollen." But Merle Loucks had insisted. His daughter didn't look swollen at all. There was no outward sign of what had killed her.

"Randy didn't want her ashes—the cremains. He just left them at the church," Merle Loucks said. "He didn't want any of the cards people sent, either. He didn't look at the flowers; there were no tears in his eyes. He just split from the church after the services."

Randy had told the elder Louckses still another story about the tragedy on the lake. "He said the 'raft just went over on us,' not only on her."

Sue Peters checked with the Lynnwood Police Department for any records they might have on Randy Roth. He had grown up there, graduated from high school there, and had two arrests in the Lynnwood files: August 25, 1973, robbery; February 14, 1975, robbery.

On August 14, Peters talked to a lawyer retained by the Pioneer Insurance Company in reference to a burglary claim Randy Roth had reported. She learned that Randy had asked for $60,000 and received a payoff of $28,500. The Pioneer Insurance Company had also filed a suit against Randy over the claim he had made after his home was burglarized in the fall of 1988. He had countersued, and both suits had been dismissed "with prejudice" on October 9, 1990.

Insurance claims popped up repeatedly in Sue Peters's and Randy Mullinax's retrospective on Randy Roth's life. They traced him back a decade, two decades. Randy's motorcycle was stolen; insurance paid off. Jan's car was stolen and then found stripped with no engine; insurance paid off. Nick Emondi, Randy's onetime good friend, had had two burglaries; insurance paid off. Jan died; insurance paid off. Randy had a burglary; insurance paid off.

And now Randy fully expected several insurance companies to pay him $385,000 in Cynthia's death.

Randy wasn't spending much time in the big yellow house in Woodinville. Perhaps there were too many haunting memories. Greg was living at Lily Vandiveer's house with Lily and Brad. Randy spent most of his evenings with Lily. Her mother was frantically worried. She called Sue Peters and warned her that she feared "Lily will be next."

But Lily Vandiveer would brook no criticism of Randy. She had stood by him before. She was not about to desert him now.

The headlines in Seattle area papers were discomfiting, both to Randy Roth and to the current women in his life. Bellevue's *Journal American* ran this headline on August 7, 1991: "Police: Drowning Might Be Homicide." It was no longer a secret that the King County Police Department's Major Crimes Unit was investigating Cynthia Roth's drowning. The article in the *Journal American* mentioned Janis Roth's accidental fall to her death a decade earlier. Randy Mullinax would say only, "We are very, very interested in this entire thing—and right now, we're particularly interested in anyone who may have been videotaping on the lake that day and may have videotaped anything about the incident, a couple in a gray raft—or even the rescue efforts."

Randy Roth, asked for a statement by reporter Cheryl Murfin, said he was shocked and confused that police had called him in for questioning: "I was emotionally and mentally shocked to have the police call me in for a statement and I was devastated to hear them tell me that the case was being investigated as anything more than an accident. I don't feel I have any concerns at this time. I volunteered the information [about the 1981 investigation] to the police. I didn't have anything to hide."

Two days later Randy called his own press conference. With his attorney, George Cody, beside him, they told reporters this would be Randy's last word to the press.

Looking stressed as his attorney repeated what had happened on July 23 on Lake Sammamish, Randy occasionally added further explanation. Cody said the Roths paddled their six-man rubber raft to the east side of the lake. They were swimming when Cynthia got a cramp in her leg. A powerboat 75 yards away had caused such a severe wake that it hit Cynthia full in the face and then flipped the sixty-pound raft over on top of her. Cynthia had been asphyxiated.

In answer to the investigators' questions about the length of time it had taken Randy to get help and about his failure to wave for help, Cody said that Randy *had* tried to wave for help. He had no explanation for why Randy had told police that he had *not* done so.

Cody pointed out that Roth had collected only a "moderate" life insurance payoff on Janis, but he refused to say how much. He also described as "small" the "$235,000" in insurance that Cynthia had and that his client stood to collect. The amount, of course, was too low by $150,000. But a quarter million dollars is hardly "small" to most people.

Randy said they had been forced to send Cynthia's children "out of town" because they were being "hounded" by the media.

Asked if he might ever marry again, Randy pondered that eventuality for the press: "It is impossible to deal with that idea at this time." He added that he and Cynthia would have celebrated their first wedding anniversary only a week before. He described Cynthia as "warm, outgoing, and personable."

Randy Roth looked directly into the cameras of Seattle's four major television stations—KING (NBC), KOMO (ABC), KIRO (CBS), and KSTW (Independent)—and viewers saw a handsome young man who seemed earnest and truthful. He had lost the woman he loved, and he was confused and miserable that his troubles were being exacerbated by a vindictive police investigative team.

Both Cody and Roth pleaded for friends and relatives of Cynthia's family to step forward to "defend" Randy's character. Randy proclaimed that he felt "in no way responsible" in the deaths of either his second wife or his fourth wife. George Cody, referring to Cynthia's drowning, said, "One would assume if there was any evidence of foul play, [witnesses] would have come forward then, or since then."

Background checks on Randy Roth with his former employers were producing interesting information. The jobs that he had left "by mutual agreement," according to him, had usually been terminated because he converted company gas or company products to his own use.

Just when the investigators had almost come to believe that Randy's first wife was probably dead too, Detective Stan Chapin found Donna Sanchez Roth. She had last been heard from in California, so Chapin checked the Department of Licenses in that state and found a listing for a Donna Sanchez in Brawley in Imperial County, close by the Mexican border. Lieutenant Bob Kuhn of the Brawley Police Department remembered Donna Sanchez: "She was a police officer for a while. I think it was for the Imperial County Sheriff's Office."

Donna's first husband, Silas Sanchez, taught at Brawley High School. Apparently, Donna *had* gone back to her former husband. Records there showed that she had worked as a jailer from 1987 to July 7, 1991.

She *was* alive. At least she had been up until two weeks before Cynthia Roth drowned, and there was every reason to think she still was. When she left the Imperial County Sheriff's Office, Donna Carlson Sanchez Roth had left a forwarding address in Washington State. By working through a series of her relatives, Chapin finally located her at a teenage crisis counseling facility in Washington where she presently worked. He left a message for her there, asking her to call him.

Late in August, Donna called Stan Chapin. Unlike Randy's other wives, Donna Sanchez did not have a bad word to say about him. She had been married to him for exactly five years—from July 4, 1975, to July 4, 1980. He had been a "take charge" kind of man, but she hadn't minded; it had made her feel secure. Their parting had been amicable. He kept Greg, but she had visitation rights; she had custody of her daughter by her marriage to Sanchez.

When Sue Peters met with Donna Sanchez she saw a very pretty, small woman with a perfect figure. Donna number one looked remarkably like Mary Jo Phillips. She too had a kind of "country" sense about her, and she seemed remarkably naive for a woman who had worked as a jail guard for years. She was very quiet and very polite. If Peters thought Donna Sanchez might talk more freely when she was interviewed by a female detective, she was disappointed; Randy's first wife really did seem to hold no grudges or bad feelings toward him. She still believed that Randy had gone to Vietnam and participated in secret missions. "Those missions weren't even *documented*," she said, lowering her voice. "They were too secret."

The end of her marriage to Randy had come as a complete surprise to Donna Sanchez. "It was right out of the blue. We came home from church, and Randy just said, 'We're getting a divorce.'" Although she had not wanted the divorce and would have liked to keep her son with her, Donna said she had given up custody of Greg willingly. She had visited her son from time to time in Randy's homes, and she never had known what had gone wrong with their marriage. There were no recriminations. In fact, Donna asked if it would be okay for her to call Randy and see how he was.

Sue Peters shrugged, thinking, *Do what you've gotta do.* Whoever Randy Roth was, he had an almost hypnotic power over women—at least at first. And with this, his first wife, his spell lingered.

16

Senior Deputy Prosecutor Marilyn Brenneman has never been a woman to whom things came easily. Brains, yes, and an ebullient sense of humor, but she has fought hard for the respect she merited in her career. Were it not for the fact that she is basically a human dynamo, she might have given up years ago. She jokes that she would choose Meryl Streep to play her if Hollywood ever made a movie of her life. Streep could do it, but she would have to quadruple her energy level. There is a physical resemblance; Brenneman and Streep have the same kind of off-beat beauty. Her chestnut hair is too thick to control. It invariably falls over her left eye, and in trial she tosses her head impatiently to clear her field of vision.

Raised on one of the small coastal islands off Georgia—Saint Simons—Marilyn Brenneman went to school on the mainland in Brunswick. She embraced the law after she saw *To Kill a Mockingbird*. "I grew up in a family who didn't hold any of the political beliefs that everyone else in town did," Brenneman remembers. She is enthusiastic about everything and talks as fast as she thinks, although she has lost all traces of any southern accent. "I thought being an attorney would be the most wonderful career possible."

There was some delay about that, however. Always there was the subtle prejudice that women law students and attorneys find rising up like an invisible wall. "I wanted to be Atticus Finch, the lawyer in *Mockingbird*, but people suggested I should train to be a legal secretary."

Brenneman left home at seventeen, after she graduated from high school in Brunswick, and went to a business college in Florida. "I got married at eighteen and had my first child at nineteen." Married to an air force pilot, she put her lawyer plans on hold for a while. When her husband left the service, he took a job with the state of Florida, and Brenneman went to the University of North Florida to get her undergraduate degree.

When it was time for her to go to law school, she and her family had moved to Washington State and she was delighted to find that the University of Washington had an excellent law school. By her third year of law school, Marilyn Brenneman had two young boys, she was separated from her husband, and was working as a law clerk. She got good grades—but not the best grades. Who had time to go to the law library?

But she made it. "When I applied for the prosecutor's office in 1978, the man who interviewed me said, 'How are you going to handle this job with two children?'"

Knowing what she had gone through to get her law degree in the first place, Brenneman snapped, "Well, a lot better than I'd handle welfare!"

She got the job. Within a short time that question was no longer permissible in job interviews.

In 1991, as a prosecutor, remarried, and now the mother of four boys, Brenneman had not come to her position in the Special Operations Unit without a struggle. She never lost sight of her ambition to be a working part of the law, despite the first marriage, which didn't work, and the second marriage (to an attorney), which worked wonderfully, despite all the juggling of jobs and babies.

But she had made it.

In the spring of 1985, when Donna Clift was marrying her perfect man, Marilyn Brenneman's youngest child was a year old, her oldest was nineteen, and she was working days and nights to close down a teenage nightclub known as the Monastery. "I don't believe in coming in on a case in the end," she explains. "I try to *be* there."

Sitting in the dark on stakeout at two or three in the morning with surveillance officers, Brenneman was appalled to see that youngsters who looked to be only twelve or thirteen were going into the seamy club that sat hard by the I-5 freeway. Further intensive investigation uncovered child prostitution, drug sales, and pornography. Hampered by the brass in some law enforcement agencies who wanted to do it their way—which appeared to Brenneman to be agonizingly slow—but encouraged by outraged parents, she was instrumental in closing down the Monastery forever.

"When I think back," Brenneman muses, trying to remember 1985, "my fall was relatively quiet in comparison. The Monastery case took months, and my cases that came after had to seem more routine."

By the spring of 1986, Marilyn Brenneman would find herself completely paralyzed from the neck down, a victim of Guillain-Barre disease. When her symptoms first began, she was frightened, wondering if she would ever be able to move again. She knew there were many diseases that she *might* have. "I went down fast, but once I was diagnosed and knew what I had, it wasn't too bad. I was lucky—I was only in the hospital, fully paralyzed, for a month."

Most sufferers of the malady eventually recover completely; some remain paralyzed. Brenneman was indeed one of the lucky ones. She had doctors who explained every facet of her illness to her and she was encouraged by their confidence in her. She did recover, and even her sense of humor came through intact. She never said "Why me?" She had seen too many people with permanent afflictions. Beyond that, Brenneman would always remember the bonus of love and support she got from the cops she had worked with, the other prosecutors, a huge circle of friends who rallied around her in a way she never could have imagined. Most of all, she had a family unit so strong that she could always count on them. Her teenage sons and her husband were rocks who never let her down; she never had to worry about what was going on at home and who was taking care of Adam, her youngest.

Although her personality, her sense of self, was stronger, perhaps, than that of the single mothers who had fallen in love with Randy Roth, Marilyn Brenneman had been where they were—alone with young children. Like Cynthia Roth, like millions of other mothers alone, she had had two little boys and been single, half hoping to find a full-time dad for them.

When she finished reading the case summary that Joe Lewis had prepared for her, Marilyn Brenneman was anxious to find some way to get Randy Roth into court.

On August 19, Detectives Mullinax, Peters, and Lewis met with Marilyn Brenneman and Dr. Donald Reay to discuss the autopsy findings on Cynthia Roth. It still seemed impossible that she could have drowned so quickly, made only that one sound—a cough or a gulp, depending on which version Randy Roth gave—and then been gone. Reay was puzzled too. They had all questioned whether Cynthia might have been drugged, but the Washington State Toxicology Lab's report had come back with no sign at all of alcohol or drugs in Cindy Roth's system. The only item the drug screen produced was caffeine. Nobody drowns because of having too many cups of coffee.

Then *why?* Why would a healthy young woman, a strong swimmer, have simply taken one gulp of water and drowned? Reay explained that he was still convinced that Cynthia had succumbed to asphyxia by drowning. He had found absolutely no internal or external indication of trauma—nothing beyond the two slight scratches on the victim's neck. However, he said it would be relatively easy to drown someone without leaving any sign at all of forced drowning on the victim's body.

The answer to all their questions might lie in that last statement. Randy Roth had bragged to any number of people that he knew how to kill someone without leaving a mark on the body.

Was Randy Roth truly a deadly killer, trained by the marines to steal into Vietnamese villages and kill every man, woman, and child? Was the stuff of his nightmares based in fact? Every one of his women had described his restless nights, the way he had cried out during his bad dreams. They had all seen the odd weapons he kept near him always—the baseball bat studded with nails, for instance. It was difficult to separate Randy's fabrications from what had really happened. Some might call him an exaggerator, some a storyteller, and some an outright liar.

But one enormous lie had already been punctured.

It was really only a matter of simple arithmetic. Ben Goodwin had always been suspicious about Randy and the Vietnam War, especially when he saw that Randy had the plaque for meritorious service exactly like the one he had seen on Ben's wall. He wasn't sure how old Randy really was, but he suspected he was younger than he claimed to be.

Randy Mullinax looked at Roth's birth date—the day after Christmas 1954. The gulf of Tonkin incident that really inflamed the situation in South Vietnam had occurred in August of 1964—when Randy Roth was only nine years old. Action in Vietnam was totally over by March of 1973. Randy graduated from high school three months *after* that. How could he have fought in Vietnam and gone to Meadowdale High School in Lynnwood, Washington, at the same time?

Detective Stan Chapin had checked with the National Archives and Records Center in St. Louis, Missouri, to see if a Randolph G. Roth had ever been in the Marine Corps. He handed Sue Peters a copy of Randy Roth's military records—a very thin folder. Roth had been in the marines all right, but that was in late 1973 and 1974. Randy Roth had never even *been* in Vietnam. It was obvious that all his knowledge of Vietnam had come from the books and magazines he collected so avidly. His only overseas duty had been on Okinawa, where he worked as a file clerk. He had never seen any kind of war action. He was mustered out of the service because his mother said it was a hardship to have him gone; he was needed at home. Randy Roth had certainly never been a member of any elite secret unit trained to kill in mysterious and bizarre ways. If he was having nightmares, they were being caused by something else.

Tyson and Rylie Baumgartner never returned to live with their stepfather. They had left with little more than the clothes on their backs a few days after their mother drowned, and almost everything they owned was still in the big new house in Woodinville. Knowing that she probably was not going to receive a hearty welcome, Lori Baker nonetheless called Randy and tried to make an appointment to get the boys' things. He wasn't cooperative. Lori and her brother, Harlan, went to the house, but Randy wouldn't let them in; he said he was sleeping.

It was Labor Day weekend, beginning Friday, August 30, when Lori, Harlan, and Dottie Baker, accompanied by Gary Baumgartner, went to rent a U-Haul trailer to pick up Cynthia's and the boys' belongings. Apparently everyone else had things to move that weekend, too, and all they were able to rent was a full-sized truck.

"I guess Randy thought we were going to take their furniture too," Lori recalled. "We weren't; that was just the only truck we could get."

Randy Roth was quietly furious. He had finally learned that he was not going to be Rylie and Tyson's guardian, and he was not happy about it. He let the Bakers into his home only grudgingly.

Dottie Baker had seen the house go downhill for a long time. During the long sad spring, Cynthia had kept it picked up, but it hadn't been as sparkling as Cynthia had always kept her home. Now, as they moved a few items aside, Dottie could see dust and dirt that had been building up for months. It looked as though Cynthia had simply given up, as if nothing had mattered to her anymore.

Randy had collected the things Cynthia had specified in her will, but he had jammed his dead wife's most valued possessions into black plastic garbage bags willy-nilly, with no concern at all for protecting them. Many of Cindy's and the boys' things were crushed and broken. Tyson and Rylie had pictures and posters that were ruined. Even Cindy's shoes had been jammed in and smashed.

When Tyson and Rylie asked if they could go into Greg's room to get some of their Nintendo games, Randy blocked their path. "You have no business in Greg's room. How do I know you won't try to take his things? You can only go in your room."

Their bicycles were gone, and so were their baseball cards and their BB guns. Randy wouldn't let them take the gloves and helmets that they had worn when they rode the four-wheelers. "They go with the four-wheelers," he said shortly.

Randy grew more and more agitated until his angry voice rang through the house. He pulled Lori Baker aside. "You have ruined my scenario," he raved. "The boys haven't had a father for seven years, and I planned to fill that spot. Now you will get the Social Security money and all the other benefits she [Cindy] had on the side and go off and you probably won't even have to work. How am *I* going to live?"

Appalled, Lori Baker just stared at him. His *scenario?* What about Cynthia's life? What about the scenario she had hoped for?

When Dottie Baker asked if they could take Rylie's piano, Randy came unglued, and they didn't push it, even though his grandparents had bought the piano for Rylie. They gathered up as many of the boys' clothes and possessions as they could and left hurriedly. They had seen that most of Cynthia's decorative touches had been ripped from the walls. *Why?*

It looked as if Randy had tried to erase every sign that Cynthia had ever lived there.

Randy put the house up for sale. He had apparently counted on the boys' Social Security survivors' benefits to pay off the mortgage, and now he knew he wouldn't be getting that money. Although he and Cynthia had paid $275,000 for the house in Woodinville and it was still in mint condition less than a year later, Randy set the price at only $225,000; he obviously wanted to be rid of it quickly.

DPA Brenneman had questions about the effect of speedboat wakes on the rubber raft belonging to the Roths. She asked that the lake experiment be repeated. On September 4, 1991, the investigative team again took the raft to Lake Sammamish. This time a detective, Laura Hoffenbacker, who was not a particularly strong swimmer, put herself in Cynthia Roth's place, and Sergeant J. K. Pewitt played Randy Roth. Once more, speedboats crisscrossed the lake, deliberately trying to overturn the raft. Sergeant Robert Cline provided his speedboat with Officers Mark Fern and S. L. Gallemore crewing, and they roared by the Sevylor raft, trying their best to tip it over.

They could not do it.

Randy Roth said he had gathered up the family's belongings that had fallen into the lake before he rowed for shore with his unconscious wife. Detective Joe Lewis carefully placed a plastic bag with clothes in it in the water. It floated. Next Lewis tried a beach towel. It sank in five seconds. Continuing to duplicate items Redmond detectives had seen in Randy Roth's vehicle on the night Cynthia drowned, Lewis took five pieces of clothing in a brown paper shopping bag, thong sandals, a department store plastic bag with two pieces of clothing, and a plastic bag with towels, and placed them in the raft. Then he deliberately overturned it. He counted off twenty-four seconds—ten to fifteen seconds less time than Randy had said the raft had been overturned—and then turned it upright. The bags of clothing and towels were strewn about in the lake and were already sinking. They were also separating and going off in many directions. The only way Lewis could retrieve them was by using a long grappling hook and by diving underwater to grab those sinking the most rapidly. Only the plastic bag and the brown bag were still floating; everything else was sinking toward the bottom. He never found the thongs.

Randy's version of Cynthia's drowning just didn't add up.

Possible Reasons to Believe Drowning Was Other Than Accidental

1. The raft wouldn't tip over, no matter how many speedboats chopped the water into strong waves.
2. When the raft was forcibly tipped, an air pocket remained underneath.
3. When the raft was forcibly tipped over a second time, the towels, clothes, thongs, and bags—which Randy had brought back sodden but intact—sank so quickly that one man could never have retrieved them all. And if his wife was drowning, why would he have even tried?
4. In his "desperate" attempt to right the raft, pull his unconscious wife from the water, retrieve all the items from the water, why had Randy not lost his prescription sunglasses? He was wearing them when he rowed back to shore. He was still wearing them in the quiet room of Overlake Hospital when he was told that his wife was beyond saving. He was so nearsighted that he couldn't see to drive—or to row—without them.

Randy was still in sporadic contact with Stacey Reese, even though he and Greg had moved out of the house he had shared with Cynthia and into Lily Vandiveer's residence.

Stacey told Randy Mullinax that Randy Roth had seemed definitely upbeat over the past few weeks. He apparently felt that the police were no longer fixing their suspicion on him. "My attorney told me that no news is good news," he had chortled to her. He said he had taken a polygraph test and that he had to pay for it, but he didn't tell her the results of the test. It sounded as though Randy's attorney wanted him to take a private lie detector test before he submitted to one administered by the police.

"Randy's going to sell his house," Stacey said. "He's going to move north."

How far north? Mullinax wondered. He didn't want to have to trail Randy Roth all the way up to Alaska if he and Sue Peters ever did get enough probable cause to arrest him. And that was a big if.

On September 19, Marilyn Brenneman, Randy Mullinax, Sue Peters, and Joe Lewis traveled to Skamania County. They met with Mike Grossie, who was now the undersheriff, and then followed the trail up the massive monolith. They climbed almost three-quarters of the way up the looming rock to the spot where Janis Roth had fallen to her death almost exactly a decade earlier. They found the shortcut between the two switchbacks, and Joe Lewis videotaped the terrain while Randy Mullinax described the area on tape. Up this high, the leaves had already begun to change. It was beautiful—but chilling— as the investigators gazed down. They were so high, they viewed the landscape and the river below as if they were looking down from a plane.

What must it have been like for a woman reportedly terrified of heights to feel herself sliding, sliding, and finally slipping over the edge? That was assuming that Janis *had* slipped, as Randy Roth had said. If she had been pushed, she would have been plummeting down, halfway there, before she realized what had happened.

Now a crew of detectives and a deputy prosecutor were re-creating that day after Thanksgiving 1981. It wasn't easy, tracking down the sheriff's men and women, the rescuers, and interviewing them ten years later. There is no statute of limitations on murder, but if Skamania County had not been able to find enough probable cause to bring charges right after Jan's death, there was no reason to think King County could do so a decade later. The one thing they had going for them in 1991—possibly—was a similar occurrence, a commonality, a *pattern*.

Randy had bragged to Stacey Reese that he wasn't worried, that nothing seemed to be happening in the investigation of Cynthia's death. But he was whistling in the wind. Randy Roth certainly had good reason to feel nervous as the summer of 1991 eased into autumn. At the request of DPA Marilyn Brenneman and the King County detectives, George Cody appeared with Roth at Sue Peters's office in the King County Courthouse. Randy was prepared to take a lie detector test. Polygrapher Norm Matzke advised Roth of his constitutional rights. He asked his preliminary baseline questions. Then he asked Randy Roth to briefly explain to him what had happened on July 23, the day Cynthia drowned.

George Cody objected. His client had, he said, already answered those kinds of questions. Suddenly the lie detector session was all over. "This is a witch hunt," Cody said. "We will not continue."

Cody and his client walked rapidly out of King County Police Headquarters.

Even so, Randy had no idea how closely Mullinax and Peters were walking behind him. He was a man who had never served more than fourteen days of jail time, who had collected on a number of insurance policies and never had to give a penny back, who had even let the U.S. government support his only child with survivor's benefits on a woman he had been married to less than a year.

Randy was ready to move on to the next chapter of his life. He had told some of his confidants that he planned to leave the area entirely. He had told others he simply planned to move one county north into Snohomish County. He had never left Greg behind before, but he had never been this spooked before. Now, Greg was armed with two phone numbers to be used in case of emergency, and Randy had settled his son in with Lily Vandiveer. If Roth rabbited, there was no telling if King County authorities could ever find him again.

17

It was October 1991. Unaware that Marilyn Brenneman had prepared a certification for determination of probable cause for his arrest, Randy Roth went to an office of the Social Security Administration on October 2.

Robbed, he felt, of Tyson's and Rylie's benefits, Randy had come up with another thought. Very quietly he made application to Social Security on Greg's behalf, asking for $768 a month in survivor's benefits. He knew from his experience with Janis that he had been married to Cynthia just long enough for Greg to qualify as her son. He explained to Candy Bryce, the Social Security Administration interviewer, that Greg's mother had drowned two months earlier. He did not mention that Greg was already collecting Social Security survivor's benefits after the death of another of his "mothers." Indeed, he said he had been married only twice—to Cynthia and to a woman named Donna Clift. He completely omitted any information on his other two wives, Janis Miranda and Donna Sanchez.

When Bryce asked if Cynthia Roth had any other surviving children, Randy said no.

"Had Cynthia been married before?" Candy Bryce asked.

"Yes," Randy answered smoothly. "Her first marriage ended in divorce."

Clearly Randy Roth did not expect to be arrested. If he had, there were many things he would not have done—not the least of which was to make the rather unfortunate application for double Social Security benefits for Greg. There were also things he might have done. He might have moved or hidden items that were not technically his own. But he was cocky. More than two months had gone by and it seemed obvious to him that the cops were chasing their own tails. They didn't have anything on him. They had no way to prove anything and they never would.

He was wrong.

On October 8, 1991, the Honorable Laura Inveen issued search warrants directing law enforcement personnel to search for and seize specified items of evidence pertaining to the crimes of murder and theft, from the defendant's residence at 15423 232nd Avenue N.E., Woodinville, King County, Washington. Each item of evidence was supported by probable cause and described with sufficient particularity to satisfy the mandate of the Fourth Amendment to the United States Constitution and Articles 1 and 7 of the Washington Constitution.

The first search warrant was for items that could be connected to the drowning of Cynthia Roth—clothing, footwear (thongs), towels, documents, financial records or writings—and for tools and other items that Randy Roth had claimed were stolen in his 1988 burglary report to Pioneer Insurance.

Everything was in place.

But first there was the matter of the arrest of Randolph G. Roth. It was ten minutes after nine on the ninth day of the tenth month of 1991. A Wednesday morning. Sue Peters, Joe Lewis, Randy Mullinax, and Sergeant Frank Kinney arrived at Bill Pierre Ford on Lake City Way. Sue Peters, who had begun this investigation on the baking hot evening of July 23, now officially arrested Randy Roth for the murder of his wife.

Randy was shocked. He stared straight ahead as Peters read him his rights under *Miranda.* He stated that he understood those rights, and he declined to make any statement. He also refused to provide the detectives with a handwriting exemplar, and he would not sign a voluntary consent to search of his home.

At that point Peters provided Roth with a copy of the search warrant. His jaw set, he said nothing. Just as he had been forced to give up his raft for police examination, he now was legally bound to let detectives search through his house.

Apparently he had not thought of that.

Roth, in his mechanic's coveralls, requested his street clothes, and Mullinax asked his supervisor to get his shoes, jacket, shirt, and pants out of his locker. Maybe Randy expected to be bailed out and wanted to have his street clothes ready. As the two detectives transported Randy Roth south on the freeway toward the King County Jail, they noticed a truck following them, the driver apparently talking to someone on a cellular phone. At length, Mullinax pulled over onto the shoulder and forced the truck to pass. He recognized Randy's best friend, Max Butts.

By a quarter to ten that morning, Roth had been booked into the King County Jail, and Peters and Mullinax drove to Woodinville to assist in the execution of the search warrant. They were understandably elated. They were perhaps halfway home. A police investigation rarely ends with the arrest; conscientious detectives are usually looking for evidence right up to—and during—a trial. Randy Roth was thirty-seven years old, and he had apparently been keeping secrets for most of his life. The two detectives had every reason to expect every room in his house to hold answers, clues, keys.

Maybe Cynthia had stumbled onto some of those answers, and maybe it had led to her death.

They were about to find out.

18

Even on real-life cop shows on television, patrolmen and detectives always seem to be bursting through front doors and yelling, "Freeze."

At the big yellow house there was no need to burst through the door; there was no hurry. Sergeant Frank Kinney, Joe Lewis, and Bill Bonair waited at the house for Sue Peters and Randy Mullinax to return from booking Randy Roth into jail. They looked at the scrubby yard that had never been landscaped and wondered why a man with the energy and obsessive need for order that Randy had had never bothered to at least throw out some grass seed. He had complained that the place was "a swamp," but that seemed an exaggeration. They could see where someone—possibly Randy—had dug a trench for drain tile and filled it in with gravel.

Someone—maybe Cindy—had placed planters with geraniums, nasturtiums, and marigolds on the front porch and in front of the triple garage. But Cindy had been dead for weeks, and no one had watered the flowers or picked off the dead leaves and blossoms; they were going to seed.

While Kinney, Bonair, and Lewis waited, they took pictures of the exterior of the empty house for the case file. When Mullinax and Peters arrived, they inserted a key in the front door and called out, "Search Warrant—King County Police."

No one answered.

Like most search warrants, this too was executed in a silent house with silent rooms. There was the thinnest layer of dust on the new oak tables, and a staleness in the air from windows and doors shut too long. There was no sound in what had once been Cynthia Roth's dream home. There were no living occupants. The only eyes left to follow the detectives as they worked were those of Cynthia's dolls, some of which still stood on pedestals in the tall oak display case at the bottom of the stairs.

Sue Peters and Randy Mullinax had come to "know" Cynthia Loucks Baumgartner Roth as well as—perhaps better than—they knew the living people in their own lives. They had talked to a hundred or more people about her. They had also come to know and sincerely like her parents, Merle and Hazel; her brother, Leon; her children, Tyson and Rylie; and her best friend, Lori Baker. They had talked to her husband.

But this was her *house*. Her essence remained in these rooms despite the fact that her widower had apparently tried to throw out all traces of her. The furniture she had chosen was still here. This was the house to which she had come full of hope, bubbling over with happiness, with a firm belief that she and her children would live here until she was old with the man she loved. Even though she was gone, the two detectives who had spent their every waking hour thinking about her for the past eleven weeks felt somehow that walking through her house was almost an invasion of her privacy. But they had to do it. There might be clues here that would explain what had led up to her death and let them see that her killer was convicted of her murder.

Dust motes floated in the sun that streamed through the multi-paned windows as Sue Peters searched the family room. Randy Roth apparently never threw any paperwork away. Peters collected stacks of it, including newspaper articles and miscellaneous papers which she found in a green plastic garbage bag. She found four books on the Vietnam War and photographed them. It wasn't hard to figure out where Randy got the material for his war stories. She knew he had told some of his other women that he was actually the subject of Vietnam books.

All lies.

At five feet three, the smallest member of the search team, Peters burrowed into a crawl space underneath the house. She saw several cases of Motorcraft motor oil from Bill Pierre Ford.

The other detectives were finding Bill Pierre items too. It looked as if Randy had brought home enough stuff to open his own garage. There were hundreds—thousands—of dollars' worth of auto parts. They had suspected that Randy might have taken unauthorized stock home from work, but nothing like this. The Bill Pierre and Ford items were not listed on the search warrant; the investigators would have to ask for an additional search warrant.

Frank Kinney found a VCR tape in the family room; someone had taped television coverage of Cynthia's drowning.

Joe Lewis bagged into evidence papers, tax records, real estate articles, an address book, bank records, telephone records, insurance, miscellaneous records, blank checks, keys, beach towels, women's thongs, and Cynthia Roth's financial and tax records.

Lewis also located scores of tools. They looked remarkably similar to the tools that Randy had reported stolen in his claim to Pioneer Insurance after the burglary in 1988.

As the searchers moved from room to room, Randy Mullinax took photographs. His search area was the master bedroom. It was still furnished, but it seemed empty of life, as if Randy had left only the most basic items to make the house more salable. The only tender touch was a teddy bear on one shelf of the wall unit; the bear wore a sweatband.

Mullinax found Cynthia's wallet and checkbook. There was no identification in the wallet, but the check register appeared to have been written by Cynthia. The last check had been written to a Safeway store for groceries on July 23, 1991—the day of her death. There were several packages of condoms next to the bed and a small magazine featuring letters about sex under the bed. Randy had told many women he'd had a vasectomy. If he had been faithful to his new wife, he should not have had any need for condoms.

The next two bedrooms were completely bare except for some empty suitcases in the closets. The fourth bedroom held the peculiar weapons that Randy had always kept close by—clubs with nails driven into them. In the closet of that room, Mullinax found a black rubber diving suit. If Randy Roth couldn't swim very well, what was he doing with a wet suit?

The upstairs rec room contained photo albums with photographs of Janis, Jalina, Randy, Greg, Cynthia, and Lori Baker. There were more clippings about Vietnam. Next to the albums were a number of Marine Corps patches. They were brand new; the sales slips were close by. Mullinax perused the slogans on the patches: "Served and Proud of It," "POW-MIA—They Are Not Forgotten," "Republic of Vietnam Service," "3rd Recon BN: Swift—Silent—Deadly." Randy also had patches from Korea, the Philippines, Camp Pendleton, Camp Delmar, Twentynine Palms, and Okinawa.

The man who had served in the marines for only a few months as a clerk had not gotten over his obsession. He had told the lies so many times to so many people that he might actually have believed he had served in Vietnam.

More likely, the stories and the patches were a part of his con technique. The older he got and the more remote the Vietnam conflict became, the better he might be able to carry off his swift-silent-deadly stories.

But not in jail. You can't con a con.

According to her sons, Randy had dumped Cynthia's makeup—blush, lipstick, mascara, and eyeliner—her perfume and nail polish, and most of her other beauty products into the garbage the day after she died. That was probably true; Mullinax found no cosmetics.

In the upstairs bathroom closet, he did find numerous family photographs, precious pictures that had obviously belonged to Cynthia Roth. There were framed pictures of Tyson and Rylie, from their earliest babyhood to more recent pictures. There was a picture of the Loucks family—Hazel, Merle, Leon, and a six-year-old Cindy—that looked as though it had been taken in the early sixties. There was a plaque from Little League that read, "Special Thanks Coach Cindy Baumgartner," and Mullinax found other plaques as well. Everything had been tossed carelessly in the bathroom closet. Those mementos should have gone to Lori or to the Louckses.

Cindy's pictures were there too, the country pictures of ducks and teddy bears, her country brooms decorated with lace and flowers, her woven baskets—so many of the little touches that she had placed around the house.

Randy had told Stacey Reese that he had gotten rid of "all that fucking mauve." Well, he had. Most of it. He'd dumped it in the bathroom closet or thrown it in the garbage.

Mullinax searched a little outside utility shed and found two Stihl chain saws, one 20-inch and one 16-inch. Those were two of the items that Mullinax remembered Randy had reported stolen to Pioneer. Either he had replaced everything he had lost—or he had never lost it at all.

Randy Mullinax found another crawl space; this one was locked. Gaining access, he found more oil, more auto parts whose boxes read "Bill Pierre."

It was a wonder that they had enough equipment back at the Ford dealership to do business.

Bill Bonair leafed through a thin book, no more than forty pages long, and the hair on the back of his neck stood up. He had found it in Randy's "macho" rec room. It was a very old book on Japanese martial arts that described in detail how to kill someone with your bare hands and never leave a mark. Most of the illustrative diagrams showed techniques to be used around the head and neck.

The detectives were all getting hot and dirty as they swarmed over the yellow house, its outbuildings and crawl spaces. Clearly, Randy Roth had not expected to be arrested on that October day. Aside from the stuff he'd thrown away, sold at the swap meet, and dumped unceremoniously into the Bakers' U-Haul truck, Randy seemed to have hung on to *everything*.

Sue Peters moved into the triple garage. It was about 12:50 P.M. and she had been searching steadily for two hours. There was a little four-drawer brown file cabinet in the garage. It didn't look important. It seemed to be stuffed with more paperwork. Searching through it all was a little like preparing to do income tax, digging through receipts, checks, letters, and miscellaneous junk that should have been organized months before.

In the second drawer Sue Peters found a wadded-up clump of what looked to be sheets of typewriter paper. She was tempted to toss it. "I don't know why I bothered with it," she would say months later. "It looked like garbage. Do I want to bother with this? I dinked around with it, and I saw 'Randy hates Cindy . . .' and I said to myself, Holy Cow!"

If Cynthia Roth had been standing right behind Sue Peters and reached out to touch her lightly on the shoulder, Peters could not have had more of a sense that she had finally broken the code. Cindy hadn't been the kind of woman to complain to friends or to her family. Peters had learned by now that Cindy was proud and private and tried her best to make things work out.

But they had not. Staring down at the crumpled sheets in her hand, Sue Peters could almost hear Cindy's voice as she read her words:

> Randy does not 'love' Cindy,
> Randy Hates Cindy. . . .
> Randy Hates Cindy's Face Make-Up,
> Randy Hates Cindy's Blush
> Randy Hates Cindy's Lipstick;
> Randy Hates Cindy's Blonde Hair
> Randy Hates Cindy's Ugly toes—
>   they're the ugliest toes he's
>   ever seen.
> Randy Hates all of Cindy's
>   5 or 6 different perfumes.
> Randy hates Cindy's cold feet
> Randy hates Cindy's cold hands.
> Randy hates Cindy's fingernails.

Randy hates Cindy's dolls in every
  room.
Randy hates Cindy's Pink Feminine
  things in every room.
Randy hates Cindy's Peach
  feminine things in every room.
Randy hates Cindy's pictures.
  Randy hates Cindy's Furniture,
  Randy hates Cindy's drawers
    because they aren't real drawers.
  Randy hates the way Cindy
    drives because she'll wreck
      the cars and trucks.
  Randy hates the way Cindy
    cooks most of the time.
      Randy hates the way
  Cindy buys groceries too
  many times every week and
    spends too much money.
  Randy hates the swamp that
  Cindy made him move to.
Randy hates Cindy's hose,
  Randy hates Cindy's things,
  Randy hates Cindy's money,
  Randy hates Cindy's
    independent nature.
  Randy hates the way Cindy
    grinds her teeth.
  Randy hates the way Cindy
    picks up his papers all
      the time.
  Randy hates the way
Cindy uses all the hot
  water to fill the huge
    tub for a bath.
Randy hates that Cindy
  drinks coffee.
Randy hates that Cindy
  eats more than all of
  the boys.
Randy hates how

Cindy decorates a house—
Randy hates Cindy
    shopping,
Randy hates Cindy
leaving the house at
    all.
Randy hates Cindy driving
    the Trooper.
Randy hates Cindy's pants.
Randy hates that Cindy
    likes to eat!! Because
    she'll get fat.
Randy hates that Cindy
    made a Cookie for
    Valentine's Day & not a
    cake.
Randy hates if Cindy
    wants to help or volunteer
        anywhere.
Randy hates Cindy having
    Lori over to our house.
Randy hates coming home
    from work instead
        of shopping or doing
            other things.
Randy hates not being able
to go shopping alone all
    the time!
Randy hates telling
    Cindy where he goes.
Randy hates Cindy's
    monthly thing and
    putting up with her
    each month.

Sue Peters sat back on her heels. The document was written as if it were a desperate poem. The writing scrawled more with each line, and she could imagine the writer sobbing as she wrote. The words had been set down in black ink with a forceful hand.

Cynthia Roth—the bubbly, giving, friendly woman—had clearly been reduced to someone who had no self-confidence left, whose every move, thought, action, and behavior had irritated the man she had loved so much. Randy Roth had beaten her down until she had little left. Nothing she did had pleased him.

And yet Cindy had still held out that last hope—that their anniversary trip to Reno would somehow renew their marriage, and bring them back to the place in their hearts where they had been in the summer of 1990.

There was no date on the "poem." It had to have been written after Valentine's Day 1991; Cindy had not yet met Randy Roth on that holiday in 1990. Her friends had seen that Cindy had seemed quietly unhappy after her first Christmas with Randy. The insurance papers had been delivered in March.

Yes, Cindy had realized full well that Randy no longer loved her, but had she been afraid of him? Afraid for her life? Probably not. If she had been, she would not have climbed into that raft with him and headed so far, far away from the crowd on the beach at Idylwood Park. She would have not left her sons alone on the beach unless she expected to be back in a very short time.

As Sue Peters sealed the desolate poem into a plastic bag and labeled it, she thought of another little note she had found in her search, a note written in the same rounded cursive script. Cindy Roth had, like all the others, believed that Randy's nightmares were triggered by his horrible experiences in a faraway Asian war. And she had been trying to help him. Peters looked at the note: "Tuesday night, 7:30 p.m.—Tell Randy about Vietnam Vet meeting. Post Traumatic Stress Disorder?"

Peters looked at the little shrine that Randy had built for himself in the front hallway. There was a picture of him in marine dress blues— a very handsome, solemn young man gazing straight ahead—and a gold-framed display of two Marine Corps emblems. And, beneath that, the bronze plaque for valor awarded to "Sergeant R. G. Roth."

Bravery and valor? Hardly. Sue Peters knew that Randy hadn't earned the plaque, that he had copied one he had seen in Ben Goodwin's house. She plucked it off the wall, handed it to Joe Lewis, and said, "Put this in evidence."

It had been a very long day. She had arrested Randy at ten minutes to nine that morning, and it was now six-thirty in the evening. "Wait a minute," Peters said. She went upstairs and got the red scrapbook with the Vietnam articles in it and handed that to Joe Lewis too.

19

As late as it was, the King County search team contacted Rick Doss from the Bill Pierre Ford agency and asked him to come and take a look at the auto parts, motor oil, and other items that might have come from the dealership. Doss arrived and made an inventory list of possible stolen agency items.

The police secured the residence at twenty minutes after seven, and by eight, Sue Peters and Bonair were downtown placing all the items they had seized in the evidence room of the King County Courthouse.

Search warrants are precise in listing what detectives may remove. In the execution of the first warrant, the King County detectives had seen countless items that clearly belonged to the Bill Pierre Ford. They immediately asked for a second warrant listing those items.

The second search warrant was issued. In lay terms, that meant that the King County detectives had the right to go back into the big yellow house and seize the motor parts, oil, gaskets, almost anything with "Bill Pierre" stamped on it.

Before they locked up the Woodinville house on October 9, Kinney, Lewis, Bonair, Mullinax, and Peters had carried and dragged the items that looked as if they had come from Randy's employer into two of the three garages. They photographed the stuff, but they couldn't really know how much it was worth, where it had come from, or if Randy was authorized to have it in his possession. The manager at the dealership that employed Randy Roth had no record that Randy had ever paid for the still-boxed products in the Woodinville home.

Armed with their second search warrant, detectives listed *ninety-five* items as they removed everything from coil springs to motor oil, gear boxes to steering fluid, brake parts to radiators, and almost everything else a man might need to rebuild cars at home. It looked as though Randy had never left work without taking something unauthorized along with him.

Max Butts arrived while the detectives spent their second day logging evidence. He picked up the Roths' dog and the motorcycles that were parked behind the house.

Sue Peters released the ninety-five items that belonged to Bill Pierre Ford to Dick Tutino of that agency.

The news of Randy Roth's arrest hit the papers on October 10, 1991. The next day, the specific charge of first-degree murder was announced. His bail was set at $1 million. Marilyn Brenneman's probable cause document ran eighteen pages and contained information that fascinated both the press and the public. For the first time, they learned about the many, many women in Randy's past—some dead, others only disenchanted. The "accident" on Lake Sammamish no longer seemed to be the result of a bitter twist of fate.

George Cody hastened to remind the media that the case against his client was purely circumstantial. Randy Roth, he said, was fully prepared to defend himself against the charge. Cody maintained that suspicions had been directed toward Roth solely because tragedy had struck him twice, that the King County prosecutors had no "smoking gun surprises" in the documents filed by Marilyn Brenneman. He called the evidence against Roth "a circumstantial web" that in no way changed his own determination to enter a plea of not guilty. He was ready to proceed to trial.

Lizabeth Roth, who had always been a shadowy, almost mythic figure in Randy's discussions of his background, called Sue Peters. Mrs. Roth explained that she was Randy's mother, and that she had been watching reports of his arrest on television and felt the situation was "unreal."

"Randy was heartbroken when Cynthia died," she said urgently. "When I hugged him at the service, he almost broke into tears."

Lizabeth Roth explained that her family was extremely religious and that they were not killers.

"Well . . ." Peters said cautiously—but there was no way to be tactful about her next question. "What about your son, David Roth? He's in prison for murder, isn't he?"

"He got a bum rap," Lizabeth Roth said indignantly. "It was a setup. He confessed by force, and the FBI is looking into it."

* * *

Randy Roth's troubles piled up. Chris Jarvis, chronicling Roth's daily troubles for the *Journal American,* reported that Roth was also under investigation for theft from Bill Pierre Ford, his employer. Randy had the murder charge and the $1 million bail hanging over his head in King County Superior Court, and Seattle District Court records showed that police had reason to believe he was also suspected of stealing more than $1,000 worth of auto parts from Bill Pierre. (The actual total was $2,254.)

Pioneer Insurance refiled charges of insurance fraud connected with the 1988 burglary of Randy's house. Randy Mullinax and Sue Peters had found too many of the things he had claimed losses for: the two Stihl saws, the Craftsman tool chest, a stereo set. For most people, it is a good idea to save receipts. For Randy, it had meant disaster. It was easy for investigators to match the dates on the receipts with the items squirreled away in and under the Woodinville house. Whatever had disappeared in 1988 had miraculously found its way back into Randy's possession.

Bill Pierre Ford fired Randy. That was the least of his troubles.

On Saturday, October 12, Randy Mullinax received a phone call from one of Lily Vandiveer's relatives. She had reason to believe that Randy had called Lily from the King County Jail. "Randy gave her a long list of things he wanted her to remove from his house right away," the woman said.

Mullinax immediately placed the empty yellow house under surveillance all weekend, but nobody appeared. It might have been too late. The same informant called him back to say that she thought Lily and a man named "Max" might already have taken things from the house that Randy didn't want anyone to know about. "I think they took them to store someplace in Snohomish County," she said. "I heard, too, that Randy gave Lily $25,000 before he went to jail."

Max Butts had had an appointment with Mullinax at ten o'clock on Saturday morning, but he hadn't shown up. On Monday the detective went to the body shop where Max worked. Butts pulled in driving Randy Roth's Ford pickup. He didn't seem particularly happy to see Mullinax.

Randy Mullinax noted that Randy Roth's toolboxes from Bill Pierre Ford were in the back of the pickup. Butts didn't want to talk to Mullinax at all, saying he had been advised by Randy's attorney not to.

"Is George Cody *your* attorney?" Mullinax asked.

"No."

"Well, I think it's very important that you talk to me about any involvement you may have had in picking up some of Randy's belongings from his house over the weekend."

Mullinax studied Butts. He saw the man was torn between loyalty to his best friend and saving his own neck.

His neck won.

Max Butts admitted that Randy had called and given him a list of things that he wanted out of his house: "He was afraid stuff that belonged to him might be taken away while he was in jail. He wanted his personal papers and other things stored for him. I took them to my house."

Mullinax called the office and spoke to Sue Peters. She had just received a call from Rick Doss at Bill Pierre. Max Butts *had* picked up Randy's toolbox, but he had also returned some large items that belonged to the Ford dealership. He had explained to the mechanic who helped him unload the equipment that Roth had "borrowed" it and Max was now returning it for him.

The items were a Walker one-and-a-half-ton bumper jack, a Weaver Acra-speed wheel balancer, and a Hunter strobe wheel balancer kit. Mullinax had seen all three of the items when he participated in the first search. The jack was in the crawl space, and the wheel balancers were under the front porch. Rick Doss said that Randy had never had permission to take either the jack or the balancers. Occasionally mechanics could borrow the heavier equipment overnight, but it was always due back the next morning.

Randy had never asked.

For a man who claimed to be as clever and competent as Randy Roth always had, his frantic return of stolen items was a little silly. He was charged with first-degree murder, and he was worrying about theft charges. But then, the theft charges were backed by physical evidence, while the murder charges really were circumstantial, just as George Cody said.

Could Marilyn Brenneman convince a jury *beyond a reasonable doubt* that Randy Roth had deliberately drowned Cynthia Roth? Could she find legal precedent that would let her bring the accidental death of Janis Roth into her courtroom? Winning or losing might all come down to that.

Sue Peters and Randy Mullinax had sensed from the very beginning that Randy Roth frightened the people whose lives touched his, that there had always been about him a subtle threat of danger. He was the man in black who prowled alone at night, the man with the nail-studded clubs hanging from his bed, the self-proclaimed expert in karate, and, the man who had carried out such vicious killings in Vietnam that he screamed out in the darkness of his dreams. And, of course, two of his four wives were dead, and violently dead.

Once Randy Roth had been arrested and was languishing in jail with a million dollars in bail keeping him there, witnesses began to speak more freely. Their fear of Randy might very well have been subliminal. He had spent most of his life perfecting his own brand of mind control.

Lori Baker had never been afraid of Randy; she had been afraid for Cynthia, but more afraid that Cindy would be hurt emotionally than physically. Marilyn Brenneman and Randy Mullinax went to Lori's home to talk with her. They showed her the four-page "poem" that Sue Peters had found in Cindy's little storage chest in the garage. If anyone could recognize Cindy's writing, it would be Lori.

Lori read through the words that showed how sad and diminished Cindy had been in her last spring. She nodded. Yes, she said, it was Cindy's writing. "She told me about writing this—all the things that Randy hated about her. I didn't know that she had saved it."

Lori would be an important witness in the case against Randy Roth, and she talked with Marilyn Brenneman about the close friendship she had had with Cindy Baumgartner. Combining their households had seemed like a good idea back in 1985, and it had been. Cindy hadn't needed Lori's $300 a month rent, but Lori had insisted. They maintained a bank account together to pay the household expenses. Lori had agreed to be the boys' guardian, but she had not expected to be the executor of Cindy's will.

"I remember when she told me that a man had asked for her phone number while she was working at the concession stand for Little League," Lori said. "That man turned out to be Randy Roth."

Lori recalled when Randy and his son Greg had come to dinner at the house she shared with Cindy. Lori had not had a chance to say much to Randy during the very short time that he and Cindy had dated; Cindy and Randy had eyes only for each other. Lori found Randy Roth pleasant enough, but his courtship was rapid and constant. She remembered that Randy kept asking Cindy to take overnight trips with him. "That was something that Cindy would never have done unless she was married to a man," Lori explained.

Cindy had been troubled that Randy was not a churchgoer. But she had been sure that she would be able to get him to attend church after they were married.

Things had not gone well after the marriage. Even though she told no one but Lori, Cindy had confided shortly after the honeymoon that her sex life with Randy was not very good. Randy had not proved to be the ardent lover she had waited for. After so many years of celibacy, it had been a disappointment. Cindy had expected that this would be a complete marriage, with both spiritual and physical love. Cindy had felt disloyal even in voicing her disillusionment about her almost nonexistent sex life. Randy had been such an impetuous suitor that she had expected him to be a warm and exciting lover. And he had not been.

"Within weeks of their wedding," Lori said sadly, "Cindy was having second thoughts."

Cindy Roth had been independent for almost six years, and she had come to value her freedom to come and go, but she told Lori that Randy wanted her to stay in the house all the time. His insistence that she was not to do *anything* on her own had quickly made Cindy feel suffocated. She was frustrated and annoyed once when she found her car wouldn't start. Lori came over to help and found that someone had deliberately disconnected a wire under the hood. "I hooked it back up," Lori said, "and she could at least do her errands."

Randy had operated under a double standard; he could join a health gym, but he didn't even want his wife to join an aerobics class if there were men in it.

Lori recalled that Cindy had been highly suspicious of Lily Vandiveer. When Randy took Lily's son, Brad, home, he would often be gone for hours. Cindy didn't trust Lily and Randy. She had begun to drive Brad home earlier in the day so that Randy had no excuse to make the trip. She hadn't been able to understand why the older woman seemed to have such a large place in Randy's life.

By the spring of 1991, Cindy had begun to mention to Lori that she had thought of leaving Randy. But Lori knew she never would have: "Her religious beliefs were too strong. She wouldn't have considered divorce."

"Do you know if Randy ever asked *her* for a divorce?" Marilyn Brenneman asked.

Lori shook her head. "I don't think so. Cindy would have told me."

Now that they knew they would be going to trial, Marilyn Brenneman needed to learn as much as she could about Randy Roth—every relationship, every detail—even those that seemed innocuous enough on the surface. Randy Mullinax was curious that

Max Butts would run so many errands for Roth. What was he to Randy Roth?

Lori had met Max several times; he was always trailing in Randy's wake. "Cindy noticed it too," Lori recalled. "She said it seemed like everywhere they went, Max showed up." He had told Lori that he didn't think Randy would marry Cindy. When he came to her house looking for Randy on the weekend the pair had eloped to Reno, Max had seemed terribly upset to hear that news.

Mullinax had seen that Roth always had had a younger male friend who was totally impressed with him, someone to run and fetch for him. Once it had been Nick Emondi; now it was Max Butts.

Emondi was ready to tell the detectives anything they needed to know; he had broken away from Randy, while Butts was still clinging to his hero.

Lori Baker said that Greg had been very fond of Cindy, although he was careful not to show how much he liked her when his father was around. Cindy hadn't known why—except that Randy was so much into marine-style macho behavior. Real men didn't show their feelings, and that went for boys too.

There was one thing that Lori had never known about: Cindy had never told her about the way Randy disciplined the boys—Greg and her own two sons. After Tyson and Rylie moved in with Lori, however, she realized with dawning horror just how bad things had been.

"He made them do squat thrusts as discipline," she told Brenneman and Mullinax. "They told me once that they were doing them in the driveway on a cold night and he turned the hose on them because they weren't doing them fast enough."

Tyson had told Lori that Randy picked him up bodily once and threw him across the room so hard that Tyson's head made a dent in the wallboard. All three of the boys had to help Randy clean the shop at Bill Pierre Ford on Friday nights. They didn't mind that, but inevitably they never worked fast enough to suit him. To hurry them along, Randy had turned the high-pressure cold water hose on them. "They had to finish cleaning and ride home with wet clothes," Lori said. What might have been a lark in the summer was miserable in the winter.

Cindy had saved Greg from serious injury at least once, the boys had told Lori. His father had been about to throw him headlong into the stone fireplace when Cindy intervened.

Marilyn Brenneman and Randy Mullinax talked alone to Tyson

Baumgartner, and they got a more fully rounded picture of what life had really been like in the picture-perfect yellow house in the country.

Cindy's older son said Randy had insisted that he and Rylie watch videos of *Platoon* and *Hamburger Hill.* Both Vietnam War movies were full of gruesome battle scenes. When the boys tried to turn away from the bloody action, Randy insisted they watch it all.

"Randy told us that he had to do a lot of the things we saw—when he was in Vietnam," Tyson said.

On some nights, when Randy was angry with Tyson or Rylie, he took out his rage on their mother. He would drive off in a spray of gravel and not come home until the early hours of the morning, or he would grab Cindy's arm so hard that she had bruises shaped like finger marks the next day.

Tyson remembered the "shop nights" at the car dealership all too well. Randy and Max, who invariably accompanied them, would laugh at the sight of the boys when they were caught in the needle-sharp spray of the high-pressure hose. The boys had just about frozen working in January or February in soaking wet clothes.

Asked if he remembered his stepfather ever bringing home "supplies" from the car dealership, Tyson nodded. He had seen Randy bring home oil and air filters and the jack that Randy Mullinax had found under the house during the search-warrant sweep. "He said he needed the jack to work on the Escort. He put the oil on shelves in the garage."

Tyson said that he had even seen Randy bringing home entire engines. One was still wrapped in plastic in a crate. He didn't know what had become of those big items. He had asked Randy once if he bought the things he brought home, and Randy had said sarcastically, "No, I did *not* buy them."

Cindy Roth's little boys were slowly coming out of their nightmare months with a stepfather who had never served in Vietnam but who behaved like a cruel marine drill sergeant. They had tried very hard to get along with him because their mother wanted them all to be a family. Sometimes Randy had done fun things with them—but mostly they had walked softly and jumped to do his bidding.

So had their mother.

20

Nineteen eighty-five had been a turning-point year for Cindy Baumgartner, Randy Roth, Sue Peters, Randy Mullinax, and Marilyn Brenneman—and for Deputy Prosecuting Attorney Susan Storey, who was chosen to be the other half of the King County prosecuting team. Because of what happened in that single year, none of them would ever be quite the same again. But, of course, not one of them had realized it. Watershed moments are only recognizable in retrospect.

When Donna Clift left Randy Roth in 1985, he became a single man and, in his own mind, a widower again. Cindy really was a widow. The two of them seemed meant, through some grim synchronicity, to meet and to marry, but for all the wrong reasons. Donna Clift would berate herself forever after for not calling Cindy to warn her. Ben Goodwin would wish he had been more convincing when he *did* warn her.

But nothing helped, and Cindy was dead. And now the most compelling murder case in King County in decades was going to trial. And it would indeed be a squeaker.

In the fall of 1985 Susan Storey was starting her last year of law school at the University of Puget Sound and working for a Tacoma law firm. Tacoma was a big city compared to Lewiston, Idaho, where she was born. She didn't stay very long in the town on the Washington-Idaho state line; Storey's childhood was peripatetic. She lived in Spokane, Seattle, and New Providence, New Jersey. She went to high school in Seattle and undergraduate school at the University of Washington, where she was an outstanding member of the crew team.

In 1985, Susan Storey had served a summer internship with the King County Prosecuting Attorney's Office in Seattle, and they had offered her a job when she graduated from law school in the spring. "I jumped at the job," Storey remembers. "I knew I wanted to practice criminal law."

Fledgling prosecutors don't get to handle much heavy-duty criminal law in the beginning, but Storey knew that. After Susan Storey graduated cum laude from UPS, she moved to Seattle and started at the King County Prosecutor's Office in October of 1986. Her first assignment was in a district court in Renton, a Seattle suburb. Next she worked in King County Juvenile Court. "I didn't come downtown until right about the end of 1988."

Dark-haired, with clear blue eyes, Storey shares Sue Peters's love for softball and served for a time as assistant commissioner of the Emerald City Softball Association.

In her first five years with the King County Prosecutor's Office, Storey moved steadily up to handle headline cases, including the Hung Tran Asian Gang case, in which the accused attempted to be tried as a juvenile after terrorizing and robbing families in his neighborhood. Forensic anthropologists used X-ray technology to determine Tran's age. He was not a juvenile.

Another memorable case for Storey was the trial of the Queen Anne Ax Murderer. Numerous homes in the historic Queen Anne Hill district of Seattle were broken into at night. At first, the pattern seemed bizarre, even kinky: the intruder would rearrange the furniture, write on the walls, or leave an ax inside the house. And then things turned deadly. A sixty-year-old woman was murdered with an ax as she slept. Detectives arrested James Cushing, who had no permanent address and rambled the streets of Seattle. He had become fixated on the Queen Anne neighborhood. Susan Storey won a conviction despite Cushing's insanity defense.

Marilyn Brenneman and Sue Storey had long since discovered, as had all female prosecutors, that the distaff members of the prosecutor's office bear an extra burden in the courtroom. Like all effective prosecutors, they had schooled themselves to remain dispassionate about the defendant, no matter what abhorrent crimes he or she might stand accused of. But it hadn't been that long since the lead prosecutor was always male, although he might be assisted by a female DPA. In the courtroom, the woman prosecutor still had to remember to walk softer. To speak softer.

"You never hear a male attorney being described as 'strident,'" Brenneman says, smiling. "Or 'bitchy' or worst of all, put them together and you have 'strident bitch!' Males don't have to think about keeping their voices modulated. *We* speak softly and calmly because we're aware that women can be fair game. Eventually this will go away too."

Petite female prosecutors could sometimes talk a bit louder and be a little more sarcastic, but Brenneman and Storey are tall women, and noticeable in the confines of the courtroom. Sometimes their height helps; sometimes it's a drawback. Brenneman, at five feet nine, is heartened to see one of Seattle's more massive defense attorneys in the opposite corner. She laughs, remembering when she was about as pregnant as a woman can get with her last child. Facing off with Tony Savage, one of Seattle's largest and most sought-out criminal defense attorneys, Brenneman quipped to the judge, "If this trial isn't over soon, I'm going to be bigger than Tony!"

She made it with a few days to spare.

Susan Storey, flushed with victory after a homicide trial, was chastened by a juror who murmured, "I know he was guilty, but did you have to be so mean to him in cross-examination?"

Although it was not deliberate, there was a certain poetic justice now in the fact that out of the prime detective-prosecutor team that stood against a man accused of seducing and killing women, three of the four members were female: Sue Peters, Marilyn Brenneman, and Susan Storey. Randy Mullinax was the lone male. Randy Roth had demeaned and abused females most of his life. He hated little girls. He was the embodiment of the kind of man who preferred his women to stay in their place, barefoot—but not pregnant.

Now he would face two smart, strong, and savvy women in the courtroom while a third, Sue Peters, would be sitting at the prosecution table as a friend of the court.

Mullinax and Susan Storey took aerial photos of Lake Sammamish and Idylwood Park. The game plan would be to re-create for the jury the events, the ambience, and the scene at the park on the day Cynthia Roth's life ended. It would not be a simple task to take that blistering hot summer day at the lake into a small windowless courtroom, to fill the jurors' senses with the sounds, sights, smells, and emotions of that awful day.

But they were going to do it. Cynthia Baumgartner Roth could no longer speak for herself; she could not say what had happened on the far side of the lake as her little boys scanned the water for some sight of their mother. But there were ways to reconstruct; Sue Peters and Randy Mullinax had steadily built a wall of probability, human memories and impressions, documents, expert opinion, similar transactions, and motivations. That wall would always have one stone missing—Cynthia herself—but it was strong enough to hold without her.

21

Contrary to a layman's view, even when a suspect has been arrested and charged, the investigation is not over. The detectives who had tracked and trapped Randy Roth worked harder, if possible, after he was arrested than they had before. He was a man whose whole life had been deliberately secretive as he carried out his schemes. Sue Peters and Randy Mullinax continued to burrow into the quagmire that was Roth's past, conferring constantly with Marilyn Brenneman and Susan Storey about the man they would come up against in court. Randy Roth had never, apparently, simply *lived* his life; he had played wicked games with everyone around him, delighting in keeping them off balance, in deluding and deceiving. Roth was a paradox. He seemed to have lied even when telling the truth might have been easier. He was not a master at Tae Kwon Do or a marine hero or a tender lover or a caring father or a score of other things he claimed to be.

He was, they were convinced, a cold and calculating con man and a killer who could walk away from his murders without a scintilla of remorse. He didn't know the meaning of the word. But he was smart—not educated smart but street smart.

Before Roth went to trial in the spring of 1992, the quartet who would face off with him had to find his Achilles' heel. They suspected that his weakness lay in the very behavior that had given him power: his lies. Given enough time, a lie invariably comes home to roost, and Randy Roth had an endless flock of lies circling him.

By sheer coincidence, Randy Roth was charged with first-degree murder exactly one year to the day after the Pioneer Insurance

Company had paid him $28,500 on his burglary claim and dismissed its court action against him—with prejudice. Sue Peters and Randy Mullinax had found two solid witnesses who told them that they knew about the "burglary" before it ever happened. Both witnesses were afraid of Roth, however. Pioneer Insurance agreed not to make any move to vacate its 1990 court action until Roth was behind bars. The witnesses who could help prove Randy had faked his burglary feared retribution. Pioneer's lawyers promised the King County detectives they would not contact the witnesses until it was safe to do so. On October 9, 1991, with Randy Roth safely in jail, Pioneer filed its motion to reopen the case against him.

One of the frightened witnesses was Nick Emondi. He signed an affidavit that his onetime best friend, Randy Roth, had told him in the summer of 1988 that he was thinking of robbing his own house.

The second witness was Brittany Goodwin. She had given a statement to Peters and Mullinax a month after Cynthia drowned, but she would not sign it until she knew Randy was behind bars.

Brittany was the daughter of the man who had been Randy's best friend for almost eight years. Both Ben and Marta Goodwin had loved and trusted Randy, and they had been disillusioned. But even at the end of their friendship, they had not realized how deeply he had betrayed them or for how long.

Brittany had been in grade school when the Goodwins met Randy, but she blossomed into a very pretty, if shy, teenager. From the time Brittany was thirteen, she had a crush on Randy. She didn't know how old he was and he would never tell her. "Let's just say I'm in a box that's over seventeen and under thirty-five," he would tease.

While it is more normal than not for teenage girls to have crushes on older men, it is *not* normal for adult men to encourage that immature adulation. At first, Randy had only seemed so handsome and so much fun. Brittany was full-breasted early and could have passed for seventeen or eighteen when she was four or five years younger, but she was really only a child when Randy began to flirt with her. There was no way she was equipped to deal with his exploitation. "He'd always help me clean up after he came over for dinner," she said. "He would pinch me on the bottom, or rub against me when he was putting the dishes away. That was the way it started."

Brittany was "kind of jealous" when Randy married Donna Clift, and then when Mary Jo moved in.

Brittany Goodwin had never been out with a boy. She was a sitting duck for a man like Randy Roth. He defined who she was, how she would act, how she would look, even how much she would weigh. And he did it so subtly that even her parents berated themselves when they grew suspicious.

"The thing is," Brittany recalls with bitterness, "that the boys were always with us. Greg and my brother Ryan would go along when Randy took me anywhere. That made it look innocent, and Randy planned it that way."

Although Brittany's weight was within normal limits, Randy always complained that she was too fat. She was not fat; she was large-breasted, but her waist and hips were slim. More than most teenagers, Brittany felt insecure and imperfect.

Slyly, Randy became a sinister Pygmalion to the fourteen-year-old girl who lived next door. "He wanted me to be thinner," she said. "He told me that every five pounds I lost, he would give me a reward—like take me skiing or inner-tubing, or he would buy me a new bathing suit. I tried, but I couldn't lose enough to suit him. I decided that if I threw up everything I ate, I would get thin, so I stuck a pencil down my throat and I just threw up all the time. I was really getting emotionally screwed up trying to be what Randy wanted me to be."

Randy kept an eye on everything Brittany ate. "He could go all day and not eat anything but an apple. He couldn't understand why I needed to eat. That was when all my problems with food and my body image started. With Randy."

While her parents believed Randy was taking an avuncular interest in Brittany, he was actually grooming her to be his lover. "He wanted me to be 'more worldly.' He wanted me to eat different foods, meet more people, and act grown-up," Brittany said. "He wanted me to be *thirty*, but I wasn't fifteen yet."

Brittany turned fifteen on February 7, 1987. On Valentine's Day while Marta and Ben Goodwin were out of town, Randy took Brittany and the boys out to dinner and then seduced his best friend's daughter. He promised Brittany that he would marry her when she was eighteen.

"He liked to talk about what my folks would say if they knew we were in love," she remembers. "He would say that maybe we could tell them we were getting married when I was seventeen and a half. He told me that I would never have to work—that he would spoil me."

Perhaps because he knew that Brittany was completely in his

power, Randy showed her more of his life than he had other women. He took her—along with Greg and Ryan—to visit his father in Vancouver, Washington. While the Goodwins trusted him, he sent the boys away so that he and Brittany could be alone. "I think Greg knew about us," Brittany said, "but Randy told him he better not say anything. If Greg told, Randy would go to prison, and if he ever got out, he'd come back and get him for telling. Greg never told."

Randy also took Brittany to see his mother. Lizabeth Roth was in the hospital in Bremerton, Washington, recovering from gall bladder surgery. Randy didn't say much to his mother, and Brittany didn't know what to say either. He took her to see his sisters, too. Brittany was surprised at the way Randy's mother and sisters looked; they all wore thick, thick blue eye shadow and dressed in a way that seemed kind of trashy to her.

Randy's physical affair with Brittany was more convenient for him when she began to baby-sit for Greg. It was almost impossible for her to control Greg. If she told him to go in his room, she would look toward the street five minutes later and see that Greg had crawled out his window and was outside playing.

But Randy could make Greg mind. "We were all afraid of him," Brittany remembers. "We all had to do what Randy said. If I didn't push in my chair after dinner, we all had to do push-ups or bends and thrusts. It seemed kind of funny to me—that Randy made love to me and then treated me like a child."

If Brittany ever argued with him, Randy would refuse to have sex with her. And at the same time, he made her feel even less desirable than he usually did.

Greg got most of the punishment, though. He was pushed into a freezing shower if he lied, or he had to stand with both hands on his bed, his pants around his ankles, while Randy beat him with his belt.

Randy took Brittany to Parents Without Partners dances, she said. "I don't know how he explained me. I guess I looked old enough. There were a lot of young women there, and I was jealous. If I didn't learn a dance step on the first try, Randy got mad. If I chewed gum, he'd tell me not to act like a teenager—but I *was* a teenager."

Randy kept Brittany completely off balance all the time. He bought her a "promise ring," and she believed he meant it when he said he would marry her. He would leave a single rose on her car windshield or at the end of her driveway where she would see it and know it was from him.

When she baby-sat, Randy would pretend to drive away, then park his truck down the street and sneak back to spend the night with her.

But she knew he was seeing other women too. She found notes from them, and condoms. He only laughed when she questioned him.

Randy particularly enjoyed touching Brittany when her father was so close it was dangerous. If Randy and Ben were working on a car, Randy would wait until Ben's back was turned and then he would blow Brittany a kiss or rub his hand over her breast. When the families went camping together, as they had for years, Brittany slept in a little tent a few feet from her parents' trailer. "Randy liked that. He liked to sneak in and have sex with me so close to where they were sleeping."

Brittany learned soon enough that Randy didn't necessarily keep his promises. She became less afraid of him but more depressed. Mary Jo or Lily would drive up to Randy's house after eleven and stay until four or five in the morning. She says, "My bedroom window was on that side, and I stood there all night, watching his dark house, trying to look in his bedroom window, until I saw them leave."

Randy seemed to take pleasure in tormenting Brittany. He flirted openly with other women when she was with him: "There was one woman who came to a wrestling match that Ryan and Greg were in. She had on those black mesh stockings, and Randy was all over her, saying, 'Can I come over to your house and count the holes in your stockings?' He knew that made me feel bad, but he always acted like that anyway."

She met Lily's daughter, Dawn,* at school, and Dawn stared at Brittany, astounded. "You *like* Randy? Don't you know he was in trouble for killing his wife?"

Brittany asked him about it, and he explained that Janis had died in a terrible accident. "He said they were on a trail and her foot slipped on a rock and she fell off. He cried when he told me about it.

"I only saw him cry twice. That time—and one time he was really worried about money. He told me that he might lose his house because he just didn't have enough money. He thought maybe he could turn it into a duplex and rent out the top half. He really cried hard because he needed money."

Randy Roth's tears came easily when he viewed his dismal financial situation, but he became annoyed with Brittany for crying when one of her favorite aunts died of cancer: "I was sitting on the lawn crying, and he told me to 'Quit crying, just quit crying. Death isn't important. Get on with your life.'"

For Randy, death was not important; money was.

Randy Roth seemed obsessed with youth. He wanted Brittany to see him as young. He liked to race "young guys" in his hot cars.

"And he was so worried about going bald," Brittany recalled. "He'd put this hair formula on his head so his hair would grow back. But it never did."

During the first year of their physical affair, Randy Roth could have told Brittany Goodwin he had hung the moon and she would have believed it. During the second, she tried tentatively to break away from the man who wanted to run her whole life, but who wanted *his* freedom to do anything. Breaking away wasn't easy; he was always there, right next door. As always, the Roths and the Goodwins had Sunday breakfast together every week. As always, Randy sneaked pinches and pats behind her parents' back to validate some dark control he had over her—and them.

Brittany was bound to Randy by her own insecurity, her passion for the first and only lover she had ever known, and by a vague fear that he could hurt her if she went too far away.

When she was sixteen and about to start her junior year in high school, she yearned for more than a clandestine affair. She didn't want to be thirty; she wanted to be sixteen. She didn't want to sneak around and hide from her parents anymore, and she knew Randy lied to her far more than he ever told the truth.

Although Randy's constant criticism of her appearance would damage Brittany's self-image for many years to come, she stopped being so afraid of him when she turned sixteen. "I got just a little bit more independent—and not so scared."

On the first day of eleventh grade, Brittany walked to her car. It was a red Ford Fiesta. Randy had the same model, only his Fiesta was burgundy. She unlocked her car, but as she slid behind the steering wheel, she saw that someone had pulled all the wires loose from behind the dashboard and left them dangling like strands of spaghetti. Frightened, she turned the key and pushed the accelerator.

Nothing happened. Randy hadn't wanted her to go to the first day of school where she might meet boys her own age. And now she couldn't get there on time.

Even though Randy Roth had held Brittany Goodwin in an invisible cage for two years, it was he who broke up with her. She does not recall the scene with her father in the driveway, but she does remember a phone conversation that might have triggered the beginning of the end. "I was upset and I called Randy. My dad was just walking in Randy's door and he heard Randy's side of the conversation. Randy hung up quickly, and so did I. But I think my father knew it was me on the other end of the line."

Even after the affair ended, Randy remained close to Brittany. "He always told me 'Semper Fi,' and he always signed his notes the same way, 'Always Faithful.' He wasn't—ever—but he let me know he would never really let me go."

Long before the summer of 1988, Randy had told Brittany, in detail, how he planned to burglarize his own house. "If we ever split up," he warned, "what I've told you has to stay between us—or I'll come and get you. . . ."

She believed him. Even when Brittany was in love with another man, Randy would put his arm around her and flirt with her in front of her new love. He enjoyed that. Creating jealousy was one of Randy's most effective ways of tormenting people and keeping them in line.

Even after Randy married Cindy Baumgartner, he stopped at his old house, which was still on the market, and called Brittany over. He looked at her in the same penetrating way and asked for her new address in Everett. "I'd like to see you again," he said quietly. "I'd like to stop by your house and see you. . . . Semper Fi."

When Cindy drowned, Brittany knew she had to come forward and tell authorities what she knew. Once Randy was safely in jail, she signed the statement she had given about her ex-lover's "burglary."

"I'm not afraid of him anymore," an adult Brittany said. "But I hate him. He had no right to do what he did to me, and it's going to take a long, long time for me to deal with it without hurting."

22

By the time Randy Roth's trial date fast approached in early 1992, Detective Randy Mullinax had interviewed seventy people; Detective Sue Peters had made 498 entries of phone calls, interviews, and actions taken in the case and produced results similar to the old Russian diminishing peasant puzzle, where each doll holds a smaller doll inside—a case within a case within a case within a case. Their investigation had gone from accidental death to possible foul play to similar "transactions" in the past to murder charges, and the two detectives had uncovered side issues of insurance fraud, robbery, child abuse, and all manner of con games. To muddy up their investigative waters, Randy Roth had proved to be a man who stepped from one phase of his life into the next as if moving through an invisible curtain. Each phase meant a new woman and often a new job, new friends, a new house. The only real constant in his life was his son Greg, whom he alternately pampered and disciplined with harshness that bordered on cruelty.

If anyone knew just who Randy Roth was, Sue Peters and Randy Mullinax did. And yet they wondered if it was possible for any human being to really know what forces drove him.

He *was* really Randolph G. Roth and nobody else; they had tracked him from his birth on December 26, 1954. He was a skilled mechanic. He had been married four times, divorced twice, widowed twice.

And he hated women. If he did not harm them physically, he left each woman who cared for him worse off in some way.

The question was, as it always was, *why?*

Gordon and Lizabeth Roth had come from Bismarck, North Dakota, to the Seattle area sometime in the late 1950's. Randy would have been five or six then. His brother David was born in Richardton, North Dakota, a crossroads with 600 citizens, three years later. No one could really say what the Roth siblings' childhoods had been like. Randy had told Ben and Marta Goodwin that he had been forced to kneel for hours on a hard floor. Were those memories *true?* Or were they simply part of the elaborate life story he had manufactured out of whole cloth? Randy's tales of childhood punishment would never be corroborated, but something had gone terribly wrong; both of Gordon and Lizabeth Roth's sons had been arrested for the murder of a woman. One had long since been convicted and the other was now awaiting trial.

The King County detective team could find little evidence of family solidarity among the Roths. Randy had shut the door against one sister and her babies on Christmas Eve. He had told so many lies about his mother that his friends really didn't know if she was dead or alive.

The Roths had apparently been staunch Catholics, but that hadn't prevented Gordon, a plumber, from leaving Lizabeth in 1971. Randy would have been about sixteen then. Gordon was ordered to pay his ex-wife $375 a month in child support. It wasn't enough; Lizabeth qualified for welfare. Randy, still in high school, worked at various jobs—in a feed store, at a gas station—to help support the family.

His one dream had surely been to escape, to become like his movie hero, Billy Jack. He feigned expertise in karate and carried a knife.

Randy joined the Marine Corps Reserves when he was a senior in high school.

Lizabeth Roth always blamed her ex-husband for quashing their children's ability to express their feelings. If they had grown up cold and lacking normal family bonds, it was not her fault—it was Gordon's.

It was hard to know what was true. When twenty-one-year-old David Roth was preparing for his trial in the strangulation-gunshot murder of the unknown female hitchhiker in Snohomish County in 1979, he had told a court-appointed psychiatrist that he counted on his mother, but that his father had beaten him.

"Whenever he wanted to do something to me or the other kids, my mom would stand up to him," David testified.

Then why had he strangled a girl he apparently didn't even know and shot her seven times for good measure?

Randy seemed to have bonded more with his father. His surviving wives and girlfriends recalled that the father and son even resembled each other physically—short, muscular, and powerful. Both were take-charge men.

At Meadowdale High School, Randy Roth moved somewhere in the middle stratum. He was an average student who hung out with guys who worked on their cars and raced down Old Highway 99. He wasn't a stoner; in fact, he was violently opposed to smoking, drinking, drugs, and anything else that would harm the body. Even in high school he was proud of his body and was pleased when the coach picked him out to demonstrate difficult gymnastics in P.E. class. He was short but muscular. He wasn't involved in extracurricular activities. He couldn't be—he was helping to support his mother and sisters. He wasn't a nerd either; he was really more of a nonentity, one of the mass of mostly forgettable students who move through three years of high school without leaving much of an impression on anyone. The impression he did leave was mostly negative. He was known as a troublemaker, the "bad dude," the unpredictable bully. His girlfriends knew better than to talk to or even look sideways at another boy, and his male friends were only those who toadied to him.

If he lied—and he often did—they pretended to believe every word. When he bragged that he had beaten up the infamous Ted Bundy "to protect my sister," they nodded eagerly.

Randy Roth's high school yearbook picture shows a young man whose face is almost overwhelmed by his thick thatch of dark hair, sideburns, a mustache, goatee and beard. He had the large, dark, slightly unfocused eyes of a myopic who wouldn't wear glasses.

In 1983 Randy attended his class's ten-year reunion. He bragged of his accomplishments in the intervening decade. He spoke of his dangerous duty in Vietnam, the secret missions carried out by the elite marine squad he belonged to, and he said he was presently involved in the operation of a huge cattle ranch. (Gordon Roth had a few horses and a few cows down in Washougal.) Randy told his former classmates he also taught martial arts classes—Tae Kwon Do, karate, and other obscure Eastern methods of self-defense. He could, he said quietly, kill a man with his bare hands and never leave a mark.

Yes, he had been in the marines—Peters and Mullinax had substantiated that—but he was only a file clerk. He spent most of his eleven months in the service at Camp Pendleton, and his mother had ended any chance he had to move up in the Marine Corps by summoning him home to take care of her two years before his enlistment was up. Would that have made Randy hate her? Perhaps.

Randy had girlfriends in high school; he usually had one steady girl for a year or more. They were all impressed with his strength—at least at first. His need to control females was evident even then. And even then Randy hated to see women cry. He hated any display of emotion.

Sue Peters eventually located all of the girls the teenage Randy had dated regularly. One was Dulcie Griffin,* who had known Randy since she was about thirteen. They had become "serious" when she was fifteen or sixteen. Dulcie recalled that Randy had an uncanny ability to use people even then. "I'm surprised that I'm alive," she commented cryptically.

"Why?" Peters asked.

Dulcie recalled a harrowing ride she had taken with Randy and one of his friends, Mike Conrad. Randy could only afford old beaters then, but he drove them as if he was racing in the Indianapolis 500. They were all laughing as Randy swerved around corners on some old road out in the country. One of the back doors flew open when he took a corner on two wheels. Dulcie started to clamber over into the backseat to shut the door and was halfway there when Randy took another corner at high speed.

"I flew out and just rolled over and over until I ended up against a curb."

She was bleeding and hurting, and she started to cry. Mike ran over to see if she was all right. Randy was right behind him—but he wasn't concerned; he looked furious. He was angry because Dulcie was sobbing, and he grabbed her roughly by the arm and hissed, "Don't you cry. Don't you dare cry! If you make any noise, I'll hit you!"

She knew he meant it, and she had managed to control her sniffling as Mike led her back to the car. "Randy didn't care at all if I was hurt," she recalled. "He just didn't want me to make a fuss."

At the time, Gordon Roth was dating Dulcie's mother, and both mother and daughter noticed how similar father and son were—hardheaded and "pushy."

Dulcie thought Randy was a little weird at times. One time as she and her mother drove up to their house Dulcie saw a man's feet disappearing through their kitchen window. It was Randy. When she confronted him about sneaking into their house, he just said he wanted to see if he could get in. All the doors had been locked.

Dulcie and Randy broke up over a silly fight. They had gone east of the Cascade Mountains to visit some of her family, and as a joke, she refused to answer him when he said something to her. He tried a few more times, and Dulcie, hiding a grin, pretended to ignore him.

She didn't know that she could have done nothing more devastating to her romance. Randy Roth, the macho man even then, could never allow a female to ignore him or make a fool of him. When Dulcie finally turned to Randy, he would not speak to her. Not then. Not for days. When he finally did, it was only to break up with her. "I don't want to go out with you anymore," he said coldly. "I'm too much like my father."

She didn't see him again until their high school reunion. At that time, he was long divorced from Donna Sanchez, and Dulcie heard him say to one of the guys, "I fired her. She wasn't working out."

For the last part of his senior year at Meadowdale, Randy worked for the Tire Mart service station in Lynnwood. His friend Jesse Akers was on duty one August night in 1973 when a short robber in a ski mask showed up with a knife. The masked robber threw Akers down, tied him up, and left him in the back room, before leaving with $240 in cash and some eight-track tapes.

Akers wasn't hurt, but he sure was puzzled. He had recognized Randy right away, and he figured it was some kind of a joke. He'd been about to say, "Hi Randy," when he sensed danger and he kept his mouth shut.

"I knew it was Randy," Akers said later. "He has the most recognizable sort of bowlegged walk I've ever seen."

Randy was not arrested. He went into the marines the next month.

Randy's next girlfriend was a girl who had helped his mother write the letter that got him out of the marines. He was disappointed with his military career; he had expected to be in battle somewhere, not pushing a pencil. He wasn't in long enough to make sergeant—despite the plaque he had made up. "Sergeant R. G. Roth" was as fictitious as "Billy Jack Roth."

Lynn Brotman* and Randy got engaged when he left the marines. Her parents had a vacant house they were selling, and they let Randy live there. Their romance went fine until Lynn found a purse in the house that belonged to someone named Donna Sanchez.

Lynn broke their engagement, and three months later someone broke into her parents' house. Television sets, tools, a stereo, and Lynn's stepfather's Purple Heart medal were missing. They suspected Randy right away, and police found the missing items—except for the Purple Heart—in a house where Randy Roth was living.

Randy confessed to the burglary, but he blamed it on Lynn's stepfather because he felt the older man was responsible for his broken engagement: "He was the only person I could think of who would have goods that I could use to sell, and I would not feel so bad about having taken them."

When Randy broke into her family's home, Lynn was mad enough to tell the police that it was he who had robbed the Tire Mart too. He had needed the money to pay for her abortion, she said.

Randy Roth, then twenty years old, pleaded guilty to second-degree burglary for the break-in. The old armed-robbery charge at the Tire Mart was dropped. Randy received a fourteen-year sentence, with all but two weeks suspended. Although he had bragged to Mullinax and Peters that he never served a day in jail, he had. He served those two weeks.

He got out of jail on June 10, 1975, and he married Donna Sanchez on July 4.

Randy's probation officer found him something of a wise-ass, but he wrote in his report that he thought the jail time had been unpleasant enough to let Roth see what could happen to someone who continued a life of crime.

It did. And it didn't. Randy Roth learned fast. The crimes he was suspected of in the future were much more subtle, more sophisticated. He apparently never stopped stealing from someone, somewhere. Sue Peters and Randy Mullinax kept checking back further and further with his former employers, and they found incident after incident where Roth had stolen equipment, gas, time, milk—whatever he could get away with.

But those were only stopgap thefts. Randy Roth—the poor boy who had been humiliated when his mother lived on welfare, when she pulled him out of the Marine Corps so he could come home and work at some other dead-end job to support her—had bigger plans.

He had learned that he could make more money with roses and sweet talk and promises he never intended to keep than he ever could with a knife and a mask. If he chose the right women, he could make them love him.

That realization gave him a sense of power greater than he had ever had in his life.

PART SEVEN

Trial

23

The road to Randy Roth's trial was not without detours. The original trial date was December 1, 1991, but the defense team asked for a delay, and it was granted. This was not at all unusual in such a high profile case.

One hundred fifty witness subpoenas were served. Just serving those documents would cost the King County Prosecutor's Office almost $2,400.

Pretrial motions began with the New Year. Defense attorneys George Cody and John Muenster argued in January 1992 that the state did not have sufficient evidence to support a first-degree murder charge against Randy Roth and asked Superior Court Judge Frank Sullivan to dismiss the charge because the only thing DPAs Marilyn Brenneman and Susan Storey could prove was that Cynthia Roth was dead and that her husband Randy had been nearby at the time—and that he stood to profit financially from her death.

"In the course of human experience," Cody argued, "many people drown." That didn't make them all homicide victims. Cody used the original autopsy findings that the drowning was probably accidental to bolster his arguments. It had been weeks before Dr. Reay had told the prosecutors that it was indeed possible to drown someone without leaving marks on the body.

Marilyn Brenneman countered with myriad other facts that Cody had not mentioned, albeit all circumstantial: Randy Roth was losing interest in his wife, he had denied knowledge of her safe-deposit box even though he had cleaned it out two days after Cindy died, and the state contended that the Sevylor raft could never have flipped over the way Randy had described.

"There is physical evidence as well," Brenneman said quietly. "It just doesn't happen to be on the body of Cynthia Roth."

Sullivan declined to dismiss the charges. The state had won the first battle of a very complicated war.

The search warrants then came under the defense's scrutiny. If Cody and Muenster could have them declared invalid, everything Sue Peters, Randy Mullinax, Frank Kinney, Bill Bonair, and Joe Lewis had found would be thrown out. The theft charges (from Bill Pierre) would be dropped. In the worst case, the pathetic poem Cynthia had left behind would be gone.

Judge Sullivan upheld the search warrants and all the evidence gathered.

The pretrial days were like walking through mine fields for both the defense and the prosecution. Naturally the prosecutors wanted to show the jury Randy Roth's whole life, all the patterns of behavior that he had traced and retraced. And just as naturally the defense attorneys would just as soon stick to the here and now.

The mines were exploding on George Cody and John Muenster. On Monday, January 27, Judge Sullivan ruled that the jurors would be allowed to know that the Pioneer Insurance Company believed that Randy had staged a burglary at his own house to collect insurance. Marilyn Brenneman stressed that alleged insurance fraud was vital to the state's case: "This is the most distinctive pattern of insurance fraud I have seen in my years at the prosecutor's office in the fraud division."

The few reporters who covered the pretrial hearing waited impatiently to hear *the* motion. Would Judge Sullivan allow Brenneman and Susan Storey to bring out the story of Janis Miranda Roth's fatal plunge from Beacon Rock in 1981? Randy had never been convicted—he had not even been arrested in that death. The two DPAs had done meticulous research and found precedent-setting cases in the Washington courts that could permit Sullivan to allow the mysterious death of Janis Roth into this proceeding. But would Sullivan agree with them?

He would. Judge Sullivan ruled that the fact that both Mrs. Roth number two and Mrs. Roth number four had been heavily insured when they died and that Randy Roth had either collected or tried to collect that insurance made the first death relevant to the case involving the second. Yes, he acknowledged that evidence relating to Janis Roth's death would be prejudicial to Roth, but its importance to the state's case outweighed the potential for damage.

John Muenster and George Cody took their argument about the rulings to the Washington State Court of Appeals. They argued that once the jurors heard about Janis Roth's death and the insurance fraud, any subsequent conviction could easily be thrown out on appeal. Because of what they considered Sullivan's "obvious and probable error," the defense attorneys alleged that the trial— scheduled to begin at the end of February—"will be a useless but extremely expensive exercise. . . . Mr. Roth wants his first trial to be a fair trial, not the second one."

On February 15, State Court of Appeals Commissioner Ellen Hudgins declined to send the defense's motion on for review by a three-member panel of appellate judges. George Cody argued that the state had no proof that Cynthia Roth had not simply drowned by accident. But Hudgins countered, "The problem I have with your argument is that no one could ever be prosecuted for a murder as long as he or she used a means that was more commonly an accident."

When a jury of Randy Roth's peers was selected, they would hear about his life, his insurance dealings, his wives, and how they lived— and died. It was a major, perhaps crippling, decision for the defense.

It would take a long, long trial to determine how crippling. As Marilyn Brenneman had said in her argument, Cynthia Roth had fallen into Randy Roth's trap "of wooing, wedding, and shedding his wives."

Could she and Susan Storey make that pattern come alive in a courtroom?

24

Jury selection began on February 24, 1992. Prospective jurors were warned that the trial would take at least five weeks and possibly as long as eight. An unusually large pool of jury candidates was provided. After more than a week, a jury was finally seated. Seven women and five men would decide whether Randy Roth was a killer or merely a very, very unlucky man. Was he a Bluebeard or simply a man who had, by the age of thirty-seven, suffered more personal tragedy than most people do in two lifetimes?

* * *

The crowds came when the trial officially began the first week in March, and there would never be a day when there was an extra spot available on one of the five long benches in Judge Frank Sullivan's courtroom. The first row was kept empty for use as a temporary perch from time to time for the attorneys' investigators; in dicey trials, where no one can be sure what the defendant may or not do, the front row also serves as a narrow safety zone.

The next two benches were reserved for family. The Louckses were there, and the Baumgartners, parents, aunts, cousins, friends. They filled the hard oak benches, gaining strength from one another.

The media clung tenaciously to the fourth bench, occasionally overflowing onto the fifth. All the newspaper and television reporters, the book writers—save one reporter who sat alone and aloof—saved seats for one another by spreading out yellow legal pads, raincoats, and briefcases. On the press bench there was always room for one more, even though it meant writing with an elbow in the solar plexus.

All together, there were only forty-eight legitimate seats. By crunching people together, sixty seats could be created. Bailiff Lori Merrick explained to spectators in the back row that those spots were reserved for the media too. They were welcome to sit there, but would have to defer to the press: "If they ask nicely, you're going to have to give up your seat."

"What if they don't ask nicely?" countered one stubborn court watcher.

"Then you can slap them," Merrick quipped. "But you'll still have to give up your seat."

Single cameramen took turns manning the television camera on the left side of the courtroom; the film would go into a pool for all the networks and independent stations. It seemed that everybody in western Washington had heard the name Randy Roth. And everyone who read a paper or watched television was curious about him.

Randy Roth sat, shoulders hunched, at the defense table. In his news conference the previous summer, he had come across as a handsome young man, strong and thickly muscled in the chest and shoulders. Now, as the defendant in a murder trial, Randy looked entirely changed, as if he suffered from some fatal wasting disease. It was more than the prison pallor that colors all men locked away in jail for months. Randy had metamorphosed into a thin, fragile-looking man with thick glasses whose balding pate shone through his graying hair.

His suit fit him tightly, creasing across his narrow back. It seemed to those who had seen him before that it was a new suit, purchased perhaps to convince a jury that Randy had *always* been a weak little man, a man incapable of holding a healthy young woman underwater until she drowned, not strong enough to push a young woman off a mountain trail.

Any good defense lawyer thinks long and hard about how he will present his client. Ladies of the night show up in court in prim dresses buttoned to the neck, motorcycle gang members appear clean-shaven in three-piece suits that cover their earthy tattoos, and chronic imbibers of alcohol take the witness stand as sober as the pope. This is fair, and it is understood in the legal profession. Put the defendant's best foot forward.

Or, in this trial, make the defendant look as close to Casper Milquetoast as possible. How Randy must have hated wearing his glasses and letting his biceps become flaccid. He, who had aimed to become a latter-day Billy Jack, a martial arts instructor and a marine hero, looked like a mild little middle-aged clerk.

Harmless.

Susan Storey rose to give the state's opening statement. Skillfully, she wove in the myriad facets of Randy Roth's life—his romances, his marriages, his widowhood, his fascination with insurance. "He married for greed," Storey said flatly. "Not for love or companionship. And he murdered for money. It wasn't hate, it wasn't fear—or even passion."

The prosecution team had discerned the distinct blueprint in Randy Roth's behavior. He had been much like the producer of a play, and he presented it over and over—changing only the cast. Susan Storey told the jurors of the "short and intense—whirlwind" courtships, where honeymoons were followed by the purchase of large insurance policies. She described Roth's demeanor after the death of two wives as "cold and unemotional . . . and on both occasions he made different and contradictory statements about what had occurred."

It was important to present the design, the repetition, the identical—or nearly identical—game plan that Randy Roth had used over and over and over again. If Storey—or George Cody, for that matter—took only one of the marriages or one of the insurance transactions and presented it as an entity in itself, it might very well have been explainable in perfectly innocent terms. But, taken all together, the configuration of Randy Roth's behavior never changed.

Pointing to a chart propped up in the witness chair, Susan Storey gave specific examples of the defendant's consuming avarice and how he had gone about filling his pockets and his bank account. Storey's pointer tapped the chart: (1) the phony theft of Janis Roth's car; (2) Janis Miranda Roth's "accidental" fall and the $115,000 payoff; (3) Randy's fraudulent application for Jalina Miranda's Social Security benefits; (4) the phony burglary of Nick Emondi's home; (5) Randy's marriage to Donna Clift and the rafting "accident"; (6) Randy's whirlwind courtship of Mary Jo Phillips, which ended when he learned Mary Jo was uninsurable; (7) the phony burglary of Randy's home; (8) Randy's whirlwind courtship of Cynthia Baumgartner, the huge insurance policies, and Cynthia's death by drowning; and (9) Randy's fraudulent application for Greg's (second) Social Security benefits.

"This man stole to feed his hunger for money nine different times," Storey said.

Susan Storey explained to the jurors that Randy Roth's onetime best friend, Nick Emondi, had finally told detectives that his burglary had never been a burglary at all—at least not in the true sense of the term. When Nick had been unable to repay his loan, Randy had suggested that Nick set fire to his home. He could then collect insurance and pay Randy back. Emondi, employed by the local fire department, did not think that was such a good idea. Next, Susan Storey told the jury, Randy came up with another plan. He would be glad to take some of the Emondis' property away—say, a television set, the stereo, and other items that could easily be liquidated. Then Nick could report a burglary to his insurance agent. Randy would keep what he had taken away *and* share in the insurance payoff.

And that was exactly what had happened. While Carrie Emondi was working the graveyard shift on her job one night, Randy came to their mobile home and removed their television, their AM-FM cassette recorder, and other things he wanted. He also partook of the insurance proceeds.

Nick Emondi's debt was marked paid.

By the time Randy met Donna Clift a few months later, he had to have been a man who believed smugly in the denseness of insurance companies. Storey told the jury they would hear from Donna Clift; she was one of two wives who had survived. Donna Clift remembered that Randy had wanted her to sign up for heavy-duty insurance policies, but she never had.

Donna knew that "Randy knew how to operate a raft," Storey

pointed out to the jury. "But on this day, he was intentionally trying to sink it."

And why would Randy have tried to drown his new bride—the one with no life insurance? Well, Storey explained, Donna Clift *did* have life insurance. She just didn't know about it. Randy had managed to insure Donna for more than $20,000, and she had been completely unaware of it—until Storey herself informed her about it.

At the defense table, Randy Roth continued to stare down at his yellow tablet. For all the reaction he showed, Susan Storey might well have been talking about someone else entirely. Even as secrets that he must have thought were long since hidden emerged, he remained stolid and calm.

He always had.

As Susan Storey talked, a huge blow-up of Beacon Rock sat on an easel behind her, and she ticked off the cold facts of Roth's increasing fortunes. It was essential for Storey and Marilyn Brenneman to *show* the jury what had happened in the defendant's life over the past dozen years. They could not take the jurors by the hand and walk them up the steep trail to the top of Beacon Rock or float them all out in a raft on Lake Sammamish, but they could, with the judicious use of audiovisual aids, re-create much of the horror.

Susan Storey replaced the bleak rock with a picture of the raft that Cynthia Roth had clung to in the last moments of her life.

There was no mystery about why Randy had deliberately drowned Cynthia Roth, Storey said. The motive was quite plain—$385,000 in insurance.

"Help was only a shout or a wave away," she said of the moments after Cynthia became unconscious in Lake Sammamish. But Randy calmly and quietly rowed to shore.

"Sixty or seventy yards from shore, no wave. . . .

"Twenty-five yards from shore. Still, he didn't yell or wave for help. . . .

"Fifty or sixty feet, he was in no particular hurry . . . He did not yell or wave for help. . . ."

And when Randy finally reached the lakeshore, he stayed quietly inside the raft, Susan Storey told the jury. He didn't appear alarmed. He didn't make a move to get help for his drowned wife until the boys ran over and saw that their mother's flesh was blue and mottled.

This man—at whom the jury now stole quick peeks—seemed so "completely uninterested" in whether his wife would survive or die that people on the shore thought he was a stranger to Cynthia.

"He made vastly different statements. . . . She'd been swimming while he was rowing. . . . They were both swimming. . . . Cynthia was under the water for ten minutes . . . she was facedown for thirty-five to forty seconds. . . .

"The boat was very close. . . . The boat was fifty to one hundred yards away. . . . The boat was east of the raft. . . . The boat was west of the raft. . . . He didn't attempt CPR. . . . He *did* try two breaths. . . . He gave her fifteen to twenty minutes of CPR."

The elements of the case that Susan Storey revealed were shocking. She described the new widower as a man so unmoved by his wife's death that he rented three comedy videos on the way home from the hospital.

If Storey's litany of years of sociopathic behavior was true, Randy Roth was a monster.

For the Roth jury, the details of Randolph G. Roth's convoluted life must have been dizzying. The gallery remained transfixed, their startled reaction heightened when someone's beeper sounded, seeming as loud as an alarm bell.

"Turn it off," Judge Sullivan growled.

Susan Storey continued without missing a beat. The defendant, was, she said, a man who at 7:30 or 7:35 P.M. on July 23, 1991, left the quiet room in the hospital where his wife had just been declared dead, where a grief counselor noted that he had shown "not the slightest evidence of distress or grief or emotion of any kind," and stopped to have dinner with the victims' sons, then picked up the videotapes. Once home, Randy Roth had placed a phone call. "He did not call relatives," Storey said. "He didn't call friends, or people from church. He called this guy to see if his red Corvette was still for sale."

Two days after Cynthia drowned, Randy Roth had told Stacey Reese that he was wondering if maybe Cynthia hadn't *wanted* to die. His biggest problem seemed to be that it would take him "fucking forever to get the mauve colors out of his house."

Randy Roth had wasted no time, Storey continued, in applying for Greg's Social Security benefits, "lying twice." He claimed that Greg was Cynthia's only child, and he did not mention that Greg was already receiving Janis's benefits.

Three weeks after Cynthia drowned, Randy rejoined Parents Without Partners, filed to collect his $385,000 in insurance proceeds, and began to sell off his assets—"everything of value—his car, his four-by-four, his John Deere front loader, two new four-wheelers. He put his house up for sale."

And why, Storey asked, did he do this? Because he had told his co-workers that he was preparing to be arrested.

She had given the jury only a summary of what they would hear in this trial. "Now you understand the number of witnesses," Susan Storey finished. There had been so many frauds, frauds pointing to Randy Roth's greed and, ultimately, explaining why Cynthia Baumgartner Roth had to die to appease that greed.

Defense attorney George Cody told the jurors about an entirely different man, a man whose traits seemed to fit the quiet, somber man who scribbled notes on a yellow legal pad in front of him. Randy rarely looked up even as his own attorney spoke.

Cody saw his client as a prudent, careful man, a caring father who wanted to be sure that his children were provided for if either he or his wife should die. Randy Roth was, Cody said, a man who had suffered a "terrible accident," the kind that could happen to anyone. (*Two* terrible accidents in point of fact, although Cody did not choose to touch on that.) The case against Randy Roth was purely circumstantial, Cody said. He disputed Storey's argument that Randy had not tried to save Cynthia from drowning when he pulled her out of the water. Indeed, his attorney said Randy had tried desperately to breathe air into her lungs from his own—but he could not do it because her gag reflex had been too strong.

George Cody outlined for the jury a luckless shadow of a man who had lost almost everything he ever loved, who, but for the grace of God, might have changed places with any man and woman in the hushed courtroom.

If Cody was right, a terrible miscarriage of justice loomed. There was nothing predictable about this trial. It *was* in large part made up of a voluminous amount of circumstantial evidence. However, that didn't mean that the prosecution could not get a conviction.

Nor did it mean that Marilyn Brenneman and Susan Storey *would* get a conviction. A fingerprint in blood is the best physical evidence in the world. A drowning in the middle of a huge lake is one of the most difficult deaths to define absolutely.

The battle lines were drawn. The windowless courtroom was hot, almost as hot as the beach had been seven and a half months earlier. Nobody moved.

Outside in the hallway, television and radio field reporters watched the trial action on small monitors they had propped up on the long oak benches. Witnesses waited there too, forbidden to enter Sullivan's courtroom before they testified. Electrical cables snaked across the worn marble floor. There were deadlines to meet—for the five o'clock news, and, if not then, for the eleven o'clock news.

Nothing was a sure thing. Nothing except that this was the biggest, most sensational trial to hit King County in a decade.

25

If there was a single trait that marked Randolph G. Roth's whole existence, it had always been secrecy. No one, *ever*, had been allowed to look into all the segments of his life. He was the man who loved to prowl in dark clothing in the stillness late at night, the man who hinted at unspeakable acts he had been called on the perform in an unfathomable war half a world away, a man who hid his own family origins, and chose women he could hold under his thumb the way he'd held the hapless frog under his sander. Randy Roth had never looked back. In his view, the dead were gone—simply gone and no longer of consequence. Yesterday did not matter. Now *he* was forced to look at the panorama that was his life, to see those whose lives he had touched—and often corroded—and it was all in a public forum.

Worse, it was literally live and on tape.

Bill Wiley, leader of the search team in Skamania County, testified about the desperate search for Janis Roth ten years earlier. Her body had been found 50 to 100 feet beyond where they expected to find her. "While anything is possible . . . it is at the far extreme and beyond anything in my experience," Wiley said, demonstrating on the giant photo of Beacon Rock where Randy said she had gone off and the spot where she had landed. She would almost have had to fall sideways to make Randy's version believable.

Sheriff Ray Blaisdell, who had been the Skamania County under-sheriff in 1981, rescuers, and hikers on the Beacon Rock trail all testified. It had taken gargantuan efforts to locate the cast of characters who swarmed over Beacon Rock on that cold day in November so long ago. Most of them remembered Randy Roth as a man who seemed unnaturally calm in the face of tragedy, although

Blaisdell said he had seen Randy cry twice after word came from the ground below that Janis Roth was dead. "At the time, he didn't say anything," Blaisdell said, but "he did show some emotion, and I did see some tears."

Marcie Thompson, a grown woman now, remembered that she had learned of Jan's death a few hours later in a pizza parlor when Randy slid the cremation receipt across the table to her as casually as if it were a menu. (Marcie had also told detectives that Randy subsequently tried to seduce her when she visited his Seattle home.) "I knew her as Jan," Marcie said, "so 'Janis' didn't ring a bell. I said, 'I don't know this person,' and he said, 'Yes, you do. Think about it.'"

Jalina Miranda, who had matured into a beautiful young woman, looked at the man who had once been her stepfather as she remembered finding the envelope her mother had told her about. "'If anything happens to me, I want you to come get this.' He took it right out of my hands," Jalina said. "He promised to use the money to buy me toys and presents."

"Did he?" Marilyn Brenneman asked.

"No. I never talked to him again."

Jalina said that her mother had been dead almost a week before she knew it. "I kept saying, 'Where's my mommy?'"

On cross-examination, John Muenster elicited from Jalina that Randy had been kind to her. It was true that her stepfather had always avoided giving her a direct answer, but he had taken her on his knee and explained about the terrible fall and about her mother being in the hospital. He had rocked her and held her tenderly while she cried.

And then Randy had answered the phone one day, and turned to her, saying, "Jalina, that was the hospital. Your mother just died."

Billie Jean Ray, Janis's mother, also admitted under defense questioning that Roth had seemed grief-stricken at her daughter's memorial service.

It was an uphill battle for the defense, however. For every witness who recalled observing some small crack in Randy Roth's austere facade, there were ten—or twenty—who described a man with the emotional makeup of a robot.

Darrel Lundquist told the jury that he had been awakened by his insurance client, Randy Roth, the day after Janis fell to her death. Randy had been anxious to collect on his policy. Shirley Lenz related how Randy had needed Janis's Social Security number that same morning because "Janis was sick."

Lily Vandiveer's ex-husband testified that Randy had had an affair with Lily after and during Randy's marriage to Janis, and that he found Randy and Lily in an intimate embrace on the floor in front of the fireplace in his own home. "I told him if he didn't stay away from my house, I was going to the prosecuting attorney."

But Vandiveer admitted he had never told the Skamania County authorities. "I was afraid of him," he said.

And so was Nick Emondi. But Nick was between a rock and a hard place. He had felt sorry for sad little Janis Roth. He suspected that Randy was seeing another woman. He had heard the Halloween conversation about "Could you kill your wife?" And then he had learned that "Janis is no longer with us."

Now Nick admitted on the witness stand that he had staged a burglary in his own home so that he could repay Randy money he had owed him. He had helped take his property to Randy's house and Randy had helped him fill out the insurance forms. They divided the $2,800 settlement, and Randy kept most of the "stolen" items. Nevertheless, the Emondis had eventually been forced to declare bankruptcy when Randy backed out of his promise to buy their home.

Nick had heard Randy describe how he would burglarize his own home—*before* the fact. He had been Randy's confidant; he had heard about all the women who didn't work out because they were "immature" and about Mary Jo's sudden fall from grace when Randy found out she'd had cancer.

Yes, he and Randy had been close friends. But Nick admitted he was afraid of Randy Roth, that he always had been.

George Cody questioned Nick Emondi persistently about the Halloween night conversation. Were not, he suggested, the two men discussing the Bible at the time? Weren't they talking about the Book of Revelation, the biblical end of the world?

That argument never went anywhere; the prosecutors objected to Cody's questions about the Bible.

Randy Roth, his panoply of invincibility shattered, was handcuffed and marched to and from court several times a day, tall court officers on either side of him. His expression never changed. His dark eyes glittered behind thick glasses, but he seemed to see no one. He could well have been shocked to find himself in the midst of a reunion that he would never have chosen to attend.

The women continued to appear, women Randy had long since dismissed from his life.

Brittany Goodwin, who had idolized him when she was a teenager, been seduced and betrayed, and who now recounted Randy's precise plan to rob his own home.

He didn't look up.

Mary Jo Phillips told of her magical courtship, of how Randy "became the man every woman dreams about." All his tender concern had shattered and fallen away when he learned that she was uninsurable.

Randy didn't look up.

Donna Clift recalled Randy's headlong pursuit of her, the lavish gifts he had given her, her perfect wedding . . . and then her bewilderment, which had turned to terror on the Skykomish River. Clift was clearly still angry at being so betrayed, and she testified not to the jury but directly to Randy Roth. She willed him with hard eyes to face her.

He didn't look up.

When Judy Clift testified that she had been afraid that her daughter would never come off the Skykomish River alive, defense attorney John Muenster asked Judge Sullivan to declare a mistrial. "Mr. Roth is on trial for something that happened in 1991," Muenster argued. "Yet he has been run through the wringer for things that allegedly happened as long as ten years ago. None of these people saw fit to report any of it until now."

Judge Sullivan refused the request, and the trial continued, gaining momentum with each day.

The Goodwins—the family that Randy had adopted as his own—testified for the prosecution. Ben and Marta and Ryan. Of all the people who had passed through Randy's life, they had perhaps cared for him the most. But they could not condone what they believed was a staged burglary—for profit. They all recalled the tools, the televisions, stereos, the Nintendos that were gone—and then were suddenly back again.

Marta had heard no sounds during that night in September 1988. Ben Goodwin knew the "tire marks" in Randy's backyard were actually the depression left by the great weight of a felled tree. Ben looked at the jury and repeated Randy's flat words, "He said, 'That's where the detective said the tires were, so that's where the tires were.'"

The burglary of 1988 had certainly come back to haunt Randy. One wondered if he berated himself now. He had asked for over $58,000, received $28,500 after a two-year legal fight, and had to give away all but $17,000 of that. Obviously the continuing testimony from so many sources about Roth's duplicity in the allegedly faked burglary was hurting him. Ben Goodwin identified several items that he recognized as having belonged to Randy both before and after the burglary.

Pioneer Insurance claims adjuster Shelly Bierman had become suspicious all on her own when she discovered that Roth had included a return slip from Sears for a Kenwood stereo radio that he claimed was stolen. Once that claim was questioned, all manner of inaccuracies had begun to emerge.

It was more than a week into trial, and still no witnesses had spoken of Cynthia Baumgartner Roth. Even so, there was the sensation of her presence there. Two rows were packed full of her family, their faces marked by grief and a kind of bleak acceptance of what they could not change. They were not vengeful people. Merle Loucks had said he did not support the death penalty—not even for the man he was convinced had deliberately drowned his beloved daughter.

And then suddenly there was another family there. Randy Roth's family—his mother, Lizabeth, and two of his sisters. The press bench murmured with speculation about who these rather bizarre-appearing women were. Indeed, they seemed at first to be strangers, more of the impatient would-be courtroom spectators who were angry at not finding a seat. There were many of those, held back by the court officers because there was not a single inch of extra space. One more body inside and the fire ordinances would be broken.

No, these women declared loudly. They were members of the defendant's family and had the right to be present. Lizabeth Roth was not what anyone had expected, at least not from her son's descriptions of her. Randy was now thirty-eight, and his mother looked no more than ten years older. Her hair was dyed a dark metallic auburn, teased and back-combed until it had become a huge helmet around her head, sprayed until it appeared brittle enough to break off if someone touched it. Her eyelids were heavily smudged with shadow and lined with kohl, her makeup resembled a thick mask, and her clothing fit her lush figure snugly. She wore a miniskirt and high-heeled pumps. A scent of heavy cologne moved with her. This was no aged mother who had been confined to a nursing home; this was Randy Roth's *real* mother.

The antipathy between mother and son was palpable. He scarcely acknowledged her presence. As Randy was led from the courtroom during a morning break, his eyes swept over his mother, who sat at the end of the second row. It was impossible to read his expression.

Randy's sisters were dark-haired too, slender and pretty. Like their mother, they had lined their eyes and teased their hair. They resembled a family of Gypsy women, exotic and flamboyant. They were outraged when they arrived so late that all the seats in the courtroom were taken. To the observer, it seemed that the Roth women had deliberately delayed their entrance so that they could cause a commotion and demand justice—at least in the seating arrangements—for their family. The victim's family slid over and made room for Mrs. Roth, and she settled down with much sighing and shifting. One of Randy's sisters sat on the arm at the end of the press row and pushed with her backside until she forcibly won a seat next to a startled reporter.

Through it all, their son and brother kept his back to them; it was as if he didn't know them at all, and certainly would not accept them as a cheering section come to show their support.

In the women's rest room where all factions of all trials meet on neutral ground, Randy Roth's sisters combed their hair and freshened their makeup beside reporters and cousins of the dead Cynthia. Randy's sisters spoke of their plans for Easter dresses.

When the Louckses and the Baumgartners had left to go back into the trial, Lisa Roth turned to a reporter and confided, "Everybody feels so sorry for *them*, but, you know, their troubles are over. Cindy's dead. It's Randy who has to suffer for the rest of his life."

The courtroom was stifling hot, and it would remain so. The King County financial office would brook no hanky-panky with its budget. The rules said that air-conditioning would not be turned on in courtrooms before April 15. It did not matter that the winter of 1991–92 had been almost balmy and that Judge Frank Sullivan's courtroom felt like August although it was March. Not only was air-conditioning officially forbidden for weeks, but the maintenance staff was cranking up the heat each morning to "take the chill off." The prize seat in the courtroom was just outside the jurors' room—the last seat in the last row. That room did have air-conditioning, and occasionally a corrections officer would prop the door open a few inches so that breathable air filtered out into the courtroom.

It was miserable, but no one left. The story of the last year of

Cynthia Baumgartner Roth's life was about to be told. Her sweet blond visage smiled back from a photograph mounted on the easel at the front of the courtroom.

She had posed next to a bush of Randy's prize red roses.

26

Until now the jury had heard testimony that certainly suggested that Randy Roth was not a very nice man, that he was neither honest nor sincerely caring about anyone. According to the state's witnesses, he had lied and cheated. And perhaps he had deliberately killed his second wife. But he had never been charged in the death of Janis Miranda Roth. A prudent juror might very well think, "If they had enough evidence to show that he was guilty, if he really did it, why didn't they charge him with murder?"

He *had* been charged with the murder of Cynthia Baumgartner Roth, and the observers in the gallery tensed as they realized the testimony would henceforth deal with Randy Roth's relationship with his fourth wife, and with her inexplicable death.

It was now the third week of March 1992, and one after another prosecution witnesses related that something was desperately wrong with Cynthia and Randy's marriage. One of Cynthia's best friends, Mary Barns, told the jury that she and Cynthia had gone to Idylwood Park on July 9; they had sat on the same beach where paramedics had worked over Cindy's body two weeks later. Cindy had confided to Mary that her marriage to Randy was deteriorating. Cindy had been concerned that Randy changed jobs so frequently; the stability she thought she had seen didn't exist. Mary added, "She said to me, more than once, 'We won't get a divorce.' It sounded like something she was trying to convince herself of because she was having doubts."

Sandra Thompson, who did Cindy's hair, said that things were not good in Cindy's marriage: "She did not want her husband to know what she was spending on her hair."

It had been the same with her nails. Randy had made Cindy explain every penny she spent.

Randy's co-workers at Bill Pierre Ford had never had a real understanding of his relationship with Cindy. It wasn't that Randy had been the only worker who complained about a spouse; it was that his remarks about Cindy had been exceptionally vicious. In truth, he never really acknowledged that he had married her. He called their relationship a "contract."

One witness recalled hearing Randy say, "Our contract's up in August, and then the bitch is gone."

Under Cody's vigorous cross-examination, the witness admitted that she did not care for Randy Roth, but she would not take back what she had heard.

Randy had complained vociferously about Cynthia at work— about everything from her cookies, "which wouldn't even soften if you dipped them in milk," to her temperament. He had gone out of his way to portray himself as a man who was trapped in a miserable relationship.

On March 18, Stacey Reese, who had quite possibly been Randy's first choice for the fifth Mrs. Roth, was a devastating witness to the defense. She too had heard about Randy's "contract" with Cynthia. She told the court, "He said it was a contract. He said they would see how it went for a year and that it would be up on August 1. And one of them would have to go."

One of them had, of course, gone.

On July 22, the day before the drowning, Randy had taken Stacey to a Lake City drive-in restaurant for lunch and told her of his doubts about his "contract." He said he was unhappy and that his and Cindy's "relationship" was almost up. He was packing his stuff, and it was "time to go."

Stacey testified to the four phone calls she had received from Randy in the four days after Cynthia drowned. She said she had become increasingly alarmed by his demeanor. The drowning had been "horrible," he said, but in a way a "relief." While Stacey listened, dumbfounded by Randy's attitude, he went on to comment about how he had always hated Cindy's pink and mauve color scheme. "He wanted to get it the fuck out of the house," Stacey said. She had been uncomfortable with his invitation in an earlier call to have breakfast with him, but she told the jurors she was profoundly shocked when he invited her to accompany him to Reno. It was clear that Stacey would have been a substitute for his dead wife—the wife who had purchased the tickets to Reno with such hope. Randy had said he didn't want the tickets to go to waste.

Mark Dalton, a vehicle maintenance instructor for Metro Transit (Seattle's bus system), took the stand to say that Randy Roth had been hired along with six other bus-fleet mechanics about a month before his wife had drowned. The first day of orientation for that job was June 17. Randy showed up, but he did not appear the next day or any day thereafter.

He had left a message on a Metro employee's voice mail system. "He said his wife had been in an accident in Idaho and he wouldn't be in," Dalton recalled. "He said it looked like she was in critical condition and might not make it."

In late June, Cynthia had not been in an accident in Idaho or anywhere else. Roth had chosen not to continue with Metro for his own reasons.

Carolyn Davidson, supervisor for Metro's vehicle-maintenance division, testified she had sent Randy Roth a registered letter on July 8, explaining that Metro could not hold his job open indefinitely. Tactfully, Ms. Davidson offered her sympathy about his wife's accident—she had no way of knowing if the woman was alive or dead—but she informed Roth that he would be fired if he didn't report for work by July 23.

Randy signed for the registered letter, but he did not go back to Metro. And of course by July 23, Randy Roth *was* a widower.

No one on the prosecution team could fathom why he had lied to Metro. Privately, Marilyn Brenneman and Susan Storey wondered if Randy had already been playing with the idea of Cindy's death weeks before she drowned.

The Sevylor raft that Randy had given up to the police so grudgingly on the night of July 23, 1991, was brought into the courtroom, inflated, and propped up against the far wall as dozens of witnesses who had been at Lake Sammamish on that date testified to memories that would never fade.

Kristina Baker, the woman who had seen the raft head out into the middle of the lake and watched its progress sporadically while keeping an eye on her children, described the tableau. She had seen two people jump into the water, and, minutes later, she had seen one of them swim away from the raft while the other trailed behind. A moment later she saw arms waving and splashes in the lake before the pair disappeared behind the raft, out of her view. She had seen a powerboat towing a water-skier slow down or stop near the raft, and she thought one of the swimmers had waved. She had turned away briefly to check on her children, and when she looked back she saw the one person dragging the other onto the raft. "It was a struggle to get the person back on the raft," she said. "You could see it wasn't an easy job."

Baker had idly watched the raft come slowly toward shore. It had taken twenty minutes. Baker saw only one figure now, but she didn't sense any danger. As it drew closer, she could see it was a man who was rowing so slowly.

Alicia Tracy had been at Idylwood Park that afternoon, and she had run to help Mike McFadden, the lifeguard. She had seen that the woman in the bottom of the raft had a blue cast to her skin and she had turned away. She saw the man she came to know as Randy Roth standing back from the raft, but she didn't connect him to the drowning. "At that point," she said, "he was just another man pulling his boat out of the water."

Needing to do *something* while the lifeguards worked frantically over the woman, Alicia had offered to help the man deflate his raft. She didn't realize who he was until a police officer had asked if anyone knew who the drowned woman was. At that point, he spoke up. "He said, 'Well, I know her. She's my wife,'" Tracy told the jury.

The officer had then asked Randy to stop deflating his raft. "He told him, 'I don't think we should be doing that—we might need it for evidence,'" Alicia said.

Randy Roth had ignored the policeman and gone right on folding up his raft.

With each witness who took the stand, the scene at the lake was painted in more grotesque strokes. The widower had made no effort at all to hurry to save his wife. He had been far more concerned about "making a scene" than he had been about Cynthia's survival. Again and again Randy Roth was described as "void of emotion," "so calm," "so normal," "had no expression."

An eleven-year-old girl had watched Tyson and Rylie Baumgartner run up to the raft where their mother lay motionless in the bottom. She said, "I saw the two boys run over to the raft and ask, 'What's happened to Mom?'"

And she testified that the man had said simply, "Go get a lifeguard, but don't make a scene."

If the testimony was shocking to strangers and press in the gallery, it was unbearable for Cynthia's family. Marge Baumgartner, Tom's mother, left the courtroom in tears when the girl on the stand described how Patti Schultz had knelt down and hugged Marge's grandsons to comfort them, and how their "father" had simply walked away from them.

"They had to hurry [to catch up]," the witness added.

Randy Roth had behaved like an insensitive automaton according to witnesses. Indeed, his behavior had been *so* cold that it might serve as an argument for the defense. If a man had deliberately planned to drown his wife, would he not have at least *pretended* to be grief-stricken? If he was truly in shock over the tragedy, might he not have acted exactly as he did—woodenly, as if he were slogging through quicksand, unable to cope with the fact that his beloved wife was gone? So stunned that he was unaware that the children needed comfort?

Or was Randy Roth a man so devoid of normal human empathy that he did not even know how to mimic it?

With each succeeding witness, the latter seemed to be more likely.

Roth had given his attorneys a great obstacle to overcome. Considered among the very top criminal defense attorneys in Seattle, George Cody and John Muenster did their best. They argued that only a fool would have chosen to commit a murder on a crowded lake on the hottest day of the summer. Of *course* he had proceeded toward shore slowly, they maintained, to avoid attracting a crowd that might interfere with rescue efforts.

Randy's own family appeared to be thorns in his side. His glance swept over them almost contemptuously as he left the courtroom in handcuffs several times a day. One afternoon he moved into the corridor to see that his mother was giving a television interview. "Keep your damn mouth shut," he muttered out of the side of his mouth. "Don't talk to them."

She ignored him. In the glow of television lights, Lizabeth Roth criticized what passed for justice in King County, Washington. She made all three network channels that night.

Redmond detective Larry Conrad was the eighty-eighth witness for the prosecution. At last, here was a witness who recalled that Randy Roth had shown emotion on the day his wife drowned—but under rather odd circumstances. Conrad said he had just told Randy he needed to confiscate his raft. "He became somewhat agitated and angry," Conrad added. "He said he felt I had no right to take it. It was the first emotion he displayed."

John Muenster objected. Conrad had not mentioned Randy's agitation in his notes or in his reports, had he?

He had not, Conrad agreed.

Although Randy Roth was the center of everything that went on in the lengthy trial, the subject of each witness's appraisal, he showed no reaction and he said nothing. Would he? Would his attorneys put the defendant on the witness stand? That is always a risky ploy because it opens up the defendant to the prosecuting team's questions. Certainly everyone in the courtroom wanted to hear Roth speak, wanted to know how his mind worked and if there was some explanation for his unemotional response to Cynthia's death.

Sue Peters and Randy Mullinax devoutly hoped Randy would get up on the stand. *They* knew that he was a most verbose man, and they wanted the jurors to know him as they did.

The defense team gave no hint as to whether Roth would testify.

D'Vorah Kost, the grief counselor at Overlake Hospital, explained to the jury that she had asked Tyson and Rylie Baumgartner if there was anyone who might help them feel better. They said they wanted to be with their uncle, Leon Loucks. But at that point Loucks had no idea that his sister was dead; Randy had not even called him.

Leon Loucks testified about the way he learned that his only sister had drowned. On the evening of July 23, another relative had called him to say that a woman with the same name as Cynthia had drowned; she had just seen it on television. At first, Leon hoped that it wasn't true. It *couldn't* be true, he thought, or he would have been notified. "We questioned the fact that no one contacted us."

Cynthia's brother called Overlake Hospital and was told only that a message would be passed to Randy Roth to call Leon as soon as possible. Dreading what he might hear, Leon Loucks waited by the phone.

No one called.

At 11:30 P.M., Loucks finally reached his sister's home in Woodinville. A very calm Randy told him that it was true; Cynthia was dead. "Why didn't you call me or someone in the family?" Leon asked.

Randy said, "I wanted to do it in person, not by telephone."

But then, Randy Roth had never liked to be the bearer of bad news. He didn't like to talk about death or think about death. Word always filtered down sooner or later.

27

Randy Roth had long claimed expertise in a number of areas, bluffing that he was a karate and Tae Kwon Do champion, that he had been trained by the marines to silently stalk and destroy. There was some areas where he *was* proficient, but he did not brag about them—especially not in the months after Cynthia drowned.

Randy was a very good swimmer. In August of 1984, he had taken a scuba diving course from Donald Johnson, a certified scuba diver and instructor. The diving course met the standards of the Professional Association of Diving Instructors (PADI) standards and followed its procedures. Before a student is even admitted to a PADI course, he or she has to demonstrate proficiency in the water by swimming 200 yards using several strokes; swimming 40 feet underwater; treading water for five minutes, four minutes with hands and feet, the next thirty seconds with feet only, and the last thirty seconds giving a distress signal with the hands. The would-be student must also be able to sustain a survival float for five minutes.

Ill at the time of trial, Johnson's recall was admitted by affidavit. Randy's scuba instructor had stressed again and again the importance of using the buddy system, "meaning you stick to your buddy like glue," and the use of hand signals in times of trouble. "Waving the arm and hand overhead is a distress signal," he said.

But not one witness had seen Randy Roth wave or signal for help while his wife was drowning.

Beyond being a strong swimmer, Randy had also taken an eight-hour CPR course in 1990. Myron Redenn, a Snohomish County Red Cross official, outlined in court what Roth had learned in that course: "I emphasize that they should start giving emergency care *immediately*. It could mean the difference between life and death."

All students in the Red Cross course had been taught that the brain begins to die if a person stops breathing for four to six minutes.

Apparently Randy Roth had committed that part of the instructions to memory; he had repeated it to Seattle Fire Department paramedic Patti Schultz as she rode with him to Overlake Hospital.

At any rate, he was not the weak swimmer he had told Donna Clift he was, the neophyte even Tyson and Rylie believed he was, a man who could not maneuver in the water unless he held on to a raft or an inner tube or stayed in the safe, shallow end of the pool.

The courtroom lights were dimmed, and the jurors' eyes left the raft propped up against the far wall and watched it on the screen in front of them. They scrutinized the first King County Police reenactment of the effect of boat wakes on the raft. Again and again, Mike Hatch's powerboat zipped by the Sevylor. The swimming "actors" were clearly never in danger.

Why, then, had the raft tipped over on July 23? Why had Cynthia, a strong swimmer, drowned so easily?

Dr. Donald Van Rossen, an expert witness, was next. Van Rossen is an aquatics safety expert and former professor at the University of Oregon. People *do* drown and laymen don't always understand why. Perhaps Van Rossen could explain what happens when humans, who are basically land creatures, enter a foreign atmosphere.

Van Rossen told the jurors that the American Red Cross recognizes two types of drowning—active and passive. Given Randy Roth's version of his wife's death, where he discovered Cynthia floating facedown when he righted his overturned raft, Van Rossen would have termed her death a passive drowning. The passive drowner "simply slips under the water immediately," he said. There are not the facial expressions of terror, the thrown-up hands, and the thrashing legs of an active drowner.

However, the Oregon expert went on, for Cynthia Roth to have drowned passively, she would have to have been suffering from some preexisting physical condition—alcohol, drugs, a heart attack, perhaps, a seizure, a stroke, or a blow to the head that could have made it impossible for her to save herself as she floated in terrible pain or, worse, unconscious.

A leg cramp? Van Rossen shook his head and said, "It's a worrisome thing, but it shouldn't lead to drowning." He had studied the autopsy report on Cynthia Roth. She had no preexisting conditions. She had suffered neither a stroke nor a heart attack. The only substance in her blood was caffeine.

Active drowning, Van Rossen explained, is quite another thing.

Susan Storey questioned Van Rossen about how a person drowns actively. He explained that the victim realizes she is in trouble and panics, trying to keep her head above water by kicking or clawing at the water's surface. "In their [attempt] to survive," he said, "they are struggling to keep their head above water, and there is a time clock that starts when panic sets in. The clock starts when the face is in the water."

Within twenty to sixty seconds after the active drowner's movements are no longer productive, the person drowns. However, the heartbeat may continue for some time. Rescue breathing, given at once, can help, but only someone wearing scuba gear could have given Cynthia two quick breaths in the water. Active CPR requires a hard surface beneath the subject.

Cynthia Roth's family sat stoically in the front rows of the courtroom, almost certainly visualizing the death of a young woman so dear to them.

Van Rossen said that active drowners are almost always poor swimmers.

"If a strong swimmer was 'in arm's length' from a raft," Storey asked, "is that person going to experience active drowning?"

"No."

There was no reason why Cynthia could not have held on to the raft or floated while she massaged the cramp from her leg.

Van Rossen turned more toward the jury. The defense's objections would not allow him to give his own assessment of how Cynthia had died, but he remarked that it was possible for one person to hold another person underwater.

"How does an individual react when . . . held underwater by another person?"

"I think their first reaction would be surprise," Van Rossen said. "Then panic sets in."

Van Rossen had conducted an experiment with two strong swimmers at the University of Oregon, and he had brought a videotape of that exercise to demonstrate his point to the jury. University student Matt Jaeger had been told to deliberately hold Allison Wade underwater. She had been given a panic signal that she was to use when she needed to come up. Jaeger testified that he had found it "pretty easy" to hold Allison under the surface with his hand on her shoulder. Her panic signal was to duck and swim away. Actually, Allison had expected she could make her way to the surface because she was such a strong swimmer. She worked out five times a week for the swim team, she was a lifeguard, and she played water polo. She had built up her lung power so that she could stay twelve feet underwater for an extended period of time.

But she couldn't get away from Matt. Allison testified that Matt's hand kept pressing her shoulder down, and at one point he missed her panic signal and she felt true panic. Everything that was happening to her was *beneath* the surface; each time she tried to claw her way upward, she was forced back down. Their experiment continued for an hour.

She was relieved when it was over, and it was only an experiment, she said.

There was a question that Susan Storey wanted very much to ask Dr. Van Rossen: "Do you believe that Cynthia Roth was murdered?"

Judge Sullivan would not permit it. He ruled it would be "an invasion of the jury's province." Only the jury could decide that.

An inanimate object—the Sevylor raft—was the subject of the next expert's testimony. Thomas Ebro of Miami was an aquatic safety consultant and an accident investigator. Admittedly, Sevylor and its parent company, Zodiac, were his clients. Ebro had gone to Lake Sammamish in January 1992 and once more carried out a reenactment of boat wakes against the Sevylor.

Did he have an opinion?

He did.

"The statements by Randy Roth did not comport or correlate [with] the reality of what really happened."

Ebro explained that inflatable boats such as the Sevylor are very stable; they are chosen for use by lifeguards and rescue teams because of their safety and stability, he said, "even in the surf with helicopter rotors above. I could not accept [that] this craft could be overturned by a motorboat wake at this distance."

The Sevylor raft was eleven feet long and five feet wide; it was designed to hold 1,100 pounds, and it had a double-chambered hull. Collapsed or inflated, its weight was about thirty-nine pounds. Even if one chamber was punctured, it would still float.

But would it overturn? Ebro was positive it would not. The Sevylor "exceeded" the criteria required for high wave conditions. "It rides like a leaf," he explained. "The waves pass *beneath* it."

The trial had been going on for weeks, and Judge Frank Sullivan's courtroom was like an oven. Randy Roth had yet to betray his feelings. He sometimes wore a gray and brown sweater, sometimes a suit and tie, and he seemed thinner and more sallow each week. At certain angles, his face looked almost skeletal. His eyes bored into photographers' lens, as if daring them to take his picture. Of course they all took the dare. If anything, he was even more Manson-like than he had been when court procedures began in February. Outside, it was April but it might as well have been December or August. Many of the witnesses who had testified were now in the gallery, listening to testimony, and the court benches were packed even tighter.

It was time for the black humor that always seizes the press section when testimony is too painful, the tragedy before them too real. Someone passed a mimeographed sheet down the row.

ROTH'S
ADVENTURE TOURS

The Thrill of a Lifetime
Rafting . . . Swimming . . . Hiking . . . Camping

If you are a single woman
Between the ages of twenty and forty
And you like EXCITEMENT
ROTH'S ADVENTURE TOURS
Is your ticket to SPINE-TINGLING FUN

Spend the day hiking on a remote mountain crag,
Shooting the rapids,
Or just lazily boating on Lake Sammamish

The Evening Ends With Pizza and Videos.
We Guarantee it Will Be a Day You Will
NEVER Forget.

Beneath a cartoon of a raft, the caption read, Randall [sic] Roth, Proprietor: Personal Insurance Required.

28

The prosecution was nearing the end of its seemingly endless witness roster.

Candy Bryce, who had taken an application from Randy for Social Security benefits for Greg as Cindy's orphaned child, recalled that Randy Roth had filed in early October. He claimed that Greg was eligible for $768 a month. He said he had been married twice—to Cynthia Baumgartner and to Donna Clift. He said that Cynthia had no other surviving children—only Greg.

"Did you ask about Cynthia's prior marriage?" Marilyn Brenneman asked Bryce.

"Yes. He indicated it ended in divorce."

The Baumgartners, sitting in the second row, gasped. Tom had died; he would never have left Cynthia any other way.

Bryce said that she had realized that Roth's claim was fraudulent when she read about his arrest a week or so later. She did a computer search and discovered that Greg was already collecting Social Security on Janis Roth's account.

Marilyn Brenneman and Susan Storey had come to some of the people who had loved Cynthia the most, those who would undoubtedly still have been a part of her life if Randy Roth had not come along.

Lori Baker recalled how she and Cynthia had met at the Silver Lake Chapel and how Cynthia's sons had become like her own. At first she had been glad for Cynthia when Randy courted her. But everything had moved too fast when there seemed no need for such impetuosity. Nobody had disapproved of Randy; they just didn't know him.

"When did you hear that Cynthia had drowned?"

"Someone called and told me it was on the news. I called Randy and asked to talk to Cindy. Randy said, 'You can't do that.'

241

"I said, 'Why?'

"He said, 'She drowned.'"

Lori said there was a family meeting in Woodinville the next day. Randy handed her the Bellevue paper, remarking, "That's pretty accurate."

About a week after Cindy's death, Lori discussed the safe-deposit box with Randy, saying, "We'll need to go together."

"He said, 'We don't have one.'

"I said, 'Yes, we do.'"

By the time Lori gained access to that box, it was empty, and all the keepsakes meant for Cindy's sons were gone. She then answered the prosecutor's questions about Tyson and Rylie coming to live with her. "At the time he gave a press conference, he [Roth] lied about where the boys were," Lori answered quietly. "I had already taken custody of the boys through the will."

It was early in August 1991 when Lori had learned she would become the boys' guardian and the executor of her best friend's estate. She told the jury how difficult it had been to get the boys' belongings back from Randy. Randy had Cindy's clothing ready, and things like the china and silver, but not the boys' prized baseball cards, especially their Ken Griffey, Jr., card. They had not been allowed to take their bikes. He had never offered her or the boys Cindy's wall hangings, bowling trophies, or family pictures.

"He wouldn't let us take all their things," Lori said. "He'd thrown what he would let them have into big garbage bags. He said, 'Take it—I have no use for it.' It was not a happy meeting."

"Randy was a little upset?" Marilyn Brenneman asked.

"Yes."

"When you told the boys—" Brenneman began to ask, but George Cody objected.

"Overruled."

"When you told the boys they would be living with you, what was their attitude?"

"Relieved."

Roth's defense team cross-examined Lori Baker, implying that she had been interested only in gaining Cynthia's estate.

April 3 was a tense day. The courtroom was full of the curious who had heard that Tyson and Rylie Baumgartner would testify, and relatives and friends who were there to support them if they did. Suddenly the fire alarm sounded. Judge Frank Sullivan's courtroom is on the seventh floor of the aged King County Courthouse, and survival-minded spectators were preparing to leave when a voice thundered over the public address system: "Everyone on the twelfth and ninth floor evacuate the building at once. The rest of you remain at your work stations."

If there were flames, they did not threaten the seventh floor. The trial ground on.

Cynthia Roth's two sons had to testify—there was no way around it. They were the only living witnesses, other than the defendant, who had been privy to what went on inside the bright yellow walls of the new house in Woodinville. Lori Baker had promised them that they would leave the courthouse behind when they were done, and fly to Disneyland. She hoped that the good memories could wipe out the bad.

Tyson Baumgartner, now twelve, took the stand first. He was a slender boy with brown hair parted on the side. He wore a bright blue shirt and tie, slacks, and Weejuns. Brenneman, the mother of four sons herself, girded herself for the questions she had to ask. Easy ones first.

"Your favorite subject?"

"Science."

"You like sports?"

"I *love* baseball."

Marilyn Brenneman asked Tyson Baumgartner to re-create, if he could, the day his mother drowned. Tyson remembered it all. He identified the towels they had taken to the beach, and he remembered that his mom had taken her suntan oil. Greg hadn't gone with them to Idylwood Park; he was at a friend's house.

Tyson said that "we all pumped up the raft. It took a half hour. And Mom and Randy said, 'We're going out on the lake. We'll be back in a little while.'"

"What time was it?"

"About one or two. We saw Joe from my baseball team. We ate chips and drank pop with him. . . . It seemed like a long time before they came back. I didn't see Mom until they got up on shore. . . . Randy was rowing really slow . . . he had his sunglasses on. I saw him first when he was twenty or thirty feet away. We got her [Mom's] stuff and went over and started waving. He just kept rowing. We ran over and Mom was laying in the bottom of the raft. . . . Randy said to go get a lifeguard without making a disturbance."

At Overlake Hospital a lady had offered counseling to Randy, but Tyson remembered Randy said he didn't need any. When the detective wanted the raft, Randy was kind of "huffy," but he gave it to the man. Tyson testified that they had wrung the water out of the towels in the hospital parking lot and then put them back in the plastic bags. He described precisely each towel, each pair of thongs, and the bags.

"On the way home, Rylie cried," Tyson recalled, "and Randy said, 'You don't really need to cry. It's over now. Where do you want to eat?' "

"I said, 'I don't really care.' We went to Burger King, but we couldn't eat."

When they were finally home, they watched the movies Randy picked out. "I thought some of it was funny." There had been a couple of messages on the answering machine, and Tyson remembered that Randy had called someone or someone had called him. He wasn't sure.

The next day, Cynthia's older son remembered, Randy had rushed to get rid of their mother's belongings, especially her makeup. "He said she had too much of it. He made us help. . . . He sold her bike at the swap meet a week later."

The boys stayed about a week with Randy, Tyson thought, and then went to their grandparents'. He remembered going back to Randy's to get their things. "He wasn't real nice to us," Tyson said. "He wouldn't let us take our Nintendo games. He said how could he trust us not to take Greg's things? He wouldn't let us take our BB gun or our rubber boots."

Tyson said he and Rylie had hoped they could live somewhere else.

"Did you want to continue to live with Randy?"

"I didn't really want to."

Rylie Baumgartner was the next witness to take the stand. He was clearly the extrovert of the two brothers. He wore a bright fuchsia shirt and a flowered tie. If anything, Rylie's memory was even more detailed than Tyson's. They had all pumped up the raft with a hand pump that didn't work very well, he said. Then they had left their bags in the raft " 'cause they could have got stolen while we were swimming."

It had been a long, long time before they saw the raft come back.

"Three hours?"

"I thought one and a half to two hours. We went and looked out from the dock. I saw the same tank top Randy had on, the same dark hair, dark glasses. I said, 'That's him,' but we could not see our mom. I came to the conclusion she was lying down suntanning. . . . Randy was rowing very casually."

"Did you see your mother?"

"She was laying down, definitely unconscious, blue in the face, blue all over. Her eyes were closed, and her mouth was open." The little boy's face was white as he recalled his horror.

Rylie remembered Randy's first concern was that they all be quiet about what had happened. "Now, don't make a scene," he said. "Very calmly go over and get a lifeguard to help us."

He also recalled that "A lady saw us crying and we said it was our mom and the lady lifeguard took us up by the shed to help us get away from the crowd . . . we went to the hospital to a waiting room. We cried harder when we heard our mother died."

Although both of the boys had been in shock, their minds had registered clear images and statements. Rylie remembered that Randy had said to the detective, "I'm not wearing these glasses to hide anything from you."

As they drove away from the hospital, leaving their mother behind, Rylie had been unable to contain his tears and Randy had seemed annoyed. "He told me there was no need to cry. 'Just quit crying.' The tears still fell down my face, but I tried to be quiet so he wouldn't hear me."

Randy had rented some movies. "He recommended a few movies—we didn't care. He picked out all comedies." Rylie described *Weekend at Bernie's* as a movie about a corpse that "two guys" kept moving around a beach. "He said, 'You'll like it. It's funny. I've seen it.'"

"Was Randy crying?" Marilyn Brenneman asked. "Was he upset?"

"Not a bit," Rylie answered. "I didn't see that much of a difference."

The boys had spent the evening trying to concentrate on the videos Randy had rented. The next day, when Randy started to clear their house of Cynthia's things, Rylie suggested they give his mother's makeup and twenty boxes of her special kind of fingernail polish to her relatives.

"He said, 'No, it's useless.'"

Rylie, who was a stocky, tough-looking boy, admitted he was afraid of Randy.

"Why?"

"The way he treated me—" Rylie shot a glance down at Randy, who stared at him from the defense table.

"How did he treat you?"

"Me and Tyson. Our punishment got worse. Under the hose in the wintertime. I couldn't breathe. We had to do exercises on the rocks and gravel outside. We had to do bends and thrusts—up to a hundred and fifty of them—on the driveway. If we weren't fast enough, he turned the hose on us. He was in the marines."

Rylie said he had been very excited to learn that he and Tyson were going back to live with Lori Baker.

At the lunch break, the court officers escorted Randy back to jail. He craned his head toward the elevator doors where his former stepsons were waiting. "Sissies," he sneered. "They're little wimps. And now they'll be worse."

On Friday, April 3, 1992, the prosecution rested. George Cody and John Muenster would now present the defense. They called a number of witnesses who testified that they thought Randy Roth had been in shock when Janis Roth fell off Beacon Rock. He had been pale and sweaty and muttering words like "wife," "fall," and "off the mountain."

On cross-examination, however, one such witness admitted that he might not be able to recall everything that Randy had said on that November day in 1981. It had been a long time.

A fellow mechanic who had gone to work at Metro at the same time as Randy had related that Randy had refused that job when he learned that Metro employees changed shifts every three months. The income was stable and the benefits would be much better than with the Ford dealer where he worked, but Randy had learned he would begin with the graveyard shift. He and Cindy had discussed his working 11:00 P.M. to 7:00 A.M. "He decided he would hold off working for Metro."

The witness said that Randy hadn't wanted to leave his family alone all night. He had returned to work at the Bill Pierre agency.

The witness was surprised to hear from the prosecution that Randy had gotten out of the job by saying his wife had been critically injured in an accident in Idaho.

Muenster and Cody were starting slowly; they seemed to be explaining small blemishes on the surface of an edifice that had suffered fatal internal damage. Perhaps they would attend to that as they progressed through their case.

Jeff Rembaugh, one of Greg Roth's two Little League coaches, described Randy as a strong volunteer who contributed much to the sport and to the kids who played: "We called him Super Dad basically—helping on the field, and coaching."

Rembaugh's wife, Patricia, recalled how impressed the other parents had been when love bloomed between Randy and Cynthia in the summer of 1990: "They were sitting there in the stands holding hands, and they were very much into each other."

Another mother, Linda Christy, concurred: "They'd stare into each other's eyes, and it was real apparent there was a lot of emotion."

On cross-examination, the Rembaughs and Christy admitted that they had no contact with the Roths since their elopement on August 1, 1990.

The defense presented their own raft-flipping video. Coy Jones, aquatics director of the Renton School District told jurors that his reenactment had proved the raft could flip over quite easily. Using two powerboats, his team had managed to flip the raft "four times in twenty passes." Prosecutors insisted the boats had made at least thirty-six passes. In fact, Susan Storey insisted the four capsizings were intentional—performed in the same way prosecution swimmers had turned the raft over by throwing themselves well up on the pontoons and grabbing the oarlocks.

Cynthia had weighed 129 pounds and stood five feet two; Jones's woman had weighed 153 pounds and was five feet six. Moreover, her wet suit had added 10 to 15 pounds. Under Storey's vigorous cross-examination, Sharine Wrigley acknowledged that she had practiced tipping the raft over in a warm pool before going out on Lake Sammamish and that her goal had *been* to tip it over.

Were the jurors satiated with boats, rafts, wakes, and waves? Perhaps. The word was that Randy Roth was going to testify. The inscrutable little man with the set jaw and dark eyes might let them see who he really was.

Neither Muenster nor Cody would say if he was or wasn't going to get up on the stand.

He was.

On Thursday, April 9, Randolph G. Roth stepped up to the witness stand. At his request, he was not filmed by the TV pool camera. He wore a tight-fitting navy blue pin-striped suit. He looked at no one but George Cody, and his speech was almost totally void of inflection and was stilted as he routinely spoke in the passive voice often used in military or police reports.

He did, of course, recall November 27, 1981, the day that his second wife had fallen to her death. The climb up Beacon Rock had been Jan's idea—a "romantic" idea.

They had taken the same shortcut to the summit they had used during the summer. "There's a slight step up that you take, and she took that step—she was perhaps three feet in front of me at this particular section—she stepped down with her left foot and the earth broke and her traction broke away and she fell at almost a forty-five-degree angle. . . . It actually looked like a cartwheel. The first contact she had with the ground was almost on her head and her shoulder, and at that point she did another roll.

"As she was falling, she was falling away from me and it was downhill. At that point she rolled to her side and disappeared over the edge . . . she hollered when she went over."

Roth testified that he had to run down the trail to find a vantage point from which he could see where Jan had landed. When rescuers finally found her, he had had trouble accepting her death; he wanted to see her body.

"She didn't look as badly damaged as one of the individuals had communicated to me. Her hair was matted down on the sides from being bloody, but other than that her face wasn't damaged."

There were apparently great blank spots in Randy Roth's memory. He didn't remember calling Janis's insurance agent the day after she died, taking the envelope of money from Jalina, or any staged burglary at Nick Emondi's house.

As for the Skykomish River raft trip that had frightened Donna Clift, that had been a misunderstanding: "Donna was uncomfortable with rowing. She wouldn't row, and I couldn't use both oars at the same time. Consequently, the raft zigzagged down the river. I couldn't steer and row at the same time."

The main outer chamber was punctured, Roth said, when he and Donna got onto the rocks and the dead trees. "Donna was upset and frightened. She thought there was something I could do. I tried to reassure her that we were all right. She was screaming. I asked her to 'Keep up! Keep up!' "

No, of course he had not shouted "Shut up! Shut up!"

Yes, Randy Roth had kept Jan's ashes, even four years after she died. Yes, Donna had questions about what to do with the cremains. "She thought they should be in an urn or in a mausoleum. They were in a very expensive wood box made by a cabinetmaker on Highway 99 to cover the plastic-coated cardboard box from the services. . . . I was still in an emotional state and couldn't bear to part with Jan's remains. . . . She [Donna] gave me an ultimatum: It was either her— or Jan's ashes. . . . I was confused and uncomfortable with the situation and didn't know how to deal with it. Instead of getting rid of the box, I took it to the attic."

Somewhat Freudianly, Randy said that the ash episode had not broken up his marriage, but "There always seemed to be some gray cloud hanging over us after she found the remains of Janis."

Donna Clift had been a problem for him, he testified, as she hung around people who drank and used marijuana. (Baffled, Donna Clift, in the gallery, shook her head.) "The real problem was an accumulation of circumstances," Randy said. "She wouldn't quit socializing with others I didn't know. She would not quit smoking. . . . I thought she might be buying marijuana." Nothing, of course, could have been further from the truth.

Randy also lied about Mary Jo Phillips. His romance with her had ended, Randy said, because she had not told him everything. It was not until she moved in with him that he had discovered she had three more children than he knew about, and over a hundred tropical birds. "I was a little shocked at this point."

Randy testified that Mary Jo also had two former boyfriends who had shown up. One had tried to run them off the road. Mary Jo's ex-love had confronted Randy. "He didn't think I had any rights to have access to his former girlfriend."

The other boyfriend had come to Randy's home. If that wasn't bad enough, Randy complained, the next shock was a woman from the IRS who said Mary Jo owed $10,000 in back taxes. Worst of all, Mary Jo had thrown Janis's remains away in a garbage can. "She felt I should be able to recover and go on with my life." There was no way he could get the cremains back. "I was upset."

In cross-examining him about these untruths, Marilyn Brenneman suggested that Randy's break with Mary Jo Phillips had really come about because he learned she'd had cancer and was uninsurable.

"I never discussed insurance of any sort with Mary Jo," he responded. "The first time I heard of cancer in relation to Mary Jo was when I was going over the paperwork for this trial."

It was a very long day of questions and answers. Randy disputed almost everything that Brenneman asked him. If not that, he answered, "I don't recall." On this day, April 14, he could not recall more than a hundred occasions of interest.

As for his 1988 burglary, Randy had been meticulous in trying to re-accumulate what he had lost. He *had* replaced many of the tools he'd lost. He had to; he was a mechanic. He had borrowed tools and purchased used tools. Almost lovingly he listed dozens of tools.

The jurors shifted, yawned, and one woman in the front row had a coughing fit. In his droning voice, Randy continued to describe saws and clamps and rachets and vises and on and on. Oddly, his

belongings seemed to evoke more feeling than the women who had
passed in and out of his life.

Lizabeth Roth no longer sat in the courtroom. In a phone interview
from her home, she castigated the prosecution for placing so much
emphasis on her son's demeanor. "Randy and his brother were
brought up by their father, who didn't allow them to show emotion,"
she said. "He was reprimanded for it. That's just the way he was
brought up. The prosecutors are presenting him as coldhearted and
cruel, but he's not."

Roth's mother claimed that she had stayed away from most of the
trial "because it's just too heartbreaking for him to see us there. He'd
rather just face it alone."

There was indeed a great deal of heartbreak in that courtroom; the
victim's family had maintained—always—a heroic kind of control,
and they continued to do so as they stared at the man accused of
deliberately drowning Cynthia Baumgartner Roth. He never glanced
at them.

Watching him, listening to him speak, was akin to observing a
specimen from some other culture or even some other planet. Randy
Roth seemed to have no sense whatsoever of his audience, choosing
to appear to be a man in complete control and of superior intelligence. What came across was a chilling lack of empathy that
permeated the courtroom. If ever emotion was called for, it was on
those days when Randy told his own story, but he offered instead a
rationale so suspect that both the media and the jury looked up again
and again as if they could not believe they had heard him correctly.

He had an explanation for every question the prosecution brought
up. If he realized how specious some of his rhetoric sounded, no one
in the courtroom could tell. He was a robot, a brilliantly programmed
robot, who seemingly had forgotten not one single word of testimony. And now he was setting everything right, arranging, adjusting,
explicating, and making clear those things that had damaged him.

The "Idaho accident" was only a misperception on the part of the
Metro staff. Cindy had bashed up the Escort in the church parking
lot. The message he had really left with Metro was this: "My wife had
an accident in our car and we need to take it in for an estimate."

Roth denied signing for a certified letter from Metro—even though
that letter was in evidence.

July 1991 had been a bad month. His uncle was killed on July 11
when a tractor fell over on him, "and, oh yeah, a close friend died of

heart complications on the fourteenth of July, and then Cindy was sick." Randy said she'd gotten wet on their previous raft trip and had come down with the flu. After a week's confinement to the house, "She expressed a desire to get out of the house—maybe go to the water."

In Randy Roth's vernacular, no one ever "said" or "told" anything to him; they always "communicated to me" or "expressed a desire."

Clearly his alleged lunches and phone calls with Stacey Reese were dangerous to Randy, and he plodded ahead to defuse them. It was Stacey who had taken an interest in him, he claimed. She had been eating lunch in a friend's car and asked him, "What's this Reno trip?"

Randy went on to say, "I told her we were celebrating our one-year anniversary by going to Reno." Stacey had asked Randy about his previous marriages, and he had told her that was "kind of personal."

"I just want to know about you," Randy quoted her.

"So I told her about Janis. I spent maybe twenty-five or twenty minutes with her. . . . I had little contact. She worked all the way in the front. We liked the coffee up there. She and Juanita joked over Cindy saying she was my wife—because I guess I didn't appear to be the type of person who would be married."

Tediously, Randy explained his work hours and his requirement to punch out on a time clock at Bill Pierre. There was no way, he insisted, that he could have taken Stacey Reese to lunch the day before Cynthia drowned; he had worked on a vehicle from 11:00 A.M. to 2:00 P.M. according to this time card. He could not have eaten lunch with Stacey, and he certainly had not complained about his marriage to her.

After five weeks of trial, Randy Roth finally gave his version of Cynthia's drowning, of the trip to the lake that had ended so tragically. Would it be his last retelling?

Cynthia, he said, had suggested a family trip on Monday night, but Randy could not get home early enough because of a turbocharger he was working on. He recalled that it was on an Escort. (He remembered cars the way most men remember women.) He had continued working on the car until "12:26" on Tuesday. He described just what he had done to the Escort's engine.

He had left work then and gone home. His wife had the boys pack up their things while he showered "to get the oil and grease off."

Randy described the plastic shopping bags, "one with snaps," and the paper bags the boys had. "I figure we left at two."

Randy testified that he had never been to Idylwood Park before.

"We parked on the upper parking lot. . . . It was almost a hundred degrees, no shade. We took turns pumping. . . . Cynthia sent the boys to the swim area. We put Rylie's paper sack into a plastic sack. . . . We paddled out across the lake. . . . It was about three or three-thirty. We had no watches."

To Cody's question, Randy shook his head. No, he had had no time frame communication.

"Cynthia had organized the trip that day . . . we proceeded to row out into the lake. There's some small grassy areas and some houses on the east side. . . . There are two sets of oarlocks. They would have been in the front. Cynthia was sitting on the floor, with the bag between us. There was no reason to hurry to the other side. I'd told the boys they could have a ride when we got back."

Randy Roth described the exceptionally heavy traffic in the sand-bar area; there were fewer boats out in the open water. A dozen jet skiers. "The water was real choppy, like Puget Sound. Real rough . . . agitated."

They got to the east side of the lake, even though it was much farther than Randy had estimated. There was an open area, and they rowed along looking for a nice place to land. They stopped in shallow water and got out, holding on to the raft so it wouldn't blow away. Randy had gotten his prescription sunglasses out of one of the sacks. He explained that he was very nearsighted "20/400 in my left eye—20/425 in my right." (A person with 20/200 uncorrected vision is legally blind.)

Suddenly Randy's voice dropped. "One of Cindy's thongs slipped off, and she swam to get it. We got in the raft and started across the very shallow water. We just stepped right into the raft. . . . There was boat activity north and south of us often. . . . We intersected all the traffic. . . . We were going west. We were on the Idylwood side. It was still fairly hot, and she asked if I wanted to get in and cool off. She put my glasses in a sack . . . she dove off and so did I. The raft was blowing around quite a bit. We stayed close. We were in the water at least five minutes. *She's* a better swimmer. She did the crawl stroke with her head out of the water. I did the breaststroke. She said she had a cramp in her foot from the cold water."

At this point Randy estimated they had 20 to 30 feet to swim back to the raft and his wife was ahead of him. "Her initial contact with the raft, she held on to the rear oarlock and the rope, which didn't keep her face out of the water. She tried to pull herself onto it. It kept bobbing up on the other side. We had never tried to get in the raft in the water. She said she couldn't use her leg to kick, and I started swimming toward the front so I could go around. . . . I got just to the bow. My back was toward her. A boat came by from behind us . . . the raft flipped over and cracked the water. I heard her cough. I heard the roar of the boat going away . . . it had been right beside us—50 to 100 yards away."

Randy Roth testified that he swam to the side of the raft and lifted it a couple of inches. "I swam to the bow and flipped it. I saw her on her face. The two plastic bags were floating. I didn't have a strong enough kick to bring her to the boat. I brought the boat to her. I held her nose and blew into her mouth. It was like blowing into a long birthday balloon where I couldn't get enough air into it. . . . I couldn't get her over the side. I let go of her and swam to the end of the raft and paddled to her. . . . I was able to get her hands and pull her over the back. I wanted to row. I needed the sack with my glasses—the one with the strings was floating deep. . . . I was headed for the lifeguard towers. In my mind, I was not more than a few minutes from the lifeguard. My arms were too weak. . . ."

The courtroom was hushed. Randy Roth said he only turned around to be sure he was rowing straight. He had told himself, "Just a few minutes . . . just a few minutes . . . to the lifeguard."

What had he told Cindy's sons?

"Run as fast as you can, but don't create a panic."

He had said that so everyone wouldn't run like they did in *Jaws* and get in the way. Above all, he had wanted to avoid a "*Jaws* effect."

If he had seemed detached, Randy explained that he was focused entirely on the efforts to save Cynthia. "I felt sick to my stomach, so I pulled all the stuff out of the raft and deflated it so I'd be ready to go."

For just an instant it seemed as though the witness might actually be crying. It was as close as he would ever come during his marathon testimony. People had been asking him questions.

How long had Cynthia been unconscious?

He thought "perhaps five minutes." He was exhausted, he wanted to be with her, he couldn't find the boys.

"*Someone said they had a pulse!*" But it had been only a CPR pulse, Randy testified. They could not get an airway in, and they had elevated Cindy with towels.

"I knew I had gotten her to shore as quick as I could, and these people were working on her, and I thought they'd be able to bring her back on the way to the hospital. I kept saying, 'I have two boys here.'"

Randy said he threw his gear in the back of his vehicle, and the boys got in the back. He drove, and the woman got in. She gave directions to the hospital. "I can't remember how fast I drove. All I had in my mind was Cindy in the aid car on the way to the hospital. The boys were really quiet. None of the three of us realized she wasn't going to be helped."

There had been many versions of what had happened after Cynthia was pronounced dead at Overlake Hospital. Now Randy gave his. He testified that he had been "preoccupied" by his conversations with Lieutenant Conrad. He had hated the thought of Cynthia's body being autopsied, but had to agree. Conrad had drawn a diagram of the lake and marked it "North" and "South," and Randy remembered having the boys wring out the towels. They had left about 8:30 P.M. He asked the boys where they wanted to eat. "They said Burger King.

"Both boys were real quiet—especially Tyson. None of us could eat. We went to a video place, and I told them they could rent two or three videos—pick a couple of comedy shows. . . . We went straight home and cleaned up. The message machine was blinking."

He had tried to call Leon, Randy testified, but the line was busy. He called the other number left on his machine. It was a man calling on an ad wanting to trade a crew cab for a Corvette. Randy spoke briefly and hung up. Between nine and ten the boys put stuff in the washer, they all took showers, and Randy made popcorn. The medical examiner's office had called wanting Cynthia's Social Security number. They had all fallen asleep on the couch and then gone to bed.

The phone had awakened Randy the next morning. He had tried his best, he explained, to keep the boys busy and preoccupied. "I had to go to the swap meet and clean out the garage, and get them larger four-wheelers."

He had not told Greg about the tragedy for a few days, as he was staying at a friend's house. The phraseology he used when he did was hauntingly familiar: "Greg couldn't really believe it. I told him that she wasn't with us anymore."

When had he talked to Cynthia's family? Cody asked.

Randy could not recall specifically when he had talked to Leon or Lori or Cynthia's parents. They had all come over. "I wanted to let them handle everything. They'd known her a lot longer than I had. They decided on the Silver Lake Chapel."

The service had been on Monday, July 29, and Randy had returned to work on Tuesday. People at work had been "very kind."

He could not recall seeing Stacey. She had called the house and left a message on the machine. How was he? How were the boys? She had left her number, and he had called and told her he was trying to distract the boys.

Yes, he had offered her the tickets to Nevada. They were prepaid and he couldn't use them. She couldn't take the time off work.

Tyson and Rylie had gone to visit relatives, and Randy testified that he had been stunned when Lori Baker called to tell him that they had located the will and that "the boys won't be coming home again."

The media had started to dog him, and he had given a press conference just to get them off his back. And then Lori had come over a day or two later with a truck. He didn't have boxes for Cynthia's things. He used sacks. Yes, he *had* protected Greg's bedroom. "I wanted to afford them all their areas of privacy and security."

Randy presented himself to the jurors—although he never looked at them—as a man bereft and robbed of the family he loved. "I guess I felt abandoned and somewhat betrayed because they took the boys away without my input."

It was impossible to discern what the jurors were thinking; some sat with their chins in their hands, some with crossed legs, but all of them were motionless and expressionless as they studied the man on the witness stand.

Randy went on to say he suspected greed on Lori's part, because the boys got about $700 apiece each month from Social Security. Randy said he earned only $2,200 to $2,800 a month and he could no longer afford the Woodinville house; he had already planned to buy a smaller home for himself and all the boys. As for the Social Security application he had made on Greg's behalf as Cynthia's surviving son, he said that Social Security representatives had practically "offered" it to him. He had never asked. *They* wanted Greg's birth certificate and other documentation. *They* sent Randy an application.

He could not "recall" ever telling them that Cindy had divorced Tom Baumgartner instead of being widowed; that must have been a clerical error. He could not recall the one check that had been sent for Greg on Cindy's account. He had been "told" it was in the bank.

Finally, George Cody had no more questions—and Randy Roth had no more explanations.

Marilyn Brenneman rose to cross-examine Randy Roth. She approached him pleasantly enough. He apparently never sensed that her questions might be troublesome, even perilous, for him. Still, he shifted in his chair to face her.

Brenneman was prepared to dismember the framework of Randy Roth's testimony section by section. She began by discussing the money that Cynthia had had in the bank.

"That money was accessed by Cindy," he answered smoothly.

"The money went to your benefit?"

"Ultimately, yes."

Marilyn Brenneman was fascinated that, until his court testimony, there had been no mention of Cindy's holding on to the oarlocks of the raft, not in Randy's statements of July 23, July 29, or August 11, and not in his press conference on August 9.

He admitted that he had spoken in "generalities" before about the drowning. "This is my first opportunity to address that."

"You have prepared yourself?"

"In a manner of speaking."

It was obvious what Brenneman was getting at; the defense reenactment video clearly showed the female swimmer holding on to the oarlocks as she tipped the raft over onto herself.

Marilyn Brenneman moved a little closer, hitting Roth with one question after another that exposed big and little lies about his past. Cody tried to stop her with a hastily called sidebar. The defense could see what was coming the moment she asked Randy what he had done after high school.

"You have investments in cattle and land?"

"None at this point in time."

"*Did* you?"

"At one point—with my father."

"How far back?"

"At least ten years."

Bit by bit Roth had to give ground. He had not been a motorcycle racer, a martial arts instructor, the owner of a successful home repair business, or a three-year college student. He didn't own vast acreage on the Columbia River, and he did not plan to purchase an exercise gym.

He had never been in Vietnam.

All the things he had listed as his accomplishments in the program from his tenth anniversary reunion at Meadowdale High School were not quite true. "Maybe somebody changed the information," he finished weakly.

"What martial arts did you teach?"

"A street version—mostly exercise, no particular style."

"Tae Kwon Do? Kung fu?"

"Basically . . . basically specific reactions to situations a person might encounter on the street . . . primarily exercise and meditation."

She asked him if he had been influenced by Bruce Lee.

"I believe . . . I was involved in a style he created."

"What was it called?"

"I don't remember."

Brenneman moved through Roth's divorce from Donna Sanchez, his alleged refusal to let Greg talk to his mother on the phone, his control over Nick and Carrie Emondi.

"How?" Roth countered. "We lived twenty miles apart."

"You had control. . . . You're a very tough person whom Nick would not cross. You showed him a weapon."

"Nick's larger than I am. . . . I had a baseball bat sawed in half with nails pounded in and painted black." Randy rocked in the witness chair ever so slightly.

"Did you invite Mr. Emondi to go with you to move your mother?"

"No. She did move three or four years ago."

"She was being held against her will?"

"No."

"You took a gun?"

"I didn't have a gun to take with me."

"Never had access to guns?"

No, he had only had his homemade weapons, and Greg had his BB gun. Still, the tall prosecutor was making the defendant nervous. He didn't know where she was going to go next.

She moved through his marriages again, and he parried each thrust. The fault had never been his. It had been in the wives, in the women who left him. He spoke of them in his curious, ponderous manner. When he talked of dancing with Janis, he didn't say they had had fun by going dancing. He said, "That was one of the sources of recreation we utilized."

And when Janis died, crushed far below the perch where they had hiked, he spoke of "damage," as if her face had been only a fender on a car.

Brenneman asked about Randy's Pioneer Insurance claims. His recovery, he said, "was very small after the attorney's fees."

Although it took a most observant person to spot it, Randy Roth tensed ever so slightly when Brenneman asked him about his lunches with Stacey Reese. No. He had only a half hour for lunch; the office staff had an hour. He didn't know Stacey well enough to take her to lunch. He had just "run into her at Dick's Drive-in."

Randy insisted he always punched in and out on his job.

"Always?"

"Always."

"Were you close with Cynthia?" Brenneman asked suddenly.

"That's part of the reason we got married."

"Any problems?"

"All relationships have problems."

"The people at Bill Pierre can't remember one *positive* thing you ever said about Cynthia."

"It's always easier to remember the negatives more than the positives."

"Did you call her a bitch?"

"I never called any woman that."

"How *did* you feel about Cynthia?"

"We enjoyed each other. I wanted to spend the rest of my life with her."

Randy speculated that their only differences might have been over the way she handled the boys. He dealt directly with their activities, he explained, while she observed.

Brenneman kept asking him for more explication, and he obliged each time, digging himself in a little deeper. He felt that Cynthia might have been envious because he spent so much money on the boys' athletic equipment. "We spent twenty-three dollars for three athletic supporters and cups."

She asked him why he had signed up as a single person at Nautilus Northwest, a gym. He didn't answer, but admitted Cynthia had "expressed her unhappiness" over that.

"You told people at work that she was restricting your freedom?"

"No."

"You disabled her car so she couldn't leave the house?"

"*She* thought so. It was a clutch. . . . I fixed it."

Item by item, Marilyn Brenneman read off the "Randy hates—" poem that Sue Peters had found during the October 1991 search. Again and again he denied that those complaints were true. The witness's face grew, if anything, blanker, and his body language became even more guarded. He didn't recognize Cindy's handwriting on the document. He spoke of his wife always in the present tense, as if she still lived.

"Did you convey any of these feelings to Stacey Reese?"

"She asked about the marriage. I assumed because she'd talked to Cindy on the phone."

"You told her it was 'shit'?"

"That's not part of my vocabulary. That was Stacey's term, not mine."

Randy acknowledged he had met Stacey for lunch one time.

"You *never* let anyone at Bill Pierre think you were not married?" Brenneman asked incredulously.

He had told Juanita Gates he was "sort of married."

"You never said you had a one-year contract and it was about up?"

"No."

Randy insisted his marriage had been very stable, with only small disagreements. Stacey's testimony was inaccurate. He had had nothing in common with Stacey except they were both single parents. No, of course he had never tried to discourage her from dating other men. He knew nothing about her personal life.

"You never said, 'Before you go out with John, think about what he wants you to give up'?" Brenneman pushed.

"I was concerned for her well-being and safety, knowing the type of person John was."

The prosecutor switched gears again, bringing out the myriad problems that witnesses had seen in Randy's fourth marriage—the time he spent with Max Butts and the long absences when he took Brad home to his mother, Lily Vandiveer.

No, he insisted. No problems. Everything had been fine.

"You remember telling Stacey Reese you didn't want the relationship to go on?"

"No."

"That Cindy was obsessive and nasty toward you, that you only had a verbal marriage?"

"No." And no and no and no.

"Did you contact Stacey Reese the Thursday following Cindy's death?"

"Yes, in response to an answering machine message."

"Did you say, 'I'm fine. Why wouldn't I be? It was a horrible thing, but a *relief*'?"

Looking directly into Marilyn Brenneman's eyes, Randy Roth replied easily that Stacey had misunderstood. "It would have been a rhyme word—like I didn't know how I would deal with my *grief*."

Randy's four phone calls to another woman in the week after his wife drowned had come back to haunt him, but he deftly deflected Stacey's memory.

Yes, he had told Stacey that the police might be developing a theory that he might be guilty of harming Cindy.

"Did you tell Stacey you were afraid they were going to come that weekend and arrest you?"

"I wouldn't have said *afraid*—maybe *concerned* about the effect on the boys."

"Did you invite Stacey to Reno?"

"No. I asked her if she had use for the tickets."

"You told Stacey you had life insurance, but just enough to pay off your home. You told her, 'It will take me fucking forever to get the pink and mauve out of my home'?"

"I don't use that word. All I did was respond to her question. Without a woman in the house, I felt uncomfortable having that much femininity in the environment around the boys."

Slowly and methodically Marilyn Brenneman was showing the dark nether side of all of Randy's previous testimony. She elicited responses that showed he had begun the very morning after Cindy's drowning to eradicate everything that reminded him or her sons of her existence. Makeup thrown away, her treasures thrown into closets, her dolls "centralized."

He explained away, again, the pesky insurance policies. Mortgage insurance, really.

The message to Metro was another "rhyme" misunderstanding. "I didn't say 'Idaho.' I would have said, '*I don't know* when I can come to work.'"

Roth was inflexible about the details of Cynthia's drowning. Anyone who remembered it differently was mistaken. He was not a good swimmer. He had not saved the life of a high school girlfriend, no matter that that ex-girlfriend had testified that he had. "It would have been impossible for me. I don't have a strong enough kick."

Despite his weakness in the water, he had done everything within his limited ability, to save Cynthia. Some things he could not remember, of course.

"You couldn't have helped Cynthia in the water?" Brenneman moved a little closer to the witness stand.

"It was not a matter of being able to help or not being able to help. It was a question of her not being able to respond to the air breaths," he answered.

"Actually, Mr. Roth, isn't it a question of whether or not you were a strong enough swimmer to be able to pull Cynthia Roth under until she drowned?"

"That wouldn't have been a part of anything that happened." He stared back at Brenneman, his jaw tight, his eyes opaque.

* * *

The two of them had been sparring for days, but it seemed more like weeks. Perhaps—outside—true summer had come again. Finally, on Thursday, April 16, Marilyn Brenneman was down to her last questions.

"Isn't it a fact, Mr. Roth, that money—insurance proceeds—is why you murdered your wife Janis?"

"That's not true at all."

"That's why you murdered Cynthia, your fourth wife. Isn't that a fact?"

"That is not a fact."

"In fact, money has been at the root of every insurance fraud scheme that you've committed, that's been testified to in front of this jury. Isn't that a fact?"

"That's totally incorrect. My life-style has never been indicative of having or controlling any large amounts of money."

"Controlling people and controlling money is what your life-style *is* all about . . . from what we've heard here. Isn't that a fact?"

"No," Randy Roth murmured.

It was over. Roth stepped down from the witness stand and walked over to his attorneys. Very few members of the gallery and none of the jury could see the expression on his face as he looked at George Cody. He smiled, the faintest of grins that looked like nothing so much as a child who had just recited before a PTA audience and had done well. It lasted only an instant before his usual mask dropped down.

Jack Hopkins, court reporter for the *Seattle Post-Intelligencer* and a veteran of more criminal trials than almost any writer in the area, summed up Roth's testimony best:

"Randy Roth, suspected of pushing one wife to her death off Beacon Rock and charged with drowning another in Lake Sammamish, spent close to 22 hours on the witness stand.

"He never unbuttoned his sport coat.

"He never crossed his legs.

"He never slumped down in his chair.

"He never looked at the jurors.

"He never raised his voice in anger or shed a tear in grief.

"For the better part of six days, he talked on and on about the past 10 years of his life, trying to convince a King County Superior Court jury the deaths of his wives were tragic accidents."

The only thing that marked Randy Roth as wary were his hands. He had held them in an almost unnatural position in front of him, and they were clenched. He was so thin his skin seemed transparent, his bones showing through. He looked to weigh no more than 125 or 130 pounds, the very image of a man who would have been too weak to save his wife from drowning and without enough stamina to row far enough fast enough to get her help.

But was he?

29

Jury selection had begun in February, and it was now the week of April 20. Time at long last for final arguments. The jury had heard well over a hundred witnesses—some who were expert, some emotional, some angry, some forgetful, some precise—and each section of testimony contributed to an almost unfathomable jigsaw puzzle, according to the prosecution. The prosecution maintained that Randy Roth was a cold-blooded killer of at least two of the women who had loved him. The defense found him only a tragic figure, besieged by loss upon loss, a victim of highly circumstantial evidence, and no more than that.

Marilyn Brenneman would present the state's final arguments, and she would do so at considerable disadvantage. Over the weekend she had been enticed away from preparing those arguments by a rollicking party to celebrate her son Adam's eighth birthday. The weather was wonderful and so was the sight of Brenneman's yardful of sons. There was a water balloon fight going on, and she chased after one of her offspring with a fully loaded balloon. As she confidently took aim and threw, she stepped in a hole and severely sprained her left ankle. The balloon missed and hit a rosebush.

A clean break would have hurt less. Brenneman would present her final argument on crutches with her ankle tightly bound up in an Ace bandage. Wearing a bright red jacket with a soft white blouse, the deputy prosecutor began a process that would take hours. From time to time, she winced slightly as she moved in front of the jury to the easel and back to a stool. For the most part, she was so involved in her intricately constructed argument that she didn't feel the pain.

Randy Roth was charged with three counts, and the jury was to debate each count separately. Count 1 was murder in the first degree. In order to convict on that count, the jury must believe that Brenneman and Susan Storey had proved beyond a reasonable doubt that Randy Roth had intentionally and with premeditation caused the death of his fourth wife, Cynthia Baumgartner Roth, and that this death had occurred in King County, Washington. The second count was theft in the first degree. To convict, the jury must believe that between September 17, 1988, and October 2, 1991, Randy Roth had gained by color or aid of deception over $1,500 from the Pioneer Insurance Company, and that that crime had occurred in King County, Washington. The third charge was theft in the second degree. To bring in a conviction the jurors needed to believe that between September 17, 1991, and October 15, 1991, Randy had wrongfully obtained by color or aid of deception over $250 from the Social Security Administration in King County, Washington.

Marilyn Brenneman was calm and deliberate, and her voice was soft. From time to time she glanced at Randy Roth as she unreeled the seemingly endless connected and similar circumstances of his alleged crimes. The jurors were fascinated; the gallery was transfixed, and even Judge Sullivan and his staff listened to Brenneman as if they had never heard all these coincidences and similar patterns before.

Direct evidence was what the jurors had heard from witnesses— those people who had seen and heard vital parts of the case with their own senses. Circumstantial evidence was what a reasonable person using common sense would deduce. For instance, Brenneman said, "If a car comes off the west end of the I-90 Bridge, common sense would tell us that it must have gone on the east side."

Almost nothing in human experience can be proved absolutely. Yes, a car could have been dropped on that one-way bridge by a giant helicopter or hoisted hydraulically from a submarine halfway across Lake Washington—but not likely. And nobody could do a U-turn on the I-90 floating bridge.

Marilyn Brenneman submitted to the jury in this seventh week of trial that "the defendant, Randy Roth, cold-bloodedly courted, married, insured, and murdered Cynthia Baumgartner Roth. That he murdered her out of greed, and that was his reason. . . . The picture before you is now clear. And it is that the defendant did indeed murder his wife . . . and he did it cold-bloodedly, making it appear to have been an accident. He did it for $385,000 in insurance proceeds, her separate property, assets, and Social Security benefits."

Scarcely glancing at her notes, Brenneman reviewed the witnesses' testimony, the direct evidence, the circumstantial evidence. She reminded the jury that not only had the victims suffered at Roth's greedy hands but so had their children and their families. This is true of all murder cases, she said, but especially of the one they now were about to consider.

"The defendant is a cold-blooded and premeditated killer who stalks his prey, not with the traditional weapons," Brenneman said, "but with a smile, flowers, and marriage proposals."

Defense attorney George Cody argued that reasonable doubt existed and that the state's tactic of linking Janis Miranda Roth's death with Cynthia Baumgartner Roth's death was unfair. "What is going on here, in large measure, is the state is saying that you should more readily accept than you would under other circumstances that Randy Roth killed Cynthia Roth because Janis Roth died in 1981. What they are saying is you should accept more easily that Randy Roth killed Janis Roth because Cynthia Roth died ten years later. I don't believe you can bounce those two things back and forth in your mind like a Ping-Pong game."

Brenneman presented the whole puzzle, pieces neatly in place, some after almost eleven years. Cody worked to present individual segments from those years.

They were both very, very good at what they did.

Randy had caught Cynthia off guard, the limping prosecutor maintained. "He was stalking Cynthia Roth and he was using those weapons that he had used before, pretending to be enamored of her, pretending to love her. How many of us could say that we would have known any different than Cynthia Roth? To be loved is a natural human desire. To be loved intensely and immediately is overwhelming, and it is wonderful when it is *real*. But this was not real. . . . He covers his real intentions behind a false front of love, and he victimizes not only those who believe those false claims but the innocent relatives and children his victims always leave behind."

George Cody acknowledged that Randy and Janis Roth had had some differences in their brief marriage, but said that did not prove he had killed her. "If it did," he said, "there would be a motive for some kind of mayhem for virtually everybody who has been married at any time."

True.

Cody insisted that Randy's lack of obvious emotion at the time of Janis's death—and, inferentially, Cynthia's—only served to confirm his innocence. "If Randy Roth was at the top of Beacon Rock, alone with Janis, and he decided to kill her, you must ask yourself why he would tell a series of stories that the state says are inconsistent and raise suspicions about the death of his wife. . . . It would be relatively simple to come up with a specific version . . . and tell it and not do anything else."

Marilyn Brenneman had the burden of proof. George Cody had only to raise reasonable doubt and Randy Roth could walk away.

Concerning Randy Roth's apparent lack of grief and emotion at Idylwood Park, Cody walked a precipice as dangerous as any on Beacon Rock. His reasoning was somewhat intricate and threatened to boomerang.

"On the day of Cynthia Roth's death," Cody said, "we are talking about somebody going through a unique situation, going through, for the second time, the same occurrence—not the second *murder*, but the second *death*. I don't know how anybody would react in that circumstance, whether they would say all the right things and make all the right moves."

For veteran court watchers, listening to and observing both Cody and Brenneman was an ambivalent experience. Each was at once folksy and intellectual, colloquial and dead-on serious. At one point George Cody actually stood behind Randy's chair and placed his hand paternally on the defendant's left shoulder. And, as if he'd rehearsed the scene, Randy Roth lifted his eyes for the very first time in the seven-week trial and looked directly into the jurors' eyes.

Cody told an anecdote about a dog sent to the pound because he had blueberry pie stains on his face and an empty pie pan under his paw. *Circumstantial.*

Brenneman told an anecdote, much beloved by attorneys, about a defense attorney who promised that the missing—and presumed dead—"victim" would walk into the courtroom; everyone looked toward the door, save the defendant.

And beneath it all, the decision to come would be ultimately serious. If Randy Roth *was* guilty but the jury did not find him so, who knew how many female and child victims lay ahead of him. He was only thirty-eight years old. If he was innocent and the jury did not find him so, he faced life behind bars. There were no smoking guns, no fingerprints in blood, no hair and fiber matches, no confessions, no living eyewitnesses. This was not an easy case.

Not at all.

As Marilyn Brenneman rose to offer her short rebuttal, the last act of this long trial, she looked steadily and frequently at Randy Roth. She pointed out that the state had offered the jurors everything—the entire puzzle with no pieces missing. The defense had offered individual pieces—pieces that could not tell them if they were looking at sky or water or clouds. Or reality.

Randy Roth's patterns were far too predictable and repetitive to be coincidental. "The parallels are just too similar, and that is because they were . . . presented by a man with a plan. And the plan said if you have gotten away with murder once with a successful story, get as close to that story as possible if you want to get away with murder twice.

"If you fool me once, shame on you." Brenneman's voice dropped. "If you fool me twice, shame on me. That's the situation we are now in. . . . If he fools us today, shame on us."

The jury filed out of Judge Sullivan's courtroom in the afternoon of April 22, 1992. They returned on the afternoon of April 23 with a verdict. They had deliberated for eight and a half hours, a little more than an hour for each week of the trial. The verdict:

Guilty of first-degree murder.

Guilty of first-degree theft.

Guilty of second-degree theft.

Randy Roth stayed true to form. Beyond a quick glance downward, he showed no emotion. His attorneys told reporters they would file an appeal.

On Friday, June 19, 1992, Judge Sullivan gave Randolph G. Roth an exceptional sentence. The state had asked for a fifty-five-year sentence. Sullivan moderated that only a little; he sentenced Randy to fifty years in prison, as he agreed with Marilyn Brenneman and Susan Storey that Roth had shown extreme greed and coldheartedness in killing his fourth wife for insurance and in leaving her two children orphans. With credit for good behavior, Roth could conceivably be released after serving thirty-four years.

George Cody and John Muenster repeated their intent to appeal the conviction, just as they had predicted they would before the trial began. Their main objection was—and remained—the inclusion of

Roth's prior behavior in his trial for a murder that had occurred in 1991.

Officials in Skamania County had been prepared to prosecute Roth in the alleged murder of Janis Roth had he not received a sentence in the fifty-year range. Such a trial, however, would have drained the county's budget. With the June 19 sentencing, Skamania County announced it would not reopen the case on Janis.

It will be years, if ever, before Randy Roth's name ceases to appear in some legal proceeding somewhere. There will be the sometimes endless appeal process. Lori Baker is suing on behalf of Tyson and Rylie Baumgartner to ask that Gordon Roth be removed as trustee from Cynthia's policies and that the money be designated only for Cynthia's sons.

In the meantime, the slender, ethereal Randy metamorphosed once again. Preparing for prison, he put on weight and restored the massive muscles that he had been so proud of. He grew a beard to go with his luxuriant mustache.

The man who had sat quietly throughout the seven-week trial never really existed. He was a character in a play that didn't succeed. The macho Randy Roth entered the Washington State Prison at Walla Walla in the fall of 1992.

Barring a successful appeal, he will be seventy-two years old when he is released.

Campbell's Revenge

"Don't the stories *you write frighten you?" It is another predictable question that I have heard two hundred times. Usually my answer is that I am rarely afraid, even though I have written about some of the most heinous criminals of the last three decades. But sometimes I must admit that a case cuts too close to the bone and triggers fears that all women have. We fear first for our children and only second for ourselves.*

Charles Rodman Campbell is a killer straight out of a nightmare. There should have been some way to keep him locked up forever. But he slipped through the loopholes of our justice system, and he was allowed freedom to stalk his unknowing victims. If ever there was a case that pitted innocence against pure evil, it is this one. He was out of his cage, and he was aware of every facet of her life, and yet his potential prey felt only a chill premonition of danger. He was a man consumed with rage and the need for revenge. Because of a neglectful bureaucracy, Campbell was allowed to take not one life—but three.

Clearview, Washington, is little more than a crossroads, a tiny neighborhood in Snohomish County, twelve miles south of Everett, the county seat. Travelers headed for Stevens Pass, one of the northern routes over the Cascade Mountains, pass through Clearview and scarcely realize it.

After it was over, Clearview residents cried, "This sort of thing doesn't happen here—not in Clearview." *Why* do people say that? Is everyone who lives outside a major metropolitan area convinced that he or she lives in a safe zone, under a kind of glass bubble where violent crimes never break through? Possibly—if the nightly news is any barometer. The cold fact is that tragedies and terror happen everywhere, no matter how sylvan the landscape, how slow the pace of life is, or how loving and protective the friends and neighbors. Psychopaths move among all of us, their motivation usually hidden behind a winning, clear-eyed smile and sincere promises. Many of them are handsome or beautiful, successful—at least for a time— and persuasive. And sometimes all of us trust too much, too soon.

He was not like the smoothly handsome predators. He frightened most women just by the way he looked. He was so big—almost six feet five—and his bushy mustache and tangled Afro hair were reddish brown and seemed to bristle with electricity. But it was his eyes that caught them in a steady, mind-altering stare. They were like the entrance to a tunnel, the dark orbs fixed above an expanse of white beneath. *Sampaku,* the Japanese call them: "eyes of death." Like Rasputin's—the mad monk who mesmerized Russian nobility, another huge man who seemed impervious to his enemies—Charles Rodman Campbell's eyes had a life of their own. They were often glazed and a little crazy. To the cons in the Monroe, Washington, Reformatory, he was a "bad-ass," and to his guards, he was trouble. To his victims, he was the devil himself.

* * *

271

Renae Ahlers Wicklund was a beautiful woman—dark-haired and big-eyed, with the high cheekbones and symmetrical features of a model. Her career was beauty—the art of bringing beauty to other women. She was kind, responsible, and gutsy. She must have been gutsy to endure what she did.

After she graduated from high school, where she was a drum majorette for the band, in Jamestown, North Dakota, Renae Ahlers moved to California and then to Washington State. When Renae met her future husband, Jack Wicklund, she was working in a beauty parlor in Seattle. She was nineteen, and Jack was fourteen years older, divorced with two children from a previous marriage.

In 1972 they fell in love and got married. Renae was expecting her first baby when they moved into their own home, a neat one-story rambler set far back in a stand of fir trees near rural Clearview. Lots were acre-sized, and being neighborly required some effort. Running across the street to have coffee meant almost a quarter-mile jog. But Renae and Barbara and Don Hendrickson grew close right away. Don was forty-three and Barbara forty-one. They had lived there for ten years, and they became almost substitute parents; their children—Peggy, Susan, and Dan—were family, too.

Jack Wicklund spent much of his time on the road, and as Renae neared term in her pregnancy, she was more grateful than ever for the Hendricksons. When she went into labor, Jack was out of town, and it was Peggy Hendrickson who drove Renae to the hospital on that day in 1973 when Renae gave birth to a baby girl she named Shannah. Shannah looked just like her mother—she had the same huge brown eyes and chestnut hair. Renae adored her, and everywhere Renae went, her baby went along.

It is impossible to know if Shannah remembered the first bad time. Probably not. She was only a year and a half old when it happened. It is likely, though, that the toddler sensed her mother's frantic terror, that the feeling surfaced in bad dreams through the next eight years. The first time, Shannah lived only because her mother did what any mother would have done to save her child: Renae Wicklund gave in to a rapist to keep him from harming Shannah.

December 11, 1974, was an unseasonably warm and sunny day for western Washington, where December usually means rain, rain, and more rain. Taking advantage of the weather, twenty-three-year-old Renae Wicklund decided to wash her windows. Knowing that darkness comes near four on a winter afternoon in the Northwest,

Renae hurried to gather rags, vinegar, and water to accomplish the task. It was about 1:30 P.M. when she carried Shannah out and plopped her down on the grass in the sunshine, talking and singing to the baby while she worked on the windows.

On that Wednesday afternoon, Renae Wicklund suddenly became aware of someone walking toward them along the long driveway that led through the trees to her house. She saw a tall figure out of the corner of her eye and turned to stare directly at a youngish man with a copper cast to his hair. When she did that, he turned and walked back out to the main road. She thought he had probably been lost and realized when he saw her that he had the wrong house.

Leaving Shannah on the grass, she stepped into the house to grab some more rags. Moments later she returned and stood at the front door. The man was coming back, and this time he was moving fast.

As she would testify later in court, "He was running. Toward the house. Up our driveway. I thought that he was after Shannah, so I ran outside to grab her. And before we could get inside the house, he was pushing the door."

Renae, dressed lightly because of the balmy December day, tried to hold the front door shut with her body, but the man was much too strong, and she had Shannah in her arms. When he burst through the door, she saw that he had a knife in his right hand. Keeping her voice determinedly calm, she asked if there was something she could do for him—thinking that if she pretended she hadn't seen the knife, it still might not be too late.

It was too late. "Yeah," the intruder said. "Get your clothes off right now or I'll kill the kid, and I mean it."

He was holding the knife terribly close to Shannah. Renae Wicklund didn't have to decide what she would do. She put Shannah down at the stranger's order and slowly removed her boots, her purple corduroy shorts, her black sweater and vest, then sat down in a chair, waiting for what she feared would come next.

But he didn't want intercourse; he wanted oral sex. While her baby daughter screamed, she complied until her attacker was satisfied.

She prayed he wouldn't hurt them and was relieved to hear him mutter "Thanks" and saw that he was leaving. Sickened, she ran to the bathroom and washed out her mouth. Then she flung her clothes back on, grabbed Shannah, and ran across the street to the Hendricksons'. Barbara Hendrickson took one look at Renae's face and pulled her inside.

"Renae said there was a man outside and she was afraid he was going to come back," Barbara told deputies later. "And she looked out the window, and I promptly locked the door and got out my shotgun."

Both Renae and Shannah were very, very upset. The women barricaded themselves inside the Hendricksons' home with a loaded shotgun and called the Snohomish County Sheriff's Office. A deputy arrived at 2:25 P.M.

Renae Wicklund was able to give a good description of the man who had sexually assaulted her and threatened to kill her baby. She said he was very tall, with frizzy reddish hair, and that he'd worn blue jeans and a red and black plaid shirt. She thought he was in his early twenties. She had detected a faint odor of alcohol on his breath.

With her description, Snohomish County detectives narrowed in on Charles Rodman Campbell, twenty, as a possible suspect. He was tremendously tall, and his hair stuck out around his head like a dandelion gone to seed. He had been in trouble since he was old enough to leave his own yard.

Charles Campbell was born October 21, 1954, in Hawaii. His parents soon moved to Snohomish County. Campbell's early problems were not his fault. He was always *different*—and in so many ways. Because of his Hawaiian descent, the kids at his school teased him. Perhaps more damaging, Charles Campbell's sister was crippled, and some of the thoughtless kids not only tormented her but teased him about it, too, shouting cruel epithets at him. He fought to protect her, and out of sheer rage. Charles Campbell's parents tired of the responsibility of children early on and had long since defected, leaving the boy's grandparents to deal with him and his sister. They didn't know where to begin, and they were not particularly interested in raising another generation of children anyway.

Charles Campbell was an angry child from the very beginning, large and clumsy for his age with a chip on his shoulder. He was always fighting or running away. Detectives at the Edmonds, Washington, police department had dealt with him since before he hit junior high school. Even then they doubted that he would stay out of prison long. He had always seen the world as out to get him.

His first arrest came when he was sixteen years old after he stole a car. According to different sources, he stayed in school either through the ninth grade or the tenth—or the eleventh. Whichever, he was not a diligent student. He was too preoccupied, apparently, with drugs and alcohol.

Chuck Campbell married when he was nineteen, eloping with a twenty-two-year-old woman. His new in-laws were not impressed with him. The couple did not celebrate even a first wedding anniversary, divorcing after ten months. One month before their divorce, his wife gave birth to a child. He was ordered to pay $75 a month in child support, but his visitation rights were revoked after a judge decreed that he "poses a serious threat to the welfare of the child and the petitioner in that he has physically abused the child and petitioner in the past and neglected them." Since Campbell went to prison shortly thereafter, his ex-wife and child were assured that he would not visit.

That was why Snohomish County police were familiar with Charles Campbell. Once you saw a man six-and-a-half-feet tall with wild reddish hair and a kind of rage that almost vibrated, you didn't forget him—especially if you were a cop. They had a mug shot of him in their files. This photograph was included in a "lay-down," which they showed to Renae Wicklund two weeks after she was attacked.

Trembling but resolute, Renae Wicklund picked Campbell's picture immediately. "That's him."

Finding Charles Campbell would prove far more difficult than identifying him. It would be more than a year before Campbell was arrested and placed in a police lineup. On March 1, 1976, Renae Wicklund looked at the line of men through one-way glass and instantly picked Campbell from the lineup. He was the man who had forced her to perform fellatio sixteen months earlier.

Campbell argued that he could not possibly have been in Clearview on December 11, 1974. He claimed that he had been living and working as a cook at a pizza restaurant in Renton, Washington, almost 30 miles away during the period in question. He insisted he had punched in to work at 3:30 P.M. on December 11 and stayed in the kitchen throughout his shift.

A closer look into Campbell's background, however, brought forth information that stamped him as more than the average hardworking pizza cook. He was wanted for a drug violation in Snohomish County in late December 1974, and he had been working in Renton under the alias Dan Leslie Kile to avoid apprehension. He had quit his job at the pizza parlor very suddenly on December 14, 1974, the day Renton police began their investigation into the apparent theft of $1,200 from the restaurant's cash register.

Campbell admitted that he could not say exactly what he had done earlier in the day that the Wicklunds were attacked, but said it was his pattern to drink in the morning—"just enough to get a buzz on"— and that he had probably done so on that Wednesday. He said he didn't even know where Clearview was for certain and that he had never had any reason to go there—despite the fact he had lived in Snohomish County for fifteen years until he moved into his mother's home in Renton a month before the sex attack.

Charles Campbell's juvenile record showed arrests for auto theft, burglary, and resisting arrest, and that he had spent time at a juvenile detention center. In 1973 he had been charged with defrauding an innkeeper, and the 1974 drug charges had stemmed from his alleged possession of sixty tablets of amphetamines. And that was just in Snohomish County. Far across the Cascade Mountains, in Okanogan County, Campbell had been arrested in the fall of 1974—before the attack on Renae Wicklund—for violation of the federal firearms act, resisting arrest, criminal trespass, burglary, two counts of grand larceny, carrying a concealed weapon, and second-degree assault. Those charges were still extant.

All in all, Charles Campbell was not someone any woman would want to see running up her driveway.

Renae Wicklund was vastly relieved when Campbell was arrested after she identified him in March 1976. He was charged with one count of first-degree assault with intent to kill and one count of sodomy. By reporting what had happened to her, she had become one of the small percentage of women who have the courage to turn a sex criminal in to the police. Law enforcement authorities agree that statistics on sex crimes are almost impossible to chart accurately, that perhaps only one out of ten victims makes a police report. Women who have been raped and sexually molested are afraid and embarrassed. They are naturally hesitant to get on the witness stand and tell strangers in a courtroom the intimate details of an aberrant sexual attack.

But Renae Wicklund reported Campbell, and she got up in court and told it all. Her neighbor, Barbara Hendrickson, went on the stand, too. There was no way they could refuse to testify and face their consciences knowing that a monstrous criminal might go free to harm other women. Still, the ordeal was agonizing.

Under our justice system, the suspect has the right to face his accusers, and Renae had to testify about the sexual appetites of her attacker as Charles Campbell stared at her, this huge man with the piercing dark eyes.

Renae Wicklund's testimony was bolstered by testimony from a young woman who had once lived with Campbell. The woman said she lived near the Wicklunds' home and that Campbell had visited her often—including the week of the rape. Campbell's former lover said that he carried a knife and that he had told her, "You never know when you're going to need it."

The seven-woman, five-man jury found Charles Campbell guilty of both the assault and the sodomy. They also found that he had committed those crimes while in possession of a deadly weapon. At his sentencing, his prior record was introduced, and the consensus was that he was not fit to be on the streets for a very long time. Campbell had already pleaded guilty to second-degree burglary in the Okanogan County cases and had received up to fifteen years in prison with a five-year minimum. In Snohomish County, Judge Phillip Sheridan sentenced Campbell to another thirty years in prison with a seven-and-a-half-year minimum for the attack on the Wicklunds.

Charles Campbell's trial in the attack on Renae and Shannah lasted only three days. It didn't even rate a headline in the Everett papers.

The headlines would come later.

Renae Wicklund went home to pick up the pieces of her life, scarred as all sexual attack victims are by a pervasive fear that never quite goes away. Her marriage to Jack Wicklund broke up, partially from the lingering emotional trauma of the sex attack and partially for personal reasons. She and Shannah remained in the modest little white house in the woods, and Renae worked hard to support them. She worked as a beautician and also as an accountant for beauty parlors. She was a very intelligent woman and a single mother who wanted to be sure Shannah had everything she needed. Her own mother, Hilda, had always worked, and Renae's life was solidly grounded in the work ethic.

Renae remained on friendly terms with Jack after he moved out. She also stayed close to her in-laws, who lived in a little town in Kitsap County across Puget Sound. Jack's parents had always liked Renae. She joined their family get-togethers happily; her own mother and her sister Lorene were more than a thousand miles away in North Dakota. Renae was a great cook and brought food to every Wicklund holiday gathering, and she was a wonderful mother to Shannah, their granddaughter. Even though Renae was divorced from their son, she made sure that Jack's parents saw Shannah often.

Once they got used to Jack's being gone, Renae Wicklund and Shannah seemed to do all right. Don and Barbara helped out with chores Renae couldn't manage, and both the Hendricksons adored Shannah.

Jack Wicklund was the one who now became a target for violence. In December 1977 he was almost killed in a bizarre attack. Wicklund was found in his West Seattle home, tied to a chair and severely burned over most of his body. He was rushed to a hospital, but it was a long time before doctors would cautiously say he might live and even longer before Wicklund could give a statement. All he remembered was that a stranger had walked into his home carrying a package and wished him Merry Christmas. He insisted he had never seen the man before. The stranger then tied Jack to a chair, poured gasoline over him, and struck a match.

Miraculously, Jack Wicklund didn't die, but he was horribly scarred and lived with constant, unyielding pain. He was forced to wear a kind of rubber suit to minimize the formation of scar tissue.

In April 1978 Jack Wicklund left his parents' home in Hansville, Washington, after a visit. They were worried about his burns, and it had been awful for them to see their son in his strange rubber suit, but he was alive. A few hours after Jack left to go home, a Kitsap County coroner's deputy came to his parents' home and broke the news that Jack had been killed in a one-car accident on the Hansville Road. His car had left the road and crashed into a tree, killing him instantly. There were no witnesses. The ensuing investigation into Jack Wicklund's death never produced any definite answers as to why the crash had occurred. After surviving what should have been a fatal torching, Wicklund had met his fate on a lonely road. The curve where the car had left the road was known to be dangerous, but Wicklund had traversed the county road countless times before, and he knew the curve was there; he should have been prepared for it. Perhaps he had been temporarily blinded by oncoming headlights. If so, the other car hadn't stopped. Perhaps he had been run off the road.

Seattle police have never solved the murder attempt on Wicklund. Perhaps he was suicidal and it took him two tries to succeed in destroying himself. Perhaps he was involved in something unsavory or dangerous—or both. Or perhaps Jack Wicklund was only a very unlucky man.

The shock of the deliberate torching of her ex-husband and then his accidental death coming so hard on the heels of the murder attempt only served to heighten Renae Wicklund's constant anxiety. The attack by Charles Campbell had made her think that the world was a terribly dangerous place where tragedy waited just ahead. She could not help but wonder if the incidents were somehow connected, if they were more than just random misfortunes. She told friends and co-workers that she lived and walked in terror that something awful was going to happen again. And who could blame her?

Still, Renae Wicklund put on the facade of a cheerful, outgoing woman who was confident that she could take care of fatherless Shannah. Maybe trouble came in threes; people always said that. If that was true, then her three were all used up: the sexual attack, the burning, Jack's fatal car crash.

Renae Wicklund didn't know much about the workings of the justice system. She knew that Charles Campbell had been sent to the Monroe Reformatory—Washington's mid-level penal institution. Security was not as tight there as it was in the state penitentiary at Walla Walla, but it was much stronger than at Green Hill Academy, the boys' training school in Chehalis. Renae didn't care where Campbell was as long as he was locked up. All together, he had forty-five years hanging over him. That seemed like a safety net. Renae assumed that Campbell would be over sixty-five when he finally got out. By then Shannah would be middle-aged and Renae would be an old woman. They would probably have moved far away, too, maybe even back to North Dakota.

To a layman, forty-five years does sound like a long, long time. However, Charles Campbell's two sentences would run concurrently, not consecutively. Although it wasn't likely, it was within the realm of possibility that he could serve only the seven-and-a-half-year minimum and be released in 1983 or 1984. He would, of course, have to have some time off for good behavior to do that.

Renae had no idea that forty-five years didn't really *mean* forty-five years.

She and Shannah stayed in their old neighborhood, and Renae worked to keep the house and yard up. Shannah grew through the toddler stage and became a pretty little girl with straight shiny brown bangs, a pageboy haircut, and big brown eyes. Tall for her age, she was quiet and a little shy. She went to the Shepherd of the Hill Lutheran Church Sunday school and they teased her fondly about being their "little missionary" because she was always bringing a new friend along with her.

Renae had played the flute as a girl, and Shannah had ambitions to master it, too. She invited Don and Barb over for "a recital," and they clapped as if she were a child prodigy. She took dancing lessons, and Don Hendrickson took pictures of her in her costumes. Her grandpa Wicklund helped her learn how to ride a two-wheel bike.

The neighborhood in Clearview was a good place for a little girl to grow up, even though it might have been easier for Renae to live in a city apartment where she didn't have to cope with leaking roofs and broken plumbing and keeping a yard clear of weeds. She really counted on her neighbors. She and Shannah shopped at the Clearview market, and everybody knew both of them. Barbara Hendrickson's grandchildren grew up along with Shannah, and they often played together.

Renae proved to be a really clever businesswoman. She operated her accounting business for beauty parlors out of her own home, and her clients were pleased with her know-how and efficiency. She was expert in helping students get grants and loans to help them through beauty school. In early 1982 Renae was only thirty-one, but she was shouldering her responsibilities with great maturity.

If she thought about the man who had broken into her home eight years earlier—and those close to her say she did—the scary memories crept up full-blown only when the moon was hidden behind scudding clouds and the wind sighed in the tall trees around her little house. He was part of a nightmare she couldn't quite forget, but his image was gone when the sun rose again.

Renae bought a large dog, an Afghan hound, more to keep her company than for protection. Afghans are not particularly territorial or effective as watchdogs. But it would bark if anyone came around her property.

Less than 25 miles away, Charles Campbell was locked up in the Monroe Reformatory. He had earned the nickname "One Punch" because his fist was so powerful. He was a bully, and weaker inmates toadied to him, fearful of that fist. Guards were aware of Campbell's drug trafficking—*inside* prison—and his infraction record grew thicker and thicker.

Renae was serene in her belief that her attacker was locked up in prison and still had years and years to go on his sentence. Nevertheless, she was super-cautious, because she knew what could happen. Charles Campbell wasn't the only man who attacked women. Renae had strong locks on the doors and windows, and she warned Shannah never, never to go with strangers.

*   *   *

It snowed in early January 1982, and Don Hendrickson noticed footprints one morning outside the side windows of his home. Later that day, Renae told Barbara that she too had found footprints beneath her windows. Since her house stood so far back from the road, the large prints in the snow upset her.

Hilda Ahlers had been visiting Renae over Christmas, as she almost always did. Renae had never told her mother about the man who had attacked her seven years earlier.

"Renae was so strong," her mother said. "I never knew. She didn't want me to worry." But with the clarity of hindsight, Hilda would come to see that something was wrong that winter. "I remember one night when Renae's dog—who normally never barked at all—went wild and began barking fiercely. I thought there was something horrid outside, but I was afraid to look."

Not long after that, the Afghan nipped a neighbor's child, and Renae decided to give it away.

Looking back, Hilda Ahlers remembered more. "Another time, I saw Renae looking out the window at the road with the strangest look on her face. I said, 'What do you see out there?' and Renae just answered, 'Oh, nothing.' She didn't seem frightened; she was just watching so quietly."

Renae didn't know that Charles Campbell had been out of prison that weekend in January. Incredibly, and despite a stack of infractions, he had somehow earned time off for good behavior. He had served less than six years in prison, and he was already going out on furloughs.

Neither Renae nor the Hendricksons were aware of that. No one had bothered to tell them. Nor did anyone tell them when Campbell was transferred a month later to a work-release facility located less than ten miles from Clearview.

Renae missed the Easter service at church on April 11, 1982. She had a terribly sore throat. Don Hendrickson finally coaxed her into seeing a doctor. "I'll go with you; I'll hold your hand," he kidded. And he *did* hold her hand while an emergency room doctor examined her. She had strep throat, and she had to stay in bed for days, taking penicillin and trying to swallow the soft foods that Barb Hendrickson brought over to her.

April 14 was a Wednesday—just as it had been a Wednesday when Charles Campbell attacked Renae and Shannah in 1974. It was sunny but blustery, and the bright periods alternated with overhanging clouds. Daffodils, dogwood and fruit trees were in bloom, and spring had almost arrived. Except for the fact that Renae was sick, everything was normal. Barbara ran over in the morning to see how she was and found her a little better. She promised she would be back in the afternoon. Renae watched television and tried to read a little.

"Barb went out to the end of our driveway to get our mail that afternoon," Don remembers. "She met Shannah coming home from school and told her to tell Renae that she'd be over soon to make Jell-O. I remember it was 4:20 when Barb asked to borrow my watch; she wanted to use it to check Renae's pulse."

Barbara Hendrickson then headed toward Renae's house. There were no loud sounds from the Wicklund home, nothing to alarm any of the neighbors. She was gone for quite a while, but Don didn't think anything of it. She and Renae and Shannah often visited for hours.

It seemed to get dark earlier than usual that evening. A gale-force wind battered the Hendrickson house. Don glanced at the spot on his wrist where his watch usually was and then got up from his chair and checked a clock. He discovered that it was almost six. His wife had been gone for an hour and a half.

Don put on a jacket and walked down his driveway, across the street, and up Renae's long driveway. He usually went in through the sliding glass doors to the kitchen area. The glass doors were partly open and he paused. *That's odd,* he thought, and then he slid the doors open more and stepped into the house.

"The house was *so* quiet," he said later. "It was unlike anything I'd ever heard before—or since. Totally still. And then, as I got further into the house, I heard something—water running from a faucet somewhere."

It was the faucet in the kitchen sink. He turned the spigot off and listened for some other sound. There should have been three of them in the house—Barb, Renae, and Shannah—and they always made enough noise for six. He listened again, but he heard nothing. Don looked around the kitchen and shuddered involuntarily when he saw that a chair had been knocked over near the dinette set. That wasn't right. Renae always kept everything so neat. The silence kept Don from calling out to his wife or Renae or Shannah.

Donald Hendrickson found them in a few moments of horror that he will never forget.

He had left the kitchen and moved slowly toward the short hallway that led to the bedrooms. He found Barbara first. His wife of thirty-four years lay motionless in the hallway, her throat slashed, the arteries severed. Even as he knelt beside her, he knew she was gone. A halo of blood soaked the carpet beneath her head and stained her beautiful prematurely silver hair. It was a scene that Don Hendrickson would never, ever be able to erase from his memory.

His wife's throat had been slit from one side to the other with a razor-sharp knife, allowing the blood to course out of her jugular vein and carotid arteries. She could have lived only moments before she bled to death.

Numb with shock, Don got up from Barbara's side and continued to make his way down the hall. He didn't want to, but he had to see what was behind the other doors. Shannah's bedroom was empty. He moved to Renae's bedroom next, pausing at the door before he made himself turn and look inside.

They were both there on the floor. Renae was nude—her body hideously bruised and her throat slashed with macabre efficiency. Shannah lay across the room from her mother. She had been almost decapitated by a knife's merciless edge. Nine years old, with her throat cut. All of them dead.

Automatically Don Hendrickson picked up the phone with nerveless fingers and dialed 911. Then he walked outside to try to make his mind function. "I heard a car engine start up," he said. "It was Renae's next-door neighbor and her daughters, and I ran out and shouted at them, 'Shannah and Renae are dead!' But they just looked at me, and then they got out of their car and ran back into their house. I think they were afraid of me because I was acting so wild."

Snohomish County deputies arrived shortly. They took one look at the carnage inside the Wicklund home and radioed in for the homicide detectives. What they encountered on April 14 would mean days of working almost around the clock. The public had no idea at first how ghastly the triple murder was. The Clearview story hit the media as a very short, deliberately succinct news bulletin. The detectives released almost no information: "Three people were found dead on April 14 in south Snohomish County. . . ."

Lieutenant Glenn Mann and Sergeant Joe Belinc would head the probe. If anyone could sort out the real story behind what had happened in the little rambler in Clearview, these men could. In addition, they would have twenty-nine investigators working on the Wicklund-Hendrickson case before it was finished. Belinc had been the driving force behind the apprehension of Washington's infamous Bellevue Sniper in the early 1970s. Now he had another headline case to work.

Someone had gotten into the Wicklund home, someone strong enough to overpower two women; the youngster could not have been much of an adversary. It appeared that Barbara Hendrickson had broken free and was, perhaps, running for help when she was struck down in the hall. It was even possible that Renae Wicklund and Shannah were already dead when Barbara Hendrickson entered the home. She might have called out to them, or she might have felt the same dread that her husband felt an hour later, might have heard the same thundering silence and been afraid—only to encounter the person with the knife and realize at the last moment that she had walked into horror.

The Snohomish County investigators spent hours at the scene, looking for bits of physical evidence that the killer might have left behind. The bodies were photographed where they lay before they were released to the Snohomish County coroner's deputies. Saddened and shocked neighbors stood at the edge of the crime-scene search area, along with cameramen from the news media who shot footage of the body bags being loaded into a station wagon–hearse for removal to await autopsy. It did not seem possible to them that Renae and Shannah and Barbara were dead. This couldn't have happened, not so suddenly and so quietly on an April day. One neighbor murmured how frightened she was, wondering if some madman was on the loose, waiting somewhere in the thick trees to strike again.

The investigators began a door-to-door canvass. They found no one who had heard or seen anything—but they did hear again and again that this was not the first time that Renae Wicklund had been the victim of a madman. Everyone knew that Renae had been attacked eight years before, and those close to her recalled that she had lived in a state of quiet terror ever since. She had feared that he might come back one day and wreak revenge upon her for testifying against him. No amount of reassurance that she had probably been a random victim, that he had probably forgotten all about her, could convince her.

She had seemed to know that she was doomed, that he—or someone—would destroy the safe walls she'd tried to build around herself and Shannah. And yet everyone described Renae as a wonderful person, a good friend, an intelligent hard worker. The extent of her friends' and neighbors' grief demonstrated just what a good person she had been. And so had Barbara Hendrickson. Once, Barbara had loaded a shotgun to protect Renae and Shannah. This time, she hadn't had the opportunity to seize a weapon to fight back. The slash wounds across each victim's throat stamped the killings as executions—cold-blooded, effective, designed to kill as if that was the murderer's only mission. He had wanted them dead. It seemed that simple. The child? She couldn't have harmed the killer, but she was old enough and smart enough to describe him, and so she had to die too. It seemed impossible that anyone could have had a grudge against a nine-year-old girl.

The detectives questioned Don Hendrickson, asking who he thought might have had reason to kill his wife and neighbors. He finally said, "The only person I could imagine that might have done this is the man who raped Renae."

At the time, he could not even remember Charles Campbell's name. Campbell was history, or he was supposed to be. But when the detectives checked on Campbell's whereabouts, they were shocked to find out that he had been living and working a short distance from Clearview, *without supervision*, almost every day.

The word from the Department of Corrections was not only startling; it was appalling. Records showed that in October 1981— less than six years after his conviction for raping Renae Wicklund— Charles Campbell had been moved to a minimum-security facility known as Monroe House. He worked there as a cook, and he was still confined, but eligible for furloughs. On February 24, six weeks before the triple murders in Clearview, Campbell moved even closer to complete freedom: he was released from the prison itself and assigned to an Everett work-release residence two blocks from the Snohomish County Courthouse. This meant that he would work outside during the day, sleep in the facility at night, and had to follow strict rules. In his case, particularly, he was to abstain from alcohol and drug use.

Even though Campbell was literally free for much of each day and within a dozen miles of the Clearview home where the 1974 attack had occurred, even though he was housed two blocks from the Snohomish County Courthouse, there was no notification to the sheriff's office. Some might say it was like dumping a fox in the chicken house without letting the farmer know.

On the night of the murders—April 14—Charles Campbell returned to the work-release residence obviously under the influence of alcohol. His blood alcohol reading was .29—almost three times higher than Washington's legal level for intoxication. Tests also detected the presence of morphine, codeine, quinine, methadone, and cocaine!

Because he had broken the cardinal rule of the halfway house, Campbell was taken back to the Monroe Reformatory. Of course, by then, Renae Wicklund, Shannah Wicklund, and Barbara Hendrickson were dead. They had neither been consulted nor informed about Campbell's early release in February. What happened to them was shocking, but the most shocking part of the horror was that it was preventable. There were so many ways the inexorable path to violent murder could have been blocked.

Back in the Monroe Reformatory, Charles Campbell was charged with three counts of aggravated first-degree murder on April 19, 1982. With the news that Charles Campbell had been charged with the three murders, citizens of Snohomish County—and, indeed, citizens all over the state—began to react with disbelief and anger. The owner of Rick's Clearview Foods, Rick Arriza, placed a petition in his small grocery store, where the victims had shopped, asking for signatures from residents demanding the death penalty for Campbell if he was convicted. People came from all around the state to sign it.

Along with the anger, there was fear. The number of women reporting rapes and other sexual assaults dropped dramatically. Women were afraid to report rapes. If they couldn't be sure that the men who had attacked them would be put away for a long time, if they had to fear violent reprisal, then they decided that it was safer just to forget what had happened—and try to live with it.

Sheriff Bobby Dodge, Lieutenant Mann, Sergeant Belinc, and their crews of detectives worked under great constraint. They had a job to do which required an orderly progression to bring a solid case against Campbell. They would not—could not—talk to reporters, and they took the flak stoically. Snohomish County sheriff Bobby Dodge did appear on television decrying the system that had allowed a man like Campbell, with all the crimes he'd been convicted of, back into the same community where the crime against the Wicklunds had occurred—and without any notification to law enforcement authorities.

On May 1, 1982, Charles Campbell, now twenty-seven, appeared before Judge Dennis Britt and entered a plea of innocent. He was ordered to undergo psychiatric testing. Possibly a defense attorney would use the results later to enter a plea of innocent by reason of insanity. The hugely tall Campbell wore handcuffs and leg irons, and spectators were searched with metal detectors before they were allowed into the courtroom. Campbell wanted to go to Western State Hospital for testing, but the roster of sex criminals who had escaped from that mental hospital to do more damage to innocent citizens was too long already. Judge Britt ordered that Campbell would meet with psychiatrists in his jail isolation cell.

The first reports on Campbell's six years at the Monroe Reformatory indicated that he had a good record there. Parole board members were aware that Campbell had made a suicide attempt in custody in 1976, and he had been watched closely by the board, but they refused to comment on the prisoner's psychiatric records. Campbell's attorneys said he had acknowledged that he had a problem with alcohol and drugs and that he thought himself a "borderline case" who "snapped" when he was drinking and blacked out.

In a case that grew steadily more bizarre, the *Seattle Times* reported that one of the witnesses interviewed by homicide detectives was a drug and alcohol counselor who had participated in a program in the Monroe Reformatory until about 1980. According to records of her former employer, the young female counselor had resigned because she had broken one of the first rules of counseling by becoming romantically involved with her "patient." The patient was Charles Campbell. The woman refused to comment, but a relative admitted that Campbell had been a visitor in their home in early 1982 while he was on a furlough from prison.

Campbell's alleged close personal relationship with the woman was borne out by a notation in the Monroe House files on January 28, 1982. Campbell had returned from a furlough and said he was in a car that had hit a pole northwest of Monroe. The car, a 1974 Volkswagen, was found, abandoned, by a Washington State trooper. It was totaled, and the pole was heavily damaged. The trooper checked with the Department of Motor Vehicles for the car's registration and found that it belonged to the woman who had been a counselor at the prison. She later told her insurance agency that it had been wrecked, but no charges were ever brought because troopers could not determine who had been driving the Volkswagen.

Campbell may have had charm for one woman, but another, his ex-wife, seemed unimpressed by his charisma. She reported to a detective in the town where she lived that Campbell—whom she, too, believed was still in prison at the time—had come to her home on Christmas Day 1981 and raped her. She said he had returned twice to rape her again. She had finally gone to the police on March 16 and attempted to make a formal complaint of rape against Campbell but the police had advised her the case seemed too weak to bring to court.

This was the man who Renae Wicklund believed was safely behind prison walls. He had only been 12 miles away, working days in a landscaping firm, apparently maintaining some kind of romantic relationship with his former drug counselor and allegedly assaulting his ex-wife. There was another factor. He had come to the attention of work-release authorities on March 18 for "having possession of or consuming beer at Everett Work Release." A female officer found a partially filled can of beer on his bed and noted that the room smelled of alcohol.

This report enraged Campbell. He hated having the female officers at the facility write him up, and he showed his resentment openly. He argued with them about even the slightest order they gave him. He said he had much more freedom in his social outings when he had furloughs from the reformatory. He felt he should have complete freedom to do what he wanted while he was in work release.

A hearing had been held about his "poor attitude and behavior" toward two women officers, but he was allowed to remain in work release. He was given a second chance primarily because of his good record while in prison.

But *was* his record that good in prison?

A look at Charles Rodman Campbell's "good behavior" was startling. For some reason, when Campbell came up before the parole board seeking work release, the paperwork that came with him cited only three minor infractions during his first year at Monroe and referred to him as a "model prisoner" thereafter. The infractions mentioned were not that bad: mutilating a curtain; possessing "pruno" (an alcoholic beverage that cons distill from yeast and any fruit or vegetable matter they can get their hands on: potatoes, apples, oranges); and refusing to allow a guard to search him for a club he had hidden under his jacket. He said he carried the club to ward off attacks by bullies in the yard.

After these minor incidents—more indicative of the behavior of a bad boy than a dangerous con—the superintendent of the state reformatory indicated to the parole board that Campbell's record was spotless.

Not quite.

After Campbell had won his furloughs and his work-release assignment, *after* Renae and Shannah Wicklund and Barbara Hendrickson had their throats slit, and *after* Campbell was charged with those crimes, the head of the guards' union at the reformatory said that Campbell had used drugs as recently as the year prior to his work release.

It was obvious that someone had been covering up for Charles Campbell. Shortly after Campbell was transferred to the work-release program, the Washington State parole board discovered that the Monroe Reformatory had failed to forward copies of prison infractions to them. Hundreds of prisoners had been released without having their behavior in prison evaluated. And Charles Campbell was one of those prisoners who had slipped through the fissures in the justice system.

KIRO-TV in Seattle managed to obtain additional infraction reports on Campbell, incidents that occurred between December 31, 1977, and June 13, 1978; these infractions were never revealed to the parole board beyond a cursory notation in a counselor's report, which mentioned that Campbell had threatened a nurse and gotten into a beef with another inmate. According to the records, the huge bushy-haired con had lunged at the nurse on New Year's Eve 1977, when she refused to give him his medication because he was an hour late reporting to the hospital. "When I refused to give him the medication late," the nurse had said, "he jumped to his feet with his fists clenched and moved toward me in a threatening manner, as though he intended to hit me."

A staff member had stepped between Campbell and the female nurse, and a guard had dragged Campbell away while he shouted obscenities at her. On May 8, 1978, Campbell had kicked another inmate in the groin and ignored a guard's order to move on in a stand-off that lasted until additional guards arrived. Later that month, Campbell had cut into the chow line and angered other prisoners. He refused to move on and broke a tray in half in his hands. The situation was fraught with tension in the mess hall full of convicts. On May 24, Campbell was discovered high on drugs. He fought guards like a tiger until they got his jacket off and found an envelope in it containing three empty yellow capsules.

A month later Campbell again balked at a body search and tossed an envelope to another con. Guards recovered it and found a syringe and needle inside. He was punished with the removal of privileges for these infractions, but even his guards were afraid of him. They asked administrators to transfer Campbell from Monroe to the state penitentiary at Walla Walla. Nothing came of this request.

None of this information was available to the parole board when it came time for Campbell's parole hearing.

When the news of Charles Campbell's actual prison behavior reached the media, Washington State legislators immediately scheduled an investigation. One state senator put it bluntly: "Somebody obviously held back information that caused the death of three people." Prison administrators argued that the parole board had asked *not* to see all the minor infractions, and that they had held back the reports for that reason.

Charles Campbell apparently scared the hell out of a lot of people, guards and fellow prisoners alike. He was so big, so muscular, and so quick to erupt into rage. Guards who had reservations about Campbell's suitability for parole didn't want their names published, but said off the record that they thought he should have been sent back to prison.

Even more frightened of seeing his name in print was an ex-convict who had served time with Campbell; the label "snitch" is a sure way to commit suicide in or out of prison for an ex-con. But the anonymous man recalled that Charles Campbell had ruled his fellow inmates with terror, forcing the weaker cons to obtain drugs for him and to submit to sodomy. Prison "prestige" belonged to the physically strong.

It is quite likely that no one will ever know what really happened on April 14, 1982. The victims are dead, and the murderer chose not to speak of his crimes.

Charles Campbell went on trial in November 1982. If he was convicted of aggravated murder in the first degree, he could be sentenced to death. To accomplish that, the state had to prove that Campbell's crimes fit within the parameters of the statute as follows:

- He was serving a prison term in a state facility or program at the time of the murders.
- The victims had previously testified against him in a court of law.
- Campbell allegedly committed the murders to conceal his identity.
- There was more than one victim and the murders were part of a common scheme or plan.

- The murders were committed along with other crimes, including first-degree rape, first-degree robbery, and first-degree burglary.

They were all true. Renae Wicklund had been raped as her stalker wreaked his revenge. Her jewelry was stolen. Allegedly Charles Campbell attempted to sell the missing jewelry hours after the slayings. The burglary charges would indicate that the defendant made illegal entry into the home—by force or subterfuge.

Charles Campbell asked for a change of venue to another state, claiming that he could not receive a fair trial in the state of Washington because of the media coverage. His request was denied.

On November 26, 1982, the day after Thanksgiving, the jury retired to debate the question of Campbell's guilt or innocence. They returned after only four hours. They had found the defendant guilty. Guilty on three counts of aggravated first-degree murder.

In the penalty phase of his trial, Charles Campbell was sentenced to death. At first he refused to cooperate with his attorneys' efforts to have his life spared. They appealed, but he said it was against his wishes.

He would spend years on death row in the Washington State penitentiary in Walla Walla, a fearsome figure who spat at Governor Booth Gardner when he had the temerity to peer through the bulletproof-glass window in Campbell's cell. For a man who one day soon might beg Gardner to stay his execution at the last minute, it was an incredibly stupid show of temper.

Campbell was visited regularly by his mistress, the ex-alcohol counselor and her child—Charles Campbell's son. They seemed a strangely mismated couple.

As the years passed and his attorneys continued to appeal his death sentence, Campbell was disdainful of their efforts on his behalf. All the while, he was drawing nearer and nearer to the hangman's noose. In March of 1989 he came within two days of being executed when his attorneys won a stay from the U.S. Ninth Circuit Court of Appeals. The three-judge panel agreed to listen to Campbell's attorneys' appeal, which contended he had been denied his right to a fair trial because he was not present when his jury was selected. (*He* had refused to come to court.)

The second issue was that having to choose the means of one's death was cruel and unusual punishment. (When Washington State added death by lethal injection to its roster of execution methods, Charles Campbell had balked. He would not choose, he insisted. In essence, the state was forcing him to commit suicide by saying which method of execution he preferred.) "That's against my religion," he said smugly.

The Ninth Circuit Court panel heard arguments in Campbell's case in June 1989, but the judges did not hand down their decision for two and a half years. In April 1992 they rejected Campbell's arguments— but later granted his request to have the same issues reheard by an eleven-judge panel. In addition, Charles Campbell and his team of attorneys filed another federal petition, his third. He lost the latter, but the second is still pending.

In the decade since his conviction, Charles Campbell has apparently come to believe that he too is mortal and that there is a fairly good possibility that the state of Washington *is* going to kill him. By the time Charles Campbell began to cooperate in the endless series of appeals, it may have been too late.

When Westly Allan Dodd, a murderous pedophile, was executed on Washington State's gallows on January 5, 1993, the state broke its thirty-five-year pattern of not carrying out the death penalty. Charles Campbell is expected to be executed before 1993 is over. Whether the execution will be by hanging or lethal injection is the only question left.

Few tears will be shed.

Renae and Shannah Wicklund are buried side by side in James-town, North Dakota, far from Clearview, Washington. Hilda Ahlers came to Clearview to settle their affairs, and grocer Rick Arriza drove her to the Clearview Elementary School to pick up Shannah's belongings. There wasn't much, because nine years is not enough time to gather much—beyond love. "I took her up to the school," Arizza recalled. "We picked up Shannah's things—glue, storybooks, an umbrella, notebooks. She just started crying."

Hilda Ahlers rarely sleepwalks anymore, but she did for years, reliving the moment she first learned of Renae's and Shannah's deaths.

"There was a light tap on my door at three A.M.," she recalls. "And I said, 'Who is it?' and this small voice said, 'It's me,' and I knew it was Lorene. I was so frightened when I opened the door, wondering which one of my grandchildren I'd lost. But Lorene was standing there holding her littlest one, and her husband, Jerry, was standing beside her with their other two children.

"I remember saying to myself, Thank God, they're all there, and then I looked behind them and I saw our pastor, and I knew it had to be Renae.

"'Airplane accident?' I asked.

"'No.'

"'Car accident?'

"'No . . . murdered.'

"My mind flew to Shannah. Who was looking after Shannah? And then I heard Lorene say, 'Shannah too.'"

The Hit Person:
Equal Opportunity Murder

The case described in *"The Hit Person: Equal Opportunity Murder" is unique, I believe, because neither the victim nor the killer was what we have come to expect. But murder, like tornadoes, earthquakes, and hurricanes, is not predictable. The pattern is forever being broken, rearranged, and mutated.*

"The Hit Person" is also a case where, even now, questions remain unanswered. The reader will have to decide if justice was accomplished, partially accomplished—or never served at all.

If one was at all inclined to believe in fate or karma or destiny—whatever word works—the story of Wanda Emelina Norewicz Touchstone would serve to validate that belief. She had come halfway around the world to start a new life. She was an immigrant, but a modern-day immigrant—vitally attractive and brilliant. The life Wanda had foreseen in America never came to pass, and she was both bitterly disappointed and frightened by the reality of her situation. Still, on August 11, 1980, Wanda was beginning to believe that she had the power to turn things around. She was only thirty-four, and she had finally begun to feel *free.*

August 11 was a warm and sunny Monday in Seattle. There is no indication at all that Wanda had reason to be apprehensive as she set out from her bachelor apartment near the University of Washington. More likely, she had every reason to believe that the pleasant weekend just past signaled that her years of worry were over. She had some errands to do, and she ticked them off in her mind as she drove along the wide tree-shaded streets of the U. District.

In truth, she had only a half hour to live.

Wanda Touchstone was born in Lodz, Poland, on Valentine's Day, 1946. She missed World War II by months and was too young to notice the havoc that war had brought to her homeland. She heard the stories, of course, as she grew up and saw the skeletons of bombed-out buildings, but the war wasn't *real* to her. Wanda grew up, went to university, and became a high school biology teacher. Despite her dark-haired beauty, she remained single, but she wasn't an old-maid schoolteacher; she was vibrant and fun, and her students loved her.

Wanda made a trip to California to see an aunt and uncle in 1975 and fell totally in love with America. She longed to stay in the United States, and she was willing to work at any job so she *could* remain. She answered a want ad in a Palo Alto paper, an ad for a housekeeper. The position was far beneath her educational and cultural background, but it was a start.

The gentleman advertising for household help was Samuel Lewis Touchstone, a.k.a. Robert Lewis Preston, age fifty-eight, a very wealthy real estate entrepreneur in the San Jose area. Touchstone apparently liked Wanda's credentials. He also stared with approval at the slender, high-cheekboned Wanda as he interviewed her. She was hired.

It wasn't surprising that Lew Touchstone's interest in the pretty Pole soon turned to more than that of an employer for an employee; he didn't want to lose her company when her temporary visa ran out. The simplest solution would have been for him to marry her. That wasn't possible, however, because Lew Touchstone was already legally married. But he did have an unmarried son, Ron Touchstone, who lived in Texas. Lew prevailed upon his son to go through a civil ceremony with Wanda, and a "paper only" marriage took place in 1976. There is no evidence that Wanda ever lived with the younger Touchstone, but their marriage was legal and it allowed her to stay in the United States while Lew Touchstone untangled himself from his current wife. When that was accomplished, Wanda was divorced from Ron Touchstone in March 1977.

In May 1977, the now-single Lew Touchstone and Wanda moved from San Jose, California, to Redmond, Washington, where Lew built them a wonderfully lavish house. Wanda had expected that she and Lew would get married right away, now that all the legal impedimenta were out of the way, but Lew found it more romantic for them to simply live together. He recalled the summer of 1977 as a "rather happy" time.

But Wanda wanted to get married. Lew recalled that he wasn't too anxious to move into a third marriage after having gone through two previous liaisons that ended in divorce. He said, too, that he was concerned about their twenty-six-year age difference, and feared that any marriage might end in divorce with a messy fight over property. It would be *his* property, his extensive land holdings and contracts, because Wanda owned nothing beyond her clothes.

Lew Touchstone remembered that it was Wanda who suggested a prenuptial agreement where what was his before marriage would remain his and what was hers would remain hers. Affidavits filed by Wanda indicated that it was Lew who wanted the agreement.

They were unable to reach a compromise, however, and the possibility that they would marry seemed remote. Wanda returned to

Poland in August 1977, a little disillusioned with her relationship with Lew Touchstone. They were never going to be able to make it work. He expected an "old country" wife, and she was a modern and intelligent woman, an equal partner, she hoped, for a husband. A month later Lew followed her to Poland and the couple discussed reconciliation, but nothing came of it, and he went back to America alone. Still, Lew Touchstone couldn't forget the woman he'd lived with for two years; he went back to Poland again in February 1978, and this time the couple decided to get married. Was it true love? Who knows? Marriages are made for all manner of reasons. Some of them work, and some of them fail miserably. In light of later events, it would seem that the marriage between Lew and Wanda was not made in heaven.

Wanda flew back to America in April, 1978, and she and Lew were married in Carson City, Nevada, on May 19, 1978. On August 1 she signed the prenuptial agreement that released Lew from granting her any of his property in case of divorce. Because she was not yet fluent in English, the wording of an agreement Lew asked her to sign was impossible for Wanda to understand. She signed it, believing that she could trust her new husband and that he would not have asked her to sign a paper that was unfair.

They seemed to get along well enough for the first year of their marriage. Lew says he gave Wanda $3,000 from one of his land sales "to show her that I loved her and was going to try to make her happy." He also presented her with a diamond ring worth almost $17,000, plus two other diamond rings of lesser—but considerable— value. Even before the marriage, Lew Touchstone had added a fifth car to his stable of vehicles, a Chevrolet El Camino pickup. He told Wanda that it was her car.

By late 1979 the honeymoon phase of their relationship was over and the marriage was in deep trouble.

Lew was clearly disappointed that the compliant young woman from Poland was uninterested in being only a housewife, dedicated to caring for him and their home; Wanda was, of course, a woman of some intellect and yearned to study for an advanced degree in microbiology. First she attended a vocational school where she became considerably more adept with the English language. She was then admitted to the University of Washington to study microbiology, and she planned to have her degree by December 1980. Her commute across the floating bridges of Lake Washington to the university and her need to study didn't leave her as much time for Lew as he wanted.

At least that was what Lew would claim in the divorce action. According to his affidavits, Wanda didn't cook for him, and they ate together only when he took her out to dinner. He had placed his original ad seeking a good Polish cook, something to remind him of his own early days. She had cooked for him when he employed her, but now that he had married her, she had no time for making kielbasa and rich stews and fancy breads. Lew complained that Wanda did only her own laundry and refused to wash the sheets from his bed. It was *his* bed alone; they had separate bedrooms. All in all, there wasn't much togetherness.

Wanda confided in letters to friends and relatives that her elderly husband was stingy, and she referred to him as a "boor" and an "old goat." She was angry because he kept taking her diamond rings back and he wanted his El Camino back, too. Whether the chicken or the egg came first is hard to determine in retrospect. Lew wanted a housekeeper, bed partner, and full-time companion, and he felt Wanda had broken her premarital promises. Wanda had apparently wanted a protector in a strange country, a college education, a companion, and had expected that they would share whatever wealth evolved through their years together.

Each had made a bad bargain.

There is no evidence that Wanda was unfaithful to Lew before she moved out in April 1980 and began divorce proceedings. She wasn't greedy in the least in her requests from him. She asked only for enough money to pay her tuition at the university and for maintenance in the amount of $600 a month. Lew Touchstone could have afforded many times that amount. Wanda also wanted her $17,000 wedding-engagement ring back. Lew had taken it away in their last argument. Wanda said her husband was "quite wealthy" and that their home in Redmond was worth well over $100,000. (In 1993 that property would be worth close to half a million dollars.)

Wanda felt Lew wanted a divorce because he was about to close a real estate deal that would net him a huge amount of money and he didn't want to risk having to share any profits with her. In fact, Wanda thought Lew was due to get almost a million dollars from his current sale. Beyond that, he would still have property in Washington and California that was worth a great deal. She listed other assets as a Caterpillar tractor and heavy equipment used in building homes.

Their parting had not been amicable, and Wanda was afraid of her estranged husband. She asked the judge for a restraining order against Lew, saying he had been violent with her before and that she feared what he might do to her now that she was asking for something for herself.

Whatever his wealth may have been, it was surely considerable; Lew Touchstone refused to list his assets or even state his income in his divorce action.

It was an untenable situation for Wanda Touchstone. She wanted to divorce Lew, but if she did, she faced deportation. Her attorney advised her to ask only for a legal separation for two years. After that, she could divorce Touchstone and remain in the country legally. Lew wanted out. Maybe.

Lew agreed through his attorney to provide maintenance for Wanda in the amount of $400 a month until December 1980. He grudgingly let her take the El Camino with her when she moved into the bachelor apartment near the university.

Some who knew them say that Lew wanted Wanda back and that he tried to court her again. He was over sixty and she was still in her early thirties. It wasn't likely he would find another woman as beautiful or as young as Wanda. He had gone through so much to make himself available to be with her, and he took the sting of her rejection badly.

But Wanda, who had written to relatives in the old country only two months after the wedding, saying, "I can't stand him anymore," certainly didn't want to go back. Once she moved to the U. District, her life became full and exciting. She was welcomed into Seattle's Polish community, where she danced the dances of her youth and ate the food familiar to her. She also met a tall, handsome bearded man who had come from Poland several years before, John Sophronski.*

John was as gentle as Lew had been aggressive, and he cared for her. They spent time together at parties in the Polish community, and they picnicked on the shores of Lake Washington. They may have begun to fall in love—but time was short.

Once she was on her own, with all the time in the world to study the demanding courses in microbiology, Wanda's progress toward her degree accelerated, and she learned she would graduate at the end of the summer quarter, 1980. With her degree, she would be able to support herself. She planned a vacation and looked at larger apartments. She was happy, not only for herself but for her sister in Sweden who had just given birth to a son.

Wanda hadn't the faintest notion that on that day in August someone was stalking her—stalking her with a specific purpose in mind: murder. As unlikely a target for execution as Wanda Touchstone was, her stalker would prove even more implausible. Even in such a chaotic event as murder, there are certain patterns of behavior that a good homicide detective can usually expect. That would not be true in this case.

The first call for help shrilled in on the 911 line at 2:15 P.M. on August 11. Patrol Sergeant Doug Fritschy was the initial officer on the scene as his patrol car, blue lights whirling, pulled to a stop in front of a walled-in parking lot between 5218 and 5214 University Way N.E. Officers Linda Whitt and Paul Gracy arrived just behind him. The three responding officers were led into the parking lot by Leon Orwitz,* the owner of an insurance company whose offices edged one side of the lot.

"There," he said in a panic. "The injured woman's over there. I found her on the ground with blood coming out of a hole in her neck. Couldn't get a pulse."

A slender dark-haired woman dressed in a blue skirt, red-and-blue-striped blouse, and white sandals lay motionless on the hot asphalt paving. She had fallen between a blue El Camino pickup and a white Valiant, and her blood had pooled beneath her and then made a meandering scarlet path down a slight incline.

Paramedics from Medic 16 were preparing to remove the woman to the hospital, but they shook their heads as they answered Sergeant Fritschy's unspoken question.

"No pulse. She's comatose. Looks like a brain wound."

As the medic's rig went screaming off toward Harborview Medical Center, the officers were joined by a crew from the Crimes Against Persons Unit in downtown Seattle: Captain John Leitch, Lieutenant Ernie Bisset, Sergeant Jerry Yates, and Detectives Danny Engle, Billy Baughman, Dick Steiner, Al Lima, and J. E. Lundin—all of whom would try to make some sense out of the scene.

The area of the parking lot was immediately cordoned off from the crowd of onlookers with the familiar yellow tape that police carry. Detectives used syringes to draw blood samples from the red pools, which were already beginning to coagulate in the hot sun. One expended slug had been located under the Valiant and given to Sergeant Fritschy, who retained it for evidence.

The driver's door of the El Camino was open, as if the occupant had intended to step out for just a moment. There was a woman's purse on the front seat.

Detectives Lima and Lundin began interviewing four witnesses at the scene. One of them was Orwitz, the insurance broker. He was able to identify the injured woman easily enough; she had just left his place of business.

"Her name is Wanda Touchstone," he said. "She had an appointment with my wife to talk about car insurance. She came in about five minutes after two. While she was giving my wife some info for the policy, I stepped out to the lot—that's my car in the first stall there—to get some papers."

Orwitz said he opened his car door and caught sight of a woman standing near the El Camino. "She just stared at me." He remembered that the woman was a blond, and fairly short and slim.

Wanda Touchstone had headed for the lot as Orwitz went back to his office. He was inside only a moment when he and his wife heard a bang, a pause, and then two more bangs.

"I thought it was a muffler, but my wife said it sounded like shots. I ran out and I saw the woman I'd seen before walking out of the lot. I almost said hi, but I didn't. I didn't see anything, and I went back inside."

Mere moments had passed.

Suddenly two women had come bursting into the agency, screaming, "Someone's been shot!" The women, university students, were also repeating a license number over and over: "UKN-524."

Leaving his wife to call 911, Orwitz ran to the lot and found Wanda behind her car, bleeding and unresponsive.

Lima and Lundin talked next to the young female witnesses, Nell Boles* and Jan Winn.* They said they had been walking past the opening to the parking lot when they heard shots and then saw a small woman in a long gray-blue dress come rushing out. "She was bent over, and she was clutching something like a black purse. She walked down the block and got into a red car," Winn said. "I wrote down the license number."

Detective Al Lima had Jan Winn initial the scrap of paper with the license number on it, and then he initialed it and dated it before retaining it for evidence.

Detectives Danny Engle and Billy Baughman were searching the El Camino. The purse left on the seat contained identification papers for Wanda Preston (Touchstone also used Preston as a surname), $38.93 in coin and currency, and the usual makeup articles most women carry. It was bagged to be checked for prints.

Nell Boles and Jan Winn had to have come very close to being eyewitnesses, and they fought to retain their composure as the investigators urged them to remember all they could. Nell Boles said she had definitely heard the victim scream.

"Then I saw this woman hurrying out. She was about five three, 115 pounds, and she had blond hair—rolled up, with a pink and white scarf tied under her chin. She might be in her mid-thirties. It just happened so fast."

The license number of the suspect's car was fed into the Department of Motor Vehicles computers by Detective Gary Fowler, and the hit came up quickly. The car was a red Datsun 200 SX, and the legal owner was the Hertz Rent-a-Car corporation. Fowler phoned the Hertz branch at Sea-Tac Airport and learned that car had been rented to a Cynthia Mahler the day before. The woman had presented a California driver's license and a credit card for identification at the time she picked up the car.

"She told us that her local address would be at the Motel 6," the Hertz representative told Fowler.

Wanda Touchstone was, for all intents and purposes, dead when the medics delivered her to the Harborview emergency entrance, and the surgery that followed was fruitless.

But why? Who would shoot a woman who was just going about her daily errands? Her purse wasn't rifled; nothing seemed to be missing. And yet from Orwitz's statement, it seemed that the killer had been waiting beside Wanda's car when she left his office—waiting to shoot her. And the person he had seen moments before the shooting was a woman.

Detectives Billy Baughman and Danny Engle, who would be given chief responsibility for the Touchstone homicide, were about to be plunged into the strangest case of their careers, a case that would set legal precedents in Washington State.

An all-points bulletin was broadcast during that late afternoon of August 11, asking every lawman in Seattle to be on the lookout for a red Datsun with license plate UKN-524, probably driven by a petite blond woman. The news of the Touchstone murder hit the media almost as fast, and citizens, too, were asked to look for the car.

In the meantime the streets of Seattle's north end were alive with patrol cars. It isn't often that detectives are fortunate enough to get witnesses with enough presence of mind to jot down the license number of a murder suspect, and every officer on the Seattle force wanted to be sure the red Datsun didn't slip through their web.

Nick Costos,* a purchasing agent for a firm in the north end, was listening to the radio that afternoon about 4:15 as he waited to pick up his wife after work on Stoneway Avenue North. Idly twisting the dial, he heard a news broadcast about the shooting and heard that the police were looking for the Datsun with UKN-524 on its plates, driven by a blond female. Something made him glance at his rearview mirror, and he immediately tensed, dumbfounded. No, it was too much of a coincidence. He saw the right car, with the right license plate, coming up behind him. Only the car was being driven by a girl with long dark hair. In fact, she reminded him of his ex-wife, the same luxuriant black hair curling over her shoulders.

In an instant the car had passed, and Costos sprinted into his wife's office and called 911. "I just saw that car you're looking for!" he said. "The red Datsun's going south on Stoneway!"

Officer Robert Boling heard the new information as he patrolled just west of the Wallingford Precinct; he was only blocks away. He searched through alleys and found the red Datsun at 4:35. It was parked in the lot of a convenience store at 3939 Stoneway North.

The car was empty.

It looked as if the woman suspect had remained within a few miles of the shooting, perhaps circling the area again and again for two hours. But she certainly wasn't in or around the rented Datsun now.

Mary Moran,* a secretary at the University of Washington, was on vacation that bloody Monday, and she hadn't heard anything about the shooting near the U. As she sat in the King's Row cocktail lounge at 3935 Stoneway North, sipping a scotch and water and playing gin rummy with a friend, she was completely unaware of the patrol cars parked near the red Datsun at the convenience store just next door.

The temperature outside was creeping toward 80 degrees, and the back door of the lounge was propped open to create a hint of breeze. Mary Moran glanced out into the glaring August light and did a double take. She saw a tiny dark-haired woman in slacks and a white blouse trying to shinny over the cyclone fence that separated the restaurant property from the row of homes beyond. The fence was almost as tall as the woman, and the petite brunette was having difficulty getting over it.

Ms. Moran thought to herself, That's really silly. The drop on the other side of the fence is about ten feet. She's going to get a big surprise if she makes it to the top of the fence.

The woman finally made it and disappeared from view. Mary Moran didn't hear any yowl of pain or see the woman again, and she turned back to her card game. A few minutes later an officer came into the lounge and asked patrons if they'd seen anything unusual.

"I did," Moran volunteered. "I just saw a tiny little woman scale that fence back there. And I'll bet she landed with a thud on the other side." She described the woman she had seen.

Weird. The detectives had started out looking for a blond woman in a long blue-gray dress, and now they were searching for a woman with long dark hair wearing slacks. But then, good sense might dictate that someone who had just pulled off an execution might have doffed her outer garments and her wig and stashed them someplace. Or was it a woman at all? Maybe they were looking for a midget with a number of wigs at his disposal. Maybe he was really blond and he was now wearing a dark wig.

Things began to happen rapidly. At 5:55, Detective Jim Parks of the Port of Seattle Police called to say that the Hertz rental booth at Sea-Tac Airport had Cynthia Mahler on the phone. "She's calling to tell them somebody stole the car she rented last night."

The Hertz clerk was instructed to keep Mahler on the line, but she had rung off, the officers learned.

Seattle detectives John Nordlund and John Boren were dispatched to the airport to keep an eye on the Hertz booth and to find out if anyone matching the description of the suspect had made reservations to fly out of Seattle. Of course, they had a choice of descriptions: female, blond, tiny, in a long gray-blue dress; or female, petite, long dark hair, dark slacks, white blouse. Their quarry probably wasn't male; the Hertz people would have picked up a deep voice on the phone.

Boren and Nordlund picked up the car rental agreement from Hertz and then checked the manifests of flights coming up from California. The car renter's driver's license gave a Hayward address. The only female flying alone from Oakland on United's Flight 468—which had landed at Sea-Tac just before Cynthia Mahler picked up the Datsun at Hertz—*and* giving a home address in Hayward, California, was a K. Adams. Boren and Nordlund raced to the United reservations desk.

"You have a Cynthia Mahler or a K. Adams booked for any flights out tonight?" Boren asked.

The clerk shook his head and then glanced at the computer. "Wait a minute! It's just coming up now. Kristine Adams, booked for the nine P.M. flight—293—to Oakland–San Francisco. She'll have to pick up her ticket by eight or eight-thirty."

Luck was still running with the police. But the two detectives didn't know if they were going to see a blonde, a brunette, or a redhead boarding the plane. If the woman had worn disguises before, she might well do it again. They had a little time to spare before Kristine Adams showed up for boarding, and they returned to the Hertz counter.

The clerk who had rented the car to Cynthia Mahler the night before remembered her. "She had a prepaid travel voucher from a travel agency in Fremont, California. We require a current driver's license for I.D., and she had one from California. The voucher was in the name of Mahler, and the name on the license was Marler, but I just figured the computer missed on a letter."

"She was alone?"

"Well, I don't know. There was a man standing behind her, and when she got the keys to the Datsun, he said something like, 'I see we finally got our car.' But she didn't say anything to him."

The Hertz supervisor who had taken the call from Cynthia Marler, or Mahler, an hour earlier—the call where she reported her rental car stolen—said that the woman said she'd already called the police and that the police had told her to inform Hertz. "She said she left it outside a restaurant, and when she came out it was gone."

The Hertz clerk said she would recognize Cynthia Mahler/ Marler–Kristine Adams if she saw her again, and went with Detectives Boren and Nordlund to the north concourse, where passengers would soon board the 9:00 P.M. flight to Oakland. She watched the passengers as they moved toward the reservations check-in point, and suddenly indicated a tiny, very beautiful woman with long black hair. The woman wore slacks and a brown tweed jacket and carried a red overnight case.

"That's her," she whispered. "That's the woman who rented the Datsun last night."

The detectives waited until all passengers had boarded, and then moved swiftly down the jetway and onto the plane. The flight attendant pointed toward the wanted woman. Kristine Adams was already engaged in animated conversation with the male passenger beside her, and the man seemed delighted to have such a lovely seatmate for the flight south.

The brunette beauty's laugh was cut short as Detective John Boren leaned over the seat behind her and clapped handcuffs on her slender wrists. She looked up in amazement as he said quietly, "You're under arrest on suspicion of murder."

Her seat companion's mouth fell open. The woman accompanied Boren and Nordlund off the plane meekly enough, half smiling, as if a ridiculous mistake had been made. As they exited, they read her rights under *Miranda*, and she nodded. There was little conversation as they waited to pick up the suitcase she had checked aboard and then drove to police headquarters in downtown Seattle.

She looked like anything but a hit woman. She barely reached five feet and couldn't have weighed more than 95 pounds. But every pound was arranged in the right spot. The woman was gorgeous.

And very, very annoyed.

She gave her name as Cynthia Ellen Marler, born May 2, 1952, and said she had grown up in Hayward and still lived there. She said she had come to Seattle for a brief vacation to visit a brother-in-law, just to get away from the burden of mothering her three children, age four, five, and twelve, for a day or so.

"Why did you fly up here under the name K. Adams?" Nordlund asked.

"A friend—Milos Panich*—booked my reservations and bought my ticket under that name," she replied, "and so I just left it that way."

Asked about the man who had been with her when she checked out the car from Hertz, Cynthia said he was someone named Felix,* a man she had met on the plane. She had offered to give him a lift to his destination in the north end.

Cynthia and Felix had a few drinks, and then she had checked into the Villa Del Mar Motel at 3938 Aurora Avenue North.

"The maid woke me about ten the next morning, and I had breakfast at a family restaurant down the street."

Cynthia Marler said she had left her keys in the Datsun while she ate and had gone out to find that the car had been stolen. She had called her friend Milos Panich in California, and he had told her to call the police. Cynthia said that Panich had also told her that one of her children was ill, and she had decided to go back to California that afternoon. She never had contacted her brother-in-law. Her visit to Seattle had lasted a little less than twenty-four hours.

Cynthia had not had enough money for a return ticket, so she had phoned Steffi Panich,* Milos's wife, who said she'd wire $160 at once through Western Union. "I was going to fly back under my own name, but I decided I might as well stick with Kristine Adams."

Cynthia had checked out of the Villa Del Mar late in the afternoon and taxied to Western Union, where she picked up the money wired by the Paniches. She had the cabbie take her to Sea-Tac Airport to board the flight to San Francisco.

The pretty suspect was incredulous that anyone might accuse her of the murder of Wanda Touchstone, whom she had never even heard of. She was adamant that she was merely a tired mother seeking a few days' surcease from the burden of child care. She was booked into the King County Jail on suspicion of murder.

The investigation would continue. Detectives Billy Baughman and Danny Engle arrived for work early the next morning and began to disentangle the convoluted case. Having learned through the victim's attorney that Wanda Preston-Touchstone was separated from her husband, Lew Touchstone—Robert Preston, they obtained Touchstone's address in Kirkland, a suburb north of Seattle.

If Touchstone was overcome with grief when the two detectives informed him that his estranged wife had been murdered, he hid his feelings well. In fact, Lew Touchstone refused to come to the medical examiner's office to identify her body until he could arrange to have his attorney accompany him.

After identifying Wanda's body, Touchstone grudgingly answered some questions for Engle and Baughman. He said he had spent Sunday, August 10, with Wanda and that they had a very pleasant day. He had met her at a hotel, and they had taken a ferry across Elliott Bay to Bainbridge Island. With the sea gulls calling and the summer breeze, it had been a lovely trip. Wanda had been affectionate, and they had held hands. Encouraged, he had asked her to come back to him, but she had refused. Still, it had been a good day and he was left feeling hopeful about their future. Wanda had been in good spirits when he left her at the hotel at 6:00 P.M.

On the day that Wanda was killed, Touchstone said he had checked into a plastic surgeon's office where he underwent a partial face-lift. He said he had spent the night at a convalescent home, doped up with pain pills, completely unaware that anything had happened to his estranged bride.

Touchstone said he didn't know any of Wanda's new friends; he suspected that she might be dating someone, but he didn't know who it might be.

In checking Lew Touchstone's background, Danny Engle and Billy Baughman did come up with one rather interesting fact. Milos Panich, the man who had paid for Cynthia Marler's trip to Seattle, was married to Lew's daughter, Steffi. The California couple now owned a farm in the Napa Valley that had once belonged to Lew, and they reportedly had interests in an auto body shop business. It seemed unlikely, then, that Cynthia had never even heard of Lew's wife.

A check into Cynthia Marler's background also elicited some facts that cast some shadows on the picture of Cynthia as a simple housewife and mother. The twenty-eight-year-old suspect had a rap sheet going back to 1971. She had been arrested on a variety of charges, including burglary, kidnapping, receiving stolen property (credit cards), theft and forgery (credit cards), conspiracy, driving while intoxicated, and reckless driving. Her husband was presently serving time for bank robbery in prison at Terminal Island, California.

Cynthia Marler had clearly talked to detectives before, even though she had pretended to be shocked that Engle and Baughman considered her involved in any way in a crime.

Detective Billy Baughman inventoried the contents of Cynthia Marler's purse. He found a key ring with two keys wired on to the ring itself, the Hertz rental agreement, an address book, a black date book with the notation for Sunday, August 10, reading, "Try for the 11th," and a piece of paper with the name Felix Misha and an address and phone number on it, $102.10 in currency and coin, and a note signed "Milos," that said, "Don't call me until I call you . . . and that will be never."

Engle and Baughman called Felix Misha,* wondering just what part he might play in this increasingly bizarre case. Misha, a tall, thin man with a wispy little mustache, said he was a concert violinist and lounge performer. He seemed genuinely aghast when he learned what had happened to the pretty woman he'd met on the plane.

"We talked on the way up, and she offered to give me a ride when she picked up her rental car. She didn't know the Seattle area, and I was going to point out some addresses to her."

One of the addresses that had interested Cynthia Marler was that of the apartment house where Wanda Touchstone lived. Misha said that Cynthia had parked beyond the apartment house entrance and told him she would be back in a short while. She went into the lobby while Misha watched, and was back within a few minutes.

"We had a couple of drinks," Misha said, "and I wrote down my address, and she wrote down hers and her husband's and gave it to me."

It was clear that the nervous musician had no closer ties with the case than a chance meeting with the suspect.

Detectives John Boatman and Mike Tando had canvassed Wanda's apartment house—with negative results. No one had seen or heard anything out of the ordinary on or before the day of her death. Her apartment seemed undisturbed; it was messy, but only the clutter one might expect in the home of a woman devoted to study. Notebooks, textbooks on biology and anatomy, and other school materials were scattered around. But there was no indication at all that any violence had taken place there.

By Lew Touchstone's own statement, Wanda had met him away from her apartment on the day before her death and had returned home alone. She didn't live to see the next day out.

Dr. John Eisele, the King County medical examiner, performed the autopsy on the body of Wanda Touchstone. The five-foot-four-inch, 121-pound woman had received two major injuries: both execution-style gunshot wounds. The first was an entry wound two and a half inches behind the right ear canal opening. That bullet entered the skull, passed through the brain, and hit the left side of the skull before ricocheting forward. The bullet was recovered, but there was no way to determine how far the gun barrel had been from Wanda's head; either the gun had been some distance away or her hair had filtered out all the barrel debris.

The second wound was an entrance wound on the left side of the neck. The skin surrounding the bullet hole was stippled with powder, indicating that the killer had held the gun one or two inches away. This bullet transversed the trachea, shattering the bone, passed through the jugular vein, broke Wanda's lower right jaw, and exited through the right cheek.

Ugly wounds. Fatal wounds.

Dr. Eisele found other injuries that were somewhat puzzling; Wanda Touchstone's body bore a number of scrapes and bruises. Large areas of skin had been abraded and contused on her right shoulder, left upper leg, inner left thigh, lower back, and right buttock. It almost looked as if someone had beaten Wanda Touchstone during the last day, or few days, of her life. The bruising was not consistent with someone falling to the pavement after being shot.

Frank Lee, firearms examiner for the Washington State Patrol Crime Lab, examined the recovered bullet under a microscope. He found its class and characteristics (the marks left on a bullet as it exits a gun barrel—lands and grooves, right-hand twist, and so forth) consistent with firing from a .38 caliber Smith & Wesson.

But there was no gun for comparison. The death gun was probably resting on the bottom of one of the many waterways in the north end of Seattle. Even so, the case against Cynthia Marler was tightening. Detectives Baughman and Engle took the key ring found in the suspect's purse with them when they returned to Wanda Touchstone's apartment house. It was a lockout apartment where, for the occupants' security, the common front door leading into the lobby could be opened only with a key provided to tenants.

One of the two keys wired onto the key ring slipped into the lockout, and the door swung open: Cynthia Marler had had in her possession a key to Wanda's apartment house. The second key was tried in the lock of Wanda's apartment itself. It did not fit. But a talk with the manager brought forth the information that Wanda had recently had the locks to her apartment changed and had added a dead bolt.

On the night Cynthia arrived in Seattle, Felix Misha had accompanied her to Wanda's address, and he had seen her gain entrance to the lobby easily. Baughman and Engle wondered if she had not planned to kill Wanda that night—with her new acquaintance waiting in the car. If she had, her plans would have been thwarted when she attempted to insert the second key into the apartment door. That key would not have worked.

That might explain the entry in Cynthia's date book on Sunday "Try for the 11th?" Had Cynthia planned to follow her unsuspecting quarry the next day until she had a second chance?

The impounded Hertz rental car was processed, but there was nothing at all in it to indicate who had driven it—no clothes, no wigs, and certainly no gun or ammunition.

The room Cynthia Marler had rented at the Villa Del Mar had been thoroughly cleaned by maids before detectives could get to it, and nothing of evidentiary value was found. The maids were interviewed and said they had found nothing in the room beyond some tourist brochures. Detectives Gary Fowler and Danny Melton had the Dumpster behind the motel loaded into a Seattle disposal truck, and the contents were spilled onto a clean area in a disposal lot where the two detectives pawed through it—an onerous and monumental task that netted nothing connected with the murder of Wanda Touchstone.

A friend of Wanda Touchstone's, who had been writing a joint term paper with her at the university, came forward and said she had met Wanda in her apartment parking lot the morning of August 11, and Wanda had worn a huge diamond ring. "I commented on it because I'd worked for a jeweler, and I could see that it was more than a carat. She just said the ring had been part of her marriage."

The ring was not on the victim's finger when she was shot a few hours later. It wasn't in her apartment either.

Detectives Engle and Baughman itemized the contents of the red overnight case Cynthia Marler had carried onto the plane where she was arrested, along with the suitcase she had checked. They wondered what a woman might take with her as she embarked on an overnight trip to commit a murder. The luggage was packed with what an average woman might take on a short vacation: makeup, a hair dryer, extra clothes (but no blue-gray dress), shoes, lingerie. There was a cross and a rosary. There was a paperback book, *Bloodletters and Bad Men,* one of a series about infamous criminals.

They found Cynthia Marler's parole papers from an earlier incarceration. And they found a wig, a blondish brown wig styled in short tight curls. There was a silk scarf, too—pink, blue, and white.

Was this wig responsible for the witnesses' description of a blond woman with a scarf, who had hurried away from the death site? Baughman and Engle thought so. She probably had stripped off the oversized dull blue dress and thrown it away during her flight. The wig would have fit in her purse. That explained why some witnesses had seen the blonde in the baggy dress and another had seen a trim woman in slacks whose hair was long and black.

And they were more convinced when Nell Boles, Jan Winn, and Mary Moran picked Cynthia Marler from a lineup of several women. This was the woman Boles and Winn had seen leaving the parking lot after the shooting. This was also the woman Moran had seen trying to scale a fence next door to where the rental Datsun was abandoned.

Working with King County Deputy Prosecuting Attorney David R. Lord, the two detectives agreed that there was enough evidence to file a first-degree murder charge against Cynthia Marler in the death of Wanda Touchstone, but they didn't feel they had the whole story. There was a chance that Cynthia might cooperate and implicate others in a plot against Wanda—*if* she was offered a plea bargain. Second-degree murder charges would mean far less prison time than first-degree, and Lord made the decision to allow Cynthia to plead guilty to second-degree murder if her allegations led to charges against others.

The case made brief headlines in Seattle, and then the media forgot about it; there were new crimes to write about. Baughman, Engle, and Lord didn't forget about it, though. Engle made many trips to California to verify information. He found the travel agent who had booked Marler's flight to Seattle and issued the voucher for the rental car. She said the trip was paid for by Steffi Panich—Lew Touchstone's daughter—who had asked for a receipt.

Cynthia Marler waited in jail. The other people close to Marler and the victim were not eager to discuss the case. Neither of the Touchstones, father or son, had much to say, nor did the Panichs.

As the weeks stretched out and Cynthia began to realize that she probably *was* headed for prison, she began to talk with Dan Engle. Rather, she began to fence with him. She had promised to reveal the whole plot behind Wanda's death, but she was adept at double-talk. This was a woman who was used to conning people, and Engle knew it. Nevertheless, he gambled that when push came to shove, Cynthia would save her own skin. For a while it looked as though she was going to.

Dan Engle and FBI Special Agent Brian Braun traveled to Pleasanton, California, to talk with Cynthia's husband, Jim. He had worked for Milos Panich before he went into prison, and he hoped to have a job in Panich's auto body shop when he was released. But this was his *wife*, the mother of his children. If she was taking the fall for someone higher up, she would go to prison for a long, long time. Engle and Braun asked Marler if he'd be willing to wear a wire the next time Milos or Steffi Panich came to visit.

Marler agreed to be wired, although he didn't seem very enthusiastic about it. Whether he was afraid of Panich or more concerned about his own future than his wife's, the body wire exercise was disappointing. Milos Panich came to visit all right, but Marler was doing everything he could to garble the transmission of their voices.

"We had told him to stay as close as he could to the door," Engle recalled, "so we could hear what they said, but he wandered back by the vending machines. It was so noisy we could only hear about ten percent of their conversation."

James Marler was walking the narrow edge of a knife. He wanted out of prison—so he didn't want to flat-out refuse to help a homicide detective and an FBI agent, but he was obviously standing so far away that his body wire sent out only static, the sound of bottles clunking down in the pop machine, and an occasional complete sentence.

Next, Dan Engle tried to talk to Cynthia again. She was the one who was in immediate danger of facing a murder conviction. If she cooperated, prosecutor David Lord would take that into account. Cynthia smiled and laughed and appeared to be willing to go halfway. Engle tried not to acknowledge that he saw a certain blankness in her eyes, the eyes of a woman who was lying.

Finally she agreed to call Milos Panich on a phone in the Seattle Homicide Unit's offices, a phone that was wired to record the conversation. It could have been the break in the case that would have let Engle and Baughman reel in two, maybe three or four more suspects in the plot to kill Wanda.

But it wasn't. Cynthia's conversation with Milos Panich was about as damaging to him as a call between two people gossiping. It seemed to Engle that caution oozed from Panich's voice and everything he said. Even Cynthia sounded stilted and rehearsed.

"Something was fishy," Engle said. "We suspected she had already called Panich from jail earlier and told him to be careful what he said when she called him later. She had been double-talking all along."

When prosecutor David Lord heard about the phone call, he said, "That's it. The deal's off entirely." Marler's cooperation had produced no substantive evidence against Panich.

Cynthia Marler would be charged with first-degree murder.

Wanda Touchstone earned her degree in microbiology; the University of Washington awarded it to her posthumously. Her grief-stricken sister arrived from Sweden to take the degree back with her, along with Wanda's clothing and a few other possessions. She expected to find Wanda's prized diamond ring, but it wasn't where she thought she would find it.

Where was it? If Lew Touchstone was the true instigator of Wanda's execution, it would have been easy for him to give her the expensive diamond ring on Sunday; he would have gotten it back on Monday when Wanda was shot.

Wanda's sister had hoped to take the body back with her to be buried in Poland, but she could not afford to transport it. She told reporters that Lew Touchstone would not pay the expense. Lew's attorney said he'd offered to pay half and that his sister-in-law had refused.

The sister returned to Sweden without Wanda's body, and Wanda was buried in a Bellevue, Washington, cemetery far from her native land.

If the public and press had forgotten about the Touchstone-Marler case, they were fully aware of it with headlines in late February. Superior Court Judge Richard Ishikawa took an unprecedented legal action. As the pretrial legal hearing opened, Judge Ishikawa barred the press and public from that hearing. When the media are barred, headlines scream. And they did.

John Henry Browne, who had advised Ted Bundy in 1975 when Browne worked for the King County Public Defender's Office, had become one of the top three criminal defense attorneys in Seattle. He represented Cynthia Marler. Pitted against him for the state would be King County Deputy Prosecutor David Lord. Worthy adversaries, just the two of them, walking carefully through a case fraught with legal technicalities. They concurred with Judge Ishikawa's decision to close and seal the pretrial hearing while the media screamed "Foul!" and the public's interest was titillated.

Cynthia Marler's part in the murder of Wanda Touchstone had allegedly been observed by eyewitnesses. It was the possibility that she was not the instigator of the execution-style murder that raised so many questions. Nonetheless, the pretrial hearing remained closed despite the pleas of lawyers from Seattle's newspapers. When the trial itself opened, TV and still cameras were allowed into the courtroom; they would pool the footage that resulted. The press bench was filled with reporters.

Who *was* Cynthia Marler?

She was certainly the camera's darling, posing constantly, directing her smile into the lens. The defendant was so photogenic that it seemed impossible to get a bad shot of her, and she made the papers almost every day of the trial. Cynthia was so tiny that spectators murmured that she certainly didn't *look* like a killer. She wore filmy white long-sleeved blouses, draped slacks, and high-heeled shoes with dainty straps across her slender ankles. As she was led into the courtroom, her wrists were encircled with specially made cuffs; her arms were too small for anything beyond a child-size measurement.

Cynthia joked with her female guard whenever court recessed, and she puffed continually on Camel cigarettes. She seemed ultimately confident, as if she had never considered that she might be convicted, as if she was only the focal point of some legal mix-up. She had thrown away her chance for a lesser charge, and yet she still seemed to expect someone to save her.

The jury consisted of nine women and three men, with two female alternates. Would the women feel sympathy for this child-woman on trial for first-degree murder, or would they judge her more objectively than a jury of men, who might have been taken with her beauty?

The motive for the murder of Wanda Touchstone was foremost in the minds of the spectators and the press, and prosecutor Lord put Detective Danny Engle on the stand—out of the jurors' hearing—to testify as to detectives' suppositions on why Wanda had died. Engle, who had lived, breathed, and slept the Marler case for months, revealed that Lew Touchstone was once considered a suspect in the case. "If we were going to talk to him about the case today," Engle said, "we'd read him his rights under *Miranda* before questioning him."

Engle said that Lew Touchstone's daughter, Steffi, and her husband, Milos Panich, had been investigated, too. Although Milos Panich admitted he paid for Cynthia's plane ticket and car rental, he said it was just a favor for her. The Panichs had not set foot in Washington State since the crime.

Lew Touchstone and his son, Ron (Wanda's first husband, a proxy spouse), were called to the witness stand to testify. They refused to answer any questions at all. Lew went first. He refused to answer such seemingly innocuous questions as "Do you have a daughter named Steffi who was married to Milos Panich?" and "How were you notified of your wife's death?" and "Did you identify the body?"

Lew read from a white card in his hand: "I decline to answer on grounds of the Fifth Amendment of the U.S. Constitution and similar provisions of the Washington State Constitution."

Son Ron followed, intoning the same Fifth Amendment response to all questions.

Judge Ishikawa ruled that Lew Touchstone would be allowed to exercise his constitutional rights under the Fifth Amendment, but that Ron Touchstone, who had never been a suspect in the bizarre murder, had no grounds for taking the Fifth. Resolute, Ron Touchstone still refused to answer any questions and was sentenced to jail for the duration of the trial. Lew and Ron stormed past strobe lights and cameras, covering their faces as they left the courtroom.

As the lengthy trial began, David Lord presented witness after witness, eliciting the information uncovered by Detectives Engle and Baughman. The case had unfolded like a movie mystery. There were the almost-eyewitnesses to the execution of the pretty Pole, the woman who had seen a petite, dark-haired woman trying to scale the fence, the man who had spotted the rented Datsun and alerted police, the pathologist, the firearms expert, the travel agent who had sold the plane ticket to Steffi Panich, the Hertz employees, the Western Union clerk who had handed $160 over to Cynthia Marler, Felix Misha, the apprehensive musician who had gone to Wanda's apartment house with Cynthia the night before the killing, and the detectives. On and on, they took the stand, painting a clearer and clearer picture of the defendant as a woman who had allegedly quite calmly traveled 900 miles to shoot another woman whom she had never known.

Invariably in murder trials the defendant looks away as the defense lawyer examines gruesome photos of the victim, taken after autopsy. Cynthia Marler did not. She studied them intently.

John Henry Browne was good. He was quick, alert, incisive, asking all the right questions on cross. But the answers he needed weren't there. If anyone could have gotten an acquittal for a client, Browne could, but the case against Cynthia Marler was as solid as cement.

There was more of a sense of things *not* said in that courtroom than of things said aloud. Questions danced around the surface of what lay beneath. At one point, Danny Engle read a translation of an ad that appeared in a Polish newspaper—*Courier Polski*, published in Warsaw. It was dated October 30, 1980, a little more than two months after Wanda Touchstone fell dead. Wanda's relatives had mailed it to Engle: "Man from America desires contact with lady around 35 years old. Knows English. Interested in house and family. Send offer to Mr. Lew Touchstone. . . ."

Wanda was gone, but Lew Touchstone apparently was determined to replace her with a mirror image, another Polish woman in her mid-thirties—but one who would stay at home with him and treat him as lord and master of the house. He had even gone to the expense and pain of having a face-lift to look more youthful. Unfortunately, he had disobeyed every instruction his doctor had given him, and his health had suffered.

After much legal maneuvering, Susan Zydak, a King County prosecutor's paralegal, was allowed to take the stand and testify regarding an interview she had witnessed between David Lord and Lew Touchstone. As the jury watched, enthralled, she diagrammed the complicated relationships among and between Lew Touchstone, Ron Touchstone, Wanda Touchstone, Steffi Panich, Milos Panich, and Cynthia Marler. For the first time, they realized that Cynthia had been sent to Seattle by the son-in-law of the victim's husband.

Incredibly, the reason Cynthia Marler might have traveled so far to shoot Wanda Touchstone was never touched upon. Money? A likely supposition. Cynthia had been living on welfare with her three children while her husband served out his sentence for bank robbery. Lew Touchstone had a bundle of money. Milos Panich apparently had enough to foot Cynthia's "vacation" away from her children.

There was no evidence that Cynthia even *knew* Wanda. No evidence that she had any reason to hate her enough to kill her. A payoff seemed a likely reason to kill, but no evidence of a payoff surfaced during her trial.

When the Western Union representative testified, he stated that a still camera routinely took photos of people picking up wired money.

Even here the case was bizarre. The number noted for the "Kristine Adams" money order was 8896. But no photo was found. Then Western Union figured that the number might have been upside down; maybe the number was 9688. They checked their files again. No photo. Finally they realized there had been no film in the camera.

Through it all, Cynthia Marler remained the coquettish beauty, smiling at her attorney and whispering in his ear, posing for the cameras. Although she looked soft in photographs, in person she occasionally looked as hard as steel. Her eyebrows were plucked to a thin line, and her acne scars were hidden with makeup. This was a woman who had obviously led a rugged life.

Would John Henry Browne put Cynthia on the stand? Would he take the chance of opening her up to cross-examination by Lord? No. Cynthia never told her story.

Browne called only one defense witness: Cynthia's brother-in-law, the man she said she'd come to Seattle to visit. She had never contacted him. He said that he and Cynthia were "estranged," that he had not seen her since 1977. However, Browne elicited the information that it would not be unusual for family members to just drop in on each other without notice. The witness smiled at Cynthia as he admitted, "We've had a beef from time to time," and she smiled back thinly.

And then it was over. The defense had lasted at most ten minutes.

It was March 10, 1981. Time for final arguments to begin.

David Lord rose to address the jury for the state. Layer by layer he built the case again from the beginning, starting with the travel arrangements for "K. Adams" to fly to Seattle. Her travel schedule was devastating to the defendant when it was first introduced; it was more devastating now as Lord's summary added bricks to the wall of probable guilt that rose around the beautiful defendant.

Lord described the petite Marler as a "cold-blooded, ruthless killer." He suggested that Cynthia's motive was a very old one: money.

John Henry Browne argued that he should be able to mention Lew Touchstone in his final argument, just as he had in his opening remarks. Browne placed the suspicion directly on Lew Touchstone who, he alleged, "had a motive to have his wife killed," the motive of a wealthy man who lived in a community-property state and was facing a divorce settlement.

David Lord felt that if Browne was allowed to mention the elusive Touchstone again, then Lord should be allowed to tell the jury why Touchstone had not testified—that he had refused on Fifth Amendment grounds, suggesting that his statements might incriminate him. Judge Ishikawa ruled that Browne could voice his thoughts on Lew Touchstone in final arguments but that he could not tell the jury why Touchstone had not taken the witness stand.

The attorney for the defense gave a philosophical argument, hitting on the essential ingredient in a first-degree murder conviction— reasonable doubt—telling the jury that it was incumbent on the state to present a case that proves the defendant guilty beyond a reasonable doubt of premeditated murder. He submitted there was still a great deal of reasonable doubt.

Browne's voice rose as he said, "I don't have to make sense out of anything. And if you think I do, then let's give up right now. I don't have to prove anything. He [Lord] has got to make sense out of [his case]." Browne was aggressive. "Our theory in this case is very simple: *prove it.*"

And then Browne raised some questions that he hoped would make the jurors wonder if they had absolute proof that Cynthia Marler had committed murder. If Cynthia had carried out a well-formed plan to kill, he asked, "Why rent a car under your own name? Why get rid of a gun, but keep a wig, and keep the keys to the victim's apartment? Why have someone make reservations for a murder trip through a travel agency? Why arrive in Seattle with no money? Not enough money to even get back home? . . . You cannot make soup from the *shadow* of a chicken. You cannot find a person guilty beyond a reasonable doubt because of *questions.*"

Browne listed seven reasonable doubts he had gleaned from the state's version of the Marler case. He found the identification of Cynthia Marler faulty—the witnesses had been confused in their descriptions of the person seen leaving the crime scene. He suggested that the defendant might have been set up to be in the parking lot, seen by witnesses while the real killer escaped. He suggested that Marler had no motive to kill Wanda Touchstone. He brought out the lack of evidence in the case. "Where is *Mr. Touchstone?* What kind of guns does *Mr. Touchstone* have? What about the bruises all over Wanda Touchstone's body?"

Browne continued with his list, hitting again and again on the elusive Lew Touchstone. (He had the advantage here, since Lord was not allowed to tell the jury that Touchstone was refusing to testify by taking the Fifth, and Lord could not explain Lew Touchstone's absence.)

Why were Cynthia's hands free of nitrate traces when they were swabbed some hours after the murder? Browne did not explain to the jury that the simple washing of one's hands can remove traces of nitrate or that smoking a cigarette or urinating can leave nitrate traces on hands.

Browne felt that there was time for a second person to have left the parking lot *before* the witness saw a woman rushing from the shooting scene. *"Time . . . time."* He questioned later witnesses' ability to accurately estimate the time they'd seen the dark-haired woman driving the red car and scaling the fence.

Browne's last "reasonable doubt" concerned common sense. He insisted common sense would dictate that no high-priced "hit lady" would leave such a well-marked trail behind her with plane tickets, car rentals, wired money, and taxis.

His scattershot technique hit the jury so rapidly that several of them were blinking. Questions. Questions—and then his repeated statement, "I don't have to explain anything; I don't have to prove anything." The young defense attorney was good; he had taken a case with evidence so damning that few attorneys would even have tried. The state and prosecutor Lord had Cynthia Marler so locked into Wanda Touchstone's execution that the press bench was making book the jury would be back within an hour of the start of deliberation, yet Browne was pulling questions out of the air.

It was an either-or situation. Either Cynthia hadn't done it or she had to have been the klutziest, sloppiest hit lady ever to sashay into Seattle.

David Lord made his final statements, stressing that Cynthia Marler—however inadequate she might have been as a paid killer—had done it, and she had done it for money, that her movements between August 8 and August 11 were far too meaningful to be mere coincidence.

The jury went out. One hour. Two. Six. Several reporters paid off on their lost wagers. It was to take ten hours of deliberation before they returned and informed Judge Ishikawa that they had reached a verdict. For the first time, Cynthia Marler seemed to have lost her bravado; she appeared to realize that she might not be acquitted after all. Jury foreman Robert Toigo read the verdict. The jury had found her guilty of first-degree murder.

The raven-haired beauty bowed her head and wept softly, as John Henry Browne leaned over to comfort her.

The foreman told the press later that the jury had spent the better part of two days going over "each and every piece" of evidence. He said one juror had fought a lonely fight for acquittal right up to the last minute. He admitted that the jurors had been confused, that they could not understand certain elements of the case. That was to be expected; Lew Touchstone, and his daughter, Steffi, her husband, Milos Panich, had been mentioned—but never produced. One possible motive for Wanda's death was the bitterness surrounding her divorce from Touchstone—but that was only one. Touchstone was more than wealthy enough to support an ex-wife without diminishing his life-style.

On March 26, 1981, Cynthia Marler was led once again into Judge Ishikawa's courtroom. She was no longer dressed in a delicate blouse, tailored slacks, and high heels; now she wore jail coveralls and sandals. She was sentenced to life in prison, with a recommendation of a twenty-five-year minimum. She murmured that she'd like to serve her time in California so she could see her children, but Cynthia Marler would serve out her term in the women's prison at Purdy, Washington.

Cynthia, the woman who had brought a rosary with her when she came to Seattle to kill Wanda Touchstone, grew angry after she heard her sentence. She balked at having her fingerprints taken in the courtroom, and her attorney had to urge her to accede. The television cameras now caught the other side of her personality—the bitter, hostile, tough Cynthia.

Her children would have no mother for perhaps twenty-five years. They had no father, either; he was serving time for bank robbery.

When the proceedings finally ended, a tall bearded man rose sadly and walked out of the courtroom. John Sophronski had seen the trial through to the finish, staring at the pretty little woman who had taken Wanda away from him. Court deputies had seen him wince during the trial, seen him clench his fists, and they had worried about what he might do. But he never said a word or made a move toward Cynthia.

The questions remained—at least officially. Detectives had been told—but were constrained from revealing—that Cynthia Marler *had* been promised payment once Wanda Touchstone was dead. The monetary amount was reportedly $3,000. As a further enticement, Marler had been assured that the title to a 1976 Chevrolet pickup truck would be put in her name. If a price could be put on a human life, Wanda Touchstone's had gone cheap. Cynthia had also been promised support if anything went wrong. Detectives believed that she never expected to go to prison, that she was convinced that those who wanted Wanda dead were so powerful that they could save her.

Perhaps that was why she played games with the police and the prosecutor's office; had she *trusted* in the manipulators behind the death plot?

Cynthia took her punishment alone. She probably was behind bars at the Washington State Women's Corrections Center at Purdy before she realized that nobody *was* coming to her rescue. At that point she was undoubtedly afraid to come forward and point her finger, at least publically. She had children on the outside. She kept her mouth shut.

For the moment.

Lew Touchstone was free, but he was a frightened man who often called the very detectives who had questioned him, asking them for protection. He was afraid that he might be the target of violence at any moment. He never was. He lives in relative obscurity with an unlisted phone number.

Cynthia Marler filed her first appeal in mid-1982. She claimed that the state had extracted a pretrial confession from her but then reneged on its promise to reduce the charges against her if her allegations resulted in charges against others. Prior to her trial, she had told prosecutors that Lew Touchstone's son-in-law, Milos Panich, had hired her to kill Wanda Touchstone and offered her $3,000 to do so. Cynthia's husband, James Marler, had allegedly been present when the offer was made. Cynthia said that Panich financed her trip to Seattle, rented her a car, and provided a photo of Wanda, a gun and ammunition, and even the keys and plans to Wanda's apartment. Cynthia also said that Panich had asked her to return to California with the diamond ring that Wanda wore.

The state had given Cynthia "use immunity," which meant the prosecution could not use these statements against her at trial. In addition, Cynthia's statements about her role as a hired killer and her husband James's implication of Milos Panich had been sealed in court records on Judge Ishikawa's orders. It took a suit by the *Seattle Times* and the *Seattle Post-Intelligencer* before that information was published, *after* the trial.

On appeal, Cynthia's new lawyer, Julie Kelser, asked the question, "Why have two men literally gotten away with murder?" King County Deputy Prosecutor William Downing accused Kelser of "Monday morning quarterbacking"; the case was more than a year old. He said the prosecution had not had sufficient evidence to charge either Touchstone or Panich.

On July 12, 1982, the State Court of Appeals affirmed Cynthia Marler's murder-for-hire conviction. The court ruled that the state had acted in good faith and had not reneged on its agreement with Cynthia Marler: it had fully investigated her statements but found no basis for charging the two men with the crime.

While Cynthia continued her life sentence for the crime of murder, there may have been others who walked free—but on egg shells, still waiting for an ax to fall.

And if it did not fall fatally, it certainly hovered menacingly in July 1986, when Cynthia again appealed her conviction for first-degree murder to the State Court of Appeals. She asked that she be released from prison based in part on her claim that one of her attorneys had a conflict of interest at the time of her trial, because he had been paid by what a news story described as "a possible co-defendant in the case," Milos Panich.

It was a most convoluted argument. The same attorney Cynthia now blamed for her incarceration was the lawyer who had negotiated a potential plea bargain for second-degree murder. For her to have received the lesser charge, she would have had to implicate Panich. Her inability to furnish sufficient evidence for the state to charge Panich, however, resulted in the heavier charge.

The appeals court decreed that her trial attorney had clearly been on Cynthia Marler's side and again rejected her bid to be released from prison.

In the end, it was Cynthia Marler's own lack of credibility that did her in. According to Deputy Prosecutor Bill Downing, her statements implicating others were too weak to use. Cynthia had failed a lie detector test and her "trustworthiness" was highly suspect. And the state found no new evidence that warranted charging others with the crime. There is, of course, no statute of limitations on murder.

Detectives proved the most important facet of their case: beautiful, petite Cynthia Marler cold-bloodedly fired two bullets into Wanda Touchstone's head and neck on August 11, 1980, and ended forever the marriage that should never have begun.

Twelve years after her conviction, Cynthia Marler remains incarcerated in the Washington State Women's Corrections Center at Purdy. The usual life term, with time off for good behavior, is thirteen years and four months in Washington State. Cynthia Marler has not been particularly cooperative while in prison, and guards call her "a tough one." She is forty-one now, her children are nearly grown, and the life she left behind has disintegrated with years and distance.

No one will ever really know why Wanda had to die. All of her secrets died with her. All but one.

Her killer took her life—but not her diamond ring. The disappearance of Wanda's diamond ring had puzzled detectives for a long time. The mystery was solved when Wanda's sister came upon it, stuck in the tow of Wanda's panty hose. Wanda might have begun to trust her ex-husband a little more after their happy Sunday together, but not enough that she didn't find it necessary to hide the ring she had just stolen back.

The Runaway

When I began my research into the inexplicable disappearance of a young teenager in Washington State, I was hesitant about approaching her family. I had always been timid about intruding on the grief of survivors of crime victims, but that changed when I met Doreen Hanson. My interview with her resulted in my membership in the Families and Friends of Victims of Violent Crimes and Missing Persons support group. Over the next seventeen years, I would meet scores of extremely brave people—survivors who were not content with the status quo and who worked tirelessly to change the system. Washington State's victims' group was one of the forerunners of such groups all over America. If their own loved ones were gone forever—and most of them were—"Families and Friends" strove to protect other people's children. I found them a most extraordinary group, and I made lasting friendships. Many years ago, when I began writing true crime articles, I agonized over my realization that I was making my living from other people's tragedies. The mothers, fathers, sisters, brothers, and grandparents in "Families and Friends" taught me that their stories had to be told, but that any writer who did so must always remember the victims too. Doreen, Janna's mother, was my first contact, and she taught me to fight for crime victims—even if the only thing I could do was to keep their memories alive.

The bleak search for thirteen-year-old Janna Hanson began on Thursday morning, December 26, 1974, in a little town north of Seattle, Washington. The Christmas just past had been an especially happy one for Janna. Her family had made it through some bad times, but they had finally come full circle and they were happy again. Janna's mother, Doreen Hanson, had divorced the father of her four daughters in the late sixties. And then in 1970 they were getting along so well that they talked of getting back together. It was not to be; Janna's father died of a sudden heart attack that year. He was only forty-one. When their father died, Gail Hanson was nineteen, the twins, Penny and Pamela, were seventeen, and Janna, the baby, was nine.

Their father's death was a blow to all the Hanson girls, but their grief had softened with the years. And this Christmas of 1974 had been good. The comfortable apartment Doreen and Janna shared had overflowed with all the people Janna loved best: her mom and her beautiful big sisters, her baby nephew, Derek. Her Grandma Hanson had traveled hundreds of miles to be with them.

Janna was as blond as her sisters, caught somewhere between childhood and womanhood. Her older sisters occasionally modeled, and Janna showed every indication that she would be as beautiful as they were. She had received almost all the presents she had asked for, but that wasn't nearly as important as just being with her family. The Hansons were—and are—a very close family.

Anyone who knew her at all well knew that Janna Hanson would never have run away. And yet, a day after Christmas, it seemed that she had been swallowed up into some other dimension, simply vanishing into infinity.

Doreen Hanson was about to enter the saddest, most frustrating period of her life. Again and again, for months, she would find her gut feelings dismissed by authorities who insisted that her daughter

had run away. That was the obvious answer when one considered the
legions of runaway teens in the sixties and seventies; it was incomprehensible to Doreen Hanson.

Janna Hanson had promised a good friend that she would check on
the girl's family's mobile home, which sat on the grounds of the Nile
Country Club, a sprawling compound near Janna's Mountlake Terrace, Washington, home. Her friend's family was away on vacation.
Janna had given her friend some plants for Christmas and had
promised to water them faithfully every day. She also was given the
responsibility of leaving a water tap turned on just enough so that an
unseasonable cold snap wouldn't freeze the trailer's water lines.

That Thursday just after Christmas, Janna left her apartment
shortly after 8:30 A.M. She wanted to finish her chores early because
she and her mother were due at her older sister Gail's home by noon
to pick up Derek. Janna was going to be his official baby-sitter, and
she was thrilled about that. Gail and her husband were flying to
Alaska for a week-long fishing trip. Janna adored her nephew and
was looking forward to caring for him. Unlike many teenagers, Janna
Hanson was completely reliable about being where she was supposed to be on time.

It was a typical December day in the Northwest—overcast and
chilly—when Janna left her home. She wore jeans, a white long-
sleeved top, a short, hooded navy blue coat, and a rust and brown
knitted scarf. The scarf was a Christmas present from her Grandma
Hanson.

It was possible to reach the Nile Country Club by going the long
way around on paved streets, but most of the youngsters in the
neighborhood took a well-worn shortcut from the apartment building. The path meandered through a thick stand of fir trees and some
Scotch broom and eventually led directly into the plush country club
grounds near the shores of Lake Ballinger. The path came out close to
her friend's mobile home. On any other day, the woods probably
would have been full of neighborhood kids, but they could sleep late
during Christmas vacation; on December 26, Janna was all alone as
she trudged through the lowering trees.

Later, the only thing that her mother could be positive about was
that Janna *had* reached the trailer safely. The walk along the shortcut
path would have taken her about twenty minutes. Between 9:00 and
9:30 Janna placed a phone call from the mobile home to a school
friend. His mother said he was still asleep, and Janna said she would
call back later.

But Janna did not answer the phone in the mobile home when Doreen Hanson called there at 10:40 A.M. It had begun to rain heavily, and her mother wanted to be sure that Janna did not attempt to walk home in the deluge. Doreen intended to pick Janna up at the mobile home at 11:20, and she didn't want Janna to walk through the storm if she happened to finish early. The phone rang endlessly. As she listened to the repeated ringing of the phone, Doreen Hanson became a little concerned, perhaps with the kind of second sense mothers possess. She tried to reason that Janna might be hesitant to answer a phone in someone else's home.

Doreen Hanson arrived at the trailer at 11:20, just as she and Janna had agreed earlier. She knocked on the door, but there was no response. She listened for the sound of a television blaring or a radio—*something*—inside that might be drowning out her knock. She could hear nothing but the rain thundering down on the trailer's metal roof. Doreen knocked louder, pounding heavily so anyone inside couldn't miss hearing her. Still no one responded.

"I went back and sat in the car, and I thought, Well, maybe she's vacuuming and she can't hear me knock, or she can't hear me because of the rain," Doreen remembers. "So I honked the car horn. She still didn't come out. I think I knew even then that I would never see Janna again."

Most mothers have it—the visceral sense that something is wrong with their children. Good detectives pay attention; those who go strictly by policy and the odds may overlook what is chillingly clear from the very beginning of a case of disappearance. It would be a very long time before attention was paid to Doreen Hanson.

Suddenly Doreen was aware of how isolated the mobile home was—at least at the moment. There seemed to be no one around, not even the maintenance personnel of the golf course. Janna's mother grew frightened. If Janna had been an irresponsible teenager, she might only have been chagrined. But she was calling for a girl who always was on time or, if she couldn't be, always called home to explain why.

The relationship between Doreen Hanson and her youngest daughter was particularly close because Janna was eight years younger than her twin sisters. Since the death of her father, it had been Janna and Doreen against the world. Although she was very popular with her peers, Janna and her mother shared many things for just the two of them. They had recently gone on a crash diet together, and the slightly pudgy teenager had emerged a glowing young woman who looked closer to seventeen than to thirteen.

Doreen Hanson shivered, and it had nothing to do with the bleak rain and keening wind. She remembered that she had seen a Mountlake Terrace Police patrol car parked near a nearby convenience store, so she drove out of the country club. The police unit was still parked where she had seen it. Officer Donald Lyle listened politely as Doreen told him of her concern for Janna and furnished him with a picture from her wallet of her newly slender, blue-eyed blond daughter.

The teenager had only been missing two hours at most. Lyle made an obligatory sweep of the neighborhood. Doreen Hanson drove to the home of one of Janna's best friends, who lived nearby. She didn't really believe Janna had gone there instead of waiting at the mobile home, but she couldn't think of anyplace else to look. Janna's friend was concerned, too, when Doreen explained the reason for her visit, and the two of them hurried back to the shortcut through the woods, hoping that Doreen's concern was the result only of missed connections. Doreen forced herself to believe that they would meet Janna coming the other way along the path; she concentrated so hard that she could almost see her. But she didn't.

As they walked, Doreen Hanson really saw the trail for the first time. She grew more worried when she realized how isolated the kids' shortcut was as it plunged into a black hole of clustered trees and continued on, shut off from the light of day. If Janna had fallen and been hurt in these woods, no one could have heard her cry for help.

But there was no sign at all of Janna in the darkness of the trees. If she had walked this way three hours earlier, there was no way of telling it now.

Doreen drove back to the mobile home, where she was met by other Mountlake Terrace officers. She explained that she didn't have a key to the trailer, and the officers had already learned that the key kept in the possession of maintenance men had been lost.

"Break in," Doreen Hanson told the skeptical police. "I will take responsibility for any damage."

The officers kicked at the lock with full force, and the front door swung open. The group moved quickly through the large mobile home. Janna wasn't there. But she had been there; her house key and the key to the trailer lay on the drainboard. A light was on in one bedroom, and there was a bag of garbage just outside the back door. It was damp but not sodden, as it would have been if it had been sitting there overnight. It was obvious that Janna had begun to clean the trailer, and something had interrupted her; a few dishes bearing the residue of chili sat in the sink. She had not finished her work. Why? In three hours she would have had plenty of time to do the dishes and vacuum.

Nothing was out of place or knocked over; there was no sign of a struggle in the trailer, and that made Doreen feel a little better—but not much. It didn't make sense that Janna had voluntarily walked away from the mobile home, leaving her house keys and the keys to the trailer behind. And she wasn't the kind of girl to leave a job half done.

Doreen went over everything that had happened since they had awakened that morning, as if she could rearrange this scene and somehow make it all right. She fought to keep her panic down. It had been only three hours—closer to four now. Periodically she dialed her own phone number, hoping to hear Janna's voice.

The vast manicured grounds of the country club were deserted. There had been nothing they could connect to Janna on the path she would have taken back home. Where had she gone?

If Janna had been a small child, forces would have been mobilized at once to look for her. But police have to make judgments about teenagers who disappear. The vast majority of missing young people come home within twenty-four hours. In any police jurisdiction in America, a widespread search for vanished adults and teenagers is rarely begun until that period has passed. That is policy. That is the widely used rule of thumb. And sometimes it is tragically wrong. Each instance is different, however. If there is evidence of foul play, the police make a judgment call.

Janna's mother and family could not wait twenty-four hours. Just sitting at home waiting for the phone to ring was agonizing. Doreen Hanson actually found herself hoping that Janna *was* a runaway, although she could not imagine why her daughter would do such a thing. She searched her mind for some quarrel, some disagreement, that might have made Janna want to leave, but there was nothing more than a slight difference of opinion on a trip Janna had wanted to take to Bremerton on a ferryboat. No, that was long since forgotten. She was grasping at anything. Doreen had already raised three girls, and she knew teenagers. She knew that she could trust Janna's good sense—*if* Janna was in a position to make a decision.

While one member of the family remained at home by the phone, Doreen Hanson and Janna's sisters, other relatives, and friends looked for her. They fanned out over the Nile Country Club golf course hunting for some trace of her. Doreen talked with Ken Burke, one of the greenskeepers. He told her not to worry, that youngsters often ran away. He had had some experience in that department, he assured her, and his own kids had always came back.

But Janna didn't.

The Christmas decorations at home, the cookies she had made, her presents, were only sad reminders that Janna wasn't there. Despite Doreen Hanson's objections, Janna Hanson's name and description were entered in statewide computers on December 27 as a runaway.

But was she? Janna had taken no clothing, no makeup, no extra money. Her school principal described her as a well-adjusted, happy student. Her close friends didn't believe she would run away. Rumors started, as they always did, sparked by casual acquaintances and even strangers, rumors that said Janna had hinted that she might run away. They were like cotton candy, evaporating because there was no substance to them.

When 1974 passed into 1975 there was no celebration of the New Year at the Hanson apartment. Doreen was certain by then that something terrible had happened to Janna, but there was no place else for her to look. She arranged to have bulletins bearing Janna's picture posted all over the area in the hope that someone might have seen her daughter.

Mountlake Terrace police, still officially listing Janna as a runaway, sent teletypes to law enforcement agencies in the thirteen western states. Doreen detested having Janna listed as a runaway, but she went along with whatever it might take to keep her disappearance in the public eye.

There *were* people who claimed to have seen Janna alive and well. They were positive it was Janna they had seen. One report came in from Lynnwood, another from Renton. But every attempt to follow up the sightings ended in failure. Janna Hanson's disappearance was becoming like an urban folktale. When police or her mother tried to find the *source* of the sighting, it was always "a friend of my cousin's next-door neighbor" or "Somebody who works down at the K mart heard a customer say . . ." There was no way to get to the source. There was never the last link in the chain. Each person contacted always had new names, and they all ended in frustration.

A casual friend was positive that she had seen Janna at a roller-skating rink. No one else had. As the posters bearing Janna's smiling likeness proliferated all along the West Coast, calls came in from as far away as Santa Barbara, California. One frightening report said that young girls were being hired to be go-go girls in Alaska in an operation that was really a front for white slavery and that Janna had been one of them. Doreen Hanson was packed and ready to fly north when that rumor, too, turned out to be valueless.

In February, divers from the Snohomish County Search and Rescue Unit, led by Sergeant John Taylor, probed the depths of Lake Ballinger for Janna's body. They found junked cars, golf balls, and every other kind of debris, but they did not find Janna Hanson. Doreen had steeled herself for a tragic discovery in the bottom of the lake, but Janna wasn't there.

On February 27 one of Doreen's former neighbors —who was unaware that Janna was missing—passed a blond girl on a down-town Seattle street and was so sure it was Janna that she nodded and said hi to the teenager she had known for years. It was weeks before she found out that Janna had disappeared. The neighbor was contrite as she talked to Doreen Hanson. Had she seen a look-alike—or Janna?

One of the oddest sightings was reported by the brother of a private investigator. He told police that he had talked to a pretty blond girl at his girlfriend's house. He had assumed she was older, and she seemed to be a good friend of his girlfriend. The girl had worn a bathrobe at the time he met her, and she had told him that she had twin sisters—as Janna did—and that she wanted to be a model, as the twins were. When he was shown a picture of Janna Hanson, he swore that was the girl he had seen. Police tracked down the girl.

It was not Janna.

One ominous development came when the family who owned the mobile home returned. As the mother of the household caught up on the washing, she gathered up a bundle of blue jeans. It was only when she started to iron one pair of jeans that she realized they didn't belong to her daughter. They were Janna's—the jeans she had worn the morning she disappeared. If Janna had slipped out of those jeans because they had gotten soaked that rainy morning, what had she put on instead? No clothes were missing from the mobile home.

The Hansons had a friend who knew a psychic in Portland, Oregon, who reportedly had incredible extrasensory powers. The psychic asked Doreen to assemble a sealed paper sack containing some of Janna's possessions. What harm could it do? Doreen asked herself. She gathered a few things, and her friend placed a phone call to the seer, keeping the sack nearby as they talked. He didn't tell Doreen what the psychic had said. It would only have made her endless vigil more difficult. The psychic had "seen" Janna in an area with trees, a pond, and fallen logs. She was almost certain that Janna was dead. If not dead, she was a great distance away from home.

It might well be true, but how could police isolate one area with trees, a pond, and fallen logs in the state of Washington? The whole state was rife with similar spots. The trouble with psychics and police investigations was that psychics frequently spoke in general terms while detectives needed something specific and precise—like a license plate, an address, a Social Security number, or a fingerprint—and in Janna's case, they had nothing at all.

Doreen didn't tell anyone beyond her other daughters, but she sometimes felt that Janna was trying to tell her something. Although she did not hear footsteps approaching, she sometimes heard someone knocking at her apartment door. When she opened it, there was no one there. The weeks had become months, and she had gone through such agony that she wondered if she was only hoping that Janna was trying to get through to her. It wasn't until a friend heard the phantom knocking that Doreen trusted her own ears.

Janna's new Christmas ski equipment, never used, remained in the Hanson apartment as the skiing season came and went. Unbelievably, *eight* months had passed without one scintilla of solid information about Janna Hanson. It was the summer of 1975, and there still was no more information about the blond teenager's whereabouts than there had been the day she vanished, despite the hundreds of teletypes sent, the scores of interviews with her friends and schoolmates, and the fact that her mother never stopped searching for her.

Not really believing that Janna was out there—that she had run away from home over some slight that Doreen had not known about—Doreen went on television, trying once again to reach her missing daughter or someone who might know where she was. Doreen reported that Janna's older sister had a new baby. If Janna knew that and *could* come home, Doreen knew she would. But there were no letters, no phone calls—not even the hollow knock on the front door.

Janna still was missing.

They found Janna Hanson on Sunday, August 3, 1975. The rural community of Maltby is about thirteen miles east of Mountlake Terrace. Close by, there was a large commune, whose members had joined together to operate a farm that would supply most of their simple needs and where they could shut out a world that marched to a different drummer. One of the residents of the commune took a walk on that Sunday afternoon and passed a large cherry tree on his way to an access road. It was a pleasant day, and he noticed nothing unusual until he returned along the same path sometime later. A human skull rested beneath the tree, on top of the earth, almost as if it had been placed there so that it could be discovered. The man picked up the skull, carried it to the commune farmhouse, and called the Snohomish County Sheriff's Office.

The skull might well have belonged to any of several missing persons in the Northwest. All during 1974, beautiful young women had vanished inexplicably until their number totaled nine. Six of them had been found—four identified by their skulls alone—and three still were missing: Janna, Georgeann Hawkins from the University of Washington, and Donna Manson from Olympia. The person who had murdered the girls, however, remained a mystery. Janna Hanson's disappearance had not fit into the pattern of the other missing girls'. She was much younger than they were.

Lawmen from several jurisdictions converged on the tranquil farm where the skull had been found, and dental charts soon established absolutely that the remains found were those of Janna Hanson, the little girl who had vanished almost eight months before. For Doreen Hanson and her family, the long search was over and the last vestige of hope was gone. The agony of not knowing was replaced with a searing sense of loss.

The task of putting the fragmented case together fell to Snohomish County investigators. There was still the possibility that Janna had run away, perhaps joined the commune, and died either naturally or some other way during the months she had been missing—but that was highly unlikely. Good detectives always view a body discovery by beginning with the supposition that they are dealing with a homicide. From there they proceed to suicide, to accidental death, and, only after they have eliminated everything else, to death by natural causes. They are trained to expect the worst.

Snohomish County detective Sergeant Doug Fraser directed the search of the area, aided by Detectives Doug Engelbretson and Ben Duncan and a huge crew of search and rescue personnel. Only Janna's skull had been found. The officers reasoned it probably had been dragged to its resting place beneath the trees by one of the two hunting dogs belonging to the commune. Somewhere in the dense woods and swamp there might be other clues.

The skull bore traces of cedar and swamp cabbage. "We're looking for a swampy area," Fraser suggested. "Someplace with cedar trees, swamp cabbage, perhaps even underwater. Look for a depression in the ground, away from the light."

Unknowingly he was directing his detectives to find a spot very like the area described by the Oregon psychic months before.

It was a big order. The area was gridded into sections a quarter of a mile square, and search and rescue officers from Snohomish County, Marysville, and Alderwood Manor, along with the King County police, literally sifted the ground cover in the grid areas.

It was not an easy search. Included in the grid pattern was a teenage parking spot, a deserted cemetery dating back perhaps a hundred years, and a cattle burial ground, plus thick woods and rolling pastureland.

Deputy Ron Cooper and his wife drove the back roads in his four-wheel-drive vehicle. After many passes, he found an area that seemed to match the criteria Sergeant Fraser had laid down: cedar trees, swamp area, and a depression in the ground. It was three-tenths of a mile from the tree where the skull was found.

Engelbretson and Duncan joined Cooper there and searched the ground on their hands and knees. They found a wristwatch, earrings, a pair of inside-out knee stockings, bits of cloth, a pair of panties, and some human bones.

Janna Hanson had lain there, in that quiet woods, for all the long months that her family and police had searched for her. Physical anthropologists from the Smithsonian Institution would confirm that Janna had been dead since shortly after she vanished.

But how and why she had died were burning questions that had to be answered. And who had brought Janna to the lonely place thirteen miles from the mobile home on the golf course and on the edge of a hippie commune? Snohomish County detectives knew they would be working at a distinct disadvantage. The optimum time for solving a homicide is in the first twenty-four hours after it has occurred. The probability of successful case closure decreases with every day that passes. And Fraser and his crew had to go back eight months and start from the beginning.

They began by questioning the seven families in the commune where Janna had been found. For a week, two hundred searchers had learned about the land; now detectives would learn about the humans who lived there. In the seventies, police and hippies were considered natural enemies, but Fraser and his detectives later spoke of the members of the communal 150-acre farm as "beautiful." The young people who lived off the verdant land did everything they could to cooperate with the investigation. But they knew very little.

They couldn't recall seeing any suspicious vehicle in the area in December of 1974. They did know that a chain that blocked a way leading into the area where the dead girl's remains were found had been mysteriously cut late in December.

One member of their group had left during the year, but he was described as a "loner" who moved on whenever he felt hemmed in by people. He had never shown any tendency toward violence; he was a gentle soul who needed quiet and space.

Detectives checked the police files for any individuals in the Maltby area with records of sex offenses. They came up with two men who had been convicted of rape in the past, but when they traced the whereabouts of the men on December 26, they found they had solid alibis: one was dead drunk in the county jail, and the other had been seen at work the whole day.

By August 25, 1975, Fraser, Duncan, and Engelbretson agreed that everything led right back to the Nile Country Club. They were convinced that Janna had met her killer there.

"We're going to take the old investigation and work right through it again from the beginning," Fraser told co-workers. "Somewhere there's the key that will tell us what happened to Janna."

The officers reread statements made by the two employees of the Nile Country Club who had been working on the day after Christmas: thirty-eight-year-old Kenneth Burke and sixty-five-year-old Sven Torgersen.* Burke was still employed as a greenskeeper, but Torgersen had retired in January. According to their statements, neither man had seen Janna that morning. Burke recalled that he had arrived at work about 6:30 A.M. on December 26. He had taken the key to the trailer from the drawer in the maintenance shack and used it to open the mobile home so that he could check the water lines at 6:55 A.M. Then he had put the key back in the drawer and gone out to check the greens and clear away debris from the storm of the night before. Burke had walked the greens instead of using a cart. He stated he hadn't seen Janna at all that morning.

Later, of course, when the Mountlake Terrace police asked him for the keys to the trailer, he hadn't been able to find them. No one but Burke and Torgersen had had access to the keys.

According to Burke, he had started to replace some trailer steps at the mobile home later, but he had mashed his finger and given it up. That would have been about 10:30 A.M., he estimated. He said he hadn't heard the phone ringing inside, even though Doreen Hanson called Janna at 10:30.

The men usually worked within sight of each other, but on that day—from 11:00 A.M. to 1:00 P.M.—Burke said he hadn't seen Sven Torgersen. He had been eating his lunch. The men's workday had ended at 3:00 P.M.

The Snohomish County detective team next looked at Sven Torgersen's statement about December 26. His account of the day concurred fairly closely with that of his partner. They had come to work before 7:00 A.M. Burke had checked the mobile home and returned the keys. Torgersen's account said he had taken the key later to use the bathroom at the trailer, but he had dropped it on the way there underneath the steps of the maintenance shed. He had not been able to find it right away, but he had found it after the police had left. Too late—they had already kicked open the trailer door. Evidently the two greenskeepers had been separated often during the day; they had been checking separate golf-course areas and had eaten lunch alone.

Fraser tapped the case file in front of him. "There are two things that bother me. This Torgersen saying he lost the key under the steps. If he knew where he lost it, why didn't he just fish down there and get it when the police needed it to open the trailer?"

"And the mail," Duncan cut in. "Burke says he picked up the mail for the trailer, and the report shows that there were some letters inside . . . some damp letters. It couldn't have been the mail from the day before Christmas. That would have been dry by the twenty-sixth. And he couldn't have picked up the mail at seven A.M. when he said he went inside the trailer. The mail isn't delivered that early."

"Right. That's the second thing that doesn't fit," Fraser agreed. "Somebody with a key went back inside that mobile home after the mail was delivered—which would put Burke there the same time Janna was supposed to be there."

On October 2, the Snohomish County detectives interviewed Ken Burke again. He recalled the day of December 26, 1974, well. He agreed that he and Torgersen were the only employees who had access to the trailer keys. He had been on vacation from December 2 to December 23, so he had not known that Janna was supposed to check the trailer, and he had checked it each day as usual. He didn't think there was any reason for Torgersen to go inside the trailer.

Ken Burke said he noticed the bedroom light was on in the trailer when he checked the pipes at 6:45 A.M. on December 26. He said there were no dishes in the sink. He didn't see any keys by the sink. His recall of time had changed ever so slightly. Was it deliberate? Did it matter? Janna wasn't there until 8:40 A.M.

Burke had been very cool as he started to talk with the detectives, but he became increasingly agitated as the conversation continued. There was a reason for that; he told them he had served time in Leavenworth prison for something that had happened while he was in the service in Korea.

They didn't press him. They could check that out themselves. Besides, Ken Burke had some theories of his own to offer about a possible suspect. He told the Snohomish County investigators that there had been a strange young man around the golf course—Rick Ames,* who earned a living as an itinerant golf ball diver. Ames traveled around the area scooping up lost balls in water traps. He was nineteen and, according to Burke, had "a dirty mind and was always after girls." Burke described the youth as six feet five inches tall; he wore size 13 shoes and had bright red hair. Burke thought Ames had been around the Nile Country Club course during December of 1974.

"Shouldn't be difficult to spot," Engelbretson commented dryly as the detectives drove back to their office in Everett.

Further checking proved that there was a Rick Ames who dived for balls in golf course ponds around the state and that he had been in Mountlake Terrace. But not on December 26. Duncan and Engelbretson traced his meanderings by interviewing a dozen acquaintances of the golf ball diver. He had been in the area before Christmas, but then he had gone to Vancouver, Washington, 200 miles south. They verified that he had been on a train on the critical day. Nevertheless, they located him and gave him a polygraph examination. He passed easily.

Ken Burke was contacted again on September 11. They told him that they wanted to talk further with Sven Torgersen, and Burke pulled out a picture postcard that bore the retired man's address in Arizona. "You'll have to travel a bit to talk to Sven. He's down there living the good life."

Duncan and Fraser studied the man before them. Burke—five feet eleven inches tall, 155 pounds—did not present a formidable image. He spoke with a slight southern drawl as he fielded their questions. He was a garrulous man, and he seemed to want to explain his prison sentence.

So they let him.

Burke told them that he had fought in the Korean War and had been threatened by his first sergeant. He'd believed the man meant it, so he had lain in wait for the sergeant when he was on guard duty. "I shot him five times with a forty-five," he said.

Amazingly, the sergeant had survived, but Burke said the corporal of the guard had been hit by a stray bullet and died. Burke said he had been convicted and sent to Leavenworth in the 1950s. He said he had been paroled in 1967 and remained on active parole until 1972. Ken Burke was clearly panicked at the thought of going back to prison. He talked too much, and he seemed to embroider his stories with too much detail. The detectives knew he was too young to have been in the Korean War. They doubted his whole story. He was hiding something.

Burke had said that nineteen-year-old Rick Ames was a womanizer. The detectives had heard much the same story about Burke from the redheaded golf ball collector. Ames had said that Burke made weird comments about girls and that he personally "would never trust" the greenskeeper around a girl.

The time had come to give a lie detector test to Ken Burke. He agreed to appear at the sheriff's office on September 25 for the polygraph examination. He did show up, but he had taken so many tranquilizers that the machine's leads might well have been connected to a department store mannequin. A new appointment was set for September 30.

The Snohomish County detectives felt that Ken Burke had lied about his activities on December 26. Among the things that bothered them were the lost key, the mail in the trailer, his claim that he hadn't seen Janna that day, and his insistence that he hadn't heard the phone ring at 10:30 when he supposedly was working on the steps just outside the mobile home. The investigators had looked at those steps and found them far too heavy for any one man to move; there was no way he could even have attempted to place them at the trailer door by himself. He would have ruined his back and had the hernia to end all hernias if he had.

The Snohomish County detectives had interviewed almost two hundred people in the Janna Hanson case, but they kept coming back to Burke. He did not avoid them, and although he was apprised of his constitutional rights before each conversation, he said he did not want a lawyer. He almost seemed to enjoy jousting with them, but his nerves always began to betray him when the conversation got too specific about Janna.

On September 30, Ken Burke showed up again to take a polygraph test. But this time he was so distraught that he could not even be linked up to the machine. He broke into tears and said, "I don't want to go back in a cage."

Burke told the detectives that he often thought about violence and death, but he didn't know why. He said he often thought about killing those closest to him, even though he loved them.

"Sometimes I think about killing people . . . all people . . . just beating their heads," he said.

Taken aback, the detectives let him talk. Words spilled out of him like lava long under pressure in a volcano. Burke recalled that he had killed his cat by beating it to death. As a teenager he had cut off his dog's head because he wanted to make a plaster cast of it. The detectives stared at him.

"Did you kill Janna?" one of the investigators asked quietly.

"I don't think so."

Asked if he'd ever had any treatment for his emotional problems, Ken Burke replied that he had "only Mickey Mouse games with ink spots in prison." Then the suspect pleaded, "Please help me." Fraser and Duncan immediately arranged for an appointment for Burke at a mental health clinic. They also consulted with a psychiatrist, outlining what they had heard, and were told that their suspect might very well be dangerous to the public and, for that matter, to himself.

The detectives were in an untenable position. They could not force Burke to accept treatment, nor did they have enough physical evidence to arrest him on a murder charge. On October 2, they talked with him again. Again he refused to have a lawyer present. Once again they retraced that long-ago stormy day after Christmas.

Burke said he ate his lunch—a sandwich—early that day, from 10:30 to 11:00, in the maintenance shed. In this latest version he said he went to the mobile home at 11:00 to fix the steps, but stopped after he mashed his thumb. He said he was having pains from an operation done three weeks earlier and that he went home to lie down until 1:00. When he returned to the country club at 1:00, he saw the police personnel around the mobile home.

He was "almost positive" that he hadn't hurt Janna. He went on to say that he got an urge to kill about once a month, but he usually "drove it off." He remembered an incident that had occurred years earlier at Fort Gordon, Georgia, where he had hitched a ride with a motorist and then attacked him with brass knuckles. "I tossed him in the palms and drove off. I never heard of him again."

Ken Burke's obsession with violence had gripped him for over twenty years. He recalled almost killing his father when he was seventeen; he had aimed a loaded gun at the sleeping man and started to squeeze the trigger when his father groaned and turned over. That had frightened Ken and he fled. Another time, he said, a young employee had "sassed" him, and Burke had headed for him with a hammer. "I smashed a bench with the hammer instead," he said.

Fraser and Duncan stopped the interview and took Burke to a hospital for a psychiatric evaluation. He was diagnosed as having a mild "situational depression" because of his involvement in a homicide investigation and his fear of returning to prison. He was not diagnosed as psychotic—crazy. Burke seemed calmer when they took him home.

On October 10, Ben Duncan was successful in placing a phone call to Sven Torgersen. Torgersen repeated much of what he had said ten months before. He said Burke had come back about 7:00 A.M. after checking the trailer. The two of them went out to clear debris, but they weren't together. He said Ken ate lunch at 9:45 while he himself went to a nearby shopping center. When he returned at 10:30, Burke was gone. Sven said he took the trailer key from the drawer just before the police got there and then he lost it. Later, Burke complained of pain and went home.

Asked what kind of tires were on Burke's car (Mountlake Terrace officer Lyle had noted snow tire tracks directly behind the trailer when he arrived on the morning of December 26), Sven said "snow tires."

"Did Burke ever talk about sex?" Duncan asked.

"Men always talk about sex some when they get together."

"Mr. Torgersen," Duncan said, "we've given polygraphs to almost everyone else. Would you be willing to take one if I can arrange it with the Phoenix police department?"

There was a long pause, then Torgersen blurted, "Well . . . about that key . . ."

"Yes."

"Well, that wasn't exactly the way it happened. When the officers asked for the key, I just stood there like a fool. I never took it, and I never had it. I guess I just made it up out of embarrassment."

Duncan's long frustration at getting vague answers broke through as he said, "Who the hell had it?"

Torgersen didn't know. "Somebody must have found it," he said. "I lied and said it was lost so I wouldn't look like an ass. Ken Burke turned it in the day after because he said he didn't want any more to do with that trailer."

On October 16, Duncan and Engelbretson talked with Ken Burke at the Nile Country Club. Burke was angry when he heard that Sven Torgersen said that he had the key on December 27. He said the key probably was in the drawer the whole time after he'd put it there early on the morning of December 26. In this new—and once again different—statement, Burke claimed that he had driven a motor scooter up to the back door of the mobile home and that it had left the wide tire marks.

He said he hadn't seen the damp garbage sack, but that Mountlake Terrace police officers had told him about it. His questioners knew that the Mountlake Terrace cops had never told him that. It was information they had all deliberately held back so they could eliminate chronic confessors.

"*Anybody* could have had a key made for that trailer," Burke insisted. He had a ready explanation for every discrepancy mentioned, but sweat beaded on his forehead as he talked with the two detectives.

On the evening of October 16 the man who had convinced a psychiatrist that he was essentially sane did something aberrant. He had given his last version of his whereabouts on the day Janna Hanson vanished. Ken Burke was found dead of a self-inflicted bullet wound in the head. He left a note disclaiming any guilt in the death of Janna Hanson. The death weapon was a .25-caliber automatic, a gun he had told friends he had "thrown in the bay" many months earlier. It was a Colt with the serial numbers filed off.

Any information that Ken Burke had about Janna Hanson's death died with him. But the investigation was not over. Duncan flew to Phoenix and observed a polygraph examination administered to Sven Torgersen. It proved the old man was telling the truth when he said he had never seen Janna Hanson and didn't know her. But he admitted he had lied about some of the occurrences of December 26.

"The first part of the morning went just like I said," Torgersen told Duncan. "But I didn't tell you that Ken left later and took the scooter. He came up from the mobile home area and told me I should go to lunch early." Torgersen described Burke as "awful nervous" and said his co-worker just sat in the maintenance shed a little after 10:30 and shook his head back and forth. When Torgersen came back from lunch shortly before 11:30, he found that Burke was gone. A little while later Ken Burke came walking up the hill from the trailer complaining of "pains." He left the country club grounds and didn't come back until one o'clock that afternoon.

Torgersen had lied about the sequence of events because neither man had spent much time working that day, and Torgersen was afraid they would be in trouble with the golf course management.

The investigators theorized that Ken Burke had come upon Janna

Hanson as she cleaned her friend's mobile home that morning. From their countless sessions with him, they were aware of the strength of his compulsion to kill. The pictures in their minds were chilling, but they knew they were right. Burke must have forced Janna to his car, parked at the back door. There had been no struggle in the trailer.

Janna's resting place in the cedar forest was a half hour's drive from the country club in midday traffic. Burke could have strangled Janna with her own scarf, hidden her body, and returned to the golf course by one o'clock.

Doreen Hanson was finally able to tell the public what she had always believed: Janna was never a runaway. She was probably already dead when her mother went looking for her at 11:20 on the morning of December 26, 1974. There was no way she could go home again to the family she loved.

Janna Hanson's memorial service at the Richmond Beach Congregational Church on August 21, 1975, was marked not by grief but by joy for the happy girl she had been.

Doreen Hanson was active for many years in Family and Friends of Missing Persons and Victims of Violent Crimes.

CAMPBELL'S REVENGE

Renae Wicklund, a beautiful drum majorette in high school in Jamestown, North Dakota. After graduation she moved to the West, where she found great happiness and stark tragedy.

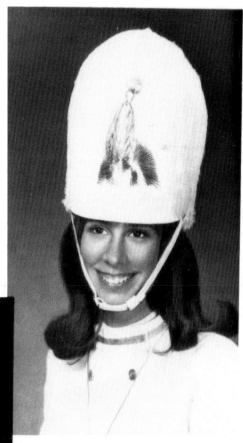

Shannah Wicklund was too young to remember the first time the huge red-haired man came to her house.

CAMPBELL'S REVENGE

Snohomish County detective Joe Belinc worked tirelessly to track down the killer of Shannah and Renae Wicklund and Barbara Hendrickson. *(Ann Rule)*

Washington State patrolmen leading Charles Campbell to the awaiting squad car that would take him to Snohomish County Superior Court, where his 1989 death warrant was issued. *(Drew Perine)*

THE HIT PERSON

Petite and beautiful Cynthia
Marler, who stood trial for an
unthinkable crime. *(Leslie Rule)*

Seattle homicide detective Dan
Engle during the trial of Cynthia
Marler. He worked for months to
connect her to the inexplicable
murder of Wanda Touchstone.
(Leslie Rule)

THE RUNAWAY

Doreen Hanson holding a picture of her thirteen-year-old daughter, Janna. When Janna vanished, local police said that she was a runaway, but her mother was filled with dread. It took almost a year for detectives to discover the truth. *(Ann Rule)*

NILE COUNTRY CLUB

A few days after Christmas 1974, Janna Hanson walked onto the grounds of the Nile Country Club (entrance shown here) and disappeared. But the answer lay here all along. *(Ann Rule)*

REHABILITATION OF A MONSTER

The hut where Richard Marquette lived in 1961 was the site of the murder of Joan Caudle.

REHABILITATION OF A MONSTER

Jim Byrnes, detective lieutenant in the Marion County sheriff's department, tracked down Richard Marquette for the second time, in 1975.

Richard Marquette was returned to the Oregon State Penitentiary after his second conviction for sadistic murder.

MOLLY'S MURDER

Molly McClure was a much-loved golden girl. Her killer left minute evidence that led straight to him. *(Ann Rule)*

MOLLY'S MURDER

Seattle police homicide detective Rudy Sutlovich (above) was the "tall" half of the brilliant investigative team that tracked down Molly's killer. He and homicide detective Hank Gruber (below), the other half of the team, will always remember Molly, even though they never knew her while she was alive. *(Ann Rule)*

The Rehabilitation of a Monster

Whenever I present *a seminar or lecture or appear on a radio or television talk show, there is one question I always expect: "Do you believe in the death penalty?" Before I researched the following case, my answer was no. I began true crime writing as the complete social worker. I believed that anyone could be rehabilitated if he or she was only given love and kindness and made to feel valued. But I learned that some human beings have no compassion, no empathy, and no desire whatsoever to change. And why should they change? They are quite content the way things are. And the way things are for them is that they have an obsessive drive to take what they want, when they want it, without a backward glance at the suffering and death they cause.*

Since I wrote about the killer in the following story, I have come upon his counterparts again and again. They all make wonderful prisoners; they are compliant, charming, and cooperative. They are almost always handsome— or beautiful—and intelligent. The people they interact with want to like them. And the charismatic sadistic sociopaths count on that. They will go along with the prison program and never give one clue about what they are really thinking.

Of course they won't reveal what is inside. They want to get out of prison. And too many of them do.

My answer then is yes. I do support the death penalty in certain instances. When a killer's first crimes are marked by such cruelty that the mass of men must turn away from the details, I don't believe he deserves a second chance. If life in prison literally meant life in prison, I would be against the death penalty. But a life sentence rarely results in life in prison, and I prefer to give the benefit of the doubt to innocent victims yet to be rather than to a proven sadistic killer.

Salem is the capital of Oregon, a beautiful city in a beautiful state. Even in December, roses bloom along the parking strips of most streets. In the spring, Salem's cherry trees are frothy pink with blossoms, and there are rhododendrons, azaleas, daffodils, and the fragrant satin florets of daphne everywhere. The huge statue of the golden pioneer towers majestically above the Oregon State Capitol beckoning new settlers. Ever since the days of the *real* pioneers, thousands upon thousands of people have come to Oregon seeking a fresh start, a new life in a faraway place. Some accomplish their dreams; some have only sought out a geographical solution to their troubles, unaware that they have brought worry and failure right along with them.

Salem is in Marion County, where all but one of Oregon's state institutions are located: the state prison, the state mental hospital, the home for the developmentally disabled, and the girls' training school—a euphemism for "reform school." Only the boys' training school is located outside the capital county. Many of the "graduates" of these institution stay on in Salem, living in a section of the city that locals call "Felony Flats." Even so, Salem does not have a markedly high incidence of crime, but when there are crimes in Salem and in Marion County, many of them are bizarre, sensational, and complicated.

Fishing should have been better than it was on that early spring afternoon of April 19, 1975. The fisherman decided to try one more spot in the slough near the Brown's Island Sanitary Landfill southeast of Salem. He had moved to a stony bank beneath a wooden bridge and was preparing to drop his line again when his eyes fixed on what appeared to be parts of a department store mannequin floating among the reeds in the shallows at the west side of the bridge. There was some clothing drifting there, too, and a white towel.

349

When the fisherman looked more closely at the mannequin's legs, however, he drew back in horror. He could see skeletal ball joints at the tops of the limbs that were undulating slowly in the water. Half aloud, he murmured, "Dummies don't have no ball joints. . . ."

All thoughts of fishing gone now, the man ran to his car and headed for a telephone. In his panicked rush, he couldn't find a phone booth right away, and he decided to go directly to Salem Police headquarters to report his gruesome find.

Salem officer R. Richie responded and soon verified that there were indeed human remains in the slough—but he noted that the area was in Marion County Sheriff Jim Heenan's jurisdiction. Marion County Sergeant Ronald Beodigheimer was dispatched at 4:14 on that Saturday afternoon, the first of a phalanx of investigators to rush to the scene: Chief of Detectives Lieutenant James Byrnes, Detective Lieutenant Kilburn McCoy, Detectives Larry Lord and Dave Kominek, Corporal Dave McMullen, Detectives Ron Martin, Carl Bramlett, and Lieutenant Ken Keuscher.

Marion County District Attorney Gary Gortmaker, known throughout Oregon's thirty-six counties as the definitive policemen's D.A., joined the investigators, as he always did.

Many of the detectives at the Brown's Island site had worked scores of homicides, but none of them had ever seen anything like the horrendous mass of human tissue that floated in the slough. Clearly, it had been a woman: two breasts bobbed near the surface. Her head, arms, legs, torso, and unidentifiable pieces of flesh were there too—all dissected as neatly as if they had never been part of an intact human form. As if the desecration of the body by amputation were not enough, the butcher who had done this had scored the limbs with a sharp instrument, laying the flesh open to the bone in wavering vertical cuts.

They made no attempt to remove the fragmented corpse from the water until the Oregon State medical examiner, Dr. William Brady, arrived from Portland. The dapper pathologist walked a circumscribed path to the edge of the slough, waded in, and pulled the torso onto the bank. It, too, had been slashed and mutilated. The breasts, of course, were nearby in the water; the genitals were completely missing, excised with gynecological thoroughness.

Strangely, only the woman's head was free of the savage mutilation. Her eyes were closed and incongruously peaceful. Her complexion was dark, suggesting Spanish, Indian, or perhaps black origin. Her eyebrows were carefully plucked and arched, her lips full. Even drenched with the muddy water of the slough, the victim's hair was still very curly and dark—more brown than black.

The investigators fished the clothing from the water. All of it seemed to be female apparel: blue slacks, a blue and gray plaid jacket top, a white sweater, panties, a girdle, and a Playtex bra cut through the middle in the front. The hook panel from the back was missing. There were shoes—black leather sling-backs with a medium heel. The clothing was tasteful, well coordinated, and handmade by a seamstress of considerable skill.

The towel was white, utilitarian—probably from a motel—and it bore distinct bloodstains, as did a flowered pillowcase.

There was one distinctly male item in the slough: a mateless sock, grayish white with a band of red at the ankle—the kind of sock a man might wear to work in the woods or to go hunting. Maybe the sock was a mistake, caught up accidentally as the killer reached into a drawer or cupboard for something to wrap his gruesome handiwork in.

Chief of Detectives Jim Byrnes took color photographs of every phase of the crime-scene investigation; there would be 120 shots when he finished, an awesome photographic record of the most sadistic homicide ever uncovered in Marion County.

The investigators worked as rapidly as they could without eliminating any of the painstakingly tedious steps of a thorough crime-scene probe. As they performed their tasks, the April afternoon sun began to deepen into twilight and they knew that precious physical evidence could drift away or sink into the silt at the bottom of the slough.

Evidently the killer had expected that the body parts and clothing would sink; perhaps he was unaware that the slough was only two or three feet deep where it passed beneath the bridge. The fact that they had not sunk might be the one advantage the detectives had.

But that was the *only* point in their favor. Identification of the victim was going to be difficult. Fingerprints were out; her hands had been so severely flayed that her fingertips were virtually destroyed. There were no rings, no jewelry at all beyond the broken strands of silver chain that had once been a necklace. Most disappointing of all, there was no purse that might have held a driver's license, a ticket stub, a scribbled note that could give a clue to who the fragmented lady before them had been.

The body parts were removed from the scene at 8:30 P.M.—more than four hours after the investigators had reached the Brown's

Island location—and taken to Golden's Mortuary in Salem for further examination by Dr. Brady and Deputy Medical Examiner Roy Patten.

According to the pathologists, the woman had been thirty to forty years old, a nonsmoker, probably a nondrinker, five feet two to five feet four inches tall, and had weighed 145 to 165 pounds. She had borne at least one child, and she suffered from gall bladder disease. There was no way to tell if she had been raped; her external and internal genitalia were completely gone, excised by the knife of what could only be a madman. The right nipple was also cut away. "He knew what he was doing," the pathologist commented quietly.

It was almost as if Jack the Ripper were still alive. The pathologists' findings were frighteningly similar to those found in London ninety years earlier.

The woman had been dead twenty-four to thirty-six hours, not from the incredible knife wounds but from manual strangulation. The intact hyoid bone at the back of her throat eliminated strangulation by ligature, and her eyes, cheeks, heart, and lungs were all dotted with the characteristic petechiae—the small burst blood vessels—of strangulation.

The victim's nails were strangely mutilated too; some had been deliberately pulled loose, while others were broken. Her face was very scarred, but they were old scars, long healed, indicating that she had suffered terrible beatings in the past.

Chief Byrnes took pictures of the dead woman's face, Polaroids that would be hand-carried at once to every law agency in the area. Other copies were rushed to the Salem *Statesman Journal* so that they could be published in the early editions Sunday morning. Later, at midnight, there would be a debriefing of investigative personnel, but no sleep; the enormity of the crime had changed night into day for the Marion County detectives.

Kilburn McCoy and Jim Byrnes checked missing persons reports that had come in the previous day; they found none that matched the description of the nameless victim. But then, she was an adult female, dead only a short time; it was quite possible that no one had seen fit to report her missing.

The second break in the mutilation slaying came in the form of a phone call to Marion County headquarters at 11:30 Sunday morning. The man who called had just read his Sunday paper. He said, "That woman—the dead woman—I can't be sure, but she looks like a woman I hired to do some sewing for me. She advertised as a seamstress, and she was very good. She was a white woman, but very dark-complected, and she had several scars on her face. She said she was from North or South Carolina. Her name was Betty Wilson. I've got her phone number. Would that help?"

Chief Byrnes told the caller that it most assuredly would.

The number was a listing in Scio, a hamlet in neighboring Linn County. Byrnes called the number and asked for Betty. The woman said she was Betty Wilson's sister—but Betty was not at home. Then Jim Byrnes explained who he was and the sister asked, "Oh, is this about the missing persons report? I just filed it at the Linn County Sheriff's Office. Betty hasn't been home since Friday night."

Tactfully, Byrnes asked the woman if she would come to Salem and attempt to make an identification of the victim. She agreed, and, by 11:00 P.M. that Sunday, the identity of the dismembered woman in the slough was confirmed. She was thirty-five-year-old Betty Lucille Wilson, late of Fayetteville, North Carolina.

Much irony may be found in murder: Betty Wilson was a woman who had spent her life looking for love and security, and she had suffered mightily in her thirty-five years. She had come to the place of her cruel death because she had run away from a life of abuse. Escaping that, she had met an even worse fate.

Betty was one of seventeen brothers and sisters. She married at sixteen and over the next nine years had seven children of her own. When she died, those children were eighteen, seventeen, sixteen, fifteen, fourteen, thirteen, and nine—all of them in foster homes in the South.

There was never much money in the household although Betty had tried to help with piecework sewing jobs. The family had lived in an old bus at the edge of a city dump in Fayetteville with none of the facilities that constitute a proper home. And Betty Wilson had claimed that she had been beaten by her husband, not once but often—which accounted for the old scars on her face; at one point, she said she had been beaten so severely that she was blinded for five days.

Betty Wilson had made her own last desperate bid for freedom in January of 1975. Her sister and family had driven away from a visit in Fayetteville and had gone many miles west when Betty popped up from the backseat. She was a stowaway, a very frightened stowaway, who begged to be allowed to go to Scio with them because she wanted to start a new life.

Betty was welcomed. Her sister's family had a lovely home, and there would be a room for her. She promised to support herself as soon as she could as a seamstress. She hoped to get situated securely enough so that she could send for her children.

Investigators Byrnes and McCoy were shown the room Betty Wilson occupied in her sister's home. She had pitifully few belongings—one suitcase, a few clothes, and some personal papers. She had made the clothes herself. "Betty could make a complete outfit in a day," her sister said sadly. "She could turn a few dollars' worth of material into a seventy-five-dollar outfit."

Betty Wilson was not a bar hopper or a party girl. She had been married since she was hardly more than a child. She didn't smoke, seldom drank more than a beer or two, and her sister said she had received no phone calls except those from sewing customers. Betty had filed for divorce from her husband through the legal aid office in Linn County.

Betty had been out at night only once since January. The second time was the evening of April 18. On that Friday evening just past, Betty's niece—who was fond of her aunt—had invited her to go along on a date. The trio planned to go to the Pepper Tree restaurant in Salem. They would have dinner and dance to the combo there. Betty loved to dance. She was thrilled to be invited and had dressed in a new blue pantsuit she'd made for herself.

Right from the start things had gone wrong. Betty's niece, who had just turned twenty, was not allowed into the Pepper Tree because she was underage. Betty had been so disappointed that the niece and her date suggested that she stay and dance for a while. They would come back and pick her up around 11:00 P.M.

"And did you?" Jim Byrnes asked the young couple.

"I went back in," the youth answered. "I could only go up to the velvet rope they had strung up there. They said they already had 250 people inside and the fire marshal wouldn't allow more. I stood there until Betty saw me and came over. She said she was having such a good time that she didn't want to leave then—said she'd meet us later at a friend's apartment in Stayton."

Questioned further, the niece's boyfriend said that there had been a man standing behind Betty who might possibly have been with her. He recalled that the man had dark hair and was about five feet ten inches tall.

"Anyway, I went back out to the car and told my girl that Betty wanted to stay. She said, 'No way. Mom will kill me. I'm supposed to look after Betty.' We couldn't find a place to park right away. When we went back, we couldn't find Betty."

The young couple looked for Betty Wilson, drove around, and notified the friend in Stayton that Betty would be coming there. But she didn't. At 3:00 A.M. they gave up and went home.

While this interview was going on, Oregon State Police technicians and divers searched the banks and waters of the slough for evidence that might show up in the light of day. They found more human tissue and, oddly, a profusion of lollipop sticks.

Lieutenants Byrnes and McCoy headed for the Pepper Tree. Maybe the missing clues to Betty Wilson's disappearance could be found there. The club was flamboyantly and expensively decorated in shades of red, from its flocked wallpaper to its padded bar and thick carpeting. It was the kind of restaurant that drew both couples and singles, always well patronized, especially on weekends. It was not a pickup spot, but strangers did feel free to dance together and "ladies' choice" dances were a regular feature.

The two detectives found the staff of twelve gathered to talk with them. The managers, bartenders, and cocktail waitresses were cooperative, searching their memories for recollections of Betty Wilson and any men she might have danced with on the previous Friday night. But it wasn't easy; there had been 250 human beings inside the Pepper Tree, dancing, drinking, and listening to the blaring rock ensemble. But several *did* recall the woman in the blue pantsuit, principally because of her pronounced southern accent. She had joined two younger women at a table first and then moved to the bar.

The barmaid in her section remembered, "She seemed to be having a good time. She had a few beers. Maybe she switched to Harvey Wallbangers later . . . I'm not sure. She paid for her drinks with a lot of change she had in her purse. She left unexpectedly. You know, people at the bar usually say good-bye or something, but she was just *gone.*"

Lieutenant McCoy stood at the padded barstool where the victim had sat and looked directly along the bar. Anyone sitting there would be in eye contact with the occupant of a stool five seats away along the curving bar. The investigators talked to the bartender in that section. Who had been sitting there? A lot of people—but he remembered one man who came into the club occasionally, a man who had mentioned he had a problem with alcohol and was on an Antabuse program (the drug when ingested concurrently with alcohol makes a person violently ill).

"This guy could handle a beer or two, though, if he spaced it out with straight water."

The bartender didn't know the man's name, but said he was

middle-aged and came in three or four times a week. He *did* remember the woman down the bar who had picked up her purse and coat and joined the man after a ladies' choice number. He had not seen them leave together.

How were they going to isolate one average-looking middle-aged man out of 250 people? They had no proof that he had even left the Pepper Tree with Betty Wilson.

Jim Byrnes wondered if Betty Wilson's husband—the man who she said had beat her—hated her enough to follow her 3,000 miles across the country to finish the job. He contacted Chief of Detectives Major Kiser in Fayetteville, North Carolina, and asked for a verification of Wilson's whereabouts during the essential time period. Kiser reported back that Wilson had punched in at his job on April 17 and 18 and was seen by a deputy who knew him well in Fayetteville at 8:00 A.M. on Saturday, April 19. There was no way he could have been in Oregon when his estranged wife was killed and dismembered.

The Marion County detectives had now gone almost thirty-six hours without sleep, and Betty Wilson's killer was almost as much of a mystery as he had been to begin with. They interviewed local residents who lived near the wooden bridge over the slough. A farmer recalled seeing a white International pickup parked there about 10:00 A.M. on the morning of April 19. He hadn't even bothered to look at the license number because the man was obviously a fisherman.

Several teenagers came forward and said their car had been stuck in mud near the bridge at 11:00 P.M. on Saturday. They hadn't seen the body in the water, but then, they hadn't looked in the water.

The tire and shoe prints Jim Byrnes had photographed at the slough bank proved useless as evidence; the ground was too gravelly to show clear demarcations.

On Sunday, April 20, detectives talked to employees in the office on the sanitary landfill dump. Perhaps they had seen the vehicle that had carried Betty Wilson's body parts to the slough. And there they found the kind of lead a detective dreams of. The personnel at the dump explained that every vehicle coming into the landfill must stop, pay, and give the name of the driver. "We have a receipt for every vehicle," one employee said. "Customers who are not on a regular contract get the original, and we keep the carbon."

The detectives asked to see the records for the early morning of April 19. The first three entries were before 7:45 A.M. when the day shift employee came on. Two were regular customers, truckers who routinely dumped large loads of trash in the landfill.

"This third one, the one with the 'sixty-nine Ford pickup-camper, was a stranger," the early morning man recalled. "I asked for his name, and he said, 'You'll never be able to spell it.' Here it is."

The investigators studied the slip. The name was Marzuette, and it was indeed unusual. Returning to the sheriff's office, they checked phone books for twelve surrounding communities and didn't come up with even one Marzuette. There was a man with a name similar to Marzuette—a man whom Detective Chief Jim Byrnes remembered only too well. He'd had occasion, as a rookie patrolman in Beaverton, Oregon, fourteen years earlier, to participate in one of the biggest manhunts in the Northwest. The man he had stalked then through the woods and brush of the Portland suburb was Richard Laurence Marquette, twenty-six, a murderer whose crime was so savage that any law enforcement officer who heard about him would never forget him.

Chief Byrnes had thought of Marquette frequently during the Wilson investigation, but it had seemed almost too pat. He hadn't wanted to focus on Marquette merely because he *seemed* right, and thereby blind himself to other possibilities. Tunnel vision in a homicide investigation could be dangerous.

Now, while thumbing through the Salem directory to see if the name Marquette was there, Byrnes thought back to the events of 1961.

It had begun on Thursday, June 8, 1961, with quiet horror. A Portland, Oregon, housewife noticed that her dog had brought home a paper bag, probably after prowling the neighbors' garbage cans. Exasperated, she called the animal over and pried the bag from its mouth. As the dog's teeth lost their grip, the bag came open and something rolled out on the grass.

It was a foot—a human foot—carefully severed at the ankle. She had to force herself to look at it. It was undoubtedly a woman's foot, petite in size, with bright red toenails.

Portland Police Chief of Detectives Byron Shields and a crew of homicide detectives were dispatched at once in answer to the woman's frantic report. Arriving and examining the foot, they agreed it was human, and they noted it had come from a body that had not yet undergone any decomposition. Even as they looked at the gruesome find, the dog scampered off again. Following the animal, they found a second package. This one contained a human hand, amputated just as neatly as the foot.

The Portland detectives called for help from uniformed patrolmen, and the area around the complainant's home was searched. There was another hand and a femur; the thigh had been boned as neatly as a haunch of beef. None of the body parts had been buried, all had been bled almost dry, and all were fresh; the pathologist, Dr. William Lehman, felt that the woman who had been dismembered had not been dead for longer than forty-eight hours. He promised detectives he would roll the fingers of the hands for prints as soon as possible.

"There is something else that might help in identification," Lehman commented. "The third and fourth toes are webbed; the cleft of the skin there is very shallow. Someone close to the victim may have noticed that."

While officers combed the neighborhood's garbage cans, vacant lots, empty houses, and thousands of other spots where a killer could hide the grisly packages, the disembodied hands were rolled for prints. Unfortunately, only a thumb and three fingers gave clear prints; the other fingerprints had been mutilated beyond recognition.

At that time—decades before computerized fingerprint matching—the FBI kept single prints on file only in the cases of the most-wanted criminals. Without a full set of prints, Portland detectives could not hope for a quick identification via the good prints—but they *could* serve to confirm identity of a victim whose prints were already known.

The detectives found no more body pieces, even though search dogs, Explorer Scouts, and jail trusties had been called upon to enlarge the sweep around the quiet Portland neighborhood.

Where the rest of the dissected woman was, and *who* she was, no one knew. Given the sketchy remains the pathologist had to work with, the supposition was that the victim was a young female, probably brunette, with fair skin, who wore a size seven shoe.

A check of missing persons records in Portland and vicinity showed that four youngish women had been reported missing in the previous week. Shields concentrated on those who had disappeared during the forty-eight hours prior to the morning of June 8. Unless the body parts had been refrigerated, they could not have belonged to anyone missing before Monday, June 5.

The first was a sixteen-year-old girl, June Freese.* She was an orphan who had moved in with an aunt two years earlier. It was hardly a surprise that the combination of a stormy teenager and a spinster who had lived alone for years had not worked. The aunt told detectives that June had threatened to run away to California many times in the past. Now, in the first week of June, with school out, it appeared that the girl had carried out her threat.

"She took her clothes, jewelry, and she had a little money. I've checked her friends, and they haven't seen her at all. I'm afraid she tried to hitchhike and someone terrible picked her up," the aunt confided fearfully.

Asked if her niece had any webbing between her toes, the relative could recall none. A check of the shoes left behind in June's closet showed them to be a good size smaller than the severed foot.

The second missing report had been filed by the husband of a Portland woman, twenty-four-year-old Joan Caudle. Her husband told the investigators that she had gone out Monday evening, June 5, to do some Father's Day shopping. The sheet-metal worker said he'd stayed home to baby-sit with their two small children. "Joan had over a hundred dollars in cash with her; I'd cashed my paycheck Saturday night, and she had most of it."

He said he had not reported his wife missing for two days because he figured she had stayed away for reasons of her own. Her mother had been very ill and was, in fact, dying. It had hit Joan hard. If she needed some time to control her emotions, he understood.

But now he was becoming frightened. He'd called her relatives and friends, but none of them had seen or heard from his pretty wife. As far as he could tell, Joan hadn't even called the hospital to check on her mother's condition.

Joan's husband couldn't say whether she had webbed toes; the Portland detectives were realizing that the toes of a loved one were not something the average person even noticed. "This is one time I wish we had a witness who was a foot fetishist," one officer commented sardonically.

The shoes in Joan Caudle's closet were size seven. That made her a "possible"—although a good 40 percent of the women in Portland wore the same size.

The third missing person report was about a thirty-year-old Beaverton, Oregon, secretary who hadn't shown up for work on Monday morning. She was quickly eliminated as a possible victim; she was back home by the time detectives called. She'd taken an unexpected trip with her estranged husband in an attempt to patch up the marriage. It hadn't worked, and she had come back to file for divorce. It had never occurred to her that anyone would report her missing.

Alma Jean Stromberg,* a nineteen-year-old farm girl, was the final missing person the detectives scrutinized. Alma Jean had been gone from her home just outside Portland for a week. Her mother said there had been a family quarrel. "She wanted to work and buy clothes," the woman said tearfully, "and her dad said she should stay on the farm and do chores and he'd see she got all the clothes she needed. . . . I pleaded with her not to go, and then I said, 'Go ahead, but at least write to me and let me know where you're at.' But she didn't. She was mad at me too."

Alma Jean wore a size seven shoe, but her mother said she had never painted her toenails. "Of course, I don't know what she'd do once she got away from her dad. He was awful strict with her."

Despite the widespread search for more body parts, none had turned up. The Portland detectives now believed that the parcels found had been tossed from a passing car. They were going to have to try to identify the dead woman with what they had.

Pathologist Lehman had done more thorough examinations on the foot and hands. He explained that they were completely free of blood in the veins and arteries.

"You don't mean the body was embalmed?" Shields asked. "It isn't a buried body dug up and hacked to pieces?"

Lehman shook his head. He explained that the body had been drained of blood immediately after the victim was dead—not unlike what a hunter or butcher would do. Somewhere—wherever the woman had been slain—there had to be a tremendous amount of human blood. Perhaps that was where they would find the rest of the victim's body.

The three missing women had never had their fingerprints taken, but there was one way to solve that problem. Technicians went to the women's homes and asked for items of personal use that the women had touched—hairbrushes, cologne bottles, compacts. In addition, they dusted countertops and doorjambs for latent prints.

Charles Hamilton, supervisor of the I.D. Bureau, compared the latents raised with the prints he'd rolled from the disembodied hand. The process was very precise and very difficult. The prints from the women's homes were old and smudged, and the delineations on the whorls and ridges of the prints from the severed hand were not as clear as Hamilton would have liked. Just as it seemed the probe had come to another of a series of dead ends, Hamilton rushed into Shields's office shouting, "We've got her!"

"Who . . . which . . . ?" Shields asked.

"Mrs. Caudle. There are more than enough comparison points on one of the prints out of her home and one finger from the hand. There's no doubt that the dead woman is Joan Caudle."

The police broke the news to Joan's distraught husband. He nodded his head as if they had only confirmed what he already dreaded. "I knew something had happened to her," he said. "Her mother died, you know, and when Joan didn't come to the funeral, I figured she had to be dead. She never would have missed her own mother's funeral."

Now detectives could home in on the activities of one woman. They asked Joan Caudle's husband to go over again the events of Monday, June 5. He was their prime suspect, although he didn't know it. The spouse is always the first suspect detectives look at.

"Well, it's like I said," the husband explained. "The stores were open Monday night, and Joan went out to get Father's Day presents. She called me around nine and said she'd be a little bit late."

Joan Caudle had not been driving a car; she would have come home by bus or taxi.

"Would your wife have stopped at a bar or a cocktail lounge after shopping?"

"She might have; it wasn't anything she did often, but she was so uptight about her mother being sick and all. Yes, she might have stopped for one drink."

It was a ticklish question, but the detectives had to explore another possibility. Did Joan Caudle's husband have any reason to think that his wife might have been seeing another man?

"No. I'm sure she wasn't. She was here with the kids all day, and she took good care of them. And I was home every night. Even if she wanted another man, there was no time when she could have met him . . . and she just wasn't like that."

What had happened to Joan Caudle between the nine o'clock call home on Monday night and the awful discoveries of Thursday morning? Her husband gave the detectives a photograph of his wife. They could see she had been a very pretty woman who stared clear-eyed into the camera, smiling slightly. She had dark hair, turned under in a pageboy. It was a good picture, and she had obviously been attractive enough so that anyone seeing her would have been likely to remember her. The picture was distributed to Portland papers and it appeared in the evening editions with a request for information.

The next afternoon, a Multnomah County jail matron called Chief Shields and said there was a young woman in her section who wanted to talk to the detectives about Joan Caudle. "She claims she saw her Monday—the fifth. It may be a bid for attention or she may be trying to work a deal, but I think you'd better see what she has to say."

The woman was very thin with Titian hair and milky skin dusted with freckles. She had clearly seen better days. Her rap sheet listed a dozen arrests for drunk and disorderly, but she was sober now and she did indeed have information for the Portland detectives. She had staked herself out on a bar stool in a lounge in southwest Portland on the Monday night Joan Caudle disappeared. The redhead said she had charmed another bar patron into paying the tab for a succession of double scotches.

"He's been around before," she said, "but the other times I seen him he looked crummy—you know, greasy clothes, dirty fingernails, the whole bit. But Monday night he looked pretty good, all slicked up. So I figure, let him buy me a couple slugs and we'll see what happens."

Investigators Shields and Tennant waited for her to get to the point. She obviously enjoyed her moment at center stage and wouldn't be rushed.

"Anyway, so me and Dick—that's all he said his name was—were hitting it off fine . . . until she walks in. You know, the one in the paper, the one they say got chopped up. He takes one look at her and it's good-bye time." She shivered slightly and lit another cigarette. "I was burned up then, but I guess I'm lucky. It could have been me."

"You're sure it was Joan Caudle? You're sure of the picture?"

"I'm sure. I looked her over good, like women do, to see what she had that I didn't. She was younger, and I'll have to admit she was pretty. I'd never seen her before in the place, and I hang out there a lot."

"And this Dick—you say he comes in regular, too?"

"Pretty regular. He's about twenty-five—say, six feet tall, 175 pounds, light brown curly hair, blue eyes. Not bad looking."

"What did he say to you?"

"The usual. He called me 'dear,' and he told me I had soft brown eyes like a deer. Pretty corny, and I told him so—but that's what you have to put up with in a bar. They all like to think they're poets."

At the mention of the word "deer," both detectives winced. They remembered Dr. Lehman's statement that the killer had butchered the body and boned it out the way a hunter would cut up a deer.

Pressed to give a clearer description of Dick, the redhead concentrated hard, closing her eyes, then said abruptly, "Hey! How about this? He was young, but I'd swear he had false teeth. He seemed to be having trouble with them. You could hear them click when he talked."

This proved to be the one detail that struck a spark of recognition in the bartender of the lounge. He recalled a young man who complained that he'd had to have all his teeth pulled. "I don't know his name, but the fellow over at the service station does."

"Sure," the attendant said when he was questioned minutes later. "That's got to be Dick Marquette. He works over in the auto wrecking yard." He gave the address.

While one team of detectives headed for the wrecking yard, another tracked down other customers of the bar. Several recalled that the missing woman had been in the bar on Monday night, and they also remembered that she'd been with a man called Dick.

"It was real strange," one patron recalled. "She came in alone, and then this fellow joined her. They were playing the Where-do-I-know-you-from? game and they thought they'd gone to high school together, but it turned out they'd both gone to the same grade school—hadn't seen each other in fifteen years. When they left, I heard him tell her that he didn't have a car but he said, 'We can walk.'"

At the wrecking yard, a worker said Richard L. Marquette had been employed there but that he hadn't shown up after Thursday, June 8. Then he added, "He's still got his pay coming."

Marquette's employee records listed an address in the neighborhood where the body parts had been discovered. There the Portland investigators found a two-room house surrounded by a yard grown high with weeds and littered with trash. The structure had only one door and one window, and both were shut tight.

They knocked on the door, not really expecting an answer, and they got none. They found that the flimsy door was unlocked. As it swung open, a cloying stench rushed out, a smell familiar to any officer who has worked homicides: the odor of death, long neglected in summer heat.

Inside, the detectives found a black sweater identical to one Joan Caudle had worn when she left on her shopping trip. Nearby they found some bloodstained lingerie.

One detective opened the door to an old refrigerator, its motor laboring in the closed heat of the house. He drew back instinctively as he saw that the compartment was jammed with packages wrapped in newspaper. It looked like a quarter of beef cut and wrapped. But it wasn't. Dr. Lehman's analysis confirmed that the macabre packages were human flesh, bled and butchered just as the first body parts had been. The head was still missing.

A murder warrant was quickly issued for Richard Marquette. His stunned neighbors described him as a rather shy, quiet bachelor who always had a friendly greeting for everyone. In an era long before the term "serial murderer" was even coined, the missing Richard Marquette drew the same accolades that all notorious killers seem to get: "He was the nicest guy you would ever want to know. Real quiet. He never bothered anyone, and he always lent a helping hand if you needed it."

On June 19, 1961, the FBI joined the hunt. Then Governor Mark Hatfield called the Caudle murder "the most heinous crime in Oregon history" and asked the FBI to take an unprecedented step and make Marquette Number 11 on the Ten Most Wanted List. The FBI agreed that this should be done, and Marquette's picture went up on a federal flier on June 29.

That very afternoon a real estate salesman in Santa Maria, California, was talking with a clerk in the office of a local credit bureau when the flier arrived. "Hey, we just got your picture in," the clerk joked.

The salesman did a double take and exclaimed, "I *know* that guy! He's working out at the old airfield. My partner and I picked him up hitching and we got him a job."

It was a rare bit of luck for law enforcement. FBI agents arrested a nonresistant Marquette at a salvage shop the next day. At first he made feeble attempts to deny the mutilation murder, but suddenly he blurted, "I was out of my head—dead drunk. That was the first time I'd seen her since grade school. . . . I didn't know her married name. I was drunk at the time, just sitting there. I don't know who picked who up."

He said he had taken Joan Caudle to his home, where she allegedly agreed to sexual relations. There was no way to tell if that was true or a fabrication on Marquette's part. From everything the Portland detectives had found out about Joan Caudle, the suspect's version of the evening sounded unbelievable. But he was the only one alive to remember. Marquette said he had sex with Caudle. After a second act of intercourse, he then choked her in a struggle. "I woke up the next morning and saw her there—dead. I panicked."

Since he had no car to use to get rid of the body of his old schoolmate, Marquette said he dragged her corpse into the shower and dismembered it. He wrapped up all the pieces but the head, which he threw into the Willamette River near the Ross Island Bridge.

Detectives later recovered it there, snagged in some brush and rotting timbers at the shoreline.

Richard Marquette's trial began on November 28, 1961. Jurors saw a young man who looked as clean-cut as a divinity student. He was actually quite handsome, and he had an almost shy demeanor. He had been charged with felony murder because the prosecution believed Joan Caudle had been murdered either during a rape or a rape attempt.

After two weeks of testimony, the jury deliberated twelve hours and returned a verdict of guilty of first-degree murder, with a recommendation for mercy. Richard Marquette received a life sentence, but he would not face an executioner. Oregon citizens relaxed in their belief that Marquette would be locked up forever. His picture appeared in the *Oregonian* a few more times as the coverage of the shocking case wound down, and then people forgot about him.

And so Richard Marquette was transported forty-seven miles to the Oregon State Prison in Salem. For eleven years he was a model prisoner. His incredible crime had long since faded from the headlines, and there was barely a ripple made when Marquette was released to parole on January 5, 1973.

Marion County Detective Chief Jim Byrnes was one of the few people who knew that Richard Marquette was out. He made it a practice to know whether most of the individuals convicted of brutal homicides in his part of the state were in or out of prison. Given the merry-go-round of arrest, conviction, prison, and parole, it sometimes seemed as though prisoners went in the front door and out the back door of the Oregon State Prison. Actually, the average "life term" was about ten years.

Byrnes had heard that Marquette was working as a plumber's apprentice for a very reputable Salem firm and living in a trailer park but he didn't know the paroled murderer's exact location. As he moved his finger along the reverse directory for mobile home parks, he found what he needed. There was a trailer court at 1865 Highway Avenue, Number 1. And that trailer park was only about 300 yards, diagonally across the street, from the Pepper Tree! Byrnes checked with the manager and verified that Richard Marquette lived there in the mobile home park.

It was 4:30 in the afternoon of April 21, 1975, when the Marion County detectives drove into Marquette's trailer park in an unmarked car. No one answered their knocks on his trailer door, and there were no sounds inside. Detective Larry Lord was staked out across the street to watch for Marquette's arrival. The probers hoped there *would* be an arrival; the last time publicity on a dismembered woman had hit the news media, the suspect had taken off.

At 6:12 P.M. Lord alerted Byrnes and McCoy that Richard Marquette had pulled up in a 1969 Ford pickup-camper. "He's sweeping out his trailer," Lord said. "You'd better hurry."

Byrnes called D.A. Gortmaker and alerted him that they would probably be needing a search warrant, and then he and McCoy drove at once to the trailer park. Marquette was almost forty now, fourteen years older than when Jim Byrnes had last tracked him. He wondered if he would recognize him. Lord pointed toward a man who stood in the doorway of his trailer. He had a mop in his hand, and he leaned on it as he chatted easily with a neighbor.

Marquette's physical appearance had changed a great deal in the years since Joan Caudle was killed. He looked older; the youthful face was gone, and he was gaunt and weathered.

But he appeared eminently relaxed as Jim Byrnes approached him and said, "I understand you're expecting us."

"No." Marquette smiled. "I wasn't."

"Well, we'd like to talk with you, if your friend will excuse us."

Still Marquette remained calm. Asked about his knowledge of Betty Wilson's murder, he said he'd heard something about it on the radio, but that was all he knew.

Byrnes asked him if he minded if they looked around. Marquette didn't demur. He gave both verbal and written consent to search, but the detectives wanted to be absolutely sure that there would be no legal loopholes; they knew the search warrant for probable cause was on its way. The two detectives and the murder suspect talked casually as they waited. Byrnes studied Marquette for any signs of anxiety or concern, and he found none.

With the search warrant in hand, the investigators moved into the small mobile home. While the meticulous search was being carried out, Marquette leaned easily against his pickup, arms folded across his chest. He was as friendly and cooperative as a man with nothing to hide had every right to be. He seemed almost oblivious to the search, and if they had expected him to follow them and peer over their shoulders, they were mistaken. Byrnes was beginning to think his hunch had been wrong and that it was only a coincidence that Marquette, a known sadistic psychopath, lived so close to the Pepper Tree.

And then he saw something that told him his suspect did indeed have things to hide. Byrnes spotted the characteristic dark mahogany stains of dried blood on the doorsill and on the hot water tap. A pair of Jockey shorts with a faint pinkish stain hung on the shower rod in the bathroom, and there was a matching stain on a pair of jeans.

Just outside the front steps, Byrnes leaned down and picked up a torn fingernail. Byrnes later commented, "A fingernail was even better than a fingerprint for means of identification. The ridges matched, the torn edges matched—even the hangnails and cuticles matched."

That nail had probably been swept out, unseen by Marquette, just before the detectives arrived.

The Marion County detectives actually vacuumed the yard outside Marquette's trailer, and then they sealed the whole vacuum bag into an evidence container so that the debris could be sorted out and evaluated.

Detective Jan Cummings spotted something glittering in the sparse grass, something the vacuum cleaner had not caught. It was a broken strand of silver chain, and it would prove microscopically identical to the other strands found in the slough with the body parts. Also swept out by the suspect's broom was the missing hook panel from the Playtex bra found with Betty Wilson's body.

And here, just as they had at the site of floating body parts, the detectives found a profusion of lollipop sticks. They had no idea what use Marquette made of them—and it didn't matter. They were one more link between the suspect and the victim. The police had come hoping for just one or two pieces of physical evidence, and they had struck a bonanza.

The searchers pried up a floor register and found a portion of clothing that didn't seem to fit the case—not then. It was the crotch of a woman's panties. All of Betty Wilson's undergarments had been found, and they were all intact.

Jim Byrnes walked out to the pickup where Marquette waited. Finally Marquette had lost some of his nonchalance as he watched officers emerge again and again from his trailer with sealed and labeled plastic bags containing evidence. He had been taken out to a restaurant for supper as the evening progressed, and although he ate heartily and chatted amiably with his escorts, the pressure was obviously beginning to build. Suddenly Marquette blurted to Jim Byrnes: "I wish I could live it all over again."

"Live *what* all over?"

Marquette hesitated and then replied, "Oh, the last twelve to fourteen years of my life." That seemed an odd response since he had spent the last fourteen years inside the prison walls.

Byrnes advised Richard Marquette of his rights under *Miranda,* and the suspect nodded that he understood—but he still wanted to talk.

"You did go to the dump on Saturday morning?" Byrnes asked.

"Yeah, I went. I had some trash to get rid of."

"How do you account for the blood we found in your trailer?"

"That's not blood."

Marquette was obviously torn between his compulsion to confess and his desire to be free.

Asked about his activities on Friday evening, he said he had gone to the Pepper Tree and had a few beers. "I'm on that Antabuse program," he told Byrne, "but I can beat it if I have a beer, throw up, and then get back to drinking." Marquette also admitted to having used amphetamines—speed.

He remembered that he had stayed at the Pepper Tree lounge until about 10:00 P.M. and then gone back to his trailer and fallen asleep on the couch. When he awakened, it was six in the morning and he made his early trip to the landfill to dump a load of siding.

Quietly Byrnes asked the important question of all, "Did you kill Betty Wilson?"

"No! No, I'm clean!" Marquette insisted.

But if ever a man was *not* clean—of murder, sadism, and unbelievable cruelty—it was Richard Marquette. At 2:30 A.M. he was placed under arrest on suspicion of first-degree murder and booked into the Marion County Jail.

As he was undressed preparatory to getting regulation jail coveralls, the detectives noted many small cuts and nicks on his body that had just begun to heal. But these cuts could never have accounted for the amount of blood found in his trailer. Oddly, both he and Betty Wilson turned out to have the same comparatively rare blood type: O Negative.

"There was a time span of fifty-five hours and fifteen minutes from the moment Betty Wilson was found until Marquette was arrested," Byrnes says. "Our team of detectives worked one stretch of forty-seven hours and thirty minutes without sleep."

Predictably, most of Marquette's neighbors were aghast when they heard he had been arrested for the incredibly vicious homicide. They said he had been a perfect neighbor. If someone needed help—a lawn mowed, a trailer leveled, anything—he was right there to assist. He had seemed like such a gentle man, devoted to his pet cats—so much so that he had built them a ramp up to the kitchen window so that they could get in out of the weather when he wasn't home.

Byrnes did talk to one rather insouciant neighborhood girl who came to visit Marquette just before he was arrested. She confided that she been "a little turned off" at first when she heard about his prison time. "I heard he killed his wife. That's not too freaky, but then I heard he cut her up . . . and I figured, 'Wow, that's a whole different trip!'"

It was that, even though the rumor she had heard was only half right.

While searching the trailer, the detectives found leather-working tools—the very best, worth $1,500—and many professionally executed leather items, including elaborate pistol holsters.

Jim Byrnes tried to trace his suspect's life as far back as possible. He wasn't surprised at what he found; Richard Marquette was almost a textbook case. He was the product of a broken home and had known many father substitutes, none of whom particularly cared to have him around. At the same time, he had been abnormally dependent upon his mother. In his teens, Richard Marquette had served in Korea in the army—ironically, as a military policeman. He was honorably discharged on October 22, 1953.

Up to that point, his relations with women appeared to have followed a normal pattern. He had become engaged (by mail) to a young woman, but when he came back to the States he found that she had married someone else. Nevertheless, she invited Marquette over to dinner while her husband was away. She later charged her ex-lover with attempted rape, although the charges were dropped after he convincingly insisted that she had invited him into her bedroom.

His pattern of violence had begun to emerge. Marquette always claimed that his victims had seduced him, that he was not responsible for the arguments that inevitably followed. He could not bear to have women reject him.

It had been that way, he said, with Joan Caudle.

Something similar had happened before Betty Wilson encountered the ultimate wrong man. Marquette had been going with a divorcée since the first part of 1975. The relationship had progressed to the point that they were considering marriage, and then the woman had broken off with him, for what inexplicable reason he could not say. He had not seen her for two weeks before he was arrested for the murder of Betty Wilson.

Had he taken out his rage and frustration on Betty Wilson?

Richard Marquette had *seemed* to be all right after his release from

prison to a halfway house. He had managed completely normal
sexual relationships with at least two women. But when the woman
he wanted to marry turned away from him, he had reverted to type.

Early in May 1975 Marquette's court-appointed attorneys announced that their client was willing to make a statement concerning
the death of Betty Wilson. Marquette agreed to be taped and televised
as he talked to detectives.

Yes, he had met Betty Wilson at the Pepper Tree and invited the
pathetically lonely woman back to his trailer. According to Marquette, Betty had been willing to engage in some physical closeness
and he had begun to make love to her on his living room couch. He
had taken off her blouse and sweater and was working on her bra
when she resisted. Betty Wilson was from a strict religious background. She had probably snapped back to reality and the fact that
she was about to have intercourse with a complete stranger. Or
maybe she had never permitted him willingly to remove any of her
clothing. At any rate, Richard Marquette said she had tried to sit up
and put her clothing back on. And he, of all men, could not stand to
have a woman fight him.

"I choked her until she was quiet."

At that point Betty Wilson had certainly recognized that she had
made a terrible misjudgment. Marquette looked into the sheriff's
department's cameras as he described how she had pleaded for her
life. "She told me she would go ahead with what I wanted—if I just
wouldn't hurt her."

But it was much too late for that. He recalled putting more force
behind his powerful hands as he choked Betty until she was dead.

The scenario might have been lifted from the original murder script
of 1961. It was clear to those who questioned Marquette that sadistic
and murderous sex was much more exciting to him than consensual
intercourse. This time, of course, Marquette had a more than
adequate vehicle to get rid of a body, and *still* he decided to cut his
victim into sections. It was part of his obsession, although he would
not admit that. Clinically, he explained that the vertical scoring of the
limbs was done to hasten blood loss. Marquette insisted that he had
no formal training in butchery, nor was he a hunter—yet he had
managed to sever the legs and arms just at the joints.

Early on Saturday morning, with what was left of Betty Wilson
wrapped in the towel and pillowcase, he had headed for the landfill.
He dumped her purse there to be buried under tons of garbage, and
placed the body in the slough, thinking it would sink like a stone.

This confession itself was more than most men—even trained lawmen—could stomach, but there was more. Marquette said he had killed still another woman in mid-1974 shortly after his release from prison. He didn't know her name or anything about her. He figured nobody had even missed her because he'd never heard anything more about her. Was this the woman whose panty crotch was found hidden in Marquette's trailer register? He would not say.

As he talked, Jim Byrnes recognized that the M.O. in 1974 was chillingly similar to that of Marquette's other two known murders. He had picked up his anonymous victim in Dubious Dudley's bar in Salem, brought her home for sex, and according to Marquette, she too had backed down at the last moment. And she too had been strangled, dismembered, and disposed of.

Marquette agreed to lead detectives to the spot where he had left the 1974 victim. On June 13 Jim Byrnes and Kilburn McCoy, along with members of the Marion County D.A.'s staff and the suspect's lawyers, traveled to the lonely, rugged area near the Roaring River Rest Stop alongside the Clackamas River. There the admitted three-time mutilation killer pointed out two graves a half mile apart. Approximately three feet below the ground they found the skeletal parts of the unfortunate lady from Dubious Dudley's. There was no clothing, no jewelry, to help in identification. Worst of all, there was no head at all. Dental records would have been the only positive means to find out who she was; fingertips and other soft tissue had long since decomposed.

She remains today simply Jane Doe, a tragic victim of a predatory killer.

Richard Marquette, faced with overpowering physical and circumstantial evidence against him, pleaded guilty to the crime of murder. On May 30, 1975, he was convicted and sentenced to prison for life. And this time, life *meant* life. Marquette is almost sixty years old and his name rarely comes up in the press. But should he ever be considered for parole, Jim Byrnes, who is now a private investigator in Salem, will remind the parole board and the public of Richard Marquette's crimes.

Molly's Murder

"Molly's Murder" *stands out in my memory for a number of reasons. When I was twenty-one and a Seattle police officer, I lived in an economy apartment whose yard backed up to the same alley Molly Ann McClure's apartment building did. Had we been born into the same generation, we would have been neighbors, ridden the same bus each morning and worked across the street from each other in downtown Seattle. There were, however, twenty-five years between us, so we were never true neighbors. Still, as I wrote about this case, I remembered being very young and very confident in my first apartment, and I felt a kinship with a young woman I never knew.*

Molly McClure's death was remarkable not only because of its senseless, stark tragedy but also because it was solved with a combination of the most sophisticated forensic science and good old-fashioned seat-of-the-pants police work by two of the best detectives I ever met: Hank Gruber and Rudy Sutlovich of the Seattle Homicide Unit.

By the time Molly Ann McClure moved to Seattle's Eastlake neighborhood, the world—and the neighborhood—had changed. Eastlake Avenue used to be the main route between downtown Seattle and the University of Washington district. By 1986, when Molly moved there, the I-5 Freeway with its multiple lanes of north and south traffic bypassed Eastlake. The neighborhood was in transition, along with most of the streets that ran parallel to Eastlake. Twenty-eight-year-old Molly found an apartment on Franklin Avenue East. There was an apartment building or two and then some private homes: a bungalow from the 1920s or a pseudo-Norman from the late thirties. Homogenous. The street was so narrow that cars parked on both sides allow only enough room for one vehicle to navigate at a time. Molly saw it would be quiet; there wasn't room for hot-rodders to race.

She could walk to the bus in three minutes, to the little corner store in two minutes. She could be at work in twenty minutes or so. Lake Union, edged to capacity with quaint-funky or half-million-dollar houseboats, was three blocks west. There were many trendy ethnic cafés and yuppie taverns down on Eastlake, ever changing in ownership and national derivation. It was the perfect neighborhood for a young career woman.

Molly Ann McClure was three weeks away from her twenty-ninth birthday when she died, a lovely, laughing golden girl who had made her parents proud, who had brightened the lives of an untold number of friends. Molly seemed the least likely person to become a murder victim. She was too good, too careful, too alive.

None of that mattered, of course. Killers choose their prey with hearts as cold as winter rain, their minds full of lust and avarice; they are not concerned with the pain they cause.

Molly McClure grew up in the perfect family of the fifties. Jean and

375

Warren McClure of the Clyde Hill section of Bellevue, Washington, had three daughters and one son, all of them wanted, all loved. Jean was a kindergarten teacher and Warren an engineer. All of their children attended the Bellevue First Presbyterian Church Sunday school, and when they were older, they went to church camp at Seabeck on Hood Canal. When Molly was in college, she worked summers at the Seabeck camp. She was petite; she never grew much over five feet. Still, she was amazingly strong. Her camp counselors remember Molly as the only girl who could heft a mattress and carry it to her cabin all by herself. If any young woman had the strength and guts to fight off an attacker, it would have been Molly . . . if she had any warning.

It is well nigh impossible to find a picture of Molly McClure where she is not smiling. In most of the shots, she is hugging a friend, giggling in the midst of a group. She was bubbly, laughing, strong, and smart. A natural winner.

Molly graduated from Bellevue High School in 1975. She attended the University of Washington in nearby Seattle first, where she pledged Alpha Chi Omega. Her sorority sisters elected her president a few years later. Molly was a young woman who focused on a goal and headed straight for it. She was intrigued with a career in hotel management, and Washington State University in Pullman, 300 miles east of Seattle, is known for its hotel program. She transferred to WSU and graduated with a degree in hotel and restaurant management in 1982.

Many of Molly's friends got married right after graduation, but Molly made up her mind to put off serious personal commitments until she was thirty. She was a rarity in the 1980s. Molly was a virgin, and she would die a virgin, unconscious and blessedly unaware of what her killer did to her.

When you are in your mid-twenties, time seems endless, with years enough and more to fit in all your hopes and dreams. First Molly would build a firm foundation under her career. Then she would marry and have babies.

Like any rookie in the corporate world, Molly went where the jobs were. She was accepted into the prestigious management program of the Westin Hotel chain. Her first job was as front office manager for the Westin Oaks in Houston. She was promoted then to assistant manager of the Westin Hotel at Tabor Center in Denver. The jobs were excellent, but the cities where Molly worked had crime rates that made Seattle seem as safe as a Sunday School picnic. In a bad year, Houston homicide detectives sometimes worked a thousand murders, twenty times Seattle's average year. Denver's violent crime statistics showed that the mile-high city had more rapes per capita during the time Molly lived there than almost any city in America.

Although her family worried, Molly survived Houston and Denver unscathed. And then with a tragic synchronicity, Molly moved back to Seattle on November 1, 1985—just weeks before her killer was due to be released from the federal prison on McNeil Island, Washington.

Molly had been offered a great job as a hotel restaurant consultant with Laventhol & Horwath, a certified public accounting firm. Delighted to be heading back to her family and hometown, she stored her furniture in Denver, with instructions that she would send for it as soon as she found an apartment in Seattle.

The man who returned from the penitentiary had slimmer prospects. But he always had an ace in the hole. He was a man who lived off women . . . in one way or another. Indulged and pampered by his women, he could turn surly when he did not get his way. Nevertheless, he held a fascination for women that belied his average appearance. Female relatives supported him; girlfriends let him live in while they paid the rent. To make ends meet, he was not averse to committing a burglary or two . . . or three. He was from a world a million light-years away from Molly McClure's.

Molly's job with the accounting firm was in downtown Seattle, in a soaring skyscraper kitty-korner from Seattle Police Headquarters. She looked for an apartment beyond the downtown area but not way out in the suburbs. She had close relatives living near Eastlake Avenue. When Molly found the apartment on Franklin Avenue East, she considered that a plus. Her aunt and cousins would be only four blocks away.

The apartment seemed a real find. The rent was only $350 for a two bedroom unit in a four-plex built in the fifties of Roman brick and cedar. The building looked neat and sturdy. Rhododendrons and camellias and evergreen trees had grown up high around the windows, allowing a sense of privacy. The vacant apartment was the lower unit on the north side of the building, 2358 East Franklin.

A careful renter, Molly called on one or two of the tenants in the other units, but nobody had complaints about the building. Sure, the owner was a little slow in making repairs, but for $350 rent in such a great neighborhood, that was a minor concern. She grabbed the apartment and moved in on Thanksgiving morning, 1985. Her furniture wouldn't arrive for three weeks, but she was willing to rough it until then.

Molly's apartment had been painted, but the metal casement windows were slightly sprung, letting cold air and Seattle's winter dampness in, and there was putty missing. Molly put a piece of cardboard up in the cracked bathroom window. Her dad, a Boeing engineer for almost forty years, dropped by several times to fix things—plumbing, electricity, and the refrigerator, which had a noisy motor.

Warren McClure was concerned because Molly's front porch light didn't work, so he bought a fixture and came over the first Saturday in January to install it. He was standing on a chair tinkering with it when one of the upstairs neighbors walked by and said hi. Molly was a little embarrassed; she didn't know the man's name, but her dad just reached out and shook hands. The men introduced themselves, and Molly went back inside.

In the short time she had lived there, Molly knew only vaguely who the other tenants were. The downstairs apartment that shared a common wall with hers was rented by a single man, a letter carrier. Right over her apartment was where the man—she found out his name was Kvay—lived with his girlfriend. A middle-aged career woman lived in the south upstairs unit. All of them seemed pleasant, and nodded and smiled when she passed them.

Molly was very busy during the first part of January. She loved her new job, and she concentrated on familiarizing herself with it. When her furniture arrived from Denver, she arranged it and added some plants and pictures to make the apartment homey. She had chosen the larger bedroom in the rear of the apartment for herself and slept in a queen-size bed she'd bought at a bargain price when the Westin remodeled its rooms and replaced the beds. The smaller bedroom became a kind of junk room. She had her childhood single bed there, a desk, her bicycle, her ironing board, books, files—everything that overflowed the other rooms.

Molly had an aversion to cats, and she sprayed her windowsills and porch with a substance guaranteed to discourage them. She didn't care if other people kept them as pets; she simply preferred not to have them prowling around her apartment. She vacuumed out the heating ducts to rid her apartment of dust and paint odors that blasted out whenever she turned on the heat. She left the vent covers off because she planned to vacuum them again.

Molly wasn't dating anyone special; she often spent her evenings at home alone or with relatives and girlfriends. She had to be up by six on weekdays, and in January, darkness settles over Seattle before 5:00 P.M. She was in a long flannel granny gown by nine on many nights, watching TV while rain pelted against the windows.

It was pitch dark at 4:00 A.M. on Thursday, January 16, when Molly's neighbor, Jack Crowley—the letter carrier—woke to hear someone pounding on his door. Half asleep, he stumbled to the door, but when he got there, he realized the knocking was not at his door but at Molly's. He stood behind his closed door and listened to voices only two feet away. He recognized one as Molly's and the other as a male's. Molly didn't sound upset, and the conversation was short. Crowley heard Molly's door shut, and he went back to bed to catch another forty winks. When he thought about it later, he was a little puzzled; his new neighbor never made any noise. No parties. No stereo creeping through his walls. Who would be knocking on her door at four in the morning?

Molly got to work shortly before 8:30 A.M. She seemed a little upset when she told her boss, Andy Olson, that she'd been awakened very early by one of her neighbors who was concerned about her safety.

"He said he was out jogging, and he saw somebody trying to get in my front window," she said. "Luckily, he chased him away."

Molly hadn't been too worried at first. She was drowsy and she had gone back to bed until her alarm sounded at six. But as she was leaving her apartment, she saw that some putty had been partially chipped away from her window frame. That jolted her.

Olson heard her calling someone about renter's insurance and took her aside, saying firmly, "Forget the insurance. First, you call the police."

She promised him that she would do that before evening. Molly worked a full day, her worry about the aborted burglary lessening with the rush of business. But when she returned home it was dark again, a storm was beginning to kick up, and a long, scary night loomed ahead.

Molly McClure was in no way a dependent, frightened woman. She was the type who took action. First she contacted Jack Crowley next door. She went over at six to tell him about the attempted break-in. She showed him the marks on her window, remarking how fortunate it was that Kvay Knight, who lived upstairs with Sondra Hill,* had come back from his morning run just in time to scare the man away.

"We exchanged phone numbers," Crowley recalled later. "And we agreed to leave extra lights on. She was concerned, but she wasn't hysterical."

Molly wanted to be sure all the neighbors were alerted. Kvay Knight already knew about the problem, of course. Molly was sure he had told Sondra. Besides, there were two of them and they lived upstairs. She would have to warn Dora Lang,* too; she knew Dora better than any of the other tenants; they sometimes had coffee together. Dora was also a woman living alone, although her unit seemed more secure because her windows weren't on the ground floor.

Molly called the Seattle Police department at 7:00 P.M. to report the would-be burglar. She didn't call on the 911 line, and she said that it wasn't imperative that an officer respond at once. It was 9:00 when Officer Gary Kuenzi appeared at her door. Shortly before Kuenzi got there, Molly had glanced out to see that Kvay Knight was picking up his mail just outside her front door, and she had invited him in to offer his impressions of the prowler to the police officer.

Kuenzi usually worked as a K-9 officer, but he was working patrol that night of January 16, 1986. He stepped inside Molly's apartment, and she pointed toward a man sitting with his back to the officer. Kuenzi wondered why the man hadn't turned around when he entered, but shrugged the thought off; a lot of people weren't crazy about policemen.

"Kvay saw him," Molly said. "I didn't. Kvay frightened him off and then woke me to warn me."

Molly's guest introduced himself as Sherwood "Kvay" Knight. He was a muscular black man of medium height. He explained to Kuenzi that he'd been jogging around 4:30 A.M. when he'd seen a figure bent over Molly's front window. The man had spotted Knight and sprinted off.

"He was either white or maybe Oriental," Knight said. "I'd say five feet six, maybe 140 pounds. He had on a black coat and blue jeans. . . . I didn't see his face, only black hair."

Kuenzi walked around the apartment living room, inspecting the windows. He suggested that Molly put screws in the handles of the front window. Idly, he noted that the apartment was neat and clean. He didn't check the bedroom.

He asked Molly if there was anyone she was afraid of. Old boyfriends? Someone who might have bothered her or come on too strong? She shook her head, but she said she'd heard that the previous tenant had had a "boyfriend problem."

Kuenzi spent about twenty minutes on the call—checking out the premises and warning Molly about safety measures. Kvay Knight was still in the apartment when Kuenzi left.

Molly had called her aunt that morning to tell her about the break-in, and she called again after Kuenzi left. "I offered to send one of my sons up to sleep there, but Molly said that she wasn't afraid," her aunt recalled. "She just wanted to be sure I didn't tell her parents, because she didn't want to worry them. She *was* concerned enough that she wanted to move. We agreed that we'd go out Saturday and look for another apartment."

Molly called out to Dora Lang to alert her when she saw Dora come home from work late in the evening. "I offered to let her sleep here," Lang recalled later. "It makes me sad that she didn't come stay with me. . . . She said, 'If you hear screams, come rescue me'—but no one heard a peep."

No one did. Dora watched the late news that night and then went to bed at 11:30. The storm that had begun as an average January downpour turned into a violent windstorm that woke Dora Lang. "That building was rocking on its foundations—it was horrible, frightening." Lang got up between seven and seven-thirty, and everything was quiet. The storm had passed.

In the apartment next door to Molly's, Jack Crowley had fallen asleep in his living room in front of the TV. The wind woke him up about midnight, and he moved to the bedroom. He slept through the night and got up at 5:00 A.M. He left for work at 6:00 and was surprised to see that Molly's porch light was off. Odd—since they'd agreed to leave extra lights on.

Dora Lang went to work a little later.

Sondra Hill hadn't gone to work on Thursday. She'd had the flu for days and still felt terrible. Besides that, the storm had started the arthritis in her knees aching. She was only thirty, but she could already predict storms in her knees. She'd been up and down all night long, taking aspirin, rubbing her throbbing knees. Kvay had slept on the couch so that he wouldn't bother her.

The second time Sondra got up, she let her cat out. She saw that Kvay had fallen asleep with the television set on. That irritated her.

Hill's alarm was set for 5:40 A.M. When it sounded, she reached over to turn it off and heard the outside door close. She assumed it was Kvay going out to jog.

At the offices of Laventhol & Horwath, Andy Olson glanced at his clock nervously. Molly was late, and that wasn't like Molly. He called her apartment, but the phone rang hollow and endless. Well, he could rationalize that. The storm had been a bad one, and she had been worried about the prowler too, so it was more than likely that she'd gone to stay the night with relatives. But nine o'clock passed. And nine-fifteen passed. And Molly didn't rush in with breathless apologies.

Olson thought about getting in his car and driving by Molly's place, but he knew she'd filed a police report on the attempted break-in, so he called the police and asked for assistance. It is a common call heard over Seattle police radios: "Check on the welfare of . . ."

Officer Harry J. Burke, with twenty-two years on the force, was working Edward sector that morning, just as he had since 1976. He knew those streets in the north end of Capitol Hill as well as he knew the floor plan of his own house. Burke was working first watch—3:30 A.M. to 11:30 A.M. Burke was "Edward 3" that morning.

Six-year veteran Charlotte Thomas had been a community service officer before becoming a patrolman. She was "Edward 4." She had gotten the "possible burglar in neighborhood" information at roll call at 3:30 A.M. Thomas had taken a swing by the 2300 block of Franklin Ave. East just before dawn. Everything looked all right. There was a light on one of the lower-unit porches. There was a streetlight right outside the four-plex. The whole block was sleeping, quiet. Thomas didn't see a living soul.

Hours later, when Burke caught the "welfare check" call, Thomas called Radio and said she would back him as she was familiar with the situation. They pulled up across from the four-plex, one patrol unit behind the other. The sun was bright now. The storm had swept everything gloomy away in its fury.

Officer Burke walked to the front door of 2358. He knocked, and the two officers waited. The drapes were pulled. He knocked again. No answer. Burke pounded on the door with the butt of his flashlight, and still no one responded. They walked around the building, but all the drapes and curtains in Molly McClure's apartment were pulled tight, and they could not see in. It was difficult to get close to the windows anyway; the dark, waxy leaves of rhododendrons and prickly holly bushes blocked their way. From a cop's point of view, the shrubbery was a hazard: the bushes would provide cover for a voyeur or a prowler.

The two patrol officers walked into the area beneath the outdoor stairway that led to the second-floor apartment on the north side. Burke clambered up onto a stair rail and tried to jiggle a side window lock loose, but the rail gave way under the stocky officer. He went back to the front door and knocked again.

But no one answered.

Burke advised Radio that he was going to try to enter the apartment. Radio said Molly's bedroom was reported to be at the back of the unit. Burke and Thomas couldn't budge that window—it was out of alignment and stuck—so Burke tried the side window. He had noted that it was stuck closed but it wasn't locked. Standing on a lawn chair, he wiggled and rattled the window until it finally slid loose.

Burke boosted himself up from the lawn chair and stepped on a rhododendron limb. He called into the apartment three times: "Police!"

It was too quiet inside.

Before he so much as touched the window, Burke looked at the wide white windowsill. He saw the print of a large shoe, the tread of a man's athletic shoe, and felt a chill. Carefully avoiding the print, he literally tumbled into the room, landing on a single bed. He could see he was in a spare room, used as a storage area.

Burke helped Officer Thomas in through the window, warning her away from the footprint. There was a pervasive hush in the apartment, somehow louder than noise. They moved cautiously out into the hall. With the drapes shutting out sun, the only light was from a little table lamp next to the couch. The living room was neat—and empty.

Burke covered Thomas as they headed down the hall toward the back of the unit, the female officer opening the doors of the long closet on their left. Charlotte Thomas peered into the bathroom at the end of the corridor on the left side and saw a dark shape behind the shower curtain. Unconsciously holding her breath, Thomas pulled the curtain aside.

A long bath towel hung there.

She stepped across the hall to the master bedroom, with Burke still covering her. There was a still figure on the bed. Charlotte Thomas thought first, *It looks like a mannequin.* But of course it wasn't. It was Molly McClure. Thomas wasn't sure if she said it out loud or only thought it: "Oh, my God."

The girl on the bed wore a blue flannel nightgown and lay facedown and diagonally across the bed, her face hidden by shiny light brown hair. She was partially covered with a pink blanket, but they could see that her hands were tied behind her.

Charlotte Thomas leaned over and gently touched Molly's carotid artery, seeking vainly for a pulse in her neck. She found none, and the flesh she touched was already cooling.

Despite her training, Thomas was momentarily overcome with emotion and she stepped out into the hall. "She's dead. She's in there dead," she whispered to Burke.

"I had to force myself to go back in the room," Thomas would testify later. "I saw a silver flashlight on the floor, and some papers on the bed. At first I thought that maybe it was a suicide note."

But when the officer picked them up, she saw that one slip of paper bore the address of Colonial Penn, an insurance company. The other listed the names and phone numbers of the tenants in the other units of the four-plex. Numbers for Molly to call for help in an emergency.

Too late.

Charlotte Thomas and Harry Burke lifted the pink blanket slightly. They could see a ligature of some kind around the victim's neck.

Burke called for homicide detectives and the King County medical examiner from his patrol car, and then he and Thomas secured the scene.

They had seen that all the heating vents were uncovered, and they wondered if somehow drugs might be involved; furnace vents were a favorite place for dopers to stash their drugs. But that thought warred with everything else they had seen in the apartment. Neat and clean, with plants and books. A young woman sleeping—alone—in a flannel nightie.

Detective Sergeant Don Cameron and Detectives Gail Richardson and Gene Ramirez responded to the East Franklin address at 10:40 that morning. According to the Homicide Unit's rotation schedule, the next detectives up for a murder case were Hank Gruber and Rudy Sutlovich. They were due in court that morning, but they were notified to respond to the McClure apartment as soon as they could get there.

Molly McClure lay facedown on the bed, her legs spread wide, her nightgown pulled high over her buttocks, which were stained with blood. Her hands were tied behind her with a cord cut from an electrical appliance (which proved to be her electric blanket control). Her head was turned to the right. When Medical Examiner Donald Reay, accompanied by forensic pathologists Corrine Fligner and Eric Keisel arrived at 11:40, they determined on their initial examination that Molly had been strangled by ligature—and probably manually, too. Her panties had been forced into her mouth until only a slight bit of cloth protruded, a cruel gag that probably had contributed to death by suffocation. A khaki wool sock was tied around her neck.

She had bled slightly from the back of her head, three linear cuts from some manner of blunt instrument. Reay found them consistent with a "striking force," which had probably stunned Molly or knocked her unconscious but would not have been fatal.

Rigor mortis, the stiffening of the joints that begins shortly after death, was well under way. In violent death, rigor is often accelerated. Lividity, a reddish purple staining that occurs when blood sinks to the lowest portions of the body, can be seen first a half hour to two hours after death and is usually fixed by six to eight hours. It, too, was evident as the investigators began their probe into Molly McClure's murder. Time of death is difficult to fix using body temperature when strangulation has occurred; rather than dropping, it tends to rise. Molly's core body temperature, using the liver as source, wavered between 99 and 101 degrees at noon, at least six hours after her death.

And the time of her death might prove to be vital in Molly's case.

Hank Gruber, nineteen years a cop, sixteen-and-a-half years a detective, with seven and a half of those in homicide, was notified at home and arrived at the scene a little after noon. His partner, Rudy Sutlovich, arrived about the same time. They were briefed by the officers present.

"Burglaries are very obvious," Gruber explains. "There's nothing subtle about a burglary. They dump the stuff all out and paw through it."

The motive here didn't look like burglary. Everywhere the detective pair looked, they saw something that any self-respecting burglar would have taken: television set, portable stereo, jewelry, Molly's purse hanging on her bedroom door. The drawers hadn't been dumped out the way a burglar would have done. The place was tidy. No, someone had come in and found Molly asleep, either because he knew she'd be there or because he broke in and found her. But why would he break in—if he didn't intend to burglarize?

Unless he intended to rape. And he knew Molly was in there alone.

The investigation had begun, and no detective who saw what had been done to Molly McClure was going to let go of it until the killer was convicted. Rudy Sutlovich tried to put into words how they felt: "There are some people who just shouldn't be murdered. . . . No, that's not what I mean. No one should be murdered. But with someone like Molly—and we have some other cases where the victims were just good, wholesome, sweet young girls—it shouldn't have happened. And then we have to go out and tell their parents what happened, how it happened, because they want to know. And we go, and we see the pain. . . . Molly McClure was one of those special cases. We'll never forget her."

Not likely. Hank Gruber and Rudy Sutlovich both have daughters.

Richardson and Ramirez had carefully gathered up possible evidence, bagging it and labeling it: the pink sheet, the mattress cover, a beige silk pillow, the two notes, a hair they found clutched in Molly's right hand, and a second hair caught in the wristband of the watch on her left arm.

In the bathroom, the detectives found a curling iron with its cord cut, but the cord was out next to the phone. Whatever purpose the killer had in mind for that, he had not used it. There was a bloodied tampon in the toilet. There were two pennies on the bathroom floor. The detectives took those, too, not sure what they meant—if anything. Better to take too much, including items of no evidentiary value, than to take too little. The crime scene would never be intact again.

Gruber asked if there had been forced entry, and Richardson said they couldn't be sure. He showed Hank the window in the smaller bedroom and the footprint on the sill. The whole case could turn on that one print, and Gruber wasn't going to take any chances. He was a man who has been known to cut out parts of walls and lug them into the evidence room—just in case. Gruber decided to remove the entire sill and wrap it safely in brown paper.

The chair that Harry Burke had used to get into Molly's apartment had been right there under the outside steps to the second floor. Neighbors said the chair had been there for a long time. Oddly, the front window—where Kvay Knight had seen the prowler the morning before—hadn't been disturbed at all. There was no sign that someone had forced his way in on a second try.

The killer had to have left by the window in the small bedroom. The front door was still dead-bolted when officers arrived; the killer could not have gotten out without a key. All the keys Molly had were quickly accounted for. The shoe print on the spare room windowsill was pointed *into* the room, as it would have been if a person had backed out of the window.

Knowing about the previous break-in attempt, learning how intelligent and cautious Molly McClure had been, Sutlovich and Gruber could not believe that she wouldn't have checked all her windows and doors on Thursday night. "No, it's got to be somebody she knows," they concluded.

To this day the detective partners feel that Molly's killer managed to talk his way into her apartment, using one ruse or another, that he came in through the front door and exited through the window so that he would not be seen after her murder.

Gruber looked into the purse hanging from a knob in Molly's bedroom. With tweezers he opened it and fished around carefully. He saw numerous credit cards and a little cash. It looked as if the killer hadn't even seen it there on the knob.

The detectives searched the apartment for the weapon used to inflict the wounds on Molly's head, but they couldn't find anything with a narrow, curving, blunt edge that matched. Nor did they find blood in any other area of the apartment.

Sutlovich worked the scene all afternoon while Gruber testified in their current court case. That night and the next, the two detectives worked in the quiet rooms until after midnight. They believed the answer was close, so close that they couldn't *see* it, or couldn't recognize it. Each night when they left, they activated a Varda alarm, which would sound in all the patrol cars in Edward sector if anyone tried to enter the premises.

Hank Gruber and Rudy Sutlovich spoke with twenty-seven-year-old Kvay Knight at Sondra Hill's apartment on that first Friday night. They took a taped statement from him as he tried to remember everything he could about the prowler he'd seen on Thursday morning. He stressed that he wanted to help; he'd called Sergeant Don Cameron to offer whatever help he could. He had told Officer Kuenzi what he remembered about Thursday night—the night right before the murder—and then he'd stayed for a while visiting with Molly. He was trying as hard as he could to bring back something, anything, that might pinpoint the "burglar" for the detectives.

Gruber asked Knight if he was familiar with Molly's apartment, and he said that he had only been in the living room. Like the other tenants in the four-plex, he had heard no cries for help, no screams or sounds of a struggle during the night.

On Saturday, January 18, Knight stopped by Molly's apartment as Gruber and Sutlovich continued their day-long crime-scene search. He had remembered that he *had* been a little beyond the living room.

"Molly was afraid of spiders," he explained, "and she asked me to look down some of the heating vents to see if there were any down there. I used her flashlight."

Ahh. That was one question answered. The silver flashlight. It had belonged to Molly. It had been dusted for prints by I.D. Technician

Marcia Jackson, but none appeared. Most of the prints Marcia found in the apartment were Molly's or "unusables," because they were fragmented or smudged. On the pictures in the living room and on a drawer in the bedroom she found some clear prints that she could not match either to Molly or her family. But then, it had only been a few weeks since movers had carried Molly's things in from their van. The investigative task was monumental; so many people had moved through Molly's apartment, both before and after she moved in, many of them strangers.

Kvay Knight told Hank Gruber that he hadn't planned to be in Molly's apartment on Thursday night, but she had asked him to come in and wait to talk to the police. He estimated he had stayed perhaps half an hour after Kuenzi left. They had talked mostly about cooking; she'd recommended a recipe and then loaned him one of her cookbooks so he could try it.

Dr. Eric Kiesel performed Molly McClure's autopsy on Monday, January 20, with Rudy Sutlovich and Hank Gruber in attendance. Kiesel found that Molly had succumbed to strangulation by asphyxia, both by ligature and manually. She had also been suffocated when her panties were jammed into her mouth, pushing her tongue to the back of her throat.

Molly had been raped, and there was slight tearing and bruising to the labia minora, the inner folds of the female genitalia. But the man who deserved no luck had been given some. Molly had been menstruating, and the semen found in her vaginal vault was mixed with menstrual flow. The semen was Type O. But Molly's blood was Type O, too. That didn't necessarily mean the killer had won; there were some very sophisticated tests that could be done on blood enzymes and subgroupings.

And there was more physical evidence, so minute that a layman would never have considered it evidence: a pill of lint removed from Molly's buttocks, a tobacco flake under the fingernail of a woman who detested smoking, a black hair from the inner portion of her left thigh, fibers caught in Molly's hand, bright blue fibers found under the pillowcase on Molly's bed, a pubic hair lifted from the panties used as a gag. There were eighteen strands or fragments of hair in all.

What did they all mean? Even a decade earlier, most of that almost infinitesimal evidence might have been part of an insoluble puzzle. However, with rapid advances in forensic science, the criminalists at the Western Washington State Patrol Crime Lab might now be able to winnow out the script of a crime from those washes of blood, semen, fibers, hairs, pills of lint. Chesterine Cwiklik is a criminalist who knows as much about hair and fiber analysis as anyone in America. Enjoying the almost impossible challenge, she went to work on the evidence that Gruber and Sutlovich had given her.

One thing was already quite obvious to the two detectives. The dark spiraling hair found on Molly's thigh at autopsy appeared to belong to someone from the black race. Chesterine would have to verify that, but Gruber and Sutlovich were already sure themselves.

The two Seattle detectives believed from the beginning that Molly had known her killer, if only casually, and that there had been no break-in. They wondered if Molly had black friends in her social circle who might have visited her.

No. Her family and friends were positive she wasn't dating a black man and currently had no black female friends. She hadn't mentioned anything about new friends; she hadn't really been back in Seattle long enough to meet new friends. Her boss said the same thing. Olson's group in the hospitality section of the company was small, and they knew each other well. Andy Olson had never seen Molly with a black man—or woman, for that matter. Neither had she ever voiced any prejudice toward other races. Indeed, Molly had a heart big enough to welcome anyone she met. Moreover, she trusted people—perhaps too much.

While evidence was being evaluated and theories explored, Molly McClure's memorial service was held at the Bellevue First Presbyterian Church that Monday evening. More than six hundred mourners packed the church and overflowed outside. Seattle newspapers published pictures of Molly, all of them, of course, smiling. She looked like a younger version of her mother. She was quite beautiful with big eyes and almost cherubic cheeks.

Warren and Jean McClure received scores of letters about Molly— from people they had known for years, from people in Molly's life, and from complete strangers who had read about their loss. They had no idea just how many lives she had touched and, in doing so, enhanced.

Jack Crowley could not bear to live in his apartment after Molly was killed; he spent only one more night there, and then he moved out, unable to shake the thought that Molly had been strangled to death on the other side of the wall and he hadn't even heard her cry out for help. *Why* hadn't he heard her? The storm, maybe. Maybe she had not had a *chance* to scream.

Rudy Sutlovich and Hank Gruber figured that Molly had been dead before 6:00 or 7:00 A.M. That was the simplest riddle to solve. If her alarm had gone off, she would have been up and getting ready for work. The shower walls had been dry, and the coffee-pot hadn't been started. Molly was found in bed in her nightgown. And the degree of rigor and lividity in her body when detectives arrived after 10:00 suggested that she had almost certainly been killed four or five hours earlier.

Gruber and Sutlovich kept coming back to one glaring fact. The only black man the detective team could connect to Molly was Sherwood "Kvay" Knight, who lived right upstairs. But he had knocked on her door to warn her once. Why would he hurt her? He had seemed more than sincere in trying to help catch her killer.

There *was* something that niggled at the two detectives. Although they hadn't yet mentioned it to him, Hank and Rudy knew about Knight's past, and it was not particularly savory. He had a record that made him a less than desirable neighbor. He had just been released from prison on a burglary conviction. He had been convicted of robbing a video store clerk after he'd tied her hands behind her with an electric cord. He wasn't the law-abiding citizen he was trying to portray. They learned that Kvay Knight had also been questioned about a rape case that occurred in Snohomish County, Washington, in December of 1984 and that he had been released for lack of evidence. An unsolved murder case in that same county bore a marked resemblance to the M.O. used in Molly McClure's death.

Knight often used the alias "Billy Williams." Rudy Sutlovich and Hank Gruber, by nature and profession suspicious men, began to see Knight's "rescue" of Molly on January 16 from a different angle.

"Suppose," Sutlovich began, "suppose he saw Molly around, found her attractive, which she certainly was, and he wanted to check out her habits. When he knocked on her door at four or four-thirty A.M., he could have found out a number of things. Number one: Jack Crowley said he heard knocking for a long time before she came to the door, so Kvay knew she was a sound sleeper. Molly told her aunt that she'd had trouble waking up when he knocked. Two: he found out she lived alone. Three: that she slept alone. Four: she normally was home—and asleep—at that hour of the morning."

There were still a lot of pieces missing. Kvay Knight lived with a most attractive woman. It would have been foolhardy of him to attack the woman who lived right downstairs—especially after he'd talked to a Seattle policeman only hours before the murder.

Or might he have counted on the investigators coming to that conclusion? Had he figured if he committed a murder almost literally right under the Seattle Police Department's noses, they would never believe he could be so stupid?

Rudy Sutlovich had done most of the interviewing of Sondra Hill. Hill, a legal secretary, had lived in the four-plex for four and a half years. Until six months earlier, she had lived in the unit right next to Molly's, which had the same floor plan, only mirror-imaged. In June of 1985 she'd moved into the upper apartment over Molly's, and Jack Crowley had moved into her old place.

Sondra said she had known Kvay Knight since February of 1979, and they had dated for six years. When he got out of prison after serving fifteen months, he had moved in with her and registered for classes at North Seattle Community College. Because he wasn't working, Sondra and one of Kvay's female relatives supported him. He had started classes in January and had an eight o'clock on Monday, Wednesday, and Friday and a nine o'clock on Tuesday and Thursday. Because he had no vehicle, Kvay had to take a circuitous bus route to get to his classes. Although his destination was north, he first had to take a southbound bus downtown and then catch a bus that would take him north again.

As far as Sondra Hill knew, Kvay had gone to school on Thursday, and then he had come home, fixed supper for her, and left to visit relatives. At 10:30 Thursday night, when he came back to the apartment they shared, he told Sondra about talking with the officer and then visiting with Molly. Kvay had been a little surprised that Molly had even called the police, Sondra said, because he told her Molly had laughed and hadn't believed him when he told her about the prowler early that morning.

Sondra and Kvay had watched the end of "20/20" and some of the eleven o'clock news. Then they had an argument, she told Sutlovich and Gruber.

"What did you argue about?" Gruber asked.

"He wanted to have sex, but I felt too lousy to be interested." She said Kvay had been grumpy and gone to sleep on the couch. Since it was a cold night, he had pulled a sleeping bag over himself, and she had added a blue afghan she had crocheted.

Sondra said she had been up half a dozen times during the night. She had heard the front door slam at 5:40, just after her alarm went off. She assumed it was Kvay going out jogging. He had suddenly become serious about running, she said, going out in the very early morning hours for two or three hours of exercise.

About twenty minutes after Sondra heard the door slam, she had heard a loud "staticky sound" coming from Molly's apartment below. That was really the only unusual aspect of the whole night; Sondra had never heard any sounds from Molly's unit before.

Although she felt rotten, Sondra nevertheless had decided to go to work. She got up, showered, and put on her makeup. She didn't hear Kvay come back, but when she went out to the kitchen at 7:10, he was there, with his hand in the refrigerator. He had smelled sweaty, she remembered, as if he had been jogging hard. He gulped down some juice and told her he was late for school.

"What was he wearing?" Sutlovich asked.

"Black cotton slacks and a gray Husky Rose Bowl sweatshirt—the same thing he had on the night before. And running shoes."

He hadn't paused to take a shower—just grabbed his notebooks and knapsack and left.

Sondra had left for work at 8:00 A.M. It was much later in the day when she received a phone call from her landlord telling her that Molly had been murdered.

Sondra Hill had been terribly afraid after that. She gave notice to the landlord that she was moving out on February 1. Even so, she had new locks installed on her apartment door for the two weeks she stayed. She wasn't fearful when Kvay was home—but he was gone so much, especially in the dark hours before dawn.

She told Rudy Sutlovich that she remembered Kvay had been in a tearing hurry the morning of January 17 because he was late for school.

As Sutlovich and Hank Gruber canvassed the neighborhood to see if anyone remembered something—anything—that was different on the morning after Molly died, they talked to Susan Stroum,* who lived in the apartment building next door. Kvay had given her the same impression that he was in a great hurry. Stroum was a woman of precise habit, and she unfailingly left for work between 7:20 and 7:25. On the morning of January 17 she had seen Knight as they walked between the buildings at precisely 7:25. She recognized Kvay; he'd lived with Sondra on and off for years. They both turned and headed south.

Susan Stroum had crossed the street, prepared to turn at East Lynn Street, and Knight continued on Franklin.

The detectives checked at North Seattle Community College and learned Kvay Knight wasn't going to school; he hadn't shown up for more than three or four classes all term. He was supposed to be taking data processing and office functions, but the college records showed he had last attended a class on January 10. Sondra didn't know that, and neither did his mother, who was giving him money.

One thing was clear. Sherwood "Kvay" Knight was a liar and a mooch. But was he a killer? And if he was, could Hank Gruber and Rudy Sutlovich prove it?

Sutlovich and Gruber felt the frustration of having to move at an agonizingly slow pace. At the crime lab, Chesterine Cwiklik and John Brown worked on the fiber and hair evidence and on the shoe print. That was really all they had. Most of the evidence couldn't even be seen by the naked eye.

The detectives returned to question Sondra Hill and Kvay Knight again—and again. With each visit they were less welcome. Kvay Knight, who had been so anxious to "help" the police, was growing surly. And so was Sondra. Hank Gruber told Kvay that he and Rudy were positive that the killer was black because of the distinctive pubic hair found during the postmortem. They needed to eliminate any innocent black males who had been around her. Knight's face betrayed shock when he heard this. No, he certainly would not want to take a polygraph test without talking to an attorney, he blurted. Why should an innocent man be subjected to such a thing?

When the detectives knocked on Sondra Hill's door on January 22 and asked for Knight, she was sarcastic. "No, he's not here. You wanta come in and look?"

On January 24, a week after Molly McClure's murder, Gruber, Sutlovich, Detective Duane Homan, and Detective Gail Richardson went to Sondra Hill's apartment to execute a search warrant. It was a search warrant based more on the gut-level hunches of two experienced detectives than on anything else.

"We spent two hours on the phone with one assistant D.A.," Gruber remembers. "Then a long time with another one. We worked over that affidavit and hand-carried it to a Judge Phil Killien. We finally convinced him. It was one A.M. when we got a search warrant signed."

Before seven o'clock the next morning, Hank and Rudy were at Sondra Hill's front door while their fellow detectives covered the back. As they had hoped, they literally caught Kvay Knight with his pants down—or rather, off.

He answered the door in long johns, shorts, and a T-shirt. It was apparent they had awakened him. The four detectives had no intention of arresting Knight at this point; they merely wanted to obtain hair, blood, and saliva samples and articles of his clothing, and to search Hill's apartment. In order to obtain blood samples, they had to take Kvay downtown to the crime lab, where the needed samples could be obtained.

A most indignant Kvay Knight was arrested—but only for investigation; they knew they couldn't hold him for more than seventy-two hours. Even if the lab should one day be able to match the hairs and fibers they had to head, temple, and pubic hair from the suspect, it might take weeks. But it was necessary to *get* those hairs, and Kvay Knight had been so adamant in refusing to voluntarily give up those samples that they had to arrest him in order to pluck his hair and draw a few test tubes of blood.

During the search, they took Knight's Husky sweatshirt, a pair of black slacks hanging over a chair, and a second pair of black slacks they found soaking in a plastic tub. They simply picked up tub, water and all. Knight wanted to wear his tennis shoes, but Hank Gruber suggested he wear another pair; Gruber wanted *those* shoes to compare with the print left on Molly's windowsill. They also took hairs they found in Sondra Hill's bathtub and in the trap underneath the stopper.

Neither Sutlovich nor Gruber wanted to balance a tub of cold, soapy water on his knees for the ride to headquarters, so they flipped for it.

Sutlovich lost. At six feet seven, he already had enough trouble fitting his long legs into a car; now he had to hold a lapful of sloshing gray water to boot. Gruber drove, grinning at his partner's dilemma.

Gruber had more to grin about than the sight of Sutlovich balancing the tub. This was the impossible case, with nothing to go on but a few pills of hair and lint, a faded footprint. But now, suddenly, it looked as though things might be turning around.

Kvay Knight gave up his blood, hair, and saliva, served his forty-eight hours, and was released.

But Chesterine Cwiklik was finding more and more trace evidence that matched. Cwiklik's specialty is akin to unraveling a puzzle, both figuratively and literally. A postgraduate student in organic chemistry, she specializes in microscopy, using a microscope to investigate very small items and to enlarge them for comparison and matching. Cwiklik was in charge of the microanalysis section of the State Patrol Crime Lab. And when she testified, she spoke of what she had discovered from those minuscule bits of fiber and lint.

A fiber is anything that is long and thin; fibers can be plastic, metal, cotton. Clothing is either *synthetic*, as in the ubiquitous polyester, or *natural*, as in jute, hemp, or cotton. The most common animal fiber is wool. With the exception of carpet fibers, most fibers are thinner than a human hair.

Once Cwiklik had a fiber, there were innumerable procedures she could choose to evaluate it. She often used a spinneret—a disk with holes of different shapes that separated and differentiated fibers. She could test for luster—a manufacturer's treatment of a surface. She could detect the differences in dye and in the stages of dyeing. She could make a "glass sandwich" with a fiber or hair fixed in a transparent mounting medium, and then gaze at it with a polarizing comparison microscope that magnified it 800 times.

Rudy Sutlovich and Hank Gruber had presented Chesterine with 237 pieces of trace evidence. It would take her weeks—months, even—to test it all. She looked at the detectives and said, "Which is the most important?"

"The stuff that was closest to the body."

And so she had begun. The black fibers found on Molly McClure's hand, buttocks, and nightgown matched microscopically the fibers from the black pants the detectives had found soaking in the plastic tub. The lint and hair pill removed from Molly's buttock contained fibers and hairs very similar to those in the pill that came from the crotch of Knight's pants; each tiny ball had cat hair mingled in it.

Cwiklik took the pant fibers several steps forward. She magnified them 1,110 times and looked at them through the polarizing comparison microscope. And there they were, each side of the screen indistinguishable from the other.

Chesterine Cwiklik knew that every human being collects bits and pieces of the world he or she lives in. Every person picks up debris—fibers, hairs, dirt—common to his or her surroundings. "Molly's environment, for instance, had rose-red and purple fibers, paint chips, natural fibers—no cat hair," she explained to Gruber and Sutlovich. "Upstairs, in Ms. Hill's apartment, there were synthetic fibers, oranges, browns, blue and green, tobacco flakes, and a great number of cat hairs."

When the fiber profile of one household intrudes into another, vital trace evidence is transferred. Molly detested cats, but someone had brought cat hairs into her bed. Molly's pillowcase bore fibers that were microscopically similar to the afghan Sondra Hill had crocheted in many shades of dark blue and white, fibers with a distinctive twist—a continual *S*, thermally bonded. There was nothing at all in Molly's apartment with those colors.

Kvay Knight had slept under that blue and white afghan the night before Molly was killed. He denied ever having been in her bedroom. But he had left signs. For Chesterine Cwiklik, it was as if the killer had signed his name and left it next to his victim.

Hair microscopically indistinguishable from Kvay Knight's was found: on Molly's left wrist, on her mattress, on her pillowcase, on her buttocks, in her pubic hair, on her inner thigh, on her sheet, in the ligature that had been used to strangle her, in the panty gag. Sondra Hill's hair—picked up in her apartment and transported—was also found in Molly's bedding. Molly's hair was found on the sole of Knight's shoes, on the blanket that Knight stood on when he removed his clothes during the search warrant, and in Knight's tub.

Good. But was it enough to convince a jury? Hair and fiber testimony is hard for the layman to understand. And it isn't absolute; it is only highly *probable* evidence.

When a case relies upon trace evidence and circumstantial evidence, the more ammunition from the lab, the better. Each "very probable" match raises the percentage of likelihood. John Brown worked over the shoe print. The pattern of the sole *could* very well have come from Knight's right sports shoe; the size was right, too, but the sole was quite common and there were no distinctive marks of wear or damage. It had rained at 2:00 A.M., but if Knight had come down from upstairs he would have stepped on only a small patch of damp earth and would not have had appreciable mud on his shoes.

The tobacco flake under Molly's nail was foreign; she didn't smoke. She hated to be around smokers, and no one smoked in her apartment out of consideration for her. The minute speck matched tobacco particles on Knight's Husky sweatshirt.

George K. Chan, an expert in biochemistry and a criminalist at the State Patrol Crime Lab, took over the testing of body fluids found at the crime scene and during the execution of the search warrant. Tremendous strides are being made in isolating blood and other body fluids, matching them to a single source. All human beings have genetic markers in tissue, blood, and body fluids. ABO typing can be done on bloodstains, and genetic markers can be isolated from blood groups, enzymes, proteins, antigens, and RH factors. Miraculous silent testimony can be extracted from blood, saliva, semen, sweat, mucus, and tears.

Over 80 percent of humans are "secretors"; their blood type can be determined from body fluids. Tests showed that both Molly McClure and Kvay Knight were Type O secretors. Chan had a problem right away, of course, when he tried to work with the vaginal swab containing Molly's menstrual blood and the semen from her rapist-killer. Both were Type O. But he knew he could do further, more probing tests.

When Chan examined the Husky sweatshirt that Kvay Knight had worn to bed on the night of the murder and when he left the next morning, the criminalist found three patches of dried blood *inside* the waistband. The sweatshirt had not been washed in the week between the murder and the search warrant. Undoubtedly Knight had no idea the blood was there.

Now the most delicate testing began. Chan determined that the dried blood was Type O. But Knight had no cuts or abrasions on his body. He had not bled. Only Molly had bled.

Chan's tests had to go beyond blood type, and he began a search for other genetic markers. The white, black, red, and yellow races tend to have certain Gm (Gamma) and Km (Kappa) markers. Even with "genetic drift" brought about by the co-mingling of the races, the signal flags remain. For instance, in Caucasians, a Gm count of 3,11 occurs in 44 percent; a Km of 3 occurs in 86 percent. In the black race, 3 is most unusual in Gm, but a 1,11 combination is common.

If a black man should bleed on his own shirt, he would almost surely leave blood with a Gm reading including an 11 but not a 3. As Gary Harmer, a forensic serologist, explained, "If you have oranges, apples, and grapes, and mix them and test them, you will get only a mixture of oranges, apples, and grapes; there will be no bananas."

The chart resulting from the test of the three bloodstains and the blood from Molly McClure and Kvay Knight looked like this:

	GM	KM
Victim (Molly)	3,11	3
Suspect (Kvay)	1,11,28	1,3
Sweatshirt	3,11	3
	3,11	3
	3,11	

Chan found *only* Caucasian genetic markers in the Type O blood dried on the inside of Kvay Knight's sweatshirt. Unknowingly, Knight had carried Molly's blood around next to his skin for a week. Had he washed the sweatshirt, the critical evidence would have been lost, but apparently he never saw the faint bloodstains, and they were almost miraculously preserved.

As Gary Harmer explained, "The bloodstains on the waistband of the shirt *could* have come from Molly McClure, but they could *not* have come from Sherwood 'Kvay' Knight."

No test yet had exonerated Kvay Knight, and the results—taken together—were building a higher and higher mountain of evidence all the time.

Molly's father was going about the sad task of closing out her bank accounts. He received her bank statement from Great Western Savings and Loan, which included all transactions she had made with her bank exchange card on an automatic teller machine. As McClure ran his eyes over the figures for the period between January 15 and February 15, he froze. *Someone had made two withdrawals from Molly's account on the morning of January 17.* It could not have been Molly; she was already dead. Moreover, Molly had only rarely used the card; she wrote checks. The withdrawals were for $100 each at 7:34 and 7:35 A.M. on January 17. The transactions were made at a Seattle First banking facility on Eastlake—only blocks south of Molly's apartment!

Warren McClure called Gruber and Sutlovich immediately.

Whatever the killer's original motive had been—rape or burglary—he had accomplished both.

At first, the detectives thought they had finally found something that would be easy to trace back to Molly's killer. Some 25 percent of the cash machines in Seattle were equipped with cameras to record the image of the person withdrawing money. But this ATM had no camera. Indeed, the bank machine was located in a facility that kept only records; it had once been a full-service bank, but was no longer. However, the money machine was still there. Whoever used it had to *know* it was there; there were no signs to mark it.

Hank Gruber and Rudy Sutlovich went to the four-plex on Franklin with a stopwatch. They would try to time a reenactment of Molly's killer's actions just after her murder. Okay, Susan Stroum had seen Kvay Knight leaving his apartment and heading south—in a hell of a hurry—at around 7:25 A.M. Gruber would have to walk it; Rudy Sutlovich's legs were so long that one of his strides equaled two of an average man's, so they couldn't get an accurate time reading from Rudy. With Sutlovich holding the watch, Hank Gruber walked the eight blocks from Molly's apartment to the cash machine.

Nine minutes. Again and again, it worked out the same. If Kvay Knight had left walking south in a hurry, Molly's cash card in his pocket, at 7:25 A.M., he would have reached the machine at 7:34 A.M.

The exact time the first $100 was withdrawn.

Then he would have had to wait a minute and withdraw the next $100.

Hank and Rudy wondered how Kvay Knight would have known the machine was there. That puzzle was solved easily. Sondra Hill admitted that she had a card that was honored at the ATM, a card that had expired only two months before the murder. Her lover would have known about the machine hidden behind what looked like a simple office building rather than a bank.

Taken individually, the blocks of evidence were not overwhelming. Combined, they defied credibility. Hank Gruber and Rudy Sutlovich believed as they had never believed anything else that Sherwood "Kvay" Knight had killed Molly McClure.

And he was getting away.

Sondra and Kvay moved out of their apartment on the first of February. Sondra went home to her parents, and Kvay was swallowed up in the mean streets of the Central District of Seattle. He was a smooth talker, persuasive and slick, and he had friends who would shelter him for a day or so before he moved on. He and Sondra kept in touch, and she was standing behind him, refusing to believe he was guilty of anything more than skipping school.

But Sutlovich and Gruber could not catch up with Kvay. He was as elusive as the wind. He surfaced here and here and here, and then he was gone again.

The detective team had become close to Jean and Warren McClure, a friendship that would last long after their investigation was over, and they wanted to be able to say, "We have your daughter's killer, and he's going to trial." But they couldn't do that. When Rudy and Hank visited Molly's family, they had to tell them that now that they had enough evidence to arrest Kvay, he had disappeared.

"But don't worry," Gruber said confidently. "Finding people is the easiest part of our job. We'll get the arrest warrant, and we'll find him."

Once they were back in their car, Rudy turned to Hank, puzzled. "What was all that about? You and I both know that finding people is the *hardest* part of our job! We're never gonna find that guy. He's gone!"

"Have faith," Gruber said. "We'll find him."

King County Senior Deputy Prosecutor Becky Roe requested bail of $250,000 when she filed affidavits on April 18, 1986, charging Sherwood "Kvay" Knight with aggravated first-degree murder. The charges were based on circumstantial and trace evidence. Roe was willing to gamble on conviction.

Knight hadn't waited around to be arrested. Rudy Sutlovich and Hank Gruber believed, however, that he was still in the Seattle area. They had a lot of places to look for their cagey suspect. They sat on stakeouts for three days, watching Knight's friends' houses.

And still their quarry eluded them.

But the news of the murder charges had been in Seattle papers, and two casual acquaintances spotted Knight sitting in a car near the Boeing Plant on East Marginal Way with a young man. Kvay was busy selling "merchandise" to the driver and didn't notice he was being observed. The acquaintances had no particular loyalty to Knight and were as repulsed by the crime he was charged with as the rest of Seattle was. They called the police.

By the time Sutlovich and Gruber arrived, the Boeing plant was ending a shift, and traffic was jammed in every direction. Finally something had come easy for the stubborn detectives. They found their suspect sitting in a police car in the middle of a traffic jam. Sherwood Kvay Knight had been arrested and handcuffed by Seattle Police Officer Al Thompson.

In October 1986, Kvay Knight went on trial in Superior Court Judge Terrence Carroll's courtroom. The twelve jurors and two alternates—six men, eight women—gazed inscrutably at the now mild-looking young man in the gray-blue suit. He didn't look very strong; he looked slender and meek. His hair was cut in a modified Afro. His two public defenders sat beside him, patting him on the shoulder, leaning over to hold whispered conferences.

All across the first two rows of the gallery, Molly McClure's family and friends packed the wooden benches. They watched and listened to horrific testimony with quiet dignity, their tear-brimmed eyes the only sign that they were far more than casual court observers. Reporters came and went, but they did not stay all day. It was not a *big* story. Jean McClure murmured, "We didn't expect reporters at all. We're just an average family who lost our daughter. We're not front page."

Only to Hank Gruber and Rudy Sutlovich. To prosecutors Becky Roe and Dan Kinerk, too, Molly McClure's death was no average case. Outside the courtroom, the October sun shone and jackhammers tore up Third Avenue as workers opened up the street for an underground bus tunnel. Inside, the courtroom hushed as an 11-by-14-inch photograph of Molly in her blue nightgown, dead, was tacked up on a display board. There is no dignity in murder; it is so important to convict the guilty that the jurors *have* to see the horror.

Testimony continued for days. Sondra Hill, looking beautiful—but pale—stared down at her ex-lover as she described the night and morning of January 16–17. Molly's family and her boss testified. And the forensic experts patiently explained what all the hairs and fibers and blood meant.

Sherwood "Kvay" Knight did not testify in his own defense. As the trial progressed, he slouched down in his seat at the defense table farther and farther as if he knew things were not going well for him.

They were not.

On October 10, the jury deliberated only two and a half hours before returning with a verdict of guilty. Becky Roe and Dan Kinerk had not asked for the death penalty. On November 3, Judge Carroll imposed the mandatory sentence: life in prison without possibility of parole. Knight stood with his hands behind him. As television cameras whirred and reporters stuck microphones in his face, he declined to make a statement.

Kvay Knight was soon swallowed up in Washington's penal system.

Kvay Knight's conviction was faint comfort to Molly McClure's family, but it put an end to one phase of their grief. "She had a sparkle about her," her aunt remarked quietly. "I don't think she had an enemy in the world. If you knew her, you loved her."

Molly Ann McClure will never be forgotten. So many gifts were given in her memory. The Molly McClure Memorial Scholarship for the College of Business and Economics at Washington State University and the Molly Ann McClure Leadership Scholarship in Alpha Chi Omega are both perpetually endowed. A tree was planted in Molly's memory in Marymoor Park in Redmond, Washington. There is a hand-carved lectern in the Fellowship Hall of Bellevue's First Presbyterian Church, and Molly's name appears in three spots in the monument at the entrance to the Downtown Park in Bellevue.

In July 1986 her parents had taken her ashes to the beach at Seaview on the Long Beach peninsula, which juts out into the Pacific Ocean off Washington's southwestern state line. "We spread her ashes, with our tears, at the water's edge. It was a favorite place of hers where she spent so many happy times with her good friends . . . and we felt she might have wanted to be returned to that place."

Jean and Warren McClure have kept their last communication from their lost daughter, a short note on pink note paper, sent two days before she died. It included a car payment and said,

1/86

Mom and Dad,

Don't know when I'll come over to drop this off. Thought
you'd rather have it sooner than later.

Dad, thanks a lot for spending your time working on the
outside light. It's working great.

See you one of these days. . . .

They never did.

YOU BELONG TO ME

and Other True Cases

Ann Rule's Crime Files: Vol. 2

From the time my memory began I have believed that policemen are among the finest human beings on this earth. Nothing has ever changed my mind. My grandfather was a sheriff and then my uncle. At the age of 19 I became a law enforcement officer myself. With the wisdom and experience of almost four decades I have learned that there will always be a minute percentage of bad cops. But they are only a tiny blot on the bravery and dedication of the mass of men and women who protect us and uphold the law.

I dedicate *You Belong to Me* to the millions of good cops out there—to those who will, and too often *do,* lay down their lives for us.

I thank them and wish them Godspeed.

Acknowledgments

When a book is *true*, as this one is, I am totally dependent on facts, documentation, and the keen memories of other people. It is also a real challenge to gather photographs from dozens of sources, all of whom furnished them to me graciously and with trust that they would receive their precious *originals* back. I cannot say how much I appreciate that. And, too, I have my front-line critics, my "first" readers who point out little slips that my eyes can no longer detect. And sometimes they have enthusiastic comments, and that's even better. They play such an important part.

As always, the names that follow are in no particular order because their lives and mine tend to cross again and again in different places on this earth and for different reasons. I think they will all understand.

Thank you Don and Susan Dappen, Phil and Margie Williams, Sandy Harris, Jimm Redmond, Pat and Fred Wessendorf, Jodi Dombroski, Carol Worley, Kathy and Gary Jacobi, Charles Steadham, Gerry Brittingham, Verne Carver, Bob and Denise Evans, Maureen and Bill Woodcock, Lisa and Martin Woodcock, Donna Anders, Bill and Shirley Hickman, Lola Linstad, "Tex" and Gene Parsons, Fay Moss, Gail DiRe, Diane Brace, Bobbi Bennett, Chuck Wright, Robert Keppel, and Greg Canova.

And thank you to John Hansen, Mark Ericks, Joe Sanford, John Boatman, Sonny Davis, Hank Gruber, Rudy Sutlovich, Don Cameron, Duane Homan, Jim Yoshida, John Henry Browne, Len Randall, Mike Baily, Ted Forrester, Joyce and Pierce Brooks, Rod Englert, Dr. Clyde Snow, Mike Tando, Craig VandePutte, Bob and Gen Lofgren, Jim Lane, Jim Swenson, Gary Svendson, Dennis Elder, Colleen and Scott Elder, Claude and Ernie Bailey, Millie Yoacham, Austin and Charlotte Seth, Erik Seth and Denise Watson, Nils and Judith Seth, and Roberta Yochim.

Thank you to Sudden Printing in Burien for living up to your name.

I am a most fortunate writer to have the backup team I do, and I appreciate them: my editors at Pocket Books, Julie Rubenstein and Bill Grose; their editorial assistants, Liate Stehlik and Joe Gram; my publicist, Cindy Ratzlaff; Pocket's sensational art director, Paolo Pepe, who always understands what I am trying to say; my gentle but determined expert in literary law, Emily Remes. And finally, my literary agents, Joan and Joe Foley; and my theatrical agents, Mary Alice Kier and Anna Cottle. Bless you all!

Author's Note

You Belong to Me, the second in my anthology series, contains one book-length new case—the title story—and five cases from my files. *You Belong to Me* took me about as far away from familiar places as I could get; I found myself on the Treasure Coast of Florida, researching what may well be one of the more bizarre cases I have encountered. While this is a case of the nineties, the emotions involved are ageless. The killer, however, was someone even I would not have suspected, which only serves to prove again, I suppose, that there is no room for preconceived ideas or haste when it comes to solving murders.

Anyone who has read my work probably has sensed that I become very involved in the lives of the people I write about. These are not simply "stories" to me; I know full well that I am writing about real people. For a time, when I have finished a book or an article, I move away from the people I have met, involved in some new project. But I always go back, and I never forget. In the five revisited cases in this book I found myself walking back into the lives of human beings I had known before. Some of them, of course, were already dead when I "met" them, and nothing has changed for them; others in their stories have gone on, as we all must in the face of tragedy. I was amazed how much I learned as I updated the five cases I once thought I knew thoroughly: "Black Christmas," "One Trick Pony," "The Computer Error and the Killer," "The Vanishing," and "The Last Letter."

If there is one thread that weaves itself through *You Belong to Me*, it is that each piece has an element of shocking revelation. Innocent people are totally unaware of the thoughts and plans of someone they know so well (or think they do) that they have no fear of him or her—*or* of someone who moves so dimly in the background of their lives that they never consider the danger there.

Some killers follow their targets with stealthy surveillance. They are like ghosts who betray their presence by the snapping of a twig or quiet breathing on the other end of a phone line. Others are omnipresent, as familiar as your own face in the mirror.

Several of the following cases, including the title story—"You Belong to Me"—deal with obsessed lovers, and yet the paths they took to snare their quarries are as diverse as the human beings involved.

Predictably, there are few happy endings.

Nor are there happy endings when a serial killer sets out to stalk— not those he has ties to, but absolute strangers who have the great misfortune to possess certain characteristics that trigger a murderer into violence.

As I look for parallels and differences I realize that almost every case in this book is about *power*, about a killer's need not only to control his own life, but to direct the lives of others. Oddly, I have never researched a killer who was *truly* powerful; every one of them was acting out of weakness. All of them were hollow and empty inside—empty enough that they went to tortuous and tragic lengths to seize power from their victims.

They are all different. They are all alike.

I suspect there are cases in this second volume of my true crime files that will astound you and catch you off guard just as they did me.

You Belong to Me

All of us wonder *how a murderer selects his victim or victims; I think about this often. What chaotic synchronicity brought them together? Sometimes they have known each other for half a century or more; sometimes they are strangers until the ill-fated instant they meet. Always I find myself thinking, "If only . . ." If the victim had left a little later or a little earlier. If it hadn't rained or traffic had been lighter or heavier. If the partners in a marriage had never met, never dated, never fallen in love and had chosen someone else entirely. If only time could be rewound and choices that turned out to be fatal could be revised.*

But of course, real life does not allow second guessing.

In the title story of this second volume, "You Belong to Me," there were so many variables that might have changed the terrible ending. The victim was, perhaps, not the woman the killer believed she was. Perhaps. The killer was the last person in the world most of us would have suspected.

PART ONE

Sandy

1

The slender woman lay on her stomach in the grove of pine trees, the hot sun baking the air; even though its rays were filtered into stripes by the pine branches above her, the sun was almost as intense in March as it would be in full summer. Where she rested her head the pines opened three or four hours a day, just enough for one steady golden ray to spotlight her cheek. Her skin was exposed, but her nakedness was hidden from the drivers and passengers riding in the trucks and cars that whooshed by on the freeway lanes that bracketed the pine grove. She was as good as invisible. The woman paid no heed to the noise of the engines or to the diesel fumes that drifted into the clean woodsy air.

The I-95 Interstate snakes all along the eastern seaboard of the United States, beginning on the border between Maine and New Brunswick, Canada, and ending in Miami. Some who have reason to know say that parts of 95 are the most dangerous stretches of road in America. It is certainly one of the busiest freeways and one of the first ever laid down across the land. Down and down 95 plunges, from the icy winter in the north to the balmy tropical always-summer of Florida. From Bangor to Boston to New York it rushes, skirting Philadelphia, passing through the heart of Washington, D.C., before it curves south through Virginia and the Carolinas. I-95 picks up the Atlantic Ocean salt wind passing through Savannah, and then hugs the Florida coastline: Jacksonville to Melbourne, Fort Pierce, Fort Lauderdale, and on into Miami, close by the sea all the way.

Families travel I-95 as they head for Disney World in Orlando and come home with their cars full of stuffed Mickey Mouses and funny hats. "Snowbirds" flee northern blizzards—and then wait until the very last moment of gently balmy Florida weather, timing their departure so that they can enjoy northern springtime and escape the thick, muggy heat of southern summers. Drug runners cruise along I-

415

95, some of them with millions of dollars worth of drugs cleverly hidden, and others as transparent and klutzy as Disney's Goofy. Many of the travelers drive straight through the 1200-plus miles from New York to Miami, senior citizens tending to drowse behind the wheel, young men fortifying themselves with alcohol, and truck drivers with No-Doz. All of them keep a wary eye out for local law enforcement and the highway patrol. Everybody's pushing a little too fast. Troopers will look the other way for five or so miles over the speed limit; after that, the ticket books come out.

Interstate 95 passes through some of the prettiest country in Florida as it bisects the eastern coastal counties in the central part of the state: Brevard, Indian River, and St. Lucie. The Indian River parallels the coast from Cape Canaveral to Port Salerno, separating the narrow coastal islands and reefs from the mainland. Here dolphins leap and the gentle giant manatees swim so ponderously that boats threaten their survival as a species. Here the land is as flat as a plain, but lush with trees and flowers that flourish in steamy heat. Orange groves and pines, crotons and palmettos. Oleanders and hibiscus. When it rains in Indian River County the hot drops literally pound the earth; when the hurricanes come they can quickly transform acres of land heavy with rows of new condominiums back into the reefs they once were.

In recent years Indian River County has been spared the more ferocious vagaries of nature. Hurricane Andrew devastated Miami, but left Sebastian, Winter Beach, and Vero Beach scarcely touched. The last hurricane to do real damage in Indian River County was Hurricane David in 1979.

Tourism is the major industry in coastal Florida, but it is still a civilized tourism in Indian River County. There is no sense of crowding or traffic jams in Vero Beach. Two Florida state troopers on each shift can handle the stretch of I-95 that passes through Indian River County. Of course, there are drugs here—there are drugs everywhere, and both the county and the local departments expect to deal with that. But a cop can still have a listed home phone number, and he doesn't have to wire his house with a burglar alarm or glance nervously over his shoulder all the time.

Although most of the travelers heading north and south on I-95 scarcely notice what goes on in Indian River County, thousands of people live out their days there, half hoping that their quality of life, weather, and natural beauty won't be "discovered," making their area a little Miami. They know one another, recognize obvious snowbirds, get married, have babies, go to the PTA, and get divorced, and some of them die there.

The Vero Beach Police Department is housed in a white stucco building with bright blue trim; the Indian River County Sheriff's Office is beige stucco, and they are both surrounded by flowering bushes and trees. The Florida Highway Patrol headquarters for the district is located on North 25th Street down in Fort Pierce. All three departments work together, their boundaries touching and intersecting. Some days, the biggest problems local cops have are the vagrants who migrate down to enjoy a warm winter, a number of whom are misfits and mental cases.

And some days, Indian River County has unspeakably horrendous crimes.

Just as in California, Oregon, and Washington, there are few natives along Florida's coastlines. Hardly anybody living there was actually *born* there. Fred and Pat Wessendorf moved down from Gloversville in upstate New York in the fifties. Fred's dad had a place in Fellsmere in Indian River County. They were young marrieds then and had a baby son, Martin. But they soon had three daughters: Kathy, Susan, and Sandra Lynn. Fred worked for the Vero Beach *Press Journal* in production and later became expert at the highly technical process of setting colored photographs. For years Fred and Pat added to their income with a paper route, stocking newspaper dispensing machines in the wee hours of the morning.

A taciturn man who listens far more than he speaks, Fred married a pretty woman who more than makes up for his quietness; Pat Wessendorf says what she thinks and what she believes to be right— whether it is tactful or not. She always has. She is very protective of her children, a fierce mother hen when she thinks they are being threatened. In the last analysis, it is probably Sandra Lynn— "Sandy"—who gets most of Pat's energy. Sandy is the baby.

The young Wessendorfs worked hard to raise their four children. They lived in the house that Fred's dad had owned, a relatively small house on a big lot full of trees and flowers. When the three girls were at an age when they needed more space and privacy, Fred built them a kind of "dormitory" out in back of the main house. The Wessendorf girls were all blond and pretty, but as different as three sisters could be. Funny that two of them would marry cops. Susan and Sandy. Even so, the men they married seemed to have nothing at all in common beyond their careers.

Although their son Martin moved back to New York, the Wessendorfs' daughters all stayed close to home. Kathy and her husband raised kids and exotic birds and pets. When she visited Kathy, Pat Wessendorf sometimes had to steel herself, wondering what might come wandering into the room. Sometimes it was an iguana, sometimes some critter she didn't even recognize. Susan worked at a bank, and Kathy and Sandy would eventually work for the same company in Vero Beach, a real estate and investment firm.

Every Thursday, without fail, Pat and her three girls tried to get together for lunch. The Wessendorfs and their grown children were the last family in the world who ever expected trouble. But then, what family ever does? They had problems, of course, the kind that everybody runs into from time to time, but not big, tragic, shocking trouble—not the kind that brings with it years of nightmares and bitter memories.

2

Fred and Pat Wessendorf's kids were all individuals and seemed more so by the late 1980s. In her early thirties, Susan Wessendorf Dappen was unarguably the *athletic* daughter. Her husband Don (Donny to his friends) was a lieutenant with the Vero Beach Police Department. Chief Jim Gabbard invited the spouses of his officers to use the fully equipped gym at headquarters. Susan was there several times a week after work. She and Don jogged, usually taking their dog, Casey, along, and swam in their own pool.

"None of us girls really ever got into cooking," Sue remarked matter-of-factly. "Not me or Sandy, at least."

Don Dappen has never minded. Sue concentrated on her very responsible job at the bank and was a great mother to their two kids. Moreover, Sue was absolutely fascinated with Don's career from the beginning. Being a policeman's wife is one of the hardest jobs in the world. Some wives don't want to know what happens on a day or night shift. Knowing makes them more frightened for their husbands. The job is easier for a policeman to handle when his wife cares, though. And Sue always did.

Don Dappen became a cop when he was twenty years old. Stocky and muscular, a friendly man—but one with a subtly unmistakable air of authority—he made detective at twenty-three.

A few years ago Don Dappen could easily have seen the end of his career—and his life—when he took a chance at foiling a major drug deal. A twenty-eight-year-old Fort Lauderdale man and his partner, a forty-eight-year-old New York resident and a licensed pilot, had loaded a twin-engine Piper Navajo plane with fifty-six bales of marijuana weighing 1,300 pounds and headed somewhat precariously north from Miami. They made the mistake of stopping at the Vero Beach Municipal Airport to refuel.

At 9 p.m. on a Thursday night the plane taxied past the Federal Aviation Administration's flight service center, and the air traffic controller noted that the numbers on the plane did not match the numbers the pilot had radioed to the tower on landing.

The controller notified the Vero Beach Police Department, and Don Dappen responded in an unmarked car. The Vero Beach dispatcher informed him that the plane currently being refueled had serial numbers N4469R—numbers that matched those of a Piper Navajo reported stolen out of a Miami airport.

Don Dappen, who would later shake his head when he remembered the incident, realizing in retrospect how it might have ended, watched as the white Navajo, loaded with two hundred gallons of fuel, began to taxi slowly down the runway. Dappen turned on his blue bubble lights, hit the siren, and he drove directly onto the airfield, deliberately cutting in front of the moving plane.

He expected it to stop, but the pilot didn't even slow down. Instead he revved up his engine. Don Dappen pulled ahead of the plane while a Vero Beach patrol car raced along beside it. The policemen intended to at least slow the stolen plane.

At that point they were going eighty miles an hour. "He came up behind me real fast," Don recalled. "He just kept going. He didn't have any intention of stopping. All I could see from the whole back of my car was his headlights. . . ."

Playing a dangerous game of near-misses, Dappen veered off the runway, and then back in front of the Navajo. The pilot became airborne—but barely—skipping over the top of Dappen's car at no more than fifteen feet.

Weighed down by the bales of marijuana, the pilot couldn't get high enough to clear a cabbage palm tree at the west end of the airport. His left wing slammed into the palm, and the plane spun so violently that it ripped apart and catapulted through the darkness into the thick undergrowth at the end of the main runway. It ended in a smoldering heap, leaking the gas it had just taken aboard. Don Dappen and his fellow officer, along with firefighters, pulled the wounded drug traffickers from the wreckage.

"It was pitch dark," Dappen said. "You couldn't see anything, and there was an odor of nothing but gasoline."

Miraculously, the wrecked $245,000 plane didn't catch fire. Just as miraculously, the pilot and his partner survived, although they needed a hospital stay to recuperate. They were charged with trafficking marijuana, aggravated assault, resisting arrest with violence, and grand theft.

"The chase didn't get to me until I got home," Don Dappen said. "Then I started to think about it. . . ."

Sandy Wessendorf met *her* cop when she was still in high school. She and Timothy Scott Harris came together like two people in a novel, their meeting as close to a woman's romantic fantasy as you can get. Sandy was only sixteen, and Tim was twenty-one, those five years a wide stretch at that point in their lives. Had they been even a few years older, no one would have raised an eyebrow. But Sandra Lynn Wessendorf was a junior in high school, and Tim Harris was already a police officer in Sebastian, Florida, the tiny hamlet where she lived.

Although Sandy didn't really approve, one of her best friends had a terrific crush on another policeman on the Sebastian force. "He was married, and he even had three kids—but he gave my friend a line that only a teenage girl would believe," Sandy recalled from the vantage point of maturity some years later. "She really thought he was going to divorce his wife and marry *her*. She wouldn't listen to reason."

Sandy's girlfriend needed an excuse to get out of the house—and Sandy was it. "I went along one night while she met this cop. He was working partners with a cop named Tim Harris. Cindy* went off in the police car with the guy she was crazy about, and Tim sat in my car, and we talked. I don't know what they were doing—not for sure—but I know that Tim and I just talked. I'm sure I noticed that he was handsome, but he seemed so much older. I wasn't really impressed. Not that first night."

The next time Sandy ran into Tim Harris it was different. She never forgot that night. It was Sunday, January 14, 1979, shortly after eleven p.m., when Sandy and Cindy were driving in Sebastian near the airport. The girls heard just the beginning trill of a siren, and Sandy saw the whirling blue bubble light in her rearview mirror. She panicked for a moment and then pulled over to the curb.

Sandy needn't have worried. The tall young policeman who walked up to her window was Tim Harris, and he was grinning. This time Sandy had to admit that he was probably the best-looking guy she had ever seen in her life. He had dark brown hair and eyes even greener than her own. Sandy Wessendorf was popular; she pretty much had her choice of boys to go out with, and she had never considered dating an "older" man. Now she did.

"Miss," Tim said in mock seriousness, "I'm afraid I'm going to have to arrest you. You've violated a municipal ordinance."

"*What?*" Sandy knew she hadn't been speeding. Her dad had pounded driving safety into her head.

"I'm sorry, but I'm going to have to write you up for violation of a 916.83."

"What's that?" Sandy still wasn't sure if he was serious or if he was teasing her.

"Resisting an officer." He was very businesslike as he filled out the complaint affidavit on his clipboard. Sandy answered his questions, giving her address on Victoria Drive in Sebastian, her height and weight: "Five feet, four . . . 110 pounds." She saw him write down "blond" for her hair, and his lips twitched a little as he filled in "Eyes—Pretty."

"I'm arresting you on probable cause, for being non-sociable," Tim told her. He tore a copy of the arrest form off and handed it to her. "You'll have to comply with the instructions there at the bottom."

Sandy read what Tim had written, and she began to smile. "Resisting this officer at the Seb. Airport. But will fix that on 1-15-79 at 7 p.m. at City Hall—This officer is off duty then and maybe Sandy would like to go somewhere, *without* Cindy."

Tim explained that she would have to report to headquarters, or the "arrest" would stay on her record. Even at the age of sixteen, Sandy Wessendorf was stubborn. She didn't report to the police station the next night.

Tim Harris wasn't about to give up so easily. He pulled her over about four days later as she drove through Sebastian. This time he refused to return Sandy's driver's license after he'd asked to see it.

"I'll be writing reports later at the station," he said. "And you can come pick up your license, and we can talk."

If she wanted her driver's license back, Sandy had no choice but to go down to Sebastian police headquarters. She spent some time with Tim, talking, although she held back from accepting an actual date with him. He was too old. He was out of school, an adult—and she still had her senior year ahead of her, and all the fun that went with that last year of school. She wasn't nearly ready to be tied down.

It wasn't that Tim frightened her. Not at all. He was a local boy, or right next door to local. He told her he had graduated from high school in 1976 in Satellite Beach, a little town about twenty-five miles north of Sebastian, built on the reef that led into Patrick Air Force Base and Cape Canaveral. Tim Harris had been a track star at Satellite High School, excelling in both high hurdles and cross country. His parents were divorced now. All Sandy knew about his family was that it sounded as though his dad had some really important job at Cape Canaveral, and his mother had a good career, too.

Sandy Wessendorf must have said "no" to Tim Harris a half dozen times, but he kept turning up in her life. Every time she looked around, Tim seemed to be nearby. No female could resist Tim Harris when he wanted something, and he certainly seemed to want Sandy.

So that January night in 1979 was really the beginning for them. Almost fifteen years later that yellowing arrest form for "resisting an officer" was still in Sandy's mementos, a reminder of that first, happy time, a wonderfully romantic meeting that didn't foreshadow all the pain, the disappointment, and the tragedies that came later.

Sandy eventually stopped avoiding Tim and agreed to meet him on a quiet road in Sebastian. He was on duty, but she was to drive her car and park it behind his. Her parents certainly wouldn't have approved if they had known the details of their sixteen-year-old daughter's romance with a twenty-one-year-old cop. But Sandy was already a little bit in love, and every time she saw Tim that emotion deepened.

When Tim finally came to call on Sandy at her home he was very polite; he called her parents "Mr. and Mrs. Wessendorf." (He always would—even after he knew them well.) Fred Wessendorf liked Tim. (He always would.) Pat wasn't so quick to warm to Sandy's suitor. But that was Pat, feisty and protective as a lioness, and she always felt uneasy about Tim. She recalled the first time she met Sandy's new boyfriend.

"Tim was weird. He was always creeping around," she remembered. "I heard the doorbell ring, but when I went to answer it there was nobody there. Tim was hiding in the shrubbery beside the house. Sandy said it was because he was shy—but for heaven's sake, he was a grown man and a policeman, and it struck me as definitely odd that he would play games like that. He was always like that, creeping around, hiding, and jumping out at you. . . ."

It wasn't a joke. That's the way Tim Harris was. He didn't come out laughing. He would walk around the house with his head hung low, like a gawky kid.

Sandy fell more and more in love with Tim Harris. She was flattered by his persistence. He simply would not take "no" for an answer, and he left her no time or space to see any other male. Tim was incredibly handsome in his uniform; he made high school boys look like kids. Sandy recalled "falling head over heels in love with him—as only a sixteen-year-old girl can."

Even so, it almost seemed as though the moment Sandy showed her love for Tim, he changed. For the first weeks that she dated Tim Sandy believed that they were going steady, even though he tormented her by flirting with her girlfriends. "It was odd," she said. "He seemed so shy, but he was always coming on to my friends. That really hurt me—and embarrassed me—but he didn't seem to care."

Besides flirting with her friends, Tim Harris was a completely undependable date. Sometimes Tim showed up, sometimes he showed up hours late, and sometimes he didn't show up at all. "He would tell me he'd been out of town—that he'd gone to see his mother."

Sandy always waited for Tim, afraid to leave the phone in case he might call. "I guess I was fascinated because he was so elusive."

Her mother was only disgusted; Pat Wessendorf hated to see any man make her daughter so miserable. One time when Tim showed up late—playing his hiding-in-the-bushes game, as usual—Pat lied and told him that Sandy wasn't home. Sandy was horrified when she found out that her mother had sent Tim away without even telling her. He *had* kept his promise to come over—if belatedly—and Sandy could always rationalize and make excuses for him.

What Sandy Wessendorf hadn't realized was that Tim was dating another girl at least as often as he was seeing her. Tim's absences finally grew to a point where Sandy couldn't ignore the obvious any longer. Too many of Tim's excuses were totally implausible. She asked questions around Sebastian and learned that her rival was a pretty Melbourne Village girl named Michelle Schrader.* Michelle was attending college at Auburn up across the Alabama border.

Sandy's hopes were completely dashed when Michelle called her and told her that she and Tim were going steady.

When Sandy confronted him, Tim grudgingly admitted that he *was* seeing someone else, but he explained that it wasn't anything serious—nothing for Sandy to give a second thought to. "We're having problems," he insisted. "I'm trying to break up with her."

Both young women were too deeply involved with the handsome policeman to simply walk away, and Tim seemed almost to enjoy the tug-of-war. It didn't take brilliant detective work for Sandy to discover that Tim was not only dating Michelle, he was engaged to her!

At one point, in the spring of 1979, Sandy and her sister, Susan, traveled up to see Michelle in Auburn, Alabama. Sandy still hoped that Michelle had been exaggerating her hold on Tim, but the visit only made seventeen-year-old Sandy Wessendorf feel worse. Michelle was wearing an engagement ring Tim had given her, and she showed Sandy and Susan her wedding gown and bragged about her wedding plans, "We're going to be married in August," she told Sandy. "I'm going to quit college to marry Tim."

Sandy was crushed. Michelle was only a few years older, but she was so much more sophisticated, and she seemed so sure of Tim.

Michelle kept talking as if she had no idea what Tim meant to Sandy, or maybe she was just rubbing Sandy's nose in *her* relationship to make a point. "I hope when we come down [to Sebastian] me and Tim can take you and one of your little boyfriends to dinner."

"Little boyfriend" indeed! The only boyfriend that Sandy had was Tim—the same man who was Michelle's fiancé. As it turned out, there was no wedding for Tim and Michelle in August, 1979, but the knowledge that Tim had been engaged and never told her made Sandy break off with him. Although it hurt her, she wouldn't talk to him or see him. What was the point? She could never trust him again.

And then on August 30, 1979, Hurricane David roared out of Cuba and Puerto Rico and headed straight for the east coast of Florida with winds predicted to peak at 150 miles an hour.

"I got a call from Tim," Pat Wessendorf recalled. "He didn't say who he was, but I knew his voice. He said, 'This is the Sebastian Police Department, ma'am. We're just checking to be sure you all know what shelter to go to if the hurricane hits us.'"

"Yes, we do, Tim," Pat answered, letting him know he hadn't fooled her. She wasn't very happy about what the phone call really meant. It meant that Tim Harris still cared about Sandy, and that he was worried about her safety as the violent hurricane roared up the

Florida coast. Pat felt almost a premonition; although Sandy would be thrilled to know that Tim still thought about her, Pat wondered if having Tim back in their lives could lead to happiness for any of them. He was handsome, he had a good job, he came from good people—and yet there was something about him that made the hairs prickle along Pat's neck. He had lied to Sandy, he always had another woman in the background, and he sneaked around like some prowler. Pat had noted that Tim would never look her straight in the eye; he wouldn't look anyone in the eye. Nobody could be that bashful—and be a policeman.

Hurricane David left a thousand people dead in its wake, but it brought Sandy and Tim back together. The night Tim called the Wessendorfs to check on their family's safety he had phoned from his apartment. Michelle was staying there with him. She overheard that call, and she knew that Tim still cared about Sandy.

Later Tim called Sandy and told her he just had to be sure she and her folks were okay. It had been three months since she had talked to him, but Sandy had wanted so much for Tim to come back to her. It had just about broken her heart not to see him or be with him.

After Hurricane David Tim was with Sandy again. But then he was still with Michelle, too. He walked a tightwire between the two girls. Tim often had to think fast to keep Michelle from realizing how much Sandy was back in his life.

Not fast enough. During Christmas vacation, 1979, Michelle saw what was happening, and she dropped out of Auburn and moved back home and in with Tim. Keeping him was far more important to her than her education.

Sandy Wessendorf was devastated. She lost weight and played her tape of "Sad Eyes" over and over again. She would have done anything to make Tim happy. "I would have jumped off a building for him if he asked me to. . . ." And there was no doubt that she meant it.

"I wanted him back so much that I started seeing him with her [Michelle] living there—at least for a little while. He bought us both Christmas presents, and he told me he would get rid of her. He was mean to her. He'd have me over there while she was there. . . . One time she jumped me. Like a cat—scratching and pulling my hair. Then she went in the bathroom and took a bunch of pills in there with her. I was frightened. What's this girl going to do? Kill herself?"

It was a histrionic gesture. Tim Harris had both Sandy and

Michelle madly in love with him, two beautiful young women. He hated confrontations, but he seemed to enjoy being the center of so much attention. He should have said good-bye to one or the other, but he didn't.

Michelle lived with Tim for six months, and then she moved out. She told her co-workers at a local hospital that it was almost a relief to be done with him. It probably was. Michelle had come to work marked with purpling bruises, but she would never talk about how she got them. When she was truly through with Tim she *did* seem to be a much happier person.

And she had no more bruises.

It was early 1980. Sandy had won in the battle for Tim Harris. In many ways, however, she had lost—and she didn't even know it.

All three of her daughters got on Pat for being nosy and interfering with their lives—most of all with Sandy's—and yet she believed she had to. She had life experience, and they didn't. Pat had been lucky in finding Fred. He was a good man and a gentle man. Sandy didn't know that all men weren't like her father. And yet even Pat couldn't put her finger on anything truly wrong about Tim. He was only twenty-two, and a lot of twenty-two-year-old men—boys, really—didn't know what they wanted in a wife. Fred liked Tim, and Fred Wessendorf could usually read people pretty well. Pat continued to feel uneasy.

When Tim Harris came back to Sandy she was older and more wary of him; he had betrayed her too many times. Still, she wanted to believe him when he asked her to forgive him. Sandy never carried a grudge, not in her whole life. If someone apologized, she would accept it in a minute—and it was over. She didn't stay mad. And she loved Tim so much.

If anything, Sandy Wessendorf was more beautiful than she had been when Tim first pulled her over with his police car. Her blond hair was very long, butterscotch-colored with natural sun streaks. She wore scarcely any makeup—she didn't need it. Actually, Sandy was the epitome of what Tim Harris had always wanted in a girlfriend. A long time later he showed her a picture of his girlfriend in high school, and she was shocked. "She looked just like me," Sandy told her mom. "Almost exactly like me. It was so weird looking at that picture. It could have been *my* picture."

From the time he was in junior high Tim Harris had always had a girlfriend, and he stayed with each girl, if not faithfully, for a year or two. All of Tim's women—save Michelle Schrader—had long blond hair. Michelle had short dark hair. Tim was always the one who initiated the breakups, moving on to the next girl he had picked out. Anyone knowing Tim well knew he would never let a woman reject *him.*

There would always be something of a paradox in the young policeman's view of women. While he sought them out continually and charmed them totally, there was a part of him that felt they deserved no respect at all. Men who knew Tim recognized a thinly veiled contempt for females, and it puzzled them.

"He could be strange," another cop recalled. "We'd be driving down the street, and he'd hang out the window and call some woman a slut or make obscene gestures at her. I mean, the guy was a cop, for Pete's sake—"

3

Tim Harris was, indeed, a cop. He had always wanted to be a policeman, and he had kept his eye firmly on that goal. When his parents divorced he lived with his father and stepmother so that he could graduate from Satellite High and stay in the town where he had more contacts that would help him get started in law enforcement.

Tim had always been a hard worker; he really had no choice. Although his father, George, had a good job as a draftsman working in the space program, and his mother, Virginia, worked as an executive secretary, Tim was only one among six Harris kids. They grew up near Washington, D.C., at 522 North Imboden Street in Alexandria, Virginia. Paul was born in January of 1957, Tim on April 26, 1958, Bethany Lea in September, 1960, Dan in June, 1961, David in June, 1963, and Sarah in July of 1964. They were all extremely photogenic children with brown hair and bluish-green eyes. Six children in seven years must have been a handful and a strain on the budget for George and Virginia Harris.

In 1965 George and Virginia moved with their young family from Washington, D.C., to Satellite Beach, where George had accepted a job in the burgeoning space program.

Tim worked whenever there were summer vacations and school breaks, usually at Disney World in Orlando. The summer after he graduated from Satellite High he worked as a busboy for a restaurant in Disney World. That fall he began to take courses at Brevard Community College in subjects he hoped would help him get a job in police work. In January, 1977, he was sponsored by the Satellite Beach Police Department to take the Basic Police Training Course at Brevard Community College. Even though he was willing to pay for the training himself, Tim had to have a sponsor. He was relieved and elated when the chief of the Satellite Beach Police Department stepped in, recommending that he be accepted in the police courses.

Tim finished the basic police course in April of 1977. He couldn't find a police job right away, so he joined the U.S. Army Reserve on July 1 and attended Military Police School from then until October. He had reached his full height of six feet, two inches, but he only weighed 175 pounds. He looked like what he was, a tall, skinny, good-looking nineteen-year-old kid, unformed and a little gawky. But he had a passion for law enforcement, and he was going to make it happen.

His counselor at Brevard Community College, William McEntee, wrote a letter recommending Tim to the mayor of Melbourne Village, Florida, as a good candidate for their minuscule police force. How well McEntee really knew Tim Harris is questionable. His letter is couched in terms that allowed him an escape hatch if Tim didn't work out.

"Apparently he [Tim Harris] will prove to be reliable, patient, and conscientious in carrying out his obligations.

"He appears to be free of self-doubt and disillusionment. Probably he will be a good team member, a good listener, and a sincere worker.

"I am willing to recommend that he be given favorable consideration."

It *was* a rather odd recommendation. Few would-be cops are tested for "disillusionment." At any rate, in November, 1977, Tim Harris was hired as a police officer for the Melbourne Village Police Department. Melbourne Village was a tiny town in Brevard County with a police force of only two or three officers. There wasn't much to do there, but it was a step on the ladder up to where Tim wanted to go; he wanted to become a Florida Highway Patrolman.

He was only nineteen, and he was a cop. That was enough for the moment.

It was in Melbourne Village that Tim had met Michelle Schrader, the girl who would vie with Sandy for him. Michelle was a high school senior when she met Tim. She was seventeen then, about the same age Sandy Wessendorf was two years later when she became involved with the handsome policeman. Tim could be charming. Michelle's parents had even invited Tim to live with them for a few months after he left his father's and stepmother's home.

Tim was voted Melbourne Village Police Officer of the Year during his abbreviated career there. Actually, it was a little bit like Sheriff Andy Taylor of Mayberry. Andy and Deputy Barney Fife made up Mayberry's sheriff's department, and there weren't that many officers on the Melbourne Village force either. The award had to pass back and forth among the skeleton police force, and Tim Harris was the only one on the force who hadn't had the honor.

In truth, the police department was troubled by reports it received about Tim Harris. There were allegations that Tim was using his badge and his status to stop young women, sometimes taking their licenses so that they would have to meet him to get them back. The kid was young and interested in women—but he had no business chasing them on the job. Moreover, Tim had allegedly arrested a motorist for having an expired temporary tag when there was a valid tag in the car's backseat. Besides that, Tim drove his squad car like a bat out of hell.

Tim Harris was given three choices: Melbourne Village's Police Officer of the Year could resign, be fired, or be placed on probation. Tim chose to resign. He wrote a short letter of resignation on July 3, 1978.

"It is [sic] regret I hereby tender my resignation from the Melbourne Village Police Department to be effective this date."

Apparently there were no hard feelings. More likely it was the closing of ranks that often happens among policemen. The rest of the world gives them a hard time; unless an offense is egregious, law enforcement takes care of its own.

The following November, the police chief, Robert Segien, gave Tim a letter of recommendation.

To Whom It May Concern:
    Timothy S. Harris was employed by this department for a period of nine months. During this time, Officer Harris' enthusiasm toward his duties gave him the extra motivations

to perform his duties in an excellent manner. Officer Harris'
willingness to accept any assignment, regardless how unpleasant, coupled with amiable attitude, proves him to be a definite
asset to any department that would require his services. He is
an individual who his superiors can rely on to get the job done
with a professional attitude. He is trustworthy, intelligent and
has a high sense of responsibility towards his profession as a
police officer.

With each new job application thereafter, Tim Harris explained
that he had resigned from the Melbourne Village department because
he "was very unhappy with the department," explaining that it did
not live up to the professional standards he had expected.

Tim was very young, and a lot of young cops mature and stop
hitting on women and driving too fast. Since the Melbourne Village
Police Department soon ceased to exist at all, whatever problems Tim
Harris had had there were forgotten. He was moving on with a
virtually clean slate.

Tim worked for a while installing aluminum doors and windows.
He told his employer—VI-CO Aluminum—that he had no intention
of staying with them for long. He was going to have a career in law
enforcement.

And he did. In 1978 Tim Harris joined the Sebastian, Florida,
police department.

The lawmen who watch over Indian River County almost all
recognize one another. When Don Dappen passes a county deputy
he honks and waves. When the Florida Highway Patrolmen pass local
cops they do the same.

Indian County Sheriff's Detective Phil Williams met Tim Harris for
the first time in 1979. And he didn't like him much. It is fairly routine
in any police jurisdiction in America for fellow officers to cut each
other some slack in traffic violations. If a cop is blatantly speeding or
driving recklessly, he's going to get a ticket like anybody else; if he's a
few miles over the limit, one of his own probably isn't going to write
him up. But when Phil Williams was on his way to a call, driving
through Sebastian, he heard a siren and saw the blue lights behind
him.

"I had just passed the Sebastian city limits—where the speed limit
goes up—and this Sebastian cop—it was Tim Harris—pulled me
over, and he actually pulls out his ticket book. I thought he was

kidding. But he wasn't," Williams remembers. "I just told him what I thought. He was out of his jurisdiction. He couldn't come after me—not unless he was in hot pursuit, and he sure wasn't. I had not been speeding in his jurisdiction.

"His demeanor left much to be desired. He began, 'I know you're a cop, but I'll write you anyway.' I peeled out and left him standing there in my dust."

Over the next decade Tim Harris and Phil Williams saw each other on the road from time to time. They weren't friends. They weren't enemies.

Sandy Wessendorf was due to graduate from Sebastian High School in June of 1980, but she didn't have to attend school for the last six months because she already had enough credits. All the Wessendorf kids worked hard. They joined their parents in working paper routes; besides covering her route, Sandy worked at the Danish bakery in a Publix supermarket.

Sandy had a good head for figures, and she saved her money. She saw very soon that Tim was not a frugal person. He was a spender. He always seemed to have something he wanted to buy. Tim didn't smoke, and he didn't drink, and he certainly didn't do drugs, but he seemed in a tearing hurry to have *things*.

He wanted to own his own home, and that struck Sandy as kind of sweet. Since his folks had divorced, Tim had never really felt he belonged anywhere. Not in his mother's home nor in his father's. Every once in a while Tim let Sandy think that they might get married someday. She wanted to believe him, but she still didn't trust him. It had only been a month since Tim broke off completely with Michelle.

Things were going pretty well between Tim and Sandy. She knew he still flirted with other girls, and she suspected he sometimes did more than that, but Sandy Wessendorf loved Tim Harris. He was her first love. He was her only love, and if Tim had some wild oats to sow, she would wait for him. She just wanted to be part of his life—the biggest part of his life—the woman who would be there when all the others were gone.

It was a lucky thing Sandy had a philosophical attitude, because one day she was visiting Tim at his apartment when she answered a knock on the door. A hysterical young woman, a waitress in a local pizza restaurant, stomped in and declared that she was pregnant—and that Tim was the father.

Sandy said nothing, but she pointed toward the bedroom, where Tim was still in bed. When he saw the sobbing waitress headed his way he put the covers over his head and wouldn't come out.

When the woman finally left, Tim started to cry. He might have been taken by surprise—but Sandy hadn't been. "I already kind of knew. I went over to his apartment one morning after he'd left for work, and I found a note. It was from her, and it said, 'Last night was great. I care about you. I want to see you again'—things like that."

Sandy was barely eighteen, but she was growing up way too fast. While Tim sobbed, terrified that the pizza waitress might be pregnant, Sandy asked him some probing questions about just *when* he'd slept with the woman. For once he answered truthfully. And Sandy thought grimly that Tim obviously didn't know anything about the female reproductive system, pregnancy, or babies.

"Well," Sandy said, "she might be pregnant—but it's too soon for her to know it yet. She's just trying to scare you."

Tim was vastly relieved.

The waitress never came back. "I wasn't jumping all over him," Sandy said. "In fact, he was so scared that I actually felt sorry for him. But he could see I was upset and that he had to straighten up a little bit."

Tim Harris was a curious mixture of little boy and macho cop. On the job he was strong and confident; with Sandy he was like a kid hiding behind his mother's skirts, letting her figure out his budget and pay his bills. A more sophisticated woman might have foreseen problems ahead, but Sandy wasn't in the least sophisticated. She was only learning to take terrible blows to the heart and keep on smiling. And keep on loving Tim Harris.

Tim was the first man Sandy had ever had sex with, and he would be the only man who made love to her for many, many years. The first time she slept with him she was only seventeen and didn't know what to expect, but she was disappointed anyway. "I was scared—and surprised when he was suddenly on top of me."

There was no foreplay and no soft kisses or loving words. No words at all. There never would be. "He threw me on the bed and that was it."

She hoped that their sex life would get better, but she didn't dream of saying that to Tim.

It wasn't long before Tim began to talk in earnest about marrying Sandy in the summer of 1980. She wasn't ready, and she didn't relish the idea of marrying Tim exactly one year after he was supposed to have had a wedding with Michelle. Sandy dragged her feet. She wanted to be absolutely sure of him before she married Tim. Naïvely she believed that Tim *would* be faithful once they were married, but she didn't want to rush it. "I really thought that once we were married, everything would change—that Tim would never cheat on me again."

By the summer of 1980 there was no question that they were a couple or that they would get married someday soon. Not only was Tim dependent upon Sandy, but she was a strikingly beautiful girl. Any other man would call him a fool for cheating on her.

In the late summer of 1980 Tim found a small house in the 600 block of Mulberry Street in Sebastian Heights. It wasn't fancy, but it was new, with maybe 900 square feet of living space and an enclosed garage. Sandy looked at it and grimaced when she saw it was *all* brown. Brown siding, brown roof, brown everything. But she was thrilled at the thought that this would be their *own* house.

Tim was making only about $16,000 a year at the Sebastian Police Department, and he didn't have the down payment on the $46,000 asking price, but he was installing some cove lighting for the contractor and managed to figure out a way to buy the little house without a down payment. He got a mortgage with Gulf Atlantic in August, 1980, and agreed to make payments of $476.00 a month. He soon had truck payments, too, to General Motors—$207.05 a month—and a Sears card, and a Mastercard.

Sandy stepped in. First she took over the management of his finances, and long before they were married she combined their money, sharing whatever she had with him. "From the time I was seventeen I was helping him to pay the mortgage."

Tim planted grass in the little yard on Mulberry Street, and Sandy added a few flowers and the ubiquitous pink flamingos of Florida landscaping. As long as Sandy made Tim's payments on time—as she always did—the house on Mulberry Street would be his in thirty years.

Tim soon grew disenchanted with his new house. It wasn't big enough, and it wasn't fancy enough. He was a man with a remarkably low boredom threshold. He wanted things so desperately until he got them, and then things and people and even animals began to lose their fascination for him.

He always needed something new and something more.

4

The woman lying in the grove of pine trees and palmettos near I-95 was still there. Ants stung her bare buttocks. Nightfall brought with it a chill breeze from the ocean. Each morning the early spring sun was hotter than the morning before. And still she didn't move, nor did anyone find her there.

In December of 1980 Tim and Sandy went together to a jeweler and picked out her engagement ring. Sandy picked a date in April, but now it was Tim who dragged his feet. "He said he wanted to wait until I was nineteen, and that would have been in October. But I was eighteen when we set our wedding date for July 25, 1981. I remember our invitations said, 'And Two Shall Become One . . .'

"I was still scared to get married. In a way it was the happiest day of my life—but in another way it wasn't."

Tim and Sandy's wedding song was Karen Carpenter's "We've Only Just Begun," and Sandy wore a traditional white gown with a high neck of sheer embroidered lace and a fingertip veil edged in lace. She carried a bouquet of yellow roses and Shasta daisies. She looked very, very young and very innocent. She wore no makeup at all. Tim wore a brown tuxedo with a ruffled Edwardian shirt and a brown velvet vest. He wore a yellow rosebud in his lapel. Sebastian Police Chief Cummings performed the wedding ceremony.

Sandy and Tim looked so happy in their informal wedding pictures, toasting each other with piña coladas.

Despite the fact that he was extremely handsome, Tim Harris always hated to have his picture taken. When Sandy insisted he would grudgingly submit and put his arm around her. He smiled for the camera, but behind her back he was pinching Sandy *hard* to let her know how he really felt.

Their sex life was no better after their marriage. "It was still 'an act'—there was no love there," Sandy said. "I used to just turn my head and cry because in the beginning I thought it should be more romantic. I always thought it was going to be. I kept hoping—but it never was. I had nine years of sex without love."

The newlyweds left on their honeymoon that Saturday evening. Tim's brother, Danny, was getting married in West Virginia the next Saturday, so Tim and Sandy drove up through Georgia and North Carolina for the ceremony. They saw the Smoky Mountains and Chimney Rock, and—except for the physical side of their marriage—they got along wonderfully. When they were alone, driving through the beautiful countryside, it seemed to Sandy Harris as if they really had a whole clean slate ahead of them. Tim would be faithful; they would have babies and spend the rest of their lives together.

They stayed with Tim's family in West Virginia, and Sandy felt uncomfortable. Tim's mother, Virginia, and one of his sisters had driven down to Florida for Tim and Sandy's wedding. Sandy met her new mother-in-law for the first time the day before her wedding. It was difficult to spend four days of her honeymoon with a family she barely knew. Danny and Debbie Harris's candid wedding shots show a very attractive, apparently very happy family. Sandy, a bride of only a week herself, sat among them trying to smile. Tim was beside her, handsome as ever but self-conscious looking. As he did in almost every photograph ever taken of him, he tilted his head up and thrust his jaw forward. "He always managed to look like Lurch, the butler in 'The Addams Family' television show, when he had his picture taken," Sandy laughed.

In the family wedding pictures Tim's right arm was behind Sandy. He was pinching her, but the camera didn't show that.

Sandy had always thought it strange that she knew so little about Tim's family. He just didn't care to talk much about them. When he did he was derisive about both his mother and his stepmother, although he was especially bitter about his stepmother. He blamed his father for divorcing his mother. Tim had lived with his father and stepmother so that he could graduate from Satellite Beach High, but he apparently was no longer welcome in their home. His stepmother appeared to hold as much enmity toward him as he did toward her. The only time Sandy ever met Tim's father was at her wedding, even though he lived only an hour north of them on Merritt Island.

The only family members Tim seemed at all close to were his younger brothers, Danny and David.

Sandy and Tim returned from their honeymoon to their little brown house at 656 Mulberry Street. "We hardly had anything in the way of furniture," Sandy remembered. "We had a table and a bed, I think. But Tim insisted on buying a high-tech, expensive alarm system to guard the house. It cost a lot more than what we had *in* the house."

At that point in their lives together Tim could have done almost anything, and Sandy would still have been wildly in love with him. She believed that they were embarking on a wonderful new life together. She had been extraordinarily patient with him while he got other women out of his system, but now they were "grown-ups" and they were together, faithful, just as it had said in their wedding vows. "I was crazy about Tim. I guess you could say that I was to the point of being obsessed with him. I would still have done anything for him."

Tim was about to see one of his lifelong dreams come true. On February 5, 1982, seven months after his marriage to Sandy Wessendorf, with his wife's urging, he applied to the Florida Highway Patrol for a position as a trooper. If ever there was an applicant who *looked* like a recruiting poster for a state trooper, it was Timothy Scott Harris. At six feet, two, he weighed 205 pounds, and it was all compact muscle. He was very handsome—more so, it seemed, with each year. He parted his dark hair on the left side, and it swept across his forehead in one thick wave. His eyes were as green as the Atlantic Ocean sometimes turned just before a storm—and as impenetrable. Sometimes Tim wore a mustache. He was twenty-three, but he could seem older. He had cut his law enforcement teeth in Melbourne Village and Sebastian, and he was far from a gung-ho kid at this point. He knew the ropes. He knew what to say and how to act.

The Florida Highway Patrol put applicants through tortuous physical, intelligence, and psychological tests. Patiently Tim filled out forms asking about his whole life, his family, his former employment. The Highway Patrol did background checks on both Tim and his family, and they didn't find a blemish on anyone's record.

Computer checks with the Clerk of Circuit Courts, the Clerk of County Courts, N.C.I.C. (National Crime Information Center at F.B.I. headquarters in Quantico), F.C.I.C. (Florida Crime Information Center), and local, county, and city law enforcement records drew no hits on the name Timothy Scott Harris. Nor should they have; Tim had never been arrested.

Nor had Sandra Lynn Wessendorf Harris, George G. Harris, his father, Virginia Ann Harris, his mother, nor Paul, Bethany Lea, Daniel, David, or Sarah.

FHP investigators talked with Sandy's and Tim's next door neighbors on both sides. All they got was "Very good neighbors" and "No problems."

Tim explained that his first police job in Melbourne Village had been a big disappointment to him because he found the department so unprofessional, and he presented the glowing letter of recommendation from Chief Segien. He had good evaluations from the Sebastian Police Department, and he had never been fired from any job. He didn't drink, smoke, do drugs—and he never had. He answered all the questions as honestly as he could. Yes, he *had* had his driver's license suspended a long time back—when he was a teenager. For reckless driving. He had sold his car to pay the fine, and he had never lost his license again.

Thanks to Sandy, Tim had an excellent credit record. He listed his debts as $34,000 to Gulf Atlantic Mortgage for his house, $250 to Sears, Roebuck, and $150 to Master Charge.

The guy wasn't a saint. Yes, Tim admitted, he had taken a "sick day" off work from time to time when he wasn't really sick. Yes, he had probably stolen a candy bar as a kid.

The FHP checked him all the way back to Surfside Elementary School in Satellite Beach, and Tim Harris was clean. He was smart; he had graduated from high school with a 3.7. He had college training in police work, he had four years of law enforcement experience, and he was active in a military police unit of the military reserve.

At the time of his application to the Florida Highway Patrol Tim had been promoted to corporal in the Sebastian Police Department, and that made him third in command in the twelve-man department.

Trooper Robert T. Weber, an applicant investigator, summed up his background check: "The field investigation has established that the applicant is well qualified for the position of Trooper. There is nothing questionable found in my investigation of his background. He is well spoken, gives a very professional impression in his uniform, and I believe would be an asset to our Department. I recommend that he be given further consideration for employment with our agency."

By May of 1982 Tim was almost through the morass of requirements he had to meet to be hired as a trooper. The hardest of all was the oral exam. Any working cop remembers what it was like to sit before a board of ranking brass and answer questions, sweating all the time and wondering if there *was* a right answer, or if they were throwing trick questions at him.

Tim Harris's ordeal was on May 5, 1982, in Lantana, Florida. He

faced an FHP lieutenant, a major, two sergeants, and a superintendent. Stone-faced, they nodded and checked their grading sheets. He
was rated on his appearance, enunciation, manner, emotional control, comprehension, logic, and coherency.

He passed. He didn't blow them away, but he didn't fall on his face
either. The rating forms were checked right down the middle. He
drew four "Recommended" ratings. He did not impress the board so
much that any of them checked "Recommended with confidence" or
"Recommended with enthusiasm," but then he didn't get any
"Recommended with hesitance" either.

Only one of the oral board members had picked up on a side of
Tim that might make him less than desirable as a member of the elite
highway patrol. Sergeant K.D. Buckner checked a box that read "Self-
conscious, ill at ease or lacks restraint," and another: "Slow in
grasping subtleties, requires explanations."

Buckner's reservations were certainly not enough to blackball Tim
Harris. He was hired. He resigned from the Sebastian Police Department and prepared to attend the Florida Highway Patrol's 65th
Recruit Training School, which would begin on May 31, 1982, and
finish August 13th. That would mean leaving his bride alone for three
months while he was up at the state capital in Tallahassee.

Tim was elated, and Sandy was proud of him. "He looked so
wonderful in his uniform," she recalled. "I always loved the way he
looked in his uniform."

That summer of 1982 may have been the most romantic period of
Sandy and Tim Harris's married life. All the while he was living at
the Highway Patrol Academy in Tallahassee, Sandy drove the
sixteen-hour round trip to see him every other weekend. She had her
job back in Indian River County, so she couldn't leave until Saturday
morning, and she had to head home again on Sunday, but the long
drive in the summer heat was worth it—just so they could be
together for eight or ten hours.

"I missed him so much while he was up in Tallahassee," Sandy
remembered. "I didn't mind the drive at all. It was worth it just to see
him for a little while."

There were fifty-five recruits in the FHP's sixty-fifth class, including ten women. They went to class from eight to five, five days a
week, and most of Saturday. The weeks were intense and packed
with information that might save the recruits' lives—or someone
else's life—when they were out on the road. Everything from First
Aid to Human Behavior, from Arrest Techniques to Courtroom

Demeanor, from Criminal Law to Crimes Against Persons. They learned how to gather and preserve evidence, how to lift fingerprints, and how to interview and interrogate. There were radar and other speed measurement devices to master. Of course, there was accident investigation. Tim Harris's main interest in law enforcement had always been traffic, and the FHP was the place to work it. Tim did very well in *every* subject at the academy, however.

His highest grade was a 99 in defensive driving, and his lowest was a respectable 88—in firearms. He excelled in criminal investigation and criminal law. Overall, his grade-point average at the patrol academy was 92.58. The FHP Academy put on a banquet and a graduation ceremony in mid-August, and Sandy Harris was in the audience, tremendously proud of her young husband.

Things worked out really well for them, too, as far as Tim's duty assignment was concerned. Although he had indicated on his application that he would be willing to be assigned anywhere in Florida, and he had meant it, both Tim and Sandy had lived in Indian River County for so long that they hated the thought of leaving. At the Academy Tim had met Lt. Gary Morgan and Trooper Byron Sickman. They knew him by sight from court hearings in Vero Beach. Both men would one day become good friends of Tim's, and back in 1982 they did him a favor.

"We knew that Tim was going to be transferred to someplace around Lake Okeechobee," Morgan recalled. "And we knew there was an opening in our Fort Pierce District, which is actually right in Vero Beach. So we looked him up to see if he wanted . . . to stay in Vero Beach . . . let him know we would . . . help him any way we could . . . to get a position right back in Indian River County."

It worked out that way. Tim worked in Lake Okeechobee for a very short time before he came back home. For the next eight years Trooper Tim Harris would be working the roads of Indian River County—roads and freeways he knew the way he knew his own face when he was shaving.

Sandy didn't have to move away from Pat and Fred Wessendorf and her sisters Susan and Kathy. They kept their little brown house, and they planned for the day they could buy some acreage and build a house big enough to raise kids in.

From the very beginning Trooper Tim Harris garnered excellent annual evaluations from his superior officers. He was consistently above average. The Florida Highway Patrol had hired themselves a superlative trooper.

"Trooper Harris is fourth in the four count district in DUI [Driving

Under the Influence] arrests, total arrests, and correction cards. . . .
He is a steady, dependable employee who requires only minimal
supervision."

". . . always displays a positive attitude . . . has aligned himself to
the goals of the Department."

"He has one of the highest DUI enforcements in the District."

"Trooper Harris . . . has been quick to volunteer for difficult
assignments and displays an enthusiasm for professional law enforcement well beyond that of his counterparts."

"Has very good relationship with local State Attorney's Office and
judges. Cases well prepared and organized in advance."

And yet it was almost as if Tim Harris lived in two different worlds:
his job and his marriage. Some things didn't change at all after Sandy
and Tim were married. He had always been something of a loner. He
wasn't interested in socializing with other couples, and he didn't
seem to have any friends of his own, nothing beyond casual
acquaintances in the Patrol. He went fishing sometimes with another
trooper, but it was the fishing that was Tim's passion—not male
bonding.

"I guess I forced him to get along with my brother-in-law, Don.
They were both cops; they should have had something in common,"
Sandy recalled. "We'd play cards with Don and Susan, but that's the
only social thing we did."

Tim didn't drink; he had an almost pathological aversion to
alcohol. Don Dappen remembers one evening he had made piña
coladas.

"Sandy told Tim, 'Just have one.' Tim drank one, and he enjoyed it.
But when I asked him if he wanted another one, he was short with
me. 'No, no!' What it was was he was beginning to feel the alcohol a
little bit, and he seemed just so afraid of losing control. . . . Tim
never even drank beer. I never saw him with a beer in his hand."

Even when they were dating, Tim had used physical force to
control Sandy. That continued into their marriage. "If I did or said
something he didn't like, he'd take my arm and twist it behind my
back. Or he'd pinch me at the tops of my thighs, between my legs,
where it really hurt—but it wouldn't show. He wanted his way, no
matter what."

Sandy had always known that Tim was extravagant and impracti-
cal. He was a man who *wanted*. He had to have the newest and best
car, the biggest boat, the newest technology. He would beg Sandy to
buy him whatever it was that had taken his fancy at the moment—as

if she were the mom and he the spoiled child. And he was relentless, nagging at her, promising, "Just let me get this, and I'll never ask for another thing."

Sometimes Sandy gave in. Sometimes she couldn't. Sandy had managed their finances for so long that she knew what they could afford and what they couldn't. And she had been with Tim for three years; she knew he would grow bored with each new toy, and he *would* ask for something again.

Sometimes she wondered where it would all end. With them in the poorhouse, probably.

Sandy made $15,000 a year, and Tim made a little over $22,000. They couldn't afford a new car every six months, a new boat, a new house, *and* a new baby on their income. And they were going to have a baby. Sandy was pregnant, due to deliver in the late spring of 1983.

Tim seemed happy enough about the baby, but he refused to acknowledge that Sandy couldn't do everything she had done before—lifting, working, sex. "You can still do this," he would insist, when she was so tired that she could hardly lift her arm. Sometimes she just couldn't keep up with all Tim expected of her. And Tim was often annoyed with her.

There was no question about what they would name the baby. Tim had long ago decided that if he ever had a daughter, her name would be Jennifer Lynn, and a son would be Timothy Jr. If he had married Michelle, it would have been the same. Those were the names he had picked out for *his* children. He allowed Sandy no input at all.

Among the things that Sandy continued to do while she was pregnant was to work full-time as a secretary *and* to deliver the morning papers on her 2 a.m. route. She delivered 250 papers in the summer, and 600 in the winter when the snowbirds were in residence. Sandy worked an area where there were apartment houses, and she had to lug two heavy sacks of the *Press Journal*, walking the whole route. She threw half the papers up to the second floor of apartment buildings and condos. "I was exhausted all the time," she sighed, remembering.

On the morning before Jennifer's birth Sandy felt some vague discomfort in her back and belly, but she had never had a baby and didn't recognize labor pains. She did prevail upon Tim to drive her on her route. When they got home he was impatient with her because she didn't know whether she should go to the hospital or not.

"I don't know," Sandy told Tim. "I don't know what to do."

"Well, make up your mind," he snapped, "because either you're going to the hospital now, or I'm going back to bed."

By the time Sandy realized she *was* in labor, she was in agony and they left for the hospital. When they neared the emergency entrance she asked Tim to let her off. But he was still angry with her because she had been indecisive, and he drove right on by, headed for the far parking lot. Sandy remembered, "I was in major, major pain, but he said, 'No, I'm going to go park, and you're going to walk, bitch.'"

And walk Sandy did. But when the ER personnel saw her they ran for a wheelchair. Jennifer Lynn Harris was born five hours later.

Tim had refused to go into the labor room with Sandy, and he had laughed when she asked him to go to Lamaze classes with her, but he seemed pleased and proud when Jennifer was born.

Tim had always called Sandy terrible names when he was angry, "slut" and "bitch." They were the same names he called out to female strangers on the street. There had never been any arguing with him; when Sandy tried to protest something he had said to her, he invariably turned on his heel and said, "Shut up, slut."

Still, she loved him. There never was and there never will be any explaining of why human beings love one another. Sandy felt bound to Tim. If she was no longer "obsessed" with him, she kept trying to please him. She figured there had to be some combination that would make him happy. She just had not come upon it yet. No one in her family had ever been divorced, and Sandy had married Tim, intending to be married forever.

For a long time Sandy was able to rationalize that Tim was different from other men. He didn't drink or smoke, and he worked hard. She knew women who were worse off.

She was sure she did.

Tim worked different shifts: 8 to 4 p.m., 4 to midnight, 11 to 7 a.m. Although Sandy had been jealous of other women before they were married, she didn't worry about that any longer. She would wait up for Tim and ask him about what had happened on his shift. "I was really interested," she remembered. "And most of the time there would have been some incident he told me about, so it seemed as though I was sharing in his life some."

Tim still flirted. "He had the eye—he had a way of looking at someone," Sandy said. "I don't think a grown woman would buy it, but I think a young girl—with the way he looked in his uniform and his green eyes . . ."

But Sandy believed that he was only flirting. He still said suggestive things to her girlfriends when they came over, but she thought that was because he resented their being there.

All in all, assuming that no marriage was perfect, Sandy Harris believed hers was about as good as anybody's. She adored her baby daughter, she loved her handsome husband, and she liked her life. She took some courses in bookkeeping at Indian River Community College so that she could get a better job, and she and Tim talked about when they would be building their new house—the house that would come up to Tim's specifications.

Tim's job with the FHP meant that they could think about selling the little house on Mulberry. They drove around Indian River County looking for land they could afford. One day Sandy found an acre lot in an area called Citrus Hideaway, the second lot from the corner off County Road 510. It was ten miles north of Vero Beach near the crossroads known as Wabbasso. There were no houses in the development yet—unless you counted the huge pseudo-plantation at the end of 75th Court: "O'Hara's Scarlett."

Sandy fell in love with the land; the acre she wanted had pine trees and palmettos and endless possibilities. It would take $15,000 to buy it, and she didn't see how they could afford it—unless *both* she and Tim agreed to tighten their belts and economize. She knew she could, but she doubted Tim would agree. Whenever she demurred at some new purchase he suggested, he got angry.

5

By the early 1980s, Phil Williams, the Indian River County deputy who had once roared away from one of Tim Harris's traffic stops, was moving up in the sheriff's office. Both Phil and Tim were men utterly consumed with their careers. They were also fairly close in age. But that was about all they had in common. Despite his protestations of poverty, Tim had grown up in relative affluence, while Phil was country all the way. When they passed each other on the road they half waved. Phil had never forgotten Tim's picayune excuse to pull him over, and he never cared much for Harris again. It didn't matter; the chance that they would ever work on the same case was remote. Phil's obsession was in solving crimes, and Tim's was catching drunk drivers.

Phil Williams was as solidly built as a linebacker, with a friendly, sometimes deceptively open face and a luxuriant mustache. His mother's folks came from Suwannee County up north near the Georgia border, where the biggest "city" was Live Oak. His father's people were from Vero Beach. "Coming up, we probably broke every fish and game law there was," Williams laughed as he remembered his boyhood. "We sure didn't have any of us in law enforcement. If I can say anything about my past and how it's helped me in investigations, I guess it's because I can figure how the bad guys are going to do something. . . . I think a person's education is not so much a piece of paper they've got hanging up on the wall, but the sum of the experiences they've lived through."

Phil's dad, Wallace Williams, worked at the power plant for the city of Vero Beach for thirty years. His mom, Audrey, worked for the First Union bank. He had two sisters, Arlene and Francine.

Growing up, Phil Williams went to elementary school with at least three future killers, a fact whose irony was not lost on him when he pondered it as an adult. "I remember Sylvan Bishop—we were in first grade together. Later he used to tell me that his number one wish was to be on the F.B.I.'s Most Wanted List. I didn't really think he meant it."

Sylvan almost made it. In September, 1970, when he was eighteen, Sylvan Bishop reported that he had discovered two decomposed bodies in a woods west of Vero Beach. The victims were eventually identified as Kathleen Phillips, nineteen, and her friend, Joanna Malandrino, twenty. They hadn't been reported missing because their families thought they were on a trip from their home in Hollywood, Florida, to see Joanna's grandmother up in New Jersey. They *had* traveled north on I-95, but they hadn't gone more than a hundred miles before they developed car trouble and stopped at a service station in Vero Beach in the wee hours of the morning of September 1.

Sylvan Bishop was the night attendant. Apparently working toward his life's ambition, Sylvan had already been to reform school in Okeechobee and Marianna, to jail in Appalachee, and in a state mental institution for six weeks. The naïve girls from Hollywood, Florida, thought he was being exceptionally kind when he offered to drive them into town at the end of his shift, and they waited until he got off duty at 6:30 a.m.

No one ever saw them alive after that. Sylvan Bishop had indeed made the "big time" in crime, and he was charged with two counts of first degree murder. When Phil Williams heard that, he recalled Sylvan's childhood goal and remembered the kid at the next desk in first grade. He realized then that killers weren't always strangers; a murderer could be someone who was so much a part of your own world that you might never suspect him—or her.

If experience counts, Williams had a doctorate in the painful side of real life, both his own and the cases he'd worked. Only one case would ever make him cry, though, and it wouldn't unfold until he was almost two decades into his career as a cop.

In the late sixties and early seventies in Vero Beach Phil Williams was a member of a rock band, playing guitar and singing. The group never made it big, although their forty-song repertoire made them much in demand at Indian River County dances and civic functions. The little band never quite made enough money to survive, perhaps because Williams refused to work bar gigs exclusively, and bands performing in church basements and fraternal lodges rarely made headlines.

When he was seventeen Phil Williams joined the army before they could draft him. He spent two and a half weeks at Fort Jackson in South Carolina, expecting to be shipped out any day for basic training. But the army didn't want him; he had an "H-3 hearing profile." That meant Williams had high-frequency hearing deafness, probably caused by his sitting in the middle of his rock band. In a time when young men were *looking* for excuses not to go to Vietnam, Phil Williams was disappointed to find himself back home in twenty days with an honorable discharge. He could hear just fine, but the army doctors thought the noise of battle might aggravate his H-3 profile, and the service wouldn't take that responsibility. Fortunately for Florida citizens, Williams never had a problem passing police physicals.

Phil Williams got married in 1971 and became the father of a son in 1975. Two years later he and his first wife divorced. "The tremendous psychological pain that I experienced with the divorce in 1977 eventually subsided," Williams recalled, "and left in its place knowl-edge that would enable me to know and feel the intense emotions of others who were experiencing the same intense psychological trauma—allow me to have compassion towards others. You might say that divorce was the hardest school I ever attended."

Williams remembered trying to find the words to tell his little boy that he wouldn't be living with him anymore. "I told him I'd always be his daddy, and I'd always be there for him—but it tore me up. I didn't know how that particular experience would help me in an investigation a long time later."

When his reconstituted band showed no sign of going places, Phil Williams took a job with Piper Aircraft in Vero Beach as a mechanic. Three years later the gasoline shortage hit, and he could see that Piper was going to be hit hard. It was economics and not a passion for being a cop that made him apply to the Indian River County Sheriff's Office. He hired on in September, 1974. Williams was as surprised as anybody when he found he loved it and seemed to have a natural ability for law enforcement.

It sure wasn't the money. Indian River County was paying its deputies $8,000 a year. Williams was remarried, and he couldn't support a wife and pay child support on that, so he started his own landscaping business in his off-duty hours. Eventually he had twenty-five accounts and hired fellow officers to help out.

His interest in growing things continued. In his own back yard he grew mangoes, two varieties of grapes, two varieties of guavas, papayas, blackberries, loquats, pineapples, and nectarines. He once saved a huge old oak tree by filling a rotten cavity with 300 pounds of concrete. It's still standing.

In 1980 Williams asked for a transfer and became an agricultural detective, part of the Ranch and Groves Unit. At that time Indian River County was having agricultural thefts of more than $150,000 a year. Sometimes it was basic old-time cattle rustling, sometimes produce. On occasion agricultural detectives had to seek the source of chemical leakage that was poisoning the groundwater. The unit also investigated drug smugglers, an avocation that was growing tremendously in Florida in the seventies and eighties. "It was not unusual to find several bales of marijuana lying on a landing strip from a botched drug run the previous night," Williams said. "I learned the different airplane modifications that were common to drug-smuggling aircraft, as well as watercraft."

By infiltrating the agricultural stolen property network, Williams and his fellow Ranch and Grove detectives were able to keep the thieves so confused about who was a real buyer and who was an undercover detective that losses dropped from $150,000 to $12,000, a $138,000 savings for Indian River County farmers and orchardists.

There was one area of law enforcement that Phil Williams was destined for, whether he realized it or not. He was about to find himself in the eye of a grisly murder probe, and it would nearly destroy his faith in friendship and loyalty. Sylvan Bishop had been, he thought, an aberration—a funny kid who thought infamy was the same as fame.

The next connection to violent death hit Williams way too close to home. Before his first marriage Phil Williams had run with two close friends—"shirttail relatives," really: David Gore and Fred Waterfield. They hunted together, dated together, went all through school together. Fred had played in the band with Phil. "David Gore's mother introduced my parents to each other fifty years ago, and all of our families were close."

Phil hadn't been that surprised to learn that Sylvan Bishop had killed two girls. But he was poleaxed to find himself investigating a bloody crime involving men who had been like brothers to him.

"Indian River County . . . was experiencing a series of female disappearances. The suspicion fell squarely on . . . David Gore," Williams said quietly. "I just didn't believe him capable of committing the murders of five women, [but] I had long ago learned to respect the suspicions of my fellow law enforcement officers. I overheard radio traffic about a man chasing a naked woman near Gore's residence. . . . I responded and [along with several other officers] surrounded Gore's residence. I found the blood dripping from Gore's automobile trunk, and I assisted in exposing the dead female that was bound by rope inside the car trunk. There was no room for suspicion; Gore's guilt was evident."

Williams was ordered to go over to Fred Waterfield's house, so he wasn't around to see the capture of his former best friend, nor the rescue of a second woman David Gore had tied up in his attic.

Phil Williams continued to relate the incredible story. "I went to Waterfield's, with whom I was equally friendly. Statements Waterfield made to me would help my department tie him into the kidnapping of the murdered girl in David Gore's vehicle, and in *six other serial murders . . . and counting.*"

Phil Williams testified at the trials of both of his friends—for the prosecution. David Gore was sentenced to death, and Fred Waterfield to sixty-five years in prison. Acknowledging that he would never have suspected them, Williams was nonetheless fascinated by what secrets humans can hide behind smiling masks. "My interest in the psychology of the criminal mind—with a specific interest toward homicide—was born."

6

In 1988 Don Dappen would work alongside Phil Williams on a multi-agency task force formed to solve one of the most heinous multiple murder cases the Treasure Coast of Florida had ever known. Tommy Wyatt, twenty-six, and Michael Lovette, thirty-one—both escapees from a North Carolina prison road-gang—burst into a Domino's Pizza parlor in Vero Beach on May 18, 1988, allegedly intending only to rob it. But the Domino's safe was rigged so that it would not open for fifteen minutes.

Wyatt and Lovette decided to wait, but they didn't just *wait*; they terrorized their hapless captives. While Lovette held a gun on them, Wyatt raped twenty-eight-year-old Frances Edwards, the store manager's wife, while her husband was forced to watch. When Wyatt was finished he put a gun to the back of her head and calmly pulled the trigger. Then he spun and shot Billy Edwards, twenty-seven, in the chest. Terribly wounded but still fighting to protect his mortally injured wife, Edwards was no match for Wyatt. Wyatt put a .38-caliber Smith and Wesson pistol to the Domino's logo on Edwards's baseball cap and pulled the trigger.

Matt Bornoosh, also twenty-seven, a driver for Domino's, dropped to his knees and began to pray. Grinning, Wyatt fired at Bornoosh's head but only grazed his scalp. He shoved the barrel of the gun roughly into Bornoosh's ear and said softly, "If you listen *real close*, you'll hear it coming . . ."

And then he pulled the trigger. Incredibly, Matt Bornoosh lived for several hours, although he never regained consciousness.

Vero Beach Police Sergeant Pete Huber thought to grab his 35mm camera and take pictures of the scene even as ambulance sirens wailed in the distance. His pictures would play a most effective part in a trial three years later. So would the new forensic technique using DNA markers to correlate semen with blood types and tracing the results to a rapist.

448

The car the killers had stolen in Jacksonville two days earlier overheated and stalled as they were leaving Vero Beach. Lovette and Wyatt parked on a side road west of town, piled tissue paper on the front seat, and torched the car. They hitchhiked west on State Road 60 after they had stashed a briefcase full of money from the Domino's under a bridge.

In a bar in Seffner, Tommy Wyatt, chubby and baby-faced and a consummate con artist, picked up a trusting young woman named Cathy Nydegger. Lovette and Wyatt headed back toward Vero Beach to retrieve their pizza loot. They found it and turned toward Tampa. Tommy Wyatt stopped the car along an isolated dirt road and signaled to Cathy Nydegger to come with him as he walked away into a field. Lovette heard some low talking and then a scuffle, and then a single shot sounded.

The two men dragged the girl's body to the bank of a canal.

Tommy Wyatt had left no witnesses behind. It would be almost three years before justice was meted out to the conscienceless killers, but justice *did* prevail. State Attorney Bruce Colton told a Sarasota jury that the task force of lawmen had gathered 82 witnesses and 155 pieces of physical evidence.

Both Tommy Wyatt and Michael Lovette were sentenced to death in Florida's electric chair. Lovette's appeal to avoid execution was successful in 1994.

The Domino's Pizza murders had every police officer along the Treasure Coast working almost round the clock in May of 1988 as they looked for suspects. This was the first time that Don Dappen saw Phil Williams in action—he noted that the county detective was like a bulldog. Phil wouldn't let go of anything until he found out what he needed to know. Dappen had no idea then how closely the two would be aligned in less than two years in a murder case that would shock both of them more, if possible, than the grotesquely cruel pizza executions.

Dappen could still laugh, though, when he recalled Phil Williams. "He *is* as down home as you can get. He isn't kidding you. He *is* a real old country boy. During the pizza manhunt we were down in some ditch looking for a gun, and I said, 'Let's go have lunch,' and Phil says, 'I'll stay right here for lunch,' and I thought he was kidding. But he took out his knife and sliced off some kind of a weed or something, and he started eating it."

Williams knew his vegetation all right, both from his boyhood and from his years as a landscaper. Given his choice, he would probably

have taken a hamburger, but he could survive on the land if he had
to. He was only half kidding.

During the early years of their marriages Sandy and Tim Harris
and Don and Sue Dappen continued to play cards, and Pat Wessendorf and her three daughters still had lunch every Thursday. Still,
Sandy was more likely to tell her sisters what was going on with her
and Tim than to confide in her mother. If she found out Tim wasn't
treating Sandy well, Pat would demand action, while Susan and
Kathy would listen and nod sympathetically. *They* saw that Tim
seemed to do things deliberately to make Sandy miserable. He even
flirted with them, although he didn't get any encouragement. Susan
told him to cut it out, and Kathy was embarrassed.

Sandy Harris kept hoping that things would improve. She loved
him so much; she still believed he would realize it and return that
love. They had so much history together—too much for her to give
up on their marriage.

Don Dappen found Tim an odd kind of guy. They were friends first
because they were married to sisters, and second because they were
cops, but Dappen sensed that Tim was basically a loner. Tim loved to
fish, and he loved boats, and he loved to catch drunk drivers. Outside
of that, it was hard to find anything to talk to him about. One thing
Dappen noticed early on was that Tim appeared to literally hate
women.

"We'd be riding down the street, and he'd see a girl walking on the
side of the road, and he'd slow up, roll down his window, and yell—I
mean *yell*—at the top of his lungs, 'Hey, slut!' and then he'd flick his
tongue in and out at the girl. I'd say, 'What's the matter with you? Are
you crazy?' and he'd just laugh.

"Sometimes Tim would pull up on the bumper of a car being
driven slowly by an old man or an old woman, and he'd just lay on
his horn—I mean for forty-five seconds or so. I cringed. And one day
we were up in Gifford—in the black section—and a black guy's just
walking down the road. And Tim just pulled up beside this guy, rolls
down his window, and yells at him, 'Hey, nigger! Where you
headed?'"

Don Dappen was appalled. Tim was a state trooper, a grown man,
and he was acting like a crude and cruel teenager. "I told him, 'Just
let me out. Just pull over and let me out here.'"

Tim Harris, of course, called his wife names as derogatory as any
he called other women. He showed no respect for anyone beyond his
superiors on the Patrol. Sandy could not understand what motivated

her husband. Sometimes it seemed as if he observed the world from an entirely different viewpoint than anyone she had ever met, as if he were looking through the wrong end of a spyglass and everything and everyone looked ugly to him.

When Tim came home after working a fatal accident Sandy saw that the tragedy of it didn't seem to touch him at all. She knew that Donny felt bad when he had to investigate fatalities, but Tim gave out tickets and pulled bodies out of wrecks with exactly the same ease.

"Sometimes he'd come home and say, 'We had a really good accident tonight,'" Sandy remembered. "He said, 'This guy flew one way out the window, and it sliced the top of his head off, and the other one flew out the door, and he made a real splat where he landed. It was neat.'"

One time Tim was called out on an accident near Fort Pierce where a little boy died, probably because he had not been wearing a seat belt. "Tim didn't care. The little boy was black," Sandy said. "And black people meant even less to him than everybody else. It was a *child*, but Tim didn't care."

Sometimes Tim and Sandy watched TV together in the evenings when he was working the day shift. Beyond sex, that was the extent of any marital togetherness. Outside of Tim's job and what happened when he was out on patrol, they never talked about anything except what Tim wanted to buy next. Still, Sandy kept trying.

"Tim was only really happy when he got something new," Sandy said. "But then he got bored with it so quickly. He had four new trucks in two years—a white Toyota pickup, a Blazer, a Chevy S-10, and a Dodge Ram."

But it wasn't just cars. Tim Harris wanted boats too. The first was a fairly modest eighteen-foot Sun Skiff. He traded up to a twenty-one-foot Well Craft.

"He always wanted a bigger, better boat than any of the other troopers had," Sandy said. "And he usually got it. He didn't have many weekends off, but when he did, the only family things we did were with the boat. We'd go down the river to the islands—either taking a picnic lunch or buying hamburgers. The kids liked that."

Sandy kept most of her marriage problems to herself. She was sure that it was *she* who was doing something wrong. And Tim liked everything to "look rosy" on the surface; he would have been very angry if she told anyone that they had problems.

In 1985 they bought the acre of land in Citrus Hideaway. They had hoped to use their equity in the Mulberry Street house to pay for the land, but when they finally sold the little brown house they didn't come out one penny ahead. Fred and Pat Wessendorf loaned them $15,000 to pay for the land. With that Sandy was able to negotiate a mortgage loan for $45,000 to build a home.

Tim sent away for the blueprints for the house he wanted, spending hundreds of dollars on the plans. He spread them out enthusiastically as he pointed out features to Sandy. She looked at the blueprints aghast. The house had 6,000 square feet! It even had a maid's room. "I was making $21,000 a year, and Tim was making $29,000. How were we ever going to pay for a house that big? Tim said that I wasn't counting on his Army Reserve pay—but that was only $160.00 more a month. He was just totally unrealistic."

They butted heads again, the dreamer and the practical bookkeeper. They had yet to pay off even one of Tim's trucks or boats before he turned them in on newer, more expensive models, and they were rapidly sinking deeper in debt.

Tim and Sandy fought over the new house plans—or rather, they came to the kind of impasse they always did when the stress level in their marriage rose too high. Tim called Sandy a slut and turned his back on her. They didn't speak for a couple of weeks.

Sandy couldn't understand why Tim chose gutter terms to call her when they had even the mildest of arguments. Sandy's fidelity was unblemished. She loved him. She never even looked at another man. Still, Tim always resorted to ugly names when he was angry with her. She hoped a home of their own would change their lives.

Finally Sandy found some house plans that she thought might work. She combined them with drawings of her own and the features that Tim wanted and came up with enough to have blueprints drawn for a home they *could* afford. It was a compromise that both she and Tim could live with. They agreed that Tim would build the house for them, saving labor costs. He was very talented with his hands—if only he didn't get bored before he was finished. They could still have almost 3,000 square feet—four bedrooms and two bathrooms.

Tim Harris *was* skilled at building. He could do everything from carpentry to intricate tile work, and he was a strong and tireless worker. He saved them thousands of dollars by working on their new house himself. When Tim wasn't on duty he was working on the place in Citrus Hideaway. It would be the first house on 75th Court— although later the street would be built up with very expensive residences. It was a great investment, a solid foundation on which Tim and Sandy could build their financial future.

Originally Sandy, Tim, and Jennifer had planned to live in a little trailer on the Citrus Hideaway property while Tim built their house, but that wasn't really practical. They had no electricity, and the trailer was small. Besides, Sandy was pregnant again, and she could barely turn around in the tiny trailer. Tim and Sandy moved in with Pat and Fred Wessendorf in the interval between leaving their old house and moving into their new one.

Just as he did with every other area of his life, Tim operated from completely opposite and contradictory ends of the scale when he built his dream house. He was both an extremely talented and precise carpenter and a sloppy and careless worker. He spent way too much on some phases of their new home and cut corners in other areas where it wasn't necessary. As he set the framework for the white stucco house he put in twice as many studs as the place needed. He had a stud every six inches. Even Fred Wessendorf, who usually kept his thoughts to himself, wondered aloud if Tim needed *that* much wood in the frame. It was almost a fortress, so heavy that no wind, no storm, not even a hurricane could blow it away. Of course, buying twice as much timber as the house plans required sent their costs soaring. Tim did a beautiful tile job in the bathrooms—but he left grout smears on the tile when he finished. By the time Sandy discovered that, the grout had dried and was almost impossible to get off. She and Tim argued "almost every day" until the house was done. "I thought he was wasting money and material.

"But I loved that house," Sandy sighed. "It was designed just like we wanted it—so everything was convenient; there was a place for everything."

And it was beautiful besides. The little house on Mulberry Street would have fit inside the double garage of their new house. It was gleaming white stucco, two-story, with a wide overhanging roof. There was a bay window in the living room and a stone fireplace with a raised hearth. The master bedroom was huge, and there was a room for Jennifer and a nursery for the new baby.

Tim worked long hours to finish up the house so that they could move in in time for Christmas, 1985. Their new baby was due around then, too.

A lot of young marriages get off to rocky starts. In December of 1985 Sandy had just turned twenty, and Tim was only five years older. On the positive side of the ledger, they both had highly responsible jobs, and they would soon have two children. With the new house it looked as though things were going to turn out all right after all. The first thing Sandy did was hang their wedding pictures beside the stone fireplace.

Maybe, if they both gave everything they had to make this

marriage work, they *could* succeed, and all their arguments would disappear. Sandy knew that other people—even her own sisters—wondered why she stayed with Tim. But nobody who hadn't been where she was could understand. When Tim was charming and sweet, no man could be sweeter. He could wipe away the bad times and make her believe in him again. Her heart still skipped beats when she saw him in his uniform. If he didn't care for her, would he have worn himself out building a house with his own hands?

And yet, despite Sandy's optimism, things were already falling apart. If it is ever possible to pinpoint an event or a moment in time when the seeds of tragedy silently take root, that Christmas season of 1985 would be the beginning of the falling down, down, and down for Tim and Sandy Harris.

7

It was December, 1985, when Trooper Tim Harris responded to an automobile accident near Vero Beach. It wasn't much more than a fender-bender. One of the passengers was a slender blond woman. Routinely Tim jotted down the names, addresses, and phone numbers of the passengers and witnesses. He had noticed the blond woman immediately, although he didn't give any indication that he had. She was probably in her early thirties, very attractive, and she stared hard at him as he went about his job.

Whether it was Tim Harris who called DeeLisa Davis* or *she* who called him—as he always claimed—an affair that would threaten his marriage began. Tim would always insist that he hadn't really thought about DeeLisa after he finished the accident report, but that she had called him at work and made it so obvious that she was available for a "fling" that he would have been crazy to refuse.

Sandy was hugely pregnant, and Tim was exhausted from driving his territory every night, building his house all day, and living with his in-laws. Most of all, he was bored.

When Tim Harris was bored he always did something to change his situation.

DeeLisa assured Tim she wanted nothing more than an interlude, and he believed her. If he had even the vaguest understanding of the female psyche, Tim Harris would have known that it is a rare woman who truly wants only a physical affair. DeeLisa was divorced, with small children, and she worked at the phone company.

She was about to fall totally in love with Tim Harris.

Tim had revealed very little about his private life to DeeLisa, and she had been careful not to ask questions. He wore a wedding ring, and she wasn't a fool. Still . . .

In early January, 1986, the house in Citrus Hideaway was finally ready for the Harrises to occupy. Sandy barely made it in time to get halfway settled before she gave birth to Timothy Scott Harris, Jr. He was born just a week after they moved in. With her second delivery Sandy had to have a caesarean, and she was in the hospital recovering for several days.

Tim brought DeeLisa to his new home, proudly showing off his handiwork. He took her into the master bedroom and drew her down with him on the bed he usually shared with Sandy. DeeLisa couldn't miss the signs that a woman lived in the house with Tim. She just had to know for sure, even though she didn't expect to like the answer. She finally asked, "A woman lives here. Probably your wife. Where *is* she?"

"She's in the hospital," Tim answered flatly. "She just had a baby."

DeeLisa drew in a sharp breath. If she had had the courage of her convictions, she would have left then. It was one thing to sleep with another woman's husband; it seemed so much more immoral to sleep with Tim in the bedroom that he shared with his wife—while that wife was in the hospital with his new baby. DeeLisa knew she should leave, but she couldn't.

She was already crazy about the man.

Sandy didn't know. She wouldn't know for a long, long, time. When she brought Timmy home from the hospital Tim was nice to her and even waited on her some while she recovered. He had wanted two girls, he had told her—and not a baby boy. But once he saw Tim Jr., he doted on his son.

They went on with their life. It was great having the new house, but its novelty soon wore off for Tim. He wasn't the least bit interested in putting in landscaping or in fixing anything that broke. It had been a new adventure for him, and now he was done with it. When one of the cupboard doors fell off its hinges Sandy asked Tim to fix it—but he never did. It hung there for years.

Tim put in Bahia grass that was easy to take care of, and he bought himself a riding lawn mower. He also bought a satellite dish.

Sandy couldn't stop him from buying one new "toy" after another. He bought a computer, but he tired of it in a few weeks and rarely used it again. He decided to build a greenhouse, and he bought several sheets of aluminum, worked on the greenhouse for a few hours, and, frustrated, threw the aluminum in a pile of junk in the backyard.

Sandy and Tim still had no friends—not the kind that they could invite over and go to parties with. They now had a house plenty big enough to have company, but Tim didn't want company.

"Tim was nice to people's faces," Sandy said. "But he called them 'those scumbags' behind their backs. He made obscene sounds at women. Everybody else's wife was a 'slut' to Tim. He hated everybody. He would never go to neighborhood barbecues. We hardly ever went to Patrol parties."

Tim didn't want Sandy to have girlfriends, either. After a while she simply stopped trying to have friends. It wasn't worth the fights or the effort. "My mom was my only friend—the only one I had to talk to."

Sandy hadn't the faintest hint that her husband was having an affair. He had, of course, the ideal profession for a marital cheat. Troopers kept their patrol cars at their own homes, and they went to work from home without ever having to report in to headquarters at the beginning of a shift. Often the radio dispatcher called them out from home when they were needed on the Interstate to help on an accident or a search.

Sandy never knew exactly where Tim was at any given time.

Sandy Harris had two babies, a job, and a house to take care of. She loved Tim still, but sometimes he was almost like having a third child. She wanted to believe he loved their kids, but he wouldn't help with them. He never bathed them or fed them. "If I called him to ask him if he was going to pick them up from day care, he would never give me an answer. He would only say, 'I might, slut—and I might not.'"

She couldn't count on him; sometimes Sandy got there and Tim had already picked up the children. "Sometimes they were waiting for me, sometimes they were home already, but I always had to stop

Patrol was nabbing with VASCAR had Fuzzbusters and were unpleasantly surprised to be stopped—because the VASCAR had no beam and emitted no signal, so the radar detectors were useless.

Patrolmen were asked to put in ten overtime hours apiece each week. That would cost the Treasure Coast patrol area a lot of money, but the counties involved, which got a portion of the speeding fines, would do well. Speeding fines were $44 for traveling 56 to 65 mph, $74 for those going 66 to 79 mph. The real speeders, Tim's "high rollers," would pay $99 plus $2 for each additional mile per hour.

Tim was the law; he was the trooper picked by Captain Dean Sullivan in the Fort Pierce office of the Florida Highway Patrol to represent the department. Sandy was proud of all the articles written about Tim, and she cut them out for her scrapbook. If ever a woman was ambivalent about her man, it was Sandy Harris. Times like that, she was glad Tim was her husband.

Other times were bad. Tim still called her and other women "sluts" and "bitches." He still refused to make friends with other couples. He still pinched Sandy high up on the inside of her thighs where no one but he would see the blackish-purple bruises. He still twisted her arms behind her back when she made him angry.

And Sandy remained completely unaware of Tim's mistress, DeeLisa Davis.

8

The woman in the pine grove was still alone. She had been there so long now that even the little animals who lived and died there were no longer aware of her. The insects no longer stung her exposed flesh. She had become part of their environment, as inanimate as a fallen pine bough, as silent as the night sometimes grew when there was no wind at all off the river.

Right through his 1988 evaluation Tim Harris continued to "exceed" what was expected of a Florida State Trooper. His superiors checked off the top box in every category. Sure, he was a quiet kind of guy, but he would stop and shoot the breeze with any of his fellow troopers. He did his job, and he did it well. He was always where he was supposed to be, and when they called him out for extra duty he never complained.

In 1987 Tim had put in a request to work as a K-9 officer, to get a dog and to be sent to K-9 training at Fort Lauderdale. The FHP was adding some more dogs so that they could be trained for their drug interdiction program. Beyond catching drunk drivers, Tim Harris was most interested in cutting down on the swath drug dealers were ripping through Florida. He was excited when he was given orders to report to K-9 school.

Tim's dog was named Shadow. Shadow was a beautiful male long-haired Alsatian who weighed ninety pounds. Tim spent weeks training with his dog, and when they came home to Indian River County the two were bonded inextricably. Tim built a chain-link pen for Shadow out beside the new house. Like most K-9s, Shadow was a gentle family pet with Sandy, Jennifer, and Timmy—but when he was working with Tim, he was ready to tear apart anyone who threatened his "partner." In fact, Shadow was exceptionally protective of Tim.

Tim was not averse to using Shadow to tease someone sadistically. It was the only kind of humor he understood. Sue Dappen happened to be afraid of dogs. One day Sue walked into her sister's house and didn't see Shadow sitting quietly in the foyer. Tim grinned and said softly, "Shadow, *watch her.*" The big dog immediately perked up his ears and started growling at Sue, and she froze in terror—as Tim had known she would. Don walked in behind Sue, saw what was going on, and said, "Tim! Cut it out!"

Tim did, but he laughed heartily.

For a while Tim was so caught up in Shadow that everything else paled. Even his enforcement percentage levels dropped, although his sergeant explained that was because he had been away at K-9 training school. "He and his canine are always available to call out."

Tim had even put his affair with DeeLisa on hold while he was down in Lauderdale training with Shadow, and neither she nor Sandy saw much of him when he came back and went to work with his dog.

Tim's actual duties didn't really change. He was still investigating accidents, arresting DUIs, and writing tickets for speeders, and he was in his old familiar district. The only difference was that from mid-1987 on, Tim had Shadow with him. The Patrol had promised to work both Tim and Shadow into a new felony program, focusing particularly on drug interdiction, but either there wasn't enough tax money to set up the program or the officials were dragging their feet, because two years went by and there was no upgrading of the felony program.

Tim Harris and Shadow made an impressive-looking pair when they stopped an errant driver: the tall trooper, made even taller in his campaign hat, and the dog who looked as though he'd like nothing better than to be released from the backseat to chomp off an arm and a leg or two. The Shadow who played with Sandy's and Tim's babies was a completely different dog than the Shadow on duty. In a way, Tim and Shadow shared that trait; each of them had two different and widely diverse personalities.

There was a brief respite of calm in the Harris's marriage after Tim got Shadow. But inevitably Tim got bored with Shadow, too. If he had been able to train Shadow to be a drug-sniffing dog and they could have worked felonies together—man and dog—as Tim wanted to do, it would have been different.

Tim took good care of Shadow at first, but then Sandy realized that he was locking his dog in his den for hours and hours when he was off-duty. She sighed. Just as with every other new toy he got, Tim no longer wanted to be bothered with Shadow, but Shadow was a living, feeling, creature, and he adored Tim. She felt sorry for the dog and tried to let him out to be with her and Jennifer and Timmy whenever she could.

Now that Tim's interest in Shadow had diminished, he grew bored again. He came to Sandy with a request that she could scarcely believe. "He wanted a helicopter! Can you *believe* that? He wanted his own helicopter. He was going to buy a kit and build it—he said it would only cost $28,000. I finally talked and talked and got him to think about getting a bigger boat instead."

A boat would be the lesser of two evils.

To make up for the lost helicopter it would have to be a really big boat. This time Tim bought a twenty-five-foot extra wide Cubby Proline 200 horsepower cabin cruiser that cost $45,000. That was when Sandy arranged for a third mortgage on their new house. Originally their monthly payment had been workable, and even the second mortgage wasn't too difficult to pay off as long as they were both working. Tim's $45,000 boat loan scared Sandy; she knew they could lose their precious acre in Citrus Hideaway so easily.

Sandy worked over their budget, and no matter how she added it up it always came out the same. The house payment was up to

$1,094, the boat payment was $329, Tim's new truck was $350, and Tim drove the truck so much that their gasoline bill was usually over $250 a month. That meant that they owed $2,023 a month before they could even think about groceries, day care, utilities, or clothes. They had no entertainment costs because they never went anywhere. If Tim was home in the evening, they watched television. They never talked anymore.

Before taxes, Sandy and Tim together brought in only $3,900 a month. Sandy was scared to death they were going to go bankrupt.

Tim didn't care; he was wildly happy about his new boat. He bought $2,000 worth of scuba equipment. He bought a $1,200 cellular phone, and the first month's phone bill was $600.

Beyond being out there in the night cruising I-95 looking for speeders, drunks, and drug runners, or sitting quietly in the daytime in one of those hidden spots troopers always seem to know about where they can observe traffic unseen, Tim loved the water. He had grown up on the Indian River and all the little islands that seemed to drift along in it. Some of the islands he whizzed by were only lumps of land too tiny to have a name, but some had docks where he could moor the big, new boat.

The Indian River could take him out into the Atlantic Ocean if he chose. Tim had no fear of the water at all. He almost dared it to drown him, although he worried about Jennifer and Timmy when they played near the omnipresent streams, rivers, and inlets. Once, when Timmy was about two and a half, Sandy was watching the children wade in shallow water, and Timmy went under and swallowed some water before Sandy could grab him and tip him upside down.

Although Timmy was never in any real danger, Tim railed at her for months for being careless. "Remember," he would intone ominously, "when our son nearly drowned—"

That always made Sandy feel guilty, although she knew there were few kids who hadn't had a noseful or two of water when they were toddlers, and she always watched the kids like a hawk when they were wading.

Tim himself was like a dolphin in the water. Now that he owned the biggest boat of all the law enforcement officers in Indian River County, he occasionally invited them to go fishing or scuba diving with him. His brother-in-law, Don Dappen, often went along.

One time Tim took several officers out in his boat to scuba dive. He volunteered to stay with the anchor line while they dived. The first man popped up from the ocean's depths and was horrified to see that Tim's boat was hundreds of yards away and drifting further. His shouts drew no response, so he swam as hard as he could, barely reaching it before it disappeared over the horizon. Exhausted, he managed to pull himself aboard. Tim wasn't there, and the anchor sure wasn't doing its job. The cop had no choice but to cut the anchor loose completely and turn the boat back to where the signal flag floated. The other men would surface soon, exhausted, to find the Cubby cruiser was gone. He could only assume that Tim had gone over the side and drowned.

Gradually the other men popped up, grateful to find the boat waiting—but shocked to hear that Tim was missing. Don Dappen wondered how he was going to break the news to Sandy. And then, amazingly, Tim Harris burst from the water. Alive and well. He laughed at their concern for his safety, but he was angry that they had cut his anchor adrift. Tim couldn't get it through his head that they might all have drowned if the boat had gotten away.

Another time Don was along on a midnight dive for lobsters. It was the opening day of the season, and they had to descend to the Indian River's bottom carefully or the riptide heading for the vastness of the Atlantic Ocean could pull them off the rope like autumn leaves in a hurricane. Tim laughed at Don's warning and said he'd go down first and look around.

"When we got down," Don remembered, "we couldn't see him. It should have been easy, because all we had to do was turn off our lights and we would have seen Tim's. But he wasn't there."

They surfaced, once again sure that Tim had drowned. The ship's radio was crackling, and there was a call from the skipper of the last boat in a long line of pleasure craft anchored out toward the ocean. "We have a man named Tim on board," the man said. "Is he by any chance off your boat?"

Tim *had* been caught in the riptide, despite his assurances that he would descend with caution. When Don put together the information from the boaters along the line he learned that Tim hadn't fought the tide at all, nor had he accepted help from the yachts he passed. He had lain back and floated as if he were home in his swimming pool while he passed dozens of boats whose owners stared in horror. At the final moment, as he drifted near the very last cruiser between himself and the open sea, the captain threw him a rope and pulled him aboard. Tim hadn't been frightened. It was almost as if he was completely unaware that he was headed for deadly undercurrents, sharks, and certain death.

It was almost as if he didn't care.

Lt. Gary Morgan, the FHP officer who had originally been responsible for helping Tim get assigned to Indian River County, became one of Tim's supervisors in 1989. Several troopers had mentioned to Morgan that Tim was very disappointed that there had been no follow-up on the promised development of the felony program. Morgan called Tim in and talked with him. Tim said he felt he just didn't have the time to train Shadow for the drug interdiction program. He wasn't getting a chance to use his dog for what Shadow had been bred for.

"I sat him down," Morgan recalled. "I promised him we would schedule a month ahead of time for him to train the dog. I would give him certain days, and I'd give him sometimes eight hours—the whole day—sometimes four hours to work his dog, take it to the different training grounds, and to take it to the vet and things like that. You know, I kind of let him have a free rein as far as doing what he wanted to do with the dog and working the dog on the Interstate with the drug interdiction program. I didn't use him to work wrecks except when I actually needed him—when all the other troopers were tied up. . . . I would call on him, and he would always go and never give me any complaints about working the wrecks. . . . I'd give him Indian River, Saint Lucie, and let him roam up and down the Interstate, working the dog."

Shadow did good work, responding to Tim in their expanded program, and man and dog spent more time together. Shadow even made the Vero Beach *Press Journal* himself in 1989. "The Shadow knows—and proved it Thursday morning . . ."

Shadow and Tim had been instrumental in apprehending a suspect in a rash of auto thefts. The suspect fled into a deep woods, and Shadow sniffed him out. There Tim found the most recently stolen car, and four more that were being stripped down.

Shadow continued to be the canine darling of the media. He and Tim posed together under the headline "Not Your Ordinary Puppy." Tim explained to the reporter that Shadow was an *official* member of the Florida Highway Patrol and had as much right as human troopers to wear a badge—and Shadow did, hanging from his collar.

Sometime in 1989 word came down that the FHP was taking applications for troopers who were interested in going into newly beefed-up felony programs. Trooper Tim Harris was one of those selected.

That wasn't surprising. He was a much-commended trooper. On August 4, 1989, Assistant Florida State Attorney Stuart A. Webb wrote to Patrol Major William Driggers and Colonel Randall Jones:

"The enclosed order is forwarded for your information and action. I must add that the defendant was forced to enter a plea due to the excellent case developed by your Trooper T.S. Harris. Although there were only traces of marijuana found, he devoted the extra time and effort to ensure success, and he made my job very easy. Trooper Harris was outstanding at every phase of the case and is a credit to himself, your leadership, and the Florida Highway Patrol."

Trooper Harris, whose last evaluation said he was "highly competent" and required minimal supervision, that he was "flexible and adapts easily to change . . . a valuable asset to the Division," apparently did not see himself that way. He was an angry, morose, and miserable man.

Who knows what it takes to make a particular man happy? Timothy Scott Harris *should* have been happy in the late summer of 1989. He had a beautiful wife who loved him even though she sometimes wished she didn't, a beautiful mistress who also loved him and who also sometimes wished she didn't, two healthy, happy kids, a fine big house he had built with his own hands, a job he had always wanted, a chance to move up, and a loyal dog who loved him, too—without reservations. Tim was movie-star handsome, healthy, and his fellow troopers respected him.

But Tim Harris wasn't happy. He had secret sexual fantasies that neither of the women in his life fulfilled. He discussed his obsessions with no one. Never a man to talk much beyond casual conversation, he certainly would not reveal those things that snaked through his mind when he traced the dark ribbons of I-95 as they curled north to Melbourne and then south to Port St. Lucie.

PART TWO

Lorraine

9

Although Lorraine Marie Dombroski Boisseau Hendricks and
Sandra Lynn Wessendorf Harris were never to meet, the two
women might have liked each other; they had a lot in common.
Like Sandy Harris, Lorraine was born in the first week of October.
Sandy's birthday was October 6th, and Lorraine's was October
3rd. Lorraine, however, was sixteen years older than Sandy, although she scarcely looked it. She was very beautiful—movie-star
beautiful. Model beautiful. She could also look like a pixie when
she eschewed makeup and high-fashion clothes—as she often did. At
the age of forty-three Lorraine looked perhaps thirty. She was five
feet, six inches tall and weighed under 125 pounds. Her chestnut-
colored hair was extremely thick, and her eyes were brown and
sparkling.

Probably the most memorable thing about Lorraine was her
ebullient love of life. She had a wonderful smile and the energy of ten
ordinary women.

Like Sandy Harris, Lorraine Hendricks had been through some
hard times, and like Sandy, she was a woman who handled problems
competently rather than collapsing into tears. Neither woman had
ever let life's misfortunes get the better of her for long. Both Lorraine
and Sandy had parents who were always there to back them up.

Lorraine was born in Stamford, Connecticut, in October of 1946 to
Frank and Josephine "Jodi" Dombroski. Frank was a career army
officer who served under General Dwight D. Eisenhower in the
European Theater in World War II.

Like all service families, the Dombroskis and their son and
daughter moved frequently. When Lorraine was five they were in
Germany; they would have a second tour there. When she was
seventeen they were at Fort Holabird in Baltimore. And there were
many, many duty stations in between until Frank retired as a major in
1965. He had served his country for twenty-four and a half years.

469

"The Major" was a strong, quiet-spoken man who adored his only daughter. Not surprisingly, Lorraine was raised to respect men in uniform. Her dad was a shining example for her.

Jodi Dombroski was a pretty woman, and Lorraine looked very much like her, although she was taller than her mother. They had the same smile, the same belief in the importance of the continuity of family. Lorraine kept a little plaque in her kitchen reminding the viewer that love and knowledge are handed down generation to generation.

The Dombroskis were strong Catholics, and for much of her life Jodi Dombroski worked as a volunteer—for the Red Cross, for hospitals, for her church—and she imbued Lorraine with the belief that those who were fortunate had an obligation to those who were not.

Lorraine was a natural athlete. She was a strong swimmer and earned her senior life saving badge when she was sixteen and her father was stationed at Fort Holabird. Her mother, wearing her Red Cross volunteer uniform, stood by, smiling proudly.

Lorraine Dombroski grew up to be an almost incandescently lovely teenager, although she herself didn't seem to realize it.

"When we were in Baltimore," Jodi said, "I remember how surprised Lorraine was when I suggested she enter a beauty pageant where the prize was a college wardrobe. She laughed and said she would never win—but she did win."

Lorraine went on to win many other beauty contests. She was Miss Stamford, Connecticut, in 1967, and then first runner-up to Miss Connecticut. In the talent contest she performed the history of drums—from jazz to rock and roll to African rhythm. "Lori" had brains, too, and she had a remarkable talent for languages. She attended the University of Connecticut. By the time she was an adult she was fluent in French, German, Spanish, and Polish. She was always especially proud of her Polish roots. When she went to classes to learn Polish she threw herself into the process, as she did in all her pursuits. In no time Lorraine was inviting the teacher home to meet her parents, to have a home-cooked Polish meal.

Although her hair would darken later, at eighteen Lorraine Dombroski was the very epitome of the lovely blonde with the perfect figure that most teenage girls long to emulate. If she hadn't been so nice, she might have aroused some jealousy. But she *was* nice. She was particularly drawn to little kids, old people, and, especially, animals.

She always would be.

Because of her tremendous kindness it would be easy to pigeon-hole Lorraine as a "goody-goody"—too nice to be true. She was much more than that. There are people who seem to accept life as it comes, never swerving from whatever path they find themselves on. Not Lorraine Dombroski. She was curious and adventurous, and she was more than a bit of a daredevil. She would try anything once—as long as it didn't go against her own moral code. She was a drummer in a rock and roll band for a while, she climbed mountains and swung off them on ropes, and she tried parachuting.

When she was younger she didn't mind being called "Lori," although later she preferred her full name. To her best friend, Carol, she was usually "Lor."

Lori Dombroski was within a semester of graduating from college when she dropped out to marry John Boisseau in 1977. Carol Worley, her friend for more than a dozen years, perhaps her closest confidante, recalled, "She put him through the rest of his college. She was very, very much in love with John, and she loved her life with him. Sometimes her friends complained that Lori was working and John was just going to school—but *she* never said a word against him. She was so happy with him. They hiked, they canoed, they camped—they rode motorcycles through the wilds of the Everglades. She loved all those things they did."

Lori and John Boisseau were involved in motocross racing, and when she was in her early twenties Lori nearly died in a crash in a motorcycle race. She ended up in an intensive care unit and then underwent emergency surgery in which much of her liver and all of her gallbladder were removed. Aside from the scar left, she scarcely thought about her injuries once she was healed. It wasn't the first time she had been injured taking part in one sport or another, and it wouldn't be the last.

John's ambition was to be a professional musician, and they lived most of the decade they were together in the Miami area. For a time Lori modeled. Her long hair was bleached until it looked like shimmering wheat, her skin was golden tan, and she posed in white go-go boots and a minidress in an ad for the Florida Highway Patrol and the Governor's Highway Safety Commission. Smiling directly into the camera, Lorraine opened the first carton of 1971–72 Florida plates that all state motorists were asked to display on their vehicles.

The plates read, "Sunshine State—ARRIVE ALIVE—Florida."

* * *

Lori and John Boisseau were divorced after eleven years. It no longer matters what they fought about, but years later Lorraine would confide to Carol Worley that in retrospect she felt she had acted too hastily—that she had let her pride get in the way of what might have been mended with counseling. "I said good-bye too quickly," Lori sighed. "I could have forgiven him." Ironically, both of their careers blossomed after their divorce.

John, once leader of the rock trio "The Better Halves," moved up rapidly in the music world, but not only as a musician; he owned a sound stage and rented trucks, cables, every kind of musical equipment musical groups that came into the Miami area for concerts might need.

Lorraine was an idea woman, creative, enthusiastic, and sparkling. Her career choice was public relations, communications, and marketing. She was a natural at innovative advertising, and she handled people with tact and sensitivity.

More than that, Lorraine Hendricks was a woman who truly *liked* people and drew them to her like a magnet. More than one friend, searching for a word to describe her, finally came up with "magical."

"She *was* magic," one associate recalled. "You could see it in her eyes, in her smile—her *aura*, I guess you'd call it. When you walked into a room with Lorraine, people wanted to talk to her. In no time they were her friends."

Not surprisingly, Lorraine's expertise and natural charm sent her rapidly up the ladder in her career. She spent fourteen years in the Fort Lauderdale area working for Jack Drury and Associates, The Communications Group, North Broward Hospital District Medical Centers, the Hospital Corporation of America, and Humana Hospitals. She had a fifteen-year association with Stubbs and Associates of Atlanta as a promotional marketing representative.

Lorraine tried skydiving, and she skied in Switzerland. She decided she wanted to learn ballet, but she refused to "go to some class with a bunch of uncoordinated women in tight leotards." Instead she took a beginning ballet class with twelve-year-olds, learning the basics. She didn't care a bit that she was taller than all the other students, that she was a grown-up and they were children. Carol Worley laughs, remembering. "Lorraine was actually in a *recital*— this big thirty-five-year-old woman with a bunch of twelve-year-old girls, and she wasn't in the least embarrassed."

When she was married to John, they taught classes in kung fu, and at one time Lorraine was nationally ranked as a black belt. Indeed, she was the first Caucasian female to reach the rank of black belt in kung fu karate in the United States. Her perfect, slender figure might have made her appear delicate. She was anything but.

Woe be unto any ordinary predatory male who looked on the exquisite and outwardly fragile beauty of Lorraine Boisseau and saw a woman who could not put up a fight. And win. Lorraine even taught self-defense to women, both those her own age and senior citizens. She was a champion of all women, but she went out of her way to help those women who had been bruised by life, women who no longer believed in themselves. If she couldn't hire them herself, she would see to it that they found jobs, and that they had nice clothes to wear until they could afford to buy their own.

Lorraine and Carol "just kind of hung out together," her best friend remembers. Carol Worley was a physical therapist at the University Community Hospital in Fort Lauderdale when Lorraine was their public information officer. They met for the first time in November, 1978. Lorraine had had a skiing accident in Zermatt and had cartilage surgery on her knee, and Carol had just come to work as a therapist at University Community. Carol ran for exercise, but only about two miles at a stretch.

"Would running help my knee heal?" Lorraine asked.

That was a new one for Carol; most of her patients favored their injured parts and moved them gingerly. Nobody ever wanted to *run*. Lorraine did.

"Yes," Carol said slowly. "Yes, I guess it would—if you don't push it."

And run Lorraine did. "And then," Carol recalls, "Lorraine came to me and said, 'Carol, I'm going to run in a *race*—7.2 miles!' She had this infectious enthusiasm that you couldn't resist—and the next thing I knew, I said, 'Well, I'm going to run with you then!' I'd never run more than two miles in my life, but Lorraine got a whole group of us from the hospital to run. It wasn't long after that that she came to me and said, 'Carol, I'm going to run a marathon!'"

And this time they both ran in a marathon. Carol was ten years younger than Lorraine, but no one ever guessed Lorraine's age correctly. "She and I ran 26.2 miles!" Carol says. "That's the way she did things. Afterward, these friends who took us asked, 'Well, are you going to run it again next year?' We took one look at each other and said, 'Not on your life!' But you know, the next year we did it again."

Whenever Carol Worley pictures Lorraine she sees her in her running clothes, with her long hair braided into pigtails, with no makeup, and with a triumphant grin on her face. "Or I *hear* her. She always wore high heels at work, and you'd hear this click-clickety-click coming down the hall, and you *knew* it had to be Lorraine—nobody else moved that fast."

Lorraine was the consummate animal lover. She found an old horse that nobody wanted, a gelding she described as having "one foot in the glue factory." Lorraine paid fifty dollars for him, adopted him, and kept his misnomer: Flicka. They were the same age—thirty. "Flicka was a big part of Lori's life for a long time," Carol remembers. "She would spend all night in the stable sitting up with that horse. She spent so much money when Flicka's hooves got infected after the pasture flooded. One time Flicka fell in the stable, and the people who owned the barn were so angry—because they thought they were going to have to take a wall down to get Flicka out. But Lori got friends and equipment, and they all went out there and hauled Flicka back up on his feet, and he lived another six or seven years!" Indeed, Flicka lived to be forty-two, an almost unheard-of age for a horse.

Lorraine visited Flicka twice a day and took care of him. "After she divorced John," Carol Worley says, "Lorraine used to say, 'Flicka's my best friend.'"

Lorraine had a birthday party for Flicka every year, and her friends brought apples and carrot cake and appropriate presents. One year Flicka made the local society pages for his birthday party, and his picture appeared. He, of course, wore a party hat. Another birthday was filmed for the eleven o'clock news in Miami.

One thing that Lorraine couldn't bear was to see dead animals left in the road. She was often late for appointments because she stopped and moved them to the grassy shoulder of the road and tried to find something to cover them. "She actually kept a shovel or something in her trunk," Carol recalls. "So she could lift them off the road and give them some dignity. If she saw an animal that had been hit in a neighborhood, she would go and knock on doors to try to find out who it belonged to and tell them so they wouldn't have to find it themselves."

Lorraine was single for two years after she divorced John Boisseau. Then she met Rick Hendricks, an executive with Eastern Airlines and a captain in the army reserve, in 1979. Lorraine quickly fell in love with Rick; they were married six weeks after they met. Their wedding was in the northwest, where Rick's best man lived, and they honeymooned at a ski resort.

Lorraine was in her early thirties by then, and she longed for a family. She was bitterly disappointed when she suffered a miscarriage. And then, when she was almost thirty-eight, Lorraine became pregnant again. On June 28, 1984, she gave birth to a baby girl by caesarean section: Katherine. Lorraine's own hair had darkened to brown, but Katherine had golden blond hair, just as her mother had once had. And as with her mother, there was a magical sense about Katherine. Lorraine adored her.

As much as her career meant to her, nothing was more important to Lorraine Hendricks than her baby girl. She took a sabbatical from work until Katherine was old enough to go to school. Six years away from such a competitive world was taking a chance—but Lorraine never considered doing otherwise.

Now, when Lorraine ran in marathons, Katherine was a part of it, too. She wore a tiny tank top with the same logo her mother's had, a little visor, athletic socks, and running shoes. In one race Lorraine actually *pushed* Katherine for 6.2 miles—not in a jogging stroller, but in a regular stroller. In a 9.2 race Lorraine was exhausted, but still she scooped up her baby toward the end so Katherine could share the joy of crossing the finish line.

Katherine Hendricks spoke Polish before she spoke English. Lorraine spoke to her baby girl in the language of her heritage, and so did the Dombroskis, knowing that it is much easier for very young children to learn a foreign language. By the time she was three or four Katherine spoke both English and Polish well. Lorraine laughed when one of Katherine's pre-school teachers called her in and said, with a perplexed look on her face, "Katherine is using words, teaching the other children—we're not sure what they are. We think they may be inappropriate—"

"Those are *Polish* words," Lorraine said. "I can assure you that they're not the least bit naughty."

Lorraine learned her grandmother's recipes for traditional Polish dishes and spent days each spring preparing an Easter feast identical to those that had graced tables in Poland a hundred years earlier. She worked with Polish families who had just immigrated and helped them set up households in America.

In 1988 Rick Hendricks was offered an excellent job as an executive with Blue Cross—but it meant a move from Fort Lauderdale to Jacksonville. It was a wrench for Lorraine Hendricks to leave her friends, but she didn't hesitate. The only thing she insisted on was that Flicka would come along, too. It was going to cost a lot to transport a forty-two-year-old horse on a six-hour trip, but Lorraine and Flicka lucked out. A man who trained race horses offered Flicka a free luxury ride to Jacksonville in his empty top-of-the-line horse trailer. Flicka—along with their corgis, Amy and Si—moved to Jacksonville in 1988, too.

Lorraine and Rick Hendricks worked to keep their marriage together. They were both nice people, but they had little in common—beyond Katherine. Lorraine was a physical woman who craved the outdoor life and the exercise she was used to. In the beginning of their marriage they had done things together—Lorraine had even learned to rappel down cliffs with Rick's reserve unit. But now Rick tended to put his energy into his career, and he preferred to stay home on weekends. In Jacksonville, for the first time in her life, Lorraine put on weight. She wasn't bored—she was never bored—but she chafed at inactivity.

In the end, despite their hope that they could stay together for Katherine's sake, Rick and Lorraine had to acknowledge that they were living separate lives long before they finally filed for divorce. They didn't live together long after the move to Jacksonville. Rick reluctantly moved into his own apartment, but he was still a big part of his daughter's life.

When Katherine was almost six Lorraine opened her own public relations business in Jacksonville. She called it Lorelei Promotions, Ltd. Lorraine listed "communications, marketing and promotions, and special events" as the services her company offered.

Lorraine Hendricks knew the meaning of "Lorelei" in folk culture; in German mythology, the Lorelei was a siren of the Rhine River whose haunting songs lured sailors to shipwreck and death. But for her, the Lorelei rock was a special place in Germany that she had loved when she lived there as a little girl. "Lorelei" and "Lorraine" sounded somewhat alike, too, so she hoped it would be something prospective clients would remember.

Lorraine Hendricks herself was the exact opposite of a "Lorelei" personality. If anything, she gave too much of herself to help other people, spread herself way too thin.

From mid-1989 to the spring of 1990 Lorraine was incredibly busy as she re-entered the business world. Her Miami-Fort Lauderdale credentials opened doors in Jacksonville. She was especially talented at putting on conventions and festivals where huge numbers of people had to be transported, housed, fed, and entertained. She thrived on the myriad details and logistics that would have daunted most people. She and her friend and associate, Ruth Straley, working with the American Society of Military Comptrollers, brought 3,000 people into Jacksonville for their annual convention. It was the largest convention ever held in Jacksonville and a huge success.

Lorraine managed a Mature Life Expo, the first of its type for Jacksonville, and her ideas helped make the 1989 Gator Bowl memorable. Lorraine orchestrated the West Virginia pre-game pep rally and a sixties vintage sock hop featuring the one and only Chubby Checker doing "The Twist" and all of his other hits.

Lorraine didn't like to travel, because it meant being away from Katherine—but wherever she was, no matter how busy she was, Lorraine never failed to stop everything at Katherine's bedtime and call home to tuck her little girl in—at least verbally. One thing Katherine knew: her mother would always be there for her.

Lorraine met the man who would become one of her dearest professional and personal friends in Jacksonville as she and Ruth Straley were working on the Military Comptrollers convention. They wanted a dynamite line-up of entertainers for the closing night of the convention and contacted Mike Raleigh,* who was—and is—one of the most successful entertainment agents and producers on the east coast. Based in New York, Raleigh often came to Florida to set up shows for conventions, clubs, posh hotels, and festivals, and he could pick up a phone and arrange for almost any celebrity a client might ask for. He had built shows around Red Skelton, Rich Little, Barbara Mandrell, Lee Greenwood, and scores of other stars.

It was May 26, 1989, when Lorraine met Mike Raleigh. They liked each other immediately. He could see that she had tremendous potential in the entertainment world, and he was supportive and encouraging, introducing her to celebrities like Joan Rivers, the Smothers Brothers, Frankie Avalon, and Jim Stafford. Raleigh could bring in country and western stars, Broadway stars, television and movie headliners. Like Lorraine, Mike Raleigh could be something of a workaholic, and they quickly developed a mutual respect.

Suddenly, in her early forties, Lorraine's whole life seemed to be changing for the better; doors were opening wide for her, and she was happier than she had ever imagined she could be. Although she hadn't expected to, didn't want to, and certainly had no time to, Lorraine Hendricks met a man with whom she would fall blindingly, irrevocably, impossibly in love. Given what was to come, his name no longer matters, and identifying him would only cause him pain. Still, he would one day remark that meeting Lorraine was the most "classically magic and romantic meeting that ever could be. . . . It came as close to undeniable true love at first sight as anything I've ever experienced."

Neither Lorraine nor the man knew if their relationship could continue as romantically as it had begun, and they moved cautiously, in awe of their feelings. In a sense, she was like a high school girl. She took her new love to Miami to introduce him to Carol Worley, and the moment she got home she called Carol and said, "Well, what do you think of him? Isn't he wonderful?"

Carol agreed that he was, indeed, wonderful. He was someone she would never have pictured with Lorraine, and yet they seemed to belong together. "But Lorraine was being careful. She had agonized over her divorce from Rick, wanting to do the right thing, and she was moving slowly, but I could tell they were so much in love."

In the meantime Lorraine plunged deeper into her growing business. Mike Raleigh helped her and Ruth Straley set up the program for the final night of their huge Jacksonville Conference. He arranged to have Gary Morris, whose operatic voice had thrilled New York audiences in *Les Misérables* and who starred on Broadway with Linda Ronstadt in *La Bohème*, headline the show. Morris is also famous for his crossover hit "Wind Beneath My Wings." The words to that song would always be special to Lorraine Hendricks.

For another event, the 1989 Night of the Stars, on New Year's Eve, Mike Raleigh and Lorraine put on a show with Jim Stafford, Joan Rivers, Danny Gans, the impressionist, and the Bill Allred Orchestra. Lorraine picked Joan Rivers up at the airport and escorted her back to the hotel before the show. Lorraine was never intimidated by celebrities; she treated them as she did everyone, with grace and warmth.

She worked on a fund-raiser starring the Smothers Brothers for the Big Brothers and Big Sisters in Jacksonville. Mike Raleigh remembers seeing tiny Katherine Hendricks in June, 1989, sitting on the late Gamble Rogers's lap backstage, giggling while he "taught" her how to play his guitar. For Raleigh it is a bittersweet memory; the beloved folk singer and songwriter would die a hero soon after as Rogers tried to rescue a drowning victim.

Some of the evenings Lorraine planned *were* extravaganzas with major celebrities like Joan Rivers and the Smothers Brothers; others were more modest. Whichever, Lorraine was adept at judging what her clients needed and coordinating the host of details for an evening or a weekend that would be memorable for both the convention attendees and their spouses and children, something to make up for the sometimes dreary banquets and long-winded speeches that mark most business conventions.

Lorraine and Rick Hendricks had parted amicably—so amicably, in fact, that theirs was a "do-it-yourself" divorce, with their legal advice furnished by a divorce kit. Neither wanted to take advantage of the other.

Their divorce was to have been final by March 4, 1990, but the judge they appeared before had asked for a modification of their divorce papers. Under child support Lorraine and Rick had written "optional," and the judge said that was much too vague a term. Although neither could envision a time when Katherine would not come first, the divorce judge thought she would be better protected if an actual amount of support or schedule of escalating support payments was specified.

Rick Hendricks could see his point, and he agreed to specify Katherine's support, and also to allow a short delay until their divorce became final. Lorraine believed, on March 4, that her divorce *was* final. She said as much to her friend, Carol Worley: "It's over; it's a done deal."

Their marriage hadn't exploded—it had just wound down until there was nothing left. Lorraine was sad about that; she had expected to be married to only one man—and forever—but her life hadn't turned out that way.

Lorraine's parents had sold their house in Connecticut and moved to a condominium in Jacksonville so that they would be on hand to care for Katherine after school.

After so many years working on her career, and despite the half dozen years she had taken off to give Katherine a good start, everything Lorraine touched turned to gold. That didn't mean she would give up her volunteer work or her close ties with St. Joseph's Catholic Church. She still taught Spanish at the church school. Lorraine was an indefatigable woman who found time for everyone who needed her.

Lorraine Hendricks was always in a hurry; she tried to crowd so much into her life. Her business wasn't something that could be worked on a nine-to-five basis. Even though she dreaded raising her daughter alone, it was a challenge she was confident she could meet.

In her mind, that spring, there was no challenge she couldn't handle.

10

It was a watershed time then for two Florida couples in 1989. Two marriages—two marriages among thousands in Florida that year—were coming to a close.

Lorraine and Rick Hendricks had already agreed to divorce when Tim Harris invited Sandy out for dinner on September 27, 1989. Although she had been pleasantly surprised, it would turn out to be a meal Sandy would never forget, an evening that would haunt her for years. It was to have been a birthday celebration for Sandy, who would turn twenty-seven on October 6th. Tim would be working a night shift on her birthday, so he told her they would celebrate early.

It wasn't a fancy restaurant, but Sandy didn't mind. It was a rare thing for them to go out without the children.

Their food had just arrived when Tim ducked his head and blurted, "I think you should know. I'm seeing another woman."

Sandy stared at him, stunned. She was taken completely off guard. Yes, Tim had continued to flirt with her friends, her sisters, practically every woman he saw. But she had had absolutely no idea that he might be having an affair. They had promised to be faithful to each other when they got married, and she believed that they had both kept their vows. They argued, certainly. And Tim drove her crazy with worry about finances because of his "toys," but Sandy had never even suspected there was another woman.

She looked at Tim and saw that he was calmly eating his meal. He glanced up and said, "Go on—eat your food before it gets cold."

She couldn't swallow. She could scarcely breathe. How could he have told her something like that and not realize what it would do to her? From the way Tim was acting, he might just as well have said that it looked as if it was going to rain.

Sandy Harris had long since grown accustomed to that peculiar flatness in her husband's manner, as if the emotions that rocked other people to their bones only drifted over him like a slight breeze. But this was truly incomprehensible to her. Tim had just told her that he was seeing another woman, told her in the middle of what was to have been a celebration of her birthday, and he was sitting across from her chewing his food as if their whole world hadn't just shifted off center and threatened to crash.

Sandy peppered Tim with questions. He wouldn't tell her the woman's name. He wouldn't tell her what she did. "All he would say was that she was a 'professional' woman, and that could have meant anything."

"How long has this been going on?" Sandy asked.

"A couple of weeks, maybe."

"You're sleeping with her, aren't you?"

Tim shook his head. "No. I've never had sex with her. It's not what you think. We just talk."

"You *talk?*"

"I don't see why you're getting so bent out of shape. We just talk."

"Then why won't you tell me who she is?"

"It doesn't matter. I'm going to keep on talking to her."

Sick to her stomach, Sandy pushed her full plate away. Forever after, when her birthday came around, she would remember that terrible night, the first time she became aware that Tim wasn't just flirting with women to tease her, he was having an affair. And that he had chosen her birthday celebration to tell her. Sandy never believed for a moment that he was seeing some woman solely for conversation. How dumb did he think she was? She was no longer the naïve sixteen-year-old that Tim once knew, but he seemed to feel he could tell her anything and she'd swallow it.

When he finally saw how upset Sandy was, Tim took her home. Quite probably he realized that he had made a terrible tactical mistake by telling her about the other woman. But it was too late.

They fought. Sandy demanded to know who her rival was, and Tim wouldn't answer. He turned away, ignoring her.

She was infuriated by his refusal to have a discussion with her. "You're just like your father."

For once in their marriage she had found words that would get a reaction out of Tim. He turned back, white-faced with rage. "No! No! I'm nothing at all like my father."

Perhaps he was; perhaps not. Sandy had seen the estrangement widen between her husband and his parents. He might look like them—those two classically handsome people—but he acted as though he were a changeling child dropped into a family he had never bonded with. Tim's brother David was the only one vaguely like Tim. David had been a cop, too, but he'd been fired from the force. What had happened while Tim was growing up to make him treat women like dirt? Sandy often wondered.

Tim, who had never been a man to grasp subtlety, was anything but subtle about his pursuit of another woman. A few days after Sandy's disastrous birthday "party" he told her he was going fishing. After he had left, Sandy discovered he hadn't even bothered to take his fishing poles.

After Tim broke his news to Sandy about his other woman he apparently expected their marriage to go on as before. Sandy's life had imploded, blown all to pieces, and she walked through the rubble, dazed. Always before she had forgiven Tim for everything. But this time she could not let it rest. She was as obsessed as every betrayed wife is, needing to know the details and yet dreading what she might learn. What Sandy did learn made her feel worse.

"I started asking questions and asking questions," Sandy said. "I finally got more information out of several different people, and everything started fitting together. Tim confessed everything to me. He'd been seeing her for four years!"

Sandy was as shocked to find out that Tim had been sneaking out to meet DeeLisa for more than four years as she had been to learn that he was unfaithful. "The only time he wasn't seeing her was when he was going through the dog training with Shadow."

This man, her husband, had been difficult to live with, but the one thing Sandy had been sure of was that he was as faithful to her as she had been to him. That commitment had been the glue that held their marriage together. It hadn't mattered what her family thought or what the neighbors thought. She and Tim had pledged their fidelity to each other, and at some point, Sandy had believed, Tim would grow up, and they would have a marriage that was an equal partnership.

Now that hope had ended. Tim Harris hadn't changed one iota from the overgrown boy he had been when Sandy herself was sixteen. Only now they had two babies and a house and cars and boats. She knew that they were going to lose everything, but worst of all, she had lost the love of her life.

Sandy found out that DeeLisa Davis was almost ten years older than Tim, divorced with young children, a woman with long bleached-blond hair, and with a slender figure not that different from Sandy's. *Why?* Sandy couldn't understand. She knew that *she* was prettier than DeeLisa, and she was certainly younger. Tim had always hated long hair—at least he said he did—and yet he had chosen to cheat with a woman who had hair very much like his wife's.

Sandy Harris tried to hide from her family the fact that her marriage was disintegrating, hoping still that there would be some way to salvage it. She knew that once she told her mother, Pat Wessendorf would never forgive Tim. And so she bided her time, but now Sandy was on the alert. Tim promised her that he wouldn't see DeeLisa anymore, but Sandy didn't believe him. Like any woman who learns she has been lied to for years, she was poised to prevent that from ever happening again.

Always before when Tim had been called out to work an accident, she had believed that that was where he was going when he roared away from their home in his patrol car. She no longer believed that. She found that Tim had often pretended that DeeLisa was a patrol dispatcher calling him out. He hadn't gone out on patrol business at all; he had simply driven over to DeeLisa's house to spend stolen hours with her.

"I took the mileage on his car, wrote it down," Sandy remembered. "One time he said he was working security down in West Palm Beach, moonlighting while they built the mall down there. Well, the odometer came out to exactly the mileage to DeeLisa's house and back."

Tim and Sandy tried marriage counseling in early November. Tim insisted that he was no longer seeing DeeLisa and that he wanted to make his marriage work. Tim was lying to both Sandy and the counselor. It didn't take Sandy long to find out that Tim was still seeing DeeLisa as much as ever.

One night Tim was called out by the "dispatcher," but his patrol car was being repaired. He told Sandy he was going to drive his truck to another trooper's house and borrow his patrol unit. Sandy waited a few minutes, then called the other trooper and asked to speak to Tim.

"Tim's not here," the trooper said, mystified. "I haven't seen Tim for weeks."

Sandy wasn't mystified. She knew Tim was with DeeLisa. Sandy finally gave up. She filed for divorce the next day. It was late November, 1989. One would expect that Tim would have been relieved. He had treated Sandy as an annoyance, an impediment, for years. Instead he was horrified. He was stunned and full of disbelief that Sandy would leave him. He pleaded with her to change her mind.

"I just want someone to care about me," he said.

"It's funny, I guess," Sandy Harris said. "He never said 'I love you,' or 'I don't want to lose you.' He just said, 'I want someone to care about *me.*'

"It wasn't so much that he didn't want to lose me," Sandy Harris said sadly. "It was that he didn't want anyone else to have me."

The day after the Harris divorce action notice appeared in the local newspaper, Sandy's phone rang at 2 a.m. The caller hung up without speaking. Sandy suspected it was DeeLisa. She didn't know where Tim was—but apparently he wasn't with DeeLisa either. The next morning, Tim phoned Sandy at work to say that DeeLisa had called him and said that if he didn't move out and stay with her, she would see that he was fired. Sandy didn't know whether DeeLisa had really said that, but Tim insisted that he didn't want DeeLisa; he wanted Sandy. "You're the only one I love," he promised.

Tim had so much of his salary tied up in payments on his boats, trucks, and cars, not to mention their third house mortgage, that he told Sandy he couldn't afford to pay rent on another place. Sandy felt sorry for him and said that he could stay in the house—but not as her husband—until they figured out some plan. She would live her life, and he would live his. The divorce was going through, she insisted, and his living in their home was only temporary.

Tim tried futilely to talk Sandy into dropping her divorce action. "He was out of control most of the time, breaking things around the house. He even broke his own expensive camera. He lost interest in everything," Sandy recalled. "I was afraid he would lose his job."

If Sandy was civil to him, Tim took her softness as a sign that she was going to drop the divorce. He saw things the way he wanted to. When he came home from seeing DeeLisa and Sandy let him know she knew where he had been, he thought that meant she cared. Sandy was resolute; her mind was made up, but Tim saw vacillation and indecision because he wanted to. He *needed* to. He was a dog in the manger, and no woman who had ever "belonged" to him had the right to leave him—not until *he* decided he wanted her gone.

In his view, Sandy belonged to him.

Sandy Harris was a beautiful woman. Suddenly Tim seemed to realize that. He was obsessed with maintaining control over her. Although *he* was free to come and go and to see DeeLisa, he didn't want Sandy going anywhere.

She wasn't *dating*, certainly; she had her hands full with her job and her two babies.

Tim railed against what he considered Sandy's family's interference in his marriage. Pat was vocal about her opinion that Sandy should get the divorce as soon as she could. In fact, when Sandy hadn't filed the moment she learned about DeeLisa Davis, Pat was furious with her daughter.

"My mom didn't even speak to me for a couple of weeks," Sandy recalled. "She thought I took too long to decide to leave Tim after I found out he was cheating."

That was Pat. She saw the world in black and white, and Tim had stepped miles over the line of what she would accept in a son-in-law.

Susan and Don Dappen knew the situation, of course. They tried to mind their own business, but the problem only grew more bizarre and more fraught with danger. Tim was jealous of Sandy, absolutely poleaxed when he realized that she was not going to take him back and that she intended to start a life without him as soon as their divorce was final.

Don Dappen had seen seemingly normal men turn into obsessive stalkers when their women left them. He had seen men who would rather have a woman dead than let her go. And he had never found Tim exactly "normal" to begin with. He was a loner whose behavior had always been unpredictable.

Dappen worried what Tim might do next. He hoped that Tim's career—which had always been so important to him—would keep him from doing anything crazy.

Tim had acknowledged to Don that he had "screwed up" when he started dating DeeLisa. He had first promised he would never see her again, but later he asked advice about how he could keep both his wife and his mistress in his life. Don had told him to make up his mind and make it up fast; he didn't tell Sandy, but he told Tim to clean up his act. When Tim realized Don hadn't said anything about it to Sandy, Tim would say later—and incorrectly—that Don "was neutral—he was fine. . . ."

On December 9, 1989, Tim's obsession with Sandy boiled over. Susan, knowing that Sandy needed desperately to get out for a while, had invited her sister to go to the UpTown Lounge in Vero Beach with her. It was a Saturday night, and Don had duty at the Vero Beach Police Department. They wouldn't be out late, and it was a hometown kind of place where the two sisters could go without being bothered.

Tim Harris—who had been a desultory father at best—had

suddenly become generous in his offers to baby-sit his children. He had asked Sandy if he could watch the children on that Saturday evening. As he recalled it, "She said 'No,' that she was going to take them over to Nana's, and I said, 'You know, I can watch the kids. I don't care if . . . if you want to go out, that's fine, you know. I would appreciate it if you just didn't go out with other guys, until we're, you know, finally divorced.'"

The handsome state patrolman was nothing if not ambiguous. His recall is that he was understanding and accommodating. His wife told confidantes a different scenario.

"Tim would come up behind me and put his hands around my neck and say, 'I could snap your neck and kill you right now.' One time I finally said, 'Go ahead and do it then.' He let go and walked away."

On the night of December 9th Tim Harris followed Sandy and Susan Dappen to the Vero Beach Police Department, where they stopped in to see Don Dappen before heading over to the UpTown. Dappen heard a commotion in the hallway and walked out to see his about-to-be-ex-brother-in-law staring strangely at Sandy. Tim began to shout at Sandy, apparently oblivious to the fact that he was in a police station hallway and that Don, in command that night, was listening.

Tim Harris was clearly out of control, blind with rage. Don had vowed to stay out of Sandy's marital troubles, but Tim had gone too far. "I always told myself that if Sandy or the kids were in *jeopardy*, all bets were off," Don said.

"Get out of here, Tim," Dappen said. "That's enough. Get out of the police department or you'll be sorry."

Tim Harris could see that Dappen meant business, and he stalked out of the Vero Beach Police Department, leapt into his truck, and burned rubber as he roared away.

Worried about his wife and sister-in-law, Dappen followed Susan's car to the parking lot behind the lounge. In moments he saw Tim running across the lot toward Sandy, shouting, "Sandy! Come home! You're supposed to be with me!"

Don Dappen jumped out of his car and started to say, "Tim—"

"Stay the fuck out of it!" Tim shouted furiously.

"No, I won't stay out of it," Dappen said firmly. "You're in a public place."

Tim Harris, who rarely swore, let loose a string of vulgarities, turned his back on his brother-in-law, and followed Sandy into the club. If Sandy had had any hopes of sitting with her sister and having a quiet drink or two, they were dashed. Tim insisted that he had to talk with her, making such a spectacle that people turned around to stare at them.

Don Dappen could see that things were escalating. *He* didn't want to have to be the Vero Beach officer who arrested Tim—if it got to that point. More than that, he sensed that Tim *wanted* to get into a physical fight with him, and Dappen wasn't going to let that happen. He called in one of his officers and explained the situation, that it was a marital hassle, that Tim was a state trooper. He asked his officer to keep an eye on the situation and keep it as low profile as possible. "If we can solve this thing peacefully, then do it. If he crosses the line, then take him. Act as you would in any other situation where you didn't know the people involved."

The young cop did a good job. Tim left, but Don waited outside, out of sight, watching.

Tim came back not once, but twice. "The guy was popping up from out of the blue," Dappen remembered. "Sandy and Sue went in the bar, and all of a sudden Tim just raced into the bar."

It was a tough situation for Don Dappen. The bar was full of people; he didn't know what his brother-in-law might do. He decided to speak to the bouncers and ask them to keep an eye on Tim, and they said they would.

"It wasn't five minutes before Tim came out of the bar with Sandy. He had his arm over her shoulder, pinning her head against him— not applying any pressure that I could see, but she couldn't move away from him."

"Sandy," Don said, "where you going?"

Sandy had given up. "I'm going home with him. I don't want to cause any more problems. I don't want him to go to jail, Donny."

Don Dappen was frustrated, but he had never been a man to stick his nose in other people's business—if he could help it. "Sandy," he said firmly, "you don't have to do this. I want you to understand you have other options."

"No," she said. "I need to get out of here."

"O.K." Dappen watched as Tim led Sandy away in a headlock; he looked back at his brother-in-law with a triumphant grin, a grin that said, See, she belongs to me, and you can't do anything about it.

"I have to admit"—Dappen grimaced—"I really wanted a piece out of him, but I didn't say anything. It was their deal."

How odd, really, that Tim Harris, for whom fidelity was a foreign

word, was convinced that his wife was cheating on him. If Sandy
Harris thought her life had been hell before, she now began to see
how bad things could be.

Don Dappen worried about his sister-in-law, and he was furious
with Tim Harris for behaving like a foul-mouthed teenager, both in
the Vero Beach police station and in the UpTown.

Dappen went back to his car and called his dispatcher, "Get me
FHP. Get me whichever supervisor is on duty, and tell him I want to
talk to him. He can come to my office, or I'll meet him someplace."

Within ten minutes Lieutenant Gary Morgan walked into Dappen's office. Dappen liked Morgan; he had known him for years.

"Gary," Dappen said. "I could have arrested Tim. You've got to
take a good look at him. The guy's unbalanced; he shouldn't be out
there stopping people on the Interstate."

Morgan knew about Tim's impending divorce, and he knew Tim
had been acting out of character—or at least out of the character he
had always presented to the Patrol. But Morgan wasn't Tim's primary
supervisor; Tim's supervisor was stationed down in Lantana, sixty
miles south. Both Dappen and Morgan talked to him by phone, and
he asked for a written report.

Don Dappen wrote that report and left it at the desk of the Vero
Beach Police Department for pickup by the Florida Highway Patrol
the next day.

"I don't know what happened to it," Dappen said. "It mysteriously
disappeared; it never made it into Tim's jacket. I don't know who
picked it up—it wasn't Gary Morgan, I know that."

The Florida Highway Patrol at least had Dappen's phone call, and
they knew that Tim Harris's job performance had dropped—but not
nearly enough for them to deem him unfit for duty. Besides, the
UpTown incident had occurred off duty, and it involved mainly a
domestic dispute—part of Harris's private life. They decided to keep
an eye on the situation, but they took no disciplinary action against
Harris.

Police work—all police work—is hard on marriages. Every working cop knows that. There are so many factors involved. For one
thing, uniforms attract some women like an aphrodisiac, and the
opportunity to cheat is always there, far more than it might be for an
accountant or an insurance salesman. Many officers want to leave the
job at the station, refusing to talk with their wives about what they
have seen during an eight-hour watch. Sometimes it's too ugly and
tragic to share and to remember. The worse things get out on the

street, the more officers want to keep their own loved ones sacro-sanct. Even though their spouses protect them out of love and concern, wives—and, with a growing number of female officers, *husbands*—often feel cut off and unimportant.

Cops form a circle that shuts out the rest of the world, and nobody who really understands blames them. They are often targets of ridicule for "civilians." Together, they all speak the same language, a language the rest of the population doesn't understand. No one who hasn't been there when the blood is still warm and gunpowder laces the air can possibly understand the stress, the pressure, the terrible sights, noises, and smells that policemen deal with. A cop's partner is often the closest human being in his life. Closer, indeed, in terms of shared experience and mutual heartache, than a cop's wife.

A lot of marriages crumble. A lot of cops are less than proficient on the job for a while. The vast majority of them emerge from divorce and are soon up to speed again.

It was ironic that Tim's dream of working on the felony program had finally come to pass just as his marriage was ending. Tim and Trooper Dean Burrows would both be working felonies under the supervision of Lt. Gary Morgan.

Even before Don Dappen's call Morgan was aware that Tim's work performance was faltering. It was obvious to Tim's fellow troopers and to his superiors that he was not the outstanding patrolman that he had been. Tim Harris had been the most gung-ho trooper in his district as he relentlessly followed and stopped speeders and drug-gers. His averages had always been way up there. They no longer were.

"His performance was definitely acceptable," Morgan hastened to point out. "But not what he was normally capable of doing."

The Patrol was between a rock and a hard place. They couldn't really take a man off active duty because his home life was chaotic, and he was still doing his job. As it turned out, their decision about the stability of Tim Harris was a tragically bad call.

Tim's unexplained absences from home were as transparent as cellophane, and Sandy, through necessity, was growing more crafty. She pushed "redial" when Tim had made a phone call before leaving the house. Invariably, DeeLisa's voice answered. And Tim's mileage *never* matched the distances he told Sandy he would be traveling.

Tim often deliberately provoked an argument with Sandy so he could storm out of the house and be gone all night. After one obvious altercation Sandy sighed and said, "Tim, I'm too tired to fight with you. If you want to visit your girlfriend, just go!"

He left, but he came back in no time. "It was no fun seeing DeeLisa," Sandy said. "Not if I knew he was there."

It didn't take a psychiatrist to see that Tim Harris was coming unglued. Twice in January, 1990, he asked for leaves of absence from the Patrol so he could work on his marriage. In all his years on the force he had rarely called in sick. Now he did—often.

By late January, 1990, Sandy Harris realized that she and Tim could no longer live in the same house. She suggested that they needed "two weeks apart" to get their heads straightened out. Maybe then they could talk together and figure out where they were going.

Reluctantly, Tim agreed to move out for two weeks. Secretly, Sandy hoped that Tim's leaving would be permanent. He seemed afraid to go it alone, and he probably would vacillate between two women until he was eighty if somebody didn't make him get off the dime. He couldn't give up DeeLisa, and he couldn't give up Sandy. Well, then, Sandy decided, let him live with DeeLisa. Sandy only wanted her freedom. She was weary of being lied to and uneasy when she sensed his car trailing behind her, feeling eyes watching her in the night.

Tim Harris's friends on the Florida Highway Patrol tried, in February, 1990, to help him get his life together. He had never been really close with any of them off-duty, and he had never talked about his private life. But all they had to do was look at him to see he was in bad shape. He had weighed about 230 pounds, and now he looked as if he had lost at least forty pounds. He had deep circles under his eyes and looked haggard. Tim's marital problems seemed to be an open secret; the formerly taciturn trooper talked of nothing but getting back together with his wife.

Lt. Gary Morgan saw that Tim was depressed. "I told him there was light at the end of the tunnel," Morgan recalled.

Over and over Tim admitted that he had "screwed up," but he had repented, he said, and all he cared about was his wife and his family. But his wife had a cold and unforgiving heart, he confided earnestly. Tim did not mention that he was still deeply involved with DeeLisa Davis.

Indeed, Tim's friends in the Florida Highway Patrol felt so sorry for him that they called Gary Morgan to see if he could find a spot where Tim could stay. Morgan owned a house on Seventh Place in Vero

Beach, but he wasn't currently living there; he was temporarily working down in Palm Beach. Morgan already had a young trooper living in his house to keep an eye on it. Sure, he said, he would ask the other officer if he would mind if Tim—and, of course, Shadow, his dog—bunked there for two weeks.

Morgan let Tim know that he had a free place to stay, and that he would leave a key under the mat for him the following Friday.

But Tim didn't show up; Lt. Morgan was at his Vero Beach house all weekend, mowing the lawn and doing minor repairs, but he didn't hear from Tim Harris. When Gary Morgan came north the next weekend he saw that Tim had apparently moved in. Harris's personal belongings were in the spare bedroom and bathroom.

Actually, Tim Harris's presence in his lieutenant's house was wraithlike. Morgan didn't see *him*. He saw Tim's things and his dog. When the two weeks were up Tim called and asked Gary Morgan if he could stay longer. "I told him it kind of messed up my weekends," Morgan recalled, "because [with him there] I couldn't come home on weekends—so he said he would stay only during the week and be out of there by Friday night."

Tim was true to his word. He was gone the next Saturday when Morgan drove up, but Tim's dog, Shadow, was there, and Morgan gave the K-9 dog food and water.

The next weekend Tim's belongings were all gone, and so was his dog. He had left a note on the kitchen table thanking his lieutenant for letting him stay.

Tim had other places to stay. He was welcome to spend some nights at his brother's house, and sometimes he slept in his new truck at one of the rest stops along I-95, or on his new boat. And of course, he was always welcome to stay with DeeLisa. She would have liked him to be with her every night.

But now Tim Harris wanted only to spend his nights with the woman he had devised such elaborate plans to sneak away from.

When Sandy had found the acre lot in Citrus Hideaway, its isolation and distance from other homes were part of its charm for her. Living there alone with her babies, aware that Tim might be out of the house physically, but that he still considered it, her, and the children totally his possessions, Sandy wished mightily for the sight of lit windows next door or across the street when dusk fell. Instead, the lots were so big that she could see only black beyond her windows.

If Tim wanted to get in, Sandy knew he could do it easily. Tim knew every inch of the house that had once been symbolic of a bright future for them. He should; he had built it himself. And now that he was banished from it—if only for two weeks—he began to let himself into the house while Sandy was at work or at her parents' house.

High up in the rafters Tim found a spot in the pink insulation and formed a depression there. Carefully he inserted a tape recorder, splicing wires so that the recorder would turn on automatically when the phone receiver was lifted. He hid a second tape recorder in the mechanism of a sofa bed. All of Sandy's calls—in or out—would now be recorded on tape, waiting for Tim to listen to them at his leisure.

She had no idea.

Tim didn't move in with DeeLisa. He stayed for a few weeks with his brother, David, and his wife, Melissa. But David's wife was expecting a baby, and it was crowded in their mobile home.

The first night Sandy heard noises against the side of the house where Tim had built a pen for Shadow, she was terrified. Jarred from her sleep, she lay rigid in bed and heard heavy footsteps moving around upstairs.

With her heart in her throat she tiptoed toward the children's rooms. In Timmy's room she saw a shadow on the floor next to his bed.

It was Tim, sleeping there beside his son. If she hadn't been through so much anguish with her husband, Sandy might have thought it sad or even touching. Instead she sighed and went back to the master bedroom.

Tim broke in almost every night after that. Sandy would hear him as he balanced atop Shadow's pen and then when he stepped onto the roof. He didn't come near her, and he was usually gone in the morning. But if Sandy got a phone call, she often heard a soft click, and she knew that Tim had lifted the receiver of the upstairs extension, that he was listening, his huge hand over the mouthpiece of the phone upstairs so she couldn't hear him breathing.

Sometimes Tim didn't sneak into the second floor window. That didn't allow Sandy to sleep any easier. Looking out in the dusk, she often saw Tim sitting in his truck back in the pines.

Just watching her.

Even when she didn't see him, Sandy knew that Tim could very well be close by. And she remembered how many times he had told her he could snap her neck in two so easily.

11

In Jacksonville, 165 miles north of Vero Beach, Lorraine Hendricks's business was doing wonderfully. Lorelei Promotions was selected to handle the opening of the Carriage Club retirement village. The opulent residences for senior citizens demanded an equally elegant grand opening, and Lorraine didn't disappoint them. She had white horses, carriages, and everyone dressed as if they were attending a magnificent ball at the turn of the century. Lorraine herself wore a satin off-the-shoulder gown, long white gloves, and a triple strand of pearls, and her thick, gleaming hair was swept into a pompadour topped with a diamond tiara.

On February 10, 1990, Lorraine assisted the Heart Guild of Northeast Florida in producing a benefit during the week of Valentine's Day. She presented the heartthrob of the late fifties, Frankie Avalon, and once again she helped to carry off a night to remember, and one that brought a bonanza to heart research in Florida.

Blissfully in love, seeing the career that she had always longed for do so well, there was nothing more in the world that Lorraine Hendricks could ask for.

In February, 1990, Sandy Harris had no idea that a tape recorder whirred away up in the attic, keeping track of every call she received and every call she made. She didn't know that Tim broke into the house during the day, too, so that he could change the tapes in the recorder. Nor did Sandy know that Tim had taken her office key from her purse and had a duplicate made.

Valentine's Day—the day meant for lovers—was a nightmare for Sandy Harris. After midnight on February 13 Tim didn't break into his own house; instead he unlocked the office where Sandy worked, an office full of private financial records. Stealthily, carefully, he spent hours carrying out a surprise he had for Sandy.

By the time Sandy Harris got to work on Valentine's Day her job hung by a thread. Her boss was furious and upset that someone had crept around their offices during the night. Bewildered, Sandy walked into her office—or as far inside it as she could get. The room was filled with red and white balloons, and there was a huge box of chocolates on her desk. As Sandy tried to move around balloons were compressed against the wall or punctured by something sharp on her desk, and they popped loudly. Numbly, Sandy looked at the curious faces of her fellow employees staring at her, and then at her boss, and she burst into tears. Her life had been reduced to this. She had no place that was private. No haven at all.

Sobbing, she walked out of her office and drove home. He was the last person on earth she wanted to see, but Tim was there waiting, grinning in happy expectation—as if he thought she had rushed home to thank him for her wonderful Valentine's surprise. She looked at him, horrified. He actually *believed* that she would be pleased by what he had done.

Sandy brushed by him and headed for the bathroom, where she could lock the door and shut him away, if only for a few minutes. She saw a tape recorder there, a machine she had never seen before. Tim hadn't expected her to come home in the middle of the day, and he had apparently been listening to something on the tape.

Sandy turned it on. Puzzled, she heard her own voice, and then it dawned on her that somehow Tim had been taping her phone calls. But *how?* She listened to an innocuous conversation she had had with her sister and heard each of them hang up. The recorder rolled on, and another call began. But this time it wasn't her own voice that Sandy heard, but Tim's. Tim was talking to DeeLisa, and he was begging his mistress to let him come and visit. He sounded every bit as desperate to be with DeeLisa as he did when he beseeched Sandy to take him back.

My God, Sandy wondered, was he crazy? All the balloons and chocolate and sneaking in every night to be in the house with her, and here was his voice pleading with DeeLisa the same way he pleaded with her.

Grimly, Sandy turned the volume up until Tim could hear his own voice calling DeeLisa. Sandy heard the sound of his feet running toward her, and then he hit the door, pounding and yelling at her to let him in. The door buckled; Tim was clearly trying to break it down.

Sandy opened it and stepped back, clutching the tape in her hand. He lunged for her, and she twisted away and ran.

"He chased me around the house, trying to get the tape. I had never, *never* seen him that angry."

Tim Harris had secrets, his own secrets—and Sandy had stumbled on one. And with that he had lost any chance at all that she would ever take him back. He hadn't changed. He still lied. All of his determined courting wasn't worth anything now that she had the proof of his continued infidelity in her hand.

Even so, Sandy found Tim's anger out of all proportion to what had happened. It wasn't as though she hadn't caught him in lies about DeeLisa before—not once, but over and over and over. Stubbornly clinging to the tape, Sandy looked back at the man who had been her husband for almost nine years, and she scarcely recognized him. His face was red and contorted, and fury surrounded him like a miasmic cloud.

Sandy Harris was a realist; she had to be. She knew that Tim's own character flaws had led them to where they were in February, 1990—but she blamed DeeLisa Davis, too. DeeLisa Davis had done everything she could to break up Sandy's marriage. The two women had never met face-to-face, although Sandy knew DeeLisa's voice and had seen her from a distance.

She was about to see her close up. Sue Dappen and Sandy took their children to the skating rink in Vero Beach every Saturday. "One Saturday," Sandy remembered, "I saw DeeLisa there. Somehow, I knew it was her—and then Jennifer said, 'Look! There's DeeLisa!' and I realized that Tim had been taking our kids over to see his mistress."

Sandy stared curiously at the woman who was sitting on a bench taking off her skates. She was much older than Sandy was, and she was attractive, but not astoundingly so. Before Sue could stop her Sandy skated over to DeeLisa Davis and waited until DeeLisa looked up.

"I guess you know who I am, but I don't know who you are," Sandy said sarcastically.

"Don't talk in front of my kids," DeeLisa said.

"Well, *my* kids know all about you," Sandy said.

DeeLisa grabbed her skates and her children and ran out of the rink. "She couldn't get away fast enough," Sandy said bitterly. It really didn't matter to Sandy anymore, but she was remembering all those times Tim had lied to her about DeeLisa.

On Saturday night, March 3, 1990, one of Sandy's girlfriends got married, and Sandy was asked to be her matron of honor. A year earlier she would have asked Tim to go with her. Now she refused his offer to go along. She had a good time—for the first time in years. She didn't stay late; she wanted to be home with the kids. When one of the groomsmen called her later to ask her to join him for a drink, she laughed and talked to him for a few minutes. She forgot that her phone was probably still wired to one of Tim's damnable tape recorders.

Sandy refused the date, but it didn't matter. Tim retrieved that tape later that evening, and he was livid that Sandy had actually defied him and gone to the wedding without him. He was sure she must have come on to the guy who called her. Every time Sandy thought Tim couldn't get any angrier, he proved to her that he could. He had held in his rage for most of their marriage, showing it only by refusing to speak to her for days. He no longer repressed his anger. She wondered if he had had that cauldron of rage inside all those years.

If she hadn't been such a nervous wreck, the double standard Sandy was living under might have been laughable. She had no interest in other men. One day she talked to one of the troopers that Tim sometimes went fishing with. When Sandy argued that Tim had no right to be sobbing and whining and furious over their divorce— not after he had cheated on her for almost five years—the trooper blurted, "Well, what did you expect him to do when he was working third watch? Just hang around the house while you were working?"

"I just hung around the house while he was on duty nights. I didn't cheat on him."

"That's different."

Why? Sandy wondered. Why was it different when Tim cheated? Why should he be so bored and horny during the daytime when she was at work? She didn't believe a man was entitled to betray a marriage any more than a woman was.

Sandy Harris was frantically trying to juggle all the problems in her life. She realized in early March, 1990, that she could no longer continue paying the huge mortgage on the new house. Regretfully and quietly she put it up for sale. She agreed to let the realtor hold an open house on Sunday, March 4th.

Tim found out. Even though the realtor didn't have a car with her company's name on it, Tim knew. Of course he knew. He was monitoring every call in and out, every conversation that took place inside Sandy's house. He had backup tape recorders. It was only a day after Tim had been so angry about the wedding she attended alone; Sandy's selling their home was, to him, the most flagrant example of her shoving him out of her life, making decisions without him.

For the first time Sandy Harris had moments of fear. Real fear. She wondered if she would ever get away from Tim. She wondered if they would both die before he let her go. . . .

12

Since Lorraine Hendricks had lived in the Fort Lauderdale/Miami area for more than fifteen years and had lived in the Mandarin area of Jacksonville for only two, she often returned to her former home. Lorraine still drove down to Fort Lauderdale to see her physician and dentist, both family friends. The trip down I-95 was over two hundred miles, but she was used to it and drove it fairly often.

Lorraine Hendricks had a dental appointment with Dr. Joe Hilton in Fort Lauderdale on Monday, March 5, 1990. She had been having extensive dental work done with Hilton. She also was scheduled to meet with Mike Lutz of Tropical Realty at 6 p.m. on that Sunday night. Along with her parents, she owned a condo on Wimbleton Drive in Plantation, and they were considering selling it.

Most important of all, Carol Worley was about to move to Washington State, and Lorraine wanted to see her before she left. "She called me Saturday morning—March third," Carol recalled. "I can hear her saying, 'Don't think you're getting out of Florida without seeing me one more time!'"

Carol said she was busy cleaning her house, and that she would finish up Sunday morning. After that she would be around the corner at her brother's house. Her phone would be disconnected, but Carol gave Lorraine her brother's number.

Lorraine said she would be in Fort Lauderdale by one the next afternoon. Carol grinned to herself; she knew Lorraine, and she doubted seriously that Lorraine was going to get out of bed by five or six and hit the road on a Sunday morning. It was a good six-hour drive. She figured Lorraine would probably come rolling in about three and planned accordingly.

Around midnight on Saturday night Lorraine talked to Mike Raleigh. She promised to call him from Miami so they could talk about a project they were working on. As always, he warned her to be careful, and as always, she assured him she would be.

In truth, Lorraine left her home on Remler Drive in Jacksonville about 8 a.m. on Sunday, March 4th. She could take care of her real estate dealings, visit with Carol, and go to her dental appointment the next day. Lorraine's busy schedule occasionally led her to drive too fast as she coordinated the many different facets of her life. She was a woman who got things done, and she could be impatient to get on to the next task, the next appointment. In fact, she had had eight speeding tickets in the previous seven years. She had commented wryly to a friend that she couldn't afford another speeding ticket. That was for sure; she was right next door to having her license suspended. She tried to drive right at the speed limit or under.

But, as everyone else does, Lorraine would daydream about the man she had come to love, or some business problem, or what the future held for her, and her foot would involuntarily press down harder on the accelerator. And then, too, she always listened to tapes when she traveled, and a fast beat tended to be reflected on her speedometer.

What Lorraine didn't know as she left on her March 4th trip was that her license actually *had* already been suspended. Her notification was in the mail but would not be delivered for a few more days.

It wasn't that big a deal. She could get it back if she went through the steps the State of Florida listed. "Before your driving privilege may be reinstated, you must do the following: Contact the court and meet their requirements. Any fine must be sent or delivered to the Duval County Court Clerk's address listed below. *Do not mail fine to this department.* Written certification that you have complied must be obtained from the court clerk and presented to any Driver's License examining office. You will be required to pay a $25.00 service fee. . . ."

Frank and Jodi Dombroski arrived early that Sunday morning in March to look after Katherine until Rick arrived from his apartment to take over. He had promised to be there at eleven, and he was.

Lorraine was dressed casually. She wore stone-washed jeans and a reddish-brown blouse, and she slipped moccasins onto her feet. Her Honda Accord was a 1982 model, but it ran well—except for the fact that its gas gauge didn't work. Rick always warned her to watch that, because she could run out of gas someplace on the Interstate miles from nowhere if she wasn't careful. He advised her to reset the odometer every time she filled up with gas, and then figure out how many miles she could go on a tank. When she saw that number coming up she should pull off and buy gas. She usually checked the oil, too, because the eight-year-old car tended to run a quart or two low.

But March 4 was a sunny, warm day, and Lorraine wasn't worried. She knew the road well, and she enjoyed driving alone with her tape deck's volume turned up and her earphones on so that she could enjoy the stereo effect of the music.

Lorraine called her father from the road about 10 a.m. to ask how things were going, and to talk to Katherine and tell her she would be home the next day. She also asked her dad to look for a slip of paper with Carol Worley's brother's number—which she had forgotten to bring along—so she could call ahead and tell her friend she was running a little late.

After that there were no more calls from Lorraine.

Lorraine Hendricks did not arrive at her friend Carol's house in Fort Lauderdale that Sunday afternoon by 1 p.m., and she hadn't called ahead, either. Carol wasn't worried. She expected Lorraine to be late, and she had no phone in the house she was moving out of. By three she was at her brother's place, expecting to see the little gray Honda come down the street any moment.

"When she wasn't there by three," Carol admits, "I got kind of angry. I thought she could at least have let me know she would be that late—or that she wasn't coming. That wasn't like Lorraine."

Carol dug through the stuff she had already packed and found the number for the condo in Plantation Lorraine was trying to sell. "I kept calling and calling there, and no one answered. And then I tried to call her home in Jacksonville—but of course, no one answered there. And then Lorraine's mom—Jodi—called *me* about five o'clock to see if Lorraine was with me. Of course, she wasn't."

Lorraine's father had taken it upon himself to call every Highway Patrol office along the Interstate. He introduced himself as "Major Dombroski"—which he was. He didn't say he was an army major and not a Patrol major. He wanted information on where his daughter might be. None of the Patrol offices had any report on her.

"Rick Hendricks finally called me at midnight," Carol Worley remembers. "No one had heard from Lorraine."

Lorraine had not met with real estate agent Mike Lutz in Plantation, Florida, at six. Nor did Lorraine show up for her dental appointment on Monday morning. Her estranged husband and her parents kept calling everyone they could think of to see if they might have heard from her.

No one had.

In almost every state in America there is a twenty-four-hour waiting period between the time an adult does not show up where he or she is supposed to be and the time he or she is legally considered to be a missing person. By Monday, March 5, 1990, Lorraine Marie Hendricks was listed in every computer system in the State of Florida. Her physical description, the clothes she had worn, her birth date, and her home address were all noted. In the unemotional language of the teletype there were nevertheless words that chilled: "Missing Adult, Endangered . . . Good Mental Condition . . . Foul Play Suspected . . ."

Lorraine Hendricks's frantic relatives tried to tell themselves that nothing could have happened to Lorraine on a sunny Sunday afternoon. She would never have picked up a hitchhiker, and she had planned no stops—except to buy gas—between Jacksonville and Fort Lauderdale. If she had been in an accident, the Highway Patrol would know, and they would have notified her family. As it was, the Patrol had answered just enough of their questions to make them desperately worried. They had found Lorraine's car. Just that. They had not found any trace of Lorraine or her purse, wallet, or glasses.

Florida Highway Patrolman Mike Transue, whose patrol district included the same long stretch of I-95 north and south through Indian River and St. Lucie counties that Tim Harris worked, was on the day shift on Monday, March 5th, and he had found her car. Shortly before noon he noted the 1982 silver Honda Accord parked on the right shoulder of southbound I-95, precisely at milepost 157.5.

Transue pulled in behind the Honda and walked around it. There was no one in the car, and he could see no one around it. It was a four-door model, and the front doors were unlocked. It was ripe for theft; he could see a number of items inside that might have tempted someone: a shiny red briefcase with miscellaneous papers inside, a 35mm camera, a blue and tan tote bag with expensive running shoes inside, a gray makeup bag, a Pulsar watch, headphones, a red suitcase, a pair of ankle weights, and a blue windbreaker jacket. With all that stuff still intact, he assumed the car hadn't been there long.

Transue called in a "Wants and Warrants" on Florida plate AKJ-65U and received word back that the last person known to be driving the Honda was a Jacksonville woman named Lorraine Hendricks, and that she had been reported missing. The Florida Highway Patrol dispatcher contacted the Duval County Sheriff's Office in Jacksonville, and Detective M.E. Hyde requested that the abandoned car be towed so that any evidence inside would be preserved.

The car was towed to the Courtesy Auto Service in Vero Beach. Transue put a hold on the vehicle until it could be processed by investigators.

After the car was towed away Transue sprayed red paint on the right shoulder of I-95 to mark the place where it had been.

Rick Hendricks, who was listed as co-owner of the silver Honda, was at home, trying to explain to his little girl why her mother hadn't come back as she had promised.

No one knew where Lorraine Hendricks was. Something unexpected had to have happened to her to make her walk away from her car on I-95. Or maybe she hadn't even been *in* the car by that time. No, something had occurred between wherever she had stopped to make that last phone call to her father, Frank, and the lonely spot on the Interstate now marked with paint as red as blood.

Something. But what?

Phil Williams, the cop who might just as well have remained an airline mechanic or a rock musician or a landscaper, the cop who grew up with three guys who became brutal killers, the cop who had become a superb detective, was about to step into one of the most unbelievable and grotesque cases any detective—anywhere—has ever encountered.

Williams had a personal credo. "I've always been willing to do whatever is necessary . . . and I mean *whatever* is necessary to solve a case."

Early on, when he was attending the police academy, the local police authorities were trying to solve the murder of a small girl. They came to the academy and asked for volunteers from the soon-to-be policemen; they were looking for the knife used to kill the child, and they needed all the manpower they could get.

"The nastiest job of all," Williams remembers, "was to get down in the ditch and wade that canal and search that black, silty water for the weapon. That's the job I took."

The alligators and the critters in the canal didn't bother Williams. "Canals like that were my playgrounds when I was growing up," he says laconically. Later, of course, Phil Williams and Don Dappen would wallow through similar ditches and overgrown waterways as they searched for the Domino's Pizza killers.

What Phil Williams had on March 5, 1990, was a missing woman, a car abandoned along a busy freeway, no sign whatsoever of foul play—nothing concrete at all. In the beginning it didn't seem to be that unusual a case. He expected that Lorraine Hendricks was probably going to show up in a day or so with some kind of explanation about where she had been. He had seen too many "missing" adults not to believe that. People disappeared for reasons of their own and came back for other reasons.

They began with the car. Williams met Florida Department of Law Enforcement Agent Bruce McMann at Courtesy Auto in Vero Beach. It was almost eerie how normal the car looked; its owner might have just stepped away for a moment. Lorraine's briefcase was in the rear seat, and it had business papers in it. There were two unopened pieces of luggage. Nothing had been disturbed, and both back doors were locked. The windows were all rolled up.

The two investigators saw the blue jacket on the front passenger seat; it was folded carefully over a headphone set and sunglasses. A box of Kleenex sat on the floorboard of the passenger seat. Beside it were both plastic and paper drinking cups. If anyone had sat in the passenger seat, his—or *her*—feet would have crushed the items on the floor and probably smashed the sunglasses. No, it seemed clear that only one person had been in the car, and that had been the driver.

As far as they could tell at this point, nothing was missing but the car keys, and the missing woman's purse or wallet . . . and Lorraine Hendricks herself.

"The usual suspicion would be she had a boyfriend," Williams says. "That she intended to meet someone. But the thing of it is, why didn't she just go on down to the Wayfarer and leave her car in the restaurant parking lot? It was only a mile from where her car was. Why just park it out there on 95?"

Bruce McMann and Phil Williams began processing the car, dusting for fingerprints, vacuuming the interior for hairs and fibers— or infinitesimal bits of dirt or debris that might prove vital at some future time. (The fingerprints would prove to be useless. Three weeks later the Florida Department of Law Enforcement lab would report that all prints with enough points to identify them belonged to Lorraine Hendricks.)

Lorraine Hendricks's father and her estranged husband Rick had called to say they were on their way to Vero Beach. Rick had a spare key for the Honda, and he thought he might also be able to tell them if anything was missing.

Williams talked with Rick Hendricks. He noted that Hendricks did not seem as frantically worried as Lorraine's father, Frank Dombroski, was. He didn't think much of that; he had been a detective long enough to know that people showed their emotions in vastly different ways. Hendricks told him soon after they met that he and Lorraine were divorcing. No hard feelings. No animosity. "Lorraine and I have agreed in most of the financial settlements already," Hendricks added. He said they shared a most important common bond, Katherine.

Rick Hendricks said that Lorraine was dating someone else, a man she had met through her business. Williams studied Hendricks's face; he detected no anger there over the other man. Apparently there was no *reason* for Lorraine to sneak around and meet some other man. She and Hendricks no longer lived together. This had all the signs of a friendly divorce, but he was taking nothing for granted until he checked it out.

As far as anything being missing from the Honda, Rick said that Lorraine's purse was gone. She usually carried a brown purse with a zipper and kept her wallet inside.

They checked the oil level in the Honda, and it registered two to three quarts low—probably not enough to make the engine freeze up. It might have been enough to make the oil light come on. Williams wondered if she had pulled over to check her oil and if someone had come along and grabbed her.

The Honda's odometer read 57.9 miles.

That might be an important clue, Hendricks explained. He said that the fuel gauge didn't work, and that Lorraine would have set the odometer at zero the last time she got gas. Williams nodded. They should be able to trace her path north and find out where she had stopped for gas exactly 57.9 miles before her car ended up on the shoulder of I-95.

"Try it," Williams said to Rick Hendricks. "See if it turns over."

Rick Hendricks slipped his spare key into the ignition, and the engine cranked up easily. There seemed to be no mechanical problems at all. Almost as an afterthought, Hendricks opened the glove box and ran his hand along the bottom. "There's something else missing. The registration is gone, too."

Williams released the car to Hendricks and Frank Dombroski, who planned to drive it back to Jacksonville. They added oil to be sure

Dombroski wouldn't have difficulty on the way home. Later Rick called Phil Williams from Jacksonville to say that he had had no car troubles at all on the drive.

Williams asked Rick Hendricks to drain three quarts of oil from the Honda and then to drive it and see if the oil light came on or if any other difficulties ensued. None did.

Retracing Lorraine Hendricks's drive exactly 57.9 miles brought easier answers than the rest of the probe would. Traveling 57.9 miles north from the red paint spot on the Interstate brought the investigators to Exit 50 off I-95.

There was an Amoco station there, and the missing woman's father thought she had probably gassed up there because she had an Amoco credit card. Detective Don Brown, with the Brevard County Sheriff's Office, checked with Amoco and found that Lorraine had, indeed, charged gas at the Amoco station at Exit 50 on the morning of March 4. The Sunshine Food and Fruits store was located there at 3580 Cheney Highway, and the manager remembered seeing Lorraine Hendricks there. She was a very attractive woman whom most men would remember. He also recalled that she had used the pay phone afterward.

The woman who had actually initialed Lorraine's gas charge slip remembered her, too. She was sure from looking at the slip that Lorraine Hendricks had been in the Amoco station between 9:45 and 10:00 that Sunday morning.

That fit. That would have been the call to her father in Jacksonville, and she might have tried to call Carol Worley in Fort Lauderdale at the same time.

Had she picked up a hitchhiker? If she had, it would have been completely against her normal pattern. Her relatives said Lorraine was too savvy to do that. Had she been *forced* to take a rider along? Maybe.

When Lorraine Hendricks was headed someplace she fixed her mind on her destination. That was one of the reasons her driving record was less than perfect. Looking over the computer printout he'd received from the Department of Highway Safety and Motor Vehicles, Phil Williams grimaced.

> 1-14-83: 65 MPH in a 45 zone
> 6-21-84: 59 MPH in a 40 zone
> 7-24-85: 57 MPH in a 40 zone
> 9-19-85: 41 MPH in a 25 zone

6-05-86: 49 MPH in a 30 zone
3-11-87: 56 MPH in a 35 zone
12-27-89: 60 MPH in a 45 zone
1-06-90: Careless or improper driving
2-06-90: 51 MPH in a 35 zone
2-16-90: Failed to pay traffic fine

Lorraine Hendricks had a lead foot.

"Who would Lorraine stop for?" Williams asked Rick Hendricks. He didn't want to mention the possibility of foul play yet. Maybe he would never have to. "Would she pick up a hitchhiker?"

Hendricks shook his head. "She stopped for turtles and cops. That's all."

"Turtles?"

"She loves animals. I've seen her pull over and go out in the road and carry a turtle out of the road so it wouldn't get hit."

"And I can see why she stopped for cops," Williams said. "She had no choice."

Hendricks shrugged. You couldn't argue with Lorraine's reputation as a speeder.

Turtles and cops. Turtles and cops.

Williams mulled over that odd combination in his mind and thought about "what ifs." What if Lorraine Hendricks had pulled over to rescue another turtle? She could have been out there in the middle of the Interstate and been hit, maybe killed. If the driver panicked, he might have thrown her in the back of his car—or truck—and taken off. Naaah. They would have some sign of a hit-and-run in the road. Blood, torn clothing, a shoe. Something.

Okay. Say she was rescuing a turtle and somebody came along, saw an astoundingly good-looking woman alone at the edge of the road, and grabbed her. That was a more likely scenario than the first. That would explain why she had left her front doors unlocked.

Whatever had happened to Lorraine Hendricks, the chance that she was alive and safe diminished with each passing hour.

Detective Phil Williams gave news releases to local newspapers so that her disappearance would be publicized by March 8th and the public might come forward with leads in a case where there were no leads at all. He had copies made of the two pictures of Lorraine that Rick Hendricks had given him—one of Lorraine with Rick and Katherine, and the other by herself. In the latter she wore a white blouse and a black jumper, and she smiled into the camera. The public certainly called in with tips and suggestions, but none that seemed to relate to Lorraine Hendricks. Nonetheless, every call was evaluated and logged.

"At that point we didn't know what was valuable and what was not," Williams explained. "We kept everything."

13

Duval County Detectives Roy Myers and Mike Robinson had now entered Lorraine Hendricks's name in the NCIC (National Crime Information Center) computers in Quantico, Virginia. If she surfaced anywhere in America, local cops would have the information in their computers.

Mike Raleigh, like all of Lorraine's friends, was stunned when he learned that she had disappeared. He told his fiancée, Alice,* that something had to have happened to her. The Lorraine he knew would never have walked away from her responsibilities on purpose. "I may have to leave," he explained. "I'm worried sick, and I might have to just go on down there, to do anything I can to help."

On Tuesday, March 6, Raleigh had a show in Orlando with Jim Stafford to oversee, but after the show he drove to Exit 50 off I-95— the last place anyone had heard from Lorraine. He arrived at 4 a.m. and got a motel room while he waited for dawn. He wasn't sure what he was going to do, but there had to be something. At first light Raleigh surveyed the businesses located at Exit 50; there was one of the south's ubiquitous Waffle House restaurants, several motels, and a couple of gas stations. He went first to the Amoco station and talked to employees who had worked the morning shift when Lorraine was there on Sunday. He carried her photograph and showed it to employees at the gas station, and then he moved on to the other businesses. He found two people who *did* remember seeing the woman in the photo.

But neither of them had noticed where Lorraine went or with whom she might have left.

Tim as a handsome young student at Satellite High School in the mid-1970s. He was a track star, and he yearned to become a policeman.

Tim as a young Sebastian, Florida, cop in 1979. This is how he looked when he stopped Sandy Wessendorf's car and gave her an intriguing "ticket." She was 16 and he was 21.

Sandy and Tim at their wedding reception, July 25, 1981. Yellow rosebuds and daisies and piña coladas and great hope for a wonderful life together.

Sandy early in her marriage. Tim said he hated her long hair, but his mistress's hair was the same. Sandy had no idea he *had* a mistress.

Shadow, Tim's attack dog, adored his master/trainer, and he was a loving family pet around the Harris home. But if anyone had threatened Tim, Shadow would have torn him to pieces.

The house that Tim built with his own hands in Citrus Hideaway. Shadow's pen was in the back of the house. After Sandy asked Tim to move out, he would sneak back in at night by standing on Shadow's fence and then crawling up onto the lower roof.

Sandy in 1993. She smiled for the camera, but she was desperately trying to pick up the shattered pieces of her life.

Tim sent this expensive angel doll to Sandy for Christmas, 1992, while he was in prison. The doll had a single "tear" seeping from her right eye. Tim sent nothing for his children that Christmas. He has never been able to set Sandy free of his possessive love.

Lorraine, 21, when she was selected "Miss Stamford" in the mid-1960s. "Lori" could have done almost anything for her talent segment, but she played the drums, giving a history of the instrument from Africa to rock 'n' roll.

In 1972 the young model posed for a safety campaign picture, sponsored by the Florida Highway Patrol and the Governor's Highway Safety Commission. The "Arrive Alive" plates, available to the public, were a sadly ironic commentary on what would happen to Lori two decades later.

Lorraine, at 33, in a 10-K marathon. She began running marathons to strengthen a knee she had injured while skiing in Switzerland. She would often carry her baby girl, Katherine, across the finish line.

Lorraine, Rick and toddler Katherine in happier days. Lorraine had longed for a good marriage and a baby. Even so, she and Rick parted as friends, and shared their love for Katherine.

Lorraine, around 40. This photo appeared in papers all over Florida after she vanished in March 1990. Several people called sheriff's detectives to report having seen her. Tragically, they were mistaken.

The palmetto and pine woods that flourished on the median between north- and south-bound lanes of Interstate 95. Detective Phil Williams made a terrible discovery here on March 9, 1990.

Phil Williams came across this drawing and a similar cartoon among the trooper's possessions when he carried out a search warrant.

Florida Highway Patrolman Tim Harris, October 1984. The years had changed the lean young trooper into a somewhat jowly but powerfully muscled man. He was highly regarded for his successful campaign against speeders and drug-runners on I-95. But underneath his professional exterior, Tim had bizarre fantasies.

The investigative team responsible for Tim's arrest. From left: Larry Smetzer, Tony Oliver, Rick McIlwain, Margy Hogan, Phil Williams and Bruce Colton.

Indian River County detective Phil Williams in 1993. He now heads the sheriff's Internal Affairs Unit and administers lie-detector examinations.

Mike Raleigh contacted a detective in Brevard County and asked what more he could do. He was especially worried because the massive annual motorcyclists' convention was taking place in Daytona Beach, thirty-five miles north of Exit 50, and Lorraine would have passed close to that area. Lorraine was still a motorcycle fan, and Raleigh was afraid she might have picked the wrong group to talk to.

The investigator studied Raleigh and finally said, "You can go home. There's nothing you can do that isn't already being done."

"I couldn't go home," Raleigh recalled four years later. "I kept driving south. I knew that her car was supposed to have been found some fifty-seven miles from there, and I spotted that red splotch of paint beside the road. That's where I met Phil Williams for the first time."

Raleigh didn't fool himself. He suspected that one of the detectives from further north had alerted Williams. "I drove up, and Phil was already sitting there in his car. He stepped out, and he didn't drop a beat. He just said, 'Hello, Mike. Let's talk.'"

Just as Raleigh wanted to know if detectives were doing everything they could to find Lorraine, Phil wanted to find out exactly who Mike Raleigh was—both to check on his whereabouts during the weekend Lorraine disappeared and to round out his own profile of the missing woman. He knew that Mike Raleigh was one of the people Lorraine had worked with in Northern Florida. He already knew Raleigh had no police record, and that no one had a bad word to say about him.

Raleigh struck Williams as a "gentleman" who looked more like a professor than an entertainment entrepreneur. He was tall and lanky and wore glasses. He looked to be in his early to mid-forties. He talked slowly and deliberately, weighing his words before he spoke.

Raleigh could easily reconstruct his own whereabouts on Sunday, March 4. He had been in his Florida office in Orlando from about two until five, and several of his employees verified that. Before that he had been with an attorney friend while they attempted to locate two lots they had purchased in High Springs. They had spoken to several residents in that area in their search for the overgrown lots.

"That evening?" Williams asked.

"I was out late in Orlando Sunday night to review a couple of acts I had working there at Pleasure Island." Raleigh said he had rented a Lincoln from Budget Rental at the Orlando Airport.

It all checked out. A witness put Raleigh at Disney World in Orlando from 8 p.m. until the wee hours. It would have been well nigh impossible for Raleigh to have been with Lorraine between eight a.m., on Sunday, March 4, when she left her home in Jacksonville, and noon the next day when Mike Transue tagged her abandoned car.

Beyond that, Williams believed that Raleigh was sincerely concerned for the safety of the woman he had worked with for less than a year. He was extremely eager to help in the investigation and tried to think of anyone who would want to harm her. Raleigh explained he had brought Lorraine along in the entertainment business and introduced her to many of the movers and shakers, feeling it was important for her to relate to the big names in the industry on a social level. Lorraine had paid her dues; she had worked for years in small cities' pageants and festivals with local talent. She was about to see her dream of working with big-time acts come true.

Raleigh listed some of the stellar names that Lorraine had booked for her benefits and festivals. He described her as a woman whose intelligence and friendliness let her fit into any situation. She was very beautiful, she dressed impeccably, and she could carry on a conversation with anyone; she was not dazzled by celebrities, and she fit into their world very well. Raleigh felt she had a real future in the entertainment world.

Phil threw out questions, "What ifs" and "What would she have done if—?" and "How would she have reacted if—?"

Raleigh explained that Lorraine was a talker. "She's a public relations person—that's what she does best. She's a salesperson, and she's a negotiator." If someone has abducted Lorraine, she is smart enough and savvy enough to be one step ahead of that person. "*If* she can keep them talking—"

Phil Williams was aware that he, too, had to pass muster. Mike Raleigh was clearly a man whose career demanded absolute attention to detail and who did nothing halfway. He searched Williams's face as they talked, as if he was judging him.

He was. "When I left that day," Raleigh recalled, "I felt absolutely that Phil would find Lorraine, that he would find out what had happened to her. I believed that. I knew it would take a very special man—one with fortitude, strength of character, and conviction—to do that. When Phil Williams assured me that he was never going to give up on finding Lorraine, that he wasn't going to drop the case, I believed him."

Phil Williams kept his promise, but the next two days passed with no sign whatsoever of Lorraine Hendricks.

Williams had to trace the movements of the new man in Lorraine's

life, the man she had fallen in love with so rapidly. Just as he had
found with Mike Raleigh, Williams discovered that Matthew,* a
Jacksonville businessman, had been far away from Indian River
County when Lorraine vanished. In fact, he had left on a plane
headed for Europe early Saturday morning, March 3. Williams
confirmed that the man had actually boarded the plane. His secretary
had informed him of the tragedy, and he was already heading back to
America.

Finally Phil Williams decided there was nothing to do but to start
back at ground zero—the last place she had been seen. Back at the
splotch of red paint beside I-95.

On March 8 the Brevard County Sheriff's Office helicopter had
circled the area, making continual passes overhead. They flew in a
spiral pattern while a spotter watched the trees and fields below. It
wasn't easy to see beyond the morass of palmettos and pines. The
helicopter search answered no questions for the investigators. If
Lorraine Hendricks was down there someplace, she was not visible
from the air.

The next day every law enforcement agency in the vicinity of
where Lorraine's car had been found mobilized for a concentrated
search of the area. She was either a thousand miles away or very
close. If she was close, Phil Williams wanted to find her. "We went
back out there and decided we were going to search up and down the
shoulders on both sides of the Interstate."

Phil Williams and his fellow detectives Larry Smetzer, Mark
Johnson, and Joe Bobrowskas and a number of Ranch and Groves
deputies began on the shoulder of the Interstate where the gray
Honda had been. They walked the shoulders and the median strip
from State Road 512 to the thickly wooded portion of the median.
The median there was about a mile from where Lorraine's car was
found. At its widest point it was about three hundred feet across.
There was a dirt road that cut through the center of the median,
designed to give state troopers a place to turn around on the
Interstate rather than having to go to the next off-ramp if they saw a
vehicle going the other way that they needed to check out in a hurry.

Literally a step at a time the ground searchers had covered 3.1
miles, hoping to find something that might lead them to Lorraine
Hendricks, missing now for five days. They didn't ask for much—
maybe a button, one of her moccasins, her purse, some scrap of paper
that they could tie to Lorraine. They found nothing at all.

State Trooper Mike Transue, working his regular shift along I-95,
stopped by and talked casually with the Indian River County

investigators. So did Tim Harris, who worked the same stretch of Interstate that Transue did. It had been Transue, of course, who had first located Lorraine Hendricks's car. The sheriff's men and the highway patrolmen talked about the baffling case, shaking their heads.

Tim Harris had Shadow in his car with him, and Williams looked over at the beautiful animal, who watched him suspiciously from his perch in the backseat of Tim's car. Shadow's teeth looked four inches long.

He turned to Tim Harris. "Your dog's a search dog, isn't he? Could we use him in looking for a body?"

Tim whirled around, and then he nodded. "Possibly. But he does better at night. It'd be a good idea, but we should wait until it cools down a little bit. Right now he'd burn out too quick in the woods. But sure, I'd be glad to help out."

Williams didn't know that much about K-9 dogs. Some dog handlers said that dogs smelled bodies up in the air and not on the ground at all. Different breeds worked in different ways. Bloodhounds were said to churn up ground scents with their long ears. The wind was whipping up pretty good, and Phil figured that Tim meant it would cool down the area by nightfall. If they hadn't found anything by evening, he would see if Harris could bring his dog out.

Tim Harris didn't mention to Phil Williams that the area they were searching was his patrol area; he probably assumed that Williams knew.

Shadow watched Williams more closely and began to bark and bare his teeth even more. The detective figured that *he* looked like a bad guy to Harris's dog.

"Call me if you need the dog later," Tim said.

While Williams talked to Tim Harris he got a call on his walkie-talkie from Deputy Joe Bobrowskas, who asked if Harris could give him a ride back to his patrol car, which was parked two miles away down underneath the bridge by the Wayfarer.

"Could you?" Williams asked Harris.

Tim Harris shook his head. "Not with my dog in there. The dog would become violent."

But Tim didn't want Bobrowskas to have to walk all that way in the heat. He drove down to where Bobrowskas was, got the deputy's keys, and said he would drive to the Wayfarer, park his unit (with Shadow locked inside) and then drive Bobrowskas's car to him "if you'll just take me back up to my patrol car." That was fine with Bobrowskas; it was steaming out.

Tim Harris was adamant that no one could ride along in his car—not with Shadow leaning over the backseat. Shadow would just as soon take a chunk out of a cop as a felon. Tim Harris said that his particular dog just didn't want anyone riding along with *his* trooper.

The sun rose higher in the sky, and the wind did nothing to cool the day. Phil Williams tried to put himself into the mind of some man whose face he had never seen. "If I were going to have sex with a girl," Williams said to Larry Smetzer, pointing to the thick clump of weeds and trees there in the wide median strip, "that's where I'd go."

The two Indian River County detectives split up, with Smetzer going one way into the median and Williams the other.

Following his hunch, Phil Williams worked his way deeper and deeper into the pine and palmetto woods that took up most of the widest part of the median between northbound and southbound I-95. He sniffed the air for the smell of death, an odor no detective ever forgets once he has smelled it.

He smelled nothing. Probably Tim Harris had been right. The wind was blowing too hard for even a dog to work the area on scent alone.

And then, as the trees behind him shut out where he had been, and the trees in front of him gave no clue to what lay ahead, as the sun-dried vegetation beneath his feet crackled too loudly, Phil Williams felt a prickling at the back of his neck. He smelled the faintest odor of death, so light on the air that he wasn't sure he smelled it at all.

But then he was sure. It was hot, but he felt cold.

He saw something but he didn't recognize what he saw. None of his senses—not smell, sight, or sound—helped. Straight ahead, just in front of a crooked pine tree, there was a long mound beneath the dried grasses and pine needles. Something dark showed at the end nearest Williams. Closer to him, he saw what looked like a woman's brown wig.

Phil Williams moved forward, his curiosity winning out over a very basic desire to go back and bring the other investigators with him. He had thought he was beyond being shocked or spooked. But here in the shadow of the trees he was definitely spooked. "I'd worked homicides—a lot of them—but there's something about finding a body out in the woods when you're alone and your buddy's looking in some other part of the area. I ran back to get Larry.

"We can call off the search," he said quietly. "She's in there."

"Dead?" The question was academic.

Williams nodded. It was almost impossible to realize that the dead woman in the pines was the same woman whose smile blazed from the pictures he had released to the press. "Yeah, dead."

She was there. She lay, they could both see now, under a thick heap of pine needles and boughs. Had he looked away for only an instant Phil Williams would have missed seeing her entirely. Someone had secreted her carefully, deep in the center of the median, and then buried her with the dried vegetation. The round dark part Williams had glimpsed first was a woman's denuded skull. The "wig" was her own hair; decomposition was far advanced, and little animals had detached the scalp and hair and pulled it about three feet away from the body.

Careful where they stepped, Phil Williams and Larry Smetzer moved around the mound that hid a human body. They could see that the woman lay on her face.

But there was something bizarre here. Someone had positioned her naked body so that her legs extended on either side of the pine tree. The tree trunk rose like some grotesque phallic symbol between her buttocks. She would not have fallen that way; that would have been impossible. No, someone extremely strong would have had to grasp her feet and drag her backward until her genitals were tight against the tree.

Phil Williams took photographs of the body site. Deputy Johnson remained with the dead woman while Williams and Smetzer went to use a pay phone at the Wayfarer. They didn't want their request for Dr. Fred Hobin, the medical examiner, to go out over the police airways where anyone with a scanner—particularly the media— could pick it up. If, as they believed, this was Lorraine Hendricks, they didn't want her family to hear the news that way.

Ron Sinclair and Anthony Oliver, identification technicians with the Indian River County Sheriff's Office, arrived at 1:15 that Friday afternoon and set up a perimeter around the body with yellow "Crime Scene—Do Not Cross" tape.

When Dr. Hobin arrived they slowly removed the pine boughs and needles hiding the woman's body. She was completely nude; if she had been wearing jewelry, it was gone now. A Band-Aid wound around one of her big toes. Because of the destruction caused by heat and insect activity, it would be impossible to identify her without dental X rays.

Her clothing and purse were gone, although the detectives did find a gold hoop earring a short distance from the body. It was real gold, expensive and classic in design. The victim was removed from the median strip and taken to Dr. Hobin's facilities to await autopsy that evening.

At 7 p.m. Dr. Hobin began his careful examination while Phil Williams and Tony Oliver observed and bagged evidence. Despite the advanced decomposition in the victim's head and face, Hobin hoped to determine the manner and cause of the woman's death. "Autopsy" means literally "to see for one's self," and the pathologist would now follow the precise steps that would tell him much about this body on the table in front of him.

Time of death was compatible with the date—March 4—that Lorraine Hendricks had vanished. The hot, humid March weather of Florida had accelerated postmortem changes, but Hobin was used to that.

The woman measured five feet five and weighed 135 pounds. Her teeth were in excellent repair, and her hair was fine and dark brown. Her skin was covered with bites from insects and ants that had probably occurred after death. At some point in her life she had undergone major abdominal surgery, and X rays revealed surgical clips in the right hepatic region. Both the entire right lobe of her liver and her gallbladder had been removed surgically.

Dr. Hobin found no broken bones, no skull fracture. There was no evidence of preexisting disease of the internal organs. He *did* find a fracture of the thyroid cartilage in the neck, a concealed hemorrhage deep in the tissues of the neck, and what he felt was a contusion injury at the front of the left shoulder.

If he had to explain those injuries to a lay person, he would say they indicated that she had been strangled. Hobin also suspected— although he could not prove it absolutely—that the woman had been beaten around the head. Injured tissue decomposes more rapidly than the rest of a body, and this victim's head was nearly skeletal, while her torso, arms, and legs were fully intact.

Identifying the body was tragically easy. Detectives didn't have to look far for Lorraine Hendricks's dentist; she had missed an appointment with him only five days before, and Dr. Hilton furnished her dental X rays at once. They matched the victim's in every way.

So did Lorraine Hendricks's fingerprints.

The detectives learned about the motorcycle accident Lorraine had been in two decades earlier. She had been gravely injured and had had to undergo surgery to stop hemorrhaging from a lacerated liver. Much of her liver had been removed at that time. Although she would have been near death from her injuries, the liver has remarkable regenerative capability, and once the hemorrhaging had stopped it had healed completely.

A sex crime kit was produced, and fingernail scrapings, scalp and pubic hair samples, pubic hair combings, and smear and swab preparations were done of the oral, anal, and vaginal cavities. A vaginal washing sample was taken. It was unlikely that they could find seminal fluid at all at this point, much less identify it as to blood type. Lorraine Hendricks had lain in the baking woods for five days. Routine blood screening proved completely negative for marijuana, cocaine, opiates, barbiturates, antidepressants, and sleeping pills.

Phil Williams had little doubt that Lorraine Hendricks had been the victim of a sexual attack. The position in which her body had been left was unmistakably sexual. Her killer had gone to great effort to arrange her legs around the pine tree's trunk in a grotesque tableau that suggested anal sodomy.

It was, perhaps, a Freudian symbolism, a final act of rage by a killer who might well have proved impotent once he either lured, dragged, or forced his victim into the shadows of the pine grove.

Maybe one day Williams would be able to answer that question—if he ever found the murderer he now knew he was looking for.

Lorraine Hendricks hadn't walked away of her own volition. She hadn't met a lover and run off with him. Something had made her stop on the right shoulder of I-95, and she had not been able to drive away again.

Ever.

14

The news that a woman had been murdered, quite probably in broad daylight, on busy I-95 triggered unreasoning fear in the hearts of scores of women who routinely traveled that freeway in Indian River County. How could it have happened? Surely there was always enough traffic out there so that it should have been extremely difficult to force a woman off the Interstate and into the dense median woods.

If it could happen to Lorraine Hendricks, that meant it could happen to any of them.

Sandy Harris was frightened, particularly since she now lived alone with her two small children only a few miles from where Lorraine had been found. But then she reasoned that she was being silly. She had spent hundreds of nights alone while Tim worked graveyard, or when he was called out to work an accident. Still, it was creepy to think that the woman they had all been looking for had been right there all the time, dead.

And so close, really, to the house in Citrus Hideaway.

Sandy wasn't sure where Tim was sleeping. Sometimes she still heard him creeping into Timmy's window upstairs. Despite their problems, having him there wasn't as scary as being in the house alone. When she heard the noises overhead now Sandy would call out, "Tim, I know you're up there!"

"I had lost all fear of him. After a while I figured if he was going to do something to me, he would do it. I couldn't be afraid of him forever."

Tim either called or visited Sandy every day. And he still wanted to come back to her. But she knew now that he was telling DeeLisa the same things he was telling her. He wanted both of them desperately, or so he said, but she suspected he didn't want either of them. He just wanted the power of having them.

When Lorraine Hendricks's picture appeared in local papers and the *Miami Herald* under the headlines reading "Missing Jacksonville Woman Found Murdered," Phil Williams's telephone lines lit up. Laymen cannot conceive of the number of tips that come into detectives in a high profile case. Scores. Hundreds. Sometimes even thousands. They are all welcome, and they all have to be checked out—sooner or later, depending on the manpower available.

At this point it seemed that everyone on the Treasure Coast had a suspect or a theory. One caller said that he and a friend had crossed under the C54 Canal on Sunday and noted a white "expensive-looking" car parked low on the bank off I-95. "At first we thought it was hunters—but then we figured the car looked too fancy for hunting. It had a chrome grille rounded in the front."

Not much help, really. No license numbers. No description of anyone around the white car.

There were no hits on the credit cards Lorraine had carried in her purse. That would have helped, but apparently her killer had taken her purse and wallet in a vain effort to delay identification rather than to use her credit cards fraudulently. That made Williams feel that she had been killed not in a robbery, but for other motives. His first instinctive reaction had been that her murder was a sex killing, and nothing so far had made him change his mind.

Rick Hendricks called Williams the next day and said that he had just received a letter from the St. Lucie County Sheriff's Office telling him that Lorraine's wallet had been recovered in that county. It had been found before Lorraine's body had, so the St. Lucie sheriff had sent it to the address inside in a routine manner, not realizing its importance. Phil Williams and I.D. Tech Tony Oliver went to the county just south of their own and talked with Detective Messina.

Messina said the wallet had been turned in by a female custodian at the Fort Pierce rest stop off I-95, about twenty miles south of where Lorraine Hendricks and her car were located. The custodian said she had found the wallet sitting on top of trash in a garbage can in the rear picnic area on the southbound side of the rest stop. She had seen no purse or any clothing, nor anyone around the area at the time she discovered the wallet.

Rick Hendricks said that Lorraine's credit cards were still inside the wallet when it was returned to him by the St. Lucie Sheriff's office, but that her driver's license and any cash she might have been carrying were missing. Fingerprint technicians could raise no identifiable prints on the wallet.

Statistically, in any given week along the east coast of Florida, law enforcement authorities expected a certain number of homicides. Phil Williams wanted to know about any of them that might have some connection to the murder of Lorraine Hendricks, and he put out his request on the police wires.

Detective Hartman of Delray, Florida, notified Williams on March 13th that he had arrested a huge and wild young man named Jack Criger.* Criger had stabbed both his aunt and his mother to death in Delray. The M.O. was nothing at all like Williams's case. However, Criger had been arrested in South Carolina on the same day that Lorraine Hendricks's body was found. He had been in South Carolina since Wednesday, March 7th. The reason Hartman was calling was that Jack Criger had traveled to South Carolina along I-95. He had left Delray on March 2—two days before Lorraine Hendricks disappeared—and had been driving a four-door white 1985 Buick sedan. Well, Williams thought, that matched the "expensive" white car.

But nothing else matched. Hartman said that Criger was a cocaine addict and that he had admitted killing his mother and aunt while he was under the influence of drugs. He insisted he had committed no other crimes. His name went back in the hopper, but he was no longer a prime suspect.

The tips continued to pour in: (1) Brevard County (just north of Indian River County) authorities advised that a young woman had been abducted from Merritt Island by two men driving a rust-red Camaro. They had subsequently dropped her off in Columbia County, and the white male suspects had become involved in a high-speed chase that went through Jasper into Lowndes County, Georgia, where they were arrested (no M.O. similarity). (2) A woman said she was northbound on I-95 on Saturday, March 3, and saw what looked like a Rhode Island State Patrol car with three antennas swing across the median. (3) A preacher at a Wabbasso church called to say that he was suspicious of a local man who drove a small gray vehicle. (4) A man said he had driven on I-95 the weekend before Lorraine Hendricks's disappearance and had seen a yellow Oldsmobile with a white male driver following a female's car, and that he had even gotten off the Interstate behind her at an exit. (5) A woman said she had seen a light tan Chrysler turning across the median near the crime scene on Monday, March 5 at about 4 p.m.

The help from the public went on and on: "Caller said he was on I-95 Sunday, 3/4, and saw 4-wheel-drive truck with loud pipes pull out of wooded area where the cops were at on Friday following. Truck was speeding. Caller never caught up." "Caller advised WM [white male] with brown shaggy hair kept bothering him at Waffle House for a hamburger . . . Caller had a funny feeling . . . might be vagrant . . . was at Exit 50, I-95, 11 to 12 noon . . . had weird personality." "Caller claims witness saw Lorraine Hendricks (ID'd by picture in papers) at Waffle House for two hours Sunday afternoon . . . (witness proves to be possible *Mental*)." "Caller advised he saw a WM about 2 p.m. Sunday, 3/4, in the Northbound Lane of I-95, just south of Brevard Co. Line . . . exited from grayish color Pontiac 4Dr . . . Older WM was driving. WM 6'2", exited and ran across the median . . . wearing bright green shorts." "Caller is Corrections Officer . . . 8:15 a.m., 3/5, subject walking with hat pulled down over his face. Was at woods line where the body was found. Subject carrying large brown suitcase that appeared heavy . . . wearing a Khaki type jacket . . ."

Detective Don Brown of Brevard County said that one of their deputies had interviewed a man in their county at I-95 and Melbourne, a man with a rather bizarre avocation. He gave his name as Rodney Marcello Martino.* He was thirty-nine, a short, rather wispy man who drove a Dodge Coronet.

"Martino told our man that he drives I-95 every day from Fort Pierce to the 520 Exit—he claims his only mission in life is to help stranded motorists. Trouble is he had a pair of handcuffs in the glove box, and he's got a rap sheet for rape."

It was beginning to sound as if I-95 was an obstacle course for trusting tourists.

Dutifully Phil Williams typed page after page of tips into his computer and followed up the most likely. The trouble was that most of them were like trying to find a certain butterfly that had flown across I-95 on the Sunday that someone forced or persuaded Lorraine Hendricks out of her car.

Williams had calls from psychics—and from psychos. He had calls from professionals and from citizens. Memory is probably the most imprecise function in the human brain. Many of the callers weren't sure of the day or time they had seen suspicious people or vehicles. Phil Williams had to prioritize, to pick those that sounded plausible and dismiss the others.

Lorraine Hendricks had either gone with someone she knew and trusted or had been taken from her car by a stranger. The question was really, *where* had Lorraine met her killer? It was possible that someone had gotten in her car when she stopped for gas way back at Exit 50.

Detective Bobby Mutter of the Titusville Police Department called Williams to say that on Saturday night, March 3, Detective Dan Carter of his department had observed a white male approaching vehicles, wandering from convenience store to convenience store. One of them had been at the Amoco station where Lorraine Hendricks was known to have stopped the next morning. Carter had stopped the man and asked for ID. He didn't have any but gave the name Erik Marshall Litton,* DOB 5-22-52. He said he was traveling south from Connecticut. Litton had been about five feet eight, 160 pounds, and he was wearing a reddish plaid shirt, dirty blue jeans, cowboy boots, and a dirty baseball cap. He had a filet-type knife with a plastic handle in a sheath at his side. Carter checked and found no wants or warrants on Litton, but he had received an emergency call and had had to leave the Amoco station to respond. The Titusville Police had had no further contact with Litton.

He might well have been at the Amoco station the next morning when Lorraine drove in.

A woman named Liane Stark* called Phil Williams to report that she had been in that Amoco station the previous summer. "I used the telephone booth, and a man—a black man—pretended to use the other phone there, but he was watching me. When I went back to my car he tried to get into the backseat behind the driver's seat. I was able to run inside and get the attendant to come back out with me. The man was gone."

If nothing else, Williams was hearing how dangerous rest stops and exit areas could be for women traveling alone. In the time a woman left her car to use the phone or the rest room, or to buy a candy bar or pay for her gas, someone could get into the backseat of an unlocked car. It *was* quite possible that Lorraine Hendricks had driven away from Exit 50 with a passenger crouched in the backseat, that she had been unaware that she was no longer traveling alone. But would the rider have waited over *fifty-seven* miles to make his move? Probably not.

Detective Greenhaigh of St. John's County just south of Jacksonville called to say that she was working a case that had possible similarities to the Hendricks case. An attractive woman had traveled to Jacksonville's Mayo Clinic on Tuesday, March 6th, two days after Lorraine vanished. After her appointment the woman had spent the day shopping around the clinic. As she traveled south toward home she noticed a man in a large gray car following her. He was tall—or at least sat "tall in the seat" of his car. Just outside Duval County he began to try to get her to pull over. He flashed his lights and pulled alongside her car, pointing at it as though she had a flat tire or some other problem. She knew there was nothing wrong with her car and pulled ahead. She turned off on US 1 and headed toward St. Augustine.

The man had followed her. "He shot her car window out," Detective Greenhaigh said. "A man who we believe is the same suspect followed a *second* victim back to the Duval County line that same night, using the same techniques to try to get her to pull over."

The tall man in the gray sedan made the mistake of trying to force an off-duty female St. Augustine detective later that night, and Detective Mary Loveck got a tag number. She checked it through the Department of Motor Vehicles and it came back to a Patrick Phillips,* WM, DOB 2/21/42, who stood several inches over six feet. The female detectives in St. Augustine and in St. John's County were checking him out thoroughly. At the moment Phillips hadn't proved to have connections further south than St. Augustine, but he was a definite threat to women traveling alone.

Greenhaigh's call was bolstered by one from a woman named Brenda Lacy.* She said she had stopped for gas at a station off I-95 outside Jacksonville, and a tall man with sandy blond hair, about six feet two, had pulled over when she did. Her car needed repairs, which had taken about two hours. Brenda, who described herself as a fifty-year-old woman and "good-looking," had been puzzled and a little alarmed that the man hung around all the while she was at the station. He bought gas and asked her to go with him to St. Augustine. She refused, but he followed her down I-95 for several miles.

When Roger Gainey of the Clay County Sheriff's Office (west of St. Augustine) called, Phil Williams began to wonder if he might be looking for a serial killer. Gainey said that his department had been working on a homicide that had occurred six weeks before Lorraine Hendricks died. The victim profile and the M.O. were too similar to be ignored. Carol Orcutt, a beautiful blonde who was five feet four and weighed a hundred pounds, and who was also a businesswoman, had disappeared within a ten-mile radius of where Lorraine Hendricks had last been seen alive. Carol Orcutt's car, a red Thunderbird, had been found—its engine still running—on State Road 21, but Carol was gone.

Carol herself was found two weeks later—on January 27th—down a little-traveled dirt road. She had been murdered, and her body had been left in a position eerily similar to Lorraine Hendricks's. On autopsy she was found to have injuries very similar to those suffered by Lorraine Hendricks. She, too, had been found nude, and her clothing was missing. Lorraine's earring had been found, and Carol Orcutt's jewelry was still on her body.

Phil Williams traveled to Clay County and conferred with Lt. Jimm Redmond, who was in charge of the investigation, and Detective Gainey. The men agreed that they had cases with too many matches to be ignored. Both women came out of the Jacksonville area just prior to their deaths; both left from within a ten-mile radius; both bodies were left in unusual and grotesque positions; and both were taken out of vehicles beside roads that were quite well traveled.

They agreed to keep in touch. But there were no quick answers for either case.

Williams and Oliver checked with tow trucks that had worked I-95 between March 4th and 9th, and with the Florida troopers who traveled the Interstate continually, their eyes out for suspicious circumstances. Mike Transue and Tim Harris had seen nothing that would help the investigation, and neither had any of the other troopers who worked other shifts along I-95.

A detective's nightmare is always that another victim will die before he can catch the killer. Phil Williams worried about that; if they were dealing with a serial killer roving between Jacksonville and Fort Pierce, there was every likelihood that he would kill again. If he was near the beginning of his obsessive fantasies, it might be months. If, like Ted Bundy, who had terrorized Florida a dozen years earlier, he was at the height of his addiction to murder, there would be another victim within days.

Phil Williams knew that the U.S. Department of Justice had set up a crime analysis program called VICAP (Violent Criminal Apprehension Program) with a computer matrix at F.B.I. headquarters in Quantico, Virginia. The program offered help to local detectives all over America who were working unsolved homicides, particularly those that involved abductions; that were—at least on the surface— random, motiveless, or sexually oriented; and that were known or suspected to be part of a series.

VICAP, the brainchild of one of the most respected detectives in America, Pierce Brooks, former captain of homicide of the Los Angeles Police Department and a chief of police in Oregon and Colorado cities, gives detectives a chance to compare their cases with similar cases around the country, and, if they request it, a profile of a what the killer might be like from Special Agents in the Behavioral Science Unit of the F.B.I.

VICAP's information forms are lengthy—fourteen pages and 188 questions, plus a narrative summary—but experts on serial murder have long since learned that seemingly trivial details of an unsolved crime may turn out to be the clues that track and trap a killer.

And Phil Williams was a detective who would try *any* route to find his man—or woman. On March 12, tediously and meticulously, he filled out the VICAP form with everything he knew about Indian River County Case 90-15640. Lorraine's case. He listed two possible related cases: the Carol Orcutt case in Clay County, 90-005374, and the St. John's County investigation of the male motorist who followed women on freeways, 90-65161.

If VICAP came up with some hits, Williams's case might be easier to solve than he expected it was going to be.

There were no hits—but he had given it a try.

In the end, Phil Williams and Larry Smetzer, who was assisting in gathering data, would check out fifty-five leads before they found the key to solving Lorraine Hendricks's murder.

Smetzer's assignment was to pick up all tickets, warnings, field interviews, and any other data from the Florida Highway Patrol and other police agencies that might reveal any unusual contacts on I-95. It was possible that Lorraine's killer had been stopped or had come into contact with police on March 4.

It was, Williams and Smetzer admitted, a ten thousand-to-one long shot.

When they took their fifty-sixth call they would open a Pandora's box with dark secrets they would have chosen never to know. The answers to their questions would bring heartbreak to many more families.

15

Tim Harris stopped by to see Sandy on Saturday, March 10th, the morning that the headlines screamed that a woman's body had been found and that she had been identified as Lorraine Hendricks of Jacksonville.

Sandy read the article and breathed, "Oh, my God! I can't believe that someone actually did this."

"And she was really pretty, too," Tim said.

Sandy studied the tiny postage-stamp-sized picture that accompanied the story. It was difficult to see what the dead woman actually looked like. She wondered how Tim could tell if she had been pretty or not, and then Sandy felt a sick roiling in her stomach, and a kind of premonition that she didn't want to acknowledge. She shook her head and took a deep breath, and the feeling went away.

While the whole county was caught up with the mystery behind Lorraine Hendricks's murder, Sandy Harris still had to cope with her own hopelessly entangled marital problems. The decision to divorce Tim had been hard. Her decision to put the house up for sale was hard. Forcing Tim out of the house had been harder. *Keeping* him out was proving to be impossible. There wasn't a day that Tim didn't come by or call—or both. Now that she was lost to him, she had become utterly desirable.

Sandy still heard Tim in the night, clambering up what had once been Shadow's pen, creaking across the roof, and then sliding through Timmy's bedroom window. It was almost creepier when she *didn't* hear him come in. Sometimes she would be talking on the phone, suddenly hear a soft click, and realize that he was in the house, and that he was listening to her conversations.

Sandy had found one tape recorder, and she and Tim had had a major confrontation over it, but she didn't delude herself into believing that he didn't have others stashed here and there. He knew too much about her comings and goings; sometimes he would give himself away, and she knew he still had devices where he could listen to her calls when he wasn't in the house. Although she certainly wasn't involved with any other man, she hated the thought that her every outgoing call was being taped. She began to fight Tim on his own level. When she got home at night she dialed the number of some business that she knew was closed and had no answering machine. Then she let the phone ring for an hour.

When Tim came during the day to retrieve his hidden tapes, all he would have would be a tape full of the sounds of an endlessly ringing phone. That frustrated him tremendously, but it didn't stop him from surveilling Sandy constantly.

He was quite open now about his tape recorders. He would deliberately pull one out of the sofa or from some other hiding place and start playing it back in front of Sandy. He liked to taunt her: "If you only knew how many nights I've spent in this house when you didn't know I was here, you might be surprised."

He wrote Sandy letters and left them behind each day, proclaiming his devotion to her. "I love you. I always will. Why can't you see that and know how happy we can be again?"

Tim also taped messages to Sandy about how much he loved her, repeating the same phrases over and over, and then left the tapes for her to play. It was as though if he said it often enough, it would be true—and all the years of cheating and abuse would vanish.

But they wouldn't. They couldn't—not for Sandy any longer.

Lt. Gary Morgan talked with Tim and tried to make him face reality. "I told him that it had been . . . six months . . . since they'd been having problems, and I thought it was about time that he got himself pulled together and went on with his life and forgot about Sandy because there was no way he was gonna make her love him if she didn't want him back. . . . I didn't realize how hard it was hitting him until I saw him sitting in front of me that day. . . . He told me he wanted to give up the felony program. . . . I told him it was something he'd worked real hard for. Working the dog—the dog was one of the better dogs . . . I told him, 'I don't think it's something you want to give up, and then six months down the road you're gonna regret giving it up . . . because it's something you're not gonna be able to get back into.' . . . I thought the best thing for him to do was to get his marriage over with, life straightened out, and to keep his current position, because that's what made him happy before the problems, and I thought it would make him happy after. . . ."

But Tim was phasing out of the felony squad despite what his superiors advised. They felt sorry for him. But of course they had heard only one side. They didn't know he was *still* seeing DeeLisa.

On March 15 Tim gave up Shadow. Sandy begged him to let her keep the dog. She and the kids loved Shadow, and they sure would feel a lot safer having him with them at night, but Tim said the Patrol wouldn't consider that. That part was true; Shadow was a working dog, and he had cost the Patrol thousands of dollars.

Tim wrote to Bobby R. Burkett, director of the Fort Pierce Division of the Florida Highway Patrol:

> I am requesting for re-assignment from Felony Canine Handler to Trooper I, Indian River County. Recent events concerning my family have prevented me from giving 100% to the program. I have been very satisfied with the program but I think in the best interest of the Florida Highway Patrol I give up my Canine Handler position. The additional duties have added to the stress to the point that I cannot give my best to the program.
>
> I am requesting that K-9 Shadow be donated to me if he cannot be re-trained to another Trooper. I will assist in any way that I can for the K-9 to be re-trained to another handler.
>
> It is with my deep regret that I request for re-assignment.

Tim's request for transfer was granted. Tim would be working traffic again and was no longer involved in any way in the investigation into Lorraine Hendricks's murder. He never really had been—nothing more than that day when Phil Williams asked to use Shadow to try to find her body, and Tim had said it was too hot and too windy.

One of Tim's lieutenants, Andy Morris, had agreed that Tim's personal life and problems had gotten the best of him, and he assisted him in getting professional help. Morris noted that Shadow was only four years old, and that he could still bond and train with another trooper. Sandy and the kids really missed Shadow when he was reassigned to another trooper.

At the urging of the Florida Highway Patrol Tim had seen a counselor in early March. He had always refused to do so before, but he went, and he told Pat Wessendorf that he was sure he could pull his marriage back together. Pat didn't think so. If he had truly regretted cheating on Sandy and had never seen DeeLisa Davis again, she would have forgiven her son-in-law, too. But she knew he was still playing games with Sandy's heart. She had seen him driving down the street with DeeLisa with her own eyes.

She thought he was acting peculiar besides. Pat was trying to help Sandy get the Citrus Hideaway house fixed up to sell. Tim had let the yard go for a long time. Pat had brought some plants out to spruce it up, and she was just beginning to work when Tim drove up. "I hadn't even started to put out the plants—I mean, they were all still in the containers—and Tim drives up and tells me how wonderful the yard looked. I stared at him, and he just seemed to be out of it—like he was sleepwalking."

Sandy Harris made tentative stabs at having a social life as a single woman. It wasn't easy. She had loved Tim since she was sixteen; now she was almost a dozen years older, and her self-esteem had suffered mightily in the interim. Sometimes she went out with her sisters, Sue and Kathy. She still had lunch on Thursdays with her mom and both her sisters. As far as she knew, Tim was living with DeeLisa—if you could call it that. During March, 1990, Tim was upstairs in *Sandy's* house almost every night. He never came near Sandy's bed, but he couldn't have been in DeeLisa's either.

Sandy wondered why DeeLisa put up with it.

And Pat Wessendorf wondered why Sandy put up with Tim's constant interference with her life. But in truth, Pat was beginning to be afraid of him. Of course, Pat didn't know about the times Tim had put his hands around Sandy's neck and threatened to choke the life out of her. She didn't know how bad things were.

Phil Williams made two more trips up to Jacksonville. Like all instinctive detectives, he knew that he would have to learn more about the victim than he knew about his own closest friends. Somewhere in Lorraine's life there had to have been something that made her temporarily vulnerable to her killer. The problem was that Williams didn't yet know what it was.

Sometimes he repeated to himself a funny little litany: "Cops and turtles—turtles and cops." When he saw turtles making their ponderous journeys across the baking hot surface of I-95 he thought of the dead woman in the woods, so compassionate that she would have stopped to save even those ugly creatures. It seemed a bitter irony that someone had destroyed *her* and left her in the slash pines alone.

On March 16 Rick Hendricks called Phil Williams at home and said that his bank had sent him a letter advising that a check for $100 on Lorraine's account had bounced. He wanted to go and get it, but Williams suggested that Hendricks wait, since he was coming up to Jacksonville in two days; he would check with the bank. It might prove to be just the lead they needed.

It wasn't. The signature was Lorraine's, and it was a check she had cashed before she left for her trip on March 4. Had she lived, she would long since have made a payroll deposit to cover it. No other checks came in, nor were there any credit card charges.

As Phil Williams worked the baffling murder case in his county the homicide rate in Florida scarcely diminished. Lou Sessa of the Palm Beach Sheriff's Office called Williams to say that they were working a murder investigation in the death of a 14-year-old girl who had been sexually assaulted and suffocated around March 18th. Williams considered it, but the M.O. was very different from the Hendricks and Orcutt cases. The Palm Beach victim was clothed, she wasn't a sophisticated businesswoman, she hadn't been left in a bizarre sexual position, and she had been found in a highly populated area rather than a quiet, lonely place.

Phil Williams still couldn't shake the "cops and turtles" image. He spoke with Bruce McMann of the Florida Department of Law Enforcement. *Could* there be police involvement? Could they possibly be looking for a rogue cop—or someone dressed like a cop? Ted Bundy had used that technique with deadly effectiveness. He had often identified himself as a policeman before he lured his victims away from shopping malls or campuses. All it had taken was the flash of a fake badge that anyone could buy through a magazine ad.

There were elements in this case that hinted that a *real* policeman or an ex-cop might be the killer. For one thing, the turnaround road through the pine woods median on I-95 was used almost exclusively by cops; few civilians even knew it was there. For another, Lorraine Hendricks's license and registration were missing. To a civilian, her credit cards surely would have been more interesting and rewarding. But a driver's license and vehicle registration were the first things every cop asked for.

But if Lorraine had been stopped by a policeman, there was no record of it. McMann ran all the available data they had through the NCIC and FCIC computers; he determined that the only time Lorraine Hendricks's car tag had been run through the system was when Trooper Mike Transue entered it at the time he found her abandoned car on March 5.

Nevertheless, Phil Williams agreed to set up a meet with the Highway Patrol brass in Fort Pierce to explore the cop theory.

And then Detective Helfer of the St. Lucie County Sheriff's Office called to say that he had been following the Hendricks case in the paper. "I want you to know that one of our detectives is working a case involving an ex-cop. He raped a woman. The interesting thing is that he grabbed her by the throat when he picked her up."

Helfer said he would try to get more specific information and call back. Oddly, Phil Williams received an anonymous letter that same day in which the writer suggested that Lorraine Hendricks might have been killed by a "deranged cop." The letter was signed "Concerned Citizen."

Phil Williams carefully carried the letter to Tony Oliver for processing. It could very well be a "catch me" letter. It wouldn't be the first time a killer couldn't wait for detectives to work through the puzzles he had left behind. Sometimes they got impatient to see their faces on the nightly news. Sometimes it was a "catch me if you can, you stupid cops" letter, a game that some murderers enjoyed.

It was the first day of spring. March 21, 1990. Phil Williams scarcely noticed.

The Indian River County Sheriff's investigators were exploring every avenue possible, no matter how ridiculous it might seem on the surface. Phil Williams and Larry Smetzer and Tony Oliver made up the main team, and Lt. Mary Hogan handled the yeoman's job of holding the press and the public at bay. This was the kind of case where reporters begged for details—and she could give them so few without jeopardizing the investigation. This was the kind of case that frightened the citizens of Indian River County, and they wanted to be assured that *they* were not in danger. Hogan walked a narrow line, always smiling, never letting the demands ruffle her. In the meantime she made sure the Hendricks case detectives received the financial wherewithal and the time they needed, unhampered by either the tight county budget or reporters. She managed somehow to assign other open cases to detectives who weren't under such intense pressure.

Phil Williams believed in listening to everyone who had a theory. "That was something I learned in my old band days. Don't ever be a one-man band; you can never have too many people. One more man may be just the one that makes the band work. That belief carried over into law enforcement for me."

The file on Lorraine Hendricks's murder was getting thicker every day.

Detective Larry Smetzer kept tracking down a number of documents from the Florida State Patrol and other agencies, including warning tickets and information about stops that troopers had made on Sunday, March 4th. Sergeant Coates of the FHP helped Smetzer with his search. It wasn't easy. Although city and county officers were required to call their dispatchers whenever they stopped a motorist, state troopers were not. Any stops the state officers might have made where they had not given out tickets or warning slips were virtually untraceable. Troopers were fairly autonomous. They kept their patrol units at their homes, they didn't report in to their headquarters at the beginning of their shifts, and they roamed their territory looking for speeders and drivers in need of help wherever they determined the traffic was heaviest.

The more people the investigators could find who had driven down I-95 on the day Lorraine Hendricks disappeared, the more likely they were to find an eyewitness—or an almost-eyewitness.

Among the warning tickets turned in to the Florida Highway Patrol was one that Trooper Tim Harris had written to a Diane Lonergan* at 10:48 a.m. on March 4th at State Road 9, not far from where Lorraine Hendricks's car had been located a day later by Trooper Mike Transue. Phil Williams was not, however, very excited about this information, as Patrol records also showed that Harris had made an actual arrest an hour later on March 4 that tended to take him out of the suspect or witness category. It was during the critical time period when Lorraine would have been driving into Indian River County, had she pursued her original plans, and it was many miles away from the wooded median.

Phil Williams also checked out the location of personnel in his own department on March 4 between 10:30 a.m. and 1 p.m. in the area along I-95. If Lorraine Hendricks had been stopped by someone she trusted because he *was* a cop—or because he was impersonating a cop—Williams couldn't avoid looking at the men who worked alongside him, as onerous a task as that might be. He was relieved to find that the area was so isolated, and "business" so slow that morning, that there had been no sheriff's cars along the Interstate within those parameters. He didn't want to find out that the cop theory was true, and most of all, he didn't want to discover that anyone working for the Indian River County Sheriff's Office was a sex killer. He had been through that before when he learned his friends were murderers. Enough pain there to last him a whole lifetime.

The contacts and calls that Phil Williams logged continued to add up. Call 53 came into the Indian River Sheriff's Office on March 24. A resident of Columbia County called to say he had read about a dead girl who was found in the back of a van. Williams contacted him for details. Nothing matched.

Call 54 was from a woman who said a gray van had tried to run her off the road on I-95.

Call 55 was from Detective Winker of the Cocoa Police Department across from Merritt Island. "A while back we had a black male driver who attempted to pull a woman over by using a blue light on his Camaro. She stopped—but she drove off when she saw he wasn't in uniform."

Call 56 came from Sergeant Carroll Boyd, and it was in reference to Sandy Harris, the wife of Florida Highway Patrolman Tim Harris.

16

Early on the evening of Friday, March 23, Sandy met her sister Susan at the UpTown for a drink after work. Tim followed her there, as he seemed to be following her everywhere. Although she didn't see him, he hid behind a post and listened as she chatted with a girlfriend in the club. She didn't dance with anyone, and she left the bar early.

Pat Wessendorf was at the house in Citrus Hideaway with Timmy and Jennifer. She was standing in the yard when Tim suddenly roared around the corner in his latest vehicle—a brand-new 1990 red Camaro. He pulled into the driveway and slid over into the yard at full speed.

"I was afraid of him," Pat recalled. "I ran into the house. Sandy could still stand up to him, but he scared me. He was screaming at Sandy that she was a barfly and a tramp. He was getting out of control."

Tim had followed Sandy home from the UpTown. He had something to give her; it was a tape he had made telling her how much he loved her, how they could be happy together again if she would only take him back. Sandy walked around the shiny new Camaro, stunned. It had only been a short time since Tim had bought his truck. "Tim," she asked in amazement, "now how are you going to pull your boat?"

"I'll buy another truck," he snapped. "Don't worry about it."

When Tim Harris left that night he had scarcely turned off of 75th onto Highway 510 when he was involved in an accident. His new Camaro's fender was crumpled, and Tim was taken to the emergency room in Vero Beach. He had a blood alcohol reading of .01. He was far from legally impaired, but for Tim Harris it was astounding that he had any alcohol in his system at all. Tim didn't drink, and he didn't smoke. Or rather, he hadn't until now.

The E.R. called, and Sandy went to pick him up, wondering why he hadn't had them call DeeLisa. They drove to a park on the way home; she thought maybe she could get through to him somehow, just *talk* to him. Tim wasn't hurt badly. It was his mind that scared her; he could not grasp that she had come to get him because there had been no one else to do it. It didn't mean she loved him or that she wanted him back.

Tim scared Sandy. She could not even make a gesture of human decency without his assuming that she had forgotten all of his betrayals over the past eleven years. He talked over her, refusing to let her tell him, for the umpteenth time, that she was going ahead with the divorce. He acted as though they were as good as reconciled.

Tim Harris was building toward some cataclysm. Sandy had no idea what he might be capable of. He had given up his goal of being in the felony unit. He had given up Shadow. His work evaluations were slipping. He was a teetotaler who had suddenly begun to drink. He had sold his new truck—which he could at least sleep in—for an expensive sports car that he couldn't afford and which he had already banged up with his wild driving. He was rocketing around Indian River and St. Lucie counties like a crazy man, sleeping in rest stops, or at his brother's, or at DeeLisa's—but mostly upstairs in Sandy's house.

Sandy felt the way she did when they were on hurricane watch. The air was heavy with danger, an ominous sense of impending catastrophe.

On Sunday night, March 24, Sandy Harris was visiting in her living room with her next-door neighbors, the Rodney Tillmans. They had been very supportive of Sandy, and they were fully aware of how scary her dealings with Tim had become. They knew she was frightened, but Sandy was a woman who fought to appear capable. Even her mother had never seen her cry during this whole divorce fiasco, and her neighbors had never seen her let down and admit how rough things were. She still got up and went to work at her bookkeeping job every day, still took care of the children, still pasted on a smile to make it look as if everything was all right.

It was dark, shortly after nine, when the trio heard a loud thump on the second floor. Both the Tillmans jumped, but Sandy only sighed. "Tim's here. It's only Tim. I know he's up there."

While her neighbors waited, half embarrassed and half alarmed, Sandy ran up the stairs calling, "Tim? Tim, are you up there?"

"He was hiding behind the bathroom door, and he had my purse," Sandy recalled. "He'd taken it from my bedroom, and I saw it open on the bathroom counter. I said, 'Tim, I know you're behind the door—I *know* you're there.' And he finally came out. I said, 'Why don't you just be normal and come downstairs? Our neighbors are here.'"

Tim Harris edged out from behind the bathroom door and followed Sandy downstairs. But he wouldn't join in the conversation. "He just sat there staring—like a zombie. Then he got up and went in his study and sat there, ignoring everyone."

The Tillmans tried to make small talk, but it was an agonizingly embarrassing situation. It was clear Tim wanted them out of there. They made excuses and left.

As soon as he was sure their neighbors were out of earshot Tim grabbed Sandy roughly and dragged her across the room, muttering, "I have a present for you in my bag."

Tim outweighed Sandy by seventy pounds or more, and there was little point in fighting him. Jennifer and Timmy were in bed, and she didn't want to wake them. This wasn't the first time Tim had been physical with her, and she let him pull her along as she frantically tried to form a plan to get free of him.

Tim wrestled Sandy up the stairs and into the master bedroom and slammed the door behind him. He reached for a shiny black vinyl bag and pulled out a pair of handcuffs. They weren't flex cuffs; they were heavy metal cuffs.

And then Tim switched off the lights.

Tim reached out for her, and this time Sandy fought. He had never done anything like this before, and she was frightened. He slipped one cuff on, but Sandy kicked and twisted so that he couldn't latch the second cuff. It seemed like forever as they tumbled around on the bedroom floor, but it was probably closer to ten minutes. Helpless against Tim's strength, Sandy ended up on the floor next to the door.

"You're going to take me back," Tim growled into her ear, repeating that phrase over and over.

"I am going to divorce you," Sandy gasped stubbornly.

"You are going to take me back," he said again, as if he hadn't even heard her. He promised her that if she didn't take him back, they were both going to die. "You are going to take me back," he said again.

"No, I am not," she said through gritted teeth. "I am going to divorce you."

Tim Harris had threatened Sandy before, and he had placed his hands around her neck and told her how easily he could break it, but he had never truly *hurt* her. He was hurting her now. The wrist in the handcuff ached as he yanked on the cuffs, trying to completely immobilize her. She had rug burns and scrapes, and she knew that Tim was deadly serious.

Sandy began to scream, even though she knew all the windows were shut.

Tim was on top of her, straddling her. She turned her face away from his, and then she saw the gun. It was a handgun, and he held it right next to her head. She had no idea if it was loaded. He beat his huge fist on the floor right next to her face, and she was afraid to look to see if he still held the gun. "This could be your face," he breathed. "Think what I could do to your *face*."

Sandy didn't doubt for a moment that Tim meant what he was saying.

Sandy's screams had awakened four-year-old Timmy, and he was banging on the door, asking her if she needed help. She didn't want her little boy to see this, and she told him it was all right—that he should go back to bed. Timmy tried to get in, but the door was locked. He started throwing things at the door, trying to save his mother.

At some point Sandy gave in. She fully believed that Tim was about to rape her and then kill her, and she feared for Timmy and Jennifer. With dull shock she knew that she had finally come to a place where she was afraid for her life. Not of being hurt. Not even of being forced to submit to sex. But of dying.

"Okay," Sandy gasped. "I'll take you back."

She didn't think Tim would believe her. "No way was he going to believe that I suddenly changed my mind like that, not after the way I had fought him."

But he did. Tim Harris actually believed that he had accomplished the reconciliation that he wanted. He was still on top of Sandy, but he wasn't hurting her. She called out to Timmy that everything was okay—that he should go back to bed.

She was very cautious, afraid Tim would flip out again. Sandy talked very slowly, very softly, as if she were calming a child. "Tomorrow we'll have a little ceremony—and we'll put our wedding rings back on," she said.

"Why don't we do it tonight?" Tim asked.

"No," Sandy stalled. "No, let's start off tomorrow—a whole new start." Slowly Tim lifted his weight off of her. She asked him if they could go downstairs so she could get a drink of water, because her throat hurt from screaming. He nodded agreeably. The back of her neck prickled as he followed her down the stairs.

Tim unlocked the cuff on Sandy's wrist. She could see that her skin was already purpling from broken blood vessels, and she knew she would have massive bruises there.

"He let me get a drink of water. He seemed to be almost back to normal, and I thought that I would be able to get him to leave. He walked into the living room and sat down, wanting to talk, trying to convince me again that we should get back together that night."

Tim was not in uniform. He was wearing a sports shirt and a pair of blue corduroy jeans. He stood up from the couch, and Sandy's heart sank. He unzipped his pants and took them off. What she saw gave her the biggest shock of her life.

Tim was wearing pantyhose and women's black lace panties with a sheer panel in the front.

"Before I go," he suggested, "why don't we do something kinky?"

"I freaked. I thought, Oh my, God! I had never, ever seen him in women's underclothes."

Sandy's veins felt icy with shock. Her huge, handsome, macho husband was standing there in women's lingerie. The panties weren't hers, and she didn't think the pantyhose were either. She never wore that color. Fighting hysteria, Sandy wondered where he had gotten them. Had he always had this fetish, and she'd never known? She kept her voice calm, although she didn't know how. Sandy watched as Tim took off the women's lingerie. He was half naked now, and wanting her to go back to the bedroom with him. But somehow she convinced him that they should put off having sex until they had their "little ceremony" and exchanged rings again. He seemed to agree with her, and she held her breath while he put his corduroy pants back on.

"Let me walk you to the door," she said, and amazingly, he went.

"Kiss me good-bye," Tim urged.

"I didn't want to. But I didn't want him to get out of control again, so I did," Sandy remembered. "I could hardly bear it, but I actually kissed him on the lips, and I turned around and walked upstairs as he left, acting as normal as I could, pretending like I was going to bed. I didn't want him to know how freaked out I was. Everything in me told me to grab the kids and run, but I didn't dare go anywhere that night, and I didn't dare call anyone for help either. There was no way of knowing how many tapes and bugs he had planted on my phones. We had that whole acre, and he always used to park out back, and I couldn't tell if he was out there or not, watching."

Sandy Harris was about to spend the longest night of her life.

"I stayed in my bed, awake, all night long, listening for Tim to crawl up the dog pen and come back in. But it was quiet. I don't know where he went."

Sandy had scheduled another open house with the realtor the next day. The woman had the key to get in. Sandy didn't wait. She grabbed her children and whatever clothes she could, and she drove to Susan and Don Dappen's house. "I was scared to death of Tim. I didn't know if I could ever go home again."

Don Dappen had tried for years to get along with his brother-in-law, but he'd been fed up with him since the scene in the Vero Beach Police Department in December. Dappen's complaint to Tim's superiors in the Patrol over that fiasco had driven the two men even further apart, though Tim had never been disciplined.

When Sandy and her children walked in that Sunday morning, Don knew what he had to do, even if it sounded cold. "Sandy," he said flatly, "you can turn right around and go back home—unless you're willing to file a complaint against Tim with the sheriff's department."

Sandy Harris did the same review in her mind that every battered wife has ever done. "I realized that the minute I did that, Tim would lose his job. How would I pay the bills and support myself and the children? I knew Don was right, though. My life was in jeopardy, and that was far more important than money. If Tim killed me, my children would be without a mother and a father."

She agreed that Don should call the sheriff, and she called her own lawyer. She wanted a restraining order so that she could go home again, although she doubted that a piece of paper would keep Tim away. She eventually got the restraining order, although her lawyer was patronizing. "Come on, Sandy," he soothed. "Your life can't be that bad."

Dappen sheltered his sister-in-law, niece, and nephew in his home. Everybody tried to pretend that life was normal, but they all knew it wasn't. Even the kids were nervous. They had an outdoor barbecue that night, and Dappen found himself glancing over his shoulder to be sure they had no unwanted company.

"I went outside later—at dusk—to shut the sprinklers off," Dappen recalled. "I caught a glimpse of 'this person' peering over our privacy fence beyond the pool, looking toward our living room. I yelled and took off after him—barefoot through the sand spurs."

Don Dappen knew it was Tim he was chasing. He ran back to the house and called the Sebastian police. They found Tim hiding on the golf course near Dappen's home. He was given a "Trespass after Warning" ticket.

Don Dappen filed another complaint against Tim with the Florida Highway Patrol. Tim Harris talked to Patrol Lt. Andy Morris. Morris had supervised Tim since he had come into the Felony Special Response Team in late 1989, four months earlier. Morris had been aware of Don Dappen's first complaint about Tim in December. That scuffle had been deemed a marital spat, and Tim was off-duty at the time. Tim's performance, while not a hundred percent in Morris's eyes, had been at least ninety percent during the past difficult months. Later Morris had given Tim time off to work out his problems with Sandy.

Morris had seen other troopers go through divorces that were far more strife-ridden than what he had seen in Tim Harris's. The psychologist Tim had been referred to had reported that he saw no signs of violence in Harris. Tim still had his job, although the Patrol made plans to take him off road duty and put him in an office until things settled down.

Tim promised to stay away from Don Dappen's house. He explained that he only wanted to see his children, and that Sandy was keeping them away from him. Sebastian police had a "Keep Watch" order on Dappen's home in case Tim showed up.

Tim didn't keep his promise. He didn't stay away from Sandy. When he saw her driving down the road the next morning he raced alongside her and then veered in front of her and forced her off the road. Don Dappen was following a little way behind her to be sure she got to work safely.

Tim was enraged at Dappen's interference. He came eyeball-to-eyeball with his brother-in-law, yelling, "Go ahead! Hit me! Hit me!"

Dappen came close; he wanted nothing more than to sock Tim until his teeth rattled. But then he backed off, knowing that that was what Tim wanted him to do. "Naw, I'm not going to hit you. But listen real close. If you bother Sandy or come near her or the kids again, or my family, I'm going to kill you. You know I'm not threatening you. I *will* literally blow your head off and not think twice about it."

"I'm going to call your chief!" Tim shouted.

"I'll give you his phone number, Tim," Dappen said evenly. "But you know I'll do it, and if you come near us again, I'm going to kill you."

Tim Harris turned and got back in his car. He didn't like Don Dappen, but he respected him, and he knew Dappen meant every word he said. He gunned his Camaro and disappeared in a haze of road dust.

Don Dappen was a man who was slow to anger, but he felt in his gut that his family was in danger. He would not allow anything to happen to them.

As Phil Williams had sifted through the pile of leads and information the investigative team had gathered so far he had come upon the ticket written to Diane Lonergan. Initially it had seemed a useless bit of documentation. But then Williams had discovered that Tim Harris had no alibi at all for the time period following that stop. When the detective called to verify that it *was* Harris who had been booking a prisoner into jail shortly after he had stopped Diane Lonergan at 10:48 a.m. on March 4th, Williams was told that Tim Harris had a *new* serial number; another trooper had been assigned the number used on the booking slip. It was the *other* trooper who had made the arrest around 11:30 on Sunday morning. Tim might very well have remained on the Interstate near the median strip. And then again, he might have been miles away when Lorraine Hendricks crossed the border into Indian River County.

Phil Williams was curious about why Harris had stopped Diane Lonergan for going only five miles over the speed limit. He located Diane at her home near Miami and called to ask her if she remembered her encounter with Trooper Tim Harris. She did indeed.

"He stopped me for speeding, and I knew I wasn't speeding. I had my Cobra radar detector on, and it had not activated. He insisted I was going six miles over the limit. I knew I was only going about sixty-four miles an hour."

Williams made arrangements to talk with Diane and her husband again. A lot of people claim they weren't speeding, but there was something hinky that bothered Williams.

It was that very night that tip 56 came in. Sergeant Carroll Boyd called Williams about Sandy Harris's problems—not because Williams was assigned to the Hendricks murder case, but because he happened to be the detective on call on March 26th.

"I just wanted to advise you," Boyd began, "that Donny Dappen says his brother-in-law is behaving like an idiot. Tim Harris has apparently been prowling around Dappen's house and threatening his wife, Sandy."

Boyd said that they were going to arrest Tim Harris if they found him.

"No," Williams said. "*Don't* arrest him. If you find him, tell him that I'm investigating whether or not he's threatening Sandy."

Phil Williams wanted very much to open a dialogue with Tim Harris. If Harris suspected that Williams was interested in talking to him about Lorraine Hendricks's murder, he was likely to be on the defensive. If he thought Williams was only investigating a domestic dispute, it would be easier.

It would be a way in for Phil Williams.

Phil Williams arranged first to meet with Sandy Harris. He didn't want to go to Dappen's house; he knew that Tim was creeping around there. And he didn't want to go to Tim and Sandy's house in

Citrus Hideaway. He didn't want Tim Harris to know that he was talking to Sandy. Sandy agreed to meet Williams and Tony Oliver in the parking lot of a high school.

Sandy already suspected that Tim might be a killer. She hadn't voiced her dread to anyone, and she tried not to think about it. Her complaint to the Indian River County Sheriff's Office about Tim's attack on her on Saturday night was officially logged as battery. Sandy was frightened by what Tim had done to her, but she was sick at heart about a deeper fear, a niggling suspicion that Tim had done something horrible, more horrible than she could ever have imagined.

By the time Phil Williams and Tony Oliver met with Sandy on Monday, March 26, the bruises on her right wrist had blossomed red and purple, and they photographed them as evidence. When she said that she had been brutally handcuffed, they believed her. They didn't want to plant any ideas about Tim's involvement in Lorraine Hendricks's death in her mind, and they were careful as they questioned her.

But she *knew*. Sandy had come to know every facet of Tim's personality. She had seen the violence, and she had heard the sweet talk. She, of all people, knew what he was capable of.

She wished mightily that she did not.

Sandy told Williams and Oliver that Tim had threatened to rape her several times while he had her pinned to the floor and partially handcuffed—that he had also threatened to kill both of them with a gun if she didn't come back to him. And she had to tell them about the women's undergarments, too, embarrassing as it was.

Phil Williams had no doubt that he was listening to a woman who had been utterly terrorized.

Tim Harris hadn't been thinking straight—especially for a cop who was well aware of the value of physical evidence. He had left the lacy black panties and the pantyhose behind.

"These aren't yours?" Williams asked Sandy.

She shook her head. "I've never seen them before. I always cut the tags off my underwear, and I don't wear brown pantyhose."

Phil Williams asked Sandy about her estranged husband's sexual preferences. Embarrassed, she revealed that Tim often asked for oral sex, something that turned her off. He also wanted to photograph her in positions that humiliated her. But his wearing the women's underwear was something new. She had been shocked.

The two detectives bagged the lingerie into evidence. They didn't know what kind of underwear Lorraine Hendricks had worn. All they had ever located of Lorraine's missing possessions were her wallet from the Fort Pierce rest stop and the single golden hoop earring near her body.

It didn't seem possible that even the kinkiest killer would put on the underwear of his victim and attempt to rape his own wife. But then it hardly seemed possible that a respected Florida State trooper with a jacket full of commendations could be the predatory killer they were looking for either. Phil Williams had to face the fact that Tim Harris merited further investigation.

Maybe he wasn't involved. They sincerely hoped he wasn't. One dirty cop blackens the reputation of all cops everywhere. But Williams and Oliver had to agree that Tim Harris seemed to be losing it. His behavior was becoming more and more bizarre, and they had to either find the evidence to convict him or look elsewhere and hope the guy got into some serious therapy.

Sandy Harris agreed to have a tape recorder attached to her phone at her office so that Tim's phone calls to her would be recorded. It was ironic; he had taped her calls for months. It probably would never occur to him that *he* was being taped surreptitiously.

She got her restraining order against Tim and moved back into her house. Every police agency in the area—city, county, and state— knew that she was afraid of Tim. That in itself might be enough protection for her.

Sandy didn't really think that Tim would hurt Jennifer or Timmy; they were his own children, and he begged to see them. There were no orders preventing Tim from seeing them, and on Monday, March 26, she let him take them out to dinner. He brought them back on time and sent a note in, thanking her for letting him spend time with his children. Sandy was cautious; she had seen him behave sweetly before—but only for a little while.

Wednesday night, March 28, Tim asked to take them overnight. Sandy said no. It was a school night, and Tim had no place, really, to take them. She didn't want them over at DeeLisa's, and there wasn't room at David and Melissa's house. Sandy asked her mother, Pat, to pick Jennifer and Timmy up after school and not to let Tim take them.

For all the times that Tim had *not* been there to pick up the children when he promised, he was there this day, and he followed his petrified mother-in-law, his red Camaro right on the bumper of her car. Pat was afraid he would take the children out of state where their mother could never find them. It was a moot point. Both Jennifer and Timmy cried when Tim tried to take them away with him, and he drove off without them.

17

A **detective** works a homicide case a little like someone untangling a seemingly impossible jumble of knots. First he must find the easiest knot and loosen that—just to find a way to get at the rest of them. Once he does that, each knot is a little bit easier than the one before. Williams had been trying and eliminating "knots" for three weeks, and now he had one that looked as though it was going to give. He had a place to focus his expertise and his energy.

He thought he had eliminated Tim Harris as a suspect early in his investigation when his serial number showed Tim had been making an arrest many miles away from where Lorraine Hendricks was killed. Now he knew that wasn't so. Another trooper had made the arrest attributed to Tim.

At this point Phil Williams knew that Harris had been acting weird, and there was nothing to show that he had ever moved from his original radar position on March 4th, a position close to where the gray Honda was found.

Phil Williams called Diane Lonergan again. She said that the trooper who stopped her had had a dog with him—an aggressive German shepherd-type dog. She had been annoyed when the officer directed her to step out of her car and walk back toward his vehicle. But when she got out his attitude had changed. "I'm pregnant—*very* pregnant now—and it was certainly obvious that I was four weeks ago. He might not have noticed that when I was in the car, but he couldn't have missed it when I stepped out."

The trooper told her that he had clocked her speed at seventy-one miles an hour, and he wrote her a warning ticket. That had irritated her, and he had said, oddly, "You can just throw that away. It doesn't mean anything."

"Were you traveling alone?" Williams asked.

"Yes. All alone." She confided that she had been suspicious of the way the officer behaved, although he had been polite and professional on a surface level. But there was something about him that made her uneasy, and she had been upset by the encounter. She knew she wasn't speeding. And the trooper had to have known that, too.

Phil Williams couldn't help but wonder if Diane Lonergan's pregnancy had saved her life. It sounded as though she *had* been stopped when she wasn't speeding, and that Harris had only told her to tear up the ticket *after* he had her out of the car and could see she was pregnant.

Stan Lonergan wasn't eager to drive his wife up to Vero Beach so that she could point out the location where she had been stopped— not until Williams said, "You're a very lucky man, you know. There's another family who have lost their wife, mother, daughter. She came driving along that same stretch of Interstate about an hour after your wife did. We think maybe she got stopped for speeding, too. . . ."

Lonergan cleared his throat, and Williams could almost hear his thoughts as the brutal truth hit him. "We'll be up," he said. "Anytime you say."

The time had come to talk to Tim Harris. Phil Williams knew him, of course. He had never known him in the context of detective and suspect, or, in a way, cat and mouse. Tim Harris was smart, he knew all the ins and outs of police work, and he would be far more savvy than the average man on the street when it came to self-incrimination.

Conveniently, Tim Harris had heard that Phil Williams was investigating the incident with Sandy. Phil didn't have to call Tim. Tim called *him* and, after a short discussion, agreed to meet with Williams at Mama Mia's restaurant in Vero Beach. He expected Williams to question him about his problems with Sandy. He had been telling everyone who would listen how broken up he was about Sandy's throwing him out. It was quite possible that he viewed Williams as another listening ear for his love problems.

It is legal in Florida to tape surreptitiously. Certainly, Tim Harris had been using tapes to follow every breath his estranged wife took. Phil Williams knew Tim had been taping Sandy, and he smiled grimly as he fit a tiny tape recorder in a hollow below his armpit and adjusted his sports jacket. There would be a kind of poetic justice if Tim Harris implicated himself in the murder of Lorraine Hendricks on tape.

They set 2 p.m. on March 27th as the time for their meeting. Phil wasn't wasting any time; it was only a day after Sandy had talked with them about Tim's bizarre attack on her.

When Tim arrived in his red Camaro Phil saw that he had brought DeeLisa Davis with him. Phil had graduated from high school with DeeLisa back in 1971. He sighed. Sometimes he wondered if it would be easier to be a cop in a big city. It seemed as though he had had to arrest or interrogate so many people who had been his friends.

Phil Williams was a master interrogator, the deceptively casual country boy who had learned a long time back that every suspect had to be treated like a human being, no matter how heinous his—or her—crime might have been. Above all, Williams had to avoid any appearance of sitting in judgment. The worse the crime, the more careful he had to be to betray no shock and no disgust. He had to put the picture of Lorraine Hendricks's body lying abandoned in the woods completely out of his mind.

That wasn't going to be easy.

Phil Williams was in no hurry. He was going to take a sympathetic approach with Harris. Tim apparently had no recollection at all of the time, years ago now, when Phil had raced away from him and his ticket book when Tim was a gung-ho young Sebastian cop.

Every word of their conversation would be recorded by the little tape whirring beneath Williams's arm.

"How are you doing?" Williams greeted Tim Harris as Tim slid into Williams's car. He saw the trooper had dark circles etched beneath his eyes and that he was thin, almost gaunt.

"Not good at all. I'm telling you, not good."

"I think you're going through hell, ain't you?"

"It's worse than hell . . . and it's not helping with the relatives. The relatives are killing me."

"Is that DeeLisa?" Williams inclined his head toward the pretty woman who waited with one of her children in the Camaro.

"Yeah."

"I went to school with her . . . nice girl, nice girl."

"She's helped out a lot," Harris said.

"Yeah. Well, at least you got somebody standing by you, right?"

Tim said he wanted to tell Phil Williams the whole story, and for an instant Williams thought it was going to be almost too easy. It wasn't. For Tim, the "whole story" was about how badly he was being treated in his divorce wars by Sandy and her mother and sisters.

And now, Tim complained, it wasn't just the women in Sandy's family. Don Dappen had turned against him. Sandy and their children had been spending all their time at Don and Sue's house.

"Donny answers [the phone] and says, 'Don't ever call her again. . . .'"

"The reason why she's staying there, Tim," Phil explained, "is that she says she's scared to death to stay at home."

Tim knew what Phil was talking about—the night Sandy claimed she had been handcuffed and almost raped. But Tim insisted that was all a misunderstanding. He said that Sandy had asked him to come over, and he had refused because she and the neighbors were drinking wine coolers and he didn't drink. He had called back a few hours later, and the neighbors were still there, and Sandy had urged him to come over. "She said, 'Well, why don't you just come on over? Maybe they will get the hint when you walk in the door.'"

Tim Harris's version of the night of March 24th was diametrically opposed to Sandy's. He insisted that Sandy had wanted a back rub, and that she had enjoyed wrestling and playing around with the handcuffs.

"I didn't put them all the way on her. . . . As a matter of fact, when she started crying and said it really hurt I took the things off. . . . I mean, I don't like talking about our sex life."

He ducked his head and wouldn't meet Williams's eyes, but Tim Harris continued to discuss in the most intimate detail his personal relationship with Sandy. According to his version, it had been Sandy who had kept luring him back to their home; it had been Sandy who couldn't make up her mind what she wanted. It had been Sandy who had suggested a number of sexual acts that she wanted to try. Tim explained that he would do anything to get Sandy back. Back rubs. Cuddling. Patting her with baby powder. Oral sex. Whatever she wanted.

Williams nodded sympathetically, but he wondered how the man before him could be so deluded or such a liar. Tim was the one with a girlfriend waiting in his Camaro, his backup woman whom he had kept on a string for five years. Tim seemed completely oblivious to any pain he might be causing DeeLisa.

Tim denied that he had brought any women's underwear to Sandy's house.

"I wonder where she got them from," Williams said mildly.

"Those are hers . . . they're all hers."

"You know, that's the only thing that worries me about her . . . making up shit, I mean, you know—" Phil began.

"I don't know what to tell you," Tim said earnestly. "You know, she's putting her panties on me . . ."

"Yeah."

"You know the sex and all that . . ."

"Yeah."

"But she didn't want sex that night, and she made it clear she didn't want it," Tim admitted. "As a matter of fact, when she started crying as far as the handcuffs go . . ."

"Ummm hmm."

Tim Harris's voice was earnest as he explained that Sandy had never been afraid of him, and that he had always agreed to do whatever she wanted. If she didn't want to be kissed on the mouth, he said "No problem" and kissed her on the cheek. If she didn't want him to stay overnight, he always left.

Phil Williams kept his face bland and friendly. Tim seemed to brighten up. "You know," he said, "this is all going to end, and, you know, things are going to work out."

"Well, what's the chance of you staying away from Don?"

"I don't have any problem with that," Tim agreed, although he said that it was Don Dappen who was mostly causing the trouble with Sandy.

"I'm the one that is kind of monitoring that situation," Phil Williams said. He knew Sandy had a restraining order, and that she was panicked at the thought that Tim might take Jennifer and Timmy away—even for an hour.

Tim Harris's conversation went in predictable circles, always coming back to his great love for Sandy, to their wonderful sex life, to his belief that they would be back together if not for her interfering family, to the "tiny little thread" he still clung to that he believed bound him to Sandy. Phil Williams wasn't lying when he said he had been through the pain of divorce himself, that he could empathize. That was true, and that was all Tim Harris chose to hear. He quickly came to view Williams as a listening ear, a fellow cop who would understand.

And yet there was an undercurrent—Tim's reticence and his body language—that told Williams Tim Harris was directing the flow of conversation away from something as dangerous to him as an alligator waiting beneath the surface of a seemingly calm ditch.

Tim admitted that the Patrol had taken his gun away. Things weren't good. Not good at all. He admitted that he knew it would break DeeLisa's heart if he went back to Sandy. But he couldn't help it if DeeLisa wanted to stick with him.

DeeLisa had been waiting for Tim for a long time, out in the hot sun—and finally Phil Williams saw her and her child get out and head toward Phil's car, where he and Tim sat talking.

Tim Harris appeared to think almost exclusively of himself and of his own feelings. He confided that he was afraid he would lose his job if he was arrested for battery. He said he appreciated Phil Williams's taking the time to talk with him about his problems.

Phil offered to be available anytime. "Just give me a call," he said easily.

They had talked for hours. Neither of them had so much as touched on the subject of the dead woman out in the pines and palmettos.

Williams wondered if Tim was for real. He seemed to be a man with the narrowest of tunnel vision. He didn't seem worried about anything beyond his obsessive struggle to win his wife back. He was concerned about the possibility of the battery charge because that would mean his job. He *was* haggard and gaunt, but men suffering unrequited love often are.

But then, of course, Phil Williams had never once mentioned Lorraine Hendricks's name. If he had, would that have made Tim Harris sweat?

Maybe next time. Williams was certain there would be a next time.

Phil Williams fully expected to maintain his dialogue with Tim Harris; he felt that sooner or later Harris was going to open the curtain that hid dark fantasies waiting somewhere behind his clear and earnest green eyes. But in order to keep his position as the sympathetic listener, Williams was going to have to have a designated "bad guy."

And that man was going to have to be Donny Dappen.

Phil Williams went to see Don Dappen. They had known each other for years, one as an Indian River County detective, one as a Vero Beach city detective. They had clambered through ditches and sloughs and fields together in the pizza murders. That was easy compared to this.

"Donny," Phil said slowly, "I want to ask you something. Would Tim be capable of killing someone?"

"You suspect him on the I-95, don't you?"

Williams just stared at Dappen, and Dappen nodded. "Yeah— yeah, I think he would be."

"Sandy has to understand that she can't tell anyone that we suspect Tim," Williams warned. "Can she do it?"

"I think so. None of us knew how bad it was for her until recently. She keeps things inside."

"And Donny," Williams continued, "I need a fall guy. I don't want to have Tim arrested on the battery charges—I have to get into a little better position with him, open him up more. To do that I have to make you the bad guy when I'm talking to him. Can you handle that?"

Dappen grinned. He knew that his brother-in-law already hated his guts. If it would help the investigation, he told Williams he didn't care what Phil said about him.

"Go ahead. Paint me as black as you want. I'll be your bad guy. I blew the whistle on him in the first place."

If Tim was guilty, he would have to be arrested. Dappen was in no hurry to have the detectives' suspicions about Tim become public. Things were ugly enough already. If Williams's hunch was right, what was going to come down would mean that their whole family would be spread all over the front page.

In the meantime Williams worked to connect Tim Harris to Lorraine Hendricks with physical evidence. It wasn't going to be easy. He doubted that Harris had ever seen Lorraine until that day she had the great misfortune to round the curve on I-95 and enter the trooper's line of sight. It would have had to have been a random thing. If she had not stopped for gas, or if she had stopped for gas and stayed five minutes longer on the phone, or if she had only left home later . . .

It didn't matter now.

Williams checked with Lorraine Hendricks's friends and her estranged husband to see what kind of lingerie she usually wore. He found that Lorraine had preferred delicate, frothy things—and that she often wore black lace panties. But no one of them could identify the black panties left in Sandy Harris's home as absolutely belonging to Lorraine. They were her size, although they were stretched out now from being worn by a two-hundred-pound man. As for pantyhose, who could say? Sandy knew they were not hers. But one pair of pantyhose looked pretty much like another.

The Lonergans drove to Vero Beach in the same car Diane Lonergan had been driving on March 4th. They accompanied Phil Williams north of town until Diane pointed out the area in the southbound lane of I-95 where she had been stopped on that vital

Sunday. "I remember the sign that said how many miles it was to the Fort Pierce Outlet Malls," Diane explained.

The wooded median strip where Lorraine Hendricks's body had lain was a stone's throw away. Diane Lonergan pointed to a spot on the shoulder of I-95 where the trooper's unit had been sitting, facing traffic, when she first observed him. Phil Williams moved to that viewpoint and realized that Tim Harris had been able to see clearly who was in the cars as oncoming traffic approached. Diane Lonergan's car had slightly tinted windows, but it would have been quite possible for Tim Harris—from his vantage point—to see that she was a very pretty woman, and that she was alone.

It was only after Tim Harris had asked Diane to exit her car and walk back to his patrol car that he would have seen she was eight months pregnant.

Phil Williams knew now that in all likelihood Tim Harris had been in the area of the median on the Interstate when Lorraine Hendricks approached it.

If *he* hadn't done anything to her, Williams thought grimly, *somebody* had pulled off a murder right under his nose. . . .

18

Sandy Harris gave her consent for Phil Williams and Tony Oliver and Lt. Greg Edwards of the Florida Highway Patrol to search her home. They found a tape recorder that she had no idea was there—the Florida Highway Patrol–issue recorder that Tim had secreted beneath the pink insulation in the attic and spliced into the phone wires. In this first sweep of the home they also found drivers' licenses and ID papers for both men and women, but none for Lorraine Hendricks.

The tape in the attic recorder had recognizable voices on it: Sandy, DeeLisa, and Don Dappen. When Williams asked them if they had known they were being recorded during those particular conversations, none of them said they had, although Sandy, at least, wasn't surprised.

The attic tape recorder indicated that Tim had continued to break into the house in Citrus Hideaway even after Sandy had fled to Sue and Don's. Williams listened as he heard Tim talk to DeeLisa, and he wondered why the woman was so steadfastly sticking by Harris. The guy was deceiving her about his feelings for her, and at the same time he was rubbing her nose in his obsessive "love" for Sandy.

"Where are you?" DeeLisa's voice asked.

"Out." Tim said.

"Are you at a pay phone?"

"Sort of."

"Where are you?"

"Just don't ask me where I am, okay? I'm not with anybody, okay?"

"Timothy?"

"What, babe?"

"Is there anything you want to tell me?"

"What?"

"About the other night? . . . You were up there with her [Sandy]. Is there anything you want to tell me?"

"Like what?"

"Did you tell me anything wrong, or did you leave anything out?"

"As in what?"

"I'm asking if you had any physical contact with her . . . if you in any way hit her or roughed her up."

"I didn't hit her, and I didn't rough her up."

Tim Harris would have known the conversation was being recorded, Williams figured, but he probably didn't think anyone would ever find the tape recorder under the insulation. Even so, he was being cagey with DeeLisa.

"I want to know what happened the other night," DeeLisa pressed.

"I came up here to talk to her."

"And . . .?"

"She asked me to come upstairs and give her a powder, and I did—"

"Give her a *powder*?"

"Yeah, it's when you lay on the bed and you put powder on her back and rub her. Do you want me to continue?"

DeeLisa had to be a glutton for emotional pain. It was obvious to everyone that she adored Harris, and yet she asked him just what he had done with Sandy. Tim repeated to her exactly the story he had told Phil Williams—all the wrestling, hugging, kissing, the "accidental" bruising with the handcuffs. "I was just talking to her about letting me come back, and she agreed; she kissed me at the door, and I left."

DeeLisa wasn't buying the story any more than Phil Williams had.

Her voice was both hurt and angry. "It's really amazing how she's gone from someone who doesn't like sex to someone who's now saying, 'Give me a powder,' and accepting oral sex. . . . Every hour that goes by, almost, I keep hearing things that absolutely astound me."

Tim's voice was alarmed. "*Who* did you hear it from?"

"It's just a clue—it's just something I've been feeling and I thought I'd just ask."

"I'm *asking* you who did you talk to?"

"Nobody."

Tim continued to deny that he was in Sandy's house. DeeLisa tricked him. Her job had taught her everything about phones. She used her three-way call system to call him on his call waiting, and he fell for it. "Hold on a second, the phone's ringing. Don't say anything right now," he told her.

After a pause he said, "Are you still there?"

"Yeah. I was just calling you, Timothy."

"Who was on the phone?"

"Me."

"*Who?*"

"*Me,*" DeeLisa said, with a trace of sad smugness. "I used my three-way calling and called you." She had fooled him by putting him on hold. She knew now that Tim was at the Citrus Hideaway house.

"You think you're smart."

"Well, I'm getting smarter."

"That wasn't very nice."

"Really? Well, I'm sick and tired of being lied to, Timothy."

Tim denied that he was lying to her about anything and insisted that he hadn't wanted any physical relationship with Sandy. "It didn't happen because I wanted it—and it didn't happen because she wanted it," he finished lamely.

"Oh, you're just both prisoners, huh? Some alien made you lay down and do it. When I asked you what happened the other night you told me that you went there and that you argued."

"We argued."

"And then, when you left, she put her arms around you and said, 'I love you'?"

"That's what she did."

"Okay. You just happened to leave out a few details."

DeeLisa hung up on Tim, and the dial tone buzzed on the slowly revolving tape.

Williams labeled the tape and recorder and placed them in an evidence bag. Tim Harris was juggling too many stories, too many women, and all the time, Williams believed, he was hiding the biggest lie of all. Phil wondered how long he could keep it up. He suggested that they leave another FHP recorder in its place, but Tim's fellow troopers didn't want to do that. Despite the case that seemed to be building against him, he was still one of their own.

Williams sighed. He had had a plan to shake Tim Harris up a little. If a recorder was still there in the pink insulation, he could have staged a phone call to Sandy, saying that he had three eyewitnesses who had "seen" Tim pull Lorraine Hendricks over on March 4th. That would have made the hairs stand up on Tim's neck the next time he checked what he *thought* was his tape recorder.

Florida State Attorney General's Investigator Rick McIlwain had come aboard the investigative team, and he agreed that they must proceed with extreme delicacy. McIlwain was a polygraphist. But like most excellent lie-detector men, he knew that often the suspect never even needed to be hooked up to the leads on the lie box. The interrogation that came first, the threat of how much the polygraph might reveal, was enough to bring forth a confession.

The man they were tracking was no civilian; he knew the game, he knew the rules of evidence, and he knew how not to get caught. And he also knew how devastatingly accurate a polygraph readout could be as it traced a subject's respiration, galvanic skin responses, blood pressure, heartbeat. McIlwain figured the lie detector would alarm Tim Harris even more than it did most civilian suspects.

Despite the plethora of items the investigators had carefully bagged and labeled, they had not come up with one scintilla—not even a hair or fiber—that could help them prove that Tim Harris had ever been near Lorraine Hendricks.

A dog hair found in the headliner of Lorraine's Honda, viewed under a scanning electron microscope, seemed to match her pet corgi at home far more than Shadow's coat. Besides, animal hair is very, very difficult to differentiate. Dog hair is nowhere near as damning evidence as human hair might be.

When Phil Williams had asked Tim Harris if he would furnish a pubic hair sample, Tim had responded by reaching down the front of his uniform trousers and plucking the sample right then and there.

The hairs matched those found in the black lace panties, but that didn't help. Tim had admitted to wearing the panties, and his were the *only* hairs found caught in the mesh of either the panties or the pantyhose.

Sandy had once found Jennifer playing with a woman's purse in the garage of their house, but it wasn't Lorraine's purse. There was no way to prove whose it was; Tim said it had been turned in as lost, and he kept it only after he had exhausted all efforts to locate the owner.

True, Tim Harris was under extreme pressure, but it might take him a long, long time to break. When it seemed prudent it was agreed that McIlwain would become Williams's partner in interviewing Tim Harris. None of them expected Harris to give it all up at once. Their technique would be to build their case against him as solid as a brick wall. Each admission would be set in mortar and dried hard so that Harris couldn't go back, and each new change in his story would build on that.

And during all that time he must never realize how high the wall was growing.

On April 2 Tim Harris called Phil Williams. He wanted to talk about Sandy. "I had problems this weekend. I went to Don's house with a court order to take the kids for two days, and they refused to turn them over. . . . She said she was gonna press charges and all that good stuff, so I was just checking to see if anything was going on."

Tim added that the Highway Patrol had taken him off the road and put him on administrative duties.

"What's that mean?" Williams asked, although he already knew.

"Paperwork."

"They got you like on a suspension-type thing?"

"Well, it's not really a suspension—it's just administrative duties."

Tim Harris said he'd like to have lunch with Phil and talk some more. Phil Williams picked him up at the Florida Highway Patrol station, and they drove along I-95. This time Phil was going to push harder; he was going to bring up Lorraine Hendricks's murder. He began by talking about Sunday, March 4th.

Yes, Tim said he remembered stopping a pregnant woman that Sunday. He hadn't mentioned it before because he hadn't considered it unusual.

On March 4, Tim said, he had spent most of his shift down in St.

Lucie County. He might have stayed near the wooded median for a very short time after stopping the pregnant woman.

"How long?"

"Probably half hour, forty-five minutes . . ."

"Then the whole thing is, Tim," Phil commented, "that you had to see *something*."

"I didn't see anything . . . out of the ordinary."

"If I found one witness that said that they saw you pull her car over?"

"The girl I stopped?"

"No, the other girl."

"You mean the girl that's dead?"

"Um-hmm."

"It wasn't me."

Williams backed off and tried another angle. He explained that he just wanted something solid from Tim so that he could absolutely clear him, get all of this over and done with.

Tim thought about the pregnant woman's claim that she hadn't been speeding and said he thought her Fuzzbuster was probably broken.

"This one works. We tested it out six different ways."

"Did you talk to her?" Tim was suddenly alert.

"I must have," Phil answered obliquely. "I'm telling you a lot of things, ain't I?"

Asked if he would take a polygraph, Tim Harris said he would. Knowing that Tim knew all the polygraphers in the area, Phil asked him to pick which one he would like to have administer his lie detector test. Tim hedged, and Phil eased off. Tim Harris had already given him permission to search his squad car; he didn't want to push him too hard too fast.

"Well, the only thing I want to know is . . . is when this investigation is over," Phil Williams said carefully. "I want to know whether you had any involvement or not and whether I'm looking at the right person or even should be looking at you at all. Okay?"

His tone of voice was easy, but his words were blunt enough.

"I'm not a murderer, Phil. I'm not out to kill people. . . . I understand where you're coming from, but I'm not out there killing people."

"And things you're doing." Phil probed deeper. "Weird shit, okay?"

Tim thought Phil was referring to his peeking in the windows at

Don and Susan's house. He said he had only wanted to see his children.

"Weird shit, too, is wearing women's pantyhose and women's underwear," Phil continued.

Tim blamed that on Sandy. All the kinky sex stuff had been Sandy's idea. Aware of how terrified Sandy had become, how she was afraid even in her own home, Phil Williams doubted that Sandy had been the instigator of all the erotica, the cross-dressing, and the bondage. He did not, however, say as much.

Phil did hit Tim with the discovery of the tape player in the attic insulation and repeated Tim's conversation with DeeLisa. Tim grew quiet. *That* surprised him; he hadn't known that Phil knew about the hidden recorder. And he surely didn't know that Williams had been recording every word of *their* current conversations from the beginning—that even now the tiny recorder secreted in Phil's armpit was rolling along.

They went round and round again. Whenever Phil Williams got too close to Lorraine Hendricks's murder Tim dug in his heels. "I didn't kill her. . . . I didn't stop her, and I didn't see her."

He recalled he had spent most of that Sunday "profiling"— looking for cars with black or Hispanic males, the types he had come to suspect as drug runners. One thing was sure: Tim said he certainly hadn't been out there looking for single women to stop.

Phil Williams regretted once again that he and Larry Smetzer and Tony Oliver had come up with exactly zip in the way of physical evidence; they had found nothing at all connecting Tim Harris to Lorraine Hendricks. They had a gold hoop earring from the palmetto grove that Rick Hendricks had identified as Lorraine's, they had the tissue, fluid, and hair and fiber samples from the autopsy (all of which had proved useless as evidence), the vacuumings from the victim's car and the possessions she had left behind, and they had also searched Tim Harris's car—with his permission—Sandy and Tim Harris's house, Tim's brother David's house, and the patrol cars of every Florida trooper who worked the I-95 corridor.

And still they had nothing they could use for probable cause for an arrest.

Phil Williams took a chance and told Tim that they had found red fibers not unlike the fibers from the carpet in Tim's new Camaro in the black lace panties and pantyhose. The crime lab *had* found several red synthetic carpet fibers as well as several dog hairs in the pantyhose Tim wore to Sandy's house the night he terrorized her.

But the red fibers really didn't match Tim's Camaro's carpet. Williams didn't tell Tim that. He was fishing, dangling some bait for Tim to jump at.

And jump he did. At that point Tim Harris suddenly remembered that he had gone through Sandy's drawers some weeks ago, taken many of her nightgowns and panties, and carried them away in his car. He didn't say why he'd done that, and Williams didn't ask him—because he didn't believe him. But his ploy had worked. Tim Harris admitted readily that he *had* worn the black panties. He said he had stolen Sandy's panties, and then he had worn them back. That would explain the red carpet fibers clinging to them.

Only they weren't the right red fibers.

Phil Williams had caught Tim Harris in a lie. The first lie. Williams turned the key in his ignition, and they pulled out onto I-95.

That was enough for this day. Let the mortar dry a bit in the wall they were building around Tim Harris.

Phil turned toward Tim, explaining in his most casual voice that he needed to clear Tim so he could get on with catching the real killer. "It's muddying up the waters as far as my investigation. . . . Like the underwear . . . I mean the things have obviously had a man in them. . . . It looks pretty doggone obvious to me that you were lying to me. Well, my question is, *Why would Tim lie to me?*"

They headed back toward Vero Beach in silence.

It was only a day later when Tim Harris called and left his phone number on Phil Williams's pager.

"Can you tell me what's going on?" Harris asked when Williams called him back.

"Just getting the polygraph set up. Looks like this afternoon at five. What time you get off?"

"About five o'clock." Harris's voice was more closed off than Williams had ever heard it.

"You mind doing that this afternoon?" Williams asked.

"I'd like to, and I told you I would," Tim said, and Phil Williams's heart sank; Harris was backing off. "Because you told me that, you know, in your mind that would help you," Tim finished in the same earnest voice that really meant "No way."

"Um-hmm."

"But I've talked to an attorney, and he suggested I don't—and not because I have anything to hide from anybody. He said, 'That's the first thing people are going to think is you're trying to hide something'. . . . But he also said it [the polygraph] can screw you over and unfairly screw you over."

Phil Williams didn't argue with Tim Harris. "It's entirely up to you. . . . It's just a chance to prove yourself innocent before God and the world."

Tim assured Phil that he was trying to cooperate, but the lie detector thing—well, he wasn't sure how accurate it would be. He was as anxious as anybody could be to get away from pushing papers and to get back on the road, but he just wasn't sure what to do.

"Well, like I said, Tim," Williams said easily, "if you could take the polygraph and pass, then I think that everything would be alleviated. If you'd take it and fail, we're right back where we are now."

"We're *nowhere*. . . . I think for right now I just don't want to take it."

"Okay. Well, let me call everybody and call it off, then."

Tim Harris's decision not to take the polygraph was almost as damning in Phil Williams's mind as if he *had* taken it and failed.

But there was something else. Tim Harris's reactions were too flat, and they were all wrong. He wasn't angry. He wasn't outraged. He didn't sound one bit like an innocent man who was indignant at being called a suspect. He should have been mad as hell. But he wasn't.

Tim sounded only like a very nervous, hesitant man.

The next day Tim Harris called Phil Williams again and asked him to come down to the Patrol office. Odd; he had to know that Williams was walking one step behind him, and yet he clung to him like a drowning man. Tim said he was getting really worried about losing his job. Lt. Greg Edwards from the Patrol was coming up from headquarters to investigate his case further. Tim wanted Phil Williams to tell him that everything was okay. But he was passive-aggressive, too; he was angry that Phil had caught him on tape on the attic recorder.

"Tim, you told *me* a lot of things," Phil said. "You bullshitted *me*. Now, you don't think that I'm going to possibly be able to set you up for a homicide, do you? I mean, what am I going to do?"

"I don't see how you can," Tim acknowledged, "because I haven't done anything."

Phil Williams had seen men about to break before, and now, even over the phone, he could hear Tim Harris beginning to come apart. They were both cops. He had used that before to explain his stubborn pursuit of the truth to Tim, and he used it now.

"You know, as far as putting the tape player back up in the attic—yeah, I wanted to see if you would go back to it. No big deal. . . . It's just as typical a tactic as when you sit beside the road and run radar. People slip into your trap. . . . You're a cop, you know what the deal is. At some point you gotta go sit down and give an official statement. You were at least in the area that day."

"There's no doubt that I was," Tim agreed.

"I don't like telephone interviews," Phil said. "We've talked casually beside the road; we've never had a sit-down—"

They were about to have their "sit-down." Tim Harris said he was ready to give a statement in person. Keeping his voice as calm as possible, Phil Williams suggested they meet at the State Attorney's Office. Tim said he would check with his captain, and if it was all right with him, he would come in. He would be there shortly before noon.

It had taken many contacts to get Tim Harris to a place where he would give an official statement. Williams called Rick McIlwain at the State Attorney's Office and told him it was about to happen. It had to happen. If Tim Harris didn't confess to strangling Lorraine Hendricks, there was every likelihood he was going to walk away. Without a confession they had nothing. Even *with* a confession conviction might not be a sure thing. It works on television, but in real life any prosecutor will choose hard physical evidence over a confession or an eyewitness.

There was always the gnawing possibility that ate at Phil Williams. Maybe Tim Harris wasn't guilty. Just because the guy treated the women in his life as if they were his property, as if their feelings were negligible, just because he liked to dress up in ladies' lingerie, just because he liked to take photos of his sex partners, just because he happened to be in the area of the murder at the time of the murder, just because he had stopped a pregnant woman and then let her go when he saw her condition—

There were an awful lot of "just becauses."

The circumstantial stuff was piling up. The search of Tim Harris's patrol car, his papers, and his possessions had revealed a man preoccupied with sex—a man with the power that his uniform and his position gave him over both the women he knew and the women he encountered out on the freeways.

Phil Williams and Tony Oliver had found the carbon copies of Tim Harris's tickets and seen where he had jotted down notes on the back of some of the thin yellow sheets: comments on female drivers' measurements, their breasts, their legs, their sexiness. And hidden among his possessions where he must never have expected anyone to find them Tim kept two cartoons. One looked as though it had been mimeographed to be passed around among good old boys and draw raucous chortles, the kind of dirty joke that junior high school boys circulated.

The other was drawn in pencil on a sheet of a yellow legal tablet, and it looked like it could well have been drawn by the same hand that drew cartoons for Tim's children—entirely different kinds of cartoons. Both of the drawings Tim Harris kept hidden involved a state trooper stopping a sports car with a pretty female driver. Both involved the woman's giving oral sex to the trooper, who stood grinning while the woman knelt and serviced him.

In the cartoon on the yellow tablet the dialogue in the balloons was personal. The naked woman kneeling at the state patrolman's feet asked, "Trooper Harris, are you sure I'm doing this right?"

The trooper, drawn wearing dark glasses, answers, "Yes. This is the new breathalyzer test."

If Tim Harris was not a murderer, Phil Williams thought he most assuredly had no business out there on the I-95 Interstate, sighting down on women as they turned a curve and came into his view. It wasn't that the average cop—himself included—didn't appreciate an attractive woman. But Tim Harris gave Williams a hinky feeling. Harris just plain didn't *like* women; he used them for his own purposes, and when one had finally had the guts to walk away from him, he became darkly obsessive about getting her back.

Sandy Harris had, Williams thought, come perilously close to death the night Tim sat astride her and held a gun close by her head. If she hadn't kept her head and lied that she would take him back, she might never have seen the next morning.

Alone with a woman, Tim would have been a formidable threat. He was such a big man to begin with. And then he had Shadow, who responded to his master's bidding without question. The power of Shadow's jaws was evident in Tim's patrol unit. When the Indian River investigators searched the car they saw where Shadow had literally "eaten" huge chunks out of the upholstery on the door panels. Maybe he had been bored at being left alone in the patrol car for a time; maybe he had been trying to chew his way through the door at some time to get to Tim.

19

Tim Harris arrived at the State Attorney's Office as he had promised. It was early in the afternoon of Friday, April 6th, four weeks almost to the minute from when Phil Williams had discovered Lorraine Hendricks's body. Phil now ushered Tim into a conference room. There was a long table there surrounded by seven white leather swivel chairs, and the walls were lined with bookcases full of law books. It was very quiet, an inner sanctum in a busy office.

Williams told Tim that Rick McIlwain from the State Attorney's Office might be joining them, and Harris didn't demur.

They began at an innocuous place. What hours had Tim worked on March 4th? Second watch. "Eight to four."

As Tim recalled, he was driving Unit 444, his regular canine unit. Shadow was with him. He started running traffic on I-95, moving his radar between the Indian River County north border and State Road 60 to the south.

Harris mostly answered Williams's questions with one-syllable answers: "Yes." "No." "Okay."

Tim said he had seen no one walking on the median, no one parked. It had just been a slow, ordinary Sunday.

At this point the door opened, and Rick McIlwain walked in smiling, extending his hand. "Hey, there," he said.

"How ya doing?" Tim responded, shaking McIlwain's hand firmly.

It was still very low key. Phil introduced the two men and continued his questioning. McIlwain listened but said nothing.

Tim recalled that he had set up his stationary radar near the wooded median strip that Sunday. He guessed it would have been between 10 and 11 a.m. He recalled that one of his fellow troopers, Carlin Parker, had come by, and they had talked for twenty minutes to half an hour.

"The warning ticket," Williams said. "Was Carlin there before that ticket—or after it?"

"I believe he was there before."

Tim denied that he had ever gone down into the woods in the median. "Not that day. . . . I've gone through there many times. . . . I take the dog through there and break him out and let him run out, doing tracks, in and out of there."

Williams asked if Tim had been in a particularly bad mood that day—feeling even more depressed and angry than he usually did, considering how he felt about his impending divorce.

"I'm probably in my worst mood right now, because of what's going on right now."

"Was there anything going on that Sunday—other than the normal?"

"I was probably better off back then, because I was still talking to Sandy, and we were still trying to get things together—back and forth."

On that Sunday, March 4, Tim said he'd just been sitting there "profiling" drivers. He could see inside the cars coming at him enough to see how many people were inside, if they were black or white, male or female, if they had tinted glass in their windows. That sort of thing. He was using an NT8 stationary radar unit, not the newer VASCAR technique. No, he would not have had the capability with the NT8 to lock in the seventy miles per hour that he said Diane Lonergan had been traveling and show the reading to her.

Tim remembered her, the "pregnant chick," remembered thinking that she might have been a policeman's wife, or maybe knew a policeman—from the way she spoke. "She was talking about the dog."

"Was she afraid of the dog?"

"I don't think she was afraid. She took note of it, because he was beating up against the window . . . and barking."

After he had written the warning ticket for Diane Lonergan Tim Harris thought he'd remained with his radar set up on the shoulder at the median for another fifteen or twenty minutes. He'd heard on the radio that Carlin Parker had made an arrest and was headed toward the jail. (It was Carlin who had been given Tim's old serial number; that arrest was the one originally attributed to Tim—the mistake that had given him a solid alibi in the beginning of the investigation.)

Tim Harris said he had left the median strip area and headed south toward St. Lucie. He hadn't eaten a real lunch, only picked up a Big Gulp and a candy bar at the Seven-Eleven on the way. The only ticket he had given that day was to a black male who was "hitting the high nineties. . . . It took a little bit to catch up with him," Tim recalled.

Tim said he had turned back north toward his brother David's house at the end of his shift. He slept there that night. He had the next two days off.

"Okay, Tim," Williams said. "Do you remember if you went into any rest areas down that way?"

"I've gone through the St. Lucie rest area—"

"Let's go back to whenever you was sleeping in there."

Tim Harris laughed. "I was in a Ram Charger—uh—the truck I used to own before I traded it in for the Camaro."

Williams skillfully wound the conversation back to the polygraph, and Tim said he just didn't want to take it. He had taken one eight years before when he applied for the Patrol, and it had shown he was being deceptive about a time he'd been stopped by a policeman. He'd been telling the truth; the polygrapher had his driving record right there in front of him, but oddly Tim's answer had come up that he was hiding something. He hadn't trusted the machines since.

They had been talking for almost an hour, and Williams began to bear down, but only a little. "Just give me—in your own words— why you don't want to take one."

"Somehow," Tim began, "I have to convince you that I'm not involved in this—"

"How you going to do that?" Rick McIlwain asked bluntly. He wasn't smiling.

"I don't know. You seem to think that my problems with Sandy or the things that stemmed from that are involved in this, and they're maybe partially involved, but they're not. I'm not out there killing people."

McIlwain questioned Tim about his law enforcement career. Gradually he had become the lead questioner in this session, asking an innocuous question, slipping in a more dangerous one, and then dropping back. He asked Tim about his experience in conducting investigations.

"You know what needs to be done. You know the things that need to be looked at. Okay?"

"I understand," Tim said.

"And here you have a homicide," McIlwain pushed ahead. "Okay—you have a woman that left Jacksonville and was coming south on I-95. We know that she was in this area around eleven— eleven-thirty. We know that would have been the approximate time when she'd been coming through on I-95. *You* know you were in this area at about the time she was coming through."

"That's correct."

"Okay. And you're a police officer. And you are a witness in this case—"

"*If* I saw something."

"You're still a witness. You know what a witness is. You know why we have witnesses, why we have people going into court. . . . You're a witness any way you look at it because you were in the area. You were working. You were running radar. You stopped somebody and gave them a warning within a time frame that would put you still right there even after you got done writing that ticket. And here's her car, sitting on a road, not a half mile south of where you saw this one woman southward bound. And here the woman's body is found back up in the area of the turnaround place. . . . You have a dog?"

"Yes, sir."

"What is your dog trained to do?"

"Narcotics—search for people."

"Okay. This lady was reported missing on Monday, the day after you finished your last day shift. The car was found sometime Monday, just south of where you were running radar. You have a dog. Did you ever take your dog back up to there? Did anyone notify you and say, 'Hey, Tim, some girl's come up missing after she left Cocoa. Monday, her car was found right here on 95 in our area'?"

Tim shook his head slowly. "No, I believe I ran into Phil that week—Wednesday, or it might have been Thursday. . . . He was walking up and down the interstate—"

"It was Friday," Phil said quietly.

Tim insisted that no one had ever told him about the missing woman. He had found out about it only after reading something in the paper. The investigation hadn't been his responsibility, and he had paid little attention to it.

For all the hours they had talked Phil Williams had let Tim see him as a buddy, a commiserater about the woes women can bring, a fellow cop. McIlwain's questioning style was entirely different. He was jabbing hard at Tim, incredulous that a working trooper, a K-9 and felony officer, would not have been aware and very interested and involved in the search for a missing woman smack dab in the middle of his regular territory.

Tim stonewalled. "You're asking me about something that I don't know anything about."

"Hey," McIlwain said. "I'm just asking—"

"Killing someone's not normal," Tim said flatly.

"True . . . it's definitely not normal." McIlwain paused for a moment. "To *think* about committing a crime is not a crime, is it?"

"But who's thinking about committing one?" Tim countered.

"You *never* thought about committing a crime?"

"No, I haven't."

"Never have? Nothing's ever gone through your mind—you never picked up the paper and read about how somebody turned around and committed a bank robbery, or committed some kind of crime, and they got caught for it . . . and you thought, 'No, *damn*, if I was going to do something like that, I wouldn't have done it that way. I'd'a turned around and done it some other way.' You never thought about anything like that? Most normal people do."

"I must not be normal, then," Tim said mildly.

There was no time in this room, cosseted and isolated by the thick barrier of law books along its walls. The three men sat there, conversing in a deceptively mild way, as if two were not hunters and one was not their quarry. No bead of sweat marked Tim Harris's forehead; he stretched his long legs out comfortably on the carpeted floor. To a casual observer they might only have been three lawmen having a friendly conversation. And yet Rick McIlwain's questions were narrowing more and more into one channel, the channel that led straight back to the murder of Lorraine Hendricks.

Tim reminded Rick McIlwain and Phil Williams that he had been cooperative with all their requests for searches. "I've done everything that you asked me to do . . . short of finding the person who killed her."

Phil Williams recalled that Tim had refused the lie box.

Phil posed a question to Tim that only a cop would understand. "If you found narcotics in a vehicle, and there's somebody in the backseat . . . does that person know there's narcotics in the front seat?"

The question gave Tim Harris a chance to admit he was peripherally involved in Lorraine Hendricks's murder, but not the man they were looking for.

"Maybe," Tim Harris said inscrutably.

He showed no distress, no tension, but he was getting a little annoyed. Tim insisted they were focusing on him only because of the battery charges Sandy had filed against him and all the other marital troubles he had been going through. "I'm not the only one going through a divorce right now."

Tim wanted to know if he was still a "witness," or had he become a "suspect"?

He was still a witness, they assured him, but he clearly didn't believe them. He reminded them that he had come in against his attorney's advice—because "I don't have anything to hide from you."

On and on they talked in circles, widening circles and then tight, cautious circles, but they always came back to the black underwear Tim insisted was Sandy's, and the fact that Tim had been working I-95 when someone took Lorraine out of her car and that he *should* have seen something.

Tim Harris continued to blame his wife for all of his problems. Sandy, he said, knew full well that the black lace panties were her own. It was *Sandy* who should be put on the polygraph, not him.

But it was *Tim* that Rick McIlwain and Phil Williams wanted to hook up to the polygraph; his growing resistance to it fascinated them. They used that resistance to nudge him off his stolid position of both innocence and ignorance concerning Lorraine Hendricks's murder.

"So people that take them [polygraphs] are automatically guilty . . . that's what you're assuming right now," Tim challenged McIlwain.

"I'm not assuming anything," McIlwain said tightly. "If you assume something, what do you do, buddy? You make an ass out of you and me. A-S-S-U-M-E . . . I'm just saying I've done cops and cops. Cops are nothing. Cops are some of the best people in the world because they know the difference between right and wrong, and when they come in there and they haven't done it there's not a damn thing for them to worry about. They could give a shit less, you know. 'Ask me what you want.' "

Phil Williams pointed out once again that the first thing a guilty man always said was "I didn't do it."

"I know you're a cop, but just in this particular incident, just you saying 'I didn't do it' does not eliminate you."

"How long are you going to keep thinking that I did?" Tim asked.

"Until you prove you didn't."

It had been more than two hours, and they had reached a kind of impasse. Rick McIlwain cleared his throat and suggested another scenario to the tall trooper in front of him. "Is there a chance you stopped her, and you let her go, and you either gave her a verbal warning or something of that nature? And you're concerned now because she was found dead, and here you're saying, 'My God . . . I stopped this woman, and I let the woman go . . . and I didn't write nothing out, and if I turn around and tell them, "Yeah, I stopped her," I'm screwed'?"

"I've never stopped that lady before."

"Do you still take your dog up there [the median crime scene] to run?"

"Not anymore, I don't."

"*Why?*"

"Because of the crime scene."

"It's over now," McIlwain said.

"It's not over with until you find somebody."

Tim Harris was far from stupid. He detected that the climate in the room had changed. McIlwain was at his throat, and he wasn't about to back off. Phil was still more understanding, but Phil was pressing him, too, wanting more, more, *more* proof.

Tim was puzzled, though, that Phil hadn't already arrested him for wiretapping in Sandy's attic. Phil could have thrown him in jail for that, and investigated Lorraine Hendricks's murder at his leisure.

Tim asked Phil why he hadn't arrested him for tapping Sandy's phone.

"What's your feelings on that?" Phil asked.

"I assumed you had stopped it [an arrest] because you didn't want me to be put in jail."

Williams nodded. "I don't like to see cops go down. But neither do I like having the suspicion on my mind that a cop killed someone either."

"How do you think I feel walking around that station," Tim countered, "knowing that people think something?"

When the questions got too pointed, when he must have begun to panic inside—although he never betrayed it externally—Tim Harris's stance was always to suggest the investigators go to Sandy. Sandy would explain that the panties were hers. They could not know how true to form he was. He had *always* run to Sandy for comfort and shelter and for someone to clean up the messes he had made in his life. She had been only sixteen when he met her, and now she was twenty-seven and he was thirty-two. Sandy had always been able to smooth things over before; she had always forgiven him or borrowed more money or bought him the newest "toy" he needed to make his life happy. She had been his buffer against the world.

And now Sandy was gone from him. He had thrown her away a number of times. This time she was not coming back. He didn't seem to know that, as he continually turned the conversation that had long since become an interrogation back to Sandy. "And I think if you talk to Sandy, and really let her know what's going on—" Tim said earnestly.

Successful interrogations are by their very nature lengthy, repetitive, and circuitous. This one certainly was. Phil Williams wondered why Tim didn't just get up and leave. Nobody was stopping him. From time to time Phil offered him a cold drink. When Tim accepted, Phil went to get the soda and took the opportunity to change the tape in his hidden recorder. He had used up three hours' worth now, and Harris was making no move to leave. Williams couldn't figure out if it was because Tim believed he was snowing them completely or because he had some subconscious need to tell them, to get the crime out of his head where it had to have been eating at him like acid for more than a month.

The calls that Tim had made to Sandy had all been taped, and he hadn't made one slip—nothing that would tie him to Lorraine Hendricks's murder. There was still always the chance that the guy was innocent—that he just happened to be a womanizer, a wife batterer, and a guy who liked to wear lady's underwear. He wouldn't be the first.

A small chance.

Tim asked how much longer they wanted to talk with him.

"Until you say 'I got to go,'" Williams answered.

"Are we going to beat a dead horse?"

Again they told him he was free to go at any time.

Tim Harris made no move to leave. He wanted something from them. He wanted them to tell him he was no longer a suspect. He wanted to go back out on the road, to have everyone forget he had ever been a suspect in a murder.

And that was something neither McIlwain nor Williams would give him. He had danced around every important question they had asked him. In three hours they had made only minuscule advances.

And yet there was a growing tension in the room. Rick McIlwain had become far more accusing and sarcastic.

"You're the good guy," Tim said suddenly, looking at Phil Williams, "and you're the bad guy," to McIlwain. It was an age-old interrogation technique. Mutt and Jeff. Good guy, bad guy.

"No, no," McIlwain disagreed. "We're not doing good guy, bad guy shit. . . . I've listened to you and listened to you and listened to you, and he's been as nice and polite as can be, and I'm a little edgy on it because I don't really know. He knows you better than I do."

Rick McIlwain and Phil Williams were closer than they realized to a break. Suddenly there was a subtle change in Tim Harris's answers, as if he was daring them to make something of the bits and pieces he revealed.

"If you got a problem, I think you better get it off your chest," McIlwain began again.

"Problem such as what?"

"Such as killing the woman."

"I told you I didn't kill her."

"Did you *stop* her?" Phillips shot out.

"What if I did? Would you think different?"

"Would that help us out?" McIlwain asked. "Yeah, it would—that would at least tell us she was in the area—"

"Suppose I had sex with her." Tim Harris said. "Would it make a difference?"

They were on the edge of something. The two interrogators scarcely breathed, but their faces betrayed nothing.

"What if you did?" Phil asked.

"Would it make a difference?"

"You got a bush bond, it would at least show what kind of lady she is," McIlwain said quietly.

"I know this girl's character, Tim," Phil Williams cut in. "One of the first things I do is character-line this person. . . . Her mother and father paint her as a nice little girl. . . ."

"Sandy's mom paints her as a nice little girl, too," Tim said bitterly.

Williams eased Tim Harris into what he sensed was coming next. He knew he could not betray even a trace of revulsion at whatever he was about to hear. If he exhibited a judgmental attitude, he would shut Harris down.

"What kind of situation was it?" McIlwain asked.

Tim began by talking in a roundabout way. They let him.

"Maybe it was perfectly normal—maybe not department policy, but maybe it was normal," Tim mused. "You leave. You think that maybe she leaves. . . . How do you think I'd feel if something like that happened and she ended up dead? Don't you think I'd feel guilty that I had a part in it?"

"Sure do," Phil said calmly. "And I think that would cause you to be worried on a polygraph."

Tim was ultimately concerned about being "normal." He had mentioned it many times over the past hours. It was a trait both McIlwain and Williams had seen before in murderers and sex offenders. No matter how heinous the crime, they didn't want to be seen as "abnormal" or "crazy."

Tim continued, almost talking to himself. "Having sex with someone that's a consenting person that is not resisting you. It's not against the law. Maybe it's not morally right—but killing somebody is. . . . I'm telling you I *didn't* kill her."

"What *did* you do?" McIlwain asked.

"I'll leave it at that."

Tim Harris had led his questioners to the edge of a precipice and then backed off. They could not, would not, drop it at this point, no matter how hard Harris dug his heels in. They were afraid he was going to leave, but he sat without moving a muscle.

"Come on, Tim," Williams urged.

"You're looking for a murderer, someone that's killed somebody. I'm not the one that did it."

"Did you stop the girl?" McIlwain pressed. "Did you have a conversation with her? Did you have a bush bond with her and let her go on down into St. Lucie County? What did you do?"

"There were bikers in that area," Tim said. "I didn't kill her. . . . I'm telling you I didn't kill her. I didn't have anything to do with that."

"Do you know who did?"

"No, I don't."

"What *do* you know?" McIlwain asked.

"Where was she when you last saw her?" Williams said.

The room crackled with tension. They were on the brink. Each of them felt it. The questions and the answers now came after agonizingly long pauses, as if each of them was feeling his way along that precipice, aware that one misstep would tumble the whole thing down. The very air in the room seemed thicker somehow. Phil Williams stole a sideways glance at Tim and noted that his forehead was free of perspiration. He watched a bead of moisture slide down Tim's empty Coke can and waited for the answer that he knew would be the key, the way in they had been looking for for weeks.

"If I talk to you about it," Tim finally said, "you're going to think I did it."

Rick McIlwain kept his voice as emotionless as he could. "Not necessarily."

Phil Williams was blunt. "I'm thinking that now, Tim."

"I know you are." For the first time Tim—who rarely looked anyone straight in the eye—was staring directly into Williams's eyes so intensely that his gaze almost burned.

"You want to tell me something?" Williams asked.

Tim Harris's answers were convoluted. "I guess people try to tell somebody something when they feel responsible for it indirectly— not actually did it."

"*How* do you feel responsible 'indirectly'?" McIlwain asked.
"I'm telling you I didn't kill her, though."

Phil Williams glanced at his watch. *Damn.* He knew his tape was just about to run out. It was the worst of all possible times to have to break the mood in the room, but if Tim was about to confess to some culpability in Lorraine Hendricks's murder, Phil wanted it on tape. They had come a long way in the four and a half hours they had spent in this room. In the beginning Tim had not even admitted to any knowledge of the case. Now he had as much as conceded he knew what had happened.

Williams signaled to McIlwain. If Tim thought it peculiar that they were pausing at this point to freshen their Cokes, he gave no sign. Phil Williams left the room, removed Tape 7, and inserted Tape 8, side A. Then he grabbed a couple of soft drinks and walked back into the conference room.

They had to backtrack from where they had been until they had once again reached the point where Tim would talk about Lorraine Hendricks. They still had not the vaguest notion of a motive for Tim Harris, whose job as a Florida Trooper was his *life*, to kill a woman driving down his sector of the Interstate. They *did* know that Tim was totally obsessed with winning back Sandy, and that he harbored tremendous rage because she no longer wanted him.

Were the two parts of his life so entangled and obsessive that they had ignited murderous fury?

Rick McIlwain mused on what might have happened, giving Tim Harris a chance to add or change details. "It could have been an accident. Maybe somebody stops to park, she's on the side of the road—somebody else came up on her. They're talking. Maybe she said something that pissed them off—"

"What would she have said to somebody to piss them off?" Tim asked.

"I don't know . . . your wife ever piss you off?"

"Many times."

"You ever hit her?"

"No."

"Struggle with her?"

"I've struggled with her."

"You ever slap her around?"

Tim would not acknowledge slapping Sandy. He had held on to her arms, her shoulders. Yes, he had put his hands around Sandy's neck, put bruises on her. "But that doesn't make me a killer."

McIlwain switched to Lorraine Hendricks. Was it possible that a cop had stopped her and she told him she couldn't take another ticket, and that she had offered a bribe? "I'll give you a little piece if you let me off this one"?

"I've had it done before," Tim said cautiously.

"Have you ever taken them up on it? . . . *What* have you done to them?"

"Sent them on down the road with their ticket in their hand," Tim answered.

Rick McIlwain tried another tack. He told Tim Harris that he was almost beginning to believe that Tim had not killed Lorraine. "We're looking at a murder, and maybe it's not even a damn murder."

"It's a murder," Tim said firmly. "I can guarantee you that."

Why would he have said that? Williams turned to stare at Tim in amazement. Rick had given him a window to escape, and he hadn't taken it.

But it was hard to make sense of what Tim Harris was saying. Over and over he continued to insist that *he* had not killed Lorraine Hendricks, but he hinted that he knew more.

"I've known you for a long time, Tim," Phil Williams said. "I don't think you have the potential for killing somebody—"

"I didn't." (Odd tense. Not "I don't," but *"I didn't."*)

"But I do think," Williams continued, "you do have the potential for getting bush bonds. What cop doesn't?"

"The thing is," Tim said slowly, "if it went down that way and I walked away and she was still alive, and now she's dead."

Tim Harris was telling them that he had had sex with Lorraine Hendricks and that someone else must have killed her. They played along, throwing out possibilities. Tim Harris was ready to open up. Whether he was willing to tell them everything was another matter.

"People have gone to jail for less things," Harris said. "I can sit here and tell you that I stopped her, and we had a conversation. She's going through a divorce, I'm going through a divorce. Things hit off real well, and we ended up in the median strip, no force involved . . . and I leave . . . and she ended up dead. Why do you think I feel the way I feel? I'm involved with some girl—I don't know her."

Again they asked him if he would take a polygraph test—just on what he had told them.

No.

Tim Harris had said he had seen no one else around the victim's car, nobody hitchhiking, no white van.

Again and again McIlwain hit on the theory that Tim was only a witness, not a suspect. A "witness" shouldn't be so leery of a polygraph.

But Tim Harris was. He was inflexible on that. No lie detector test. And no written statements with his signature on the bottom.

"Tim," Phil said, "if I was you, if I was you, I'd follow this thing through and let us go ahead and see who *did* kill her."

"You telling me *I* didn't?"

"I believe you," Williams said. "Okay?"

Rick McIlwain eased back in his chair; he had done his job. Now he would let Phil Williams build on the rapport he had established with Tim Harris.

"I might have stopped her, and I might have seen her, and I might have talked to her," Harris began tentatively.

"I know you talked to her. . . . What kind of girl was she?"

"She was a nice girl."

"Did you look at her picture?" Phil asked.

"She's a lot younger—a lot younger; she didn't look her age."

"Did she tell you she could speak Spanish and all those languages?"

"No. She had a little girl, Phil. How could I kill someone that's got a little girl?"

"She tell you she could not afford another ticket?"

"She wasn't stopped for speeding."

"Why then?"

"She was wearing headphones."

Bingo! No one but the investigative team knew that Lorraine Hendricks routinely listened to music through headphones while she drove. No one else knew they had found her headphones in her car. That information had never been published in any paper.

No murder victim ever gets to tell her—or his—side of the story. Only physical evidence, prior reputation, and holes in a suspect's story can speak for them. Now Tim Harris, whose disdain for women was legendary, told Rick McIlwain and Phil Williams that Lorraine Hendricks had been so starved for sex that she had offered to have both intercourse and oral sex with him, "because she hadn't had any for a while because of her divorce."

Tim Harris's version of his meeting with Lorraine seemed like nothing so much as those letters college boys write to *Playboy* and *Penthouse*. "I stopped her for the headphones, figured it would be an easy warning."

"Did she agree to go down there where you were?"

"She did. She was in a hurry, though." Harris explained that the woman had been headed toward Fort Lauderdale to see her little girl. "She had a time frame. She said she had to be down in Fort Lauderdale, I believe by six. She knew about my divorce. I talked to her about it. She was going through what she had done as far as her divorce—talking about the kids. I hate to say it, but I think she felt sorry for me."

"She was a compassionate person," Williams offered.

"Beg your pardon?"

"She was a compassionate person?"

"She seemed to be."

Lorraine had, Harris said, been interested in Shadow and asked about him. I'll bet she did, Williams thought. Shadow, with his fangs bared as they always were when someone approached Tim, was as scary an animal as he had ever seen.

"Where did the sex occur—in your car or her car?"

"In the palmettos." They had both backed their cars in there, behind a tree.

Harris described Lorraine Hendricks's clothing as long pants, a red outfit, a shirt—"some kind of university type—and loafer-type shoes."

Phil Williams held out a drawing of the turnaround and asked Tim to point out where he had had sex with Lorraine Hendricks.

"When you left, which way did you go?"

"I came out toward the west and then went south, and I assumed she was right behind me."

Phil held out an 8 x 10 photograph he had taken of the median and the Interstate. "Did you ever see her pull down into this area here, turn around or anything? . . . Did you ever look in your rearview mirror to see if she was coming out?"

"There were other cars coming. I just assumed she was right behind me—"

"Any possibility she could have gotten stuck?"

"She was worried about going across the median strip the first time when we crossed, and I told her to follow me."

At the very least, Trooper Tim Harris had been no gentleman. If his story of consensual sex was true—which Williams doubted—Tim had not paused to see that Lorraine was safely out of the woods and the median strip and headed south before he cleared out.

Tim said he had no idea why Lorraine's driver's license and registration were missing. He had given them back to her right after he glanced at them.

"What kind of panties was she wearing?" Williams asked.

"Cotton . . . they weren't fancy ones, nothing sexy or anything."

Asked about what had happened to Lorraine's warning ticket, Tim said he had thrown all copies away—the white original, the driver's pink copy, and the yellow carbon copy. He insisted he hadn't done it to keep from being connected to her; she already knew his name from his nameplate. They had even discussed seeing each other when she returned from Fort Lauderdale.

Phil Williams and Rick McIlwain asked Tim a dozen times if he felt comfortable about taking a polygraph now that he had gotten the "truth" out.

He did not.

Rick McIlwain held the pictures of how Lorraine Hendricks had looked when she was found five days after she died. Both he and Williams noted how violently opposed Tim Harris was to looking at them. He had been a trooper for eight years, he had worked horrible fatal accidents and seen things that would make normal men vomit and pass out.

But he turned his head firmly away from the photographs.

"I've got to live with it for the rest of my life, knowing that I've done something with this girl, and now she's dead. Maybe I could have prevented that if maybe I'd stayed there and waited, or turned around and gone back and maybe seen if she really did get out of there. I could just imagine what that picture looks like that you want to show me, and I don't want to see it."

"These pictures are the result of what happened."

"I'm fixing to walk out this door in about two seconds," Tim threatened.

He would not look at the photographs in McIlwain's hand. He was as agitated as he had been in the entire five hours they had been closeted in this room together.

"That's the result of what happened when she died," McIlwain began.

Tim Harris was on his feet, knocking the white leather chair back, and in two strides he was out of the room. The door banged behind him.

Rick McIlwain turned to Phil Williams. "I say he doesn't want to see those pictures. . . . He's got a guilty conscience because of what happened."

Phil Williams nodded, pulled out his tape recorder, and turned it off. He had five hours of interrogation on the fragile brown ribbons of tape, five hours that chronicled a masterful police interrogation. The

man who had just bolted from the room had begun the session
intending to tell them nothing, and he had ended on the verge of a
complete confession.

They were so close now.

20

Rick **McIlwain** and Phil Williams knew that they could not let
Tim Harris cool off overnight. They still had too many unanswered
questions. It just didn't make sense that Lorraine Hendricks's gray
Honda should end up back on the shoulder of I-95 in the exact spot
where Tim Harris said he had pulled her over. They didn't believe
that she had ever driven it down into the wooded median. They
suspected she had been taken down there under some kind of
duress—whether Tim Harris had used his dog to frighten her into
submission or his gun (as he had with Sandy two weeks after
Lorraine's murder), or simply the authority his position and uniform
gave him.

They gave Tim thirty minutes. They were sure he would head for
DeeLisa's house. As much as he seemed to despise women, he always
went to them for comfort, and they knew Sandy wasn't about to let
him in. DeeLisa was standing by him, figuratively and literally
holding his hand.

They were right. Tim was at DeeLisa's, and they asked him if he
was ready to continue the interview he had left so precipitously. No,
he didn't want to. "I'd rather not talk to you anymore right now,"
Harris said.

There was nothing they could do. They couldn't force him to talk.
The guy was about ready to blow and spill everything. They knew it,
but they couldn't hurry it, and they couldn't make it happen.

If there was one person Tim Harris respected, it was his captain,
Dean Sullivan. Sullivan was advised of the situation and said he
would be willing to speak with Tim if he came back in. He would do

the best he could for his trooper. If Tim was guilty of murder, he would have to continue talking to the investigators. If he was innocent, he needed to cooperate with them to clear himself.

An hour and a half after their first visit to DeeLisa Davis's house Williams and McIlwain returned. DeeLisa had just come back from Gainesville, where her young son had had surgery earlier in the day. She probably had not had a worse day in a decade. She looked exhausted and apprehensive. She greeted Phil Williams, her old classmate, and apprehensively agreed to get Tim.

"Tim," Phil said, "you need to come on back down there and finish talking with us."

Not surprisingly, Tim didn't want to go. He changed his mind when he learned that Captain Sullivan had come in to talk with him and was waiting.

"Are you going to let me come home after I talk to you?" Tim asked.

"You take your car up there. It still stands the same way. You want to leave, you leave," McIlwain said.

But Tim Harris knew. Even as he headed back down to the State Attorney's Office he took DeeLisa with him. If he could not drive his car home, if he should be arrested, she could drive it home for him. And Tim wanted DeeLisa with him when he spoke to his captain. The trio remained behind closed doors for half an hour or more.

When they emerged it was obvious that this was a different Tim Harris. The proud stance of the trooper was gone, and he seemed utterly deflated. He was ready, finally, to talk in detail about Sunday, March 4. He had only one request. He wanted someone to send for Sandy.

He needed Sandy.

DeeLisa's face was a sad mask. She obviously loved Tim Harris, no matter what he had done, no matter that he had humiliated her once again—this time in front of a room full of detectives and state attorneys. No one watching doubted that she would have held Tim's hand all through his upcoming session with State Attorney Bruce Colton if Tim needed her.

Bruce Colton was in charge of the State Attorney's Office in Florida's 19th Judicial District; that included Martin, St. Lucie, Okeechobee, and Indian River Counties. Tim had made it clear he no longer wanted to talk with Phil Williams and Rick McIlwain. They had winnowed the truth from his protestations of innocence, and he was sick of the sight of their faces and the sound of their voices.

Besides, Tim wanted somebody as high up on the state judicial ladder as he could get. If he gave a full confession to someone as powerful as Bruce Colton, Tim Harris obviously harbored the hope that he might make a deal.

Colton had agreed to come in to take an official statement from Tim.

When the door had closed behind Tim and Colton, Phil Williams asked DeeLisa what Tim had told her, and she said she had asked Tim if Lorraine's death had been an accident. "And he said 'no.' I asked him if he had done it, and he said it wasn't the Tim Harris I knew who did it—not Tim Harris, the trooper. . . ."

Phil Williams had alerted Don Dappen earlier that evening that something big was probably going to come down. Don knew they were grilling Tim. "I think Sandy half believed that Tim was guilty in Lorraine Hendricks's murder," Dappen recalls. "But she didn't *want* to believe it was true. Phil called up and said he had a favor to ask of me. He said that Tim had agreed to tell everything that had happened—but he wanted to talk to Sandy first. Just one more time."

Dappen groaned when he heard that. He figured Tim Harris wanted to leave something with Sandy, some horror that she would never forget—or some guilt she would carry for the rest of her life. But he promised Williams that he would talk to Sandy and call back. She might not be willing to come in; she had been through so much already.

Don Dappen talked to Sandy, explaining that he felt Tim was going to pull something—that he would not let her walk away without feeling that somehow she shared his guilt. "It's up to you if you want to go down or not."

Sandy said nothing for a long time, and then she looked up. "I'll go."

Dappen called Phil Williams and told him that he and Sandy would be there in about fifteen minutes.

It was April 7, very early now on Saturday morning, but it was still warm. Even so, Sandy's arms were covered with goose bumps. As much as she had tried to prepare herself for what she had feared would come, she was not ready. There was no way she would ever be ready.

Tim sat alone now in Bruce Colton's office, facing the state attorney. It was smaller than the conference room where Tim had spent the whole afternoon with Phil and Rick. There was only Colton's desk with a phone, a jug of sharpened pencils, a Scotch tape dispenser, and two pictures of the state attorney's family. There was a typewriter and a little table with a lamp whose base looked like a globe. Incongruously, two stuffed animals—a tiger and a white Scottie dog—sat beside the lamp. There were no pictures on the wall, nothing for Tim Harris to look at except Bruce Colton's eyes.

As Bruce Colton entered the room Phil Williams shoved a microrecorder into Colton's suit jacket.

Tim sat in one of the two black leather chairs in front of the desk, his head down.

"Phil called," Colton began, "and Sandy's coming. Okay? He hasn't explained a whole lot to her, just that you're here and you want to talk to her."

"Can I talk to her?"

"If that's what you wanted me to do."

"I appreciate it."

Before they even touched on the subject that lay between them like a sleeping lion, before they roused all the ugliness and tragedy that had to be in Tim Harris's brain, Colton made it impeccably clear that he could promise Tim nothing at all. "I don't even want you to tell me anything because you're thinking that 'Sure he's telling me he can't promise me this—but I know if I tell him, that he will do this or that for me.'"

"I know what your job is," Tim said. "I know what you're expected to do."

Tim had been asked again if he wanted Phil or Rick or Captain Sullivan in the room while he gave his statement to Colton, and he shook his head when Colton asked him again.

"I don't want them."

"All right."

"They treated me right. I don't have any hard feelings toward them."

It was time.

None of the detectives, none of the state attorney's men, had been able to understand *why* this heretofore "perfect" state trooper had turned killer, although they all believed that he had. He had had everything a man could want, and he had systematically thrown it all away. Hell, a lot of cops—a lot of *men*, period—had tossed out perfectly good marriages when they went out chasing women. That part wasn't hard to figure out. But until now the investigators had no motive at all for Lorraine Hendricks's murder.

They knew Tim had stopped Lorraine for wearing headphones while she was driving. Only her killer would have known about the headphones. They had heard Tim's story that she offered him sex in exchange for tearing up her ticket, that she had willingly turned her car off a busy freeway into the green darkness of the pine and palmetto grove in the median. They had listened and avoided commenting or arguing with him about that—no matter their strong belief that it had not happened that way at all.

Tim had finally made some oblique reference to *why* he committed murder in his preliminary conversation with Bruce Colton. He had mentioned how much Lorraine had resembled Sandy.

Bruce Colton began his formal questioning at that point. "Did you tell her that she reminded you of Sandy?"

"I think I *called* her Sandy several times."

"Did she seem puzzled by that?"

"Yes."

"Did there ever get to be a point where it appeared to you that she was afraid of you?"

"Yes."

"Was that before you had sex?"

"After."

"Do you think it was a look in your eye—or did you say something to her that caused her to suddenly become afraid?"

"Don't think so."

"Did she try to run when she got afraid?"

"No. She was laying down."

Tim explained that he had been on top of Lorraine. "I told her I didn't want to hurt her."

"But something happened then, right?"

"I lost it."

"Did you choke her with your hands? Or was it like a chop to her neck, or did you like grab her around the neck? I know this is the part that's hardest to say, Tim."

"Mr. Colton, I'm going to think about this for the rest of my life."

"I know, and you have got to deal with it. How did that part happen? I'm not asking you why that part happened. I'm not asking you to give me an explanation. I'm asking *physically* how did that part happen?"

Tim Harris began to cry.

"Tim?" Colton urged.

"I don't want to remember."

"What is upsetting you is that you *do* remember. . . . Does it hurt you more to say it even than it hurts to remember it?"

"It hurts deep inside."

Tim Harris, the muscular man who loved arresting speeders and druggers, who controlled one of the most vicious dogs in the K-9 Unit, who had punched and pinched and choked and tormented women who loved him, cried like a child—like a spoiled child who had been called into the principal's office to explain why he had been naughty.

Bruce Colton waited, and the tape recorder catching this confession rolled on silently for a long time. Finally Harris's tears ebbed, and he was ready to answer more questions.

"You two were both still on the ground. She was completely undressed, right?" Colton asked.

Tim said he had his pants down and so did his victim, and that her blouse was pulled up.

"You had taken your holster, your gun belt off?"

"Yes."

"Did she get scared because you forced her to have sex?"

"No," Tim insisted. "There was no forcing the sex."

"Okay. Was there part of the sex that she agreed to, and then did you want to do something she didn't agree to? Is that what scared her?"

"No."

"When she died, Tim, was it fast?"

There was no sound at all in the room, save for the mechanical clickings of the air conditioning system. The two men sat frozen for what seemed like an hour.

Finally Tim spoke. "No . . . I wanted to stop it . . . I just couldn't stop, you know."

Tim Harris resisted giving details, no matter how Bruce Colton phrased his questions. "You're at the hardest part right now, Tim. Don't hold back."

"It's not quite that I'm gonna feel good about it."

"I'm not saying that you're going to feel good about it . . . you're going to feel better if you can tell me what happened."

"Am I crazy, Mr. Colton," Tim asked, "or am I just losing it?"

Bruce Colton explained again that it was not his place to say what was or was not wrong with Tim Harris. "The medical examiner can tell us the cause of death [of Lorraine], but *you're* the one that has to fill in the details. . . . We can't just leave that to speculation."

They sat silent again for minutes. Finally Tim Harris heaved a great sigh and said, "I think I killed her with her own underwear. Put it around her neck."

"You mean like her underpants or her bra or what?"

"Her underpants."

"Did you put it around her neck and then pull on it . . . tighten it, squeezing it?"

This was like pulling teeth for Bruce Colton. Tim Harris would either not talk at all or would nod or shake his head. He finally acknowledged that after oral sex he had told Lorraine to remove her panties.

"At that point was she already getting afraid, do you think?"

"She didn't understand what was going on, I don't think."

"Did you ever pull a gun on her?"

"No."

"How about the dog? Did you ever threaten her with the dog?"

"No . . . I just asked her to take her clothes off."

"Okay. Well, after she took her pants off, did you immediately start to choke her, or was there much conversation first?"

"She rolled over on her stomach."

"Did you tell her to?"

"Yes."

"Did you have sex with her that way? Or did you attempt to?"

Again there was a long, long pause.

"Did you attempt to, Tim?"

"I rubbed up against her. I was on top of her."

"At that point do you feel that she had started to become frightened yet?"

Tim nodded.

"Why do you think that was—that she started to become frightened? Do you think you were becoming more aggressive or more forceful in telling her things?"

"I was talking to her like I was talking to Sandy. I kept calling her 'Sandy.'"

"Okay. When you say you were talking to her like you were talking to Sandy, was it as though you were angry at Sandy?"

"I asked her why she was divorcing me."

"What did this girl say?"

"She said, 'I know that you're hurt.' [She said] that she's not the girl I think she is."

"This girl said, 'I'm not the girl that you think I am'? . . . And did that just kind of set you off? Or did you just more and more—in your mind think this was Sandy?"

"I think that's what I thought. . . . I know she wasn't."

"Was she then laying on her stomach when you put the pants around her neck . . . and then how did you do it? Did you like sit on her or what?"

The tape rolled silent again.

"Come on, Tim," Colton urged.

"I wish you could read my mind."

"I know. But I can't. I can only depend on you to tell me what happened."

Tim Harris either could not or would not speak. Possibly the enormity of his crime had finally hit him. More likely he was weighing what a full confession would do to him. For thirty-three years his whole focus had been on himself. He knew his career was gone. He didn't want to go to prison. He had spent so many hours in court as a witness for the prosecution; he knew how much difference intent and time elapsed and mental capabilities could make in the length of a sentence.

"Were you still laying on her when you were pulling the pants around her neck, or had you sat up or gotten on your knees or what?"

"I was sitting up."

"On top of her still?"

"Yeah."

"By the time that you stopped choking her, were you sure she had stopped breathing?"

"No."

"Did you choke her for a long time, though? I mean until she stopped struggling and moving around?"

"Yes."

"What did you do then, Tim?"

Again Tim just stopped speaking. He seemed to be in a world of his own, his eyes averted from Colton's, his hands limp in his lap as if they had no part of him, and certainly no part of strangling the life from a beautiful, vibrant woman who had tried in vain to make him understand that she was not Sandy; she was not the woman he said had deserted him. The woman had shown compassion for him—a man who didn't know the meaning of the word.

"So what did you do?" Colton asked again.

"Stared . . ."

"After you realized that she had stopped breathing, what did you do next?"

"Went to help her . . . I couldn't do anything for her. . . . I couldn't do anything for her."

"You realized that she was dead?"

"Think she was . . . I didn't know what to do."

"What *did* you do, though?"

"Covered her up."

"With what?"

"Pine needles."

"What about her clothes?"

"I took her clothes off."

"Why . . . what were you thinking about that?"

"I don't know."

Tim Harris insisted through intensive questioning that he had no idea where Lorraine Hendricks's clothes were. He thought he must have taken them away in his patrol car, but he didn't know what he had done with them after that. He admitted that he had moved Lorraine's body.

"I moved her probably ten or fifteen feet from where we were doing things."

He recalled a "bunch of trees," but he could not remember what position he had left her in, whether she was face up or face down. "I couldn't look at her face anymore. . . . I didn't want to hurt that girl. I didn't want to hurt her."

The investigators knew that Tim had switched from his regular patrol car to a Mustang around the time of Lorraine Hendricks's murder. They also knew that someone had broken into that Mustang in the police garage, but Tim denied doing it. He didn't know where the clothes were. Yes, he had thrown Lorraine's wallet in the trash dumpster at the Fort Pierce rest area. He had put her driver's license and registration back in her purse, and he didn't know where her purse was.

Bruce Colton was fascinated with Tim's insistence that he had confused Lorraine Hendricks with Sandy. "It was when you started seeing her as Sandy that the problem occurred. . . . Was it almost from the time you were with her that she was reminding you of Sandy?"

"She looked a little bit like her. She doesn't have the same color hair, but the way she acted."

"But as you got into having sex with her, she more and more reminded you of Sandy?"

"I don't hate Sandy. I don't know why."

Tim insisted he had not gone back through the turnaround in the days before Lorraine was found. "I didn't go anywhere near it."

"Have you tried to confide in anybody else?" Colton asked.

"I tried to tell DeeLisa, but I can't talk about it."

Bruce Colton reminded Tim that there was another trooper in the area that Sunday morning.

"He's not involved," Tim said firmly.

That wasn't what Colton meant. "How did you know that he wouldn't ride up on you when this was occurring?"

"I didn't."

"Well, you knew he went to take a prisoner to the jail. . . . You heard that on the radio?"

Tim acknowledged that that was true. He had known exactly where Carlin Parker was.

"Have you ever had sex with anybody on the job before? I'm not saying that you forced them to, but has anyone voluntarily done it before?"

"That's how I met DeeLisa."

But Tim insisted there had been no other women; none of the beautiful women he had stopped over the past eight years had ever been sex partners—willing or unwilling.

Lorraine Hendricks was dead. She could not refute Tim Harris's words as he talked more freely now, soiling her reputation, describing her as a woman who willingly offered him sex to save herself a traffic ticket. Tim Harris didn't know that Phil Williams had already established Lorraine's pattern of behavior when she was stopped for speeding. She had taken her tickets sometimes quietly, sometimes a little sullenly. But she had never, never offered to exchange sex for a pass on a traffic ticket. All of her life Lorraine had had respect for a uniform—ever since she first saw her beloved father in his.

Interestingly, the trooper who kept cartoons and drawings of pretty girls performing fellatio on "Trooper Harris" as part of the "new breathalyzer test" insisted that he had "happened" to come upon just such a woman.

No, and no, and no, Tim Harris insisted to Bruce Colton. The girl in the Honda had not been afraid, and it was she who had initiated the idea of sex. She had performed fellatio upon him not once but twice, quite willingly. She had submitted to intercourse voluntarily. He was sure of that.

If Lorraine had been so willing to have sex with a complete stranger she had met on the Interstate, why had there been a strong indication on autopsy that she had been beaten around the face and head? Dr. Fred Hobin had told the investigators that the very rapid decomposition of her head—compared to the rest of her body—

suggested that the victim had suffered severe trauma, probably from some kind of blows to her face. The investigators all wondered if Tim Harris hadn't slugged Lorraine to make her do what he wanted.

But Tim Harris insisted to Bruce Colton that the "girl" had become frightened only when he had her pinned to the ground on her face in the pine needles and when he began to call her by his wife's name.

"What did you say you asked her—thinking of Sandy?"

"Why she was divorcing me."

"And what did the girl say?"

"She said she wasn't Sandy."

"Was there any more talk between you before you started choking her—in other words, was the last thing she said, 'I'm not Sandy,' or was there anything after that?"

"No."

"Was it because you were choking her and she couldn't? Are you saying yes, Tim?"

"Yes."

And that was, tragically, when Tim Harris had "lost it." He had sat on Lorraine Hendricks's back, pinning her arms with his knees, and tightened her panties around her neck until she died. And then he had stripped her of her clothing, dragged her against the tree trunk (although he would not admit that part), and covered her with pine boughs and needles.

And returned to patrolling his district.

Sandy Harris waited outside the interview room. Bruce Colton asked Tim if he still wanted to see his estranged wife.

"Yes, I'm not going to hurt her."

"I'm not concerned about that. I just don't want you to feel that I'm forcing her on you."

"I want to see her, and I'm going to tell her I love her."

Sandy Harris would rather have been anywhere else. She stood in the doorway looking at the man who had terrorized *her* so recently. "Tim," she said softly. "Do you want to talk to me?"

"Can you hold me for a few minutes?" He threw his arms around her waist and tried to pull her close to him.

"Tim—" She stood rigid. Sandy didn't want to touch Tim. She couldn't believe he wanted her to, but then she remembered he had always been like this. He had believed her instantly when she told him she'd take him back, even though he had her handcuffed and forced to the floor with a gun next to her head. He would always believe what he wanted to.

"Are you going to talk to me?" she asked.

"Can you hold me for a few minutes?" he asked again.

"Please. Tim, *don't.* Tim, it's hard on me, too. I can't believe it—"

"Where's Timmy and Jennifer?" he asked.

"They're at Don's house right now. Tim, do you want to talk to me at all?"

"Can't you put your arms around me for a long time?"

Tim wouldn't speak to her with Bruce Colton in the room, and he asked to be alone with Sandy. There was no way Colton could risk that, not after hearing what he had heard in Tim's confession. Sandy had just learned that Tim had called the dying woman by *her* name, that his rage at her divorcing him had apparently sent him out looking for her "image" to destroy.

"Tim," Sandy implored. "Why did you do it? Whatever got into you to do that anyway, Tim . . . did you tell her it was me, and that's what you were trying to do to me? Do you wish it was me? Is that why you did it, Tim?"

"No."

"You kept telling me that you could do that to me, and you did it to someone else."

"You were my world," he said softly. "And I lost it."

"Tim, you threw it away, and you know it. You cheated on me for four years, and you sit there and tell me about it."

"I don't want to. I belong to you."

"You lost it a long time ago, Tim."

"I'm trying to put it back together."

Sandy Harris was shocked and frightened and angry. Tim had never played by other people's rules—only his own. Even now, even when he had just confessed to a terrible murder, he was sitting there and telling her that he was trying to put things back together.

"No," Sandy said. "Why did you do that to her, Tim? Why did you kill her?"

"The person that loves you didn't kill her. I need help. You were always there when I needed you, you know that. I won't have to call you anymore. . . . Don't think bad of me. I wish I could change it."

"Tim," Sandy said, with more awful possibilities dawning in her mind, "you didn't hurt anybody else, did you? Did you do it to anybody else?"

"No. I'm trying to get help."

"You don't do things like that when you need help, Tim. You've been threatening me for months. Like why didn't you get it [help] before then? Because back *months* ago—why didn't you do something before?"

"I thought I could control it."

"I gotta go, Tim." Her voice was washed of all feeling.

And Sandy Harris walked out of the room and out of Tim Harris's life. He had expected her to fix this, too, just as she had always fixed things for him. She had forgiven him a hundred times over. She no longer could.

Tim asked Bruce Colton if he could go, too. He knew it meant to jail. "I wish I were dead," he cried.

He didn't want his mother or father to know what he had done. He wanted to go someplace where "I can get help."

"Please don't let me go somewhere and rot," he said to Colton.

There was a grim irony in Tim Harris's request. That was exactly what he had meted out to his victim. He didn't know it, nor would he probably have cared, but the woman he left in the woods had cared so much for every living creature that she could not even leave a dog or cat dead in the road. It was as if the most unselfish human in Florida had, through a terrible synchronicity, crossed the path of the most selfish.

Sandy and Don Dappen still waited outside Colton's office. Dappen looked around at the men who waited with him. They were lawmen and attorneys whom he had known for almost two decades. And it was his own brother-in-law who had just confessed to one of the most heinous crimes he himself had ever encountered. They waited in awkward silence.

"They brought Tim by to go to the bathroom. He looked at Sandy and he looked at me," Dappen recalls. "A few minutes later he comes back by. You understand, by that time I *hated* the guy, but he was about to get me one more time. He stopped. He looked me right in the eye, and he leaned over and he whispered in my ear, *'Please take care of my kids.'* He walked away, and I busted out crying. Here I am—in front of all these guys I've worked with. And the guy got me. One last time."

It was the kids. Don Dappen realized in that one moment that this was all real, and that it was going to be the kids who would hurt the most. Not just Jennifer and Timmy, but Don's own kids, Chris and Charlene; Kathy's kids, Gary Jr., Freddie, and Michael; and even the sisters' niece and nephew, April Rose and Ryan, Martin's children in New York.

Most of all, Katherine Hendricks's whole life would be diminished; her mother, who had loved her so, was dead because of Tim Harris.

Phil Williams had written the arrest affidavit, and he served it on Tim Harris at 2:20 a.m. Although it was akin to bringing coals to Newcastle, Phil read Tim his Miranda rights. Tim answered after each sentence that he did, indeed, understand. Anything he said *could* be used against him in a court of law, and he did have the right to an attorney, and if he didn't have money to afford one, one would be appointed for him. It was almost psychedelic—reading a veteran cop his rights. But it was the law.

On the way to the Indian River County Jail, with Indian River County Sheriff's deputy Pete Lenz accompanying them, Phil asked Tim a question that had been nibbling at his mind ever since he had discovered Lorraine in that single heart-stopping moment.

"You remember, Tim, how she was," Phil began. "The way you dragged her and put her legs around the tree?"

Tim looked straight ahead, silent.

"Why?" Phil asked. "Could you tell me why you left her that way?"

"No reason."

"You got to admit that was a strange position. Did it mean something to you? Was there a reason?"

"I don't know."

When Phil Williams walked Tim Harris into jail to book him for murder the jailers' mouths fell open. At first they almost thought it was a joke. They had seen Tim, the tall, handsome trooper in uniform, as he ushered hundreds of prisoners in to be booked. He had waved at them, stopped to talk with them, been one of the massive team that was law enforcement in Indian River County. He had been one of them. And now it was Tim himself who wore the handcuffs.

It was no joke, and Phil Williams felt no sense of triumph. He was glad it was over, relieved that Tim was no longer free to rove the freeways, but he didn't feel like shouting and clapping his team of investigators on the back. None of them did. Instead tears stung his eyes. One dirty cop sullies the reputation of thousands of good cops. Beyond that, there was so much pain for innocent people. Donny Dappen was a tough cop, but he had cried, and Phil felt his own eyes fill with tears.

And this was only the beginning of the pain. Phil hoped they could block the details of Tim's confession from the media for a little while at least. This was going to hit the wire services with a bang, and he knew they could expect a circus. Mary Hogan could only hold reporters at bay for so long.

21

During the previous week Don Dappen had taken Sandy and Susan and all their kids to Disney World in Orlando for an overnight trip, not so much to keep Tim from harassing them or trying to take Jennifer and Timmy away, but just to help them forget for a little while. He was glad he had; there would be no forgetting now. Not for weeks, months, years—not for the rest of their lives.

Tim's family was shocked and devastated. Phil Williams called David Harris Saturday morning to let him know that his brother had been arrested. David and Melissa were out, so he had no choice but to leave a message on their answering machine. Melissa watched her husband's face as he walked into the living room after playing his messages.

"David didn't believe it. . . . We didn't know what the problem was. We thought it had to do with Sandy. . . . We tried Sandy's house, and there was no answer."

Both David and Melissa had gone over to the jail to visit with Tim. David went in to see his brother, and Tim clung to him and sobbed, "Don't leave me."

Melissa remembered that David walked out in "total shock. He just kept saying, 'I can't believe it, I can't believe it,' and he was crying hysterically when he walked out."

Tim's mother flew down on Sunday to see him. She sat in her son's cell, holding him for fifteen or twenty minutes, neither of them saying a word. Tim's father came to Vero Beach, too, but he balked at going in to see his son. According to family members, the two men had not spoken for a half dozen years; Tim and his stepmother were engaged in a feud. At length Tim's father turned around and went home, saying that he refused to go to the jail and see his son in that position.

David Harris tried to explain that to Phil Williams. "My dad doesn't have anything to do with us."

Tim Harris was being held without bond and in isolation. There were reasons for the latter; cops don't always fare well when they find themselves on the other side of the bars. And *no* woman killer is respected in prison. Tim was both. For his own protection Tim was placed well away from the other prisoners. Jailers logged his behavior and movements every fifteen minutes.

The press found out about Tim Harris's arrest quickly; they had been watching the activity around the sheriff's office avidly, and they picked up on the tension. It was too big to keep under wraps. Harris's case was headlined in the *Miami Herald* and the Vero Beach *Press Journal* on Sunday, April 8, 1990. Columns and columns of details emerged, whetting the appetites of the tabloid television world.

The *Orlando Sentinel* headline read, "A Woman Is Slain, a Trooper Confesses, a Fear Festers"; the *Miami Herald's*: "Descent into Darkness—From Success to Suspect in Murder: State Trooper 'Snapped'".

Two women came forward after reading about Tim Harris's arrest and told Rick McIlwain that they didn't believe he had suddenly snapped. They had had the misfortune to deal with him months before, in July, 1989, and they characterized Harris as a "walking time bomb."

"He acted like he hated women," said forty-seven-year-old Sandy Horne. She recalled that she and twenty-three-year-old Mary Turney had been southbound on I-95 about three in the afternoon when Tim Harris had come speeding up behind them near the Okeechobee Road exit in Fort Pierce. They saw no lights and heard no siren, and they began to pass the car in front of their truck. At that point Tim Harris had turned on his blue bubble lights and pulled them over. He didn't ask for their licenses or registration; he was obviously furious about something.

"He said, 'You're in my way, and I was in a hurry,' " Sandy Horne said. When the women began to protest he shouted at them. Horne said she had figured there was something wrong with the trooper—his rage was out of all proportion to the situation—and she slid her eyes down to read his name tag. He caught her looking at it, and he was enraged.

"He went wild," she said simply. He said he could cite her for littering because a plastic milk jug had flown out of the back of her pickup truck a half mile down the road near some woods.

"I went to get out of my truck to see if it had blown out," Horne said, "and I had one leg out, and he leaned against the door, and it caught my leg. He said, 'Where are you going?'"

She had explained that she wanted to check the back of her truck to be sure the three milk jugs she had were still there. Tim Harris would not allow it. Instead he ordered her to walk back along the Interstate and then down into the wooded median and retrieve the jug he said had flown out.

"I said I wasn't going down in the woods, and he said that six times at least." But she wouldn't go. The woods were dark and "spooky."

Horne said she had come forward because she was tired of reading in the papers that Tim Harris had just "snapped" recently.

"He had a bad temper a long time ago," she said. "We've never been treated so rudely in all our lives . . . I thought, 'God, I'm going to jail over a milk jug.' But he was a walking time bomb that day. I'm glad I didn't go [into the woods]."

There were several aspects to Tim Harris's confession that rankled Phil Williams. Tim had been so insistent that Lorraine Hendricks had readily agreed to have sex with him—what Florida lawmen referred to irreverently as a "bush bond." Everything that Phil had learned about Lorraine in his five weeks of investigation warred with that. To begin with, Phil had talked to several of the officers who had given her speeding tickets earlier, asking them about how she had acted— what kind of woman she seemed to be.

One thing she definitely was not was a flirt, according to the other officers, and she appeared anything but "easy." She had been businesslike with one Jacksonville policeman, and she had been annoyed and downright snappish with another. Why then would she have been so compliant with Tim Harris? It just didn't make sense.

A lot of things didn't make sense. Tim said that Lorraine had driven her car across the Interstate and down into the median strip— as had he—where they would be hidden in the trees. If that was true, Williams figured he and Larry Smetzer and Tony Oliver would have found some signs that two cars had been parked down in there. More than that, when Lorraine's car was processed they would have found weeds, pine twigs, palmetto leaves, and other debris from the median in the undercarriage of her Honda when they put it up on the rack. But they hadn't. The bottom of her car looked like that of a car driven on main roads and freeways.

If Tim Harris was telling the truth, he would have had to drive Lorraine's Honda back to where he had first pulled it over, park it on the Interstate, and then *walk* a mile along I-95 to get back to his patrol car. A tall trooper in uniform walking along the Interstate would certainly have drawn attention. Someone would have remembered seeing him. Phil didn't believe Tim would have taken that chance.

Lorraine's car had been found with both front doors unlocked and her belongings still inside, including her briefcase with important business papers. Everyone Phil Williams talked to said she had been a cautious woman—a woman who never would have left her car unlocked for more than a moment or two, and certainly not with her things inside.

The only way Lorraine would have walked away from her unlocked car would have been if Tim Harris had asked her to step back to his patrol car for a moment. This is a fairly standard procedure in Florida and elsewhere. Officers have the driver sit in the patrol unit while they have their dispatcher check "Wants and Warrants," and while they write tickets.

Lorraine might very well have complied with that request, thinking she would be back in her car in a few minutes. Common sense said that she would never have left her car unlocked and willingly accompanied a perfect stranger down into the darkening wood for sex.

Lorraine hadn't been hard up for sex; she had a lover. Williams knew Lorraine so well by this time; he had talked to almost everyone who had ever cared about her. She was a loving, passionate woman when she was in a permanent relationship. She had never, ever engaged in casual sex.

Her friend Carol Worley recalled Lorraine as modest—so modest she didn't even undress in front of other women in a health club locker room. Asked if Lorraine would have offered sex to get out of a speeding ticket, Carol's eyes flashed. "Never. *Never.* There is just no way. That was not Lorraine. . . . At one time Lorraine could have had a huge promotion—an executive came to her hotel room at midnight and suggested they could be more than friends. She was shocked, and she was mad. She sent him away. She didn't care how it might hurt her career."

No, Phil Williams believed that Lorraine Hendricks had been thinking about getting to Fort Lauderdale as quickly as she could to see her friend, get her dental work done, and take care of her real estate business so she could get back to her little girl in Jacksonville.

She did have a lousy driving record, but she didn't even know that her license had been suspended, and she could have gotten it reinstated by paying a fine or two. A woman with her class and her commitment to her child wouldn't be likely to barter sex for a free pass on a ticket. The women in Tim's *cartoons* would, and Phil Williams believed those women had taken over Tim's imagination so much that he had written his own scenario, filling in Lorraine's response so that it fit.

The dog. Shadow was quite possibly a part of Tim's power. Don Dappen thought about that, too. He would remember how Tim had said, "Watch her, Shadow," to torment Susan. Once Lorraine Hendricks had entered Tim's car, or even *approached* Tim's car, if Tim had said, "Watch her" to Shadow, Lorraine would have been as helpless as if the trooper held her in his gun sights. It wouldn't have mattered that she had a black belt in kung fu. How could she have stood off both a trained attack dog and a 200-pound state trooper? It was ironic for a woman who loved animals so much that a dog—a good dog under the control of a deranged master—might have helped hold her captive.

Williams knew that killers confess in diverse ways; some tell the straight truth, but more often they tend to slide over the parts of their crimes that either eat at their consciences the most or make them seem most guilty. The result is a self-serving confabulation.

Phil had no doubt that Tim Harris had stopped Lorraine or that he had talked with her. He knew too much about her. He knew she was getting a divorce, he knew she was headed toward Fort Lauderdale, and he knew she had a little girl. Tim had said repeatedly that she was going to *see* her little girl, while in reality she had left Katherine at home. It was possible that Lorraine had even said she was hurrying toward Katherine so that he would let her go.

It was highly unlikely that Lorraine Hendricks had agreed voluntarily to have sex with Tim Harris. However, once he had forced her into the woods and cuffed her around to demonstrate his strength, she would have realized that she might very well die if she didn't obey the trooper's commands. At that point she might have stopped struggling. She was, above all, a mother, and mothers down through the ages have sacrificed themselves, done whatever they had to for their children. Katherine was Lorraine's whole life. If she had to submit to the hulking trooper so that she could get back to Katherine, she probably would have done so. From what Phil Williams had learned about her character and her personality, he figured that was the way it had happened. Lorraine Hendricks, already bruised and injured, had believed Harris would release her after he was finished with her.

Too late, Lorraine must have realized that the trooper had trapped her and that he never intended to let her go. When she heard him calling her by another woman's name she had cried out, "I'm not the woman you think I am! *I'm* not Sandy!" *That* statement from Harris had the ring of truth.

There would be one slight comfort that Phil Williams could give Lorraine's family and friends. Death by strangulation is almost always very rapid. Once the carotid arteries leading to the brain are shut down with a ligature, unconsciousness follows almost immediately. In his rage Tim Harris might have continued to choke Lorraine Hendricks, but she would not have felt it or known. She would already have been in a safe place, a place fitting for a woman who had spent her whole life helping large and small creatures and making other people's lives richer.

A public defender was appointed to represent Tim Harris. Assistant Public Defender Clifford Barnes would defend him on charges of first-degree murder. The State of Florida was seeking the death penalty. Assistant State Attorney David Morgan said that he was not even considering a plea bargain that would keep Harris from joining the long roster of prisoners at the Florida State Penitentiary in Starke, Florida, who were awaiting their fatal moment in the electric chair.

"We're definitely pursuing first-degree murder," Morgan said, explaining that the state would rely on two aggravating circumstances that would make the first-degree charges stick—even if the defense could prove that Tim's crime wasn't premeditated.

In jail Tim Harris continued to cry much of the time. He was monitored by the closed-circuit television camera, although jail authorities did not consider it a suicide watch. DeeLisa Davis visited him faithfully, but Sandy did not. She was trying to cope with telling her children where their father was and to protect them from the teasing of their friends. She had to go to work every day and face her friends and co-workers. Vero Beach and Sebastian were basically small towns, and there were no secrets.

Major Frank and Jodi Dombroski tried to accept that their wonderful daughter was gone from them forever. Rick Hendricks had a little six-year-old daughter who would never again see her mother. Mike Raleigh had lost the business associate he'd found so brilliant. The man Lorraine had come to love had lost her before he really found her; he would remember her the rest of his life.

For Tim Harris it was as if Lorraine Hendricks's death was old business, something that had happened in the past, something that was not nearly as important in his mind as winning Sandy back. He was crying because he had lost Sandy, and for himself because he was locked up in a cell that he told visitors was filthy and disgusting.

Sandy was the one thing that had been denied Tim in his adult life, and he would not accept that she was gone. He wrote to her constantly, in pencil on lined jail-issue paper.

Tim sat in jail and sobbed as he wrote to Sandy, a letter carefully constructed to make her feel guilty and miss him and come back to him. But when it came to human feelings and compassion or even to understanding life from someone else's point of view, he just didn't get it.

Looking at the letter Tim sent in the last week of April is akin to viewing the same situation from both sides of the looking glass. Sandy had been so embarrassed when Tim broke into her office the night before Valentine's Day that she had gone home in tears. Tim had reconstructed that day in his memory, and it came out completely changed.

"I just wanted you to know," Tim began, "last night I cried myself to sleep. . . . It's dumb, I know, but I was thinking about Valentine's Day. Did you ever think to ask DeeLisa what I did for *her* on that day? Nothing. I think about those balloons, and how many trips it took me from my truck to inside, wondering if I was going to get caught. I kinda impressed myself. . . ."

He mused that he had thought about buying her some sexy outfit, but that Sandy knew he could never do that on his own—he had always had to have his daughter or some of the guys at his reserve camp with him.

"I don't ever want to see another Valentine's Day again," he wrote. "And to think you never even said, Thank you. *I love you.* . . ."

Tim Harris had received a fan letter from a woman who had read about his arrest, and he wrote to Sandy about that. "I figure if some lady that doesn't know me can write, why can't my wife? Maybe you don't want to be my wife? Wife and Husband are suppose to stand up for each other. . . . I want you to come see me every week. I want you to write me. I want the kids to write. I want you to love me. I want you to care about what happens to me. . . . Since you may not testify, why don't you sit with me in court? If you were in trouble—no matter how mad I was at you—I'd be there. . . ."

"I want . . ."

Again Tim Harris begged Sandy to take him back, to put his ring on her finger.

In May Tim sent Sandy a Mother's Day card. She had not written to him, and he didn't understand why. He seemed truly unable to grasp *what* might have happened to send her fleeing from him.

"I still can't figure out why you won't come to see me or write. You don't break a eight and a half year marriage off just like that. I can assure you that if we end up in a divorce, it will be because you wanted it. . . . Pretending I don't exist doesn't help. I never thought *you* were that type of girl. Your emotions . . . are hurt, so are mine. . . ."

Although one wondered how Tim thought he was going to escape his present legal troubles, he wrote to Sandy as if he were in jail for nothing more serious than a traffic violation. "I think I might want to move after this. Are you interested in coming with me?"

Tim sent Sandy articles condemning divorce. He sent her Robert Fulghum's *All I Ever Really Needed to Know I Learned in Kindergarten.* He quoted an article called "It's Never Too Late." The sentiments were meaningful and on target—except for the fact that Tim Harris was completely avoiding the huge black chasm that separated him from Sandy, the chasm that held infidelity, brutality, and murder.

Painstakingly Tim Harris drew pictures for Sandy and Jenny and Timmy. A single red rose, a Snoopy dog, and every letter ended with "Love Always" and his signature in a flourishing sweep of his pencil.

Sandy had to sell everything to keep going—Tim's boat, his car, their house. She was shocked to find that Tim had signed his income tax refund over to DeeLisa. And still his letters poured in, full of his undying love and his terrible fear that Sandy might date other men, and that his children would forget him. He warned her not to let them see his picture in the paper when he went to court.

Tim's letters had a stultifying sameness. Before Sandy opened them she knew what they would say. He still loved her. They should be together. He loved the children, and he wanted to hear from all of them, have visits from all of them. When he didn't hear from Sandy he suspected the jail was keeping her letters from him. He simply would not accept that she was through with him, that in some instances it *was* too late. Sandy read the letters, refolded them, and put them back into their envelopes. She didn't throw them away, and she didn't know why.

Finally she found a buyer for the house on 75th Court. Her family helped Sandy move out of what had once been her dream house. While Don Dappen was helping Sandy clear some stuff out of her house he checked all the closets for things she might have missed. Far back in a closet he found several pairs of nylons—with their feet cut off. They were not Sandy's, and they had been pushed back behind other clothes on the top shelf of a closet. Sandy had never seen them. For whatever reason, Tim must have put them there.

Sandy was able to build a much smaller place for herself and the children. She stayed in Indian River County, although there were times she thought of moving someplace far away, someplace where no one had ever heard of Tim or of her. But she had a good job, she had her family close by, and people were kind to her. Nobody was rubbing her nose in the scandal.

It might get worse when Tim was actually on trial, when all the details were spread across the papers again. But Sandy stayed. Her kids had their Uncle Don and their Grandpa Fred, and she had her mother and her sisters, Susan and Kathy.

22

Tim Harris's trial on charges of first-degree murder was set for October 9, 1990. The week before, Sandy would have her twenty-eighth birthday, and Lorraine Hendricks would have had her forty-fourth. Only a year earlier Tim himself had started the tumbling down of his life when he took Sandy out for her "birthday dinner" and told her bluntly that he was seeing another woman.

If he ever thought of that, it didn't matter now. It was a year later, and he stood a good chance of going to the electric chair. On September 19 the defense lost on a major point. Clifford Barnes's main defense stratagem was that Tim had been coerced and tricked into confessing. More than anything he wanted to keep Tim's taped statements to Phil Williams and Rick McIlwain and his confession to State Attorney Bruce Colton kept out of his trial.

This hearing was vital. If Judge Vocelle left the tapes in, Clifford Barnes would have little recourse but to try to convince a jury that his client was guilty of second-degree murder or manslaughter—but not of first-degree murder. "It doesn't look like the insanity defense will work," Barnes admitted. His interviews with his client had shown him a man eminently sane who had probably been sane at the time of the crime.

There was always the far-out possibility that if Judge Vocelle suppressed the tapes, the whole case could be thrown out, and Tim Harris would walk free. That seemed incredible, but State Attorney Bruce Colton testified that if Tim Harris had not confessed to the Hendricks murder, "I didn't feel we had enough probable cause to arrest him for murder."

Public Defender Barnes insisted that Tim had been taped under oppressive circumstances. "They constantly fostered his fear of being arrested," he said. "This was a masterpiece of psychological coercion. They did a heck of a job of breaking him down. The fact that he's a cop doesn't mean he doesn't have constitutional rights."

It was a risky stance at best. Tim Harris had carried a Miranda Warning card in his wallet for eight years; he probably had read those rights aloud to thousands of motorists. He knew all along that he didn't have to talk with Phil Williams or Rick McIlwain or Bruce Colton. Indeed, Phil Williams had him on tape saying "I can walk out that door and tell you to drop dead and not talk to you anymore." And Bruce Colton had Tim on tape saying "I'm here because I want to [be]" as he made his official confession.

The courtroom was hushed as the tapes made on April 6th and 7th were played. Tim Harris's voice was clotted with tears as he described the murder of Lorraine Hendricks and his confusion over whether he had been strangling Lorraine or his wife, Sandy.

The real Tim Harris—the one in the courtroom—was stone-faced as he listened, his arms folded in front of him on the oak defense table. Photographers waited to catch some trace of emotion on his face, but they were disappointed. He had not talked to reporters in the five months since his arrest, and he was not about to give the photographers a good shot. Occasionally he shut his eyes, as if by doing so he could shut out the ugly details of Lorraine's death.

Wearing red jail coveralls, Tim Harris looked as if he had lost weight, but all of the media shots the lensmen *did* get showed a man handsome enough to be playing the *role* of a murder defendant in a movie or on television. An errant lock of his thick black hair fell over his forehead.

After a tense waiting period Circuit Judge L. B. Vocelle commented, "We're not dealing with a novice." He remarked that Tim Harris's eleven years of experience in law enforcement and extensive training were "obviously items the Court should take into consideration."

The tapes were in. Jurors in Tim's trial would hear both the interrogation of the afternoon of April 7 and his confession.

Harris showed no disappointment. He had not expected the tape to be thrown out. As a working cop he knew that he had been legally "Mirandized." He had known what he was doing when he talked to Williams and the two men from the State Attorney's Office.

Barnes said he expected the worst. "It's a first-degree murder charge. It's a terrible crime. It's a small town, and it's an extremely complex issue." He was confident, however, that an appellate court would disagree with Judge Vocelle and said he planned to appeal the ruling after the first trial if Harris should be convicted.

Phil Williams remarked that even if Tim Harris had continued to deny killing Lorraine Hendricks on that long day of interrogation back in April, he would not have given up. "I would have taken him on a fishing trip," Williams said. "Nobody but me and him and the tape recorder."

As it turned out, there would be no murder trial for Timothy Scott Harris. On Friday, September 28, 1990, Tim broke his silence. Lorraine Hendricks's parents, alerted by Assistant State Attorney David Morgan, were present in Judge Vocelle's courtroom to hear Tim Harris admit that he had killed their only daughter. Major Frank Dombroski was stoic, and Jodi Dombroski fought to hold back tears.

Dressed in red jail coveralls, with his hands cuffed to his belt, Tim Harris entered the courtroom. He would not plead guilty to murder, but he would plead no contest to the first-degree murder charges. That would save him from the electric chair.

Harris stood before Judge Vocelle, his face blank. "I'm not going to be able to forget what happened," he said. "And I know there's nothing I can say to make things change. . . . I am truly sorry for her family and friends and the hurt I caused. I've hurt a lot of people, and I won't forget it. . . . I don't deserve to live."

Referring to Lorraine Hendricks's family, he said, "I wish they could forgive me. In time, I hope they will."

The Dombroskis stared at Harris, as if he were speaking in another language.

Tim talked of how much pride he had taken in his career as a policeman; he had never expected to find himself standing before a judge as a defendant. "I just hope law enforcement is not tarnished by what I've done, because law enforcement's not that way."

Judge Vocelle heard Tim Harris out, and then he sentenced him to life in prison.

For Lorraine's parents it was a tragically light sentence. They would have preferred to have known that Tim Harris was going to die himself for what he had done to Lorraine. Still, there was a closure now to all they had been through. "We'd just like to have a finality to the situation," Major Dombroski said. "If the appeal process was used, it could go on for the next ten to twelve years. I don't feel that, emotionally-wise, we would survive."

Jodi Dombroski was clearly fighting to maintain control, but she had words she needed to say. She wondered about the bleak coincidence that her daughter, who had posed as Florida's "Arrive Alive" model in 1971, should now be dead at the hands of a member of the very agency that had sponsored the program.

"How sad it is that this deranged murderer could tarnish the slate of the honorable officers that serve this country and try to do their best to protect us, not destroy us," she told reporters. "Let him start his punishment. He'll live with it, day by day. Our whole family has suffered because we all loved her dearly. And all our friends will pray that each day he's not going to forget how he made her suffer. That each moment of his life he'll wish he was dead."

Sandy Harris was not in the courtroom. She gave a brief statement on the phone to reporters. "It was what he deserved," she said. "Does anyone deserve the death penalty? Life is worse than the death penalty. If I killed someone, I wouldn't want to live my life in jail."

Sandy had taken her children to see Tim in jail two days before—but only so they might understand why their father never came to see them anymore. She hoped never to have to see him again, and that she could forget him.

Tim Harris had come within a hair's breadth of getting the death penalty; that was the only reason his legal advisors had agreed to the plea bargain. He had no right to appeal, and he would have to serve, under Florida law, at least twenty-five years in prison before he could become eligible for parole.

Within hours of hearing himself sentenced to life in prison Tim Harris was transported from the Indian River County Jail to the Orlando Receiving Center, where he would be processed and assigned to the prison where he would live out, quite possibly, the rest of his life.

Shortly thereafter he was sent to the Baker Correctional Institution in Olustee, Florida. Trooper Timothy Scott Harris had become Inmate Timothy Scott Harris, 139009.

Afterword

At the Baker facility Tim Harris joined 1,600 other inmates. He was assigned as a clerk for a math and GED teacher. He joined the prison Jaycees and began to go to church, something he told reporters he had not done before he was sentenced to prison.

DeeLisa Davis visited him faithfully for the first six months of his incarceration. Sandy did not—nor did she answer the letters Tim sent. He would not be easily dissuaded. He still wrote to both DeeLisa and Sandy, assuring them both that he loved them.

On March 12, 1991, Tim Harris carried out his last act for the Florida State Patrol. He was transferred from prison to Fort Pierce so that he could testify as a witness for the State in a case where a drunk driver in a panel truck collided with a car, killing two people and injuring three others. It was, in fact, the case in which the little black boy was killed in 1989. He was not permitted to wear his uniform, but for part of a day Tim Harris was once again a "trooper" on the witness stand—and not a prisoner.

And then he was returned to Baker.

Cut off from his children, Tim Harris had finally become the complete father, wanting nothing more than a chance to be part of their lives. He sent them questionnaires about their lives—asking about everything from their favorite foods to what made them afraid to what they thought, dreamed, felt, and yearned for. He asked Sandy to help the children fill out their answers. One questionnaire, sent to seven-year-old Timmy, had 148 questions—some with many sections—for the little boy to answer.

Sandy tried to comply, but Timmy and Jennifer grew tired and frustrated. They wondered why they had to spend hours revealing every detail of their worlds. Even as children they recognized the invasion of their private, secret selves. Harris's curiosity was voracious—*invasive*.

One nine-page letter sent to Timmy asked, among other questions,

"What animal scares you the most? What kind of jelly do you like on your toast? If you caught a fish, would you let it go—or eat it? Are you afraid of sharks? Do you like caramel-coated apples?"

In a sense, it was almost as if Tim Harris was trying to be a little boy again, perhaps trying to relive a childhood by picking at Timmy's brain.

"Have you ever shot a bow and arrow? Have you ever shot a gun? Do you like grilled cheese sandwiches? Do hurricanes scare you? Have you ever gotten seasick? Do you believe in ghosts? What's the name of a famous ghost? When you take your lunch to school, what does Mom put in your lunch box? Do you have a girlfriend? What's her name? Name some things that your mom does that you are glad she does for you. How many times a day do you tell your mom you love her? What's one thing that you would like to do that you don't get to do—or are not allowed to do? And why?"

Tim Harris asked his son to list seven things that scared him and seven things that made him happy. He asked for six examples of things that Sandy did for him that made him glad. He asked, "Have you ever seen a bad car accident?" and "What does a shrimp look like?"

Few adults could have handled so many questions. One seven-year-old boy certainly could not.

Tim's handwriting on his traffic tickets had been scrawling and almost illegible. His letters to his children, and subsequently, the legal documents he filed—acting as his own attorney—were printed as precisely and neatly as if done in a calligrapher's hand.

In the end, Tim Harris's whole purpose in life seemed to be to force his ex-wife, by court order if necessary, to bend to his will and come to visit him in prison with Jennifer and Timmy.

Tim Harris had agreed to a plea bargain that would save his life. He broke that promise in 1991 when he requested an evidentiary hearing on his allegations that his attorneys had not adequately represented him when he pleaded no contest. Assistant State Attorney Lynn Park did not object to the hearing. "There are some allegations he's made that will require testimony from his attorneys," Park commented.

It would be a convoluted hearing legally. Public Defender Philip Yacucci and Chief Assistant Public Defender Clifford Barnes would be on the other side, testifying for the State. Tim Harris alleged that an insanity defense was tossed out three weeks before trial because his psychologist didn't have time to render an opinion. He also claimed he was erroneously told that he would only have to serve half of the minimum mandatory twenty-five years of his sentence.

Both the State *and* his own former lawyers said he knew full well that he would give up his right to appeal when he pleaded no contest. Tim wanted Stuart (Florida) Attorney Robert Udell to be appointed to represent him in his appeal. Udell was the defense attorney in the Ft. Pierce court where Tim Harris had testified in the hit-and-run case.

On June 6, 1991, Tim Harris wrote a letter to the Vero Beach *Press Journal* complaining about the insensitivity of the State Attorney's Office.

After his sentencing, he wrote, he had requested a public disclosure file in reference to his case. It was sent to him.

There were numerous documents that I never saw until I received the files. . . . The State Attorney's Office saw fit to send me a picture of the victim in my case. I think it was very distasteful and served no purpose. Why did they send it? If it was to remind me of the victim, I am reminded of it every minute of my life. . . . Is this not a common practice that the State sends a person a picture of his victim? They seem to forget that there are a number of victims in this case. . . .

I believe in punishment for a wrong. It's true that nothing will bring back an innocent person. I'm not like some. I do care and I do have feelings. I'm not the "cold-blooded murderer" that some people want to make me. . . .

Prison is bad enough. I think the picture idea is cruel. . . . I'm being punished in the worst way. Please don't make it worse.

Tim had never wanted to see a picture of Lorraine Hendricks's body; he had stayed away from the median strip and kept his dog away until she was found. He had walked out of his interrogation session with McIlwain and Williams when they started to show him a photograph. His letter to the *Press Journal* enraged readers.

Lori Brenton of Vero Beach wrote:

Poor Tim Harris. He receives a photo of the victim . . . and feels it is "cruel treatment." I did feel sympathy when I read his letter; unfortunately, it wasn't for him, but for his victim and her family. Wake up, Tim! That life you took will never again have the opportunity to look at anything . . . never see another sunset or the smile on a child's face. . . .

You are right about one thing; if they do it for one, they

should do it for all. Every murderer should be forced to look at his victim and imagine the dreams and hopes he ended. . . .

Mary Ann Layman and Linda Furrows agreed.

Our hearts go out to him, sitting in an air-conditioned cell . . . Hopefully he had eaten dinner before he saw pictures of his victim. . . . Did Lorraine Hendricks's death have a purpose? Did she have a chance? Harris doesn't deserve to live. . . .

"Good grief, poor Tim Harris," wrote Rindy Reardon.

He murdered an innocent woman and wants everyone to feel badly because he was sent a picture of the victim—that same picture that is boldly etched in the minds of her family and friends.

And he says prison is bad enough—that is just really heartbreaking, isn't it? Well, it makes me want to throw up. . . .

Clearly, Tim Harris still didn't get it.

On Tuesday, December 17, 1991, Judge Vocelle quashed Tim's motion to have his murder conviction overturned. Earlier Tim had told reporters that being a cop in prison wasn't as dangerous as he thought it would be, and that he hadn't needed any special protection from the state. He said that being unable to see his kids and his dog, Shadow, was far more depressing than he had expected. "It's tough," he said. "It's no fun, for sure. But I'm making it."

Judge Vocelle's ruling didn't make Tim any more cheerful. As he was led away, Major Frank Dombroski stood and shouted, "Harris, may you rot in hell!"

Tim Harris went back to prison to continue serving his twenty-five years.

He was not, however, finished with his legal manueverings. Tim sued to have his divorce modified so that he would have more contact with his children. He asked the court to grant him at least two phone calls a month to his children; letters from his children to him in prison; partial parental responsibilities for "catastrophic events," including notification of the children's medical problems; access to their school and medical records; visits with the children in prison.

He asked that either his family or court officials bring the children to see him for their birthdays and on Christmas.

In his letter to Judge Vocelle Tim said, "I came from a family where my father and mother divorced when I was young. I don't know a father like a son should know a father. . . . It does have an effect on you in the long run." No one would ever know exactly what Tim Harris's childhood had been like; he had never said, and he was not specific at this point.

Even though Tim had gone for months without contacting his children; even though the calls he made—collect—to Sandy had been to talk to *her;* even though he sent Sandy a very expensive angel doll with one teardrop on her cheek for Christmas, and no presents at all for his children, he was granted his request to see them. The only hitch was that he had to provide money to transport Timmy and Jennifer to Baker. And Tim Harris had no money. (He succeeded in early 1994 in getting a judge to order Sandy to bring his children to prison to see him, at her expense.)

On February 16, 1992, Rick Hendricks filed a wrongful death suit on behalf of Lorraine Hendricks—against the State of Florida and the Department of Highway Safety and Motor Vehicles (which oversees the Florida Highway Patrol). Seeking damages "in excess of $5,000," Hendricks asserted that the FHP "failed to discover the fact that [Harris] had been asked to resign from another agency for improper conduct, and that [Harris] had exhibited a pattern of socially deviant behavior demonstrating that he was psychologically unfit to be a highway trooper assigned to road patrol duty."

That suit was heard in the last week of February, 1994. Once again Lorraine and Katherine Hendricks played together, but this time they were only moving shadows on a videoscreen as jurors in Courtroom D of the Indian River County Courthouse watched silently while the little girl and her mother laughed into the lens of the camcorder.

Rick Hendricks testified about Katherine's uncanny reaction as he began to tell her the sad news about her mother. She had interrupted him and said, "My mom's not coming home, is she?"

When he had to say that was true, Katherine was silent for a few seconds, and then she began to cry and say, "I won't live without Mama. I won't live without Mama. . . ."

Attorneys for Lorraine's and Katherine's estates elicited information from an expert witness that the estates had lost between $588,153 and $898,000 in projected wages and household support when Lorraine was murdered. This, of course, did not—*could not*—

include the emotional losses, which were incalculable. However, lawyers for the Hendricks family were asking $3 million for Katherine's pain, suffering, and loss of parental companionship.

Lt. Andrew Morris of the Florida Highway Patrol testified that he had taken "what steps I felt necessary" after Don Dappen brought Tim's inappropriate behavior in December, 1989, to his attention. "I brought the conduct to his [Tim's] attention and told him he may be disciplined by the department for that type of conduct."

For the Hendricks family to win, they would have to prove that the state was liable and had been able to foresee what Tim Harris was going to do. Quite literally, the six jurors would have to believe that the Florida Highway Patrol's failure to act was a cause of Lorraine Hendricks's murder.

On February 25, 1994, the jurors found that the FHP was not liable for having Trooper Tim Harris on road patrol the day he strangled Lorraine. It took them less than ninety minutes of deliberation.

FHP Lt. Jim Howell felt the verdict was fair. "I just think that under the totality of the circumstances, this was not a foreseeable act. We could not have foreseen what happened." He emphasized, however, that his department felt a great deal of sympathy toward the Hendricks family, that the FHP, too, had been "betrayed" by the actions of its former trooper.

Tim Harris remains incarcerated at the Baker Correctional Institution. He is reportedly a model prisoner who sometimes teaches in the prison school. For most of his life he had tried to *own* both people and things.

But in the end, Tim Harris owns nothing at all.

Rick Hendricks has remarried; Katherine will be ten years old this year, and she has a loving stepmother. She visits her maternal grandmother, Jodi Dombroski, often.

Major Frank Dombroski died in September, 1993, after a long battle with cancer. He and Jodi had become active in a new Florida victims' rights group: STOP (STOP Turning Out Prisoners). They handed out scores of postcards addressed to Florida Governor Lawton Chiles that said "I'm mad as hell about crime, and I'm not going to take it anymore. Please stop the release of violent criminals." Jodi Dombroski volunteers at the Veterans' Hospital where her husband died. It fills some of her days and helps her show her gratitude for the wonderful care given her husband; it does not take away the memories of what she has lost.

Mike Raleigh works, as he always has, fourteen-hour days as he produces shows all over the United States.

The man who loved Lorraine at first sight, the man she loved almost as quickly, has never forgotten her. He loves her still.

Ruth Straley, who worked with Lorraine Hendricks in the wonderful days of 1989 and the first months of 1990 in Jacksonville, has moved to Europe, and Lorraine's dear friend, Carol, has moved to Washington State. Life, as it will, has gone on, but I encountered no one who can speak about Lorraine without tears.

Flicka, Lorraine's beloved horse, died a year before Lorraine herself did.

Sandy Harris remarried on New Year's Eve, 1993. She and her children will live far away from Indian River County.

Don Dappen still works for the Vero Beach Police Department.

The Wessendorfs still live in Fellsmere in the winter and New York State in the summer.

Phil Williams has realized his longtime ambition to become a polygraph operator. Like Rick McIlwain, he attended the National Training Center of Polygraph Science in New York City, and he now heads the Indian River County Sheriff's Office Internal Affairs Unit and is an expert at giving lie-detector examinations. He is currently working on his master's degree.

The murder of Carol Orcutt in Clay County, Florida, remains unsolved, four years after the day that she was found. Lt. Jimm Redmond of the Clay County Sheriff's Office, working with Phil Williams, was able to establish that there was no way Tim Harris could have been in the area of her murder at the time she died. Redmond welcomes any new information on the case.

At the time of her murder Lorraine was thrilled to have been assigned to oversee the Micanopy Fall Festival in North Florida. The Micanopy Merchants' Association had met with her several weeks before her last, fatal, trip to Fort Lauderdale and hired Lorelei Promotions to produce the entire festival. Lorraine's enthusiasm was contagious, and many of the association members were excited about the festival for the first time in years.

Lorraine never got to see her plans come to fruition, but she had done such a superlative job at laying the groundwork that Ruth Straley was able to take over the project and see it through so that it would go off smoothly on schedule.

The Sixteenth Micanopy Fall Festival was a great success, and it was dedicated to the memory of Lorraine Hendricks.

"We have chosen to dedicate this festival to her memory so she can be remembered publicly for her accomplishments and the special feeling about life and living that she left behind with everyone whose life she touched—if even for a very short while."

Lorraine Hendricks was many things to many people. She was the pigtailed marathon runner, the fine lady in the satin gown and pearls, the cook who spent days cooking Polish Easter dinner, the self-assured and confident businesswoman, the daughter who made her parents proud, the beloved of one man, the daredevil athlete, the listener who became a mentor for frightened women who didn't think they could make it in this world, the animal lover. Probably, most of all, she was Katherine's mother.

Irony so often touches all of our lives. And it was so with Lorraine Hendricks. When Jodi Dombroski searched through all the pictures that she had saved to remember different phases of her daughter's life, she came across the one from Lori's days as a model. Lori had been so young and so very beautiful when she had posed in 1971 as part of a safe driving campaign for the Florida Highway Patrol.

Lori smiled as she held up a license plate that read "Arrive Alive!"

Black Christmas

This story *is one of many that I never wanted to write. I wanted to turn my head and walk away. It is too sad and too blindly senseless. If crazed, cruel murder could destroy these victims, then should we not all be afraid? The answer is "Of course." But then we must balance that by knowing that our lives would be stunted and boxed in if we lived daily with fear and anxiety. Somewhere in the middle there has to be an answer. Cautious awareness that there are those with skewed minds who march to bleakly perverted drummers can help us to stay a little safer. None of us can assume that every knock on our door is a threat. None of us should trust completely that each knock is powered by the hand of a friend. All of us could benefit by becoming more familiar with the arcane forces that empower humans like the oddly clear-eyed killer in this case.*

No one ever deserves to be murdered. However, we often read about homicide victims who seem to have programmed themselves for violent death—the woman who goes home with a stranger from a bar, the careless hitchhiker (and, yes, the careless driver who picks up hitchhiking strangers), the drunk who flashes a roll of bills—those who do not take care. We are not like that, we say. It is more comfortable for us to suggest that the victim is partially responsible for his own fate.

"Well, that would never happen to me," we say confidently. "I don't go to those places," or "See what happens when you don't use common sense."

It takes the inexplicable slaughter of innocents to knock away the crutch of smugness—"My God!" we realize. "If it could happen to them, it could happen to me. . . ."

Charles and Annie Goldmark and their sons—Derek, twelve, and Colin, ten—seemed the least likely family to encounter a killer. Although Charles, forty-one, was a partner in a successful law firm, he didn't practice criminal law. He was a civil attorney dealing with comparatively dull points of law, civil suits, an occasional divorce case, maybe, but nothing that inspired the need for vengeance by the litigants involved. He was brilliant, thoughtful, and kind. Annie (pronounced Ann-*ee*) was a lovely woman at forty-three. She was sparkling and vivacious. Because she was a native of France, Annie often flew with her sons to her homeland during summer vacations so they would understand her roots as well as their father's.

The Goldmarks epitomized what was good about the American family. First above everything, the four of them loved one another and their friends devotedly. They were involved in the concerns of their community, and they were successful—not only financially, but in the more ephemeral things of life. They lived a healthy life, and they were consummate nature lovers, often taking advantage of all that the Northwest had to offer.

Annie was beautiful; Charles was handsome. The little boys were delightful, bright children. Derek was only twelve, but already he played a skilled game of bridge. Ten-year-old Colin sang in the school choir at The Bush School, the private school both boys attended. They were the furthest thing in the world, though, from being snobby rich kids. Their heritage was one of public service and concern for those less fortunate; it was instilled in their genes. The Goldmarks were not unlike the Kennedy family in the days of Camelot.

Charles Goldmark had long been active in Democratic politics. He served as the party's legal counsel in Washington State and led Senator Gary Hart's presidential campaign in Washington State when Hart seemed to be the great hope of the Democratic party, the next "Kennedy" in the White House.

In essence, each of the four Goldmarks had infinite potential to change the world around them, to make it a better place for those citizens who had fallen through the cracks of life.

Although the Goldmarks seemed to have a secure future as 1984 drew to a close, and the promise of a long, good life, Charles had once known the emotional pain of being slandered and ostracized. Long before he met Annie, Charles's family was subjected to cruel and exaggerated publicity.

The story of the smear campaign against his father, Washington State Senator John Goldmark, and his mother, Sally, was so outrageous and convoluted that it became the subject of a book by U.S. District Court Judge William L. Dwyer: *The Goldmark Case: An American Libel Trial.* Dwyer's book was a tribute to Sally and John Goldmark, who had stood firmly behind what they knew was right even though they risked being destroyed.

What happened to John and Sally Goldmark had a direct bearing on what happened to their son, Charles, and his family many, many years later. And all of it was based on lies, mistakes, half truths, misconceptions, and hate. When the first domino fell, all of the others toppled, creating havoc and death.

Charles's mother, Sally, was a native of New York, born to German immigrant parents. When she entered school in World War I she was quickly shunned because she spoke German. As a very young child she felt the sharp bite of prejudice. She was a vibrant, sensitive child with an IQ in the genius range. She would never forget how it felt to be singled out for torment for something for which she was in no way responsible. Her given name was Irma Ringe, but, when she was old enough she changed the German-sounding Irma to the more American name Sally.

All her life Sally Ringe Goldmark was devoted to helping people; she was particularly drawn to the underdog. After only one year of medical school the Great Depression of the 1930s forced Sally to give up her dream of becoming a doctor. She moved to Washington, D.C., where she worked for the National Youth Administration. It was the era of Franklin D. Roosevelt, and she was caught up in the excitement of the "New Deal." There *was* a way, she saw, to help those less fortunate. When the Work Projects Administration (W.P.A.) was formed in 1935, she saw that jobs were being found for hundreds of thousands of desperate men who had been broken by the Depression, and she realized the power of politics.

Sally Ringe aligned herself for brief periods with any number of causes and groups, always looking for the right channel to help mankind.

At the beginning of the Second World War Sally met a young attorney—John Goldmark. They got married, and John went off to war to serve with bravery and distinction in the U.S. Navy. When the war was over he and Sally struck out for the West, even though Sally had always been a city girl. She went willingly wherever her young husband would be happy. John and Sally Goldmark were about to fulfill their dream of adventure and country living, far from hustle of the East Coast.

In 1947 Charles Goldmark's parents settled on a wheat and cattle ranch on the Colville Indian Reservation in north central Washington State. The ranch flourished, and so did their two sons, Charles and Peter. Yellowed newspaper clippings show the Goldmark boys posing proudly on their ranch. The Goldmarks had become so much a part of the West that it was hard to imagine their origins in the East. The Okanogan country was the best of all possible worlds in which to raise two sons.

In 1956 John Goldmark was elected to the Washington Senate, where he would serve for many years. He was defeated in the mid-1960s after a rumor-filled campaign. Someone in the opposition party had discovered that Sally Ringe Goldmark had once belonged to the Communist Party. Although McCarthyism had reached its peak in the mid to late 1950s, Senator Joseph McCarthy's hearings had frightened and sensitized people to the threat of communists. Many careers were destroyed, often unjustly.

It was true. Sally Ringe had been a member of the Communist Party—for about as long as it took to blink an eye. It had been a long time before, when she was hardly more than a girl, filled as so many young people were in the twenties and thirties with sometimes misdirected fervor in their efforts to help mankind. Sally had quickly become disenchanted with the Communist Party. Her name remained someplace on the yellowing rosters of early communist followers. It was more than enough to provide fodder for the candidate running against her husband decades later. Far more devastating than John Goldmark's defeat at the polls was the damage done to his family's reputation. The rumors grew and became more scurrilous with each telling. This family, who had done so much for others, suffered mightily. The idyllic ranch life Charles and Peter Goldmark had always known was tainted now.

Those who took the trouble to seek truth at the source understood. But others believed the rumors that Sally Goldmark was, at the very least, a lifelong devotee of communism and therefore dangerous. Her name was on "their" lists; that meant she was one of "them." Too many forgot who Sally Goldmark really was and painted her with the black brush of vicious rumor.

The Goldmarks sued, charging libel. They won, but John Goldmark's political career was already smashed. In 1965 they moved from their beloved ranch to Seattle, where John Goldmark practiced law. Sally, her heart still in the vast Okanogan country, gave a family inheritance to the Omak town library so that they might commission an artist to carve the massive library doors. Books and people had always been her loves, a devotion handed down to her sons and her grandchildren.

John Goldmark died in 1979, and Sally lived on for six years. When she died she left behind letters filled with her memories of the Goldmarks' wonderful years of ranch life in the Okanogan. One paragraph was to take on macabre meaning in light of the tragedy of Christmas Eve, 1985. Sally wrote, "There is a great thing in the mechanism that pulsates in every beast and human, a heart that pushes out the juice and heat. It needs feeding, but it creates spirit, and the human angle is a joke, the kid, the banter, which lightens the spirit and warms the heart."

She could not have known about a man whose heart also demanded feeding, but feeding of quite another sort. Where Charles and Peter Goldmark had had it all—or as much as John and Sally could give their beloved sons—this man, this killer with a face like a mask, had had virtually nothing in life. Or at least it seemed that way to him, and he was always searching; while he searched he let hate suffuse him and burn away whatever conscience he once might have had.

When Sally Goldmark died on May 31, 1985, old friends and new mourned her, as did her sons, their wives, and her grandchildren. Only later would someone say, "Thank God Sally died before it happened; she couldn't have borne the grief."

Perhaps so. Barely six months later a disaster of cataclysmic proportions would strike her beloved family.

In December of 1985 the Seattle Homicide Unit was made up of fifteen detectives, three sergeants, a lieutenant, and a captain—all of whom would have preferred not to work on Christmas Eve. For as long as anyone could remember, there had always been approximately fifty to sixty murders a year in Seattle—not a particularly high rate per capita for a city whose environs were home to a million people. So far in 1985 the toll stood at fifty-five; the detectives who investigated murder were hoping it wouldn't climb any higher in the last week of the year. But they also knew that family beefs often exploded into violence during the holidays.

Some families were never meant to get as close to one another as the distance across the Christmas tree.

Detective Hank Gruber, who was also a graphic artist, made the murder charts each year. The 1985 chart was tacked to the wall in the captain's office. With his perfect, precise printing Gruber listed date, victim, sex, age, cause of death, location, and, hopefully, the name of the person charged with the crime. There was very little room left at the bottom of the chart for any additions.

Sergeant Jerry Yates's night crew of detectives was slated to work until midnight on December 24th, and the officers were pleased to find everything blessedly quiet during the early evening. Not a squawk on the phone, nothing from radio—not even a family fight. If they could just make it to the witching hour, they could go home and celebrate Christmas the way civilians did. After midnight Detective Sergeant Joe Sanford and Detectives Hank Gruber and Rudy Sutlovich had volunteered to be on standby to cover any calls that might come in between 12 and 7:30 a.m., when the Homicide Unit offices were closed. In fact, filled with holiday spirit, Sanford decided that Gruber and Sutlovich would start early—at 9 p.m.

It remained quiet on Christmas Eve on the fifth floor of the Public Safety Building through 7, 8, 9 p.m. Finally Sergeant Yates told his men to go home and have dinner with their families. They turned off the lights and locked the office door; if something *should* happen, radio would call standby detectives.

"I got a call from Joe Sanford at 9:30," Hank Gruber remembers the beginning of Seattle Police Case 85-551331. For the Homicide Unit it would be H85-365. "Standby had started earlier than we'd gambled on—Joe had a murder. I said, 'What is it?' And he said 'Well, from what I can gather, it was some kind of a Christmas party, and it sounds like somebody got in an argument and they started shooting, and they've got some people in Harborview [King County's hospital]—and one is deceased. We can handle it. You and I can just check it out, see what gives.'"

Reports often come in that way. Not garbled, exactly, but piecemeal. Sergeant Sanford sent Hank Gruber to the address furnished to try to get a fix on what had happened.

"I really expected to go up there and find it was some family beef, arguing how to carve the turkey or something," Gruber says wryly, remembering. "When I got up there, of course, I saw that we had something entirely different—and I needed help. Joe ended up calling Rudy in. And later we had to call a whole lot of the guys in."

The address given was on 36th Avenue in the Madrona District of Seattle overlooking Lake Washington. It was a good address in an upper-middle-class neighborhood. There was a breathtaking view of the huge lake from the rear windows of all the houses on the street. The home was like so many built in the 1930s in Seattle; it was a modified Norman cottage with two stories on the street which became three floors at the back as the yard fell away. Hank Gruber saw the police patrol units parked in front and lights on inside the house. Colored Christmas tree lights glowed in the front window.

Patrol Officer Dane Bean, the first officer at the scene, briefed the detective on what he knew so far. The call for help had come in from friends of the Charles Goldmark family. They had come to the house that evening to attend a Christmas party, but no one had answered their knocks. Puzzled and a little worried, they had gone home and telephoned the Goldmarks.

"Nobody answered," Bean said, "so they came back over. They thought they heard someone calling out or crying very faintly inside. They had a key and went in."

What the Goldmarks' friends had found was beyond anything they could have imagined. All Bean knew for sure was that everyone inside had been injured. He thought there was one fatality.

"The aid car took the man and the boys in," Bean explained. "The woman is upstairs. We haven't moved her—or anything in the room."

Gruber stepped into the home. There was something unreal about this; this home simply didn't look like the scene of a homicide. Everything was immaculate. The house was decorated festively for Christmas. There were stockings hung on the fireplace and a poinsettia plant on the coffee table near the tree. In the dining alcove there was a table impeccably set with fine china and red napkins, with a centerpiece made of candles and holly. Places were set for ten people.

The kitchen bar was crowded with candles, chips and dip, hors d'oeuvres. Gruber sniffed and turned toward the kitchen. The oven was still on; the burners had been turned down to simmer while pots of food cooked. Everything smelled wonderful; nothing had even begun to burn. Where was the cook who had prepared all this? She had to have stepped away from her kitchen only a little while ago.

A *party*. That's what the neighbors had said to Dane Bean. They were going to celebrate Christmas Eve at a festive dinner. Gruber sighed and carefully switched the burners and oven to off.

The name Goldmark didn't mean anything special to him; Hank Gruber was a New Yorker, a transplant into the Northwest, and he was not up on Seattle history. He had long since learned that a clean and classy house was certainly no guarantee that domestic violence wouldn't occur, but his gut feeling said no. This didn't look like a domestic violence call.

Besides, Bean said the husband was injured to the point of unconsciousness, too, and the friends who'd called the police insisted this was a happy family. A happy, loving family. No way could this be a papa-kills-mama case.

Gruber's glance at the dining room and kitchen had taken only twenty seconds at most. Now he moved toward the stairs.

Rudy Sutlovich arrived just then and followed him up. The house was very still.

On Christmas Eve, 1985, they climbed the stairs to the home's top floor, walking softly on the thick beige carpeting, still feeling somehow that they were intruding. The detectives had only to walk across a narrow hall to be in the master bedroom, a huge room that measured 15 feet by 19 feet. They stood just inside the doorway, silent for a moment, taking it all in.

The room was a little cluttered with the last-minute rush of Christmas. There were wrapping paper, ribbons and seals, boxes covered with shiny blue paper, other presents waiting to be wrapped. There was a damp towel at the entrance to the master bath, either carelessly or hurriedly dropped.

Hank Gruber looked toward the bay window with its curving window seat, and his chest tightened. He forced his eyes down to the rug and saw that it was spattered in spots and drenched in other places with both bright red and partially drying dark red fluid. The little boys had been there, Bean was saying.

The woman lay on her side, her hands pulled behind her, her slender wrists handcuffed. Even in death she was beautiful. Her robe had been pulled off her shoulders, leaving her partially nude. That didn't necessarily indicate sexual attack; the robe would have slipped as her hands were yanked backward.

The detectives could see that she had suffered a deep stab wound to her chest, a fatal wound.

This would be Annie Goldmark—a beautiful woman who looked to be a decade younger than they had been told she was. Someone had dealt terrible crushing blows to her skull, apparently as she lay helplessly manacled. She lay with her feet pointing toward an antique organ and her head toward the bed.

The probable murder weapons still rested beside her—a steam iron with its plastic handle broken off by great force, the plate blood-stained, with hairs caught in it. A long, narrow knife was there, too, a kitchen knife. It looked as if the killer had found his weapons in his victims' own home.

One of the patrol officers produced a ring of handcuff keys, and he tested them until one fit the cuffs on Annie's wrists. The officer slipped them off and slid them carefully into a plastic bag to be checked for fingerprints. A gold bracelet still encircled Annie Goldmark's wrist, and an expensive diamond ring remained undisturbed on her finger.

The investigators stepped carefully past the debris left by the Seattle Fire Department's Medic One crew: bandages, hypodermic needles and plastic tubing, packets of dextrose solution emptied of their fluid. Fourteen paramedics and fire personnel had rushed to the Goldmark home. It was apparent that the fire department medics had fought desperately to save the injured.

For both medics and cops the rule is always, "First of all, protect life."

The Seattle Fire Department has been a front runner in emergency medical care. If any paramedic team would be able to save the Goldmark family, Medic One was it. They had raced time and stanched blood from terrible wounds to save as many lives as they could on what had become a bleak and tragic Christmas Eve.

The Seattle detectives didn't know how Charles Goldmark and his sons were doing, but here in this lovely room there was no life left to protect. Dr. Corinne Fligner, from the King County Medical Examiner's Office, examined Annie Goldmark's body. She found that her left ear had been lacerated and that there was a deep puncture wound just behind the ear, in the neck, as well as the chest wound.

Annie's body was removed by the M.E.'s office, and the investigators were alone in the pleasant bedroom that had become an abattoir.

Bean pointed to a large bloodied spot in the entrance of the room. "The man was there when we got here, with his legs pointing toward the stairway."

Hank Gruber and Rudy Sutlovich could tell that the victims had all been down on the floor when they were struck with whatever object had been used to bludgeon them—probably the steam iron. "We could see that from the blood spray pattern," Gruber explained. "So it wasn't like people were running around and trying to get away; they were hit when they were down, helpless."

Rudy·Sutlovich looked at the spot where the children had lain and saw a trace of brain tissue. He glanced at Gruber and saw something in his partner's eyes. They were both thinking the same thing. There was every chance the kids wouldn't make it—or maybe worse, that they'd survive terribly brain-damaged. Had the parents seen their children being bludgeoned? Or had the kids had to watch as their mother and father were attacked?

The investigators didn't have to think about that now; they were grateful that they had work to do. The first major puzzle was who had done this and why. And the second was how one person could get control of four people. Perhaps there had been more than one killer.

The detectives peered into the bathroom. The tub was wet; there were more wet towels on the floor, and fresh clothing—a woman's party outfit—was laid out on the bed. Annie Goldmark had obviously just taken a shower and was preparing to get dressed when the intruder—or intruders—grabbed her and handcuffed her.

The patrol officers said that Charles Goldmark had been fully dressed. His neighbors had already managed to cut the handcuffs off his wrists by the time the police arrived. Colin and Derek had also been fully clothed, but someone had yanked their sweaters up around their shoulders and necks to restrain them.

All four Goldmarks had suffered severe battering wounds to the head. Someone had to have been in the grip of rage to carry out such a frenzied, brutal attack.

But *why?*

By 10:45 that night, Sutlovich, Gruber, and Sanford were joined in their investigation by Detectives Sonny Davis, Duane Homan, and Jim Yoshida. Teams of investigators would be either at the crime scene or at the hospital until six or seven on Christmas morning, gathering evidence, bagging it, labeling it, asking questions. They wouldn't be asking questions of the three surviving victims, however; they were comatose and in critical condition.

Detectives had assured themselves early on that there was no forced entry. One of the Goldmarks had to have let the killer in. Searching through the house, the police found the path of exit. The back door in the basement was standing wide open. It had a lock that was dead-bolted on both sides. No one could get in or *out* without a key.

"We assumed the killer had taken the keys," Gruber recalled. "We didn't know how many cars the victims had at that point, so we wondered if the killer might have left in one of their vehicles."

But then they found signs that someone had tried unsuccessfully to get into the detached garage. Unless he found a car on the street he would have had to slip away on foot through the sloping backyard. That was the likeliest possibility. He would have had little time between the attacks and the arrival of the first of the Goldmark's invited guests. He would have been a fool to appear at the front of the house. Indeed, he was probably going out the basement door as friends pounded on the front door.

Dr. Michael Copass, head of the Medic One program, told Detectives Jim Yoshida and Duane Homan that Charles Goldmark had not only been battered on the head; someone had deliberately inserted a thin knife into the brain itself, through the skull fractures made by the iron. The little boys had both been battered and stabbed in the head. They were in extremely critical condition.

The investigators wondered if the killer had been someone they all knew; he seemed to have gone to great lengths to assure himself that even the children would not be able to speak and identify him.

Or *her*. Nobody knew at that point whether they were looking for a man, a woman, or several people.

Back at the Goldmark home Sutlovich and Gruber took *everything* from the bedroom that might conceivably be helpful. "It's kind of an interesting thing," Gruber explains. "Before you figure out the crime, it's hard to know what's important and what isn't—so you end up taking things, and you really don't know why . . . You just say, 'Well, we'll take it—and see if it matters.' So one of the things we found was a handkerchief near her—kind of bloodied up—and we found some handkerchiefs and paper towels over where the kids were, too. It just didn't make sense at the time. What's with the handkerchiefs? They surely weren't able to hold them to their own wounds—and why would the killer do that? We found out later that they were soaked with chloroform. The lab brought it out—in blood studies and from the handkerchief—but by the time we got there you couldn't smell it. That would explain why the victims were down and why they didn't fight."

Indeed it would. Had someone chloroformed the Goldmarks to subdue them and then bludgeoned and knifed them when they were unconscious? If so, it was small comfort to those who loved them. They would not have known what was happening to them.

The most difficult thing of all for the detectives to try to get a handle on was a motive. The place had not been ransacked. The Goldmarks had two computers, several television sets, antique guns on the wall, presents under the Christmas tree, paintings, jewelry, objects d'art, stereo equipment, all the things that any professional burglar would have taken. But nothing had been touched. The only thing the investigators found that pointed to robbery was Charles Goldmark's wallet. It lay on the bedroom floor, and all the credit cards were fanned out on a shelf, as if someone had riffled through them, searching for particular cards. The detectives couldn't tell which, if any, cards were missing. They would have to check later with friends or family members to see what cards Goldmark had.

While evidence was being gathered Sonny Davis, Duane Homan, and Jim Yoshida talked with the friends of the victims, who had gathered anxiously on the ninth floor of Harborview Hospital.

Everyone was so shaken by the shock of Annie's murder and the attacks on her husband and children that detectives had been hesitant to ask much about the Goldmark's background. Now Homan and Yoshida (who were referred to at Seattle Homicide as "Ho" and "Yo") realized how well-known the victims were. Chief of Police Patrick Fitzsimmons was there in the hospital waiting room, and so was Bill Dwyer, who had written the book about the elder Goldmarks, and Jim Wickwire, an internationally famous mountain climber and one of nine partners in Goldmark's law firm.

Jim Wickwire explained that Charles Goldmark's clients were strictly civil litigants—as was the whole firm's practice. Charles had represented Seattle's historic Pike Place Market, the Seattle Art Museum, and the Flight Museum. There had been absolutely no hassles, no resentments, no threats—nothing—in Goldmark's caseload.

One friend, Janet Lilly,* said she was a very close friend of Annie's. They talked every day, either in person or by phone. They had stored Christmas presents at each other's homes to keep them away from snoopy children, and they had planned to exchange them on Christmas Day. Lilly had talked to Annie several times on December 24th, the last time at twenty minutes to six.

Lilly said that the Goldmarks had two cars at present—a BMW and an Alpha Romeo. They also owned a Volkswagen Rabbit, but Charles's sister-in-law had borrowed it to drive back to eastern Washington when she missed a flight.

"Chuck was in a wonderful mood, very festive," Janet Lilly said as she recalled the afternoon of Christmas Eve. "Annie always cooked a traditional meal for Christmas Eve, and she was probably going to put on her traditional Swedish gown, as she always did."

Lilly shook her head at the question of marital problems. No, she was positive Chuck and Annie were happy together. If not, she would have known about it.

Homan and Yoshida talked next to Allie Chambers.* She had gone to help Annie at noon that day, and they had set the table together. "I left at a quarter to five to run over to my house and change clothes for dinner—that was to be at seven. Chuck was wearing a red velour shirt and Levi's, and Annie was wearing jeans, a red sweater, blue turtleneck, and blue apron. She was going to change into her Scandinavian dress after she took a shower."

An hour and fifteen minutes after Allie Chambers left she had returned with her family. She had been a little surprised to find that the porch light was off and that only the kitchen light was on inside. They knocked and then banged and rattled the door—but no one came.

"I thought they were playing a joke on us or something," she said sadly, "so we sat at the outside picnic table on the deck waiting for them. We finally left a note and went on home."

Once home, Allie phoned the Goldmarks and found the line was busy. Puzzled and beginning to be worried, the Chamberses returned to the Goldmarks' twenty minutes later. Allie Chambers thought she heard a faint sound through the peephole in the front door. She called to her husband, Leif.* Frankly worried, the couple went to mutual friends—the Ben Walkers*—who had a key to the Goldmark house.

With that key they had opened the front door. They followed the sounds to the upstairs master bedroom and, horrified, found their friends on the floor.

Leif Chambers had heard Charles Goldmark calling "Leif . . . Leif . . . hurts . . . hurting . . ." He was trembling and complaining about the handcuffs, and, in shock themselves, Walker and Chambers could think only of getting those handcuffs off.

The telephone in the residence was dead. Chambers and Walker worked with tin snips and a hacksaw to cut the cuffs off of Charles Goldmark. As they worked they saw that someone had tossed a blanket over the little boys—as if even the killer could not bear to look upon what he had done to them.

Two patrolmen had ridden in the ambulance with Charles Goldmark on the slight chance that he might be able to identify his family's attacker. Detective Sonny Davis continued still to sit beside Goldmark's bed at the hospital, but he was either silent or incoherent.

One of the Goldmark boys was undergoing a CAT scan, and the other was in the operating room.

At Homan's and Yoshida's request, Ben Walker and Allie Chambers searched their memories for anything unusual that might have happened in the neighborhood during the hour before the party. All they could come up with was that they had seen a 1975 green Datsun pickup truck drive by the Goldmark house several times. There were two men in it, and they were laughing.

The ninth floor waiting room was jammed with people, and everyone tried to help the detectives. Almost all of Charles Goldmark's law partners were there. None of them could recall that Chuck Goldmark had an enemy. The only thing they could think of that might have sparked animosity was that the firm had many applicants for jobs. The partners often sent rejection letters on the firm's stationery and signed their own names.

Canvasses of the 36th Avenue neighborhood elicited information from a woman who lived next door. She had opened her door to a stranger earlier that evening. The man had carried a white box, and he slurred his words as he asked for "Charles . . . somebody." She had told him she didn't recognize the name.

She remembered the "delivery man," though. It was his eyes that stayed with her. The man was tall, dark-haired, and he'd had light eyes, strangely penetrating—almost crazy eyes. She described the man to Detective Al Smalley, and the sketch he drew was chilling to look at. It was the eyes that made it so. They were blank, inscrutable—unforgettable.

Ordinarily, someone delivering packages would be easy to trace. But it was Christmastime; everybody on the street was receiving package deliveries. The investigators found a number of packages in the victims' home, but no plain white package.

Nobody on the Goldmarks' street had the heart to celebrate Christmas. Silently, neighbors walked up and left flowers on the doorstep of the house where nobody lived anymore. A little shrine grew there. Vases full of flowers stirring in the rainy wind. But a sad, macabre shrine it was, bordered with yellow plastic ribbons that signified police barriers not to be crossed.

The word from the hospital wasn't good. The three surviving members of the family were not expected to live. Brains so insulted by bludgeoning and knives swelled against the hard plates of the skull, doing more damage, even though physicians had operated to remove sections of the skull to allow more room. And infection was a constant danger. Charles and Colin and Derek could neither hear nor speak.

The Seattle homicide detectives working the case were quick to admit they were in trouble. They had no evidence at the scene that was going to help them—unless they came up with a suspect to link it to. The handcuffs had been brought to the victims' home; the weapons were already there. They had isolated a single fingerprint, but it wasn't any good unless they had prints to compare it to. AFIS—Automated Fingerprint Identification System—was still a few years away. The killer had apparently worn gloves for most of the time he carried out his ghastly work. This appeared to have been a stranger-to-stranger crime, the hardest kind to solve.

And they still had no motive. They would need help from the public. Or a confession. Or some luck.

In Seattle's Broadway District, however—a few miles west of the Goldmarks' house—things *were* happening.

Max Stingley* was a highly educated black man who lived in an apartment in the Broadway District. He was a kindhearted man who had been known to help somebody down on his luck, and Christmas-time is a bad time to be down and out. When Stingley heard a knock on his door he was a little surprised to find a man he knew only as David. He knew David slightly as a member of a group he belonged to called the Fox Club.*

The Fox Club was a rather loose organization. It was basically a discussion group whose purpose was "promotion of the strict adherence to the Constitution of the United States." As far as Stingley had been able to tell, the Fox Club was a peaceful enough organization, although its members felt that their rights as citizens were steadily being taken away from them because officials weren't sticking to the Constitution. It was not a militant group; it was a rather homogeneous bunch of people who liked to get together in a restaurant over cups of coffee and discuss political philosophy.

Stingley confided that he was a bit wary of the members, however. He sensed they weren't fond of Jews, and he wondered if blacks might be next.

But here was this kid—David, the one who lived with the lady doctor, Suzanne Perreau*—at his door, saying he had been wandering the streets for seventy-two hours, and that he was cold and needed a place to crash. Stingley had reluctantly invited him in.

David had always been pale with dark circles under his eyes, but on Christmas night he had really looked wasted. Stingley was tired himself and told his impromptu guest that he was going to bed. When he left, David was sitting on the couch in the living room.

It was what Stingley found on the coffee table before dawn the next morning that made him nervous enough to call the police—even though he wasn't sure what it meant. He had seen the kid scribbling on a tablet the night before, but he couldn't figure out if the scrawled words were supposed to be true or some kind of creative writing. Whatever it was, it made the hairs stand up on the back of his neck.

TO WHOM IT MAY CONCERN, I AM THE PERSON YOU ARE LOOKING FOR IN THE GOLDMARK CASE.

I KNOW WHAT I DID WAS A VERY TERRIBLE THING. THAT IS WHY I AM AS YOU SEE ME NOW.

I WANT IT PERFECTLY UNDERSTOOD THAT NO ONE ELSE HAD ANYTHING WHATSOEVER TO DO WITH WHAT I DID. I WENT TO GREAT LENGTHS TO MAKE SURE OF THAT.

THE PERSON THAT I LIVE WITH DOESN'T EVEN KNOW THAT I AM WANTED ON A DIFFERENT CHARGE, SHE RECIEVED [*sic*] A COUPLE OF MESSAGES ON HER MACHINE, BUT I ERASED THEM BEFORE SHE GOT TO THEM.

I DID NOT USE THE RIFLE THAT I PURCHASED A FEW WEEKS AGO. INSTEAD, I FOOLED THEM WITH A TOY PISTOL WHICH YOU WILL FIND IN THE STORAGE LOCKER. I THREW THE RIFLE AWAY A COUPLE OF WEEKS AGO.

AGAIN, I WANT IT UNDERSTOOD THAT NO ONE KNEW ANYTHING ABOUT THIS, SO PLEASE DO NOT CAUSE ANY UNNESESSARY [*sic*] SUFFERING TO INNOCENT PEOPLE. I THINK THAT I'VE ALREADY DONE ENOUGH.

I GUESS I SHOULD TELL YOU WHY I DID WHAT I DID. THAT WAY, YOU WON'T HAVE TO ASK OTHER PEOPLE ABOUT IT.

MY LIFE IS A MESS. IT HAS BEEN SINCE MY WIFE LEFT. SUE HAD BEEN TRYING TO HELP ME STRAIGHTEN IT OUT BUT . . .

That was all. Either David had been working on a rough draft and decided to start agian when he woke up, or he really didn't want to reveal exactly *why* he had done what he had done.

Max Stingley had never heard the name Goldmark. What with the holiday and all, he hadn't read a paper for a couple of days or had the

TV news on. He read the note again, glanced at David, who was still asleep, and puttered about making coffee while he decided what he should do. The man he knew only as David was definitely acting weird.

His guest woke up and was sitting on the couch watching television when Stingley said he was going out to get a pack of cigarettes. Stingley crossed the darkened street to a club he belonged to at 11th and Union. Still troubled, he asked a few early birds there if they had heard about some shooting or something having to do with a Goldmark.

They looked at him, astounded. Everybody in Seattle must surely know about the Goldmark attack by now. Where the heck had Stingley been, they asked. Somebody held up the front page of the morning *Post-Intelligencer* for December 26. The name Goldmark was spread all over it.

Stingley felt sick. The note he had found on the table in his apartment wasn't fiction at all. He had just slept through the night with a probable killer in his apartment.

Rudy Sutlovich had arrived to work the day shift in Homicide shortly after 7 a.m. on December 26. There was no one there except the two secretaries. The phone rang, and Sutlovich reached for it; it was Elizabeth Eddy, the chief radio dispatcher. "I've got a citizen on the 911 line who says his name is Max Stingley—he's at 11th and Union. Says he's got a guy watching TV in his apartment who says he killed the Goldmarks. What should I do?"

"Get a uniform up there," Sutlovich said urgently, pulling his coat back on. "I'm leaving right now."

Sutlovich ran for the police garage; Gruber coordinated with Dispatch. Sonny Davis and Sutlovich headed up the hill toward Broadway. By the time they reached Boren and Madison they could hear sirens, and the radio picked up sounds of a foot chase nearby.

"You don't suppose that's our man, do you?" Sutlovich kidded Davis.

Davis shrugged. "No way. That would be too easy."

But it was.

Stingley had been talking to the uniformed officers in front of his club when his guest happened to glance out the window and see the conference. David deduced correctly that they were talking about him. He realized that Max Stingley must have found the note he had been trying to write.

David didn't wait around for the officers to come knocking on the door. He ran out of the apartment building and headed north on 11th

Avenue. Stingley saw him and pointed him out to the officers. Patrolmen R. P. Cuncan and Peter Hogan raced after the tall, slender man. Feet pounding, they ran north on 11th, halfway around the block, and then south on Braodway, where the two officers began to close the gap. They saw the suspect had a vial of something in his hand. They watched him lift it to his lips and then toss it away.

In the next instant they had him, and they forced him to the ground and handcuffed him. Just at that moment Rudy Sutlovich and Sonny Davis drove up.

Sutlovich walked over to where the cuffed suspect lay, all the fight seemingly gone out of him. Hunkering down from his considerable height, Sutlovich looked for the first time into the face of the man who gave his name as David Lewis Rice. Sutlovich advised him of his rights under Miranda.

"Why did you run from the officers?" Sutlovich asked.

"I don't want to answer that."

Rice was young, only twenty-seven. He had straight black hair, a luxuriant mustache, and a neat beard. He might have been considered handsome, despite his pasty complexion, but there was something odd about him. His movements and his speech were stilted; he seemed almost like a store mannequin—not real.

"It was his eyes," Sutlovich recalled.

"I looked in those eyes, and I remembered the picture Al Smalley drew from the Goldmarks' neighbor's description. It was as if I were looking into the eyes in that picture. She said she'd never forget those eyes, and I could see why. They were very distinct—faraway, yes— vacant."

Rice had not struggled at all once the policemen caught him. They crawled into the Dempsey Dumpster to retrieve the vial he had tossed there in his flight and asked him what it was.

"Nicotine," Rice replied. "Liquid nicotine."

Could nicotine kill you? Sonny Davis and Rudy Sutlovich wondered about that. Rice seemed to be all right. It had probably been some kind of grandstand play.

Sonny Davis took custody of the prisoner and headed back to the homicide offices. Rudy Sutlovich wanted to talk more with Max Stingley.

Stingley said he really didn't know David Rice—that he hadn't even known his last name until a few minutes before. When Sutlovich asked about the note, which seemed now to be a confession, Stingley said he guessed it was back at his apartment.

Fortunately, it was still there, and Sutlovich retrieved it for evidence. Detective Sergeant Don Cameron, Sonny Davis, and his partner, John Boatman, could use a copy of it in their interrogation of David Rice.

The case was officially assigned to John Boatman and Sonny Davis. It was their task now to try to get a complete confession or, at the very least, some explanation for the baffling attack on the Goldmark family.

David Rice had been advised once again of his rights under Miranda. Indeed, Sonny Davis had him read those rights aloud. The detectives had obtained an attorney for Rice—one of Seattle's veteran defense attorneys, Bill Lanning, had come to headquarters and conferred with the suspect.

Still, Rice said he thought he wanted to tell them his story, attorney or not. Sonny Davis asked Rice if he was ready to do that, and David Rice hesitated, saying he was not sure yet. Asked to empty his pockets, the suspect laid items on the table. Among them were two key rings, rings that each carried handcuff keys that would open the cuffs found on the victims.

Sonny Davis showed the copy of the note from Max Stingley's apartment to David Rice and asked him if he had written it. He acknowledged that he had. Asked if he cared to finish the letter, Rice nodded. Davis gave him a pen and left him alone, but when he returned he saw that Rice had written nothing. He didn't want to write about it; he wanted to *tell* the detectives what had happened in the Goldmark house on Christmas Eve.

It was December 26, 13:07 hours in police lingo, 1:07 p.m. on the clock, when the suspect began to talk, fully aware that a tape recorder was rolling and catching all his words.

It was a backwards kind of case. The investigators believed that they had the killer in custody, but this twenty-seven-year-old man with the empty eyes was not what they had expected. What *had* they expected? How could anyone know what kind of a killer could plot the monstrous crime against the Goldmark family?

It was hard to imagine Rice in Charles and Annie Goldmark's world. He had not robbed them. Why, then, had he struck them down? He *had* been looking for them specifically. He had asked for them by name. But why had he sought them out? And who was he?

David Lewis Rice was born on November 11, 1958. Armistice Day. He had two older brothers and a sister who remembered that he had never fit in—almost from the time he could walk. He had been raised in Arizona, and he had been a child who was always alone. His brothers teased him and laughed at him because he was an easy target.

When David was eleven, his brothers heard a peculiar thumping sound coming from his room. When they forced open the door they found him hanging by the neck, unconscious. He was already turning blue. They cut him down, and his skin recovered a pink hue as he regained consciousness. His mother took him to a doctor, but he received no therapy of any kind.

Things went on as before. David Rice's brothers were embarrassed to be associated with him because he was such a klutz. Later one brother rather ruefully remembered pushing him out of a tree.

"He never fought back."

Surprisingly, David had dated, gotten married, and fathered a child—but the marriage didn't last. Nothing lasted for him. He had no talent for life or for getting along with people or for holding a job. He began to feel more and more that the world was against him.

David Rice moved to Seattle in the early 1980s, perhaps to be closer to his brothers, who lived in Washington. Despite the way they had teased him when they were all children, they did care about him, and they urged him to come north. For a time he worked as a welder for a steel company. He was the lead man in his shop, and he made good money. But then the business he worked for went bankrupt, and he, along with the other men he worked with, was shorted on his last paycheck.

The injustice of it all seemed to trigger overwhelming hatred in David Rice.

He became strongly anti-communist in the early spring of 1983. Communism was something he could focus his hate on. Despite his skills as a welder, he couldn't seem to find a job. He lived on the edges of life, subsisting on unemployment and through the kindness of strangers from the summer of 1984 until his arrest. For eighteen months he had roamed Seattle, full of a malign hunger for vengeance. He wasn't really sure what it was he hated. He was angry at the big-business bosses who had fired him and shorted him on his paycheck. But then he hated communists, too, and he didn't seem to understand that he was at cross-purposes.

Literally on the streets in early 1985, David Rice met Dr. Suzanne Perreau, who was a podiatrist. She was several years older than he.

Dr. Perreau belonged to the Fox Club, and she introduced David to
the group. He was enthusiastic about the club's discussions, although
he sometimes seemed to go on too long when he had comments to
make, his voice rising and saliva gathering at the corners of his
mouth. The Fox Club was tolerant of him, though. He believed, as
they did, in the sanctity of the U. S. Constitution.

David Rice was also fascinated with guns, survivalists, explosives,
soldiers of fortune, paramilitary activities, and, of course, with the
need to fight communist invasion.

At some point after he lost his job Rice read an article that changed
his world, and, eventually, the world of many others. He concluded
that that article identified Charles Goldmark as a leading communist.
It is far more likely that David Rice's mind was not tracking well. The
only link Charles Goldmark ever had with communism was his
mother's short-lived membership in the party more than a dozen
years before he was born.

"Do you know the Goldmarks?" Sonny Davis asked him now as
they sat in one of the tiny interview rooms in the Homicide Unit.

"Only by history," Rice answered vaguely.

"History from where?"

"Newspaper clippings and so forth . . . In today's paper it mentioned that Charles Goldmark was a prominent figure in the Democratic Party. What it doesn't mention is that he was also a prominent
figure in the Communist Party. . . . I had found out that he had been
brought before the Senate subcommittee on Un-Americanism . . ."

"*This* Mr. Goldmark?" Boatman sounded puzzled.

"Right."

Charles Goldmark? Davis asked.

David Rice nodded, as if the detectives were woefully uninformed.
"Charles Goldmark . . . nothing had been done. He was at one time
the regional director of the American Communist Party."

Rice said he didn't think he had kept any of the articles he had read
that had told about his victims' "past." He thought he might have
some of his notes.

"How did you know where the Goldmarks lived?" Davis asked.

"A newspaper clipping. It showed that he had just moved into a
house on 36th." Rice said he thought he had read that in an issue of
the *Seattle Times* sometime in March, 1983.

"You're talking a couple of years ago, then. Has the Goldmark
family been on your mind, then, for some period of time?"

"Yeah, I'd say in the last six months."

David Rice said he had to get himself mentally set to do what he planned to do.

"What were you going to do?" Boatman asked.

"I was going to kill the Goldmarks."

Detectives Davis and Boatman and Sergeant Cameron watched the tall, thin man across the interview table, wondering if he really could explain the virtually unexplainable to them.

David Rice's confession took seventy-seven pages when it was transcribed from tape. He told a bizarrely tragic story, shocking even to detectives who had seen and heard all manner of horror.

By mid-1985 Rice decided he had to kill Charles Goldmark. He believed that Goldmark was both a Jew and a Communist. In actual fact, of course, Charles Goldmark was neither. But to David Rice, Goldmark represented the enemy.

Rice's first reason for destroying Goldmark had been political, but he had some "financial reasons," too. "I assumed that he would have an amount of cash on him. I didn't know how much, but it would be enough to get me by."

By Christmastime, 1985, David Rice was in difficult financial straits.

Although Dr. Perreau had allowed him to live with her, she began to doubt her judgment. She began to find David irritating. She returned home one day to find her television set was missing. She asked David where it was, and he said he had taken it.

"Why?" she asked.

"For the money. I pawned it for ten dollars."

The final straw, however, was more serious. In late October Dr. Perreau found a rifle that David had purchased and hidden. She took it out of her apartment and gave it to a friend. She was leaving for Florida for a vacation over Christmas, and she gave David an ultimatum. She told him that he must be completely out of her apartment when she returned from her trip on December 28th.

Unknowing, Dr. Perreau had unleashed hellish forces. David Rice's financial picture was getting worse and worse because he wasn't working. He was spending his days searching for "enemies" in the library, and he had no time to bother with work. Soon he would have no place to go. He blamed the communists.

The answer to all of his problems had seemed simple to him. He would go to Charles Goldmark's home and steal money from him. This would alleviate Rice's precarious financial condition, which he felt was caused by the Goldmarks and people like them.

He would also obtain from Charles Goldmark a list of the other leading people in the Communist Party, because, as Rice explained to the detectives, they weren't, "after all, listed in the phone book."

After that, David Rice said, he would kill Charles Goldmark and his wife. He hated them with a passion, although he had never seen them—although he hadn't researched much about them or asked questions. He didn't dare; he didn't want to raise any eyebrows.

Of necessity, Rice worked alone. He didn't know what the Goldmarks looked like. He didn't know how old they were. He didn't know they had young sons. He knew virtually nothing about them. He knew only that Charles Goldmark was an attorney, and attorneys, he knew, weren't always on "the up and up."

The world had always cheated David Lewis Rice, and he was about to get even.

On Christmas Eve day David had gone to Dr. Perreau's house to water her plants, just as he had promised he would. He was storing some of his belongings there, and he wanted to get his green parka. Its many pockets would make it well-suited for what he planned. He was wearing blue jeans, a red sweater, and a pair of work boots. He also grabbed a pair of white cotton work gloves.

"I took a toy pistol. I had bought the rifle earlier, which I was going to use, but I figured . . . it would just make a lot of noise."

Rice admitted to Davis and Boatman that he had purchased an M-1 carbine from the Central Gun Exchange but said he had thrown it away two weeks before Christmas Eve because it was too big and too bulky. It was hard to carry around. He hadn't planned to shoot them anyway, he said. He said he had wanted it to keep them under his control. He didn't mention the gun Dr. Perreau had given away.

"When was it, then," Davis asked, "you bought the toy pistol?"

"That was Christmas Eve."

"Was it a realistic-looking pistol?"

"Yes . . . probably the closest it would come to would be a detective's special."

"A snub-nosed revolver . . . black?" Davis asked.

"Uh-huh."

"Thirty-eight-type caliber?" Boatman asked.

"Mmm-hmm."

David said he had purchased it at the Toys Galore store on Christmas Eve, paying three dollars for it. He had also bought two pairs of handcuffs at a Big 5 Sporting Goods store—but that had been a long time ago, maybe four months. He had stuffed the gun, the handcuffs, the gloves, two rags, and two bottles of chloroform in the pockets of his green parka and then taken the number seven bus downtown, where he could transfer to a number three that would take him to the Goldmark's neighborhood.

He had only taken two bottles of chloroform and two rags, he explained, because he expected to confront only two people: Mr. and Mrs. Goldmark.

"Is there any way that evening that you prepared yourself with—" Davis asked.

"No, no drugs," Rice cut in. "No alcohol. I was stone sober."

He hadn't needed drugs or alcohol; David Rice had been preparing himself mentally for six months to carry out his plans. Sometimes he hadn't thought that much about the Goldmarks, but inside he had known that it would be only a matter of time until he did what he meant to do. That it happened on Christmas Eve was just a coincidence, he said.

"Did you include Mrs. Goldmark?" John Boatman asked.

"Yes."

"Did that include anybody who was there—who appeared to be a Goldmark?" Davis said.

"Yes."

"How did you know you had to take a certain bus to get to the area where the Goldmarks lived?" Davis asked.

"I had been there twice before. . . . The first time was, I believe, about the first of November. . . . I went there just to see what kind of house it was and just check out the neighborhood."

This, then, was the man who appeared at the front door of the Charles Goldmark residence a half hour before they were to host a Christmas Eve dinner. David Rice was an angry man. A desperate man. A man who, perhaps, viewed the world more than a bit off-center.

When David Rice went to the house in the Madrona District on Christmas Eve he said he had expected to find only a couple, an older couple. He had not expected to find children. Quite clearly, David Rice had read or heard something about the furor—now a quarter of a century in the past—over Sally Goldmark's brief days as a member of the Communist Party, and perhaps of John Goldmark's troubles because of it. And Rice had confabulated and rearranged that information. Detectives listening to him realized that Rice had gone to kill Sally and John Goldmark, who were both long dead.

His careful plans had been wrong from the start. Sally and John

Goldmark were not communists; their son Charles was even further removed. David Rice had set out to kill the wrong people for the wrong reasons.

Dressed in his green parka, he had taken the bus to the Goldmarks' home. He carried the toy pistol and the two pairs of chrome-colored handcuffs.

Nobody paid any attention to him. He was another face in the busy Christmas Eve shopping crowd as he rode the buses.

Rice said he had no idea what Charles Goldmark or his wife looked like. He didn't know what kind of cars they drove. He had returned during the first week of December, again by bus, hoping to peek in the windows to see what Goldmark looked like, but the house was dark. He had stayed on the street for an hour or so to watch the house, but neighborhood kids were playing outside; he was afraid someone would notice him, and he left. He did go around to the back of the residence to see that there was an alley and a garage there. He saw there was no handle on the garage door and realized he had no easy entry there. He figured that it was operated by an electric eye.

As the detectives' questions probed deeper, David Rice admitted that he had also gone to the building where Charles Goldmark had his law offices. But he had never even gone into the reception area. Still, there was no question that Rice had been stalking Charles Goldmark—ineffectively, yes, but determinedly.

On Christmas Eve, Rice explained, he had decided to go ahead and approach Charles Goldmark. Yes, he had carried an empty white box with him. He had inadvertently gone to the wrong house first and said he was from Farwest Cab and had a package for Charles Goldmark. "The woman told me I had the wrong house. I just said thanks and left."

The box had been part of his preparation for the assassination. It was empty. "I wanted to use the box to get them to open the door."

Even though the three detectives listening were relieved that they had Annie Goldmark's killer in custody, and that he was quite willing to confess his crimes to them, they dreaded hearing what they knew was coming next. They had seen the results of his visit in colored crime scene pictures. His odd, stilted voice continued, filling in the gaps of what had happened that night.

David Rice recalled that he had walked up to the Goldmarks' home a few minutes after seven. He knocked on the door, and a young boy answered it.

"I was surprised, because I assumed that there were only two—

Charles Goldmark and his wife—but I went ahead and I said, 'I'm from Farwest Cab, and I have a package to deliver for Charles Goldmark,' and so he called him. Charles came downstairs."

The little boy had seemed about eight or ten to Rice. He stood there as his father walked down the stairs. Rice pulled out the toy pistol he had hidden behind the box.

"I flashed it in front of him . . . and I grabbed him [Charles] by the shirt and turned him around and told him to get down on the floor. . . . The boy ran out. He ran into the kitchen."

David Rice kicked the front door shut behind him. Now no one on the street could see in.

He held Charles Goldmark down on the floor just inside the doorway. Goldmark had been shocked into immobility at first; he had expected to come down the stairs and greet his party guests. Instead he had encountered a man with a gun.

"I told Mr. Goldmark to call his son and he did . . . and so he came in, and I took them upstairs."

"Why did you decide to go upstairs?" Sonny Davis asked.

"I asked him, 'Where is your wife?' and he said, 'Upstairs in the shower,' and so I said, 'Let's go upstairs.'"

Then he marched the man and the boy up the stairs, the realistic-looking gun pointed at their backs. Charles Goldmark, a peaceful, nonviolent man, was undoubtedly thinking frantically about what would be the best way to save his family.

David Rice continued his statement: "He asked, 'Do you want money?' and I said, 'Yes, I can use all you got,' and he said, 'I don't have much. What I have is upstairs,' and so he showed me there was fourteen dollars and some change."

Rice had also spotted a wallet and gone through that. There was no money, only credit cards and a SeaFirst bank card. "I asked him his identification number."

Rice described the upstairs of the Goldmark home perfectly. He recalled the placement of the doors, the bay window, the location of the bathrooms. There was no question that he had been there.

"And we got upstairs and he [Goldmark] said, 'Honey, could you come out here?' and she said, 'What?' and he knocked on the door. He poked his head in the bathroom door and said, 'Put something on and come out here,' and so she put on a robe and came out."

"What color robe was she wearing, David?" Sonny Davis asked.

"It was a striped robe. It had a lot of different colors, red and green."

Rice had ushered the family into the master bedroom. Only then had he noticed there was a second boy.

At this point in the questioning David Rice asked to stop for a while. He had a cup of coffee and a cigarette, and then he began again. He explained that he had stopped because he thought that what he was about to say might be too rough for the detectives to hear. His own voice was flat and void of emotion.

"Okay, when we entered the bedroom I told everybody to get on the floor face-down and had them face away from me so that they couldn't see that it was just a toy pistol. Then I handcuffed Charles and his wife."

He had handcuffed Charles first, with his hands behind his back and his face pressed to the beige carpet. Then he did the same to Annie Goldmark.

"Do you remember Charles's clothing? The best you can," John Boatman asked.

"It was a tan sweater with, I believe . . . a brown shirt. . . . I think he was wearing gray slacks."

David Rice had been confused. He had expected Charles Goldmark and his wife to be much older, and he hadn't expected to find two children there. "I had to stop for a minute. I was getting a little rattled because there were two kids, and so I stopped and thought and . . . then I just figured, 'I'm in it now. I can't stop.'"

Rice described where the Goldmarks had lain, all of them helpless now on the floor of the master bedroom. He had intended to get some "information" from Goldmark, but he found there was no point at which he could ask questions. There had, Rice recalled, been very little conversation. Charles had told him, "I want to tell you that we're expecting company, and they'll be here at 7:30."

It might have scared off an assailant less obsessed with his "mission." It only made David Rice work faster. He said he had poured chloroform on a rag and pressed it to Goldmark's nose until he became unconscious. Then he bent over Annie Goldmark. She jerked her head away from him, but he held her fast, and she, too, passed out. "She didn't like it. It's got a pretty nasty smell to it."

Sonny Davis asked quietly, "Did the children struggle?"

"No. The one with the glasses moved his head a little bit."

Both vials were empty, and the family lay still. Only about ten minutes had passed since Rice had entered the Goldmarks' home. He glanced at his watch and figured he had five or ten minutes before the company arrived.

BLACK CHRISTMAS

Derek Goldmark (left), 12, and Colin, 10. They were fatally injured on Christmas Eve, 1985, at the hands of a man who stalked the wrong family for the wrong reasons.

Derek and Colin's father, Charles Goldmark, 41, also fatally injured on Christmas Eve by David Lewis Rice, who thought he was attacking Charles's father.

David Lewis Rice, 27, stalked the Charles Goldmark family, believing he was wiping out communists. He had the wrong generation and the wrong information.

ONE TRICK PONY

Donna Bennett, around 1950, a few years before she met her future husband, Noyes "Russ" Howard. Her sister felt they had little in common, but Russ's charisma caught Donna, and she forgot her dreams of marrying a cowboy. She married him, knowing she was taking a chance on love. *(Bobbi Bennett)*

The Bennet sisters in the early 1950s. They were as close as sisters could be. Donna is on the left, and Bobbi is on the right. *(Bobbi Bennett)*

ONE TRICK PONY

This is how Russ Howard said he had found Donna after he'd returned from town with warm doughnuts and a new mailbox. Note the "paintbrush" swipes of blood just above her left elbow. Lt. Rod Englert, nationally renowned blood-spatter expert, said these were made as someone repositioned Donna's body, not by medium-velocity blood spatter from a horse-kick wound. Donna's shirt and jeans are pulled up as if she had been dragged by her boots.

Noyes "Russ" Howard on trial in 1986 for the murder of his wife, Donna, a dozen years after her death. The years since Russ met Donna are etched on his face.

ONE TRICK PONY

Washington State senior assistant attorney general Greg Canova, who successfully prosecuted Russ Howard for the murder of Donna Howard.

Bob Keppel, investigator for the Washington State Attorney General's Office, who would not quit until he uncovered what *really* happened to Donna Howard.

THE COMPUTER ERROR AND THE KILLER

Vonnie Stuth as a teenager.

Vonnie and her mother, Lola Linstad, on Vonnie's wedding day in May 1974. Although Lola could not save her own daughter, she went on to co-found "Families and Friends of Victims of Violent Crimes and Missing Persons" to help other families.

THE COMPUTER ERROR AND THE KILLER

When Vonnie was a little girl, shown here holding her dog and with her sisters, Gary Addison Taylor was already roving the Detroit area searching out women to rape and bludgeon.

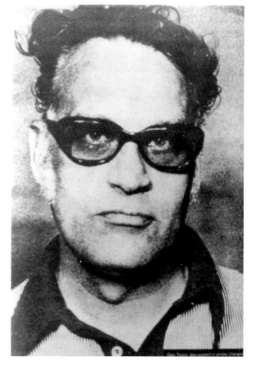

Gary Addison Taylor, convicted killer of Vonnie Stuth, confessed to the murders of a number of other females from Michigan to Texas. In the early 1970s he was supposed to be reporting, for counseling and medication, to a Michigan clinic for criminally insane felons. Through a tragic oversight he was never listed as a parole violator. He was free to roam America because the "wanted" information on him was not entered into law enforcement computers until it was far too late for Vonnie and his other victims.

THE VANISHING

On July 9, 1979, Stacy Sparks vanished from the I-5 freeway north of Seattle. The answer to what happened to her didn't come until September 14, 1981, and the truth was the one possibility no one had considered.

Detectives in Washington State circulated this picture of a Plymouth Arrow, a car just like the one Stacy had last been seen driving. Her car wasn't found until she herself was found.

Jackie and Bill Brand. He pursued her for years, but when he won her for himself he still wasn't happy.

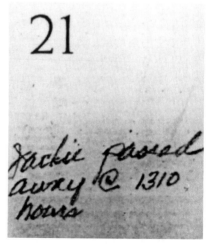

21

Jackie passed away @ 1310 hours

Bill Brand was nothing if not precise. He noted the minute of Jackie's death in military time.

He realized that he wasn't going to get the information on other "communists" now. He still intended to kill them all. . . .

Sonny Davis proceeded cautiously with the questioning. He and Boatman now had to elicit details they didn't really want to know. "They were there at your 'disposal,' as it were?"

"Right."

"Now . . . now you've got to determine how?"

"Right."

"What went through your mind, and what did you come up with?"

"Well," David Rice answered, "first I went downstairs into the kitchen, and I was looking for a knife. . . . I found a filleting knife. It was in the drawer right next to the island."

"Could you describe what you mean by a filleting knife?" Sonny Davis asked.

"It's a knife that's got a twelve-inch blade. It's about a half-inch wide. It had a white wood handle."

"You still had your gloves on during this?" John Boatman asked.

"Yeah. What I was looking for was a . . . one of those meat hammers."

"Why?" Davis asked.

"I didn't like the idea of using a knife."

"Cutting?"

"Uh-huh."

"You wanted to beat as opposed to cut?"

"Right."

But David Rice had no luck looking for a hammer. He moved from the kitchen to a storage area near the front door, found nothing suitable there, and went down the basement steps. All the while his victims lay bound and unconscious from chloroform upstairs.

"I found an iron . . . a regular clothing iron."

"Okay," Sonny Davis said evenly. "This appeared to suit your purpose."

"Yeah. That's the closest I could find."

Carrying the iron with the blue plastic handle, Rice ran upstairs. He estimated that it had taken him four or five minutes to find his weapons. He felt comfortable with the chloroform. "It works for about fifteen or twenty minutes."

"Had you ever tried it before to know what the effects were?" Sonny Davis asked.

"Yeah, I timed myself."

"On *yourself?*"

"Uh-huh."

When Rice reached the master bedroom he found all four of the Goldmarks still in the same positions, still unconscious.

"Like I said," Rice continued, "I knew I didn't have much time, so I had to get it over with. And so I took the iron, and I hit Mr. Goldmark on the head—on the back of the head. I think I hit him about four or five times."

"Then what?" Davis asked.

"Then I hit Mrs. Goldmark. I hit her on the side of the head, and she started moving. I figured the chloroform was starting to wear off, so I hit her a couple more times, and then she stopped moving."

Stealthy, deadly, David Rice had bent over the children. They were still unconscious. He hit "the child with the glasses" five or six times in the head with the iron, and the other youngster four times.

The listening detectives fought to distance themselves from emotion. They had to get this information if they were going to convict the man in front of them. They could not afford to think of the little boys lying in the midst of Christmas presents and gift wrapping.

"Then I went over and checked Mr. Goldmark. I checked his arteries in his neck—"

"For a pulse?" Davis asked.

"Right. And it was still beating, and I checked Mrs. Goldmark, and hers was still beating, and so I decided to complete the job with the knife, so I inserted the point of the knife into the skull where it had broken from the iron."

Sonny Davis struggled to keep his voice empty of anger or judgment. "This is Mr. or Mrs. now?"

"Mr."

"How many times?"

"Just once, and I kind of stirred it around."

"How far did you put the knife in?" Boatman asked quietly.

"Maybe five inches. It slipped right in."

"Then what?" Sonny Davis asked.

"Then I did the same thing to the other three."

"Stirred it around once to each, the mother and the two children?" Davis asked, hearing his voice tremble despite himself.

"Well, actually, I didn't . . . I didn't find a . . . a place on Mrs. Goldmark, so I entered it into the chest area. . . . I just had to put a little pressure on it."

And so Annie Goldmark died there. The other three were surely going to die. David Rice had quite literally tried to destroy their brains. It seemed a miracle they still lived at all.

His description of committing what he believed to be four murders was so workmanlike. He hadn't been angry or afraid when he did what he did; he had done it because it needed to be done.

Now David Rice continued in his strangely empty voice, his blank eyes staring. He had seen there was blood on his green jacket and on his blue jeans. His left boot was covered with blood, and he wiped it with a blue T-shirt and stuck the shirt in his pocket. His gloves were covered with blood from stabbing Annie. He stuffed them in his pocket, too. It was time to leave—to get out of there before the partygoers arrived.

It was almost twenty minutes past seven.

He didn't look around for more money; there was no time. He had killed "the communist," and that was his first priority.

"I was looking for the back door, which I did not find for quite a while. It took me about three minutes to find the back door . . . down in the sub-basement. As I was leaving I turned out all the lights."

He went through the steel-covered door in the basement, through another small room, and out a set of glass doors. David Rice was outside.

He was out and down the walkway, turning the knob to open the back gate to the alley. He intended to go back to Dr. Perreau's house. He didn't dare take a bus; he walked. It was a long way, over two miles, but he knew his clothes were too stained with fresh blood to risk taking a bus.

"But about halfway there I realized that I'd forgotten my handcuffs—so I went home and changed clothes and put the stuff down in the basement . . . and went back over there."

"To the house?" Davis asked, surprised.

Incredibly, David Rice *had* returned to the scene of his crime. Rice said he had taken a cab to 26th and Union and then walked back to the Goldmark house, arriving between 8:30 and 9:00. He had thought that the victims might not have been discovered yet. He walked along an ivy-clotted bank across the street from the Goldmark house, watching.

"I heard radios and so forth, and so I just kept walking . . . police radios . . . I didn't see a [police] car. There were a few lights on in the house, though, and I assumed that, you know, that it'd been discovered."

So the killer had walked on by, the detectives inside the house completely unaware that the man who had created this carnage was within fifty feet of them for a moment or so.

"I thought, Well, I'm caught now. . . . They've got my fingerprints on those handcuffs."

Rice remembered that he had made another stop on his way home right after the attack. He had stopped at the SeaFirst Bank cash machine, armed with the ID number Charles Goldmark had given him. He had written it down. David Rice was furious when he realized that Charles Goldmark had tricked him. The number was no good. He walked three or four blocks further and tossed the paper with the number, the credit card, and a set of keys into the ivy of someone's yard.

Davis and Boatman wondered if the items were still there, sodden now with rain and fog. It would be more physical evidence, and the more the better.

The second time David Rice left the Goldmark home he walked back to Suzanne Perreau's empty apartment again. He stopped at a market and bought a tablet (the same tablet he wrote his "confession" on), some soda pop, and a candy bar. But when he got back to Dr. Perreau's residence he saw someone standing in the garage, and he was afraid the police were on to him. "I just turned south and went downtown."

He had never been back to Suzanne's place since. He had stayed with Max Stingley until his arrest.

"What items did you put in the storage shed [at Dr. Perreau's apartment]?" John Boatman asked.

"Let's see—in a paper sack there was my coat, my pants, that shirt, the gloves in with it." The chloroform vials and rags were in a closet inside the apartment. He had placed the toy .38 in a storage locker that belonged to Dr. Perreau. Oddly, he hadn't attempted to throw all those things away in some spot that could not be connected to him. Every bit of the evidence linking David Rice to the inexplicable attack on people he didn't even know was still in the apartment of the woman who had forced him to move out. Perhaps he had left it all there—either deliberately or subliminally—to embarrass her and involve her in his crimes. He had even left the white box he had carried to the Goldmarks, the "delivery" that had gained him entrance into their home.

It was almost three in the afternoon on the day after Christmas. Sonny Davis stared at David Rice. "Okay—we're getting close to wrapping up this session. For the purposes of this interview, do you have any remorse or sorrow or feeling about what you did to the Goldmark family?"

"The children. I—I didn't expect them there, and I wouldn't have been there if they had been."

"You're sorry about the children?"

"Yeah."

"Did it ever occur to you to just say, 'Okay—they're down and out; let me turn on my heel and walk out of this house and forget it'?" Davis asked.

"They had already seen me. It was too late."

Much too late.

Colin Goldmark died two days later on December 28, 1985.

Charles Goldmark died at 9:47 in the morning of January 9, 1986.

Derek Goldmark died on January 30, 1986.

They were all gone, all of them who had made up that sunny, brilliant, kind family.

David Lewis Rice's trial began in May, 1986. He was represented by Tony Savage and Bill Lanning, two of the very finest criminal defense attorneys in Washington State. King County Deputy Prosecutor Bill Downing would represent the State. He was a young—but tough—opponent. The defense sought to prove David Rice insane under the law, and therefore not responsible for his crimes.

Bill Downing stressed the care with which David Rice planned his attacks, the cruel savagery with which he carried them out, and how cleverly he executed his escape. None of Rice's actions before or after his crimes indicated he was legally insane. Bill Downing also read a list of Rice's future victims; the defendant had apparently not intended to stop his killing swath with the Goldmarks.

It was a long and grueling trial, almost a month of testimony. Through it all a pale David Rice sat as calm as death itself. His relatives cried in the gallery. So did friends and relatives who had loved the Goldmarks.

Perhaps the most telling argument of all for conviction was the playing of the tape made of Rice's confession to John Boatman and Sonny Davis on December 26, two days after the murders. On tape David Rice sounded intelligent, coherent, and completely without remorse. His voice filled the courtroom and made listeners shudder.

On June 5, 1986, the jury of six men and six women retired to deliberate. Less than five hours later they were back with a verdict; they had rejected Rice's insanity plea and had found him guilty of four counts of first-degree murder. Rice took the news serenely. However, as he walked to the jail elevator, he told reporters, "The scum lied about everything. He said I lied to save myself when in actuality the lie was to kill myself." (He did not say whether he was referring to Deputy Prosecutor Downing or to his associate, Bob Lasnik.)

In the bifurcated trial, the next phase was to decide whether David Rice would serve life in prison or go to his death.

On June 10 the jury announced that they had agreed that Rice should be put to death. "It's not easy to play God," Jury Foreman Joel Babcock told reporters. "It's a very emotional thing to have to do something like this. Mr. Rice may very well be insane right now, but we're dealing with December 24. I could be insane if I killed four people and sat in a jail cell and thought about it long enough. I think Mr. Rice has some character disorders, but I think the prosecution showed he was able to think about what he was doing and do this step by step by step."

In the meantime, David Rice had once again gulped a mixture of tobacco and water and been rushed to Harborview Medical Center. And once again he showed no ill effects. He would not respond to the news of the death penalty, nor would he speak to his relatives, who had come to comfort him.

Within days, however, David Rice was talking and eating.

On August 15, 1986, he was ordered to be transferred to the Washington State Penitentiary in Walla Walla. The appeal process lay ahead. Everyone expected it would be years before David Rice's death sentence might be carried out.

On 36 Avenue, the lovely home the Goldmarks had shared remained "an open wound" to their neighbors. All the Goldmarks had done was open their own front door on a happy Christmas Eve.

It would not be stretching the truth to say that a political dirty trick designed to discredit Charles Goldmark's father and mother had set the stage for this tragedy. The lies about Sally Ringe Goldmark that had been whispered three decades earlier had ruined her husband's political career. Even when the elder Goldmarks were vindicated, the lies hadn't really died. They had only slumbered. Somewhere in the dusty shelves of the public library David Lewis Rice, full of hate and looking for someone to blame for the shambles his life had become, had seized on an old article. His delusion had grown and burgeoned and eventually become an obsession.

David Rice had actually believed that he was killing *John* Goldmark. John Goldmark had never been a communist. It had all been such a stupid, tragic mistake.

The entire Charles Goldmark family died by mistake. But they are just as dead as if cruel delusion hadn't followed vicious slander.

Charles, Annie, Colin, and Derek Goldmark were never allowed to realize their tremendous potential for good. The Charles and Annie Goldmark Family Foundation was established in their memory, a living foundation to advance the values of democracy, freedom, understanding, and civic participation they believed in.

The tragic story of the Goldmarks' murders did not end in 1986. The man who had destroyed them was still alive. Although David Rice had killed mother and father and two little boys quite calmly, *he* did not want to die. He began to explore the legal avenues of appeal open to him.

His appeal to the U.S. Supreme Court asked that his death penalty sentence be overturned because his execution would violate the constitutional ban on cruel and unusual punishment. Through his attorneys, David Rice claimed to be suffering from "substantial mental illness."

The appeal argued also that he had been denied the right to a fair sentencing because the prosecution team had asked the jurors to put themselves in the shoes of twelve-year-old Derek and ten-year-old Colin Goldmark, and because the jurors had been shown pictures of the boys taken before the attack that killed them.

On June 19, 1989, the Supreme Court rejected those arguments and refused to overturn David Rice's death sentence.

King County Deputy Prosecutor Robert Lasnik, who, with Bill Downing, had won the guilty verdicts against Rice, said he knew that a death date could be set for David Rice—but warned that there were several more pathways for appeal through state and federal courts. He predicted that it might be as long as three years before a final execution date would be set for David Lewis Rice. In truth, it has been longer.

No one had actually been executed in Washington State for almost three decades, anyway. Not since 1963, when Joseph Chester Self was hanged for the murder of a Seattle taxi driver.

That changed, however, on January 5, 1993, when Westly Allan Dodd, a sadistic pedophile, went to the gallows in Walla Walla for the murders of three little boys.

Despite a number of horrendous homicides since David Rice took his place on Death Row in Walla Walla, his name was still familiar to almost everyone in the state, his crimes as crystalline in the minds of those who remembered the black Christmas Eve of 1985 as if they had happened yesterday.

The public was shocked on August 6, 1993, when U.S. District Court Judge Jack Tanner threw out the death penalty that was imposed on David Rice. Tanner ruled that Rice would not die because he had not been in the courtroom when the jury that convicted him pronounced the death sentence.

Appalled, Assistant Attorney General Jack Jones argued, "Rice was not there because he had swallowed several packs of tobacco mixed with water and had been taken to Harborview Medical Center to have his stomach pumped. He did that *twenty minutes before the jury was to announce its decision.* Rice's counsel waived Rice's presence."

The State plans to appeal Judge Tanner's decision, which ruled that David Rice's absence violated his constitutional rights under the Fifth, Sixth, and Twenty-fourth amendments. The attorney general's office accused Tanner of refusing to hear the State's arguments.

If Tanner's decision is upheld, David Rice will face a mandatory sentence of life in prison without possibility of parole.

One Trick Pony

Most of us believe that there is no such thing as a perfect murder. And we have good reason to; literature down through the ages has told us that. Shakespeare said it in many of his plays: "How easily murder is discovered!" "Truth will come to light; murder cannot be hid long." "Murder, though it have no tongue, will speak."

Cervantes wrote in Don Quixote that "Murder will out."

In the seventeenth century John Webster wrote, "Other sins only speak; murder shrieks out."

Not really. There are, unfortunately, hundreds of perfect murders. Some are never discovered. More are never solved.

Donna Howard's death was listed as accidental in dusty records for a dozen years. But Donna didn't die the way detectives and coroners originally believed she had, and it took the determined efforts of her own sister, Bobbi, to bring belated justice. Bobbi Bennett never gave up until the truth about Donna's death was exposed to light like the underside of a muddy rock turned over in the bright sun. With a singleness of purpose that defied fatigue and despair, Bobbi fought to avenge Donna. Only when she did could she go on with her own life.

This case, I believe, is a classic example that things are not always what they seem to be—particularly when it comes to murder.

The state of Washington is cut in half by the Cascade Mountains; Seattle and its environs are termed "the coast" by eastern Washington residents, even though the actual Pacific coast is many miles away. The west side of the state is moderate and lush, green, often sodden with rain. Eastern Washington has fertile fields, arid desert, the rolling Palouse Hills covered with a sea of wheat, and orchards as far as the eye can see.

Ellensburg and Yakima are in the middle of orchard country, of horse country. You put an apple or cherry twig in irrigated land there and it will take root overnight. Or so it seems.

These are western towns where even the bankers and the grocery store managers usually wear cowboy boots. There are rodeos, horse shows, and county fairs. Just as it does in every medium-sized town in America, an occasional scandal surfaces. Sometimes the scandals are homegrown: a love triangle exploding into deadly violence, or a family fight that ends in death. The shock waves that follow seem to occur only in small towns. Perhaps it is simply that big cities have so much violence that individual crimes don't stand out as much as they do in small towns.

Donna Bennett was born on Flag Day—June 14, 1932; a few years later, her sister Blodwyn—who would always be called Bobbi—came along. Their parents were older, at least for that era, both over thirty when their girls were born. The Bennetts and their forefathers had lived near Ellensburg at the upper edge of the Yakima Valley for generations. They were horse people—not fancy-schmancy horse people, but genuine cowboys.

Possibly because they had waited longer to have children, Donna and Bobbi's parents adored their two little girls. The Bennett girls were pretty, with shiny brown hair and huge brown eyes. Both Donna and Bobbi were born to ride horses, galloping joyously with the smell of sagebrush and apple blossoms in their nostrils. They grew up together, as close as sisters are meant to be.

Donna was already standing bareback on a horse at the age of three, her balance perfectly attuned to the horse's gait.

When Donna was five she was chosen the "best-dressed junior cowgirl" at the Ellensburg Rodeo parade.

Donna and Bobbi attended Ellensburg High School. Donna was in the class of 1950, and her friends from those days remember her as clearly as if they had seen her only yesterday. She could be very serious and a little straitlaced, but when she was your friend, she was your friend forever. She didn't have a lot of time for after-school activities because she had chores to do on the farm. She usually rode the bus right home after school, and she didn't date much in high school.

But Donna's dad had played the drums, and she did, too—the slender girl marching along in the Bull Dog band, keeping time on the bulky drums. Jean "Tex" Turner Parsons was the drum majorette, and Fay Griffin Moss and Gail Kelly Sether were flag twirlers. They were Donna Bennett's best friends. Fay and Donna had known each other since fifth grade. They would stay close for all of her life.

All through high school and for years afterward Donna and Bobbi rode their horses in parades. "They rode in the Ellensburg Rodeo—and in the other parades," Fay Moss remembers. "They were never in the royal court, though. I think it's because their family wasn't rich—and that's what it took to get in the court. But they were so classy, sitting straight in their saddles. They were *real* cowgirls."

When she was eighteen and graduating from Ellensburg High School a local newspaper picked Donna as the graduate with the prettiest eyes. It was true; she had huge doe-like eyes.

Donna and all her closest friends exchanged pictures. On the one she gave to "Tex" Turner she wrote, "Hi Tex, I can't forget all the good times we've had. Parties and the jokes on our band trips. I wish you all the luck and happiness in [the] future and be good!! Love and Kizzes, Donna."

Summertimes and after she had graduated high school, Donna performed as a trick rider at rodeos all over eastern Washington. She was wonderfully talented. Beautiful and slender, Donna wore bright satin shirts in rainbow colors, with sequined embroidery and pearl studs, tight pants, boots, and cowboy hats. Her picture brightened up many a county fair poster.

But Donna wasn't just pretty; she was a superb equestrienne. An action photo from those days in the fifties shows Donna standing *atop*

Bobbi's white steed, Dana, her perfect body leaning tautly into the wind, her arms flung out exultantly as she performs a stunt called "The Hippodrome." Bobbi is on the horse, too, her feet hooked into the stirrups as she drapes herself *backwards* down over Dana's hindquarters, so close to the ground and the horse's hooves that her long hair actually trails along the ground of the arena.

Both Bennett girls were as confident with horses as most people would be with a puppy. They were alternately atop, underneath, dragging, and cavorting as the horse trotted so fast that the wind whipped their hair. They were exquisitely coordinated, in their glory.

But they weren't daredevils. They knew that horses could be skittish, and they took no chances. "Donna knew that you never put your head down to work on a horse's hooves," Fay says. "That you *back* up to a horse and present your least vulnerable part."

Donna figured she would meet a cowboy one day and settle down. That was her world, and she met dozens of handsome young men at the rodeos. But another kind of man came along, and Donna Bennett was attracted to him in spite of herself, and in spite of her friends' and family's reservations. She met Noyes Russell Howard at Yakima Valley Community College and began dating him sporadically.

Russ Howard was handsome then—not a big man, but he had a good, compactly muscled build. He was about five feet nine—two inches or so taller than Donna. He combed his thick hair into a wave in front. The best thing about Russ was his gift of gab; he was a riot at parties. You could never predict what Russ would do next.

"He was fun, and he was crazy," Fay Moss remembers. "I could see how she could be attracted to him."

Donna and Russ dated off and on. For a while in 1954 Donna and Fay moved to Seattle and lived together in a little apartment on Republican Street—on what would become the site of the 1962 World's Fair. Donna got a job as sales clerk at Best's Apparel in downtown Seattle. By the time Best's became the flagship store of Nordstrom's, Donna had moved back over the mountains. Her picture often appeared on fashion pages in the *Yakima Herald.* She was so photogenic that department stores often asked her to pose, wearing their newest lines.

After college Russ worked in a number of jobs—selling shoes at first. Eventually he worked, in one capacity or another, with seeds, sometimes as a salesman for a seed company in the Yakima Valley and later as a seed inspector for the State Department of Agriculture. He was only two years older than Donna, but far more worldly. When they met Russ was already a pretty good drinker, and that put

Donna off. She didn't drink at all and didn't want to raise a family with liquor in the home. She was young; she thought he would change his bad habits in time.

When Russ proposed Donna hesitated. But she kept going out with him, and it was soon obvious that the quiet rodeo rider was in love with the glib party guy. They were very different, but often opposites *do* attract. Donna finally said yes, and though she delayed the wedding a few times, Donna finally married Russ Howard as the fifties eased into the sixties. She was almost thirty; all of her friends had been married for years.

Donna's family smiled determinedly at the wedding, but they worried. Donna's friends could see that she wanted desperately to make a go of her marriage, and that she ached for a secure home in which to have children. Apparently it took her a long time to feel secure; Donna Howard was into her thirties before her two daughters, Lisa and Marilyn, were born. Even though things weren't perfect and Russ was drinking, she wanted so much to have children.

Donna's family, well-known and respected in the valley, helped the young couple buy a home and some acreage on Galloway Road a few miles northwest of Yakima on the Naches River. Yakima is only about forty miles south of Ellensburg, so Donna still saw her family often. There was room for a stable; Donna couldn't imagine living without a horse or two.

Russ's job with the State of Washington meant he had to be on the road a good deal. That gave him the opportunity to imbibe away from his wife's disappointed eyes. It also gave him the chance to date other women. He would one day refer rather obliquely to his wife's "changing sexual needs" as the impetus that "drove" him into affairs with at least eight other women. It was an easy and ambiguous excuse for him, and Donna never had a chance to tell her side of the story.

Did Donna know that Russ was cheating on her? Probably. But she was loyal, and she was a very private person. Many women would have run crying to friends or, in Donna's case, to family. But for years Donna Howard kept her problems to herself. Her pride wouldn't let her admit how hellish her marriage had become.

Why any man would want to cheat on Donna Bennett Howard was a puzzle in itself. She was warm and friendly, and her family came first with her. Into her late thirties and early forties she remained a startlingly beautiful woman. She was as slender as she had been during her days as a rodeo queen, her face unlined, her eyes as lovely as ever, and her hair free of gray strands. Russ, on the other hand, had begun to show the effects of years of hard drinking. His face was seamed with deep wrinkles. But he had taken up weight-lifting, and that made him as strong as a man twice his size. He was still a barrel of laughs at a party or in a bar, however—and it was true that he had little difficulty attracting women.

The class of 1950 of Ellensburg High School stayed in close touch. Originally there had been 107 in that graduating class. Although their numbers dwindled, at least half of them showed up at the class reunions they held every five years.

"Donna only came once," "Tex" Parsons says. "And she came alone. I think we all knew that she was afraid that Russ might get drunk and embarrass her. As much as she wanted to come to our reunions, she missed most of them."

"Tex" and Gene Parsons, who had moved to the Seattle area after they got married, stopped by to visit the Howards once when they were in Yakima for a Toastmasters convention. Russ seemed the same as he always had—maybe a little bit cockier. Gene Parsons, who stands well over six feet, found Russ something of a swaggering show-off. "He had several guns, and he took me out on the porch to show me what a marksman he was," Parsons recalls. "He would toss aspirin into the air—ordinary aspirin tablets—and then blast them to pieces before they fell. He was good, and he must have been practicing a lot. It never rains over in Yakima, and his yard was sprinkled with all those little white bits of aspirin. Must have been a thousand or more of them."

Donna Howard apparently tried every means she could think of to save her marriage. She prevailed upon Russ to go to an alcoholic treatment center. He went, but he began to drink again after he was back home. Feeling that his friends exacerbated his drinking problem, Donna put her foot down and barred them from her home, and that irritated Russ. She herself joined Al-Anon (the group for families of problem drinkers), and she talked almost daily with members of the group, seeking some way to help Russ stay sober. When nothing seemed to work she went so far as to consult an attorney about a divorce. But she changed her mind. She worried that she couldn't support her daughters alone, and she really wanted them to have a father as well as a mother.

If there was one thing that the Howards were both concerned with, it was their daughters. The little girls were eight and ten, and Russ and Donna loved them.

Even so, his children were not enough to keep Russ Howard home much. Donna never knew where he was for sure. Once she was injured in a car accident, and nobody could find Russ for hours to tell him she had been hurt.

When Russ was in town he was a frequent patron at the bar at the Yakima VFW Club. The bartender there had been the attraction for a year or more. She was a cute little blonde with a sprinkling of freckles across the bridge of her nose and just the beginning edges of hardness. Her name was Sunny Riley,* and she was about a dozen years younger than Donna.

Sunny and Russ Howard had been involved in a sizzling affair for a year. Sunny liked the same characteristics in Russ that had drawn Donna to him twenty years earlier: he was fun, he was exciting, and he made her laugh. She wanted to marry him. But of course, he was already married. Sunny turned the screws a little. She simply told him that if he didn't get a divorce, he'd better not expect her to wait around; she was going to date other men.

By December, 1974, Donna Howard could no longer hide the strain of living in a house torn apart. Here it was the Christmas season, and her family was living a sham. Russ was hardly ever home; he'd slacked off the alcohol treatment and gone on as before.

Donna had tried so hard to do whatever Russ seemed to want, hoping that they could get along better. One of the things he had wanted was to buy a new house. Donna hadn't wanted to move, but she'd gone along with it. They bought a house on Tieton Drive, and they would be moving in January. It seemed ridiculous when the marriage was so shaky, but she thought a new house *might* shed a happier light on the marriage—kind of a geographical remedy to a seemingly insoluble situation.

In mid-December Russ got home very late one night, and he was drunk. An argument ensued, and he hauled off and belted Donna twice in the head, practically knocking her out. That scared her. When her head stopped spinning she called the sheriff's office and filed a report. Donna told the officer responding that she was going to see her lawyer the next day, that she would be filing for divorce.

Russ hitting her was the deciding factor. Her lawyer was worried about Donna. He had advised her to file many times before, but Donna had always backed out. Now she was determined to divorce Russ and seek sole custody of her two daughters. She told Bobbi that she was resolute. "I was positive in my heart," Bobbi remembered, "that she was going ahead and getting the divorce."

Fay Moss suspected things had come to a breaking point, too. "Donna was always the kind that never complained. *She* was the one who would always go up to the rest of us, look us square in the eye, and say, 'How are you? How are the kids?' and she really wanted to know. But this one time in late December I said to her, 'Donna, how are *you, really?*' She just broke down and cried and responded, 'Not good. Just not good.'"

Russ Howard was between the proverbial rock and a hard place. If he didn't divorce Donna, Sunny was going to dump him. If Donna divorced him—as she was threatening to do—he might lose his kids, and the equity in their new home as well. Since the original down payment for the old house had come from Donna's family, he suspected a judge would award Donna the new house.

Perhaps to punctuate that she, too, meant what she said, Sunny had broken up with Russ as 1974 turned into 1975. Both women in Russ's life were fed up.

What he really wanted were his kids, the new house, and Sunny. On January 9, 1975, Russ Howard had a long talk with Sunny, and he confided an idea he had. She didn't really believe him; she thought it was the liquor talking.

On that same January 9th Donna's friend Fay Moss was visiting in Ellensburg. "I was talking to a friend who went to Yakima often, and I said, 'Ellie, call Donna. She *really* needs a friend right now.'"

Fay remembered her phone conversation with Donna Howard in December, and it had left her with anxiety over her old friend. Donna had cried during that call, and Donna *never* cried. "She had told me that she was sorry that she hadn't been able to make it over to Seattle to visit. Then she said, 'I'm changing a few things in 1975. We're moving to Selah on January first. This should prove very interesting. I'll let you know more.'"

Fay Moss didn't think the real changes in Donna's life had anything to do with the new house. She knew Donna, and Donna was talking about something that would mean far more upheaval in her life than simply changing addresses. It had something to do with her marriage. Fay worried about Donna all day on January 9th, and she made up her mind to drive on down to Yakima and see her the next day. "But I didn't. A winter storm blew in, and the roads were so bad that I turned around and came home. When I got home I learned that Donna was dead."

Donna Howard was forty-two years old when she died on January 10, 1975. It happened so quickly; it was 9:27 on that bitter, icy morning in Yakima, Washington, when Russ found her. Emergency medical technicians pronounced her dead at 9:47.

How ironic that Donna Howard of all people should die in a stable, when she had loved horses since before she could walk. It just didn't make sense. It would take almost a dozen years before it did.

Donna and Russ and the girls hadn't quite finished moving everything out of the house on Galloway Road. Russ and Donna took their girls to school, and then they headed back to the old house. They passed some of their neighbors, and Russ and Donna waved.

Russ told the medics that they had put on a pot of coffee, and a little later he went into town to the hardware store to buy a mailbox for their new house. Then he stopped at a doughnut shop and picked up a dozen fresh doughnuts, explaining that he was taking them back to share with Donna. He talked to a number of people at the hardware store and the doughnut shop that morning. He had even written a check at the hardware store. Always talkative, Russ had seemed particularly gregarious.

His call for help came in just minutes before 9:30. A woman had been injured out on Route 8, Box 741. A fire department medic responded along with Yakima County Sheriff's Office Patrolmen Jerry Hofsos and Ron Ward.

A worried Russ Howard led them out toward the loafing shed where the family's two horses were kept. He explained that he and Donna were doing some last-minute moving and repairs. He had gone into town to get some supplies they needed, and he'd thought he would surprise Donna with some fresh doughnuts. But she hadn't been in the house when he got back, nor had she responded to his shouts. He figured Donna was over at the neighbors' house because she often visited there—but they hadn't seen her either. He felt as if he had wasted precious minutes looking in the wrong place.

When Russ trudged through the deep snow out to the barn area he had found Donna. She lay in the loafing shed, just as she still was— except for the quilt, which he'd placed over her. The fire department medic knelt beside her and removed the quilt.

Donna Howard lay on her back with her left arm raised, her face turned to the left. Her right hand was pinned palm down beneath her right buttock. The medic felt for a pulse in the carotid artery in the neck. There was none. Donna Howard's eyes were slightly open, but the pupils were already fixed and dilated. Her body was warm, but she was dead.

The immediate cause of death seemed to stem from some manner of head injury; there was blood streaking Donna's forehead, running back into her thick brown hair, which was virtually soaked with blood from some terrible head wound. Mere inches from her head one wall of the two-sided shed had thick scarlet stains, as if someone had taken a paint brush and daubed on two swaths. Almost directly opposite and a foot or so above Donna's left elbow one swath was horizontal, the other vertical.

Donna wore bell-bottom jeans, rubber galoshes much too big for her feet (unzipped), a white sweater, a dark quilted jacket (open), and gloves. Her sweater was pulled up, exposing flesh at her waist. Her jeans were wrinkled oddly, too, pulled up slightly toward her knees. Her clothing looked almost as if someone had dragged her by her feet. Her galoshes nudged a salt block placed there earlier for her two horses.

"I found her like this," Russ Howard explained. "I covered her with a quilt, and I called for the medics." He had not moved her at all, he said, fearful of injuring her further.

The fire department and the responding deputies had, of course, called detectives for backup. In all cases of violent death—accidental or deliberate—detectives must investigate. Detective Sergeant Bob Langdale and Detective Ray Ochs responded to the scene to assist in the initial probe.

The sheriff's men took pictures of the scene, but that was all. The barn and the house were a good distance apart. There was nothing in the house that seemed out of place. There wasn't much to photograph. The cause of death seemed obvious: one of Donna Howard's beloved horses had spooked and kicked her in the back of the head. She had lain there until Russ returned.

Pictures remaining in police files show a pretty woman with a lithe, perfect figure lying stretched out on the icy ground of the loafing shed. Over toward the slatted open side there is a plaid quilt and a Bekins Movers' blanket. Beyond, a blizzard has kicked up, and the snow and sky meet in never-ending white.

Neighbors rushed to comfort the bereaved widower, who blamed himself for not being home when Donna needed him. "One of her horses must have kicked her," he said. He couldn't describe his feelings. "I don't know how you describe something like that. I felt a combination of grief and rage, not knowing where to vent the rage."

One of the first things Russ did after Donna's body was removed was to contact Sunny Riley. He told her that Donna was dead, and he explained the events of the morning. Sunny was appalled, even terrified by what he related. But Sunny still loved Russ despite what he had told her. She kept her knowledge to herself.

Donna's family was stunned by the news of the tragedy. That Donna should be killed by the very animal she loved was incomprehensible to them. She had been around horses her whole life; she talked to them in some unspoken language, and she trusted them more than she trusted most people. Moreover, she was no neophyte who didn't know how to approach horses.

Dr. Richard Muzzall, the Yakima County coroner and a local surgeon who had gone to Ellensburg High School with Donna, performed her autopsy on January 11th. Although he was a board-certified surgeon, Muzzall had no special training in forensic pathology. He noted the back of the skull where it had been shattered and found the damage consistent with a blow from a horse's hoof. He also found a second fracture of the skull, on the upper right side, a small ovoid (oval-shaped) depressed fracture. That puzzled him, given what Russ Howard had told him about the accident. Muzzall was not as sure about the cause of that wound as he was about the occipital fractures, and he made a note to go to the loafing shed and find out what had caused that.

When he went back to the horse shed Muzzall spotted three stacked railroad ties that made up part of the wall adjacent to where Donna Howard's body was found. The top tie had been broken off raggedly at some time and had a sharp, jagged piece of wood protruding. That might have caused the small single fracture.

Muzzall deduced that Donna had been bending over, cleaning a horse's hoof, and that she had been kicked by one of the horse's other hooves, knocked headlong into the tie, and then propelled backward, her head sliding across the side of the shed, leaving the two bloody swipes. She had finally come to rest flat on her back with her legs stretched out. That scenario might explain how her skull was fractured both in the back and on the top, and why the smaller top fracture's shape bore no resemblance to a horse's foot size.

Muzzall's postmortem report was only a page long, and the conclusion was death from multiple skull fractures due to horse kick. He noted the two areas of fracture and a third finding—a bruise on the webbing between the thumb and forefinger of the right hand. That bruise bore the imprint of the fabric of the glove Donna had worn. At the bottom of the autopsy report the summary diagnosis listed the fabric-pattern bruise as having been found on the *left* hand. A minor oversight, but one that would have been *very* important to a forensic pathologist.

A bruise in the webbing between the thumb and the forefinger is a classic defense wound. What part of a horse could have given Donna

Howard such a bruise? And why hadn't Muzzall proofread the autopsy report?

Outside of major metropolitan areas there are few trained forensic pathologists, and even the best sometimes disagree with one another on a close call. Indeed, in many rural and thinly populated areas coroners are not even required to be physicians. Muzzall had drawn his conclusions from the information available at the time and with the training that he had. Later several forensic pathologists would agree with him; others would not.

Neither Detectives Langdale and Ochs nor Yakima County Prosecuting Attorney Jeff Sullivan could come up with enough probable cause to arrest anyone for killing Donna Howard. It was, they were forced to conclude, a tragic and ironic accident.

Donna was buried, and Russ Howard and his daughters pulled their lives together, living in the new house. There wasn't much insurance on Donna's life—only $17,000—but Russ would receive social security benefits for the minor children.

Only Donna's family could not accept the cause of death on the death certificate. Nothing added up. One might attribute the family's doubts to grief and denial. And yet . . .

Bobbi Bennett sought—and found—refuge in her religion, but her growing faith only heightened her conviction that it was her duty to Donna to see that the real killer was punished. Bobbi knew how unhappy Donna had been, knew of her decision to divorce Russ, and knew that he had physically attacked her sister less than a month earlier—an attack so violent that Donna had been left almost unconscious. Bobbi Bennett was convinced that Russ Howard had killed Donna, but she had no idea in the world how to prove it.

With her family's backing, Bobbi hired a private detective.

One of the startling pieces of intelligence the private investigator reported was that a young woman named Sunny Riley was living with Russ and his daughters. Donna was barely in her grave when Sunny moved in during February. Ostensibly she had been hired as a baby-sitter to care for the girls. Since Russ was a traveling seed salesman, it made sense that he had to have household help, but Donna's family was suspicious. The private investigator pretended to be a real estate agent and talked with Sunny. There was no question that she was living in Russ's home full-time. And she didn't strike him as the baby-sitter type.

Four months later, in June—the month when Donna would have

celebrated her forty-third birthday—Russ Howard and Sunny Riley were married, ending the arguments among townspeople over whether Sunny was a baby-sitter or a girlfriend.

There were reasons that the June wedding was not as romantic as it might have been. Sunny Riley was a woman tortured by conflicting emotions. She *did* still love Russ no matter what her suspicions were, and she had wanted to marry him for a long time. But she was frightened, too. Russ had confided things to her that she wished she had never heard. Whatever he might or might not have done, Sunny was absolutely convinced that she was just as responsible under the law as he was. Indeed, Russ often reminded her of her complicity, and she believed him when he said she would be in terrible trouble, too, if she ever revealed what he had told her.

She had been afraid to marry him and afraid *not* to marry him. She had gone along with the wedding plans, she would say later, because she kept hoping something or someone would intervene before she and Russ made it to the altar. For his part, Russ was quite aware that a man's wife cannot be forced to testify against him in a court of law.

No one intervened, of course, and the wedding went off without a hitch. Sunny did her best to block her fears out of her mind; at times she was able to completely submerge her doubts. Once they were married Russ didn't seem to worry much at all about the law. He seemed quite secure. The coroner had agreed with his version of Donna's death, and so had the prosecutor and the sheriff. Let the past bury the past.

But Donna's sister Bobbi was not about to let that happen. She knew nothing about how to investigate a murder when she began her quest, but she read voraciously, and she soon gleaned a great deal of information. One afternoon while she was sitting in a beauty parlor chair she read about Thomas Noguchi, then chief medical examiner of Los Angeles County.

Bobbi Bennett got in touch with Noguchi and asked him and an associate to review Donna's case. After doing that they agreed that it at least warranted a more complete autopsy.

Yakima County D.A. Jeff Sullivan agreed to an exhumation order, and a second postmortem examination was performed on Donna Howard's body in late 1976. Forensic pathologist Dr. William Brady—then the Oregon state medical examiner—performed the autopsy with Dr. Bob Bucklin, an ex-assistant medical examiner for Los Angeles County, assisting. Dr. Muzzall, Jeff Sullivan, and Sergeant Langdale observed.

At length Dr. Bucklin concluded that he could not say with *absolute medical certainty* that the damage to her skull had not been caused by the kick of a horse. His inclination, however, was to *disagree* with Dr. Muzzall's findings.

Dr. Brady prefaced his written report with the comment that pathological conclusions must take into account what was known to have been at the scene of a death—i.e., common sense combined with autopsy findings. A badly fractured skull and horses would tend to go together; unless other circumstances were known, Brady said he could not say what had caused the damage to Donna Howard's skull.

The lack of a definitive decision on the part of either pathologist was a crushing disappointment for Donna's sister. She had fought so hard to get the exhumation order and the second postmortem examination. It had been agonizing to go through, too—and now it seemed all for nothing.

For D.A. Jeff Sullivan there was still not enough probable cause to issue an arrest warrant charging anyone with murder. For the second time he declined to prosecute.

The world moved on. Donna Howard was dead, and that's the way it was—to everyone but Donna's family. Her parents grew older, their will to live weakened by the loss of their beloved daughter. Donna's father would not live to see the end of the case.

Bobbi Bennett, however, never gave up. She read. She phoned. She wrote letters to anyone who might help her avenge Donna's death. "Some people might say it took over my life," she would recall later. "I made up my mind that I was not going to let her go until they did something."

Over the years Donna's family would spend thousands of dollars on the case, a case everyone else seemed to consider closed.

The marriage between Sunny and Russ Howard was a bumpy one. Perhaps it was inevitable that it would be. Sunny had fallen in love with Russ because he was fun, and she loved fun. But there was little hilarity once they were married; Sunny was scared and guilty about what she knew, Russ was gone a lot, and he continued to drink a great deal. For all intents and purposes the marriage ended in 1978.

Sunny left Russ and ran off with another man. But Sunny was adept at picking the wrong men. She found herself in an abusive relationship. Periodically things got so bad that Russ looked good, and she would phone him and beg him to come and rescue her. He would pick her up, bring her back, and help her get set up in an apartment or in his house. Until 1979 Sunny and Russ had some manner of a relationship, however tenuous.

Donna Howard had been dead for almost five years, but Sunny's conscience still bothered her. If her niggling doubts hadn't gone away by then, she figured they weren't going to. In early July, 1980, Sunny went to a Yakima County deputy sheriff, an old friend from high school, and asked him a hypothetical question: "If I knew information about somebody that was going to be murdered, and then they were, and somebody told me more things—and I never said anything—would I be in trouble, too?"

Her deputy friend stared at her quizzically for a few moments, and then he assured her that *she* would not be the focal point of a sheriff's probe.

Sunny replied that in that case, she had some things to say. However, she told him that if she *did* get charged with a crime, she was going to deny everything. Her friend took her down to the county detectives, who took a taped statement from her.

Bob Langdale had retired, but Ray Ochs was still in the detective unit, and Jerry Hofsos had moved up from patrol. What Sunny Riley had to tell them was riveting, to say the least.

Sunny began by reviewing late December, 1974. She said Russ Howard had told her that he planned to kill his wife. He had told her he was going to lure Donna out to the barn of their old house on the pretext of making some repairs that had to be done before the new tenants moved in. It would be only natural, he had said, for him to have a hammer with him. Then he planned to strike Donna with the side of his hammer because he thought that would make a wound resembling a horse's shoe. His alibi would be that he had been in town at the time Donna died. He would go to town right after the crime, and he would make sure people in town remembered him.

On the day Donna died Russ had told Sunny he'd done it—but he said it had been more difficult to kill his wife than he expected. He confided that he'd had to hit Donna in the head three times before she died. The rest of his plan had been carried out just as he had outlined it to Sunny earlier.

The information that Sunny gave might well have been enough to indict Russ Howard for the murder of his wife. There were some problems, though; the things he had told her before marriage would be admissible in a court of law, but the confidences after marriage probably would not be. And then there was the fact that Sunny had gone right ahead and *married* a man she believed to be a murderer. A jury might wonder about that and find her a less than credible witness.

A polygraph exam administered by an expert from the Washington State Patrol indicated that Sunny Riley was telling the truth.

The Yakima County Prosecutor's Office continued to mull over whether to charge Russ Howard. So much of the original physical evidence was gone. Donna's bloodstained clothing, the quilt, the Bekins blanket had all been destroyed. The loafing shed had been repainted, obliterating the blood smears there. No investigator had ever found a hammer or, for that matter, even looked for one.

The railroad tie that Dr. Muzzall believed to be the instrument that made the oval fracture in the victim's skull was now anchored in cement, part of a fence. No one had ever searched the barn or the house thoroughly for signs of violence; it hadn't seemed important back in 1975 when the autopsy decreed accidental death.

Now it was too late.

Sunny ran scared. She moved around from place to place, fearful of reprisal from Russ. She moved to California with a new man and waited for word from Yakima authorities. Impatient now, she couldn't wait for Russ to be arrested. But months passed, and nothing happened—at least nothing she could see.

The case was already more than five years old, and authorities were doing their best to make it as solid as possible before they moved on it. They figured Russ Howard wasn't going anyplace.

It was 1981. Sunny was worried, and she was drinking. A few more drinks and Sunny was not only worried, she was angry, too. Russ had her furniture. She called him one night and suggested that they get married again. She pointed out that he was going to be charged with murder sooner or later, and if they were married, she couldn't testify against him. Sunny figured this might make him give back her furniture. After the trial was over they could split up again, she reasoned.

The next day Sunny was sober, and she changed her mind about the plan that had seemed so good the night before. Russ had rejected her proposal anyway. But she had tipped him off that something might be happening that he didn't know about. Still, he didn't move from the Yakima area. He didn't seem the least bit worried.

Russ Howard continued to have bad luck with women in his life. In the early 1980s he was living sporadically with a new woman and working part-time at a local tavern. One afternoon the couple came home together and talked for a few moments with Russ's daughters and a friend of theirs who was visiting.

Russ left a little while later to go to work at the tavern, and his girlfriend went upstairs, apparently to take a nap.

A few minutes later the three teenagers heard a loud noise upstairs. They went up to investigate and found the woman dead on the bed, shot in the stomach. She clutched a gun in her hand.

The nearly hysterical girls called Russ at work, and he rushed home, managing to arrive even before the police did. When the police got there they found Russ standing next to the dead woman, the gun in his hand.

The bartender at the tavern told investigators that Russ had been there when the phone call came in from his daughters. His most recent girlfriend's death was ruled a suicide.

This was the situation when two of the Washington State justice system's most prominent figures entered the case. A special investigative unit of the State Attorney General's Office was mandated by a new law in 1981 to conduct independent inquiries into criminal cases around the state, to offer assistance to counties, and indeed to prosecute in some instances. (At the request or with the concurrence of the governor or the county prosecutor.) It was to be basically a two-man operation, but those two men were quite probably the equal of a half-dozen less-skilled investigators and prosecutors. Greg Canova would head the unit as senior assistant state attorney general, and his sole investigator would be Bob Keppel, late of the King County Police's Major Crimes Unit.

Greg Canova worked as a deputy prosecutor in the King County Prosecutor's Office from 1974 to 1981, ending up as the senior deputy criminal prosecutor in that office. Canova was brilliant, honest, and persistent. He rarely lost a case, and he garnered respect from both conservative and liberal factions. Greg Canova had helped draft Washington State's new capital punishment law. Tall and handsome, with a luxuriant mustache, a quick legal mind, and a deep, confident voice that served him well in the courtroom, Canova had been so successful a prosecutor that he was already something of a legend at thirty-five. Canova candidly attributed some of his wins to luck. "Luck plays a part. In the past I've won some cases I probably should have lost and lost some I figured to win. You can never be sure with juries.

"I always go in thinking I can win. If you don't think you can prove guilt beyond a reasonable doubt, then you shouldn't ever file a case."

The other half of the new team—Bob Keppel, Canova's investigator—is one of the smartest detectives this reporter ever knew, respected all over America for his intellectual approach to investigation. A former track star, Bob Keppel was a young homicide detective in the King County Police Department with only one case under his belt when he found himself plunged into one of the biggest cases of his—or any other homicide detective's—career: the "Ted Murders" that began in the Northwest in 1974 and ended in Florida in 1978.

("Ted" turned out to be Ted Bundy, who died in the electric chair in Starke, Florida, on January 24, 1989. Just a day before he died, Bundy, who was suspected of murdering anywhere from twenty-five to three hundred young women all over America, confessed some of those murders to Bob Keppel. He viewed Keppel as his intellectual equal, and the two had jousted many times. Indeed, many experts suspect that Bundy's offer to "advise" Bob Keppel and several F.B.I. special agents on how to second-guess serial killers was the basis for *Silence of the Lambs*. Keppel let Bundy *think* he was a respected advisor—just to keep dialogue open between them.

In 1975, using what now seems to be an archaic computer system, Keppel narrowed a field of 3,500 suspects in the "Ted Murders" to only five, and Ted Bundy was one of those five. Keppel's methods were right on target when Bundy was arrested for similar crimes against pretty dark-haired women in the Salt Lake City area. The rest is, of course, criminal history.)

With the expertise he gained in being one of the lead detectives in the "Ted Task Force," Bob Keppel has been called upon by probers in dozens of serial murder investigations in this country. When Canova recruited Keppel away from the King County police, he knew what he was doing. Even so, he had to lend Bob Keppel back to the Green River Task Force for two years.

Greg Canova and Bob Keppel were just what Donna Howard's family had needed for a long, long time; they had become disheartened by years of butting their heads into bureaucratic brick walls. Bobbi Bennett would not give up until someone was convicted for what she believed to be Donna's murder.

Bobbi carried her campaign to reopen the investigation into Donna's death to the governor's office, and her arguments were cogent and persuasive. Then-Governor John Spellman asked the Attorney General's Office (specifically Canova's unit) to look into the Howard investigation in late 1981.

At that time it was a moot point. Canova *had* no investigators. In March, 1982, Bob Keppel came aboard, and the probe began in earnest. Keppel would practically wear a groove in the I-90 Freeway across the mountains to Yakima, interviewing and re-interviewing.

He talked to the original detectives, and to Ray Ochs and Jerry Hofsos, who were more than eager to continue the probe. He questioned the paramedic who had been at the scene of Donna's death. He found neighbors and hardware store employees, and perhaps most important, Keppel questioned Sunny Riley.

Meticulously Bob Keppel reconstructed a case that was already seven years old and seemed to be as dead as the victim. In truth, it was about to have a whole new life.

The problem, Greg Canova felt, had begun with the first autopsy. The report was only one page long, and that page stated that the wrong hand bore the defense bruising. Moreover, it had not been a complete autopsy because her death was deemed accidental. The investigating stopped, any physical evidence was tainted or obliterated, the body was buried, and the case collapsed like a straw fence in a windstorm.

What Greg Canova and Bob Keppel *did* have was a witness who had passed the lie detector test with no signs whatsoever of deception. Sunny Riley had come forward even though she was scared to death of being implicated. She was a woman whose life-style had changed from hedonistic to responsible. Sunny knew she would probably face some uncomfortable questions from Russ Howard's attorneys—if this case ever got as far as a courtroom—but she was prepared to answer them.

Bob Keppel's efforts to talk with Russ Howard himself were met with scorn. "I was amused," Howard said later. "I never dreamed it would get this far, that anybody would take Sunny seriously."

Howard confided to reporters that he felt he had antagonized Greg Canova and Bob Keppel by "laughing at them."

Not so. He only intrigued them more.

The physical evidence came down to a few precious items that remained. There were the pictures taken by investigating officers that icy morning of January 10, 1975. Blow-ups of the photographs and the recall of the Yakima deputies who were there indicated that there had been absolutely no hair, blood, or human tissue on the sharp end of the railroad tie. Some experts felt that since the ovoid fracture was a depressed fracture, the instrument causing it would have pierced the brain itself, however briefly, and probably come away with blood and tissue residue, and probably some hairs from the victim's head.

Beyond that, Dr. Muzzall's re-creation had Donna Howard kneeling to clean off her horse's hoof. If that was true, why didn't the pictures show dirt or snow on the knees of her jeans? In the photographs the knee portion of her jeans was clean.

Greg Canova and Bob Keppel had a picture in their minds now of how and why the murder had occurred. Russ Howard had wanted out of his marriage and had wanted to keep his children and his financial assets. So, as he had told Sunny, he had, indeed, managed to get Donna out to the loafing shed on some ruse. There he had struck his wife once with the flat of the hammer, expecting her to go down. But Donna had fought him, fending off the hammer with her right hand, protecting her head. The force of the hammer's blows against the webbing between her thumb and forefinger had been so strong that it was not only bruised, but the actual weave of her glove was imprinted on her flesh. Twice more Russ had crashed the hammer against Donna's head.

Then he would have dragged her body along the frozen ground on the Bekins blanket, arranging the corpse in the loafing shed where the two horses were. If Donna Howard had been kicked and simply fallen back, her shirt and jeans would not have been pulled up as they were in the pictures. That rumpling was exactly what would happen if someone had pulled her by her feet.

Donna's body was warm when the sheriff's men and the paramedic arrived, covered tenderly with a quilt. Russ had probably done that deliberately—to keep her warm while he was in town creating his alibi. Either that, or he had gone to town first and returned to carry out the rest of his plan.

The problem for Greg Canova and Bob Keppel in 1982 was how they were going to prove their theory of what happened in 1975 to a jury's satisfaction.

The main piece of physical evidence was Donna Howard's skull. Cleaned and dry and reconstructed, it would be examined now by some of the most expert forensic pathologists in the country.

Dr. Donald Reay, chief of the King County Medical Examiner's Office, examined the skull in July, 1982, and agreed that the damage did not seem to be from a horse's hoof. The back of the skull, maybe—it had been shattered in nineteen pieces, and all manner of force could have done that. However, the much smaller ovoid fracture on the top right side of the skull was very unusual. An oval piece of bone had been broken clean through and forced through the skull against where the brain had been.

The skull was sent next to the Smithsonian Institution, where it was examined by a chief forensic anthropologist. He thought that the top single fracture looked as if it had been caused by a hammer. However, he said, "There's someone who knows a lot more about this kind of injury than even I do—and that's Clyde Snow."

Clyde Collins Snow, Ph.D., forensic anthropology consultant and something of a legend. Big, gray-haired, and deceptively casual, Snow lives in Norman, Oklahoma, but he is rarely there. He may be in South America working over skeletons or in the Philippines reconstructing skulls of massacre victims. He is a witty and jovial man whose manner belies the grimmer aspects of his profession. Snow can tell all manner of things from a skull.

Dr. Snow is not averse to checking out his findings with other experts, and in this case Snow showed Donna Howard's skull to Dr. Bob Kirschner of the Cook County (Chicago) Medical Examiner's Office, to Kirschner's associates, and to Dr. Fred Jordan of the Oklahoma State Medical Examiner's Office. They all agreed with Snow's conclusion that the small oval fracture had been caused by a hammer. Kirschner particularly pointed out that he felt the wood from the railroad tie would have left splinters in the wound, and the wound would have left tissue on the railroad tie.

When Clyde Snow reported his initial findings to Bob Keppel he commented, "This case shines like a herring left too long in the hot sun." That was Clyde Snow's way of saying things were not as they had been reported to be.

After a meticulous examination of Donna Howard's skull Dr. Snow sent a letter to Bob Keppel and Greg Canova. Donna Howard had not had a thin skull, easily shattered. Rather his exam had shown it to be slightly thicker than normal.

Snow noted, too, that the wood of the railroad tie would have been far too soft to have done the damage found in the ovoid fracture. "The fracture was caused by an object of high density with a flat face and a circular upper margin."

Snow continued, "The critical feature of the cranium is the depressed fracture of the right fronto-parietal region. It is a classic example of a 'fracture à la signature' of a hammer. To me, this finding reduces the arguments about the remainder of the injuries to academic quibbling. Whether it was the first or last blow, or whether there was one, two, or three blows is of little significance. . . . Of course, one might speculate that a horse kicked the victim and then administered the coup de grace with a hammer. I don't know about Washington horses, but Oklahoma horses have not shown that degree of dexterity. . . ."

Snow felt that the back blow (probably two blows, according to what Russ Howard had allegedly told Sunny) had been delivered while the victim was still standing, and from the rear, where she could not see it coming. The depressed frontal fracture had occurred when she was lying on her back with her head turned to the left. The killer would have been standing over the victim at that point, and she could well have tried to cover her head with her hand.

Snow's findings made a gruesome and pathetic mind picture.

Photographs of the blood patterns on the loafing shed wall were blown up to 11 x 14 prints and sent to Lt. Rod Englert of the Multnomah County Sheriff's Office in Portland, Oregon. Englert is one of the most respected experts in the United States on blood patterns. He spends much of his time traveling to testify in homicide trials and has presented over three hundred seminars on blood spatter analysis. Lt. Englert teaches detectives how to determine myriad facts from the silent testimony of blood—if blood is "high velocity" (gunshot wounds), "medium velocity," or "low velocity." Among the concepts he teaches are "bloodstain transfer" and "blood swipe." In both of the latter, bloody objects come into contact with a surface not previously contaminated with blood and leave distinctive patterns.

Englert examined the pictures of Donna Howard's body and the loafing shed and weighed the blood patterns he saw with the story told by Russ Howard and with the reconstruction of the "accident" by Dr. Muzzall.

Lt. Englert's opinion was that Donna's death simply could not have happened the way Muzzall had perceived. Donna Howard's curly brown hair had been sodden with blood from the head wounds. But *had* she been kicked, had she bounced off the jagged railroad tie and then fallen backward, the blood patterns would have been higher, more diffuse, and well beyond the body. The pictures didn't show that.

Instead, the two thick, bloody swaths in the picture looked as if they had been left as someone was lowering and re-positioning a body on the ground. Donna's hair, so heavy with wet blood, would have left exactly those marks photographed on the wall: one swipe up and down and another side to side. The laws of motion would not have allowed Donna Howard to have been kicked into the railroad tie with enough force to penetrate her skull and then let her fall back so gently that her hair left those two solid stains on the white wall a foot away. A powerful kick from a horse would have sprayed blood in a diffuse pattern all over that wall.

The layman would never have thought of that. A surgeon, trained for other kinds of medicine, might not have seen what Rod Englert saw.

Donna Howard might not have known what was about to happen

to her. One would hope she was not frightened by the steps behind her as she concentrated on something in the barn. The first blow might have knocked her unconscious as her skull shattered, and the second might have come hard upon the first. Perhaps she fell neatly on an already-spread Bekins blanket, only to be smashed once more on the top of her head because she still breathed. Perhaps she was still able to use one hand to try to block the hammer coming down.

No one would ever know that except for Donna and her killer.

On November 8, 1984, the Washington State Attorney General's Office charged Noyes Russell Howard, fifty-four, with first-degree murder in the death of his first wife almost nine years earlier. Attorneys Susan Hahn and Wes Raber were appointed to defend him.

But the murder case was to be kept from the courtroom even longer. Challenges were made in pre-trial hearings asking who was going to pay for the defense, challenges that were ultimately appealed to the State Supreme Court. Eventually the state and not Yakima County was found liable for the cost of Russ Howard's defense since it was the state that had filed the murder charges.

In 1986 Washington's state legislature appropriated $50,000 to pay for Russ Howard's defense.

The trial finally began on October 13, 1986, in Superior Court Judge James Gavin's courtroom. Greg Canova was the sole prosecutor, and most of the State's witnesses would be experts in forensic science.

The only civilian witness Canova called was Sunny Riley. She made an excellent witness as she testified for hours. Yes, she had been told by Russ before the murder that he planned to kill Donna with a hammer and make it look as though a horse had kicked her. And yes, he had called her on the day of the murder and told her he had done it. The courtroom was hushed as Sunny related that Russ had complained it had taken him three blows with the hammer to do the job. Sunny said she hadn't wanted to believe it was true, and when she did allow herself to believe it she said she thought that something would happen to prevent her from actually marrying Russ. Yes, she acknowledged softly, part of her had still loved him even then.

In the end Sunny said she could not live with the thought that Donna Howard's murder had never been discovered.

Each side had its forensic pathology witnesses because the burden of the case rested ultimately on one small skull, its battered occiput reconstructed from nineteen shattered pieces.

It was hard going all the way. The defense would not even stipulate that the skull in evidence belonged to Donna Howard.

The forensic pathologists and anthropologists for the State agreed that the massive crushing at the back of Donna's skull *might* have been caused by a hammer, but that the fracture in the front of the skull *definitely* had been.

The defense team called Dr. Muzzall (then practicing in Alaska), Dr. William Brady, and Cyril Wacht, a world-famous forensic pathologist from Pittsburgh. They disagreed with the absolute statements the State's doctors had made. "Our position was," Defense Attorney Susan Hahn said, "[the injury] does look like a hammer [caused it]. But that's not the only thing that could cause that kind of injury, and the explanation that was originally given was still the best explanation."

Greg Canova questioned Dr. Muzzall carefully about the original autopsy. He asked Muzzall to step down from the witness stand and demonstrate just how the injuries could have occurred given the original autopsy's scenario. Greg Canova argued that a contortionist could not have gone through the sequence that Donna Howard's body was alleged to have completed. Dr. Muzzall resolutely disagreed, and maintained his original stance.

Seventeen days after the trial began the jury retired to deliberate. They went out on the evening of October 30, 1986, and returned in the early afternoon on Halloween. It took them eight hours to find Russ Howard guilty of premeditated first-degree murder.

"I had a feeling the jury wanted to find a way to find the man innocent," the jury foreman commented later. "Then there was the feeling, as one juror said, 'I know he did it, but . . .' We talked about what would follow that 'but.' There was nothing there."

Judge Gavin sentenced Howard to life with a twenty-year minimum term. That would make him eligible for parole in thirteen years and eight months, around the turn of the century—when he was almost seventy. Noyes Russell Howard, fifty-six years old in 1986, continues to maintain his innocence, as do his daughters, and he continues to appeal his conviction.

As this is being written it is January, 1994, almost two decades since Donna Howard walked out to the stable for the last time. In her case, the wheels of justice ground exceedingly slow—but they *did* grind. Without Bobbi Bennett's determination and dedication, without Greg Canova and Bob Keppel, Donna would have lain unavenged throughout time.

The Computer Error
and the Killer

It is not *"news" when a criminal who should have been locked up for earlier crimes re-offends. It happens so often that we have come to take a kind of ho-hum attitude toward this unfortunate phenomenon of criminology. Still, sometimes there are cases that are so deplorable that we have to shake our heads. How on earth could anyone even have considered letting such prisoners walk free when they have proved over and over that they are more dangerous than the most vicious predatory animals?*

One case keeps running through my mind. This man was a walking bomb; he had been designated criminally insane for seventeen years before his last terrible swath of killing. By his own reckoning, he had wanted to hurt women for thirty years, ever since he was in the third grade. His compulsion to destroy and torture females was not a hidden fantasy; he had acted on it again and again and again. But he was as free as you or I, because of an unbelievable series of "clerical errors." Before he was caught he would wreak incredible damage on a number of women who did not recognize the smoldering dynamite beneath the charming exterior—at least not until it was far too late.

I include this case because I think that it demonstrates how charming and benign the sadistic sociopath can be when he wants to appear that way. Sadly, it also shows what stark tragedy can come of trusting the mask he wears.

When lovely, blond Vonnie Stuth and her husband were married on May 4, 1974, the future looked as bright as a Northwest sunrise. And well it should have. They were very much in love, he had a good job, and Vonnie planned to work as a volunteer case aide at the Youth Service Center in Seattle. Both were youth leaders in the Highland Park United Methodist Church, the church where they were married.

In the summer of 1974 the couple moved into a small house in the Burien area just south of Seattle, and Vonnie settled happily into her role as a housewife. Todd Stuth worked the swing shift at a Seattle foundry, and that meant that they were apart most evenings, but Vonnie's parents and her younger sisters lived nearby, and so did a lot of her friends, so she wasn't lonely.

On Wednesday evening, November 27, 1974, Vonnie was preparing for the Thanksgiving feast the next day. This would be her first Thanksgiving as a married woman. Her contribution to the family gathering was to be a Jell-O salad. She dissolved the Jell-O in boiling water and set the other ingredients out on the kitchen counter while she listened to the television blaring from the living room.

At 10:30 her sister phoned, and the two talked for a while. At one point in their conversation Vonnie mentioned that she had to answer the door. When she came back to the phone she said it had been a man from across the street who wanted to give them a dog. "I told him he'd have to come back tomorrow when Todd is home," she said.

At 11 p.m. Vonnie's stepbrother pulled into the Stuth's driveway to pick up something from a car parked there. He glanced into the house and saw Vonnie on the phone, but he didn't go in to talk with her.

Todd came home at a quarter after one in the morning as usual. He found the door was unlocked, and the television and all the lights

671

were on. He called out to Vonnie, but no one answered. Concerned, he noticed her purse on the desk and the salad preparations, half-done, on the counter. Vonnie had had $150 in her purse, and he could see it was still there. Puzzled, Todd Stuth checked the closet and saw that Vonnie's gray hooded coat was gone.

But there was no note. It was incomprehensible that Vonnie would have gone out so late without leaving him a note. He called relatives and friends to see if she had left on a spur-of-the-moment errand, perhaps to borrow something she needed for Thanksgiving preparations. No one had seen or heard from her.

Vonnie Stuth, nineteen, was simply gone, and there was immediate terror in the hearts of those who knew and loved her.

There were eight other young women who had been reported missing in the Northwest, all of whom had vanished just as inexplicably as the young housewife. The media had been flooded with information on those cases: Lynda Healy, Donna Manson, Susan Rancourt, Roberta Parks, Brenda Ball, Georgeann Hawkins, Denise Naslund, Janice Ott. Janice's and Denise's skeletons had been found in mid-September.

They were all between eighteen and twenty-two years old, slender, with long hair parted in the middle. All pretty. Vonnie matched the physical characteristics of the missing girls. Brenda Ball and Denise Naslund had both lived in the Burien area; indeed, Vonnie and Denise had known each other in school. And Janice Ott had worked at the Youth Service Center, too. Was it mere coincidence or part of some awful conspiracy?

King County detectives were worried, too. Vonnie's disappearance had all the earmarks of an abduction. Vonnie's family described her as a cautious young woman who always kept her door locked. She wouldn't have opened it to anyone she didn't know.

Todd Stuth spent the next few days either in the homicide unit, talking with King County Police detectives, trying to offer some clue that might help them find her, or in his house, waiting for a call from Vonnie. He was adamant that they had had no quarrel; there had been nothing at all that might have made Vonnie want to run away. "It's weird," the twenty-one-year-old foundry worker said. "She was definitely taken. There's no doubt in my mind. If a nut took your wife, you'd be worried, wouldn't you?"

Assured that there seemed to be no direct links to the other eight girls who had vanished, he tried to agree: "I hope not. Because I don't want my wife dead. I'm not leaving this house until I find out what happened to her."

There was nothing in the Stuth house that indicated a struggle. Detectives found no signs of blood or a scuffle. Nothing. For some reason Vonnie Stuth had unlocked the front door, and something or someone had persuaded or coerced her to leave the house.

The only clue investigators had was Vonnie's comment to her sister about the man from across the street who had offered to give her a dog. But which man? Detectives talked to neighbors, but no one recalled—or admitted—talking to Vonnie on the night before Thanksgiving.

The house directly across the street was empty, recently vacated. Stuth said they hadn't known those tenants well at all. He recalled that a couple approaching middle age had lived there. They had driven a van. One neighbor had seen that van parked in the driveway of the vacated home for about ten minutes on the night Vonnie disappeared.

Detectives checked the vacant house and noted that there was a great deal of trash left behind. Pawing through garbage is one of the more onerous tasks of criminal investigators, but trash can yield a gold mine of information, too. Among other items, the King County detectives found a number of snapshots torn into pieces. When they were fitted together the pictures were of a dark-haired woman, attractive enough to be a model, who was posing nearly nude. Neighbors recognized her as the woman who had lived in the house. Other bits of paper bore the address and name of Gary A. Taylor. Neighbors thought that sounded like the name of the man who lived there.

The Taylors had kept to themselves. No one knew what Taylor did for a living or where he and the woman came from. They had lived in the home only a few months. As far as anyone remembered, they didn't have a dog. Taylor was about thirty-five or forty, maybe a little over six feet tall, with light brown hair graying at the temples. He had worn dark-rimmed glasses.

Of course, they couldn't be sure that *he* was the man who had come to Vonnie's door with a dog. Any stranger could have come to the Stuth's door, pointed to a nearby house, and *pretended* to be a neighbor. Vonnie hadn't told her sister *who* the neighbor was. She had talked to someone, shut the front door, and come back to the phone. She certainly had not sounded upset. Her stepbrother had seen her safe at eleven, a half hour after that.

But the man could have returned, perhaps even urged Vonnie to come out and look at the puppy so she could describe it to her husband. She had been firm about not going outside on the first visit;

could she have been persuaded to do so later? She hadn't screamed. Neighbors were sure they'd heard nothing. But then the neighborhood where they lived was almost directly under the flight path of giant jets just before they landed to the south at Seattle-Tacoma Airport. When the jets roared in for a landing all other sounds were drowned out.

Detective Sergeant Len Randall and Detective Mike Baily worked on the case, which had been officially designated as a missing person case. But they didn't feel it was only a missing person case as the days passed and no word of Vonnie came.

They felt the same frustration they had felt in the cases of the other missing girls. Even if they had a red-hot suspect they would have to handle him with great tact and discretion. There was no corpse to make anyone a homicide suspect. A suspect could cry "harassment" and "false arrest" and play the snowy-white innocent. There was as yet no crime. There was only a missing person, an adult who might have left of her own free will.

Mike Baily and Len Randall located a forwarding address for Gary Taylor and saw that he had moved to an isolated three-acre ranch near Enumclaw, Washington, deep in the southeastern portion of King County. They put out a request for information on Taylor through the NCIC (National Crime Information Center) computer, which programmed all data on wants, warrants, and records of criminals.

It was 1974. Computers were in their infancy, and they were horse-and-buggy, technically, compared to what they can do in 1994.

There were no hits on the name Gary A. Taylor. According to information relayed back to King County, Taylor was not currently wanted in any jurisdiction in America, nor did he have a record that might make him a prime suspect in the Stuth case.

On December 6th the detectives located the isolated farm where the Taylors had moved and talked to Gary Taylor in person. He wasn't exactly delighted to see them, but he seemed agreeable enough. He said he would go back with them to the county police offices in the King County Courthouse in downtown Seattle. There he was routinely informed of his rights under Miranda, and Randall told him he was a suspect in the disappearance of Vonnie Stuth.

Randall and Baily studied the tall man. He was visibly nervous. Beads of sweat stood out on his forehead as he denied having any connection with Vonnie Stuth's disappearance. He didn't even know her, he assured them. Still, both detectives had the gut feeling a good investigator senses when he faces his quarry. This guy was antsy, far more that the normal anxiety they saw in an interview situation. But the days of holding a suspect because it felt right were long gone. They could hold Taylor for a few hours, but there were absolutely no legal precedents that would let them book Gary Taylor into jail. They had no probable cause to arrest him.

Technically, there had been no crime. They had no victim. They had no crime scene. And their check through NCIC had failed to show that Taylor was wanted for even a traffic warrant.

Len Randall drove Gary Taylor back to the little house in the woods near Enumclaw. He elicited a promise that Taylor would come into the homicide unit on Monday, December 9th, to talk further and to take a lie-detector test. Once out of the atmosphere of the detectives' office Gary Taylor became relaxed, even affable, and he assured Randall he would be in on Monday to straighten everything out.

Monday came—but Taylor didn't. He was gone. The house in Enumclaw had been vacated hurriedly, and the whereabouts of the Taylor couple was anybody's guess. Belatedly, King County detectives learned who Gary Addison Taylor really was. And the information that came in from authorities in Michigan left very little hope that Vonnie Stuth would ever come home again.

Somehow there had been a horrendous glitch in the system. Somehow a monster had slipped through an escape hatch and been let free to prowl once again.

Gary Addison Taylor was born in 1936 in Howell, Michigan, a small town between Ann Arbor and Lansing. As in most small midwestern towns, there were few secrets—everybody knew everybody else. Gary lived in Howell with his parents and one brother until he was fifteen. School friends recalled him as a physical fitness enthusiast with a lightning-quick temper, and also as a very talented trumpet player. The only trouble he had with the law in Howell could have been considered a boyish prank: Gary shot out windows in downtown stores with a pellet gun.

In 1951 the Taylor family moved to St. Petersburg, Florida, where they managed a motel. Taylor's first arrest took place on Christmas Eve, 1954, when he was eighteen. He was accused of attacking a thirty-nine-year-old St. Petersburg woman, a theater cashier, with a wrench as she stepped off a bus. He didn't know her. Police said at the time that they believed Gary was responsible for sixteen or seventeen other attacks on women in the area. Mindless, motiveless episodes of violence against females. He was tried on a single charge of assault with intent to murder and acquitted by a jury.

Later Gary Taylor told three Michigan psychiatrists he "felt lucky" that he hadn't killed the theater cashier because he "might have."

Shortly after Gary was acquitted in Florida the Taylors moved back to Michigan—this time to Royal Oak near Detroit, where the elder Taylor opened up a dry goods store. Gary joined the navy.

He lasted eleven months. He was discharged because he complained of chronic migraine headaches.

Gary Taylor had been home in Michigan only a month and a half when he was arrested once again for terrorizing women. With each incident the crimes of which he was suspected grew more ominous. The Detroit papers had been full of headlines about "The Phantom Sniper of Royal Oak." Someone with a rifle had been hunting women as if they were deer.

Gary Taylor's arrest came after a nineteen-year-old woman was shot as she walked home from a bus stop. Police spotted him as he fled, and he was captured following a wild three-hour chase through four Detroit suburbs.

Taylor confessed to shooting the woman, as well as to fifteen other sniping attacks on females. Four of the victims had been wounded; no one had been killed—but that was only through sheer luck. One of the victims was an eleven-year-old girl. Gary Taylor hadn't known any of the girls and women he had shot at; their only crime had been that they were females. He told psychiatrists that he had bought the .22-caliber rifle "expressly for the idea of shooting women." He said he aimed at them above the waist because of impulses he couldn't control. He appeared to have derived terrific pleasure from the shootings. Sexual pleasure.

He admitted that he had had "a compulsion to harm women ever since I was in the third grade." He told examining psychiatrists that he had gone to prostitutes since he was only fifteen and that he had enjoyed seeing the fear on their faces as he beat and robbed them.

Why had he picked women as his targets and his quarry? Why did he hate them so? The psychiatric team was fascinated with this young man who seemed so intelligent but whose affect was so cold. Like the biblical Samson, Gary Taylor explained that he found that women were "a source of weakening him, and possibly all men," and he felt that threat fully justified his shooting at them.

Although a teenage Gary Taylor had struck out at females with sheer brute force or through the sights of a gun, an older Taylor had learned that he had only to put on a kind of mask to make women trust him. He was a handsome young man, tall and muscular, and he enjoyed presenting himself as a nice guy, a witty guy good for laughs; he liked seeing the reaction he got from women. It was a kick for him to play a part, to be an actor on the outside while inside he laughed at them, and worse.

Warming to his subject, he told detectives about the waitresses he had encountered who were "flirty." He explained that he would always smile back at them. "They'd think I might be flirting with them. If she only knew what I was thinking, she'd be scared to death because I might be thinking something like, 'Boy, I'd like to shoot you.'"

After the Royal Oak phantom snipings Gary Taylor was deemed to be psychotic—criminally insane. Dr. Abraham Tauber told a Michigan court that Gary Taylor was "so unreasonably hostile toward women, this makes it very possible that he might very well kill a person—and probably a woman—if he were allowed free in the community."

On March 28, 1957, Taylor was committed to the Ionia State Hospital for the Criminally Insane. He was one day away from his twenty-first birthday.

Some 2,500 miles away, Vonnie Stuth was one week away from her second *birthday.*

In 1960 Gary Addison Taylor was transferred for treatment to the Lafayette Clinic in Detroit. He had apparently shown improvement during his three years in Ionia. At any rate, he was given passes outside the clinic to attend classes in arc welding at the Wolverine Trade School.

Over the years he had learned a lot more than arc welding; he had become the complete sociopath. He had a story for every occasion. He could be anyone he chose to be—and be so most convincingly. His charm was as superficial as the thin glaze of ice on a pond in autumn, but how he made it work for him.

At Christmastime Taylor was allowed to be away from the Lafayette Clinic on temporary leave. He posed as an Internal Revenue Service agent as he knocked on the door of the west side Detroit home of a former beauty queen. Earlier he had watched her and followed her home to see where she lived. Once inside he set down his empty briefcase and raped the woman. Perhaps as an afterthought, he robbed her of $13 on his way out the door.

Gary Addison Taylor was twenty-four that year.

Vonnie Stuth was in kindergarten.

Given more and more freedom because he was apparently doing so well at the Lafayette Clinic, Gary Taylor roamed the Detroit area with ease. His savage obsessions had not changed. Four months later, in April, 1961, he was arrested by Detroit police after he assaulted a rooming house owner and her daughter with an eighteen-inch machete.

As he always did, Taylor had a ruse to get into the homes of his chosen victims. He had rented a room in the victims' house, and of course they let him in when he returned several hours later. This time he attacked them.

When the news of Taylor's arrest broke, a twenty-six-year-old Detroit woman who owned an art import store called police and identified Taylor as the same man who had choked her into unconsciousness in her store in January. She had been horrified to see the smooth connoisseur of paintings and sculpture change into a man filled with rage and lust. In only a second the "mask" had dropped, revealing the monster beneath.

There was a great deal of negative publicity in Michigan about Gary Taylor in 1961, and a resounding response from the public. People asked loudly why he had been transferred out of Ionia in the first place. He was whisked back to the hospital for the criminally insane without ever going to trial in the 1960–61 cases. Then Michigan Attorney General Paul L. Adams launched a three-month investigation into Taylor's transfer to the Lafayette Clinic and concluded that patients should be paroled *only* through court hearings instead of simply being released from mental hospitals in the state.

It would have seemed that premise should always have been followed.

Twice more, in 1966 and in 1967, Gary Taylor and his family requested his release from Ionia through court orders. Both times the requests were turned down on the grounds that he was still dangerously mentally ill.

Like many once-high-profile offenders, Taylor no longer made headlines. The public forgot about him.

In 1970 Taylor was transferred from the prison for the criminally insane in Ionia to the Michigan Center for Forensic Psychiatry in Ypsilanti, a relatively small city between Detroit and Ann Arbor. Without fanfare he was released from inpatient care in July of 1972— with, of course, the stipulation that he return periodically for treatment. Dr. Ames Robey, the center's director, said he believed Taylor was no longer mentally ill and would be dangerous only if he failed to take his medication. Even in therapy Gary Addison Taylor could be convincingly sincere, a man who said all the right things.

Gary Taylor was now thirty-six years old. Vonnie Stuth was seventeen; she had grown to be a beautiful young woman, but she was still safe, still 2,500 miles away from Taylor.

For about a year Gary Taylor returned sporadically for treatment to the forensic psychiatry center in Ypsilanti, but in mid-1973 he stopped showing up for his appointments.

He was not listed as an escaped mental patient for three months, not until November, 1974. And then, to compound the mistake further, through some human error or some temporary aberration of the teletype network that crisscrossed America, Taylor's name was not entered into the national law enforcement communication system.

After more than a year Michigan authorities discovered the mistake and asked that any law enforcement agency in America take Taylor immediately into custody if he was located. This urgent notification to all agencies was *supposed* to have been issued on November 6, 1974, but was not, because of an oversight.

That made *three* tragic oversights.

There would be a fourth. Indeed, Gary Taylor's name was not entered into the nationwide computers until January 13, 1975— seven weeks after Vonnie Stuth vanished.

Would the correct notifications have saved Vonnie? The first three almost certainly would have; if anyone in authority had known Taylor was a walkaway from his treatment, he would have been picked up and locked up. If the November 6, 1974 "urgent" bulletin had been disseminated on time, he might have been arrested in the twenty-one days between the bulletin and the night he encountered Vonnie.

One thing was certain: the last mistake kept county detectives from holding Gary Taylor in jail after they talked to him on December 6. But they had checked the system to see if there were any "wants" on him and found none. By January 13 Vonnie was still missing, and Taylor was nowhere to be found.

Detectives had searched the Enumclaw property where Gary Taylor last lived for some trace of Vonnie. It would have been an ideal spot to hold her captive. Although modern homes fronted the main road on each side of the property, the white frame house Taylor rented sat six hundred feet back on the rugged farm, accessible only by a winding dirt road through a thick stand of evergreens. There were many outbuildings—a double garage and sheds—all hidden from the road and from the neighbors' view. Behind the house the property dropped away a hundred feet or more, ending in the rushing Newaukum Creek. The ground was frozen solid in December and January; there were no obvious gravesites.

Short of digging up the whole three acres—an almost impossible task in winter—there was no way for the investigators to be sure Vonnie was there somewhere. Gary Taylor had moved on in his van and might well have taken Vonnie, or her body, with him.

He had had hundreds of miles of lonely spots where he could hide Vonnie.

King County detectives knew that he had gone south, but they didn't know how far south. They had managed to trace Taylor to Portland, Oregon. A woman who said she was his wife, Emily* Taylor, had rented an apartment there with him from December 6 to December 16. His van was found in Portland, where it had been repossessed by a finance company.

The van was processed, and a long blond hair, similar in class and characteristic to Vonnie Stuth's hair, was found inside. There was no way of knowing how long it had been there. And there was no way of proving that it actually *was* her hair.

By the time King County detectives traced him to Portland, Gary Taylor had left; he was rumored to have departed Portland in a Ford Pinto, leaving his wife behind. He was seen in several small Oregon towns, alone, but he moved on before authorities could catch up with him. Taylor's wife left Portland in late January, 1975, and drove the couple's Chrysler to Tucson, Arizona, where a relative of her husband's lived.

The house in Tucson was staked out, but Taylor himself did not appear in Arizona. However, a court-ordered phone tap of calls to the residence in Tucson indicated that calls were coming in from various areas in the Southwest. Gary Taylor was on the move again.

Houston, Texas, special assault detectives were dealing with an elusive sexual predator in March and April of 1975. The four victims were all women managers of large apartment complexes, and they had all been attacked by a man who had shown interest in renting a unit.

The tall, good-looking would-be tenant was described as being quite charming at first, but his charm had quickly vanished when he was alone with a woman in an empty apartment. In each case he had held a chrome nine-shot revolver on the women and demanded sex. But he hadn't raped the captive women. He had been unable to achieve an erection, and he had demanded that they perform fellatio on him.

The female victims all described their attacker as a man in the grip of a white-hot rage. He had shouted terrible things at them, threatened to kill them, and screamed "bitch" at them as if he loathed them.

Two of the Texas victims had been assaulted on March 11th, the other two in late March and early April. One of the Houston women told her attacker that she had multiple sclerosis and managed to pull away from his grasp as he seemed momentarily hesitant. She fell down a stairwell in her flight and screamed as loud as she could. The man fled, leaving behind his chrome revolver. Disappointed police found no prints on it; the suspect had worn black gloves during all the attacks.

There was one more victim in Houston whom detectives felt might be part of the pattern. A smooth-talking man managed to get inside the home of a pregnant sixteen-year-old housewife. She had been alone there with her eighteen-month-old baby. After sexually assaulting her in her house the man ordered her to go with him to a motel, and she complied, fearful for her baby's safety. He allowed her to take the youngster along with them.

This time the attacker was not impotent and succeeded in raping the terrified young mother. The girl managed to escape when her attacker fell asleep. She crept out of the room with her baby and took a cab home, then called the police. She told them that the man who had raped her seemed very drowsy, and she thought he was high on drugs. His clothing had smelled of marijuana.

Houston police rushed to the Ramada Inn but found the rapist gone. But he had made a mistake, his normal attention to detail dulled by drugs. He had registered as "Sarge" Taylor and had given a Michigan license plate number. Houston checked the number with NCIC, and this time the proper information had been programmed.

The plates belonged to Gary Addison Taylor, an escaped mental patient from Michigan, also wanted in Seattle for suspicion of homicide in the 1974 disappearance of Vonnie Stuth. The four other Houston victims identified mug shots of Taylor. They were positive he was the man who had attacked them.

Once again Gary Taylor was gone. The pressure to arrest Taylor was tremendous—especially when a busload of girls and several motorists were fired on by a sniper with a .22 rifle in Sherman, Texas, on May 16.

A month after the attack on the young mother in the Ramada Inn Houston police received an anonymous tip that Gary Addison Taylor was working in a Houston machine shop. He had learned arc welding long ago when he was on leave from one of the Detroit clinics; he had also, of course, attacked women after he left class.

The Houston informant whispered that Taylor would be taking a particular route from his job to the duplex he was renting. He was stopped and arrested by police at 3 a.m. on May 20, 1975.

Vonnie Stuth was still missing.

Once Gary Taylor was safely in jail in Texas, Emily Taylor surfaced through her attorney in San Diego. She had much to tell authorities. Her fears and suspicions had grown to the point where she had fled from Taylor, whom she had married three years earlier without knowing his true background.

She told the attorney, Frederick A. Meiser, that she believed her husband had been involved in several murders. Whenever he was drunk, she said, he had talked of killing people. "He would get drunk and say, 'Hey, you know those people. I killed them and buried them outside our house in Michigan.' " Emily Taylor also thought that he had killed Vonnie Stuth and buried her in their yard in Enumclaw.

The Gary Taylors had lived in the hamlet of Onsted, Michigan, near Ann Arbor and Jackson, when he had last reported at the Forensic Center in Ypsilanti. Even as Houston detectives began to unravel cases that might be traced to Taylor in Texas, Washington and Michigan authorities were alerted to the possibility that murder victims might be buried on properties where the Taylors had lived in those two states.

Sheriff Richard Germond of Lenawee County, where the Taylors' Michigan home was located, gathered a search crew on Thursday, May 22, 1975. King County, Washington, authorities were doing the same.

Germond's crew worked in the yard of the little house where the Taylors had lived in the early seventies. The home was located twenty miles southeast of Jackson near the Irish Hills. They had been instructed that they would find four bodies. They found only two bodies and a quantity of women's clothing, buried almost underneath the Taylors' former bedroom window. The decomposed bodies were encased in plastic garbage bags and the clothes stuffed into two other bags. A cursory examination of the corpses, which had been buried naked and were bound with electric cords and rope, seemed to indicate the victims had died of gunshot wounds to the head. The remains were transported to Lansing, where forensic pathologists would do postmortem examinations.

A library card in one of the bags was for Lee Fletcher, twenty-four, with a Toledo, Ohio, address. The Ohio city is just south of the Michigan border, and Michigan authorities were aware that two women had been listed as missing from a bar in Toledo since late April, 1974.

The women, both alleged to be prostitutes, had last been seen leaving the bar with a tall man who drove a van with Michigan plates. Lee Fletcher was one of the women. The other was seventeen-year-old Debbie Henneman. A male friend of the two, concerned about their disappearance, spotted a van that matched the description of the one in which the women had left. He checked the license plates and found it registered to Gary A. Taylor. He had gone to Taylor's home and searched for Lee Fletcher and Debbie Henneman but had been unable to find them.

Now, at last, they had been found.

Lenawee County detectives got a search warrant for the house where Gary Taylor and his wife had lived. Their initial search of the home was unremarkable; it was just a house like any other. However, when they got to the southwest corner of the residence's basement they found a small room that could only have been a soundproof torture chamber. Even though more than a year had passed, the investigators found blood and human tissue on the floor, ceiling, walls, and pipes.

According to the path of the Taylors' travels that police all over the country were retracing, the couple had left Onsted, Michigan, in the spring of 1974 and traveled west.

In Enumclaw the search for Vonnie Stuth's body began on Thursday, May 22, and lasted through Friday and Saturday. Seven King County officers, forty Search and Rescue Explorer Scouts, several National Guardsmen and a German shepherd search dog went over the grounds of Taylor's former home literally inch by inch.

Wildflowers dotted the grass beneath the cedar trees now, and rhododendrons and wisteria planted by a former owner softened the grisly search somehow. The Newaukum Creek at the back of the farm property ran high along its banks, and birds sang.

Vonnie had been spirited away in the depths of winter. Now it was spring, and the thaw had softened the ground. Even so, the searchers ended each day with no sign of Vonnie. When they had finished a section they marked it with sticks with strips of plastic attached. By the third day the backyard was almost filled with the little sticks and their tiny multicolored banners fluttering in the wind.

The searchers paused along a dike area between a small pond and the creek. The underbrush was very thick, but one of the team detected just the tip of what appeared to be a shoe protruding from the ground.

Now the Explorer Scouts and non-police personnel were relieved of their duties, and they moved away. Carefully, meticulously, detectives removed the sandy dirt from the gravesite. A body lay buried fourteen to twenty inches beneath, a body clad in jeans, a gray hooded coat, and small brown ankle-high boots. The body had long blond hair.

On Monday, May 26, the King County Medical Examiner, using dental records, positively identified the remains found buried beside the Newaukum Creek as those of nineteen-year-old Vonnie Stuth. She had died of a gunshot wound to the head and appeared to have been dead for six months. There was no way to determine if she had been sexually assaulted.

Just as a pebble dropped into a still pool makes endless rings in the water, the ramifications of Gary Addison Taylor's urge to kill grew and grew. In Houston, Homicide Detectives Carol Stephenson and Theresa Pierce were asking the suspect about the death of a twenty-one-year-old go-go dancer, Susan Kay Jackson. There was a singular irony in the fact that this man who detested women had his case assigned to two female detectives.

Susan Jackson had disappeared from the Three Thieves Bar, where she worked, on May 14, 1975. Four days later an elderly heart patient, out on his prescribed daily hike, stumbled over her blanket-wrapped body in an isolated area thirty miles from downtown Houston.

Gary Taylor made no pretense of innocence. Yes, he had killed Susan Jackson, he confessed. He said he had picked her up in the bar and taken her to his duplex, where he had suffocated her. He had then wrapped her feet and legs with one garbage bag and her trunk and head with another, swaddled her in a blanket secured by chains, and driven her body to the spot where it was found.

He also confessed to the killing of Vonnie Stuth, and to murdering the two women from Toledo, whose names, he said, he never knew. He did not ask for an attorney, even though he had been told repeatedly that he had the right to one. He signed confessions to the murders but confessed only orally to the sexual attacks in Houston.

Informants told Michigan police that Gary Taylor had bragged of killing yet another woman in that state as well as a man who had worked with him in Ypsilanti. In Ann Arbor Police Chief Walter Krasny and Detective Bernard Price were most interested. They had been investigating the disappearance of thirty-three-year-old Sandra Horwath, a mother of three, who had dated Taylor. Mrs. Horwath, employed by an Ann Arbor building firm, vanished in October of 1973.

The male alleged murder victim surfaced, alive and well, a day later in Garden City, Michigan. He said he had no idea he was the man supposed to be buried along with the three women. He had known Taylor only casually. Sandra Horwath, however, remained missing.

No one knew how many unsolved murders might be linked to Gary Addison Taylor. In one of his sanity hearings Gary Taylor had told a psychiatrist, Dr. Ivan A. LeCore of the Pontiac, Michigan, State Hospital, that he fantasized about killing a woman skier. "He thought of sniping at women on a ski jump and went so far as to procure a rifle and a telescopic sight, but after a personal trip to a ski jump he decided that he would not do this for some reason or another," LeCore recalled.

Taylor's wife remained secluded in San Diego. She was asked how she could have lived with the suspect and not realized he was a killer. "I tell you he's a very cunning person, and he acts completely sane, and all the time he probably wants to kill."

Houston Detective Carol Stephenson was inclined to agree. She felt that there were more victims than anyone knew about. Taylor denied that there were any crimes other than those he had confessed to, but Stephenson shook her head and added, "I don't feel he would confess to anything he thought we knew nothing about. He was asked that and said he wouldn't."

She described Taylor succinctly as "mean," but also as "very intelligent."

"I feel like he is far and away the most dangerous person I've ever talked to in the fourteen years I've been in this work," she said, adding that he would be charged for the Texas crimes. "His 'irresistible urge' won't hold water in this state."

Detective Stephenson said Taylor had told police in Houston that he had decided to move there in December, 1974, after reading want ads from several papers in major cities to check job opportunities. He was hired by the Houston machine shop two days before Christmas and more than three weeks before he ever actually made national "wanted" networks. He had listed three Michigan men as references. The addresses he gave for the men were nonexistent.

Nobody checked.

Taylor had also listed his father as a reference. In mid-March he asked for a leave of absence to attend his father's funeral in Tucson. His father was alive and well. When he was contacted by a Detroit paper the elder Taylor reportedly said that he had not seen his son in five years and wanted nothing more to do with him.

Gary Taylor was indicted by a Harris County, Texas, grand jury on May 28, 1975, on five counts of sexual crimes: three of aggravated sexual abuse, one of aggravated rape, and one of attempted rape. He was held in lieu of $340,000 bail.

Taylor complained to a Houston judge that city detectives had beaten him and threatened his life at a city park before he signed statements confessing to the murders in Texas. Detective Theresa Pierce denied that either she or Carol Stephenson had beaten Gary Taylor. She said Taylor was not mistreated, and he had never been taken to a park.

On May 29, 1975, Gary Taylor was formally charged with first-degree murder in the death of Vonnie Stuth in an affidavit filed by King County Senior Deputy Prosecutor Phil Killien.

All hope had ended for Vonnie Stuth's family when her body was found on the lonely acreage in Enumclaw after six months of waiting. They had kept the top layer of her wedding cake frozen on the slight chance that she might be home to celebrate her first anniversary on May 4th. There would never be such a celebration, and her mother, Lola Linstad, quietly disposed of the cake.

Memorial services for Vonnie were held on Sunday, June 1, 1975, in the church where she had been married thirteen months before. Lola Linstad, a co-founder of Families and Friends of Victims of Violent Crimes and Missing Persons, remained active in the group. "There was still a job to do. It was important to me that other families, if at all possible, be spared this kind of tragedy."

There was some faint comfort for Vonnie's family. They knew that she had been dead for a very long time. They had some closure, and they could go on. They did not know, however, how long Gary Taylor had held Vonnie captive after he lured her out of her home to look at a dog. They agonized over that.

"It would have been hard to do," Lola Linstad said when a reporter suggested that Vonnie might have been alive for several days after she was abducted. "She was a fiery girl, and in his confession Taylor said he got her outside to look at a dog he wanted to give her, but when it wasn't in his van she got mad."

Everyone who knew Vonnie Stuth wanted to believe that she had been shot in the back of the head as she broke free of Taylor and ran from him when they arrived at the Enumclaw farm. The fact that she was still dressed when her body was found seemed to substantiate that. When he appeared before King County Superior Court Judge William Goodloe in Seattle, Taylor pleaded guilty to second-degree murder. It was a way for him to escape trials in Texas and Michigan. Deputy Prosecutor Joanne Maida urged the minimum recommendation of life in prison. Judge Goodloe sentenced Gary Addison Taylor to up to life in prison. "If I had the power to do so, I would recommend a *second* term of life."

But he didn't have that power. Actually, the mandatory minimum for second-degree murder was not less than five years in prison. The King County prosecutor recommended that the Washington State Board of Prison Terms and Paroles not parole Taylor for at least fifteen years.

After hearing his sentence Gary Addison Taylor said he wanted to express his "regrets" for Vonnie Stuth's death. He appeared very calm, and he had smiled as he entered the courtroom. After he heard his sentence he shook hands with his attorney. All in all, he had fared well. The King County Prosecutor's Office had little choice but to accept the plea bargain. Taylor had confessed to Vonnie's murder before her body was found. There had been questions about how his confession was obtained, and there was the likelihood that evidence against him would be suppressed. There was also the issue of a speedy trial on the sexual assault cases in Texas, and he might, *incredibly*, have been set free without the plea bargain of second-degree murder.

No one knows why Gary Addison Taylor felt that women were his enemies, Delilahs and Jezebels who drained men of life and strength. Perhaps this man who chose Adolf Hitler as his hero *was* insane.

But for an insane man, he was able to stay away from the scores of detectives who were seeking him for an incredibly long time.

Gary Taylor had admitted to killing four women and assaulting five more, but this was only in his final reign of terror across America. This did not include the myriad attacks on women that had begun when he was in his mid-teens. There *were* some victims that he could not claim—the women who disappeared in Washington and Oregon in 1974. Lynda Healy, Donna Manson, Susan Rancourt, Roberta Parks, Brenda Ball, Georgeann Hawkins, Denise Naslund, and Janice

Ott were not murdered by Gary Addison Taylor; they had the terrible misfortune to cross Ted Bundy's path. Both serial killers had been prowling in Washington State in 1974.

Gary Taylor *was* imprisoned in the Washington penitentiary in Walla Walla, but only for eight years. Washington State correctional computers—which are far more sophisticated and dependable than the computers of two decades ago—indicate that Taylor went out of the Washington penal system in 1984 and was transferred to another state. He remains behind bars as this is written. Although his status is reviewed every few years, the earliest possible release date for Gary Taylor is May 17, 2036. If he survives, he will then be a hundred years old and, one would hope, no longer dangerous.

But in 1994 Gary Addison Taylor is fifty-eight years old. If she had been allowed to live, Vonnie Stuth would have been thirty-nine.

Lola Linstad pondered a question I asked her, not out of curiosity, but from my admiration for her strength: "How have you survived? How have you been able to bear losing Vonnie the way you did?"

"Vonnie was such a happy person, and she would have wanted us to be happy," Lola answered. "If we had spent the rest of *our* lives grieving and mourning for her, I know it would have made her so sad. She would have wanted us to go on celebrating Christmas and laughing and living. We will always miss her, but I know we are living as she would have wished us to. . . ."

The Vanishing

Back in the late 1950s, when the author was a Seattle policewoman, it was something of a rarity to have a teenager disappear or even run away. In the whole city of Seattle there were perhaps two or three girls missing at any given time. In the decades since, the problem of missing youngsters has, of course, reached epidemic proportions. Every police department of any size has dozens of runaways listed on its books.

The vast majority of missing teenagers have left of their own accord, and while they often become involved in unsavory situations, most of them are alive and well. One day most of them will come home, sadder and, hopefully, wiser. Sometimes, however, there are disappearances so totally unexpected, so inexplicable, that even seasoned police investigators shake their heads.

Stacy Sparks's disappearance was one of those.

Stacy vanished under the strangest circumstances—vanished so completely that it was difficult for a rational mind to understand how it could have happened.

Stacy's story has an ending. No one of us who searched for her could ever have guessed what that ending would be. Of all the possibilities, the truth was one that no one ever considered.

On July 9, 1979, Stacy Sparks's life was not only completely normal, it was filled with happy plans. She had a new job and a steady boyfriend, and she was looking forward to the realization of a longtime dream: Stacy was going to Hawaii. Eighteen years old and a recent high school graduate, Stacy had less reason than most young women to run away voluntarily. And yet something changed the pattern of Stacy's life that long-ago night in June, something that no one who knew and loved her could explain.

By midnight Stacy had disappeared. In fact, both Stacy and her beloved new car seemed to have been swallowed up by the earth itself. Detectives found it hard to believe that her car, at least, had never turned up.

When Stacy awoke on July 9 she was happy. In the weeks and months after she vanished, her mother and stepfather—Peg and Mike Haley—went over and over that day, trying to think of some small signal they might have missed, something to indicate that she had a problem. They came up with nothing at all.

Stacy left their home in the Ballard area of Seattle on her way to have breakfast at Sambo's Restaurant a mile away. Stacy had worked at Sambo's for a long time but had recently taken a job as a waitress at the Little Pebble restaurant at the Shilshole Marina, which was also in Ballard. The Little Pebble was the coffee shop portion of the elegant Windjammer restaurant, and the new job meant more pay and an opportunity in the future for Stacy to be promoted upstairs, where the tips were usually lavish. She liked the new restaurant, and she liked the job.

Stacy worked her daytime shift that Monday, wearing the little nautical outfit the café furnished. She did the uniform proud. At five feet, two inches, her 115 pounds gave her a perfect figure. Her ash-blond hair was streaked with lighter blond from the summer sun, and her brown eyes sparkled. Stacy was vivacious and unfailingly

691

friendly. It was rare to see her without a smile, even when her feet hurt at the end of a long shift.

Stacy finished her shift about six that evening and walked to the car that was her pride and joy. It was a light blue 1978 Plymouth Arrow with four-inch-wide white racing stripes along its sides.

Stacy Sparks drove next to the Ballard apartment of two friends, Kim Turner* and Polly Gunderson.* Polly was due to go to work that evening at the Raintree restaurant and lounge in Lynnwood, a suburb north of Seattle. The three girls chatted while she got ready to leave. Kim and Stacy stopped at Stacy's while she changed into blue jeans and a yellow T-shirt with a large rose appliqued on the front. Stacy loved roses; she always wore a necklace with two carved white roses with gold leaves surrounding them. She slipped into thong sandals.

Stacy and Kim had never been to the Raintree before July 9, but they headed next for the popular spot where their friend worked. Stacy carried a change of clothes with her because she planned to spend the night in West Seattle, where her boyfriend lived.

On the drive to the Raintree Stacy talked enthusiastically about her trip to Hawaii. She already had her round-trip ticket to Honolulu for August 1st. The Hawaiian trip had been a dream for Stacy and the three girlfriends who were going with her since they were fifteen. Now she was working hard to save enough spending money so that she could see and do everything possible in the islands.

At the Raintree Stacy parked her Arrow just outside the main entrance in the crowded parking lot. It was 8:30 p.m.

Stacy's boyfriend, Ron Bates,* had to work late in the auto supply firm where he clerked. She had promised to be at his home in West Seattle at nine so that he could call her and have her pick him up at work.

But when Ron called at nine there was no answer. There is no mystery about that; Stacy had simply dawdled at the Raintree and realized there was no way she could get to West Seattle by 9 p.m. She figured Ron could get home all right.

Ron gave up trying to reach Stacy and, somewhat annoyed, caught a bus for home, figuring she would probably be there by the time he got home. He had promised to take her out to dinner.

Stacy and Kim had several drinks at the Raintree, chatted with their friend, Polly, and talked to some young men at the bar. Sometime around 9:30 Stacy left—alone. She had perhaps five feet to walk to her little blue car in the parking lot. All things being equal, she would have quickly reached the I-5 freeway heading south into Seattle, driven through the downtown section, and then exited at the

West Seattle off-ramp and driven west to meet Ron. The drive should not have taken more than half an hour to forty-five minutes, even though it was pouring down rain.

Stacy never got to Ron Bates's home. First he was mad, and then he was worried; he waited up all night for her. Her parents weren't concerned that night or the next day. They hadn't expected Stacy home Monday night, and they assumed that she had gone directly to work at the Little Pebble on Tuesday morning.

But Stacy didn't come home Tuesday night, and a call to Ron Bates brought forth the frightening news that he hadn't seen her at all on Monday night.

Nor had she shown up for work at the Little Pebble on Tuesday.

Stacy's parents contacted everyone they could think of who might have seen her. The last direct contact anyone had had with her was at the Raintree.

On July 12, 1979, Stacy Sparks was officially listed as a missing person, and the file was flagged "suspicious circumstances." It was the beginning of one of the most massive searches that the Seattle police and the Lynnwood police had ever carried out, and the case file would grow over the next months until it consisted of two bulging folders several inches thick. Detective Bud Jelberg, head of the Missing Persons Unit, worked it first, and it was subsequently handled by the Homicide Unit, with Detectives John Boatman and Mike Tando spending untold hours on it. Since she had last been *seen* in Lynnwood, detectives there coordinated their efforts with the Seattle police.

A check on the WASIC (Washington State) computers failed to bring a "hit" on any accident, impounding, or police stop involving Stacy's little blue Plymouth Arrow. The investigators knew she wasn't lying injured and unconscious in any hospital in the state; her car had not been involved in an accident.

Information on Stacy and the missing car was broadcast in every county in Washington, and then to every law enforcement agency in a seven-state area. The hunt became widespread.

Stacy's family was sure of one thing: If anyone had grabbed her, she would not have gone quietly. She was a fighter who would have kicked, screamed, and scratched. However, the walls of the Raintree facing the parking lot were windowless. And the Raintree, which catered to a young crowd, featured disco music at top volume. If the parking lot had been temporarily empty of everyone but Stacy and an attacker, no one inside could have heard her cry for help.

It seemed frighteningly obvious that Stacy Sparks had not left voluntarily. She hadn't picked up her last check from Sambo's, she hadn't touched her savings account, and she would have had no more than $25 in her purse the night she vanished.

Seattle Police Sergeant Craig VandePutte and Detectives Boatman and Tando contacted Kim Turner. She recalled that Stacy had stayed about an hour at the Raintree, leaving about 9:30. They had talked to two Oregon men in their twenties at the bar—Ken Brinks* and Ralph Lawrence.* The men hadn't come on strong or said anything offensive. Stacy had left first—to go to West Seattle to pick up her boyfriend—and Ralph Lawrence had left shortly after. After Stacy and Lawrence had left, Kim had played a game of backgammon with Ken Brinks, and then they had left—but not together.

VandePutte contacted Brinks in Portland. The man, married, admitted that he and Lawrence had talked with Kim and Stacy, and he agreed with Kim's recall of that night. They had talked with the girls but hadn't seen them outside the tavern. Brinks stayed with an aunt when he was in Seattle on business, and Lawrence, who was divorced, stayed at his parents' home. VandePutte felt that Brinks was giving him a straight story. The men had arrived at and left the Raintree in their own cars.

A waitress at the Little Pebble recalled Stacy's last day at work to the detectives: "She was very happy. She was looking forward to spending the evening with her boyfriend."

The waitress described Stacy as a very friendly girl. "She was almost too friendly. She would talk with just anyone, and she wasn't afraid of anyone."

The detectives checked out the alibis of both Ken Brinks and Ralph Lawrence and found that there was no way either man could have abducted Stacy. They were seen by relatives within half an hour of leaving the Raintree. There was simply no way they could have kidnapped Stacy and hidden her car so thoroughly that no one could find it in half an hour.

Both Polly and Kim said that Stacy had had only two or three beers and was not even slightly intoxicated when she left for the drive to West Seattle.

"Would Stacy ever consider picking up a hitchhiker?" Mike Tando asked.

"Yes," Kim said. "She might. She's a really sweet person. She'd pick up a hitchhiker . . . if they looked all right."

It was the only viable theory going. The detectives knew that hitchhikers who look "all right" often turn out to be monsters, but they didn't say that to Polly and Kim.

On July 14th a man came into the homicide offices. He'd seen the papers full of articles about Stacy Sparks, and he had a strange story to tell. "Some guy where I work has been telling this story about something that happened on the night of July 9th. He was driving on I-5 during the evening, and he saw this naked girl lying in the freeway. She was badly injured. He stopped to help, and so did some others—including a doctor or a nurse or something. It wasn't a car wreck; the girl was just out there in the middle of the freeway up by the Snohomish County line."

Sergeant VandePutte immediately began calling hospital emergency rooms checking for the possible arrival of a "Jane Doe" injured on the freeway on July 9. He came up empty at Seattle's Harborview Hospital, where Seattle Medic One paramedics take their emergency patients, and in the Shoreline district north of Seattle. However, when he called the Sno-Com line in Snohomish County he found that there *had* been such an incident. VandePutte was directed to the paramedic who'd made the run.

"Yeah, we picked her up," the medic recalled. "We got the call at 11:18 p.m. We responded to I-5 northbound at 228th. There was a nude white female, about twenty-one, lying in the road with multiple leg injuries and other trauma. While we were working on her she kept asking. 'What happened to my friend?'"

The injured woman had been taken to Stevens Memorial Hospital and placed in the intensive care unit. It sounded as if the mystery of Stacy Sparks had been solved. However, a check with the hospital brought disappointment. The woman was not Stacy, and she didn't know Stacy. She had been hurt in an accident, and there was absolutely nothing linking her to Stacy Sparks.

On the slight chance that Stacy had somehow managed to fly to Hawaii despite the fact that her ticket was still in her parents' home, detectives contacted the airlines. No one had tried to use the reservation or to change it. There had been no attempt to redeem the ticket.

On July 15, an anonymous caller rambled on and on, saying that Stacy's body was probably at a rest stop on Blewett Pass. The area was searched—to no avail.

Stacy's blue Arrow hadn't turned up on any of the computers, nor had it been located in a search of used car lots.

Police divers couldn't very well search waterways for the little Plymouth without having some idea of where it might have gone in. To get from Lynnwood to West Seattle via I-5 Stacy would have had to cross two bridges: first the University Bridge over the Lake

Washington Ship Canal, and then the West Seattle Bridge over the Duwamish Waterway. Helicopters did flyovers in these two areas. If Stacy's car had been in the water, spotters could have discerned it from the air in fifteen to twenty feet of water when it could not be seen any other way, but no pilot or spotter detected the blue car below.

The fact that Stacy's car had vanished as completely as she had was a continuing puzzle. It is always easier to find a car than a hidden body.

Peg and Mike Haley, Stacy's parents, and her friends and relatives distributed hundreds of pictures and flyers describing her and her car to stores, bowling alleys, Laundromats, and other public places all over King and Snohomish counties. Her face was familiar to thousands of people who had never known her—but still there were no early solid reports of sightings. In desperation the Haleys turned to psychics, hoping that there might be a message from the spirit world that could let them know what had become of their daughter.

Some psychics have proved eerily accurate in finding the bodies of crime victims, but others can fill families full of both false hope and deep anxiety.

One Seattle psychic held the earrings that matched the carved rose necklace Stacy was wearing when she vanished and, according to Peg Haley, described Stacy's purse and its contents—something that he could not have known.

But his "vision" of Stacy was unsettling, to say the least. He "saw" the missing teenager in a deserted cabin near Snoqualmie Pass. He described a candy factory (Swiss type) and a dirt road leading away from it. There is a Swiss chocolate factory outlet near the pass, a very well-known store. The psychic said that three people were involved, one of them a man named Tom who was part Indian. The psychic gave Stacy only three days to live because she was being injected with heroin.

The Haleys could think of three Toms that Stacy knew—one an Indian, the other two part-Indian. One was quickly ruled out, the second was out of the area, and the whereabouts of the third was unknown. Because her parents were so upset by the psychic's visions, King County police units were contacted, and they carried out a fruitless search in the mountain foothill area. Issaquah police—whose jurisdiction covered the cabin location—were alerted, too, but they found no cabin matching the seer's description. Relatives and friends searched the region, too, frantic to find Stacy before her three days ran out. And when all the searching was finished they found not one trace of her in the little mountain foothill town.

The police searchers continued their probe into Stacy's disappearance through more realistic channels. More and more bulletins bearing Stacy's picture were printed and distributed. A clerk at the Washington State Department of Motor Vehicles volunteered to hand-search all vehicle impound forms in the state for one on a blue Plymouth Arrow that might have been missed in the computer checks. It was a tedious task, going through all the impounds back to July 9—but the little Plymouth wasn't there.

A man in his mid-forties, Jeff O'Dell,* called Detectives Mike Tando and John Boatman and said he had talked to Stacy Sparks twice on July 9. He said he was a longtime customer at Sambo's. He said he'd seen Stacy at Sambo's that Monday morning and talked with her then. O'Dell said she had confided in him that she had a boyfriend who was getting serious, but that she was a long way from being ready to settle down. She had invited O'Dell to drop into the Little Pebble sometime.

"Did you?" Boatman asked.

"Yeah, I went over that night for dinner. Stacy waited on me, and then she got off work just as I was leaving. I showed her my new van, and she told me she was going out with friends that evening."

The man had no new information; he only verified what the detectives were hearing again and again—that Stacy Sparks was a cheerful, friendly girl who seemed to have no real problems at all. She had told O'Dell that she wasn't ready to settle down, but she hadn't been so concerned about that that she would run away to avoid marriage. Detectives already knew that she didn't want to get married. Ron Bates had told them that he and Stacy had broken up for a week after he had proposed to her, but they had reconciled when he told her he wouldn't press her for a commitment. The trip to Hawaii was to have been a chance for Stacy to "gain new experiences and a new outlook on life," according to Ron.

Detectives Boatman and Tando had alerted the Canadian customs stations at the northern border of Washington, and they, too, were watching for the missing girl and her car. Had Stacy turned north instead of south on I-5, she would have been at the U.S. border in two hours.

On the off chance that Jeff O'Dell might have had more interest in Stacy than the avuncular affection he proclaimed and that he might even have followed her to the Raintree, the Seattle detectives checked out his movements for the night of July 9th. They found that he had attended an AA meeting with a married couple and that the couple could verify that he was with them continually until hours after Stacy had vanished.

Two of Stacy's former co-workers at Sambo's had left Seattle for California within a day or so of Stacy's disappearance, and the investigators wondered if it was possible that Stacy had joined them. It would have been completely out of character for her to do that, but the timing was perhaps more than coincidental. When the women returned to Seattle they were shocked to hear that Stacy was missing; they hadn't seen her at all.

The public's response to the intensive campaign to find Stacy was overwhelming. One of the more interesting leads came from a woman who lived in Kent, Washington, a small town south of Seattle:

"I was driving on I-5, headed south, on July 9th or 10th. When I was on the southern edge of the downtown section my attention was drawn to a medium blue small car with a girl driving. She looked just like the pictures I've seen of Stacy Sparks. There was a man sitting in the backseat right behind her—thirty-eight to forty, white, dark-haired. The girl kept staring at me, and I stared back. She looked at me for so long that our cars almost nudged each other. Then the man in the back sat forward. He leaned against her, and he stared at me. Our cars were going about sixty miles an hour at the time. I looked at her because she seemed to be staring at me so intensely. When I saw the picture of Stacy on TV tonight I was sure it was her."

This report made sense in light of the theory that Stacy might have either picked up a hitchhiker or been forced into her car by a man waiting in the parking lot of the Raintree. Perhaps she had been trying to get the woman's attention and help by staring so fixedly at her.

On July 19 Detective Deardon of Lynnwood reported that a pair of girls' jeans and women's panties had been found two blocks west of the Raintree. The jeans were Levi's brand with an elastic band made of variegated colors. The jeans were extremely dirty but in good condition. The panties were white with a green floral print.

Detectives asked for a more thorough description of the jeans Stacy had worn when she vanished. Kim Turner didn't know if Stacy had worn panties or not because Stacy hadn't changed clothes in front of her on July 9, but Kim knew her jeans well; she had given them to Stacy. "They were high-waisted, size 30, probably. I don't think they had any elastic band with colored thread. I think they had a strap around the waist which buckled in front."

The jeans found on the dirt road near the Raintree were not Stacy's.

An older couple who had been vacationing called to say that they were positive they had seen a light blue car with a white stripe on July 10 at 5 p.m. near Mud Bay, some seventy miles from Seattle. "It passed us, speeding and wavering erratically. We could only get a partial license number: UCX—."

Stacy's license number was UCX-487!

"Did you notice anyone in the car? Who was driving?" Tando asked.

"We couldn't see. It went by too fast," was the disappointing reply.

A woman from Olympia, Washington, sixty miles south of Seattle, reported that she had seen Stacy's car on Martin Way in that city, which was only ten miles from Mud Bay. "I know it had a UCX prefix, because our car does, too, and I noticed it."

Again she could not identify a driver or any passengers. The sightings—if they were actual sightings—of Stacy's car had all taken place on a route leading south out of Seattle and heading toward the Pacific Ocean.

In the meantime, Seattle detectives gathered items that might help to identify the missing girl if she eventually turned up as a homicide victim. Kim was asked to purchase a pair of jeans identical to those she had given Stacy, and she did that, bringing in a pair of jeans with a belt fastening in front. Stacy had carried her hairbrush in her purse, and it was missing along with her, but strands of her hair were retrieved from a hair dryer's brush attachment. Even as they gathered these identification items Mike Tando and John Boatman hoped that it was still possible that Stacy had left of her own accord.

But they no longer believed that. Everything they'd learned about the missing girl told them she would never have put her family through such agony. Her stepfather, Mike Haley, had resigned his job and was now spending all his time looking for her. On foot, by four-wheel-drive vehicle, and from a private plane he had scanned the acres of wilderness east of the city, trying to spot a glint of blue or a sheaf of blond hair. Stacy's mother, brother, aunts, uncles, grandmother, and dozens of friends spent their days delivering bulletins, asking questions. Always searching. They were trying to raise funds, too, to consult another psychic.

The Haleys contacted Peter Hurkos, the famed Dutch psychic who was living in California. His services, he explained, would cost $6,000. Although the psychics who had tried to help them so far hadn't charged at all, and the Haleys didn't have that kind of money, they thought Hurkos might be able to tell them something more than the clairvoyants they'd consulted in the Seattle area. They determined that somehow they would find the money.

People who cared about Stacy began the Stacy Sparks Search Fund, and high school students fanned out across Ballard, a close-knit, basically Scandinavian community. They collected donations, they had rummage sales—anything to raise the money needed for the psychic whose books detailed his many successful searches.

By the end of July the donations given to help in the search for Stacy reached $3,500. On July 30th—two days before Stacy would have left for her long-planned trip to Hawaii—Peg Haley and Polly Gunderson boarded a plane for Los Angeles. Their mission was to persuade Hurkos to help them for half his usual fee. Stacy's mother had a cashier's check for $2,000 and $1,900 in bills and rolled coins in her purse.

After pondering it for a while Hurkos agreed to help them. He placed a picture of Stacy, turned facedown, on a table, and after concentrating in silence for several minutes he described her. He seemed able to tell Peg Haley things about Stacy and their family that he couldn't have known. In three subsequent sessions he said he had divined that:

   —Stacy had been having an affair with a man in his thirties. (Polly Gunderson said that Stacy had referred to such a man, but she had never told Polly his name.)
   —Stacy had stopped at a gas station on the night of July 9.
   —Although Hurkos could not see how, when, or where Stacy had been abducted, he perceived that three men were involved— one of them Stacy's secret lover, a man who was jealous of Ron Bates and resistant to Stacy's trip to Hawaii. Another was a younger white man. The third was probably of Indian descent.
   —Two of the men took Stacy away in one car, while the third followed in her blue Arrow. Hurkos thought the missing Plymouth Arrow was hidden in a garage in Tacoma, Washington.
   —Stacy had fought and had been subdued by an injection of heroin.

The vision Hurkos saw was similar in many ways to the Seattle psychic's and not a pleasant one; he too felt that Stacy had overdosed on the heroin injection and been dumped in a ditch.

Hurkos furnished Mrs. Haley with a map that showed a Y-shaped road in front of a mountain range with three prominent peaks. Near the bottom of the left corner he drew a small airfield. The gas station at the Y had a trailer parked beside it. There was a residential area near the right foothill of the mountains, and a narrow road veering off from the main road. At the end of this road was a falling-down cabin, its yard filled with junked appliances and an old trailer. Stacy's body, he pointed out, lay in a ditch nearby, covered with leaves. Hurkos circled three areas on a Washington map—all of them near Everett in Snohomish County, just north of King County, and, incidentally, close to the Raintree. He instructed Peg Haley to check the area near Lake Stevens first.

As soon as Peg Haley and Polly Gunderson returned from Los Angeles on August 2 their family and friends geared up for another search. They located a pilot in the Lake Stevens area who studied the map for a few seconds and then said he knew the area depicted on the hand-drawn map: "It's Highway 92 leading to Granite Falls!"

The searchers headed into the brush. They worked until dusk and found . . . nothing. The next day it was the same story. For the next three weekends they searched every side road in the Granite Falls area and found no trace of at all of Stacy. They still felt sure that Hurkos held the answer, but the area circled was just too big.

Peter Hurkos had assured Peg Haley that if Stacy wasn't found by October, he would personally come to Seattle and lead them to her. But when Peg phoned him for more information he never returned her calls.

For a long time Stacy Sparks's family went out on searches for her, given new hope each time by psychics who were sure they could "see" her body.

The police, too, thought twice that they had, indeed, found Stacy.

On September 26, 1979, the skeletonized body of a young girl was found off a dirt road in Kent, Washington. Dental records proved it was not Stacy, but Jacqueline Plante, a visitor to Washington from Utah, who had been missing since early June. On December 7th, Bellevue, Washington, police found a skeletonized body in that city, which was much closer to the area cited by psychics. Dental comparisons showed this second tragic victim to be fifteen-year-old Teresa Sterling, a runaway from Georgia. With the discovery of each body Stacy Sparks's family spent anxious days until they learned that neither of the victims was their daughter.

One man was convicted of the murder of Jackie Plante, and another in the killing of Teresa Sterling.

A year later police were no closer to knowing what had happened to Stacy Sparks than they were a day after she vanished. It was not from lack of trying. There simply was no place else to go with the investigation, nothing beyond asking for help from the public. After a while the posters and fliers with her picture became weather-worn and tattered. It was hard to make out what they said:

> Stacy Sparks is five feet two inches tall and weighs between 115 and 120 pounds. Her eyes are deep brown. Her hair is probably blond or its natural light brown. Her birthday is January 25, 1961. Her work experience is principally as a waitress. If she is alive, she may well be in Hawaii.
>
> Stacy's car is pictured on this flier. There are black louvers on the rear hatchback window, and there is a tassel hanging from the rearview mirror. The license number is Washington UCX-487. The VIN number is VIN.7H24U84300830.

Something terrible had happened to Stacy Sparks; that seemed almost certain. It was possible that she had walked away from the lights and laughter in the Raintree tavern on that warm Monday night in July, 1979, out to a dark parking lot where she met someone she couldn't get away from. It was less likely that she picked up a hitchhiker who was not what he seemed. It was doubtful—but possible—that she had undergone a psychic shock that caused amnesia. It was vaguely within the realm of possibility that she chose to leave for reasons of her own.

There are thousands of young women who vanish every year, and many of them are never found. Stacy Sparks was not to be one of those missing forever. She disappeared on a Monday—July 9, 1979—and she was found on a Monday—September 14, 1981—two years and two months after she vanished. She was where she had been all along, where no one had ever searched.

Seattle, Washington, is flanked to the west by Elliott Bay and to the east by Lake Washington. Until 1940, when the first Lake Washington Floating Bridge was dedicated, there was no way to get to eastern Washington from Seattle without driving *around* the huge lake. Lake Washington is so deep that a standard bridge wouldn't work, and so the very innovative floating bridge was constructed. The Lacey V. Murrow Bridge floated on pontoons and had a bulge in the middle that opened to allow small craft and sailboats to pass through.

The Floating Bridge was nowhere near Stacy Sparks's route from Lynnwood to West Seattle along I-5; she would have had to go exactly opposite the direction of her destination to come anywhere near the bridge that led to Mercer Island and then on to Bellevue along the I-90 freeway.

And she had done just that. For what reason, no one will ever really know.

On Monday, September 14, 1981, the Floating Bridge was closed from midnight on while workmen removed the bulge in the center and replaced it with a straight section. Any number of fatal accidents had been blamed on that bulge, which had caught a number of motorists unaware in the forty years it existed. Workmen for the General Construction Company were hooking cables to the new straight portion of the bridge when they found something snagged on the bulge cables far beneath the surface of Lake Washington.

Lake Washington is very cold and very deep. In its deepest regions the bottom is two hundred feet down. Under the bulge in the bridge the steel cables stretched at least eighty feet into the dark water.

Divers found what was snagging their cables. It was a blue car with white racing stripes. A Plymouth Arrow. At 8:25 a.m. it was winched to the surface by a crane on a barge and taken to the west end of the bridge.

There was a body inside, a body wearing blue jeans, a shirt with a rose, and a necklace with two carved roses. It would take a check of dental records, however, to be certain that this was Stacy Sparks.

The Plymouth Arrow had extreme front-end damage, which included sharp dents in both front wheels. The roof was smashed flat, almost to the top of the seat. The driver would almost certainly have died instantly as the car became airborne, flipped over, and cleared the concrete bridge rail. Water can be as hard as steel on impact.

It was Stacy they had found. The license plate and the VIN (Vehicle Identification Number) matched her missing car. Dental records matched the remains exactly. There was some sense of closure, some relief, finally, for her parents. "I know now that Stacy wasn't murdered," Peg Haley said, "that she wasn't tortured . . . that she didn't suffer."

But the questions remained. They probably always will. Was it raining so hard that Stacy became confused and turned off on a ramp that led to the Floating Bridge? That seems unlikely; she knew the trip to West Seattle by heart.

Had she been more affected by the few beers she drank at the Raintree than anyone realized? Possibly.

But there was the most puzzling element of all. When the Washington State Patrol reconstructed the accident—and they did believe it was an accident—they determined that Stacy had not been headed eastbound *toward* Mercer Island when she hit the bulge at high speed; she had been coming *from* Mercer Island and was heading toward Seattle. Westbound.

One possible answer is that the older man that Stacy had talked about to her friends lived on the Mercer Island side of the bridge, and that she had decided on a sudden whim to go to meet him—instead of meeting her young boyfriend in West Seattle. If Stacy Sparks did take that detour, if she did see the unknown man, had they had an argument? Had she been upset when she raced back across the bridge, her vision blurred by tears and the pelting rain? This was pure conjecture. No one would know that but the man himself—if, indeed, such a man existed.

Kenneth Irwin, the Washington State trooper who investigated the accident two years after it occurred, set an arbitrary time for the crash—2 a.m. on July 10, 1979—mostly because that was when the summer storm was at its peak. And that was the time the bridge had had the least traffic. In truth, no one saw it happen. No one could really know the exact time Stacy lost control of her car.

Irwin estimated that Stacy's car had been traveling well in excess of the forty-five-mile-an-hour speed limit when it failed to negotiate the bulge and jumped the concrete bulkhead on the bridge's north side. It hit nothing above the waterline. That would account for the absence of broken glass or any other debris on the bridge; that was why no one was aware at the time that there had even *been* an accident. But it *was* an accident—not a murder. Had anyone else been in the car with Stacy, he—or she—would have ridden to the bottom of Lake Washington, too. No one could have jumped out before the car cleared the cement railing.

The Arrow, like its namesake, had taken wing for a short, soaring space before it plunged down and down and down into the depths of Lake Washington, crushed like a tin can.

Many homicides are carried out so cleverly that they are written off as accidents. In the case of Stacy Sparks, what had been investigated as a murder was, in truth, only a tragic accident.

The Last Letter

No one who knew them through the decades of their relationship would ever deny that Bill and Jackie were in love. Their years together—and apart—were full of longing and wonder, jealousy and ecstasy. They were, indeed, two people who embodied the kind of emotion we hear about in love songs. Songs of love lost, love regained, and sometimes love destroyed—forever. But popular songs seldom mention a kind of supremely selfish "love" that can hurt innocent people and smear even the most romantic love affair with blood.

This story haunts me. Why? I suppose it is because the ending was so pointless, so totally unnecessary. Quite probably thirty years of happiness were thrown away because one of the partners did not believe in love. And the other believed—and trusted—in love too much. There is an old adage: "Be careful what you wish for—because you just may get it, but your wish will never come about exactly as you planned . . ."

Detectives from the Bellevue, Washington Police Department, of necessity, viewed the "Bill and Jackie" story first as a forensic puzzle. Only later could they allow themselves to delve into the reasons why Bill and Jackie Brand's romance ended as it did. They had a bit of a head start. One of the principals in the love affair had written their story, possibly believing that theirs was a relationship too momentous not to be shared with the world, possibly feeling the need to explain what was unthinkable.

In 1958 Bill Brand lived in Fairbanks, Alaska, with his wife and small daughters. He was in his early thirties, a tall, sandy-haired man who was handsome in a rugged way that seemed to fit Alaska. He was involved in lumber and construction and was already on his way to a considerable fortune. Brand had had the foresight to see where Alaska was headed and had dug himself a solid foothold in the building supply business there. When Alaska became the forty-ninth state on January 3, 1959, Bill already had it made. The largest state in the union had the smallest population, but it was about to boom, and housing was in great demand. As the years went by Bill Brand would become an extremely wealthy man.

Jackie Lindall* was seventeen, pretty, dark-haired, and slender when she met Bill Brand for the first time. She had moved from her Minnesota home to go to the University of Alaska in 1958, leaving behind small-town life and a large, loving family. She had a sister two years older than she, and two brothers, seven and twelve years younger. Although it was hard for her to travel so far from home, a spirit of adventure burned within Jackie. And Alaska was about as adventurous a spot as Jackie could imagine.

Wherever she went, Alaska—or rather, what it meant to her—would always call her back and back and back.

Her family didn't worry about Jackie as much as they might have because she was going to live with the Brand family instead of in a college dormitory or apartment. She would be a nanny for the little girls and help around the house to pay for her room and board.

Bill Brand apparently found the willowy teenager absolutely enchanting. To a seventeen-year-old a man over thirty must have seemed far removed from her social sphere, and yet it is likely she found him a little exciting; he was dynamic, and much smoother than the college boys she met. Indeed, Jackie may well have had a crush on Bill.

707

Whatever Jackie's and Bill's relationship may have been in the late 1950s and early 1960s, nothing openly marred the surface of the Brand marriage. Although his work meant he was always busy and often away from home, Bill was a devoted father, and seemingly as devoted a husband. He and his wife had a third baby girl.

After a few years of living with the Brands Jackie graduated from college and returned to Minnesota. Jackie moved out of Bill's life. Or rather, she tried to. Bill Brand always managed to know where Jackie was and what she was doing. He never really let her go.

With her personality, poise, and beauty, Jackie Lindall quickly found a job with Northwest Orient Airlines. Jackie went through flight attendant's training in Minneapolis in 1962. (She was called a stewardess in those days.) Her first home base was in Washington, D.C.—all the way across the country from Bill Brand.

In 1963 Jackie shared an apartment with another stewardess from her training class, and she was caught up with a new social life, dating, and making friends. She refused, however, to date pilots or other airline employees. More experienced stewardesses had warned her that it usually brought only grief. But then, she didn't need to; Jackie met scores of men on every flight. One businessman, Dan Barret,* who flew regularly between Detroit and Washington, introduced her to his roommate in Washington, D.C., Cal Logan.* Jackie fell in love with Cal, and they were soon engaged. For a while she was able to relegate her life in Alaska to her past, and she was excited about her wedding plans.

Only months before her wedding day Cal Logan was killed in an automobile accident. That was the first time violent death wiped out Jackie's plans. Dan Barret had lost his best friend, and Jackie had lost the man she planned to marry. They comforted each other, and it strengthened their platonic friendship. For years Dan was special to Jackie—but she never loved him in a romantic way.

Whatever might have happened between Jackie and Bill back in Fairbanks, it was pivotal in his life. He had never forgotten Jackie, and he missed having her as a part of his life. She was no longer a schoolgirl. She was a grown woman now, and drifting farther and farther away from him. He had no intention of letting that happen. Bill Brand wanted Jackie—possibly he had from the first time he saw her—and he detested the thought that another man might touch her. Even though he remained in his marriage he kept tabs on her, calling her often, questioning her when she wasn't home for his evening calls. Brand comforted himself for a long time, convinced Jackie wouldn't have sex with anyone else because she had such a solid midwestern religious background.

It did not seem to occur to him that an affair with a married man— himself—might be far more alien to her moral upbringing than intimacy with a single man.

Jackie's friendships with the other flight attendants were solid, and she would keep in touch with many of them for the next two decades, just as she remained close to the friends she had grown up with in Minnesota, and with her brothers and sisters and parents. She was a very loving young woman; Jackie was "down-to-earth," according to friends. Despite her tragically short engagement to Cal Logan, most of her close girlfriends had realized even then that Jackie's real longing was for Bill Brand. Few of them would ever actually meet the man Jackie spoke of in such glowing terms.

Jackie compared every man she met to Brand, and none measured up. But instinctively she tried to pull away from the big man she had left behind in Alaska. Although she had probably loved Bill Brand since she was in college, Jackie wanted security. She wanted a home and a husband who could support her without worrying about bills. She had exquisite taste, and she hoped one day to be able to have the home she wanted without considering the cost.

Bill had taught her that. He had told Jackie over and over that *she* was like royalty—that she should never consider riding a bus or streetcar. That was for ordinary women, and she was special. She never believed that part—but subtly, cunningly, Bill had instilled in Jackie an appreciation of and desire for expensive clothes and lovely homes.

After Cal died Jackie began to date often, but in the back of her mind there was always Bill. And Bill was not free to marry her. Bill Brand was not an option for her.

After she had spent a few years in the East, Northwest Airlines transferred Jackie to Seattle. It was a promotion; now she would have a chance to fly to the Orient as well as the States. One of her best friends was transferred with her. They had lived a block apart in Washington, D.C., and they were delighted and surprised to find they had taken apartments just as close in Seattle.

Bill Brand would later claim that Jackie became pregnant in the summer of 1965. He suspected the father was either an Alaska state trooper or an airline pilot. He told people the "pregnancy" was aborted while Jackie was on a flight to Tokyo. The alleged father of that child was rumored to have committed suicide in Anchorage, Alaska. It was all very nebulous. It may have been true; more likely it was a vicious figment of Bill Brand's jealous imagination. Years later, as he looked back upon his life and Jackie's, he saw indiscretions that had never happened, and he hated vehemently anyone he thought might have come between him and Jackie.

Friends who knew Jackie Lindall since kindergarten and others who remember a younger Bill Brand believe the physical affair between Jackie and Bill probably began in the mid-sixties. He was, of course, still married, but his obsession with Jackie had continued undeterred by time or distance.

Although far apart in miles, Alaska and Seattle seem right next door to northwesterners, and commuters fly back and forth all the time. Brand frequently had business in Seattle, or he *made* business in Seattle. Jackie was flying out of Seattle, and he saw her as often as he could, seething with jealousy over her other suitors.

And still he did not plan to divorce his wife or leave his children. He offered Jackie nothing more than an affair. For the ultimately selfish man, it worked out well. Jackie would have her job to fill much of her time, and she would wait for Bill in the meantime. Brand couldn't see that she might need a life beyond that; he liked the thought of her in her Seattle apartment, waiting for his call.

He made vague promises to Jackie from time to time. Someday, perhaps, they *could* be married, but not until his children were grown. He missed Jackie when he was away from her, but he was a very busy man, continuing to build his fortune in Alaska's booming construction era.

For Jackie it wasn't as easy; she wanted a *life*. She could see her twenties passing by with no man who was really her own, and she dreaded spending her life that way. Bill was always showering her with presents—but presents were cold comfort over lonely weekends.

Friends remembering Jackie recall that, of all things, Jackie seemed to need security the most—emotional security and financial security. Bill Brand was not in a position to give her either.

At that point, in the mid-sixties, Jackie probably truly loved Bill Brand. She clung to the same dream every "other woman" has—that someday Bill would be divorced and they would marry. He was even more attractive at forty than he had been when she first moved into his home, and he was quite powerful in the business world, making money hand over fist. As one of Jackie's friends said later, Jackie would have left any man for a chance to marry Bill Brand. "He personified all the things she admired in a man."

Jackie turned down scores of dates to keep her promise to be faithful to Bill.

But finally there were just too many days and too many long nights alone. Maybe Jackie intended to force Bill's hand; maybe not. More likely, in the end she simply couldn't bring herself to break up another woman's home. Jackie met another man, a good man who was free to be with her. Jud Jessup* was divorced and had custody of his two children. Worst of all for Bill Brand, Jessup lived on the East Coast.

By 1967 Jackie was twenty-six, and she had decided to marry Jud and help him raise his youngsters. It was a decision that Bill Brand deplored. He was incredibly vicious when he spoke of Jessup and his children. He could not imagine why Jackie would leave him to raise what he termed "another man's idiots." As he remembered the situation, the events were cunningly rearranged to suit his obsession. It was almost as if he believed that Jackie had been somehow *forced* to marry Jud Jessup, and that Bill had tried vainly to save her.

Bill Brand was a man who kept diaries, marked dates on calendars; writing down his thoughts helped him remember those things that were of great importance to him, both in business and in his relationships. He would one day write a long, long letter, the pages chronicling so many years of his feelings for—and about—Jackie. Many of his recollections were about the many rendezvous the pair had had.

During October, 1967, Jackie and I got together in Anchorage. I was there on business and she was on her way through on a trip to the Orient, and when she arrived, she found that we were staying at the same hotel. So she left word for me to call her. I did, and that night we went to dinner together at the hotel. Luckily, the next day her flight was delayed for twelve hours which gave her the chance to recover and we made plans to meet in Portland on December 12th.

I arranged for a suite at a hotel in Portland for that day, and that evening Jackie flew in from Seattle after having worked a flight from Tokyo that day. She was absolutely exhausted. . . . We went back to the room, she in one [bed] and I in another, and she immediately fell asleep. . . . During dinner that night at the hotel, I told her that I really loved her. There wasn't much of a response to that, but that night she came into the room where I was sleeping and laid down on the bed next to me and asked, "What are we going to do?" I knew that she was to be married, but it wasn't until then that I understood that the date was hard and fast.

Brand would not accept Jackie's marriage to another man.

The next day she turned, put her arms around me and told me that she felt she was in love with me . . . we had decisions to make.

My position was that I would proceed immediately with the business of a divorce because nothing would ever be the same between my wife and I. She objected to that, saying that was nothing for me to do because the girls were too young and their absence would make my life miserable for me. The indignity of aborting her wedding plans and the subsequent explanation to her family were repulsive to her, so much so that she would rather cast her lot with a life of unhappiness. It later developed that the decision was almost disastrous. . . .

Bill Brand had waited too long to be with Jackie. She had simply decided to take her life off hold and marry a man who loved her and was free to do something about it.

She must have had doubts. After a decade of being bound to Bill she must have wondered if she was doing the right thing. Even as she prepared to marry another man, Jackie gave Bill a silver letter opener inscribed "Somewhere, Someday, Somehow." Bill interpreted that to mean they would eventually be together.

Maybe she did mean it that way. Maybe she knew how Bill was hurting over her defection from their relationship, and she wanted to ease his pain. But she still went ahead with her wedding.

"The saddest day of my life took place while I was a continent away," Bill Brand wrote of Jackie's wedding day. "The marriage wasn't going to amount to anything from the beginning."

Despite the fact that she was married to someone else, Bill called Jackie Jessup three times a week. He gloated, "She was in his bed, and I was on his phone talking to her three times a week. . . ."

Jackie's best stewardess friend was married in late 1969, with Jackie as matron of honor. Bill planned to fly to meet her, but at the last minute his business in Fairbanks "went to hell" and he didn't go. He reminisced later, "Jackie felt betrayed. That pack (her new family) had been giving her fits, and she badly needed a renewal of hope."

That was only Bill's perception, and in retrospect at that. Jackie's stepchildren liked her, and would always remember her as "a 'mother' and our friend."

Bill considered Jessup a monster and his children "genetic cripples." They were impediments to his true love for Jackie. He fought constantly to break up her marriage. He urged Jackie to meet him and arranged to fly back to her home on the eastern seaboard to see her. In Bill Brand's mind Jackie was being driven nearly insane by her marriage and her separation from him. In actuality it was quite the other way around.

If Jackie was upset, it was undoubtedly because she was being pulled in two directions. Now that he could not have her, Bill Brand *would* not let go.

In October, 1973, Bill Brand was forty-eight years old. He was admitted to a Seattle clinic for a procedure designed to prevent a stroke. Tests had shown that his left carotid artery—the artery that carries blood to the brain—was ninety percent occluded (blocked). He had episodes of tingling and numbness in his hand and trouble with one eye. There was the very real possibility that his mental functions might also be compromised by the lack of oxygen to his brain. Delicate surgery removed the fatty plug that blocked the vital artery, and he recovered uneventfully.

In the years to come Brand would have frequent checkups and take a vast array of medications—to help him sleep, to relieve depression, and to control ulcers. He was clearly not a happy man; his ailments were those often triggered by anxiety and depression.

How could he be happy? Jackie was married to someone else, and even though so many years had passed he still struggled to find a way to bring her back to him. He called and wrote and sent tapes, cajoling, pleading.

She still cared about him, as much as she fought it. Time after time Bill's campaign to draw her back worked. He sent Jackie money to come to Seattle to talk with him in April of 1974. He rented a suite at an expensive hotel; he always got accommodations in the very best hotels. But he recalled later that Jackie's visit was not as wonderful as he had expected. Bill was convinced he had caught her in an assignation with another man—an airline friend she had known for years. Bill Brand was becoming shockingly paranoid in his thinking, at least when it came to Jackie. There were so many men he suspected of being Jackie's lovers.

There were not enough hours in the day for Jackie to have had that many lovers.

One day Bill Brand would document his years with the woman he loved so possessively in a missive he called "The Bill and Jackie Letter."

"The reason that I mention this incident," he wrote many years later, "is because she displayed a vulgar capability that was so totally foreign to me according to my moral values."

Bill Brand was so righteous. He saw sin wherever he looked—if Jackie was involved. In reality, he manufactured sin out of whole cloth. Except for her meetings with Bill, Jackie was faithful to her husband.

"The week was memorable," he wrote of the 1974 visit, "and was the foundation for our being together. There were no hard and fast dates set because things in Fairbanks needed attention but things in Maryland were coming apart pretty fast by then and arrangements in Seattle were in order. . . ."

Bill constantly urged Jackie to leave Jessup as soon as possible and to come to Seattle to live. He would set her up in an apartment and take care of her completely. Then, in time they would be married.

Jackie Jessup was, as the song goes, "Torn Between Two Lovers." She was thirty-three years old in 1974, and whichever man she chose to be with she fully expected to *stay* with until she died. If she expected to have children of her own, she didn't have that many years left. Bill clearly wasn't going to go away unless she did something convincingly decisive. But did she truly *want* him to go away? She loved Jessup—but not with the fiery passion she felt for Bill. She had been in love with Bill for so long that he was part of who *she* was. And now, for the first time, he was promising that he really would marry her. He tugged at her continually, and finally he pulled her free of her husband.

He wrote proudly in "The Bill and Jackie Letter" that he had convinced her to leave Jessup and her stepchildren, and how "re-lieved" she was when he instructed her to be in Seattle by November, 1975.

Jackie really had no choice at that point. Jud Jessup had finally discovered Jackie's other love when he found a bunch of cassette tapes with long messages to Jackie from Bill. Not surprisingly, he gathered up his youngsters and left.

"He had gone into a rage and otherwise behaved like a jerk," Brand wrote happily. "He must have realized long before that his days with her were limited. . . ."

Jackie's marriage had lasted a little more than seven years. In reality, it never stood a chance. By sheer force of will Bill Brand had not allowed it to succeed.

Bill Brand was gleeful. He had won. He had his Jackie back. She packed her things and shipped them to Seattle.

"Then she got herself on an airplane and headed to Seattle to arrive here late in the day on November 1st. There was a suite ready for us at the hotel. We needed to stay there until we decided just where in the Seattle area it would be that we wanted to live."

Bill was a bit premature. They would not actually live together for a long time. Bill Brand was still married and living with his family in Fairbanks.

But he had wrenched Jackie free of her marriage, and she was once again waiting for his visits. Now she no longer had her career as a flight attendant to fill her time. Bill could not be with her for Christmas or New Year's, of course; he had his family. He bought her a ticket to fly to Minneapolis to be with her family.

Bill Brand had become her sole support. Jackie was his mistress. She loved him. She was faithful.

On November 14, 1977, Jackie Jessup moved into the apartment where she would live for the next eight years. It was a lovely three-bedroom unit in Bellevue, Washington, one of Seattle's posher bedroom communities. She signed the lease and listed her occupation as a "buyer's assistant" for a Fairbanks, Alaska, corporation. It was, of course, one of Bill Brand's corporations. In reality, Jackie didn't work at all.

She was a quiet tenant, and her landlady soon became familiar with the handsome man who often spent time with Jackie. "It was my observation over these years that Jackie was beautifully courted by Bill Brand," she recalled. "Although I didn't know the Brands socially, I was never aware of any domestic strife between them. I knew Bill Brand as a very gentle man with a gruff exterior."

Bill Brand still nursed his paranoid fantasy that Jackie was not true to him. For all his blustery gloating, he felt deep down that his main attraction for Jackie was his wealth. He believed that she wouldn't stay with him unless he could support her better than any other man. It was a premise that wasn't even remotely true. He was her "prince," her perfect man. She adored him. All Jackie sought was honesty and commitment.

The two things Bill would not give her.

Brand later recalled:

> During late February, 1980, Jackie and I had some problems communicating. I wasn't spending enough time in Seattle, and according to her, I wasn't moving fast enough to get things done in Fairbanks so that we could get on with our lives. I was in my office one afternoon when the phone rang. She was on it, asking if I was sitting down because she had just checked into an inn in Fairbanks. The purpose of the visit was to talk and get our stuff together. She stayed overnight and the better part of the next day, and then left for Seattle.

The problem was simple enough. Bill Brand wouldn't make the break with his wife. Even so, he was furiously jealous when he found a rough draft of a letter on one of Jackie's legal tablets. She had written to a man—a friend of one of her brothers—thanking him for buying her dinner when they met accidentally in the airport. This had been the night she returned from her trip to urge Bill to divorce his wife. In the letter she invited the friend, his wife, and his daughter to stay in her apartment in Bellevue if they ever found themselves passing through Seattle.

"I never mentioned anything about it to her," Brand wrote in his "Bill and Jackie Letter"—"but it's another example of her morally loose style of life and her need to have something going on. I have no way of knowing how often he stayed with her, but I do know that she's spectacular enough in bed that any man would rig more than one Seattle trip to be with her if he was invited."

Bill Brand saw shadows of sex everywhere. If Jackie went to the beach with a friend and her husband during the time Bill was home in Fairbanks, he imagined kinky threesomes. He even suspected Jackie of having incestuous relationships with a male member of her family. He perceived her hand touching a man's as she passed a cigarette lighter as an overtly sexual signal.

It was all in Bill's own distorted perception, but frightening in its intensity. As he wrote out his evaluation of Jackie's morals, the skewed convolutions of his thinking show in his tangled prose.

> She has always had traces of the hedonistic approach to things such as, "If it feels good and the consequences aren't

that bad, do it." Sex to some people is like shaking hands, no more consequential than that. The most disturbing matter to this is that while I have been aware of it, I have never exposed my resentment to her behavior, expecting to be accepted on a normal social and moral level, while, because she isn't going to say anything different, she doesn't, in fact, belong at *any* level. When it's considered the number of men she has had sex with in her lifetime and then demands and receives acceptance of a moral and social level that most people have to earn, there is something very wrong.

There *was* something very wrong. Jackie Jessup had no hint of the rage in her lover. Bill never mentioned his jealousy to her. He never gave her a chance to convince him of her fidelity, of the truth. Jackie didn't realize Bill considered her "morally loose"; she would have been appalled had she known what was really festering in Bill's mind.

Bill Brand finally obtained a divorce and came to Jackie at last a single man.

On April 23, 1982, almost a quarter of a century after they first met, Jackie Jessup and Bill Brand were married. When Jackie married Bill she virtually gave up friends, family, and all outside interests. Jackie's role—a role she accepted gladly—as defined by her bridegroom was to live for Bill, and only for Bill. Their life together, realized after many years of frustration, was supposed to be one long honeymoon; the peak phase of Bill Brand's ecstasy must never be allowed to settle into a pleasant, comfortable marriage. It must be romance, romance, romance.

A devastatingly impossible goal.

Bill finally moved into the Bellevue apartment he had rented for Jackie so many years earlier. He opened a business, Alaska Marketing Industries, and rented an office on 116th N.E. in Bellevue.

It should have been a happy ending. It was anything but.

Bill wanted to know where Jackie was every minute, and who she was talking to. He resented it if she spent too much time with anyone else—even her own family. She had made scores of friends—but Bill was annoyed when they passed through Seattle and called her. If she did arrange a brief lunch with a girlfriend, he paced and grumbled until she came home again. She always seemed to be on edge during those quick meetings, explaining that she had to hurry home. She was too jumpy to enjoy herself.

Bill's pervasive jealousy was ridiculous. Jackie loved him; she never cheated on him. The only thing that could have made her leave her marriage to Bill Brand would be her death. She had given up so much to be with him, and she appreciated what he had given up for her. A quarter of a century of longing had finally led to their marriage, and she treasured it above anything else.

Barring an accident, however, Jackie Brand wasn't likely to precede Bill in death; she was much younger than he was—forty-three to his fifty-nine—and it was Bill who had a number of health problems.

All things being equal, Jackie would outlive Bill. That was a possibility she had considered and found unimportant when she married Bill in 1982. Whatever time they might have together would be worth the pain of widowhood later.

On February 22, 1985, Bellevue Police Lt. S.M. Bourgette received a phone call from the police dispatcher. They had received a worried call from Regis Caulfield,* Bill Brand's insurance agent. Caulfield had been alerted by another business associate of Brand's, Thomas Donley.* Both men had reason to be concerned; they had each received long identical letters from Brand which also contained his last will and testament. Caulfield had only recently tried to talk Brand out of changing his will. Bill had wanted to exclude Jackie completely and leave everything to his daughters instead. Besides that, Bill Brand had taken out an additional half million dollars worth of insurance.

After they received the bizarre letters from Bill Brand both Donley and Caulfield had attempted to phone his apartment, but no one answered. They had then contacted the apartment house manager. The manager went to the Brand apartment and knocked, and finally Bill Brand, his hair tousled, had come to the door. He assured the manager everything was "fine." The manager hadn't seen Jackie Brand but reported back that nothing was wrong at the apartment.

Not satisfied, Regis Caulfield had driven to Bellevue. It was nearly 4:30 when he got to the Brands' apartment house. Both Jackie's and Bill's cars, a Plymouth Arrow and a Mercury Cougar, were parked outside. He knocked at their door, but no one answered. He went to the manager's office and used the phone there. This time Bill's answering machine picked up his call.

Worried, Caulfield had called the Bellevue Police Department. Both he and Tom Donley had received an odd ten-page typewritten letter, with "Bill and Jackie" scrawled in Brand's handwriting across the top. It was mimeographed, and it was a scalding exposé chronicling the couple's twenty-five-year relationship, but mostly decrying Jackie Brand's lack of morals and her betrayal of Bill. Even to a layman's perception the letter was sick and full of rage. It was as if Bill Brand had attempted to obliterate Jackie with words, revealing the most intimate things about her to virtual strangers.

But what alarmed Caulfield and Donley were not the slurs on Jackie's fidelity. The document had ended, "Inasmuch as my wife has died with me, I direct that she shall be conclusively deemed not to have survived me."

Lt. Bourgette and Patrol Officer Dennis Dingfield arrived at the Northside Apartments at 5:30 p.m. on February 22nd. The day had been gloomy and cloudy, and it was almost full dark out.

Regis Caulfield pointed out the Cougar and Plymouth Arrow parked in the lot. "The first time I looked through the window," Caulfield said, "I saw a glass with some liquor in it—when I came back twenty minutes later, it had been moved. Somebody's in there."

Bourgette and Dingfield noted that the Brands' apartment occupied the entire lower half of the south side of the building. Apprised of the floor plan of the apartment by the manager, they could see light in the kitchen, the dining/living room area, and a back bedroom. And then they saw someone walking around inside. It was a tall man with silver hair.

Dingfield asked the police dispatcher to try to call the apartment and gave both of Brand's numbers. The phone rang, but the man inside didn't answer. The second number was the answering machine. The dispatcher left a message that the police were outside and wanted Brand to come to the door. Bourgette, watching, saw the man inside walk to the machine, rewind it, and listen to the message.

But he did not come to the door. The lights inside were turned off now, save for one in the back bedroom and a stove clock light.

Bourgette called for backup and got a key from the manager. He could still see someone walking around inside the apartment, and then the tall man drinking from a glass.

He could not see a woman.

The Bellevue Police thought they might have a hostage situation, and they quickly surrounded the apartment building. Armed officers covered all its perimeters. Hostage negotiators Tom Wray, Cherie Bay, James Kowalczyk, and E.O. Mott, led by Lt. Mark Ericks, were briefed on the situation.

Thomas Donley, still surprised that he had been designated the executor of Bill Brand's estate, was convinced that Brand's will meant

"There will be no tomorrow." Caulfield, the insurance agent, knew very little about Bill Brand. He knew only that Brand was married to a second wife, that he was a "self-made, very hardheaded man" whose huge Alaska business empire had collapsed, and that all he had left were real estate holdings. Brand was described by both informants as an awesome drinker.

They waited. Minutes and hours passed. If Jackie Brand was inside, perhaps unable to get past Bill and come out, they didn't want to rush the apartment and give Brand a chance to carry out the promise in his "will."

Dennis Dingfield had not taken his eyes off the dimly lighted rooms inside the apartment for even a minute. After hours of observation he spotted the man inside crawling on his hands and knees. He would crawl for a while and then either lie or fall down. He appeared to be injured, or perhaps about to pass out from an overdose of some kind. He no longer looked capable of harming anyone. Bourgette called for an aid car.

At the same time, 2126 hours (9:26 p.m.), the TAG (Tactical Arms Group) team advised over police frequencies that there was a Code 4 at the Brand residence. Code 4 meant that everything was stable. It did *not* necessarily mean that everything had turned out well.

And then the TAG team went in. The man inside was standing as they went through the door, but only with great difficulty.

It was Bill Brand. He was alive—but extremely intoxicated.

Dennis Dingfield looked beyond the man frozen in the TAG team's flashlights. Dingfield's breath caught in his throat. Beyond the man, down the hallway, Dingfield spotted someone else, a woman lying motionless on the carpet. There was a dark red circle spread out around her body.

Too late.

Maybe it had been too late four hours earlier when they first surrounded the apartment building. It would have made the police feel better, somehow, to know that.

Dingfield cuffed Brand and led him to a police car to drive him back to headquarters, where E. O. Mott and Tom Wray were waiting to talk to him.

The investigation at the apartment was handed over to the detectives. Sadly, there was no hurry now.

Detective John Hansen had worked some of the more bizarre homicide cases that had begun to proliferate in Bellevue, the sleepy little town of the 1940s that had become one of Washington State's largest cities. Hansen was a stubborn, even dogged, instinctive investigator with flashes of brilliance. Tall and husky, with a voice like a bear, Hansen rarely smiled—unless the conversation turned to hunting dogs or his wife and children. In repose his face was handsome, but closed off; no one ever knew what he was really thinking.

Bill and Jackie Brand and John Hansen moved in different worlds, even though they all lived in Bellevue. Hansen was active in his church and spent whatever time he wasn't on duty with his family.

However, Hansen now began to be intimately acquainted with the tangled story of the Brands' lives, probably *better* acquainted than anyone else ever had. He would be the principal investigator assigned to Case No. 85-B-02260.

Hansen had stood outside the Brand apartment since 6:30. One paramedic from the Bellevue Fire Department had been allowed in to confirm that the woman inside was beyond human help, and then the scene had been sealed. As soon as Bill Brand was taken out Hansen and Detective Gary Felt stepped in.

The woman lay facedown on the hallway carpet. She wore a brown plaid skirt, a yellow silk blouse, and a brown corduroy jacket. She was also wearing high heels, stockings, and black gloves. Her makeup was perfect. A brown and tan comforter, which the fire department medic had lifted from her body, lay at her feet. A shiny briefcase was there, too.

John Hansen touched the calf of one of the woman's legs; the flesh was icy and stiff. The victim had been dead a long time. Hours at the very least.

The dead woman looked as though she had been headed for a trip; a camera on a red strap, a key ring, and a large blue purse rested on the floor beside her. A tweed suitcase was further down the hall. A capped container of tea lay where it had dropped from her hand. Her feet pointed toward the front door. She looked as if she had fallen straight backward, felled instantly by someone or something.

She could not have known she was about to die.

Although a layman might wonder why it was necessary to have permission to investigate what almost surely was a murder, the detectives needed a search warrant to move freely around the apartment. Hansen immediately listed his reasons for a search warrant and obtained one via telephone from District Court Judge Brian Gain. With this in hand Hansen and Detective Gary Felt began to search the apartment.

* * *

The apartment was impeccably furnished, as if it had been done by a designer—or by someone with natural talent and a loving hand. The living room was done in shades of red and white, with objets d'art, pillows, and paintings all carrying out the same theme.

Someone had apparently been sleeping on the floral and satin striped couch. There was a rumpled quilt there. A glass of scotch, its ice not yet melted, was leaving a ring on the shiny waxed surface of the teak coffee table. Beside the glass there was a cocked handgun. A .357.

Ironically, the walls of the hallway where Jackie Brand lay dead were hung with gentle pictures of children and fields of flowers. All the furnishings were expensive. All the pictures were of flowers and children and, of course, of Bill and Jackie.

Bill had been proud of his affluence and his expensive tastes; he had discussed that in "The Bill and Jackie Letter" that Regis Caulfield and Tom Donley had turned over to the investigative team. The letter would answer many questions, but it would leave more unanswered. Brand had written of the Bellevue apartment and of the time when Jackie first agreed to live there and wait for him to "take care of things in Fairbanks."

"We found the apartment that suited our needs, leased it, and headed for downtown Seattle to shop for the furniture to furnish it. On one day, we bought for three bedrooms, a devan [sic], patio furniture, and a new car. When we got home, she threw up because we spent so much money."

Bill Brand seemed to have liked to communicate by writing—of one kind or another. The apartment was littered with notes. Felt and Hansen gazed around the apartment and saw them. They were everywhere. Notes from Bill to Jackie hung from door jambs, and fluttered where they were taped on cabinets. Brand had even taped them to the wall above her body.

They were love notes of a sort. Some of them were requests for sex; others were weird affirmations of Brand's devotion to the woman who had apparently been his wife for almost three years, his lover for twenty.

One note dated February 11, 1985—ten days earlier—read: "My weekends are great because of you. Monday comes and that means I have to leave you—I hate that. I can barely wait for the next weekend. That tells you what my life is all about. Love is what you and I are all about and that's what makes us go. I'll see you this noon. Be kinky—wear it to lunch. Bill."

The detectives shook their heads. What had he meant? Probably some Frederick's of Hollywood piece of lingerie he had bought Jackie. If the note had been there ten days, that probably meant that no one but Jackie and Bill ever entered this apartment. They couldn't imagine that she would have left such an explicit note for someone else to read. She must have felt like a prisoner.

Hansen and Felt moved around the apartment. Hansen noted a scuff on the hallway of the kitchen area, just a slight gouge in the plasterboard, probably a bullet ricochet. He saw an ashtray and a calendar on the dining room table. Bending to read, he felt the hairs rise on the back of his neck. The last entry on the calendar was penciled neatly into the block for February 21st. Yesterday.

"Jackie passed away at 13:10 hrs."

There was a half-empty bottle of Johnnie Walker Red Label scotch and an empty bottle of Bulloch scotch in the kitchen, and at the other end of the counter a long row of vitamin bottles next to a pack of Winstons. That must have been Jackie Brand's choice. A last cigarette, a Winston, was stubbed out in a crystal ashtray, its filter scarlet with fresh lipstick.

Liquor, cigarettes, and vitamins. Everything in this place was a contradiction. Guns, flowers, blood, love notes.

Trying to look at it all rationally and with as little emotion as possible, John Hansen deduced what had probably happened. For whatever grotesque reason, Bill Brand had shot his wife in the back of the head as she was walking ahead of him toward the front door. The cup of tea in her hand indicated she had been totally oblivious to the danger behind her.

After she was dead Brand had apparently calmly jotted down the time of her death on his calendar, as if he were marking some business appointment.

Then he would have hit the scotch, trying, perhaps, to get the courage to shoot himself, too. He had indicated in the letters he sent out that they would *both* be dead by the time the letters reached their destinations. The .357 Magnum six-shot revolver was cocked and ready there on the coffee table, with three cylinder chambers empty.

Deputy Medical Examiner Corinne Fligner checked for the wounds of entry and exit. She determined that two .357 slugs had struck Jackie's head; one on the right side had entered between her ear and the top of the head and penetrated her brain. A fatal wound. At the back of the victim's skull a shot had simply grazed Jackie's head.

Barring an eyewitness, it is impossible to reconstruct *exactly* how any homicide occurs—but John Hansen could almost visualize what had happened here.

The location of the wound at the rear of the head—plus the gun debris that surrounded it—indicated that this was the first wound, fired from a short distance away. The shooter would have been just behind Jackie in the hall. This bullet appeared to have deflected off the back of her skull and lodged in the hallway ceiling directly ahead of her.

The direction of fire of the fatal wound was different. Its path went from front to back, right to left and very slightly downward.

When the first shot was fired and it grazed Jackie Brand's head its force would probably have spun her around to face the man with the gun. Her Bill.

The second bullet was fired from farther away but had pierced her brain, killing her instantly. Would she have had time to form a thought? Had she looked into her killer's eyes when she spun around?

No one would ever know.

At Bellevue police headquarters Detectives E. O. Mott and Tom Wray observed Bill Brand. His face was flushed, and he appeared intoxicated. He wore a white dress shirt with blue pin stripes, buttoned at the cuffs and tucked into his dark blue slacks. His clothing had clearly cost a great deal; the labels showed the garments had been purchased at Seattle's best stores. He was shoeless, but he wore dark socks.

Alone with the detectives in the interview room, Brand suddenly began talking about football and the Seattle Seahawks as if nothing unusual had happened at all. More likely, he didn't want to remember the tableau he had left behind in the apartment he shared with Jackie.

Mott introduced himself and Wray and waited for directions from Lt. Mark Ericks before they proceeded. The guy seemed so drunk, they wondered if they would be able to get any sense out of him. Ericks and John Hansen called from the crime scene to ask that Bill Brand's hands be "bagged" and that he remain handcuffed until a neutron activation analysis test could be performed to determine if he had indeed fired the .357. They also asked that a nitrate test be done to see what would show up on swabbings of his hands, and that a breathalyzer reading be taken before Wray and Mott proceeded with any questioning.

Gary Felt had advised Brand of his rights under Miranda before he was driven away from his apartment. However, when Brand suddenly blurted to Mott and Wray that he had shot his "beautiful wife," both detectives tried again to advise him of his rights to be absolutely sure that he understood.

Brand commented that he understood his rights but said he was quite willing to talk and answer questions. He said he was sorry for shooting his wife. He had shot her, he recalled, about noon the day before. She had been headed for the front door, and he was following her when he shot her twice. She had fallen to the floor, and he had left her there.

"Why did you kill her?" Mott asked quietly.

Brand did not answer directly.

"He only indicated that she was a very beautiful woman and that I wouldn't understand things about her, nor would I understand things about him," Mott wrote in his report.

"I got nothing to hide," Brand blurted. "I murdered my wife. I shot the most beautiful woman in the world."

And then he had begun to drink scotch.

Bill Brand was still drunk, twice as drunk as required in order to be considered legally drunk in the State of Washington. His blood alcohol was .20; his breathalyzer was .19.

He rambled on about killing his "beautiful wife," interspersing his memories of Jackie Brand's murder with a chillingly calm discussion of football. He shook his head back and forth, and his eyes filled with tears. He acknowledged that he was intoxicated and promised he would give a written statement when he sobered up—"tomorrow."

Brand stared at Detective Tom Wray and blurted that Wray looked just like a Seattle Seahawks football star. Then he sat silent for long minutes, tears welling up and beading at the corners of his eyes. Brand finally looked up at Wray and said, "I murdered my wife about twenty-four hours ago. I just got bombed—Johnnie Walker Red. . . . I used a .38 or a .357 and shot [pointing his left index finger under his chin]. I loaded five rounds—.38s, I think. There are three left, the gun's on the table, you know. . . . Who were those guys who barged into my home?"

Brand confided to Wray that he had kept drinking because that was the only way he could sleep. He had slept on the couch, waking up every three hours or so and drinking more.

"I can't believe I really messed things up. She didn't deserve this. . . ."

Bill Brand was coming down from his alcoholic binge, and he began to confront the horror of what he had done.

None of the detectives yet knew why.

Back at the Brands' apartment Hansen and Felt, along with Ericks,

Oliver, and a police photographer, worked until almost four in the morning gathering evidence.

Gary Felt found a single spent bullet lying on the ceiling light trim, just beyond where it had passed through the wall. They had to saw a square of plasterboard free to get at that one. Ericks discovered a small lead fragment on the hallway carpet. They knew that Brand had blown a .19 on the breathalyzer—that he had been legally intoxicated when he was arrested. But had he been intoxicated thirty-three hours earlier when Jackie Brand died?

The tenant who lived in the apartment above the Brands told Hansen and Felt that she had heard a "thud-like sound, like someone had dropped something heavy" the day before, confirming that Jackie had been dead more than twenty-four hours when police entered her home.

John Hansen realized he would have to work this case backwards. He knew who the murderer was; the killer had been waiting for the police. And the evidence they had gathered during the long night after Bill Brand was arrested only served to confirm what had happened. The question was why. Why on earth had Bill Brand shot his "beautiful wife" in the back of the head?

Some of the answers began to come in from a dozen or more people who had received "The Bill and Jackie Letter." With each passing day that monstrous document showed up in more and more mailboxes across the country. Bill Brand had spewed out his jealousy and suspicion, so long repressed, in the ugly letter, and then he had sent it to everyone he could think of that Jackie had known—her family, her friends, even men he suspected had cuckolded him. It was not enough that he had killed Jackie; he had wanted to destroy her image, too. He had tried to wipe away every trace of the real, loving woman. Most of those who received the letter were horrified and sickened. Some were disgusted. Some—who had barely known Jackie Brand—were merely bewildered.

In talking with her relatives and friends, John Hansen found nothing to substantiate Jackie's alleged infidelities. Rather, friends who had received the letter gave statements that were just the opposite. Whenever they had come to Seattle and tried to spend some time with Jackie, her ex-stewardess friends said, she was always looking at her watch, anxious to get back to Bill. On the very rare occasions when they did meet Bill he was pleasant enough, but disinterested, obviously bored with their company.

"Jackie told me Bill unplugged their phone—so they wouldn't be bothered by outsiders," one woman remarked.

Bill had cloistered Jackie, keeping her just for himself, but she hadn't seemed to mind it. Hansen didn't find one witness who could remember that Jackie ever complained about her husband's suffocating affection. She still loved him. Nor could Hansen find anyone who believed Jackie had cheated on Bill Brand.

Two of Jackie's girlfriends had spoken to her a day or so before she died, and she had told them that Bill was going to fly to Alaska on the 21st—and that she would be taking him to the airport. That made sense. The suitcase found next to Jackie's body was packed with men's clothing.

Hansen read "The Bill and Jackie Letter" again and again. It was apparent, even with Brand's exaggerations, that the two had been a part of each other's lives for a long, long time.

They had, indeed, finally been married. Happy ever after.

It wasn't going to be easy for Hansen to ferret out what had gone wrong. Sobered up in jail, Bill Brand declined to talk. He would only say—as if John Hansen could give him some answers—"I'd just like to understand why it all happened."

Hansen was silent, and the room seemed to hum with tension. If anyone should know why it happened, it was the man in jail coveralls, the man who had known Jackie for almost three decades. But Bill Brand just shook his head as if he, too, was bewildered. Perhaps he was. Perhaps he was beginning to try to save his own skin.

Finally Brand sighed and said, "I'll be able to sort it all out in a few hours." And then he said he wanted an attorney. John Hansen ended the interview.

As John Hansen interviewed Jackie's friends and Bill Brand's business associates he was told that Brand had once been extremely wealthy in Fairbanks. At some point, however, his fortune had begun to slide. He had suffered severe business reversals in the late seventies when high interest rates began to cripple the construction business. Bill Brand had finally been forced to file for three separate bankruptcies—a personal bankruptcy due to his guarantees to his bank and supplier debts on behalf of his companies, and two business bankruptcies. Along with his own financial disaster, Brand's first wife sacrificed most of her holdings to settle Brand's debts.

From 1977 on, Bill Brand had suffered continual financial reverses. His vast fortune dwindled. The Alaskan oil pipeline had gone on line in 1975, and Brand had counted on a natural gas pipeline to follow. It never happened, though, and interest rates kept climbing.

Amid the ashes of what had once been a thriving business Bill divorced his first wife, moved to Seattle, married Jackie, and began a business that was scarcely more than a front to conceal his growing desperation. He had begun with high hopes that he could earn a good living again by helping Washington businesses that wanted to branch out into Alaska. He still had savvy; he still had contacts. But the only real money Brand had coming in was from leases he held in Alaska.

Jackie had no idea how bad things were. Bill had always showered her with jewelry and presents, and he worried that she would leave him if she found out how close he was to financial disaster. So he didn't tell her. Even though he wasn't doing any business at all, he left their apartment each day, carrying a briefcase. At the office he phoned friends or read magazines. Sometimes he chatted with people in neighboring offices. In truth, Bill simply marked time until he could rush home to Jackie.

If only he had confided in her, she would have understood.

Jackie knew they were living off his prior investments, but Bill had always had so much money, she assumed he had a stake that would see them through any hard times.

But failure bred failure. Bill Brand, stressed to the breaking point by his business losses, by the fact that he had almost reached the limit on his many credit cards, by his overriding fear that he would lose Jackie, became impotent.

Although she had seldom confided in anyone about her marriage, Jackie did mention Bill's sexual problems to one of her two Seattle friends. She also said it was no big deal. "I like so many other things about my Bill that it really does not matter to me."

One friend told John Hansen that Jackie Brand had always struck her as a woman so straight and puritanical that she was "almost sexless," and that she couldn't imagine Jackie in the role of the harlot Brand described in his final letter. No, she assured Hansen, a husband who could no longer make love wouldn't have been the end of the world for Jackie. Not at all.

But it had been for Brand. He had consulted sex therapists, trying to regain his potency. Hansen found a desk planner in Brand's office that went back two years, and its pages were full of coded notations about business meetings and about sex. He had listed both his failures and his successes. Bill Brand had been obsessed with his sexual performance. Perhaps in an attempt to prove himself, he had been unfaithful to Jackie, even during the times in his marriage when he had accused *her* of cheating on him.

Bill Brand's sexual notations and the derogatory notes about Jackie were all written in red ink. Every sexual encounter, however brief, had been noted in Brand's books. There were also a number of references to pornographic movies Brand had seen, right down to the titles and the dates he had viewed them.

Along with all of this Hansen read through medical records that showed that Bill Brand had consulted physicians more and more frequently, worried about his eyes, his lungs, his heart, his blood pressure. The business and sexual performance strain Brand felt had quite clearly converted into physical symptoms. Beyond that, there was the very real possibility that Brand *was* falling apart physically. He overindulged in everything; that had worked when he was younger, but he was almost sixty, and his body was failing him.

It was easier now for Hansen to see what had gone wrong. Bill Brand had feared he was losing those things that *he* perceived Jackie wanted from him—money and sexual performance. He was no longer the vigorous young man she remembered from 1958.

Brand had been gripped in a nightmarish midlife crisis blown all out of proportion. Despite all the years they had been involved with each other, Brand clearly hadn't known Jackie at all. He didn't know his wife well enough to trust her with his pain. And she obviously had known virtually nothing about what was going on in his head.

Something had to happen, some explosion, some end to it.

And tragically, something had.

John Hansen met another of Jackie's friends a week after Jackie died. This friend had known Jackie, she said, since they grew up together in Minnesota. She said she had not approved when Jackie married Bill. He had been overly possessive, and rude and overbearing toward her family and friends.

"I realized I could not enjoy Jackie's company when Bill was around. I resorted to meeting her for lunch or talking with her on the phone. But if you called and left a message for her with him, he wouldn't pass it on."

Jackie had called her friend at 5:00 p.m. on either the 19th or 20th of February to say that Bill was flying to Fairbanks on Thursday for business and wouldn't be back until Sunday. Jackie had invited her friend over to the Bellevue apartment for dinner, but the woman said she had other plans. They had agreed to meet at a restaurant for lunch the following week.

Instead of having dinner with Jackie Brand in her apartment on February 22, the friend had received "The Bill and Jackie Letter" by Priority Mail and read it with growing horror.

Two of Jackie's other friends said that they had always felt that Bill treated his wife tenderly. One friend had last seen Jackie only six days before she died. During this last meeting she had been a little surprised when Jackie commented, "I would like to have had somebody more handsome, but you know, Bill is so good to me."

It had been almost as if Jackie was trying to convince herself that she *had* made the right choice when she committed her life to Bill Brand.

This friend received the letter on the 22nd, too. "When I read it I knew instinctively that Jackie was dead; I immediately called their house, starting at 6:25. I left messages on the tape machine, but never got an answer. . . ."

February 21, 1985, had been Bill Brand's cutoff day. He had told Jackie he would be flying to Fairbanks. He bought a ticket, but he never really expected to fly to Alaska that day. He had hoped against improbable hope that he would make a deal, extend a lease, do *something* so that Jackie wouldn't know they were flat broke. If nothing happened by the 21st, they would both have to die. To Bill Brand it was that simple.

Nothing happened. All Brand's money was gone. He couldn't even charge a meal on a credit card. Jackie didn't know. He had lived a lie for so long that Bill was able on this one last day to paste a serene look on his face so that she *wouldn't* know. He mailed his hate-filled letters, a dozen or more of them.

There was no turning back now.

When Thursday morning came they both dressed. Jackie packed Bill's bag, stubbed out her cigarette, grabbed a cup of tea for the ride to the airport, and walked down the hall ahead of Bill on her way to drive him to SeaTac Airport.

Bill raised the gun. He fired. Jackie spun around, a look of pain and shock on her face, and Bill thought for one crazy second that she might be having one of her headaches. She had terrible headaches. He fired again.

And Jackie died. She never knew that Bill had no more money. For a man who had failed at so many things, Bill Brand had managed to succeed in this one tragic effort. This one useless, senseless act of cruelty.

Bill's note to his executor was succinct. He wrote that he had supported Jackie since November 1, 1975.

> It was Brand money that purchased all the furniture and appliances that are in the apartment. That includes a Maytag washer and dryer and a Sears freezer. . . . Also, I brought to the marriage a Unigard policy. . . . At the time we were married, I made my wife beneficiary, but on the 12th of

December, I signed the enclosed change of beneficiary statement. . . .

I should make clear to you . . . that my wife never adopted the Jessup children which will severely limit any claims they might think they have for any of her possessions. . . .

Bill had never accepted Jackie's stepchildren. He saw them, too, as interlopers, and he wanted to be sure they got nothing. He wanted his body cremated and sent to relatives. He left Jackie's remains to her family.

Bill Brand would have preferred that Jackie's family received nothing more. But John Hansen made a decision to give the victim's family the few pieces of gold jewelry that the medical examiner had removed from her body. That was all they would have left of her—that and the despicably savage letter from Bill.

It was over.

But of course, it really wasn't. Bill Brand had had the courage to kill the woman he claimed to love beyond life itself, but he had not had the courage to commit suicide.

John Henry Browne, his defense attorney, had Bill Brand examined by a psychiatrist to see if he had been, under the law, responsible for his actions on February 21, 1985.

Brand's diagnosis was that he was in the grip of a major clinical depression and that his responses were indicative of a narcissistic personality disorder. The former was understandable, given the circumstances; the latter had probably been a part of Bill Brand his whole life. The narcissist focuses always on himself. He is not crazy, either legally or medically; he simply cannot empathize with other human beings. He expects special favors and views those around him as extensions of himself—his to summon or to send away at will. Jackie's main job was to admire Bill and offer him unconditional support. As all narcissists do, Bill alternately overidealized and devalued her.

Jackie made Bill whole. He owned her, and he could not let her find out that he was a failure. "Unconsciously," his examiner wrote, "his need to kill her represented his need to protect himself from her harsh judgment. His life . . . was dominated by her attentions and approval, from which he sustained his major—if not his sole—emotional support."

No one would ever say that Jackie had not done her best to make Bill Brand happy. She shut herself away from everyone but Bill. It wasn't enough. Nothing ever could have been.

Bill Brand had a profound personality disorder, and he was

depressed—but he was not crazy. His examiner, a physician from the University of Washington School of Medicine, determined that Bill Brand had indeed been aware of his actions when he shot his wife in the head, and that he had had the ability to distinguish right from wrong. He could not hope to plead innocent by reason of insanity.

Bill Brand was convicted of second-degree murder in King County Superior Court Judge Jim Bates's courtroom in February, 1986. Sentencing was delayed as Defense Attorney John Henry Browne argued that medical tests had revealed a degree of brain damage. It was a defense that might have worked six or eight years later, when medical experts understood how devastating steroids could be to both the physical and mental health of men who took them. Bill Brand, panicked by impotence, had been taking steroids. He had also been taking Halcyon pills to sleep. The synergesic (cumulative) effect of combining those drugs—not to mention his excessive use of alcohol and other medications he was taking—might well have heightened the paranoia he felt over losing Jackie.

It would have been an interesting courtroom battle. Crimes committed while someone is under the influence of so-called recreational drugs and/or alcohol do not usually go unpunished. A "diminished capacity" defense doesn't usually work because the defendant has *chosen* to render himself less than capable. Might an insanity plea have convinced a jury, given the new information that has come out on steroids? Perhaps. But then there was the whole quarter of a century of background of Bill Brand's possessive hold over Jackie—a thread going back to the days when he was young and alert and vigorous.

At any rate, John Henry Browne, who is one of Seattle's most sought-after defense attorneys, did not yet have the final decision on the negative effects of steroids to argue with in 1986.

In the late summer of 1986 Bill Brand was sentenced to thirteen years in prison. Due to his increasingly poor health and diminishing mental capacity his sentence was appealed, and he was released on October 11, 1991. He was suffering from chronic obstructive pulmonary disease, better known as emphysema.

In the summer of 1993 Bill Brand, now sixty-eight, was admitted to the Veterans Administration Medical Center in Seattle. He died there at ten minutes past eleven in the evening on July 16th. Brand's death certificate listed him as a widower, and he was indeed that. Jackie had been dead for eight years.

Jackie had told him long before that they would ultimately be together. And they were—but for such a bitterly short time.

"Somewhere, Someday, Somehow" had come and gone.

A
FEVER
IN THE
HEART

and Other True Cases

Ann Rule's Crime Files: Vol. 3

For my friend
Olive Morgan Blankenbaker, born 1910,
and
for my mother,
Sophie Hansen Stackhouse, 1906–1995,
two brave women who lost their only sons
much too soon.

They taught me how to survive tragedy and loss
and how to grow old with grace and dignity.

Acknowledgments

This book has been more than twenty years in the making. Down through those years, so many people have helped me research, understand, and find documentation for *A Fever in the Heart* and the other five cases included. No one ever forgets murder cases where tragedy and betrayal are linked so closely, and time does little to dull the pain. Because of that, I particularly appreciate the many people who talked to me during the trial, and later searched their memories to help me.

And so I thank: Olive Blankenbaker, Vernon Henderson, Yakima County Prosecuting Attorney Jeff Sullivan and his staff, Mike McGuigan, the Yakima Police Department, Robert Brimmer, Mike Meyers, Marion Baugher, the late Mike Brown, Lonna K. Vachon, "Pleas" Green, the *Yakima Herald-Republic* (especially Librarian Donean Sinsel and Reporter James Wallace), the Yakima Valley Regional Library (especially Janna Davis and Jacob Warren), Mike Blankenbaker, and John Sandifer.

Chuck Wright, Joyce Johnson, the Seattle Police Department's Homicide Unit, Bernie Miller, Roy Moran, Benny DePalmo, the late Dick Reed and George Cuthill, the Pierce County, Washington, Sheriff's Office, Walt Stout, Mark French, the Oregon State Police, the Marion County, Oregon, Sheriff's office, Jim Byrnes, Dave Kominek, Mel Gibson, the King County Police Department, Ted Forrester, Roger Dunn, Columbia County, Oregon, District Attorney Marty Sells, Phil Jackson, Herb McDonnell, the Bellevue, Washington, Police Department, Gary Trent, Mark Ericks, and scores more detectives, patrolmen, deputy prosecutors, and corrections officers whose dedication helped to apprehend, convict, and supervise the "anti-heroes" in these cases from my crime files.

I would also like to commend the many winesses who had the courage to come forward and testify in court.

* * *

737

Although it often seems as though I never see *anyone* but my two dogs and two cats and my computer screen, I am always aware of my own private cheering section out there, and that helps! My gratitude goes to my editors: Bill Grose (who conceived the idea of Ann Rule's True Crime Files); my constant and caring editor, Julie Rubenstein; Molly Allen, my quick-thinking and sharp-eyed line editor; and Leslie Stern, who helps organize our creative chaos. Also, Paolo Pepe, who works with me so graciously to create our book covers, and Gina Centrello, our president and publisher.

Despite the fact that I seldom come up for air, I find I still have friends, and I appreciate them doubly because they *do* understand deadlines. To: Donna Anders, Gerry Brittingham, Tina Abeel, Lisa and Bryan Pearce—and Taryn and Ashlyn, Ruth and Greg Aeschliman— and Kirsten, Peter and Brad, Anne and Haleigh Jaeger, Sue and Joe Beckner, Maureen and Bill Woodcock, Martin and Lisa Woodcock, Lola Cunningham, Mary Lynn Lyke, Susan Paynter, Bill and Shirley Hickman, Ione and Jack Kniskern, Austin and Charlotte Seth, Clarene and Jan Shelley, Millie Yoacham and Eilene Schultz, Peter Modde, Bill Hoppe, Jennie and Harley Everson, Hank Gruber, Nils and Judy Seth, Erik Seth, Bill and Joyce Johnson, Verne and Ruth Cornelius, Barbara Easton, Jeanne Hermens and Jack Livengood, Mike Shinn and Kari Morando, Kalen Thomas and Amy Lowin, Dan "The-Sausage-Man" House, Verne Shangle, Betty May and Phil Settecase, Sue and Bob Morrison, Jennifer and Siebrand Heimstra, Bill and Ginger Clinton, Hope Yenko, Lois Duncan, Joe and Jeannie Okimoto, Carol and Don McQuinn, John Saul, Edna Buchanan, Anne Combs, Michael Sack, Judine and Terry Brooks, and Margaret Chittenden.

With the age of being "on-line," I have made a host of new friends whom I may never see in person. Still, they have been wonderful to "talk" to. So thank you to the Time-Warner True Crime Forum, the Author's Forum, and the CNN Forums. Thank you, Darlah and Nathan Potechin, Madeleine Kopp, Karen Ellis, Deanie Mills, Pat Moses-Caudel, Emily Johnston, Joseph Carey, William Diehl, Lowell Cauffiel, Joe Bob Briggs and Clark Howard.

To my family: Laura, Leslie, Andy, Mike, and Bruce. Rebecca and Matthew, Ugo, Nancy, and Lucas Saverio Fiorante. To all of Chris Hansen's descendants who have scattered to the four winds: Michigan, Wisconsin, Nevada, California, Florida, and the Northwest, and to the Stackhouse Clan that began in Nankin, Ohio. I love you all.

If it had not been for Joan and Joe Foley, my literary agents, and Mary Alice Kier and Anna Cottle, I would still be writing in my flooded basement in Washington State. Thanks for the dry feet and the roof over my head!

And now I thank all of you who read my books. You cannot know how much it means to hear, "I stayed up all night reading." That is music to an author's ears. If you are not already on the mailing list for my quarterly newsletter, and you would like to be, please write to me at: P.O. Box 98846, Seattle, Washington 98198.

In tragic life, God wot
No villain need be! Passions win the plot;
We are betrayed by what is false within.

—George Meredith, *Modern Love*

Author's Note

It has been said that there are no new stories under the sun. Even those dramas and tragedies that are true are only a reprise of something that has happened before. I suspect that is an accurate analysis.

In this third volume of my true crime files, I note that I have either subconsciously or inadvertently chosen four cases that share a common theme: personal betrayal. Since I am a great believer in the premise that we do nothing *accidentally*, it must be the right time to contemplate homicides that occur because the victim or victims have been betrayed by someone they have come to trust. In most of the following cases, the victims have believed in their killers over a long time; in one case, the victims have put their faith too quickly in the wrong men. There is something especially heartbreaking about love and friendships betrayed. The thought that some of the victims in this book must have recognized that betrayal at the very last moments of their lives may be difficult to cope with.

In the final two cases, the system trusted a criminal's rehabilitation—and innocent people paid for this mistake.

All serve to remind us that things are seldom what they seem. And to be wary.

The title case in *A Fever in the Heart* occurred very early in my career as a true crime writer, so early, in fact, that I felt I had neither the courage nor the technical skill to undertake a book. To be truthful, I admit that I was afraid to attempt a book; I could not even imagine myself turning out three or four hundred pages.

Even so, I attended the entire trial that resulted from an intensive police investigation in Yakima, Washington. Because of a change in venue, the trial took place during one uncharacteristically hot summer in Seattle. I was there in the courtroom every day, utterly fascinated by the havoc wrought by one man's "love" for a beautiful woman. But this was not the kind of tender, romantic love we usually think of. This was obsessive love, a consuming passion that ate at a theretofore well-adjusted man as surely as acid eats into metal, until all the values he had believed in eroded.

I saw all the "characters" in this modern-day classic tragedy in person, and became friends with some of them. This was not simply a case of multiple murder; it involved the bonding and later disintegration of many families. Anyone who wrote about it would have to go back decades to even begin to explain the extent of the loss. I knew that the story needed to be told, and close family members asked me to delve deeper, but after some agonizing debates with myself, I let it pass. I didn't think I could do it justice.

I would be years before I undertook my first book, *The Stranger Beside Me*. After my view of the Ted Bundy story was published, I wrote a dozen more books but I kept coming back to "A Fever in the Heart." During all that time, I kept my notes, the pictures my daughter took in the courtroom, and those given to me by relatives of the victims. I think I knew that someday I *would* write the whole story, because I moved all the paraphernalia of "A Fever in the Heart" with me every time I changed residences.

Two decades later, I still find this chillingly ironic story of murder in Yakima, Washington, full of the most compelling series of circumstances I have ever encountered. Everyone involved was a winner— intelligent, physically attractive, charismatic, athletically gifted, and surrounded by love.

What on earth went wrong? It will take a whole book to try to sort it out, and I am finally ready to do that.

In addition to "A Fever in the Heart," you will find five other cases that I have never forgotten: "Mirror Image," "Black Leather," "I'll Love You Forever," "Murder Without a Body," and "The Highway Accident."

I hope you enjoy them all!

A Fever in the Heart

The holiday season *can be something of a letdown—even if the celebrations are successful and families manage to get together without allowing half-forgotten slights and old wounds to bubble to the surface. In New York City and in Yakima, Washington, and in every city and hamlet in between, families who coexist all year tend to become dysfunctional with the pressure of holiday emotions. Perhaps humans expect more out of life during the festive season. Those over the age of ten are usually disappointed.*

1

In **1975** the Friday before Thanksgiving was icy and bleak. In the spring, Yakima, and all of Yakima County, is scented by what seems like a continuous froth of apple and peach blossoms from a thousand orchards; in the summer, it is rich with growing things, and in the autumn, the tree branches are pregnant with fruit. However, in the last dark week of November 1975, Yakima was bitterly cold with lowering clouds that promised snow all day but never quite delivered by the time night fell.

Saturday would mark the twelfth anniversary of one of America's most stunning catastrophes. November 22, 1963. The day President John F. Kennedy was assassinated in Dallas while he was at the peak of his powers, dead-shot to the brain before he had time to sense the presence of danger. The date was the first in a series of grim similarities, albeit on a smaller stage.

Even though newly hung Christmas decorations were up on the light poles, it was hard to feel festive in Yakima. On that night of November 21, 1975, the sun set far too soon. For those people whose memories made their hearts heavy with sorrow and loss, there was the usual sense of apprehension about two major holidays ahead to live through. Thanksgiving first—and Christmas would arrive hard on its heels.

It was so cold.

Gerda Lenberg lived in a duplex at 506 East Lincoln in Yakima. Many streets in town were named after numbers or letters or names of presidents, and most of them had alleys that ran behind backyards, slicing the blocks in two, and allowing residents to park off the main streets. Gerda always described where she lived precisely: "On the right-hand side on the corner of Sixth or Lincoln—or of Lincoln and the alley."

The latter was more accurate. Gerda lived in a semibasement level

747

apartment; her bedroom window was set in a well, and located smack-dab on the alley.

Most evenings, Gerda sipped a bourbon and water, ate dinner, and then watched television until ten when she went to bed. She followed her pattern that dark Friday night of November 21, 1975. She turned out her lights, and then raised the bedroom window to get some fresh air. She wasn't afraid of burglars; it was a good neighborhood with lots of apartments, private homes, and churches nearby. In the daytime, there were dozens of older people who walked south down the alley to church activities.

Gerda could never be absolutely sure of the order of events that happened later that night. Either she woke up from a disturbing dream in the middle of the night or something she heard outside awakened her. She lay there trying to decide whether to get up. Later, she was fairly certain that she was already wide-awake when she heard footsteps running in the alley. "And I thought," she said, "well, that's kind of odd this time of night, because it was so quiet so I knew it was past midnight. And then it sounded like somebody bumped a garbage can or something . . . kind of a 'metal' sound."

Gerda Lenberg lay there, not disoriented but curious and a little apprehensive, as she heard "firecrackers" popping beyond her window. "It was three or four, like you light them right in succession."

It might have been a few minutes or a little longer before she heard running footsteps again, this time heading in the opposite direction—north—and coming from a short distance away, thudding directly above her window, and then fading. She was positive the person was running. She was used to hearing the faltering steps of elderly people walking through the alley to church. This was nothing like that.

"It was kind of a hollow sound like they might have had heavy soles or clogs," she remembered.

That wouldn't mean much later in helping to identify the person running. In the midseventies, practically everyone under thirty wore shoes with improbably built-up soles and Cuban heels—just as they wore polyester leisure suits with stitching on the lapels, plaid sports coats, bell-bottom pants, and "poor boy" sweaters.

Gerda Lenberg didn't believe she had heard anything that unusual or frightening. Only firecrackers and someone running in the chilly night. She glanced instinctively at the clock on the wall next to her bed. It was a decorative clock with Roman numerals, fancy rather than functional. She was never really sure exactly what time it was, but she could see it was somewhere between five or ten minutes after two in the morning. She turned over and was asleep in a short time.

"The next morning," Gerda recalled, "I remarked they were sure starting the Fourth of July early because somebody was shooting off firecrackers."

Dale Soost lived several buildings down the alley from Gerda's duplex. They had never met; he didn't know many people in the neighborhood of his apartment house at 208 North Sixth. He was employed by the State of Washington as a systems analysis programmer and was working on a project to automate the Superior Courts in the state. This phase of his contract had brought him to Yakima County.

Soost retired about midnight that Friday before Thanksgiving. He knew he wasn't going to get much sleep because he had to be up at four to go deer hunting. As it was, he got even less sleep than he expected; he was awakened suddenly in the hours before dawn by the sound of shots. As a hunter he was familiar with both rifles and pistols and he knew a gunshot when he heard one. "It was one shot," he would say later. "One shot, followed by two in rapid succession . . . *bang* . . . *bang–bang.*"

Soost looked out his window to see if he could see anything. The shots sounded as if they had come from the other end of his apartment house. His unit was on the alley, and the noise seemed to have come more from the street side. He thought they had been fired closer to Sixth Street. It was long before the era of "drive-by shootings," and Soost wasn't particularly concerned. He put it down to somebody shooting in the air.

He crawled back into bed and caught another few hours of sleep. By five A.M., Soost was on the sidewalk in front of the brick-facaded apartment house where he lived, dressed in hunting gear, and waiting for his companions to pick him up. It was still that impenetrable black of a winter's predawn and he jumped a little when a man walked toward him on the sidewalk. Then he saw it was another resident of his apartment complex, a man he often nodded to, but who he didn't really know. It turned out that the man, Rowland Seal, was going hunting too—duck hunting. He was also waiting for his ride.

Seal was a body and fender mechanic by trade, but his avocations kept him so busy he didn't normally have time to chat with his neighbors. He was filled up every hour of every day, and although he recognized people who lived in his apartment house and knew where most of them worked, Seal didn't socialize, considering idle conversation a waste of valuable time.

While they looked up Sixth Street for approaching headlights and paced back and forth to keep warm, Rowland Seal and Dale Soost made small talk about the noises they'd both heard in the night. Seal said he too had been awakened by the sound of shots. He was a most precise man and he knew the exact time. His digital watch and the digital clock next to his bed had both read 2:05 A.M.

Eventually they agreed that while it was true they lived in town, Yakima wasn't that big and it *was* hunting season. Somebody must have gotten a little anxious to get started. There were a lot of would-be Nimrods out there.

Since it was so early and so cold, both men immediately noticed the woman who emerged from the big frame house next to the apartment house. At first, they figured she was coming out in her robe to get the morning *Yakima Herald-Republic.* But she crossed the frosty porch and then walked slowly down the front steps and onto the lawn dusted half-white from a desultory snowfall. Almost as if she were walking in her sleep, she disappeared around the side yard toward the alley.

Suddenly, the silent icy air was shattered by screams. The woman was calling out the name of the man Rowland Seal knew she lived with. "Morris! Morris!" she cried over and over.

Soost and Seal were caught off-guard. For a long moment, they stared at each other. A few seconds later, the young woman ran back into view and disappeared into her house.

Seal murmured, "Morris's dog must have got shot last night."

Soost didn't know the neighbors, but he figured Morris was the woman's husband or maybe her boyfriend. If someone had shot his dog, he was going to be upset. The woman had certainly seemed shaken. While the two hunters stood awkwardly, hesitant about what they should do, the woman next door ran out of her house again. She was still screaming and she seemed on the verge of complete hysteria, "Oh, my God! He's *dead.* Oh, my God!"

Rowland Seal was the kind of man who stepped up when he saw an emergency, and he was sure he was seeing one now. While Dale Soost hung back, Seal hurried over to her and said, "We'll call an ambulance." It seemed the right thing to say, but he didn't even know if you *could* call an ambulance for a dog.

The woman didn't seem to understand what he was saying to her.

Seal had no choice but to bring her back to reality with firm words. "I wasn't too gentle or too courteous," he recalled, "but I said, 'Get in there and call an ambulance,' and so she did."

While the young woman was in the house, Rowland Seal walked along the side of the thin wire fence separating the apartment house property from the lawn next door. The fence was more of a psychological barrier than a physical one, not much more than chicken wire. Seal felt the hairs prickle at the back of his neck. It was still dark but he could see that it was not a dog at all—but a man— who lay on his back in an open gate between the area where the people next door parked their cars and the side yard of their house. The man lay in the shadows and it was so dark near the gate that at first Seal could see only a white shirt and a white face. But there was more. He *could* make out scarlet stains—*blood?*—on the man's face. He couldn't be sure who it was, but it was a big man. That and the blood were all he could see for certain. Peering from his side of the fence, Seal was unable to get any closer than five or six feet from the body.

He forced himself to conquer his shock and headed back to the sidewalk. The young woman had emerged from her house again and this time two small children and a large dog trailed after her.

Leaving the children and dog on the porch, she ran back to the body crying, "Oh, my God, he's dead. He's been shot. My God. He's shot. He's dead. . . ."

Rowland Seal saw that the woman was getting more and more frantic, and he didn't want the kids to catch her hysteria. He instructed her very carefully to take the children into the house and to call the police.

For a moment the scene on the porch seemed eternal, a frozen tableau, until the slender, dark-haired woman turned and headed into the house. "And then," Seal remembered, "a police officer came and then another one and then another one. When the third one came, I thought everything was under control, and I gave my name and address and told him I was going duck hunting and he could find me at my address."

Rowland Seal was nothing if not pragmatic; he went ahead with the day he had planned. He could do nothing to help the man who lay in the snow. Nor could he help the woman. The police would take care of it.

A shaken Dale Soost went ahead with his day too.

And so did Gerda Lenberg. She had no idea at all that anything earthshaking had occurred in the dark hours between Friday night and Saturday morning. It wasn't until Sunday morning when she read the paper that she looked up and said slowly, "Oh, my lord, that wasn't firecrackers at all. . . ."

2

It never should have ended the way it did. There are some people whom destiny smiles upon, human beings blessed with wonderfully classic good looks, intelligence, and talents and skills that far surpass the average—people who grow up surrounded by love and high hopes. In Yakima, Washington, in that window of time in the 1970s, there were four people like that, an oddly assembled quartet of players whose lives would grow so intertwined and hopelessly entangled that they could never seem to pull apart. The very "oxygen" of their freedom to live and breathe was soon compromised by their closeness. The obsessive desire of one player damned the happiness of the other three forever.

Possibly the end of the game had been fated decades before; certain choices each of them made had brought them to this place.

Olive Morgan Blankenbaker was one of four daughters born to Esther and Ray Morgan, who named all their girls somewhat whimsically (and horticulturally): Hazel, Fern, Olive, and Iris. Their maternal grandfather, Ernst Skarstedt, was a writer of some note in his native Sweden and his intelligence and sensitivity came through undiluted to his descendants.

Olive was born in 1910 near Wapato in Yakima County. She would spend all of her working years in the court systems of Washington. She began as a court secretary, but her true goal was to be a court reporter. This was long before the era of stenotype machines or computer disks. Court reporters wrote in beautifully executed script.

It was also long before television was anything more than a scientific phenomenon demonstrated at world's fairs. Radios were the home entertainment in vogue when Olive was a young woman in her twenties. Huge console radios with shiny mahogany cabinets and ornately carved facades were the status symbols of the thirties. Franklin D. Roosevelt had his "fireside chats" over the radio, kids listened to "Jack Armstrong, the All-American Boy," and "The Lone Ranger," and dance bands from a ballroom "high atop" some hotel far away enchanted late-night listeners.

Olive Morgan met Ned Blankenbaker in Yakima where he worked as a radio salesman in a radio and musical instrument store. She was a slender, beautiful young woman with marcelled curls and a sweet smile. Ned always seemed to be standing outside the store to catch a little sun just when Olive came walking downtown on her way to lunch. He was a short, stocky man with thick wavy hair and interesting eyes. Those eyes followed Olive as she passed by, and she knew it. He would stand on his tiptoes to make himself look taller when Olive walked by.

"Some other girls I knew knew him and they introduced us," Olive says. "I liked him the moment I met him."

It wasn't long before Ned and Olive began to talk, and then he asked her to go dancing. That's what all the young people did then. There were dance halls with lanterns swaying in the wind, and everyone tried to emulate Fred Astaire and Ginger Rogers. "Ned was a great dancer," Olive remembers. "We'd go out to Bock's Café where you could dance. It was just up the street from the music store. We knew everyone."

Songs like "Blue Moon" and "Anything Goes" were popular. FDR was in his first term in office and Social Security had just been voted in. The night before Olive Morgan married Ned Blankenbaker on September 25, 1935, Joe Louis took away Max Baer's heavyweight crown. Huey Long had been assassinated in Louisiana two weeks before, and war clouds were lowering in Europe. But all that was so far away. Yakima, in the center of Washington State, was seemingly insulated from the world outside. Olive was twenty-five years old when she married Ned, and she expected her marriage would last forever.

Ned and Olive Blankenbaker were married seven years before they had their only child. Morris Ray Blankenbaker was born on December 16, 1942. Thirty-two-year-old Olive was transfixed with love for this sturdy baby boy who made her holiday season the best she had ever had. As it almost always is, it was a "White Christmas" in Yakima. Although the world was at war and everything was rationed, everything in Olive's life at that moment was perfect.

A half-century later, looking back she would ask, "Why should it be that way? When people are so happy, why does it all have to disappear?"

For Olive's wonderful world did disappear. Somehow, the Blankenbaker marriage didn't work very well after Morris was born. In all, Olive and Ned were married nine years; Morris was barely two when Olive was left to raise him alone. Over the years, his father would remain a part of Morris's life and pay regular child support, but Ned fathered two more sons—Morris's half brothers, Mike and Charles. It was Olive who was always there for Morris Blankenbaker. Her love for him was so unselfish that she encouraged him to spend time with his father and his younger brothers. They would become an important part of his life.

Olive could easily have smothered Morris and made him a mama's boy, but she didn't. Morris was a natural athlete, a kid who was always running and leaping and playing ball. He had plenty of scrapes, bruises, and sprains, but Olive just sighed and bound up his wounds. She bit her lip when she felt she was about to ask him to give up the sports he adored. She knew it wouldn't do any good, anyway.

Olive signed up for a correspondence course to learn how to use the stenotype machine. She and Morris were living with her family in Wapato, and she managed to combine her studying with camping trips with her son. "I'd fix a big pot of stew and put it over the campfire, while Morris and his two friends—Indian boys from the Wapato Reservation—would go exploring in the forest. They could take the dog and have fun and I could study."

In the meantime, Olive was working as a court reporter, using Gregg shorthand. She sat through everything from divorces to murder trials, taking down all the proceedings in her fine hand. She worked in the Yakima County Superior Court, and then transferred over to Federal Court in Seattle, where Federal Judge Bowen, an elderly man who disliked change, was delighted to discover that there was still one court reporter in the Seattle area who could transcribe courtroom proceedings with a pen. "When he saw me writing with a pen on a notebook, he set up a whole bunch of proceedings for me to cover. He hated those little black machines," Olive remembered. "I never told him that I *could* write with one of those little black machines. We went all up and down the Washington coast from Bellingham to Vancouver hearing cases."

Judge Bowen was ninety-three and still on the bench when he asked Olive if she would consider working in Yakima, and of course she agreed readily. That was home. She and Morris moved back into her mother's house just outside town, and Olive worked days and evenings to keep up with the punishing schedule of cases that were filed into Judge Bowen's court.

Morris always came home for lunch to his Grandmother Morgan's house. "You could see him coming a block away—running," Olive said. "And he took her picket fence with a high jump every day. My mother loved to see that boy eat."

Morris Blankenbaker was a handsome child with tight blond curls and brown eyes. When he was five, he posed proudly for his mother's Brownie camera in his cowboy shirt, tooled belt with the silver buckle, and western boots. He was a Cub Scout, and into more athletic events with every year. He went out for tumbling and scrambled up to the top of the pyramid of bodies. "He broke his arm, of course," Olive recalled. "That was Morris."

One summer, when Morris was seven, Olive took him for an automobile trip all across Canada. "We stopped wherever there was a swimming pool," she said. "Even at seven, he swam like a fish, and he could dive off the high board, doing somersaults in the air. People used to gather around to watch him."

Olive was running her own kind of marathon in the Yakima Superior Court. "I kept up for a long time, but I finally had to quit," she said. "I was just about breaking down, because I was working for the most effective judge, and everyone was filing their cases in his court."

As common as it is in the 1990s, a single mother raising a son was a rarity in the 1940s. There were fathers who were away during the war certainly, but divorced mothers were far from the norm and it wasn't easy for Olive. She kept trying to find a job that would give her more time with Morris. She moved to Vancouver, Washington, where Morris went to Fort Vancouver High School.

Later, they moved to Spokane, ". . . to a big court with a lot of cases."

Back in Yakima again, Morris went to Washington Junior High and then Davis High School. He was the golden boy who could do anything. He was on the "A" squad of the track, baseball, football, and wrestling teams. He played the trombone and the French horn, marching in the Davis High band, carrying the huge horn as lightly as a feather. His mother remembers the band triumphantly playing "Bonaparte's Retreat" as they marched down the field.

It hardly seemed possible that one kid could participate in so many activities—but Morris did. He played baseball, ran track, and wrestled, and he was the star fullback on the football squad. The crowd shouted his name again and again as he made touchdowns. *"MORRIS BLANK-EN-BAKER! MOR-RIS BLANK-EN-BAKER!"*

In the summertime, Morris worked as a lifeguard in Yakima parks. From his teens well into his twenties, he always had an audience of adoring girls who carefully spread their towels out so they would be directly in his line of vision. He appreciated the view, but Morris didn't date much. He scarcely had time. In the end, there was only one girl he ever went steady with. Only one girl he ever really loved.

Jerilee. *Jerilee Karlberg.**

One of Morris's coaches at Davis High School during his senior year in 1961 was Talmadge Glynn Moore. Of course, nobody called Moore by his full name, and very few people called him "Glynn"; everyone knew him by "Gabby." Morris had known Gabby since he and Olive came back to Yakima in the midfifties—ever since junior high. He figured Gabby had coached him in about every sport there was at one time or another: wrestling, football, track. Gabby was almost exactly nine years Morris's senior. Morris's birthday was on December 16, and Gabby's was on the twenty-first. But when Morris was a schoolboy, Gabby was a grown man, married with a family, and their worlds were completely different. Morris always called Gabby "Coach"; he always would, even after he too was an adult.

When Morris graduated from Davis High in 1961, he took home just about every athletic honor. He received the Traub Blocking and Tackling trophy, and he was voted "Best Athlete of the Year." Best of all, Morris was offered a four-year football scholarship to Washington State University in Pullman. All he had to do was keep his grades up and do what came naturally as an athlete.

Olive was living and working in Spokane then, and Morris visited on holidays and weekends when he didn't have a game. Morris was playing right halfback for the Washington State Cougars. His mother didn't have the time or money to get to his games, but she did manage to get to Spokane to watch him play once.

"That was when Washington State played the University of Washington," Olive said. "They played in Spokane at night under the lights. I got to go to that game. It was so terribly cold. We were wrapped up in blankets with long underwear and everything. I even remember the date—it was November twenty-fourth, 1962. It was a real good game, and he played all the way through. I was so proud of him," Olive remembered. "He was so handsome and they kept shouting 'Morris Blankenbaker! Morris Blankenbaker!'"

Even so, for the first time in his athletic career, there were other halfbacks at Washington State University who made the starting lineup more often than Morris did. He was 5'11", tall and 175 pounds. That was plenty big enough in high school; in college, there were players who dwarfed him. Dennis McCurdy, Herman McKee, and Clarence Williams were playing halfback for the Cougars too and they were 6'1", 6'3", and 6'2" respectively, and they all weighed over 190. Morris's dreams of becoming a professional football player before he started a coaching career seemed less realistic than they once had.

Besides that, there was Jerilee. Jerilee Karlberg was three years behind Morris in school, and she attended the other public high school in Yakima: Eisenhower High. Morris barely knew her when he was in high school but he got to know her well when he went back to Yakima to visit his hometown. He had always been a guy who dated casually. As far as any of his friends remember, Morris was never serious about any girl in high school.

Jerilee Karlberg was another story. Outwardly, she seemed to be what every teenage girl in the sixties yearned to be. She had a perfect figure: slender, but full-breasted. She had clouds of dark hair and blue eyes and she wasn't just pretty; she was beautiful. Her skin was flawless and her features were enchanting. She was petite and entirely feminine. And of course she was a cheerleader for Eisenhower High.

"Jerilee was everything we wanted to be," one of her peers remembered. "She was pretty and slender and popular—so popular with boys. Her father was Henry Karlberg* and he had his own real estate company. He let Jerilee drive his new Cadillac whenever she wanted. While we all *yearned* after the 'jocks,' Jerilee *married* Morris Blankenbaker, the super athlete of them all. We envied her . . . I suppose some of us hated her. Or at least *resented* her. It's hard to put into words. Maybe you had to have lived in Yakima in the sixties to really understand."

Jerilee Karlberg may have appeared to have had everything, but her life was no more serene and perfect than any other teenager's was. She had her insecurities in high school and often smiled when she didn't feel like smiling. It was true that she came from an affluent family and she *was* gorgeous—but her world wasn't ideal. She longed to have a boyfriend of her own, someone she could count on.

She wanted to go steady; she didn't want to date different boys all the time, even though she was besieged with offers. Basically, Jerilee wanted to marry young and have a family.

Morris was something solid for her to hold on to and she loved him for that more than for his prowess on the football field. She wasn't really that interested in sports. She could see that everyone liked Morris, and he seemed to have scores of friends. Morris was handsome and built like a young Greek god with bulging biceps and a "washboard" stomach that rippled with muscles. He was a college man and he made the boys at Eisenhower High look like wimpy kids. There was no question that Jerilee was completely in love with Morris.

Jerilee was still in high school when she started dating Morris, and she begged him to come to Yakima to take her to her proms. She didn't want to miss the most memorable social events of any teenage girl's school years, yet she refused to go with anyone else. For Morris, it was almost a four hundred-mile round-trip, but he made it willingly. He posed with Jerilee who wore lovely formal gowns with the corsages he'd given her. Sometimes, the long trips back to Yakima cut into his study time and his grades suffered, but it didn't matter. Morris Blankenbaker was in love for the first time in his life.

Jerilee certainly had the intelligence to go to college, but she didn't want that; she wanted her own family. On August 28, 1965, three months after she graduated from Eisenhower High School, Jerilee and Morris were married. She was just eighteen. He was twenty-two.

"They had a big church wedding in the Presbyterian church," Olive remembered. "With a huge reception at the Chinook Hotel in Yakima. They served food and had liquor and everything . . ."

Henry Karlberg had put on a wonderful wedding for his daughter. Had it been up to her, Olive would have chosen not to serve liquor at the reception. It was just one of the things that carved a chasm between Olive and Jerilee's family, one that they all crossed tentatively for years to come. Olive and Morris had not exactly lived a hardscrabble existence, but nothing had ever come easy. No big houses and certainly no fancy cars.

For decades after that wedding in 1965, Olive and Jerilee Blankenbaker would have an ambivalent relationship. It was to be expected. They both loved Morris. He was Olive's only child, the son she had struggled so hard to raise, and he could do no wrong in her eyes. She had wanted so much for him to graduate from college before he got married, and Jerilee had detoured him from that goal. For her part,

Jerilee at eighteen was perhaps a little spoiled. She was not nearly as expert at either housework or a career as Olive was. Eventually, however, the two women would come to have a kind of grudging respect for one another.

The newly married Mr. and Mrs. Morris Ray Blankenbaker moved to Tacoma, Washington, where Morris planned to obtain his bachelor's degree at Pacific Lutheran University. He hadn't given up on his ambition to get his degree and become a coach. It would just take a little longer.

Morris had dropped out of Washington State and joined the Marine Corps Reserves before the draft could scoop him up. This meant that he had to train in the desert outside Coronado, California, for a few weeks each year, and risk being called to active duty in Vietnam. He was lucky; he didn't have to go to war and eventually he made lance corporal. Four years later, in February of 1969, he was honorably discharged from the Reserves.

3

Talmadge Glynn "Gabby" Moore had coached at Davis High School in Yakima since the 1960–61 school year. Like Morris, he was a Yakima boy, although he wasn't a native. Gabby was born in the depths of the Depression in Missouri—four days before Christmas, 1931. His family moved to Yakima when he was a child and Gabby attended school there, graduating from North Yakima High School in 1950. He too was a sports hero. He received North Yakima High's football inspirational trophy. But Gabby Moore, like so many teenagers graduating in the early fifties, went off to the Korean War instead of to college. He served in the Air Force from 1951 to 1955.

When he was discharged, Gabby came back to Yakima. He was a very handsome young man then with straight blond hair and heavy-lidded dark eyes. Gabby Moore, who looked like the jock that he was, clean-cut and in great shape, wanted to be a high school coach. He went to college on the GI Bill—first to Yakima Valley Community College, and then to Central Washington State College (now Central Washington University) in Ellensburg where he got his BA in 1958. Two years later, he received his master's degree at the same college.

Gabby's education wasn't easy; he taught and coached while he was going to college. He had married by then, to Gay Myers, and during the time Gabby was getting his education and beginning his career as a teacher they had three babies: Sherry,* Kate,* and Derek.* Gay, who was startlingly attractive with smoky blond hair and a lithe figure, eventually became a physical education teacher herself.

As they are in most small towns in America, sports were king in Yakima, and the Moores were so much a part of the fabric of the town, of its educational system and its sports circle. Gabby Moore had taught in tiny Union Gap first, and then at Washington Junior High in Yakima. He moved steadily up the career ladder. In 1960 he was hired to teach and coach at Davis High School where he stayed to become a much-admired fixture. Gabby taught math and driver training and was the track coach and the assistant football coach. One year he was the head football coach.

But the gridiron wasn't his forte; it was at wrestling that he excelled as a mentor. He became, arguably, one of the most outstanding wrestling coaches in America. He could have moved on up to college coaching—he was certainly skilled enough—but he had sunk deep roots in Yakima.

Gabby Moore was the impetus behind bringing "kid wrestling" to Yakima. The town's boosters were pleased, and the Yakima Junior Chamber of Commerce honored him for that program by giving him the trophy for "Outstanding Physical Education Educator" for 1969. Moore's wrestling team took the Washington State Championship in 1972. He was a member of the selection committee in the Washington Cultural Exchange with Japan, where wrestling is a major sport. Gabby found a way to travel to the Orient with his star athletes so that they could wrestle with the best.

Athletes from many graduating classes had passed through Gabby's wrestling programs and they never forgot him. He could take a boy with no particular aptitude for sports and turn him into a champion. He could, and he *did*, not once but many times. His athletes loved Gabby, and he cared deeply for his boys.

Beyond his solid place at Davis High, Gabby Moore had other compelling reasons to prefer Yakima to one of the college towns on the "coast" near Seattle or to the east: Pullman or Moscow, Idaho, where Washington State and the University of Idaho were located.

He and Gay had an extended family in Yakima with a closeness that anyone would envy, a tight circle of love and emotional support.

Gabby's father-in-law, Dr. A. J. Myers, was an osteopathic physician and surgeon who owned and operated the Valley Osteopathic Hospital on Tieton Drive in Yakima. "Doc" Myers had practiced medicine in Yakima for more than thirty years and in 1952 he built Valley Hospital.

"Doc" and Gabby met for the first time shortly before Gabby married Gay, and they soon became fast friends. Myers was Gabby's doctor and his friend, a relationship that existed outside of Gabby's marriage.

In those days Gabby Moore was a family man and a revered coach. He was twenty-seven when Morris Blankenbaker graduated from high school, and they kept in touch, although only sporadically. There was no reason to think that their lives would touch again in much more than a tangential way.

While Morris Blankenbaker was an Adonis of a young man who was everyone's friend, Gabby Moore's popularity came from his compelling, persuasive personality. As he aged, his appearance changed from that of a good-looking young coach to one of an average-looking man who seemed older than he really was. All coaches at every level are under pressure to win. Gabby didn't handle stress well. The pressure to win—much of it self-driven—got to him and he developed primary hypertension in his early thirties. Gabby's high blood pressure was serious enough to concern his father-in-law. A. J. Myers did his best to convince Gabby that elevated blood pressure was nothing to ignore, but his warnings usually fell on deaf ears. Gabby Moore continued to demand too much of himself and of his athletes. When he concentrated on something, it was with every fiber of his being; he did nothing halfway.

With the years, Gabby's hair thinned and he was beginning to resort to "comb-overs" and deliberately careless bangs over his forehead. By the time he was in his late thirties, despite his sports activities, Gabby had a burgeoning paunch that his wrestlers teased him about. He wasn't the handsome young coach he had been in his twenties; Gabby had come to look like a thousand other high school teacher-coaches in America.

But that hardly mattered. It was his personality that shone through. An alumna remembered that, as a teacher of driver's training, Gabby was so calm—so patient.

"I had Gabby for driver's training," recalled the woman, who worked in the Yakima County District Attorney's Office, twenty years after graduation. "I *liked* him. We all did. I remember he always told us to 'Look for a way out'—to expect trouble, and be ready to get out of the way. He wasn't temperamental. He wasn't mean. He was a great guy . . . I still can't understand what happened. . . ."

For most of his years of teaching and coaching, Gabby Moore was a dynamic, charismatic man who could make anyone believe anything. And if *he* believed, his listeners believed. If he said a kid from Yakima could make it to the Olympics and bring home a gold medal, then, by golly, the kid would go for it. He would not listen to excuses. "If you got a problem," Gabby would say, "you eliminate the problem—and you win." While Gabby was known to have a short fuse on occasion, it didn't affect his job or his status at Davis High School.

Gay Myers Moore was a beautiful woman and, unlike Gabby, she grew more attractive as she approached middle age. Gay was teaching girls' physical ed at Lewis & Clark Junior High. Both Moores were busy with their teaching schedules and raising three youngsters, but they made a great couple. Their marriage seemed as solid as Gibraltar.

No one really *knows* how things are in a marriage, though, not from the outside looking in. Maybe Gabby focused too much on his wrestling squads and forgot that his family needed him too. He not only had after-school practice, he usually brought some of his wrestlers home for practice-after-practice. There weren't enough hours in the day for him to have had much time to spend with his wife—at least during wrestling season.

In 1965, just after Morris and Jerilee got married, he and Gabby Moore had no closer a relationship than Gabby did with any of his ex-athletes from Davis. They sometimes saw one another in Yakima when Morris and Jerilee came home to visit their relatives on holidays or during the summer, but that was about it.

Morris had precious little free time. The curriculum at Pacific Lutheran University was far more demanding than the classes he had taken at Washington State. PLU attracted students with the highest academic records. And Pacific Lutheran is a private university where the tuition is a lot higher than a state school. This time, Morris had no football scholarship—he didn't have time to play football. Both he and Jerilee had to work so that they could make it financially.

Jerilee might have *looked* like a fragile, dependent girl who needed a man to look after her, and, yes, maybe she had played that role a time or two because boys seemed to like it. Inside, though, she was strong and smart; she just wasn't used to letting it show. She was the kind of woman who combined a kittenish quality with profound sensuality—a Brigitte Bardot or a Claudine Longet kind of woman. Physically, Jerilee resembled Longet a great deal.

Jerilee Blankenbaker was highly intelligent. She and Morris needed the money she could bring in, and she was determined to get a job. She applied at a bank in Tacoma even though they hadn't advertised for new employees. She simply strode in and said, "I want a job."

The bank manager drew up a chair and asked her to sit down.

"The bank had a test they gave to everyone," Olive Blankenbaker recalled. "They handed Jerilee this great big stack of checks, and they said, 'There's one forgery in there. See if you can find it.' And do you know, *she* found it—and nobody ever had before. She is really bright. You've got to give her credit."

Jerilee was hired at once. Not only was her appearance an asset to the bank, but she was obviously smart. They hadn't guessed wrong on her. Although she had no training and was fresh out of high school, she was a quick study and she proved to be a very valuable employee. She began as a clerk, but she rose rapidly to a position of trust officer.

Morris found a job at Western State Hospital in Steilacoom, Washington's state institution for people who are profoundly psychotic. He worked the late shift from three to eleven P.M. It was a demanding job. He was at work for the evening meal and then he helped medical personnel get patients settled down for the night with a variety of medications. He always had to be ready for trouble. The most placid patients sometimes had psychotic breaks with no warning at all. Morris knew that one of the reasons he had been hired was his muscular build. But Morris's innate kindness and his calm manner seemed to soothe the more disturbed patients at Western State.

No matter how difficult the night's work had been, Morris still had to study when he got home close to midnight. While he worked nights, Jerilee worked days. Her "banker's hours" ended just as his job began. In the little time they had together, they got along well. If they argued at all, their discussions were about money or in-laws. Jerilee had assumed that Olive would continue to send money to Morris until he got out of college, while Olive figured that he was a grown man now, and a married man as well. She had looked forward to cutting back on the heavy workload she had carried since he was a baby.

Jerilee was upset about that, Olive remembered, but it wasn't a big problem. Mostly, Jerilee was homesick for Yakima and for her own mother and sister. She didn't know anyone in Tacoma, and she spent most evenings alone because Morris was working. She was uneasy too; sometimes people escaped from Western State Hospital. PLU's campus had a lovely sweeping greensward and scores of huge trees, but the streets nearby quickly disintegrated into high-crime areas. When Morris was gone, it seemed to Jerilee that every sound was magnified.

Morris had hoped to finish college at Pacific Lutheran, but Jerilee was so miserable and homesick that he finally agreed to move back to Yakima, find a job there, and attend Central Washington State College in Ellensburg on a part-time basis. A move would mean that his degree would take a year or two longer than he had hoped. In truth, it would be six years before Morris Blankenbaker graduated from college.

Back in Yakima, Morris took a "temporary" job with the phone company as a telephone lineman. It wasn't his ultimate goal, but he liked scampering up poles with spiked boots and the camaraderie of the crews he worked with. And he was happy being back in the county where he was raised, back with his good friends. He had grown up in the big old house where his grandparents lived and he often stopped in for his coffee break, bringing his whole crew with him. His grandmother Esther looked forward to fussing over Morris and his fellow linemen, and she usually had something baking in the oven just in case.

All the while, Morris plugged away at his college degree at Central Washington College. It was only thirty-five miles to Ellensburg, but it was a rough thirty-five miles before the freeway was built: across the Twin Bridges, and then along the riverbanks outside of Yakima and across great stretches of barren land and winding roads through hills that were more like mountains, past squared-off buttes. Eastern Washington is not at all like the rainy and mild western half of the state. In winter, blizzards often made State Road 821 virtually impassable while, in summer, sand storms full of tumbleweeds blinded drivers who headed north out of Yakima toward Ellensburg. It was a great road for sightseers, as it curved along the Yakima River, but it was a student commuter's nightmare.

Gabby Moore, Morris's old track coach, was taking classes at Central Washington too, and he and Morris often car-pooled. They renewed their friendship, but it was a different kind of friendship now; they were both adults. In the spring of 1969, Gabby's and Gay's three kids were growing up and Jerilee was pregnant with her first baby.

Sometimes, Gabby and Morris went hunting or spear fishing together on weekends. They often went whitewater rafting and boating on the Yakima River. Theirs was a male friendship; the Moores and the Blankenbakers didn't socialize. Jerilee scarcely knew Gabby.

Rick* Blankenbaker was born on May 5, 1969, and Jerilee was swept up in first-time motherhood. Amanda* was born a little over a year later on September 1, 1970. The young Blankenbakers had it all: a happy marriage, a little boy, and a little girl. Old photographs show Jerilee and Morris posing happily with their babies: Morris hoisting his chunky young son high with one muscular arm; Jerilee riding on Morris's shoulders on a whirligig as the family plays in the park; Jerilee and the kids proudly presenting Morris with a birthday cake. Looking at the photos, it seems impossible that it could not have gone on that way forever.

The young Blankenbakers had every reason to believe that they would grow old together and watch their children and grandchildren live out their lives in Yakima too.

Olive Blankenbaker was in her midfifties when Morris married Jerilee. It seemed to her that it was too late then to find anyone marriageable who appealed to her. More out of habit than anything else, Olive kept up much the same heavy work pace she had set for herself so long before. She did, however, stop court reporting and accepted an offer to go to work for J. P. "Pete" Tonkoff of the Yakima firm of Tonkoff and Holst. It proved to be the best job she had ever had, a steady—if intense—schedule, with more benefits than any of her other positions.

Pete Tonkoff, a native of Bulgaria, was a "great attorney," dynamic and dramatic in the courtroom. He was not in the least impressed with city lawyers. He once subpoenaed Eleanor Roosevelt as a witness in a case he was bringing against Fulton Lewis. Olive would work for Pete Tonkoff for ten years, driving in from her family's old homestead near the Yakima River in an "old jalopy." She loved the challenge of working for Tonkoff. She admired his brilliance, even his occasional bombasity.

The years passed. Olive was in her sixties, but she was as efficient as ever and indispensable to Tonkoff and Holst. At some point, Pete Tonkoff took one look at the car she drove through blizzards and summer heat alike and bought her a new one, gruffly saying he didn't want her missing work because her old car had broken down.

Olive's ideal job ended suddenly on July 18, 1973, when Pete Tonkoff was lost and presumed dead after the Beechcraft he owned and was piloting disappeared over Lake Pontchartrain in Louisiana. Tonkoff had been flying in to handle a New Orleans case. He had been coming in for a landing when the tower ordered him to make another go-round because the runway was occupied. He never came back. Later, his plane was found deep in the lake. His death was only the first blow that Olive Blankenbaker would suffer in the mid-1970s.

"Up until then," she said, "everything was good. I thought it would last forever."

4

All too often the falling-down of lives is like dominoes tumbling. When one falls, it knocks over the next, and the next, and on and on until everything is flattened. In the early 1970s, Gabby Moore was at the very peak of his profession, with his athletes winning more honors every year. His own son, Derek, made the football team at Davis, and another generation of Moores played for the Pirates. His daughters, Sherry and Kate, were pretty girls and good students.

Who can say what detours human beings from a smooth road ahead? The "midlife crazies," maybe. Unfulfilled dreams? On occasion, it is a near-tragedy that serves as a wake-up call that life doesn't go on forever.

Gabby Moore came so close to dying one summer day that he may well have reevaluated his life and realized that he had slid into middle age without ever seeing it looming on the horizon. Had it not been for Morris Blankenbaker, Gabby Moore never would have made it much past forty.

It happened on one of the river trips that Morris and Gabby often took. The day began like any other. The two men had parked one of their cars near Olive's place close by the Yakima River and driven the other up to Ellensburg. There, they pushed off in a boat and headed downriver toward Yakima. They had made this trip dozens of times before. But this time something went wrong, and their boat capsized in a powerful undercurrent, scattering its occupants and their gear alike.

Both Morris and Gabby were plunged beneath the surface of the river, sucked deeper and deeper, down where the sunlight was swallowed up and they had to dodge floating debris and sunken logs in an underwater obstacle course. Morris was the strong swimmer and he quickly fought his way to the surface. Somehow Gabby ended up beneath the bank along the river's edge, his feet entangled in the clutch of vines and roots that flourished in the deep water. There was no way he could ever have gotten out of their death grip by himself and he was virtually invisible from the surface of the river.

Morris wasn't worried about himself; he was like an otter in the water. As a younger man, he had tormented his friends and his mother by swimming underwater so long they were sure he had drowned. But he was only "counting" until he was confident he had broken his own record for holding his breath. Satisfied, he then would burst up triumphantly just as they were all running for a lifeguard to pull him out.

Now, in the whitewater that overturned their drift-boat, Morris dove again and again, looking for Gabby. Finally he saw him flailing his arms helplessly, his feet held in the vise of the underwater vegetation. Morris wrenched Gabby free and took him to the top. Gabby flopped on the bank like a dying fish, throwing up. But he was breathing and he was alive.

"I wish he'd never made it," Olive Blankenbaker would say with quiet bitterness many years later. "I wish Morris had left him there in the river."

Olive would remember that she had felt an aversion to Gabby Moore from the first time she met him out there at her river place. She never said anything to Morris, because she couldn't put her finger on what it was about Gabby that set her teeth on edge.

Morris was unaware that his mother didn't like Gabby. The two men remained fast friends. They hunted and fished and sometimes worked out at the YMCA together. Morris was flattered when Gabby sought his advice on football plays. Morris attended a number of

Gabby's teams's wrestling matches and he sometimes helped coach the heavyweight wrestlers. The two men talked often, almost every day.

In December of 1973, Gabby confided to Morris the shocking news that he and Gay were getting a divorce. He said he would be moving out of his family home after Christmas. Morris was stunned. Gabby and Gay had been married almost two decades, and Morris had had no idea they were having problems. From what Gabby told him, it was Gay who wanted out of the marriage, and Gabby who was fighting to keep it together.

Gabby asked Morris if he might move in with him and Jerilee for a few weeks, just until he and Gay tried to settle their problems. Morris was all for it if it would help Gabby salvage his marriage. A "time-out" might be just what Gabby's marriage needed.

Jerilee Blankenbaker was definitely not enthusiastic when Morris approached her with the suggestion that they invite Gabby to stay with them until he pulled himself together. His divorce was hurting him bad and he wasn't taking it well, Morris explained. Gabby was lonesome and lost outside the family he had been used to.

Jerilee didn't really know Gabby Moore. At twenty-seven she had two little children to take care of, not to mention her full-time job at a Yakima bank; she had more than enough to do without helping Morris baby-sit his old coach. It wasn't that she was selfish or uncaring, it was simply that she and Morris were just getting their own lives on track. Morris had his college degree, and he was teaching at last. She couldn't envision bringing Gabby into their home without incurring problems. She didn't have time to cook and clean up after another man, to do his laundry, and she didn't feel like giving up her privacy.

Morris argued that it wouldn't be for very long. Gabby was probably going to be getting back with Gay; if he didn't, he would soon be looking for his own place. Morris said he just couldn't turn the guy away in good conscience. And that was typical of Morris. He *had* a conscience, and he cared a lot about Gabby.

A future prosecuting attorney named Jeff Sullivan was Gay Moore's divorce attorney. Much later, Sullivan would scarcely recall the divorce proceedings, which led him to believe that the dissolution of the Moore marriage was uncomplicated. "No-fault" divorces had just come into effect in Washington State at that time and Sullivan cannot remember if Gabby was any more reluctant than the average man to get a divorce. In fact, it was Sullivan's impression that Gabby *wanted* the divorce. In any case, the proceedings were calm enough that they did not stand out in his mind.

That was not the way Gabby described it to Morris, however. Bereft, Gabby confided in his athletes and in his friends. He seemed lost, frightened of the future, and angry at the same time. Of all of Gabby's friends, Morris Blankenbaker was the one who worried the most about what would happen to Gabby when he didn't have Gay any longer. At first, it didn't occur to Morris that he was hearing only one side of the story: a side that showed Gabby in the best light.

Morris had saved Gabby's life once, and he was ready to do it again. It was almost as if he were living out the Chinese proverb that says that once you save someone's life, it belongs to you forever after and you remain responsible for that person. Gabby was in bad shape and Morris was not a man to ever walk away from any of his friends when they were as down as Gabby seemed.

Gabby had other friends, and his about-to-be ex-father-in-law was still close to him, but that didn't make the long nights alone any easier. He needed to be around people. Morris saw Gabby as a victim, and Gabby did nothing to dissuade him. There were many things that Gabby did not confide in Morris. Certainly, Morris had no idea how much Gabby was drinking or how insanely jealous he was of Gay.

Had Morris known, he might have rethought his offer to Gabby to move in. But he didn't know, and he worked hard to convince Jerilee that Gabby needed a place to stay where people cared about him. Finally, she gave in, and Gabby Moore moved in with the family in January of 1974.

Whatever Gabby was doing to effect a reconciliation, it wasn't working. Gay Moore went ahead with her divorce action. She wasn't divorcing Gabby because there was another man; she just wanted a different kind of life. Gabby's moods were too unpredictable and he was almost paranoid, believing that she *was* interested in someone else. With a teaching job and three teenagers to raise, Gay had no time to think about a new relationship.

Although Jerilee Blankenbaker had been against Gabby Moore's moving into her home, she soon changed her mind. She could see why Morris and he were such good friends. He was a nice guy, and he was fun to have around. More than that, though, Gabby's old charisma that had always drawn people to him was still working. When he wanted to be, he was the most charming man in the room, full of anecdotes and jokes, confident and bristling with goodwill. He was compelling, a man who seemed taller, handsomer, and more successful than he really was. He brought that force of energy to the Blankenbaker house, and when his eyes met Jerilee's, she found it almost impossible to look away.

No one could ever say when Jerilee began to view Gabby in a new light. Sharing a house with someone is an intimate experience— sometimes pleasant, sometimes uncomfortable. Gabby was there in the morning with his eyes sleepy and his hair tousled, and he was usually there as they all went to bed. In truth, Jerilee was living with two men, one her husband and one an interloper. But he was a disturbingly fascinating interloper. She knew that he drank a little, but she had no idea how much. Gabby was careful to be his most charming when he was with Jerilee. If there was an early hint that she found him special, perhaps it was the way she called him "Glynn" instead of Gabby, as everyone else did. She didn't like his nickname.

It was *Morris* who began to see his best friend with more critical eyes. He saw traits in Gabby he had never noticed before. "Morris said he could just see a change in Glynn," Jerilee said much later. "And Glynn would drink for two or three days without sleeping and do things that were unlike his character. He took a gun up to his ex-wife's house and he made threats toward her, and Morris could just . . . well, he lost his respect for him."

But Morris didn't immediately confide in Jerilee about the negative things he was seeing in Gabby. Since she hadn't known him at all well before he moved in with them, she couldn't see the alarming change.

"I didn't know Glynn Moore that well previous to that," she admitted. Morris didn't tell Jerilee how much Gabby was drinking, or how bizarre his behavior became when he *did* drink. He didn't tell her about the obsessive, almost psychotic jealousy Gabby was exhibiting toward Gay.

Later, Jerilee would see the other side of Gabby, the one that made Morris pull back from the friendship. But by the time Morris distanced himself from his old coach, it was far too late to stop what was happening in his own home.

Someone who wasn't there cannot possibly say when things began to go awry in the Blankenbaker marriage. One can only conjecture.

Jerilee and Morris had been married eight years, and they had long since grown accustomed to each other. Gabby Moore was a new element in the equation. He clearly found Jerilee enchanting. He listened to what she had to say, and he was quick to jump up to help her clear the dinner table. It soon began to seem natural to have him there; he was like part of the family. And then it was more than that—he *was* part of the family.

Gabby Moore needed to talk about his feelings, and Jerilee listened. Gabby was, as a song popular in that era said, "a giant of a man brought down by love"—a condition that is ultimately appealing to most women. At first, Jerilee probably felt sorry for him as she listened to him talk about his lost marriage. The only side to Gabby she had ever seen—and that was at a distance—was the macho coach, the sportsman, her husband's friend. Now, as he poured his heart out to her, she must have sensed that he had emotional depths she had never realized. Jerilee was undoubtedly touched when she saw how the end of his marriage had diminished his joy in life and in his successes. He would have made it seem that he was telling her secrets that no one else knew, that he trusted her enough to reveal weakness that he would show only to her.

Jerilee must have realized why Morris had felt so sorry for him. His heart was broken, his children were lost to him, and every day was a challenge. Yet, somehow he gathered the strength to go on, to paste a smile on his face and go off to school to teach and to coach.

The stage was set for disaster. Before he was aware of all the circumstances and the many-faceted sides to Gabby's personality, Morris had invited a predator into his home. He had thought nothing of leaving Gabby alone with Jerilee. He was disgusted when he realized how much Gabby was drinking—disgusted and disappointed in the man he had once idolized, but Morris wasn't worried and he wasn't wary.

He should have been. At some point Jerilee's relationship with Gabby had metamorphosed. Gabby no longer grieved for his lost wife and family; he was in love with his best friend's wife. Although he didn't tell her right away, watching Jerilee may have made Gabby glad he was free. His wholehearted pursuit to win her love suggests that he didn't even reflect on the fact that *she* was not.

At first glance, it seemed highly unlikely that Gabby would be attractive to Jerilee. He was forty-two years old, and nowhere near as handsome as Morris. Morris had put on some weight but, underneath, he was still solid muscle. Gabby was soft and out of shape. He was not in good health, although the Blankenbakers didn't know how precarious Gabby's physical condition was. But Gabby had one big advantage: He was an unknown quantity to Jerilee. She had been with Morris since she was seventeen, and at twenty-seven she was no longer an immature teenage beauty queen. She was a lovely woman who had made a place for herself in the business world.

To Morris, Jerilee was still Jerilee. They had achieved the comfortable familiarity of a long-term marriage. Morris loved his wife devotedly but he was used to having her around. The exhilarating, breathtaking romance of a new relationship just wasn't there any longer. How could it be?

Gabby played on that; he pushed back any thoughts he had about the ethics of what he was doing to Morris. He had moved into his friend's life and he felt comfortable there. He wanted it all for himself. Gabby had always gone against the odds in sports. He was now prepared to beat the odds when it came to love. He wanted Jerilee Blankenbaker and he was ready to be whoever he had to be to win her away from Morris.

Morris and Jerilee's home now housed a three-adult family. If Morris noticed that Jerilee no longer complained about the nuisance of having Gabby live with them, he didn't mention it. He just hoped that Gabby would make other living arrangements as soon as possible. He wanted his old life back.

Morris may even have been relieved that Jerilee didn't complain any longer about the loss of their privacy or about the extra work it was to have Gabby live with them. Gabby seemed to enjoy being around five-year-old Rick and four-year-old Amanda too.

Apparently, Gabby never tired of looking at Jerilee. His eyes followed her appreciatively as she moved around her kitchen fixing supper and when she got her toddlers ready for bed. Although she was very intelligent, she was not an aggressive woman. She bent with seeming ease to the needs and requests of the men in her life. Jerilee had looked for so long to Morris for protection and approval. Now, subtly, it appears that she began to lean on Gabby. Although she had good female friends, she was a man's woman, soft and pretty and sweet.

No one but the participants knew just when the balance finally shifted in the Blankenbaker household. The change was cataclysmic, but it occurred so silently that it was as if a deep fissure in the earth had crunched one seismic plate against another and cracked every wall in the house. The marriage *looked* sound, but a gypsy wind blowing across the land could have flattened the whole thing. Obviously, Jerilee began to feel as if she were sleeping with the wrong man when she went to bed with her husband. She must have thought of the man in the guest bedroom, who was unquestionably thinking of *her* and seething at the situation.

No one who knew them or who encountered them later believes that Jerilee had planned to fall in love with Gabby, and it would probably be fair to say that he had not expected to fall in love with her. He had simply switched his obsession with Gay to Jerilee, with barely a pause in between. Even Gabby—who was quite used to having his own way—must have seen the shame of stealing the woman who belonged to the man who had literally saved his life, who had rescued him from drowning. Undoubtedly, Gabby recognized what he was about to do, but it didn't deter him.

It was Jerilee he wanted now and he was going to have her.

Gabby led Jerilee to believe that his financial picture was far brighter than it really was. He promised her that once they were married, he would buy her a wonderful brick house and that she could furnish it however she liked without ever worrying about the cost. The lifestyle he painted for her sounded secure and happy and without any problems at all. Gabby seemed to love her with a passion and a fervor that the more taciturn Morris had never demonstrated. Morris made commitments and kept them—that was the way he showed his love. Gabby was all fire and promises.

The very fact that Gabby was fifteen years older than Jerilee may have drawn her to him.

His charisma and his ability to inspire confidence drew her to him—just as he inspired his athletes. He seemed a dependable rock, a kind of half lover/half father figure. He was such a hero at Davis High School and in Yakima itself. Morris had a teaching job too, of course, but he hadn't begun to achieve the status that Gabby had.

Whatever it was—chemistry, pragmatism, true love—Jerilee had become completely mesmerized by Gabby Moore. When he asked her to leave Morris and marry him, she accepted. It could not help but seem that she threw away her marriage with scarcely a backward glance.

Gabby had nothing to throw away; he was already figuratively on the street with a suitcase when Jerilee and Morris took him in. It wasn't that he was destitute—he had money—but he was not a man who could live by himself. He never had been.

Once they had admitted the obvious, there was apparently no going back for Jerilee and Gabby. It was spring in Yakima and the apple trees were blossoming. They were in love and they were not going to turn away from the overpowering emotion that swept over them. It had all happened in less than three months. . . .

When Jerilee told Morris that she was leaving him for Gabby, he was poleaxed. She was the only woman he had ever loved. But like many powerfully built men, Morris was gentle and not the kind to rage and threaten. He was too hurt. If Jerilee wanted a divorce, he would give it to her. There was nothing else for him to do. He let her walk away from him with one proviso, though. He made it clear that he still loved her. If she ever needed him, if she ever came to her senses, he would take her back.

Morris wasn't in a position to ask for custody of his children. Rick and Amanda were preschoolers. How would he take care of them? Olive couldn't be expected to take on the daily care of two little kids, and, besides, she was still working full-time. He knew that Jerilee would let him see them whenever he could, and so he didn't fight her for them. In his heart, he believed that she and the children would be coming back to him.

It happened with such swiftness. When 1974 began, Morris Blankenbaker had considered himself married for life. By March, only a little over two months later, Jerilee had filed for divorce. Since uncontested divorces in Washington State take ninety days, she was a free woman by June. She and Morris would have been married for nine years on August 28, but, of course, they never made it that far.

Coincidentally, Morris's marriage had lasted almost exactly as long as his parents' marriage.

Jerilee came back to Morris once, but only for a very brief time. She was pulled in two directions. Her conscience and the familiar warmth and dependability of the man she had left drew her back. But when she was living with Morris again, Gabby wouldn't let her alone. He was the most persuasive person she had ever encountered. He kept reminding her that *he* was the one she loved, and that he could not go on living without her. He played "their" song, and her resolve melted.

Lay your head upon my pillow,
Hold your warm and tender body close to mine.
Hear the whisper of the raindrops falling soft against the
  window,
And make believe you love me one more time. . . .

Unlike most men in his situation, Morris was remarkably civilized. Although he was crushed by the betrayal of both his wife and his best friend, he actually allowed Gabby back in his house to discuss their dilemma. The three of them, each side of the hopeless triangle, had stilted, awkward discussions. Sometimes, Gabby would show up at suppertime and they all sat together at the table again, unspoken thoughts heavy in the air. It was as if there were some solution to be found, some ending where all three of them could be happy, and yet they all knew there was none. Whatever happened, one of them was going to lose.

Of them all, Morris was the strongest, heartbroken as he was. Gabby was full of bluster and persuasive arguments but he held on to Jerilee like the drowning man he had once been, and Jerilee was torn, caught in a situation she could never have imagined a few months earlier.

Olive Blankenbaker, still troubled by the tableau she encountered two decades ago, recalled an evening when she inadvertently walked in on one of those meetings. "I took two steaks over to Morris and Jerilee . . . and Moore was there. I said, 'I guess I should have brought *three* steaks. I didn't know you had company.' Gabby just hung his head and looked away. I even felt kind of sorry for him, but that was before I realized what he had done to Morris."

Years after it had all been played out, Olive could not speak of Gabby as anyone other than "Moore," and she could not keep the disgust and rage from her voice. For all of her life, she had worked to make her son happy and there had finally come a time when she had no power whatsoever to ease the searing pain he was suffering.

Hammering away at Jerilee with skewed logic and raw emotion and relentless pleas, it wasn't long before Gabby Moore had convinced her to leave Morris once again and come back to live with him.

This time, Morris realized his marriage was truly over.

When his life disintegrated, Morris Blankenbaker could not bear to be in Yakima any longer, despite the fact that his mother, his brothers, his children, and his friends were all there. Everywhere he went there were reminders of Jerilee. Worse, there was every likelihood that he would actually run into his wife with her new husband. Yakima wasn't big enough to avoid that.

Gabby Moore *was* Jerilee's new husband; he married her almost before the ink on her divorce papers was dry. He couldn't risk the possibility that she would change her mind.

On September 14, 1974, Jerilee Blankenbaker became Jerilee Moore. Along with Amanda and Rick and Gabby's sixteen-year-old son, Derek, she and Gabby formed a new family. As he had promised, Gabby bought a house for them all to live in. It wasn't quite as lavish as he had promised, but it was a nice house.

Morris's and Jerilee's children were very young. They must have been confused to find themselves in a different house, without their daddy, and to see their mother living with the man who had come to stay with them after Christmas.

The swiftness with which Morris's marriage had vaporized stunned everyone who knew him. In a big city, the exchange of marital partners might have gone relatively unnoticed, but in Yakima, Washington, everyone seemed to be talking about the scandal.

Morris moved to Hawaii, a long, long way from his memories of the year just past, from a dozen years of memories of Jerilee. The weather was tropical, the vegetation lush and exotic; nothing looked or smelled or felt the least bit like Yakima, Washington. He figured that maybe there he could forget Jerilee. But this geographical solution to a shattered world didn't work. Morris was still alone. His pain had followed him every mile of the way.

Knowing how lonesome Morris was, and missing him, a bunch of his friends withdrew their savings and booked passage to Hawaii to visit him. They had barely arrived when Olive was rushed to the hospital back in Yakima. She warned Morris's half brothers and her own sisters not to tell Morris she was sick and they promised that they wouldn't. But Olive's ex-husband, Ned, came to visit her and he misunderstood the doctors' assessment of her condition. Ned thought they had said that her condition was terminal.

"He got on the phone to Morris, and said, 'Come right home. Your mother is dying.' I was disgusted," Olive recalled. "The whole lot of them got on a plane with Morris and came back to see if I was okay. They all came home, after the kids had only been there for one day in Hawaii. Even Morris's half brother, Mike, sold his car—the only car he'd ever had—so he could go with them and cheer up Morris. I didn't even want Morris to know I was in the hospital . . . I wasn't that sick, and I would have been fine. It spoiled their whole trip."

Morris Blankenbaker had grown up in the icy winters of eastern Washington, and in Hawaii he felt like an alien in a foreign land. His world had been turned upside down and it wasn't better in Hawaii—

it was worse. Someday he would have to accept that Jerilee was lost to him. It might as well be sooner as later. He missed his kids. He missed Yakima. He packed up and moved back home.

Morris found a big house on North Sixth Street, and he rented the extra bedrooms to some of his male friends. It wasn't the same as living with his own family, but he was a lot less lonely than he had been in Hawaii.

Morris was given a contract as a physical education teacher at Wapato Intermediate School. He was finally doing what he loved to do, but it was all ashes. Jerilee was gone. He only saw Amanda and Rick on sporadic visits. All the things he had worked for so long were gone.

His friends urged him to start dating—to stop being such a hermit—but he couldn't do it. When he tried, he felt as though he were an imposter. The only woman who meant anything to him was his wife—only she wasn't *his* wife anymore.

5

In September 1973, Jerilee Blankenbaker barely knew Gabby Moore; a year later she was divorced from Morris and married to him. Sometimes even she had trouble understanding how it could have happened.

At first, being with Gabby was romantic. There was no question that he adored Jerilee. She liked his son, Derek, and she thought that probably she and Gabby could make their new his-and-hers family work, although it was only natural that it would take a while for all of them to adjust to each other. Where Morris had been easygoing and predictable, Gabby was moody and mercurial. That had been part of his attraction—in the beginning. The very excitement and the passion of being with this man whose emotions seesawed so wildly had drawn her to him. He had promised her so much. He had talked about their future and their love. His plans were grandiose and breathtaking. She had believed everything he told her. She had no reason not to—not at first.

In the mid-seventies Gabby Moore was still a very popular and respected man in Yakima. Townspeople crowded in to see his team's wrestling matches; he had put Yakima on the map with his wrestlers. He made a good salary; he had been at Davis High a long time, almost fifteen years. He was an institution, a tradition, and being his wife made Jerilee proud. Of course, there were those who whispered about how her second marriage had come about. But she held her head high. Her choice had been agonizing, but she had made it and she planned to stick by her new husband.

Even so, it wasn't long before Jerilee realized that some of Gabby's moods could be frightening. He revealed a side of his personality that she had not seen before. And many of his promises never came to fruition. He had led her to believe that he was very well fixed financially—and he wasn't. He had his salary, and that was about it.

In a sense, Jerilee was back where she had begun—married to a coach, raising a family, working full-time. Only the role of her husband had been recast.

One thing, however, was vastly different: Gabby Moore's consumption of alcohol. Morris had said something about it, but he had held back from telling her everything. Jerilee had not known that Gabby drank so heavily. Now she saw what she had not seen before. "He drank so very much. When he drank he became hostile toward anybody. . . . He yelled, and he grabbed hold of whoever was close and shook them."

Jerilee had never known anyone who could drink as much bourbon whiskey as Gabby Moore. In a voice still full of disbelief, Jerilee remembered how bad it became. "He even kicked his own family, *his daughter and his son,* out of the house on Christmas Eve.

"He drank very heavily," she would recall in her light, feminine voice. "Within a two- or three-hour period, he would drink a fifth of bourbon or whatever."

And Gabby's consumption of a bottle of whiskey in a few hours was not a sometime thing. Three or four times a week, he would sit with a bottle beside him, steadily downing shots until it was empty. Jerilee saw now that his moods had a direct correlation to the amount of liquor he put away.

"He loved you a lot one minute," she remembered ruefully. "And the next minute he would just kick you out of the house and I was getting a little bit scared of him."

Actually, Jerilee Moore was getting a *lot* scared of her second husband. Like most women married to alcoholics, she soon learned to chart precisely the progression from high spirits and loving sentimentality to suspicion and paranoia. When Gabby got close to the bottom of the whiskey bottle, he was a mean drunk. More than once, she found herself locked out of her own home. More than once, she must have wondered what on earth she had gotten herself into. Gabby could be insanely jealous. Perhaps he felt that she would leave *him* as easily as she had been lured away from Morris—that some other man could turn her head just as he had. He had stolen her; now he feared someone would steal her from him.

Three times, Jerilee did leave Gabby, even though she still felt a powerful attraction to him when he was himself. She was a woman torn by conflicting emotions. He could still make her cry when he put on his record that began, "Lay your head upon my pillow . . ."

But living in the center of a constant emotional hurricane was far different than the excitement of a rapid courtship, and Jerilee probably found herself longing for Morris's loving predictability. She saw Morris when he picked up Amanda and Rick or when she dropped them off. She talked to him on the phone, which was only natural since they still shared the responsibility for their children. They had such a long history together, and the longer she stayed away from Morris, the more Jerilee appreciated her first love and his steadfast devotion to her.

She had cut off so many ties that she almost felt obligated to make a go of her marriage. And that was not an easy task. When Gabby was out of control and full of rage he actually made her afraid for her life and for her children's lives. When he threw her out of the house, muttering the imprecations of a befuddled drunk, she had to find somewhere to run. To her family. To friends. Sometimes, she came back later in the night when she figured he would be asleep. Sometimes, she stayed away, hoping she would have the strength not to go back. Gradually, Jerilee began to make tentative moves away from Gabby. At first, she came back after a few days. Once, she managed to stay away for two weeks.

Each time Jerilee walked away from Gabby, he was instantly contrite. He turned on the charm and worked hard to convince her that he would never mistreat her again. She wanted to believe him.

It was a familiar pattern, but one that Jerilee had never had an occasion to understand before she fell in love with Gabby Moore. His tears and remorse were so utterly real to her. He knew her weaknesses and her tender heart. If he had been able to win her away from Morris and cut her neatly out of her marriage—and he had—he certainly was adept now at keeping her tied to him. He was her husband. Time after time, Jerilee believed his promises about a new start. Time after time, she went back to him.

All that spring of 1975, Jerilee vacillated. Outside, it was so like the spring a year before when she was falling in love with Gabby, when she was so transfixed by him and the way he painted their future together that she had forgotten everything else. But now, she was seeing the Gabby behind the charming mask and she was afraid.

Gabby had always been caught up in his coaching and his athletes. Having lived with Morris, Jerilee understood that. Coaches were a different breed. But Gabby didn't even care about sports any longer. Almost every other day, when he got home from work, he pulled a fifth of whiskey out of a brown bag. He usually drank it straight, out of a glass. Sometimes, he added a little Pepsi to the bourbon but it didn't keep him from getting drunk and argumentative. The worst thing was his unpredictability. Jerilee watched him warily, never knowing what to expect.

From the moment she fell in love with him, Jerilee had never even imagined she might want to leave Gabby. She had sacrificed her marriage for him; she had betrayed Morris when she committed herself to Gabby. But there came a moment when she listened to his importuning and only stared back coldly. She no longer believed that he was going to change. She had heard his promises too many times, and too many times had watched him turn and reach for his bottle of bourbon an instant later.

When all the periods of their actually being together were added up, it wasn't much time at all. Less than a year. Jerilee had married Gabby in September 1974. She left him for good in July of 1975. So when she filed for divorce this time, she would have two divorce decrees within eighteen months.

Jerilee Blankenbaker Moore had made an appalling decision when she left her first husband, and she saw that with the terrible clarity that the truth can bring. When she finally realized what she had done, she rushed to rectify her error. The longer she had been away from Morris, the more she had missed him and come to realize what a good man he was, that *he* was the man she loved. She had been momentarily bedazzled, but her eyes were open now.

In a sequence of events right out of a soap opera script, Jerilee left Gabby Moore's home and bed and moved back in with Morris

Blankenbaker. It was a move that seared Gabby's soul, one that drove him nearly insane with jealousy. He drank to salve his pain, and drinking made him even more paranoid.

By 1975—if not earlier—Gabby Moore had come to a point where he saw everything that happened in the world in terms of how it affected *him*. He had no empathy, no sympathy. He had no rational or emotional ability to step back and view a situation from another person's point of view. If he had ever felt any guilt over betraying Morris, he fought it down before it could bubble to the surface of his mind. He could not now admit that Jerilee had been Morris's to begin with and that she had gone back to her husband and the father of her two little children. He could only beat his breast and cry out that he had been deeply wounded. The startling thing about Moore's position was that he believed that he was absolutely within his rights— that *he* was the injured party. He would have been astounded had anyone suggested otherwise.

His great love was gone, and he could not allow that to happen. The campaign that Gabby Moore mounted to win Jerilee back was prodigious—he used all of his considerable weapons.

When Jerilee and the children moved back in with Morris, he was still living in the big frame house on North Sixth. All of his roomers except for one had moved out, and he made plans to move soon. Morris, Jerilee, and the children occupied the downstairs until then.

If Jerilee had believed that Gabby would let her go without a fight, she soon found out she was mistaken. He called her every day—at the Pacific National Bank in Selah, Washington, where she worked and at the house where she lived with Morris. He made several trips to the bank to confront Jerilee at work. She had a good job as a loan interviewer, and it was embarrassing when one of her coworkers announced that Gabby Moore was waiting to see her.

She knew what he was going to say. He would ask her, "When are you coming back?" and "Won't you give me just one more chance?"

He told Jerilee that he wasn't going to make it without her, and she caught the manipulative threat. He was telling her that if he couldn't have her, he didn't want to live. When she refused to come back to him, he got more specific. He was going to kill himself, he said, and he wanted her to watch—to see what she had done to him.

Perhaps frightened by his threats of suicide, and worn down by his pleas, Jerilee may not have taken a strong enough stand with him. She may have agreed to meet him to talk more often than she would later admit to. There were those in Yakima who blamed her for being too "wishy-washy," and for not making the clean break that they felt would have kept Gabby Moore from pining after her.

Despite his drinking and his depression, Gabby had any number of people who loved him devotedly. His two daughters and his son came to Jerilee as emissaries from their father. Amanda and Rick had always followed Derek Moore around like puppy dogs, and they were thrilled when Gabby sent Derek over to take the children out for an ice-cream cone.

"I let them go," Jerilee said. "They thought a lot of Derek."

Gabby's daughters phoned Jerilee. They asked her what she thought she was accomplishing by leaving their father all alone. They blamed her for his pain.

"They asked me wouldn't I please go back and give their dad another try?" Jerilee recalled, and she said she simply could not go back to him again—ever.

She felt sorry for Gabby's children, and she could understand why they had come to her pleading his case. But there were things they didn't know. Once she was free of him, there was no way she was going back. She tried so many times to explain that to Gabby. She and Morris made plans to remarry shortly after her divorce from Gabby was final on November 10. They hoped to be married by Christmas. In time, she hoped that the whole episode with Gabby would be only a distant memory.

"I asked him very definitely to quit bothering me, [told him] that I was trying to start a new life; I wanted my family all back together and would he please quit harassing us."

Gabby had just stared at Jerilee as if she were speaking to him in a foreign language. He was never going to let her go. Didn't she know that? Whatever it took, he would do it. Whatever she wanted, he would get for her. He would not accept that all she wanted from him was her freedom.

He just didn't get it. "He would say," Jerilee recalled, " 'If it wasn't for Morris, you would be back with me.' "

But there *was* Morris, and she was grateful that he was still there for her. Nevertheless, she would not have stayed with Gabby even if Morris had turned his back on her. She could no longer live with Gabby's rages and his volatile moods.

In one of their conversations, Gabby told Jerilee—almost with a flourish—the depths to which she had made him sink. "I'm losing my job," he told her, "and it's because of you."

He told her that he had been asked to resign from Davis High

School and that he had been told his contract would not be renewed after the 1975–76 school year. In June of 1976, he would be through. He told her that he had been fired because he'd lost his temper with some of the student drivers, that he'd grabbed them and shaken them when they were driving and made a mistake. *That* must have stunned both the students and the administrators. Gabby had always been the soul of patience with his driver-training kids.

Jerilee suspected that it was more than his behavior in his driver-training sessions that had led to Gabby's dismissal. Yakima was too small a town for the school administrators not to know about his drinking and his profound personality change. Even so, he was such an institution at Davis that it seemed impossible they would ever ask him to leave. He would have had to do something pretty bad to get fired. But, if Gabby had expected her to come back to him because he'd been fired, he was mistaken. *He* was the one who had ruined his career.

Jerilee was afraid of Gabby. He asked her to postpone their divorce date, to give him some time before she finalized it, but she was adamant that she was going ahead. When November 10 came, both Jerilee and Gabby were in the courthouse. One of the things she had requested in her divorce was that she have the name "Blankenbaker" back. When Gabby Moore heard that, he was visibly upset.

She had rejected even his name.

Jerilee got Morris's last name back and she got her divorce, but Gabby didn't go away. In fact, he became even more aggressive and insistent that he couldn't live without her *after* their divorce than he had been before.

It would be impossible to explain the siege Jerilee Blankenbaker was enduring to anyone but another woman who has had a man fixate on her. It is akin to being in a glass house where none of your movements are entirely free, where someone is always watching.

Both Jerilee and Morris were working; in fact Morris was working *two* jobs. He taught at Wapato Intermediate School and he worked three evenings a week at the Lion's Share Lounge as a bouncer. That meant leaving Jerilee alone at night, but they had "Hike," their big black Labrador who was very protective of Jerilee and the children.

Gabby had come three times to Morris's home in his desperate battle to get Jerilee to come back. Morris wasn't really worried that Gabby would do anything crazy. Despite everything, Gabby was still "Coach" to him. Morris figured that in time everything would work out.

Late one night in mid-November when Morris was working at the

Lion's Share, Jerilee woke to hear someone walking around inside the house. There were no locks on the exterior doors. In a big city, that would have seemed foolhardy, but this was Yakima, where the crime rate was low. People didn't lock their doors, even when they lived—as the Blankenbakers did—only a few blocks from the downtown business district. Morris and Jerilee had a lock on their bedroom door though, to keep the kids from walking in.

Now, Jerilee, her children asleep beside her, lay frozen in bed as she heard heavy footsteps and crashing sounds. She was grateful for the bedroom door lock as she heard someone call her name and then unintelligible grumbling and muttering.

It was Gabby.

"He had been drinking," Jerilee remembered, "and he threatened if I didn't come out into the living room area that he would kick in the door and come after me. He wasn't very rational at the time; he was quite drunk."

She had a phone in the bedroom and she reached for it quietly and dialed the number at the Lion's Share.

"Morris," she whispered, when he came to the phone. "Gabby's here. He's out in the living room and he's threatening to kick my door in."

Morris left the Lion's Share and headed for the house on North Sixth. It wasn't far; the bar was on Second Street.

Jerilee stayed quiet in her bedroom, listening, expecting to hear the crash of a foot through the thin bedroom door at any moment. She knew how Gabby could be when he was this drunk, and she was afraid, remembering some of the threats he had made.

It had become very quiet in the living room. Jerilee hoped that Gabby had given up and left. But then, suddenly, there was a banging crash on her window. Gabby was outside, yelling at her through the closed window. He was determined to get to her, to talk to her, to hold her in his arms.

Maybe this was the night he was going to kill himself in front of her. . . .

Joey Watkins* had known both Morris and Gabby for a long time. Seven or eight years before, when he was at Davis, Morris was an assistant coach on the teams Joey turned out for. Joey was a big guy—one of the heavyweights that Morris had helped coach. And, of course, Gabby was head wrestling coach when Joey wrestled.

Later, Joey, twenty-two, recalled the incident that night in November. "Well, I was sitting in the Lion's Share with Morris and we was talking, and like here the phone rang and a lady answers and said, 'It's for you, Morris,' and so Morris got the phone and it was his wife and she said that Mr. Moore was banging around on her house and stuff, and he said he would be over and he asked me to go with him, so I went over there with him. . . . Mr. Moore was 'bamming' on the windows."

It was apparent that Gabby Moore was drunk, and Joey Watkins half-expected Morris to start fighting with him. After all, it was Morris's house, and Morris's woman, and she had sounded scared half to death when she called the Lion's Share.

"Morris got out of the car and went over there. But he said to me, 'Joey, you know what? I would hit him in the mouth, but he was my coach too. I can't do it.' So they just went over there and started talking. Mr. Moore and Morris was talking, and I guess Morris told him something and he just left."

Joey Watkins stared at his former coach. Gabby was so intoxicated that he had been staggering as he moved from window to window, beating on the glass with his fists. Like most of the young men who had turned out for sports at Davis High, Watkins had been flabbergasted at the change in Gabby.

"He was my football coach and wrestling coach ever since I was a sophomore in high school. . . . I seen Mr. Moore the first time [in a bar] when I was in the Lion's Share and he was wild, you know . . . like he just changed from the coach that we used to see because he was strict, you know, on us. He wasn't the same person. For one thing, his hair was longer and he just didn't dress like he used to."

After Joey saw Gabby in the bar the first time, he had seen him often. Gabby had always been with a crowd of friends, and he was drinking like there was no tomorrow. That just wasn't the coach Joey remembered. Gabby had always demanded that his athletes train hard. "If you got beat," Watkins said, "he knows why—because you didn't work out hard enough."

Joey Watkins couldn't hear what Morris had said to Gabby, but whatever it was it was effective. He saw Gabby stagger away, and then he heard the sound of a car starting up. He knew the sound of that engine; it was Gabby's little caramel-colored MG sports car.

Inside, Jerilee had listened to Morris's voice trying to reason with Gabby. She could make out only the faint mumble of deep voices and then the sound of a car leaving.

"Morris and Joey Watkins came into the house," Jerilee said. "And then Morris called the police department and told them the story and they said they would send a patrol car just to go by off and on during the night. Morris went back to work."

And, apparently, Gabby went home to sleep it off. No one seemed to take the incident too seriously. Half the police department had taken a class from him, or played ball for him, or wrestled for him. Some had gone to school with him when he was a star himself. Gabby wasn't a threat—not really. Gabby was "Coach" and one of the finest teachers Davis High ever had.

He just had to get hold of himself.

6

Everyone who knew Gabby Moore believed that he would come to his senses. He had far too much to lose to let himself go over a woman. There were plenty of women in Yakima who would have been delighted to go out with him. But he wasn't interested any more than Morris had been interested when he was left alone the year before. When men fell in love with Jerilee, they didn't seem able to forget her.

That bitter fall, Gabby was living in an apartment with his son, Derek, out on South Eighteenth Street. He didn't want to live in the house where he had lived with Jerilee, and put it up for sale. The apartment he shared with seventeen-year-old Derek wasn't fancy, but it worked for two guys "batching it." Derek had the small bedroom off the kitchen. They ate what meals they took at home at the kitchen counter that separated that room from the rest of the apartment. Gabby turned the living room into a combination bedroom/living room by putting his bed in there and blocking the front door with a wardrobe. They parked out in back on the alley side and used the back door as the only entrance.

Gabby was still coaching and teaching although his contract would be up at the end of the school year. He was almost "phoning in" his participation at school, simply going through the motions, and mostly he didn't even bother with that. Gabby's wrestling team still turned out for practice and showed up at matches even if their coach wasn't the fireball he had once been. Sometimes it seemed they almost coached themselves, but they loved Gabby and covered for him.

In an unspoken pact, some of the athletes who had graduated from Davis started showing up after school to take over Gabby's duties. He had made his wrestlers champions and they would do anything for him. Between the alumni and the kids on the squad, the wrestling matches went on—mostly without Gabby.

Derek Moore was doing well in school, and he was a first team starter for the Davis High School "Pirates" football team. Any other time, his father would have been bursting with pride over his accomplishments in the athletic world. But now, nothing mattered to Gabby but getting Jerilee back.

Derek cut his dad a lot of slack. Like everyone else who knew Gabby Moore, he believed that things were going to be better in time. Derek was a strong kid who had a lot of emotional support—his grandparents, his mother, his new stepfather Larry Pryse, who was an assistant football coach at Davis.

At seventeen, Derek Moore's whole world was wrapped up in Yakima, in high school athletics, and in his girlfriend. Loyally, he lived with his dad and hoped for better days.

Dr. Myers, Gabby's former father-in-law, was extremely concerned about him. A.J. had been treating Gabby for hypertension for a decade, and he suspected that he wasn't taking his prescribed medication—a beta blocker and a diuretic. Gabby would take the medicine Myers prescribed all right, but then he would begin to feel better and, like many patients with high blood pressure, he would stop taking his pills. It was a vicious circle. Hypertension is a silent disease with few symptoms. A lot of patients die of strokes or heart attacks because they "feel fine" and they have no hint that the push of blood against fragile blood vessels has become critical. Sometimes, extremely high blood pressure causes headaches. Not often. The only sure sign of trouble is a nosebleed. If that happens, the patient is lucky. It is far better to bleed from an artery in the nose than to bleed, silently and lethally, from an artery in the brain.

Gabby was drinking heavily and he was stressed to the maximum. In addition, he wasn't taking his medication. Dr. Myers met him for lunch in November and tried to talk some sense into him. He warned him that he was going to blow out an artery if he didn't pay attention.

But Gabby Moore didn't seem to care. All he could talk about was Jerilee. If he couldn't have her back, he didn't want to live, anyway.

Myers nodded. It didn't matter that his daughter was Gabby's first ex-wife since she was happily remarried. Now they were just two men talking as friends, and it was Gabby who was left out in the cold and in seeming agony over it.

Myers hoped it wasn't going to flat out kill him.

It looked as though it might, when on the 18th of November, a few days after the incident at Jerilee and Morris's house, Gabby showed up at Dr. Myers's office and asked for an appointment.

"He reported to me that he had had repeated nosebleeds for the past twenty-four hours—a total of four of them—which were difficult to stop," Myers said. "He appeared at my office following one of these. . . . Because of his blood pressure and the history of four nosebleeds in twenty-four hours, I decided to hospitalize him."

It wouldn't be the first time that Gabby's hypertension became critical; Dr. Myers had been treating him for high blood pressure for ten years. He had had to hospitalize him for the same condition five years earlier, almost to the day. Now, Myers was really concerned; he could see that there was a clot on the arterial opening in the midsection of Gabby's left nostril. Gabby was going to be in trouble if he didn't get his blood pressure lowered and right away.

Gabby didn't want to go to the hospital; he just wanted Dr. Myers to give him something to stop the nosebleeds. Myers wouldn't listen to his arguments—not with such sky-high pressure registering on his sphygmomanometer. It didn't matter that Gabby was only forty-four, he was in danger of dying—and soon. With Gabby complaining all the way, Dr. Myers checked him into his own hospital, the Valley Osteopathic Hospital, at 3003 Tieton Drive.

From November 18 until November 22, Gabby Moore stayed in his hospital bed in a room just across the hall from the nursing station. He tried to check himself out earlier, but Myers would not allow him to go.

Jerilee knew that Gabby was in the hospital. His mother had called to tell her after he had been there for a day. Although she felt bad for his mother, she had disconnected emotionally from Gabby.

In a way, Gabby's illness and hospitalization gave Morris and Jerilee Blankenbaker a respite from his harassment. For two blissful days, he didn't call and he didn't show up to pound on windows or demand to be let in. They were back together for their first big holiday in this, the second phase of their marriage.

Thanksgiving would mean so much more to them this year. They were fortunate to have salvaged what had been a good marriage, to be able to forgive and forget, and to start over.

Morris taught all day, and then he was due at his moonlighting job at the Lion's Share. Jerilee had to work all day at the bank, and Morris stayed home and looked after Rick and Amanda. He was so happy to have his kids back, to have her back. They needed time, but they would regain the comfortable, secure world they had known before Gabby moved in with them.

While Jerilee didn't know if Gabby was still in the hospital, she hadn't heard from him and that was a good sign. "When I got home from work about six-thirty," she said, "Morris and the children and I went out to Shakey's for dinner, and Morris then took us home and dropped us off before eight o'clock."

Jerilee had planned to stay home all evening on Friday, but a friend, Helen Crimin, dropped by around nine and asked her if she wanted to go and listen to Helen's husband play in his band. He was an officer on the Yakima Police Department and he and some fellow policemen had formed a band that was playing at a cocktail lounge called the Country Cousin. Helen's invitation sounded like fun. Jerilee called her mother-in-law and Olive said she'd be glad to look after Rick and Amanda if Jerilee would bring them over to her mobile home. Olive had bought the double-wide trailer to use as an office, and now she made her home there.

"We stopped by the Lion's Share before we went to the Country Cousin so that I could tell Morris that I was going over there," Jerilee recalled. "We left about a quarter to ten. Then my girlfriend and I went down to the cocktail lounge and listened to her husband play . . . oh, probably ten songs."

Although she went to the clubs with some trepidation, Jerilee was relieved to find that Gabby wasn't in either of them. She and Helen had a good time and she began to breathe a little more easily. "We left and went to my mother-in-law's to pick up the children and then we went straight home to Sixth Street. It was about eleven o'clock when we got home."

When Helen Crimin's car pulled up in front of the Blankenbakers' house, everything looked normal. Still, Helen sensed that Jerilee was a little nervous, and she walked her and the children to the front door to be sure they got in all right, and that nobody was hanging around.

The house was quiet. Everything was just as Jerilee had left it. Hike seemed calm as he padded around, following her as she got Amanda and Rick ready for bed, a good sign that nobody had been in the house.

Still, Jerilee felt a little jittery with Morris at work, and she tucked the children in bed with her. She could move them after two when Morris got home. She didn't set an alarm clock; she knew she would wake up when she heard Morris come home.

Something woke Jerilee at two. Some loud noise. She wasn't sure what it was, but she rolled over and looked at the clock next to the bed. It was right around two. "I realized Morris would be coming home soon," she said, "so I took the children out of the bed and put them in their own beds. Then I went back to bed myself."

It was cold, and she snuggled under the blankets. She didn't fall back to sleep because it was only a few minutes before she heard Morris's car drive in back in the alley, its tires crunching on the frozen ground. "I heard our car door shut. And then I thought that I heard two more car doors shut, and Morris didn't come in."

She wasn't worried. They had had three days without any trouble at all, and Morris had so many friends. Hike hadn't even barked, as he would if a stranger were outside. She assumed that someone had asked Morris to go out for a couple of drinks after work and that they had followed him home to pick him up.

She heard male voices coming from the back of the house someplace out toward the alley. They were excited sounding, high-pitched. She strained to hear what they were saying. It wasn't much—maybe ten words or so.

"I stayed in bed about a half hour," Jerilee remembered. "And then I got up and went to the back window and looked out, and I saw that our car was there. So then I went outside and went to the car and looked inside the car, and nobody was there so I went back in the house—went back to bed."

Morris had actually been driving *her* car that night—the forest green Chevy Malibu. It was parked there, and it looked just the same as always. She didn't expect Morris to be gone very long. While she was outside, Jerilee hadn't looked around very much; she was very nearsighted and she had removed her contact lenses, so it wouldn't have done much good to look around. But she did see her car parked in the back, and the Volkswagen that Morris usually drove was in the carport. They were both there, and that was enough to ease her mind.

It was dark and it was cold and she could barely see her hand in front of her face. Once inside, Jerilee shivered at the thought of going back outside. Vaguely uneasy, she read for a while until she fell back to sleep. The children slept peacefully in the other bedroom, and Hike snoozed on the floor beside her.

At five, Jerilee woke with a start. She was cold, and the other side of the bed was empty. *Where was Morris?* This wasn't like him. She tried to remember if he'd said anything about going somewhere after work, and she couldn't remember a thing. She was positive he had planned to come home after the Lion's Share closed.

She couldn't very well call the police. What would she tell them? That her husband was three hours late getting home? There were probably a lot of husbands in Yakima who were a lot later than that.

But Morris would have called her.

Jerilee dialed the number she had for Mike Blankenbaker, Morris's half brother. "I called Mike and asked him if he knew what Morris had planned to do after work," Jerilee said. "He said that he was going to come straight home to me. So then I was worried and I said, 'Well, the car is here but he hasn't come in.' And Mike said, 'Well, just stay where you are and I'll come down and check things out.'"

Jerilee was beginning to feel a little less nervous. She said that she would take Hike with her and look around outside the house. "I think it will be okay," she told her brother-in-law. He promised to wait on the phone while she checked.

Jerilee's hand was steady as she put her contact lenses in. There had to be a simple explanation for where Morris was. It wasn't like him to drink too much, but, if he had, he was probably asleep at a friend's house.

"I went out the front door and the dog ran ahead of me and started growling and barking at something on the ground. I couldn't tell right then what it was," she recalled quietly. "But when I got there, I saw that it was Morris. . . ."

Shock—the kind that congeals the blood and makes the heart race out of sync—also dulls the senses. When something bad happens, so bad that the world will never, ever be the same again, the human mind cannot take it in all at once. Jerilee Blankenbaker had not yet acknowledged that *her* world had changed forever. At that moment, as she moved toward the man who lay facedown on the snowy ground, she had the tremendous strength that comes with an adrenaline rush. He lay just inside the gate, his feet pointed back toward the alley. He had fallen forward in an almost perfectly straight line.

"I rolled him over," Jerilee said, speaking of a man who weighed

210 pounds. "And tried to pull him toward me. I felt his face and I thought I felt something on his face. I thought it was mud at that time. And he was really heavy. I mean, he didn't help me at all. . . ."

A long time later when she spoke about it, Jerilee Blankenbaker's voice had the thinnest layer of calm over the remembered terror of that moment. "I took a hold of his jacket on his right side and rolled him toward the house, which would be north, and then I pulled him into a sitting position toward me with his jacket. . . . And I think that I tried to hear a heartbeat . . . and then I laid him back down."

Jerilee remembered running inside the house and picking up the phone where her husband's brother still waited on the line. "Mike," she cried. "Come quick. Morris has blood all over him."

Within a few minutes, Mike Blankenbaker was on his way to help Jerilee, and, he prayed, to help his brother. And so were the Yakima police.

7

Dennis Meyers had been a patrol officer for the Yakima Police Department for six years, and he was working the early shift—four A.M. to noon—on November 22. He got a call from the police dispatcher at 5:03 that morning to proceed to 210 North Sixth Street "in regards to a subject at that location being covered with lots of blood."

That was all Meyers knew at that point. He half-expected to find some drunk with a bloody nose. He was seven blocks away from the location when he got the call, and he was there in a few minutes. Meyers saw a woman standing in front of the house. "She was standing there and crying."

The officer walked up to the woman who led him around to the south side of the house and showed him a man lying on his back. It was still almost dark and Meyers used his flashlight to examine the "man down." The fallen man wore jeans, athletic shoes, and an open down jacket. His right leg was crossed almost casually over his left, and his arms rested on the ground. There was a great deal of blood on his face and seeping into the grass and snow next to his left hand.

Meyers didn't recognize the man, but the woman told him that it was her husband: Morris Blankenbaker. Everyone in Yakima knew Morris, but it would have been hard for anyone to recognize him with so much blood on his face.

More police began to arrive and Meyers tried to calm Jerilee Blankenbaker, who was still sobbing and nearly hysterical, as Officer Terry Rosenberry knelt beside the supine man and checked for signs of life. None were discernible.

While Meyers and Rosenberry and Patrol Sergeant Pleas Green waited for Sergeant Robert Brimmer, the Yakima police's chief investigator of homicides and a nineteen-year veteran of the department, they did not approach the body. Time seemed to stretch into hours, but it was actually only fifteen minutes until Brimmer arrived. The patrol officers led him back to the body, and he noted that the blood on the ground was clotted; whatever had happened had occurred some time before the police were called.

It was an eerie scene in the gray half-dawn. An empty Budweiser beer bottle nudged the dead man's right foot and a section of Lincoln log lay near the body, left behind, probably, by the victim's small son.

A dark green Chevrolet was pulled up beyond the gate area, near the alley. Brimmer directed Meyer to check it out, and he found that Morris's keys were still in the car, dropped on the floor on the driver's side. His bank statement lay on the seat. Just as Morris had no locks on his exterior doors, he didn't bother hiding his keys. He had not expected trouble.

Don Washburn of the Yakima Ambulance Company was also a deputy coroner. Actually, the ambulance service had gotten the first call for help from the Blankenbaker house, and it was the ambulance company that had called the police. Washburn had driven in around 5:25 A.M. It was he who officially pronounced Morris Blankenbaker dead. He had been dead for hours; rigor mortis—the condition where a human body "freezes" into position after death—had begun. The victim's jaw and shoulders were already hard to move. It was difficult to be certain with so much blood, but he seemed to have been shot in the face. There appeared to be a bullet wound—an entry wound—through his upper lip.

It was the ambulance attendants who put a sheet over the body—

not police procedure because evidence can inadvertently be transferred from the body to the sheet and vice versa. Brimmer wasn't happy to see this and removed the sheet carefully so that they could take photographs of the body. Two decades later, sheets would be flung over the bodies of Nicole Simpson and Ron Goldman. It is a natural reaction to shelter the dead from prying eyes. Morris Blankenbaker, Yakima's football hero and a friend to scores of people, was lying dead, staring blindly as snowflakes dotted his body. With his "wife" sobbing hysterically and his small children inside the house, it had seemed the decent thing to do. Then with the help of the investigators, the ambulance attendants lifted Morris's body to a gurney and put it in the ambulance for the short trip to the St. Elizabeth's Hospital morgue to await autopsy.

The police at the scene searched the grounds for more evidence. Brimmer, Rosenberry, and Lt. Bernie Kline combed the area at the south side of the house, along the wire fence between the yard and the apartment house, and moved on to the back where Morris's car was parked, and then into the alley itself. They had to use their flashlights at first. Sometimes, the refracted beam of a flashlight can help find minute bits of evidence as it hits the shiny side of a shell casing, a bullet fragment, a key, something that might lie hidden on the lawn or beneath a bush. The grass hadn't been mowed and it was three or four inches high. They searched trash cans in the alley in the faint hope that someone had tossed the murder gun away in his—or *her*—flight.

They found nothing.

They desperately needed to find some piece of physical evidence that could lead them to Morris Blankenbaker's killer. His executioner, really. They already had part of a possible scenario. Morris Blankenbaker had arrived home, stashed his keys on his car floor, and strolled through the gate of his yard. Quite probably, the open beer bottle had been in his hand. A man in fear of his life would not have been carrying a bottle of beer. His ex-wife had found him lying on his face and had somehow managed to turn him over. It would have taken the kind of strength that lets women lift cars off their children; Morris was a big man, a solid man, and she was such a delicate woman.

The blood on the ground would have come from his facial wounds; he had bled profusely in the moments before he died. In her vain attempt to save his life, Jerilee had managed to flip Morris over; the blood marked where he had lain.

Maybe an autopsy would give them some information. Maybe

there was a bullet in Morris's head that they could trace to a gun. From the appearance of the wounds, Brimmer's long experience suggested to him that the gun had been a small-caliber weapon— possibly a .22.

Carefully, as a pale sun cast light on their cheerless work, Brimmer's team measured every inch of the Blankenbaker yard and the porch, and then measured again from one set point. Later, this would enable them to triangulate their findings and place the body and all the bits and pieces of evidence—so few—in the exact spot where they had been found.

Their precise work kept them from facing the terrible question that kept echoing. Who on earth would shoot Morris Blankenbaker? *Everybody liked Morris. . . .*

The word that Morris Blankenbaker had been murdered spread throughout town to almost everyone who had ever known him, and that was half of Yakima. Long before the headlines hit, everyone who mattered knew.

Olive Blankenbaker will never forget the way she heard the worst news of her life. From the moment he was born, she had worried about her only child, but she had fought her natural inclination to warn him to be careful. All through his football days, and then when he was in the service, and working in the mental hospital, and climbing telephone poles in all kinds of weather, she had worried, but she had determinedly kept her mouth shut. In the end she had raised a man's man, but a gentle sensitive man too.

Olive was asleep in the early morning hours of November 22. She didn't know that the police and Mike Blankenbaker were trying to locate the best person to inform her that her son was dead. "They finally went and got my sister. Hazel came and got me out of bed," Olive remembered. "She just said it right out, 'Olive, Morris has been shot.' And I said, 'Is he dead?' and she said, 'Yes.' I just wanted to know, to get it over with in a hurry. I knew he was dead from the moment she took ahold of my hand. I really thought that I was going to die right on the spot. I thought 'This is *too* bad. Nothing this bad has ever happened to me before, and I can't take it. I'm not going to survive this. I'm going to die tonight.' "

Wild with grief, Olive Blankenbaker asked silently why it had to be Morris, her only son. Why couldn't it have been someone else's son—someone who had ten kids—it might be easier for them. She knew that wasn't true, and that wasn't the way she usually thought, but she could not bear the idea of living her life out without Morris. She had no husband, her sisters had their own lives, the boss she'd loved to work for was dead in a plane crash. Now the future yawned ahead of her empty of everything she had ever cared about.

Olive had no idea who had shot Morris; she couldn't conceive how anyone could have wanted to hurt him, much less kill him.

Robert Brimmer returned to the police station, and he and his investigators started their incident report procedure. "At that time," he said, "we started contacting witnesses or people to talk to. They started coming in after eight-thirty that morning."

Brimmer, a tall, lanky, laconic man in his forties, whose smiles were infrequent, was in charge of almost every major crime that came into the Yakima detective unit: homicide, arson, assault, armed robbery. If he was occasionally short-tempered, he was always fair and he treated every man who worked for him equally.

Some of the information Brimmer had elicited thus far in the Blankenbaker case was no help at all, some might prove to be, and some was startling. It would take a while to check it all out, but first there was the postmortem examination to attend.

The word *autopsy* by definition roughly means to "see for one's self." Everyone who attended Morris Blankenbaker's autopsy would be there to see what had happened to him—medically, clinically, ballistically. They could not allow themselves to consider the emotional aspect of this crime. Not now.

Dr. Richard Muzzall was the Yakima County Coroner. In Washington State, counties can choose whether they want to have a medical examiner or a coroner. Yakima and many of the smaller counties have coroners who are medical doctors but have not had extensive training in the science of death examination. In the old days, some counties didn't even require that coroners be doctors. Muzzall, however, had more experience than most coroners. He had worked as a deputy coroner in the Minneapolis area before moving to Yakima. By the time he stood over Morris Blankenbaker's body, he had performed approximately 150 autopsies.

It was ten o'clock in the morning on November 22; Morris had been dead about eight hours, his body had been discovered only five hours before. Just the evening before, he had been laughing with Jerilee and their children as they ate pizza at Shakey's. They were looking forward to Thanksgiving dinner together. And within the month, he and Jerilee would have remarried and the scars of the past two years would have begun to heal over.

Now that was not to be.

Three men stood in the autopsy room with Dr. Muzzall: Sergeant Brimmer, Eric Gustafson, a Yakima County Deputy District Attorney, and a young detective named Vern Henderson. Henderson swallowed hard and fought to maintain a professional distance from the dead man before him. It wasn't easy; Vern Henderson and Morris Blankenbaker had played football together at Davis High School. More than that—so *much* more than that—they had been best friends since they were thirteen years old. If any detective on the force had a special reason to want to find Morris's killer, it was Vern Henderson. Brimmer glanced covertly at Vern to see if he could handle this and, satisfied that he could, looked again at the perfect athlete's body on the table.

Vern Henderson had long since learned to hide his feelings, and his face was without expression. "I had been to a lot of autopsies by then, even to some where I knew the person. But I'd never been to one where the subject was such a good friend as Morris was. It was hard on me to go, but I wanted to know everything that had happened to him," Henderson said. "Because, see, I knew in my own mind that if they didn't find him [the killer] right away, I was going to have to look. I wanted to know what happened and you can only know if you go to the autopsy. I wanted to know the facts, so when I heard things, I'd know if it really happened that way or not."

Before the body was undressed and washed, photographs and measurements were taken. The four men took notes and observed minute details that would not have been significant to men in other professions.

Morris had always had a thick head of hair, and he had recently grown a mustache and a short beard. His face and beard were still stained with dried blood. When he was undressed and examined, it was clear that there were no injuries to his body. All the damage had been done to his head.

That he had been shot was evident both in the appearance of the wounds and in the gun barrel debris that was still present in his hair and on his skin. Muzzall pointed to the wound he felt had been the first, a shot fired while Morris was standing. It had pierced the upper lip at the center line and knocked out two front teeth before it embedded itself against the base of the spine just below the spot where the occipital portion of the skull joined the spinal column. The mouth wound itself, Muzzall felt, would not have caused death. However, the area where the spinal cord joins the brain is the control center of the human body. It regulates breathing and heart rate, and a bullet striking there might well have caused respiratory arrest. At the very least, this shot would have knocked the victim off his feet.

Morris had been lying on his face when Jerilee found him. Either the shooter had been in front of him, or the force of the first shot had spun him around as he fell. Muzzall pointed out the "freckles" of unburned gunpowder that had tattooed the victim's face. Tiny black dots extended up to the forehead, into the hairline and down into the beard for a distance of about three and a half inches from the lip wound. This meant that the killer had stood quite close to Morris when he fired and hit him in the mouth.

The second and third wounds had been delivered when Morris was down. They entered just behind the left ear and traveled horizontally through the brain, causing fatal damage. The second bullet had lodged against the skull on the right side, traveling at a slight upward angle. The third bullet entered the head just below the second and traveled forward and again slightly upward, ending in the frontal lobe of the brain. This third wound had dark gunpowder rimming it; it had almost been a *contact* wound. Each of these two shots could be considered "execution style" wounds. The killer had leaned over the prone man and held the murder weapon very close behind the victim's ear. Each was a fatal shot.

Whoever had shot Morris Blankenbaker had wanted to be very sure that he was dead. Morris had probably seen the first shot coming, if only at the last moment, Muzzall explained. He lifted Morris's right hand. It was flecked with dried blood. "This is blowback," he commented. "Here on the back, side, and even the palm of his hand. I would say the first bullet to strike him was the one to the mouth. . . . He would have had to have been in an upright position, to be raising his hand in front of his face, to get this blowback of blood from the lip wound. If he had been shot behind the ear first, he would have fallen on the ground, and his hand would not have been in a position to catch this blowback."

Morris had no other wounds beyond a small scratch on his nose, probably sustained when he fell. There was the characteristic bruising around his eyes almost always present with a head shot—quite consistent with the brain damage and bleeding behind his eyes. His knuckles were smooth. He hadn't hit anyone. His clothing wasn't torn. All he had time to do was hold up his hand in a futile attempt to protect his head from the gun he saw in his killer's fist. Morris had been a tremendously strong man; given a chance, he would have put up an awesome fight for his life.

Vern Henderson knew that. He had never seen anyone take Morris—not in a fair fight. Morris was—*had been,* he told himself— as strong as a bull moose.

But he clearly had not been given any warning. Brimmer and Henderson knew that the victim was due home shortly after two, and that Jerilee thought she had heard his car about then. She hadn't heard gunshots—although others had—and had probably mistaken the shots for "car doors slamming." His dog hadn't barked. Whoever was outside was someone familiar to the victim's black Lab. Hike was a guard dog, but he was as friendly as a pup to people he recognized.

Someone must have known Morris's habits, or someone had followed him from the Lion's Share. Whoever it was, Morris hadn't been afraid when his killer came up to him. He was probably carrying the open bottle of beer in his hand, a bottle that fell at his feet when he was shot. He hadn't shouted out a threat or a warning. He hadn't called out for help.

Muzzall routinely took a blood sample, which he would send to the Washington State Toxicology Laboratory at the University of Washington in Seattle for analysis.

Muzzall removed some battered slugs and a number of bullet fragments from the victim's skull. Their combined weight suggested strongly that they were .22s. Robert Brimmer marked them into evidence and locked them in a file cabinet in his office until he could mail them to the Washington State Police Crime Lab for testing. The casings (or shells) that had once held them had not been found. If the murder gun was a revolver, the cylinder would have retained the casings until the shooter deliberately tipped them out. If the gun had been an automatic, it would have ejected the shell and slid a new bullet into firing position after every shot.

They couldn't be sure which kind of gun they were looking for. If the gun was an automatic, there should be shells at the crime scene. The investigators hadn't found any yet, but they had had to search in dim light in high grass with patches of snow on the ground. For all they knew, the bullet casings were still lying somewhere on the Blankenbaker's lawn.

Sergeant Brimmer had locked the Budweiser bottle and the Lincoln log in the evidence vault on the second floor of the Yakima Police

Department. He dusted the brown bottle now with light fingerprint powder, but he could bring up nothing but smudges; there were no distinctive loops, ridges, or whorls that might give him the information that either the victim or the killer had held that bottle.

One of the most convoluted murder investigations the Yakima detectives had ever known—an intricate murder probe that *any* big city detective would have found baffling—was just beginning.

One of the people Brimmer talked to early on was a staff member at Davis High School. For the first time, he learned that there "was an indication of hard feelings between Morris and Mr. Moore."

It was like the first little wisp of smoke from a smoldering hidden fire. Brimmer knew Gabby, and he couldn't imagine the beloved coach would do something like shoot a friend in the face and the back of the head. But he would have to look into it.

When Jerilee came out of the worst of her shock and hysteria, she thought of the only person she knew who had resented Morris. As impossible as it seemed—even to her—she began to wonder, and she felt she had to mention her doubts to the police. Gabby had always told her that she would come back to him, if it weren't for Morris. She knew that Gabby didn't just love her; he was totally obsessed with her. He had let his job slide, he had let his athletes down, and his relentless drinking had made him turn on his own children. He blamed it all on her, and then on Morris.

She didn't even want to think what she was thinking. Gabby had threatened so many times to kill *himself* in front of her, but he had never said anything about hurting Morris. Morris had always been so kind to Gabby. Even after what she and Gabby had done to him, Morris *still* treated Gabby with respect. He still called him "Coach," and he had told her he couldn't bring himself to hit Gabby a week before when he had broken into their house.

No, she couldn't imagine Gabby Moore killing Morris. But then, she couldn't imagine anyone else killing Morris. Of all the things she had been afraid might happen, that was one eventuality that had never crossed her mind.

Sergeant Brimmer called Gabby Moore and requested that he come down to the police station, asking him to bring any firearms he might own with him. Gabby did come to the station on that first Saturday afternoon, but he did not come prepared to talk to Brimmer. Instead, he said that anyone who was interested in talking to him would have to talk to his attorney. He had nothing to say.

8

Detective Vernon Henry Henderson had broken through barriers of one kind or another all of his life. Like Morris Blanken-baker, he had grown up in Yakima. But Morris was *born* there, and Vern arrived at the age of five, coming from the South to a world entirely different from the one he had known.

"My mother, my sister, and I came from Shreveport, Louisiana," Henderson said. "My grandfather was living up here already, and he called and told us to come on up here—that it was a better life. He owned some houses in Yakima and told my mother she could probably get a home up here. We moved up, and we *were* able to get a home."

It wasn't easy; Vern's mother, Leona, would work in a Yakima cannery her entire life. She was everything to her son—just as Olive was all things to Morris. Henderson's sister, Joanne, died when she was only twelve, and he was working by that age thinning apples in the orchards, picking fruit when the trees grew heavy with ripe produce.

As hard as they all had to work, the move *did* bring Leona Henderson's family a better life. "When I was growing up, you could leave your house open," Vern recalled. "And no one would go in it. And if someone did, we all knew who it was. We *knew* who the bad people were. Later, when I was on [police] patrol, I *knew* who the bad kids were, but now, you *don't* know who they are, and that makes it real hard to investigate."

There was no father in Vern Henderson's world, and while Morris Blankenbaker did have his father, Ned, in town to go to in a pinch, basically both Morris and Vern were being raised by their mothers. Athletics and the friendship of two of his peers, Les Rucker and Morris Blankenbaker, filled in most of the empty spaces in Vern's life. They were *family* to him.

"I met Morris at Washington Junior High," Henderson recalled. "He showed up in either seventh or eighth grade."

That would have been when Olive left her court job in Vancouver, Washington, and headed back to her hometown. Vern said that Morris lived with his mother and his grandmother out near the river. Morris had always been blind to the color of anyone's skin. He had played with Indian boys when he was smaller, and if you had asked him what color Vern Henderson and Les Rucker were, he probably would have had to think a moment to come up with "black."

There weren't many blacks living in Yakima four or five decades ago. Vern remembered that he was one of only six at Washington Junior High and that there were eight black students at Davis High School when he attended.

Over the years, many races would move into Yakima, but in the midfifties, there were very few Mexicans and the Indian population mostly lived south of town in Toppenish on the Yakima Indian Reservation. At Davis High, when Morris, Vern, and Les attended, out of the three hundred teenagers registered there was a total of twenty mixed-race students: blacks, Indians, and, perhaps, two or three Chinese. Yakima was a typical small-town orchard and farming community where it was "normal" to be white, and unusual to be any other color, unless you happened to be there to harvest the fruit or work in the fields, and then move on to another migrant worker camp. But the migrant kids rarely got a chance to attend school; they headed south with the first cold snap.

While Morris treated everyone the same and didn't notice that his school was mostly white, Vern Henderson did; he had come out of the Deep South to a far better life, just as his grandfather had promised, but he was still aware that he was a member of a minority race, and that he was *truly* in the minority at Davis High School.

His mother had found them a house in the northeast area of town, an exclusively Caucasian section of Yakima. "Everything *north* of Yakima Avenue was white then," he said. "South was where other races lived. . . . I even played on a baseball team where I was the only black, because all my friends were white."

In Yakima, Catholic teenagers went to Marquette High School, and all the rich kids who went to public school went to Eisenhower High School. Jerilee, several grades behind Vern and Morris, would go to Eisenhower. Later, Vern Henderson remembered that she had lived in a big house up near Thirty-second and Inglewood. "There were *no* poor people up there."

Morris and Vern met Gabby Moore for the first time at Washington

Junior High. He was the assistant wrestling coach then and they viewed him as the hero figure that most boys see in their coaches. They were twelve or thirteen, and Gabby was about twenty-one. The near-decade between them, of course, made a tremendous difference at that stage in their lives. Vern and Morris were awestruck by everything Gabby told them.

"I remember," Vern said, "that he taught us to always look our opponent in the eye to let him know what we were thinking, and that we weren't afraid of him, and that we could beat him."

When Morris and Vern moved up to Davis High School, Gabby was their coach there too; he had a better job, coaching on the high school level. "Morris and I both weighed one hundred eighty-five pounds," Vern said. "Gabby didn't need two of us competing in that heavyweight category, and he made Morris lose ten pounds so he could wrestle at a lower weight.

"Me and Morris were just about even," Vern said. "He was the only one I could go hand-to-hand with and come out even—anyone else, I could just tear apart."

Despite his prowess as an athlete, Vern Henderson never forgot what it felt like to be a kid who never had a father in the bleachers cheering him on, one who didn't have a dad to take him to the Father-Son banquets or to the awards ceremonies. Lots of times, Morris's dad couldn't come either, and both Vern and Morris had mothers who were working so hard to support them that they couldn't take time off. Vern and Morris and Les Rucker were a triumvirate against the world—more than friends—closer even than relatives.

"Morris and Les were always there for me," Vern recalled. "We were all there for each other."

Morris and Vern hung out together. You rarely saw one without the other. They didn't go to each other's homes that much, mostly because they were always playing football or wrestling or driving around town. Vern didn't have a car, but Morris had a little white Volkswagen that Ned Blankenbaker had bought for him. Olive laughed, remembering it. "Those great big boys weighed that car down so much when they were all in it, they looked like they were sitting on the street!"

Vern knew both Olive and Ned. "Morris's dad had the music store and sometimes we'd go over and see him at the store. He was a solid, stocky man." Morris's half brother, Mike, was just a little kid then, a kid who idolized Morris.

Like Morris, Vern belonged to the Lettermen's Club and was on the "A" Squad of the baseball and football teams, as well as turning out for Gabby Moore's wrestling squad. Vern and Morris were together so much that they actually could almost read each other's minds. "I knew what Morris was thinking and he knew what I was thinking." Vern smiled, remembering. "We could understand each other without talking. He knew if I was going to fight somebody, and he would walk up and stop me. And I'd walk up and stop him. We just knew each other. We *knew* each other."

Morris was not only a tremendously strong athlete, he also had an easygoing nature and reasonable turn of mind. He could always see the other guy's point of view. When he saw that Vern, who kept so much inside, was about to blow, he could step in and calm him down with a word or two.

Davis High School played in the AAA Football League and went up against Wenatchee and Richland, and, of course, Eisenhower. Vern played left halfback, Les Rucker played right halfback, and Morris played fullback. Dutch Schultz was their head coach, and Gabby assisted.

Even though the three musketeers would scatter—Morris and Les to Washington State University, and Vern to Central—Gabby Moore was a hero to all three through their high school years, and after. Lives in a small town are closely interwoven. Almost everyone knew each other and secrets weren't really secrets. Back then, Gabby seemed like the last man in the world to have secrets. He was a straight shooter, a good teacher, and a good coach whose athletes looked up to him. And he didn't live by a double standard. If the boys couldn't drink—and they couldn't—he didn't drink. If he ordered his wrestlers to diet, he dieted right along with them.

Vern Henderson and Morris Blankenbaker took his every word for gospel.

The friendship between Morris Blankenbaker and Vern Henderson only became stronger as the years went by. Vern laughed as he recalled that he was "serious about every girl I ever met—but not Morris," he said, suddenly sober. "I never saw him serious about anyone but Jerilee. Oh, he'd talk to girls at the movies or something, but Jerilee was the only one for him."

Vern and Morris both went off to college, working evenings and summers to pay for it. Vern married young, the first of their group to do so. He fathered two sons. He was working for the City of Yakima, driving a garbage truck while Morris was working nights in the state mental hospital.

They both had dreams. Morris had always wanted to become a teacher and a coach. Vern Henderson dreamed of being a policeman and one day a detective. "I always thought I wanted to be a policeman because I thought that would be nice—working and helping people," Vern recalled. "But I really thought that I never had a chance to be in law enforcement, if you want to know the truth. Back in those days, you didn't see any black policemen, not in Yakima. I wanted to work in the juvenile section; that's where I wanted to be, working with kids."

When Vern graduated from Davis and went to Yakima Valley Community College, and then Central Washington University at Ellensburg, he held on to that ambition. "A lot of my friends were becoming policemen. Jim Beaushaw—who was a quarterback and was a couple of years ahead of us—he became a police officer. And then a few others. Jim said, 'Vern, it would be a good job for you. You relate well with people.'"

Vern Henderson told Jim he would give it a try. He took the test for patrolman. "They had one opening," he remembered. "And the first time I took the test, I didn't pass high enough. And then I said to myself, 'Wait a minute. I can do better than this. I know these guys are not smarter than me.' I went back and I studied, and eight guys took the test and they had one opening again. This time, though, I came out number one."

That was in 1968. Chief Robert Madden hired Vern Henderson— the first black police officer ever in Yakima. It was the fulfillment of Vern's impossible dreams.

In 1968 Gabby Moore was bringing glory to Davis High with his wrestling squads. Morris and Jerilee had moved back to Yakima from Tacoma and she was pregnant with her first child. And Vern Henderson was a young patrolman, cruising the streets of Yakima.

Eighteen months later, Vern was sent "upstairs" to try out as a detective working in the juvenile section. "They were having a lot of problems with juvenile black gangs," he said. "They knew that I knew a lot of the kids. After I stayed there for three or four months, I went back down 'on the line.' But I was only there for thirty days. I'd made so many arrests in juvenile that they said, 'You're going back upstairs,' and that's where I was for the next ten years."

Over those years, Vern Henderson would work five years in juvenile, and then in the "regular" detective unit. He worked all manner of cases: burglary, auto theft, and homicides. His being black often gave him a leg up with many of the informants and suspects.

In the juvenile division, Vern could speak the same language as many of the kids who were brought in. "I understood them and I could talk to them. They knew I was serious when I said they could trust what I said."

Whenever there was a problem in the black community, it was Vern Henderson who was sent to represent the Yakima Police Department. He felt very confident then; it was only decades later that he marveled at his temerity in thinking he could handle the emerging gang problem single-handedly. It was decades later too when he would look back with some regret on a decision he had had to make—a decision that would weaken forever the link he had forged with members of his own race.

By 1974 both Morris Blankenbaker and Vern Henderson were almost thirty-two, and they had realized their goals. Morris was teaching sociology at Washington Junior High School and expecting to coach there too. The two men were still close friends, possibly closer than ever.

One day the Yakima City water line sprung a leak somewhere beneath the surface of the Yakima River. Someone had to dive down and try to locate the break. Both Vern and Morris were skilled SCUBA divers. "They couldn't pay me," Vern recalled, "because I was *already* on the city payroll, so I went and got Morris. We tied a rope around him and I stayed on shore and held on and he swam out and dove until he found the leak."

Morris was still strong as a bull, and a natural swimmer. Symbolically, one or the other of them was always holding the "rope" for the other, as if they could somehow keep each other safe.

Although Vern and his wife didn't socialize much with Morris and Jerilee, Vern had gotten to know Jerilee when he visited Morris, and he found her a gracious hostess, a pretty woman who kept a neat house. She seemed devoted to Morris. And Morris clearly adored her.

When Morris told him that Gabby Moore was moving in with him and Jerilee for a while, Vern didn't think much about it. Everyone knew that Gabby was having a rough time over his divorce from Gay. The word was that Gabby had begun to drink—something that none of his athletes had ever seen before. Vern was soon aware that Gabby became unreasonably jealous and suspicious when he drank, and heard the rumors that Gay Moore couldn't leave the house on the most innocent of errands without Gabby suspecting she was on her way to some romantic assignation. No marriage could survive long under that kind of pressure, and Gabby's hadn't.

It never occurred to Vern Henderson that Gabby would pose any threat to Morris's marriage. He was astonished when Morris stopped by the police station one day in the early spring of 1974 to see him. Morris didn't look very happy, and Vern led him to a quiet corner of the detective unit.

"You'll never guess who Jerilee's moved in with," Morris said.

Vern thought he was kidding. "What do you mean *'moved in with'*? Jerilee isn't going anywhere."

But then the look on Morris's face stopped him. He was dead serious. "She's left me and moved in with Gabby."

"With Gabby?"

It was the most unlikely thing Vern Henderson could ever have imagined. He stared at Morris, expecting him to break into a grin at any moment and tell him that it was all a joke. Why on earth would Jerilee leave Morris for Gabby? Gabby was on the skids, and Morris was younger, handsomer, and more dependable. Morris would have given Jerilee the moon if he could have pulled it down for her. Vern shook his head, trying to picture Jerilee Blankenbaker living with Gabby Moore.

In time, Vern accepted that impossible circumstance. And, like all Morris's friends, Vern tried to cheer him up. Nothing much helped, of course. Morris's wife and his two little kids were gone from his home. His life had been turned inside out, and now *he* was the one who was all alone.

Vern Henderson was relieved when he heard that Jerilee was back for a trial reconciliation with Morris. He expected that it would work out for Morris after all. But then he learned that she had gone back to Gabby. It seemed as though the woman were torn between her first husband and her second, and that her indecision was driving all three of them crazy. Finally, in the summer of 1975, Morris told Vern that Jerilee was truly back with him—that she had filed for divorce from Gabby and that they were going to remarry as soon as they could.

Vern Henderson was happy for his old friend. Morris had always been so kind to everyone that it ate at Vern to think of the pain his friend had endured. Vern was not so serene, however, when he spotted Jerilee's car and Gabby's little brown MG parked close together near a city park.

"There I am in a detective's car going up Lincoln Avenue and I see Jerilee over in a parking lot on the West Side with *Gabby*. They were sitting in one of the cars—talking," Vern said. "And I'm saying to myself, 'Why is she talking to him? What she was doing was giving him a ray of hope yet.' I saw them a couple of times, and I thought,

'Can't the woman make up her mind? She's got no business talking to Gabby and giving him any kind of idea that she might go back to him.'

"I didn't mention anything about seeing them to Morris. For one thing, I didn't know what she was talking to Gabby about. It wasn't my business. For another, I learned a long time ago that you don't get involved in somebody else's relationship. I liked Jerilee and I *loved* Morris. Me and Morris were kind of like brothers. . . . You side with one or another—or you tell what you've seen—and then they get back together, and they're *both* mad at *you*."

Everyone who had ever known Gabby knew by then that he was carrying a torch for Jerilee that could light up a whole street. Vern felt that Jerilee should have cut it off clean, and never agreed to meet or talk to Gabby. Vern knew how stubborn Gabby was; he had always taught his athletes never to quit. And Vern worried because it didn't seem like Gabby was about to let Jerilee walk away from him.

Still, it never crossed Vern Henderson's mind to worry that there would be any *physical* confrontation between Morris and Gabby. "There was never any thought that Gabby would do something at the house—not with the kids there. Morris still respected Gabby as his coach. Morris was not going to fight Gabby unless he had to. That's the way Morris was. He would never have hurt Gabby," Vern said. "And Gabby—he knew that Morris was so strong he would destroy him. He was too smart to ever take Morris on."

Vern could see that there might be more heartbreak on the horizon for his best friend and his former coach, but he never thought either of them was in danger.

Never.

Two decades later, a cloud passed over Vern Henderson's face as he remembered the night of November 21, 1975. Apparently Morris had had more misgivings than he himself had had. Vern remembered a conversation he had with Morris, one he had sloughed off at the time. "Morris said to me about a month and a half before he died, 'If anything should ever happen to me, Vern, you be sure you check out Gabby.'

"I told him, 'Don't be talking this stupidness because this is not going to happen.' I didn't want to visualize anything like that happening. I said, 'You two guys—you gotta get straight with each other.'

"The thing is," Vern remembered, "I drove *right* by Morris's house that last night. It was five minutes after one in the morning, and I drove by and I looked at the house because I'd heard Gabby had been coming over, but everything was fine. And an hour later, Morris was dead—shot."

One got the sense that Vern Henderson had lived with some unnecessary guilt, a vague feeling that if only he had stopped to see Jerilee that night, if only he had parked and waited for Morris to get home, if only . . .

When Morris Blankenbaker was buried on November 25, 1975, Vern Henderson was one of his pallbearers. So was Les Rucker. The service in the Shaw and Sons Chapel was conducted by Priest Charles Benedict of the Reorganized Church of the Jesus Christ of Latter-Day Saints, and the chapel was full to overflowing. Neither Olive nor Morris were Mormons, and many years later, Olive wasn't sure just why Morris had a Mormon funeral. That terrible week was a blur in her mind.

The news stories described Jerilee as Morris's ex-wife, but the funeral notices all omitted the "Moore" from Jerilee's name and listed her as Morris's widow, Jerilee Blankenbaker. And she would have been Morris's wife again within a matter of weeks if someone had not shot him execution style in his own backyard. Now, Jerilee was left in a kind of never-never land. She was legally free of Gabby, but nothing mattered much anymore. There would be no marriage ceremony and no future with Morris. Her children would have no father to guide them as they grew up.

Olive Blankenbaker didn't die, although her grief was so over-whelming that she wanted to. When Vern Henderson visited her to offer his condolences, she took his hand and looked into his eyes, "Vern," she said, "I know *you'll* find out who killed my son."

Vern looked back at her and made a promise he had every intention of keeping. "Yes," he said quietly and convincingly, "yes, I will."

The newspapers noted that there were "no suspects" in Morris Blankenbaker's murder. That wasn't technically true. The investigators were looking hard at Gabby. The very fact that Gabby Moore refused to talk to detectives and said he would not take a lie detector test made him a suspect in the investigators' minds. That didn't mean they could arrest him. Far from it. They had no physical evidence linking him to the crime scene, and they certainly had no eyewitnesses.

Since Vern Henderson was still with the Youth Division, he was not assigned to the investigation of his good friend's murder. Even so, Vern had been notified of Morris's shooting at five A.M. on the morning of November 22 by Sergeant Green. Pleas Green knew how close Vern and Morris were and he didn't want him to hear it on the radio.

Vern had steeled himself to be at Morris's autopsy. Vern owed Morris that—not that Morris knew any longer that his friend was there for him, just as he had always been. More than that, Vern Henderson had wanted to know *how* Morris had died, and then maybe he would know why. It wasn't his case, it wasn't his assignment, but he had left the postmortem knowing that there was a good chance that there might be some .22 bullet casings lying somewhere in Morris's yard or close by. He didn't know if the gun was an automatic or not. If it was an automatic, he didn't know if it ejected casings to the right or left. But he knew that casings ejected from an automatic would be left with very distinctive, individual marks both from the extractor and the ejector. That would be a start. Still, even if he found the casings, they would be of help only if they could be matched to a specific weapon.

A lot of people have guns, especially around Yakima. Most of them are unfamiliar with the science of ballistics and the damning evidence that can be detected in slugs, casings, pellets, wadding, gunpowder, the lands and grooves of a gun barrel. Bullets, once fired, are not unlike fingerprints, rife with unique individual markings.

If Morris Blankenbaker's killer wasn't arrested immediately and if a confession didn't follow soon after, it was likely that it would take direct physical evidence to find and convict the killer. And the only really compelling evidence Henderson hoped to find was a couple of bullet casings.

But Vern Henderson wasn't assigned to the Blankenbaker case and he didn't try to insert himself into other detectives' investigations. He went back to the Youth Division and the cases waiting for him there. But he didn't forget. In fact, the more time that passed, the more he remembered that Morris's killer was walking around free, perhaps smug in the belief that he had pulled it off.

9

Sergeant Robert Brimmer continued to direct the probe into Morris's death. He and his detectives learned from Jerilee that Morris had been working at the Lion's Share that Friday night. They checked to see if there had been any trouble at the tavern in the hours before Morris's murder. But there had been nothing unusual—just the regulars and a few quiet strangers. Someone thought that two young men had been asking for Morris or talking to him an hour or so before the Lion's Share closed for the night.

What Brimmer learned from Jerilee that was the most intriguing were the details of her brief marriage and quick estrangement from Gabby Moore. In talking with Jerilee, and with others, it soon became evident to Brimmer that Moore had been totally beset by his passion for Jerilee. The Yakima police investigators and the new Yakima County Prosecutor, Jeff Sullivan, thought it quite possible that he had killed Morris in a jealous rage. It wouldn't be the first time that they had seen jealousy spark murder.

But that theory lost some plausibility when Jerilee told detectives that Gabby was in the hospital most of the week before Thanksgiving. She wasn't sure when he was released. Nor did she think he was capable of shooting Morris. Pressed, she said she just didn't know anymore.

The Yakima investigators knew that Morris had been shot at approximately 2:05 A.M.—give or take five minutes—on November 22. They were betting that Gabby Moore had been out of the hospital by then. They had witnesses who would testify that Moore had come to the Blankenbaker house a week earlier in the middle of the night in a drunken attempt to talk to Jerilee. Perhaps he had come back again.

It was easy enough to check on Gabby Moore's hospitalization. Brimmer and Sullivan went to the Valley Osteopathic Hospital and asked to see records on Moore's most recent stay there. Dr. A. J. Myers produced them at once.

"He was hospitalized on November eighteenth," Myers said, explaining that he was concerned about his former son-in-law's severe nosebleeds and he had advised him to go into the hospital until his blood pressure came down within normal limits.

"How long did he remain in the hospital?" Brimmer asked.

"Until November twenty-second."

For a moment, the detective's interest flared, but then he reminded himself that the twenty-second had been twenty-four hours long. Morris had been shot two hours into the day, in the wee hours of the morning, and most hospitals discharged patients around noon. He asked Dr. Myers just when Gabby Moore had checked out.

"He wanted to leave the night before—Friday—but I insisted he stay over to give me at least another night's rest on the blood pressure problem. So he went out on the morning of the twenty-second with my knowledge and permission."

"And what time *did* he check out?"

"I would say in the neighborhood of around nine-thirty, a quarter of ten o'clock that morning."

That meant that officially at least Gabby Moore had been a patient at the Valley Osteopathic Hospital at the moment Morris Blankenbaker was shot to death. However, that didn't mean that he had not *left* the hospital sometime during the night and returned later.

Brimmer asked if Gabby had been confined to bed during his stay.

"A large part of the time. I would say the last thirty-six hours I got him up. I was trying to hold him pretty quiet because I was having difficulty getting the blood pressure down."

Dr. Myers said he had changed his patient's blood pressure medicine, but it would take ten days to see if it would be effective. The best thing he could do short-term was rest. "He spent most of the day reading and he was up to go to the bathroom. He visited the nurses at the desk, but most of the time he was reading or watching television."

"Did he have a phone in his room?"

"No. We have room service for a telephone. Phones can be brought to the bedside, but they are not left in the room."

There was, however, a public phone at the far end of the corridor near the emergency entrance. Gabby could have walked down there and used it, but he would have been observed doing so.

Bob Brimmer and Jeff Sullivan asked for a tour of the hospital, with a special trip to the room that Moore had occupied.

The hospital, which Dr. Myers had had built in 1952 and which he had remodeled four times, faced Tieton Drive to the north. On

Thirtieth Avenue South, there was an emergency entrance and the Central Services Area with a waiting room and hospital offices. On the west side of the building, the patients' rooms opened off a wide corridor. There was an entrance from the waiting rooms on the south end of the hall, and a fire exit at the north end. There were a number of ways to get *out* of the hospital—perhaps even without being detected because no alarm would sound—but there were precious few ways to get back in. And all of those were monitored or alarmed.

They could see that no one could come into the area of the patients' rooms except from the waiting room. The fire exit on the north end of the same corridor was locked on the interior side with a bar. "There's no way to open this from the outside," Myers demonstrated, "with a key or otherwise." In case of fire, all a patient had to do was push on the door and it would swing open. But then the bar lock inside would click back in place.

There was another door to the outside through the kitchen and dining room area, but that too was locked unless an actual delivery was being made.

"The nurses' desk is here at the apex of the ell in order that all of the rooms are under observation from the nurses' desk—in addition to communication—so that there is an unobstructed view to the waiting room's inside door," Myers pointed out. "And an unobstructed view in this direction down to where you go out of the exit."

"Where was Mr. Moore's room?"

"His room was directly across from the nurses' desk," Myers said. "This just happened to be a vacant bed I put him in."

Myers said that there had been three nurses on duty on the night of November 21–22, at least one of whom would always be at the desk. It began to sound almost impossible for Gabby Moore to have left his hospital room without a nurse or hospital employee observing him. The corridors were brightly lit and well within the nurses' line of sight.

"What about the emergency room door?" Brimmer asked, speculating on another egress and reentry for the suspect.

Dr. Myers said that they had had a problem with theft of equipment when the ER door was left open. "That's locked now throughout a twenty-four-hour period, and it's not opened except by signal. There's a two-way speaker there. That door can be opened immediately from the inside, but not from the outside."

The visitors' room door was locked after 8:00 P.M. and no one could get *back* into the hospital from the outside after 8:00 P.M.

Myers repeated that it would be highly unlikely that a patient could slip out. "With three nurses on duty, you have one at the desk to watch the monitoring equipment and for patient calls, to write orders as they are telephoned or brought in, to chart the care . . . this desk is seldom unoccupied."

The investigators reasoned that *even if Gabby somehow managed to leave the hospital unobserved, there was no way he could have gotten back in without someone seeing him. No possible way.*

If Gabby Moore had wanted to get out of the hospital, it looked as though the only way he could have done it and be sure he wasn't observed would have been to go through the window in his room. But that proved to be impossible too; when Brimmer checked the outside of the hospital, he saw that the patients' windows were locked from the outside with a cylinder that slipped into a slot and was then held firmly by a screw.

Unless Gabby Moore had perfected the art of astral projection, the most viable suspect in the murder of Morris Blankenbaker had just been eliminated from the list of possibles. Gabby might have resented Morris and blamed him for Jerilee's departure, and he might have refused to talk to the police, but he couldn't have pulled the trigger on the gun that killed Morris; he had been in the hospital under medical watch at two A.M. on November 22. He had been there until 9:00 or 9:30 the next morning, seven hours after the murder.

Jerilee and her children moved in with her parents. She couldn't imagine staying in the house on North Sixth, not with the memory of Morris lying there in the snow, his blood staining the ground.

As far as Jerilee was concerned, the fact that Gabby had been in the hospital when someone killed Morris didn't lessen her suspicions one bit. But as much as she thought about it, she couldn't come up with one person, other than Gabby, who had a reason to want Morris dead. He had said often enough that Morris was the only reason she wouldn't come back to him.

Morris had only been dead a week when Jerilee learned that Gabby was trying to manipulate people so they would convince her to come back to him. It was as if he didn't care that Morris was dead. He couldn't even wait for a decent period of mourning. It didn't really matter to Jerilee how long he waited, though; she was never going back to him. Somehow, in some way that she didn't yet understand, she knew that Gabby was the cause of Morris's death. She would never forgive him, much less consider being with him again.

The thought made her skin crawl.

Jerilee's sister Kit* owned the apartment where Gabby was living with his son, Derek, and she lived close by. There wasn't even a proper street that separated their residences; it was more of a "lane," and Kit could not avoid seeing Gabby. It seemed as though he were always there, wanting to talk to her.

Moore wanted Kit to reason with Jerilee. He asked her all the time to try to persuade her sister to reconcile with him. When she stared at him, appalled, he looked back uncomprehendingly. Both Kit and Jerilee were horrified at Gabby's easy assumption that it was completely logical Jerilee should come back to him now that Morris was dead.

Gabby had a theory which he propounded to anyone who would listen. He suspected that someone wanted both him and Morris out of the picture. He said he had had unsettling incidents himself—odd phone calls at all hours of the day and night. He said he couldn't identify the voices. Some sounded Caucasian and some sounded black. But the gist of the calls was plain enough; the voices threatened him with death.

He told people that he had found a windowpane shattered and it looked as though the damage were done with a bullet.

Gabby told his intimates that *he* intended to find and expose Morris's killer, and that he figured he must be getting awfully close because someone was trying to silence *him* before he "scored." He was especially worried, he said, that one of his daughters had gotten a threatening call, and so had his mother.

That was much too close for comfort, and he said he didn't know what would happen next. He was a fatalist. He was going to do what he had to do without giving in.

Gabby even went into great detail with his older daughter about plans for his funeral in case the person who was stalking him succeeded in killing him. Gabby described what kind of funeral he wanted, but when his daughter started to cry, he would laugh, as if he had been kidding all along. One can only imagine the emotional impact on a teenager who loved her father.

Jerilee wasn't buying any of it. "*I* thought he had something to do with killing Morris," she recalled. "Just from different things he said. He had told my sister that he knew people that would do anything for him. All he had to do was ask. I just felt that *he* felt that if Morris wasn't there, I would be back to him; he was very confident that I would be back."

Gabby Moore was so confident, in fact, that he continued to phone the now-widowed Jerilee as the Christmas season approached. He wanted her back. He needed her, and now, he pointed out, she really needed him too. Jerilee refused to talk to him. She would have her mother or someone else answer the phone and tell him that she was unavailable.

Sometimes, Gabby would have his mother call. Jerilee would talk to her. She had nothing against Gabby's mother. But then the older woman would say suddenly, "Just a minute, Glynn wants to talk to you."

And then Jerilee would immediately say, "I'm sorry," and hang up. Always before, Gabby had been persuasive enough to get her to meet him "just to talk." No more. He had tried to confuse her in his campaign to get her to leave Morris. She was no longer confused; the bleak specter of Morris's death had made everything all too clear. She could not afford to talk to Gabby.

Finally, he stopped calling her parents' home and her office every day. He no longer tried to speak to her in person, but she knew he hadn't given up because he continued to send messages through his family.

Only once after Morris's murder did Jerilee agree to speak to Gabby on the phone. It happened approximately two-and-a-half weeks after Morris's murder—in the middle of December. Gabby told her that the police were bothering him, that they had asked him to take a polygraph test. He didn't tell her that he had hired an attorney.

Jerilee couldn't hold back her feelings. She told Gabby flat out that she believed he was involved in Morris's murder.

"He said he couldn't have done something like that," she recalled. "He insisted that he just couldn't have done it. I didn't believe him."

She told him it didn't matter anyway. She would never come back to him, and he had to accept that. As always, he countered with what he wanted her to believe. He told her that he could *prove* to her that he had absolutely nothing to do with the murder. Before he could begin to expand on the weird threats he was receiving, she cut him off.

She told him again that made no difference. She wasn't coming back to him. He kept repeating that he could prove what happened to Morris might be connected to him, but that it had nothing to do with his feelings for her. He *loved* her. He suspected that there was someone who had been after *both* him and Morris, and he had reason to fear for his own life. Something strange was going on.

Jerilee hung up. That was the last time she spoke to Gabby before Christmas. He sent messages through her sister, or through his relatives, but she would never speak to him again.

After Christmas, everything in Jerilee's world would change once more. It was as if she had entered a "House of Horrors" at the county fair—only it was all real. With every step she took, something even more ghastly popped up.

Bright lights lit up houses and lawns all over town, and deep snow fell. It got colder and the icy wind blew across the hills and plains of Yakima County, howling like the hounds of hell.

There *was* someone following Gabby Moore, someone just beyond his awareness. It wasn't anyone for Gabby to fear—at least not physically. But Vern Henderson was curious about Gabby Moore. He thought he had known the man; now he was not so sure. Although Vern wasn't officially working Homicide, and he was not assigned to Morris's case, he had promised Morris's mother he would find her son's killer.

In his own mind, he had promised Morris too.

From time to time, Vern spotted Gabby's MG or his Jeep weaving through town. Sometimes, Vern followed him. On two occasions, Vern followed Gabby as he drove up to the Tahoma Cemetery where Morris was buried. While Vern watched undetected, Gabby stood looking down at Morris's grave, his face a blank mask. What was he thinking? Vern wondered why he had come here to stand silent in the cold.

"He looked as though he felt bad," Vern remembered. "And I wondered if he had really loved Morris, his old friend, but maybe he'd wanted the woman more."

Inside the apartment Gabby Moore had rented with his sixteen-year-old son, there were no Christmas decorations. The two had been batching it for two months in an apartment that was nothing like the comfortable homes they were both used to. This was not a home; it was a stopping-off place for two males on their way to someplace else. They both had sports practice after school and games and wrestling matches. But Derek had a girlfriend, and his father had no one.

When he was alone, the sound of Gabby's stereo echoed through the empty rooms. He played the same record over and over and over again.

"Lay your head upon my pillow, put your warm and tender body close to mine. . . ."

It was one of the saddest—and most popular—of the country-western hits that year, Ray Price singing of lost love. The lyrics were far more accepting that the love affair was over, however, than Gabby was.

"I'll get along; you'll find another," Ray Price sang, "and I'll be here in case you ever need me. Let's just be glad we had some time to spend together. We don't have to watch the bridges that we're burning . . ."

Gabby had played "For the Good Times" so often that the record sometimes skipped where the needle had worn deep grooves. He was living almost entirely in the past, but he was planning for the future he was determined to have with Jerilee.

10

Although Jerilee could no longer be counted among that group, there were still many, many people who loved Gabby Moore. His three children tried to help him deal with his lost love. His ex-in-laws made him welcome, and Dr. A. J. Myers made an effort to keep track of Gabby's health. Looking at Gabby's bloated body and flushed face, Myers worried. He was clearly drinking too much and not eating right, and he didn't appear to have been taking his medication. He looked like a heart attack looking for a place to happen.

Perhaps more than anyone, Gabby's athletes—past and present—kept close tabs on him, making sure he wasn't alone for too long, trying to stop by and visit with him. He was "the man" to his boys. He was the coach that had lifted many of them from mediocrity and made them champions.

When Gabby was too distraught or too ill or even too intoxicated to show up for wrestling practice and wrestling matches, some of the star wrestlers who had graduated from Davis made sure that *they* were there to see that things ran smoothly. It was getting pretty bad.

They had seen Gabby step out of the gym and go to his car and take a swig out of a bottle he kept there. They had often smelled alcohol on his breath inside Davis High School at practice.

Still, not one of them could believe that the Davis High administrators would really fire Gabby. Sure, he said that he wouldn't be teaching or coaching at Davis after next graduation, but that seemed impossible. When push came to shove, it couldn't happen. Gabby was part of Davis, and Davis was part of him.

Gabby was as low as they had ever seen him. He was getting more reclusive, and he spent a lot of time in his apartment. Gabby's boys didn't see him around town in his snappy little MG sports car as much as they used to. Sometimes he showed up at the bars and the lounges, but not often. He bought bottles and took them home to drink. Gabby urged his former athletes to come over to his apartment. That meant they would have to have a drink with him and listen to him talk about Jerilee. They had heard about how wonderful Jerilee was and how beautiful and how she was meant to be with Gabby so many times that they could practically recite chapter and verse, but they listened attentively and tried to say something that would make their old coach feel better. They urged him just to "give the woman some time," because he wouldn't listen to them when they suggested he should forget her and find a woman who appreciated him. He would not allow them to say one word against Jerilee.

Nothing could make him feel better. Gabby wallowed in self-pity and in his memories. He had albums full of pictures of himself and Jerilee when their lives together were happy, and he had the record of their song. At some point during the long evenings, when he had just enough bourbon in his system to blur the emotional pain he felt, he would pore over his photographs and tell himself that Jerilee *would* be coming back. She didn't have any reason not to now. She had no husband, and no other boyfriend. Gabby still believed she was meant to be his.

On Saturday, December 13, Yakima Officer Michael Bartleson received a radio call to an address on South Fourth Street. It was one A.M. He was to meet officers in a two-man unit at the address. En route, they got a second complaint, "Possible child neglect at this address."

The officers had had calls to this address before and they knew that a teenage girl was baby-sitting her younger brothers and sisters while their mother was at work. When the girl answered the door, she appeared to have been drinking.

"Everything's all right," the girl mumbled.

"Is there anybody else in the house besides you and your brothers and sisters?" Bartleson asked.

"Maybe two . . ."

"Does your mother know that?" he asked.

"Yeah, she doesn't care," the girl said.

Bartleson doubted this, and he asked the station to call the mother and tell her that things didn't look good at home. She said she was on her way. The worried mother arrived after the patrolmen had been there for about half an hour. She wanted to go inside, and Bartleson went with her while Officers Ehmer and Beaulaurier circled around and waited at the back door on the alley side of the house.

As Bartleson and the mother went through the front door, they heard loud running sounds headed for the back door and something crashing in the rear of the house. "The two subjects—three subjects actually, were stopped at the back door by Ehmer and Beaulaurier," Bartleson recalled. "There was one young white male about fifteen or sixteen who was a cousin of the family, and a Kenny Marino* and a Glynn Moore—known to us as 'Gabby.'"

Marino was carrying a half-gallon of Ten-High whiskey, and the coach the officers all knew well was so under the influence that he didn't recognize them. "He was very intoxicated," Bartleson said with regret in his voice. "Leaning against the side of the house. He had no shoes on, in his stocking feet; there was snow on the ground. His pants were unbuckled, snapped at the top and unzipped . . ."

Inside the house, the teenage girl had gone to bed in the basement. She was fully dressed, and there was no indication that she had been harmed.

Still, it was a disturbing incident. It was just one more step down for Gabby Moore, shocking to the officers who had confronted him.

Jerilee tried to pull some kind of Christmas together for the children. They knew their father was gone, but they were far too young to understand that he was never coming back. Their grandparents tried to help, even though everyone was heartbroken. There is never a good time to lose someone to a senseless murder, but the holiday season is somehow worse than any other; none of them would ever see a Christmas tree again or a Thanksgiving turkey without thinking of Morris. Morris should have been with them for another fifty years.

Christmas Eve was the hardest. For everyone. The year before, Gabby had been with Jerilee, their only Christmas together. And now he was alone again. On Christmas Eve afternoon, Gay—Gabby's first ex-wife—came over to the apartment on Eighteenth Avenue and cleaned it up, doing the dishes, vacuuming, and trying to make it look a little more livable. Her son lived there too, of course, but even she felt sorry for Gabby. Gay had gone on with her life, but Gabby still seemed to be caught up in his obsessive jealousy; only the object of it had changed.

The Christmas before, Olive had had her son; the holidays had always been a happy time for her because Morris had been born just before Christmas.

Derek Moore stayed home with Gabby and watched television during the early part of Christmas Eve. Gabby had no plans to celebrate the holiday, but Derek was going to go to his girlfriend Janet Whitman's family to join in their Christmas Eve festivities. Her grandmother lived in the hamlet of Union Gap, a ten-minute drive from Derek's apartment, and Janet had arranged to pick Derek up in her car around eight.

Derek wasn't sure what his dad was going to do. He probably would call Derek's sisters who would be over at their grandparents, the Myers.

When Derek and Janet left the apartment, Gabby was alone. Later, when Derek tried to remember, he said he didn't think his father was drinking. It was kind of sad, though, leaving him behind in the apartment. No Christmas tree. No decorations. It could have been any other night in the year.

No one in the family heard from Gabby that evening until sometime between eleven and midnight when he called over to Dr. Myers's residence and talked to his eighteen-year-old daughter, Kate. They spoke for about fifteen minutes, a conversation that obviously upset Kate. After she hung up, she tried four times to call her father back. Each time, the line was busy. She wasn't looking at the clock, but it seemed to her when she tried to remember later that her last attempt had been at about 12:15 A.M.

What Kate didn't know was that her father had called her back after their first conversation, and that her grandfather had picked up the phone. He expected it to be his son, who was late in arriving for their Christmas Eve festivities, but when he heard Gabby's voice, he decided to talk to him to forestall any scenes. He didn't know until later that Kate had already talked to her father.

All over America, families were tiptoeing through the holidays, avoiding confrontations about old resentments and grudges. Alcohol only adds to the potential for trouble, and Gabby Moore's drinking was scaring his family.

"I decided to occupy his time on the telephone with me, rather than to have any problem . . . to disturb Christmas Eve," Dr. Myers remembered. "I visited with him and we made a date for the day following Christmas for him to appear at my office—it would be closed. . . . I wanted to examine him, and I suggested that I take him to lunch."

Gabby hadn't asked for Kate and he thanked Dr. Myers for remembering his birthday three days before. Dr. Myers assumed that that had been the purpose for his call. As close as Myers could tell, it was about 11:30. He was becoming quite concerned about his son, worrying that he might have had car trouble or a flat tire, so he had been glancing at the clock.

Myers couldn't be sure if Gabby was drinking. "He generally hid that pretty well from me. . . . He told me he wasn't drinking and I rather suspected that he might be bending the truth a bit with me," Myers recalled. "That particular night, he gave very little trace of drinking except toward the end of the conversation. And I asked him then, and he said, 'Oh, just a little bit.'"

If Gabby had been imbibing, he did an excellent job of hiding any slur in his voice. It was easy for Myers to believe that he had had only a few drinks and that things would be all right. He would get Gabby into his office, check his blood pressure, take him out for a good lunch and they could talk things out. Gabby wasn't even forty-five; he had so many good years ahead of him. He would pull out of this depression and get his life together.

That night there were no more calls from Gabby Moore.

Derek Moore and his girlfriend, Janet, had a great time at her family's Christmas Eve, and it was late when they left Union Gap to head back to Derek's apartment. Derek was driving Janet's car and he estimated that he pulled into the backyard parking spot sometime between one and one-thirty.

They noticed right away that the back porch light was off; Gabby *always* left it on.

"Derek," Janet said, "I think something is wrong."

"We better get out of the car," Derek answered. He had seen that both his dad's MG and his own Jeep were parked in their usual spots. "I'll look in the house," he said, while Janet reached in the backseat to gather up his Christmas gifts.

As Derek walked up to the back door, he noticed that the screen door in the back, which Gabby hadn't gotten around to replacing with a storm door for winter, was propped open, held by a white brick.

It hadn't been that way when they left.

Derek saw that someone had closed the kitchen window blinds during the time he'd been gone. They were always open, but now there were just thin slices of light coming through. Vaguely uneasy, he peered through the glass in the back door, and then he spun around with a premonition of trouble, and yelled to Janet who had been waiting tensely in her car. "My dad's not in there!"

"Then he looked at the floor," Janet remembered, "and he said, 'Janet, Janet! Come here!'" As Janet rushed up the steps to join him, Derek cried, "My dad is laying on the floor!"

Janet looked in and saw Gabby lying there. They both acknowledged that Derek's father drank a lot, but they had never seen him on the floor and that frightened them.

"We didn't know what the deal was . . . we didn't know that he was passed out or anything," she said. "We just kind of stood there, didn't know what to do, and then Derek said, 'Come on, I'm going to my mom's—to get her to come down with us,' so we went to his mom's and she wasn't home, so we went to the assistant wrestling coach at Davis—to his house—and *he* wasn't home, so we went to the Seven-Eleven and I called the police."

Most people don't have to work on Christmas, but cops do. Police departments never close down—especially not during the "amateur drinking" season when holiday parties send intoxicated drivers out on the roads and trigger family brawls. Patrolman John Mitchell was working one of the least desirable shifts that Christmas in Yakima. Third shift—from eight on Christmas Eve until four o'clock Christmas morning. It was very cold, the ground was covered with snow and the streets were a glare of ice.

It was nearing two A.M. that Christmas morning when Mitchell's radio suddenly crackled, "Respond to eight-one-six South Eighteenth Street . . . Unattended death . . ."

It was an especially sad call at Christmastime. An unattended death. Probably some elderly person, alone and ill, who had died all alone on Christmas Eve. It was a police matter in a sense, but it would probably prove to be a natural death. A stroke. A heart attack. Mitchell drove toward the address on South Eighteenth but he didn't use his whirling bubble lights or siren and he didn't speed over the slippery streets. Whatever had happened had already happened and there was no need to rush. He pulled his police cruiser up in front of the small frame house. He had been told someone would meet him there and he saw a young couple waiting in a parked car. They introduced themselves as Janet Whitman and Derek Moore.

They appeared to be in their teens and they both looked frightened. The boy said, "I think my father's dead. We have to go around to the rear to get into our place."

Mitchell followed Derek Moore's car as he drove around to the back alley and parked. The screen door in the back of the place was held open by a large brick or building block.

"He's in there," the boy said.

Mitchell walked up the steps and peered through the window in the door. There was a light on in the kitchen just beyond the door. A counter, which seemed to serve as an eating area, ran parallel to the back wall. Mitchell could see a man lying on the floor. He had fallen just where there was a passage between the counter and the wall, and his legs were toward the back door. Mitchell couldn't see the upper portion of the man's body because it extended into some room on the other side of the breakfast bar.

Cautiously, the officer stepped into the kitchen. The apartment was quiet. He leaned over the fallen man, who was lying on his left side. Mitchell touched the side of the man's neck, just over the carotid artery. There was no encouraging pulse there, and the skin beneath his hand was already faintly cold. There were no signs of life at all. It looked as though the man had suffered a seizure of some sort and fallen forward, probably dead when he hit the floor. There was no blood, and no sign of struggle.

The call seemed to be as the dispatcher had said, "an unattended death."

Mitchell stepped outside and saw that the young girl—Janet—was waiting close by, while the boy was standing back by their car. "I'm afraid Derek's father is dead," he said quietly, and then he watched while she went over to the boy, put her hand on his arm, and spoke to him.

John Mitchell was startled to hear Janet Whitman say, "Derek, they've shot your father."

Why would she say that? As far as Mitchell knew, the man inside had died a natural death; he certainly hadn't seen anything to indicate that there had been a shooting. Janet was probably on the thin edge of hysteria, and, like all kids, she had undoubtedly seen too many violent movies.

Mitchell didn't know at that point that Gabby had been telling everyone around him that he feared for his life, that someone was threatening to shoot him just as they had Morris Blankenbaker.

Mitchell walked up to Derek Moore. The boy was shocked, but he was able to answer questions.

"Did your dad have any medical problems that might have caused his death?"

Derek nodded his head slowly. "He had high blood pressure, but he was feeling fine tonight when I left. He was in good health . . ."

Puzzled, Mitchell went back into the kitchen. He looked around the room and he caught a glint of light reflected from something on the floor. Leaning over, he saw that it was a .22 caliber brass cartridge. He didn't touch it. He looked beyond the kitchen counter into the living room and noted that the telephone receiver was off the hook, and that a glass next to it had been tipped over.

Still, the place seemed fairly normal. The dishes had been done and the rooms looked neat. Mitchell glanced around the kitchen. There was a broiler pan on the kitchen counter, but it wasn't sitting flat; it rested on a pair of eyeglasses.

That was odd.

Back outside, Mitchell learned that the man who lay dead on the kitchen floor was Glynn "Gabby" Moore, the coach from Davis High School. That made the second coach in Yakima to be found dead at two A.M. in less than five weeks. What were the chances of that happening? Mitchell radioed for his sergeant, Mike Bamsmer, to respond to the scene. While he waited, he advised the watch commander, Lt. Roy Capen, that he thought he might have a possible homicide and requested a detective team too.

Since Moore was lying there in a white T-shirt and there wasn't a speck of blood on him, Mitchell still believed that Gabby had died of a heart attack. The bullet casing on the floor was a little out of place, but it could have been lying there for a long time. The phone off the hook and the glass being knocked over didn't concern Mitchell. If Moore had felt the first twinges of a coronary, he might have tried to call for help, left the phone off the hook, knocked over the glass, and then staggered toward the kitchen—maybe to open the door for the ambulance attendants. Of course, he *had* fallen with his head in the living room and his feet toward the back door, and it seemed as if he should have fallen in the other direction if he had been coming from the living room.

During the fifteen minutes it took for the detectives and his

supervisor to arrive, Mitchell planted himself at the back door to keep
the scene from being contaminated.

Sergeant Robert Brimmer and Detective Howard Cyr had been
wakened from sleep and they had hastily thrown on their clothes to
get to Gabby Moore's apartment as quickly as possible. When they
arrived at 816 South Eighteenth Avenue, they saw Sergeant Bamsmer
and a Dr. A. W. Stevenson standing out in the street on Arlington on
the south side of the residence. Stevenson was very active with the
athletic teams in Yakima, and Derek Moore had called him to tell him
that his father was dead. He had gotten dressed and come over to
help in any way he could.

Bob Brimmer stepped into the kitchen and observed Gabby Moore
lying on his side between a counter and a wall in the kitchen. His feet
and legs were up against the south wall of the kitchen and his back
was against the end of the counter. There was a small throw rug
beneath his body.

As Brimmer started to enter the kitchen, Mitchell warned him not
to step on the shell casing lying on the floor just inside the door about
two feet from Moore's feet. The casing was already slightly crimped
as if someone had accidentally stepped on it. Mitchell was sure he
had not. It was impossible to say how long the casing had been there.

The death scene was photographed, a not entirely silent tableau,
because Brimmer became aware of the sound of a record someplace
in the apartment, a record that had come to the end, with a needle
still wobbling on it: *bi-bipp . . . bi-bipp . . . bi-bipp . . .*

The apartment looked like any bachelor pad that lacked a woman's
touch. One end of the living room was being used as a bedroom,
blocked off from the rest of the room by a chest of drawers. The king-
sized bed was unmade, and a television set and a pair of trousers
with the belt still in the loops rested atop the tangled covers.

Brimmer saw that there was a photo album lying open on the floor
beside the bed. Bending closer, he recognized pictures of Gabby
Moore and Jerilee Blankenbaker Moore. Someone had apparently
lain on his stomach on the unmade bed and gazed at the photographs
of a once-happy couple—as a record played.

As Brimmer's eyes and camera swept over the room in segments,
recording everything, he saw a series of file cabinets that were stuffed
with wrestling records and coaching plans. There was a solid cabinet
blocking the front door, an overstuffed chair, a couch, a small coffee
table. There was a single bathroom, and a small bedroom near the
kitchen where sixteen-year-old Derek Moore apparently slept.

The wallpaper was patterned like a simulated old-fashioned piece-work quilt, and there were knickknacks here and there and a few prints on the walls; the decor seemed to be a combination of what a previous tenant might have left and the necessary items that Moore and his teenaged son had moved in. Above the bed was a Renoir print of a long-ago Parisian woman with a shadow-box of miniatures beside it—hardly something Gabby would have placed there.

There was a concrete building block beside the rumpled bed, with a box of Kleenex on it, a shoe rack with men's shoes lined up with a precision that seemed ironic now, an alarm clock, and a stack of paperback books.

The phone receiver was on the floor. A portable stereo sat on a table in a corner. The record still revolved, but the arm and needle were at the inside center groove, so that no music played any longer. The record on the turntable was Ray Price's "For the Good Times."

Brimmer found two guns in the bedroom section of the living room. A loaded shotgun leaned against the wall, and a 30-30 lever-action rifle, a Marlin, was lying under the bed. It too was loaded.

"I unloaded both of the weapons," Brimmer said later. "I smelled the barrels. There were no empty rounds in the chambers, and there was no odor of fresh burnt gunpowder in either."

All the while the detectives moved around the Moore apartment, taking pictures, measuring, Gabby Moore's body lay on the little throw rug. They all assumed he had suffered a fatal heart attack. But, because of the recent murder of Morris Blankenbaker, they were taking extra care as they processed the apartment.

They looked in a trash can in the kitchen and saw the Ten-High whiskey bottle with perhaps a "finger" of liquor in the bottom. Brimmer was unable to bring up any usable prints, only prints on top of other prints that left unreadable smudges.

Brimmer and Detective Howard Cyr stood over Gabby Moore's body. He looked quite peaceful now in the darkest moments of the long Christmas Eve-Christmas Day night. Whatever had killed him, he had died, it appeared, almost instantly. It was time to have his body removed. Chances were that there might not even be an autopsy—not with his history of high blood pressure. Brimmer knew, of course, that Gabby had been hospitalized for hypertension only a month before.

"We had taken measurements, we photographed the scene, and there was absolutely no evidence," Brimmer recalled, "and then I got down on my hands and knees and I was looking at this small rug on which he was lying—and *I detected a small spot.*"

Brimmer enlisted Cyr to help him roll Gabby's body over so that he could investigate the speck of red on the rug. Probably catsup or something.

"We moved Mr. Moore from his original position," Brimmer said. "At that point in time, a quantity of blood oozed from the body through this opening in the left shoulder area."

The detectives, who were rarely startled by anything, were shocked. Even with their combined years of experience in investigating deaths, they couldn't believe that there could be this much free blood and not one spot on Gabby Moore's white T-shirt. They could see now, however, what had happened.

Gabby Moore had been shot in the side beneath his left armpit. As long as he lay on the cold linoleum floor of his kitchen with his own considerable weight compressing the wound, the blood was walled back. There had been no sign at all that a bullet had pierced his body. But once they changed the position of his body, the huge amount of blood inside his chest had begun to seep through the wound beneath his left shoulder. It didn't gush as it would from a live person whose heart's beating would pump it out in geysers. The blood only leaked as any fluid would through an inanimate object with a hole in it.

Somewhere along the way, the tangled skein of Gabby's and Morris's personal relationships seemed to have caught them up and trapped them until they had come to a place where they could not get free.

And now neither of them ever would.

11

It was eleven A.M. on Christmas Day. But it did not seem like a holiday in the clean white room where a bright light illuminated the metal table and the air smelled of dried blood and disinfectant. Dr. Richard Muzzall bent once again to perform an autopsy on a most unlikely murder victim. Thirty-three days to the hour since Morris Blankenbaker's postmorten exam, it was Gabby Moore's turn.

Some of the men in the room had been there on November 22: Besides Muzzall, there was Sergeant Brimmer and Detective Vern Henderson. Detective Howard Cyr was there too, and Jeff Sullivan joined them now. The young prosecuting attorney had been elected to office the year before. He and his seven deputy prosecutors took turns being on call to attend autopsies. Sullivan knew it was vital that someone from his office be present at postmortems. When Bob Brimmer had called him before dawn on this Christmas Day, he had elected to forego a celebration with his family. Moore's death astonished him as much as the rest of them.

"Up to that point," Sullivan recalled, "I felt that Gabby was somehow involved in Morris's death, but I'd been out to the hospital and I knew he couldn't have done it himself. We figured maybe he had hired someone to do it. When Gabby was shot too, I didn't know *what* to think."

All of them watched intently as Muzzall lifted his scalpel and made the initial cut. Muzzall's first gross examination of the body of Gabby Moore, forty-four years and three days old, was that he had sustained a gunshot wound to the left posterior, lateral chest. That was all; there were no other injuries.

Muzzall made the first Y-shaped incision from shoulder to shoulder, and at the midpoint, a vertical cut down to the pubic bone. There had clearly been tremendous damage to the organs in the upper part of Moore's body and it was necessary to remove the front ribs and the breastbone so that the coroner could examine the dead man's heart and lungs.

Gabby Moore had died from a massive hemorrhage "secondary to a bullet wound passing through both chest cavities and the heart," Muzzall explained. "After entering the muscles of the left posterior chest, the bullet struck the fourth rib—here—on the left," he said, pointing. "Then it deflected. That changed the angle of its course so that it traveled transversely through the chest passing through the left lung, entering the left side of the heart—what we call the pulmonary outflow tract where the right ventricle pumps blood into the lungs."

Seldom had any of the men in the quiet room seen such damage from a lone bullet. Muzzall showed them where the slug had passed out the right side of the heart and through the right lung, lodging finally underneath the fourth rib on the victim's right side.

"There are approximately two thousand cc's of blood in the left chest," he said. "That's about four pints. I'd say fifteen hundred cc's—three pints—in the right chest, and another three hundred cc's in the pericardial sac—the membranous sac that surrounds the heart."

Half the blood in Moore's body had gushed out into his chest cavities, and yet only a slight fleck of red had stained the rug beneath him. Muzzall likened the bullet's effect on Moore's heart to cutting a garden house with an ax. "You hemorrhage out exceedingly rapidly," he said. "I'm sure that he lost consciousness within less than a minute and was probably dead in three or four at the most."

Pathologists often use metal probes to figure the angle at which a bullet enters a body. Dr. Muzzall inserted the probe and showed the investigators watching that the bullet had entered directly below the victim's left armpit at the fourth rib, a shot into his "side" in laymen's terms. Had the bullet continued down at the angle it entered, forty-five degrees, Muzzall said that he doubted that it would have been a fatal wound. It probably would have gone through a portion of the left lung, but in all likelihood would have missed the heart and come out somewhere in the front of the chest. However, once it hit the fourth rib, it deflected. The probe went horizontally across the chest, following the path of the bullet that had penetrated the heart and both lungs.

At this point, Muzzall's conclusions didn't seem as important as they would later. What did it matter the angle at which a bullet had entered? Or that it had traveled inside the body? Gabby Moore was dead; he had been dead almost from the moment he hit the kitchen floor.

Muzzall retrieved only one bullet, a .22 caliber slug, that was very distorted after it had smashed into the fourth rib on the left. These bullets are notorious for their unpredictability. They are small caliber and if they pass only through soft tissue, they do minimal damage. However, .22s cut through the air with such velocity that they have been known to kill a target a half mile away. A larger caliber bullet stops a victim in his tracks and knocks him down, doing tremendous damage. The speeding .22 slug is given to tumbling when it hits a bone and is far more likely to ricochet than a larger bullet. A .22 slug that comes into contact with a bone is like a car without a driver— bouncing heedlessly from one obstacle in its path to the next.

Gabby Moore had been alive at eleven P.M. the night before— Christmas Eve. He had been alive, according to his former father-in-law, at 12:15 A.M. when Dr. Myers talked to him on the phone and the two planned a lunch date for December 26. He was dead when his son came home an hour to an hour and a half later.

What had happened during that vital and mysterious time period? Had someone forced his—or her—way into Gabby's apartment, pulled down the blinds to hide what was going on inside from the neighbors, leaving the back door propped open with a brick to assure a quick and fluid getaway?

Ever since Morris Blankenbaker's murder, Gabby Moore had been telling intimates that someone was stalking *him* too, and that he was afraid for himself and his family. No one had taken Gabby very seriously when he insisted that someone was trying to get to him, just the way they had got to Morris. He had tried to tell Jerilee about it, to convince her that not only was he innocent of any implication in Morris's death, but that he was in danger too. He had sworn to Jerilee that he would prove to her he was not involved in any collusion in Morris's murder. Had he had to die to prove his innocence to her? Or was it possible that the real answers to two seemingly senseless murders were more bizarre than anything a fiction writer could possibly dream up?

Now Gabby was dead too, murdered too. The answers were not going to come from him.

Although both of the victims were coaches, both had been shot with a .22 caliber gun, both had been married to the same woman, and both had been killed during the holidays, there were dissimilarities too. Just as he had during the Blankenbaker autopsy, Dr. Muzzall had removed a blood sample from Gabby Moore to check for any alcohol content. Morris had had no percentage of alcohol at all in his blood; Gabby's reading was almost .31. In Washington State, as in most states, .10 is considered evidence of intoxication.

Gabby Moore had done a remarkable job of convincing Dr. Myers that he had had only a "little" to drink. It was amazing that he was still standing when he was shot. For a person unused to drinking, much beyond .30 is life-threatening; Gabby had undoubtedly developed a tolerance to liquor over the past few years, but even so, .31 was startling.

The killer had had the advantage over both victims; Morris had quite likely been taken by surprise. Gabby would have been too drunk to fight back.

On Friday, December 26, the *Yakima Herald-Republic* headlined the news that another popular local coach had been murdered: "Tied to Blankenbaker Slaying? Davis Mat Coach Moore Shot, Killed."

Dr. Myers was as shocked as anyone. After all, he had spoken to Gabby within an hour or so of his death. Now, he remembered an odd question that Gabby had asked him once—something that had no meaning at the time. Gabby had wanted to know if there was any place on the human body where a person could be shot—not in an arm or a leg, but part of the torso—where it wouldn't be fatal. Myers had pondered the question for a moment and then said that most people could probably sustain a gunshot wound in the shoulder blade and it probably wouldn't hit any vital organs. From what he understood, Gabby had been shot somewhere near his shoulder. It was odd and troubling to think that what he had taken to be a casual conversation might have had a purpose, although for the life of him he couldn't imagine what that purpose might be.

To the media's frustration, Prosecutor Jeff Sullivan was playing his cards very close to his vest, and anyone outside the investigation was getting very little information. "It's a real tragedy," Sullivan said. "I'm very concerned. The police are working on it. So far we have nobody in custody, no answers."

And, indeed, there did not seem to *be* any answers. From all reports, Gabby Moore had been his own worst enemy. Neither the Yakima Police nor the Yakima County Prosecutor had any idea who had reason to kill him. He had lost a lot of his credibility but not his popularity. Revenge for Morris's murder seemed an unlikely motive. Everyone who knew Gabby well knew he had been in the hospital when Morris died. It seemed unlikely that anyone would be so convinced that Gabby had a finger in Morris's murder that he had murdered Gabby in reprisal. Moreover, Morris Blankenbaker's friends were good solid guys—athletes—some the men who had worked climbing telephone poles with him, some who had gone to school with him. No, detectives couldn't believe that any of them had killed Gabby for revenge. They had no proof. Even if they had had evidence linking Gabby to Morris's murder, they would have gone to the police and not taken justice into their own hands.

The obituaries for Gabby Moore were all glowing, reminding Yakimans of what he had done for sports in their town. No mention was made of the fact that Gabby Moore had been asked to leave Davis High School at the end of the school year. In death, he had somehow regained the respectability that he had lost in life. The quotes from his superiors made it sound almost as if the administration regretted firing him.

Yakima School Superintendent Warren Dean Starr told the press,

"We're shocked. He's been a fine employee and an outstanding wrestling coach. The administration is just sick about it."

Funeral services for Gabby Moore were held on December 29, 1975, in the Central Lutheran Church in Yakima. Dr. Charles Wilkes of the First Church of the Nazarene officiated. Gabby's family suggested that memorials be given to the Davis Wrestling Team or Yakima Youth Baseball. There was a decent-sized group of mourners, but not nearly as many as those who had come to pay their respects to Morris Blankenbaker five weeks before.

The apartment on Eighteenth Street that had become a shrine to Jerilee was vacated. Derek Moore went to live with his mother, sisters, and stepfather.

Jerilee Blankenbaker looked for a way to pick up the fragments of her life. If she was afraid, few would blame her. Both of her husbands had been murdered within five weeks, and the police had no idea who the killer was. It was easy to imagine all kinds of frightening scenarios. She wondered sometimes if she *did* have a phantom admirer, someone even more obsessed with her than Gabby had been. What if there was still someone out there who was watching her, now that the men in her life were dead? What had happened already was beyond comprehension. She could no longer believe in a safe, protected existence; she knew that the whole world could blow up without warning.

For her, it had done so. Twice.

Two coaches. Two murders. One at Thanksgiving. One at Christmas. There was no way that anyone was going to write this off as coincidence.

What on earth did it mean? Who would have a reason to hate both of the dead men enough to kill them? A disgruntled former athlete? Some other man who was fixated on Jerilee—from a distance, perhaps—and seethed to see her with Morris and Gabby? No, that was fictional plotting. It didn't fit in Yakima, and it didn't fit with Morris Blankenbaker and Gabby Moore. That didn't stop the rumor mills from churning out motives both plausible and utterly ridiculous.

One tale that circulated around Yakima County was that there was a "drug connection," that both of the victims had known too much about illegal narcotics operations in the area. Another strong rumor was that "organized crime" was involved.

Lt. Bernie Kline told the press that the Yakima police had found nothing that suggested either motive. Nor had they found any connection at all between Morris and Gabby's murders and the shooting death of Everett "Fritz" Fretland, a restaurant owner in nearby Selah, Washington, who had been found shot to death on September 6. Aside from the parallels in time and place, Fretland's murder had nothing at all to do with those of the two coaches.

Kline would say only that Prosecutor Jeff Sullivan and the police were making progress on Blankenbaker's and Moore's murders, although neither would give any details. "I have every confidence that both killings will be solved," Sullivan said. "The investigation is proceeding and progress is being made. We are looking into a number of possibilities. It is just a process of putting them together."

12

In truth, Sullivan and the others were baffled—but only for a short time. Then they dug in hard to solve this seemingly insoluble double-murder case. In the years ahead, Sullivan would prosecute dozens of felonies and supervise many times that number, but he would never forget this case, a baptism of fire.

In 1976 Prosecuting Attorney Jeff Sullivan was thirty-two years old, the same age as Morris Blankenbaker. Indeed, they both graduated from high school in Yakima in 1961, but Morris had gone to public school at Davis and Sullivan had attended parochial school: Marquette. Basketball was Sullivan's sport; football was Blankenbaker's. Sullivan would come to know Morris Blankenbaker—and Gabby Moore—better in death than he had ever known them in life.

Jeff Sullivan was very handsome, a tall man with a thick shock of blond hair, who bore more than a passing resemblance to John F. Kennedy. After winning the election in November 1974, Sullivan was just embarking on the first of six terms as the elected prosecutor of Yakima County. He was a native Yakiman, the son of a family who had run a dry cleaning business in the area for many years. Sullivan had worked long and hard to achieve the responsible position he held at such a young age. His BA degree was from Gonzaga University in Spokane; he had a Bronze Star from his service as a first lieutenant in Vietnam where he was platoon leader and executive officer.

Returning from Vietnam, Sullivan, who had a wife and two children by then (a family that would swell to four children), worked a full-time job as a trust officer of a Spokane bank during the day and attended law school at Gonzaga at night. Despite his punishing schedule, he graduated third in his class in the spring of 1971. Two months later, he was a deputy prosecutor in Yakima. The next year, he changed hats and worked as a public defender.

The first case that Sullivan won was against J. Adam Moore (no relation to Gabby). He managed to get the second-degree murder charges against his client reduced to manslaughter. "Well, *I* think I won." Sullivan laughs. "Adam Moore claims *he* won."

Adam Moore and Jeff Sullivan would continue to meet on the legal battlegrounds of Yakima County over the next three decades.

During trials, their friendship was always there—but on hold. Sullivan considers Moore "the premier defense attorney in Yakima County—probably in the whole state of Washington."

The two attorneys had no way of knowing in December of 1975 how challenged both of them would be by the Morris Blankenbaker–Gabby Moore homicide case.

Gabby Moore's death left a huge void in the lives of his current and former athletes. His connection to them had been so much more than that of a teacher to his students. Coaches—good coaches—shape the lives of their athletes forever after. They are often the father figures that some boys and girls never had. They can instill a sense of self-worth and an inner confidence that lasts a lifetime. Teenagers may be cocky on the outside, but most of them are unsure of their own capabilities, tough or sullen because they are scared inside. Sports bring discipline and the courage to keep going when it looks as though the athlete has no more heart, muscle, or breath left.

For most of his life, Gabby had been a superlative coach; only the last few years had sullied that image. Gabby had coached both football and wrestling, but, like most coaches, he excelled in one—and that was, of course, wrestling. Wrestlers have to practice more self-denial than participants in almost any other sport. In order to "make their weights," most wrestlers diet or fast the last few days before a match. They may also "sweat out" water weight in saunas. A football player can still play his position if he goes into a game weighing 195 instead of 190; a wrestler cannot. His sport is one-on-one; in a match, he is on his own: just the wrestler and his coach against another team's wrestler and *his* coach. And, of course, almost to the end of his life, Gabby Moore had been there with his boys all the way.

Gabby had recruited his wrestlers when they were in junior high. In Yakima, many of them had the choice of attending either Eisenhower or Davis High School, and Gabby had scouted for up-and-coming young athletes when they were way back in the seventh or eighth grade. With his chosen boys, he became a large part of their lives from that moment on. Little wonder, then, that his murder left dozens of young men shocked and grieving. Gabby Moore had been invincible to them, the strongest, toughest man they had ever known. If something could happen to Gabby, their own mortality suddenly stared back at them when they looked in their mirrors.

Hurting the most were the handful of young men who had counted on Gabby for advice and inspiration and friendship, who had continued to see him on an almost daily basis, even when his life had blown all to hell over a woman who didn't love him anymore. Now they were left free-floating with no anchor.

All of the massive media coverage of Gabby's mysterious death and his obituaries had mentioned that his Davis wrestling team took the Washington State Championship in 1972. That was his dream team. The stars were Kenny Marino, Greg Williams, J. T. Culbertson, Mike McBerb, and Angelo Pleasant. Angelo was probably the most outstanding athlete Gabby had ever coached. Together, that 1972 team had shown what small-town athletes with a superb coach could do. Those were glory days, days that none of them forgot.

And now all the glory was ashes.

Angelo Pleasant was the shining star of the 1972 Davis wrestling squad. His family was proud of him, just as he was proud of them. The Pleasant family had carved a place for themselves as one of the most respected families in Yakima. Coydell Pleasant and her husband, Andrew, ran the Pleasant Shopper Market on South Sixth Street. In order to make ends meet and see that his children all had a good education, Andrew also drove a garbage truck for the city of Yakima. In the summer, when Vern Henderson was between college terms, he and Andrew Pleasant had worked together on the garbage routes, and the two became good friends.

The Pleasant Shopper Market was a typical neighborhood grocery store with a little bit of everything from canned goods to dairy products to produce, and even had a small line of clothing. The Pleasants' strength was that they gave a lot of personal attention that customers didn't find at chain supermarkets. They went out of their way to help customers find what they wanted, they were unfailingly friendly and they were just plain nice people. A black family in a small town populated mostly by Caucasians and a few Hispanics, the Pleasants worked long hours themselves and so did their three sons and three daughters. A close family, they were highly respected for what they had achieved.

"We were always close," Coydell recalled of the good days. The two younger boys, Angelo and Anthony, who were two years apart in age, were especially tight. "They never really fought much. . . . They did things together," Coydell remembered. "They hunted, they fished, picnicked . . . bowling."

The boys were always tussling around and wrestling with each other. They were in Boy Scouts together—in Pack 22 to start with. Later, they both wrestled for Gabby Moore.

One of the things the elder Pleasants preached over and over to their children was the value of education. "I have always taught the kids," Coydell emphasized, "to listen and do what their teacher tells them because the teachers that's teaching them have their education, and they [the kids] are there to try and get theirs. . . . We were really wanting them to go and get an education and that was the only way to do it. They would have to listen to their teachers and learn."

By 1975 the Pleasants had been in business for a decade and their children were just about grown, ranging in age from eighteen to twenty-nine. They had all either completed their higher education or were in the process. The boys all had "A" names: Andrew, Jr., Angelo, and Anthony. The girls had pretty "S" names: Sarita*, Sondra*, and Selia*. Andrew, Sr., and Coydell were proud of all their children, but it was Angelo who had truly excelled in sports. Andrew and Anthony were good, but Angelo was championship material. Gabby Moore had dropped by the store and told the elder Pleasants that he couldn't see that anything would keep Angelo down; in fact, he figured that Angelo might even make the Olympic Team.

Angelo worked hard in the store. His parents loved to fish, and when they took short vacations, he took over the market and ran it for them. He was an energetic shelf stocker too, and good at getting his friends to help him. Angelo was the kid with the biggest smile and the broadest shoulders. But it was Angelo who had given his parents the most grief too. Every family with more than one child has its problem kid—or *kids.* If one of their children was going to be in trouble, the Pleasants knew it would be Angelo. He was tremendously strong and he was as quick to fight as he was to laugh. He did a lot of both. Schoolwork was harder for him than it was for his older brother, Andrew, or for his sisters. And it was Angelo who chafed most at his father's strict guidelines for behavior.

To his everlasting regret, it was Angelo who once raised his fists to his own father.

Eventually, all three of the Pleasant sons went out for wrestling at Davis High School and wrestled under Gabby Moore's tutelage. Angelo and Anthony admired their older brother, Andrew, and they wanted to follow in his footsteps.

In keeping with his pugnacity, Angelo had a nickname that made his complete name sound like an oxymoron; everyone called him "Tuffy"—Tuffy Pleasant. Only on formal occasions did anyone call Angelo anything but Tuffy.

Tuffy was a good-looking kid with a wide smile. You had to like him when he grinned. He was born on January 28, 1954, in Yakima and spent most his school years there.

"I was in the sixth grade at Adams Elementary School," he remembered, "when my parents went into the grocery business."

Tuffy Pleasant went on to Washington Junior High, and that was where he first met the man who would become his hero. Tuffy was in the ninth grade. Everyone knew Gabby Moore, and when he showed up in the gymnasiums of middle schools, it was like a Broadway producer showing up at a college play. There was a buzz.

"The season was about half over," Tuffy remembered, "and I saw him at certain matches, but I still wasn't wrestling varsity until after Christmas. I finally made the first string and then a couple of people on the team told me that he was the coach at Davis High School and he was down looking for prospects for the years coming."

Tuffy had planned to go to Eisenhower High, but Gabby changed that. "He was down there to talk to me as a coach and asked me to, you know, wrestle for them—that I had potential and to give him a chance as a coach."

Actually, Gabby wasn't the first coach who had tried to recruit Tuffy Pleasant. Even in the ninth grade, the kid had something extra. It wasn't that he was that big; he grew to be 5'7" and he only weighed 138 pounds in his sophomore and junior years in high school, but even way back then he just wouldn't quit.

From the beginning, Tuffy liked Coach Moore. Gabby seemed to take an interest in his wrestlers not just as athletes but as *people*. "You know, it kind of went beyond a coach and a student. It's kind of hard to explain," Tuffy said many years later, half-smiling. "But [it gets so] you know you are pretty good . . . you *are* pretty good, and you just get pretty tight with that coach, especially if you're one of the main starters and he had a lot of interest in you. . . . You want to do good for your coach and your school."

Tuffy did remarkably "good" for his school *and* his coach. He and Gabby had a truly symbiotic relation. Gabby could see that Tuffy was the most outstanding wrestler on a squad of top-grade athletes and that Tuffy would represent him well. A coach's "work product" is the athletes he brings along. Tuffy Pleasant had one of the best wrestling coaches in the state, and a friend/father-figure who had been there for him for years and who would continue to be there. Tuffy already had a wonderful father in Andrew Pleasant, but Gabby painted pictures of a future for Tuffy that Andrew might never have imagined. Gabby promised Tuffy the whole world.

Gabby was Tuffy's football coach too. "He was our head coach on defense." Tuffy had the most challenging position on the football team. "I played 'monster back,' the toughest position on defense," Tuffy remembered. "You can get trapped sometimes. They double-team you, they *triple*-team you—and you got to be tough to handle the position. . . . I was mostly on the off-side of center—either on one side or the other of our defensive tackle."

Tuffy played football two years at Davis High School, but wrestling was his real love, his avocation, the very center of his existence. He didn't mind the strict training rules Gabby Moore laid down.

"No drinking," Tuffy recited the forbidden activities. "No late hours whatsoever, and, if you can restrain yourself from it, no 'physical contact' with any type of lady."

Gabby didn't like his athletes to have girlfriends. "I tried to observe his requirements," Tuffy said with a grin. "To the best of my ability." Since Tuffy had always been a ladies' man, the "best of his ability" was none too pristine when it came to sex.

It was probably natural that Tuffy Pleasant and Gabby Moore were already more than coach and athlete while Tuffy was in high school. Gabby visited a few times at the Pleasant family home, and he still dropped by the Shopper Market often. The man and the boy went out to dinner where Gabby preached to Tuffy about what his future could be. "He talked to me," Tuffy said. "He told me to keep on moving. 'Don't let your education stop here,' he said. He told me to carry it on through, and I could probably be the head coach here at Davis myself."

Head wrestling coach at Davis! The very thought of something so wonderful made Tuffy's chest swell. That became Tuffy's ambition, the goal he looked toward all through college. One day, he would pick up the torch that Gabby handed down.

Looking back, Tuffy said he considered Gabby a "second father," who was always there for him. "I would go over to his house. I would get the best treatment, and I felt like he just treated me like one of his own kids."

During Tuffy's senior year in high school, he was wrestling in three or four matches a week. Gabby, Gay, and their three children shared a big two-story house, and Tuffy was often invited to stay in the basement guest room. There was a wrestling mat down there, and after a workout, the young champion and several of the others on the squad—Kenny Marino and Joey Watkins, and some of the others— would head for Gabby's house where they would go through another workout. They were young, in peak form, and tireless. They *and* their coach were eating, breathing, and sleeping wrestling.

There was no drinking. Not even beer. The teenagers on his squad got caught drinking beer once and Gabby had a fit. "He just wouldn't allow it," Tuffy said. "Because you get to messing with all of that stuff and you can't get in as good a shape as you need to be for that type of sport."

Gabby himself wasn't drinking then either. None of them could even picture Gabby drinking. When his boys had to "cut weight," he did too. Tuffy smiled again, remembering. "He would have him a little stomach too, you see, and he would lose weight right along with us. We had to have our hair cut; he would cut his."

Sometimes the wrestlers, including Tuffy Pleasant, had trouble with their grades. Gabby saw to it that they had tutors to help them. And if they needed extra credits, he made them "assistants" in his driver-training classes. How much actual work they did is questionable, but they made up for lost credits. It wasn't that he made life too easy for them though. It was more that he was always there to solve their problems, to make them feel confident, to tell them that their hopes for the future *were* attainable. He was a benevolent tyrant, far more benevolent than tyrant.

In 1971 and 1972 Gabby Moore seemed to his athletes to have it all, everything that they hoped to have one day. He had a beautiful wife and a long-standing, apparently happy marriage. He had three great kids and a nice house. And he had the job that most of them thought would be the best job in the world.

Most of them wanted to be just like him.

The peak experience of Tuffy Pleasant's life and his athletic career to date was in the summer of 1972. He had just graduated from high school and was looking forward to college. Four wrestlers—the best in the state of Washington—would be chosen to go to Japan and Hawaii in the exchange program that Gabby had worked so hard on. Tuffy yearned to be one of them.

Tuffy had put on some weight—not much. By his senior year, he was wrestling at 158 pounds. There would be only one wrestler in that weight category chosen for the Japan trip. It was going to be difficult to pick *the* best from the whole state of Washington. All the contenders went to wrestling camp in Moses Lake, Washington. Tuffy roomed with his best friend and teammate, Kenny Marino, knowing how much both of them wanted to win the trip to the Far East.

Kenny made it to the semifinals and then he was dropped. Tuffy made it all the way. He was on top of the world. He had a memorable time in Japan and Hawaii, and then came home to a hero's welcome in Yakima.

He was proud—and happy. No matter what happened to him later in his life, he would always talk about his shining moments in the summer of 1972. "[I was] very happy and always will be too," he would say, almost defiantly.

Tuffy soon came back to earth after the glory of his triumph in Japan. The rest of the summer of 1972 he worked for the Yakima City Sanitation Department hauling brush, to save money for college. With Gabby's hearty recommendation, he had been recruited by the wrestling coach at Columbia Basin College in Pasco, Washington.

Tuffy attended Columbia Basin from September 1972, through the winter quarter in 1975. His best friend, Kenny Marino, started *his* freshman year at the University of Washington in Seattle. Tuffy's brother Anthony was still in high school.

Gabby kept track of his "boys" even after they were in college. "He would come down and see me," Tuffy said. "He was interested in how I did. When I left high school, he called my college coach and asked 'How's Pleasant doing?' If 'Pleasant' was not doing this well, [he'd say] 'Have him do this,' or if 'Pleasant' is not responding to that, 'Well then, have him do that—and he'll respond.'"

It was as if Tuffy had team coaching. Gabby was always around or on the phone to be sure that he was wrestling to his peak ability. It made Tuffy happy to know that his old coach was still guiding him. They were as tight as ever.

Tuffy had not cut himself off from Yakima ties, even though he was living in Pasco. He made the 160-mile round trip twice a week—once in the middle of the week, and again on the weekends.

Kenny Marino, who hadn't gone back to the University of Washington after his freshman year, was living in Yakima. "As soon as I would hit town, he [Kenny] would probably be the first person I would look up," Tuffy remembered. "Before I even went to see my family."

Kenny Marino was like another brother to Tuffy. "I loved him just as much," he said. But neither Kenny nor Tuffy's brother Anthony seemed to have the ambition that Tuffy did. He and Kenny Marino had a social life together, but they didn't talk much about the future. And Tuffy saw that his younger brother Anthony's main ambition was to "become another Jimi Hendrix." Anthony was very good with the guitar, but Tuffy knew what the odds were and sometimes he thought his younger brother was a dreamer.

Anthony had dropped out of school, and both Tuffy and Gabby were trying to get him back in. "Gabby was talking to the principal and some of his teachers trying to get some of his grades straightened out, and the classes straightened out."

In college, Tuffy's road suddenly developed detours. Although he had been a phenomenon in high school, Tuffy Pleasant never quite saw his dreams of wrestling championships in college come to fruition. "I did good," he said of his career at Columbia Basin. "Except that I never did finish up at 'State' because every time it got right down to it, something all the time happened to me—not grades—it was either injury or sickness."

But his grades weren't superior; Tuffy had a hard time in college, and he didn't have Gabby close by to find tutors for him.

In the spring of 1975, as Jerilee Blankenbaker Moore was trying to get up her courage to leave Gabby, Tuffy Pleasant had decided to drop out of college for a quarter. He stayed on in Pasco, though. He had a job with the Washington Fish and Game Department. "We planted fish, salmon, steelhead at certain dams," he explained. "We would go up the river and plant fish, and then we would go down the river to a lower level dam and wait and count how many came through."

Tuffy planned to continue his college at Central Washington

University in Ellensburg. He had enough credits to enter as a junior. He planned to bring his grades up so that he really would have a shot at being a teacher and coach back in Yakima. Gabby had told him he could do it. In September 1975 Tuffy would move to Ellensburg and share an off-campus apartment with two roommates at 1501 Glen Drive.

With the new freeway between Ellensburg and Yakima, Tuffy could be in Yakima in thirty-five or forty minutes. And he had a number of reasons to make the trip often. For one thing, he had never been able to adhere absolutely to Gabby's "no girlfriends" rule. Tuffy was engaged to a young woman named René Sandon*. *More* than engaged, really. They had a three-year-old daughter and René was pregnant again by late fall 1975, due to deliver in June.

Tuffy's second reason to travel often to Yakima was that he realized that Gabby Moore needed him. Gabby had been keeping an eye on Tuffy's college wrestling, but Tuffy had not visited Gabby's home as he used to. He knew that Gabby and Gay were divorced, and he knew about the merry-go-round involving Morris and Jerilee and Gabby, but he was shocked when he moved back closer to Yakima to find that Gabby had completely fallen apart after Jerilee left him.

Beginning in August 1975, Tuffy saw Gabby more often. "Usually," Tuffy said, "I started seeing him other summers toward the end—seeing how he's doing and talking to him about his team for the coming year, and about football."

But this summer was different. Sometime in August, Tuffy went by the house that Gabby had bought to share with Jerilee and her children. He was surprised to find that Gabby didn't live there any longer. He set out to find him.

"I kind of felt he would be the same old Mr. Moore," Tuffy recalled. But he had heard rumors that Gabby's teams weren't doing well at all, and some of the wrestlers had told him, "It's Mr. Moore— it's not us."

Tuffy had wanted to see for himself, and he found that the scuttlebutt was all true. Gabby was doing a lot of drinking, sitting there in front of Tuffy and the other guys and pouring one drink after another. Gabby had always told Tuffy and the other athletes, "I don't care what you do out of season, but *during* season I care a lot what you do."

Now, Tuffy tried to tell himself that it wasn't as if school had started. Gabby wasn't really coaching yet, and when September came and the wrestlers turned out, he would shape up. Tuffy was sure Gabby would quit drinking then.

From the moment Tuffy Pleasant renewed his contacts with Gabby Moore in the summer of 1975, he saw him every day for a month. It seemed essential to Gabby that Tuffy be there—to listen. Gabby was morose; all the old spark had gone out of him. He told Tuffy that he was selling the house he had just bought the year before. No reason to keep it. He had only bought it for Jerilee and her kids. He couldn't live in it alone. He thought it would sell quicker if he put in a concrete driveway. Laying concrete was at least something solid Tuffy could do to help Gabby, so he and a couple of his cousins put the driveway in. "We finished it off after Labor Day."

School started and Gabby kept right on drinking.

Tuffy and Kenny Marino and some of the other members of Gabby's earlier teams talked it out and set up a schedule where they could cover for him at after-school practice and even at wrestling meets. They knew that if they weren't there to oversee things, the school administration would see how bad things really were with Gabby.

There are few things more shocking for the very young than to discover that their heroes have feet of clay. Gabby Moore had been everything to them, and he had had it all. Now, their old coach didn't have the perfect life any longer. Both his marriages were history. His first wife, Gay, was married to one of the football coaches at Davis. Gabby's marriage to Jerilee had been over before it began. And soon his athletes heard that, despite their help, Gabby's job was in jeopardy. This news only made them redouble their efforts to save it for him.

Sometimes Gabby showed up for practice, and sometimes he didn't. It was really better when he *didn't*—better than the occasions when he had liquor on his breath, or when he went out to his car to sneak a drink from a bottle he kept there. He just hadn't seemed to care anymore about anything except getting Jerilee to come back to him.

Gabby's athletes had tried to save him. If it was a matter of trying and wanting and wishing on their parts, he would have somehow come around to being his old self again. Right up to the end, they had been visiting him and trying to cheer him up.

But now Gabby Moore was dead, and none of that mattered anymore.

13

Vern Henderson had not been officially assigned to the
Morris Blankenbaker murder case, but now, with Gabby Moore's
murder, Vern was transferred to the homicide team investigating
both the Blankenbaker and Moore murders. There was no way that
Vern could keep from working on the growing mystery. He couldn't
stand on the outside any longer. He had to be there to find the answer
to what was proving to be a more and more inscrutable puzzle. But
first, he needed some key to find his way in—some piece of physical
evidence that could start him in the right direction.

The loss and grief Vern had felt when Morris Blankenbaker was
murdered had not diminished, and it never would until he found his
friend's killer. "I don't have many friends," he said. "No, that's not
what I mean—I *know* lots of people—but people who really *know*
me, know how I'm feeling, no . . . I don't let many people get close to
me. Morris was like that. Rucker was like that too. We had *bonds.* Just
some people you get the feeling with and others you don't. . . . I
always learned you *can't* let people get that close to you because then
they know your weaknesses. In a fatherless home, you learn to grow
up quick; you don't really have a childhood. . . . Morris's mother and
my mother kept telling us, 'You gotta do something with your life.
You can't just be running around the streets.'"

Both Morris and Vern had been aware that people said mothers
couldn't do a good job of raising sons, and they strived to excel to
prove them wrong. "I always wanted to do something to make my
mother proud of me," Vern Henderson said.

Now Vern would never be proud of himself, not really, until he
found Morris's killer. Morris had been so kind to everyone. "If Morris
Blankenbaker liked you, he would do anything for you. He was like a
bull on the football field," Vern said. "He could run right over
anybody. He could have whipped half the school, but he wasn't a
bully; he wasn't like that."

Everyone on the Yakima Police Department wanted to solve the bizarre double murders of the two popular coaches, but not one of them felt the impetus to do so in his gut the way Vern Henderson did. In that dismal period between a bloody Christmas and a cheerless New Year, Vern thought about all that had happened and wondered where to start. Which brick could he remove from the wall that a killer had built up around himself? How could he make that wall tumble?

Bob Brimmer was Vern's sergeant upstairs in the detectives' office. He was an old-school investigator with decades on the job. He would work the case his way, and Vern would work it his. He knew what his strengths were. He was a "listener" and he had spread out a network that snared information during his years investigating juveniles. He counted on his network now. Yakima was a small town, and people talked. Sooner or later, some names were going to work their way back to Henderson. At a time when he had the *least* inclination to be patient, that was just what he was going to have to be.

Vern Henderson, always taciturn, became doubly so as the old year passed away and 1976 dawned. Somebody knew who had shot Morris and who had shot Gabby. It might be the same man—or woman. It might be two different men—*or women.*

Even though Gabby Moore had begun as the prime suspect in Morris Blankenbaker's murder, Bob Brimmer and Howard Cyr had established that he could not have killed Morris—not with his own hands.

But then who had?

When Vern Henderson said everybody in Yakima liked Morris, he wasn't overstating it. Everybody had.

It's an old rule of thumb in homicide investigation that detectives look for the killer among those closest to the victims. Family first. Then friends. Then coworkers, and out into a continually widening circle. There had been no obvious reason at all for strangers to kill either Morris or Gabby. They hadn't been robbed. Neither had been involved in a fight or altercation with anyone. Their only "enemies" were one another.

And their main "connection" was Jerilee. All of the witnesses who had seen Jerilee the morning she found Morris's body agreed that this was a woman in deep shock and excruciating grief. She was never a serious suspect. Why should she be? If she had wanted to be free of Morris a second time, he would have let her go as gently as he had the first time. But she hadn't wanted to leave the father of her two little children; she loved Morris, and she was looking forward to remarrying him.

She had no gun.

She had no gun debris on her hands.

Her recall of events of the night/morning of November 21/22 dovetailed perfectly with witness statements and with the detectives' reconstruction of events.

Morris had stuck close to home when he wasn't teaching, coaching, or moonlighting at the Lion's Share. Gabby had stayed in his apartment in the last weeks of his life. His closest companions had been his son, his daughters, and the former athletes who had tried to comfort him and to cover for him so he wouldn't lose his job.

Even in the weeks when he had not been officially assigned to the Blankenbaker case, Vern Henderson had gone over Morris's last moments a hundred times in his mind. "He knew who it was," Vern said. "The reason I know Morris knew who it was was because there were no defensive wounds. I looked for that when I was at his autopsy."

Vern Henderson knew Morris's habits almost as well as he knew his own. Morris would have driven into the alley behind his house, parked his car next to the carport, and headed for the side gate.

"He had gotten through the gate," Henderson surmised. "And he was probably shutting it, and someone called, 'Morris!' and he turned around. He knew who it was. As good as Morris was, you might have killed him, but not without his having some defensive marks, unless he knew who it was. As close as the shooter was, it made me know it wasn't an 'enemy' who shot him, to get that close to Morris— because Morris was too good at hand-to-hand combat. No, he knew him."

There would always be times when Vern Henderson regretted that he carried the visual memory of Morris lying on the autopsy table, but that was the price he had to pay. He had needed to *know* that there were no defensive marks on his friend at all, to *know* how close the shooter had gotten to Morris. It helped him to picture who he was looking for. "I knew that Morris not only knew the person who shot him—he had to have trusted him—to let him get that close."

Now, at last, Vern was right in the middle of the investigation not only of Morris's murder but also of Gabby's. He had watched Gabby from a distance during the last weeks of his life. "I expected that Gabby had had something to do with it," he said. "I knew he didn't shoot him [Morris]—as far as that point, but naturally he was a suspect."

One encounter kept coming back to Vern. After Morris's autopsy, he had been downstairs in the radio room just as Gabby Moore was coming down the hall headed for Brimmer's office on the second floor. "He was coming around there and I wanted to see him, because that would tell me something for my own self.

"He came down the hall and I'm standing at the end of the hall waiting on him. And he kept his head down. He would not look up at me," Vern recalled. "And he got right even with me and he says, 'Vern, I . . . I . . . just didn't do it,' but he never would look up and look at me dead in the face. And he went on and I kept looking at him. I said, in my own mind, I *know* he didn't shoot him, but he had someone do it."

Vern Henderson shrugged. "And there was no evidence. And all I could think of was when we were back in junior high school and he was our wrestling coach. How he always said, 'Look your opponent dead in the eye. Let him know what you're feeling, and that you're going to beat him.' But Gabby wouldn't look at me."

Sometimes now, Vern wished he had gone up to Gabby as he stood over Morris's grave and asked him some questions. Vern hadn't known how short the time was. He had always thought that there would come a time when he could talk to his old coach—where maybe careful conversation would allow the whole truth to come out. He remembered the old Gabby, and how he had loved his athletes— how he had loved Morris. He had figured that somewhere deep inside, Gabby had to be feeling pangs of conscience. That was why Gabby had driven up to the cemetery in the bitter wind of winter. That was probably why Gabby had increased his prodigious consumption of alcohol. At the end of his life, Gabby Moore had been as self-destructive as any man Vern Henderson had ever seen. Whatever had happened on Christmas Eve, there would never be a time now for Vern Henderson to sit down and talk with Gabby Moore. He would have to figure out a way to tap into the minds of the killer or killers, living or dead.

How were Bob Brimmer and Vern Henderson and the rest of the Yakima detectives going to find the concealed fragments that made up the crimes? How were they going to get solid evidence that Jeff Sullivan could take into a murder trial? Tips and leads were called into the office, and Brimmer fielded those. Henderson was more a believer in the gifts of information that could be gleaned out in the streets.

Henderson had made a point to find out who Gabby's closest associates were when Morris was killed. Now, the Yakima investigator set out to see who Gabby Moore had spent his time with in the last week or so of his life. It didn't take long for him to find out that Gabby had had almost daily visits from a number of his athletes. Names mentioned to Vern Henderson and Bob Brimmer were Joey Watkins, Angelo "Tuffy" Pleasant, Tuffy's younger brother Anthony, and Stoney Morton*.

Joey Watkins told Brimmer and Henderson that several of the guys had visited Gabby often in December. He knew for a fact that Tuffy and Anthony Pleasant and Stoney Morton had stopped by to check on him on Christmas Eve.

Vern couldn't believe that the Pleasant brothers or Joey Watkins or Kenny Marino would have hurt Morris. They were Morris's friends. Vern had seen Morris teach Tuffy some wrestling moves, and the Pleasants and Joey sometimes visited at the house on North Sixth Street.

"I called all my friends," Henderson said, "and asked if they had heard any rumors, and my one friend said he had heard that Joey Watkins and Tuffy Pleasant had been in the Lion's Share talking to Morris a little while before he got off work."

That information didn't make much of an impression on Henderson. He knew that both Watkins and Pleasant often stopped by the Lion's Share; it wasn't as if they had suddenly shown up someplace where they had never been. In fact, it was Joey Watkins who had gone home with Morris to back him up the night Gabby broke into Morris's house while he was working and Jerilee had been frightened.

When Vern checked at the Lion's Share, he learned that Tuffy and Joey had been in on Friday night, probably between nine and eleven, at least two hours before Morris got off work.

Tuffy Pleasant interested Vern more than Joey Watkins, though. "I thought, 'Now Tuffy hung around with Gabby all the time.' I'd seen him driving Gabby's little MG around town."

Back in November, Vern had turned that information over in his head but he never could make it fit. Sure, Tuffy had two sides to him. He could be the kid with the wide-open grin who was everybody's friend, but he could also be a fighter. Vern knew that Tuffy had put his own father in the hospital once. "His dad never turned him in," Vern recalled. "But I knew about it because we worked on the garbage trucks together way back and we got to be friends."

Joey Watkins was a big guy, but Vern had never known him to be threatening off the wrestling mat. Naaww . . . he couldn't see either of those "fools" shooting Morris. He put it out of his mind and concentrated on his own assignments.

But now he was working two homicides and on occasion his thoughts turned back to the tight relationship Gabby and Tuffy had had. Vern wondered if Tuffy had wanted Gabby to be happy bad enough to shoot Morris. That conclusion was too mind-boggling and Henderson shook it away. Tuffy was a hothead sometimes, but Vern couldn't picture him as a killer.

And then there was the question of who had shot Gabby. Tuffy Pleasant owed everything to Gabby Moore. He loved his coach and his friend. There was no way he would have harmed a hair on Gabby's rapidly balding head.

Vern Henderson always ended up right back where he'd started with his maddeningly circular theorizing. When it came right down to it, he had no idea who had killed either Morris or Gabby.

Bob Brimmer and Vern had gone to the Pleasants' South Sixth Street grocery store several times. They now asked Tuffy's mother, Coydell, if she would have Tuffy contact their office.

On Saturday, January 3, 1976, Tuffy Pleasant came into the Yakima Police Station for an interview. He was not read his rights under Miranda because he was not considered a viable suspect. Yes, he said he had visited with his former coach early on the evening of Christmas Eve. He said he had asked Moore if he'd like to go out someplace and have a couple of drinks and Gabby Moore had agreed and started to clean up. But then, Gabby had received two phone calls and whoever it was had seemed to upset him. Tuffy said he had changed his mind about going out. He wanted to stay in his apartment and have some drinks. And so Tuffy had left to go to some of his own family's Christmas celebrations. When Tuffy left, he said Gabby had been fine. Tuffy had apparently been as shocked as everyone else to learn the next morning that Gabby was dead.

Pressed, Tuffy admitted that Gabby had been talking kind of crazy about getting rid of Morris Blankenbaker earlier in the fall. He had told Tuffy that he would be willing to pay five hundred dollars, or even more, if someone would shoot Morris. Tuffy had said he wouldn't even consider killing Morris. To get Gabby off the subject, to placate him for the moment, he had suggested a name he plucked out of the air as a possible hired killer, someone who could furnish "a cold gun." He said he had described this potential hired gun as someone who "likes leather clothes."

"The whole idea behind the [proposed] shooting of Morris," Tuffy told police, "was for the love of Jerilee."

Gabby was up and down emotionally all fall, Tuffy said, but he seemed to be at his lowest ebb a few days before Christmas. Tuffy told Brimmer and Henderson that he had a strong alibi for the night Morris Blankenbaker was shot, although he couldn't say just what Joey Watkins had done that night.

He said that he and Joey had gone to the Red Lion and then Joey "split" and went off by himself. Tuffy said he had stayed all night with a girl at the hotel, and then had gone to an address on North Fourth in Yakima and spent the rest of Saturday and Saturday night with the girl there. On Sunday, he said he had moved his belongings out of Joey Watkins's house and that was the last time he had had much to do with him.

Although the Yakima detectives were not entirely convinced that Tuffy had told them the truth or *all* of the truth, they had no evidence to tell them differently. Tuffy left their offices.

Tuffy Pleasant's whereabouts on the night Morris Blankenbaker was shot had to be traced. Hard facts were essential, even though Tuffy made an unlikely suspect. No matter how many questions the Yakima detectives asked, they couldn't find anyone who said Tuffy had anything against Morris. It was common knowledge that Gabby had been his hero, his mentor, for years.

Bob Brimmer and his detectives had gone over the yard where Morris Blankenbaker had been shot a number of times. They figured that, with three shots, there should be three bullet casings lying somewhere in the area, unless the death gun had been a revolver. An automatic or a semiautomatic would eject the spent casings once the slug had been fired at a target. Morris hadn't mowed the grass before the snow fell, and there were also tall weeds in a lot of spots. It wasn't likely that the killer had taken the time to stop and look for bullet casings so he could pick them up before he fled down the alley. The detectives had even used metal detectors, painstakingly working over the grass and parking area in a grid pattern.

And they had found nothing.

With Gabby's murder, they *did* have a bullet casing. The .22 shell was crimped on the open end, probably where the killer had stepped on it as he left by Moore's back door. The casing's worth was minimal *unless* or *until* they found a gun to match it to, or they found a casing from the Blankenbaker shooting to compare to it. At least they knew now they were looking for an automatic .22 caliber weapon.

If they were lucky enough to find a casing on the Blankenbaker property, they could establish what everyone involved in the probe already believed—that both Morris and Gabby had been shot with the same gun. If they could prove that, and if they could somehow locate that gun—a tremendously big "if"—they might just be back in business.

In the meantime, Vern Henderson continued his "playing tag," as he put it. He talked to his friends who had talked to their friends who had talked to others. Everyone seemed to have his or her own slightly unique hypothesis about who the killer was.

Vern kept hearing Joey Watkins's name. Vern's gut still told him that it wasn't Joey Watkins he was after. Joey was talking too much for a man trying to hide something, and Vern just couldn't see him as a double murderer.

But Joey Watkins and Tuffy Pleasant were friends, and they had occasionally shared living quarters. In fact, they had lived together right up to the night Gabby died. Tuffy and Gabby had been "tight." Both Tuffy and Joey Watkins had been seen with Morris within hours of his murder, and over the last few months of his life they had been regular visitors to Gabby's apartment.

Joey Watkins and Tuffy Pleasant had been close friends since grade school. Joey nodded when Vern asked about that. Yes, Tuffy had lived with him on and off during the previous autumn when Tuffy came home from college on the weekends, except when he was staying at his girlfriend's house. Joey told Vern Henderson that he *was* with Tuffy for the first part of the evening on November 21, until Tuffy joined some people at the next table in the Red Lion—two women and a man.

Joey said he had gone home, visited with his girlfriend, and then gone to bed. He said he really didn't know *when* Tuffy came home, or *if* he came home during the night. Tuffy often went to his girlfriend René's house to stay overnight. He had his own key to Joey's place, so Joey couldn't say yes, no, or maybe about where Tuffy had been after he last saw him at nine P.M. on the night of November 21.

However, Vern found it interesting that by Christmas Eve, Tuffy no longer stayed with Joey Watkins on weekends. In fact, Joey said, they rarely saw each other after Morris's death.

Joey agreed that he had seen Gabby Moore on Christmas Eve. Moore had come over to his house around 6:30 or 7:00 that evening. He had been looking for Tuffy and Kenny Marino because they had his sports car. The coach had sat down and watched a football game with Joey for a while, and then Joey said he had driven Moore down to North Fourth Street where Kenny Marino lived. "Gabby's car was parked out there."

Joey said that was the last he saw of Gabby; he had picked up his girlfriend and gone out to Harrah, a tiny hamlet south of Yakima, where she worked at a halfway house for mentally disturbed adolescents. "We stayed there until Christmas morning," Watkins said.

Joey said he had no idea that Gabby Moore had been shot until the next morning. "I stopped at Mrs. Pleasant's store and I was going to get something to eat and I just saw his picture in the headlines."

In January, Sergeant Richard Nesary, the Yakima Police Department's polygraph examiner, ran four lie detector tests on Gabby Moore's associates—including Tuffy Pleasant—in an effort to see if red flags might pop up. Nesary read the resulting strips and came up with only inconclusive readings.

Despite Tuffy's protestations that he had no idea who had shot Gabby Moore, Vern Henderson had heard enough through the grapevine to be more interested in the results of Tuffy's polygraph than in the others. Tuffy had been the closest to Gabby Moore by far. Tuffy Pleasant had always called Gabby Moore "The Man." And that was exactly what Gabby had been to Tuffy for the greater part of their relationship—the perfect example of what a man should be. If Tuffy had wanted one thing in this world, it was to go to college and graduate and be just like Gabby Moore. Vern heard that often enough as he asked around town. "It wasn't Joey Watkins who was driving around in 'The Man's' car all the time," Vern said. "It was Tuffy in that little MG."

Then how *could* it be Tuffy who had killed his hero? Everyone Vern talked to said that Tuffy would have done anything to help Gabby. Vern Henderson realized *that* might be the answer to only half of the puzzle, and that if Tuffy had killed Morris for Gabby, it made some kind of bleak sense. The other half didn't make any sense at all. Tuffy might have killed *for* Gabby, but he would have died, Vern thought, before he would kill Gabby himself.

Vern had begun following Tuffy's car occasionally as he drove through Yakima. He knew that Tuffy had gone up to Gabby Moore's grave—just as Gabby had been seen standing silently over Morris's grave. Was Tuffy's grief a normal sense of loss or was it combined with regret and guilt?

Polygraph examinations can produce all kinds of results. Four recording "pens" glide smoothly along moving graph paper at the rate of six inches a minute. A subject's blood pressure, respiration (number of breaths per minute), galvanic skin response (sweating), and pulse are generally good indicators of reactions to stress-producing questions. All polygraph questions are answered either "Yes" or "No," and the operator establishes his subject's "normal" responses by asking innocuous questions such as "Do you live in the United States?" "Is it Wednesday?" and "Is your shirt green?" He often will ask a deliberate lie question to check to see how a particular subject will react when he gives a dishonest response.

With every decade, polygraph machines become more sophisticated just as their operators learn to look for more subtle signals. Beyond the accepted physiological reactions, there are minute chemical changes that today can alert a polygrapher that a subject may be evading the truth.

When Tuffy Pleasant went on the polygraph on January 10, 1976, Dick Nesary was using what was then a near-state-of-the-art system: a 1971 Arthur II polygraph machine. Nesary always double-checked the machine beforehand. Nesary explained his check-out procedure. "Well, it's very simple. You take a pop bottle and wrap the blood pressure cuff around it, pump up the pressure to eighty and leave it sit for five minutes and see if the pressure goes down. If it doesn't, then there's no leaks in the system."

On January 10, as Nesary gave the lie detector test to Tuffy Pleasant, he built up gradually to the vital questions: "Did you shoot Morris Blankenbaker?" and "Did you shoot Gabby Moore?"

In Nesary's words, the results were "unreadable."

"My opinion was that he had knowledge of the situation, but I could not arrive at an opinion as to whether or not he was the actual one involved in it."

Those January results dampened Vern Henderson's enthusiasm for Tuffy Pleasant as a viable suspect, at least until he talked again to Joey Watkins. Watkins wasn't happy about becoming even a long-shot murder suspect, and he was quite willing to talk with Vern. He pointed out that *he* was not the one who had always been seen with Gabby Moore—that it was Tuffy who was Gabby's buddy. "Who do you think was running around with Gabby?" Watkins asked Henderson. "It was Tuffy, not me. I didn't run around with that man."

"That's true," Vern agreed. "You didn't."

Vern Henderson realized, however, that Joey Watkins might be the vital link between himself and Tuffy Pleasant. With every meeting he had with Watkins, Vern learned more. "Tuffy didn't know what Joey Watkins was saying to me," Vern recalled. "But from talking with Watkins, I knew that when I eventually got to Tuffy, he would be able to tell me what had gone on."

Joey Watkins had taken his time about trusting Vern Henderson, and he had debated how much to tell him. Finally, he blurted out information that was of tremendous importance to the double-murder probe.

Vern remembered the moment. "Joey said, 'Hey, look—Tuffy—I saw Tuffy with a *gun*.' And I said, 'What kind of a gun?' and he said, 'A German-type twenty-two with a long barrel and a long handle that was wrapped with tape.'"

Vern asked Watkins if the gun had been an automatic, and Watkins nodded. "Yeah, one of those German Luger type guns."

"But I heard *you* had a gun like that," Vern hedged.

"It was in my house, all right," Watkins agreed, "but it wasn't mine. It belonged to Tuffy."

Watkins said he didn't know where the gun had come from and he had no idea where it might be at the present moment.

Although he desperately wanted to solve Morris's and Gabby's murders, Vern Henderson had been halfway hoping that he wouldn't hear information that placed Tuffy Pleasant squarely as the focal point in his investigation. He would far rather have had the suspect be a stranger. There were too many ties between them, these two young black men in a town where they were in such a minority. Vern and Tuffy were both athletes who had excelled and made their school and their town proud. Vern liked Tuffy, even though he could be a wiseguy at times, and Vern deeply admired Tuffy's father, Andrew Pleasant, Sr. The last thing Vern wanted to do was humiliate and grieve that man who had struggled so hard to see his children do better in the world than he had. Andrew had worked two jobs all his life and he had just about seen his dreams come true; all but one of Andrew and Coydell's children were in college by the midseventies.

But the word was out that Tuffy Pleasant might be a suspect in the two shootings—not officially, but in an undercurrent of gossip—and Andrew, Sr., came to Vern, just as Olive Blankenbaker had once come to him. They were each pleading for justice for their children, and their requests left Vern Henderson torn in two.

"When Morris's mother asked me to find who had killed him, I told her that I would," Vern said. "I didn't know what else to say. It was very emotional, and I just wanted to hug her. It was the same with Tuffy's father.

"Tuffy's father came to me and he said, 'Look, Vern, you're working this case. I want to know if my son actually did this or not. I know we can trust you.' I knew right then that I was going to be in trouble because who *really* wants to know that his son committed murder? I knew right then that if I found out Tuffy had something to do with it, our friendship would be over.''

It was a solid friendship going back to when Andrew Pleasant came to watch Vern play football and continuing when they worked in the Sanitation Department while Vern was going to Yakima Valley Community College.

Vern didn't know Tuffy Pleasant as well as he did Tuffy's father, but he was about to. He drove up to Ellensburg and went to the rooming house where Tuffy was living while he was going to Central Washington University. Tuffy met him outside, and the two began what would be a tentative, edgy, continuing dialogue.

From that point on, Tuffy Pleasant would always sense that someone was waiting and watching his movements. He could count on seeing Vern Henderson often. He suspected—correctly—that Vern was somewhere around, even when he didn't see him. It didn't matter that Tuffy had walked out of the lie detector test with an unreadable graph, leaving the polygrapher Dick Nesary shaking his head. It didn't matter that Tuffy felt he had aced his meeting with Brimmer and the other detectives in January. He still felt uneasy. It seemed to Tuffy that Vern knew too much about him, and that he wasn't ever going to leave him alone until he proved it.

The hell of it was that Tuffy kind of liked Vern Henderson. In other circumstances, he would have been glad to talk with him, but, for the moment, Vern made him nervous.

And that was exactly the reaction Vern was trying for.

14

Morris's big old house on North Sixth Street had renters again, and life went on. Every time Vern Henderson passed the house, memories came back, good memories of visiting with Morris and Jerilee, of being welcome in their home and of his own pleasure at seeing Morris happy again. But in the end the bad memories always prevailed. Vern had not seen Morris lying there in the snow on that awful night when he died, but he had seen the pictures. He could half close his eyes and see just the way it had been. There had to be some evidence left in Morris's yard or in the alley, something that hadn't been found yet.

The pressure to come up with enough evidence to charge a suspect had been incredibly hard on Sergeant Bob Brimmer. It was Friday, January 16, when he took his first day off in a long time and prepared to go fishing for three days just to get away from the case for a short time.

Sitting in the detectives' office alone, Vern Henderson felt an overwhelming urge to do *something*. He threw on his coat and headed out to North Sixth Street. He knew from talking with Joey Watkins that Tuffy Pleasant had had the German automatic in his possession during November and December. *If* Tuffy was the guilty man, and *if* he had used that gun to shoot Morris, there would have to be some casings somewhere near where Morris had fallen. Henderson decided to literally put himself in the shoes of the shooter.

He walked south on Lincoln down the alley behind the apartment house at 208 North Sixth Street where Gerda Lenberg had heard the sound of someone running the night of November 21. Her duplex was right where the sidewalk on Lincoln met the alleyway.

Several houses down, Vern came to the parking area behind what once had been Morris's house. The little Volkswagen would have been in the carport, and the Chevelle that Morris had driven to work that night had been pulled right up onto the grass of the backyard. There were different cars there now, but Vern saw only the way it had been in November.

The new apartment house where Rowland Seal and Dale Soost lived was very close to Morris's yard, probably not more than ten feet from the property line.

"First, I walked up to the fence where I knew—where I thought Morris would have been standing," Vern remembered, his eyes focusing on some time long ago. "I knew how the body was, because I knew how the bullets had entered—from seeing the autopsy . . . and I'd seen the photographs."

Now Vern Henderson *became* the shooter. He never doubted that there had only been one killer; Mrs. Lenberg was positive she had heard only one set of feet in clunky shoes running down the alley, and then, after the "firecrackers," back up the alley. Vern stood where the man whose face he couldn't yet know had stood facing Morris.

It was almost as real to Henderson at that moment as if he had actually been there two months earlier. "I knew it was an automatic. I said to myself, those guns will kick to the right. I'd read in a book that the casings could kick up to fifteen to twenty feet when they eject out of that thing depending on what kind of spring it had in there. That shell could pop fifteen to twenty feet and it could go in either direction, directly back or out to the side. Well, so I said to myself, let's do a triangle. You're standing here when you shot him, so it went over to the right."

Vern turned his head slowly and looked to the right. He saw the four-foot-tall chicken-wire fence that separated the apartment grounds from the lawn of Morris's house. There was a cement path with a curb just beyond the fence. He figured the fence was about ten feet from where he stood. Almost as if some hand were guiding him, Vern drew an imaginary arc in his mind to the right, and then he walked over to the fence. To himself, he muttered, "It should have landed right here."

He looked down at a spot between the path and the fence on the apartment house side. And there it was. The shell lay in a puddle in the shadow of one of the cement posts, its shiny surface dulled now from lying out in the weather.

Vern Henderson felt his heart beat faster as he crouched and picked up the single shell casing. It was more precious to him than if it had been made of solid gold. He knew in his gut that it had been there all along—from the very moment Morris died. The slug from this casing had entered his best friend's head and shattered, and the casing had sailed through the freezing night air and landed so that it was hidden in plain sight.

Cradling the shell carefully, Vern Henderson slipped it into an evidence envelope and drove to his sergeant's home. There, Bob Brimmer looked at it and said that he thought it would turn out to be almost identical in make and in markings left by the firing pin, extractor, and ejector to the casing found on the kitchen floor of Gabby Moore's apartment on Christmas Eve. They would have to send it to the state lab to be sure.

Both men were excited but cautious. They didn't have a gun yet, but if the casings matched, they would know that the two shootings were connected. However, they still wouldn't know whose gun had fired them.

Vern Henderson took the shell back to the Yakima Police Department. He compared it to the casing from the Moore murder. That

Morris Blankenbaker, about 6, shows off his new cowboy outfit. *(Olive Blankenbaker collection)*

Morris Blankenbaker at graduation from Davis High School. He won a number of athletic awards and a football scholarship to Washington State University. He dated, but there was no special girl—not then. *(Olive Blankenbaker collection)*

Morris celebrates a fish
catch on the Yakima River.
He and Gabby Moore often
fished and boated. On one
trip, Morris saved Gabby
from drowning. *(Olive
Blankenbaker collection)*

Morris trains in the desert
with his Reserve unit. He
and Jerilee were newly
married and he hated
leaving her for weeks
every summer. *(Olive
Blankenbaker collection)*

Morris Blankenbaker at his peak at Washington State University. He had everything in the world to live for. *(Olive Blankenbaker collection)*

Jerilee, Rick and Morris Blankenbaker in late 1969. Morris was trying to finish his college degree while working as a lineman for the telephone company. The couple had been married four years. *(Olive Blankenbaker collection)*

Jerilee, Rick and Morris Blankenbaker. They were very happy in the early seventies in Yakima. *(Olive Blankenbaker collection)*

In the good years just before their breakup, Jerilee Blankenbaker rides on Morris's shoulders on a "whirligig" in a Yakima park with Amanda and Rick riding along. *(Olive Blankenbaker collection)*

Amanda and Rick Blankenbaker play outside their grandmother Olive's mobile home the spring before their father was murdered.
(Olive Blankenbaker collection)

The winning wrestling squad from Davis High in 1972. Gabby Moore is on the far right. Tuffy Pleasant is third from left, back row. Everything worked for Gabby's wrestlers that year, culminating in the Washington State Championship and a trip to Japan and Hawaii for his top wrestlers.

Gabby Moore when he was a revered coach at Davis High—before his long decline over a lost love. *(Yakima Herald-Republic)*

Morris Blankenbaker in July 1975—four months before his murder. He had just come back from a trip to Hawaii. *(Olive Blankenbaker collection)*

The front of the house on North 6th. Morris Blankenbaker parked his car in the back (visible at left) and walked toward the gate beyond. Someone he trusted met him with a gun. *(Court photo)*

Morris and Jerilee lived in the house at left. Witnesses Dale Soost and Rowland Seal lived in the apartment at the right. Vern Henderson found the vital .22 shell beneath the fence in the far center of the picture. *(Ann Rule)*

Morris had driven Jerilee's car on the night he died because they needed the bigger car to take their children out for pizza. Jerilee saw the car and thought he had come home . . . safe. *(Court photo)*

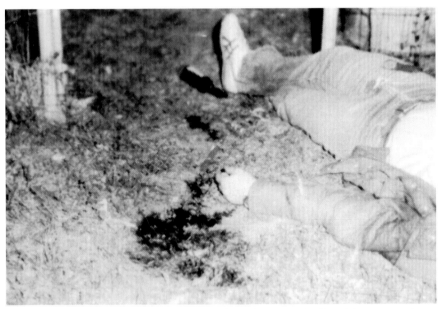

Morris's body lies in his own yard. With almost unbelievable strength born of desperation, Jerilee managed to turn him over and tried to save his life. It was too late. *(Court photo)*

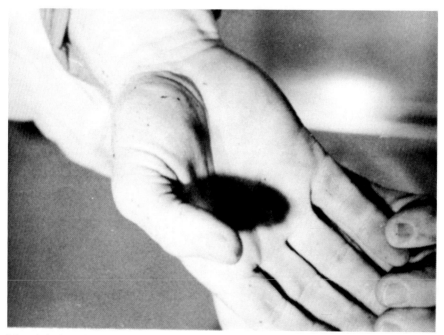

Morris's hand showed the blow-back of blood spatter from the wound in his mouth. Dr. Robert Muzzall said this proved he had had time only to fling his hand up in a hopeless gesture to stop a fatal bullet. *(Court photo)*

Gabby Moore's bedroom. He lay on the bed, listening to a song of impossible, lost love and pored over a photograph album on the floor next to the bed. Detectives found loaded guns beneath his bed. *(Court photo)*

Jeff Sullivan (left), 32, the new prosecuting attorney of Yakima County, is interviewed outside of the Blankenbaker/Moore trial by John Sandifer, anchorman for KOMO-ABC, Seattle, in the summer of 1976. *(Leslie Rule)*

Angelo "Tuffy" Pleasant grinned as he walked into the Blankenbaker/Moore case trial in Seattle. *(Leslie Rule)*

Yakima police sergeant Robert Brimmer, who processed both Morris's and Gabby's crime scenes and oversaw the investigations, awaits his turn to testify in the Seattle trial. *(Leslie Rule)*

Vern Henderson, 32, the young Yakima detective who vowed to find the person who had shot his best friend. *(Leslie Rule)*

Defense attorney Adam Moore (left—no relation to Gabby) who, with Chris Tait (right), represented his client well in the trial, which drew so much publicity that it had to be moved from Yakima to Seattle. *(Yakima Herald-Republic)*

Loretta Scott, Tuffy Pleasant's cousin, waits to testify. She would admit that she unwittingly provided the death gun to the person who killed the two Yakima athletic heroes. *(Yakima Herald-Republic)*

Yakima police officer Dennis Meyers (left) studies the witness list as Jerilee Blankenbaker Moore Littleton prepares to testify. *(Yakima Herald-Republic)*

Defense attorney Chris Tait stands behind his client as he fervently argues with the Court over an evidentiary ruling. *(Yakima Herald-Republic)*

Vern Henderson in 1996. After two decades he still works in law enforcement—as an investigator for the State Attorney General's Office. He will never forget the tragic solution to a pair of tragic murders, or the best friend he lost. (Ann Rule)

Yakima prosecuting attorney Jeff Sullivan in 1996. He has served an almost unprecedented six terms in office. The Blankenbaker/Moore case remains one of his most unforgettable. (Ann Rule)

Olive Blankenbaker in 1996 at 85. *(Ann Rule)*

shell was shinier, but that didn't matter. What mattered were the extractor and ejector marks made by the gun mechanism—and the firing pin mark.

"They both had that moon-shape on the bottom," Vern remembered. "Just alike."

He tagged the casing from the apartment fence and locked it in his desk. On Monday, Bob Brimmer would send it to the lab to verify what both he and Henderson had seen with their naked eyes.

When—and *if*—the murder weapon was located, the casing from the bullet that had killed Gabby Moore could be matched to the lands and grooves inside the barrel. Not so with the weather-beaten shell Vern had found ten feet from where Morris died. But the marks left by the gun on its base would be enough.

Henderson suspected that the other two casings from bullets fired at Morris had ejected to the right too, but had traveled farther than this one; they probably had landed on the well-traveled path and been stepped on or kicked aside long ago by residents of the apartment house. He didn't need them. Even so, he and another detective returned to North Sixth Street with a shovel and a screen. They pulled up grass and weeds and dug up shovelfuls of dirt and sifted them through the screen on the off-chance they would find the other shell casings.

They didn't find them. They never would.

The chance of finding the gun that had killed both Morris Blankenbaker and Gabby Moore was minute. Whoever the killer was, he would have been a fool not to have gotten rid of it after the second murder. There were so many places around Yakima to dispose of a weapon. Canyons, endless miles of barren desert, mountains, rivers. There was a huge military training reservation east of town where thousands of Washington State National Guardsmen, reserve officers, and troops from Fort Lewis went on maneuvers. For that matter, the gun could have been sold or given to someone on "The Coast"— a term residents of eastern Washington use when referring to Seattle.

The latter assumption seemed the most likely. The *Yakima Herald-Republic* reported that Yakima County authorities were arranging for divers to search for the missing .22 in rivers and lakes on "The Coast."

As it turned out that wasn't necessary. Some unseen force seemed to be dictating that there would be justice in this murder puzzle. The discovery of the missing weapon was too perfect; any editor in his right mind would have penciled it out of a fictional murder mystery. But this was real life.

On February 21, five weeks after Vern Henderson had walked unerringly to the shell beneath the fence, John and Paul Klingele, aged fifteen and sixteen, went off to pursue their favorite hobby— fishing. They headed for the Naches River just where it flowed into the Yakima River right under the Twin Bridges, two double green steel arches over both the north and south lanes where Interstate 82 now heads north toward Ellensburg out of Yakima, or south into Yakima itself.

John Klingele would remember that day for a long time, not because of the fishing, but because of what he found in the river. The rains and melting snow runoff had been heavy that winter and the river had actually rushed in a tumult over a little island that sticks out into the Naches beneath the Twin Bridges. But now, the water had receded until it was very shallow and John was able to wade underneath the bridges from the west side to the east. It was about noon when he looked down and saw a cylindrical metal object in the water. Peering closer, he realized it was the long barrel of a handgun. He called to his brother, Paul, who was fishing about fifteen feet away.

The boys pulled the gun from about three inches of water and saw that the grips were wrapped with white masking tape. The gun was a .22 caliber automatic. They washed it off in the river and Paul checked to see if it was loaded. The clip was empty. Still curious, they unwound the tape.

John Klingele was more interested in fishing than in guns, and he gave the .22 to his brother to take home. They would ask their dad about it when he came home for lunch. Wayne Klingele, a printer for the *Yakima Herald-Republic*, knew a lot about guns. He was a hunter and a trapshooter, and he kept his own guns in good shape.

The elder Klingele was not too happy to hear that his teenaged sons had been fiddling around with a gun. He looked at it, saw it was unloaded, and recognized it as a .22 Colt Woodsman with a six-inch barrel. It was an older model, somewhat rusted from being in the river. He supposed it could have been in the Naches for years.

Klingele had to go back to work, but he was dead serious when he instructed Paul to put the gun high up on the Klingele trophy shelf and to remember that neither he nor John were to touch it. Wayne had no idea where it had come from, but he knew what he was going to do about it. Wayne Klingele kept guns in the house—shotguns and rifles—because he was such an avid trapshooter. In fact, he would be trapshooting the next day, Sunday, with Jack La Rue, the chief of police of Yakima.

When Klingele mentioned the gun from the river to La Rue, he found the chief was extremely interested in seeing it. Klingele promised to bring it to the station the next morning. "I took it down on Monday morning and Chief La Rue was waiting for me and took me right up to the second floor to see Sergeant Brimmer. I handed the gun to him."

Brimmer and Henderson were fascinated with the gun that had lain in three inches of water where the Naches lapped up over the island. The caliber was right. The long barrel was right. It was an automatic. When they heard that the Klingele boys had unwrapped white tape from the grips, they began to grin. But cautiously.

Now they had two casings from two murder scenes—casings that had tested as having been fired from the same gun—*and* a .22 caliber, long-barreled, automatic Colt Woodsman with vestiges of white tape on the grips. The crime lab would be able to tell them if the river gun had fired those bullets.

They also had to try to trace the peregrinations of that weapon before it landed in the river. Whoever had tossed the gun into the Naches had probably been headed toward Ellensburg or was coming back from Ellensburg. And they surely had not known about the way the little island below projected out into the river. Had they known, they would have pitched the gun with a lot more force.

Instead, the rusty old gun had just been waiting there for someone to find it, its barrel moving slightly with the tug of the current. It was almost eerie, when one considered how the bullet casing had been waiting for Vern Henderson to discover it. And now the gun had been found almost as easily. Murder sometimes does will out, after all.

In this case, it was beginning to look as though luck were walking with the Yakima police. Still, the detectives had no way of knowing how convoluted this case would become. They had some promising ballistics evidence. They had a lot of rumors, but they had no idea what the motive behind the two murders was. That had all blown up on Christmas Eve when their likeliest killer had turned out to be their second victim.

15

Prosecutor Jeff Sullivan met with Bob Brimmer and Vern Henderson. The gun might prove to be vital to the case. At this point, they had no idea who that gun belonged to or through whose hands it might have passed. But they suspected someone out there would be sweating if he—or she—knew that the weapon was now in the hands of the Yakima police. Most people have seen enough television mysteries to know that guns can be traced, but they don't understand the finer points of forensic ballistics.

For the moment, the gun was mentioned to no one outside the investigation. But when a reporter from the *Yakima Herald-Republic* made his usual police department rounds on that Monday, February 23, he asked, as always, whether there was anything new on the Blankenbaker-Moore case. There wasn't much, but Chief Jack La Rue casually mentioned that someone had brought in a .22 that had been found underneath the Twin Bridges.

That news story galvanized at least three readers into a panic. Each felt that the police would know who had thrown the gun in the river as surely as if they had scratched their names and addresses on the side of the barrel.

In the meantime, Vern Henderson was wearing a groove in the road up to Ellensburg. Tuffy Pleasant was growing used to looking up and seeing Vern heading his way. It bugged him that Vern seemed to know what was going on in his head. And the detective had picked up a lot of things on the streets in Yakima, rumors and remarks made by some of the guys Tuffy ran with.

Henderson had felt for weeks now that Tuffy was somehow connected with the two shootings, but he wasn't sure how or why. When they talked, they talked in circles, fencing and feinting. Sometimes, Vern thought he saw sweat bead up along Tuffy's forehead, especially when Vern confirmed that they had, indeed, found a .22 in the Naches River.

862

"I told him how much we could tell from a gun," Henderson recalled. "He didn't know we couldn't trace it unless someone came forward, and he believed me that we were right next door to knowing who the killer was."

Tuffy had brazened it out. He told Vern that he had talked to a lawyer, and he "knew his rights. I don't have to talk to you or Brimmer if I don't want to."

"That's right."

"What would you do if you were in my position?" Tuffy asked suddenly.

"Well," Vern Henderson said slowly, "if I was in your position, I don't know just what I would do. I might—I *would* get myself an attorney and I wouldn't say anything."

Henderson figured he'd just put his foot in his own mouth, but the kid asked him, and he answered him straight. Tuffy stared back at him, weighing something in his mind.

"No," Tuffy said. "I want to talk with you. I want to help clear this up."

And they kept talking until it grew cold and dark and Vern had to head back to Yakima. Whatever Tuffy had been about to say, he didn't say anything definitive. He just wanted to know more about what police could tell from a gun.

Driving home, Vern was convinced Tuffy knew who had killed both Morris and Gabby. He wondered if Tuffy had done it himself. And then, as always, he wondered, if he did, *why?*

Actually, the Yakima investigators were both further and closer than they suspected from finding the gun's owner. They didn't know it yet, but the old Colt had come back from Vietnam and there was virtually no way to trace it. It was of no more use than a "drop gun," a gun deliberately left at the scene of some crimes to throw police off because the person who left it behind knows it has no identifying marks. They might be able to show that the deadly bullets had been fired from the gun in the river, but unless the investigators could find a link between the gun and Tuffy—or whoever the shooter was— they couldn't prove he had used it to commit murder.

During that third week in February, a very attractive twenty-seven-year-old woman named Loretta Scott* read the paper and felt her heart constrict. She had been panicky since Christmas Day, worrying about that gun, although she had nothing whatsoever to do with killing Morris Blankenbaker or Gabby Moore. She hadn't even known them except by sight.

But Loretta Scott had been drawn into a most bizarre sequence of events, all because she wanted to help out a relative. Now Loretta was apprehensive as she contacted a public defender and said she might have a legal problem. She told him that she might know something about a gun that had possibly been involved in a murder. She didn't want to believe that it was, but she confessed that she and her brother had thrown it into the Naches River.

"Could I be in trouble?" she asked.

The public defender pulled no punches. "You could. I think you should tell the prosecuting attorney what you know."

First, though, the attorney from the Public Defender's office placed a call to Jeff Sullivan and gave him the plot of a theoretical set of circumstances involving a bystander who had inadvertently become involved in a murder—or two murders—"after the fact."

The Yakima County prosecutor understood immediately what he was hearing. They had just hit paydirt. He asked the attorney to bring his client into the courthouse.

Together, Loretta Scott and her attorney appeared at Jeff Sullivan's office in the Yakima County Courthouse. Tall and slender with huge sloe eyes, Loretta could have been a model. But not on the day she came in to tell her story; she was trembling too badly.

Loretta Scott explained that she was Tuffy Pleasant's first cousin on his father's side. For seven months of the previous year, she had lived with her three small children in Walla Walla, Washington, over a hundred miles southeast of Yakima. She said that she and Tuffy had been close growing up but she had seen little of him in the past few years. The Pleasant clan was large and cherished family loyalty, but Tuffy hadn't been around much, and then she had moved out of Yakima for a while herself.

Loretta said she had been surprised when Tuffy visited her in Walla Walla around Halloween. He had not called her first; he just showed up on a Thursday afternoon. She was startled, but she was happy to see him too.

"We sat down and rapped and went to the store and got some food and ate . . . and then," she continued, "and I don't know how the conversation really came about—he asked me, 'Hey, Cuz, do you have any weapons? Do you have a gun?'

"I said, 'Yeah, I have a gun,' and he asked, 'Can I see it?'"

Loretta Scott said she had an old .22 that someone had given to one of her brothers and then he had given it to a friend, who had given it to her. She had been having trouble with an old boyfriend who wouldn't let go. Having the gun around made her feel a little safer. She had no idea where it had come from in the beginning. When she had bad times with her ex, somebody gave it to her. When Tuffy asked about a gun, she retrieved it from where she kept it hidden from her children and showed it to him.

Asked to describe it, Loretta remembered that the gun had a long barrel and some kind of white tape around the grips. Tuffy had told her that he might buy it from her, but he would have to test it first. He told her that he needed it for "protection."

"You can have that old gun for thirty-five dollars," Loretta told him.

Tuffy had played with her kids and visited and then stayed the night at her home. Just before he left for Yakima the next day, he asked her if he could try the gun out. Then he asked for a potato. She had looked at him as if he were crazy, but she handed him one.

"And so we went out into the backyard," she said, "and he took the potato and held it in his hand and he fired the gun off into the potato to see how much power it had."

"What happened to the potato?" Prosecutor Jeff Sullivan asked.

"It went all over. It hit me in the eye."

Tuffy had tried shooting a potato twice and then, satisfied, he said he would buy the gun. He didn't give her any money at the time, but offered to pay her later. Loretta didn't know what he needed a gun for, and he didn't offer any explanation. He was a good kid who'd never been in any trouble, so she wasn't concerned.

Loretta said she had never checked for a serial number on the gun, but she remembered it had a clip in it, and that she had given Tuffy some bullets that came with it.

On November 10, Loretta Scott had moved back to Yakima. Sometime in the next few weeks, she had seen Tuffy again over at her sister's house. He didn't have the gun with him, and he had never paid her. Thirty-five dollars wasn't that much, but he *had* promised. On November 29, Loretta decided to confront him about getting either the gun or the money back, and she went to the apartment he shared with his girlfriend when he was home from college.

Tuffy was outside working on his car when she drove up and he grinned at her and sauntered over to her car.

"I went over there and I said could I have it back?" Loretta said. "He gave the gun back. He went to his car and wrapped the gun up in a cloth and gave it to me."

Loretta said she had stuck it in her purse and then put it in a closet at her apartment. That seemed to be the end of the matter. She wasn't mad because her cousin hadn't paid her for the gun and she had it back. As far as she knew, he had just wanted to carry it to look like a big man. He was going to college, he wasn't in any trouble, and the whole transaction was no big deal.

Loretta Scott paused as she answered the detectives' and the prosecutor's questions. She was still nervous, but she felt better now that she'd started to tell the story.

"Okay," Jeff Sullivan asked her, "did Angelo [Tuffy] ever come to you again asking for the gun?"

"Yes, he did," she said. "On the twenty-fourth . . . Christmas."

It was Christmas Eve and she and her sister were alone when he came over and said, "Can I get that from you again, Cousin?" He didn't say the word *gun* at first but she knew what he meant. She asked him what he wanted it for, but he didn't really answer. All he would say was, "You'll read about it in the paper."

She stared at him. That didn't sound so good. But he seemed to be in a hurry, and he was Tuffy—her "Cuz," her longtime friend. She gave him the .22 again and he asked about ammunition. "I told him I only had one bullet left—in the bathroom in the medicine cabinet. We were in there already and I just had to turn around to get it for him."

She remembered that she had put the lone bullet in a medicine vial when she cleaned the cabinet. It was there with a single aspirin, a bobby pin, and a penny.

When Tuffy left, her sister had looked at her and shook her head. "You shouldn't have done that, Loretta," she said flatly.

Loretta had wondered briefly why her sister hadn't objected while Tuffy was in the house. Whatever he wanted the gun for, it was too late now. She moved about her kitchen, getting ready for a family Christmas Eve party.

All over Yakima, people were celebrating the holiday.

The first time Loretta Scott had given Tuffy her gun, she had had to go and ask for it. That's probably why Loretta's sister had told her she had done a dumb thing. Oddly, she didn't have to ask for the gun this time. Tuffy was back before she knew it.

Loretta had been bewildered to see Tuffy again at about 1:30 A.M. Christmas morning. Her Christmas Eve party was in full swing when he and his girlfriend, René, showed up unexpectedly. But he hadn't come to the party; he had come to give her the .22. She thought that was kind of strange—his bothering to come to her house on Christmas Eve.

"Did you have any conversation with him?" Jeff Sullivan asked Loretta.

"No, he just gave it to me. I put it in a drawer."

Loretta had no idea what Tuffy had wanted with the gun that he had kept for only five hours. Not, at least, until Christmas morning.

"We had opened our Christmas gifts and we were supposed to have dinner at my mother's house," Loretta said nervously. "When I came in the door, my sister said, 'Loretta, I have something to tell you.'"

Loretta Scott had thought her sister was just joking and she moved toward the buffet to fill her plate. But her sister was adamant that she stop and listen to her news before she ate.

"*Okay,*" Loretta said. "Before I fix my plate. *What?*"

"Mr. Moore is dead."

"Aww, girl, go on." Loretta laughed.

"No," her sister said urgently. "He's dead. He was shot last night."

Suddenly, Loretta Scott had lost her appetite and any Christmas spirit. "*He was shot last night?*" she whispered.

"Yeah, he was shot last night with a twenty-two."

"*With a twenty-two?*" Loretta repeated like an automaton. She kept hearing Tuffy say, "You'll read about it in the paper."

She stayed at her mother's house so her children could enjoy the day, but her mind had been going ninety miles an hour. She could not believe that Tuffy had had anything to do with shooting Mr. Moore. Mr. Moore had made Tuffy a champion. Still, on Monday, she was waiting for the paper boy at five. She took the paper in carefully but was afraid to open it. She set it down on the kitchen table. "I let it sit there until about eight-thirty and I started thinking. I was trying to get my mind clear."

Loretta still could not imagine that Tuffy would hurt anyone, much less Mr. Moore. She turned to her boyfriend, "G," and the look on her face made him ask, "What's *wrong?*"

"I've got a gun," she answered. "And I've got a feeling something is wrong."

Loretta picked up the paper and started reading about Gabby Moore's murder. "When I got to the twenty-two-caliber part, I panicked."

The paper said the bullet had been a .22 caliber long bullet, and that was the same kind of bullet she had given to Tuffy. She asked "G" if she could borrow his car, a brand-new Oldsmobile.

He handed her the keys. Whatever was going on, he didn't particularly care to know the details.

"I went to my mother's house," Loretta told the investigators who were listening to her recollections avidly. "I had forgotten that she had left and went to Seattle, and there was no one there but my brother, Charles. He was having a little party. I called him into the bedroom, and I said, 'Chucky, I did something terrible. I don't know what to do about it. I'm panicky and I'm scared and I don't want to believe it. I think it's a dream.'"

Seeing how upset Loretta was, Chucky Pleasant was scared too.

"He panicked right along with me," Loretta said. "We started talking about, 'Let's bury the gun,' and we started acting like Columbo—trying to pick apart a puzzle and everything. And so we got into the car and so we decided to throw it in the river."

"Where did you throw it in the river?" Jeff Sullivan asked.

"The Naches."

They had been heading south toward Yakima when they approached the Twin Bridges. If they hadn't been so frightened and if the reason for their mission hadn't been so deadly serious, their efforts to get rid of the .22 might have been humorous. It was like a snake lying between them on the car seat, and neither of them was adept at stealthy games.

Chucky Pleasant, nineteen, who was also Tuffy's first cousin, had flung the gun from the car, aiming at the Naches River. Instead, he hit the bridge railing and the gun bounced back into the road. Loretta told him to get out and throw it far, far out into the swiftest, deepest part of the river. She would circle around and pick him up on the other side of the road.

It was very dark and cold. December 26. They were both scared to death that someone would see them. They didn't want the gun, but they didn't want to implicate their cousin in a murder. It was almost as if they could throw the gun away, the whole ugly business could be over and forgotten.

Chucky picked up the gun and threw it where it looked like the river was deep and running fast. He didn't know that he had only tossed it onto the little island below the bridge where the water would not be deep for long.

It was ironic, Jeff Sullivan realized. If Chucky Pleasant hadn't missed with his first throw, the gun *would* have gone into such a deep part of the river that no one would ever have found it. The second throw was the one that hit the water over the island.

Loretta Scott was still afraid as she poured out her story, but telling it to the police and the prosecutor made her feel a little better. She still fully expected to go to jail.

She said her brother hadn't told her exactly where he had thrown the gun, but he had assured her it was "deep."

"What did you do after you threw the gun in the river?" Sullivan asked.

"I went home and went to sleep."

Loretta had read the papers, seen all the stories about Mr. Moore and Mr. Blankenbaker, but she had tried to put it all out of her mind. She didn't want to know what had happened. It was exactly two months later—a few days before she came to the prosecutor—Loretta said, when her cousin Tuffy had showed up at her new apartment.

He was the last person she wanted to see. He seemed jittery. He *was* jittery, and that just wasn't like Tuffy. He always had fun and saw the happy side of things. But he had been having too many visits from Vern Henderson, and Vern had told him how much the police could tell if they ever found the gun that shot Gabby and Morris. And Tuffy had read about the Klingele boys finding a .22 automatic in the Naches River. He wanted to make sure that it wasn't *the* gun.

Tuffy and Loretta talked around the subject. They had known such happy family times together in the past, and each of them wanted so much to go back to those days. But it was too late. Finally, Tuffy blurted out a question, "Where's the gun?"

Loretta studied his face, and she knew she had to find out what had really happened to Mr. Moore. Feeling a little guilty, she told Tuffy a lie. "Oh, I gave it to some dude who lives down in Florida. I just gave it to him."

Instantly, Tuffy's face gleamed with relief. "Oh, Cousin, thank you," he said. "I love you for what you did."

Tuffy asked her if she had read in the papers about the little boy who had gone fishing and had pulled a gun from the river. He had been so worried when he read that, afraid it was the .22 she had loaned him. But now he was relieved.

Softly, Loretta continued her story to the Yakima investigators. "I saw the joy and the love he had for me on his face because he thought I had done this [sent the gun to Florida] and I said, 'No, Cuz, that's a lie I told you.' And I sat him down on the couch and I said I had thrown the gun away in the river."

All the relief had drained from Tuffy's face, Loretta said.

"How did he act when he found that you *had* thrown the gun into the Naches River?" Bob Brimmer asked.

"*Time* . . ."

"I don't understand."

"Time. He was talking about, you know, what he was going to have to go through."

"Go through?"

"Time" meant time in prison. Vern Henderson had convinced Tuffy so completely that if that death gun should ever be found, it could be traced directly back to the man who shot Morris and Gabby. And at this moment, Tuffy Pleasant was reacting as if all of his dreams of glory in wrestling, all his hopes and plans to be a teacher would evaporate.

"All he could see was hard time," Loretta said.

Loretta said that Tuffy had told her that a "white boy" had shot Mr. Moore as part of a plan that was supposed to pay off five thousand dollars. She didn't know if the shooter was supposed to get the money or if Mr. Moore was supposed to—because Mr. Moore wasn't supposed to be killed; he was only supposed to be wounded.

The men listening exchanged glances. It sounded like a peculiar plan indeed. Tuffy had mentioned Joey Watkins and Kenny Marino as part of the plan, and he had said Mr. Moore was supposed to sign a piece of paper and give somebody five thousand dollars.

Tuffy had never admitted anything incriminating to Loretta. He hadn't told her that *he* had held the gun himself or that he had shot it at anyone.

And *who* did he mean by the "white boy" who had shot Mr. Moore? Kenny Marino? Or someone they had never considered before?

It was time for more lie detector tests.

16

Olive **Blankenbaker** tried to keep busy, but the walls of her mobile home were closing in on her. She waited for Vern Henderson to come and tell her that he had solved Morris's murder. It wouldn't bring Morris back, but it would help some.

Morris's half brother, Mike, who resembled Morris and Ned, their father, so much around the eyes that he made Olive catch her breath whenever she saw him, was very good to her. He stopped by often to see if she was managing all right, even though he knew she would never really get over losing her only son.

In the early months of 1976, Olive thought about how Mike had sold his car so he could go to Hawaii and comfort Morris when Jerilee divorced him. *When was that?* It seemed to her that a dozen years had passed, but she realized it had been less than two years ago. That was hard to believe when so much had happened.

Olive arranged to buy Morris's Volkswagen from his estate. She wanted Mike Blankenbaker to have it; it would make up for his giving up his first car for Morris, and it would be something of his big brother's that he could cherish.

Jerilee Blankenbaker-Moore-Blankenbaker, in some ways a double-widow now, kept working at the bank. If she moved through her days in a blur of shock, no one could fault her. She was brilliant on the job; it was a way to shut the world out for a while. Her children were small and they needed her, her own family was supportive, and so the months rolled by. She was very lonely at first, adrift really. She had been married since she was eighteen years old, albeit to two men, but she had never been truly "single" during the past dozen years. One marriage had moved so seamlessly into the next that she had never learned to live alone.

There was—there *had* to be—a distance between Morris's family and Jerilee. Although no one ever said it aloud, the thought was always there: If Jerilee had not fallen in love with Gabby and gone off with him, if he had not become obsessed with her, Morris's family believed that Morris would be alive. They had no proof. Even the police had no proof. But it was just common sense. Except for the normal problems everyone has from time to time, all of their lives had moved along so smoothly until Gabby Moore moved in with Morris and Jerilee. In time, maybe they could work out their differences with Jerilee, but it was hard for Olive to look at her and not think of losing Morris.

Olive didn't know exactly what had happened, but she vowed she would find out before she died. And Olive had learned that she probably *would* die soon. At sixty-five, she had been diagnosed with lung cancer. Wasn't that just her kind of luck? She didn't even smoke. Sometimes Olive wondered why she had had to take so many heavy hits in her life. She had lost her only husband, her only child, the best friend-and-boss she had ever had, and now it looked as if she were going to be one of the small percentage of nonsmokers to die of lung cancer.

Yet there was a strength in Olive Blankenbaker that few women have. Maybe it was rage, and maybe it was only an ability to accept the unthinkable and go on. She planned her little garden for spring and was pleased that her cat was going to have kittens.

Olive loved life and she was not going to give up easily. She knew what the odds were—the doctors had told her—but it didn't matter that much to her any longer. "I just figured I wasn't going to live to be an old woman," she said quietly.

Olive was determined, however, to stay alive long enough to attend the trial of Morris's murderer—whoever that turned out to be. Vern Henderson wasn't telling her anything specific; he just kept reassuring her that he was working on the case, and for her not to worry.

"I didn't sit around and cry," Olive said. "I went back to work. As it turned out, I worked for years after Morris was killed. If I hadn't had my work, I don't know what I would have done because when I wasn't busy, I sat around and thought about Morris. I went back to work as a court reporter in federal court cases. They brought a lot of them down from Spokane, and I was kept busy."

Olive was completely unaware that Jerilee had begun to date again. Had she known, she would have been shocked, even though she expected that one day, in the future, Jerilee would remarry since she was only thirty. Olive certainly did not consider that her ex-daughter-in-law would even think of another marriage anytime soon.

While the *Yakima Herald-Republic* was barely mentioning the Blankenbaker-Moore murders anymore, there had been a great deal going on below the surface. District Attorney Jeff Sullivan, Sergeant Bob Brimmer, and Detective Vern Henderson had been working feverishly to build the strongest case possible against the man they now believed to be the shooter in at least one of the murders. And that was the man who had borrowed the death gun shortly before each of the killings: Angelo "Tuffy" Pleasant.

Brimmer, Henderson, and Jeff Sullivan were about to make a move. With the visit from Loretta Scott and her linking of the .22 to her cousin, Sullivan agreed that they had probable cause now to arrest Tuffy Pleasant. On February 27, 1976, Sullivan issued a warrant charging Tuffy with aiding and abetting first-degree murder, and for commiting second-degree murder.

The warrant was sent up to the Ellensburg Police Department with a request to arrest Tuffy Pleasant and to inform Yakima County detectives when he was in custody. It didn't take long. Tuffy wasn't hiding. He was going to class during the week, and he was coming home to be with his friends on weekends. It was that same Friday, in the late afternoon, when word came that Tuffy Pleasant had been arrested and was being held in the Kittitas County Jail in Ellensburg.

The weather was bitter. Snoqualmie Pass, the main route through the Cascade Mountains between Seattle and Yakima, had already been closed down twice and motorists who were finally allowed to risk going through were warned to watch for avalanches and rolling rocks. There were twelve inches of snow on the ground in Yakima and more coming down.

Bob Brimmer and Vern Henderson checked out a city car and headed north in the roaring blizzard to pick up their prisoner. When Tuffy saw Vern and Brimmer, he half shrugged. Whatever the game was, it was over—or it had entered another phase. Brimmer advised Tuffy of his rights under Miranda. *This* time, Angelo "Tuffy" Pleasant *was* a suspect. He got in the backseat of the patrol unit with Vern Henderson while Brimmer drove. The snow was so thick as it pointed icy darts at the headlights that it was hard to see the road. But all of them were used to this kind of weather. It was a typical February in eastern Washington.

Just to be doubly sure that his prisoner understood his rights, Vern pulled the little Miranda card from his pocket and read the warnings again. Tuffy nodded that he understood he didn't have to talk to them, but he was willing to do so.

As a cop, Vern Henderson was elated; they had hooked a big fish. As an athlete, a black man, a human being, he pondered how sad this all was. Andrew Pleasant had been so proud to see his son get a hero's welcome when he came back from Japan in 1972. Tuffy Pleasant was never going to make "State" now, and he was never going to the Olympics. He wasn't going to get a college degree in education and become head wrestling coach at Davis High School. He had had the whole world almost in his grasp.

That was all gone now.

"I didn't shoot anyone," Tuffy told Vern. "The only thing I did was furnish the gun."

"Who did you give the gun to?"

"To Gabby. I picked it up from him a week after Morris was shot."

"What about Christmas Eve?"

"I . . . I went and picked the gun up again and gave it to Gabby."

Vern Henderson asked him how he got the gun back after Gabby was shot, and Tuffy said that the "shooter" and he had agreed on a "rendezvous spot" where he would retrieve the gun on Christmas morning.

"And where was this rendezvous spot supposed to be at?"

"Over by Eisenhower High School by the golf course."

Vern said nothing, but none of it made any sense. All that nonsense about Tuffy running around borrowing a gun and picking it up and borrowing it again. And why was Gabby Moore sending out for a gun to have himself shot, and then arranging to have Tuffy pick it up? Why would he care *what* happened to the gun after he was dead? Had he so wanted to convince Jerilee that he too was the victim of an unknown stalker that he was willing to literally *die* to do it?

The winter wind howled around their patrol car and it felt as though they were being lifted off the road and set down again. They barely noticed; the questions on their minds preoccupied them. But Vern Henderson and Bob Brimmer were going to have to wait to find out the rest of the story—if they ever did. Tuffy didn't want to talk about the murders anymore.

Ordinarily, they could have made the drive back to Yakima in about half an hour, and it took them only a little longer in the snowstorm. Tuffy stared out the window at the white on white on white. Vern wondered what he was thinking about.

Time, probably. That's what his cousin Loretta said he was afraid of, *doing time*.

And he had good reason to be afraid.

As they drove into Yakima, Vern realized that it was too late for Tuffy to get anything to eat at the Yakima County Jail. He asked his prisoner if he was hungry.

"Yeah . . ."

"Well, the best you might get in the jail this time of night is a cold sandwich," Vern said. "You got any money on you?"

Tuffy shook his head.

"The only people I treat to free meals are pretty women, and that's not you," Vern kidded him. "I'll *loan* you the money for a hamburger and a Coke."

They stopped at a drive-in and Vern bought the food for Tuffy. It was dark and late when they booked him into the Yakima County Jail. It was too late to start an interrogation into what they knew were two very complicated murder cases. Tuffy was placed in a single cell.

Brimmer and Henderson had waited three months to find out why Morris Blankenbaker had been murdered, and two months to solve the riddle of Gabby Moore's death. They felt they were right on the brink of knowing, but one more night wouldn't make any difference.

"You want to call anyone, Tuffy?" Vern asked.

Tuffy shook his head.

The two detectives left him there and walked away from the jail smells of stale cigarette smoke, sweat, urine, and Pine-Sol disinfectant out into the blessedly cold, clean air. Their feet crunched on the snow. They didn't talk. Both Brimmer and Henderson felt as if they were in a state of suspended animation.

Tomorrow would—tomorrow *might*—bring the explanations that had eluded them. They both felt they had the right man—at least on Morris's murder. They still didn't believe that Tuffy could have killed his hero, Gabby Moore, but they figured he knew who had.

17

At 9:30 on Saturday morning, February 28, Bob Brimmer and Vern Henderson took Tuffy Pleasant from the Yakima County Jail back to their offices. Again, Brimmer read him his rights and explained that Tuffy could waive his rights to have an attorney present during questioning. The detective sergeant was careful to assure himself that his prisoner understood what "waive" meant. Tuffy did and said he wanted to talk with Brimmer and Henderson.

But if they had expected that he would tell them what they had waited so long to hear right away, they were disappointed.

Since January 3, they had both been convinced that Tuffy knew the motivation for the two murders, and now they knew from talking to his cousin, Loretta Scott, that he had arranged not once, but twice, to furnish the death weapon. What they wanted to know was the entire story, and the name of the actual shooter.

Tuffy talked around the subject for an hour or more. It was obvious that he wanted to tell them the real truth after all the false starts and half truths he had told before. It was also obvious that he knew that once he told them what was fighting to get out, there would be no going back.

Half an hour past noon, Tuffy Pleasant agreed to dictate a statement about the death of Gabby Moore. The long descent of what had once been the finest example of a coach-athlete relationship into a sinister manipulation would be caught on the slowly turning tape recorder.

Tuffy gave his birthday, January 28, 1954, and his address, 1501 Glen Drive, Ellensburg, Washington, Apartment 12, Executive House.

He listened quietly, poised to speak, as Vern Henderson once more read him his Miranda rights. As the last clause echoed in the room, and after Tuffy had indicated that he understood every one of his legal options under Miranda, he declined to have his attorney present. He looked at Vern Henderson and he began to talk.

"Christmas Eve night," Tuffy said, "after I did a little visiting, I decided, you know, to go up and see Mr. Moore. . . . Okay, so apparently he had just gotten home. He just got home so we just started talking and I asked him if he would like to go out—you know, get a drink, go visit, whatever. And he said, 'Yeah'—we'd go check it out after he got cleaned up. But then the phone rings. I think it was Kenny Marino on it and he said I was there. . . . Okay, then he hangs up and we start talking . . . about everyday things, mainly about wrestling. About half an hour later, there is a second phone call. And then I notice something pretty strange about it."

Tuffy explained that Mr. Moore usually told him who was on the phone, but on this night, he hadn't explained anything about the second call, and the call had seemed to upset Moore.

"Then," Tuffy continued, "he started acting strange and then he broke out his bottle. He started drinking—drinking everything straight. Then he started to talking crazy. He started saying, 'Tonight's the night.' He asked me if I could go get the gun. . . . I told him no. Then he said, 'Look, if you don't go get that gun, I'll see to it that your neck is on the chopping block for Morris Blankenbaker's death.' And I says, 'It don't make no difference because I didn't do it.'

". . . Then he ran it down to me. He said, 'It's not that you did it or not; it's just that you did have a part in it because you committed [sic] this gun to me the first time.' And unaware, *myself* unaware the gun was going to be used."

. Tuffy said he had resisted Gabby's plan. "So then I says, 'Well, look—that gun is a long ways from here.' And he says, 'Well, can you get it tonight?' and I says, 'No.' He says, 'Well, we can gas up my car and we can go get it wherever it's at because I want to have it tonight.'"

Tuffy Pleasant's face glistened with sweat as he relived that last ghastly Christmas Eve in Gabby Moore's apartment. "And then I told him I wasn't going to do it. But then he threatened me again, and he showed me the police department's number on the phone book, and he dialed all four numbers—four, five, and then four numbers—and he said, 'You sure you don't want me to dial this last number? Think about it.' And then he went on and dialed that last number."

There was remembered desperation in Tuffy's voice as he stared at Vern Henderson. He sighed. "Then I told him I could get the gun. That was the end of the phone call to the police department, so he said, 'Well, you go get that gun.' He gave me fifteen minutes to get that gun."

His coach, whose word had always been law to him, had ordered him to do something he dreaded doing. But Tuffy had finally said "All right." Gabby told him to get the gun and come back with it. "I was supposed to come back and honk twice—to let him know I had the gun."

Vern Henderson thought he knew what was coming next; Loretta Scott had told them about Christmas Eve, but he wanted to see if Tuffy's version of the evening meshed with her recall.

Just at that instant, the tape recorder ground to a halt, and tensely Henderson and Brimmer checked it out, while Tuffy waited, wanting—and not wanting—to continue his statement.

"We got everything going again, now," Vern told him.

"Okay," Tuffy continued. "So I went and got the gun. I went to my cousin's house. She was having a little party, so I had a drink or two and then I asked her if I could get the gun and she didn't ask me for what or nothing. You know, my cousin is unaware of what is going on.

"So I got the gun from her and I went back by Mr. Moore's place and I honked twice. He was supposed to be ready, see, and he was supposed to come to the door, drunk, you know—trying to get drunk so he wouldn't feel too much pain."

Henderson was hesitant to slow down this outpouring of confession, but he wanted to be sure that he understood what Tuffy was talking about. Why would Gabby have wanted Tuffy to shoot him in the first place? He had to have known it was going to hurt like hell.

Tuffy Pleasant had known about Gabby's plan to make Jerilee believe that someone was after him, trying to kill him—just as they had killed Morris. Gabby had seen that she suspected him of being behind Morris's murder, and he believed he had to convince her otherwise or she would never marry him again. Tuffy knew that Gabby had told Jerilee about mysterious phone calls and broken windows. He knew she hadn't believed a word of it, and that she had hung up on Gabby, making him more despondent.

On Christmas Eve, in his obsessive, desperate fool-for-love state, Gabby had demanded that Tuffy help him carry out a wild, ill-conceived, tragic plan.

Gabby had had it all figured out. If he were to be shot—not actually *killed*—but just injured by a bullet fired from the gun that had killed Morris, then he was sure Jerilee would relent. He would become a victim himself, and no longer a suspect. He didn't care how much it hurt; nothing could hurt him more than being without Jerilee. Besides Gabby planned to drink enough while Tuffy was picking up the gun so that the pain wouldn't get to him.

Jerilee. Jerilee was why Gabby had threatened Tuffy and sent him out into that icy Christmas Eve to find the .22 that had killed Morris. If Loretta hadn't moved from Walla Walla back to Yakima the month before, it would have been impossible to carry out Gabby's plan. Walla Walla was at least a four-hour round trip. Tuffy could never had retrieved the gun and come back to Yakima before Derek Moore got home from his date.

But Loretta was only blocks away, and Gabby had convinced Tuffy that he would turn him into the Yakima police and say he had shot Morris *unless* Tuffy did exactly what he ordered.

Vern Henderson could sense that Tuffy Pleasant must have been driven by two tremendously compelling and powerful emotions that night. He loved Gabby Moore—his coach, his alternate father, the man who had told him he could do anything and be anything he wanted to be, the man whose guidance had already taken him to heights of glory he could never have imagined. He must have wanted to bring back the old Gabby again, the happy, joking, confident Gabby. He had seen the man's heart break over the loss of Jerilee, and he wanted Gabby to have her. After months of listening to his coach talk about Jerilee and break down in tears, Tuffy had finally believed that *nothing* else was going to make him happy. Tuffy couldn't see it, he'd said, but Gabby Moore was a one-woman man.

Tuffy's second emotion was probably even stronger—the instinct to survive that bubbles to the surface of any human being in danger. Gabby had scared him when he picked up the phone and dialed the police. If Gabby turned him in and said he had shot Morris, Tuffy knew they would come and arrest him, and he would do heavy hard time.

When Gabby was drunk, there was no telling what he would do. And he was drinking heavily on Christmas Eve.

And so, Tuffy had gone to get the .22 from his cousin Loretta. He explained Gabby's plan in more detail.

"He was trying to get drunk so he wouldn't feel too much pain. [He would] come to the door, and I was supposed to hit him in his left shoulder. I was supposed to hit him—just *nick* him in his left shoulder." (Tuffy had no way of knowing about Gabby's conversation with Dr. Myers. He didn't know Gabby had researched just where the bullet should go in so it would wound but not kill him.)

There were tears in Tuffy's eyes as he moved through the scene in Gabby's apartment on Christmas Eve in his mind. He shook his head almost imperceptibly as he brought it all back, as if he could not believe that it had really happened.

"So I banged on the door," Tuffy remembered. "But it didn't come to that. What happened was I *couldn't do it*. I couldn't do it and I tried to talk to the man. I tried to talk to him, so we went inside. He had a few more drinks and I kept telling him—talking to the man. I said, 'Look, *I* can't do it.'"

Vern Henderson tried to picture what it must have been like. He knew that Tuffy was a womanizing, party-going mischief-maker. He knew he had given his parents any number of gray hairs. But Tuffy wasn't naturally a mean guy, and he had loved Gabby Moore like he loved Andrew, like he loved his natural father. Could Tuffy have fired a bullet into his own father? *No.* Could he have fired a bullet into Gabby?

Maybe, but it must well-nigh have killed him to do it. Vern waited while Tuffy took a deep breath and kept talking and the tape recorder lead circled around and around.

"He said, 'You are *going* to do it, whether you like it or not.'"

"But what it was supposed to be," Tuffy said desolately. "It was supposed to have just been a hit and a miss, and therefore the hit and the miss [would have meant] he could get to the phone and call up his girlfriend named Cathy so she could call the ambulance and then things start from there. There was supposed to have been only an *attempt* made on his life."

Tuffy said that Gabby kept insisting that he had to shoot him, and that he realized his own neck was "on the chopping block" for Morris Blankenbaker's murder.

"So, therefore, I took the gun, you know . . . I shot him, you know. I pointed the gun, you know. As soon as he turned his back—right here in his left shoulder. . . . As he turned, I shot him in the shoulder, high in his left shoulder. Okay, well, it happened he turned and stumbled, but then I guess I hit him low and then that was it. I just left and took the gun back to my cousin."

Tuffy Pleasant made a point of releasing his cousin Loretta from any complicity in Gabby's death. He stressed that she knew nothing at all about it.

Henderson believed him. It was odd, he thought, the points of honor in the delicate dance around the crime of murder. The detective did not believe, however, that he had heard the true version of Gabby's death. Tuffy had waffled too much over the sequence of events. He offered him another cup of coffee, and they changed the tape on the machine.

There is a rhythm to an effective interrogation. Henderson fell back now into simple questions and answers. The emotion in the room was about to choke them both. He would have to back off and let Tuffy build up to the actual killing again. Bob Brimmer sat back, silently; he could see that Vern Henderson was doing a good job of drawing out Tuffy's confession.

"Okay, Angelo," Vern said, "going back to the beginning of your story. You were talking about being over there Christmas Eve, the twenty-fourth. You were at Mr. Moore's address on Eighteenth Avenue, right?"

"Yes."

"How did you get there?"

"My car. I drove."

"Where did you park?"

"I parked out front on the street."

"The reason I ask you this is isn't it kind of normal that everybody comes around and parks in his backyard? Is that right?"

"Yeah."

"A lot of people?"

"Yes."

"Students?"

"Yes."

"Now, during the time that you were sitting there talking to Mr. Moore, did anybody else come and go from there?"

"Yes, my brother Anthony and Stoney Morton."

The story was already changing slightly. Vern Henderson's voice betrayed no surprise.

"About what time were they there?"

"I would say they were there between nine-thirty and ten-thirty."

Tuffy said that he had stayed on visiting with his coach after the other two left.

"Now had you already gone and got the gun by the time your brother and Stoney got there? Was the gun in the house at that time?"

"Uh . . . yes."

"Where did you put it?"

"It was on the other side of his daveno—in back of it."

"Okay. Now then, did you go out in your car and toot the horn or had you already done that?"

"That was already done. It was supposed to come down after I honked the horn twice. I was supposed to wait five minutes and then knock on the door, and he was supposed to come to the door and then I was supposed to shoot him."

"Okay. Now what happened in the kitchen? There was a curtain pulled loose and the screen door was propped open by a cement block. How did this all come about?"

"He did it."

"He wanted to make it look like a big deal?"

"Yes, he did that himself."

"Did he ever say he had made any phone calls to himself or to his relatives about being threatened. Did he ever tell you anything?"

"Yes," Tuffy said. "He told me he had. There were a couple of phone calls about threats being made on his life."

But Tuffy said he really didn't know if Gabby had made the calls himself or not.

On Christmas Eve, Tuffy thought there had been a phone call for Gabby about 10:15. Vern knew that would have been Gabby's daughter, but believed she had called him a little later.

They were approaching Gabby Moore's horrific death again, and the room crackled with tension.

"Okay then," Vern began, "did you go over and pick up the phone after you shot him?"

"No. He took the phone off the receiver."

"He did? This was *before* you shot him? Why? So there wouldn't be any phone calls or something?"

"I don't know. I don't know," Tuffy said, distressed. "But I think it was because that way it was off the receiver and all he had to do was dial the number like he planned. He could take the shock and just crawl to the phone and just dial with one hand. That way he wouldn't have to fumble with the receiver. . . ."

It wouldn't have worked, of course. After twenty seconds or so, the phone would have lost its dial tone and Gabby would have had to hang it up. That would have been harder for him than to leave it on the hook all along. It sounded crazy, but maybe he didn't want the sound of a phone jangling as he braced himself for the bullet he had apparently ordered Tuffy to fire into his body.

But Vern knew that Gabby had done one more thing before he prepared to stop a bullet. He had turned on his stereo, set the needle on his record of "Lay Your Head Upon My Pillow," and turned the volume up high. Ray Price's words of lost love had floated through his apartment long after he died—until the needle wore a groove it couldn't get out of.

"The whole plan revolved around the fact that he wanted Jerilee to come back?" Vern asked again. "Is that right?"

"*Jerilee.*" Tuffy Pleasant made the name sound like a swear word. "Yes. He wanted to prove the fact that he had nothing to do with Morris Blankenbaker's death and that he wanted her that bad— enough to go all the way."

"After you shot him and he fell to the floor, how did you leave the place?" Henderson asked.

Tuffy looked down at the floor. Then he gazed straight into Vern's eyes. "Uhhhhh. I didn't shoot him and he didn't fall on the floor. I shot him when he was already *on* the floor in what we call in wrestling terms the 'referee position,' both hands on the floor with your palms down."

The room was silent for a full minute. What a travesty of everything that the shooter and the dead man had been to each other and to the sport they had both loved. Gabby Moore had taught Tuffy everything he knew about wrestling. In the end, in the last moment of time they would spend together in this lifetime, Gabby had dropped to his hands and knees, drunk from a full bottle of whiskey, and assumed the "referee position"—after instructing Tuffy exactly where to shoot.

It made an awful picture, but it explained more how Gabby could have lain there without so much as a tiny spray of blood on his T-shirt. The .22 that went in beneath his left armpit had done its damage as he dropped the last few inches to the floor and his full weight compressed his chest, holding back the quarts of blood that were already drowning his ruined heart and lungs.

"How far away were you when you shot him?" Henderson asked.

"How far is that table, there?"

"Two feet," Vern answered, and then understanding what Tuffy meant, he asked, "You mean from where you are sitting from the wall of this room? Oh, we are talking about seven feet—or something."

Tuffy indicated that he had been six or seven feet from Gabby when he pulled the trigger, with Gabby's voice repeating, "Shoot . . . shoot . . . shoot . . ."

"Did you point the gun, aim the gun, or just pull it up and shoot?"

Vern knew that Tuffy had had only one bullet. Only one. If he had missed, in all likelihood Gabby would still be alive.

"I pointed it at his shoulder," Tuffy said. "But then he moved. . . . I believe he fell against the refrigerator . . . I guess from the effects of the alcohol."

"Are you sure he was down on his hands and knees?"

"Yes."

"Did you try to bend over to shoot him?"

"Yes."

"You didn't just walk up and shoot straight down, did you?"

"No . . . I was off to the side."

"And did he just fall to the floor?"

"Yes."

"Did you say anything to him?"

"No."

"You just got out of there?"

"Yes."

"Was this the plan after you shot him? You were to run out of there and leave?"

"Well, it wasn't a plan. I just did it."

Vern Henderson asked the next question quite deliberately. He needed to know which emotion had prevailed in the end: Gabby's power over Tuffy, or Tuffy's own fight to survive as a free man? "Now, did you do this because he had you up against the wall or did you do this because this was the plan he had?"

"I mainly did it because he had me up against the wall. I really believed he had me. . . ."

With those words, Tuffy Pleasant probably sealed his own fate.

When Tuffy left Gabby's apartment, he could not have known if Gabby was alive or dead. He ran into the frigid night with the music still playing behind him, "Don't look so sad . . . I know it's over. Let's just be glad we had some time to spend together. There's no need to watch the bridges that we're burning. . . ."

Vern Henderson and Bob Brimmer knew what had happened; they had been present at Gabby's autopsy. That single .22 bullet had hit a rib and gone crazy. All of Gabby's planning and careful questions to Doc Myers had been for nothing; you can't trust a .22 slug to go where it's intended anymore than you can throw a knife with your eyes closed and expect it to hit a target.

Tuffy Pleasant was drained. He knew that he would have to tell Bob Brimmer and Vern Henderson about the night that Morris Blankenbaker died.

But that could wait until tomorrow. In his mind, he had to be seeing the kitchen where Gabby Moore lay, unmoving, and hearing that song again, over and over and over . . .

18

Even under ordinary circumstances, February 29 is a special date, but on this Sunday, February 29, Vern Henderson and Bob Brimmer were about to experience—at least, they hoped they were—the culmination of an intensive investigation, the last answer to the last question. Who had shot Morris Blankenbaker?

Angelo "Tuffy" Pleasant sat once more in the interrogation room of the Yakima Police Department. They began by talking, the pas de deux that takes place in every well-orchestrated interrogation. Almost always, everything in the suspect makes him want to keep silent. Often he is appalled at what he (or *she*) has done. It is difficult when the words finally burst forth, to be frozen forever on a tape recorder. Tuffy's confession to shooting Gabby Moore had been hard, but it was obvious that he had been cajoled, ordered, blackmailed, and threatened to shoot by the victim himself. There was every reason to think that he had shot in the belief that he would only wound—that he never intended to kill his hero.

When Tuffy Pleasant had confessed to shooting Gabby Moore, he had conveyed his shock and his grief. When he said that Gabby had had him "up against the wall," it was apparent that Tuffy meant just that. At the time of the shooting on Christmas Eve, he had felt he had no other choice.

But Morris's death was something else again, something to be ashamed of. The victim had not participated in his shooting, and he hadn't braced for the bullet. Vern knew from the blood "blowback" on Morris's hand that all he had had time to do was throw up that hand, a flesh-and-blood barrier against death, and he only did that at the last moment when he finally recognized his enemy. Morris's murder had been the result of a cowardly and treacherous plot.

It had been the ultimate act of poor sportsmanship, something that both Vern and his prisoner deplored. It was no wonder that this was the murder that was hardest for Tuffy to discuss.

They took their positions across the table from one another: Vern on one side and Tuffy on the other. Way back in the beginning of the probe, Vern had told Tuffy that he would eventually find out the truth, and he had compared their verbal jousting to a "game." It was a game of deadly seriousness, and they had now come to the last period of play.

Once again, Vern would do the questioning. All three of the men in the room acknowledged why Tuffy had shot Gabby Moore. It was simple and terrible: Gabby had had Tuffy backed into a corner. Tuffy had told them the day before that he feared he would take the fall for Morris's murder, even though he hadn't done it.

Well then, *who* had? Maybe now they would know. Vern thought he already did. "I was always honest with Angelo," he recalled. "I told him the things that I knew to be true, and I said, 'This is how I knew you did it.'"

Off the tape, Tuffy admitted that he had tried to tell Morris to leave Jerilee alone—for Gabby's sake. He had confronted Morris that night in his yard and tried to reason with him. "He told me he wasn't going to leave her alone," Tuffy said, "because Jerilee was *his* wife."

He told Vern that he had lied to Morris and told him that he had run out of gas. Tuffy was edging closer and closer to the whole story, and he had not yet mentioned that anyone but he and Morris had been present when Morris died.

Even so, it took two and a half hours before Tuffy was finally willing to commit his statement to tape. At 12:20, Bob Brimmer set the tape recorder up.

"Okay," Vern said, "let's go back to the beginning of a situation which involved Morris Blankenbaker. Angelo, you tell us in your own words how it came about, and what happened on that night, please."

Henderson had to remind himself that this was his job, an interrogation about a murder. He couldn't allow himself to think of the Morris he had known, of all the football games in the autumn nights, all the problems and the confidences they had shared, of riding around with Morris and Les Rucker in the little white Volkswagen. Whatever he was about to hear, he had to remember that it was over. It had happened. For Morris, the pain was gone.

But Vern Henderson had to know.

Tuffy Pleasant was silent, wondering where to begin—far more nervous about this statement than he had been when he spoke of Gabby Moore's death. He had already told Vern a great deal. It shouldn't be this hard to tell it all.

"Well," Vern said, "just tell us about before the night it happened—tell us a little bit prior to that."

"Well . . ." Tuffy finally spoke, rambling at first: "I'll just start. It was for a class. It was for a credit for this wrestling coaching class I was taking up there at Central Washington State College in Ellensburg. I needed to assist in a coaching class on a team, so I confronted my former head coach, Mr. Moore. So I saw him off and on there for a while. I was seeing him two or three times a week. And I noticed in this time the changes he was going through. We were tight, and like in my book he was Number One and I would do anything in the world for the man, you know, not to see him hurt—just not to see him hurt."

Henderson didn't doubt that Tuffy was telling him the truth about that.

"So he was talking about his wife most of the time. He was really upset over his wife, Jerilee. Jerilee this. Jerilee that. He was really caught up in her. And what really hurt him before their final divorce was when she moved back and started living with Morris again. That really broke him up. He couldn't see it. Because he didn't have that last chance, you know—that second chance he was always talking about."

Tuffy said that Gabby had begun to talk the way he did in

coaching, about eliminating problems. "'You eliminate your problems,' he said, 'and then you take it from there.' So his problem was Morris, number one, because the second problem was Jerilee and she was *with* Morris. So therefore both problems were together so you eliminate one to get the other."

Tuffy laughed nervously, a harsh sound in the quiet room. He said that Gabby hadn't been himself for a long time. "Every time I saw him he was just losing it. *He was just losing it.* And we were so close, [I felt] like what he felt. He shed a tear—I shed a tear. . . .

"And so then he started talking about who could he find to eliminate Morris and how it was [to be] done—to waste him . . . about who could I find? First, he wanted to see if I could find a hit man for him and he asked for a couple of names, and I gave him one name: Max Phillips.* He asked me where he was, and I told him the last time I heard Max was in Wenatchee doing his thing, whatever it might have been at the time."

That had satisfied Moore for a while. He had a name of an alleged hitman, but he became restive when he couldn't get Tuffy to contact Max. Gabby had begun to talk about Stoney Morton and Joey Watkins—two of his former wrestlers—as possible hired killers. That was a ridiculous idea, and Tuffy said he had just kept stalling, waiting for Gabby to turn to some other harebrained scheme. But all the while, he was still feeling Gabby's agony. Even with the slight relief he achieved through alcohol, Gabby Moore was a walking, talking broken heart. Tuffy, who appreciated a good-looking female, was baffled that a man as strong as Gabby could be so humbled by the rejection of just one woman.

"Okay, so then that dies out. This man, this man, he's just tore up—he's just not himself. He's just bleeding inside and I could see it and I could feel it."

Vern believed him. Tuffy had loved Gabby. Gabby had been on him, Tuffy said, to find a gun. He delayed that too, as long as he could. "Time elapsed," Tuffy continued, "so much has been said I couldn't really say right now—not to the fact I don't want to—that I can't really remember it all word for word. . . . He said if I could find somebody, he would offer them seven hundred dollars, but five hundred dollars was all he could handle right at that time. Okay, so then he offers it to *me*, and I says, 'No five hundred dollars.' I couldn't take no life for that amount of money or any amount of money for that fact."

Tuffy said he was beginning to dread the visits with his old coach.

He explained he had no choice but to go on seeing Gabby. He wanted to see him because he was worried about him, but he also was taking the coaching course and he needed the credit. More important, Gabby had simply allowed Tuffy to become the "head coach." Tuffy didn't feel competent to handle it all on his own, and even though he got no backup from Gabby, he still felt better talking with him. Sometimes in the first hour or so of their conversations—before Gabby was really intoxicated—they still talked about the sport they both loved.

"He never showed for the matches," Tuffy said. "I helped take out the mats. I'd even make the starting lineup. I had that much authority . . . and," he admitted, "I was digging it."

For a little while, Tuffy was living his dream—the dream that Gabby had promised him. If he got his college degree, Gabby had said, Tuffy *would* be the head coach. He *would* take Gabby's place one day.

Sitting in the interrogation room, Tuffy kept talking with little prompting, his words flowing out as if they had finally been released from tremendous pressure. Tuffy had held them in for a long time, and it seemed a relief to him to be telling it all. He told Brimmer and Henderson about getting the gun from his cousin, Loretta, and test-shooting it into a potato.

"I took it . . . and brought it back and took it to Mr. Moore. Then we tried it out. If you go up there to the house, you will see, between his bedroom and a divider and the living room, there is a hole right there in the rug. What we did was I went outside to listen for the shot, and he took a wastepaper basket full of water and set it right down there in that spot and shot it a couple of times. I was listening for the noise outside and he was seeing how fast and how deep it would go—how powerful the gun was altogether. Well, you couldn't hear it too good outside, just like a cap gun. And so we figured that would be the gun."

Suddenly, Tuffy Pleasant sighed deeply. *"And I just did it for the man. . . ."*

Vern Henderson managed to keep his voice steady as he asked, "Did you get any money for it?"

"No, I didn't get any money for it."

"You did it for him *as a favor*?"

"It was for him, *the man*," Tuffy said. "He mentioned the fact of money, but he said I would never have to worry about money again."

"That he would give you things?"

"Yeah, whatever. Over a long-term situation."

They had not yet come to the moments just before Morris had died, and Vern knew he had to get there.

"Was a plan ever mentioned to you about perhaps sneaking up on Mr. Blankenbaker in the morning and shooting him while he was in the bathroom or someplace in his house, like it was a burglar or something like that?"

Tuffy said that Gabby Moore had thought up and then discarded several plans; he was always refining the method of his "problem's" death. He had suggested that Tuffy knock on Morris's door, and he thought that Tuesday would be a good day. Then he changed his mind again.

"Every Tuesday he [Morris] went to the 'Y,' and so it was when he went to the 'Y' that he wanted him to be hit. He had the time schedule down, see, and what it was. He wanted the hit in front of Rick [Morris's little boy]. . . . I was supposed to do it right there, and I was supposed to snatch his wallet and make it look like a robbery."

A brazen daylight robbery in downtown Yakima on a weekday was a remarkably stupid plan, and even Gabby Moore in his drunken scheming had realized that. He devised another scenario and then another.

"Who came up with the idea of waiting for him by the garage when he got off work at the Lion's Share?" Vern asked.

"He did. Everything was his idea."

"Mr. Moore had this plan laid out, right?"

"Yes, he had it all laid out. To the bone. *To the bone.*"

Vern Henderson moved to Friday, November 21. "The night Mr. Blankenbaker was shot, okay now, in detail. Whatever time it was, were you actually with Joey Watkins?"

"Yeah, I was with Joey Watkins."

"From that point on, tell me in detail."

As Tuffy spoke, Vern could see Morris's house on North Sixth— the alley, the gate, the picture of Morris lying there in death, his eyes unseeing as the snow fell. Vern had stood where the shooter—had it *really* been Tuffy?—stood. Vern had walked to where the bullet casing landed. If Tuffy wasn't leveling with him, he would know it in an instant. He didn't *want* to hear the details, but he had to hear them.

"Well," Tuffy began again. "About nine-thirty, we took off—Joey Watkins and I, Angelo Pleasant—we took off to go girl chasing, but not to go girl chasing because we figured we looked good enough for them to chase us." Pleasant grinned as if this had been any other night, but his voice was taut. He had had two agendas that night.

"We hit the Lion's Share a little after nine-thirty. Joey went in for a few minutes and then he came out and said it was kind of slow. So we left there and went to the Red Lion for a while. We were there for about an hour or so. Then we parted company, and I was invited to this other table."

Tuffy said he had to back up a little. He had been at his girlfriend's house (the mother of his child, pregnant with his second baby) earlier in the evening. "He [Gabby] has the number to my girlfriend's house and he called earlier that night. He called about seven, and I was there. He was in the hospital—"

"Gabby called you?"

"Yeah, he called from the hospital. And he said, 'Well, if you are going to do it, tonight is the night'—while he was up there—for an alibi."

Of course. It was the perfect alibi. According to Dr. Myers, Gabby hadn't wanted to be hospitalized, and he'd gone in dragging his feet. But, once there, he must have realized that nobody could accuse him of murder if he could prove he was in the hospital.

Since Gabby hadn't called for someone to bring the phone to his room, Henderson figured he had strolled down the hall to the public phone.

Tuffy Pleasant had gone on out, obviously with his mind always focused on Gabby's orders. He and Joey Watkins had cruised around, looking for pretty women. Maybe Tuffy had even told himself that, if he got lucky, that would be a sign that he wasn't meant to carry out Gabby's plan.

And Tuffy *had* gotten lucky. A couple with an extra woman in tow had introduced themselves to him and pulled out a chair at their table. It could have been a reprieve for Tuffy—and for Morris. Vern tried not to think about that.

"So, okay," Tuffy continued. "I was invited to this table with these other people. This single lady, you know. I was there maybe about ten minutes, and I told them I would be back, to excuse me. [They were] unaware. They didn't know what I was going to do or where I was going. I went to my folks' house and got a little money from my mom, and I went back to the Red Lion and reunited with the people who invited me over to their table. We went from there to the Holiday Inn, and we went to the Thunderbird, and back to the Red Lion. Then we parted company just a little bit before two o'clock A.M."

Thinking about it years later, Vern Henderson commented, "He left because he had a job to do for Gabby. Any other night, I can't imagine he would walk away from a willing woman who was ready to stay the night with him. He must have been looking at his watch.

He left the Red Lion a little before two o'clock A.M. He had something he had to do."

A little after 2:00 o'clock A.M. was when Morris was due to drive into his parking space off the alley after he had finished his Lion's Share job.

"You know, I wasn't going to do it if I didn't have time, because I was going to party," Tuffy said softly, perhaps regretting his final decision. "My intentions were that I had caught a lady for the night, and I was going to be with the lady the rest of the night, see, but we happened to part company before two . . . and I just went on over to Lincoln and waited until Morris came up the alley. As soon as he was coming up the alley and pulled in his yard, I ran up the alley and drew his attention. I drew and fired and ran back down the alley and took off. . . ."

Vern wasn't buying it, not the whole package. He believed now that Tuffy had shot Morris but he did not think for one moment he had heard the whole story. It was too simple, and Tuffy had glossed over it too quickly as if he were ashamed to linger over the deliberate deception that had thrown Morris so completely off guard. Vern knew that Morris had to have been completely relaxed. Otherwise, he would have tried to defend himself.

No, Tuffy had slid too rapidly over the actual murder. Vern had been there at Morris's autopsy, and he had made himself look at every bit of it. Now, he would make himself listen to every word about the last few moments of Morris's life.

Once again, he backed up a little. "Okay, now you and your friends parted down at the Red Lion shortly before two, and then you drove down and parked your car where? On Lincoln Avenue? Or Naches?"

"Lincoln."

"Lincoln Avenue—right up by the alleyway there?"

"Right by the alley."

"By the apartments—the redbrick apartments?"

"No, no—*Lincoln*. Okay," Tuffy corrected himself. "There *is* a little apartment there, yeah."

That was right, Vern thought. It wasn't the redbrick apartment next door to Morris's house that was on Lincoln; it was the little duplex where Mrs. Lenberg lived.

Tuffy denied that he had run into a garbage can as he ran down the alley, but Vern wondered if he would have even remembered in his state of panic, knowing what he was about to do.

"What kind of shoes were you wearing?"

"Platform type."

"Had a little bit of heel on them?"

"Yeah, a little bit of heel."

So far, Tuffy Pleasant's version of the night of the murder was meshing with Gerda Lenberg's statement. Most of the young guys wore platform shoes, Afros, flared plaid trousers, and leather jackets. Those shoes made a heck of a lot of noise.

"So you ran down the alley when you saw Morris's car come up the alley?"

"Yeah . . . like a trot."

"Okay, just a jog or whatever. And did you approach him from behind the garage?"

"No."

"You came right up behind his car?"

Vern could see it. He could see it in his mind, but he didn't dare look away. Maybe he could forget it . . . sometime.

"Yes." Tuffy nodded. "He was almost all the way up to the front of his house, and I called him back. I said, 'Morris! Morris!' you know."

"He walked back?"

Too late now to shout out a warning, but the impulse was there. *Morris, Morris, keep going—up the front steps. Shut the door behind you. Don't turn around. Don't go back. . . .*

Tuffy Pleasant shifted uncomfortably. "Yes, he walked back, and he had a bottle of beer in his hand, and the gate was open. And he walked back, and had just, you know, kind of closed the gate. And I said, 'My car stopped on me down the street,' you know. And he says, 'I can't hear you.' I says, '*My car stopped on me down the street.*' Just to wait until I got close enough. Then I got close enough and I unloaded on him."

Amazingly, impossibly, Vern heard his own voice speaking in a calm, professional manner. "Okay, so actually when you shot him, it was at most a matter of like you and I are sitting here across the table, just a matter of inches really?"

"Yes."

"And then he fell to the ground. Did you shoot him after he went down on the ground?"

"No." Tuffy said that he had just aimed at the big part of Morris's head.

He was lying. Vern knew that Morris had been shot once in the mouth to knock him down, and twice more behind the ear as he lay helpless on his stomach, dying. Vern didn't call Tuffy on the inaccuracies—not then.

toward Tuffy with as much trust as he would have walked toward Vern himself. Tuffy Pleasant would have been the last person in the world that Morris would have expected to point a gun at him.

But it didn't matter. Morris was just as dead as if he had been shot by a complete stranger.

19

Angelo Pleasant's arrest was headlined in the *Yakima Republic*. It was the end of the dreams Coydell and Andrew held so long for their children. All of their years of work. Andrew had asked Vern to find out the truth, the surface—just as Vern had feared—he

remembered, "but

"... When he was standing up. Okay, now then, you ran back down the alley and got in your car, and then where did you go?"

"I went back to Ellensburg."

"What did you do with the gun?"

"I kept it."

"What happened to the clip?"

"I don't know. I lost it somewhere."

"And then you returned the gun to your cousin's place some days later?"

"Yes."

"The reason you did this, Angelo, is you talked to Gabby for a long time and you had these plans to shoot Morris. Is that right? You used one of his plans? Or did you think of this by yourself?"

"It was his. It was all his idea."

Tuffy said he had received no money at all. None of it had been about money.

"You did it for him as a *favor* because you liked him?"

"Yeah."

"You were going to help him out? Ease some of going through about losing his wife?"

"Yeah."

Even knowing how close

promise of forty-five thousand dollars more if he should not show up for hearings. That was an awful lot of money to raise, and nobody close to Tuffy came up with it. He remained behind bars.

His arraignment was set for March 1.

Every article about Tuffy's arrest reprised his glory days as a champion wrestler, just as Jerilee was mentioned in each retelling as having been married to both murdered coaches. The scandal burned brightly in Yakima.

At Tuffy's arraignment, Yakima County Superior Court Judge Howard Hettinger revised the charges against him; he was now charged with two counts: first-degree murder in the shooting of Morris Blankenbaker and second-degree murder in T. Glynn "Gabby" Moore's death. The first-degree murder charge stemmed from the "premeditated" aspect of Morris's death, whereas Gabby Moore was deemed to have died while his killer was engaged in a felony, to wit: second-degree assault. Hettinger also revoked Tuffy's bail and appointed two attorneys to defend him: Wade Gano and Chris Tait.

Angelo Pleasant's trial date was set for April 19, less than two months away. Court watchers predicted that there would be delays.

There were those who murmured that the man who was ultimately to blame for the double murder was not the man locked up in the Yakima County Jail. But that man could no longer be made to answer for any misdeeds: Gabby Moore was dead, and the kid who had listened to his every thought and his every word so avidly now stared out through bars at a world that no longer held any promise at all for him.

Angelo "Tuffy" Pleasant soon had three attorneys. Adam Moore, arguably the best criminal defense attorney in Yakima County, was appointed by Judge Hettinger as chief defense counsel. He had more experience in murder trials than either Gano or Tait, and Tuffy was going to need as much legal help as he could get. Adam Moore and Jeff Sullivan had once again switched places. Now Sullivan was the prosecutor and Moore was the defense attorney.

As Jeff Sullivan explained, "Many of the players in our county's trials are the same over the years—only the scripts change." Sullivan viewed Adam Moore as a worthy adversary; he always would, no matter how many times they met on the legal playing field.

Loretta Scott had been granted immunity from prosecution on any charges stemming from her involvement with the suspect Colt .22, which was still undergoing ballistics tests.

It seemed that there would be no more surprises. Almost routinely, Tuffy's attorneys asked that he be examined by a psychiatrist to see if he was mentally competent to stand trial. Dr. Frederick Montgomery asked Tuffy the usual questions and gave him tests designed to point out any aberrance that would indicate that he did not know the difference between right and wrong at the time of the two shootings or currently.

After Montgomery's evaluation, there was no further mention of an insanity defense. It was possible that Tuffy had been partially brainwashed, but he was not insane under the law or clinically.

20

There was startling news about the Blankenbaker-Moore murders in the March 19 edition of the local papers. After listening to additional statements purportedly made by Tuffy Pleasant, Yakima detectives arrested his younger brother, Anthony Pleasant, nineteen. He too was booked into the Yakima County Jail, charged with first-degree murder in Morris Blankenbaker's death and held without bail.

Dick Nesary, the Yakima police's polygrapher, had run a number of lie detector tests on the men awaiting trial. Nesary, who had administered over eighteen hundred polygraphs, had reported that Tuffy Pleasant's first tests in January had been inconclusive. On March 18, Tuffy was put on the polygraph again and had implicated his own brother in Morris's murder. Adam Moore and Chris Tait thought another polygraph might verify that accusation; *this* test was done at the request of the defense team.

With Vern Henderson, Chris Tait, and Jeff Sullivan observing out of eye range, Nesary administered a Backster Zone Comparison Test to Tuffy—basically asking one question in two different ways, with control questions in between.

Nesary had never talked with Tuffy before the January 10 polygraphs, although he was aware of Tuffy's athletic fame. In January he had found Tuffy talkative and friendly. Now, two months later, he found himself talking to a different man.

"When I first started to run him on March 18," Nesary said, "he was a rather quiet, subdued type of person, and I had to pull things out of him to get him to talk in the pretest part."

Nesary listened as Tuffy told him who had shot Morris; it was a different story than he had told Vern Henderson. "He stated he was there and so was Anthony and Anthony was the one that had actually shot Morris Blankenbaker," Sergeant Nesary said.

Tuffy had worked hard in his life, and his hands were callused, not the best mediums for the Galvanic Skin Response test because they would not produce the classic "sweaty palms" reaction. Nesary also noted that Tuffy's breathing patterns were irregular. But he didn't think either condition would change the results of the polygraph significantly.

The results of the March 18 lie detector on Tuffy Pleasant surprised Nesary and caught the prosecution team off guard. Although Nesary was a Yakima police sergeant, he read the three charts he had taken on their own merit. Tuffy had told him that his brother Anthony shot Morris Blankenbaker, and Nesary said that his responses seemed to support that.

"In my opinion, he was truthful to the questions asked pertaining to the shooting situation. . . ."

Jeff Sullivan had had no choice but to order an arrest warrant for Anthony Pleasant, and on Thursday, March 18, Anthony was arrested. Later that day, Nesary got a call from Vern Henderson. "Come on down here," Vern said. "We want you to run Anthony."

Wanting to be absolutely certain that his reading was as accurate as it could be, Nesary ran six charts on Anthony Pleasant. Anthony too had "breathing problems," irregular respirations brought on perhaps by nervousness and the shock of having just been arrested.

In the end, Nesary's findings provided more shockers. "On the question, 'Did you shoot Morris Blankenbaker?' when the subject answered 'No,' it's my opinion that he was untruthful."

Vern Henderson, Bob Brimmer, and Jeff Sullivan were set back on their heels. All of their investigation thus far had indicated that Tuffy—and not Anthony—was the shooter in both murder cases. Now one of the city police department's *own* sworn officers was telling them that his read of the polygraph tests indicated the reverse.

Nesary himself was startled; he had made mistakes in his readings of lie detector results only rarely, and that was because he had worded control questions incorrectly or because he had been given the facts wrong. Usually, he said, mistakes tended to favor defendants rather than hurt them.

Undoubtedly, the defense would attempt to enter the reversely weighted polygraphs into Tuffy Pleasant's trial. Just as surely, Prosecutor Sullivan would fight to keep them out. It would be impossible, however, for the results of lie detector tests to be admitted into evidence and presented to a jury, *unless* both sides stipulated to their admission.

On March 30, Tuffy Pleasant reneged on his confessions and pleaded not guilty to both charges during his pretrial hearing. Vern Henderson was nonplussed. He had heard Tuffy's confessions; Vern *knew* that Tuffy knew things that only the killer could have known. But it was more than that. There had been a despair in Tuffy's words as he told of shooting two men he had cared about, emotion that Vern didn't think could be manufactured. If Tuffy was scared and having second thoughts, that was understandable, but Vern didn't believe they had arrested the wrong man.

Among the defense motions entered that day was a request for a change of venue. Tuffy's attorneys argued that there had already been so much publicity about the cases that it would be impossible for him to get a fair trial in Yakima County.

Adam Moore said that radio, television, and newspaper reports had been "highly inflammatory" and that there was no way an impartial jury of twelve people could be picked. Mike Brown, an investigator for the public defender's office, said that he had taken an unofficial survey of community attitude toward the case, although Brown's techniques might not have been considered sophisticated in a large city. He said he had checked the pulse of opinion in Yakima. He had been to "three barbershops and three beauty parlors" within the city limits. His survey of employees showed a unanimous response that they had all heard rumors about the double murders. Brown said he had also interviewed twenty-eight people in The Mall and fourteen people in Sunnyside—twenty miles southeast of Yakima. Of those forty-two, only nine said they had not heard of the cases. Of those who did know of it, however, just three had formed opinions as to Tuffy's guilt or innocence.

According to Brown, they all thought Tuffy was guilty.

"This case stands like a Goliath over previous county murder cases," defense attorney Adam Moore told reporters as he explained his request for a change of venue. "Drugs, romance, and jealousy are the fabric upon which this motion is woven."

Prosecutor Jeff Sullivan demurred, citing other cases just as sensational which had been tried within Yakima County.

Judge Carl Loy ruled that he felt that Angelo Pleasant could get a fair trial in Yakima and that he would not move the trial to Seattle, Spokane, or some other city in Washington. "The publicity has been factual rather than evidential," Loy commented succinctly. He said he had seen no signs of prejudicial reporting and that media versions of the cases' progression had, in his opinion, "met bench-bar-press guidelines." Although Loy agreed that there had been a great deal of publicity in the Blankenbaker-Moore case, he attributed that to who the victims *were* and to the bizarre circumstances of the killings.

It was clearly not the kind of case that local reporters were going to bury on the back pages. However, given the gossip circulating through the Yakima Valley, the newspapers had been remarkably circumspect.

Still, reading the papers, Vern Henderson shook his head. Romance and jealousy . . . and now drugs. The whole case, as it appeared in the headlines, was beginning to sound like a regular soap opera.

The rumor mill ground on, fueled with no other ammunition than speculation, imagination, and half truths.

On April 8, there were more headlines and yet another suspect under arrest. Kenny Marino, Tuffy Pleasant's best friend and also a member of the 1972 championship wrestling team, was arraigned on charges of second-degree murder in Gabby Moore's death. While both Pleasant brothers were being held without bond, Marino's bail was set at fifty thousand dollars.

Prosecutor Sullivan would give no details but said only that the investigation was continuing. If things went on as they had, it seemed as if the murder case were going to tarnish every wrestler close to Gabby Moore.

Now two of Coydell and Andrew Pleasant's sons were charged with murder. Anthony was to go on trial May 3, two weeks after Angelo's trial was to begin. None of it made much sense to the public who could only speculate on their alleged motives for murder.

With the burgeoning list of murder defendants and arguments over when and where the trials would take place, little official attention was paid to an event that took place in that strange spring of 1976.

On April 18, Jerilee Blankenbaker Moore Blankenbaker quietly married for the third time. Where Gabby had been fourteen years older than she, and Morris three years older, Jerilee's new husband was seven years younger. He was Jim Littleton*, twenty-two. Littleton worked in the grocery business. A handsome young man, his lifestyle and interests bore little similarity to either Morris or Gabby, except that, like them, he was very protective of Jerilee. His ambition was to be a successful businessman. He had no interest in playing sports or coaching.

Olive was shocked to learn of Jerilee's marriage. So was Vern Henderson. He remembered that Littleton had been one of the pallbearers at Morris's funeral services, although Henderson had no idea who Jim Littleton was or what his connection to Morris and Jerilee had been.

It was not that Morris's family and friends didn't want Jerilee to go on with her life; it was just that it seemed too soon. Morris had only been dead five months and Gabby four when the woman who had been married to both of them appeared to have stepped completely out of the mess she had made of her life over the past few years. Of course, she would still have to testify in the trial—or *trials*—coming up.

People wondered if hers wasn't a rebound marriage. And maybe it was in the beginning. Jerilee had been searching for a secure family unit ever since her parents divorced when she was in high school. Now, even before the first daffodils bloomed on Morris's and Gabby's graves, Jerilee had a new husband and a new family. There were a few snide comments in Yakima about "the merry widow," and "I wonder how long *this* one is going to last?" but Jerilee and Jim kept such a low profile that the gossip and jokes soon died.

It wasn't just Jerilee who had been through hell. The double murders had left a number of women emotionally adrift. Olive Blankenbaker had withstood blows before and come back, and she now proved that she could do it again. She was back at work, back in the midst of life. She would not allow either her illness or the loss of her son to destroy her. She didn't care what the doctors had told her—she was going to survive.

Tuffy Pleasant's girlfriend, René, was six months pregnant and already raising a toddler. Although Tuffy had not been the most constant of lovers, she had always figured they would be together for good one day. Now René didn't know what was going to happen, but she feared she might be left all alone after Tuffy's trial.

And Coydell Pleasant was trying to adjust to the horror of having two sons in jail awaiting trials on murder charges.

The March polygraph test results and the subsequent arrests of Anthony Pleasant and Kenny Marino meant that Vern Henderson had to find more witnesses, enough so that they could *absolutely* account for both Tuffy's and his brother Anthony's movements on the nights of the murders. Tuffy had given them a reprise of his movements on November 21, but they needed someone who had seen him on his peregrinations that Friday night. And, with accusing fingers also pointing at Kenny Marino, there was yet a third suspect to backtrack on. The investigators devoutly hoped that there would be no more suspects in this increasingly convoluted investigation, but it was within the realm of possibility that Anthony Pleasant and Kenny Marino *had* been present just before—or even *during*—the murders of Morris Blankenbaker and Gabby Moore. However, the Yakima County investigators doubted it.

Prosecuting Attorney Jeff Sullivan and Yakima Police Detective Vern Henderson were about to become partners in a sense—if improbable ones.

Both Tuffy Pleasant and Joey Watkins had mentioned the name of one of the three people whose party Tuffy had joined at the Red Lion on the night of November 21. There had been two women and a man that Friday, and Tuffy said he had "caught a lady" that night.

Armed with the name of the man in the party, Sam Berber,* and the information that the trio had come from Pasco, Washington, Vern Henderson and Jeff Sullivan headed for the Tri-cities area, which had burst from the desert with the advent of the Hanford atomic power project during the Second World War. (Pasco, Kennewick, and Richland are rarely referred to separately by Washingtonians.)

Henderson's and Sullivan's investigation led them into a mostly black neighborhood in the Tri-cities, where the black detective and the blond Irish prosecuting attorney drew a lot of attention. "They used to take one look at us and say, 'Here comes Shaft and young Mr. Kennedy.'" Vern Henderson laughs. "They'd never seen a black detective before and Jeff *did* look just like John Kennedy. We made quite a pair."

They found Sam Berber, twenty-eight, in Pasco. He worked for Standard Oil and said he rarely had occasion to travel to Yakima, which was eighty miles away. However, on November 21, he had volunteered to drive a friend, Sally Nash,* to Yakima to see her brother who was in the Yakima County Jail. Sam, Sally, and her girlfriend, Melodie Isaacs,* arrived in Yakima about 8:15 that night, only to find they were too late for visiting hours at the jail. They left some money for Sally's brother at the booking desk and then ventured out on the town.

When Sullivan and Henderson asked Berber about Tuffy Pleasant, Sam said he did know the man, but not well; they had met way back in November. In fact, Sam could name the date easily. It was November 21, 1975.

Berber explained that he and his two female passengers had been left with time on their hands after they missed visiting hours in the jail. They had looked for someplace in Yakima to have a few drinks and maybe dance. They went first to the Cosmopolitan Chinook Hotel and the Red Lion cocktail lounge there.

Berber said he and the ladies with him were interested in finding clubs that catered to blacks where they might find some music other than the standard hotel lounge canned music. They had noticed a young black man sitting at a table with another man.

"I approached him and asked him if there were some places we might be able to go . . . and he offered to show us around," Berber recalled. "He had asked if the lady with us was with someone, and I told him she wasn't and then he asked if he could come over and sit at the table with us."

Berber had then invited the man, who introduced himself as Angelo Pleasant, to join their party. The man who had been sitting with Pleasant left. They had sat there in the Red Lion until Pleasant told them to follow him; he would lead them to a place that might be livelier. It wasn't. "We just stayed long enough to have a drink and leave," Berber said, "because it was just as dead as the place we had just left." Henderson nodded. That would have been the Holiday Inn, according to what Tuffy had said in his confession.

Their new friend had then suggested that they go to the Thunderbird. They had stayed there until almost closing time, and Pleasant had asked if they were anxious to leave for Pasco, or if they would be interested in some after-hours parties.

"He took us past a couple of places," Berber said, "and there was nothing going on, so we just took him back to his car."

"Where was his car parked?" Brimmer asked.

"At the Chinook."

"And about what time did you get back to the Chinook?"

"I imagine it had to be just right around two A.M. because people were leaving . . . from the bar. That was about it. We invited him to

Pasco and told him if he ever came around to give us a call or try to get in touch with us and we would try to return the evening."

Sam Berber wasn't sure if he could positively identify the man. But he had introduced himself as Angelo Pleasant and told them that he used to live in Pasco while he was attending Columbia Basin College.

Berber hadn't looked at the clocks in the bars they visited. He based his recall of when they dropped Pleasant off on his date's comment. "My young lady was in the front seat and she had fallen asleep and she had to get up and lean forward to let him out. We were right under a light, and she looked at her watch and said, 'It's two o'clock—we better head on back home.'"

Melodie Isaacs, who had been Tuffy Pleasant's date for the evening, remembered meeting him, a good-looking man in a black leather jacket. They had had three or four drinks and some dances between nine P.M. and a little before two and then they had let him out of the car at two A.M. She had given him her phone number in case he ever came to Pasco, but he hadn't called her.

Sullivan and Henderson knew that the Chinook was only a few blocks, a few *minutes*, from Morris Blankenbaker's house. Neither of them said what they were surely thinking. If the quartet *had* found an after-hours place open that night, would Tuffy have decided not to carry out Gabby's instructions? If it hadn't been that night, would it have been another night? Or would both Morris and Gabby still be alive?

While the Pasco witnesses had placed Tuffy only a few blocks from Morris's house a few minutes before Morris was killed, the investigators had to find witnesses who could either involve, or eliminate, Anthony from the shooting. One witness they found was ideal; the others they located were less desirable but made up in sheer number for their inherent lack of credibility. Eventually, they would find a plethora of witnesses who placed Tuffy's younger brother, Anthony, far away from the shooting scene and, moreover, in no condition to walk, much less commit murder.

Vern Henderson thumbed through the November 21–22 FIRs (Field Investigation Reports filled out by patrolmen for every incident on every shift). He was elated to find an officer who had had occasion to contact Anthony Pleasant that night. Patrol Officer Allen D. Bischoff of the Yakima Police Department was working C-Squad that Friday night from eight P.M. to four A.M. He told Brimmer that he had responded to an incident on La Salle Street—a "possible disturbance" shortly after ten P.M.

Bischoff and his partner found several young black men, a young white woman, and an older white female. The men were arguing. Bischoff said they had been a little wary about going to the call; there had been some threats against the lives of police officers, particularly in this area. Since it came in with an "anonymous" citizen reporting, they had wondered if it might be a setup, and Bischoff was actually rather relieved to find that he knew one of the young men. It was Anthony Pleasant, whom he did not consider a threat. Bischoff talked to Anthony, shined his flashlight in his face to check his eyes for signs of drinking (police officers know that there is an involuntary shifting of the pupils in the eyes of someone under the influence), and concluded that Anthony had, indeed, been drinking. The fight seemed to be over after Bischoff talked to Anthony and his partner talked to the other combatant.

"I told him to leave . . . and go directly home," Bischoff told Brimmer.

Anthony had gotten into a Chevrolet sedan and left the scene. As Bischoff went on the air to clear the complaint, it was approximately ten minutes to eleven. He assumed that Anthony had gone home as he directed, but he could not be certain of it.

However, Anthony did not go home, as Henderson found when he located a number of teenagers who told him about almost-weekly "floating" parties where the guest list was whoever showed up. The refreshments were beer and marijuana. Henderson might have wished to have witnesses whose memories were a bit more crystal-line than those he found, but eventually, he did discover some party-goers who remembered the night of November 21 very well.

More importantly, they remembered exactly where Anthony Pleas-ant had been that night between the fight in the street and dawn. Most particularly, they remembered where he had been around two A.M.—the time when his big brother claimed Anthony had been shooting Morris Blankenbaker.

Although the party on the night of the murder had been full of drop-ins and drop-*outs*, there were a few people who remained in the home of the young woman who was the hostess that night. Everyone agreed that one couple had disappeared into a bedroom and stayed there. There was a girl who had had an argument with Anthony Pleasant, and there were several other people who had laughed to see Anthony passed out cold on a couch.

One of the best sources Henderson found was an eighteen-year-old girl named Casey Lynn Anderson.* She was a recent graduate of Davis High School and was working as a cook and waitress at the

Cosmopolitan Chinook Hotel. Casey and her sister, who also worked at the Chinook, went to the party-of-the-week on November 21. Casey said she had "babied a beer" all night, and she had had no marijuana at all.

She was upset with Anthony Pleasant because he had been in a fight with a friend of hers over a girl. (This was the "incident" that Bischoff had just investigated.) Anthony had returned to the party, and Casey said she had given him a good lecture about fighting. "I was trying to tell him that he was stupid," she recalled. "And then he told me I didn't know what I was talking about—that he had his reasons and he was man enough to take care of himself."

Casey said she found Anthony's arguments almost unintelligible because he was very, very drunk. "He was standing up—he was *trying* to stand up against the wall—and I remember telling him, 'Sit down before you fall down,' and he told me to shut up."

As far as Casey was concerned, her longtime friend Anthony was in no condition to remember anything about their argument that night. "He looked like he was ready to just say 'good night' to the world."

A number of people at the party confirmed that Anthony had fallen asleep on a large couch in the living room. A girl had vomited on the couch sometime earlier, but Anthony had been so out of it that he hadn't noticed. People watching had thought this was hilarious.

"What time?" Henderson asked again and again of those who had been at the Friday night party. "What time did you see Anthony Pleasant passed out on the couch?"

The consensus was that it was well before two A.M. Since two A.M. was the magic hour to buy beer and they were running low, a group left to buy more. When they left, Anthony had already been almost comatose and the subject of many giggles and guffaws.

One girl said that she had been there both when the beer-buyers left, and when they came back—without finding any stores open. She had stayed awake until three-thirty or four. When she and her friend finally did get tired enough to sleep, they had a problem.

"Okay," she explained, "we were laughing at him [Anthony] because he was on the couch and he was passed out. Me and a girlfriend were getting tired and we wanted to go to sleep, but he was on the double couch . . . and so we rolled him off the couch and he just fell right on the floor, and he was just *blah*. And we sat up for a while longer and kind of laughed at him, and then he crawled over to the chair and sat in that and fell asleep."

Under ordinary circumstances, Anthony Pleasant, nineteen, might have been chagrined that he had made such a fool of himself by getting passed-out drunk, and becoming "the main part of the night, because we were all laughing at him." However, the number of witnesses who recalled absolutely that he had not left the party between eleven and dawn would eventually save him from murder charges.

Vern Henderson reported to Jeff Sullivan that he now knew where Anthony had been at two A.M. on November 21, and where Tuffy had been.

They knew where Tuffy had been on Christmas Eve, but they still had to check on where Kenny Marino had been. Once more, it was the memory of teenaged girls that provided alibis. Kenny Marino had invited three girls to come to his parents' home that night for Tequila Sunrises, a curious Christmas libation. One of the girls told the detectives that she had to plead with her mother to go out, and only got permission when she promised to be home by midnight.

At midnight, while the others were raptly watching a horror film on television, the witness realized she wasn't going to make her deadline. In fact, it was 12:30 before she could convince Kenny Marino to drive her home. It was close to one when she got home, and her mother was waiting up for her. Kenny Marino and the other two girls returned to his house.

Over on Eighteenth Street, miles away, someone had just shot Gabby Moore. Figuring the times and the distances and the witnesses, there was no way Kenny Marino could have been the shooter.

Although Tuffy Pleasant would go into his trial still claiming to have been only an observer at the murders of Morris Blankenbaker and Gabby Moore, Jeff Sullivan had his witnesses in place, ready to show that Anthony Pleasant and Kenny Marino could not have been the killers.

Tuffy agreed to waive his right to a speedy trial (within sixty days of his arrest) and was given a new trial date in early June. Anthony Pleasant and Kenny Marino had their trials joined at the request of Marino's attorney. *Their* new trial date was now May 24.

With less than two weeks to go before their trial, Judge Howard Hettinger ordered that the Anthony Pleasant/Kenny Marino pretrial hearing be held in secret. No one in Yakima knew *what* was going on. Hettinger said that he would release a statement on the closed-door hearing as soon as a jury was sequestered. After defense attorneys argued that any reporting of the pretrial motions would "seriously jeopardize" their clients' right to a fair trial by an impartial jury,

Hettinger issued an order excluding the press and public from the pretrial hearings.

Tuffy Pleasant's hearing, presided over by Judge Loy, had been open to the press although they agreed not to report on it—beyond change-of-venue arguments—until a jury was sequestered.

Interest in the trials was at fever pitch among Yakimans. Court Administrator Charlotte Phillips said that the trials themselves *would* be open to the public and that the press could expect special seating arrangements in the largest courtroom in the courthouse. The trials would run continuously, including weekends, partly because jurors would be sequestered.

Newspapers announced that security would be tight in the courtrooms. No one knew exactly why. No one beyond the principals involved and the police, attorneys, and prosecuting team knew the whole story, but everyone in town was curious.

And then, four days before Anthony Pleasant and Kenny Marino were to go on trial, Prosecutor Jeff Sullivan moved for dismissal of the charges against them. The defendants' jaws dropped; they hadn't been expecting this. Sullivan would have preferred to postpone their trial, rather than have it dropped, but, in the interests of justice, he said he did not have sufficient evidence to bring them to trial. (Sullivan said later that the dismissal of charges against Tuffy Pleasant's younger brother and his best friend not did not affect the case against Tuffy at all.)

Jeff Sullivan was between a rock and a hard place. He was not entirely convinced that Marino and Anthony didn't have some guilty knowledge, before or after the shootings, but he could not produce evidence linking them to the crimes. They each had witnesses who could prove that they were nowhere near the murder scenes at the time the shootings occurred. Although he did not want to reveal that information in this venue, Sullivan had asked for "dismissal without prejudice," meaning that he could refile the charges should the investigation come up with new evidence. Defense attorneys did not object.

Thirty minutes later, smiling broadly, Anthony Pleasant and Kenny Marino walked out into the sunlight. Anthony had been in jail for sixty-two days, and Kenny Marino for forty.

"What's it like to be in jail?" a reporter called out.

"God, I can't say," Marino said. "You'd have to go through it. I had nightmares and nightmares . . . every night."

For them, at least, it was over. For Tuffy Pleasant, a trial lay just ahead.

21

Despite everything, there was still a grudging respect between Tuffy Pleasant and Vern Henderson. Vern didn't exactly feel sorry for Tuffy. How could he when Vern knew that Tuffy had shot his best friend and, for that matter, *Tuffy's* best friend. But Vern sensed the waste, the tragedy, the loss for so many people, all because Gabby Moore had been ready to sacrifice anything and any*one* so that he could regain what *he* had lost: *Jerilee.*

When Tuffy's girlfriend, René, gave birth to her second daughter—to Tuffy's second daughter too—it was Vern who took Tuffy from the Yakima jail up to the hospital so that he could hold his new baby. It was a bittersweet moment. Although Tuffy's murder trial had been continued for a second time, until July 19, it loomed ahead like a dark tunnel. If he should be convicted, Tuffy might not be around to see either of his children grow up.

When Tuffy Pleasant had waived his right to a speedy trial, he had allowed Jeff Sullivan the time he needed to bring the fragments of this peculiar case into some kind of order. Sullivan remarked that each "fact uncovered led to another." He wanted to be very sure that the person (or persons) who had shot Morris and Gabby was the one on trial. There were more witnesses to locate. It was becoming clear, however, that the state could never try the person who had instigated the shootings even though statute made that person just as guilty as the one whose finger pulled the trigger.

That person—Gabby Moore—was dead.

The public didn't know that, of course. Every facet of the case had been shrouded in secrecy. Adam Moore, Tuffy's attorney, had agreed to the continuance, saying inscrutably, "When the truth is finally known, a lot of questions will be answered."

Loretta Scott was a vital witness for the prosecution. Sullivan needed her testimony to show the transfers of the murder weapon

908

from herself to Tuffy and back again. She would be granted immunity from prosecution on the weapons charges. It was possible that Kenny Marino and Anthony Pleasant, once suspects themselves, would end up being state witnesses too.

In late June, without fanfare, Prosecuting Attorney Jeff Sullivan and Defense Attorney Adam Moore flew to Germany. "We left Sunday morning," Sullivan recalled, "and although we went to Worms, Frankfort, and Heidelberg, we were back on Wednesday."

Although they were on opposite sides in this case, both attorneys had questions about the Colt .22 *and* about unconfirmed rumors that they needed answers for. Working on minimal sleep, Moore and Sullivan took depositions from David Pleasant, Loretta Scott's brother, who was serving in the army in Germany, and from Anthony Pleasant's girlfriend at the time of Morris Blankenbaker's murder. Her stepfather was also in the army in Germany. One of the most rampant rumors around Yakima was that she had been told the "real" truth about the double murder, and David was supposed to know where the gun had come from. As it turned out, Anthony's girlfriend knew nothing about the killings.

In his deposition given in Frankfort, Germany, on June 22, David Pleasant verified that he had once owned the .22, and that he had given it to his sister, Loretta, when he went into the army. He had gotten it from a friend who had gotten it from a friend. The gun had come from Vietnam, and it was virtually untraceable.

Had Loretta not panicked, the gun could never have been connected to her—and through her—to Tuffy Pleasant.

Jeff Sullivan had now found out everything he ever would about the death weapon, and about Anthony Pleasant's movements on November 21, 1975.

It was time to move ahead.

On July 8, Tuffy Pleasant's pretrial hearing was held in Yakima, and the possibility that Anthony and Kenny Marino would move to the state's side of the chess game that is the law became reality. It was not a good day for the defense camp. Shortly before the hearing began, Tuffy's attorneys learned that Jeff Sullivan was amending the charges against their client; instead of first-degree murder in Morris Blankenbaker's death, and second-degree murder in Gabby Moore's, the charge in Moore's death was also *first*-degree murder.

Appalled by what they termed "eleventh hour" tactics, Adam Moore and Chris Tait asked for more time. And they had other motions. They renewed their request for a change of venue, and for two *separate* trials. They told Judge Loy that Pleasant could not get a fair trial if the two murder charges were heard by the same jury. They argued that the alibi witnesses the state intended to call to corroborate the whereabouts of Anthony Pleasant and Kenny Marino at the moments of murder would "sandbag" a jury.

The philosophical question naturally arose: If a man is guilty of two murders, should a jury not hear the connection between those murders? And, then again, if a man is innocent of two murders, or of one of the murders, should the same jury hear about both crimes? Defense attorneys always choose to separate charges; prosecutors always prefer to let a jury see all the possible ramifications—the similar transactions—of conjoined crimes.

As it was, this trial promised to be one of the most expensive ever to hit the taxpayers of Yakima County. It would take an estimated three weeks, and jurors would be sequestered. That meant, of course, hotel costs and meals for the jurors on top of all of Tuffy's lawyers' fees and money for the defense's private investigator. It was true, as Adam Moore argued, that "There is no place on the scales of justice for dollar signs on one side and fairness on the other," but moving the trial to another city would be even more expensive than the projected fifty thousand dollars to hold it in Yakima. (Today fifty thousand dollars wouldn't pay for half a day of a headline big-city trial such as O.J. Simpson's or the Menendez brothers, but fifty thousand dollars would cut a huge chunk out of the Yakima County budget. As it was, legal fees for Anthony Pleasant and Kenny Marino had cost thirteen thousand dollars.)

In the end, Judge Carl Loy's rulings were split. He would grant the change of venue; he would not separate the two murder charges into two trials. The two murders had so many similar transaction aspects that Loy could not justify severing them.

Tuffy Pleasant smiled when he heard that there would be a change of venue, but Yakimans who had planned to attend every day of the sensational trial were disappointed. If they wanted to watch all the action, they would have to travel 140 miles west across the Cascade Mountains to Seattle. Some of them would; King County promised to provide an adequate courtroom.

Besides the family, friends, press, and gallery, there would be more than fifty witnesses traveling from eastern Washington for the trial in Seattle.

In the end, the question of sequestration of the jury would be moot. The murders in Yakima might well have happened 14,000 miles away rather than 140; Morris Blankenbaker, Gabby Moore, and Tuffy

Pleasant were celebrities in their hometown, but very few residents of King County had heard of them or of the murders. Seattle and the county it sat in had its own homicides to think about. It was almost shocking to realize that out of the fifty-member jury pool of King County residents brought in for the Pleasant jury, only *one* had ever heard of the case, and that was because she had friends in Yakima. Bitter tragedy and shocking double murder in eastern Washington had not filtered through at all. Perhaps murder is an insular phenomenon, its impact diminished by distance and geography almost as if the looming Cascades that separated Yakima from Seattle had absorbed the shock and pain.

But the pain would come brilliantly alive again on August 16 and continue through the weeks of trial in Seattle. The case would be featured not only in the *Yakima Herald-Republic* but in the *Seattle Times* and the Seattle *Post-Intelligencer*. James Wallace, a *Herald-Republic* reporter, would file daily stories from the courthouse so that hometown people who could not make the trip could monitor the trial.

Olive Blankenbaker and her sister would attend every session of the trial. A long time later, when she remembered those weeks, she would sigh, "It was so hard—so hard."

Ned Blankenbaker, Morris's father, his face reddened with emotion and unshed tears, would sit nearby. Andrew Pleasant, Sr., Tuffy's father, and Tuffy's grandmother would be there, all of them at once linked and divided by the enormity of the crimes Tuffy stood accused of. Many family members were barred from the courtroom because they would be called as witnesses.

Tuffy Pleasant would be housed in the King County Jail, a two-story elevator ride to King County Superior Courtroom West 1019. He would be accompanied to court each day by Yakima police officers Dennis Meyers and Marion Baugher.

Seattle's media, caught up in the drama of this case, were prepared to be on hand. John Sandifer, anchorman for the nightly news of the ABC affiliate in Seattle, KOMO, marked off two weeks on his calendar, and photographers from the *Seattle Times* and the Seattle *Post-Intelligencer* did too.

Defendants and witnesses alike would walk the gauntlet from the elevators, through the marble-walled corridors, to the King County courtrooms.

Jeff Sullivan, Mike McGuigan, his deputy prosecutor in this trial, Vern Henderson, Court Reporter Lonna Vachon, and the rest of the entourage from Yakima County had trouble simply finding a place to stay in Seattle; there was a huge convention in town that August.

Eventually, they found enough rooms at the old Roosevelt Hotel, which was more than a mile north of the courthouse and had yet to be refurbished.

The sheer logistics of getting witnesses to Seattle to testify was a challenge. Jeff Sullivan was grateful for the transportation provided by the Yakima Police Department. "We had a number of teenage witnesses," he recalled. "We tried to bring them over in the morning and get them back home in the evening, so we didn't have to worry about their staying over in Seattle without adult supervision."

22

And so it began. This long-awaited trial that might reveal the seemingly inexplicable reasoning behind the deaths of two most unlikely murder victims.

Tuffy Pleasant invariably grinned at the cameras, as insouciant as a rock star passing through a crowd of fans. Female photographers got an extra-large smile. He spoke with the Yakima officers who escorted him as if they were old friends and they talked just as easily with him.

Were it not for his hands cuffed behind him, it would have been difficult to pick Tuffy out as the defendant. He looked like the young athlete he had been until his arrest for double murder. His shoulders were broad and thickly muscled, his waist trim, his ears were the "cauliflower ears" of a longtime wrestler. Despite his situation, he seemed optimistic and smiled easily for photographers.

Would he testify? Murder defendants usually don't, but Tuffy Pleasant had such an outgoing manner about him. He might make a good witness for himself, and then again, if he took the stand, he would risk opening himself up to Jeff Sullivan's fierce cross-examination. Time would tell.

Would Jerilee testify? And what about Anthony Pleasant and Kenny Marino? They were rumored to be potential witnesses for the state.

The players took their positions in the courtroom. Judge Carl Loy sat on an unfamiliar bench in Department 27 of King County. The six who would be present for the whole trial were seated at a long oak table. J. Adam Moore and Christopher Tait sat on either side of their client, Angelo Denny "Tuffy" Pleasant. Yakima County Prosecuting Attorney Jeffrey C. Sullivan sat at the far end of the table next to Vern Henderson who would be the "friend of the court," the detective responsible for bringing in evidence and being available for consultation on the investigative facts. Deputy Prosecutor Mike McGuigan sat to Henderson's right.

First, a jury had to be selected. Monday, August 16, passed and only eight jurors were chosen. It would be Tuesday at noon before a full jury was seated. Eight women and four men, and three alternates—two men and a woman. Potential jurors who had demurred had done so because they didn't want to be tied up for two weeks or possibly three, not because they had formed opinions on the case.

Adam Moore asked interesting questions of potential jurors. "If 'A' wants someone removed and he goes to 'B' and asks him to do the job, what kind of judgment would you make about 'A' and 'B?'"

Moore asked one juror a question that spurred Sullivan to ask for a sidebar conference: "Have you ever known a man who became extremely jealous over a woman?"

After the sidebar with Judge Carl Loy, there were no more questions in that vein from the defense.

Moore also asked a potential juror, "Have you ever known anybody, who, out of loyalty, took the blame for something he did not do?"

Jeff Sullivan shifted uneasily at that line of questioning, but he did not object.

At 1:30 P.M. on August 17, Jeff Sullivan rose to begin his opening statements.

If ever opening statements were diametrically opposed regarding the facts of a case, those of Prosecutor Jeff Sullivan and defense lawyers Adam Moore and Chris Tait were. Sullivan's voice was disdainful as he paced in long strides in front of the jury box. He promised the jurors that the state would offer them proof that Angelo Pleasant was guilty of two murders, and that they would actually *hear* him confess to those murders on tape.

Sullivan told them that the defendant had killed Morris Blankenbaker "in cold blood" at the urging of his mentor and former coach. Then, Sullivan said, Pleasant had killed Moore himself because Moore "had a claw in him."

There was no one else involved, Sullivan said bitingly. Only Tuffy Pleasant. Jeff Sullivan was succinct as he gave the jurors two terrible scenarios of murder—the first of the night Morris was killed and the second of the Christmas Eve shooting of Gabby Moore. The prosecutor spoke for thirty-five minutes, as a hushed courtroom listened avidly.

It was the first time Olive Blankenbaker had really heard her son's death described. It was difficult to listen, but she could not *not* listen; this was what she had come to Seattle to do, to hear all the evidence and, hopefully, to see justice done.

Sullivan explained how Gabby Moore had told Tuffy Pleasant on November 21, "If you're going to do it, tonight's the night."

The prosecutor described Morris's arrival home after work, the familiar voice calling to him from the alley, and then the shot that hit him in the mouth, knocking out several teeth, before it lodged in his spine. The second bullet had struck him behind the left ear, and the third in the back of the head.

Sullivan said that on Christmas Eve, Gabby Moore had coerced Tuffy into retrieving that same gun by threatening to turn him in to the Yakima Police, his finger poised over the final digit of the police number. Tuffy had gone back to his cousin's, Sullivan said, retrieved the .22, and returned to Moore's apartment later. According to Sullivan, he had found his brother and Stoney Morton there, although they didn't stay long. A short time later, Tuffy had shot Gabby Moore from a distance of nine inches.

There should be no going back, the prosecutor stressed. Tuffy Pleasant had confessed *twice*. Within days of Tuffy's arrest, he had described both murders—and on tape.

More long-winded and perhaps a bit more histrionic, Adam Moore and Chris Tait painted Tuffy Pleasant as an innocent man, almost a saint, a family man who had confessed to two murders only to protect his younger brother and his best friend. For an hour and a half, the defense team gave *their* version of the murders. Yes, they readily acknowledged, Tuffy *had* known about Gabby's plan to kill Morris, but he had absolutely refused to have any part in it.

Chris Tait agreed with Jeff Sullivan's chronology of events on November 21, but only up to a point. Tait said that when Tuffy left the Red Lion, he was with his brother Anthony. The Colt Woodsman

.22 was under the front seat of Tuffy's car. In this scenario, the two brothers drove around for a while and then Anthony had said he wanted to go visit Morris. Tuffy had obliged him and parked on Lincoln Avenue, a half block away from Morris's house.

Yes, Tuffy had seen his younger brother take something from beneath the seat, but he thought it was only a beer. That's what Anthony had been drinking during the evening. When they saw Morris's car pulling up, both brothers had gotten out of their car.

Here, the script for murder changed radically as it played out in the defense case. When they were a few feet apart, it had been *Anthony* who told Morris he wanted to talk to him about Jerilee. According to Chris Tait, Morris had said he didn't care to discuss her and had walked menacingly toward Anthony.

It was at that point, Tait said, that Anthony Pleasant had pulled out the gun and shot Morris. Running away, the Pleasant brothers had driven off, promising never to tell anyone. They were "very close," Tait said.

Later, when Tuffy was arrested, he was "willing to take the rap." It was not until detectives bore down on him, saying they did not believe that he had acted alone that Tuffy had changed his story and admitted to them that Anthony had killed Morris. His first confession had not been the truth, only the words of a brother trying to save a younger brother.

Adam Moore rose to continue the defense's opening remarks. He explained how Gabby Moore had been killed. Moore listed four themes that sparked murder: jealousy, manipulation, loyalty . . . and irony. Gabby Moore had been living in a "fantasy world, consumed with the intent to get Jerilee back. It was more than he could hold up to . . . the loss of her . . ."

But, Moore said, Gabby's fantasy had "backfired." Jerilee had added up the facts and she suspected her ex-husband had had a hand in the murder of Morris, her once and future husband. Adam Moore gave Gabby grudging credit for being "clever in a bizarre way" when he planned his own shooting—to take the suspicion off himself. Yes, on Christmas Eve he *had* demanded that Tuffy go and get the same gun that had killed Morris and shoot him. But Tuffy had refused adamantly. Yes, Tuffy had stayed on talking with Gabby after Anthony and Stoney had left Gabby's apartment. Gabby had received a phone call and that call, said Adam Moore, was from Kenny Marino. Gabby had not wanted to discuss it with Tuffy, but Tuffy had said he was upset by the call.

Later in the evening, this rendition of the "facts" went on, Kenny
Marino had come over to Gabby's. By this time, Adam Moore said
that Tuffy had returned with the gun he had borrowed for the second
time and he had given it to Gabby. When Kenny Marino came over,
Tuffy had urged Gabby to take a walk in the backyard with him to
clear his head and to help him forget his wild plan about wanting
Tuffy to shoot him.

Apparently unconvinced, Gabby had walked into the house, while
Tuffy stayed outside, turning the situation over and over in his mind,
trying to find some solution to Gabby's problems—and his own.

And then, according to Adam Moore, Tuffy had frozen in horror as
a shot sounded inside. When he ran in, he had seen his best friend
standing over their coach with the pistol in his hand. Gabby was
lying on the kitchen floor with blood covering his T-shirt.

"Merry Christmas, everyone," Adam Moore said sarcastically,
with a wave of his hand.

But Moore wasn't quite through. According to the defense attorney, Tuffy had promised Kenny Marino that he would take the rap for
him too. Tuffy had said since he had no previous record, the court
would go easy on him.

The jurors sat expressionless—as all jurors, everywhere, always
do. What could they be thinking? The two versions of the murders
were so disparate. Was it possible that the young man at the defense
table was so good-hearted and generous of spirit that he would risk
giving up years of his own life to keep his younger brother and best
friend out of prison?

Or was it possible that he really had shot an old friend in cold
blood and then turned on the coach he had once loved in a panic that
he might be discovered?

The jurors had weeks of testimony to listen to. Maybe the truth
would filter out like clear water from a silty stream.

Adam Moore had either misspoken in the last part of his dramatic
opening remarks, or he was not aware of the details of the crime
scene that Sergeant Bob Brimmer and Detective Howard Cyr had
noted. Kenny Marino could not have been standing over a body
dressed in a bloody T-shirt. There had been no blood on Gabby's T-
shirt—not a speck of it—not until Brimmer and Cyr had lifted his
body to turn it over.

Then it had gushed out, quarts of it.

But, by then, the killer—or killers—were long gone.

* * *

The prosecution began its case. Whenever possible, a good prosecution case begins with witnesses whose words can reconstruct the ambiance of the crime scene, using exhibits and evidence that will draw the jurors back in time to the moment of murder. It was the middle of an unusually hot summer in Seattle. To step from the marble halls of the King County Courthouse into the late afternoon heat was akin to walking into a sauna.

What Jeff Sullivan had to do was summon up the icy dawn the November before in Yakima, and then the snowy Christmas Eve that followed. He had to make the jurors shiver involuntarily, even as they perspired in fact. He needed to let them feel the shock Morris's apartment house neighbors had felt when they heard Jerilee scream. They had to "hear" the screams themselves.

Gerda Lenberg, Dale Soost, and Rowland Seal were only the first of dozens of witnesses who would make their way across the mountains to Seattle so that they could fill in their personal "segments" in a giant mosaic of murder.

Since the jurors were from the Seattle area and not familiar with the streets of Yakima, Jeff Sullivan provided an easel with a large sheet of white paper so that addresses, streets, and directions could be drawn in by witnesses. Gerda Lenberg picked up a crayon and made the first marks on the pristine white.

"Five-oh-six East Lincoln," she said, drawing in the location of her duplex. "That's Lincoln Avenue there and the alley runs north and south down here like this. (She drew a line south from her home to the other end of the alley, marking Lincoln Avenue where it ran east and west.) This would be 'B' Street here."

"Okay," the prosecutor nodded. "Would you draw the duplex in?"

"Right there on the corner . . . right on the alley." (She drew a rectangle where the alley connected with Lincoln Avenue.)

Gerda had heard the footsteps and the "firecrackers" between "five, six, seven minutes after two."

She had heard only one person running. She was sure of that.

Adam Moore rose to cross-examine, and the tone of the defense soon became evident. Tuffy Pleasant's attorneys would attempt to convince the jury that the police and prosecutors had unduly influenced witnesses. It is a standard and often effective technique. Any prosecutor, or defense attorney, will talk to his witnesses before trial, but nervous witnesses can be made to feel that they should not have spoken to anyone.

"In your statement," Moore asked, "on March second . . . you don't say how many people . . . were making footsteps, do you? Since then have you talked to Mr. Sullivan or any policeman about this?"

Mrs. Lenberg gave an odd non sequitur answer: "Just when I shut my eyes and looked back on the night, and I can hear the echo because of the close proximity of the buildings . . . and I just heard one echo."

"My question was: Did you talk to Mr. Sullivan or any of the policemen before getting on the stand about how many footsteps you thought there were?"

Gerda knew what she knew, and she said she had told that to one detective. Moore cut her off, asking about gravel and the interval between one foot and then the other hitting. It was not gravel, she said, but blacktop.

She was a good prosecution witness.

So was Dale Soost. He had heard three shots sometime between midnight and 4:15 A.M. He had not looked at the clock. He had heard the woman scream as he waited on the sidewalk around 5:00. He had not spoken to her or looked at the victim's body.

"No questions," Moore said.

Rowland Seal spoke rapidly but with infinite precision. "I'm an auto body and fender mechanic," he said in answer to Sullivan's initial question. "With a great many very busy hobbies. . . . I manage a couple of duck clubs. I am a professional roller skating instructor, I teach trapshooting, shotgun shooting . . . I have friends in the Game Department and I do photography work for them, and keep track of wildlife counts, big game, birds and such as that."

Sullivan had Seal draw the apartment house at 208 North Sixth on "State's Identification –2." (His and Soost's apartment house was on the opposite end of the alley from Gerda Lenberg's.)

"Were you awakened sometime during the night?"

Where Soost had been vague, Seal was right on the mark. "A few seconds before two-oh-five in the morning—"

"How did you know it was a few seconds before two-oh-five?"

"Well, I have a digital watch and digital clock next to my bed that I cross-checked the next morning . . . and I heard three shots—*bang, bang–bang,* and I and my wife both looked at the clock immediately, so I would say I was awakened a few seconds before—the length of time it takes you to come back down on the bed and turn over and look at the clock."

Seal had peered from his window, but he said he could not have seen Morris Blankenbaker lying dead in his side yard. The cones of lights from the porches and the alley all ended before they came to that part of the yard.

Rowland Seal had walked along the apartment house side of the wire fence and seen the dead man, and he had tried to talk with the screaming woman, who could not be comforted.

"She was very hysterical," he testified. "That's why I was rather blunt with her to kind of get her to do something and get her settled down. . . . She was in front of the house and I said, 'Get in there and call the police or I will.' And I said, 'Well, if you aren't going to do it, I will.' So I started into the house—started toward the steps—and the dog wouldn't let me in."

Rowland Seal was an excellent witness. His recall was obviously as set as Jell-O, and Chris Tait said quietly, "No questions."

The first three witnesses had described how it was in the wee hours of the Friday night/Saturday morning when Morris Blankenbaker died. Each had heard something slightly different, but their testimony meshed. Gerda Lenberg spoke of hearing the "firecrackers," and the sound of running feet with hollow-sounding heels in the alley just outside her bedroom window.

Dale Soost had heard shots and gone back to sleep. Rowland Seal, punctilious and precise, knew the number of shots, the exact time he had heard them.

Both men had seen the slender woman emerge from her home and run through the snow, only to run back, screaming, "Morris! Morris!"

Despite the August heat, it *had* grown cold in the courtroom. Sullivan had been successful in turning back time and season.

Shortly before nine the next morning, Wednesday, August 18, the word that the woman at the center of the triangle was going to testify buzzed through the tenth floor.

"*She's here. . . .*" The murmuring passed along the oak benches outside the courtroom. Witnesses waited there. Family sometimes retreated to the benches when the testimony grew too graphic, while the reporters came and went. Today, they packed the press rows inside the courtroom and their cameramen waited outside for a glimpse of the woman who had bedazzled two men—one enough to forgive her for what many men would find unforgivable—and the other enough, allegedly, to both kill and die for her.

She *was* beautiful. There had been no exaggeration about that. Jerilee had a wonderful figure, slender and full breasted. She wore a tight-fitting striped shirt over a black turtleneck top and black bell-bottom slacks. Her hair was dark brown, parted in the middle, and fell to her shoulders. She had huge eyes under carefully arched brows. Her eyes were lined with kohl, which made them appear even bigger. Despite everything that she had been through, she seemed younger than twenty-nine.

Outside the courtroom, Jerilee posed willingly for the cameras and talked to reporters. Yes, she was nervous, but she was prepared to testify.

Only when Jerilee moved toward the witness chair to be sworn in, did her real anxiety show. She would now have to relive the most horrendous three years of her life. There was a quaver in her voice as she answered Jeff Sullivan's questions.

"First, Jerilee," he said, "I want you to sit up as close to the microphone as you can and speak loudly to all of the jurors, and so counsel can hear you. Would you please state your full name and spell it for the record?"

"Jerilee Littleton. J-e-r-i-l-e-e . . . L-i-t-t-l-e-t-o-n."

Vern Henderson stared at her from his spot at the prosecution table. Later, he commented somewhat sardonically, "Everybody was looking to see Mrs. *Blankenbaker* or Mrs. *Moore,* and neither of them showed up. Mrs. *Littleton* came to court. Most people were surprised to find that out."

The witness gave her address in Yakima, and said she was a loan interviewer at the Pacific National Bank. "Since October . . ."

"Jerilee, when were you married to Morris Blankenbaker?"

"August twenty-eight, 1965."

"Did you and Morris have any children?"

"Yes, we did—a boy, Rick—he's now seven, and a girl, Amanda, and she's five."

"Now, how long were you and Morris married?"

"It would have been nine years in August of seventy-four; we were divorced in June."

"After you divorced Morris, did you remarry?"

"Yes . . . Glynn Moore."

"Does Glynn Moore have a nickname?"

"Yes, it was 'Gabby.'"

"Now, when were you and Gabby Moore married?"

"September fourteenth, 1974."

"How long did you and Gabby Moore live together?"

"Till July of 1975."

"Less than a year?"

"Yes."

"From September to July, did you and he ever separate?"

"Yes, about three times."

"What was the longest separation?"

"I think about two weeks."

"Why did you and he separate during that period of time?"

"Well, he was a very unpredictable person. He would—he loved you a lot one minute and the next minute he just kicked you out of the house, and I was getting a little bit scared of him."

"Did he actually throw you out of the house on occasion?"

"Yes."

"What about his drinking habits during the time you were married to him?"

"He drank very heavily."

"When you say 'very heavily,' can you give me some idea of the amount?"

"Well, within a two- or three-hour period, he would drink a fifth of bourbon or whatever."

Jerilee testified that this level of drinking occurred three or four times a week, but she said she didn't think Gabby had used drugs.

"Not that you are aware of?"

"No."

"Now, were you separated in July?"

"Yes."

"When you left, where did you go?"

"I went back to my first husband, Morris Blankenbaker."

There was a slight murmur in the courtroom. What had been well-chewed gossip in Yakima was news to most of the spectators in this Seattle trial.

Jerilee kept her eyes on Jeff Sullivan. He was being gentle with her. She didn't know what kind of questions Adam Moore and Chris Tait might ask.

"When did you file for divorce from Glynn Moore?"

"In July."

"So when you moved out of Gabby's house, you moved back in with Morris? And where were you and Morris living in July of 1975?"

"At two-ten North Sixth Street in Yakima."

Jerilee answered questions about Gabby's obsession to have her back.

"Did you have any contact with Gabby Moore?"

"He would call daily and he stopped by a couple of times. He would call me at work and he would call me at home . . . he came out to the bank . . ."

"When he called, what was the general nature of his conversation?"

"He would just ask when I was coming back and wouldn't I give him another chance. He wasn't going to make it without me."

"Did he ever talk about Morris?"

"Not really that I recall."

"Did he ever threaten to do bodily harm to Morris?"

"No."

"Did he ever threaten to do bodily harm to himself?"

"Yes. . . . He would often say that he would like to commit suicide in front of me so that I would be on the fifth floor of Memorial—which is the psychiatric ward."

Jerilee testified that Gabby's children had all spoken to her on their father's behalf and begged her to give him another chance.

"Did you tell Glynn Moore that if Morris wasn't around that you would go back to him?"

"No, I *definitely* didn't."

"Did he ever ask you what you would do if Morris wasn't there?"

"I don't believe he did."

At the prosecution table, Vern Henderson listened and watched. He knew that Jerilee had met with Gabby Moore—he had seen them. From the distance at which he had observed them, he had no way of knowing if Jerilee had given Gabby any mixed signals. He wished that he had talked to her. Talked to Gabby. Done something. But he had kept out of it; he had followed his own rule not to mess in anyone else's relationship.

Jerilee told the jury about the night Gabby came into her house, and of how Morris and Joey Watkins had arrived to send him away.

"Do you remember where he [Morris] was teaching?"

"He was teaching physical education at the intermediate school—in Wapato."

"And sometime later in the fall, he took on another job; is that right?"

"Yes, he checked ID at the Lion's Share, at the door."

"And what is the Lion's Share?"

"It's a tavern, located on Second Street, I believe, in Yakima."

"How long had Morris been working at the Lion's Share?"

"He worked three days a week, and I believe this was his second week."

Jerilee's voice trembled more as she recalled the last night of Morris's life. They had had pizza with their children, and then he had gone off to work. She and a girlfriend had gone out to hear her friend's husband's band playing at the Country Cousin. They had stopped by to see Morris. The last time she had seen him alive was about a quarter to ten that night. Later, she had picked up Rick and Amanda from Olive's mobile home and taken them home where they'd all gone to bed. At two A.M., she had wakened, realized Morris would be home soon and she had moved the children from her bed into their own.

"Did you just wake up at two or did you have an alarm set?"

"I just woke up at two o'clock."

". . . How did you know it was two?"

"I have a clock by the bed. I took the children out of the bed and put them in their own beds. Then I went back to bed myself."

"Did Morris come in, come home?"

"He came home—just a few minutes after I put the children in bed."

"Tell us what happened then," Jeff Sullivan said.

"I heard our car drive in and I heard our car door shut. And then I thought that I heard two more car doors shut—and Morris didn't come in."

"What did you do when he didn't come in?"

"Well, at the time I didn't do anything because I had thought some fellows had asked him if he would like to go for a couple of drinks after work. So I thought the car doors that I heard later were the fellows picking him up, so I didn't do anything. I just remained in bed."

"Did you hear anything else, Jerilee, when the car doors closed?"

"I heard some voices . . . from the back of the house . . . toward the alley. . . . They sounded rather excited, kind of high-pitched."

"Did you recognize any of the voices?"

"No, I didn't."

"Could one of the voices have been Morris's?"

"Could have been, but I didn't recognize it at the time."

"How long did this conversation or these voices last?"

"Not long, maybe ten words."

Jerilee could not remember the sequence of the car doors slamming and the voices. She didn't know which had come first.

"Okay. How long did you stay in bed before you decided you better see what's going on?"

"About half an hour. Then I got up and went to the back window and looked out, and I saw that our car was there. So then I went outside and looked inside the car. Nobody was there so I went back in the house, went back to bed."

"How far was the car parked from where Morris's body was found the next day?"

"Maybe thirty feet, about."

"Is it dark out there?"

"Where Morris's body was . . . it was."

"Do you wear glasses?"

"I wear contact lenses."

"If you take your contact lenses out, how far can you see?"

"I can't see hardly at all."

Jerilee had taken her contacts out when she went to bed, and she had gone out to look in the car without them. She was nearsighted and had difficulty seeing at a distance. She had been able to see that both their cars were parked in their usual places, but not much more than that. She had gone back to bed, read for a while, and then slept fitfully until five A.M.

"You have a large dog, do you not, or did at that time?"

"Yes, we did—a black Lab."

"Where was he?"

"In my bedroom."

"Did he make any noise at two o'clock?"

"No, he didn't."

"Did he usually bark when there were strangers outside the house?"

"Oh, yes . . . he's very, very protective."

"To the point where you didn't have your mail delivered if he was outside? Is that right?"

"That's right."

"Did he bark when Morris came home—usually?"

"No, he pretty much could recognize the footsteps, I believe, because he never barked at anybody familiar."

At five A.M., Jerilee had called her brother-in-law Mike, who had offered to come over. He knew that Morris had had no plans to go anywhere after work.

"I said, 'Well, I think it will be okay,'" Jerilee testified. "'Rather than have you come down, I'll take Hike and we'll go around the house' . . . so I left Mike on the phone and took the dog and went out the front door. Before I did that, though, I put my contacts in this time. The dog ran ahead of me and started growling and barking at something on the ground. I couldn't tell right then what it was, but when I got there I saw that it was Morris."

Jerilee could no longer contain the tears that brimmed up in her eyes, trying as she obviously was to blink them back.

This was the worst part, but she kept answering Jeff Sullivan's questions.

"Was it dark?" he asked softly.

"Yes."

"How was Morris lying when you first walked over to him?"

"He was lying on his stomach, facedown—his feet pointing toward the alley—that would be west."

"And his head?"

"East toward Sixth Street."

"Where was his body, Jerilee, in relationship to your fence and the gate?"

"It was just inside the gate—just right inside the gate, and—" Her voice shook, thick with tears.

"What did you do then?"

"I rolled him over and tried to pull him toward me. I felt his face and I thought I felt something on his face which I thought was mud at that time. And he was really heavy. I mean he didn't help me at all. And I think I tried to hear a heartbeat. I don't remember exactly. . . . I took ahold of his jacket on his right side and rolled him toward the house, which would be north, and then I pulled him into a sitting position toward me with his jacket.

"And then I started screaming. . . ."

23

The summer morning in Seattle was lost to everyone in Judge Loy's courtroom. They were too caught up in listening to Jerilee Littleton recall a dark dawn in November. She explained to Prosecutor Sullivan how she had run to the phone where her husband's brother waited. "I just ran inside and picked up the phone and said, 'Mike, come quick. Morris has blood all over him!' And then I went back outside and I was screaming—and then two neighbor people came over and asked me if I had called the ambulance, and I said no, and they told me to do that—so I went in and called the ambulance. And by the time I went back outside, the police had arrived then and I went back inside and stayed."

There were photographs to be introduced into evidence. Sullivan began with the least upsetting. He handed Jerilee pictures of her car, the carport on North Sixth, the back of her house, of Morris's car, the side yard.

"The gate was always open," Jerilee said. "I don't know if the hinges weren't working right or—"

"Jerilee," Jeff Sullivan said gently, "I'm handing you what's been marked as Identification eight. Can you tell me what that is, please?"

Her breath caught, but she managed to answer, "The fence and Morris's body on his back."

"Does that picture fairly and accurately portray the position of Morris's body?"

"Yes."

Sullivan changed gears and asked Jerilee about her sister's conversation with Gabby Moore. "What did he talk to her about?"

"He would ask her to influence me or persuade me to go back to him."

"And, in that regard, Jerilee, was there ever a time after you left him in July that you indicated to him that you would come back to him?"

"No, I didn't."

"Did you encourage him in any way?"

"No," she said firmly.

"After Morris was killed, did you believe that Glynn Moore had something to do with it?"

"Yes, I did—from different things he said. He had told my sister that he knew people that would do anything for him. All he had to do was ask. I just felt that he felt that if Morris wasn't there, I would be back to him; he was very confident that I would be back with him."

This was a peculiar trial, indeed. Angelo "Tuffy" Pleasant was the defendant, certainly. But Talmadge Glynn "Gabby" Moore was also on trial. The prosecution had to show how Gabby had cajoled, pleaded, sobbed, and, finally, blackmailed Tuffy into killing Morris and wounding himself. The defense didn't really disagree with the portrayal of Gabby Moore, but they had to paint Tuffy as the self-sacrificing hero and lay the blame on Anthony and Larry.

The "ghost of Gabby Moore" was going to take a verbal beating in this courtroom, even if the man himself was beyond human reach.

Chris Tait cross-examined Jerilee. "After Morris's death and before Christmas, did you talk with Gabby about his possible involvement in Morris's death?"

"Yes, I talked to him once on the phone."

"Did you tell him you thought he was involved?"

"Yes, I did. . . . He said 'No way.' He couldn't have. He just couldn't have done it."

"Did you believe him?"

"No, I didn't."

"Did you tell him that you would never come back to him so long as you thought he was involved in Morris's death?"

"I told him I would never go back to him, no matter what."

"Regardless?"

"That's right."

And, Jerilee testified, Gabby had insisted he could prove to her that he was innocent of any complicity in Morris's murder. He told her he had ways, but he didn't go into details. She told him again she didn't care. Nothing would make her go back to him.

Nothing.

Tait elicited the dates of Jerilee's three marriages, and then turned away from her as she said she had married Jim Littleton on April 18.

"April of *this* year?"

"Yes."

"Thank you, Jerilee. I don't think I have any further questions."

Again, the courtroom was filled with a murmur of indistinguishable voices, whispers of shock that the witness should have married again so soon after her husbands' deaths.

Sullivan's redirect dealt mostly with having Jerilee draw a diagram of her house and yard for the jury. He could see that she was shaken and about to break into tears.

Just as Jerilee thought her ordeal on the stand might be over, Chris Tait rose with more questions. He wanted to know more about her marriages. How old was she when she married Morris?

"Eighteen."

"And how old are you now?"

"Twenty-nine."

"And how old were you when you married Gabby?"

"Twenty-seven."

"And how old was Gabby when you married him?"

"Forty-two, I believe."

"You had moved back with Morris. . . . Did Gabby threaten you in any way?"

"Not me, no."

"Okay. Did he threaten you the night he came to the house and got inside because there weren't any locks on the doors?"

"No."

"What did you mean," Tait pounced, "when you said that he told you that if you didn't unlock the door and come out of the bedroom into the living room that he was going to kick the door in and come in after you?"

"That's just what he said. I don't—"

"Was he threatening you when he said that, do you think?"

"I was scared, yes."

"I can imagine you were. What was Gabby's attitude about having you come back—did it seem important to him?"

"Yes—*very* important."

"Did you think it would be fair to say that it was probably the most important thing in his life?"

"He seemed to make it that way at that time, yes."

"Talking about his blood pressure and the nosebleeds and the medication—did you ever know him to quit taking his medication on purpose, so that he would *get* nosebleeds?"

"No, he didn't."

Tait had put that thought into the jurors' minds, however, to show how manipulative Gabby had been—to the point of hatching a convoluted murder plot.

Tait asked about the disintegration of Morris's relationship with Gabby: these two men who had hunted together, worked out at the YMCA together, and discussed coaching together, these men who had faced death on the river together. Jerilee recalled that Morris had become disenchanted with Gabby sometime after December 1973, when Gay Moore had begun divorce proceedings. It had not been too long after Gabby had moved in with the Blankenbakers.

"After the divorce with Gay," Tait asked, " . . . the relationship between Morris and Gabby started to deteriorate? Did they see each other often after that—or not at all. How would you characterize it?"

A lot of Yakimans expected Jerilee and Jim to move away to Seattle or Spokane, but they had no plans to do that. The best way to deal with the rumors and disapproving stares was simply to stare back. After time had passed, maybe people would find something else to talk about.

24

The most avidly awaited witness had already testified, but the trial of Tuffy Pleasant had weeks to go, and there were surprises yet to come. The battle plans were clear now, and Adam Moore and Chris Tait would have an uphill battle if the jury was allowed to hear Tuffy's own voice confessing to murder.

In the meantime, Jeff Sullivan continued laying out the state's case in neat progression. Dennis Meyers, one of Tuffy's escort officers, was also one of the first Yakima police officers who had responded to the scene of Morris Blankenbaker's murder. He testified to what he personally had observed. He listed the other police personnel who were there: Officer Rosenberry, Sergeant Green, Sergeant Brimmer, Sergeant Beaushaw, and Lieutenant Kline.

Adam Moore cross-examined, asking questions designed to make the police crime scene investigation appear inept and bumbling. It was standard defense stuff, and he did nothing to shake Meyers. Moore wanted to know when the body had been photographed, when it had been covered with a sheet, how dark it was as they searched for the missing bullet casings.

Sullivan sat implacably, unruffled. He knew the crime scene probe had been properly executed.

"Did you take custody of any objects, any evidence?" Moore asked Meyers.

"Only the objects I took from the car."

"That was a bank statement and . . ."

"A set of keys."

"To the car?"

"Yes, sir."

"Were the keys in the ignition or were they in a more subtle place."

"They were laying on the floorboards on the driver's side."

"All right. Did you find any weapons? I assume you didn't?"

"No, sir," Meyers replied. "I did not."

The jury was relegated to their quarters for forty-five minutes after lunch while Adam Moore and Jeff Sullivan argued a point of law before Judge Loy. Loretta Scott, Tuffy's cousin who had loaned him the death weapon twice, was to be the next witness. Moore argued that Jeff Sullivan had overstepped his authority on February 27 when he had granted Loretta immunity from prosecution for disposing of the gun. He asked that Loretta be informed that she could be prosecuted at some future time by some future prosecutor because she had not *truly* had immunity when she gave a forty-page statement to the investigators in February.

Sullivan argued that giving Loretta Scott such a warning would undoubtedly frighten her and serve to make her a reluctant witness. He asked Judge Loy to compel her to testify, but at the same time, to grant her permanent immunity. She had not known about any of the murder plans beforehand, and she had come forward voluntarily to tell Sullivan and the Yakima detectives about the gun. Furthermore, she had had two attorneys with her to protect her rights at the time.

Without Loretta Scott, Sullivan pointed out, the state probably would never have been able to trace the gun to Tuffy Pleasant. He asked Judge Loy to grant her immunity to testify now and to restrain the defense attorneys from alarming her with scare tactics that would make her think she could go to jail at some time in the future because she attempted to dispose of a murder weapon.

Loretta Scott sat on one of the long oak benches in the hall, unaware of the argument inside the courtroom. In truth, she had no immunity from prosecution until the court granted it.

Judge Loy said that he would need time to rule on the motions.

Loretta's testimony was skipped over, and she was told she didn't have to wait in the hall that afternoon. But she would be back. It had been her visit to the prosecutor's office that had resulted in Tuffy Pleasant's arrest for murder several hours later. She was a *very* important witness. Good for the state. Potentially devastating for the defense.

Sullivan's prosecution plan was to connect Tuffy to the death weapon, and also to connect Tuffy to the murder sites by tracing his movements on the nights in question. The state's next witnesses were the trio from Pasco who had met a single guy in the Chinook Cosmopolitan's lounge.

Sam Berber and his girlfriend, Sally Nash,* and Melodie Isaacs testified that they had met a man who introduced himself as "Angelo Pleasant" in the Chinook that night. To Sullivan's question about absolute identification, Berber said he could not honestly swear that the man at the defense table was the man he had met, but he remembered the name well.

Sally Nash couldn't be positive either.

Melodie Isaacs *was* positive; she had been Tuffy's date that night.

"So you recognize that man today?" Sullivan asked.

"Yes, I do," she said, and pointed to Tuffy Pleasant. Melodie was as positive as Sam was that it was right at two a.m. when Mary looked at her watch as they let Tuffy out of Sam's Cadillac at the Chinook Hotel.

"Yes, she [Sally] told me it was two o'clock and she better head back home."

"Did you have a baby-sitter at home too that you had told you would be home a little earlier than that?"

"Yes. I told my daughter—I have a fifteen-year-old daughter."

Adam Moore hit on the trio's drinking that evening, on Sam and Sally's failure to absolutely identify Tuffy, and he even managed to confuse Melodie.

"And there's no doubt in your mind that our man is Angelo Pleasant, the guy you met *nine months ago?*"

"I really don't know, but I'm saying it's him," Melodie vacillated suddenly. "I wouldn't know him, you know—"

"Does he look like the same man?"

"He don't to me. He had a little more hair."

"He had more hair then?"

"Yeah."

"Any other differences?"

"He looked like he gained a little weight—that's about it."

"*Could* this be the man? Is it possible?"

"Yes."

"You said he was the man when Mr. Sullivan was asking you."

"Yeah," Melodie, a nightmare of a witness, equivocated. "I'm sure it's him now since I seen him again."

Melodie was certain, however, that they had dropped her date off that night at two a.m. at his car at the Chinook.

Joey Watkins, Tuffy's former housemate and wrestling buddy, was the next witness. Joey might knit up the raveled mess of uncertainties the previous witnesses had left. That is the excitement of a trial. Players leave gaps, misinterpretations, outright lies, and prejudiced statements in the fabric of the case, and the attorneys must rush to present other players who will undo the damage, and maybe even push their side a few lengths ahead. Nothing is ever a given—nor should it be. Smug, overconfident trial lawyers can be humbled in an instant.

Joey Watkins, an extremely tall young man, took the stand. He recalled knowing Tuffy since grade school and living with him for six weeks in the fall of 1975. Tuffy, he said, was back and forth from college classes in Ellensburg, helping coach Gabby Moore's high school wrestlers.

"Did you know Morris Blankenbaker?"

"Yes. I knew of him when I was in school because he was like assistant coach to us."

"So you knew both Morris Blankenbaker and Gabby Moore; is that right?" Sullivan asked.

"Yes."

"Were you going up and assisting at the wrestling practices?"

"Angelo asked me to go up to get ahold of the heavyweights and teach them, because they were kind of slow in learning things. . . . I was helping him out."

"Angelo was up [at wrestling practice] all the time. Is that right?"

"Yeah, I believe he was."

Joey recalled going up to Morris's house the night Gabby broke in. Gabby was outside when they got there and he was "bamming" on the windows.

"What happened? Was there any kind of a fight or anything?"

"No." Joey shook his head. "Morris got out of the car and went over there. He says, 'Man, Watkins, you know what? I would hit him' but he says it was his *coach*. . . . They just started talking and I guess Morris told him something and he just left."

Joey was the friend who had been with Tuffy in the Red Lion in the Chinook Hotel on the night Morris was murdered. He remembered it extremely well. "Me and Angelo were at the Lion's Share messing around. We went to the Red Lion. That's where he met these three people. We were sitting down drinking . . . Angelo looked over and saw these people sitting over there, so he went over and talked to them. So Angelo came back over to the table and told me that he was going to be with these people tonight—and so he took me home."

"Now, once you got home, do you remember what you did?"

"Well, I just stayed at the house and laid back on the couch. Then my woman came by and we just sat and talked."

"Did you ever leave home again that night?"

"No."

"How did you find out Morris Blankenbaker had been killed?"

"Well, Angelo's mother and father were going fishing to Moses Lake. . . . Me, Anthony, and Angelo were all out at his parents' house cleaning up the yard, and I just happened to see the newspaper and saw his picture in there."

"What day was that?"

Joey wasn't sure. He knew it was on the weekend, and thought it was probably on the Sunday—November 22.

Back to the Friday night/Saturday morning when Morris died—the witness said he had gone to sleep between twelve or one a.m. and he hadn't seen Tuffy-Angelo at all that night.

"Now, Joey." Sullivan's voice was strong. "Did *you* have anything to do with the death of Morris Blankenbaker? Were you there when he was shot?"

"No."

"Did you drive the car for Angelo?"

"No."

"You had *nothing* to do with it? You were nowhere near the scene?"

"No."

"Did you ever see Gabby Moore give Angelo money?"

"When we were wrestling, he probably gave him, say, about thirty-five, forty, fifty dollars."

Joey didn't know what the money was for, or exactly when Gabby gave it to Tuffy. "I imagine he gave it to Angelo for helping him out with the wrestling practice."

As for the Christmas Eve when Gabby was shot, Joey testified he was down at the home for handicapped children with his girl-friend—down in Harrah.

"Had you been down there before?"

"Yes."

"You worked for a while at another place that took care of mentally retarded children, didn't you?"

"Yes, the Yakima Valley School."

"Last year . . . and what did you do with these small kids?"

"I was a rec leader and what we did with the kids was have recreation planned like carnivals and games with them."

"And you worked in that capacity for six or eight months?"

Joey Watkins came across as a gentle giant and the least likely of the wrestling squad alumni to have committed two murders.

On cross, Chris Tait elicited answers from Joey Watkins that showed the last time he had seen Gabby Moore on Christmas Eve was in Kenny Marino's apartment.

Tait wanted to hear more about the change that had come over Gabby Moore in the months before he was killed.

"How long had you known him?"

"Since I was a sophomore in high school."

"You had known him for five years or so?"

"Yeah."

"Did you ever experience any change in Mr. Moore?"

"Well, the only time I really saw Mr. Moore was the first time when I was in the Lion's Share and he was wild—"

"Can you tell us what you mean by that?"

"He was—I mean—like he was just changed from the coach that I used to see—because he was strict on us."

"Are you saying he wasn't the same coach—you mean he wasn't the same kind of person?"

"He wasn't the *same* person."

"How was he different?"

"Well, for one thing his hair was longer and he just didn't dress like he used to."

Joey recalled a coach who had demanded strict adherence to training rules from his athletes.

"Do you know if Mr. Moore was the sort of person who drank quite a bit?"

"No. I never knew him to drink that much until I saw him in the Lion's Share."

Joey had been baffled by a long-haired, intoxicated coach who kept trying to grab his beer. He had been horrified to see Moore trying to break into Morris's wife's window, so drunk that he couldn't walk a straight line.

With one more witness denigrating Gabby Moore, Chris Tait moved on to show that Tuffy and Joey had known Morris too as a coach.

"How close were you to Morris Blankenbaker?"

"Not really close. I didn't really know him because he was like an assistant coach when I was a sophomore and he taught me little things—moves and stuff in wrestling."

"Was Morris older than you?"

"He was thirty-two."

"And you are twenty-two. So he was ten years older?"

"Yeah."

"You said that Morris was the assistant coach?"

"He just came in there to show us things."

"He wasn't formally the coach?"

"No."

"He just showed up at the practices and kind of taught you things? Was that when you were playing football or wrestling—or both?"

"Wrestling."

"Tell us, if you can, a little bit about the wrestling experiences that you had with Angelo."

"*Well*, Angelo was—to me—the best on the team."

"Did he win most of his matches?"

"Yeah."

"Do you remember going to tournaments together?"

"No, because I never made it to the tournaments."

Joey said that Angelo-Tuffy had, and that he usually took firsts. Tuffy Pleasant had been the best there was; Gabby Moore had coached him to be a champion.

Tait asked Joey about playing football. He said he had had bad experiences, losing experiences in that sport. He and Angelo had been the best players on the Davis squad.

"Were you the biggest?"

"Well, I *was* the biggest," Joey said, "but Angelo was the tough man for scrape lineback."

"No further questions."

Jeff Sullivan rose to ask some questions on redirect.

"When you say Angelo was tough, was he a good linebacker?"

"Yeah."

"He liked to hit people?"

"Yeah, he stuck people."

Sullivan half smiled. "If he's going to be a good linebacker, you have to stick people, don't you?"

"That's right."

There was a sense of regret in the courtroom as the afternoon lengthened. Tuffy had lived years of sports glory. He had almost always been first, and now he sat hunched over the defense table, his huge shoulders at their muscular peak. Like Morris before him, Tuffy was a perfect physical specimen. One could imagine him and Joey in the arena—the huge gentle witness—and the scrappy defendant.

No more.

Fifteen-year-old John Klingele and and his father, Wayne, were the last witnesses of the day. John told the jury how he had found the Colt Woodsman .22 in the Naches River under the Twin Bridges. His father testified that he had put it up on a shelf and told the Yakima Police Chief about it the next day.

Judge Loy dismissed the jury at 4:30 and reminded them not to watch television, read the papers, or discuss the case. The Seattle media had begun to report this murder trial in more depth with every day that passed. It had transcended a hometown story in Yakima, Washington.

25

At 9:30 the next morning, Judge Loy said he was prepared to rule on Jeff Sullivan's motion to grant immunity to Loretta Scott and her brother, Charles "Chucky" Pleasant, for their involvement with the murder gun. "The state's motion to grant immunity from prosecution to Loretta Scott and Charles Pleasant in return for their testimony in this case is granted."

It was a big boost for the state's case.

Loretta Scott, a beautiful woman, wore a white tunic dress, a wide-brimmed dark hat, and giant gold hoops in her ears for her day in court. She did not mind the cameras in the hallway and smiled for James Wallace, the *Herald–Tribune* reporter who was covering the trial and doubling as a news photographer.

Loretta's memory was excellent, and she was a compelling story-teller as she recalled her cousin Tuffy's two visits to her home to borrow the gun and her horror when she realized what it had been used for.

Her recall of the hysteria she and her brother, Chucky, had felt as they tried to throw away a gun that kept bouncing back off the bridge made the Christmas Day event sound like a Keystone Kops episode.

Chris Tait asked her if Tuffy had ever told her what had happened, and she said he had told her about the death of Gabby Moore.

"Well, he told me a white boy did the shooting."

"Okay. What did he tell you happened?"

"I'm just trying to gather my thoughts. He told me that Mr. Moore and he had a plan that he was supposed to have been shot, but he wasn't supposed to be killed. He said that he was supposed to get five thousand dollars out of this—that he was just supposed to wound Mr. Moore, but he wasn't supposed to die and that the white boy did the shooting."

"Did he tell you where it happened at Mr. Moore's?"

"They were in the kitchen."

"Did he tell you about anybody else being involved in these two killings?"

"He mentioned a Joey Watkins and Kenny Marino."

"And what did he tell you about how they were involved?"

"He didn't actually say. He just said Blankenbaker, Moore, [somebody was] driving a car, and Joey Watkins and Marino. . . . He told me that Joey Watkins was on the list of suspicion for murder."

"Now, who was going to get this five thousand dollars? Was Angelo to get it or was Mr. Moore going to get it?"

"I don't know who all was supposed to get this money. He said they were supposed to receive five thousand after he was supposed to have been shot. He was supposed to sign a piece of paper and supposed to get five thousand dollars . . . When he died, everything went."

Tait sounded as mystified and confused as the gallery. "But when Mr. Moore died, it all went down the drain?"

"Right."

Loretta had a few skeletons in her own closet, facts that Chris Tait dragged out of her over her extended time on the stand. He wondered why Tuffy would think to go to her for a gun.

"Well, if you want to know the truth about it, when I lived in Seattle a long time ago, he used to come over and we were always having revolvers around the house."

"I'm sorry," Tait said, "I can't hear you."

"When I lived in Seattle, we always had revolvers around the house."

"Loretta, isn't it a fact that you used to *live* with a man who dealt in stolen guns?"

"Yes, I did."

Tait homed in on her drinking habits. "Do you drink often?"

"When I feel like I want to indulge, I will."

"How many drinks does it take before you start to feel the effects?"

"About three."

"Isn't it a fact that you had four drinks on Christmas Eve?"

"That was the beginning."

"How many was it in the end?"

"I wasn't counting."

"Were you intoxicated?"

"I was feeling nice."

Loretta said she had made a Christmas punch of McNaughtons and vodka.

"It must have been quite a punch," Tait said with a smile.

Loretta Scott was on the witness stand for a very long time, much of it while the defense attorneys and the prosecutors wrangled over what areas the defense could cover. Loretta had had a gun because she was afraid of an old boyfriend, but that had nothing to do with this murder trial. She was a colorful, often humorous, witness, but she was not swayed from the central testimony about her cousin Tuffy and the borrowed gun, or about throwing it in the Naches River when she learned it might well be a murder weapon.

On redirect, Sullivan asked Loretta once again the specific questions that mattered and only those. She was positive that:

- She gave the .22 to Tuffy in October 1975.
- That she took it back from him on the Saturday after Thanksgiving.
- That he came to borrow it again on December 24.
- That he told her she would read about this in the newspaper.
- That he brought the gun back to her late on Christmas Eve.
- That he came to her house on February 26, 1976, to ask what she had done with the gun.

Nothing else really mattered as far as the outcome of the trial.

Mike McGuigan questioned Chucky Pleasant, who was a last-minute participant in getting rid of the gun. Chucky proved to be the kind of witness who scarcely needs an attorney's questions to elicit information. He began by playing both roles.

"What did Loretta ask of you?"

"Well, she came in and she said, 'Chuck, I think I know who killed Mr. Moore.' And I said, 'You do! Who?' And she told me that it was Angelo. And I said, 'No, you are kidding.' I just couldn't believe it. And then she said, 'Yeah, it's true.' And I said, 'How do you know?' and she said, 'Because I gave him the gun.'"

Chucky Pleasant said he had been totally shocked. He testified that he had gone along with pitching the gun in the Naches, which proved to be more difficult than it looked. On the day before his cousin Tuffy was arrested, Tuffy had called him in his dorm in Ellensburg.

"He just said, 'Chuck, are you sure that you threw the gun in the river?' And I said, 'Yeah.' And he said, 'Did you have gloves on when you did it?' And I said, 'Yeah, I had some gloves.' And he had asked me, 'Don't you know you might get involved in all this stuff?'"

The plan that the state alleged Gabby Moore had forged had clearly spread its poison until it infiltrated the Pleasant family, a tightly connected extended clan. Even so, Loretta and Chucky's testimony was almost lighthearted in contrast to what the afternoon witnesses would say. Much of the rest of that day would be taken up with forensic pathology and toxicology, and the evidence found at the autopsies of the two dead coaches.

The participants in the Pleasant trial—the attorneys, law officers, witnesses, and the defendant himself—were in a strange city, in an unfamiliar courthouse, yet the halls were becoming familiar and so were the jurors' faces. The trial had taken on its own rhythm now, as all trials eventually do. The case had found its flow.

Olive Blankenbaker's sister lived in Seattle, so Olive had planned to stay with her, but the trip to downtown took so long in the morning and the rush-hour traffic going home was so bad that they rented a hotel room in the center of the city so they could walk to the courthouse. There was such a sense of urgency, a kind of anxiety that they might miss something, some bit of information, that could never be found and then there would never be any closure.

Although this was a trial marked with many sidebar arguments— one where the jurors were often banished to their chambers for an hour or more at a time—it moved along. Court started promptly each morning at 9:30, with a 10:15 midmorning recess, a noon to 1:30 lunch hour, an afternoon break, and then dismissal by 4:30 P.M. Because Judge Loy had noticed that the jurors often rode the same elevators as the gallery and were sometimes blocked by corridors thick with spectators, reporters, and family, he had ordered that the jurors were to arrive first and leave first.

Thursday afternoon began with Dr. Ted Loomis, who was the Washington State Toxicologist. Loomis testified that he had had occasion to analyze blood samples taken at the postmortem examinations of both Morris Blankenbaker and Gabby Moore. He said that Morris had had "essentially no alcohol" content in his blood. Gabby, on the other hand, had had .31.

Asked by Jeff Sullivan to comment on what impairment this much alcohol in the bloodstream would cause, Loomis answered, "All people with a blood alcohol level of point thirty-one would have very significant impairment with respect to judgment and reasoning, with respect to vision, with respect to hearing. They would have some impairment with respect to speech, but it might not be particularly noticeable. Some people, but not *all* people, would be impaired significantly with respect to their gross body muscle activity; that's walking, turning, standing, or sitting. Some people are so affected at .31 that they are actually out of contact with reality—they are in a comatose state."

"But it is possible that somebody in that condition would be able to speak . . . and somebody else not feel that they were intoxicated? Is that correct?"

"Possible for them to speak fairly well."

"Some other people's speech would be slurred?"

"Yes, and some people would be out cold."

Dr. Richard Muzzall, the Yakima County Coroner, testified next. His voice was matter-of-fact as he explained the terrible damage done by the old .22.

"Mr. Blankenbaker suffered three small-caliber wounds to the head—one passing through the upper lip and embedding itself against the base of the spine just below the skull, the other two entering behind the left ear, transversing the brain and lodging within the skull. Death, of course, was caused by extensive brain injury hemorrhage. I think it's more likely that death was caused by the two behind the ear."

Because of the gunbarrel "tattooing," Muzzall estimated that all three of the wounds were the result of a gun held at almost point-blank range, and one was a contact wound.

Olive kept her face expressionless, although she felt like screaming. Ned Blankenbaker's normally ruddy face was bright red with pain.

Each of them had loved their boy so much. It still didn't seem possible that it was Morris that Muzzall was talking about.

The coroner moved on to the complete autopsy he had performed on the body of Gabby Moore. Gabby has asked Dr. Myers where it was safe to take a bullet, but the shot to the ribs under his left arm had gone chaotically awry, and he had drowned in his own blood.

"Somebody who had sustained that kind of wound," Sullivan asked, "would it be possible to save him surgically?"

"No, I think it would be extremely unlikely, even if it happened right in the hospital."

On cross-examination, Adam Moore wondered what kind of wound Gabby would have had if the .22 bullet had not deflected and tumbled.

"If it had continued at forty-five degrees after penetrating the rib," Muzzall answered, "it would have gone through the part of the left lung, would, in all likelihood, have missed the heart and come out somewhere in the anterior [front] chest."

"I see. Uh-huh. You thought that if it hadn't been deflected by the rib, it would have been a nonfatal wound?"

"The chances it were nonfatal would be much higher."

Dr. Muzzall said he had not noticed any powder tattooing on Gabby's T-shirt, and he knew there was none on the skin itself.

Adam Moore asked Muzzall to talk about the specks of dried blood found on Morris's hand. "Your inference is that the hand was raised in a defensive—"

"It would be the only explanation . . . to explain the blood on the hand. . . . In other words, the hand had to be somewhere in front of his head where blood could get on it. . . . Blood would shoot out of the wound . . . in the direction of a cone, just as any spray from a spray can."

"In your opinion, was the gun closer to the circular wound by the ear with the dense powder patterns or the lip wound?"

"Of the two wounds, the one in the mouth would be the farthest away."

This did not seem to be information that a defense attorney would want to bring out. All of it seemed to bear out the state's theory that Morris had been lured toward someone he trusted, shot in the lip and then twice in the back of the head—at near contact range—by someone who must have wanted to be sure he was dead. He had thrown up his hand in a vain attempt to stop the first slug.

Eight photographs of the shooting site, Morris's body, and the blood flecked hand were entered into evidence over the objections of the defense who called them "inflammatory." Every defense attorney, *everywhere*, every time, objects to pictures of the victims as "inflammatory and of no probative value." Some get in. Some don't. For the average juror, unused to the sight of *any* dead human being, the photographs they must view are often the most jarring part of a murder trial.

But what had happened had happened, and the jurors would need to *see* the crime scenes in order to make their decisions about the guilt or innocence of Angelo "Tuffy" Pleasant.

26

Well into the first week of Tuffy Pleasant's trial, Jeff Sullivan called John Anderson, the Director of the Washington State Patrol Crime Laboratory in Spokane. Anderson had testified in more than nine hundred trials; he was a brilliant criminalist and an expert in firearms examination. Sergeant Bob Brimmer had sent the bullets and casings retrieved from the victims and the crime scenes in the Blankenbaker-Moore murders to Anderson. He had performed his forensic alchemy and connected that evidence to the Colt .22 found in the river.

Anderson gave the jury a quick lesson in the way guns propel bullets. "Except for shotguns, which are essentially smoother bore weapons, if you look down the barrel, you will see a series of circular patterns. These are caused by indentations made by the cutting implement making the barrel. The land and groove is a high point and a low point . . . and gives the direction of twist. When a cartridge is fired and the bullet is forced down the barrel, the direction of twist and the land and groove impart a spin to the bullet, putting it on a truer course."

He pointed out that the lands and grooves in a gun barrel are designed to prevent a bullet from emerging and "flip-flopping," going off course when it hits the friction of the air.

The soft metal of a bullet is marked by these high and low swirls in the gun barrel, leaving striae. These are highly individual markings. The same tool making a half-dozen gun barrels will itself be worn down imperceptibly so that no two barrels are ever exactly alike, and the bullets propelled from each barrel will have slightly different striae.

Bullets are compared in two ways: for *class* characteristics and for *individual* characteristics. Some are so battered that they meet the former criteria but not the latter. In this case, the bullet taken from Morris's head and that from Gabby's body were alike in class characteristics—each with six lands and grooves striae and with the same dimensions. Anderson, however, testified he could not say absolutely that they had come from the same gun.

However, when he compared the shell casings—the one Vern Henderson had found at the edge of Morris's yard, and the one found on Gabby's kitchen floor—he *had* been able to match them conclusively in *both* class and individual characteristics. "When a round is chambered in the barrel," Anderson said, "the *extractor* is a piece of metal that wraps around the cartridge case itself. As it is fired, the extractor will pull the empty shell case from the breech. Another piece of stationary metal hits the shell case—that is the ejectory and that will force the empty shell case out of the weapon."

Each of these actions leaves its mark on the base of the casing. Sullivan asked Anderson how he had concluded that the same gun had fired both bullets.

"I found an ejectory mark at 'eight o'clock,' holding the firing pin impression at 'twelve o'clock,'" he said. "At 'three o'clock,' there was an extractor mark."

These marks were identical on both bullet casings—from each murder. Combined with the same firing pin mark stamped on the bottom of each shell, this left no doubt at all that the same gun had been used to kill both Morris and Gabby. And that was the gun found in the river. Everything dovetailed perfectly.

Vern Henderson had not been exaggerating when he told Tuffy how much evidence can be detected when a crime lab has both a gun and bullets for comparison.

Further, John Anderson testified that his test firings indicated that the person who shot Gabby Moore had been *nine inches or, at the most, twelve inches away.*

That warred with Tuffy's taped confession to Vern Henderson where he said he had been *six or seven feet* away from Gabby when Gabby had ordered him to shoot him. In reality, Tuffy had been very,

very close to Gabby when he fired. Gabby's bloodied T-shirt with a bullet hole just beneath the left armpit was entered into evidence.

It was Friday, August 20, 1976. For the casual observer and the media too, trials are fascinating to watch. For the families of those involved—both victims and defendants—a trial is an ordeal to be gotten through, a reminder of horror and loss.

Derek Moore took the witness stand to testify about how he found his father dead before dawn on Christmas morning. His girlfriend, Janet Whitman, followed him on the stand, and then his sister, Kate, and his grandfather, Dr. A. J. Myers.

All of them related their memories of the final night of Gabby Moore's life, remembering the last time they had ever talked to someone whom they had truly cared about, but someone they could not save from his own obsessions.

Everyone in Judge Loy's courtroom was caught in those hours between sunset and the first glimmers of light on Christmas Day, trapped, somehow, in the tiny apartment on Eighteenth Avenue, along with the dead man.

And then Jeff Sullivan skillfully elicited testimony which summed up more of the weeks and months of investigation into the two murders. The jury had heard from all the police personnel who were present at the scene of Morris Blankenbaker's murder, and now they heard about the scene at Gabby Moore's apartment—right from the call: "Unattended death."

Adam Moore and Chris Tait knew that the time when Sullivan would introduce the tapes of Tuffy Pleasant confessing to the two murders was approaching. They could not stop the tapes from being heard, but they sensed that Jeff Sullivan was about to wind up the state's case, and they were adamant that they did not want the jurors to adjourn for the weekend with those confessions ringing in their ears.

If they expected an argument from the prosecutor, Sullivan surprised them. He was not finished with his case, he said, and he had no objection to the tapes being played on Monday rather than Friday.

The day was far from over. Adam Moore made a motion for mistrial, arguing that the state had made promises to Tuffy Pleasant that they would not use a portion of the statements he had made against him if he should ever be tried for murder. In Brimmer's testimony, he had mentioned that two other people (unnamed) had been arrested and charged with murder before being released. The defense insisted Brimmer had breached their agreement and demanded a mistrial.

The motion was denied, although Loy ordered the jury to disregard Brimmer's statement.

"You cannot unring a bell," Moore said ominously.

As an offer of proof, Jeff Sullivan prepared to call Stoney Morton, one of the coterie of young wrestlers who had made up Gabby Moore's social circle. Chris Tait objected on the grounds of hearsay and irrelevancy. Morton's testimony would not be a happy thing for the defense. He had accompanied Gabby Moore on a visit to Tuffy in Ellensburg the previous October. At some point, Gabby and Tuffy had told Stoney to go out and "start the car." He had done so, but as the two had come out of the dorm, Stoney had overheard a conversation.

"I got out of the car," Stoney had told investigators, "and I heard Tuffy say, 'But they will *know* it was a black man.'"

"No," Gabby had said, "not if you wear a full-faced ski mask."

The defense prevailed, at least for the moment, and Stoney Morton was sent back to Yakima, to testify, perhaps, on another day.

Although the jury was unaware of decisions being made over the weekend of August 21-22, those days marked the most agonizing part of the whole trial for Prosecuting Attorney Jeff Sullivan. And it all concerned lie detector tests.

At the time, only three states in America allowed polygraph results into a trial without stipulation (agreement) by both the prosecution and the defense. Several lie detector tests had been given to both Tuffy and his brother by Dick Nesary, the Yakima police polygrapher. And, ironically, the tests tended to suggest that Tuffy was telling the truth and Anthony was not.

The defense team wanted Sullivan to agree to a stipulated polygraph, one whose results could be presented to the jury—no matter what the outcome was. They were prepared to call in an out-of-state polygraph expert, Dr. Stanley Abrams, to administer the test to Tuffy. Adam Moore and Chris Tait were obviously confident that Tuffy would pass this *fourth* and *stipulated* polygraph test, confident enough to offer the results to the jury.

Jeff Sullivan's first impulse was to say no to the stipulated polygraph. His case was flowing well, each witness building on the foundation laid down by the witness before. Unless Sullivan agreed to allow the fourth polygraph in, there would be no mention of any of the lie detector tests. A prosecutor's political reputation is built on his win-loss record, and this was a huge case, particularly for a thirty-two-year-old newly elected prosecuting attorney.

But, for Jeff Sullivan, there were other factors more compelling than winning for the sake of winning.

"I was in the middle of a trial," Sullivan recalled, "and I knew I could lose it all. But, morally, I could not risk convicting an innocent man."

After wrestling with the dilemma all weekend, Sullivan agreed to the stipulated polygraph. Everything in him agreed with Vern Henderson that Tuffy's taped confessions *were* the real truth and that the polygraph by someone totally unconnected with the case or the Yakima Police Department would substantiate that. And yet, if Tuffy should *pass* the lie detector test, Sullivan's case would be dead in the water.

It was an awesome risk. But not as awesome as the prospect of convicting an innocent man without giving him every opportunity to prove his innocence.

Jeff Sullivan's decision proved to be the correct one. Dr. Abrams, a defense witness, was impressive. It was Abrams who had given a lie detector test to Patty Hearst (although the results were not allowed into her trial). His credentials were impeccable.

Abrams had examined the lie detector test results that Dick Nesary had administered to Tuffy and Anthony Pleasant. He had found that the first two tests given to Tuffy were "inconclusive" and he thought the third was leaning "slightly toward the truth." Like Nesary, Abrams found Anthony's test more untruthful.

It was all moot. The jury never heard Abrams testify. They lingered all of Monday morning in the jurors' room, curious about what was going on in the courtroom.

Dr. Abrams was to have administered a fourth—and definitive—polygraph examination to Tuffy Pleasant that morning. However, after the pretest conversation with Abrams, Tuffy asked for some time to think. After fifteen minutes, he spoke to his attorneys. He had decided he didn't want to take the polygraph from Abrams, after all.

The defense team, who had been so anxious to have Prosecutor Jeff Sullivan stipulate to this polygraph, now backpedaled. They went back into the courtroom and told Judge Loy that *they* would not now—or ever—stipulate to a new polygraph test.

"We will not agree to it," Adam Moore said.

The jury never heard a word about polygraph tests. Sullivan heaved a discreet sigh of relief. He had gambled on the side of his conscience and it had been the right way to go.

27

The state's case was drawing to a close. Vern Henderson testified just before the two taped confessions were played. Adam Moore and Chris Tait cross-examined Vern fiercely, suggesting that the witness had tricked Tuffy into confessing.

It didn't fly. Vern Henderson was perfectly willing to discuss his friendship with Morris Blankenbaker. There had been no vendetta on his part. All he ever wanted was the truth. He told of finding the casing ten feet from where Morris lay dying.

Chris Tait questioned why Tuffy had been put in a private cell the night of his arrest, and why he had given his confessions on two separate days. He suggested that Vern and Bob Brimmer had told Tuffy they were going to "pretend they were in court" and that a jury was listening to the story Tuffy was telling about the murders.

"Yes, sir," Vern said quietly. "He did say that to him." Vern did not remember every word of the conversation between Brimmer and Tuffy before the tape was turned on.

"Isn't it a fact that Sergeant Brimmer told him they would never buy his story, and that he didn't believe him?"

"Yes, he did say that."

"What did Angelo say about this game of 'pretend'?"

"What do you mean what did he say, sir?"

"How did he react to it?"

"He was telling him what happened—that's how. . . . He told a story and Sergeant Brimmer told him that there weren't any facts to back it up. . . . He couldn't tell us where he was between two o'clock A.M. and three o'clock A.M." [the night of Morris Blankenbaker's murder].

"And you told him 'There aren't any facts to back up your story'?"

"We told him to *give* us some facts to back up the story."

Chris Tait had a slight touch of sarcasm in his voice as he questioned Vern Henderson, but he didn't shake the young detective.

949

Vern had a cleanness in his testimony that no amount of cross-examination could sully.

Yes, Tuffy had trusted him, but Vern had promised nothing, ever. He had bought Tuffy a hamburger and a Coke, but Tuffy had repaid him.

"Did you loan him more money?"

"Bought him a Coke out of the pop machine. . . . Loaned him a quarter."

"Why was it that you didn't participate in this pretending session that Sergeant Brimmer was the jury and Angelo was telling his story?"

"Because *he* was talking to him, sir. He was the chief investigator. He didn't need both of us talking to him at the same time."

"You didn't take any part in that at all. You were just kind of along for the ride, sir?" Tait mimicked Henderson.

"I wasn't along for the ride, sir. I was sitting there listening."

"Did you call *Angelo* 'sir' every time he answered a question the way you are to me this afternoon?"

"I really doubt that, sir."

The gallery laughed, and Judge Loy rapped for order. There had been so little to laugh about in this trial.

Tait kept trying to box Vern Henderson into a corner, to get him to say that Tuffy had been tricked—promising him that he could continue his education in prison. "Tell us about that conversation," Tait directed.

"He was concerned about he was going to have to go to jail and lose out on all of the things that he really wanted in life—that he was working hard for his school and stuff."

"Did you tell him that you would help him with his education?"

"He was told by Sergeant Brimmer that there were programs he might get into . . . we would try to make a request . . . if it was possible. That's all."

Scornful, Tait asked, "Did you tell him to trust you?"

"No. I didn't use the words 'Trust me.' *He* used the word that he trusted me."

The tapes that Tuffy Pleasant and his attorneys now wished to recant played to a hushed courtroom. This was powerful direct evidence, the sound of Tuffy's voice speaking of the coach he had once revered. "We were tight. In my book, he was Number One. . . . I would do anything for the man, just not to see him hurt."

Tuffy's voice detailed the last moments of Morris Blankenbaker, and then the last moments of the man who had planned both murders. These tapes that had long since become familiar to the attorneys and the detectives were riveting and horrifying to the gallery. The jurors' faces remained unreadable.

"Everything was his idea." Tuffy Pleasant's voice cracked.

"Mr. Moore had this plan laid out, right?" Vern Henderson asked.

"Yes, he had it all laid out. To the bone. *To the bone.*"

"How do you feel?" Vern Henderson's voice asked, as the second tape came to an end.

"I don't," Tuffy said stoically. "Because I really just did it for him."

"What else?"

"I was under the influence of him all the time, you know," Tuffy said wearily. "I was on *his* mind track. I wasn't on mine."

As a defense, would it have flown? Murder by brainwashing? Mind control? Perhaps. Perhaps not. But it might be too late now. Adam Moore and Chris Tait had gone with a straight "Our client is innocent" defense.

Now, Adam Moore leaped to his feet and asked for a dismissal of the murder charges in the death of Gabby Moore—or, at the very least, a reduction to manslaughter.

"The facts before the court clearly proclaim the involvement of Gabby Moore as the prime mover behind this whole sordid mess, this whole sickening sequence. He's the grand artificer about everything that we've heard in court. He brought it all about. There isn't a scintilla of evidence that Angelo Pleasant intended the death of that man, not a bit, not a scrap, not a tidbit, nothing."

Chris Tait argued that Gabby Moore had never intended to die, and that the defense believed that Tuffy never intended to administer a fatal wound.

"He was supposed to *live.* That's why the telephone was off the hook, so that Mr. Moore could crawl across the floor with the bullet wound in his shoulder and call for help. We know that he wanted to live because it was with the bullet wound, the attack on his person, that he hoped to convince Jerilee that he was innocent of his prior involvement. . . . He was *supposed to live.* He wanted very much to live. He wanted to get Jerilee back. . . . [Even] taking it in the light most favorable to the state, it's got to be by some magical, mysterious process that we turn it into evidence of premeditation. It isn't by any logical process that any of us are normally acquainted with. It's by some other process that I will never understand as long as I live. That's not premeditation."

Ahh, but it was.

And Jeff Sullivan had the evidence in the defendant's own words. Tuffy Pleasant had been afraid of the power Gabby Moore held over him.

"It seems to me," Sullivan began, "there are a number of logical inferences from the evidence that indicate that Glynn Moore was killed premeditatively and Angelo Pleasant intended his death. . . . Glynn Moore contacted Angelo on Christmas Eve. Angelo came up there and he threatened him. *He threatened him.* He said, 'Angelo, go get that gun and shoot me or I'm going to turn you in for the death of Morris Blankenbaker.' So he went and got that gun. I think his exact words were, 'I will put your neck on the chopping block if you don't do what I say.'"

Sullivan pointed out that the defendant was supposed to shoot Moore high in the left shoulder. "He also told the police that the shot came from six or seven feet away. I submit, Your Honor, that Exhibit fourteen shows the bullet hole of entry in the body of Glynn Moore not high on the left shoulder but seven or eight inches *below* the left shoulder. The testimony of Dr. Muzzall is clear—from twelve inches or less."

> VERN HENDERSON: Well, this is the plan?
> TUFFY: Well, it wasn't a plan. I just did it.
> VERN HENDERSON: Now, you did this because he had you up against the wall, or did you do this because this was mainly a plan he had?
> TUFFY: I really did it because he had me up against a wall. I really believed he had me.

"Angelo realized," Sullivan said firmly, "that if he didn't eliminate Mr. Moore he was going to be able to use this threat of exposing him for the death of Morris Blankenbaker, and he would keep it over him for the rest of his life. And he adopted some of Mr. Moore's philosophy: *'If you got a problem, eliminate the problem,'* and he eliminated him. As soon as he shot him, did he try and help this man that he loved so much? No, he didn't help him. He ran."

Jeff Sullivan submitted that the evidence of premeditation was in place to support the first-degree murder charges.

The prosecution rested.

At nine the next morning, Judge Loy ruled that he would not reduce the charge against the defendant in Gabby Moore's death.

Coydell Pleasant began the defense case. She was in an untenable position. If she stood up for her son Angelo (Tuffy), she endangered Anthony. And vice versa. She testified that Anthony had only visited Angelo once in jail, and he said he was "nervous" after Angelo was arrested. She said she and other family members had encouraged Angelo to tell the police everything.

In tears, Coydell Pleasant said that Angelo had told her about Anthony during one of her visits to the Yakima County Jail. "He told me, 'Mom, it's going to hurt you, but Daddy raised us up to tell the truth.'"

It was almost as if Coydell believed that if *two* of her sons shared the guilt of the murders, each would pay only half the penalty. Her testimony was clearly a desperate—and heartbreaking—attempt to protect both Tuffy and Anthony. In the end, her words had little impact.

It was Tuffy Pleasant who would be the main defense witness. Handsome, with a broad grin that seemed completely without guile, Tuffy proved at times to be a garrulous, even charming witness, as he recalled his rise to fame under Gabby Moore's tutelage and his glory days. Despite the fact that he had been in jail for six months, he was still in peak condition. If he had been brought down by the long months of waiting for trial, he did not betray it. It was almost as if Tuffy Pleasant believed he were going to walk away from the courtroom a free man.

To do so, of course, he would have to implicate his own brother and his own best friend.

Adam Moore clearly wanted the jurors to get to know his client as a person, rather than as the defendant in a double murder case. Tuffy obliged by recalling the high points of his life. "My senior year I took second in state. Coming up my sophomore year and my junior year, I was a two-time state champion in freestyle wrestling."

"In what weight class, Angelo?"

"My sophomore year, it was one hundred thirty eight and two pounds on would be one hundred forty. As a senior, I wrestled at one hundred fifty eight pounds."

"Would you say that the height of your athletic career [was] going to Japan?"

"Japan and Hawaii, yes."

"And you fellows competed for the honor of being on that team to represent Washington?"

"Yes—the best in the state."

After Tuffy had established his commitment to sports, Moore asked him about Gabby. "Now, how did your relationship with Talmadge Glynn Moore develop during your high school years? You have said that he recruited you as a small boy from junior high school and he developed you into a wrestler good enough to go to Hawaii and Tokyo. How did your relationship with the man grow—*if* it did grow during this time?"

"I feel that it was a tight relationship."

"'Tight'? Was that the word? What do you mean by that?"

"By 'tight' I mean that it went a little further than just teacher and student or coach and student. I could visit him and we visited as friends."

Tuffy likened Gabby to a father—a *strict* father figure who demanded that his athletes, including Tuffy, stuck to spartan training rules. He said that Gabby had continued to oversee his wrestling progress even when he went off to Columbia Basin College.

Moore asked about Tuffy's children with René Sandon.

"We have two." Tuffy smiled.

"Names and ages?"

"Reneshia Naomi Pleasant* is four years old . . . Melenae Tonyia Pleasant* is two months old."

The dark shadow of two murders lingered at the edge of the courtroom as Moore asked questions that were easy to answer. Slowly, he moved into Tuffy's relationship with his brother Anthony. This too Tuffy characterized as "tight." He could not say how his younger brother felt about him.

The logic of Moore's question was emerging. Tuffy was the older, self-sacrificing brother. Anthony was heedless and greedy.

"We went out together quite a few times. But whenever he needed a car, he would always come and ask for mine, or else my older brother—but usually it would be mine. I would let him have it."

"You would let him use your car?"

"Yes, I would cancel my night just so he could have fun on his night because I felt there's always time for me to do my thing, so he can go on and do his thing."

"Did you ever talk to him the way Mr. Moore was talking to you about direction in life and motivation and that kind of stuff?"

"Yes. *Yes.* I always tried to steer him forward and I felt he could be better than me and his older brother and our cousins, you see, because I felt that he had a lot better potential."

"Did you ever talk to Mr. Moore about Anthony in this vein?"

"Yes, and we felt the same, that he could be the best of all of us if he just put his mind to it, and really strive for it and work for it."

"If he just put his mind to it?"

"If he just put his mind to it."

"But he didn't stay in the program, did he?"

"No, he didn't."

"He strayed from the path that you followed, didn't he?"

"Yes, he did."

"Did he keep the training rules?"

"No, he didn't. . . . I just tried to help him out. I said that's not really the way to do it, and I tried to give him explanations why not. . . . I never held nothing against him."

Was it possible that Adam Moore had gone a bit too far? Some gallery watchers rolled their eyes, as if a chorus of Salvation Army singers were about to emerge and say "Amen, brother." Tuffy was being painted with a very, very broad brush of goodness.

Kenny Marino, Tuffy's longtime best friend, whom he had also fingered as a murderer, was the next subject discussed by the witness. Moore asked about how close Tuffy and Kenny had been after they were in college.

"Were you tight then? Were you close?"

"Yes, I would say we were very close. I took him in as another brother; I loved him just as much."

"You had accepted Mr. Moore as kind of a second father and Mr. Marino as a substitute brother?"

"As *another* brother," Tuffy corrected.

But Moore elicited testimony that Kenny Marino had dropped out of school and seemed to Tuffy to have no goals in life.

Once Anthony's and Kenny's characters were found lacking by Tuffy as he sat on the stand, Moore moved on to the disintegration of Gabby Moore's ethics and values. There was no question at all of the defense strategy. They were attempting to let all blame slide off Tuffy Pleasant's broad shoulders.

It was a plan, but was the defense underestimating the jurors' intelligence? Jeff Sullivan had been mightily impressed with this jury. He studied them, wondering as always what they were thinking, and realizing as always that he would not have a definitive answer to that until they came back with a verdict.

Tuffy was telling them now about his shock at finding Gabby Moore "on the skids" in the autumn of 1975, of how he had tried to help him by putting in a driveway for him and helping to coach the high school wrestling team. This testimony sounded sincere. There seemed to be little question that Tuffy Pleasant had cared about Gabby Moore, that he had been slowly drawn into Gabby's madness.

"He was telling me that they [he and Jerilee] had gotten a divorce. He started telling me about the good times they had, and that she had left him and went back to stay with her former husband—that he had hoped she would make up her mind pretty soon. Maybe in a couple of weeks, she would make up her mind and she would be back with him."

"Was he optimistic that she might come back to him?"

"Yes."

"But he was planning to sell the house?"

"Yes."

"Because she left him?"

"Yes."

"Would it be a fair statement that he was unsure whether she was going to come back or not?"

"I don't know. I don't feel I could answer that."

"You don't know what was in the man's head at that time?"

"No, I don't."

"Did you notice a change in him between Labor Day and Thanksgiving?"

"Yes. He was changed. He wasn't like Mr. Moore, the one I used to know, and I could hardly ever talk to him unless he was drinking. Usually what was on his mind was Jerilee, and he always would talk about Jerilee. . . ."

This jury of Seattlites had never heard of either Gabby Moore or Morris Blankenbaker before the trial. Skillfully, Adam Moore sketched in all the connections between Gabby and Morris and Tuffy and Morris and Gabby. Tuffy said he had met Morris years before when Morris was the lifeguard at the Washington Pool. He had talked to him there and known him through the years at wrestling practice. Tuffy acknowledged that relations between Morris and Gabby had not been good.

"Mainly it was Moore toward him [Morris], wasn't it?"

"I felt it was, yes."

"Now, Moore started talking about Blankenbaker being in the way and that sort of thing. Did he talk about actually killing him?"

"Well, he talked about a problem, see, and that Morris was presenting a problem to him at the time. And so then he started talking about eliminating the problem."

Apparently, Tuffy had forgotten that Jeff Sullivan had used that "eliminating the problem" quote from his taped confession the day before when the prosecutor was successful in keeping first-degree murder charges in force against Tuffy.

"Did you know what he meant by that?" Adam Moore asked, unruffled.

"No," Tuffy answered. "Not until later. I was still trying to understand where he was coming from as a matter of speech."

"You didn't understand he meant having him killed?"

"Eventually, that's what he meant."

"What was your position on that?"

"Well, my position was I felt that he should forget about it—because he was an older man. . . . Eventually he could forget about the situation and latch on to another lady, form another relationship with another party."

"Did you tell him that?"

"Yes, I did. He said all he wanted was Jerilee. That's all that was on his mind."

Tuffy described the impasse he and his former coach had come to in late October. Gabby drank and talked about Jerilee. "He had him a few glasses down and he started talking about Jerilee. And I told him he should just try to forget about the woman—like I was repeating myself also. And then he started getting down. He would break out his pictures—"

"Pictures?"

"Yes."

"Was this the album Sergeant Brimmer was talking about? There were two albums found in the bedroom there. Is that what he meant by pictures?"

"Yes, and then he would play some music that he would say he and Jerilee had a good time to. It stood out in his memory and he played the music over and over."

"What else happened this particular night?"

"Then he started talking about Morris. Then he came out and he finally told me—he was finally to that point to have Morris eliminated."

The facts had not changed from the statement Tuffy had given to Vern Henderson, the facts the jury had heard on the tape. It was up to Adam Moore now to work his rhetorical magic and turn his client, the defendant, into the hero of this American tragedy instead of the shooter.

It would be a gargantuan task even for the best criminal defense lawyer in Yakima County.

But that would wait until the morning. It was five P.M., and Judge Loy was strict about letting the jurors go home at a reasonable time.

The trial was in high gear though, and he announced that he would begin court a half hour earlier in the morning.

Tuffy Pleasant was back on the stand the next day. Adam Moore asked him to relate the events of one Sunday in the first part of November—a few weeks before Morris Blankenbaker's murder.

"How long were you at his [Moore's] house that day?"

"About a couple of hours—two hours."

"Okay. Just tell the jury about everything that you remember about that two hours, will you?"

"I got there and Mr. Moore was drinking. He asked me when I stepped through the door, 'Why don't you go ahead and pour yourself a drink?' So I went ahead and poured myself a shot or two. Then he watched TV and he turned the TV down and then he started talking.

"And he started talking about Jerilee again. And I was just listening, you know. I wasn't going to tell him too much. I was already trying to talk to him. I was just waiting until he finished because he just continually kept talking and then you kind of interrupt him. I noticed at the time I interrupted him he would get mad and jump right back at me and say, 'Well, I'm talking. Just wait until I'm through talking and then you can give me your response.' But then he kept carrying on and he finally said, 'Well, I can't find nobody to do it.' And then he asked me if I would do it. I told him, 'No,' I wouldn't do it. I wouldn't even think about doing it. I felt that he was a grown man, and I said, 'You are a grown man and you are asking me to do this for you. Now, I would do a lot for you but shooting somebody—that's something else.' "

Gabby had gotten angry, Tuffy testified, and he had tried to calm him by giving him the name of someone who might do it, just to stall.

"I felt I was trying to talk him out of it."

In this new recanted version of events, Tuffy said that Gabby had said he would try to get in touch with this man—another former wrestler of his, but a few years older than Tuffy. Then he had suggested that Joey Watkins might do the shooting.

"He was talking about having a professional hit man come in and do the job, and I says, 'No, you are really getting carried away with this.' "

Tuffy testified he left, only to return a week later to find Gabby more obsessed with his plan to kill Morris. "I said 'No—and don't ask me again,' and he didn't ask me again."

"Okay. Up until which time?"

"Up until the night Morris got shot."

On that Friday night, Tuffy's revisionist version was that he had come home from college, met Joey Watkins and agreed to a blind date with Joey's girlfriend's friend. He then went back to his fiancée's house. (Tuffy apparently saw nothing wrong with having a pregnant fiancée, and a daughter—*and* a blind date with another woman.)

While he was at René's house, he *had* received a call from Gabby who was in the hospital. "He wouldn't tell me what was wrong with him. I asked him three or four different times. He said, 'I'm in the hospital and tonight would be a good night to shoot Morris—if you know what I mean.'

"I says, 'Well, I have got other things planned for tonight. I'm going out tonight for myself and you are just going to have to take care of yourself, and I'll see you later.' And I hung up on him."

Tuffy testified that he had asked his fiancée to find out which hospital Gabby was in so he could go up and visit him. Then he had kissed his fiancée and left for his blind date. But even though he had met Joey Watkins, he said they had only spent ten minutes talking to the two women. Later, after several trips to Watkins's house, the Red Lion, the Lion's Share, and around Yakima in general, Tuffy testified he had met the trio from Pasco and joined their party.

Joey Watkins had said, "Well, man, things are pretty slow tonight so you might have you a catch over there—so why don't you just go on. I can take care of myself."

There were refinements to Tuffy's recall of Friday, November 21. Now, he testified that when he had gone home sometime in the evening to borrow some money from his mother, he had met up with his brother Anthony for the second time that night. He said that he told Anthony about Gabby's phone call instructing him to shoot Morris, and Anthony had agreed with him that it was "odd."

Back with the Pasco group now, Tuffy testified they had all gone to the Thunderbird to dance. "We were dancing and I met some people—schoolteachers. Mr. Pryse and another schoolteacher— Mrs. Pryse. She used to be Mrs. Moore."

"Anything significant between you and Gay Pryse at this time?" Adam Moore asked, trying to keep this peripatetic story in some kind of order. "Just some small talk, wasn't it?"

"Small talk, yes."

"You didn't communicate to her how her husband was acting—or ex-husband, I mean?"

"No."

The quartet had returned to the Red Lion, Tuffy said, and he had finally parted from them after looking for an after-hours place. He had then gone back to Joey Watkins's house. He was packing his clothes to return to Ellensburg when his brother Anthony came to Joey's.

"I saw he had about four cans of beer, and he asked me what I was doing and I told him I was figuring to leave and go up to Ellensburg to a party. And, well, he asked me, 'Why don't you—Let's go riding for a bit and let's go have a drink.' . . . I said, 'Okay, I will go riding; I will drink a beer with you.'"

Adam Moore suddenly backed up. He had not asked Tuffy Pleasant about the gun! Now, he did. Tuffy nodded and agreed that he had gotten a gun from his cousin Loretta. But his version of that transaction was vastly different from her statement *and* from his taped confession. Tuffy testified that he had gone to see Loretta, bought her some groceries, spent the night, and been awakened by— ironically—"firecrackers going off in the back."

"I went to the backyard and she was there looking at the garage door. I saw a couple of holes she was looking at. I don't know if they came from the gun or not. I saw some potato peelings on the ground and I saw some smashed on her face. Then I asked her whatever she was doing, and she said she was just shooting the gun. . . . I looked at the gun, and says, 'Well, I will buy it from you' because earlier in the night she told me she was in debt. . . . She needed money pretty bad to pay some of her debts."

"Did you buy it?" Moore asked.

"No, I didn't. I just took it from her and I told her I would pay her later. I thought I would make some money in Yakima, you know, make a few extra dollars."

"Sell it?"

"Yes."

Tuffy said that he had slipped the gun under the front seat of his car. Under the driver's side.

"Did your brother know that?"

"Well, he knew I had the gun. Earlier when I was down at my girlfriend's house, I had showed it to him and asked him if he knew anybody that was interested and he said yes, he did."

Tuffy specified that Anthony had seen the Colt .22 under the bucket seat of his car a week earlier.

Adam Moore had brought it all together. The gun. The car. The two brothers. And now, Tuffy explained how he had suddenly become aware that they were "apparently" driving up to Morris Blankenbaker's house.

"Why do you say 'apparently'?"

"Because my brother asked me to slow down. Eventually, as time went on, I found out it was his house.

"He asked me to slow down. He says he wanted to see if Morris was home. I says, 'This time of the morning, you know, nobody is going to be up. You don't go visiting at this time in the morning.'"

But Tuffy said Anthony said he and Morris were "pretty tight" and that he would get up.

"He saw that the car was missing, and that 'Morris isn't home, so apparently he's at work.'"

"What happened next?" Adam Moore asked.

Tuffy gave a long answer about his younger brother's concern with Gabby and Jerilee—saying that Anthony wanted to talk to Morris about it. He had just assumed that Anthony knew Morris better than he himself did. They had driven by the Lion's Share and saw Morris come out to his car. And then, at Anthony's insistence, they had returned to North Sixth Street.

"We went down the alley and . . . I saw Morris going through the gate. We were walking a little bit faster, a lighter trot. We were coming around the back of his garage and I had seen Morris just about up to the front of his house and I had called him. I called him, and apparently—"

Adam Moore cut in quickly. Tuffy Pleasant had unconsciously slipped into the first person.

"*Okay.* You called Morris then—or you *had* called him?"

"I called him then."

Tuffy's attorney let it go; it was better than drawing attention to the slip. "What did you say?"

"I said, 'Morris—'"

"And what happened next?"

"Apparently I took it he didn't hear me, and my brother hollered at him. He said, 'Morris! Morris!' . . . Morris turned around and he saw us and he came back. He said, 'How are you guys doing?' And I said, 'I'm doing all right. How are you doing?' He said, 'I'm doing pretty good.' And I didn't hear my brother say anything, and then he asked Anthony, 'How are you doing, Anthony?' He said, 'I'm doing all right.'"

The courtroom was very quiet. Everyone listening knew what was going to come next, and no one wanted to hear it. Whoever had been there, whoever had pulled the trigger, the ending was going to be the same.

"And then," Tuffy went on testifying, "there was just a little light conversation. Morris had kind of relaxed himself on the gate and Anthony said, 'Well, it's about Jerilee.' And then Morris kind of stiffened up and told him, 'Well, I don't want to hear nothing from you or nobody else about Jerilee, and if I hear anything from you or anybody else about Jerilee, I will see to it they don't say nothing else.' And then he kind of stiffened up and took a step toward us."

"Did he have anything in his hand?"

"He had a beer bottle in his hand."

"And then what happened, Angelo?"

"Well, when he took the step, next thing I know it, I heard the shot. I saw some fire, and I saw him turn, I saw his head turn."

"Who was holding the gun?"

"My brother Anthony . . .

"I don't know if I saw the second shot or not, but I saw some fire and I took off running . . . down the alley, headed north toward my car."

"Where was your brother?"

"He was right behind me. Well, probably not *right* behind me but I heard his footsteps."

Tuffy's voice was full of emotion as he described how shaken he had been. "I didn't turn on my car lights. . . . I was scared and I just took off from there and went on down First Street. And I was telling my brother, I said, 'Look, I don't know what happened back there. Just don't tell me nothing,' and I took the gun from him and I told him, 'Just don't tell me nothing, but I'm not going to be able to vouch for you tonight. If you say anything to anybody that I saw you tonight about this time I'm not going to be able to tell them nothing.'"

"Did you say anything to him about taking the blame?"

"Yes, I did. I told him if it came down to it, and if my name came up first that I would take it."

"Take what?"

"The blame."

Jeff Sullivan had written steadily on the long yellow legal pad in front of him as Tuffy testified. He had seen slight flaws and then widening tears and finally huge gaps in Tuffy's latest version of the death of Morris Blankenbaker. If Tuffy had been so anxious to protect his younger brother and his best friend, why was he telling it all now, placing the blame squarely on their shoulders?

Sullivan was anxious for the time to come for cross-examination.

28

Before Jeff Sullivan could cross-examine Tuffy Pleasant about this new scenario on the death of Morris Blankenbaker, he had to sit through a new script about the shooting of Gabby Moore on Christmas Eve. Tuffy said he had still visited Gabby and heard the same obsessive discussion about how Gabby would win back Jerilee, the conversation becoming increasingly maudlin as his coach drank bourbon mixed with Pepsi or Kool-Aid—or straight, if he had nothing else. The more he drank, Tuffy testified, the more hostile Gabby became. Interestingly, Tuffy himself seemed to have become hostile too—hounded as he was by Gabby.

"Angelo, how would you characterize Gabby Moore's demeanor when he would discuss with you his situation with Jerilee?"

"I would say it wasn't working out too good. . . . You couldn't say nothing to him. He would just get upset or holler at you."

"Did he cry?"

"I saw him cry one time—one time earlier. And then the night that he was shot."

"Okay, let's talk about Christmas Eve. Let's start in the morning."

Tuffy moved through his day, going into agonizing detail about all of his visits with René, his family, his cousins. He finally arrived at the evening hours when he was at a party at Stoney Morton's house.

"Who was there?"

"Stoney, his lady friend, my brother Anthony, Stoney's younger brother . . . I was there. . . . We were sitting down and looking at a game on TV and drinking a little bit. There was this knock at the door . . . and it was Kenny Marino."

"Then what happened?"

"He came in. He didn't say 'Hi' or nothing. He just said, 'Angelo, Mr. Moore would like to see you up at his house as soon as possible.' And I told him, I says, 'Look, now don't be ordering me like that. I'm out here trying to visit people and I'm just not going to up and run and go visit somebody else just because they ask somebody to come see where I'm at.' And he said, 'Mr. Moore would like to see you as soon as possible.' And I said, 'Well, I see him when I get around to seeing him. . . . I'm not going to rush for nobody.' "

He testified that Kenny had left after "cussing him out." Tuffy said that Mr. Moore had called him at René's house, saying, "Tonight's the night if you know what I mean."

"I said I didn't know, and he says, 'Why don't you come up and find out?' I was getting ready to take my lady friend out, but it was eating away at me, so I talked with my lady and then I left and went on up to Mr. Moore's house."

"What time did you get there, Angelo?"

"Between eight-thirty and nine."

Gabby had been dressed nicely, Tuffy testified, and he had kicked off his shoes and told Tuffy to pour himself a drink. Tuffy testified that Moore had said that he couldn't wait any longer, that this was the night he wanted *himself* shot.

"He asked me if I would do it. . . . I told him, no, I'm not going to do it. And he says, 'Yes, you are. You're going to do it.' "

"How did he want himself shot?"

"High in the shoulder, left shoulder. He wanted an attempt to be made on his life. He figured that was the only thing—if it was made on his life like it was made on Morris, he figured he could get Jerilee back in a couple of weeks or even before the first of January."

Although Tuffy had insisted he would not shoot Gabby, he testified that Gabby said, " 'Well, I'll see to it that you get the blame for Morris Blankenbaker's shooting.' And I didn't tell him I didn't do it. I didn't want nobody else to know [about Anthony] not even him—*nobody.* . . . And he says, 'Well, I will see to it that your neck is on the chopping block for Morris's death.' And I says—well, I don't know what I really said. I was kind of quiet. He asked me if I knew where the gun was—was it close, and I said it was nowhere around here. And he said I was lying. . . . I said, 'I don't know where the gun is—it's gone. It's a long ways from here. . . .' "

Gabby had said he would gas up his car, Tuffy testified. "I said, 'It's a long way from here and it's buried.' " That, he said, didn't stop Gabby, who said they could take a shovel. When Tuffy still refused, he said Gabby had picked up the phone book and showed him the police number.

"He dialed the digits down to the last one. He asked me if I was going to do it. . . . I said, 'I'm not going to do it,' and he dialed the last digit and so I says, 'Okay, I will do it.'"

Tuffy said he still thought he could talk Gabby out of it until he dialed that last digit, and then he realized his old coach "wasn't playing."

Vern Henderson had heard this before. He wondered what spin Tuffy was going to put on it this time. So far, it was almost verbatim with that was on the tapes. Yes, Gabby was going to "put down" a lot of whiskey while Tuffy went for the gun—just as it had been in the first confession.

"I told him," Tuffy was saying, " 'You can't take the shot, because I don't think even I could,' and I felt I was a little bit stronger than he—just on street strength-wise. But he was a bigger man than I was and I told him, 'I don't think you could take the shot.' I was trying my best to talk him out of it. And he said, 'No, this is what I want and this is the only way to get Jerilee back.' "

Gabby had accused Tuffy of stalling for time. Gabby had ordered him, "Go get the gun."

"Did you go get the gun?"

"Yes, but I told him that he was talking crazy, completely crazy."

Now, as Jeff Sullivan and Vern Henderson listened for the slightest straying from the tapes, they heard Tuffy veer off.

"What happened then?"

"I had parked in front of another car, and I was waiting, talking to myself. I says, 'Well, I'm not going to do it no matter what, but I will take the gun in and show it to him anyway, just to see if it would calm him down—and see if I can talk to him a little bit more.' "

But while he was waiting, Tuffy said he honked twice, and he had seen his brother Anthony and a friend drive by. Then they went in Moore's house.

"Did you go in the house?"

"Yes."

In this version, Tuffy said that he had tried to get his brother and his friend to help him get Gabby out of the house, to go visiting or to a tavern. But it didn't work. Gabby was "as drunk as I've ever seen him. He was swaying back and forth. He could hardly stand."

After the others had left, Gabby took off his shirt, his shoes, and started talking about Jerilee. He broke out his photo albums. He was single-minded about what he wanted done.

Emotions washed across Tuffy Pleasant's face as he testified. There was little question that he was remembering a desperate night. There *was* a question about whether he was confabulating—taking a real event and rewriting it so that it emerged in a manner favorable to him. He could not have been making this monologue up; he didn't seem that sophisticated. But it was quite possible he was weaving self-serving "memories" into what had really happened at Gabby Moore's apartment on Christmas Eve.

The phone rang twice, but Gabby wouldn't say who it was. Tuffy said that Kenny Marino had appeared a short time later. But Kenny had stayed in the house while Tuffy was walking Gabby around the backyard. Tuffy testified that he'd managed to get his coach out in the backyard for air only to have Gabby order him to shoot him there. Tuffy said he refused and Gabby stumbled back into the house.

"Where was the gun?" Adam Moore asked.

"In the house—on the right side of the daveno on the floor. I was kind of upset because he [Gabby] saw where I put the gun because he was looking right at me when I put it down there. I don't know if he was in a daze or looking past me."

Tuffy said he was thinking then of "bookin'" (leaving) and letting his friend Kenny deal with their old coach. But then he had remembered the gun was in the house. "I can't leave without the gun. My keys are in the house, my coat was in the house, so I says, I'm going to go back in there. I'm going to talk to this man one more time and if he doesn't come around, I'm leaving."

"And so," Tuffy continued, his voice taut, "as I went stepping through the door—I just opened the door—there was a shot. Mr. Moore was on the floor and Kenny was just lowering the gun."

In hours and hours of testimony, Tuffy had explained away all of the blood on his hands. His brother Anthony had killed Morris; his best friend Kenny had killed Gabby. He himself had just happened to be in close proximity to both murders.

Pleasant's attorneys called for the noon break, and Judge Loy agreed but cautioned the spectators in the gallery to sit in their seats and say nothing until the jury filed out.

When the jury room door was shut tight, Adam Moore and Chris Tait voiced their concern about the way Jeff Sullivan would present testimony on the defendant's recanting of his original confessions. Without the jury present, Tuffy took the stand again and said he felt that Vern Henderson and Jeff Sullivan had been dishonest with him by pretending to believe him when he implicated Anthony and Kenny as the guilty ones. Now, he felt he had been tricked.

Sullivan reminded Tuffy he had always told him that—if he was not telling them the truth—Tuffy would be tried for the murders. The defendant's attorneys had been present and aware of every step of the case. Faced with Sullivan's questions, Tuffy backed up, admitting that he had been warned what would happen if he was lying to the detectives and the prosecuting attorney.

In truth, Jeff Sullivan and Vern Henderson *had* believed Tuffy's recanting, enough so that Anthony Pleasant and Kenny Marino had been arrested. But, as witnesses and forensic evidence failed to validate Tuffy's version and did nothing to connect the other two suspects, they had changed their minds.

Tuffy Pleasant's direct testimony continued for hours. Adam Moore ended it on a poignant, dramatic note. He asked Tuffy to tell the jury about Gabby Moore's trophy case.

"[He had] wrestling trophies, trophies he had received from different teams that were sentimental to him as a coach, pictures of his different teams, pictures of his different companions throughout the years that he was coaching there at Davis High School. Pictures of his son, the baseball team he played on and their national team that they had last summer."

"What did Gabby tell you Christmas Eve about the trophy case?"

"He said, 'Some people live and strive for what I have here'—and he pointed to his trophy case—'to have a lot of trophies to really make something out of themselves, but I have a whole trophy case full and I have what I wanted in that department and in my other department I would like Jerilee.' What he wanted was Jerilee; that was his biggest goal."

"How old were you at the time?"

"I was twenty-one."

"How old was he?"

"Approximately forty-four."

"Did you shoot Morris Blankenbaker?"

"No, I did not."

"Did you at any time intend for him to die?"

"No, not at any time in my mind did I intend for Morris Blankenbaker to die."

"Did you know that your brother was going to kill him?"

"Not at no time did I know that my brother, Anthony Pleasant, was going to shoot Morris Blankenbaker."

"Did you shoot Talmadge Glynn Moore?"

"No, at no time did I shoot Mr. Moore."

"Did you want Mr. Moore to be dead?"

"No, I did not."

Angelo Pleasant and his attorneys had taken a calculated risk when he decided to testify. Now, the danger was at hand. Jeff Sullivan rose to cross-examine Tuffy.

There were so many lies and half truths to cut out of the defendant's direct testimony and hold up for the jury to see. Within the first few minutes of Sullivan's cross-examination, the first lie popped up. Tuffy admitted that he had lied to police about the time he had left Gabby Moore's house on Christmas Eve.

"Actually," Sullivan moved in, "the first three or four or five contacts that you had with the police you admitted whatever you thought they already knew. Is that right?"

"Yes."

Regarding the February 27 and 28 taped confessions, the prosecutor asked, "Anybody beat you or force you to make those statements?"

"Didn't nobody beat me."

"Did they force you to make the statements?"

"No force."

Grudgingly, Tuffy answered questions about Gabby Moore's plans for murder.

"He talked to you about those plans, didn't he?"

"He talked *at* me."

"But you listened, didn't you?"

"I was there in his house."

"He had a plan to kill Morris Blankenbaker when he came home from work, didn't he? . . . How many other plans did he have?"

"Two other plans. Every Tuesday, Morris went to the 'Y' with his son—and to have him shot in front of his son, Rick, but if Rick wasn't with him to just shoot him going to the 'Y' and to take out his wallet and make it look like a robbery. And another one that I remember was that Jerilee and Morris went to work about five minutes apart in the morning. After Jerilee went, [I was] to park off of Naches and to walk up to the house . . . and knock on the door."

"And actually shoot him at the front door?"

"Or step into his house . . ."

The final plan had been the one that transpired. Only Tuffy denied that he had been the shooter. He was certainly familiar with all the details. "He suggested to me that *whoever* did it—that he would like him shot once by the heart and once—if he fell, then to walk up to him and put one in the back of his head."

"And you shot him in the head?"

"No."

"He *was* shot in the head?"

"Yes."

"I mean he was shot just like that plan, wasn't he?"

"He wasn't shot in the heart," Tuffy blurted, "so I feel that's not exactly like what he was talking to me about."

"I see," Sullivan said sarcastically. "Just three times in the head. Is that right?"

Sullivan's cross-examination was adroit; at the first sign of an opening, he pounced. The defendant was so busy straining at gnats that he forgot to show "appropriate" emotion where he should have. The gallery could see that, and surely the jurors could.

And the lies and semi-lies. There were so many.

Tuffy admitted he could have easily reached Morris's house from the Chinook Hotel in five minutes. He knew there had been three shots in Morris's murder, but he could not remember how he knew. He gave three or four scenarios, weakening his impact with each new reason. He couldn't remember what he had said in his taped confession. In retelling, he confused the order of his own statements.

Jeff Sullivan was like a boxer looking for an opening. When he found one, he jabbed. He caught every hesitation, every contradiction. Tuffy Pleasant was on the ropes, confused and wobbling.

"You are trying to tell me that he [Gabby] didn't have it planned very well?"

"I felt he didn't—I'm right here this very day on charges."

"Oh, I see. I see. Your conception of the plan is that it is very good if you don't get caught?"

"No. I did not do it."

"He told you where he wanted the man shot . . . and he told you where you could park your car. . . . And he told you the layout of the back of that house? Right?"

"Yes."

"But he didn't tell you *where* the house was. Is that right?"

"Well . . . he *mentioned* where it was."

"Why did you testify here today . . . that you didn't know where he lived? That it wasn't until Anthony told you that you found out where Morris lived?"

"I did not exactly know which house he lived in."

Suddenly, it was five o'clock. Sullivan would have happily continued all night, but Judge Loy would not. The rhythm was broken, but the prosecutor would pick it up in the morning.

29

And so he did. If Angelo Pleasant had been engaged in a wrestling match, he could have detected where his opponent was going to move next. But he was not a debater and he seemed to have no inkling of when Jeff Sullivan was about to catch him up in yet another inconsistency in his testimony. Time and again, Sullivan winnowed out a lie.

Adam Moore finally stood up and complained that he didn't want Sullivan reading from Tuffy's earlier statements and then pointing out that his client was lying. Judge Loy asked Sullivan to rephrase his questions.

It didn't matter. With each slip, Sullivan repeated what Tuffy had said—and repeated it incredulously, or derisively, or with amusement—and sometimes with a question mark. The carefully reconstructed events of Tuffy's testimony began to buckle. It could be only a matter of time before the whole construction imploded and fell back on Tuffy.

From time to time, Sullivan had Tuffy read his earlier confession silently to himself. Sweat beaded on the defendant's forehead. There was no way to mesh what he had once said with what he was now claiming.

"Angelo," Sullivan said, "are you saying that this statement was not true?"

"Yes, I'm saying that."

"Even though you were telling your lawyers and telling me that this was the truth?"

"Some of it."

"Some of it. Some of what you told us after you were arrested then was not true; is that what you are saying?"

"Well, I was still on my own, Mr. Sullivan, wasn't nobody looking out for me but myself."

"So you chose to tell us something that wasn't true?"

"Well, I don't know what my thinking was at the time."

Sullivan had elicited testimony that seemed to suggest that Tuffy had felt nothing about Morris Blankenbaker's death but fear that he would be caught. But Gabby was another matter entirely. His coach had been so much a part of the defendant's life for so long. Sullivan needed to focus on a heedlessness, a failure to grieve, on Tuffy's part as Gabby lay dying.

"Angelo," he began, "at that time Glynn Moore was lying on the kitchen floor, you didn't know whether he was dead or alive. You indicated to us he was one of your best friends, and you were no *more concerned* than just to go to a party. Is that right?"

"Yes, I was concerned."

"But you *went* to a party?"

"Later on, yes."

"Angelo, as you saw Mr. Moore lying there after '*Kenny* shot him,' why didn't you try and help him?"

"Mr. Sullivan, I was scared and I didn't want to be caught in the house; I had the gun in my hand."

"But you didn't shoot him, did you?"

"No, I didn't, but I had the gun in my hand."

"You didn't call an ambulance for him?"

"No."

". . . Now, Mr. Moore's plan was that he would be wounded with that same gun, but he was supposed to get to a doctor soon, wasn't he? So that he wouldn't get injured seriously?"

"He was going to call one of his lady friends—or he felt that he was strong enough to take the shot and go across the street and talk to the lady who owned the house—"

"That was Jerilee's sister?"

"Yes . . . I was telling him, 'You can't do it.' "

"He's laying there on the floor—not moving. Didn't you say that you heard him groan or something?"

"When I was leaving."

"When you were *leaving*?"

"I heard a noise."

"Did you look back to see what was happening?"

"No, I was trying to get out of there."

Stubbornly, despite being confronted with his oft-repeated statement that Gabby Moore had "his neck on the chopping block," Tuffy denied that he had thought about the danger of Gabby exposing him as a killer. "I did not shoot Mr. Glynn Moore," he insisted.

"You intended to kill him, didn't you, Angelo?"

"I did not kill Glynn Moore. And it hurts me just to sit up here and to listen to you, Mr. Sullivan—with all due respect to you—and keep accusing me and accusing me and I didn't do it. I really loved that man. But at the time when I did leave, when Kenny did shoot him, I was scared and confused and I just thought of leaving and not being caught on the premises."

When Jeff Sullivan turned away at last from Tuffy Pleasant, he had effectively revealed the truth. Tuffy had shot Morris and he had shot Gabby. But had he shot Gabby, intending to kill him? Or had he merely been following Gabby's orders? It was still impossible to tell. But he had left. That much was clear. Perhaps Tuffy could not look that fact straight in the face. Perhaps he could not allow himself to recall stepping over Gabby's body, hearing his last gasps for life, and walking away.

In the end, Tuffy *had* deserted "The Man," his mentor, his hero, his friend, his role model. In a sense, Gabby had deserted Tuffy too. Together, they had made wrestling championships their only goals. But Gabby had no longer cared about the glory of winning.

On recross, Adam Moore asked Tuffy again about Gabby's complete defection from all they had believed in.

"Well, he was talking about the trophy case," Tuffy answered. "Some young men—also some young ladies—[he said] who are pretty good in sports and have pretty good ability to achieve, all they had to do was try hard. He said he was forty-four years old and that he felt he was over the hill. That trophies didn't mean nothing anymore—his biggest goal and trophy in life was Jerilee . . . and that I was pretty young and I didn't know what he meant, but when I was older, and time went on, I would realize what he meant."

Tuffy Pleasant had been on the witness stand for three days. He had clung to his position that his brother and best friend were the true killers, but their testimony and the rebuttal testimony of more than a dozen witnesses would place both Kenny Marino and Anthony Pleasant well away from both crime scenes. Jeff Sullivan knew that, and he was not concerned.

When Tuffy had stepped down from the stand, the trial began to wind down rapidly.

On Saturday, August 28, Adam Moore and Chris Tait and Jeff Sullivan made their final arguments. Two weeks before, they had promised the jury that they would give them certain facts. And they had all stayed close to their opening statements.

Prosecutor Jeff Sullivan's voice boomed through the small courtroom and bounced off the walls as he reconstructed the entire trial, the evidence that had, he said, pointed to only one man. Sullivan focused on Tuffy's taped confessions. "He learned from Glynn Moore that when you get a problem," Sullivan said, "you *eliminate* the problem." The prosecutor called Morris Blankenbaker's murder a "contract killing."

"Gabby Moore was killed to shut him up."

Despite Tuffy Pleasant's open and affable appearance, Jeff Sullivan said he was cold. "A man who could shoot two people and then go to a party . . . that's callousness. That's why he could come into this courtroom and say what he did. This man would have us believe that he missed [hitting Gabby high up in the shoulder] from twelve inches away. He shot him . . . and then where did he go? He picked up his girlfriend and went to a Christmas party."

Adam Moore for the defense said he had "utter contempt" for Gabby Moore for drawing Anthony and Angelo Pleasant and Kenny Marino "into the sewer."

Moore's face and words were full of rage as he characterized Gabby as "vile and despicable." Everyone in the courtroom jumped as Tuffy's chief lawyer bellowed, "GOD! The worst tragedy of this is that he isn't sitting here today. I blame him for the whole mess."

Adam Moore literally vibrated with anger. "I have for two weeks seen the prosecutor stand before you and tell you to convict this man on two counts of first-degree murder. . . . I could puke," Moore said as he slammed his fist on the table in front of him.

The gallery jumped again.

Adam Moore, an attorney with a courtroom demeanor that long predated the antics of a Johnny Cochran, grew suddenly calm. He walked to Tuffy Pleasant and placed his hands on his client's shoulders. "I apologize for the emotion, but it's real," he said with his voice cracking. "It's the way I feel."

As he asked for an acquittal on both counts, Moore pleaded, "Let it be done with. Let Gabby Moore's end be his just reward."

It was over for the gallery, for the regulars who had shown up for the trial every day. Many of them would probably not have enough forewarning of the verdict to get to the courtroom in downtown Seattle in time to hear it read.

Fourth Avenue, just outside the King County Courthouse, was quiet. It was a Saturday, and Saturday trial sessions were a rarity. Few cars headed north up the one-way street. There were no pedestrians. The courthouse was closed except for the trial just ended. It was still hot but the sun was blocked by the courthouse, and its warmth came up only from the sidewalks where it had baked all day while the lawyers inside talked on and on of death and blood and guilt.

It didn't seem possible that two weeks had gone by. All trials are engrossing, but this one had been more compelling than most, and the gallery straggled out, reluctant to have it over. All the players had been unknown entities when the trial started. Now, they were almost as exposed as family members sometimes are. So many secrets told.

At the corner of Fourth and James Street, the sun blasted through the gap in the buildings built along James up from Eliott Bay, but the air suddenly felt sweet and cool.

High up in his cell in the jail, Tuffy Pleasant waited to hear what his future would be. He thought of "time."

The eight-woman, four-man jury retired that Saturday evening and deliberated for close to five hours before stopping for the night. Judge Loy had instructed them that they had several options. They could consider first-degree *and* second-degree murder in the murder of Morris Blankenbaker. In Gabby Moore's killing, they could choose between first-degree and second-degree murder, *and* manslaughter.

Unless they came back with the two acquittals that Adam Moore had asked for, Tuffy would, indeed, be doing heavy "time."

The jurors were sequestered in a hotel that Saturday night. They began deliberation again on Sunday. They had an awesome task, and they knew that whatever their verdicts, no one would win. They deliberated all day Sunday and, shortly before six in the evening, they signaled that they had finally reached a verdict.

It was obvious that several of the jurors had been crying. Not a good sign for the defense. And it was not. Jury Foreman Earl Willey read the verdicts. The jurors had found Tuffy Pleasant guilty of first-degree murder in the death of Morris Blankenbaker and guilty of manslaughter in Gabby Moore's shooting.

Tuffy was impassive when the verdicts were read, but his mother and his fiancée burst into tears as did many of the jurors. He would not be sentenced on this night, but he faced a maximum sentence of life imprisonment on the murder charge and twenty years for manslaughter. He was returned immediately to his jail cell on the tenth floor of the courthouse.

Jurors, waiting for the elevator, hugged Coydell Pleasant. "This was the hardest day of my life," one juror said, and another sobbed,

"I'm sorry . . . I'm so sorry," as she put her arms around Tuffy's mother.

"Just as long as you were honest," Coydell Pleasant said, "Just as long as you were honest, that's all I can ask."

One juror, an airline flight attendant, leaned against the marble wall and cried uncontrollably. Another, who also had tears streaming down her face, told a reporter, "It was the law. We had to do it. It was the law. It was the goddamned law."

Other jurors led the woman away, and a bus took them all back to the hotel where they had stayed the night before. They had come to trial knowing nothing about Tuffy Pleasant or Morris Blankenbaker or Gabby Moore. Now, they would never forget them.

Sentencing was set for Friday, September 10, 1976, in Judge Carl Loy's Yakima County Superior Courtroom. Under Washington statute, Loy could, technically, still grant Tuffy probation, or he could sentence him to the maximum. For first-degree murder, the maximum would be twenty years with one-third off for good behavior, meaning that Tuffy would have to serve thirteen years and four months before he would be eligible for parole. The maximum for manslaughter (while armed with a deadly weapon) was also twenty years. Jeff Sullivan said that he would ask that the sentences be served consecutively, rather than at the same time.

After hearing arguments, Judge Loy sentenced Angelo "Tuffy" Pleasant to the maximum on each count, but acceded to the defense's request that the sentences run concurrently. In the best of all worlds for Tuffy, he could be released by late 1989.

On September 17, Tuffy was taken from the Yakima County Jail in chains and delivered to a prison bus which would take him to the Washington State Prison facility in Shelton. He flashed his familiar grin to newsmen as he left the jail.

Afterword

Since books on criminal cases usually follow hard on the heels of a conviction, readers seldom find out what happened "later." One advantage of my lack of confidence in my ability to write a "whole book" back in 1976 is that I came to know the rest of the story—or "stories"—over the intervening years. Life *does* go on, even after the most horrendous tragedies, even after so much heartbreak. When Talmadge Glynn "Gabby" Moore fastened his obsessive eye on Jerilee Blankenbaker, his hell-bent manipulations ultimately changed the course of many lives. Nothing was ever the same again, but people went on, following the new paths that loss and grief had cut out for them.

Vern Henderson continued working for the Yakima Police Department. He regretted that Tuffy's father, Andrew, Sr., blamed him for everything, but he was not surprised. He had known it would be this way, but he had had no choice.

One of the cases assigned to Henderson in the late seventies involved a robbery ring. He solved that case and saw the perpetrators convicted. They swore they would get revenge. And they did. Vern's house was firebombed and reduced to rubble. He didn't care about the furniture and other replaceable items, but he lost a lot of photographs and sentimental possessions. It was too much. Just as his house had burned, Vern had "burnout."

In 1978 Vern Henderson resigned from the police department and accepted a job working security on the Alaska Pipeline. He spent eighteen months in the vastness of Alaska. It proved to be a healing time for him. He dealt, finally, with losing Morris and with having his world blown up both literally and figuratively.

In 1980 Vern came back to Yakima where he would spend the next decade as an investigator for the Public Defender's Office. Since the early 1990s, Vern Henderson has worked for the Attorney General's Office in both Washington State and, currently, in a southwestern state. At present, he is assigned to fraud cases, white-collar crime, and internal investigations.

The little kid from Shreveport, Louisiana, has carved out a remarkable career and is a credit to law enforcement. He is in his early fifties—as Morris would be, had he lived.

Sergeant Bob Brimmer is retired from the Yakima Police Department and, at last, has time to go fishing whenever he wants.

Yakima County Prosecuting Attorney Jeff Sullivan has held that office for six terms. He is a past president of the Washington Association of Prosecuting Attorneys as well as being one of the most reelected prosecutors in the state of Washington. Yakima County has burgeoned and Sullivan now supervises thirty attorneys and seventy civilian employees. Somehow he found time along the way to help his wife raise four children, to coach AAU basketball teams—both boys and girls—Grid Kids Football, and to be a lector in his church. His thick blond hair is now thick white hair and he is a grandfather. His oldest son is an accountant; his youngest an army lieutenant. One daughter is a successful television producer and the other a civil attorney.

Although Sullivan has tried many, many cases since the Pleasant trial, it remains "one of the top ten of all the cases I've handled in over twenty years. It stands out as a highlight of my career. There was so much involved," he comments. "A good blend of scientific investigation, good detective work, interesting legal aspects—particularly the polygraph question." Sullivan acknowledges that the local celebrity of the principals and the "love triangle" helped to make the case unforgettable. "This has always been one that you remember. I've tried to explain this case to people and they just stare at me. They can't believe it really happened. But then truth *is* stranger than fiction. In the end, the reason we were able to solve it was because 'People don't keep secrets.' You can count on that."

Sullivan's deputy prosecutor, Mike McGuigan, practices law in Hawaii.

Adam Moore is still one of the best criminal defense attorneys in the state of Washington, and he and Sullivan cross swords regularly. As this is written, they are preparing to meet in court once again. Neither could tell you how many trials this will make. Adam Moore is also a longtime friend of Vern Henderson's. At the time of the Tuffy Pleasant investigation and trial, no one knew it, but Adam and Vern ran together every noon. By tacit agreement, they did not discuss the case they were each immersed in.

Despite gossips' smug predictions that Jerilee's marriage to Jim

Littleton would never last, they have been happily married for more than twenty years. They lived in Yakima for many years after they were married. Jerilee became a successful stockbroker while Jim built a huge wholesale produce business. Eventually, the Littletons moved over to "the coast." In Seattle, Jim's enterprises expanded even more.

It wasn't really surprising to me that Jerilee was reluctant about an interview to talk of the tragic events of the midseventies. Finally, we did meet briefly, and I saw that she had changed from the vulnerable, shocked young woman I had watched testify at Tuffy's trial. She was still beautiful, but it was a sophisticated, mature beauty. She stood straighter and she seemed taller, with her shining dark hair drawn into a French roll atop her head. She had clearly become a woman in control of her life, a world away from the teenager who had walked into a bank in Tacoma in 1965 and asked for a job.

Jim Littleton accompanied Jerilee to our meeting. He had grown handsomer as he reached forty and he was obviously very much in love with Jerilee. He was not eager, however, to have his wife recall bad days of long ago. Although they had never had children together, they had raised Jerilee and Morris's children, Rick and Amanda. Rick, taller than Morris by six inches and as attractive as a movie star, had gone into business with Jim. Amanda was going to college in Seattle, studying to become a teacher. Both of the children had grown up to be happy, well-adjusted adults.

I did not blame Jerilee for demurring when I asked about her feelings after the murders of Morris and Gabby. Those days were all in the past for her and whatever regrets she might have had, she chose to keep private. She said that she might want to talk to me in depth one day. I never heard from her again, however.

Amanda and Rick remained close to Olive Blankenbaker, their paternal grandmother. Married and living once again in Yakima, Amanda gave birth in February 1996. The baby would have been Morris's first grandchild.

Mike Blankenbaker, Morris's half brother, joined the Yakima Police Department. Although there were no blood ties between Mike and Olive, he gradually became her son too. He understood how much she missed Morris, and tried to be there for Olive.

René Sandon, Tuffy Pleasant's fiancée and the mother of his two daughters, gradually distanced herself from the lover who had never been entirely faithful to her. With new confidence, she went to college, earned her master's degree, and became a school counselor. Tuffy's daughters grew up to be fine young women.

Joey Watkins, the huge but gentle wrestler who had been so much help to Vern Henderson in the investigation, also went to college and is now a teacher.

Kenny Marino, Tuffy's best friend *once*, has vanished from Yakima. No one can say where he is or what he is doing today.

Coydell and Andrew Pleasant, Sr., held their heads up proudly in Yakima, but nothing was ever the same for them. Their son Anthony lives in the house next door. Their other children finished college and prospered. A few years ago, Andrew, Sr., nearing seventy, put a ladder against his store so he could climb up and fix the roof. While he was working, the ladder fell. Always a robust man who was used to working hard and being in good shape, Pleasant didn't call for help. Instead, he attempted to jump from the roof onto the bed of his truck. He fell short and was badly injured. He died in the hospital without ever seeing his middle son again as a free man.

Angelo "Tuffy" Pleasant, who had dreamed of being a teacher and a coach, did not get out of prison in 1989. He served six years more, spending almost twenty years in prison. Given the choice, one wonders if he would not have traded his few moments in the sun as a state champion for a normal life—a free life. Gabby Moore had filled his head first with ambition and hope, and then with paranoid plots. When Gabby fell to earth, so had Tuffy.

Two decades ago, Gabby had told Tuffy, "You don't understand what I'm feeling now, but when you are middle-aged—over the hill—you may." And now, Tuffy Pleasant is forty-two years old, one year younger than Gabby Moore was when he declared that Jerilee was the only trophy that mattered to him. *Does* Tuffy understand? Perhaps. Perhaps not. No one would blame him for being bitter toward his old mentor. Gabby, at least, had a life, a wife—*two* wives—children, a magnificent coaching career. Tuffy, who "hurt" when Gabby "hurt," has had twenty years behind bars. How many times must he have realized that "The Man" cared nothing at all about *his* future or *his* dreams?

Out of prison, but on probation, Tuffy scarcely resembles the perfectly muscled young athlete he once was. Twenty years of prison food and confinement have piled on untold pounds. No one looking at his newspaper photographs in 1976 could recognize Tuffy Pleasant today. Probation authorities have noted Tuffy as "a good candidate for rehabilitation," and have recommended schools and programs.

Olive Blankenbaker lived to see her son's killer sentenced to life in prison. She had not asked for any more time than that. In trying to convince me to write this book, she gave me a number of her precious photographs of Morris. I accepted them, but I told her I didn't think I would be able to sell a book to a publisher as I had no track record. She said she understood.

I didn't hear from Olive over the next few years, and I concluded, sadly, that she had succumbed to lung cancer; I knew she had accepted her "terminal" diagnosis. Ten years later, I was giving a lecture at Yakima Valley Community College. By that time, I had published six books and I spoke often on topics such as serial murder and high-profile offenders. Afterward, I was signing books in the school library when I glanced up to see a woman who looked quite familiar. I stared at her, thinking, "No, it can't be. She looks so much like Olive Blankenbaker."

As the woman came up to the table, she smiled at me and said, "Yes, it's me. I didn't die after all."

Olive had one request beyond a signature; she still wanted me to write the story of her son. I promised that I would try. Over the last ten years, I have visited with her often in her mobile home in Yakima. She still grows flowers and she pampers a family of cats. Olive and Jerilee have long since made their peace with one another. Jerilee, Rick, and Amanda are in close contact, worrying about her and helping out when they can. When Amanda moved back to Yakima, she became her grandmother's strongest support.

Mike Blankenbaker still drops by often to see Olive, and pictures of Mike in his Yakima police uniform sit on Olive's piano next to wedding pictures of Olive and Ned, childhood photos of Morris, and photographs of Olive's grandchildren.

Nevertheless, Olive never forgot her pleas to me to write "Morris's story."

And so, at last, I have kept my promise. After twenty years, it wasn't easy to track down people who once lived in Yakima, Washington, some scattered to the four winds. For this book is not just Morris's story—it is the story of many others as well.

Yakima's houses, buildings, and streets are all still in place—some a little shabbier—some freshly painted. Only last week, I walked down the alley behind the big frame house on North Sixth, walked south from where Tuffy Pleasant parked his car on Lincoln, past the window where Gerda Lenberg heard the hollow heels of a running man, and into the backyard where Morris Blankenbaker died in the snowstorm. The wire fence where Vern Henderson found the vital bullet casing is, amazingly, still there.

I could almost hear a voice calling, "Morris! Morris . . ."

Olive Blankenbaker is eighty-five years old. I am grateful to her for waiting for me. This is for you, Olive.

The Highway Accident

There is such a thing as a perfect murder. Any detective will admit that some homicides are never recognized for what they are. All of the popular sayings such as "Murder will out" and "There's no such thing as a perfect crime" are the stuff of fictional mysteries. Although the advent of the space age of forensic science is shifting the odds to the side of law enforcement, there will always be murderers who are never caught. And there will always be murders that are written off as something else.

The rule of thumb followed by an experienced homicide detective investigating an unexplained death is that he must look skeptically at what may very well be a crime scene. First, he must suspect murder, and next suicide, and then accidental death. Only when he has exhausted all other eventualities should he decide he is looking at a natural death.

Even so, some cases of murder do slide through savvy investigators' tightly woven nets of suspicion. The case that follows, one of Oregon's most memorable investigations, might never have come to the attention of homicide detectives if sharp-eyed state policemen and apprehensive neighbors had not raised questions. The incredible story that evolved shed harsh light on a marriage that seemed happy despite the fact that its very fabric was riddled with lies and betrayal.

The sounds coming through the bedroom wall in the duplex apartment in suburban Salem, Oregon, were too loud and too disturbing for anyone to sleep through. It was very early in the morning on February 25, 1976, when both Marilee* and Doug Blaine* had the same dream, or rather, the same nightmare. Wrenched from deep sleep in the dark winter night, they sat up in bed. Doug fumbled for a light.

They could hear a woman screaming over and over, "No! No! Don't!" Then there was only silence, which was followed by a softer sound that was almost like a moan. That was suddenly cut short.

Blaine looked at the clock beside their bed and saw it was three A.M. He and his wife discussed what they should do. Although they had never heard the couple in the adjoining duplex fight before, they agreed that they were probably overhearing a domestic squabble. They hated to interfere in something that was none of their business. What should they do—go knock on the door in the next unit and ask, "What seems to be the problem?" Maybe pound on the wall? They couldn't phone because they didn't even know the last name of the people next door, much less their telephone number.

There were no more screams, now. They tried to get back to sleep, but Doug Blaine was troubled and he tossed and turned, watching bare tree limbs bend grotesquely over the streetlight outside as the wind pushed them.

After awhile, he thought he heard someone open the front door of the adjacent duplex. Blaine got out of bed and, without turning on any lights, crept to his living room. Feeling somewhat like a busybody, he eased out of his front door silently and stood in the frigid dark where he knew he was hidden by his car. Everything seemed perfectly normal. Both of the neighbors' cars were parked in the driveway: a Volkswagen bug and a Chevy Vega. Far off, a dog barked and the trees creaked in the wind, but there was no other sound.

Back inside, Blaine heard nothing but the ticking of clocks and the furnace blower. He crawled back in bed and he and his wife tried to go back to sleep.

It was quiet for about twenty minutes, but then they heard drawers being opened and shut next door, closet doors squeaking, and bedsprings settling. Beginning to feel like a fool, Blaine looked out his front window once more. This time, the man next door was carrying what looked like laundry or bedding to the Vega. He made several trips back and forth to the car. Then he got in and started it up. Without pausing to let the engine warm up, he backed out, accelerating as he disappeared down Cedar Court.

Wide-awake, the Blaines discussed what they should do. It looked as if their neighbors had had a spat and the husband had left to cool off. They didn't know the couple except to nod and say "Hi" when they happened to meet. The wife was always friendly, but her husband seemed aloof. If they didn't even know the couple's names, they certainly hadn't the faintest idea about the state of their marriage. The only times they had heard any loud noise from the other side of the wall was when the couple had parties, and that had not happened very often.

It was after 4:30 A.M. when the Blaines finally decided they should notify the police; they couldn't forget the screams they had heard. If the girl next door was all right they would feel a little foolish, but feeling foolish was worth peace of mind.

Their call came into the Marion County Sheriff's radio room at 4:47 A.M. Corporal Tim Taylor and Deputy Ralph Nicholson were dispatched to Cedar Court. They knocked on the door of the neat duplex, but there was no response. Since the Blaines didn't know their neighbors' last name, Taylor gave the radio operator the license plate number on the Volkswagen parked there and asked for a check on the registered owner. The owners came back as Lori Susan* and Walter Louis Buckley.* Taylor asked the operator to look up the Buckleys' phone number and telephone the residence. Soon, he heard the lonely sound of a phone ringing again and again in the empty apartment.

It there was anyone inside, they either would not—or could not—answer the phone.

The Blaines were positive that the woman who lived next door had not left with her husband in the Vega. They pointed out that her car, the Volkswagen, was still parked there. Tim Taylor contacted the man who owned the duplexes. Even though it was still very early in the morning, he said he would be right over with a key to open the door for the deputies.

The door to the Buckleys' duplex swung open and the deputies stepped in. They saw that the place was immaculate. Tentatively, the two sheriff's officers peered into each room, calling out the Buckleys' names. No one answered. There wasn't that much to look at; there was a living-dining area, a kitchen, and two bedrooms. The southeast bedroom looked as if it were being used for storage. A drawer had been left pulled out in one chest. Oddly, there was a pile of walnuts on the floor in front of it.

The master bedroom—the southwest bedroom—was the room that shared a common wall with the Blaines' bedroom. It was as neat as the rest of the house. The queen-sized bed had been stripped of sheets, and clean sheets rested atop the mattress as if someone had begun to change the bed linen.

There were no visible signs of violence. The missing bedding was something of a puzzle, but then Doug Blaine had said it looked as if Buckley had been carrying laundry to the car. Well, that's why twenty-four-hour Laundromats stayed in business. People did their laundry at all times of the day and night.

Even though he hadn't found anything suspicious inside the empty duplex, Tim Taylor radioed in that he felt there should be a recheck of the premises in daylight. "The occupants will probably be back by then," he said.

Taylor left his business card on the dining room table with a note asking the Buckleys to call the sheriff's office on their return. Then they could write the complaint off in a simple FIR (Field Investigation Report).

But there were no calls from the Buckley duplex. Six hours later, Deputy Bernie Papenfus returned to the Cedar Court address and knocked on the door. There still was no response. But now in daylight, Papenfus noticed a faint red spot on the front step. It looked very much like dried blood. Once again, the landlord, who had also felt strangely troubled since he had opened the door for the deputies at five that morning, produced a key.

Their voices hushed, Papenfus and the landlord entered the duplex. It was bright and airy; the sun was shining through the windows. The home had been decorated with charm and good taste, with paintings, plants, and a wine rack with bottles of homemade wine bearing the Buckleys' names. Wicker lamps and end tables complemented the furniture. There was nothing out of place in the living room—not even a magazine or newspaper.

They moved to the master bedroom. Papenfus's trained eye noted another reddish stain that was barely visible on the rust carpet in the bedroom. Still the room looked normal enough.

But cops see things that other people don't. Papenfus's throat tightened a little as he saw that the blue-flowered mattress was not sitting square on the springs. He raised it. The underside was a mass of bloody stains. Blood had soaked into the surface and it was still damp.

Hurrying now, Papenfus looked for more signs that something violent had taken place in this little duplex unit. He didn't have to look far. There were more dried scarlet streaks on the towel cupboard and on the entryway into the kitchen. The stains on the carpet were blurred, as if someone had tried to rub them out.

Deputy Bernie Papenfus had seen enough; something terrible had happened here during the night. Careful not to use the phone in the Buckleys' duplex, he radioed Sheriff Jim Heenan's office and asked that detectives respond to what could now only be considered a "possible homicide."

Lieutenant Kilburn McCoy and Sergeant Will Hingston left their offices in Salem and headed for the address on Cedar Court. Lieutenant James Byrnes, chief of detectives, and Detective Dave Kominek had left Salem very early to attend a narcotics conference in Portland. Enroute, McCoy radioed Byrnes to stand by because the circumstances at the Buckley home were most suspicious.

Byrnes would not be going to Portland, after all.

Kilburn McCoy learned that Lori Buckley, who was twenty-six, was employed as a sixth grade teacher at the Highland Elementary School in Salem. It was possible that she was in her classroom, teaching. That would explain why she was not in the apartment at eleven A.M. on a Wednesday morning. He called the school and learned that Lori Buckley was not there. However, she had arranged to have a substitute because she had a dental appointment scheduled for Wednesday morning. She was not due at school until the afternoon sessions. The school office staff didn't know her dentist's name. They gave the detectives the phone numbers for Lori Buckley's relatives, suggesting that they might know her dentist.

While they waited to hear from Lori Buckley's family, the Marion County detectives moved around her home. They found more and more bloodstains marring the otherwise immaculate apartment.

Whatever had happened here, the scene had to be protected.

Hingston and Papenfus strung heavy rope, cordoning off the entire property from the sidewalk back, and posted a sign that read, POLICE LINE: DO NOT ENTER. They half expected Lori and Walt Buckley to come driving up and ask them what in the world they were doing. But no one came by except curious drivers who gawked at the rope and the sign.

Finally armed with the name of Lori Buckley's dentist, McCoy called his office, only to find that Lori had not shown up for her appointment. It was to have been a preliminary session for a long-term teeth-straightening procedure. Lori's dentist was concerned when she didn't keep her appointment or even call. He said she was always thoughtful about calling to cancel if she could not make an appointment.

Lori Buckley's family arrived at her duplex, worried and completely mystified. They talked with detectives outside, since no one but police personnel could go in until the place had been processed. Her family said that Lori and Walt had been happily married for four years. Lori had been teaching since her graduation from Oregon College of Education. Walt was attending Oregon State University in Corvallis. He was about to graduate with a degree in accounting. Lori's folks commented that Walt had recently applied to become an FBI agent. He had told them about the fifteen-page form he had to fill out, laughing about what specific details the Bureau wanted to know about every facet of his background.

Asked if it was possible that Lori and Walt had gotten into a brawl, her family was aghast. They could not imagine such a thing. That just wasn't possible. Lori and Walt just didn't have that kind of a marriage. They had never known them to have *any* kind of physical confrontation.

The Marion County detectives wondered if it was possible that someone had entered the Buckleys' duplex during the night. Doug Blaine had admitted he didn't know the neighbors that well. He had seen a man going out to his neighbors' car and he thought it had been the man who lived next door, but he admitted he could have been mistaken. Could the Buckleys have been abducted by someone who had injured one—or both—of them?

Doug Blaine said he hadn't seen Lori Buckley at all. Just her husband with his arms full of laundry.

In whatever manner Lori had left her duplex, she wasn't there now. A thorough search of the apartment proved that. She wasn't in the closets or in the crawl spaces. She and her husband were both missing.

The detectives shook their heads. How could that be? How could the Blaines have heard screams on the other side of their bedroom wall at three A.M. when Lori was in an accident so far away? If they had been men who believed in ghosts, which *very* few detectives are, they might have come up with some otherworldly scenarios.

It took the Marion County detectives a number of phone calls before they established that Walt Buckley was alive but had been injured in the accident that killed his wife. The Oregon State Police said he had been taken to a hospital in Lincoln City in Lincoln County.

The next report that seemed connected to the increasingly peculiar case was a call from Sergeant Lee Miller of the Polk County Sheriff's Office. Polk County lies between Marion County and Lincoln County and the Buckleys would have had to pass through it to get to Lincoln City. Miller said a hiker had found a pile of bloody bedding—sheets, blankets, a bedspread, and a mattress pad—among the forest undergrowth along Mill Creek Road in Polk County. Jim Byrnes checked the description of the bed linen against that of the list of the bedding found in the Buckleys' duplex. He found many similarities.

Byrnes and Dave Kominek left Salem and headed over to the coast. Crime lab technicians went to Polk County to pick up and bag the blood-soaked bedding found along a narrow dirt logging road.

When Jim Byrnes and Dave Kominek arrived at the scene of the fatal traffic accident, the Buckleys' Vega had already been towed away. They parked at Mile Post 14 on Highway 18 at 4:20 P.M., aware that there was precious little daylight left. But they could see where the Vega had gone off the shoulder of the road. It had crushed vegetation when it went over the bank and then dropped about twelve feet through a thick stand of fir trees. The two Marion County investigators commented to each other that there were no skid marks or torn-up areas on the shoulder of the highway; there were only parallel tracks in the soft dirt and grass.

Oregon State Troopers Michael Luka and Wayne Price had been the first to respond to the report of the accident. A log truck driver had called for help over his CB radio. The trucker told the troopers that he had seen a man lying beside the road shortly after eight that morning. He had managed to call for an ambulance by relaying his emergency request through two other CB-ers.

"Then I got out of my rig and ran to help the guy in the road."

"Did he say anything?" Luka had asked.

The trucker had shaken his head. "He kept repeating, 'Lori. Lori.'

Then I looked down through the trees and spotted the green car down in there."

Luka and Price told the Marion County detectives that they found Lori Buckley lying outside the Vega. Her feet had been partially under the right door, and her head was resting on a pillow. Someone had covered her with coats. But Lori Buckley had been dead for a long time when the troopers got to her.

They had photographed her body where it lay in the fir forest, and then released it to a mortuary. Her husband, Walt Buckley, had been rushed to Lincoln City for treatment.

There was no question that the Walt and Lori Buckley who had been in the accident along the Van Duzer Corridor were the same Walt and Lori Buckley who lived on Cedar Court. But Jim Byrnes and Dave Kominek were still trying to figure out just *how* they ended up miles away, almost at the Pacific Ocean.

Walt Buckley had given statements about the accident to Trooper Price—both at the scene and at the hospital. According to Price, he had explained that he and his wife had left Salem the afternoon before. They had planned to drive to the coast for dinner. They had eaten at the popular Pixie Kitchen in Lincoln City. He said they had decided to drive south a short way to have an after-dinner drink at the lounge in the plush Salishan Lodge. Buckley told Price he and his wife had left for Salem about midnight. They were on their way home when the accident occurred.

Buckley said they had lain in the ditch beside the highway all night waiting for help. He had done what he could to make his wife comfortable and to keep her warm.

The ambulance attendant who had transported Walt Buckley told the detectives that Buckley had been very tense—so tense that he had held his arms tight against his chest. Both of his fists were tightly clenched and full of dirt and grass. He had kept his eyes closed and mumbled incoherently as the EMT checked him for injuries. Although he had appeared to be seriously hurt, his injuries had proved to be only superficial.

It had looked like a normal, if tragic, accident. At her husband's request, Lori Buckley's body was scheduled to be embalmed as soon as possible. However, the mortician who removed her body from the accident scene had been busy that Wednesday afternoon and several hours passed before he began the embalming procedure. He had just made the first cut—an incision into the femoral artery of the thigh— when the phone rang and Dave Kominek told him to stop immediately. *Nothing* was to be done to the body until the accident investigation was complete.

Kominek went to the mortuary and viewed the corpse of Lori Buckley. He noted immediately that she had suffered many, many deep cuts around her face and shoulders. It would take a complete postmortem examination to establish the cause of death, but her injuries seemed far too severe to have been sustained in a car wreck in which the vehicle was damaged as slightly as the Vega had been. There had been only minimal damage to the right front fender and grill. The windshield on the right, where Lori had reportedly been sitting, was shattered in a wide "spiderweb," but it had not been broken clean through. It was safety glass with no sharp edges that might have cut her face and upper body. Odd.

Kominek received the clothing that Lori Buckley had worn when she was found. He looked at the blood-soaked blue-and-white checked blouse and the jeans. There were no cuts or tears in the clothing.

Marion County detectives questioned even what seemed obvious. They interviewed personnel at both the Pixie Kitchen and the Salishan Lodge about the evening of February 24 to see if anyone remembered serving the Buckleys. The Pixie Kitchen, which was usually jammed with lines of people waiting to get in, had been rather quiet on Tuesday night, but none of the waitresses remembered serving the couple. One waitress said she would have remembered Lori particularly because she had been saving to get braces for her daughter and she noticed anyone with a similar dental problem. The Pixie Kitchen cashier said there had been no out-of-town checks or credit cards used by customers on Tuesday night.

The cocktail waitresses and the bartender at Salishan Lodge were positive they had not served drinks to the Buckleys.

It would be days before the widespread investigation could be coordinated and evaluated. Lieutenant Jim Byrnes wanted to talk to Walt Buckley. Maybe Buckley would have some explanation as to why the edges of his story didn't come together cleanly.

Byrnes talked first with the emergency room nurses at the Lincoln City Hospital. They had treated Walt Buckley at nine A.M. when the ambulance brought him in. One nurse said that his arms were stiff and shaking and that he had appeared to be in shock. He had cried out the same phrases over and over: "Lori—where is she? I couldn't stop. Lori yelled. I couldn't stop the bleeding," and "It's my fault."

"If he was acting, he sure was a good actor," the nurse commented. She said that Buckley had stared into space and cried intermittently as he was being treated.

One thing had been a little odd. Walt Buckley's feet had been very cold, as they would expect in someone who had lain out in the cold of a February night for hours. But his *body* was warm—so warm that his temperature was up one degree above normal. The staff had thought it was strange that he hadn't shown signs of hypothermia.

They had sedated Walt Buckley and he had grown a little calmer. He had talked of how he and Lori had gone out to have a nice dinner. He told them he was a college student, majoring in accounting. He had explained that Lori was supposed to be in Salem that morning so she could have braces put on her teeth. But when the nurses asked, "Was Lori your wife?" he had started to cry again.

Jim Byrnes had to wait until almost six before he was allowed to talk with Walt Buckley. A local physician checked Buckley to be sure that he was well enough to talk to Byrnes. As the doctor left Walt's room, he nodded his consent and said, "He wants to talk to you and is very alert."

Jim Byrnes had a fairly good idea what had happened to Lori Buckley. He didn't believe that Lori had been alive when the accident occurred; he felt she had either been dead or very badly injured when the Vega had pulled away from the duplex on Cedar Court at 4:30 in the morning.

Now, as Dave Kominek stood by, Byrnes read Walt Buckley his rights under the Miranda ruling, and the widower signed the MIR card as Byrnes questioned him casually about subjects unconnected to the accident. He wanted to be sure that Buckley was alert enough to be questioned about his wife's death. Byrnes was surprised to find him as stable as the doctor had indicated.

Asked what he remembered about the night before, Walt Buckley first repeated a version of the evening's events that, in essence, corresponded with what he had told troopers earlier. He said Lori had been very tired when she came home from school the day before. He had suggested that they go out to dinner so that she wouldn't have to cook. Lori had agreed happily to that, so they had driven over to the coast, leaving about six. He estimated that they had eaten dinner about eight at the Pixie Kitchen in Lincoln City.

"What did you order?" Byrnes asked casually.

"I had the salad bar plate, and Lori had the combination plate."

Then, Buckley said, they had gone to Salishan Lodge where they had after-dinner drinks and walked on the beach. Oregon beaches are wonderfully smooth and wide when the tide is out, and tourists walk on them all the time. But Byrnes wondered how many people might have wanted to be out there after ten at night with a cold February wind blowing.

He said nothing about his thoughts.

It had been very late, Buckley said, when they started home. Much too late, really. He hadn't realized how exhausted he was. He sighed heavily as he said that he had fallen asleep at the wheel.

"The last thing I remembered was Lori yelling 'Walt!' and then the car ran off the road."

Walt Buckley had tears in his eyes as he recalled how he had tried to help his wife. He had covered Lori up the best he could and tried to talk to her, but she hadn't responded at all. Finally, he had crawled up the bank to get to the road. He had hoped a car would come by and he could signal for help. But they had lain there for hours before the log truck stopped.

Jim Byrnes let silence fill the hospital room. Neither he nor Kominek said anything as Buckley stared down at his own hands. And then Byrnes told Walt Buckley that the sheriff's office had sent deputies to his home early that morning—and what they had found there. He asked Buckley if he and his wife had been lying next to the wreckage of their car after midnight, who was it who had been screaming and moaning in their duplex at three A.M.? Whose blood had stained their mattress and left telltale spatters around their house?

Jim Byrnes, whose flinty blue eyes had intimidated scores of suspects, watched Buckley's reaction. Despite the sedation, Buckley was nervous. Sweat dotted his forehead and he sighed deeply. Even so, while Walt Buckley began to modify his version of his wife's death in the accident—attempting to make his recall fit the facts he now realized the detectives knew—he refused to give a complete statement.

Instead, he talked *around* what had happened, coming close to something terrible and then veering off into extraneous detail. He admitted a great deal without really admitting anything. He said that he hadn't meant to hurt Lori. He talked about putting her in the back of the car, but then he mentioned that he thought he had heard her moan once as he drove through Salem.

The *back* of the car? *Salem?* Buckley had finally changed his story from that of the highway accident fifty miles from Salem, and Byrnes realized that he was talking about what had happened on Cedar Court.

"I drove to a doctor's office by the freeway but the lights were out," Buckley said weakly.

As Jim Byrnes and Dave Kominek stared at him, Walt Buckley repeated over and over again, "I was going home."

What did he mean by that? Had Buckley actually driven to the Oregon coast with his dead or dying wife and then changed his mind and headed toward his home? That was possible.

Walt Buckley was scared, worried about what would happen to him if he told the whole truth.

Byrnes asked him if he knew District Attorney Gary Gortmaker. (Gortmaker had arrived at the hospital a short while before. Gortmaker went to the scenes of homicides and worked side by side with detectives.)

"I don't know him but I've heard of him," Buckley said.

"Do you want to talk to him?"

Buckley nodded, and Byrnes and Kominek left the room.

Gortmaker pulled a chair up to Walt Buckley's bedside and answered his questions about the legal ramifications of the situation. After they had talked quietly for several minutes, Gortmaker stepped into the corridor. He told Jim Byrnes and Dave Kominek that Walt was ready now to tell them what had really happened to Lori Buckley.

The story that Walt Buckley told proved once again that no one can really know what goes on behind the closed doors of a neighbor's home. The most serene facade can hide turmoil beyond our most wild imaginings. What appears to be an ideal marriage can be, in reality, a bomb waiting to explode. As Walt Buckley spoke, the detectives quickly perceived that the neat and tastefully decorated duplex on Cedar Court had not been a real home at all, but only a stage where a massive deception was played out.

Walt Buckley admitted there were things in his marriage that even Lori had never known. He said he had managed to live two lives, not for weeks or months—but for years.

Their families, their friends, and Lori's school associates had been under the impression that they had had a perfect marriage. The Marion County detectives had already learned that in their preliminary interviews. Everyone they had talked to when they were searching for the missing Buckleys had described them as a loving couple.

Lori Buckley had always seemed happy at school and was a well-liked and competent teacher. She often talked about Walt's upcoming graduation from college. Although she loved her job, Lori had been eager for Walt to begin *his* career so she could resign from teaching and start having a family. Still, she had never seemed to resent the fact that she was the sole breadwinner in the marriage. She had not only paid the bills with her teacher's salary, but she was putting Walt through college.

And she had never mentioned any quarrels—not to her family, her friends, or other teachers.

As Walt Buckley began to talk about his *real* life, the detectives listening remembered that his and Lori's friends had described them as "a beautiful couple." They had both loved to play tennis, and several friends had recalled that Lori and Walt often did things on the spur of the moment, including drives to the coast. They had taken carefully planned vacations too; during the summer of 1975, they had gone off on a junket to Europe.

Everyone they had interviewed had told the investigators that Lori had been as cheerful as always on her last day at school. She would have been tired—just as Walt said in his first statement—because she had stayed late working on a chili dinner for the school. Detectives knew that she had left for home around 4:20.

No one—*no one*—had described Walt Buckley as a man with a temper or as an abusive husband.

However, as he spoke now, it became rapidly apparent he had kept many secrets from Lori. Yes, she had been paying his tuition and supporting him. She had believed that he was about to get his bachelor's degree in accounting. She had been so proud of him, and thrilled that he might become a special agent with the FBI.

But it had all been an incredibly intricate sham. In reality, Buckley had been dropped from Oregon State University in 1974—an academic suspension. He had then enrolled in Linn-Benton Community College, but anyone who checked his records would see that he hadn't completed any courses. He hadn't even paid his tuition. He had left home each morning with his briefcase as if he were going to school, but he didn't go to college classes. And he hadn't had schoolbooks in his briefcase; he had carried copies of *Playboy* and *Penthouse*. He spent his days as he liked, returning home at the right time had he been going to college in Corvallis which Lori believed.

There was more to Buckley's machinations than Detective Kominek already knew. In looking through papers in the Buckleys' duplex, seeking some clue as to where the couple might have gone, Kominek had discovered that Walt Buckley had been playing games with Lori's bookkeeping and their household accounts. It was apparent that each month, after Lori had written checks for the proper amount of the bills, she had given them to Walt to mail. But he hadn't mailed them; instead he had made out *new* checks for smaller amounts. This had left most of their bills only partially paid, with a growing accumulation of debt. Kominek had found many overdue accounts, and he had also seen where someone had altered the bills that came in so that this wouldn't be apparent.

It looked as if Walt Buckley had been "skimming" money from their joint bank account, but that was puzzling too, because he hadn't removed the money from the bank; he'd only written duplicate checks for lesser amounts. There was no explanation for that double-ledger bookkeeping, although he might have been planning to withdraw a very large sum at some future time.

Walt Buckley *had* filled out a fifteen-page application to the FBI, just as he had told everyone, and it was dated February 19, six days before he killed Lori. But he had never submitted it.

Of course Walt Buckley knew that the FBI wouldn't hire him. He had no college degree in accounting. He hadn't been going to college for two years.

Buckley continued his confession, describing the house of cards that had just grown higher and higher until it was bound to tumble. It may have been on the last night of her life that Lori Buckley finally discovered Walt had dropped out of school. There would be no degree for Walt, she would not be able to stop teaching, and there would be no babies. Worst of all, she discovered that the man she trusted implicitly had been lying to her for *years*.

Buckley said Lori had been angry at him that Tuesday night when she walked into the living room and found him "wasting his time watching television."

That's how it had started, at least in Walt Buckley's memory. The argument had been over television. He had fallen asleep on the couch watching the set, and she had turned it off and called him a "rotten whore." When he had fallen asleep, Lori had been sewing. He wasn't sure what made her so angry.

How long she had known the truth was debatable. It must have been a sickening shock for her to discover that all her plans had evaporated. They were behind in their bills and she wondered where all the money had gone. She had bragged to everyone about how well Walt was doing in college; she had even been planning a party for his graduation.

Walt said that Lori had been furious with him—angry enough to threaten to leave their home at three in the morning and go to her mother's house. When he walked into their bedroom, she had been slipping on her shirt. "When she told me she was going to her mom's house, I picked up the quart bottle and hit her until it broke."

"What kind of bottle?" Byrnes asked.

"I hit her with a Tab or Safeway Diet Coke bottle."

He wasn't sure just what kind of bottle it was. He said he recalled only that it was a clear quart bottle. "I don't remember if the bottle broke the first time I hit her or not."

He did remember that Lori had been sitting on the bed, and the bottle had been on the dresser.

"She was mad and wanted me to stop watching TV and go back to school. I didn't want to disappoint her. I got mad and hit her. I put pillows over her to stop the bleeding. Blood was everywhere."

Buckley said he had carried Lori and the stained bedclothes out to the car and headed out of town. But he was sure he heard her moan when they were driving on Cherry Avenue. He said he stopped in a parking lot, but when he checked her, she was dead. He knew he couldn't go home, so he had headed toward the forest in Polk County. He had planned to leave both Lori's body and the bedding deep among the fir trees.

"I couldn't leave her there," he said regretfully. Instead, he said he had dumped all the bedding and some bags with the broken bottles near Buell, Oregon. But he couldn't bring himself to leave his wife's body there or in the river.

Buckley said he couldn't face what he'd done and that he had taken a bottle and tried to kill himself. But he didn't have the nerve. And so he had driven farther and staged an automobile accident, deliberately driving his car off the road and over the embankment.

The windshield had not broken in the accident, so Buckley said he had broken it himself. Then he had lifted his wife's body and positioned it near the car. After that, he had crawled up to the road. He admitted he had told the troopers that he had fallen asleep at the wheel.

"Had you been drinking—taking drugs?" Jim Byrnes asked.

Buckley shook his head. "I only had one drink all day. I've never taken speed or barbiturates."

He had no excuse for killing his wife, not really. He said he had no medical problems, and he had never suffered from blackouts—he just knew there had been an argument.

Jim Byrnes arrested Buckley at 8:25 P.M.; a guard was placed outside his hospital room for the night until he could be returned to the Marion County Jail.

Part of the puzzle was solved. Lori Buckley's killer was under arrest, but the investigation wasn't over. The question of why Walt Buckley had struck out at Lori so violently bothered the detectives.

Dave Kominek attended Lori's autopsy. State Medical Examiner Dr. William Brady and Dr. Joseph Much, the Marion County Medical Examiner, performed the postmortem exam. Lori Buckley had suffered a number of deep, gouging wounds to her scalp, forehead, neck, nose, and shoulders and left upper back. There were no wounds below her breasts except for defense wounds on her hands and arms where she had tried valiantly to fend off the cutting edges of the broken bottle.

Lori would have been left terribly scarred from these wounds and she would have lost a great deal of blood, but, according to Dr. Brady, she would not have died. None of the bottle wounds were fatal. Death had come from suffocation or asphyxiation, but not from manual strangulation. The hyoid bone at the very back of her throat was not cracked and there were no finger or ligature marks on her throat. It was more likely that Lori's killer had held a pillow over her face. Her lungs were fully expanded and discolored, which indicated trapped air. Perhaps Walt Buckley had been trying to stop her screams.

Walt Buckley came very, very close to getting away with murder. If no one had heard Lori's two screams, if the neighbors had not been at home, there might not have been such a careful investigation of the automobile accident. Lori Buckley would have been embalmed and buried, and her widower would have been the object of concern and pity. He would have had plenty of time to return to their apartment and destroy the blood-soaked mattress, throw away the bits of broken bottle and wipe up the bloodstains. Since everyone, even their closest friends and relatives, thought their marriage was so loving, questions might never have been raised.

But questions *were* raised, and a thorough investigation followed. The Vega probably would not have been checked had the state police not been forewarned. When the car *was* processed, it held many clues that warred with the theory of an accident. Technicians found that the passenger side of the windshield *had* been broken from the inside, but the force had not come from a round, yielding object like a human head. Instead, some sharp, hard instrument had been used, centering the focal point of force in a small area.

The backseat was folded down and there was Type A blood in the far rear inside floor as well as in the wheel well. A gold rug in the back was stained with blood. Lori had not ridden in the front seat on her last ride; she had been in the back, already dead.

Her blue sneakers and a broken Tab bottle were on the floor in the front, along with a bloody hand towel.

When it was coordinated with what was already known, the cache of bedding found in the forest in Polk County was very important. Alone, without being linked to all the other information detectives and criminalists had unearthed, it would have been almost impossible to identify and might never have been connected to a fatal "accident in another county." As it was, the flowered sheets were found to be identical to bedding back in the Buckley duplex. The bloody bits of a broken bottle were stained with Type A blood, Lori's type. A dishcloth wrapped around a chunk of broken bottle matched Lori's dishcloths. In all, twenty-two items had been taken from the woods and tagged into evidence.

Walt Buckley was returned to Salem by Sheriff Heenan and Undersheriff Prinslow and arraigned on murder charges.

Lori Buckley was buried on Monday, March 1. Lori had been an outdoor education enthusiast and she had frequently organized trips for sixth graders to Camp Cascade. A memorial fund was set up with contributions to the "Camp Cascade Memorial Fund in Honor of Lori Buckley."

When detectives developed a roll of film they had found in the Buckley duplex, they found prints of a happy family gathering, obviously a celebration honoring Lori and Walt. There were a number of pictures of the couple. Walt was handsome with a luxuriant dark mustache; Lori was winsomely pretty. In one shot, Walt held his arm protectively around his smiling wife; in another, the two held a basket of flowers and champagne.

Lori didn't live to see those pictures.

Walt Buckley had been living a lie for a long time. Perhaps he was afraid Lori would leave him. Perhaps he truly loved her, in his own way. Maybe he only thought of losing the cushy life he had led. He may have panicked, or he may have been maniacally angry when she impugned his masculinity and scorned him for letting her carry all the responsibilities while he did nothing.

Walt Buckley pleaded guilty to murder charges during the first week in April 1976, and was sentenced to life imprisonment.

Sheriff Jim Heenan commented on the case: "One thing I know. I don't think any of us who worked on this investigation will ever look at an automobile accident again without having second thoughts."

In prison, Walt Buckley was depressed and morose for weeks. In time, he became a model prisoner. After a little more than a decade, he was released on parole. He remarried, had a family, and found a job with the State of Oregon. Ironically, he now lives the life that Lori dreamed of.

Murder Without a Body

Despite its *frequent misuse by mystery novelists, the term "corpus delicti" does not mean the corpse itself; rather, it means the "body of the crime," the physical evidence, the tangible proof that a crime has been committed. A defendant can be convicted of a murder without the discovery of his victim's body, but only if there is enough of this tangible evidence to prove that a murder has been committed. And then the detectives and prosecutor must be able to connect the suspect to the victim at the time the crime occurred. However, there are few prosecutors in America who have the temerity to go into a courtroom with a murder charge when they have no body and no autopsy report to show to the jury.*

Oregon's last murder conviction in which the body was never found was in 1904. It would be seventy-two years before a young district attorney in Columbia County prepared to attempt such a feat again despite advice from more cautious legal heads who doubted he—or anyone—could carry it off.

The victim was a lovely young woman who thought she could judge human nature. She trusted the man who followed her and longed for her because she thought she was the one who controlled their relationship. Her own flawed judgment betrayed her.

Marty Sells is the District Attorney of Columbia County, Oregon. It would seem to be one of the least likely spots in America where the solution to a murder would be a textbook case of forensic science. Columbia County extends northwesterly so far above the rest of Oregon that it almost seems as if it is a piece of Washington that broke off as the Columbia River coursed through it. It isn't a big county, 744 square miles, thirty-one thousand total population. Sells is a former teacher who fulfilled his dream of becoming a lawyer the hard way. He went to law school nights and supported his young family during the day. Sells, whose sense of humor belies his profession, would be the district attorney in Columbia County for more than two decades and serve as president of the Oregon District Attorneys' Association.

In the second week of February 1976, Marty Sells was faced with his greatest challenge.

Rainier, Oregon, is a little town with fewer than two thousand residents. It sits at the edge of the Columbia River amid forested countryside, some twenty miles north of the county seat at St. Helens. A deceptively fragile-looking bridge connects Rainier to Kelso-Longview on the Washington side of the great river. Until the events of February 9, Rainier was seldom in the news; it was like any small town, with its share of gossip and secrets, where everyone knew one another.

Hilda Victoria "Vicki" Brown lived in Rainier. She was a tall striking blonde whose Finnish origins were evident in her bright blue eyes and high cheekbones. At 5'9½" and 140 pounds, Vicki was not the helpless type; she was slender but strong and could work beside any man. And she had to work. She was only twenty-five, but Vicki had a nine-year-old daughter to support. Her teenage marriage had failed years before. Vicki worked as a school bus driver, wrestling the huge yellow vehicles around the winding back roads near Rainier.

Vicki was buying a house in Rainier, where her mother, to whom she was emotionally close, also lived.

Vicki Brown didn't lack for male companionship. Her vibrant good looks and sensual nature attracted men easily. She wrote her dating experiences down in a black diary, something that might have given some of her suitors pause had they known of her penchant for keeping records. But she was a good mother, and never left her daughter alone. If she planned to go out, she either left her child with her mother or with the family of Myron Wicks,* who, with his twin brother, Byron,* oversaw the bus barn for the school district. Byron was the boss, and Myron the chief mechanic.

On Monday, February 9, 1976, Vicki left her little girl at Myron's house while she drove the after-school activity bus. It was the last school bus of the day and she transported high school students who stayed late for after-school sports and other extracurricular activities. The run lasted from five to six-thirty, and the Wickses expected Vicki to pick her daughter up shortly after that.

When seven, and then eight o'clock, came and went, they decided that Vicki must have had an unexpected date. They took her daughter over to Vicki's mother's house for the night. Vicki's mother was vaguely worried; it just wasn't like her daughter to go off without making special preparations or leaving word with someone. But then, Vicki knew that the youngster was safe at the Wickses and that they would take her to her grandmother's house if they couldn't care for her.

When Vicki did not show up for work on Tuesday morning, it was a different matter entirely. Vicki Brown *always* arrived at school on time for her bus routes. Her bus was there—parked in its place in the six-stall bus barn just behind the high school. But where was Vicki?

A highly reliable senior at the high school recalled that he had seen Vicki bring the bus in the night before around 6:30. He was sure it was Vicki. He had even waved at her, and she waved back. He had ridden with her often enough so that he recognized her, even from a distance. Asked if he had seen her leave the barn after she parked the bus, he shook his head. "I walked into school after I waved to her, so I didn't see her leave."

Vicki's worried relatives and friends checked her house, hoping against hope they would find her. But she wasn't there. Inside, everything seemed completely normal, as if she had stepped away for just a short time. There was a brown-paper package of almost thawed frozen steak on the counter. Vicki had obviously left it there because she had planned to be home to fix supper the night before. But they found no indication that she had been home at all after she finished her late bus run. Her mother could locate no one who had seen Vicki *leave* the bus barn after she parked her bus in stall 21.

Vicki's family notified the Rainier police as soon as they left her house. The Columbia County Sheriff's Office and the Oregon State Police were also alerted. It would take twenty-four hours before Vicki, an adult, could officially be considered a missing person. It was still possible that Vicki had found someone whom she really wanted to spend a few days with, someone who had swept her off her feet so completely that her normal predictable patterns were tossed aside. Possible, but not very likely.

It became even less likely later on February 10 when one of the mechanics saw a peculiar stain on the inside wall of the bus barn. The barn was dim inside and badly lighted. When the work crew came to work that morning, they had found it was even dimmer; the main light was out. Someone had unplugged its extension cord at the wall.

Dexter Bryson,* another mechanic, looked at the smears on the wall and scoffed, "Oh, that's just oil."

It was later in the afternoon when someone noticed a pool of some liquid right outside the doors to the mechanics' office on the far end of the barn. The ground was graveled there, and the sticky, mahogany-colored substance looked suspiciously like blood. But then, everyone was spooked by Vicki's disappearance and they soon realized that it might only be transmission fluid.

Determined to find out, the mechanics did a comparison test. They poured transmission fluid over the gravel. It spread out immediately and practically disappeared into the gravel. It didn't seem to have the same properties as the thick clotting stuff they had found and it was a different color.

They found Vicki's green Mazda parked in front of the high school wood shop just next to the barn. The hood wasn't warm; it had been parked there a long, long time, probably since the night before.

As the search for Vicki continued, police noted all the cars around the bus barn. Dexter Bryson's vehicle, a gray-green '51 Chevy pickup, sat parked just outside the double doors on the other side of the mechanics' office.

When Rainier police were notified of the pool of red fluid and the smears inside the bus barn, they asked for help from the Oregon State Police. (In Oregon, the state police work felony investigations as well as traffic accidents.) Captain V. L. Kezar assigned Lieutenant George Winterfeld and Criminal Investigator Dean Renfrow to assist in the search for Vicki.

Columbia County Sheriff Tom Tennant put his chief investigator,

Captain Bruce Oester, at the disposal of the investigative crew. D.A. Marty Sells felt that Oester could aid most in deploying the search of the area, while Winterfeld and Renfrow would handle the scene at the bus barn and interview any witnesses who might turn up.

Criminalists from the Oregon State Police Crime Lab in Portland would test the fluid found in the bus barn to see if it was, indeed, blood, and, if it was, to determine if it was animal or human.

As night fell, Vicki had been missing more than twenty-four hours; her fellow bus drivers and employees of the bus barn were baffled. They searched the area around the barn, the high school, and the athletic field and found nothing.

Dexter Bryson volunteered to walk up into the fir and alder sapling forest behind the barn. He was back in only minutes, holding what looked like a woman's water-soaked purse at the end of a stick.

"It's Vicki's. I poked the stick in just enough to see her wallet with her name in it," he said. "I found it floating in a little pond back there."

The twenty-three-year-old mechanic hadn't found anything else that belonged to Vicki in the woods. Still it didn't look promising. The fact that her car and her purse were both located so close to the bus barn made investigators feel that Vicki had not left the area of her own accord.

If Vicki Brown had been injured, she had to be found quickly. Daylight ended early and February nights were cold. She would surely die of exposure—if not from wounds she had suffered—if she wasn't found soon. Explorer Search and Rescue Scouts, Coast Guard helicopters, the National Guard, the Civil Air Patrol, search dogs flown down from Seattle and Tacoma, the Argonauts (a diving group), and local groups with picturesque names like "The Stump Humpers" and the "Over-the-Hill-Gang" from Mount Hood joined every lawman in the area who could be spared from other duties.

But there were so many places to look: forests, caves, wells, ravines; even the tumultuous Columbia River was searched, at least to the degree that it *could* be searched. The Oregon State Police team concentrated first on the bus barn. With every discovery they made, hope diminished for Vicki Brown.

Using powerful floodlights, the troopers could see that something—or some*one*—had been dragged or carried along the front wall of the barn, leaving great splotches of dried blood on the rough wood. The attack, and surely there had been an attack of awful ferocity, appeared to have begun in stall 21. That was where Vicki Brown had parked her bus. It looked as though she had either been dragged or had run into the end stall, Number 20. The bus parked in that spot was encrusted with dried blood.

There was blood on a fender over the tire, and there were a few strands of long blond hair caught in it. In the corner of that stall, they found a huge puddle of blood at the bottom of a two-by-six beam. Farther up, they noted a spray pattern of blood flecks. One investigator said softly, "It's just as if someone had sprayed it with an aerosol can."

The physical evidence left behind gave investigators the basis to form a tentative scenario. It looked as if Vicki had been assaulted by someone waiting for her as she drove her bus into the barn around 6:30 on Tuesday night. But how could that be? The bus barn was not an isolated building; it was right in the middle of the high school complex. The wood shop teacher held night classes right next door, although, admittedly, the noise of sawing and hammering might well have drowned out screams.

But then again, there had been a play practice for the senior play in the high school. Students and teachers were wandering all over. Before the investigation was finished, every student in the school would be questioned. However, while this was being done, the detectives were finding more and more evidence, and it was grim. They discovered a partial dental bridge caught under the door of stall 21.

No woman would run away with a lover without her teeth. If the bridge belonged to Vicki Brown, as they feared it did, her dentist would be able to give them a definitive answer.

District Attorney Marty Sells coordinated the entire case with his chief investigator, Phil Jackson, who had retired after many years in the Homicide Unit of the Portland Police Department. Neither man had ever had a case like this one.

State police detectives Dean Renfrow and George Winterfeld interviewed students and teachers at Rainier High School. They talked to the senior boy who had waved at Vicki Brown at 6:30 on the night of the ninth. They found a girl student who had been waiting for play practice to start. It had been a little before seven when she stepped out on a rear balcony to sneak a cigarette. From that vantage point, she had had a clear view of the bus barn behind the school. She had seen nothing unusual, but she had *heard* something—sounds of scuffling or fighting coming from the barn. It hadn't lasted long, and she had not been alarmed enough to report it to anyone at the time.

One of the female teachers had pulled her car into the circular driveway between the barn and the school five minutes later. She parked next to gas pumps there and headed into play practice. She remembered seeing the girl smoking on the balcony. "I called out, 'Snuff that cigarette!'"

And then the teacher had heard a dissonant sound. She recalled that it had been a sharp report like a gunshot. She had stood listening for perhaps fifteen seconds, but there was nothing more. She had finally decided it must have been a car backfiring. She was sure of the time: 6:55 P.M. She had glanced at her watch.

Things were beginning to fall together. A male student said he had driven into the driveway a little after seven. He parked his van behind a pickup near the bus barn. "I knew I wouldn't be blocking it because I recognized it as the school's pickup, and they wouldn't need to get out until morning."

It had been a green-gray 1951 Chevrolet, and it *had* been the school's property until a few weeks before. One of the mechanics, Dexter Bryson, had bought it from the school, but the student didn't know that.

The boy had then walked into the school; he said he had heard nothing and seen nothing unusual. Minutes later, one of his friends had walked out of the high school. As he neared the bus barn, he saw his friend's van, lights out, coasting down the driveway. He looked inside, expecting to see his friend driving. Instead, he saw a stranger—a man wearing a black stocking cap and a dark jacket. He had a droopy Fu Manchu mustache and long sideburns. The boy ran inside the school to tell his friend that someone was trying to steal his van. When they came out the van was there, but the pickup was gone.

The boy who owned the van told detectives he was still angry. He had his van back, but someone had broken his wing window to get in. There had been blood on the window, on the steering wheel, and the gear shift. He had assumed the car thief had cut his hand on the window. He had used a paper towel to wipe the blood off. Fortunately, he was able to show the state police investigators where he'd thrown the towel, and lab tests proved it was human blood.

The description of the man seen coasting the van matched Dexter Bryson exactly. And Bryson had been one of the prime searchers for Vicki. Every time they looked around he had been there helping out. It was he, of course, who had found her purse, after he walked almost unerringly into the woods to the pond where it was floating.

When they went to talk with him, the detectives noticed that Bryson seemed upset. There could be at least two reasons for that. He might simply be truly concerned about Vicki's disappearance. And then again, he might have a more malevolent reason for being so jumpy. Experience has taught detectives that some killers—and arsonists—get a thrill out of putting themselves in the center of an investigation, of playing games with the very men and women who are trying to solve the crime.

Dexter Bryson became decidedly nervous, however, when the investigators asked him to sign a consent to search his truck. He told them he didn't see what good that would do, and they explained casually that since his truck had been parked near the bus barn when Vicki vanished, the killer might have touched it or thrown some bit of evidence in the truck bed. Bryson finally gave his permission for them to search his truck, albeit somewhat reluctantly.

There were some plywood sheets, wood chips, a tire, and a steel cable in the bed of Bryson's truck. Some dark stains were visible along the bottom edges of the plywood, and they noted that some of the wood chips were discolored too. There was another dark splotch in the center of the bench seat in the cab. Oregon State Police Criminalists Bonnie Garthus and Ray Grimsbo processed the truck. The stains were human blood. They found a human hair caught in the tailgate and another on the rear bumper.

It suddenly became important to know more about Dexter Bryson's movements on February 9 and detectives asked him to give them a statement. If he had been seen by other witnesses working in the mechanic's office at the time Vicki disappeared, someone else could have used his truck to stash her body temporarily.

According to his statement, however, Bryson had left work before five on the day Vicki vanished. He said he had gone to see his mother at Alston's Corners five miles away. She had offered to split a load of Presto Logs with him. He said he had picked up his half and his brother had helped him load them into the pickup. Just then, it had begun to rain. He said he had rushed to get home before the sawdust logs disintegrated. He lived, he said, in a mobile home parked on a Christmas tree farm.

Dexter Bryson had a remarkably precise memory of his movements on the night Vicki Brown disappeared. About six, he continued, he had stopped at a little grocery store to get gas and a six-pack of beer. Then he had driven his pickup to a shed next to his trailer, stacked the logs, and washed out the truck bed to get rid of any wood chips.

Bryson said that he was married and living with his wife, but they worked different shifts. She worked the swing shift at a grocery store across the bridge in Longview, Washington, so he had reheated some chili for his supper.

"What did you do after that?" a detective asked.

"I watched television and shaved. Then I saw that my clock had stopped, and I called my mother to ask the time. It was seven thirty exactly." Bryson had also asked what his share of the cost of the Presto Logs was. At *exactly* eight fifteen," he had called his mother again. He said he was concerned because a white Chevrolet truck had pulled in in back of his trailer and someone had jiggled his doorknob. He said he had been alarmed because he had been "hassled" before. He lived in a very isolated area and there was no one nearby to help in case of trouble.

He asked that his brother come over to back him up. His brother had come over, but the truck was gone by the time he got there. Then the two had driven into Rainier to call on Bryson's best friend, Rex Simcox.* It was about nine then, Bryson said, and his friend wasn't home.

Then, as it happened, they had driven by the bus barn. Bryson said he had been concerned because he noticed that the double doors into the mechanics' office were not securely closed. He had gone in and looked around for any sign of vandalism. He said he had called his boss, Myron Wicks, to tell him about the open doors. Wicks had told him not to worry—just to lock everything up. Bryson had checked for signs that anyone had been inside and found nothing amiss, so he said he had locked the doors securely and left.

"I told my brother then," Bryson said, "that I thought I'd seen Vicki's green Mazda still parked there."

Bryson said he had thought something was funny. He and his brother had driven back to Simcox's house and found him home this time. He asked Rex if *he* had seen the open door to the shop, and Rex said he hadn't. Nor had he noticed that Vicki's car was still there.

Dexter Bryson was either a most conscientious employee or he was a little paranoid. He said he had brought a gun—a .44 Magnum—to work with him the day after Vicki vanished. He was nervous because Vicki had disappeared, the double doors had been open, and because someone in a white truck had tried to get into his mobile home.

"Why do you think you need protection?" he was asked, and he shrugged. It wasn't because he had any information about Vicki's disappearance, he insisted, it was just that so many unexplainable things had happened on Tuesday night.

Bryson was released from questioning after he gave his consent to have his mobile home on Fern Hill Road searched. The Oregon state police investigators and criminalists headed for the mobile home on the Christmas tree farm. Bonnie Garthus noticed that Bryson had what appeared to be fresh blood on his thumb, but when she asked him about it, he said it was from his own bloody nose. She took scrapings from his fingernails. They were dirty but that would be expected on a bus mechanic's hands.

If the state investigators had hoped to find Vicki Brown in Bryson's trailer, they were disappointed. However, they noted things that only increased their suspicions. In the bedroom Dexter Bryson and his wife shared, they found dress boots with splatters of blood on them. In the spare bedroom, they found a black vinyl motorcycle jacket. (It had been recently washed, yet lab tests would show that it had been soaked inside and out with human blood.)

While the search went on, the state police saw that Bryson was attempting to push something out of sight in his bedroom. When they checked, they found a pair of black leather gloves soaked inside with blood and with a hair similar to the one they had found on his truck. Bryson looked at the gloves and said he had never seen them before. He said that he always marked his gloves inside and these had no marks.

Bonnie Garthus had found a holster in the bedroom and asked where the gun was that fit it. Bryson walked over to a plastic box that sat on the kitchen counter near the sink and pulled out a .22 Ruger. Investigator Winterfeld stepped forward quickly and took it from him. There appeared to be blood on the exterior muzzle. The Ruger would join a growing cache of possible evidence slated for crime lab tests.

Dexter Bryson had become a prime suspect—but in what crime? *Kidnapping? Assault with intent to do bodily harm? Murder?* There was no victim. Someone's blood had stained Bryson's clothes and his truck—but whose? The case was not as simple legally as common sense made it appear.

All the authorities could do was place Bryson under constant surveillance while they continued their investigation on many different levels. The search team still worked against time to find Vicki Brown. No one said what they all were thinking. They were looking for a body now.

Regular duty hours meant nothing. Officers from every department in Columbia County donated unpaid overtime. They searched 127 square miles of forests, fields, water, and land in Columbia County and used 7,023 manhours.

Detectives weighed the variables they had to work with. Only three people had had keys to the bus barn. One was Dexter Bryson, and the other two were the twin brothers: Byron and Myron Wicks. Myron Wicks was a middle-aged man with a family and it had been Myron who took Vicki Brown's daughter to her grandmother the night Vicki vanished. As a matter of course, both twin brothers were asked about their whereabouts on the night in question. Each of them had a sound alibi; many people had seen them elsewhere at the critical time.

Myron Wicks, however, admitted ruefully that he was one of the men in Vicki's black book. He said they had had a brief affair. His wife knew about it and had already forgiven him. With astounding frankness, he said he had only had sex with Vicki once. He had tried twice more, he said.

"What do you mean you tried?"

"I couldn't get it up," he confessed with a shrug.

The investigators looked at each other. The man had to be telling the truth; no man is going to lie and say he is impotent. It would have been more realistic if he had lied in the other direction. This man wasn't boasting—he was being honest.

Yes, Myron Wicks said he would testify to the "affair" in court if it came to that, although he hoped it wouldn't.

Vicki Brown's close confidantes said that she had one man whom she really wanted, but he was far away from Rainier. He was in Alaska. The rest of Vicki's suitors had merely filled her time while she waited for him. Reportedly, none of the men she dated expected anything more. Detectives didn't uncover even one rumor that any of Vicki's casual dates had been jealous.

There *had*, however, been a disturbing incident the previous November. One evening while Vicki was out, someone had broken into her house. The intruder, who was never caught, had entered through a broken window. Once inside, he (they *assumed* it was a "he") had pawed through Vicki's negligees, bras, and panties. He had also snooped through her personal diary and papers. Nothing was missing except two bras and a pair of panties. A bottle of beer had been taken from her refrigerator, emptied, and thrown into the toilet bowl.

Odd. Frightening? An underwear thief is usually a man with some sexual aberration, a step beyond the window peeper. Laymen consider voyeurs, exposers, and those who collect undergarments—fetishists—among the most harmless of sexual offenders. Experts in sexual deviation know these offenders often escalate their fantasies to a point where they include rape—and even murder.

To prove probable cause to bring charges against Dexter Bryson, District Attorney Marty Sells had to first establish that the person injured in the bus barn had been Vicki Brown. It seemed obvious, but it had to be proven absolutely. Although the Oregon State Police crime lab had found enough blood to type for a dozen victims, there was a problem. When the investigators checked, they could not find Vicki Brown's blood type on file anywhere. The doctor who had delivered her daughter had noted only that her blood was RH negative but had neglected to jot down the type. For some reason, none of the medical procedures she had undergone had required blood-typing.

Dexter Bryson had Type O blood, RH positive. The blood in the bus barn, his pickup, his jacket, his gloves, and on a shovel found in a search of Bryson's property, was all Type O.

District Attorney Sells feared that the blood found at the crime scene and on Bryson's clothing would be useless if extensive tests were not done at once and so he asked that the crime lab proceed with the tests.

The O blood was broken down to its enzyme components. It had DCc and E factors. The small "c" factor indicated that the person who had lost that blood was RH negative—just as Vicki Brown had been.

Dexter Bryson's blood broke down to DC, with no small "c" or big "E" factors. None of the blood found could have come from *his* body.

The next step in proving who had been attacked in the bus barn was to retrieve some hair from Vicki's brush and rollers and compare it microscopically with the hairs found matted in blood on the bus fender, the tailgate of Bryson's truck, and inside the bloody gloves in his trailer. The crime lab technicians found thirty points of microscopic similarity in class and characteristics with the comparison hairs. Although hair cannot be considered as individual as a fingerprint, or DNA matches (not yet in use at the time), thirty points of similarity made it very likely that the hair found stuck in dried blood was Vicki Brown's.

Vicki's dentist examined the bridge found in her bus stall. "It's Vicki's," he said firmly. "It's what we call a cantilevered bridge. Until she came in, I hadn't seen one in ten years. They aren't done anymore because they put too much strain on adjacent teeth. That's why she came in. I had to modify it with a drill and affix tabs to make it fit better. There were all kinds of x rays. I still have them."

The dentist's drill fit perfectly into the holes in the bridge.

There were no fingerprints to check. They had found only smudged marks along the inside of the bus barn. Criminalist Bonnie Garthus said they had been left by someone wearing blood-soaked gloves.

The investigators looked into Dexter Bryson's background. He had no criminal record at all. He had graduated from high school and then served in the Marines. He was 5'10" tall and weighed 170 pounds. Vicki at almost the same height, even thirty pounds lighter, would probably have given him a good fight if he had tried to grab her in the bus barn.

Although Bryson was married, he had not confined his attentions to his wife. The investigators learned that he had had a couple of girlfriends. One was rumored to have married and moved away. The other was still in town.

Witnesses described Dexter Bryson's demeanor at his job the day after Vicki vanished as out of character. He had shown up very early, long before he was due to check in. When someone asked him why he was there so early, he had answered, "Oh, one of the drivers might not come in. I might have to fill in for them. . . ."

His thumb had been black-and-blue. He had explained that away by saying a "giant Presto log" had fallen on it. He was in so much pain from it that he couldn't pull the hand brake on a bus or change a tire.

Packing his .44 Magnum for protection, Bryson had later tried to convince fellow workers that Vicki had been kidnapped, saying with conviction, "She was snatched."

One of the other women bus drivers, who was initially suspicious that Vicki had simply taken off on a fling, had said to Bryson, "Wouldn't it be nice to live like that—a free life?"

Bryson had snapped, "No!" curtly to her comment, startling the woman with his vehemence.

Like all small towns, Rainier, Oregon, was rife with rumors and Dexter Bryson's name was at the top of the murder suspect list for some residents. Others were convinced a homicidal maniac was loose. Special guards were posted at the bus barn and on the school buses to allay the fears of worried parents.

Someone who believed that the bus mechanic was responsible for Vicki Brown's disappearance painted "Bryson's a Killer" on the street in front of the school. Bryson himself painted it out. Then he spray painted a whole wall of the bus barn where there had been bloodstains.

His efforts did not impede the investigation. The vital sections of the wall had already been cut out and sent to one of the leading criminalists in America—one of the foremost authorities on the patterns that blood can make *after* it leaves the body. He was Herbert L. McDonnell, adjunct professor in criminalistics at Elmira College and Corning Community College in New York State. McDonnell is the director of the Lab of Forensic Sciences and has an MS degree in chemistry. Over the years, among the hundreds of cases he worked on were the Dr. Sam Sheppard case and the assassinations of Bobby Kennedy and Martin Luther King. (One day, he would testify in the O.J. Simpson trial.)

Both the barn beam with the blood spray pattern on it and the Ruger found in Bryson's kitchen had been sent to McDonnell and he was analyzing them as the investigation continued three thousand miles away.

Dexter Bryson had no idea of how closely he was being watched. If he had begun to feel that he was home free, he had not reckoned with the combined forces of the Oregon State Police, the Columbia County Sheriff's office, and District Attorney Marty Sells. The organized search for Vicki was suspended after a month, but the hidden investigation continued unabated.

One of the most interesting pieces of information detectives discovered was that Dexter Bryson had been obsessed with Vicki Brown. There had been nothing he wouldn't do to gain her approval. He had fixed her stove and made repairs on her house—all for free. On the very day she disappeared, he had fixed her car. For all of his efforts, he had received nothing more than a smile and a thank you.

Marty Sells figured that Bryson must have been disappointed and frustrated, perhaps even angry that Vicki had no interest in sleeping with him. Sells had confirmation of his suppositions when the probe led to one of Bryson's former lovers, a girl who had married and moved away to Mississippi, and was now the nineteen-year-old wife of an airman. She gave a statement to police that it had been Dexter Bryson who had broken into Vicki's house in November. She said he had found her diary and read about the other men who had enjoyed Vicki's favors. Bryson, who had done so much for her, had always been rejected. He had been enraged to find he had been such a patsy.

"He gave me two bras and a pair of panties he took from her house," the girl said. "I still have them. He said he broke in because he wanted her to suffer. He was angry because he'd fixed things for her and she rejected him."

Detectives found it hard to contain their elation. Here was the motivation the investigators had looked for all along. Dexter Bryson's ex-girlfriend agreed to mail Vicki's stolen lingerie to Oregon.

When Vicki's small daughter viewed the bikini panties mailed from the East Coast, she cried, "Oh, you've found my mom."

She identified the panties by the strawberry pattern on them. "They're my mom's," she said, nodding vigorously. "Hers are pink and her friend has the same kind, only the strawberries are orange on hers."

It all fit. Dexter Bryson had probably been seething over his latest rejection. Now, the investigators knew that he had fixed Vicki's car on the afternoon of the ninth. He had probably decided to take what he considered his right. If Vicki had not submitted willingly, and they doubted that she would have, then Bryson must have attempted to force her.

It was easy to imagine him as he waited in the darkened bus barn. He would have known Vicki was due in from her run at 6:30. All the other drivers would have come and gone by that time. When Vicki alighted from her bus, unaware, Bryson would have had the upper hand. Or maybe he had expected it would be easier to subdue her than it was. She might well have put up more of a fight than he had foreseen. Struggling and kicking, the pair must have scuffled through the empty barn. That would account for the sounds the girl smoking on the balcony had heard.

And the one gunshot—the sound heard by the teacher a few minutes later—would have ended the fight. And then Vicki Brown, dead, would have had to be disposed of as rapidly as possible.

The bloody smudges on the wall could be explained. Vicki's killer would have had to drag her inert body, or lift her in a fireman's carry over his shoulder. They believed that someone had moved her body along the length of the barn, swabbing the walls with streaks of blood as he went. In his panic to avoid detection, it wasn't likely that he would have noticed that Vicki's dental bridge had fallen out.

If Dexter Bryson had planned to put Vicki in his pickup truck, he must have been appalled when he had found it blocked in by the student's van. He had had to break the wing window and release the brake. He must have cut himself—that would account for all the blood in the van, and maybe his bruised thumb. Then Bryson would have had to get into the van and steer it while it coasted far enough so that he could move his truck. Had he realized that someone saw him in the van? Probably not. In his panic to hide the body of his victim, he had undoubtedly been totally focused on getting away from the high school.

Reconstructing the scenario of the crime, the investigating team could almost hear Bryson's ragged breath and smell the fear in his sweat. He would have been terrified that he would be discovered on the high school campus with Vicki Brown's body in the bed of his pickup truck. He had to get her away, and he had to cover his own trail.

Police were convinced that Bryson *had* picked up the Presto Logs from his mother—just as he had called her at precise times, making sure that he commented on the time so that she could, albeit unaware of the truth, substantiate an alibi he was constructing.

The Oregon State Police investigators, the sheriff's detectives, and the district attorney's staff believed they now knew what had

THE HIGHWAY ACCIDENT

When Marion County detectives developed film found in a camera in the victim's home, they found photographs of a happy couple. Within a few weeks, they would be separated forever. *(Police file photo)*

Bloodstained bedding found many miles from the duplex on Cedar Court matched sheets in Lori and Walt Buckley's home. *(Police file photo)*

When Detectives Jim Byrnes and Dave Kominek arrived at the fatal accident site along the Van Duzer Corridor between Salem, Oregon, and the Pacific coast, they were surprised to find there were no hesitation marks where the Buckley's Vega left the road and crashed over a bank and into the forest. *(Police file photo)*

MURDER WITHOUT A BODY

District attorney Martin Sells successfully prosecuted the first murder case in Oregon in 73 years in which the victim's body was never found. *(Courtesy of D.A. Martin Sells)*

Herb McDonnell, blood spatter expert from the Laboratory of Forensic Science in Corning, New York, is one of the definitive experts in his field in the world. He was able to show that Vicki Brown had died of a gunshot wound, even though her body was never found. *(Gill Photographics)*

MURDER WITHOUT A BODY

The victim's blood and hair were left on the walls of the bus barn, and that convicted her killer. *(Police file photo)*

Pretty Vicki Brown, whose body was never found, was school bus driver for the district. *(Ann Rule collection)*

From a magazine, "Dr." Anthony Fernandez raises a glass of champagne to toast his new bride, Ruth Logg. Their perfect love did not survive for long. *(Ann Rule collection)*

Roger Dunn, King County, Washington, homicide detective, worked with Detective Ted Forrester to prove that Ruth Logg had not died in a tragic driving accident. *(Ann Rule)*

Anthony Fernandez was so angry at Detective Ted Forrester for pursuing him on a murder charge that he sued Forrester for a million dollars. He did not collect. *(Ann Rule)*

BLACK LEATHER

Pierce County homicide detective Walt Stout looks into the black van owned by Larry Hendricks, a counselor in a sexual psychopath therapy program. Hendricks had outfitted the van as a traveling torture chamber. *(Ann Rule collection)*

Two of Larry Hendricks's guns. The young soldier he abducted turned the tables on Hendricks and shot him with his own guns. One of Hendricks's guns was later tied to two murders in the San Francisco area. *(Ann Rule collection)*

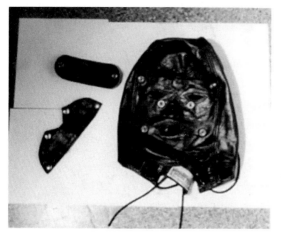

Niels Honegger, Hendricks's intended victim, was kidnapped and blinded with this black leather mask and gag. Pierce County detectives found this and other restraint devices in the killer's van. *(Ann Rule collection)*

MIRROR IMAGES

James Ruzicka, one half of the bizarre duo who referred to themselves as "Troy Asin." Ruzicka changed his appearance constantly. *(Ann Rule collection)*

Sex Crimes detective Joyce Johnson, Seattle Police Department. Johnson found the rape suspect she sought in a most unusual location. *(Ann Rule collection)*

MIRROR IMAGES

Carl Harp, known as the infamous "Bellevue Sniper" and the other half of the "Troy Asin" persona. Harp and Ruzicka had ironically similar backgrounds.
(Chuck Wright collection)

Penny Haddenham, 14, was on her way home when she met a convicted sexual psychopath. Days later, detectives work in the woods where her body was found. They didn't believe she had committed suicide.
(Police file photo)

MIRROR IMAGES

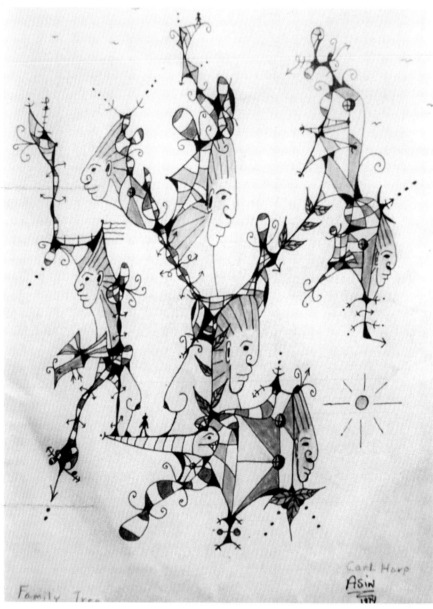

Carl Harp, convicted as a rapist and as the "Bellevue Sniper," drew this enigmatic "Family Tree" in 1974. He signed it with the alias he shared with James Ruzicka. Chuck Wright, of the Washington State Department of Corrections (8635 Evergreen Way, Everett, WA 98208), would like to hear readers' thoughts on Harp's vision of his "family." *(Chuck Wright collection)*

happened to Vicki Brown, but they were no closer to finding her than they had been the first night. Perhaps Bryson had left her body somewhere while he went about his errands and his coverups. He might well have returned later to dispose of it. But, in the meantime, he had been busy. He contacted his brother, his best friend, his boss—all to set up his red herring story about the mysterious white truck behind his mobile home, the open doors at the bus barn. He had even made a casual comment that Vicki's car was still parked near the barn.

It would have been feasible for Bryson to hide Vicki's corpse in the dark woods behind the bus barn. That would allow him to return at his leisure to bury it or hide it somewhere where it would never be found.

The question of whether he had enough to charge Dexter Bryson still sat heavily on D.A. Marty Sells's mind. "Can you charge a man with murder when you have no body?" If he went ahead, Sells knew he would be fighting heavy odds. He had checked the law books and he knew that there had been no successful prosecutions in similar cases in Oregon in seventy-two years. The defense would be sure to suggest that Vicki Brown had had her own reasons to disappear.

Still, Sells was morally certain he had his man, and so were Renfrow, Winterfeld, Oester, and Phil Jackson. If Sells didn't risk losing in court, he would be betraying every lawman in the county who had worked so long and so hard gathering information.

With all the negatives he was facing, Sells nevertheless had an ace in the hole: He had Herb McDonnell as a prosecution witness. Sells was convinced that McDonnell's testimony would blast any defense case right out of the water.

When Sells called in the investigative crew and handed out the arrest warrant, there were satisfied grins all around. The time had come to jar Bryson's self-confidence. He was shocked when he was arrested on April 6, 1976. Vicki Brown had been missing for eight weeks and three days and no one expected that her remains would ever be found. Even so, her suspected killer was going to go on trial.

Dexter Bryson's trial began on September 8 in Judge Donald L. Kalberer's courtroom in St. Helens, Oregon. As expected, the courtroom was jammed with spectators. Bryson had been given a choice of facing a jury or letting Judge Kalberer decide his fate. He waived the jury. Judge Kalberer would make the final decision.

District Attorney Marty Sells had scores of potential witnesses, but he chose only thirty local ones, the most convincing, to build his case:

the students who had been on the school grounds on February 9, the teacher who heard the shot, the state police criminal investigators, and, finally, Vicki Brown's own little daughter, who made a good, strong, credible—if tragic—witness.

Herbert McDonnell, the criminalist from Elmira, New York, was the key witness even though he had never been in Columbia County, Oregon, before, even though McDonnell had never seen Vicki Brown in life, and had certainly never had occasion to see her body. McDonnell's special expertise allowed him to describe what had happened seven months before in the high school bus barn as accurately as if he had been hiding in the shadows and watching. It was eerie to comprehend the true meaning of "Blood will tell."

Professor McDonnell first held a pointer to blown-up photographs of the distinctive spray pattern of blood on the corner of the bus barn. This was the blood that looked as if someone had aimed an aerosol can full of red paint at the wood. McDonnell said that the diffuse specks indicated that they were "high velocity impact blood." This blood could only have resulted from a gunshot wound. He estimated that the gun had probably been held less than three inches and probably closer to one inch from the victim. The bullet had probably penetrated the victim's head.

McDonnell explained that if the blood had been the result of bludgeoning, it would have left an entirely different kind of pattern. A club or hammer would have "cast off" blood in much larger drops with "tails" that showed the direction of force. Cast-off blood is nothing like the pinpoints of sprayed blood. There was no question in McDonnell's mind that whoever had been injured in the bus barn had been shot.

McDonnell then addressed himself to the .22 caliber Ruger gun found in Bryson's trailer. There had been blood on the exterior of the gun when it was found. The surface of the weapon had been "tacky" with it. Blood had also been found inside the muzzle and the cylinder wall. This, McDonnell explained, was entirely in keeping with his findings after examining the two-by-six beam. High-velocity blood is drawn back into the cylinder of the gun. The terrific energy released from the gun breaks the blood down and it speckles the surrounding area. Herb McDonnell said that the high-velocity blood hit the beam and the interior of the muzzle at the same time. As the hot gases from firing the gun begin to cool almost instantly, the victim's blood was pulled back into the barrel of the gun. The blood *inside* the gun was what led McDonnell to deduce that the gun had been held less than three inches away from the victim.

Dexter Bryson shifted uncomfortably in his chair at the defense table. He had had no idea that his victim had connected him and his weapon to her murder, even as she died. *She had marked his gun with her blood!*

Through Herb McDonnell's expertise, the method of murder was exposed. By itself, the testimony of the teacher who heard the loud report would not have been enough to prove absolutely that a gun had been fired in the bus barn, had hit a human being, and that that human being had been severely injured—perhaps killed.

The sheer amount of blood at the crime scene had been measured and a careful comparison with its percentage of Vicki Brown's entire blood supply had told the investigators that she could not have survived long.

Herb McDonnell's testimony was electrifying. Anyone listening could almost see the awful struggle in the darkened barn. As Dexter Bryson realized that he could not overcome Vicki with his strength and that rape was out of the question, he also must have realized that she would report him. He had turned to the gun he carried—just in case. Vicki Brown had been trapped in the corner with nowhere left to run when he held the gun against her head and fired. Then she had slid down the wall, either dead or dying. From there, the defendant had carried or dragged her body along that wall.

The inexorable parade of physical evidence continued: Vicki's hair samples and the hair found on Bryson's truck, her blood type, her dental bridge, Bryson's bloodied clothing, Vicki's stolen strawberry panties, Bryson's bloody shovel.

And then Marty Sells pointed out the many disparities in Bryson's story. The clock in Bryson's trailer was not broken; it was an efficiently working pendulum type clock, which incidentally, Bryson could have seen from his phone. No one other than the defendant had seen the "phantom white truck" whose occupants had allegedly tried to break into his trailer. Another woman bus driver had seen Bryson in town at nine P.M., the time he said he had been at Rex Simcox's house. Finally, Rex Simcox himself testified that he had called Bryson back after *he* had checked the bus barn that night. And Bryson had *not* been at his mobile home. No one knew where he had been on the night Vicki Brown vanished.

Marty Sells presented other possible "suspects" before the defense could bring them up. Myron Wicks fulfilled his promise to testify to his brief affair with Vicki and, predictably, the gallery gasped at his frank testimony about his impotency. No defense attorney was going to touch that.

Vicki's former husband was mentioned as a suspect in her disappearance, but Marty Sells quashed that. Vicki's ex could not have murdered her, even if he had had a motive. He had been in a hospital miles away from Rainier on the night of February 9.

Investigator Renfrow testified that he had been discussing Vicki Brown's disappearance with Dexter Bryson and his wife when Bryson suggested that whatever had happened to Vicki "had to have been an accident." How could he possibly have known that, if he himself had not been there when she died?

There was more than enough testimony to titillate the courtroom watchers. In an effort to show that Vicki Brown had vanished of her own volition, the defense tried to show that Vicki was lonesome for her boyfriend in Alaska, that she had disliked her job, and that she had been unpopular with the other female bus drivers. They even brought in an interesting witness, one "Skip Tracy," the alias of a private detective who said he was an expert witness on people who simply chose to run out on their responsibilities for their own reasons.

Tracy cut a rather bizarre figure as he entered the courtroom, dressed immaculately in suit, tie, and high-top tennis shoes. He regaled listeners with tales of adults who simply took off, stepping out of one life and into another where no one knew them. He recalled that he had located one woman whose apartment was found soaked with blood. "She wasn't dead at all," he finished firmly. "We found her in Las Vegas."

When Marty Sells cross-examined Skip Tracy, he asked, "Have you read *this* case? Do you know anything at all about Vicki Brown? Do you know if she is dead or alive?"

"No, sir, I do not," Skip Tracy admitted.

It was a long trial, seventeen days. On September 25, Sells rose to make his final arguments. "Mr. Bryson—" he began. "When he went out there that night, he took away from Vicki Brown the most important thing that any human being can possess, the most important *right* that any human being can possess, and that is the right to be, the right to exist, to live. He took that away from her and he did it intentionally, and he did it unlawfully, and we ask the court to find him guilty."

Judge Kalberer did not deliberate long. When he returned to confront Dexter Bryson, he explained that he had three factors to consider in his decision. "I must decide if Vicki Brown is dead, if she has been murdered, and if you did it. I am satisfied beyond any doubt, Mr. Bryson—beyond all possible doubt—that she is dead, (that) she was murdered, and that *you did it.*"

Dexter Bryson stared back at Judge Kalberer. His expression did not change, his posture was erect, and he did not tremble. It was almost as if he hadn't heard at all.

Bryson was sentenced to life in prison. He appealed his life sentence and lost. Under Oregon law at the time, he was technically eligible to ask for a parole hearing after serving six months in prison. He served more than six months, of course, but he did not serve life. "Life in prison" is a deceptive term. In most states, it means anywhere from ten years to eighteen years—unless the sentence is *mandatory.* Even then, new administrations, new governors, and new laws can mitigate the length of what seemed at the time to be endless years in prison.

Dexter Bryson has been a free man for some years now. Vicki Brown has never been found and quite possibly Bryson is the only one who knows where she is. And he will not say.

Perhaps one day a camper will find a skeleton or a fisherman in the Columbia River will discover some small fragment of bone or clothing. It is no longer likely that that will happen. But time reveals all things in one way or another.

Vicki Brown's murderer was convicted even though her body was never found. And there is a kind of poetic as well as legal justice in that. Vicki was a good mother, good daughter, dependable on her job, and she had every reason to look forward to many years ahead. That ended for her in a darkened bus barn when a rejected would-be lover's frustration and rage exploded.

As Marty Sells pointed out in his final argument, Dexter Bryson had made one clumsy mistake after another when he murdered Vicki. "The only clever thing he did was to hide the body."

And because of the silent testimony of Vicki Brown's own blood, that just wasn't enough.

I'll Love You Forever

I learned about this story of ultimate betrayal long after it was too late to save the victim. Ruth Logg's daughters and other relatives could not save her either, but they prevailed and saw a certain kind of justice done in a landmark court decision.

This is the kind of nightmare case that haunts every woman on her own. Each of us can identify with Ruth Logg. Each of us would like to think that we would never fall for the blandishments of a man like Ruth's "Tony." And yet, inside, I think we must admit that any woman who hopes to find permanent love risks meeting the perfect liar instead of the perfect lover.

When I researched this case many years ago, I found Ruth Logg's "perfect lover" so sinister that I actually changed my usual pen name to a completely different pseudonym so that he wouldn't be able to find me.

I think you will see why as the story of the man who promised to love Ruth "forever" unfolds.

When her life was viewed in terms of worldly goods, Ruth Logg had everything. The lovely blond widow had been well provided for by her late husband, Les. She lived alone for several years after Les's death in her sprawling house in Auburn, Washington. The grounds were impeccably maintained and there was even a huge swimming pool. Ruth's home was valued in the early seventies at $85,000. Today, it would be worth well over a million dollars. Les Logg's business holdings had amounted to something over a quarter of a million dollars at the time of his death. Again, that $250,000 would be worth ten times as much in the economy of the nineties. Ruth herself had a good business head. She had moved smoothly into her new place as owner of a business.

Unlike many women who are suddenly widowed, Ruth Logg was able to manage. Her two pretty teenage daughters, Kathleen and Susan, lived with her and she loved them devotedly. But Ruth was only in her early forties, and she sometimes dreamed of finding a man to share her life. She was lonely and the years ahead often seemed to stretch out bleakly.

Ruth knew that her girls would soon be moving away to start their own lives, and that was as it should be. She accepted that. But she couldn't bear the thought of rattling around her huge house alone once Kathleen and Susan were gone. In March of 1971, she put the house on the market. Perhaps she would buy a condominium or take an apartment where she wouldn't have to worry about yard work. Her personal safety was on her mind too. A woman in a house alone wasn't as safe as one who lived close to other people in a security building.

Most single women hold on to a romantic dream that a special man will come along one day and change their lives. Ruth Logg was no exception. She was far too young to give up on love, even though her prospects looked slim. She hated the idea of dating services or Parents Without Partners, or blind dates set up by well-meaning friends. She sometimes wondered why it had to be so difficult to meet someone.

And then Ruth Logg *did* meet someone in such an unexpected way. It was a blustery March afternoon when she first encountered the man who would suddenly launch her world in exciting new directions. A sleek luxury car pulled up in front of her home and a compactly muscled, impeccably dressed man emerged and knocked at her door. He had a great voice. He introduced himself as "Dr. Anthony Fernandez."

No one would have described Dr. Fernandez as handsome, and yet he had an undeniably charismatic quality. He had wide shoulders and thickly muscled arms and wrists, and he looked at Ruth with warm dark eyes under thick brows. Ruth could sense that he was gentle. His manners were wonderful; he was almost apologetic for interrupting her schedule, but he did want to see her home. Ruth assured him that she would be delighted to show him through the house.

Dr. Fernandez explained that he was forty-eight years old and divorced. He said he had just opened a family counseling clinic in the Tacoma area and that he was hoping to buy a house within easy commuting distance to his business.

Ruth Logg was quite taken with Dr. Fernandez, who urged her to call him "Tony." They talked as she led him through her home and he seemed impressed with the floor plan, the way she had decorated the rooms, and with the lawn and gardens. It wasn't long before they stopped talking about the house; they discovered that they shared many interests. Dr. Anthony Fernandez asked Ruth Logg if she would join him for dinner and she accepted, a little surprised at herself for agreeing to a date with someone she really didn't know.

Tony and Ruth had such a good time on their first evening that they both knew they would see more of each other. More dates followed and Ruth suddenly found herself caught up in a whirlwind courtship. After so many years at the edge of other people's lives, she found it incredibly exciting to have this fascinating man pursuing her. And Tony Fernandez *was* pursuing her. At first, Ruth questioned her great good fortune, but then she accepted it. She was, after all, a good-looking woman with a lush figure and a pretty face. She had forgotten that in her years as a widow. Now, Ruth became even prettier with her newfound happiness.

It never occurred to Ruth that Tony might be interested in her because she was wealthy. In fact, she believed that what she had was chicken feed compared to what he owned; Tony had told her that he was a man with substantial assets. He spoke of timber holdings and real estate, and, of course, he had his counseling practice. He didn't *need* her money.

Ruth didn't know that the plush car Tony drove was rented, nor did she know much about his life before they met. None of that mattered. Ruth Logg was totally in love with Anthony Fernandez.

Ruth's family and friends were not as enthusiastic about Tony. They wanted her to be happy, of course, because she had devoted so many years helping other people, but they were worried. They had checked into Tony's background, and they soon heard rumors that "Dr." Fernandez had spent time in prison for fraud. They doubted that Ruth would believe the rumors, so they pleaded with her to check into Fernandez's background before she considered marriage.

Ruth only smiled and reassured them that she knew all about Tony. He had told her that he had had a little bit of trouble in the past. He had been honest with her, she said, and his past didn't matter to her. Ruth's philosophy was that everyone deserves a second chance. Why should she dredge up unhappy memories? Ruth's sister was particularly persistent in trying to coax Ruth off her rosy cloud.

When Tony Fernandez discovered that, he told Ruth's sister that if she didn't like his plans with Ruth, then she could just consider herself excluded from their social circle and future family gatherings. Amazingly, Ruth went along with Tony's decision.

No one is blinder than someone in the first stages of romance, and Ruth refused to listen to one detrimental word about Tony. By September of 1971, Ruth and Tony were engaged. She gave up all thoughts of selling her house; she and Tony would need it to live in. At his suggestion, Ruth and Tony drew up new wills. Although the will Ruth had drawn up three years earlier had left everything she owned—$250,000 plus her home—to her daughters, her new will left it all to Tony. She was confident that if anything should happen to her, Tony would provide for her girls. In turn, Tony left everything he owned to Ruth in his will.

What Anthony Fernandez actually owned was debatable. Despite his grandiose boasting to his fiancée, Tony's assets were negligible. When he met Ruth, he had seventy-five hundred dollars in the bank, a thousand-dollar bond, and some mining claims and real property that would one day sell at a tax sale for less than four thousand dollars. Beyond that, Tony had substantial judgments filed against him. His financial statement would have been written entirely in red ink.

Despite objections and pleadings from the people who truly loved Ruth Logg, she and Dr. Tony Fernandez flew to Puerto Rico on January 5, 1972, where they were married. She had only known him ten months, but it seemed as if they were meant to be together. They toasted their new life with champagne, and Ruth was blissfully happy. Her honeymoon with her new husband was everything she had hoped. She was confident that, in time, her family would come to see Tony for the wonderful man he was.

While she had left Tony everything in her will, she didn't plan on dying for at least four more decades. She had too much to live for now. When Tony casually mentioned that it would be easier for him to help her manage her affairs if he had her Power of Attorney, Ruth didn't hesitate. They went at once to a notary and Ruth gave her husband the power to sell her property or do any other business in her name.

In retrospect, it is easy to see that Ruth Logg Fernandez knew pitifully little about this man who was her husband. Even her worried family had no idea.

It would not have been difficult for Ruth to have found out about Tony's recent and remote past. Reams of newspaper copy had been published about Tony Fernandez's checkered career. In his home territory, he had been at first famous—and later *infamous.*

In the early 1950s, Tony Fernandez had been an important player in the timber industry of Washington and Oregon. When he was in his twenties, he had made a killing in the logging business. He operated mainly out of Longview, a city of twenty thousand in southwestern Washington. The Longview *Daily News* frequently carried reports of Fernandez's new and massive timber buys. Some of his deals involved millions of dollars worth of virgin timber.

Tony Fernandez was listed as a partner in many companies, and he was considered one of the more solid citizens in Longview. He was headline material: "Fernandez Buys Timber at Dam Site in Oregon" (this was on July 19, 1954, when Tony had purchased 40 million board feet at thirty-two dollars per thousand feet); "Chinook Region Logging Planned" (this was on October 4, 1954, when he had bought eight million board feet); "Fernandez Buys Pacific Timber" (on March 9, 1956, when Tony Fernandez estimated his newest contract would eventually cost $300,000).

At the time Tony Fernandez was only thirty-one, but he was on a roll and he didn't stop at timber. On March 22, 1955, the Longview *Daily News* told of a new mining company being incorporated in Cowlitz County, Washington. Tony Fernandez was its president. The purpose of the company would be "to mine, mill, concentrate, convert, smelt, treat and sell gold, silver, copper, lead, zinc, brass, iron and steel." The new company also expected to obtain oil rights. Stock valued at $100,000 had been authorized.

Tony Fernandez maintained a high profile. He drove new Cadillacs. As an honorary deputy sheriff, he was allowed to install a siren in his car. He lived in a big house on the hill above Longview with his wife and four children. He was a Boy Scout leader and a Longview city councilman.

In April of 1957, Fernandez announced that he was branching out into Canada and that he had purchased a *billion* board feet of timber—an early land grant by the British Royal family—near Nelson, British Columbia for $1,500,000. He said he was considering setting up a branch office near the Canadian border.

In reality, Tony's business empire seemed to have been built on shifting sands. Several huge timber companies brought suit against him, saying that he had logged off areas long after his contracts had expired. He was also accused of selling sections of timber by misrepresentation; he had identified the wrong sections of trees to prospective buyers. They thought they were buying acreage thick with timber when in reality Tony had simply shown them property that he didn't own. They had signed purchase agreements without checking legal descriptions.

It wasn't only the big corporations who were after Tony Fernandez. Several elderly landowners claimed they had been cajoled into signing their names to blank contracts, only to find to their regret that they had signed quit-claim deeds to their timberland.

Tony Fernandez couldn't juggle his books forever. By July 1958 the IRS began to look at him with a jaundiced eye. The Internal Revenue Service filed notice of a tax lien of $95,246.31 against him for taxes that he hadn't paid in 1951, 1952, and 1953. The IRS filed what was known as a "jeopardy assessment" against Fernandez's assets. This amounted to a lien against all his property. It followed two Superior Court memorandums saying that the wheeler-dealer logger had to pay two logging firms over half a million dollars as the result of civil suits.

Still, Tony Fernandez drove his Cadillacs, lived in his nice house, and kept up the facade of a highly successful businessman and a pillar in Longview.

Individuals who had done business with Fernandez were nothing if not confused. An Oregon man, Bill Belcher, was foggy about a trip he had made to Nelson, British Columbia, with Fernandez in March of 1958. Tony had offered to "fly over" his timber holdings there so Belcher could have a look. But the clouds had been so thick that Belcher couldn't tell whether he was looking at fir, pine, spruce, hemlock . . . or tumbleweed. When they attempted to reach the woods later by Jeep, they were forced back by deep snowdrifts.

While they pondered their predicament, Belcher stepped behind the Jeep to light a cigarette. The next conscious memory he had was of lying beside a railroad track; his head felt as though a train had run over it. He was found by railroad workers who called for medics. Belcher was hospitalized with severe head injuries for ten days.

Later, he learned that Tony Fernandez had returned to the guest cabin where the two men had been staying. He had told the managers that Belcher had decided to stay up in the woods in a miner's cabin.

The Royal Canadian Mounted Police notified Bill Belcher's family that he had been critically injured. His wife left at once for Canada. After assuring herself that he would survive, she followed Belcher's instructions to retrieve his briefcase in which he had carried important papers and money. She found the briefcase but Belcher could not explain a logging contract that had been tucked inside. There was also a receipt for $40,000 in payment for some land.

Bill Belcher had no memory whatsoever of what happened to him after he stepped out of Tony Fernandez's vehicle to have a cigarette alongside a snowy road. However, he was adamant that he would never have bought timber he had not even seen, and he would not have given someone $40,000 for trees hidden in fog.

While Belcher had lain unconscious, a bank officer in Grants Pass, Oregon, where Belcher had an account, received several phone calls from a man who identified himself as Bill Belcher. The caller directed the banker to transfer $40,000 to a Gresham, Oregon, bank to the account of the "Fernandez-Belcher deal."

Belcher, who had never suffered blackouts, fainting spells, or anything akin to them before his mysterious "attack" behind the Jeep in the snowy Canadian timberland, eventually recovered thirty-six thousand from Tony Fernandez's company in an out-of-court settlement.

In 1959 Tony Fernandez faced charges of another kind. He was arrested in March of that year and charged with three counts of carnal knowledge and indecent liberties after a teenage girl alleged that he had forced sex on her two years earlier. After many delays and a change of venue to Clark County, Washington, Fernandez was acquitted of the charges.

Tony Fernandez continued to remain active in timber commodities. In the latter part of April 1961, another bizarre incident took place when John Casteel, an elderly Cresswell, Oregon, lumberman, flew over the Canadian timberland with Fernandez. It was almost a replay of what had happened with Bill Belcher. Casteel couldn't see well enough to judge the quality or kind of timber far beneath him. All the while, Fernandez kept talking, mentioning that the syndicate he represented had recently purchased 1,800 acres in Wasco County, Oregon, for two million dollars. Casteel craned his neck to try to see the trees that Fernandez wanted to sell him, but the plane was much too high and the weather didn't cooperate.

After the abortive flight, Fernandez and Casteel stayed in a Spokane hotel and Tony said it would take about $100,000 to protect the rights to the Canadian timber. Casteel said he didn't have that kind of money to invest in timber at the moment and wasn't interested. Tony knew, however, that the elderly man had plenty of money; earlier, Casteel had given Tony a three-day option at a price of three million dollars on some timberland Casteel owned.

When the two returned to Longview, Fernandez invited the old man to look at a tract of timber twenty miles east of Longview. After they had looked at one stand of trees, Tony suggested they check out another forest which grew at the end of a logging road.

They viewed the trees and Casteel wasn't very impressed. On the way out of the deep woods, Tony Fernandez had suddenly shouted that he had lost control of the Jeep.

"When I looked up, I saw Fernandez bailing out," said Casteel, who proved to be more resilient than Tony had figured. "He was still hanging on to the steering wheel."

Casteel himself had had no choice but to ride the out-of-control Jeep to the bottom of a sixty-foot grade, "bouncing like a rubber ball" inside the closed cab. To his amazement, he was still alive when the Jeep finally stopped against a tree trunk. He had clambered out of the wrecked Jeep and made his way painfully up the slope.

Fernandez was waiting at the top, towering over him as he climbed hand over hand. Casteel wasn't sure if he was in trouble, but Tony had snorted and said only, "You're a tough old devil—I couldn't kill you with a club."

Casteel hoped Fernandez wasn't about to try.

The two hitched a ride into town on a logging truck and Casteel drove himself two hundred miles to his home, where a doctor found he'd survived the crash with only some torn ligaments.

Later, when John Casteel opened his suitcase to show a friend a map of the Canadian timberland, he found copies of a memorandum of agreement between himself and one of Fernandez's companies. He had never seen it before, yet it was a deed conveying Casteel's timberland to Fernandez in consideration of an option on Tony's Wasco County property, *and* an assignment of the Canadian timber asserting that Casteel had offered $400,000 for it.

John Casteel was a sharp businessman and he immediately set about clouding the title to his three-million-dollar stand of timber so that Fernandez could not take it over. He eventually paid Tony fifteen hundred dollars to release all claims and considered himself lucky to have lost only that much.

It would take a book-length volume to describe the intricacies of Tony Fernandez's timber dealings. One would suspect that he had some successful incidents where would-be buyers "signed" papers without being aware that they had. There may even have been other "accidents" in the woods that were never reported.

Fernandez's financial world blew up finally in April of 1962 when he was indicted by a federal grand jury on charges of engaging in a multimillion-dollar timber swindle. It was the culmination of a four-year investigation into Fernandez's business machinations. The incidents involving Belcher and Casteel were cited in the charges along with many others.

Tony Fernandez was convicted of seven counts of interstate fraud and one of conspiracy in Judge William G. East's Federal District Courtroom in Portland, Oregon, in December 1962. Two months later, he was sentenced to eleven years and eleven months in prison. That April, his remaining property was sold to satisfy judgments against him. Despite appeals, Tony Fernandez remained in the McNeill Island Federal Prison until his parole on January 15, 1970.

Tony was far from idle during his years on the bleak prison island in Puget Sound. In 1968, claiming status as a taxpayer in the state of Washington, he sued Washington's Secretary of State Lud Kramer and U.S. Representative Julia Butler Hansen for a hundred thousand dollars on the grounds that Ms. Hansen was not qualified to serve in Congress because she was a woman. The suit was capricious, not to mention chauvinistic, and it got nowhere. However, it netted Tony Fernandez more headlines and he liked that.

Six months after he was paroled, Fernandez was awarded a degree from Tacoma Community College's extension program. He became the first convict in the State of Washington to earn a college degree through an innovative program that allowed prisoners to take courses while they were in the penitentiary.

And so, in 1970, Anthony Fernandez was free—both from prison and from his twenty-three-year marriage. His wife had divorced him in 1965 while he was in prison. Surprisingly, she said she had no ill feelings toward Tony. He had always been a good provider and never mean or abusive. She did mention his wandering eye, however. She just hadn't wanted to be lied to any longer. It had been a most civilized divorce. *So* civilized, in fact, that when Tony was paroled, he often brought his new girlfriends to visit his ex-wife.

Scattered accounts of Tony Fernandez's postprison activities boggle the mind. He reported to hometown friends that he was a senior at Pacific Lutheran University in Tacoma, majoring in psychology and ecology. This wasn't long after his release from prison. As part of his studies, he joined a student tour to Arizona and New Mexico to study Navajo Indian history, culture, and economy. In an article in the Longview *Daily News*, it was also noted that Tony was enrolled simultaneously in an MA and Ph.D. program in a Florida university. (As it happened, all this "college" required its students to do to get a "diploma" was to write a thesis of unspecified length.)

Tony Fernandez's doctorate had been awarded simply because he had submitted a paper entitled "The Innovated Navajo." And *voilà!* Tony Fernandez became Dr. Anthony Fernandez.

When he was heard from next, *Dr.* Fernandez reported he was attending the North American College of Acupuncture in Vancouver, British Columbia. Tony is quoted as saying he attended classes in Vancouver three times a week and would be spending fifteen weeks in Hong Kong and sixty days in Peking as part of his training.

It wasn't that Fernandez believed that acupuncture was particularly important in the Western world. "It is," he pontificated, "at best, a fad. But I'm going into this with the point of view that it is most likely a psychological tool. And even if I never use it, the experience and knowledge will be a benefit."

On March 30, 1971—the same month he met Ruth Logg—a small item appeared in the Longview *Daily News*. "Anthony Fernandez, formerly of Longview and a recent Pacific Lutheran University graduate, will open a counseling office complex next month at 8815 S. Tacoma Way. He is also negotiating for property in Kelso on which to construct a family counseling clinic."

Dr. Fernandez promised to provide a twenty-four-hour answering service and said he had contracted to evaluate welfare recipients for the Tacoma office of the Department of Public Assistance.

On June 10, 1971, "Dr." Fernandez's picture appeared in the Wenatchee, Washington, *Daily World* beside an article about his plans to establish a "rehabilitation center" for drug addicts and alcoholics on eighty acres he owned in the rural town of Alstown. He promised that he would build a modern clinic but retain the flavor of the historic old cabins on the eastern Washington property. He assured nearby residents that his patients would not be "turned loose" in the community. He did not mention, of course, that he himself was a parolee from a federal prison.

None of Fernandez's new endeavors ever got off the ground. He didn't need them. He had Ruth Logg and the fortune her late husband had left her.

This was the man with whom Ruth fell madly in love. This was her soft-eyed, warm-voiced hero who was going to make the second half of her life a wonderful time of love and companionship. She had never known anyone with no conscience at all; she was naive about the world of the con man. Les had loved her and protected her.

Once married to Ruth, Tony Fernandez was kept busy overseeing her business interests and fortune. He encouraged Kathleen, her older daughter, to move out almost immediately after his marriage to her mother. He told Ruth it would be good for Kathleen to have an apartment of her own. Ruth's younger daughter, Susan, lived with them but was involved with her own friends.

At first, the Fernandez marriage seemed idyllic. If Ruth's former friends and relatives didn't call often, she didn't notice—she was so caught up in loving Tony.

The marriage turned bitter and disappointing far too soon. While Tony's first wife had turned a deaf ear to rumors of his infidelities, Ruth could not. She suspected he was seeing other women. It tore her apart.

In May of 1974, when she had been married to Tony for just over two years, Ruth took a trip to Texas—alone. Tony remarked to one of her daughter's boyfriends, "When she comes back, she'll have to shape up or ship out."

While Ruth was gone, Fernandez used Ruth's Power of Attorney and sold some of her property without her knowledge for $100,000—far less than its actual value.

Only six months before, Ruth and Tony had vacationed at a plush resort in Mazatlan, Mexico, where they had impressed other couples as an "ideal couple." But that had evidently been the last try on Ruth's part to make the marriage work. One reason for the end of the perfect romance—and a good reason at that—was the fact that Tony reportedly had another woman he was seriously involved with. She lived in Centralia, Washington. Although Ruth didn't realize it, he had used *her* money to give the other woman an expensive fur coat and a diamond solitaire. He told the woman that they would be married soon.

While Ruth Fernandez was on her lonely trip in May, Tony also took care of some other pressing business. He took out a $100,000 accidental death insurance policy on Ruth through Mutual of Omaha. There was never any concrete evidence that Ruth signed the application for that policy.

To her everlasting misfortune, Ruth still loved Tony. She still believed she could win back his love and that he would be faithful to her. During the third week of July 1974, she was excited about a camping trip they were going to take together. It would be like another honeymoon. They had rented a fully equipped Winnebago Brave motor home from a local dealer, and also took a four-wheel drive vehicle with them.

On Sunday afternoon, July 26, Ruth and Tony Fernandez stopped at the Mount Si Golf Course restaurant in North Bend, Washington, for cocktails and lunch. They lingered in the picturesque spot for a long time.

Just beyond North Bend, the I-90 freeway and back roads head east swiftly up toward the summit of Snoqualmie Pass. The land drops away steeply at the edges of the byroads. The Fernandez's campsite was eight miles up the mountain from North Bend.

According to witnesses, both Ruth and Tony had seemed somewhat affected by the drinks they had with lunch. They left, saying they were headed for their campsite. At 4:15 that July afternoon, the Fernandezes visited the Snoqualmie office of the Weyerhauser Lumber Company on a business errand. Employees there recalled that Ruth seemed to be unhappy and a little querulous, while Tony was reflective and quiet. Neither of them, however, seemed to be intoxicated. When they left, they said they were going on up toward Snoqualmie Pass to the place where they were camping.

The first hint that something might be wrong came at 8:30 that Sunday evening. Tony called the waitress at the Mount Si restaurant to ask if she had seen Ruth. She had not. Next, he called the Little Chalet Café in North Bend, asking the staff there if they had seen Ruth. They knew her, but they hadn't seen her that evening.

At 8:36 P.M. Tony called the Washington State Patrol station in North Bend, expressing his concern for Ruth's safety. When the trooper on duty asked him why he was worried, Tony said first that Ruth had left the campsite for a walk in the woods alone and she had not returned. But then he changed his story. He said she had driven in the Winnebago, and he thought she had been heading for their home in Auburn.

"I followed her twenty minutes to half an hour later in my four-wheel drive Scout," he said. "But I couldn't find any sign of her."

Coincidentally, Susan Logg and her fiancé, Don Stafford, had headed up the Granite Creek Road toward the campsite between 8:30 and 9:30 P.M. that Sunday night. They had passed neither Ruth nor Tony along the way. When they got back to the big house in Auburn at 10:40 P.M., they encountered Tony, who had just emerged from taking a shower. He told them he had no idea where Ruth had gone off to. He figured she would come driving up any time, and there was no use to go looking for her. It was too dark.

The long night passed with no word at all from Ruth. The next morning, Don Stafford and Tony Fernandez drove back to North Bend and officially reported Ruth as a missing person to the State Patrol. Then they drove up the Martha Lake Road to the Granite Creek Road along the route to the vacated campsite. There was no sign of the Winnebago along the roadway. Suddenly, Stafford spotted some tracks in the dirt shoulder next to the Granite Creek Road. The tracks appeared to disappear over the cliff's edge. When Stafford pointed them out, Tony Fernandez asked him, "Do you think I should look here?"

Stafford volunteered to look. He walked to the edge of the precipitous cliff where rock had been blasted out, making it an almost sheer drop. Bracing himself, he looked down. Far, far below, he saw the crumpled mass of metal that had been the Winnebago.

Before he turned back to give Tony the bad news, Don Stafford forced himself to look along the cliff side between the wrecked camper and the top. About halfway down, he saw a body and he knew it was Ruth Fernandez.

In a very short time, the sunny mountain road was alive with King County Police and Washington State Patrol troopers. The wreckage was three hundred feet below. The investigators were able to approach it only obliquely by using a logging road farther down the grade. When they finally got to Ruth Fernandez, they confirmed that she was dead, and that she had been for many hours. Rigor mortis was almost complete. She appeared to have suffered massive head injuries. Oddly, her clothing was remarkably untorn for someone who had ridden the hurtling camper off the embankment and then one hundred fifty feet down the hill before she had fallen out.

Tony Fernandez complained about the hours the police were spending at the scene. It was perfectly obvious what had happened. He muttered to Don Stafford, "They are just creating red tape." Tony asked Stafford to leave with him. He didn't want to stay around there any longer, watching from above as the cops worked over his dead wife.

There were aspects of the accident that puzzled and bothered the investigators. Trooper Don Caughell of the Washington State Patrol's Fatality Investigative Unit looked with his discerning eye first at the road and then at the shattered motor home. The road had no defects that would make control of a vehicle difficult; there was no breaking away of the shoulder area where the rig had gone over. This indicated to him that the Winnebago had been moving slowly and that no one had stomped on the brakes in a desperate attempt to keep from plunging over. "Why?" he wondered. Why hadn't Ruth Fernandez tried to save herself?

Although the motor home itself was thoroughly crumpled, there was no sign inside it to indicate that a body had bounced around during the terrible drop. No blood, no torn flesh, no hair. Ruth Fernandez had been wearing a loosely woven blouse which would have been likely to catch on *something* during the terrible bucketing down the steep hill. But her blouse had no tears or snags at all.

Ruth Fernandez's body was lifted with the use of a carefully balanced litter, from the side of the cliff and taken to the King County Medical Examiner's Office in Seattle to await autopsy.

The postmortem examination showed that she had suffered two severe injuries, neither of which was typical of a victim who had ridden a vehicle down a slope for almost two hundred feet. The first wound was caused by some kind of blunt object striking her omentum—the fatty, apronlike membrane that hangs from the stomach and transverse colon in the abdominal cavity. The omentum is rich in blood vessels. Ruth's second wound—and the fatal wound—was a fractured skull. She had died sometime between 11:30 A.M. on the 26 and 11:30 A.M. on the 27. The best clue to time of death is when the victim has last been seen. As Ruth was known to be alive at 4:30 P.M. on the Sunday she disappeared, the time-of-death period could be cut to nineteen hours.

According to autopsy findings, she could have lived a maximum of six hours without treatment and a minimum of one hour. Blood alcohol tests indicated that Ruth had been legally intoxicated at the time of her death, that is, she had at least .10 of alcohol in her bloodstream.

Tony Fernandez was Ruth's sole heir, and he applied almost immediately for her insurance benefits. Mutual of Omaha declined to cut him a check, however, because there was an ongoing investigation into her death. Indeed, King County Police homicide detectives Ted Forrester and Roger Dunn would spend months in their initial probe of the strange circumstance of Ruth Logg Fernandez's death. Those months would stretch into years.

Circumstantial evidence indicated that some outside force had caused Ruth's Winnebago to plunge over the cliff. Forester and Dunn suspected Tony Fernandez of killing his wife, but they could not prove it.

What did happen between 4:30 and 8:30 P.M. on July 26, 1974? No one but Tony saw Ruth during that time, and he insisted that she first took a walk in the woods and then decided to drive home alone from their campsite.

He liked to imply that Ruth had been out of control, hysterical, irrational—a woman who should not have been driving the big Winnebago rig. Tony even suggested obliquely that Ruth might have been suicidal. But was it consistent with human psychology that a healthy, forty-four-year-old woman, slightly intoxicated, perhaps upset at her failing marriage, would deliberately drive herself off a cliff? She had two daughters who needed her, family, friends, a considerable fortune. If she was so angry at Tony that she wanted to die, would she have done this knowing that it was Tony and Tony alone who would inherit everything she owned?

Probably not.

The case dragged on. No criminal charges were filed against Tony Fernandez. Fernandez himself pooh-poohed the theory that he might have killed his wife. He remained in the family home and gave frequent interviews to the media, appearing often on the nightly news television programs. He appeared affable and confident.

Tony Fernandez was *so* confident, in fact, that he began to date publicly. He was a grieving widower, yes, but a man got lonely.

In February of 1976, a year and a half after Ruth Logg Fernandez died, her daughters, Mrs. Kathleen Logg Lea, twenty-two, and Susan Logg, nineteen, brought civil suit against Tony Fernandez, charging that he was not eligible to inherit any of Ruth's fortune. Under the Slayer's Act, no one shall inherit benefits resulting from the death of someone whose death they have caused.

Ruth's daughters were so frustrated to see Tony Fernandez going blithely on with his life that they felt they had to do something. Ted Forrester and Roger Dunn had explained that they had not yet come up with enough physical evidence to take to the King County Prosecutor's Office so that criminal charges could be brought. Criminally, guilt must be proved beyond the shadow of a doubt. *Civilly*, however, a judgment can be made on the "preponderance of evidence." Testimony on "prior bad acts" (of which Tony Fernandez had plenty) could be introduced.

Ruth's daughters decided to go for it.

Enraged, Tony Fernandez brought a million-dollar lawsuit against Ted Forrester.

It was a marathon four-week trial and received more press coverage than most criminal trials. Superior Court Judge George Revelle's courtroom became a kind of microcosm of the lives of Tony Fernandez and Ruth Logg Fernandez. Ghosts of Fernandez's past reappeared. John Casteel, the man who had bounced in a Jeep sixty feet down a cliff after Fernandez bailed out, was there. So was William Belcher, who wound up with a head wound in the snowy wilds of Canada. Neither man came right out and accused Tony of violence—they merely related what had happened to them.

Tony's ex-wife testified—for the defense—saying he was faithful "in his own way" and that he had never thrown his other women in her face during their marriage. She smiled at him as she testified.

After the background of the couple's meeting, romance, and marriage was presented, both sides called experts in forensic pathology to the stand.

Dr. F. Warren Lovell, Chief Pathologist of Northwest Hospital, testified for Fernandez's defense. Lovell, who specialized in the study of fatal accidents and designed the autopsy program for the NASA flight project, said that it was likely that, when the Winnebago went over the cliff, Ruth Fernandez's body became an essentially weightless object, thrown against the motor, which would have yielded on impact. This, Lovell testified would explain why Ruth's injuries were not more extensive. He also said it was not unusual that her clothing was untorn.

On cross-examination, however, Dr. Lovell conceded that the fatal skull fracture could have been caused by a man taking her by the hair and striking her head on a rock. "But it would be very hard to do," he added.

Dr. Lovell did not agree with the plaintiffs that the injury to the abdomen was consistent with a blow from a fist. He said that it could have been caused by Ruth's belly hitting the steering wheel.

Detective Roger Dunn, however, testified that he had examined the steering wheel of the Winnebago and found no damage consistent with a great force pushing against it.

Dr. Gale Wilson, who had been the King County Medical Examiner for forty years before his retirement and who had done over seventeen thousand autopsies, testified that, in his educated opinion, Ruth was not in the motor home when it left the road. He was convinced, rather, that she had died from a blunt instrument applied with great force to her head. Dr. Donald Reay, the current medical examiner, testified that Ruth had died of a skull fracture and that it was possible—but not very likely—that she was in the motor home when it left the road.

The options open to the deciding judge were essentially this:

1. Ruth Fernandez, distraught and a little intoxicated, drove accidentally off the cliff without even applying the brakes of the motor home. Her body fell out halfway down.
2. Ruth Fernandez drove deliberately off the cliff and her body was thrown out halfway down.
3. Someone bludgeoned and beat Ruth Fernandez, pushed the motor home off the cliff and flung Ruth down after it. *Or* someone carried her body halfway down to make it look as if she had been in an accident.
4. Someone pushed the Winnebago over and persuaded Ruth to go down to it to help retrieve valuables. That someone then killed her where she was found.

Tony Fernandez himself did not testify in the trial.

Arthur Piehler, the attorney for the Logg sisters, summed up the plaintiff's case dramatically: "Tony Fernandez *did* fall in love when he met Ruth in 1971. He fell in love with her house, her five acres, her swimming pool, her stocks, her bonds, and other assets."

Piehler recalled that medical experts had testified that Ruth would have had broken bones, multiple cuts, lacerations, foreign objects in wounds, and torn clothing had she been in the Winnebago when it crashed. He theorized that Fernandez had somehow crashed the motor home and then persuaded Ruth to walk down the mountainside with him to recover items in it. It would have been easy for him to hit her on the head and in the stomach, and leave her there to die alone.

Piehler contended that Fernandez had forged Ruth's signature on the one-hundred-thousand-dollar accidental death policy two months and six days before she died. He said Tony had probably become concerned that his wife was considering a divorce. "He could see all his lovely property drifting away from him." Piehler told the court about the other woman Tony was seeing, the woman who had received the diamonds and furs.

John C. Hoover, Fernandez's attorney, argued that the couple had been happy and that they had taken a week's camping trip together. The Winnebago had crashed, he said, only because Ruth had had too much to drink. Hoover insisted that Ruth had been completely content with all the property agreements between herself and her husband. If she had not been satisfied with their arrangement, she had had plenty of time to change it.

In March 1976, Tony Fernandez's fortune evaporated when Judge Revelle read his oral decision to a packed courtroom, a decision in which he found the defendant without credibility. "I do not believe anything he says," Revelle began succinctly.

Revelle read his thirty-one-page decision and concluded, "I have examined many possibilities and numerous high probabilities of the cause and method of her death. Each such probability requires the participation of the only person I know who was with her; that's Anthony Fernandez. One of those methods or probabilities is a method suggested by Mr. Piehler, but I can't say that's it. I just know that under the burden of proof here—even stronger than necessary to be found—Anthony Fernandez, I conclude, participated as a principal in the willful and unlawful killing of Ruth Fernandez."

In his conclusions of law, Judge Revelle said, "Anthony Fernandez, as the slayer of Ruth Fernandez, shall not acquire, in any way, property or receive any benefit as the result of the death of Ruth Fernandez. Anthony Fernandez is deemed to have predeceased the decedent (under the Slayer's Act) Ruth Fernandez. All property which would have passed to or for the benefit of the defendant, Anthony Fernandez, by the terms of the Will of Ruth Fernandez, or any agreement of the defendant and Ruth Fernandez, under the provisions of RCW 21.16.120 shall be distributed as if the defendant had predeceased Ruth Fernandez."

With that, Tony lost the financial ball game. But he did not lose his freedom. He had only lost a civil case.

It took another court order to get Fernandez to vacate the home in Auburn. He had lived there since July of 1974 when Ruth died. Tony was ordered not to attempt to remove furniture, appliances, or anything of value that would be part of the estate. Judge Revelle also restrained Fernandez from using credit cards drawn on the estate. Counsel for Sue and Kathy said, "Fernandez has been dissipating everything he can get his hands upon and has spent about $155,000 that was part of the estate." Even as the trial had progressed, Tony was said to have been involved in a $200,000 land purchase.

Finally, Tony moved from the home that now belonged to Ruth's daughters. But, in the end, there was little of the estate left for the two orphaned young women. After lawyers' fees and Tony's free spending, they obtained less than 10 percent of the money their parents had put aside for their futures.

On June 3, 1976, Fernandez was charged in Lane County, Oregon, with forgery and theft by sale of timber valued at nearly $75,000 and was arrested on a federal parole violation warrant. He was not inside long. Yet another woman besotted with Tony Fernandez put up his bail.

On August 12, 1977, Fernandez was charged with seven felony counts in Thurston County, Washington—second-degree theft, two counts of unlawful issuance of bank checks, and four counts of first-degree theft alleging unlawful sale of timber rights that he claimed were his to a third party. These violations were said to have occurred in Thurston County in the winter of 1976–77. Convicted on all these counts, consecutive sentences could net him fifty-five years in prison.

On September 1, 1977, the charge for which Ruth's daughters and loved ones had waited so long was made. The King County Prosecutor's Office charged Anthony Fernandez with first-degree murder in the death of Ruth Fernandez. His trial, scheduled for January 9, 1978—almost four years after Ruth died on the lonely mountainside—was one where the evidence was mostly circumstantial, one of the most difficult cases for a prosecutor to press. It was lengthy, and full of surprises. Tony Fernandez's mistress, wearing her fur coat, was present at his trial every day.

Tony Fernandez was convicted of Ruth Logg Fernandez's murder in February 1978, and sentenced to life in prison. And that was exactly what he served.

On Christmas Day 1995, Anthony Fernandez, seventy-three, enjoyed a hearty holiday meal in prison. And then he dropped dead of a massive heart attack.

Who was the real Tony Fernandez? Was he a timber baron, a doctor of psychology, an acupuncturist, a historian of Navajo culture, a master of city government? A lover—a studied conman—or a methodical killer?

It doesn't matter anymore to Ruth Logg Fernandez. The man who promised to love her forever betrayed her. She lost her hopes for the perfect romance in the darkness on the steep mountainside along Granite Creek Road. She will never see her grandchildren and never know her daughters as mature women.

Perhaps she knows, however, that those daughters saw their quest through to the end and gave her the only gift they could: justice.

Black Leather

The cases *that follow next—"Black Leather" and "Mirror Images"—
are companion pieces, a close look at the injustice that resulted when those
who should have been paying attention looked the other way.*

*The first case, which allows a rare insider's look at the crimes of a sexually
aberrant criminal, is ugly; it may be offensive to some readers. Still, it
demonstrates more than any other I have written how ridiculously dangerous misplaced trust in a sexual psychopath can be. This case will lead you
into the next in the natural order of unnatural behavior—if such a thing is
possible.*

*Larry Hendricks, the murderer in "Black Leather," was a sexual psycho-
path. So are the two killers in the case following this one. They shared one
identity between them; Larry Hendricks was two people all by himself, a
man with a respectable facade and a secret life so dark and so sick that his
crimes left even experienced Pierce County, Washington, detectives, who
have seen their share of grisly murders, shaking their heads.*

*This killer was trusted far beyond limits that anyone might imagine,
trusted by the system that released him into society, and he betrayed that
trust in a series of unspeakable crimes.*

It was a little after eight A.M. on Monday, the first of May, 1979, when Sam Brand, a farmer who lives in an isolated, wooded rural area near Roy, Washington, heard someone pounding frantically on his front door. Drop-in visitors at Brand's farm were a rarity and he was a little ill at ease when he heard the insistent beating on his door.

He was more alarmed when he opened the door and saw a young man, apparently badly beaten and drenched in blood—some of it dried, some freshly glistening. The man was shouting almost incoherently. In New York City or Detroit or Chicago—and probably even in downtown Seattle—Brand would probably have slammed his door and called police. But this was the country where neighbors helped neighbors and even strangers.

"Hey, I need some help!" the youth cried.

Sam Brand opened the door wider, beckoning the boy in. "Yeah . . . it sort of looks like you do."

"A guy took me out in the woods, and he beat me. And there was another body there already," the youth blurted. "I shot him. I *had* to. He was going to kill me too."

Brand didn't doubt that the young man had been beaten. His fair hair was scarlet with blood, one arm dangled awkwardly, and he winced as if every movement caused him pain.

"He kidnaped me," the man babbled on. "I was finally able to overpower him and I shot him with all the guns. They're back there. I just drove until I found someone."

Still not convinced that the injured man wasn't under the influence of hallucinatory drugs, Brand moved to the phone and called to ask that the Pierce County Sheriff's Department and an aide car respond. He offered the stranger something to eat, some coffee, but all he would accept was water.

The location of the Brand farm was so obscure that only deputies who worked the region were familiar with it. It was deep in the southern end of the county about eight miles east of the crossroads town of McKenna. Deputy Greg Riehl and Rescue Squad Number 15 arrived simultaneously at 8:51 A.M.

Sam Brand had set a mattress on the ground outside his garage so that the injured man could lie down while three emergency medical technicians worked over him. Riehl noted that fresh blood continued to seep from a wound at the back of the man's head.

The victim quickly identified himself as Private Niels Honegger,* twenty-one, and said he was stationed at Fort Lewis. He produced a military ID card with his picture on it.

Honegger talked so rapidly that the deputy could barely understand him; he repeated over and over that he had had no choice but to shoot. Gently, Riehl asked the young soldier to start from the beginning and try to slow down.

Honegger said that he had been waiting for a taxi back to the base at about 3:40 that morning when a man driving a black van stopped. At first he had beckoned to Honegger to come over to the van, and then the stranger had pulled a gun and ordered him into the back. The rest of his story was so terrifying that it sounded like it had happened in a nightmare.

"He put some kind of black leather hood over my head and drove around for hours," Honegger said. "Then he drove out to some logging road, made me take off all my clothes, and then he handcuffed me and put leg irons on me. He forced me back in the woods. That's when I saw the body. He said the same thing was going to happen to me."

He said the man had been dressed entirely in black leather. Once Honegger was handcuffed, his captor beat him with a billy club. Realizing that he was in the hands of a sadomasochistic crazy man, who was probably planning to subject him to a sexual assault, Honegger said he had feigned unconsciousness while he tried to think of a way out of his predicament.

The young soldier said he had waited for his chance. When the man in black had bent over to unhook his leg irons, he had been able to break free. The man had several guns.

"I shot him," Honegger said. "I shot him with all the guns. Then I beat him with the gun barrel until I was sure he was dead."

The paramedics and Riehl stared at the wild-eyed young soldier. Could this be true, or was he in the grip of some delusion?

Honegger said he had thrown on his clothes, and then he had

driven the stranger's black van until he found a house. "I was so scared I drove right through the gate. Then I found I couldn't find a road in so I parked the van and walked down. This man let me in."

Riehl advised Niels Honegger of his rights. He had just admitted to shooting a man to death, and it was procedure that he should be read his rights under Miranda. Honegger shook his head impatiently and said he understood all of that and waived his right to counsel. He repeated his story again, and it was exactly as he had told it before.

More deputies arrived and looked for the area where Honegger said he had left two bodies—one his captor's, and another that had been there when they drove in at dawn. The woods were so thick on the property, which was owned by the Weyerhauser Lumber Company, that they doubted they could find the location of the attack without help from Honegger.

"I marked it when I left," the soldier told them. "I took an empty six-pack out of the van and put it by the road so I could find it again."

The medics nodded when asked if Honegger's condition was stable enough for him to give assistance in searching the area. They drove over the narrow roads in Deputy Riehl's patrol car until Honegger spotted the six-pack marker he had left.

"They're in there," he said quietly.

Deputies went over a deadfall fir tree that blocked access to a dirt road that wound up and then disappeared into the woods. When they returned a few minutes later, they looked sick.

"He's right," one said. "There are two bodies back there. I've never seen anything like it."

Detectives Walt Stout and Mark French were notified at sheriff's headquarters in Tacoma and they left at once for the site. They arrived at the Brand farm as Niels Honegger was being loaded into an ambulance for the trip to Madigan Army Hospital. A full statement would have to wait; the young soldier was clearly going into shock.

Briefed by Riehl, Stout and French accompanied him and the other deputies deep into the woods and the body site. The area was thick with new-growth timber and crisscrossed with logging roads. Each one looked much like the last, and it seemed a miracle that Honegger had been able to find his way out and to the Brand farm.

It was a brilliantly sunny spring morning—May Day, in fact—and birds sang in the grove of fir trees, an ironic contrast to the grotesque scene the investigators found.

Detective Walt Stout came upon the first body which lay sprawled in the undergrowth of Oregon grape, sword ferns, and salal. The body was that of an extremely short white male; he was so chubby that he looked oddly like an overgrown infant. But there was nothing childlike about the man's outfit. He was dressed entirely in black leather: a motorcycle jacket, pants, pull-on boots, gloves. Even a billed cap of black leather lay near the body's head. A black turtleneck sweater completed his grotesque outfit.

Although he was clothed from head to foot in leather, the dead man's genitals were exposed. His tight pants had a square of black leather which could be unsnapped at the crotch, not unlike the codpieces worn by men in the fifteenth and sixteenth centuries. The Pierce County detectives had heard of this kind of gear, but they had never actually seen it before. The body's penis and testicles had a kind of "penis ring" or "penis harness" looped around them, a strange rig of black leather thongs.

The man had been shot many, many times in the head and body and had apparently had his skull cracked by blows from a blunt instrument.

The investigators found a second body twelve feet away from the first. It was that of an extremely tall and lanky man who was completely nude. His general physique was all they could tell about him. Most of his face and head had been obliterated, probably blown away by a large caliber weapon. The dead man had a second wound to the left groin area which had torn away much flesh from his genitals and his thigh.

The second body had obviously been in the grove of trees for several days.

The detectives gazed at an assortment of macabre equipment that lay scattered in the undergrowth. This was gear that could only have been intended for bondage and torture: handcuffs, leg irons, several dogs' choke chains on black leather leads, a billy club. Walt Stout and Mark French had no trouble now believing the strange story that Niels Honegger had told.

This quiet woods had been turned into a torture chamber for someone whose sexual fantasies were apparently fulfilled through sadomasochistic rituals.

After measuring the scene, the investigators began to pick up and bag items into evidence. There were enough weapons scattered around for a small revolution: a Winchester double-barreled shotgun, a Colt Python .357 revolver, a Smith & Wesson Airweight 9mm revolver, a Smith & Wesson .44 Magnum revolver, another Smith & Wesson .44 Magnum, and a Browning .25 caliber automatic. The body in black leather still wore two gun belts, two holsters, and a handcuff case and ring for the nightstick that dangled from one belt.

Almost all of the torture gear was bloodstained; the nightstick bore bits of hair and blood, and one of the dogs' choke chains appeared to have been tightened around the neck of someone who was bleeding profusely.

Stout and French found a pair of silver-colored opaque sunglasses lying near the leg irons, all of the items blood-flecked and resting under a sword fern.

As the detectives worked, they didn't talk much. Sadomasochism was something they had learned about in training classes on abnormal psychology, but they could never recall actually *seeing* anything as grotesque as this. They marveled that the stocky young soldier had ever emerged from this thicket of torture alive.

When Pierce County Deputy Coroner Casey Stengel arrived, a closer examination was made of the two bodies. The squat, little man in the black leather suit had a smashed nose, bullet wounds to the left ear and temple, and there were also numerous bullet holes in the leather jacket.

The second victim lay on his back, his legs straight and together, his arms behind his back as if he had been handcuffed when he died. Marks around his ankles indicated that his legs had been shackled for some time.

After the bodies were removed to await autopsy, Deputy John McDonald arrived with his K-9 dog, Duke, and worked the entire area to see if there might be more physical evidence hidden in the woods, but nothing more was found.

Detectives Stout and French left to look at the black 1978 Dodge van that Niels Honegger had driven in his desperate escape. It was still parked on a hill overlooking the Brand residence. Identification Officer Hilding Johnson processed it as the detectives looked on.

They found a registration slip which showed the vehicle was being leased by a Larry Hendricks at an address on North G. in Tacoma. Johnson photographed the rig inside and out and dusted for latent prints before the trio moved in to check for more evidence.

Inside the van, Stout and French found a brown leather bag jammed full of ammunition, some live and some spent cartridges. There was also a black leather hood much like the kind that executioners wore in days of old. The hood had snaps on the front where covers for the eyes and mouth could be attached. The blinder attachment and the mouthpiece were nearby. The mouthpiece had a hard rubber protuberance designed to effectively gag the person who wore the hood.

The hood, which had a label from "The Trading Post" in San Francisco, could be laced tightly up the back and secured at the neck.

The traveling torture chamber also held a black dildo and a black crotchpiece, probably from the leather pants the short dead man wore.

There were some "normal" things too, that seemed out of place: empty beer bottles, cigarette butts, cigar butts.

ID Officer Johnson moved along with Detectives French and Stout, filming every step of the processing. Then he went to the morgue to fingerprint the near-headless corpse in an attempt to identify the man.

Detective John Clark was dispatched to Madigan Army Hospital where he would wait until medics gave the okay for him to take a complete statement from Private Niels Honegger.

In the meantime, Stout and French drove to the apartment house on North G. where the man named Larry Hendricks had lived. They were sure now that Hendricks was the man in the black leather suit. When his clothing was removed in the coroner's office, his driver's license was there, and the picture on it matched. The round, almost childish face was the same. Hendricks was thirty-two years old.

If they had been expecting to walk into quarters designed by the Marquis de Sade, they were to be surprised. Using keys they found on a ring in the van, they entered an immaculate apartment furnished entirely in exquisite antiques. There was nothing at all that might indicate that the apartment's occupant was into kinky sex. Rather, it looked like the home of a wealthy interior decorator. There were pieces of perfectly restored furniture, tapestries, paintings, silk rugs, vases, and lamps. The place might well have come right off a page in *House Beautiful.*

They looked further, however. There was a black vinyl case on a desk in the two-room apartment. Inside, they found nine one-hundred-dollar bills. And, when they opened a closet door, they found a number of items that suggested they had the right man. Either Larry Hendricks had unusual sexual hang-ups or he owned several dogs. There were three black leather dog collars on choke chains in the closet, but no dog dishes, no dog hair on the plush furniture, nor any other sign that Hendricks had pets.

The detectives also found a vinyl shoulder weapon case that would fit the Winchester shotgun found at the scene, and a box of .38 caliber ammunition. There were no kinky magazines in the apartment, but there were two issues of *Soldier of Fortune,* a somewhat militant paramilitary publication for avid gun collectors.

Tenants had storage lockers in the basement of the building, and Larry Hendricks had kept some of his possessions there. Walt Stout and Mark French found several holsters for handguns—both hip and shoulder type, another billy club, and a box of 16-gauge shotgun shells.

What a paradox—a man living in delicate luxury in an antique collector's paradise—but also a man who collected guns and ammunition as if he expected a civil war.

At Madigan Hospital, Detective John Clark was finally allowed to enter the emergency room where Niels Honegger was being treated for his extensive wounds. The youth's broken right arm was splinted and in a sling, and the thick turban of bandages around his head was stained with still-seeping blood. His back was covered with ugly red welts from a beating and burn marks, round and vicious looking, dotted his skin. Honegger's ankles and wrists had abrasions where the handcuffs and leg irons had cut into the skin.

While a military policeman stood by, Niels Honegger agreed to a tape recording of his statement.

He told John Clark that he had gone into Tacoma the previous evening—Sunday night—to see friends, but he hadn't found them at home. He had had one or two beers and then gone to an all-night grocery store where he called a cab to take him back to Fort Lewis.

"I was standing out front, waiting, when this black van pulls up and the driver says, 'Well, what are you doing?' "

As Honegger had peered into the van, he said the driver had pulled a gun and ordered him inside.

"He made me lie down in the back and he put handcuffs on me. I wasn't about to argue with him. He had the gun. He drove for a while and stopped someplace and he put some manacles on my ankles, and then this black leather hood over my head. He tried to put that mouthpiece thing on, but I fought him."

Honegger said that the gun the man had pointed at him in the kidnaping had been one of the .44s.

"My arms were cuffed behind me. I tried to work out of the cuffs, but they were too tight. The manacles had about eighteen inches of chain between them so you could walk, but then he had this little bar with hooks on it and he fastened that on and you couldn't move your legs more than six inches apart."

Honegger said that his captor had driven him around for a long time, until he could see daylight through the eyeholes of his mask. He couldn't be sure but he thought it had been about 5:30 A.M. when they arrived on the lonely logging road. He had heard the stranger moving his guns around, and then the sound of him uncapping a beer bottle.

Next, the man in the black leather suit had come back into the van and demanded that Honegger strip, all the while holding a gun on him.

"He unlocked the manacles on my feet, took off my shoes and socks, and then pulled my pants off. Then he locked those manacles back up, unlocked my handcuffs, and held the gun to my head, telling me to take my shirt off. Then he handcuffed me again."

The man in black leather had then loosened the leg irons so that Honegger could walk and forced him out of the van. He had placed the dog choke chain around his neck, pulling it tight, and prodded Honegger deep into the woods, all the time holding the shotgun to the back of his head.

"He made me say 'sir' all the time—'Yes, sir,' and 'No, sir.' He told me where to go and I guess we walked about twenty-five meters back into the woods. We ended up right by the other body. I thought it was a dog at first, and then I realized it was a man. He wanted to shock me. I was scared as hell, and shivering from the cold. He told me I was going to die and he kept calling me 'Punk.'"

Honegger said that his captor had begun to beat him with the nightstick and that he had been helpless to resist because he was still handcuffed and shackled. Even though he was much bigger and had had combat training, he had been caught and bound up by the little man in black leather before he was aware of what was happening.

"I thought my arm was broken," Honegger said. "He hit me on the head too. He hit me a couple of times in the stomach but I've been trained how to take a stomach punch and I breathed out when I saw it coming so it didn't hurt."

Honegger said that he had tried to make his captor believe he had passed out from the pain, but that had only infuriated the man in leather.

"I lay there and he started burning me with cigarettes and cigars. He put them out on my back and on my nipples. I just couldn't take the pain so I had to get up."

During all this time, Honegger hadn't really seen the other man's face. The black leather cap was pulled down over his eyes and he had worn dark sunglasses that were like mirrors. Honegger, who was a solidly built 5'5" tall, said he had thought his abductor was taller when he had been picked up. He realized now that the man had been much shorter than he was. "I guess the guns made him seem taller," he said, somewhat ruefully.

Hendricks had demanded that his captive perform fellatio on him, but the plucky youth decided that he would rather die than submit to that. "He hit me a couple more times with the nightstick when I refused."

Honegger had reconciled himself to the fact that he was going to die. He told Clark that he had been an atheist up until that point, but he found himself praying and the face of his grandmother kept flashing through his mind. He was shivering from cold and shock, and he was getting dizzy from loss of blood. At that time, Hendricks had told him he was about to die.

"He unlocked my arms first," Honegger recalled. "And then he bent over to unlock the leg irons. I was sitting there watching him and wondered if I ought to do something. He didn't have any of his guns out. After he unlocked my right leg, I leaned back and kicked him as hard as I could. I tried to aim for his face, but I can't remember if I hit it. He fell over backward and I jumped on top of him. I hit him with my right arm—and it hurt me pretty bad—but I kept on hitting him until I saw his nose flatten out and start bleeding."

Honegger's combat training and instinct for survival had given him superhuman strength despite his injuries. Hendricks had tried to pull a gun from the holster he wore and it had gone off twice in the struggle. One bullet had come so close to Honegger's hand that the gunpowder burned it.

"I hit him first, and then I started shooting him." Niels Honegger's eyes closed; he was clearly back once again fighting for his life. "I couldn't tell if I'd hit him or not. He was still moving. When I got done with the first gun, I picked up another one. I shot every single round into him."

Almost hysterical with terror and pain by then, Honegger said he had picked up another weapon and emptied that into his tormentor. He recalled that the man in the black leather suit had assured him quite calmly, "Hey, man, you've *killed* me." But he had kept on firing almost automatically.

For a sadomasochist, receiving pain is almost as pleasurable as inflicting pain, but Larry Hendricks had finally gotten more than he had bargained for. When he stopped moving, Niels Honegger said he had scrambled to the van, thrown his clothes on, and headed for help. But first, afraid he would never find the path to the carnage in the woods, he had stopped to leave the six-pack marker so that he could lead police back to the scene.

Completely unfamiliar with the lonely area, Honegger had driven quite a while before he had seen Brand's farm and barreled the van through the gate in an effort to get help.

"Finally I parked the car at the top of the hill and walked down to the house. And the guy—a real nice guy—looks at me, sees I'm all covered with blood, and he let me into the house."

It was a chilling account, but Detective Clark had no doubt that the soldier was telling him the absolute truth.

Honegger had survived, and Hendricks was dead, but the case was far from over. At headquarters, Walt Stout and Mark French met with Chief Criminal Deputy Henry Suprunowski and ID Officer Johnson concerning the identity of the second victim at the scene. Johnson said that he had a tentative identification from fingerprints he'd taken off the body.

"He only had a minor arrest on a traffic warrant in Port Angeles, but it was enough to get his prints on file. His name is Michael Bertram Zahnle, born June twelfth, 1956. Six feet two, one hundred sixty pounds, red hair, green eyes. His last address is in Tacoma, but they don't know anything about him there."

They agreed that they would give Zahnle's description to the news media in the hope that someone would have more information about him.

Walt Stout received a phone call from a retired firefighter who said that he knew Larry Hendricks. "I deal in antiques and that's how I met him. He has a business he called 'The Merchant Prince' and he does—*did*—quite an antique business. I saw him last night about a quarter to one when he came by my place to talk business."

"How was he dressed?" Stout asked.

"Casual . . . a shirt and slacks, I think."

Hendricks had apparently gone home and dressed in his prowling outfit of black leather before encountering his victim in front of the all-night grocery.

The Pierce County investigative team immediately placed the information on the incident on teletype wires to the eleven western states. They doubted that Larry Hendricks had just begun his bizarre prowlings; the labels on his kinky gear indicated they had been purchased in San Francisco.

But there was a lot more they didn't know about Hendricks. If the case was not already shocking enough, the further revelations into his background would prove almost incomprehensible to the detectives working the case.

They were not particularly surprised to find that Hendricks had been arrested for robbery, assault, and sodomy by the Seattle Police Department in 1969 and sent to the Sexual Offender's program at Western State Hospital. A man who had refined his prowling to a fine art had not done it overnight. He had the van equipped to take prisoners and was well supplied with bondage gear.

What absolutely stunned the case-weary detective veterans was that Larry Hendricks had "graduated" from the Western State Sexual Offender's program after two years—only to be *hired* as a therapy supervisor by the same institution.

There was no question that Larry Hendricks was brilliant. He had graduated with a degree in English literature from the University of Washington, and his friends described him to the detectives and the press as personable and articulate. He had evidently been adept at keeping his straight life separate from his secret world of stalking and sexual aberration.

Larry Hendricks had passed an extensive battery of psychological tests and had been deemed "completely reliable" during his six months work-release period from the mental hospital before he was given the job as counselor.

As a counselor rather than a patient, Hendricks had been promoted steadily until he reached a position where, as a therapy supervisor, he was responsible for a group of twelve to fifteen patients. He monitored their progress, sat in on group therapy sessions, and was responsible for recommending patients' promotions from one stage to the next.

According to hospital spokesman Sidney Acuff, Larry Hendricks's patients were rapists, child molesters, and voyeurs. Embarrassed, the hospital's administrators stressed to the press in a rather obvious statement that Hendricks would never have been employed at Western State for six and a half years if they had known of his bizarre activities.

"Of course, you never know about the private lives of individuals," Acuff said. "But there was never any indication of anything like that."

However, there were those who claimed that there was, indeed, evidence that Larry Hendricks was absolutely unsuited to be a counselor. Even though he had reorganized the hospital's drug treatment program and become director of the new unit he had established, Larry Hendricks behaved inappropriately both at his job and in his private life.

Several residents of the drug program signed sworn affidavits that were released to the media on May 2 when the news of Hendrick's suspected crimes hit the press. One eighteen-year-old patient, who had been transferred to Western State after being raped several times in Alabama State Prison, stated that Hendricks had read about his background in his file. "As soon as he saw the data on the rapes, he started rubbing my leg. Once, he started feeling me all over. I got upset and Larry said if I did that one more time, I would be sent back to prison."

A twenty-two-year-old patient said Hendricks had made a pass at him, telling him he had dreamed of putting his arms around him.

One outspoken critic said, "I threatened to quit if (administrators) didn't deal with Hendrick's rapacious verbal attacks on other staff members." He claimed that instead Hendricks was given even more power and responsibility. Two months later, the employee who had complained about Larry Hendricks resigned in disgust.

Larry Hendricks wasn't particularly unique in his "qualifications" to work as a therapist. At least five members of the paid drug unit at the hospital were reported to have been graduates of the sexual psychopath program.

Larry Hendricks had left his job at the hospital of his own accord in September of 1977 when the drug unit was transferred out of Western State. He had gotten married, but it hadn't lasted. In March of 1978, he returned to his former position of Therapy Specialist III and worked as a ward attendant until the end of July when he started his antique store, "The Merchant Prince."

The Pierce County Sheriff's detectives didn't have to wait long to hear from detectives in other areas. On May 2, they received calls from Captain Bill Cashdollar of the Tehama County Sheriff's Office in California and Sergeant John Robertson of Napa County. They had two unsolved homicides that fit the pattern.

One California victim had been Tom Gloster, a comptroller of the California School of Professional Psychology in San Francisco. His nude body had been found on February 9 in a remote area of Tehama County. Witnesses said they had seen a black van speeding from the scene. Gloster had been shot many times with either a Colt .38 or a .357 Magnum.

The second victim was Larry Harland Niemeier, thirty-two, who had disappeared on February 5 and been found in Napa County. He had been shot with the same gun as Gloster, although the exact caliber and make would have to be determined by microscopic ballistics tests. He too was found naked. A piece of orange carpeting and a cigarette butt were found at the scene. The latter was the same brand found at the scene where Hendricks attacked Niels Honegger.

A thorough search of Larry Hendricks's apartment had turned up credit card slips indicating that he was in the San Francisco area at the time of these slayings, his van had orange carpeting, and he smoked the same brand of cigarettes. Several packs of that brand were found in the apartment wastebaskets. Oddly, each pack was thrown away with a single cigarette remaining—apparently a compulsion with the man.

Mark French contacted an auto body shop whose business card had been found among Hendrick's belongings. The shop confirmed that Hendricks had had the van in the shop from April 16 to April 19 to have bullet holes repaired. Bullets had been fired into the left front door post, the left rear double door, the left side of the van, and the left side of the driver's door.

"He had covered them with black electrical tape," the owner said. "He told us he got into a beef in a parking lot of a bar in San Francisco."

On May 4, Captain Cashdollar and Sergeant Robertson arrived from California to discuss their cases. Both of their victims had last been traced to a bar in San Francisco—"The Brig," an S-and-M–oriented bar—and both men had been dressed in "leathers" similar to Hendricks's outfit when last seen.

Larry Hendricks had apparently suffered a grazing bullet wound sometime before the first of May. Detectives had found eight used bandages in his apartment. And, on autopsy, a similar bandage was found on his body. Dr. J. Cordova said a bullet had grazed the suspect's back on the right side.

It left a question. Had the bullet holes in the van occurred during the killings of Gloster and Niemeier or had there been another victim yet unaccounted for?

On May 6, the results came back from ballistics. Hendricks's Colt Python .357 matched the bullets used in the California killings. He was now linked absolutely to three murders and one attempted murder.

The saddest of all was the murder of Michael Zahnle. On May 3, Detective Art Anderson had received several calls from relatives of Zahnle. They said his parents lived in California and that he had come up to live in Washington about two years earlier. Zahnle was married, and his relatives knew he lived in the Tacoma area but they didn't have his present address.

At 6:15 P.M., after Zahnle's driver's license picture had been shown on the evening news, Anderson received a call from his wife's sister. She said that Michael Zahnle had been missing since April 27, and her sister had moved in with her while waiting for word of his whereabouts.

On May 4, Zahnle's widow came in to talk with Detective John Clark. The grief-stricken woman had had to bear more tragedy in a short time than any young woman should. On April 20, the Zahnles had lost their baby son, who was only eleven days old when he died. The grieving parents had been coaxed to go out with relatives on Friday, April 27, to try to forget for a while. But a few drinks had made Michael Zahnle more morose than ever. In tears, he had left the restaurant in Puyallup, Washington, on foot. Zahnle, a carpenter, had been unemployed. The young couple had no car of their own.

"He hitchhiked a lot, but he was very good at martial arts," his wife said. "And he always got himself out of any situation he got into."

She said her husband had been wearing a yellow pullover, a shirt with "California" on it, blue corduroy pants, and black zip-up boots when he left the restaurant. He had a ninety-two-dollar income tax refund check with him, and a key ring with a picture of their baby on it.

She was adamant that her husband had never shown any homosexual tendencies at all. Moreover, he had been scornful of anyone who was "into weird sex." If Michael Zahnle had gotten into Larry Hendricks's van, it would have been because he needed a ride home. He might not have been as alert as usual because he was upset about the loss of the baby.

The Pierce County detectives talked to others who had known Larry Hendricks, or who *thought* they knew him. The woman who had bought out his interest in "The Merchant Prince" said he was very knowledgeable about antiques but was somewhat strange. "Two or three weeks ago, I went to his apartment on a Saturday," she said thoughtfully. "When he opened the door, I saw two spots of blood on his forehead that had run down from his scalp. His face was flushed and his eyes were glazed. He said he'd been looking at an apartment to buy and he'd struck his head on some nails in the basement. I didn't believe him. I suspected he was into some kind of sexual deviancy, but I let it drop."

A relative of the man who had been addicted to sadomasochism tried to explain what might have caused Larry Hendricks's lifestyle. He knew that Hendricks was gay and said his marriage had lasted only two months. Hendricks had served in Vietnam, but not as a combatant—he was a courier for the military police.

As a child, Hendricks had been very gentle and had never shown the least sign of sadism. When he was seven or eight, he had suffered severe head injuries after being struck with a chunk of concrete. He had had to have brain surgery, and the relative thought this might have caused some of his later deviant behavior.

Larry Hendricks had had a peculiar childhood, dysfunctional in every sense of the word. His mother had dressed Larry in baby clothes until he was well past six. If her baby did not grow older, perhaps she thought that she too would remain young.

When Hendricks was ten, his parents separated and later divorced. Larry had hated his father, blaming him for the divorce. In later years, he was able to forgive his father, but, apparently, the traumas of his youth had scarred him.

Hendricks was an extremely small man. His gun collection, his macho clothes, all the sadistic gear he secreted in his fantasy world might have been part of his almost-psychotic obsession to be a big man.

In an ironic twist, Private Niels Honegger was awarded a $2,500 reward collected by a gay tavern association and "leather" motor-cycle clubs in the San Francisco area for information leading to the arrest of the killer of Tom Gloster. A spokesman for a San Francisco gay group said, "We intend to pay Private Honegger the $2,500 for acting as judge, jury, and executioner. We admire his courage and stamina."

Honegger, on leave, had no comment.

A $1,000 reward collected for information leading to the killer of Richard Niemeier was not sent to Honegger but went instead to establish a memorial reward fund to be used in future killings involving homosexuals.

The backlash to the program that let prisoner-patients free to wander was sharp and biting. At least three King County Superior Court judges and local probation and parole officers said that their primary concern with any sex offender program is security.

Superior Court Judge Barbara Durham (now a Washington State Supreme Court Judge) said, "The potential for danger is so great that security has to be the first concern and treatment second. However, I have a feeling that the program is too amateurish—anyone who gets too difficult is bounced out. In California, there is a sexual psychopath unit separate from the hospital that has fantastic security. It has the highest rate of success in the country."

The laissez-faire program at Western State did not survive the scandals, and its policies tightened up. Two decades later, sadistic sexual predators are housed in a new prison where they have no freedom to roam Washington or any other state. They have no parole dates and some may never get out of prison.

Private Niels Honegger never considered himself a hero. He is a victim like all the others—albeit a victim who survived. What he endured in his fight for life is a memory that no young man should have to carry. And he *does* carry that nightmare for the rest of his days.

Mirror Images

Everything is cyclical—even the death penalty. In most states capital punishment is on the ballots every decade or so. It often takes horrendous crimes to wake up a complacent public. On November 2, 1976, only one referendum passed overwhelmingly in the Washington State elections. Voters, outraged and sickened by a wave of brutal murders, voted to restore the death penalty by a margin of two-to-one, and the governor of Washington signed the death penalty into law in June 1977. It was the backlash of a public surfeited with stories of coddled offenders—particularly sexual psychopaths—who had been paroled, furloughed, and work-released until they could virtually come and go at will. Many ex-convicts reverted to type when they found no walls around them and no eyes watching. Too many innocents died. It seemed that the inmates were running the asylum.

While some argued for mercy for convicted killers, particularly since Washington executions harkened back to the days of the Old West and murderers would be hanged, one mother of a teenage murder victim faced television cameras and said quietly: "Has anyone thought that the deaths our children died were easy . . . or pleasant to think about?"

And so for the next two decades murderers feared the gallows in Washington State. Hanging is not an easy death, not something that the average man on the street cares to contemplate for very long. In the end, Washington hung only two killers: Charles Rodman Campbell and Westly Alan Dodd.* Although both were sexual offenders who had tortured their victims, the public nonetheless blanched at the details of their last moments. There will be no more hangings in Washington State. In the future, executions will be administered by lethal injection.

---

*Charles Campbell killed a young mother, her nine-year-old daughter, and their neighbor to wreak revenge on the women for testifying against him in an earlier rape trial. (See Ann Rule's Crime Files: Vol. 1.) Westly Alan Dodd, an admitted sadistic pedophile, tortured and killed three small boys.

James Ruzicka and Carl Harp were convicted killers of the 1970s—and rapists too—several times over, but they never faced the hangman's noose. Both their crimes and convictions occurred in time to get them in under the wire. Since the death penalty cannot be invoked retroactively, they were home safe. In the preceding case— that of Larry Hendricks—justice was done without the help of the authorities.

The fact that Ruzicka and Harp should in all likelihood have been executed is not why I chose their stories for this book. Rather, they are remarkable in the way that their formative years were almost mirror images of one another. Their eventual destinies were bleakly similar. When they met, they recognized the commonalities that bound them together. At one point, they actually used the same pseudonym: "Troy Asin." These men were basically loners who shared their bizarre fantasies for a time.

When "Troy Asin" was cut in two, however, and James Ruzicka and Carl Harp parted, each of them continued his personal rampage of rape and murder. Neither should have ever been released to prey once more upon society. Each of them had the capacity to be as charming as any Don Juan and as harmless-appearing as a lost puppy. Behind their masks, they were full of betrayal and black purpose.

Their story is one of the strangest I have ever encountered.

Carl Lowell Harp was born in Vancouver, Washington, on March 8, 1949; James Edward Ruzicka was born almost exactly a year later on March 24, 1950, in Port Angeles, Washington. Were one to set out to find early case histories that would almost guarantee that the subjects were headed for trouble, Harp and Ruzicka would make "ideal" focal points.

There is an awful fascination in reading such case histories, akin to watching an out-of-control train barreling down the tracks. We can see what is going to happen, but there is no way in the world to stop it.

Public records describe Carl Harp's father as "a young, emotionally unstable carnival roustabout," his mother was only sixteen years old. By the time Carl was a year old, his parents were divorced. His mother remarried at least once and then moved on to a half-dozen common-law relationships. The child, Carl, could not count on any permanent father figure. When he was not committed to one or another mental institution, Carl's natural father had to live with *his* parents, his mental illness forcing him to be dependent.

Carl trailed after his mother, a small, thin boy with blue eyes and blond hair that would later turn brown. He and his mother lived on welfare in California, Arizona, New Mexico, Texas, Oklahoma, Alaska, Oregon, and Washington. In time, his mother descended into alcoholism, and Carl lived in such terrible conditions that authorities moved in and took him from her custody. He was placed first with a maternal uncle and aunt.

Carl Harp left a home where promiscuity and drinking were the norm and was suddenly plunged into one that was as staid as a church picnic. His uncle's affiliation with the Salvation Army barred booze, sex, swearing—and rowdiness of any kind. Carl would recall later that he was mistreated and punished severely. He was expected to attend religious services, and when he balked, his uncle forced him to go.

Not surprisingly, Carl Harp didn't last long in his uncle's house. He moved on to live with one of his former stepfathers. There, he finally found someone to love and connect with—his half sister. She was an epileptic and he was very protective of her. But by the time he was twelve Carl was a handful. He had committed uncountable curfew violations, petty thefts, burglaries, and even one car theft.

When Carl Harp was about fourteen, he was hit in the head while playing basketball. Another player struck him so hard with his elbow that Harp's temple bone was actually fractured. After that, his behavior changed markedly; he suffered excruciating headaches and blackouts. During one blackout, Carl choked his beloved half sister and almost killed her before someone pulled him off. Later, he would have no memory of the incident.

When he was fifteen, he was admitted to the Napa State Hospital in California in June of 1964, for a ninety-day observation. When the three months were up, he was voluntarily committed to the hospital. His diagnosis at that time was that of a "borderline psychotic," and the staff psychiatrists' impression was that he suffered from "schizo-phrenic reaction—chronic undifferentiated type." It was an ominous diagnosis.

All in all, Carl was considered amenable to treatment during the ten months he spent at Napa State. Although he did walk away one night, he returned the next morning. He was released on April 15, 1965.

Carl Harp completed the ninth grade at Castro Valley High School and entered Mount Whitney High in Visalia. He didn't finish high school, however. Indeed, it would be years later before he got his GED degree while in prison. Despite his unstable genetic heritage, Carl Harp was intelligent and quite artistic. He drew strange but intricate pen-and-ink pictures and wrote poems.

In January 1966, Harp was arrested for car theft and burglary and committed to the Preston School of Industry in Ione, California, where he stayed for a little over a year.

Two states away, there was another teenager whose life history had been almost a mirror image of Carl Harp's. James Edward Ruzicka was born 228 miles from Carl Harp's birthplace. Ruzicka's mother, Myrtle, would type a summary of the births of her children for authorities one day, a sad little list of tragedy upon tragedy. She had been only seventeen when she had her first child. Thereafter, she gave birth every year—save one—until she had borne ten babies. She knew the precise details of each pregnancy and delivery. She wrote:

1. John Ruzicka, born 5/16/48—deceased 5/16/48. Cause of death was placenta came first and also a 5½-month pregnancy.
2. Stanley Edward Ruzicka, Jr., born 3/2/49—deceased 3/17/49. Seven-month pregnancy and child born with pancriest [sic] which caused death.
3. James Edward Ruzicka, born 3/24/50 . . .

James Ruzicka was the first of his mother's children to survive and she was amazed when he lived a week, two weeks, a *month*—and then continued to thrive. However, Myrtle's next child—her fourth—was born with a congenital heart defect on November 19, 1951; Linda Marie died in July 1957, three days after surgery to correct a flawed pulmonary artery.

Myrtle's fifth child was born on October 20, 1952. He was healthy enough, but she noted that he was in prison by the time he was in his early twenties. "On the honor farm," she added, almost proudly. The list continued:

6.   Basil Arthur, born 9/4/53—deceased January 1954. The doctor and the autopsy diagnosed it as a combination of drowning and strangulation. A curd of milk lodged in his throat during the night, forcing the fluid down into his lungs. The doctor said he did not have a chance to utter a whisper or cry.

7.   Wayne Allen, born 7/27/54.

8.   Myrtle Elaine, born 8/7/55.

9.   Christine Louise, born 10/20/56—deceased 10/27/56. Cause of death was pancriest [sic].

10.   Morris Lee, born 7/16/58.

Myrtle Ruzicka had lost five of her ten children to premature death, a series of losses almost unheard of in the 1950s in America.

Who can say if her troubles with her son James caused her more pain than the deaths of five of his siblings. Myrtle was a woman who did her best to gloss over problems. "In all honesty," she wrote, "my children got along better than some families."

Perhaps. Just as Carl Harp's father disappeared from *his* life through divorce when he was a year old, Myrtle Ruzicka recalled that she divorced Jimmy's father when the child was one. Stanley Ruzicka was a longshoreman, and he continued to visit until Myrtle remarried. When he stopped coming, Jimmy was bereft. He complained to his mother that his daddy didn't love him. Although she tried to explain that he did, Jimmy said that wasn't true. If his father loved him, he would take him to his house or come and see him.

It is questionable if Ruzicka was, indeed, Jimmy's father. He would one day completely disown him in a letter to Jim's parole officer, suggesting a chronology that supported his argument. "James Ruzicka is not my son. I gave him my name only. Was married to his mother at one time. He was born thirteen months after she left me. Know nothing of his childhood days. You'll have to get in touch with his mother."

One thing was certain. Jimmy Ruzicka never had much in the way of paternal approval. Myrtle's second husband, Sam, used him as his whipping boy when he wanted to get back at Myrtle about something. He would either ignore him or spank him or slap him. Since Jimmy was the only child who survived Myrtle's first marriage and all the others were Sam's children, he resented the boy. Jimmy Ruzicka tried to make his stepfather love him, even after he'd been beaten. "As soon as he quit crying," Myrtle wrote, "Jimmy would crawl up on the easy chair or daveno and put his arms around his neck and say, 'Daddy, I love you.'" But Sam really didn't care for his stepson. He told him he was stupid and that he didn't know "a damn thing."

Myrtle remembers Jimmy as "kind, affectionate, and good-hearted . . . a hard worker, friendly and outgoing to everyone—including strangers."

The Ruzicka family barely made it financially; Myrtle was the sole support of her five children much of the time, working as a clerk for $1.25 an hour. "We had necessities," she explained, "and that was it. No Saturday matinees, ice-cream or candy money. No weekly allowance or bikes or trikes like the other playmates."

Of necessity, she was away from the family home much of the time. Jimmy had been especially close to his sister Linda and was inconsolable when she died at the age of five. "He was only seven or eight," Myrtle recalled, "and he would comment that she was an angel in Heaven with God, and he picked the brightest star a couple of times and said, 'There's Linda.'"

Although James Ruzicka's mother remembered his good qualities, she was also aware that something was wrong with him. He had chronic tonsillitis from the age of one to three when his tonsils were removed. When he was two, he had convulsions and had to be hospitalized. A year or so later, he had convulsions again and there was no definitive diagnosis as to their cause. "He was rigid and completely out," his mother said. Jimmy Ruzicka was delirious for three days with chicken pox. He had weak eyes and wore thick, magnifying glasses from the time he was about five.

As late as 1972, when he was in his early twenties, he fell to the floor, turned blue, and stopped breathing. His brother had to smack him hard in the back to get him breathing. (This latter attack could have been a drug reaction, however.)

But it was not his physical problems that alarmed his mother the most. Rather, it was his premature and obsessive interest in sex play. He molested his younger brother and even his sister, Linda, when he himself was only six or seven. Myrtle thought perhaps it was her fault; she had taken hormones during her pregnancy for James to ensure that she would carry him to term. She wondered if they were responsible for his unhealthy interest in sex.

She took him to a series of doctors. They all found him very restless, but they disagreed on what was wrong with him. One doctor told her Jimmy had brain damage; another found no brain dysfunction.

James Ruzicka was a hyperactive child, and probably would have been diagnosed today as having ADHD (Attention Deficit Hyperactive Disorder). He could not sit still to watch television and had to be doing *something* all the time. Sometimes his activities were constructive. (He could make tepees of gunny sacks and sticks when he was four or five and amuse his younger siblings.) Sometimes they were not.

"As Jim got older," his mother wrote, "he masturbated in his sister's slips and panties from the dirty laundry hamper. On different occasions, he asked his sister to let him look at her genitals. . . . At the age of nineteen or twenty, he tried to get his sister, Myrtle, to have sex with him. When she told me, he became almost wild—denying it, screaming, yelling, and accusing me of calling him a liar. His eyes were odd and the look on his face, I must admit, scared me, even though I didn't let on."

As an adult, James Ruzicka recalled a home life that was not nearly as idyllic as his mother remembered. He described a constant marathon of divorce, remarriage, divorce, ad nauseam. "There were always fights . . . it was all one big turmoil."

He said his weak eyes were discovered early and he had glasses before he was five. He remembered that he ran into a tree limb and knocked them off a few days after getting them and that he lost them. He recalls that his mother beat him severely for that.

When James Ruzicka was nine, he stole bicycles to ride. When he was finished with them, he either hid them or destroyed them. Later, he began to shoplift. Sex—aberrant sex—had become a part of his life at an age when most young boys were only concerned with baseball and marbles. Besides his sexual interest in his own half sisters, he had also begun molesting little girls his own age when he was ten. During that period, he experimented with having sexual relations with animals.

James Ruzicka was thirteen when he went "into the system" for stealing and was sent to the Washington State juvenile center at Fort Worden in Port Townsend. He spent his time there trying to run away—and learning about marijuana. Before he was eighteen, James Ruzicka would try LSD, mescaline, cocaine, heroin, speed, and alcohol. On one authorized home visit, he became so violently angry at his brother over a minor incident that he choked him hard enough to leave fiery red marks on his throat. His mother had him returned to Fort Worden.

When he was sixteen, Ruzicka was paroled from Fort Worden. He stayed free for six months and eventually was sent to a youth camp in Mason County after a burglary conviction. Still, he tried to run away, and after a year, was transferred to the Green Hill State School for Boys in Chehalis.

The runner still ran. During one of his escapes, he was involved in three burglaries. They were penny-ante stuff; he stole $160 from a Texaco station, $400 from a dry cleaners, and broke into a drugstore—but fled before he could take anything. He pleaded guilty to one charge and the other two charges were dropped. In July 1968 he was sentenced to fifteen years at the state reformatory at Monroe.

A month later, Carl Harp was arrested and sentenced to the Monroe facility. Harp's path through his teenage years had not been that different from Ruzicka's. Neither had had secure home lives, and they had both been involved in drugs and thefts. Harp resented women and referred to them in obscene terms. He felt the world had treated him badly—which, indeed, it had—and he cared about no one.

Harp's first adult arrest was on December 30, 1967, in San Luis Obispo, California, when he was charged with possession of stolen property. He was eighteen years old. On August 11, 1968, he was arrested by Seattle police after he robbed a grocery store in the south end of the city. He had held a .22 caliber starter's pistol to the head of a small boy while he ordered the clerk to "Give me the bills, or I'll blow his head off."

Carl Harp, who also used the aliases "Troy Asin" and "Carroll Lowell Trimble," was sentenced to the Monroe Reformatory despite his plea that he was a drug addict and had needed money for a fix.

And so it was that, in the winter of 1968–69, James Ruzicka and Carl Harp met—two men of almost the same age and of remarkably similar backgrounds. Each was a smoldering cauldron of rage that transcended anything we might imagine. They came to prison on robbery and burglary charges, but any forensic psychiatrist who reviewed their case files could have warned that their potential was for violent sexual crimes.

Although the two convicts both wore thick glasses, that was the only physical similarity they shared. James Ruzicka was 6'1" tall and weighed 155 pounds. Carl Harp, who was only 5'8", weighed 162 pounds. Ruzicka *looked* like a poet with his finely hewn features, while Harp's face was flat and bland. But it was Harp who *was* the poet. He was probably the smarter of the two; Ruzicka had tested at 100 to 109 on the Otis IQ scale, which put him squarely at "average." Both men were cunning and manipulative.

In the worst possible sense of the term, Ruzicka and Harp were kindred spirits. No one but the men themselves can know what they talked about in their moments in the yard or when they worked on the kitchen crew, but at some point Harp shared his prized alias with Ruzicka. From that point forward, they agreed that if they should get free and if they were stopped by the law, they would each give the name "Troy Asin." That would be their private joke and it would certainly confuse the damned cops.

There is little question, though, that the two men spoke of rape and of the pleasures inherent in controlling women absolutely through fear and intimidation. The little boys who had followed their mothers through a series of marriages and who had been buffeted about from one home to another had grown up resentful of females and obsessed with sex.

James Ruzicka and Carl Harp had a plan to be free. All they needed was an opportunity. Ruzicka recalled that opportunity for prison authorities sometime later.

"I escaped from the Honor Farm. Harp and I left together. I would guess it was about seven-thirty P.M. on November twentieth [1970], when we took off. I didn't really plan it, but I had thought about it several times when I was on the farm. I had heard earlier that evening that several guys were going to jump me and beat me up because I had been flushing the toilet all hours of the night and this had upset them. I guess it kept them awake. I had found some Pruno [prison liquor made from fermented potatoes or fruit and yeast and hidden from the guards] out in back of the kitchen, and after I had some of it, I suddenly decided I just had to get out of there. I guess Harp had been thinking about taking off too, so when he saw I was going to escape, he came with me. We cut across the field behind the kitchen, then crossed the railroad tracks and on into the brush. We spent the first night near the fairgrounds, right outside the town of Monroe. The next day, we found an old abandoned house and sort of holed up in it. Harp and I separated at that time and we met again, later, in Seattle.

"I finally got to Seattle late that night and went directly to the University District. I stayed in the district for about three weeks. I slept where I could—at whatever 'crash pad' I could get into."

While he was free, he met a pregnant woman who had a little girl. He considered her his fiancée. She was one of the few women he ever felt compassion for. "One day I took my fiancée and my little daughter [not his child, but the daughter of the woman] to Bremerton to see my stepdad because I wanted his permission so I could marry my fiancée. The woman my stepdad was married to excused herself from the house and left. A few minutes later, the police were at the front door. I heard them ask if I was there so I ran to a back bedroom. The police came in the house so I jumped out the window, and they pounced on me."

Ruzicka had been gone two months before he was arrested. After he was caught and returned to prison, he married the woman and felt proud to give her unborn baby his name. Their marriage lasted just a year. The breakup of this marriage only served to substantiate Ruzicka's belief that emotional involvement with a woman was an open-sesame to getting hurt. "You get to know each other and then the bottom drops out," he said. "That's why I don't want to get emotionally involved with anyone for fear of getting hurt."

Despite his escape, James Ruzicka was paroled from Monroe on November 4, 1971. He was con-wise, and a decade of perverse sexual behavior had blossomed into a need for violent sex. Carl Harp, also recaptured, was paroled from Monroe two weeks after his friend. Essentially lone wolves, they went their separate ways, but, in a sense, they followed the same trail.

"Troy Asin" was loose.

It was January 18, 1973 when Nina Temple*, a twenty-one-year-old department store clerk, left her job in downtown Seattle around 4:30 and headed to the bus stop where she would catch the bus to her Capitol Hill apartment. She was tired, her feet hurt, and she thought longingly of getting home. While she waited, a tall, bushy-haired man asked her for directions and she pointed out the bus he should take. It happened to be the Number 9 bus she was taking. "You can catch it here," she told him.

When Nina exited through the rear doors of the bus, she didn't notice that the man got off too. She bent her head against the north wind that was blowing rain against her face. It was only five in the afternoon, but it was already dark and she hurried as she walked away from the lighted storefronts of the Broadway District. Huge homes, once single-family dwellings, had long since become apartments and boarding houses, their gardens gone to weeds except for stubborn laurel hedges and a few rosebushes.

Nina Temple was unaware of the man who kept pace with her as he walked on the opposite side of the street. She didn't see him at all until she opened the door to her apartment house and stepped in out of the driving rain. Suddenly, there he was—right in the lobby with her. He murmured something about knowing someone in the building, but he didn't seem to know where his friend's apartment was.

Before she could even move, he pinioned her with a strong arm around her waist and pressed the sharp edge of a four-inch knife against her neck. Then he wrestled her down the dark stairs to the basement.

In the black abyss beneath the stairs, he held her close as he told her that the "pigs" had shot his brother. "He's bleeding to death," he panted. "He sent me to get a girl to help."

"But why?" she blurted. "Why me? I don't know anything about first aid."

The bushy-haired man said that his brother was on parole and that he couldn't risk calling a doctor, and he shoved his knife harder against her flesh to coerce her to come with him.

There was nothing she could do. She was afraid to scream and she let him lead her back up the stairs, across a street completely empty of traffic, to another rooming house. It was a large, turreted house with leaded glass windows, a "Peace" symbol drawn on cardboard was tacked on the door's frame. Hopeless, she saw that the lobby of this house was empty too. The man pointed to stairs leading to the basement. "My brother's in there."

As he dragged her down the steps, she looked where he gestured. There was nothing but padlocked storage bins made of wood slats, designed to hold tenants' belongings. There was no brother. She was alone in the basement with the man and his knife. Nina prayed that she might hear the voices of someone coming, but there was no sound at all but her captor's heavy breathing.

"I'll have to tie you up, of course," he said. He bound her wrists with rope until it cut into her flesh. And then he carefully crossed one of her feet over the other and tied her ankles. He took off his T-shirt and gagged her with it. She could smell his perspiration and fought to keep from vomiting. While she lay there helpless, he urinated in a corner of the basement.

Returning to Nina, the stranger yanked her slacks and panties to her ankles and pulled her bra up to her shoulders, exposing her breasts. Then he stared at her as she lay helpless, naked, and trembling. He straddled her body but he was unable to achieve an erection; his impotency sent him into a violent rage.

Nina managed to choke out some words past the gag, taunting him. "Why don't you just kill me?"

"Don't worry," he answered. "I *will*."

And then he set about trying to do just that. Again and again, more than a dozen times, his closed fists thudded against Nina Temple's jaw. She could feel her head bounce off the concrete floor and then slam into it again. The pain in her jaw was so intense that she almost lost consciousness.

When he stopped hitting her, she felt his strong fingers close around her throat as he began to choke her. Pinpoints of light exploded behind the darkness in her eyes. She went limp and pretended to be dead.

Oddly now, Nina's would-be killer became concerned; he patted her cheeks gently and talked to her, urging her to live. But as soon as she responded, he became violent again. She realized that he was actually *kneeling* on her neck, using his entire weight to suffocate her.

Nina decided she had nothing left to lose. She wasn't going to let him kill her without a fight. Although her hands and legs were still bound, she managed to raise her feet high enough to kick some metal bedsprings that leaned against one wall. The springs clattered and clanged, distracting the man who was intent on raping her. Using her teeth and her tongue, she loosened the gag enough so that she could scream—and she did—over and over.

The sound of running feet thundered overhead and the bushy-haired man suddenly leaped off her. When she opened her eyes, he was gone.

Nina Temple saw the flash of a match above her head, and then heard a different male voice gasp, "Oh, my God." Gentler arms picked her up and carried her from the basement. An ambulance rushed Nina to nearby Harborview Hospital. ER doctors found that she had suffered a broken jaw and severe contusions all over her face, a badly cut lip, and rope burns on her wrists and ankles. Her face was so swollen that she was unrecognizable.

While Seattle Police Sex Crimes Detective Joyce Johnson waited for Nina Temple to emerge from deep shock, the young man who had rescued her said that he had passed a man running up the basement steps as he ran down. "I drew a sketch of him right after the ambulance took the girl away. Would that help?"

Johnson assured him that it would, and he handed her a pen-and-ink sketch of a thin-faced man with thick curling hair and a drooping mustache.

Once Nina Temple was able to talk, she was a good witness. She described the tall, thin man with the deceptively gentle face and thick glasses. She too remembered his distinctive mustache. He had told her his name was Jim.

When she left the hospital, Nina viewed a dozen mug-shot books of sex offenders' photographs, but she didn't find "Jim." Joyce Johnson was worried. The man who had attacked Nina Temple seemed to harbor tremendous rage against women, far more than most rapists. She was afraid they were going to hear more from him.

She was right. Only a month later—on Valentine's Day—the man with the mustache surfaced again. This time his victim was a nineteen-year-old girl—Tannie Fletcher.* Tannie and her husband, Jon*, hadn't been married long, but with him, she finally felt safe after a childhood marked by continual upheaval. They had found temporary living quarters with a friend in the University District of Seattle, but they both hoped to get jobs so they could have their own place.

Tannie soon found that local papers required payment in advance for "Work Wanted" ads, so she printed up several cards and tacked them on bulletin boards in coffeehouses and supermarkets around the district. She said she was seeking work as a housekeeper/nanny. Only one person responded. The man who called her explained that his house was difficult to find by the address alone. She agreed, therefore, to meet him on a corner of N.E. Fiftieth and Fifteenth Avenue N.E., near where she lived, at eight P.M. on Valentine's night.

Tannie waited nervously. She had assumed that he lived in a house on one of the nearby corners, so she knocked on the door of one of the houses and asked if someone there needed a housekeeper.

"Right on," a woman said with a laugh. "But we can't afford one. You've probably got the wrong address."

Tannie nodded and went back to the corner. She began to feel as if she were the target of a practical joke when, suddenly, she saw a man just beyond the streetlight's circle of yellow. He was tall and thin and wore a ski jacket.

"Tannie Fletcher?" he asked in a pleasant voice.

"Yes," she said with relief. "I thought we'd missed connections."

As he moved into the light, she thought he looked very young to require a housekeeper, but she needed a job badly, so she agreed to follow him down an alley that he told her led to his home. He said he had a very large house and he needed a full-time housekeeper. She darted a look at him and wondered if he was telling the truth; he wasn't dressed very well.

The alley opened onto another and then another. After about eight blocks, Tannie realized that she had been duped. There was no house. There was only a cold knife held now against her side. Tannie didn't know it, but she was hearing the same story Nina Temple had heard a month before, "My brother's hurt bad in the park. The pigs shot him and you have to help me stop the bleeding."

The petite girl was forced deep into Cowan Park at knifepoint. Tannie kept protesting that the sight of blood sickened her and that she couldn't possibly help her captor's wounded brother. Finally, he looked at her with an odd smile and said, "If you ball me, I won't make you look at my brother."

She wanted to stay alive. Thinking rapidly, she asked, "If I say yes, will you throw the knife away?" The man responded by flinging the knife into the bushes, but he said coldly, "Be nice. I still have a razor."

Fighting her revulsion, Tannie Fletcher submitted to rape. When the man had climaxed, he let her put her clothes back on. Perversely gallant now, he walked her back to within a block of her home. She thought he must be crazy. He talked to her as if they were truly lovers, as if she had made love with him willingly. "I want to be with you again," he said in a soft voice.

Tannie kept walking, nodding as if she agreed with him. He told her he had been in the Monroe Reformatory from 1968 until 1971, and that he had been married but was divorced. She lied, telling him she had once been in a girl's training school.

Expansive, taking Tannie Fletcher's conversation as approval, he became even more talkative. He bragged about his extraordinary job. He told her he was part of a research project at the University of Washington—one where he was given massive doses of vitamins every day and received seventy dollars a week just to let them study him. "It's some research deal, ten dollars a day for doing nothing but swallowing pills." He showed her a card with some medical phrases on it. It was too dark for her to read much of it, but she saw the name "Jim R."

Tannie felt a hysterical giggle rise in her throat. Was her abductor so revved up on vitamins that they had turned him into a rapist? Had she just gone through the worst ordeal of her life because the scientists at the university had given him too much Vitamin C or something?

She said nothing when the man told her he would call her the next day, but she couldn't control a shudder as he removed a pendant from his neck and placed it around hers as a memento of their meeting. All that mattered now was that she believed he was going to let her go. She wanted to get home alive.

Terrified that he would come after her, Tannie Fletcher made herself walk normally as she headed away from him. If she ran, he would know she was frightened.

Tannie's husband found her crying hysterically, covered with mud from head to foot. At the University Hospital, physicians verified that she had been raped.

While Tannie and her husband were at the hospital, two phone calls came in from a man who said he wanted to "apologize" to Tannie. He told the people who owned the home Tannie and her husband were sharing temporarily to tell her that "Jim Otto" had called.

Detective Joyce Johnson studied the almost identical MOs used in the two attacks, reading first one victim statement and then the other. This "Jim" had to be the same man who had attacked Nina Temple. Everything fit. Johnson suspected that the "vitamin guinea pig" story was as false as his ruse about his brother being shot by "the pigs," but it was all she had to go on. The pendant the rapist had given Tannie Fletcher was a disappointing piece of evidence; it proved to be a mass-produced bit of jewelry that could never be traced.

Joyce Johnson telephoned the University Hospital and, to her surprise, she found that there was indeed such a vitamin research program. In fact, the next massive vitamin administration was to be given that very afternoon at one P.M. Johnson alerted University of Washington police and asked them to stand by when the test subjects reported.

Sure enough, the officers spotted a tall, slim man with bushy reddish brown hair, thick glasses, and a drooping mustache. His name was Jim. However, it wasn't Jim Otto; it was James Edward Ruzicka. And he had had his last massive dose of vitamins.

Ruzicka was charged with one count of attempted rape while armed with a deadly weapon, one count of second-degree assault, and a second count of rape. He gave a five-page statement to Joyce Johnson. Yes, he agreed, he had met Tannie Fletcher when he asked her for a cigarette. Then she had asked him to have sex with her, and, according to Ruzicka, he had obliged and accompanied her to a nearby alley.

But Tannie had said "Jim" had forced her into a muddy park. And detectives found footprints in the ground there that *exactly* matched the bottom of Tannie's "waffle-stomper" shoes.

Although both rape victims identified Ruzicka as their attacker, he finally admitted only to the rape of Tannie Fletcher. He was subsequently convicted and certified as a sexual psychopath. His ten-year sentence was suspended on the condition that he take part in the sexual psychopath program at Western State Hospital.

This sexual offenders program may well have been one of the reasons that Washington voters restored the death penalty. It was a program that allowed its participants incredible freedom. The premise was that locked doors suggested that the hospital staff did not trust the sexual psychopaths. Counselors argued that unless the inmates felt affirmation and trust from their captors, they would never get well. The program featured frequent passes on the grounds and then into Steilacoom where the hospital was located, and finally into other Washington cities. Of course, the patients had to "prove themselves" before they were given more freedom.

Viewed in retrospect, this philosophy of the midseventies was an almost Utopian "feel-good" therapy approach, in tune with the times where everyone did their "own thing."

James Ruzicka stayed nine months at Western State. After some months inside where he attended group therapy faithfully and participated in a appropriate manner, he was granted a number of leaves.

On January 31, 1974, he failed to return to the hospital after an unsupervised twelve-hour pass.

On Friday, February 15, sixteen-year-old Nancy Kinghammer stormed out of her West Seattle home shortly after six in the evening. She and one of her sisters had disagreed over which television show to watch. It was a relatively minor sibling disagreement, but Nancy was angry. Her family assumed she had walked down the block to visit friends and would be back in a few hours.

But Nancy did not come home. By three-twenty the next afternoon, her worried father had called all her friends and even contacted West Seattle High School administrators where she was a junior. No one had seen her. Her father was convinced she had not run away; she had taken neither extra clothes nor money with her when she left.

The tall, brunette teenager was simply gone.

It was even less likely that fourteen-year-old Penny Marie Haddenham should vanish from *her* home several blocks from the Kinghammer residence six days later. The red-haired, freckled youngster hadn't even had a tiff with anyone. In fact, she had been laughing the last time her father had seen her. That had been at 6:30 in the evening of February 21 in a West Seattle restaurant. Penny had needed twenty dollars to buy material for a pantsuit she was making in home economics at Madison Junior High School.

Penny was a strong "B" student at Madison and her father had been glad to give her the money. The last time he saw her she was headed toward the fabric store a few blocks away. A friend's mother saw her about 8:30 that evening. Nancy had stopped in to see the friend, who lived only four blocks from her own home and had been told she'd already gone to bed. Penny had been in good spirits then. She had said she was going home.

But, like Nancy, Penny had not gone home. And there was no way in the world her parents would believe she'd run away. She was too happy at home, too dependable, too concerned with her friends and schoolwork.

For the next three weeks, police, family, and friends looked for Penny and Nancy in vain. Seattle police detectives wondered if there could be any connection between Penny's disappearance and Nancy's. The only link they could find was the proximity of the girls' homes. They had not known each other, they went to different schools, and they traveled in different crowds. Now, they were linked only by terrible speculation.

Penny was found first. On March 12, a newsboy cut through a woods edging the Fauntleroy Expressway in West Seattle. The woods was made up of deciduous maple trees with only a few clusters of evergreens, and the ground was covered by a deep carpet of brown leaves. Although the freeway was close by and there were several houses at the edge of the woods, the wooded area itself was as isolated as the center of a forest.

The boy stopped in his tracks, transfixed with horror at the sight in front of him. A girl hung from a tree, her neck bent sharply to the side. It was so quiet that the boy's own involuntary cry and the pounding of his heart seemed to echo and reecho through the trees.

Police patrol units soon responded to the boy's phone call. The officers looked at the body of the red-haired girl hanging from the bare limb; it was obvious she had been dead for some time—days at least. They made no effort to approach closely, but called for homicide detectives.

Seattle homicide detectives Roy Moran and Bernie Miller noted that the girl's feet were almost touching the ground, her body leaning back against a slight embankment angling down from the tree. She was not bound; there was just the rope around her neck attached to the limb. The petite girl was dressed in jeans, a yellow nylon jacket (whose right pocket was turned inside out), and platform boots. Her purse was nearby and some items spilled from it were not far away in the leaves. A thorough search of the area turned up a pantsuit pattern envelope and some gray wool and gray silk yardage.

Could it be a suicide? If this was Penny Haddenham, and her description matched that of the body in the woods so closely, it seemed impossible that she would have taken her own life. She had been such a happy girl. But it isn't unheard of for teenagers to take life's small problems very, very seriously. Teenagers think they will live forever, and sometimes they make dramatic gestures and find that they cannot turn back.

As darkness descended, the body was carefully cut from the tree— not at the noose—but farther along the rope so that the direction of the fray marks could be studied. If the girl had committed suicide by hanging, the fraying would point upward; if someone had killed her first and then *hoisted* her up over the tree limb, the fraying would slant downward.

Uniformed officers guarded the scene all night. With the first light of day, there would be a further search. There was no doubt now that the body hanging from the tree was Penny Haddenham; the state of decomposition indicated she had been there for a week or more. The question was *how* she had gotten there. How could a smiling, joking fourteen-year-old girl end up a suicide? Or, more likely, how had some sadist enticed her away from her own neighborhood and forced her into the woods to die this lonely death?

The postmortem examination on the 5′2″, 110-pound girl quickly eliminated any possibility that Penny had killed herself. She had died from hanging—asphyxiation—but she had been raped before she died. Her underclothing and jeans were soaked with semen. Her killer had obviously redressed her after the attack and then hanged her to make it look like suicide.

Once again, detectives went over the scene where Penny had been hanged, where she had waited for ten days for someone to come and find her. It was not an easy scene to search with the thick leaf carpeting obscuring the ground, but they found some interesting items. The most damning was a fishing knife, its point honed to a fine edge. It lay half under a cover of leaves, its tan taped handle blending in with the leaves. The killer had probably dropped it and been unable to find it in the dark. It had not been out in the elements long, no longer than Penny's body had hung there.

Penny should have had seven or eight dollars left in her purse when she headed home after purchasing the material (and two forbidden packs of cigarettes, according to her best friend), but her purse had had no money at all in it when she was found. The cigarettes had been found, sodden with rain, on the ground beneath her feet.

When Penny Haddenham's body was found, the fear that Nancy Kinghammer was dead—murdered too—was exacerbated. On Saturday, March 16, detectives, patrol officers, and sixty Explorer Search and Rescue Scouts scoured the neighborhood where Nancy had vanished. They searched through empty houses, woods, vacant lots—anyplace where a body could have been secreted. Penny had not been far from home; detectives didn't feel that Nancy was either.

Police helicopters took aerial photographs on the chance that a body with bright enough clothing might show up from that vantage point. Throughout the day, the search proved fruitless. It was almost five and growing dark when one detective returned to a vacant lot at the corner of Andover and Avalon. The lot had become a very convenient, if unofficial, dumpsite for the community.

Unerringly, almost as if he had some kind of psychic clue, Detective George Cuthill walked through the blackberry brambles and garbage until he came to a pile of boards, cardboard, and junked furniture. "I think she may be under here," he muttered.

Bit by bit, as the pile of junk diminished, the remains of a human being were exposed to the fading sunlight. It had been five weeks, and the nearly nude corpse was much deteriorated, the only seemingly alive part of it the long brown hair and the bright rings still glittering on the fingers. A green scarf was tied around the neck of the body, which had been wrapped in white drapery material and towels, fabric that seemed too new to have been part of the debris dumped in the lot.

Dental charts, the rings, and a watch gave absolute proof that the body was Nancy Kinghammer's. There was no way now to find *what* had killed her; the method vanished with her flesh. But a sexual motive was apparent because Nancy was found naked.

Two girls had been raped and murdered in less than a week in a quiet family neighborhood. Residents asked what kind of prowling animal was loose in West Seattle? Detectives had a knife, a towel, and a strip of white drapery to tie the killer to the bodies, but where could they start looking? There was nothing in either girl's background that indicated they might have known their killer. He had probably been a stranger who waited on a dark street until they were alone.

An arrest in Beaverton, Oregon—almost two hundred miles south of Seattle—brought some answers, but more questions. Washington County, Oregon, detectives called the Seattle Police Department with a request for information on a man named Troy Asin.

The man in the Washington County Jail was tall, slim, and had dark red, bushy hair.

The Oregon offense which had landed "Troy Asin" in jail sounded familiar to Detective Joyce Johnson. A thirteen-year-old girl had phoned the Washington County Sheriff's office to report that she had been raped. She and a girlfriend had met her bushy-haired, mustachioed man and his friend near a penny arcade in Portland. After talking with the junior high school girls for a while, the men said they had decided to ride the bus out to Beaverton, a suburb of Portland, with the teenagers. Once in Beaverton, they had all gone to a pool hall restaurant for something to eat. The man with the mustache, the one who said his name was "Troy," had offered to walk one girl home.

She didn't get home; instead she was raped at knifepoint in a churchyard and when "Troy" finally let her go, she had stumbled out sobbing to call the sheriff. "Troy" was apprehended almost immediately as he walked near the pool hall; his thirteen-year-old victim pointed him out to a Beaverton patrolman.

In the Washington County jail, he gave his name as Troy Asin. The Oregon officers were slightly suspicious of his identity as he had no papers in his wallet that listed that name. "Troy Asin" had given a home address in the West Seattle area of Seattle, however, and a routine request to verify Asin's identity had reached Seattle detectives shortly after Nancy Kinghammer's body was found.

When Beaverton detectives questioned Asin about the rape, he maintained an attitude of calm disbelief. He insisted that the thirteen-year-old girl had been completely willing—even *grateful*—for the act of intercourse in the churchyard. In fact, he said that she had told him she was glad she wasn't a virgin anymore because her friends had been calling her a prude. "When I asked her if she wanted to ball, she didn't say yes or no so I figured she wouldn't mind," he said easily. Asin seemed to be puzzled that the girl had called the police.

The name "Troy Asin" baffled Seattle detectives at first. "Moniker files" brought up the name all right, but it was one used by a parolee from the Monroe Reformatory named Carl Harp. He had used that alias, or variations of it, for years. But Harp's physical description was nothing like that of the man in custody in Oregon—not unless he'd grown a half a foot and dyed and permed his hair. "Troy Asin" wasn't exactly "John Smith." There couldn't be two men who had accidentally picked such an unusual pseudonym.

The mystery of the identity of the man charged with rape in Oregon was solved when Seattle detectives checked the address "Asin" had given. The home, occupied by a married couple and two other women, was only a block from the lot where Nancy Kinghammer's body had just been found. The woman who lived there said that the man in Oregon sounded like her ex-husband: James Edward Ruzicka.

In a remarkable show of civility, her new husband had allowed Ruzicka to stay with them after he had walked away from the sexual psychopath program at Western State Hospital. "He was here from February first to February twenty-fifth," she said.

When the detectives asked Ruzicka's ex-wife if anything was missing from her home, her answer was one of the biggest jackpots of information any homicide detective ever hit. Yes, she answered, she *had* found that some towels, some white drapes, and a fishing knife were missing. She added that Ruzicka had asked her to leave the back door unlocked on March 3, and when she returned home, she found $37.95 in cash missing. Ruzicka had not returned after that, and she hadn't heard from him since.

The ex–Mrs. Ruzicka was asked about any memory she might have of the night of February 21, the night Penny Haddenham vanished. She recalled that night well, because "Jim" had left at 6:30 absolutely broke. When he returned after 10:30 P.M., his coat had been covered with mud. He had had seven or eight dollars when he came home (exactly what Penny Haddenham's change from the twenty-dollar bill her father gave her would have been after she bought material and two packs of cigarettes).

"He told me that a man had given him the money for helping him change a tire," Ruzicka's former wife said. "That was how his clothes got all muddy."

She identified the knife found at the scene of Penny Haddenham's hanging site as the one missing from her house.

It looked as though James Ruzicka, "The Guinea Pig Rapist," had cut a leisurely swath of terror since he'd left the grounds of Western State Hospital. His alibi in Beaverton, Oregon, about merely obliging a willing girl sounded familiar to Detective Joyce Johnson. "Jim Otto James Ruzicka" had also claimed that Tannie Fletcher had propositioned him. He either suffered from some delusion that women found him sexually irresistible, or he chose to gloss over the fact that he had actually forced himself on his victims.

James Ruzicka's trail, from Western State Hospital to West Seattle to Oregon, was traced as closely as possible. He apparently had made at least two trips south into Oregon. In Eugene, a hundred miles south of Beaverton, a forty-eight-year-old housewife told police that she remembered him all too well. The mother of eight children, she had quit her job so she could take care of her husband who was terminally ill.

A tall man with wildly curly hair had come to her door and asked for a ride into Eugene. "He called himself 'Jack,' " she recalled, "and when I told him I couldn't take him anywhere, he held a knife to my throat, tied me to my bed . . . and raped me."

Then "Jack" had stolen money from her children's rooms and, still holding the knife to the woman's neck, demanded that she drive him to downtown Eugene. "Along the way, he told me a story about some friend of his leaving a knapsack beside the road for him. I knew it was just an excuse to get me into the woods so he could rape me again."

She had had no choice but to let him lead her into the woods. All she wanted to do was survive and her mind raced feverishly as she submitted to a second sexual attack. "Then I told him I had lost my car keys on the ground," she told police. "I guess he believed me because he went back to the road and started hitchhiking. I had my keys all along, and I ran to my car and headed in the other direction. He told me if I called the police, he would come back and kill me and my family."

Few would question that James Ruzicka's diagnosis as a sexual psychopath had been accurate. Now, all circumstantial and physical evidence pointed to the conclusion that he was also a merciless killer. Detectives believed that he had murdered Nancy Kinghammer exactly one year and one day from Nina Temple's rape in the basement of the Capital Hill rooming house.

While James Ruzicka was locked up, awaiting trial, the first "Troy Asin" was still free.

Carl Harp had left the Monroe Reformatory a few weeks after his friend James Ruzicka. He presented a bland, cooperative facade to his parole officer and was given a "conditional discharge from supervision" on April 2, 1973. By this time, his "other half" had raped two women—at the very least.

Harp had a good job working as a shoemaker and repairman at the

Bon Marché department store in South Center, a huge mall in south King County. Like his "twin," Harp had had unsatisfactory experiences with women, finding them untrustworthy. His first marriage ended when he discovered his wife was working in a body painting studio in Seattle, and that she had been arrested for prostitution while he was in prison. His second wife simply left.

Carl Harp lost his job in the shoe department when a female employee complained that he was writing her obscene letters. He feigned amazement; he had only been trying to "create a relationship" with her.

While James Ruzicka was out of circulation and temporarily out of the headlines, Washington State was jolted by a terrifying sniper attack along one of its freeways.

May 14, 1973, was a Monday, a wonderfully sunny spring day in Bellevue, Washington; drivers could finally roll their windows down without fear of being blasted in the face with rain.

Interstate 405 freeway runs along the east side of Lake Washington from Renton on the south to Mountlake Terrace beyond its north shore. It has always been a tremendously busy freeway, day or night; workers in the Renton Boeing plant clog 405 during morning and afternoon rush hours.

But at three in the afternoon as he headed back to his office, Abraham Saltzman, fifty-four, who sold houses for a living, was enjoying relatively light traffic. He had gone out as a favor to give another realtor a jump start when his battery went dead. Abe, a short man with a bald head and a heart of gold, had a wife, daughter, a sister, and brother who loved him, and he had a list of former clients who swore by him. He was the kind of realtor who would rather let a commission go by than sell the wrong house to the right people.

Now, the middle-aged realtor drove his dark Plymouth Fury skillfully beneath the 520 overpass. As his sedan emerged into the bright sun, Abe Saltzman's world exploded. A bullet he neither saw nor heard ended his life. He died at once, his hands on the wheel; his car veered sharply to the left, across traffic lanes, into a ditch and then hit the grassy embankment.

At the same time, John Mott, another motorist, was driving with his left elbow on the doorjamb of his car. He heard nothing—just felt a flash of white-hot pain. His head whipped to the left and his mind numbed with shock as he saw that his elbow was virtually gone. Somehow, he managed to get his car stopped.

Other motorists heard *ping-ping-ping*s against their cars. Only luck saved them from taking the bullets.

Someone was standing high up on the hill that looked down on the freeway—someone who was methodically aiming and firing with a bolt-action rifle.

In the space of a few minutes, that section of 405 was alive with emergency vehicles, Washington State troopers, Bellevue police detectives, and paramedics who tried to calm the wounded and the terrified. Some motorists, stunned, had simply stopped their cars on the freeway. Some had hit the accelerator and raced past danger.

John Mott was treated and rushed to Overlake Hospital. A young man in his early twenties, he would never again be able to fully extend his left arm, but at least he was alive.

Abe Saltzman was not. There was no rush to remove him from his vehicle, no longer any need to hurry.

Investigators figured the angle of fire and headed up the hill. They didn't know if the man with the rifle was still there or not; he could have had them fixed in his gunsight as they climbed the steep bank. They found the place where he had stood, the grass and weeds stomped almost flat. With a metal detector, they found the brass casings ejected by a .308 bolt-action rifle.

The rifle itself was gone. So was the shooter.

There is a special kind of venom toward society that inspires someone to shoot anonymously and erratically at cars full of strangers. The shooter—male or female?—could have killed mothers, babies, entire families. As it was, those who escaped with only bullet holes in their cars were grateful for their lives.

It could have been so much worse. But that didn't help Abe Saltzman's family, or the dozens of people who called him friend.

The man—and it *was* a man—who had fired the rifle had made it safely away from the brushy area above I-405. He smiled as he found a good hiding place and wrapped the .303 bolt-action rifle in oiled plastic to keep it in good working order. He might need it again.

On June 21, 1973, a little over five weeks later and some twenty miles northeast of the sniper shooting scene, two female camp counselors met a stranger on the trail. The young women, Lia* and Brook*, both twenty-one, were counselors at a religious camp for children near May's Creek Falls in the isolated wilderness in the Snoqualmie National Forest. In keeping with their religious beliefs, both were virgins, something of a rarity in the sexually permissive seventies; they intended to stay chaste until marriage.

On this Thursday afternoon, the counselors had been given some time off and decided to go for a hike along a forest trail. It was the first day of summer and the longest day of the year, which meant, in Washington, that it would be light until ten P.M..

But it was only three when Brook and Lia were startled to see a man who was apparently camping near the trail. He was of medium height, blond, and wore glasses. From all appearances, he must have been in the woods for a long time. They nodded and said "Hi," as they headed up toward the trail head where they had parked their car.

They were even more startled a little later when they saw the same man *ahead* of them on the trail. They couldn't understand how he had managed to get so far ahead. He hadn't passed them; apparently he knew the woods so well that he had taken a shortcut. He seemed harmless enough, though, and made idle conversation as he walked along with them. But some sixth sense made them uneasy. They exchanged glances, each girl letting the other know silently that she was nervous.

When they got to the parking lot, Brook's eagerness to find her car keys was obvious. She rummaged around in her backpack, willing the keys to be there. And then, quietly but firmly, the man said, "Hold it."

Lia and Brook turned around as if they already knew what was going to happen. The man held a revolver in his hand, and he gestured toward a steep bank off the parking lot. "Go down there," he said.

"Don't hurt us," Brook said. "We'll do whatever you want."

"Don't kill us," Lia echoed. "She means it. Tell us what to do."

The stranger ordered them to walk over to a tree. They did as he told them.

"Now take your clothes off," he said. "You can leave your shoes on."

He used Lia's belt, looping it tightly around her neck *and* the tree itself so that she could not move without choking. He told Brook to lie on the ground near the tree.

There was little question now about what he was going to do. They prayed silently that he wouldn't kill them as they watched him take off his shirt and unzip his pants. And then he orally sodomized one of the counselors and raped the other.

They were so far from help that they knew it wouldn't do them any good to scream, and so they used their powers of reasoning. They told him he wasn't a bad person—that he just needed help. Lia offered him a copy of the New Testament, saying, "Jesus can help you more than we ever could."

The rapist backed away, shaking his head, almost as if the Bible frightened him. They were sure he was going to shoot them. Instead, he turned around and disappeared into the woods.

Lia and Brook drove back to camp and immediately called the Snohomish County Sheriff's office. They made excellent witnesses; they could describe the man perfectly. They remembered every one of his tattoos, his T-shirt, the way his blond hair flopped across his forehead. He was back in the woods, but he was going to have to come out at some point. The sheriff's department made sure that every law enforcement officer in the county, every state trooper, and every city patrolman working along Highway 2 had his description.

Mark Ericks, then a deputy marshal in the tiny hamlet of Gold Bar, Washington, in the foothills of the Snoqualmie Mountain Range, was patrolling along Highway 2 when he saw a hitchhiker just west of town.

Ericks felt the hairs stand up on the back of his neck. He *knew* who that hitchhiker was. "You couldn't miss him," he remembered. "He had the T-shirt, the tattoos. He was the guy."

The young deputy marshal whipped his car around and headed back. The blond man with the glasses knew he had been spotted. "He started pulling his gun to shoot me," Ericks recalled. "But I already had my gun on him and I'd made up my mind I was going to shoot."

For seconds that seemed like hours, the two men looked at each other, and then the hitchhiker threw his gun down. It was a .36 caliber Navy percussion pistol, an unusual gun that was a cap and ball replica, but it was fully capable of firing, and it was loaded. The prisoner said he used it only for target practice. A search of his belongings also produced several joints of marijuana.

And his name. Carl Lowell Harp.

Interviewed in the Snohomish County Jail, Harp vehemently denied that he had raped the camp counselors. He remembered meeting two girls at the May's Creek Falls, but said they were mistaken in thinking he had been a threat to them. "I was cleaning my gun at my campsite and it was lying on the ground when they walked by."

Harp said it was the women who had talked to him, asking questions about the area. Yes, he had walked a short ways with them along the trail, talking. If they had been raped, he insisted he wasn't the man who had done it. "I did see a guy farther up the trail that day—he looked a lot like me, you know—height, weight, coloring, even had glasses. *He's* your rapist, not me."

Detectives weren't about to buy that convenient explanation.

What surprised the Snohomish County investigators *and* Bellevue Police and the Washington State Patrol, however, was that Carl Harp had had a very good reason to be camping out in the woods. When the news of his arrest on rape charges hit the media, Harp's ex-wife came forward with shocking information. She led authorities to a .308 bolt-action rifle that belonged to him.

Tests on the weapon, which was perfectly oiled and ready to fire, proved that it was the same gun that had been used by the "Bellevue Sniper."

Carl Lowell Harp aka Troy Asin aka T. Asian aka Carroll Lowell Trimble, who had once been a little boy nobody wanted, was paying the world back—both individually and collectively.

The odd story of two men from such similar dysfunctional backgrounds seemed to be winding down. Both halves of "Troy Asin" were now behind bars.

James Ruzicka was convicted in Oregon on rape charges involving the thirteen-year-old. He received a ten-year sentence. He then went on trial in Seattle in August 1975, on charges of first-degree murder in the deaths of Penny Haddenham and Nancy Kinghammer.

King County Senior Deputy Prosecutors Jon Noll and Ron Clark had a powerful battery of physical and circumstantial evidence to present to the jury in Judge Horton Smith's courtroom. There was the fishing knife, the moldering white draperies which had served as Nancy Kinghammer's shroud, the towels—all taken from Ruzicka's former wife's house—all identified by her in court. And there was devastating testimony from a cellmate of Ruzicka's during his stay in jail.

The witness recalled a conversation with the defendant when Ruzicka bragged of raping and killing two girls. The defendant had told him, he testified, that he liked to "collect" knives. Ruzicka had said that he had hung one of his victims from a tree after he raped her, and that he had lost his knife at that scene. But, according to the witness, Ruzicka had not been concerned about the knife because it had tape on the handle and he knew no fingerprints could be gleaned from tape.

Ruzicka himself did not testify. He sat quietly throughout the trial twisting a gold ring on one finger. He was considerably discomfited by the presence of one of his former victims in the courtroom. Nina

Temple, the pretty store clerk whose jaw he had broken when he had tried to strangle her two and a half years before, sat in the gallery section, listening to every word of testimony. Ruzicka's defense counsel cried "Foul" at the girl's presence and asked to have her barred from the courtroom. However, Judge Horton Smith ruled she had the right to stay.

It took the jury only four hours to find James Ruzicka guilty on two counts of first-degree murder.

After his conviction, Ruzicka granted an extensive interview to a Seattle reporter. Chain-smoking, he commented that no one really knew him as a person, that he was actually shy and lonely. He said he had placed ads in underground publications seeking pen pals. He said he was currently corresponding with nineteen women and sixteen men. He readily admitted that he was a sexual psychopath and had difficulty relating to women, yet he hoped one day to marry again and have children. He had met a blind woman, a woman who loved him devotedly, and she was a faithful presence in the courtroom for all his legal proceedings. "She's very nice," he said. "I felt the least I could do, out of respect for her, is learn Braille."

James Ruzicka continued to see himself in a rosy light that had little to do with reality. He said he was positive that even if he were to be released immediately, he would not be dangerous. "I wouldn't rape anyone," he said. "I'd try to get into some kind of treatment program. I want help."

He denied adamantly that he killed either Penny Haddenham or Nancy Kinghammer. He claimed that the thirteen-year-old girl rape victim in Oregon was a willing participant. "There was no knife."

The tragic fact remained that James Ruzicka *had* been granted an opportunity for help—given counseling, understanding, trust, freedom, in the sexual offenders program. And he walked away from it. Fifteen days later, Nancy Kinghammer died a horrible death and her body was cast aside on a junk heap. Twenty-one days later, Penny Haddenham was raped and hung from a tree like an abandoned rag doll.

Their parents successfully sued the state of Washington for allowing James Ruzicka a second chance *and* an unsupervised leave from the sexual offenders program. The Haddenhams and Kinghammers gave a large portion of the proceeds of their suit to the Families and Friends of Victims of Violent Crime and Missing Persons. Families and Friends had helped them survive emotionally when they lost their daughters.

Ruzicka's self-serving version of his life and crimes, which appeared in Seattle papers, omitted a great deal. Chuck Wright, a veteran of the Washington State Department of Corrections and an expert on human sexuality, did the presentence report on Ruzicka. The convicted rapist/killer was more expansive in discussing his activities with Wright than he was with local reporters.

Chuck Wright found James Ruzicka a fascinating study in denial. Ruzicka listed fourteen former employers on his questionnaire, but said he had never worked for any of them long enough to get a social security number. He said he was "definitely" not a criminal, although he admitted to using many more aliases than "Troy J. Asin."

"I think I'm getting screwed," Ruzicka insisted. "I didn't get a fair trial. I am determined to get out, get a job, and settle down. I want to get married."

James Ruzicka was attempting to portray himself as just an ordinary guy. But he was striving to con the wrong man. Wright knew that Ruzicka had demonstrated a bizarre and precise MO in his sexual attacks. Beyond the use of a knife held against his victims' throats and his ruse about his "wounded brother," he usually removed *one* of the victim's shoes. He had bragged to fellow inmates that he was a necrophile who revisited the bodies of the girls he had killed.

Assuming that Wright's nonjudgmental facade indicated approval, James Ruzicka bragged that he had had "sexual contacts" with at least three hundred different women. He was vehement that he had never had any homosexual encounters beyond his molestation of his younger brother.

As far as other crimes went, Ruzicka admitted a thousand shoplifting episodes, a hundred burglaries—all unsolved.

He said that knives had always been important to him. He had needed to have a knife under his pillow when he was a child—or he couldn't sleep.

For Chuck Wright, who had evaluated countless convicted felons, James Ruzicka was one in a thousand, dangerous beyond reckoning. Wright sought to find some treatment which, while it might not change Ruzicka's mind-set, might at least protect future victims.

"I brought up the question of the possibility of his being castrated," Wright recalled. "He appeared to be very angry and stated, 'They can *try*. If they do that, I'll do myself in. I'd rather rot in prison.' I informed him there was a process in which an individual can be *chemically* castrated and that it was reversible. . . . I informed him that we would probably be recommending that he serve two life sentences to run consecutively, and that he be chemically castrated. He seemed quite calm at that time."

On September 30, 1975, Judge Smith ordered Ruzicka to first serve his sentence in Oregon and then to begin serving two *consecutive* life sentences in the killings of Penny Haddenham and Nancy King-hammer.

"I just do not believe this court should operate a bargain basement for murder—allowing two murders to go for the price of one," Smith commented. He said that when Ruzicka arrived at the Washington State Penitentiary in Walla Walla, he would be placed among the one hundred most dangerous criminals, for whom maximum security was paramount to all other considerations.

Consulting psychologist Dr. John Berberich had found Ruzicka "extremely dangerous and untreatable" and, like Chuck Wright, he thought that castration might be wise.

Chuck Wright had fought hard to have chemical castration considered in James Ruzicka's case, mindful of Ruzicka's history of escape. "Ruzicka is like a lot of cons," Wright recalled. "He always denies everything. I can't emphasize enough that if this man ever gets on the street, he will kill someone. He is very devious and life means nothing to him. He lied to us from the time he walked in the door to the time he left."

At this writing, James Ruzicka is still locked up in the Washington State Penitentiary at Walla Walla. He is now forty-six years old. There was massive publicity at the time of his sentencing in the midseventies. However, other murderers have supplanted his image in the minds of the public and it is important that the memory of his crimes remain fresh. Although it is extremely doubtful that James Ruzicka will walk the streets again until he is an old man, it is not impossible.

It is still questionable whether chemical castration (with the administration of female hormones) can achieve the desired effect; some of the most vicious sex killings in modern history have been accomplished by men who were physically or psychologically impotent. Their anger at their inability to perform only increased their homicidal rage. In several cases, their victims made the fatal mistake of laughing at them.

And chemical castration only works as long as the subject takes the hormones meant to quell sexual violence. One wonders how long a rapist, once free, would choose to continue taking female hormones.

Carl Lowell Harp, the "other" Troy Asin, was convicted on counts ranging from first-degree murder to sodomy/rape to felon in possession of a weapon. The maximum he could have received was five life sentences, one twenty-year and two ten-year sentences. After a number of violent and obscene outbursts—particularly at female parole officers—Harp admitted that he acted "crazy" because he wanted to go to Western State Hospital so he could be examined by experts and proven "a normal person." Instead, Carl Harp went directly to the penitentiary at Walla Walla to begin serving consecutive life sentences. Because, at that time, a "life" sentence in Washington usually meant thirteen years, four months, the "consecutive" stipulation assured he would never be free.

A new statute was enacted after Carl Harp carried out his "sniper" crimes. If a future sniper should act "with utter disregard for human life" as Harp did, he would be tried for first-degree murder.

Carl Harp was not out of the headlines long. In May 1979, he and two other inmates took ten hostages and held them inside a prison office, rigged with two pipe bombs made with plastic explosives. Harp and the other convicts—convicted kidnapers—were armed with knives. Their hostages—including three women—were eight prison counselors, a guard, and a legal aide who worked outside the penitentiary. Harp listed thirty grievances the prisoners had and said the captors would give themselves up if at least three were satisfied. The prison maximum security unit was overcrowded, Harp maintained, and prisoners had no due process for their complaints.

Harp's insurrection was short; the hostages were released at one A.M. on May 10 after they had been held for eleven hours. They were not injured. But Carl Harp was a constant thorn in the side of prison officials. Calling himself an "anarchist," he said, "I am nonviolent. I'm not out to be a hero. I abhor violence. I've been treated like s—. I've been beat, tortured, and maced. I'm not a slave. I'm not an animal and I'm not subhuman."

Of all the men in the world who might have an opportunity to find romance, one would think that Carl Harp, a convicted rapist and sniper, sentenced to life-after-life sentences, locked away in maximum security, might be far down on the list. But that wasn't true. Carl Harp wrote letters constantly, and one went to an "underground" newspaper in Bellingham: *Northwest Passage*. A pretty eighteen-year-old college student had read Harp's letter in 1974 and begun a correspondence with him.

"I wanted to offer friendship and moral support," Susan Black* said later. She had believed what Harp said in his letter—that he had not been given a fair trial.

Susan and Carl began to write to each other often. They exchanged literally hundreds of letters and poems. It was a platonic relationship at first. When Susan got married to someone else, Carl Harp sent one of his drawings as a wedding gift.

Susan's marriage only lasted two years. When she was divorced in 1979, Harp asked her to marry *him*. It wasn't a very romantic proposal, given the location. They were having a "no contact" visit, separated by thick wire mesh. Harp didn't know if he would ever live to be out of prison; he told Susan that he was afraid he might be killed by enemies inside. But she loved him, and she agreed to marry him. He was thirty and she was twenty-three. She had dark sloe eyes, perfect features, and shimmering long black hair. He was the same bland-looking man he had always been; she adored him and believed that he had never hurt anyone.

After the hostage situation in Walla Walla, Carl Harp was transferred to San Quentin prison in California. On September 2, 1980, Susan went to San Quentin to marry him. They lived for the possibility that they might be allowed conjugal visits so that they could consummate their marriage. They wanted to have children.

Susan was happy being married to Carl, and she believed that he was happy. Still, his drawings were filled with images of death. One was a black-and-white sketch of thirteen men and one woman, all of them hanging from nooses, their hands tied behind them.

In July of 1981, Susan and Carl Harp had their first—and only—conjugal visit. He had been returned to Walla Walla from San Quentin. They were allowed to have some privacy in one of the trailers that the Washington State Penitentiary maintains so that married prisoners can be with their wives.

The two sat in the kitchen and stared at one another. "We almost didn't know how to act after all these years of no contact and no privacy," Susan Harp told *Seattle Times* reporter Erik Lacitis. "(We) sat around and laughed, just acting silly."

And then they made love.

Susan Harp remembers her hours in a trailer behind the walls of the prison in Walla Walla as very romantic. She says Carl wrote to her about his memories of that time. "He was so enthused about the next visit," she said.

"I love you, Wife, in case you didn't know that. . . . Just think, by this time tomorrow if all had worked out, where we would be—sigh." They were to have had a second conjugal visit, but there was a lockdown at the prison and all such visits were cancelled.

"Everything is going to be fine, you watch and see, and our love is going to grow and grow. Think ONLY positive, Susan . . ."

There was never another visit. At 6:42 P.M. on September 5, 1981, when a guard brought Carl Harp's evening meal, he found him with his wrists slashed, slumped on the floor with a television cable cord around his neck. The other end of the cord was tied to a clothes hook on the cell wall.

It took four months for Carl Harp's death certificate to be entered into the Vital Records of Washington. Interestingly, his occupation was given as "self-employed artist." On the line where cause of death was to be specified, the Walla Walla County coroner listed "asphyxiation and strangulation." Under "Accidental?" "Suicide?" "Homicide?" or "Undetermined?" he chose the latter.

Carl Harp had written to his attorneys that a sympathetic guard had warned him that there was a "contract" out on his life because he was not wanted in the prison. But he had told another attorney that he was "ill with mental exhaustion. I am locked in my cell twenty-three hours a day and when I lie down, I fall into a coma. My whole being is tired."

His widow believed that he had been murdered.

But there was no indication on autopsy that someone had strangled Carl Harp and arranged his cell to make his death look like a suicide. The injuries to his neck were commensurate with death by hanging. The cuts on his arms were not deep enough to cause death. The suicide note was in his handwriting: "I did myself so blame no one for any reason at all." There was, however, a shredded note in the commode in his cell. Although it was pieced together by authorities, its contents were never released to the media.

An enigma he lived, and an enigma Carl Harp died. Detectives and medical examiners know how easy it is to hang oneself, and that it is not necessary for a body to drop from a considerable height. They have seen people sitting under tables who have merely leaned against a rope—and died. Carl Harp could have stood up if he had chosen to do so.

Perhaps he did not choose to stand up and take the cable off the clothes hook. Perhaps the image of Abraham Saltzman in his gunsight came to haunt Harp in his prison cell.

And perhaps he *was* murdered. He had annoyed the prison administration and he wasn't much loved by his fellow prisoners. No one will ever really know *how* Carl Harp died.

It is almost as difficult to choose *which* of two reflections of the mirror image killers was the true leader, the true madman. Was it Carl Harp? Or was it James Ruzicka? When they were separated, they simply went along their own killing and raping paths. And, in the end, could not they both have been considered "madmen"?

Note: Chuck Wright has never forgotten the two "Troy Asins." One is locked away, perhaps forever. The other has been dead for fifteen years. When the unclaimed possessions of Carl Harp were gathered up for disposal, Wright saw a drawing that intrigued him. It is one of the hundreds of sketches Carl Harp did. This sketch (reproduced in the picture section) is entitled "Family Tree, 12/10/74" and signed "Carl Harp *Asin*". (Wright would like to hear critiques of "Family Tree" from mental health professionals, artists, and laymen. There may be subtleties, symbolism, and clues in this drawing that no one has yet detected. Those who have comments are asked to contact Chuck Wright, Washington State Department of Corrections, Suite 100, 8625 Evergreen Way, Everett, Washington, 98208-2620.)